POSITION	PRIMARY RESPONSIBILITIES	REQUIREMENTS	FOR MORE INFORMATION
Judge	Apply the law through hearings and trials, ensuring that they are conducted in fairness to all parties, issuing sentences and penalties to guilty parties. Judges hear the facts and evidence of each case from prosecution and defense counsels to decide whether a trial is necessary.	> Bachelor's degree > Juris Doctorate degree > Practicing attorney experience	www.fjc.gov www.judges.org
Attorney	Attorneys practice in either criminal or civil law as prosecution or defense counsel. Activities include researching and examining evidence and facts of each case and interpreting the law based on the purposes of the laws and prior judicial decisions.	> Bachelor's degree > Juris Doctorate degree > Passed the state Bar exam.	www.usajobs.opm.gov
Paralegal	Research laws and prior cases, investigate facts and evidence, write legal documents and briefs, coordinate communications, keep records of all documents.	> Varies among firms and employers > Generally a college degree or paralegal certification required. Certification requires an exam.	www.nala.org
Corrections Officer	Monitor prisoners, enforce rules, maintain order, inspect correctional facilities and prisoners for illegal substances and weapons.	> 18 years of age > U.S. Citizen > High school diploma or equivalent > Federal Bureau of Prisons requires one of the following: Bachelors Degree, three years' work experience, or combination of undergraduate experience + work experience.	www.corrections.com
Probation Officer	Counseling and rehabilitating criminal offenders without the use of incarceration. Probation officers also assist in sentencing by preparing presentence reports. Monitor and keep records of the offender's behavior for the Courts.	> Bachelor's degree and/or experience in probation of intermediate corrections. > U.S. Citizen > Valid driver's license > Must pass drug, medical , and psychological screening.	www.appa-net.org
Parole Officer	Responsible for legal custody of offenders following release from incarceration and ensuring adherence to conditions of parole.	> Bachelor's degree or prior work experience in parole or probation > Written and oral exams typically required.	www.appa-net.org

> THIRD
EDITION

Criminal Justice in Action

Larry K. Gaines
California State University—San Bernardino

Roger LeRoy Miller
Institute for University Studies
Arlington, Texas

THOMSON

WADSWORTH

Australia • Canada • Mexico • Singapore • Spain
United Kingdom • United States

THOMSON

™

WADSWORTH

Editor-in-Chief, Criminal Justice: Eve Howard
Criminal Justice Editor: Jay Whitney
Development Editor: Sherry Symington
Editorial Assistant: Jennifer Walsh
Technology Project Manager: Susan DeVanna
Marketing Manager: Terra Schultz
Marketing Assistant: Andrew Keay
Advertising Project Manager: Stacey Purviance
Project Manager, Editorial Production: Jennie Redwitz
Art Director: Rob Hugel
Print/Media Buyer: Judy Inouye
Permissions Editor: Joohee Lee

Production Service: Ann Borman
Text Designer: Lisa Buckley
Art Editor/Illustrator: Ann Borman
Photo Researcher: Anne Sheroff
Copy Editor: Patricia Lewis
Proofreader: Suzie De Fazio
Indexer: Bob Marsh
Cover Designer: Lisa Buckley
Cover Images: Scales, Premium Stock/CORBIS; Fingerprint:
    Ed Bock/CORBIS, other: PhotoDisc
Compositor: Parkwood Composition
Text and Cover Printer: Transcontinental Printing/Interglobe

Printed in Canada
1 2 3 4 5 6 7 08 07 06 05 04

For more information about our products, contact us at:
Thomson Learning Academic Resource Center
1-800-423-0563
For permission to use material from this text or product, submit a request online at **http://www.thomsonrights.com.**
Any additional questions about permissions can be submitted by email to **thomsonrights@thomson.com.**

Library of Congress Control Number: 2003115694

Student Casebound Edition: ISBN 0-534-62901-6
Student Paperback Edition: ISBN 0-534-62903-2
Instructor's Edition: ISBN 0-534-62905-9

Thomson Wadsworth
10 Davis Drive
Belmont, CA 94002-3098
USA

Asia
Thomson Learning
5 Shenton Way #01-01
UIC Building
Singapore 068808

Australia/New Zealand
Thomson Learning
102 Dodds Street
Southbank, Victoria 3006
Australia

Canada
Nelson
1120 Birchmount Road
Toronto, Ontario M1K 5G4
Canada

Europe/Middle East/Africa
Thomson Learning
High Holborn House
50/51 Bedford Row
London WC1R 4LR
United Kingdom

Latin America
Thomson Learning
Seneca, 53
Colonia Polanco
11560 Mexico D.F.
Mexico

Spain/Portugal
Paraninfo
Calle Magallanes, 25
28015 Madrid, Spain

Contents in Brief

Contents

>Chapter 4<

Inside Criminal Law 106

Part Two: The Police and Law Enforcement

>Chapter 5<

Law Enforcement Today   136

Challenges to Effective Policing 170

> Chapter 7 <

Police and the Constitution: The Rules of Law Enforcement   214

CHAPTER SEVEN FEATURES

Part Three:
Criminal Courts

> Chapter 8 <

Courts and the Quest for Justice   252

CHAPTER EIGHT FEATURES

> Chapter 9 <

Pretrial Procedures: The Adversary System in Action   286

CHAPTER NINE FEATURES

> **Chapter 10** <

The Criminal Trial 322

Punishment and Sentencing   360

Part Four: Corrections

> Chapter 12 <

Probation and Community Corrections 402

CHAPTER TWELVE FEATURES

> Chapter 13 <

Prisons and Jails 434

Part Five: Special Issues

> Chapter 15 <

The Juvenile Justice System   504

> Chapter 16 <

The Ongoing War against Illegal Drugs   540

CHAPTER SIXTEEN FEATURES

> Chapter 17 <

Terrorism, Cyber Crime, and the Future   570

CHAPTER SEVENTEEN FEATURES

International CJ
> British Intelligence   577

You Be the Judge
> Does the U.S. Constitution Apply to "Terrorist Organizations"?   586

CJ and Technology
> Scriptkiddies and the "Do It Yourself" Web Attack   591

Criminal Justice in Action

> **Child Pornography and the Internet**   599

Chapter Summary > Stories from the Street > Key Terms > Questions for Critical
Analysis > Test Preparation Online > Web Resources > Search Online with InfoTrac
College Edition > Suggested Readings > Notes **603–607**

Preface

Simply stated, criminal justice is one of the fastest-growing majors in American higher education. Criminal justice programs across the country are offering more students than ever a combination of theory, practice, and topics that present a unique perspective on issues that dominate today's headlines. The practical benefits of the criminal justice major are also evident: a "foot in the door" to dozens of professional fields such as law enforcement, corrections administration, and probation and parole, as well as a strong foundation for a graduate degree in law or a career in crime-based research and data analysis. Especially in the wake of the events of September 11, 2001, the practical applications of a criminal justice degree are far-reaching and immediate.

In this, the third edition of *Criminal Justice in Action,* we continue to blend the bedrock theoretical principles of criminal justice with up-to-date research and high-interest examples of what is happening in the world of crime and crime prevention right now. Students just entering the discipline of criminal justice are facing a dizzying array of challenges in a field that has seen epochal changes in the past few years. Consider the following:

> With the creation of the U.S. Department of Homeland Security and the reorganization of the Federal Bureau of Investigation, the "war on terror" has led to the most extensive shift in how the federal government views and fights crime since World War II. These changes have affected every level of the criminal justice system, including local police departments, which must now take responsibility for areas of law enforcement that had previously been handled by federal agencies.

> For the first time ever, those incarcerated throughout the United States exceeded 2 million, and the number is rising. In many states, prison and jail overcrowding has reached the point at which administrators are forced to release criminals, some of whom have been convicted of violent crimes, because they cannot afford to imprison them.

> New technologies have influenced nearly every aspect of the criminal justice process. DNA techniques have allowed police to solve more crimes, sometimes years after they have occurred, but have also provided evidence that many people have been wrongly convicted and imprisoned.

> The public's view of the criminal justice system is being increasingly molded by how the popular media portray it. Have the media been accurate? If not, is there anything we can do about it? How do we teach our students to become more critical consumers of the media?

These are the kinds of issues that face students going into the field of criminal justice today. Undoubtedly, as this nation faces the challenge of terrorism on our soil, the role of the criminal justice system will expand and evolve. What is certain is that major new questions involving the trade-off between increased security and diminished civil liberties will be at the forefront of the public debate.

A Complete Learning Experience

While the text of *Criminal Justice in Action,* Third Edition, is filled with numerous eye-catching, instructive, and penetrating features, we have not stopped there. You will notice that the first page of every chapter starts with the chapter outline and learning objectives. The following page has an introduction in the form of a case study and an appropriate photo. The pedagogy continues all the way through to the end of each chapter, with the pedagogical devices listed below:

> **Criminal Justice in Action:** Every chapter ends with this important feature. It deals with major issues and controversies that require several pages to explain.

> **What Works:** While much criticism of our criminal justice system continues in the press and elsewhere, there are numerous instances of great ideas being carried out by industrious members of that system that actually work! In these features we highlight and analyze what works, and why.

> **You Be the Judge:** Students are put into the position of a judge in a hypothetical criminal case (based, though, on an actual court case). The facts of the case are presented with alternative possible outcomes. The student is asked to make a decision as if he or she were the judge. What the courts actually ruled in each case can be found by the student in Appendix B at the end of the text.

> **International CJ:** Because it is sometimes easier to teach by comparison, in this feature we present students with information about how our criminal justice system compares with those of other countries.

> **CJ and Technology:** Since the criminal justice field is changing so rapidly because of technology, we made sure that the student could not miss learning about the important technology issues confronted by practitioners in the field today.

> **CJ and the Media:** Many aspects of the criminal justice system have invaded the media. We felt that this feature was important to reveal these "invasions" while at the same time commenting on their accuracy.

> **Careers in CJ:** Most students reading this book are planning a career in criminal justice. We have provided them with an insight into some of these careers by offering first-person accounts of what it is like to work in the criminal justice professions.

> **CJ in Focus:** This generic feature title covers important topics such as excerpts from significant Supreme Court cases and the age-old struggle between the need to protect society and the rights of individuals.

> **Mastering Concepts:** This feature helps students to master essential concepts of criminal justice. Because it is often important to compare and contrast two similar concepts to help the student understand them, many of the concept summaries are based on comparisons.

> **In-Margin Online Features:** Our teaching/learning package offers numerous opportunities for using online technology in the classroom. In the margins, you will find InfoTrac® citations that lead students to very important research

articles in this powerful private, password-protected, online database. In addition, there are relevant Web citations in the margins of every chapter. Each chapter also starts with a *Concept Builder* that leads students to an interactive critical-thinking exploration of a key topic. Finally, when appropriate, there is a CD-ROM logo displayed to show that a career feature is available in the text's companion careers CD-ROM.

Challenges for the Future: Terrorism and Cyber Crime

Because of the growing and obvious importance of terrorism and cyber crime in the criminal justice system, we have devoted most of Chapter 17 to these issues. The discussion will focus on the steps taken by American law enforcement personnel to combat these threats, as well as efforts to protect the public against terrorists and cyber criminals while at the same time protecting the nation's commitment to civil liberties. Chapter 17 also provides a "wrap" of the course, closing the textbook with a brief look to the immediate future of the criminal justice system.

The Supplements

Our entire team—the two authors plus numerous individuals at Wadsworth—have put together a complete teaching package. In this package you will find:

FOR THE INSTRUCTOR

Instructor's Resource Manual with Test Bank and *CNN Today* DVD   One of the most comprehensive resource manuals to accompany *Criminal Justice in Action*, this manual includes detailed outlines, chapter summaries, key terms, student research activities, and a test bank containing over 1,400 questions. The accompanying DVD features selected video from the *CNN Today: Introduction to Criminal Justice* Video Series along with teaching tips on incorporating it into lectures.

Criminal Justice Video Library   Qualified adopters can select from a variety of videos, including exclusive *CNN Today* videos for Introduction to Criminal Justice, Criminology, Juvenile Delinquency, and Corrections, as well as *America's New War: CNN Looks at Terrorism*, Volumes I and II, all of which are tied to chapters of the selected texts; an exclusive *Introduction to Criminal Justice* video from the Films for the Humanities, Volumes I and II; sixteen dynamic *Court TV* videos profiling some of the most famous and current cases in the judicial system; the *A&E American Justice Series;* ABC News and MPI Home videos; and the *National Institute of Justice Crime File* videos.

***Criminal Justice Faculty Development: Teaching Professors to Teach*, Second Edition**   This completely revised booklet provides valuable tips on teaching the introduction to criminal justice course with suggested articles, work sheets, and sample syllabi.

Introduction to Criminal Justice 2005 Transparency Acetates   Enhance your lectures with full-color acetates that highlight some of the most important concepts in criminal justice.

ExamView®   This fully integrated suite of computerized test creation, delivery, and reporting tools enables you to help students enhance their test performance, and allows you to deliver tests that can be customized to fit your needs.

WebTutor Advantage on WebCT and Blackboard   Designed specifically for *Criminal Justice in Action,* Third Edition, WebTutor Advantage is an online resource that gives both instructors and students a virtual environment that is rich with study and communication tools, including an e-Book.   For instructors, WebTutor Advantage can provide virtual office hours, post syllabi, set up threaded discussions, and track student progress.   WebTutor Advantage can also be customized in a variety of ways, such as uploading images and other resources and adding Web links to create customized practice materials.   For students, WebTutor Advantage offers real-time access to many study aids, including flash cards, practice quizzes, online tutorials and Web links.

Multimedia Manager for Criminal Justice 2005: A Microsoft® PowerPoint® Link Tool   The Multimedia Manager for Criminal Justice is an important instrument that instructors can utilize to prepare for class lectures.   More than 450 color images are included on this invaluable reference to aid instructors in visually representing to students the main concepts and ideas contained in the text.

FOR THE STUDENT

Web Site to Accompany *Criminal Justice in Action,* Third Edition   Students and instructors will have access to the book-specific Web site that includes chapter links, discussions, Internet projects, homework, quizzes, scavenger hunts, and instructor resources. **http://www.cjinaction.com**

Careers in Criminal Justice Interactive CD-ROM (automatically included with the hardback version of the book)   This engaging self-exploration provides an interactive discovery of careers in criminal justice. The CD-ROM furnishes personalized results from a self-assessment of interests and strengths to help steer students to careers based on their profiles. Students gather information on various careers from job descriptions, salaries, employment requirements, and actual video profiles of criminal justice professionals.

The Wadsworth Criminal Justice Resource Center   Designed to help students easily locate the latest and most relevant information in the field of criminal justice, this Web site features fascinating links, conference and job listings, grant information, links to book-specific sites with additional student resources, and much more. **http:// cj.wadsworth.com**

Crime Scenes CD-ROM   An interactive CD-ROM featuring six vignettes that allows students to play various roles as they explore all aspects of the criminal justice system such as policing/investigation, courts, and sentencing and corrections. Awarded the gold medal in higher education and silver medal for video interface by *New Media* magazine's *Invision* Awards.

Study Guide   Includes chapter objectives, outlines, summaries, key terms and concepts, and a multitude of test questions in true/false, multiple-choice, matching, and essay formats.

InfoTrac® College Edition   Students receive four months of real-time access to InfoTrac® College Edition's online database of continuously updated, full-length articles from nearly five thousand journals and periodicals. By doing a simple key-word search, users can quickly generate a powerful list of related articles from thousands of possibilities, then select relevant articles to explore and/or print out for reference or for further study.

The Criminal Justice Internet Investigator III   This colorful trifold brochure lists the most popular Internet addresses for criminal justice–related Web sites, including URLs for corrections, victimization, crime prevention, high-tech crime, policing, courts, investigations, juvenile justice, research, and fun sites.

***Internet Activities for Criminal Justice*, Second Edition**   This guide teaches students the best practices for utilizing the Internet for research and includes criminal justice–specific activities.

***Internet Guide for Criminal Justice*, Second Edition**   Intended for the novice user, the first half of this eighty-page booklet explains the background and vocabulary necessary for navigating the Web, while the second half is customized for criminal justice–related Web sites as well as Internet project ideas.

***Seeking Employment in Criminal Justice and Related Fields*, Fourth Edition**
This new edition is designed to help students develop a job-search strategy and provides information on résumés, cover letters, and interview techniques; it also furnishes extensive details about a wide range of criminal justice professions.

Acknowledgments

Throughout the creation of the three editions of this text, we have been aided by literally hundreds of experts in various criminal justice fields and by professors throughout the country, as well as by numerous students who have used the text. We list below the reviewers and survey respondents for this Third Edition, followed by the class-test participants and reviewers for the first two editions. We sincerely thank all who participated on the revision of *Criminal Justice in Action*. We believe that the Third Edition responds even more to the needs of today's criminal justice instructors and students alike because we have taken into account the constructive comments and criticisms of our reviewers and the helpful suggestions of our survey respondents.

REVIEWERS AND SURVEY RESPONDENTS FOR THE THIRD EDITION

We are grateful for the participation of the reviewers who read and reviewed portions of our manuscript throughout its development, and for those who gave us valuable insights through their responses to our survey.

David L. Anderson
Louisiana State University—Shreveport

Tammy Anderson
University of Delaware

Thomas E. Baker
University of Scranton

Shannon Barton
Indiana State University

Lee Roy Black
California University of Pennsylvania

John K. Bordell
Kansas Wesleyan University

Sandy Boyd
College of Marin

Robert Boyer
Luzerne County Community College

Frank W. Budd
Weber State University

Frank Butler
Temple University

Charles Chastain
University of Arkansas at Little Rock

James J. Chriss
Cleveland State University

Ellen G. Cohn
Florida International University

William Crawley
Grand Valley State University

Chris De Lay
University of Louisiana at Lafayette

Dick De Lung
Wayland Baptist University

Jo-Ann Della-Giustina
John Jay College of Criminal Justice

Frank J. Drummond
Modesto Junior College

Michael T. Eskey
Troy State University

Peter Galie
Canisius College

Donna F. Gaughan
Prince George's Community College

Paul Gregory
Western Michigan University

Deborah Henderson
Arizona State University

Nancy A. Horton
University of Maryland Eastern Shore

G. G. Hunt
Wharton County Junior College

Al Ingham
Western New England College

James M. Johnson
Virginia Union University

Howard Jordan
Hostos College

Joseph Kibitlewski
International College

Lloyd Klein
Bemidji State University

Francis Kollmann
Suffolk County Community College

David Kotajarvi
Lakeshore Technical College

Betsey Wright Kreisel
Central Missouri State University

James Lasley
California State University Fullerton

Deborah Lauferweiler-Dwyer
University of Arkansas at Little Rock

Larry Linville
North Virginia Community College

Neal W. Lippold
Waubonsee Community College

Arnold C. Lyerly
Community College of Southern Nevada

Larry Mays
New Mexico State University

James J. Mazza
Middlesex Community College

Joe Morris
Northwestern State University

Thomas R. O'Connor
North Carolina Wesleyan College

Peter Parilla
University of St. Thomas

William R. Parks II
University of South Carolina—Spartanburg

Mike Penrod
Kirkwood Community College

Heather Perfetti
Murray State University

Michael Polakowski
University of Arizona

Byron Quivey
Chipola Junior College

James T. Santor
Community College of Southern Nevada

Jim Smith
West Valley College

John Song
Buffalo State College

Sally Velzen
Itasca Community College

Ross A. Wolf
University of Central Florida

Kevin C. Woods
Becker College

Thanks to the Career Education Criminal Justice Advisory Board for their valuable inputs and contributions to the Wadsworth Criminal Justice Team:

Adell Newman
Chair, School of Criminal Justice
Kaplan College

Nancy Oesch
Criminal Justice Department Chair
Florida Metropolitan University

Kathryn Sellers
Criminal Justice Program Director
Virginia College

Jim Walney
Criminal Justice Program Director
ICM School of Business & Medical Careers

CLASS-TEST PARTICIPANTS

We also want to acknowledge the participation of the professors and their students who agreed to class-test portions of the text. Our thanks go to:

Tom Arnold
College of Lake County

Paula M. Broussard
University of Southwestern Louisiana

Mike Higginson
Suffolk Community College

Andrew Karmen
John Jay College of Criminal Justice

Fred Kramer
John Jay College of Criminal Justice

Anthony P. LaRose
Western Oregon University

Anne Lawrence
Kean University

Jerry E. Loar
Walters State Community College

Phil Reichel
University of Northern Colorado

Albert Sproule
Allentown College

Gregory B. Talley
Broome Community College

Karen Terry
John Jay College of Criminal Justice

Angelo Tritini
Passaic County Community College

Gary Uhrin
Westmoreland County Community College

Robert Vodde
Fairleigh Dickinson University

REVIEWERS OF THE FIRST AND SECOND EDITIONS

We appreciate the assistance of the following reviewers whose guidance helped create the foundation for this best seller. We are grateful to all.

Angela Ambers-Henderson
Montgomery County Community College

Judge James Bachman
Bowling Green State University

Tom Barclay
University of South Alabama

Julia Beeman
University of North Carolina at Charlotte

Anita Blowers
University of North Carolina at Charlotte

John Bower
Bethel College

Steven Brandl
University of Wisconsin—Milwaukee

Charles Brawner III
Heartland Community College

Susan Brinkley
University of Tampa

Paula Broussard
University of Southwestern Louisiana

Michael Brown
Ball State College

Joseph Bunce
Montgomery College—Rockville

James T. Burnett
SUNY, Rockland Community College

Ronald Burns
Texas Christian University

Paul Campbell
Wayne State College

Dae Chang
Wichita State University

Steven Chermak
Indiana University

Charlie Chukwudolue
Northern Kentucky University

Monte Clampett
Asheville-Buncome Community College

John Cochran
University of South Florida

Mark Correia
University of Nevada—Reno

John del Nero
Lane Community College

John Dempsey
Suffolk County Community College

Tom Dempsey
Christopher Newpoint University

Joyce Dozier
Wilmington College

M. G. Eichenberg
Wayne State College

Frank L. Fischer
Kankakee Community College

Frederick Galt
Dutchess Community College

James Gilbert
University of Nebraska—Kearney

Dean Golding
West Chester University of Pennsylvania

Debbie Goodman
Miami-Dade Community College

Donald Grubb
Northern Virginia Community College

Sharon Halford
Community College of Aurora

Michael Hallett
Middle Tennessee State University

Mark Hansel
Moorhead State University

Michelle Heward
Weber State University

Dennis Hoffman
University of Nebraska—Omaha

Richard Holden
Central Missouri State University

Ronald Holmes
University of Louisville

Marilyn Horace-Moore
Eastern Michigan University

Matrice Hurrah
Shelby State Community College

Nicholas Irons
County College of Morris

Michael Israel
Kean University

J. D. Jamieson
Southwest Texas State University

James Jengeleski
Shippensburg University

Paul Johnson
Weber State University

Casey Jordan
Western Connecticut State University

Matthew Kanjirathinkal
Texas A & M University—Commerce

Bill Kelly
University of Texas—Austin

John H. Kramer
Pennsylvania State University

Kristen Kuehnle
Salem State University

Karl Kunkel
Southwest Missouri State

Barry Latzer
John Jay College of Criminal Justice

Deborah Laufersweiler-Dwyer
University of Arkansas—Little Rock

Paul Lawson
Montana State University

Nella Lee
Portland State University

Walter Lewis
St. Louis Community College—Meramec

Faith Lutze
Washington State University

Richard Martin
Elgin Community College

Richard H. Martin
University of Findlay

Bill Matthias
University of South Carolina—Columbia

William J. Mathias
University of South Carolina

Janet McClellan
Southwestern Oregon Community
College

Pat Murphy
State University of New York—Geneseo

Rebecca Nathanson
Housatonic Community Technical
College

Michael Palmiotto
Wichita State University

Rebecca D. Petersen
University of Texas, San Antonio

Gary Prawel
Monroe Community College

Mark Robarge
Mansfield University

Matt Robinson
Appalachian State University

Debra Ross
Buffalo State College

William Ruefle
University of South Carolina

Gregory Russell
Washington State University

John Scheb II
University of Tennessee—Knoxville

Ed Selby
Southwestern College

Ronald Sopenoff
Brookdale Community College

Katherine Steinbeck
Lakeland Community College

Kathleen M. Sweet
St. Cloud State University

Lawrence F. Travis III
University of Cincinnati

Ron Walker
Trinity Valley Community College

Gregory Talley
Broome Community College

Kimberly Vogt
University of Wisconsin—La Crosse

John Wyant
Illinois Central College

Karen Terry
John Jay College of Criminal Justice

Robert Wadman
Weber State University

Others were instrumental in bringing this Third Edition to fruition. We continue to appreciate the extensive research efforts of Shawn G. Miller and the additional legal assistance of William Eric Hollowell. Sherry Symington, our development editor, provided equal parts elbow grease and creative energy; it was a pleasure to work with her. Editor Jay Whitney supplied crucial guidance to the project through his suggestions, recommendations, and direct orders. Editor-in-chief Eve Howard and CEO Susan Badger provided key support. At the production end, we once again feel fortunate to have enjoyed the services of our tireless project manager, Ann Borman, who oversaw virtually all aspects of this book. How she was able to make all of the schedules on time never ceased to amaze us. Additionally, we wish to thank the designer of this new edition, Lisa Buckley, who has created what we believe to be the most dazzling and student-friendly design of any text in the field. Photo researcher Anne Sheroff went to great lengths to satisfy our requests, and we greatly appreciate her efforts. We are also thankful for the services of all those at Parkwood Composition who worked on the Third Edition, particularly Debbie Mealey. The eagle eyes of Pat Lewis, who did expert double duty as copy editor and proofreader, and Suzie Franklin DeFazio, proofer extraordinaire, were invaluable.

A special word of thanks must also go to the team responsible for the extensive multimedia package included in this project, including technology project manager Susan DeVanna, writers Robert C. De Lucia of John Jay College of Criminal Justice and Kelli Stevens of Texas Christian University, Larry Bassi of SUNY Brockport, and Carolyn Dennis of Mount Olive College. In addition, we appreciate the work of Joe Morris of Northwestern State University who developed the Instructor's Resource Manual and Student Study Guide, as well as the help of editorial assistant Jennifer Walsh, who pitched in to ensure the timely publication of the supplements. A final thanks to all of the great people in marketing and advertising who helped to get the word out about the book, including marketing manager Dory Schaeffer, who has been tireless in her attention to this project; Joy Westberg for her excellent writing skills; and advertising project manager Stacey Purviance for keeping everything on track.

Any criminal justice text has to be considered a work in progress. We know that there are improvements that we can make. Therefore, write us with any suggestions that you may have.

L. K. G.
R. L. M.

Dedication

This book is dedicated to
my good friend and colleague,
Lawrence Walsh, of the Lexington,
Kentucky Police Department.
When I was a rookie, he taught me
about policing. When I became a
researcher, he taught me about the
practical applications of knowledge. He is truly an inspiriting
professional in our field.

L.K.G.

In loving memory of
Lillian S. Miller.
I owe it all to you,
wherever you may be.

R.L.M.

>Chapter 1<

Criminal Justice Today

>chapter objectives<

After reading this chapter, you should be able to:

1 Describe the two most common models of how society determines which acts are criminal.

2 Define crime and the different types of crime.

3 Outline the three levels of law enforcement.

4 List the essential elements of the corrections system.

5 Explain the difference between the formal and informal criminal justice processes.

6 Describe the layers of the "wedding cake" model.

7 Contrast the crime control and due process models.

8 List the major issues in criminal justice today.

A Sniper among Us

The first shot from the Bushmaster XM15 shattered a storefront window in Montgomery County, Maryland. The second, fired forty minutes later, killed a program analyst in a nearby supermarket

parking lot. Five more shots on the following morning killed five more people, and suddenly the residents of the Washington, D.C., area were thrown into a state of fear and confusion.

Washington, D.C., area sniper suspects John Lee Malvo, left, and John Muhammad.

Over the next three weeks in the fall of 2002, bullets from the high-powered rifle killed four more people and injured three others. All the victims were shot in public, turning a simple trip to the grocery store or gas station into a nerve-racking experience. The heavy law enforcement presence—squad cars at major intersections, military spy planes and helicopters in the sky—seemed to heighten feelings of tension rather than calm them. "I can't believe what's happening here," said a local woman on Day Twenty of the ordeal. "They're not going to get this guy."

Finally, however, they did get him. In a message to the police, the gunman had bragged about a crime he had committed in Montgomery, Alabama. This led investigators to an unmatched fingerprint on a magazine from a liquor store in that city. The fingerprint belonged to a seventeen-year-old named John Lee Malvo. Law enforcement agents announced that Malvo has been spotted in the D.C. area, traveling with a friend named John Muhammad in a blue Chevrolet Caprice. On October 24, thanks to a tip from a motorist who recognized their car, Muhammad and Malvo were arrested at a rest stop near Frederick, Maryland. Though a SWAT team smashed the windows of the Caprice and used a blinding device known as a "flash bang" to stun the two suspects, it was a relatively easy operation. Both Muhammad and Malvo were asleep at the wheel—literally.

> **Once John Muhammad** and John Lee Malvo were in custody, it seemed that law enforcement officials had an open-and-shut case. After all, the ballistics evidence linked eleven of the thirteen shootings to the same Bushmaster XM15, and the rifle was found in the back seat of the car in which Muhammad and Malvo were arrested. Furthermore, Malvo confessed to committing several of the attacks himself, and implicated Muhammad in the others.

In the days and months following the suspects' arrest, however, a number of loose ends emerged concerning their fate. Malvo's lawyers claimed that Fairfax County, Virginia, police did not follow proper procedure in questioning their client, leaving open the possibility that his confession could not be used in court. We will discuss the rules that police must follow in this and other situations in Chapter 7. Furthermore, Muhammad and Malvo were eventually linked to murders not only in Washington, D.C., Maryland, and Virginia, but also in Alabama, Louisiana, Georgia, and Washington State. In Chapters 8 and 9, we will learn who decides where a person is charged for committing a crime and how that decision is made. Finally, how were Muhammad and Malvo to be brought to justice? Law enforcement officials chose to seek the death penalty for both suspects. As we shall see in Chapter 11, capital punishment is one of the most hotly debated topics in the United States today, and it becomes even more controversial when applied to a juvenile such as Malvo, a subject we will explore in Chapter 15. (Muhammad was eventually convicted of murder and sentenced to death. Malvo's trial was ongoing as this textbook went to press.)

As you proceed through this textbook, you will see that few aspects of the criminal justice system are ever simple, even though you may have clear opinions about them. In this first chapter, we will introduce you to the criminal justice system by discussing its structure, the values that it is designed to promote, and the most challenging issues it faces in the first decade of the new century.

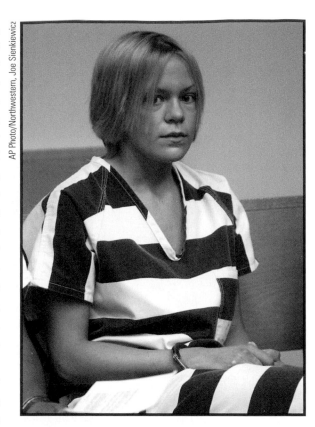

In 2003, seventeen-year-old Kristen Cleaver was charged with first-degree intentional homicide and hiding a corpse. According to officials in Oshkosh, Wisconsin, Cleaver gave birth in her bathtub, watched the child drown, and then hid the body in her bedroom closet. Why does society need to punish this kind of behavior with criminal sanctions?

What Is Crime?

During the preliminary stages of his trial, John Muhammad's lawyers informed the judge that their client had been exposed to nerve gas while serving as an army engineer in the first Gulf War in 1991. By suggesting that his mental health might be impaired, the lawyers were raising the possibility that Muhammad might not be fully responsible for his actions. As we shall see in Chapter 4, to commit a crime, a person must be sane enough to intend to take part in criminal activity. Thus, even though Muhammad may have pulled the trigger, he might not be guilty of murder. This is not the only instance in which the taking of a life is not considered murder. Homicide may be justified when the offender is protecting himself or herself, a situation also discussed in Chapter 4. In some circumstances, described in Chapter 6, law enforcement officers may kill in the line of duty without invoking criminal penalties. The state may sanction killing in times of war or as punishment.

When, then, is homicide considered murder? The easy answer is: when it meets the legal conditions that designate it as such. Therefore, a *crime* can be defined as a wrong against society proclaimed by law and, if committed under certain circumstances, punishable by society.[1] The problem with this definition, however, is that it obscures the complex nature of societies. A society is not static—it evolves and changes, and its concept of criminality evolves and changes as well. Different societies can have vastly different ideas of what constitutes "a wrong." In Singapore, for example, until recently the sale of chewing gum was illegal, a law that many Americans found incomprehensible.

CONCEPT BUILDER
Society has become less tolerant of crime, and especially of certain types of crime. Visit www.cjinaction.com for an interactive exploration of how such intolerance affects crime policies.

To more fully understand the concept of crime, it will help to examine the two most common models of how society "decides" which acts are criminal: the consensus model and the conflict model.

THE CONSENSUS MODEL

The **consensus model** assumes that as people gather together to form a society, its members will naturally come to a basic agreement with regard to shared norms and values. Those individuals whose actions deviate from the established norms and values are considered to pose a threat to the well-being of society as a whole and must be sanctioned (punished). The society passes laws to control and prevent deviant behavior, thereby setting the boundaries for acceptable behavior within the group.[2] Use of the term *consensus* implies that a majority of the citizens agree on what activities should be outlawed and punished as crimes.

The consensus model, to a certain extent, assumes that a diverse group of people can have similar *morals;* that is, they share an ideal of what is "right" and "wrong." Consequently, as public attitudes toward morality change, so do laws. In colonial times, those found guilty of adultery were subjected to corporal punishment; a century ago, one could walk into a pharmacy and purchase heroin. Today, social attitudes have shifted to consider adultery a personal issue, beyond the purview of the state, and to consider the sale of heroin a criminal act. When a consensus does not exist as to whether a certain act falls within the parameters of acceptable behavior, a period of uncertainty ensues as society struggles to formalize its attitudes as law. (For an example of the consensus model at work, see the feature *International CJ—Doctor-Assisted Death and the Dutch.*)

THE CONFLICT MODEL

Those who reject the consensus model do so on the ground that moral attitudes are not absolute. In large, democratic societies such as the United States, different segments of society will inevitably have different value systems and shared norms. According to the **conflict model,** these different segments—separated by social class, income, age, and race—are engaged in a constant struggle with each other for control of society. The victorious groups exercise their power by codifying their value systems into criminal laws.[3]

Consequently, what is criminal activity is determined by whichever group happens to be holding power at any given time. Because certain groups do not have access to political power, their interests are not served by the criminal justice system. To give one example, the penalty (five years in prison) for possession of 5 grams of crack cocaine is the same as for possession of 500 grams of powder cocaine. This 1:100 ratio has had widespread implications for inner-city African Americans, who are statistically more likely to get caught using crack cocaine than are white suburbanites, who appear to favor the illicit drug in its powdered form.[4]

AN INTEGRATED DEFINITION OF CRIME

Considering both the consensus and conflict models, we can construct a definition of crime that will be useful throughout this textbook. For our purposes, crime is an action or activity that is:

Doctor-Assisted Death and the Dutch

In 2001, the Netherlands became the first nation to legalize physician-assisted suicide and euthanasia ("mercy killing"). The new law simply formalized practices that had been taking place since 1973, when this European nation's courts decided that doctors can help terminate a patient's life if certain conditions are met: the patient must explicitly request such an action, the request must be voluntary, and the patient's suffering must be unbearable and without any hope of improvement. The law requires youths aged twelve to sixteen to obtain parental consent before requesting assisted suicide. From the age of sixteen, all patients have the right to discuss the matter with their doctors without obtaining their parents' approval.

In explaining why the Netherlands accepts actions that many other countries would consider objectionable, observers point to several characteristics of Dutch society. First, doctors hold exalted positions, and their actions are rarely questioned. Not only are doctors authorized to terminate "meaningless" lives, but they are also expected to do so. Second, the country lacks a strong religious influence, which might place the question of assisted suicide in a different moral perspective. As it is, hopelessly ill patients who fail to request euthanasia are seen as adhering to outdated ethical values. Third, and most important, is the Dutch emphasis on personal autonomy; the choice to die is considered the responsibility of the individual, not of the state.

In 1998, an elderly Oregon woman whose breast cancer left her unable to breathe easily became the first American to

AP Photo/Serge Ligtenberg

On April 10, 2000, thousands of protesters gather outside the Upper House of Parliament in The Hague, Netherlands, as Dutch government officials debate the legalization of euthanasia.

legally commit suicide with the aid of a doctor. Oregon's Death with Dignity Act—which is modeled in many respects after the Dutch system—was upheld by a federal court ruling in 2002 that reconfirmed each state's authority to legalize assisted suicide. To date, 129 people have ended their lives with a physician's help in Oregon, the only state that allows such a practice.

FOR CRITICAL ANALYSIS
What social attitudes make it unlikely that physician-assisted suicide and euthanasia will become widely accepted in this country?

1 Punishable under criminal law, as determined by the majority of a society or, in some cases, a powerful minority.
2 Considered an *offense against society as a whole* and prosecuted by public officials, not by victims and their relatives or friends.
3 Punishable by statutorily determined sanctions that bring about the loss of personal freedom or life.

TYPES OF CRIME

The manner in which crimes are classified depends on their seriousness. Federal, state, and local legislation has provided for the classification and punishment of hundreds of thousands of different criminal acts, ranging from jay-walking to first degree murder. For general purposes, we can group criminal behavior into six categories: violent crime, property crime, public order crime, white-collar crime, organized crime, and high-tech crime.

Violent Crime   Crimes against persons, or **violent crimes,** have come to dominate our perspectives on crime. There are four major categories of violent crime:

Violent Crime
Crimes committed against persons, including murder, rape, assault and battery, and robbery.

At the Cannabis Buyers' Cooperative in Oakland, California, "bartender" Pamela Powers picks out a marijuana muffin for quadriplegic Ken Estes. In the mid-1990s, voters in California approved Proposition 215, which allows those with a physician's approval to purchase marijuana for medical purposes. The U.S. Department of Justice declared Proposition 215 illegal, as it countered federal drug laws that prohibit the production and sale of marijuana. U.S. District Judge Charles Breyer agreed, ordering the closing of the Oakland Cannabis Cooperative. In response, the city kept the Cooperative open, with an official telling the federal government to "butt out." How does the debate over medical marijuana reflect the consensus model (see p. 6) in action?

Property Crime
Crimes committed against property, including larceny/theft, burglary, and arson.

Public Order Crime
Behavior that has been labeled criminal because it is contrary to shared social values, customs, and norms.

White-Collar Crime
Nonviolent crimes committed by corporations and individuals to gain a personal or business advantage.

> *Murder,* or the unlawful killing of a human being.

> *Sexual assault,* or *rape,* which refers to coerced actions of a sexual nature against an unwilling participant.

> *Assault and battery,* two separate acts that cover situations in which one person physically attacks another (battery) or, through threats, intentionally leads another to believe that he or she will be physically harmed (assault).

> *Robbery,* or the taking of money, personal property, or any other article of value from a person by means of force or fear.

As we shall see in Chapter 4, these violent crimes are further classified by *degree,* depending on the circumstances surrounding the criminal act. These circumstances include the intent of the person committing the crime, whether a weapon was used, and (in cases other than murder) the level of pain and suffering experienced by the victim.

Property Crime   The most common form of criminal activity is **property crime,** or those crimes in which the goal of the offender is some form of economic gain or the damaging of property. Pocket-picking, shoplifting, and the stealing of any property that is not accomplished by force are covered by laws against *larceny/theft. Burglary* refers to the unlawful entry of a structure with the intention of committing a serious crime such as theft. *Motor vehicle theft* describes the theft or attempted theft of a motor vehicle, including all cases in which automobiles are taken by persons not having lawful access to them. The willful and malicious burning of a home, automobile, commercial building, or any other construction, known as *arson,* is also a property crime.

Public Order Crime   The concept of **public order crimes** is linked to the consensus model discussed earlier. Historically, societies have always outlawed activities that are considered contrary to public values and morals. Today, the most common public order crimes include public drunkenness, prostitution, gambling, and illicit drug use. These crimes are sometimes referred to as *victimless crimes* because they often harm only the offender. As we shall see throughout this textbook, however, that term is rather misleading. Public order crimes may create an environment that gives rise to property and violent crimes.

White-Collar Crime   Crimes occur in the business world too. Business-related crimes are popularly referred to as **white-collar crimes.** The term *white-collar crime* is broadly used to describe an illegal act or series of acts committed by an individual or business entity using some nonviolent means to obtain a personal or business advantage. Figure 1.1 lists various types of white-collar crime; note that certain property crimes fall into this category when committed in a corporate context.

White-collar crime costs corporate America about $600 billion annually.[5] Some observers see the relatively light penalties given to wealthy white-collar criminals—in contrast to harsher penalties for poorer "blue-collar" (or street) criminals convicted of burglary, larceny, and the sale of illegal drugs—as supporting the conflict model of criminality. Following a series of high-profile corporate fraud cases in 2002, President George W. Bush tried to change the perception of law enforcement's "slap on the wrist" mentality toward white-collar crime by signing a bill that greatly increased the criminal penalties for a variety of types of business-related wrongdoing.[6] (See the feature *CJ in Focus—A Question of Ethics: The Boom in White-Collar Crime* on page 10.)

Organized Crime White-collar crime involves the use of legal business facilities and employees to commit illegal acts. For example, a bank teller can't embezzle unless she is hired first as a legal employee of the bank. In contrast, **organized crime** describes illegal acts by illegal organizations, usually geared toward satisfying the public's demand for unlawful goods and services. Organized crime broadly implies a conspiratorial and illegal relationship between any number of persons engaged in unlawful acts. More specifically, groups engaged in organized crime employ criminal tactics such as violence, corruption, and intimidation for economic gain. The hierarchical structure of organized crime operations often mirrors that of legitimate businesses, and, like any corporation, these groups attempt to capture a sufficient percentage of any given market to make a profit. For organized crime, the traditional preferred markets are gambling, prostitution, illegal narcotics, and loan sharking (lending money at higher-than-legal rates), along with more recent ventures into counterfeiting and credit-card scams.[7]

High-Tech Crime The newest typology of crime is directly related to the increased use of computers in everyday life. The Internet, with approximately 200 million users worldwide, is the site of numerous *cyber crimes,* such as selling

Organized Crime
A conspiratorial relationship between any number of persons engaged in the market for illegal goods or services, such as illicit drugs or firearms.

FIGURE 1.1 White-Collar Crime

Embezzlement	A form of employee fraud in which an individual uses his or her position within a corporation to *embezzle,* or steal, the corporation's money, property, or other assets.
Pilferage	A less serious form of employee fraud in which the individual steals items from the workplace.
Credit-Card and Check Fraud	The unauthorized use of credit cards costs billions of dollars annually. This form of white-collar crime involves obtaining credit-card numbers through a variety of schemes (such as stealing them from the Internet) and using the numbers for personal gain. Check fraud includes writing checks that are not covered by bank funds, forging checks, and stealing traveler's checks.
Insurance Fraud	Insurance fraud involves making false claims in order to collect insurance payments under false pretenses. Faking an injury in order to receive payments from a workers' compensation program, for example, is a form of insurance fraud.
Securities Fraud	This area covers illegal activity in the stock market. It includes stockbrokers who steal money from their clients and *insider trading,* which is the illegal trading in a stock by someone (or on behalf of someone) who has inside knowledge about the company in question.
Bribery	Also known as *influence peddling,* bribery occurs in the business world when somebody within a company sells influence, power, or information to a person outside the company who can benefit. A county official, for example, could give a construction company a lucrative county contract to build a new jail. In return, the construction company would give a sum of money, also known as a *kickback,* to the official.
Consumer Fraud	This term covers a wide variety of activities designed to defraud consumers, from selling counterfeit art to offering "free" items, such as electronic devices or vacations, that include a number of hidden charges.
Tax Evasion	The practice by which taxpayers either underreport (or do not report) their taxable income or otherwise purposely attempt to evade a tax liability.

> The Boom in White-Collar Crime

"The business pages of American news-papers should not read like a scandal sheet," lectured President George W. Bush to a group of Wall Street professionals. "At this moment America's greatest economic need is higher eth-ical standards." During the summer of 2002, it did seem as if the world of commerce was suffering from an ethical crisis. Corporate fraud involving billions of dollars had been uncovered at giant companies such as Enron, Xerox, Adelphia, and WorldCom. One in five American workers said they knew of colleagues who had lied on expense reports, stolen items from supply cabinets, accepted personal gifts from clients, or skimmed money off of cash sales. The country appeared to be suffering from an epidemic of white-collar crime, causing many to believe that we were somehow less ethical as a people than we used to be.

Such generalizations rarely tell the whole story. As we will see in the next chapter and throughout this textbook, an impor-tant aspect of understanding crime is understanding the condi-tions that contribute to criminal behavior. White-collar criminals, for example, are generally older and better educated than those who commit "street" crimes. Thus, as society ages and its edu-cational level rises—two factors that currently exist in the United States—corporate crimes should increase. Furthermore,

AP Photo/Ron Edmonds

On February 12, 2002, Kenneth Lay is sworn in before a U.S. Senate committee. Lay had been the head of the Enron Corporation, a giant energy company, when it went bankrupt in December 2001, causing thousands of shareholders in the company to lose their investments. Enron's downfall was blamed on a series of illegal and unethical business practices that provided executives such as Lay with healthy profits. The Enron scandal, along with evidence of other misdeeds in American boardrooms, created intense pressure for stricter laws punishing white-collar crime.

the Internet offers opportuni-ties for perpetrating financial crimes that were not possible even a decade ago. When com-pared with the risks that one runs in committing a petty crime such as purse snatching, stealing a credit-card number online seems a safer alternative, not to mention that, if caught, the punishment generally is less. (We will examine crime on the Internet in Chapter 17.)

FOR CRITICAL ANALYSIS
In general, the rise in the white-collar crime rate has coincided with a decline in violent and property crimes, such as assault and theft, since the late 1970s. How might the higher average age and greater educational levels in America during this time period contribute to these trends?

INFOTRAC KEYWORDS

computer crime

For more information, use this search term with InfoTrac College Edition, your online library at www.infotrac-college.com

pornographic materials, soliciting minors, and defrauding consumers with bogus financial investments. The dependence of businesses on computer operations has left corporations vulnerable to sabotage, fraud, embezzlement, and theft of pro-prietary data. (See Figure 1.2 for several types of cybercrimes.)

↗ ONLINE REVIEW *Go to the book's Web site for an interactive review of this section*

The Criminal Justice System

Defining which actions are to be labeled "crimes" is only the first step in safe-guarding society from criminal behavior. Institutions must be created to apprehend alleged wrongdoers, determine whether these persons have indeed committed crimes, and punish those who are found guilty according to society's wishes. These institutions combine to form the *criminal justice system*. As we begin our examination of the American criminal justice system in this introductory chapter, it is important to have an idea of its purpose.

See the UCLA Online Institute for Cyberspace Law and Policy for a wealth of information on cyber crimes. Find this Web site by clicking on *Web Links* under *Chapter Resources* at www.cjinaction.com

THE PURPOSE OF THE CRIMINAL JUSTICE SYSTEM

In 1967, the President's Commission on Law Enforcement and Administration of Justice stated that the criminal justice system is obliged to enforce accepted standards of conduct so as to "protect individuals and the community."[8] Given this general mandate, we can further separate the purpose of the modern criminal justice system into three general goals:

1 To control crime

2 To prevent crime

3 To provide and maintain justice

Though many observers differ on the precise methods of reaching them, the first two goals are fairly straightforward. By arresting, prosecuting, and punishing wrongdoers, the criminal justice system attempts to *control* crime. In the process, the system also hopes to *prevent* new crimes from taking place. The prevention goal is often used to justify harsh punishments for wrongdoers, which some see as deterring others from committing similar criminal acts. The third goal—of providing and maintaining justice—is more complicated, largely because *justice* is a difficult concept to define. Broadly stated, justice means that all citizens are equal before the law and that they are free from arbitrary arrest or seizure as defined by the law.[9] In other words, the idea of justice is linked with the idea of fairness. Above all, we want our laws and the means by which they are carried out to be fair.

Justice and fairness are subjective terms; different people may have different concepts of what is just and fair. If a woman who has been beaten by her husband retaliates by killing him, what is her just punishment? Reasonable persons could disagree, with some thinking that the homicide was justified and she should be treated leniently, and others insisting that she should not have taken the law into her own hands. Police officers, judges, prosecutors, prison administrators, and other employees of the criminal justice system must decide what is "fair." Sometimes, their course of action is obvious; often, as we shall see, it is not.

Society places the burden of controlling crime, preventing crime, and determining fairness on those citizens who work in the three main institutions

FIGURE 1.2 Types of Cyber Crimes

Cyber Crime against Persons

> *Obscene Material and Pornography:* The selling, posting, and distributing of obscene material such as pornography, indecent exposure, and child pornography.
> *Cyber-Stalking:* The act of using a computer and the Internet to continually attempt to contact and/or intimidate another person.
> *Cyber-Harassment:* The harassment of a person through electronic mail, on chat sites, or by printing information about the person on Web sites.

Cyber Crime against Property

> *Hacking:* The act of using programming abilities with malicious intent.
> *Cracking:* The act of using programming abilities in an attempt to gain unauthorized access to a computer or network.
> *Piracy:* Copying and distributing software or other items belonging to someone else over the Internet.
> *Viruses:* The creation and distribution of harmful computer programs.

Cyber Crime against the Government

> *Cyber-Terrorism:* The use of a computer and/or the Internet to further political goals of terrorism against a country and its citizens.

Source: Susan Brenner and Rebecca Cochran, University of Dayton School of Law at www.cybercrimes.net

of the criminal justice system: law enforcement, courts, and corrections. In the next section, we take an introductory look at these institutions and their role in the criminal justice system as a whole.

THE STRUCTURE OF THE CRIMINAL JUSTICE SYSTEM

To understand the structure of the criminal justice system, one must understand the concept of **federalism,** which means that government powers are shared by the national (federal) government and the states. The framers of the U.S. Constitution, fearful of tyranny and a too-powerful central government, chose the system of federalism as a compromise. The appeal of federalism was that it allowed for state powers and local traditions while establishing a strong national government capable of handling large-scale problems.

The Constitution gave the national government certain express powers, such as the power to coin money, raise an army, and regulate interstate commerce. All other powers were left to the states, including police power, which allows the states to enact whatever laws are necessary to protect the health, morals, safety, and welfare of their citizens. As the American criminal justice system has evolved, the ideals of federalism have ebbed somewhat; in particular, federal involvement has expanded significantly. Crime is still, however, for the most part a local concern, and the majority of all employees in the criminal justice system work for local government (see Figure 1.3).

Law Enforcement   The ideals of federalism can be clearly seen in the local, state, and federal levels of law enforcement. Though agencies from the different levels will cooperate if the need arises, they have their own organizational structures and tend to operate independently of one another. In addition to this brief introduction, each level of law enforcement will be covered in more detail in Chapters 5, 6, and 7.

Local Law Enforcement   On the local level, the duties of law enforcement agencies are split between counties and municipalities. The chief law enforcement officer of most counties is the county sheriff. The sheriff is usually an elected post, with a two- or four-year term. In some areas, where city and county governments have merged, there is a county police force, headed by a chief of police. The bulk

Federalism

A form of government in which a written constitution provides for a division of powers between a central government and several regional governments. In the United States, the division of powers between the federal government and the fifty states is established by the Constitution.

FIGURE 1.3 Local, State, and Federal Employees in Our Criminal Justice System

Source: Bureau of Justice Statistics, *Justice Expenditure and Employment Extracts, 1999* (Washington, D.C.: U.S. Department of Justice, 2002), Table 5.

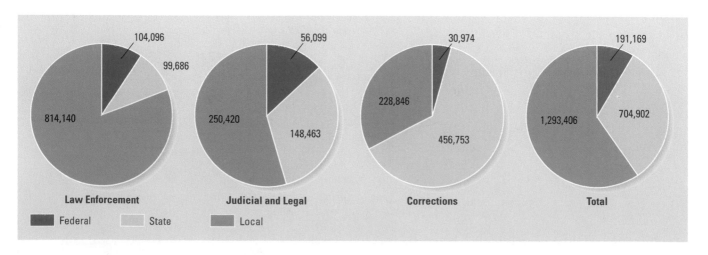

Law Enforcement — 104,096 / 99,686 / 814,140

Judicial and Legal — 56,099 / 148,463 / 250,420

Corrections — 30,974 / 228,846 / 456,753

Total — 191,169 / 704,902 / 1,293,406

■ Federal   ■ State   ■ Local

of local police officers—nearly 500,000—are employed by municipalities. The majority of these forces consist of fewer than ten officers, though a large city such as New York can have a police force of more than 35,000.

Local police are responsible for the "nuts and bolts" of law enforcement work. They investigate most crimes and attempt to deter crime through patrol activities. They apprehend criminals and participate in the trial proceedings, if necessary. Local police are also charged with "keeping the peace," a broad set of duties that includes crowd and traffic control and the resolution of minor conflicts between citizens. In many areas, local police have the added obligation of providing social services such as dealing with domestic violence and child abuse.

State Law Enforcement Hawaii is the only state that does not have a state law enforcement agency. Generally, there are two types of state law enforcement agencies, those designated simply as "state police" and those designated as "highway patrols." State highway patrols concern themselves mainly with infractions on public highways and freeways. Other state law enforcers include fire marshals, who investigate suspicious fires and educate the public on fire prevention, and fish, game, and watercraft wardens, who police a state's natural resources and often oversee its firearms laws. Some states also have alcoholic beverage control officers plus agents who investigate welfare and food stamp fraud. (To see how one state deals with the challenges of law enforcement, see the feature *CJ and Technology—Weathering the Storm in Alaska* on the following page.)

Federal Law Enforcement The creation of new national gun, drug, and violent crime laws over the past thirty years has led to an expansion in the size and scope of the federal government's participation in the criminal justice system. Federal agencies with police powers include the Federal Bureau of Investigation (FBI), the Drug Enforcement Administration (DEA), the U.S. Secret Service, and the Bureau of Alcohol, Tobacco, Firearms, and Explosives (ATF). In fact, almost every federal agency, including the postal and forest services, has some kind of police power. On November 25, 2002, President George W. Bush created the Department of Homeland Security, which combines the police powers of twenty-two federal agencies in order to protect the United States from terrorist attacks. The crucial law enforcement role of this new department will be examined in detail in Chapters 5 and 17.

The Courts The United States has a *dual court system;* that is, we have two independent judicial systems, one on the federal level and one on the state level. In practice, this translates into fifty-two different court systems: one national court system and fifty different state court systems (including the District of Columbia). The federal system consists of district courts, circuit courts of appeals, and the United States Supreme Court. The state systems include trial courts at the local and state levels, intermediate courts of appeals, and state supreme courts.

The *criminal court* and its work group—the judge, prosecutors, and defense attorneys—are charged with the weighty responsibility of determining the innocence or guilt of criminal suspects. We will cover these important participants, their role in the criminal trial, and the court system as a whole in Chapters 8, 9, 10, and 11.

> Weathering the Storm in Alaska

Few states face the law enforcement challenges found in Alaska. Covering more than 586,000 square miles, the state is filled with mountains, glaciers, millions of lakes, and thousands of rivers and has a coastline of more than 6,600 miles. Its law enforcement personnel must cope with blizzards, avalanches, and winter temperatures that average twenty degrees below zero. "Snow is a big problem," says one officer. "When everything is white, it's impossible to get your bearings." Shutter releases on cameras often stop working in the cold, severely hampering efforts to photograph crime scenes. To prevent oil and transmission fluid from freezing, police vehicles must be left running, but that makes them susceptible to theft. To make things worse, nearly 30 percent of Alaska's population lives in communities inaccessible by road or ferry, making it arduous not only to reach many locations, but also to transport suspects back to police stations.

To deal with these challenges, Alaska has the fewest law enforcement personnel of any state in the Union—around 1,200 sworn officers. As a result, many of the crime-fighting technologies that will be discussed in this textbook are crucial to police work in Alaska. Portable crime-processing kits are necessary to gather clues at remote crime scenes. Geographic information systems (GISs) allow officials to "map crime" and place resources where they are most needed. Satellite tracking and electronic monitoring permit correctional officials to supervise nonviolent criminals in their own communities, saving the cost and trouble of transporting them to, and housing them in, jails. Finally, using thermal imaging devices that measure heat, officers can "see" in the dark and through snowstorms. "If it's thirty-eight below and a moose walks through town," notes the police chief of Wasilla, Alaska, "we can find the heat signature in the snow two hours later."

Photo courtesy of the Alaska State Troopers

To cover a territory one-fifth the size of the continental United States, the Alaska State Troopers, pictured here, must rely on a variety of forms of transportation. Many isolated communities can be reached only by airplane or snowmobile. Obviously, environment plays a large role in law enforcement on a state and local level.

In the Future

One of the greatest difficulties in policing large areas such as Alaska is communication. If various agencies are not able to transfer information to one another, the quality of law enforcement will inevitably suffer. Alaska is in the process of creating an integrated criminal justice information system that will connect police departments, courts, district attorneys' offices, probation departments, and social services agencies, allowing them to exchange data no matter how geographically isolated they may be.

 For more information on hi-tech police gear and other CJ technologies, click on Crime and Technology under Book Resources at www.cjinaction.com

Corrections Once the court system convicts and sentences an offender, she or he is delegated to the corrections system. Depending on the seriousness of the crime and their individual needs, offenders are placed on probation, incarcerated, or transferred to community-based corrections facilities.

> *Probation,* the most common correctional treatment, allows the offender to return to the community and remain under the supervision of an agent of the court known as a probation officer. While on probation, the offender must follow certain rules of conduct. If probationers fail to follow these rules, they may be incarcerated.

> If the offender's sentence includes a period of incarceration, he or she will be remanded to a corrections facility for a certain amount of time. *Jails* hold

> Patrick Connolly | Supervisory Special Agent, FBI Coordinator, Joint Terrorism Task Force

In the course of my 23 years with the Federal Bureau of Investigation, I've held many jobs with many titles, with my most recent being Supervisory Special Agent and Coordinator for the Joint Terrorism Task Force. The FBI clearly has an important mission to prevent another attack like that of September 11, 2001, which is why the antiterrorism function of the Bureau is so important. However, the FBI is not alone in this mission. In fact, the Joint Terrorism Task Force includes representatives from more than 30 agencies—including federal, state, and local intelligence and law enforcement agencies.

The training of the FBI members selected for the task force is not different from the standard training. The Special Agents go through 15 to 16 weeks of training at the FBI Academy at the U.S. Marine Corps base at Quantico, Virginia. I went through the Academy early in my career but now the training has been refocused to increase the emphasis on international terrorism issues. There is also a great deal of emphasis on providing timely and relevant training on current terrorism issues to all members of the task force.

In my work with the Bureau, I've been responsible for investigations in every area of FBI jurisdiction—including terrorism, organized crime, drugs/alien smuggling, violent crime, white-collar crime, and civil rights. Most of these investigations were long term and targeted criminal enterprises. We used sophisticated investigative techniques, such as wiretaps and undercover operations. In addition, I've served as a hostage negotiator, police instructor, legal adviser, and crisis management coordinator.

I also oversaw our FBI Detainee operation at the military prison at the U.S. Naval Base at Guantanamo Bay, Cuba. There, hundreds of individuals who had been involved with the Taliban and the war in Afghanistan were detained for questioning. Working at Guantanamo made it especially clear to me how important the FBI's role was in preventing attacks in the U.S., although there has since been controversy over the appropriateness of detaining so many for so long. A key challenge in the area of antiterrorism is to balance individual liberties with national security. This is always a fine line but I feel that the FBI in general and the Joint Terrorism Task Forces in particular have been very successful at achieving that balance.

My background includes a law degree (J.D.) and experience working as a prosecutor in Howard County, Maryland. Before that, I had spent about seven years in other jobs and two years in the Army. All of these experiences helped me in making the career switch from attorney to FBI Special Agent.

What is the hardest part about my job? Paperwork can be a challenge since everything has to be so carefully documented. You may eventually have to turn over records for legal proceedings. Also, all FBI employees are subject to a high level of scrutiny by FBI management, the judiciary, the media, and Congress.

Patrick Connolly

What advice would I give a job seeker looking for a position in the FBI?

Get a college degree in any subject that interests you because the FBI is looking for individuals with expertise in a wide range of areas. For example, if you're interested in fields that range from criminal justice, biology, psychology, to business administration, there are relevant jobs in the FBI. Also, if you're especially interested in terrorism, you can access much unclassified information to educate yourself. For example, just exploring the Web will yield much information about terrorist groups, ideologies, and tactics. Of course, it's necessary to evaluate this material carefully, and to use a variety of resources.

Most positions in the FBI now require at least a Bachelor's Degree and three years of full-time related experience. However, given the number of applicants for each position, you would have a better chance with a Master's Degree. You must also have the highest ethics not only because that's a core value, but you may end up testifying under oath at a trial.

Overall, I have found the job very fulfilling. Every day is different and the FBI is involved in important matters ranging from informing policy on a national level to vindicating victims. I retired very recently from the FBI and now teach Administration of Justice at MiraCosta College in Oceanside, California.

 Go to the Careers in Criminal Justice Interactive CD *for more profiles in the field of criminal justice.*

those convicted of minor crimes with relatively short sentences, as well as those awaiting trial or involved in certain court proceedings. *Prisons* house those convicted of more serious crimes with longer sentences. Generally speaking, counties and municipalities administer jails, while prisons are the domain of federal and state governments.

> *Community-based corrections* have increased in popularity, as jails and prisons have been plagued with problems of overcrowding. Community-based correctional facilities include halfway houses, residential centers, and work-release centers; they operate on the assumption that all convicts do not need, and are not benefited by, incarceration in jail or prison.

The majority of those inmates released from incarceration are not finished with the correctional system. The most frequent type of release from a jail or prison is *parole,* in which an inmate, after serving part of his or her sentence in a correctional facility, is allowed to serve the rest of the term in the community. Like someone on probation, a parolee must conform to certain conditions of freedom, with the same consequences if these conditions are not followed. Issues of probation, incarceration, community-based corrections, and parole will be covered in Chapters 12, 13, and 14.

THE CRIMINAL JUSTICE PROCESS

In its 1967 report, the President's Commission on Law Enforcement and Administration of Justice asserted that the criminal justice system

> is not a hodgepodge of random actions. It is rather a continuum—an orderly progression of events—some of which, like arrest and trial, are highly visible and some of which, though of great importance, occur out of public view.[10]

The commission's assertion that the criminal justice system is a "continuum" is one that many observers would challenge.[11] Some liken the criminal justice system to a sports team, which is the sum of an indeterminable number of decisions, relationships, conflicts, and adjustments.[12] Such a volatile mix is not what we generally associate with a "system." For most, the word *system* indicates a certain degree of order and discipline. That we refer to our law enforcement agencies, courts, and correctional facilities as part of a "system" may reflect our hopes rather than reality.

Just as there is an idealized image of the criminal justice system as a smooth continuum, there also exists an idealized version of the *criminal justice process,* or the procedures through which the criminal justice system meets the expectations of society. Professor Herbert Packer, for example, compared the idealized criminal justice process to an assembly line,

> down which moves an endless stream of cases, never stopping, carrying the cases to workers who stand at fixed stations and who perform on each case as it comes by the same small but essential operation that brings it one stop closer to being a finished product, or, to exchange the metaphor for the reality, a closed file.[13]

As Packer himself was wont to point out, the daily operations of criminal justice are not nearly so perfect. In this textbook, the criminal justice process will be examined as the end product of literally thousands of decisions made by the police, courtroom workers, and correctional administrators. It should become clear that, in fact, the criminal justice process functions as a continuous balancing act between its formal and informal nature, both of which are discussed below.

The Formal Criminal Justice Process   In Packer's image of assembly-line justice, each step of the process "involves a series of routinized operations whose success is gauged primarily by their tendency to pass the case along to a successful conclusion."[14] These "routinized" steps are detailed in the fold-out poster in this chapter.

The Informal Criminal Justice Process Each step described in the fold-out poster is the result of a series of decisions that must be made by those who work in the criminal justice system. This **discretion**—which can be defined as the authority to choose between and among alternative courses of action—leads to the development of the informal criminal justice process, discussed below.

Patrick Downs/Los Angeles Times

Discretionary Basics One New York City public defender called his job "a pressure cooker." That term could apply to the entire spectrum of the criminal justice process. Law enforcement agencies do not have the staff or money to investigate *every* crime; they must decide where to direct their restricted resources. Increasing caseloads and a limited amount of time with which to dispose of them constrict many of our nation's courts. Overcrowding in prisons and jails affects both law enforcement agencies and the courts—there is simply not enough room for all convicts.

The criminal justice system uses discretion to alleviate these pressures. Police decide whether to arrest a suspect; prosecutors decide whether to prosecute; magistrates decide whether there is sufficient probable cause for a case to go to a jury; judges decide on sentencing; and so on. (See Figure 1.4 on page 18 for a rundown of some of the most important discretionary decisions.) Collectively, these decisions are said to produce an *informal criminal justice system* because discretion is informally exercised by the individual and is not enclosed by the rigid confines of the law. Even if prosecutors believe that a suspect is guilty, they may decide not to prosecute if the case is weak or if they know that the police erred in the investigative process. In most cases, prosecutors will not squander the scarce resource of court time on a case they might not win. Some argue that the informal process has made our criminal justice system more just. Given the immense pressure of limited resources, the argument goes, only rarely will an innocent person end up before a judge and jury.[15]

Of course, not all discretionary decisions are dictated by the scarcity of resources. Sometimes, discretion is based on political considerations, such as when a police administrator orders a crackdown on public order crimes because of citizen complaints. Furthermore, employees of the criminal justice system may make decisions based on their personal values or morality, which, depending on what those personal and moral values are, may make the system less just in the eyes of some observers. For that reason, discretion is closely connected to questions of *ethics* in criminal justice and will be discussed in that context throughout this textbook.

Although discretion is absolutely necessary in the criminal justice system, it can be abused. Several years ago, Damien "Pookie" Burris, above with his young son, spent more than five months in a Los Angeles jail for a murder he did not commit. Witnesses to the killing said the assailant was nicknamed "Pookie," and, after several identified Burris from mug shots, he was arrested by the police. Burris claimed he was in church at the time of the murder, an alibi detectives chose not to validate. In fact, it took the discretionary intervention of a patrol officer to prove that Burris had in fact been in church and the police had arrested the wrong "Pookie." How can criminal justice procedure be seen as a system of "checks and balances" in which discretionary errors are eventually corrected?

Discretion
The ability of individuals in the criminal justice system to make operational decisions based on personal judgment instead of formal rules or official information.

FIGURE 1.4 Discretion in the Criminal Justice System

Criminal justice officials must make decisions every day concerning their duties. The following officials must decide whether or not to make the following decisions, or how to make them.

Police	> Enforce laws
	> Investigate specific crimes
	> Search people or buildings
	> Arrest or detain people
Prosecutors	> File charges against suspects brought to them by the police
	> Drop cases
	> Reduce charges
Judges	> Set conditions for pretrial release
	> Accept pleas
	> Dismiss charges
	> Impose sentences
Correctional Officials	> Assign convicts to prison or jail
	> Punish prisoners who misbehave
	> Reward prisoners who behave well

Source: U.S. Department of Justice, Bureau of Justice Statistics, *Report to the Nation on Crime and Justice,* 2d ed. (Washington, D.C.: Government Printing Office, 1988), 59.

"Wedding Cake" Model

A wedding cake-shaped model that explains why different cases receive different treatment in the criminal justice system. The cases at the "top" of the cake receive the most attention and have the greatest effect on public perception of criminal justice, while those cases at the "bottom" are disposed of quickly and virtually ignored by the media.

Felony

A serious crime punishable by death or by imprisonment in a federal or state corrections facility for more than a year.

Misdemeanor

Any crime that is not a felony; punishable by a fine or by confinement for up to a year.

The "Wedding Cake" Model of Criminal Justice

Some believe that the prevailing informal approach to criminal justice creates a situation in which all cases are not treated equally. They point to the highly publicized O. J. Simpson trial of 1994, during which the defendant was treated differently than most double-murder suspects. To describe this effect, criminal justice researchers Lawrence M. Friedman and Robert V. Percival came up with a **"wedding cake" model** of criminal justice.[16] This model posits that discretion comes to bear depending on the relative importance of a particular case to the decision makers. Like any wedding cake, Friedman and Percival's model has the smallest layer at the top and the largest at the bottom (see Figure 1.5).

1   The "top" layer consists of a handful of "celebrity" cases that attract the most attention and publicity. Recent examples of top level cases include the trials of Scott Peterson, accused of murdering his pregnant wife Laci; John Muhammad, the Washington, D.C., area sniper suspect; and professional basketball player Kobe Bryant charged with rape.

2   The second layer consists of "high-profile" felonies. A **felony** is a serious crime such as murder, rape, or burglary that in most states is punishable either by death or by incarceration for a period longer than one year. This layer includes crimes committed by persons with criminal records, crimes in which the victim was seriously injured, and crimes in which a weapon was used, as well as crimes in which the offender and victim were strangers. These types of felonies are considered "high profile" because they usually draw a certain amount of public attention, which places pressure on the prosecutors to bring the case to trial instead of accepting a guilty plea for a lesser sentence.

3   The third layer consists of "ordinary" felonies, which include less violent crimes such as burglaries and thefts or even robberies in which no weapon was used. Because of the low profile of the accused—usually a first-time offender who has had a prior relationship with his or her victim—these "ordinary" felonies often do not receive the full formal process of a trial.

4   Finally, the fourth layer consists of **misdemeanors,** or crimes less serious than felonies. Misdemeanors include petty offenses such as shoplifting, disturbing the peace, and violations of local ordinances; they are usually punishable by fines, probation, or short jail times. More than three-quarters of all arrests made by police are for misdemeanors.

The irony of the wedding cake model is that the cases on the top level come closest to meeting our standards of ideal criminal justice. In these celebrity trials, we get to see committed (and expensive) attorneys argue minute technicalities of the law, sometimes for days on end. The further one moves down the layers of the cake, the more informal the process becomes. Though many of the cases in the second layer are brought to trial, only rarely does this occur for the less serious felonies in the third level of the wedding cake. By the fourth level, cases are dealt with almost completely informally, and the end goal appears to be speed rather than what can be called "justice."

Public fascination with celebrity cases obscures a truth of the informal criminal justice process: trial by jury is relatively rare (only about 3 percent of those arrested for felonies go to trial), and most cases are disposed of with an eye more toward convenience than ideals of justice or fairness. Consequently, the summary of the criminal justice system provided by the wedding cake model is much more realistic than the impression many Americans have obtained from the media.

↗ ONLINE REVIEW *Go to the book's Web site for an interactive review of this section*

FIGURE 1.5
The Wedding Cake Model

Values of the Criminal Justice System

If the general conclusion of the wedding cake model—that some defendants are treated differently than others—bothers you, then you probably question the values of the system. Just as individuals have values—a belief structure governing individual conduct—our criminal justice system can be said to have values, too. These values form the foundation for Herbert Packer's two models of the criminal justice system.

CRIME CONTROL AND DUE PROCESS: TO PUNISH OR PROTECT?

In his landmark book, *The Limits of the Criminal Sanction,* Packer introduced two models for the American criminal justice system: the crime control model and the due process model.[17] The underlying value of the crime control model is that the most important function of the criminal justice process is to punish and repress criminal conduct. Though not in direct conflict with crime control, the underlying values of the due process model focus more on protecting the rights of the accused through legal constraints on police, courts, and corrections.

The Crime Control Model   Under the **crime control model,** law enforcement must be counted on to control criminal activity. "Controlling" criminal activity is at best difficult, and probably impossible. For the crime control model to operate successfully, Packer writes, it

> must produce a high rate of apprehension and conviction, and must do so in a context where the magnitudes being dealt with are very large and the resources for dealing with them are very limited.[18]

In other words, the system must be quick and efficient. In the ideal crime control model, any suspect who most likely did not commit a crime is quickly jettisoned from the system, while those who are transferred to the trial process are convicted as quickly as possible. It was in this context that Packer referred to the criminal justice process as an assembly line.

The crime control model also assumes that the police are in a better position than the courts to determine the guilt of arrested suspects. Therefore, not only should

Crime Control Model
A criminal justice model that places primary emphasis on the right of society to be protected from crime and violent criminals. Crime control values emphasize speed and efficiency in the criminal justice process; the benefits of lower crime rates outweigh any possible costs to individual rights.

judges operate on a "presumption of guilt" (that is, any suspect brought before the court is more likely guilty than not), but as few restrictions as possible should be placed on police investigative and fact-gathering activities. The crime control model relies on the informality in the criminal justice system, as discussed earlier.

Due Process Model

A criminal justice model that places primacy on the right of the individual to be protected from the power of the government. Due process values hold that the state must prove a person's guilt within the confines of a process designed to safeguard personal liberties as enumerated in the Bill of Rights.

The Due Process Model   Packer likened the **due process model** to an obstacle course rather than an assembly line. Rather than expediting cases through the system, as is preferable in the crime control model, the due process model strives to make it more difficult to prove guilt. It rests on the belief that it is more desirable for society that ninety-nine guilty suspects go free than that a single innocent person be condemned.[19]

The due process model is based on the assumption that the absolute efficiency that is the goal of the crime control model can be realized only if the power of the state is absolute. Because fairness, and not efficiency, is the ultimate goal of the due process model, it rejects the idea of a criminal justice system with unlimited powers. As a practical matter, the model also argues that human error in any process is inevitable; therefore, the criminal justice system should recognize its own fallibility and take all measures necessary to ensure that this fallibility does not impinge on the rights of citizens.

Finally, whereas the crime control model relies heavily on the police, the due process model relies just as heavily on the courts and their role in upholding the legal procedures of establishing guilt. The due process model is willing to accept that a person who is factually guilty will go free if the criminal justice system does not follow legally prescribed procedures in proving her or his culpability.[20] Therefore, the due process model relies on formality in the criminal justice system. *Mastering Concepts* compares and contrasts the two models.

WHICH MODEL PREVAILS TODAY?

Though both the crime control and the due process models have always been present to a certain degree, during different time periods one has taken precedence over the other. The twentieth century saw an ebb and flow between them. The influx of immigrants and problems of urbanization in the early 1900s caused somewhat of a panic among the American upper class. Considering that most, if not all, politicians and legal theorists were members of this class, it not surprising that crime control principles prevailed during the first half of the century.

As the nation became more secure and prosperous in the 1950s and 1960s, a "due process revolution" took place. Under the leadership of Chief Justice Earl Warren, the United States Supreme Court significantly expanded the rights of the accused. Following a series of landmark cases that will be referred to throughout this textbook (some of which are featured in the timeline on the back of the fold out poster at the end of this chapter), suspected offenders were guaranteed, among other things, that an attorney would be provided to them by the state if they could not afford one,[21] and that they would be notified of their right to remain silent and retain counsel on being arrested.[22] The 1960s also saw severe limits placed on the power of the police, as the Court required law enforcement officers to strictly follow specific guidelines on gathering evidence or risk having that evidence invalidated.[23]

Rising crime rates in the late 1970s and early 1980s led to increased pressure on politicians and judges to get "tough on crime." This certainly slowed down the

> Crime Control Model versus Due Process Model

CRIME CONTROL MODEL	DUE PROCESS MODEL
Goals of the Criminal Justice System:	**Goals of the Criminal Justice System**
> Deter crime.	> Protect the individual against the immense power of the state.
> Protect citizens from crime.	> Rehabilitate those convicted of crimes.
> Incapacitate criminals.	
> Provide quick and efficient justice.	
Goals Can Best Be Met by:	**Goals Can Best Be Met by:**
> Promoting discretion and limiting bureaucratic red tape in criminal justice institutions.	> Limiting state power by assuring the constitutional rights of the accused.
> Making it easier for police to arrest criminals.	> Providing even guilty offenders with full protection of the law, and allowing those offenders to go free if due process procedures are not followed.
> Reducing legal restrictions on proving guilt in a criminal trial.	> Assuring that all accused criminals receive the same treatment from the law, regardless of class, race, gender, or sexual orientation.
	> Protecting the civil rights of prisoners.
Favored Policies	**Favored Policies**
> More police.	> Open the criminal justice process to scrutiny by the media and public.
> More jails and prisons.	> Abolish the death penalty.
> Harsher penalties (including increased use of the death penalty) and longer sentences.	> Limit police powers to arbitrarily search, interrogate, and seize criminal suspects.
	> Limit discretion and formalize criminal justice procedures so that all suspects and convicted offenders receive the same treatment.
	> Increase funding for rehabilitation and education programs in jails and prisons.
View of Criminality	**View of Criminality**
> Wrongdoers are responsible for their own actions.	> Criminal behavior can be attributed to social and biological factors.
> Wrongdoers have violated the social contract and can therefore be deprived of many of the rights afforded to law-abiding citizens.	> Criminals can be rehabilitated and returned to the community.
Case in Point	**Case in Point**
> *Ohio v. Robinette* (519 U.S. 33 [1996]), which allows police greater freedom to search the automobile of a driver stopped for speeding.	> *Mapp v. Ohio* (367 U.S. 643 [1961]), which invalidates evidence improperly gathered by the police, even if the evidence proves the suspect's guilt.

due process revolution and perhaps returned the principles of the crime control model to our criminal justice system. In 1984, for example, three Supreme Court cases restored to police some of the freedoms they had enjoyed in the first half of the century. Even if evidence was obtained illegally, the Court ruled, it could be admitted at trial if the police officers could prove they would have obtained the evidence legally anyway.[24] Furthermore, the Court created the "good faith" exception to evidence-gathering rules, which basically allowed illegally obtained evidence to be admitted if the police officers were unaware that they were acting unconstitutionally.[25] According to many criminal law experts, this trio of cases resulted in the values of crime control gaining undue leverage.[26] (The role of the Bill of Rights in determining police power will be covered in Chapter 7.)

The values of the criminal justice system are reflected not only in court decisions, but also in public policy. Six weeks after the September 11, 2001, terrorist attacks, President George W. Bush signed the USA Patriot Act into law.[27] In an effort to prevent future strikes, the new law strengthens the ability of federal law enforcement agencies to investigate and incarcerate suspects; thus, it represents a dramatic shift toward the crime control model. The USA Patriot Act has, as we shall see in Chapter 17, been strongly criticized as going "too far" and endangering the due process rights of many Americans. If these measures do indeed represent the will of the public, as expressed by its elected officials, crime control values will continue to dominate the criminal justice system in the immediate future.

↗ ONLINE REVIEW *Go to the book's Web site for an interactive review of this section*

Trends and Issues in Criminal Justice Today

In this textbook, we will concentrate on the structural and theoretical aspects of the criminal justice system. We cannot lose sight, however, of the system's place in the "real world"—how it affects and is affected by the citizens it serves. This final section of the introductory chapter offers a preview of the trends and issues that dominate the crime debate and thus provide the context in which the criminal justice system operates.

THE RETURN OF CRIME

"Crime is like cutting grass," a politician once noted. "Just because you cut it down doesn't mean that it's going to stay there."[28] To continue the metaphor, it appears time to get out the lawn mower, as crime rates have begun to rise for the first time in more than a decade. Indeed, perhaps the most significant trend in criminal justice in the 1990s was the decline in crime rates. The murder rate dropped nearly 50 percent from 1992 to 1999, and the overall rate of serious crimes declined each year during that span.[29]

Then, according to data gathered by the FBI, in 2000 crime rates remained steady, causing some observers to predict that the crime drop had ended.[30] The forecasts proved correct. Violent crime rates rose 2 percent in 2001, the first major increase since the early 1990s.[31] The overall rates dropped by less than 1 percent in 2002, though rapes, burglaries, and homicides continued to escalate. As we shall learn in Chapter 2, experts who study crime rates, known as criminologists, have a number of theories as to why crime rates rise and fall. Many believe that the recent upturn can be attributed to a slow economy and the rising number (about 600,000 in 2002) of inmates released from prison—a segment of the population with a relatively high probability of committing crimes.[32] While not losing sight of the fact that the crime rate is still quite low compared to the peak year of 1992, criminal justice professionals believe that the system should prepare for a period of higher crime rates. "The great 1990s crime drop ended with the 1990s," says James Alan Fox, a professor of criminal justice at Northeastern University. "[W]e can't be complacent about crime levels. We have to reintensify our efforts."[33]

JUVENILE CRIME: HOW BAD IS IT?

Many criminologists believe that demographics have a significant effect on crime levels, and they point to the growing teen-age male population in this country as a possible danger signal. About 17 percent of all persons arrested for violent crimes each year in the United States are juveniles, making them the age group most likely to be involved in such crimes.[34] Like general crime rates, however, juvenile arrest rates declined sharply in the 1990s; the number of juveniles arrested for murder in 2002 was about one-third what it was in 1993.[35]

This is not to say that juvenile wrongdoing has become any less important to our criminal justice system. Because juvenile offenders often become adult criminals, preventing delinquency is a crucial aspect of crime prevention strategies. We will devote Chapter 15 to the subject of juvenile justice, paying particular attention to the problem of youth gangs. Even as other indicators of juvenile criminal activity have dropped or remained level, the number of youths involved with gangs and gang-related crime has consistently risen, particularly in the nation's largest cities.[36]

Fifteen-year-old Andy Williams appears in El Cajon Superior Court on March 26, 2001, in El Cajon, California. Williams went on a shooting spree at Santana High School in Santee, California, killing two and injuring thirteen. Does this single incident reflect growing rates of juvenile crime in the early 2000s?

FEAR OF CRIME

In the mid-1990s, public worries about a sharp spike in juvenile criminal activity were spurred by the use of the catch phrase "superpredator" to describe the new breed of young criminals. As a result of these concerns, a number of states passed laws making it easier to prosecute juveniles as adults and send convicted juveniles to adult prisons and jails. Today, although the "superpredator" theory has been largely discredited, the juvenile justice system is still marked by a willingness to treat juvenile offenders as adult criminals,[37] as we shall see in Chapter 15.

Thus, fear of crime can have a significant effect on public policy, even when the fear is based on a faulty assumption. Indeed, fear of crime has often operated independently of crime data. For example, even after nearly a decade of declining crime rates, more Americans were afraid to walk through their neighborhoods in 2000 than in 1999, and one in six admitted to curtailing normal activities because of fear of crime.[38]

Media and Fear Most academic discussions of the public's fear of crime begin with the role of the media. More than half a century ago, when the modern media were in their infancy, researcher Edwin H. Sutherland noted the ability of mass communications to increase fear through the dissemination of publicity.[39] The propensity of the media—especially television—to condense any act into its most graphic aspects without providing any context has had a much-discussed effect on public perception. For example, polls show that most parents believe that random shootings are a serious threat to their children's safety at school. In fact, as we shall see in Chapter 15, the chances of a student being injured by gunfire at school are minuscule. A report by the Building Blocks for Youth singles out intense coverage of school shootings as having a particularly strong effect on perceptions of juvenile crime.[40]

"The fear of burglars is not only the fear of being robbed, but also the fear of a sudden and unexpected clutch out of the darkness."
—Elias Canetti,
Austrian novelist (1962)

INFOTRAC KEYWORDS

risk and criminal victimization

For more information, use these search terms with InfoTrac College Edition, your online library at www.infotrac-college.com

The media can also distort reality by the subjects they choose to cover. One survey of a hundred local news programs found that seventy-two began their broadcasts with a crime-related story and that one-third of all stories concerned crime or crime control.[41] Widespread coverage of violence on such local programs can have a particularly strong effect on fear of crime, as it gives viewers the impression that their communities are unsafe.[42]

Crisis Situations and Fear   Are Americans being manipulated into an irrational fear of crime? Not necessarily. Especially during high-stress situations, rising levels of fear are to be expected, as are changes in behavior.[43] During the 2001 anthrax attacks, for example, when the poison was delivered via letters, many people were afraid to open their mail. In 2002 and 2003, a number of women in Baton Rouge, Louisiana, stopped leaving their homes, began carrying Mace in their purses, and even dyed their hair blonde to avoid being the victim of a serial killer who targeted brunettes. Thousands of residents of Washington, D.C., Maryland, and Virginia took evasive measures to lessen the risk of encountering the snipers who terrorized that area in the fall of 2002.

In each of these situations, the fear of being victimized by the particular crime was out of proportion to the actual risk of being a victim. In fact, the risk was much less than that posed by everyday activities. Every year, more than 13,000 Americans die falling out of a bed, chair, or other piece of furniture, and almost 1,000 are fatally electrocuted at home.[44] It is unlikely, however, that we will stop sleeping in beds or plugging in television sets. "We don't like risks that are imposed on us, versus risks that we take on our own," points out Baruch Fischoff, an expert in risk perception at Carnegie Mellon University.[45] Crime is most certainly a risk that is imposed on us, and thus we feel more vulnerable to it.

THE TERRORIST THREAT

Of course, the terrorist attacks on New York and Washington, D.C., on September 11, 2001, introduced a type of fear into the daily lives of many Americans that they had never before experienced. Broadly defined as the random use of staged violence at infrequent intervals to achieve political goals, **terrorism** has traditionally been viewed by most Americans as an international, not a local, problem. The 2001 attacks certainly changed that perception. Gun and ammunition sales rose nearly 10 percent in the three months after the attack, reflecting the belief of many citizens that protection against terrorist threats starts at home.[46] (In fact, one Maine lawyer stored 81 guns, 20,000 rounds of ammunition, hand grenades, and rocket launchers in his basement to fight off any invaders.)

Fear of a terrorist attack has had other, far-reaching consequences. Public opinion polls show considerable support for measures that, before September 11, 2001, would have struck many as being overly intrusive into the privacy rights of Americans. Such measures include more power for law enforcement agents to listen in on phone conversations and greater access to personal computer systems. Given the focus on Arab or Muslim males in the wake of the attacks, members of this group have found themselves the particular target of efforts by the FBI and other law enforcement agencies. These and other antiterrorist strategies threaten many basic civil liberties, and the question of how to balance security and personal freedom will

Terrorism
The use or threat of violence to achieve political objectives.

See Foundations of Inquiry: Terrorism for information concerning federal, state, local, and international efforts to combat terrorism. Find this Web site by clicking on *Web Links* under *Chapter Resources* at www.cjinaction.com

be addressed throughout this textbook, particularly in Chapters 5 and 17. The impact that efforts to combat terrorism have had on the criminal justice system is the subject of the *Criminal Justice in Action* feature at the end of this chapter.

NEW DIRECTIONS IN LAW ENFORCEMENT

Of all the segments of the criminal justice system, the law enforcement community was most affected by the events of September 11, 2001. To a certain extent, those attacks served as a "wake-up call" for those agencies and individuals whose duty it is to thwart future attacks while at the same time fighting conventional crime. Law enforcement agencies are searching for new strategies to help them become more efficient at fighting domestic and international crime. Increasingly, officials are turning to the following three approaches to achieve that goal:

> *Cooperation.* One of the greatest hindrances to effective crime fighting has been the unwillingness of federal, state, and local law enforcement agencies to cooperate with each other. In the past several years, however, federal agencies such as the FBI and the Central Intelligence Agency (CIA) have begun sharing information to a much greater extent, and "antiterrorist task forces" combining federal, state, and local police agents have become popular. Databases have allowed agencies to share important information with each other as well.

> *Globalization.* With American security being threatened by persons and groups that operate outside our borders, law enforcement agencies have been forced to broaden the scope of their operations. The FBI has engaged in numerous searches for terrorist suspects in countries such as Pakistan and Afghanistan, while New York City police officers have been assigned to the Middle East to protect New York from future attacks.

> *Militarization.* For most of this nation's history, the idea of the U.S. military becoming involved in crime prevention has been rejected as improper, dangerous, and even unconstitutional. Now, however, the "war" against terrorism has led to a reconsideration of this stance, though many observers are still uneasy with the prospect of a military police force.

AP Photo/Carmen Taylor

The moment of impact as United Airlines Flight 175 crashes into the World Trade Center south tower at 9:03 on the morning of September 11, 2001. To the left, the World Trade Center north tower burns after being hit by American Airlines Flight 11 approximately fifteen minutes earlier. The New York City landmarks would eventually collapse. This attack, along with a simultaneous one on the Pentagon in Washington, D.C., cost more than three thousand lives and brought the horrors of terrorism into the lives of all Americans. What freedoms do you think the nation would be willing to give up to prevent such attacks in the future?

The general motto of the American police is "To protect and serve." As one observer noted, in the past several decades, with the advent of community policing, the emphasis has been placed on the "serve" portion of the motto.[47] Since September 11, 2001, the emphasis appears to have shifted, with protection moving to the forefront. In Chapters 4 and 5, we will examine the community policing "revolution" of the 1980s and 1990s and discuss how the three factors mentioned above, among others, represent a "counterrevolutionary" force in law enforcement.

STAYING TOUGH: CRIME AND PUNISHMENT

While law enforcement agencies have recently moved to "get tough on crime," our nation's courts—prompted by our lawmakers—have been heading in that direction for nearly two decades. During that time, the federal government and a majority of states have passed tough new sentencing laws. Discussed in detail in Chapter 11, these laws include "three-strikes-and-you're-out" statutes, which require judges to sentence those persons convicted of a third crime to life imprisonment, and other mandatory sentencing laws, which place a floor on the length of a sentence for a particular crime.

Alone among Western nations, the United States also continues to rely on the death penalty as punishment for the most heinous crimes. By August 2003, the government had executed 273 convicts in the new century. Opposition to capital punishment is at its highest levels since the 1970s, however, and in Chapter 11 we will discuss important legal and social changes that threaten the death penalty as we know it.

THE GROWING PRISON POPULATION

The mandatory sentences mentioned in the section above have contributed to one of the most consistent trends in the criminal justice system—a steadily rising number of inmates in American prisons and jails. As Figure 1.6 shows, the prisoner population in this country has increased steadily for the past twenty years, reaching its latest peak of 2.1 million in 2002. Tough sentencing laws are only one reason experts offer for this increase. More stringent laws against illegal drugs—addressed in Chapter 16—have also had a large impact. In fact, drug offenders now represent more than half of all inmates in federal prisons.[48]

FIGURE 1.6
Prison and Jail Populations in the United States, 1985–2002

Sources: Bureau of Justice Statistics, *Correctional Populations in the United States, 1995* (Washington, D.C.: U.S. Department of Justice, June 1997), Table 1.1, page 12; and Bureau of Justice Statistics, *Prison and Jail Inmates at Midyear 2002* (Washington, D.C.: U.S. Department of Justice, March 2003), Table 1, page 2.

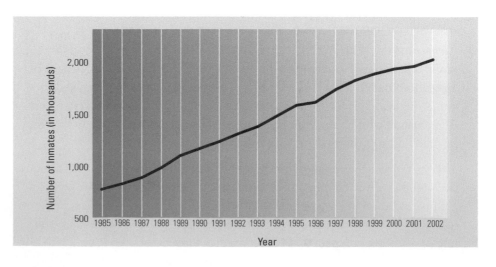

During the 1990s, states and the federal government were willing to spend seemingly limitless amounts to house the steady flow of inmates. The bleaker economic climate of the 2000s, however, has had a dampening effect on the prison boom. Keeping a person incarcerated is not a cheap proposition, with construction costs of a prison cell at $100,000 and annual housing, feeding, and caring for an inmate reaching $200,000.[49] A number of states have decided to grant early release to nonviolent prisoners, not because of a change in the political climate, but because their budgets cannot accommodate "tough-on-crime" public policies. We will examine our nation's prison and jail situation and the ramifications of this new form of leniency in Chapters 13 and 14.

INFOTRAC KEYWORDS

prison population

For more information, use this search term with InfoTrac College Edition, your online library at www.infotrac-college.com

QUESTIONS OF RACE AND GENDER

One of the most disturbing aspects of the boom in our prison population is that it seems to be disproportionately affecting African American males. Even though blacks make up only 13 percent of the general population in the United States, the number of black men in state and federal prisons (586,700) is significantly greater than the number of white men (436,800).[50] Furthermore, about 10 percent of all black men in this country between 25 and 29 years of age were in prison or jail in 2002, compared with 1.2 percent of white men and 2.4 percent of Hispanic men of that age.[51]

Even with those somewhat staggering figures, African American males are not the fastest-growing demographic group of the inmate population. That dubious honor goes to women. Since 1980, the number of women in prison has increased nearly twice as quickly as that of men. That year, there were about 12,300 women in state and federal prisons; by 2002, that number had spiked to 96,000.[52] Many different criminal justice experts have many different theories on why the incarceration rates of African Americans and women behave in such dramatic fashion. We will investigate a number of these theories throughout this textbook, particularly in Chapter 11 when we discuss sentencing policies.

TECHNOLOGY: FIGHTING AND FUELING CRIME

Finally, as technology has become more advanced, high-tech crime has become big business. According to the annual Computer Crime and Security Survey, 90 percent of large corporations and governmental organizations polled reported that the security of their computer systems had been breached within the past year, with 80 percent suffering financial losses as a result.[53] The Internet has become a veritable web of criminal activity, as users have learned to take advantage of the anonymity and access it provides as cover for illegal drug and weapon sales, terrorist activity, gambling, and child pornography. In 2002, an estimated $36.5 billion was spent on black market Internet activity, compared to $39.3 billion spent by consumers in the United States on legitimate online transactions.[54]

At the same time, however, technology offers law enforcement agents a wealth of crime-fighting devices to combat both high-tech and conventional crime. Almost every chapter of this textbook will contain some information on technology and the criminal justice system, and we will explore the subject in great depth in Chapter 17.

ONLINE REVIEW *Go to the book's Web site for an interactive review of this section*

> Criminal Justice and the War against Terrorism

I t would be difficult to overestimate the impact that the terrorist attacks of September 11, 2001, have had on the way many people think about fighting crime in this country. According to one official at the U.S. Department of Justice, the attacks "introduced a new era in criminal justice in this country and around the world."[55] As this "new era" dawns, efforts to protect the United States against further acts of aggression have affected every major component of the criminal justice system—law enforcement, the courts, and corrections. In this *Criminal Justice in Action* feature, we will provide an overview of these changes and begin to answer the question of whether they will help the system be a more effective weapon in what has become known as the "war against terrorism."

Traditional Methods Rejected

To a certain extent, the criminal justice system was equipped to combat terrorism before September 11, 2001. In 1993, for example, a car bomb exploded in the basement of the World Trade Center in New York City, killing six people and injuring more than one thousand. Following an intense investigation, law enforcement agents were able to identify and apprehend the members of the fundamentalist Islamic group responsible for the act. Foreign governments provided aid in the worldwide hunt for those suspects who resided outside the country; in fact, police in Pakistan arrested Ramzi Yousef, who planned the bombing, and handed him over to U.S. authorities to stand trial in the United States. Though one suspect remains at large, the remaining perpetrators were tried, convicted, and sentenced in the U.S. District Court for the Southern District of New York.[56]

Theoretically, then, those responsible for hijacking the four commercial airliners and killing 3,021 in New York City, northern Virginia, and rural Pennsylvania in 2001 could have been brought to justice in a similar manner. The attacks were, indeed, criminal acts, involving premeditated murder, piracy of civilian aircraft, and

AP Photo/Amy Sancetta

Residents of New York City seek safety after a group of terrorists flew a commercial airplane into the World Trade Center on September 11, 2001. The incident, along with simultaneous crashes in northern Virginia and rural southwest Pennsylvania, has transformed the American criminal justice system.

destruction of private and government property.[57] Furthermore, they satisfied the elements of the federal law which defines the crime of terrorism, and thus were punishable by life in prison or the death penalty.[58]

It was clear, however, that a traditional response to the events of September 11, 2001, would not be acceptable. Given the scope and carnage of those attacks, most of the American public saw them as an act of war as much as an act of terrorism. The federal government, under the direction of President George W. Bush, responded accordingly, launching military operations in Afghanistan in 2001 to rid that country of its Taliban leadership and in Iraq in 2003 to remove Saddam Hussein and in the process seek out elements of al Qaeda. Both groups are recognized as supporters of international terrorism.

Communication Breakdowns

The response in domestic law enforcement circles has been no less dramatic. Several weeks after September 11, 2001, Attorney General John Ashcroft, who as head of the Department of Justice is the "top cop" in the U.S. government, promised a "wartime reorganization and mobilization" of all federal law enforcement agents under his control.[59] In practical terms, this has meant that agents from the FBI and the Bureau of Alcohol, Tobacco, Firearms and Explosives (ATF) have spent less time on local crimes and the continuing struggle against illegal narcotics and more time on antiterrorism activities.

Such proclamations, though perhaps comforting, did not address some of the fundamental problems with our criminal justice system that may have contributed to the nation's lack of preparedness. Given that terrorist networks are spread across the globe and consist of an ever-changing roster of "foot soldiers," efforts to contain them rely heavily on information. Prior to September 11, 2001, information sharing within federal law enforcement agencies, among the various agencies, and between federal and local agents was, in many instances, woefully inadequate.

For example, in July 2001, an FBI agent based in Phoenix, Arizona, sent a memo to his superiors warning that Osama bin Laden—considered the mastermind behind the September 11, 2001, attacks—had begun sending operatives to flight training schools in the United States. A number of these American-trained operatives wound up piloting the planes used as weapons in the attacks, but officials at FBI headquarters in Washington, D.C., did not see the memo until after September 11.[60] Furthermore, although the CIA suspected in March 2000 that Khalid al-Midhar and Nawaf Alhazmi, both of whom were on the plane that crashed

President George W. Bush shakes hands with Secretary of Department of Homeland Security Tom Ridge, left, during a welcome ceremony for the employees of the newly formed agency in Washington on February 28, 2003.

into the Pentagon, had ties to al Qaeda, the agency did not share this information with the FBI and other federal agencies until three weeks before the attacks. Consequently, as the CIA does not operate extensively within U.S. borders, nothing was done to limit the movements of these two men as they operated on American soil.[61]

The Department of Homeland Security

In an effort to break down this "wall" blocking the free flow of crucial information among law enforcement agencies, the Bush administration has carried out the largest transformation of the U.S. government since the Department of Defense was created in 1947. The centerpiece of this reorganization is the Department of Homeland Security (DHS), which began operating in the winter of 2003. The DHS, under Secretary Tom Ridge, is designed to coordinate the terrorism-fighting activities of twenty-two different federal law enforcement agencies, including the U.S. Secret Service, Coast Guard, Bureau of Citizenship and Immigration Services (previously known as the Immigration and Nationalization Service), Federal Emergency Management Agency, and segments of the FBI and CIA.[62] We will discuss the DHS and its impact on the criminal justice system in much greater detail in Chapter 5.

The USA Patriot Act

Many law enforcement officials also believe that their antiterrorism efforts have been hindered by legal restrictions on their ability to watch, stop, and interrogate suspects. As an example, they point to Zacarias Moussaoui, who was eventually the first person indicted by the federal government in connection with the attacks on New York City and the Pentagon. Moussaoui's suspicious behavior at a Minnesota flight school during August 2001 attracted the attention of the FBI, but the only legal violations they could find at the time were visa violations. While Moussaoui was in the custody of the U.S. immigration service, FBI agents tried to get a warrant to search the hard drive of the suspect's computer. Legal experts at the Department of Justice, however, did not think the agency had enough evidence to establish probable cause that Moussaoui had committed any crime, and the warrant was never obtained. Today, the U.S. government claims that information in Moussaoui's possession could have possibly included clues to the eventual terrorist attacks.[63]

The Bush administration and the U.S. Congress addressed these concerns by passing the controversial 342-page USA Patriot Act in 2001.[64] Among other measures, this legislation:

< Creates a new crime of "domestic terrorism," defined as acts that "appear to be intended . . . to influence the policy of a government by intimidation or coercion."

< Expands the definition of "engage in terrorist activity" to include not only the use of weapons but also the provision of material support by such activities as fund-raising for suspected terrorist organizations.

< Allows for easier detention and removal of noncitizens. (About 1,200 immigrants were detained in the nation's jails without being charged with committing a crime in the months following September 11, 2001.)

< Gives law enforcement agents greater ability to use surveillance and wiretap methods, conduct searches, track Internet use, and access private records when investigating terrorist activity.

< Reduces the amount of suspicion law enforcement agents need before apprehending a terrorism suspect (which would have allowed the FBI to seize Moussaoui before September 11, 2001).[65]

We will examine the USA Patriot Act in more depth in Chapter 7, when we discuss the "rules" of being a police officer.

Questions Remain

Other segments of the criminal justice system have also been affected by the war on terrorism. In 2001, President Bush created special tribunals to try suspected terrorists.[66] These military courts would operate without many of the procedural and other protections that are provided to defendants in the regular court system. The U.S. military has also created a new prison for those suspected of having ties to the Taliban or al Qaeda at its naval base at Guantanamo Bay, Cuba. As of January 2004, nearly 700 people were detained at the base.

How successful have these efforts been in protecting the American public from terrorist attacks? The Bush administration can point to several acheivements. The Buffalo Joint Terrorism Task Force, which included agents from the Customs Service, the Federal Drug Enforcement Administration, the FBI, and local police, was instrumental in the arrest and conviction of the "Lackawanna Six" for providing material aid to terrorism. The group consisted of six Americans with Yemeni backgrounds who took part in exercises at a training camp operated by Osama bin Laden in Al Farooq, Afghanistan. In the summer of 2003, Iyman Faris—a truck driver from Columbus, Ohio—confessed his involvement in an al Qaeda plot to destroy the Brooklyn Bridge, a case that Attorney General Ashcroft said "highlights the very real threat that still exists here at home."[67]

Many observers have been quite critical of the Bush administration's moves, however, saying that the political and legislative actions go too far in limiting freedoms long cherished by Americans. U.S. District Judge Gladys Kessler summed up the challenges facing the criminal justice system when she acknowledged that the "first priority" of the government is protect its citizens, while at the same time noting that it should "operate within the statutory and constitutional constraints which distinguish a democracy from a dictatorship."[68] The tension between security and civil liberties will receive a great deal of attention in this textbook, culminating with an explicit exploration of the subject in Chapter 17.

MAKING SENSE OF THE CRIMINAL JUSTICE SYSTEM'S ROLE IN THE WAR ON TERRORISM

1 Do you feel an overhaul of the criminal justice system was required after the terrorist attacks on September 11, 2001? What arguments might be made to the effect that the existing laws were sufficient to bring those who carried out the attacks to justice?

2 Why might various federal law enforcement agencies such as the FBI, CIA, and ATF not automatically share information concerning terrorists with each other?

3 Do you think that those who "materially aid" terrorist activities—for example, by participating in a training camp in Afghanistan or plotting to blow up a major bridge—should receive the same punishment as those who actually carry out terrorist attacks? In what ways would making the punishments equal deter terrorism in the United States? What problems arise when you punish someone for a crime that has not yet been committed?

Chapter Summary

1 **Describe the two most common models of how society determines which acts are criminal.** The consensus model argues that the majority of citizens will agree on which activities should be outlawed and punished as crimes; it rests on the assumption that a diverse group of people can have similar morals. In contrast, the conflict model argues that in a diverse society, the dominant groups exercise power by codifying their value systems into criminal laws.

2 **Define crime and the different types of crime.** Crime is any action punishable under criminal statutes and is considered an offense against society. Therefore, alleged criminals are prosecuted by the state rather than by victims. Crimes are punishable by sanctions that bring about a loss of personal freedom or, in some cases, fines. There are six groups of crimes: (a) violent crimes—murder, rape, assault, battery, robbery; (b) property crimes—pocket-picking, shoplifting, larceny/theft, burglary, and arson; (c) public order crimes—public drunkenness, prostitution, gambling, and illicit drug use; (d) white-collar crime—fraud and embezzlement; (e) organized crime—crime undertaken by a number of persons who operate their activities much as legal businesses do; and (f) high-tech crime—sabotage, fraud, embezzlement, and theft of proprietary data from computer systems as well as cyber crimes, such as selling child pornography over the Internet.

3 **Outline the three levels of law enforcement.** Because we have a federal system of government, law enforcement occurs at the (a) federal and the (b) state levels and within the states at (c) local levels. Because crime is mostly a local concern, most employees in the criminal justice system work for local governments. Agencies at the federal level include the FBI, the DEA, and the U.S. Secret Service, among others.

4 **List the essential elements of the corrections system.** Criminal offenders are placed on probation, incarcerated in a jail or prison, transferred to community-based corrections facilities, or released on parole.

5 **Explain the difference between the formal and informal criminal justice processes.** The formal criminal justice process involves procedures such as booking, setting bail, and the like. For every step in the formal process, though, someone has discretion, and such discretion leads to an informal process. Even when prosecutors believe that a suspect is guilty, they have the discretion not to prosecute, for example.

6 **Describe the layers of the "wedding cake" model.** The top layer consists of celebrity cases, which are most highly publicized; the second layer involves high-profile felonies, such as rape and

STORIES FROM THE STREET

Go to the Stories from the Street feature at www.cjinaction.com to hear Larry Gaines tell insightful stories related to this chapter and his experiences in the field.

Chapter Summary continued

murder; the third layer consists of property crimes such as larcenies and burglaries; the fourth layer consists of misdemeanors.

7 Contrast the crime control and due process models. The crime control model assumes that the criminal justice system is designed to protect the public from criminals; thus, its most important function is to punish and repress criminal conduct. The due process model presumes that the accused are innocent and provides them with the most complete safe-

guards, usually within the court system.

8 List the major issues in criminal justice today. (a) The return of rising crime rates; (b) juvenile crime; (c) the fear of crime; (d) terrorism and how law enforcement is changing to combat it; (e) the political "tough-on-crime" aspects of our system; (f) the growing prison population; (g) questions of race and gender; (h) the role of technology.

Key Terms

conflict model 6
consensus model 6
crime control model 19
discretion 17
due process model 20
federalism 12

felony 18
misdemeanor 18
organized crime 9
property crime 8
public order crime 8
terrorism 24

violent crime 7
"wedding cake"
  model 18
white-collar crime 8

Questions for Critical Analysis

1 How is it possible to have a consensus about what should or should not be illegal in a country with several hundred million adults from all races, religions, and walks of life?

2 Why are criminals prosecuted by the state, through its public officials, rather than by the victims themselves?

3 Why are public order crimes sometimes referred to as victimless crimes?

4 At what political level is most law enforcement carried out? Relate your answer to the concept of federalism.

5 Assume that all of the officials involved in the criminal justice process were deprived of most of the discretion they now have. What might some of the results be?

6 What effect do the media—particularly local news coverage—have on the public's perception of crime and fears concerning crime?

7 How can a weak economy influence the number of people kept in prisons and jails?

8 What is the name of the new federal department designed to fight terrorism? In what ways will this department aid efforts in that direction?

▶ TEST PREPARATION ONLINE

Go to www.cjinaction.com for tools to aid you in studying for your exams. Click on *Online Reviews* under *Chapter Resources* for an interactive review of each major section of this chapter. Under *Chapter Resources*, you will also find the *Chapter Outline, Chapter Summary, Flashcards, Glossary, Learning Objectives, Lecture Presentations, Concept Builder, Essay Questions*, and a *Tutorial Quiz*. You can also test yourself with a game of *Concentration* or the *Crossword Puzzle*.

Go to www.cjinaction.com for a wealth of online resources. Explore the *Internet Activities* and *Class Project*s under *Chapter Resources*. Check out the *Web Links* to access the Web sites mentioned in the text, as well as many others. You can also access recent perspectives by clicking on *CJ in the News* and *Terrorism Update* under *Course Resources*. If you'd like some mentoring, click on *Board of Mentors* under *Book Resources*.

For additional information, explore InfoTrac College Edition, your online library that offers complete full-length articles from thousands of scholarly and popular publications. Click on *InfoTrac College Edition* under *Chapter Resources* at www.cjinaction.com for a list of key words and InfoTrac exercises. Use the passcode that came with your book.

Hesalroad, Mary, *Law Enforcement Career Starter*, 2d ed., New York: Learning-Express, 2001. This paperback "how-to" guide provides a detailed look at the best way to get the law enforcement job that interests you. It offers helpful explanations of various careers in the criminal justice system, along with practical suggestions concerning the educational opportunities, internships, and work-study programs that can be the first step to a career in criminal justice.

Penzler, Otto, Thomas H. Cook, and John Berendt, eds., *Best American Crime*

Writing 2003: The Year's Best True Crime Reporting, New York: Vintage Books, USA, 2003. This anthology offers a variety of angles on criminal behavior while covering some of the most important crime stories of 2002. The collection focuses not only on criminals, but also on victims and their families and, in some cases, the wider sociological implications of the criminal act. Included are pieces on Webcam pornography, the murder of *Wall Street Journal* reporter Daniel Pearl, and the clues to be found in rotting corpses.

Notes

1. Kenneth W. Clarkson, Roger LeRoy Miller, Gaylord A. Jentz, and Frank B. Cross, *West's Business Law: Texts, Cases, Legal, Ethical. Regulatory, and International Environment*, 6th ed. (Minneapolis/St. Paul, MN: West Publishing Co., 1995), 165.

2. Herman Bianchi, *Justice as Sanctuary: Toward a New System of Crime Control* (Bloomington: Indiana University Press, 1994), 72.

3. George B. Vold, *Theoretical Criminology* (New York: Oxford Press, 1994), 72.

4. United States Sentencing Commission, *Special Report to Congress: Cocaine and Federal Sentencing Policy* (Washington, D.C.: Government Printing Office, 1995), 184–187.

5. *2002 Report to the Nation: Occupational Fraud and Abuse* (Austin, TX: The Association of Certified Fraud Examiners, 2002), 5.

6. Sarbanes-Oxley Act of 2002, Pub. L. No. 107-24, 116 Stat. 745 (2002).

7. Chicago Crime Commission, *The New Faces of Organized Crime* (Chicago: IL: Chicago Crime Commission, 1997).

8. President's Commission on Law Enforcement and Administration of Justice, *The Challenge of Crime in a Free Society* (Washington, D.C.: Government Printing Office, 1967), 7.

9. John Rawls, *A Theory of Justice* (Cambridge, MA: Belknap Press of Harvard University Press, 1971), 60–61.

10. President's Commission on Law Enforcement and Administration of Justice, 7.

11. John Heinz and Peter Manikas, "Networks among Elites in a Local Criminal Justice System," *Law and Society Review* 26 (1992), 831–861.

12. James Q. Wilson, "What to Do about Crime: Blaming Crime on Root Causes," *Vital Speeches* (April 1, 1995), 373.

13. Herbert Packer, *The Limits of the Criminal Sanction* (Stanford, CA: Stanford University Press, 1968), 154–173.

14. *Ibid.*

15. Daniel Givelber, "Meaningless Acquittals, Meaningful Convictions: Do We Reliably Acquit the Innocent?" *Rutgers Law Review* 49 (Summer 1997), 1317.

16. Lawrence M. Friedman and Robert V. Percival, *The Roots of Justice* (Chapel Hill, NC: University of North Carolina Press, 1981).

17. Packer, 154–173.

18. *Ibid.*

19. Givelber, 1317.

20. Guy-Uriel E. Charles, "Fourth Amendment Accommodations: (Un) Compelling Public Needs, Balancing Acts, and the Fiction of Consent," *Michigan Journal of Race and Law* (Spring 1997), 461.

21. *Gideon v. Wainwright*, 372 U.S. 335 (1963). Many United States Supreme Court cases will be cited in this book, and it is important to understand these citations. *Gideon v. Wainwright* refers to the parties in the case that the Court is reviewing. "U.S." is the abbreviation for *United States Reports*, the official publication of United States Supreme Court decisions. "372" refers to the volume of the *United States Reports* where the case appears, and "335" refers to the page number. The citation ends with the year the case was decided in parentheses. Most, though not all, case citations in this book will follow this formula. For general information on how to read case citations and find court decisions, see the appendix at the end of this chapter.

22. *Miranda v. Arizona*, 384 U.S. 436 (1966).

23. *Mapp v. Ohio*, 367 U.S. 643 (1961).

24. *Nix v. Williams*, 467 U.S. 431 (1984).

25. *Massachusetts v. Sheppard*, 468 U.S. 981 (1984); and *United States v. Leon*, 468 U.S. 897 (1984).

26. James P. Fleissner, "Glide Path to an 'Inclusionary Rule,'" *Mercer Law Review* 48 (Spring 1997), 1023.

27. Uniting and Strengthening America by Providing Appropriate Tools Required to Intercept and Obstruct Terrorism (USA PATRIOT) Act of 2001, Pub. L. No. 107-56, 115 Stat. 272 (2001).

28. Joseph Biden, quoted in Dan Eggen, "Major Crimes in U.S. Increase," *Washington Post* (June 23, 2002), A01.

29. Federal Bureau of Investigation, *Crime in the United States, 1999* (Washington, D.C.: U.S. Department of Justice, 2000).

30. Fox Butterfield, "U.S. Crime Figures Were Stable in '00 after 8-Year Drop," *New York Times* (May 31, 2001), A1.

31. Federal Bureau of Investigation, *Crime in the United States, 2001* (Washington, D.C.: U.S. Department of Justice, 2002).

32. Eggen, A01.

33. *Ibid.*

34. Howard W. Snyder, *Juvenile Arrests 2000* (Washington, D.C.: Office of Juvenile Justice and Delinquency Prevention, November 2002), 1.

35. Federal Bureau of Investigation, *Crime in the United States, 2002* (Washington, D.C.: U.S. Department of Justice, 2003), table 33, page 239.

36. Arlen Egley, Jr., and Aline K. Major, *Highlights of the 2001 National Youth Gang Survey* (Washington, D.C.: Office of Juvenile Justice and Delinquency Prevention, April 2003), 1.

37. David S. Tanehaus, " 'Owing to the Extreme Youth of the Accused': The Changing Legal Response to Juvenile Homicide," *Journal of Criminal Law & Criminology* (Spring/Summer 2002), 641.

38. *Are We Safe? The 2000 National Crime Prevention Survey* (Washington, D.C.: National Crime Prevention Council, 2001), 11–12.

39. Edwin H. Sutherland, "The Diffusion of Sexual Psychopath Laws," *American Journal of Sociology* 56 (1950), 142–148.

40. Lori Dorfman and Vincent Schiraldi, *Off Balance: Youth, Race, and Crime in the News* (Washington, D.C.: Justice Policy Institute, April 2001), 1.

41. Paul Klite, Robert A. Bardwell, and Jason Salzman, *Baaad News: Local TV News in America* (Denver, CO: Rocky Mountain Media Watch, 1997), 23.

42. Ted Chiricos, Kathy Padgett, and Marc Getz, "Fear, TV News, and the Reality of Crime," *Criminology* (May 2000), 755.

43. David Ropeik and George Gray, *Risk: A Practical Guide for Deciding What's Really Safe and What's Dangerous in the World around You* (Boston: Houghton Mifflin, 2002), 2.

44. National Security Council, "What Are the Odds of Dying?" at http://www.nsc.org/lrs/statinfo/odds.htm.

45. Sheryl Gay Stolberg, "When Risk Ruptures Life," *New York Times* (October 20, 2002), Section 4, 1.

46. Lionel Van Deerlin, "Clippings from a Society with a Gun in Every Home," *San Diego Union-Tribune* (January 2, 2002), B7.

47. Marie Simonetti Rosen, "2001: A Year in Profile," *Law Enforcement News* (December 15/31, 2001), 1.

48. Curt Anderson, "States Face Growing Prison Population," *Charleston Gazette & Daily Mail* (July 28, 2003), 7A.

49. The Sentencing Project, "Incarceration," at http://www.sentencingproject.org/issues_01.cfm.

50. Paige M. Harrison and Allen J. Beck, *Prisoners in 2002* (Washington, D.C.: U.S. Department of Justice, July 2003), 9.

51. *Ibid.*

52. *Factsheet: Women in Prison* (Washington, D.C.: The Sentencing Project, May 2003).

53. *Computer Crime and Security Survey* (San Francisco: Computer Security Institute, 2003).

54. Ira Sager, Ben Elgin, Peter Elstrom, Faith Keenan, and Pallavi Gogoi, "The Underground Web," *BusinessWeek* (September 2002), 67.

55. Deborah J. Daniels, "The Challenge of Domestic Terrorism to American Criminal Justice," *Corrections Today* (December 1, 2002), 66.

56. *United States v. Salameh,* 152 F.3d 88 (2d Cir. 1998).

57. "Responding to Terrorism," *Harvard Law Review* (February 2002), 1219.

58. 18 U.S.C. Section 2332(b) (2000).

59. Quoted in John Cloud, "General on the March," *Time* (November 19, 2001), 63.

60. Eric Lichtblau, "9/11 Findings Raise Terror War Doubt," *International Herald Tribune* (July 26–27, 2003), 1.

61. Toby Eckert, "New Details Emerge on SD–Based Hijackers," *San Diego Union-Tribune* (September 27, 2002), A1.

62. Department of Homeland Security, "DHS Organization," at http://www.dhs.gov/dhspublic/display?theme=1.

63. Mark Fineman, "A Case of Where, Not What," *Los Angeles Times (*March 20, 2002), A1.

64. USA Patriot Act of 2001.

65. This summary provided in Lisa F. Abdolian and Harold Takooshian, "The USA Patriot Act: Civil Liberties, the Media, and Public Opinion," *Fordham Urban Law Journal* (May 2003), 1430–1431.

66. Military Order of November 13, 2001: Detention, Treatment, and Trial of Certain Non-Citizens in the War Against Terrorism, 66 Fed. Reg. 57,833 (Nov. 13, 2001).

67. Jonathan Riskin and Jack Torry, "Al-Qaida among Us," *Columbus Dispatch* (June 20, 2003), 1A.

68. *Center for National Security Studies v. U.S. Department of Justice,* 215 F.Supp.2d 96 (D.D.C. 2002).

Chapter One Appendix

HOW TO READ CASE CITATIONS AND FIND COURT DECISIONS

Many important court cases are discussed throughout this book. Every time a court case is mentioned, you will be able to check its citation using the endnotes on the final pages of the chapter. Court decisions are recorded and published on paper and on the Internet. When a court case is mentioned, the notation that is used to refer to, or to cite, the case denotes where the published decision can be found.

State courts of appeals decisions are usually published in two places, the state reports of that particular state and the more widely used *National Reporter System* published by West Group. Some states no longer publish their own reports. The *National Reporter System* divides the states into the following geographic areas: Atlantic (A. or A.2d), South Western (S.W., S.W.2d, or S.W.3d), North Eastern (N.E. or N.E.2d), North Western (N.W. or N.W.2d), Southern (So. or So.2d), and Pacific (P., P.2d, or P.3d). The *2d* and *3d* in these abbreviations refer to the *Second Series* and *Third Series,* respectively.

Federal trial court decisions are published unofficially in West's *Federal Supplement* (F.Supp. or F.Supp.2d), and opinions from the circuit courts of appeals are reported unofficially in West's *Federal Reporter* (F., F.2d, or F.3d). Opinions from the United States Supreme Court are reported in the *United States Reports* (U.S.), the *Lawyers' Edition of the Supreme Court Reports* (L.Ed.), West's *Supreme Court Reporter* (S.Ct.), and other publications. The *United States Reports* is the official publication of United States Supreme Court decisions. It is published by the federal government. Many early decisions are missing from these volumes. The citations of the early volumes of the *United States Reports* include the names of the actual reporters, such as Dallas, Cranch, or Wheaton. *McCulloch v. Maryland,* for example, is cited as 17 U.S. (4 Wheat.) 316. Only after 1874 did the present citation system, in which cases are cited based solely on their volume and page numbers in the *United States Reports,* come into being. The *Lawyers' Edition of the Supreme Court Reports* is an unofficial and more complete edition of Supreme Court decisions. West's *Supreme Court Reporter* is an unofficial edition of decisions dating from October 1882. These volumes contain headnotes and numerous brief editorial statements of the law involved in the case.

State courts of appeals decisions are cited by giving the name of the case; the volume, name, and page number of the state's official report (if the state publishes its own reports); and the volume, unit, and page number of the *National Reporter.* Federal court citations are also listed by giving the name of the case and the volume, name, and page number of the reports. In addition to the citation, this textbook lists the year of the decision in parentheses. Consider, for example, the case *Miranda v. Arizona,* 384 U.S. 436 (1966). The Supreme Court's decision in this case may be found in volume 384 of the *United States Reports* on page 436. The case was decided in 1966.

Causes of Crime

>chapter objectives<

After reading this chapter, you should be able to:

1. Explain why classical criminology is based on choice theory.

2. Contrast positivism with classical criminology.

3. List and describe the three theories of social structure that help explain crime.

4. List the six focal concerns that dominate disorganized community existence.

5. List and briefly explain the three branches of social process theory.

6. Explain some of the links between income level and crime.

7. Identify some of the reasons criminologists give to explain the high rate of delinquent and criminal behavior by adolescents and young adults.

8. Discuss how social conflict theory can be used to explain the disproportionate number of minority group members who are arrested for committing crimes involving illegal drugs.

9. Identify the problem that criminal justice practitioners have with crime researchers, and discuss what can be done to resolve it.

Like Father, Like Son?

The news report jolted Ruth McCarty. Law enforcement agents had finally discovered the fate of twelve-year-old Ashley Pond and thirteen-year-old Miranda Gaddis. The two girls, who had vanished from the same apartment complex in Oregon City, Oregon, about six months earlier, were found on the property of Ward Weaver III. Miranda's corpse was found in a box in a shed behind Weaver's house, while Ashley's remains were buried inside a barrel under a concrete slab in his backyard.

McCarty could not believe her ears. Twenty years earlier, Ward Weaver, Jr.—Weaver III's father— had pulled his truck off the road near Bakersfield, California, and clubbed a stranded motorist to death. He then raped and strangled Barbara Levoy, the motorist's fiancée, before burying her underneath a concrete slab in his backyard. Barbara was twenty-three years old at the time of her murder, a crime for which Weaver, Jr., is still on death row in San Quentin prison in northern California. She was also McCarty's daughter.

Shortly after the bodies of Miranda and Ashley were unearthed, a grand jury indicted Weaver III on charges of aggravated murder, rape, and abuse of a corpse, among other crimes. "Two in the same family," wondered McCarty. "I wouldn't have thought it was possible."

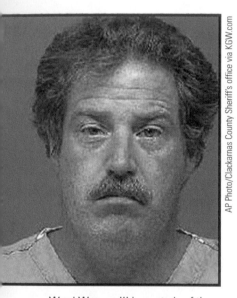

AP Photo/Clackamas County Sheriff's office via KGW.com

Ward Weaver III in custody of the Clackamas County (Oregon) Sheriff's Department.

> **Is the eerie similarity** between the two crimes a freak coincidence, or did the fact that Ward Weaver, Jr., committed a violent crime make it *more* likely that his son would do so as well? (As a point of fact, Weaver III's own son, Francis, was sentenced to juvenile detention in 1999 for shooting and wounding another teen-ager.) According to Allen J. Beck, a researcher at the Bureau of Justice Statistics, 47 percent of all inmates in state prisons have a parent or other close relative who has spent time behind bars.[1]

Does this mean that criminal tendencies are passed along genetically from generation to generation, like blue eyes? The question divides those who study crime. Some, such as scientist David Comings, believe that that it is "pretty clear

CONCEPT BUILDER
To what extent should a person be held responsible for his or her behavior. Visit www.cjinaction.com for an interactive exploration of this ideal in relation to causes of crime.

[that] there's a significant genetic component to antisocial behavior."[2] Others, including Dina Rose, a director of New York's Women's Prison Association and Home, hold that the cause of crime is found in social factors such as poverty, poor schooling, and broken families.[3]

The study of crime, or **criminology,** is rich with different theories as to why people commit crimes. In this chapter, we will discuss the most influential of these theories, some of which complement each other and some which do not. We will also look at the various factors most commonly, if not always correctly, associated with criminal behavior. Finally, this chapter will address the question of relevance: What effect do theories of why wrongdoing occurs have on efforts to control and prevent crime?

Criminology
The scientific study of crime and the causes of criminal behavior.

Exploring the Causes of Crime

Generally speaking, the different theories as to the root causes of criminal behavior can be separated into two categories: those causes found in the individual and those causes found in society.[4] In the incident described above, we might believe that Ward Weaver III's criminal tendencies (past transgressions included attacking a baby-sitter with a brick of concrete and raping his son's girlfriend) are the result of a "crime gene" passed down from his father. We might also consider that crime may be its own reward for Weaver III—serial killer John Wayne Gacy claims to have "realized that death was the ultimate thrill" after murdering the first of his more than thirty victims.[5]

Or the causes of Weaver III's wrongdoing may lie in the social context rather than in Weaver III himself. Perhaps his unsettled, fatherless childhood, or his lack of educational opportunities, or bad role models, or something else in his environment contributed to his criminal activities. Research shows at least a *correlation* between each of these factors and violent criminal behavior. Researchers who study the causes of crime, known as criminologists, have not, however, been able to reach a consensus on the *cause* of violent criminal behavior. Correlation between two variables means that they tend to vary together. Causation, in contrast, means that one variable is responsible for the change in the other. Research shows, for example, that ice cream sales and crime rates both rise in the summer. Thus, there is a correlation between ice cream sales and crime. Nobody would seriously suggest, though, that increased sales of ice cream cause the boost in crime rates.

This is the quandary in which criminologists find themselves. One can say that there is a correlation between criminal behavior by a father and similar behavior by his son. But we cannot say that the father's criminal behavior caused the son's actions. Consequently, the question that is the underpinning of criminology—what causes crime?—has yet to be fully answered. Certainly, criminologists have uncovered a wealth of information concerning a different, and more practically applicable, inquiry: Given a certain set of circumstances, why do individuals commit certain crimes? Various schools of criminology have developed numerous theories of crime causation, the most widely recognized of which we will examine in the following sections.

Choice Theory

A school of criminology that holds that wrongdoers act as if they weigh the possible benefits of criminal or delinquent activity against the expected costs of being apprehended. When the benefits are greater than the expected costs, the offender will make a rational choice to commit a crime or delinquent act.

Classical Criminology

A school of criminology based on the belief that individuals have free will to engage in any behavior, including criminal behavior. To deter criminal behavior, society must hold wrongdoers responsible for their actions by punishing them.

For the purposes of the American criminal justice system, the answer to why a person commits a crime is rather straightforward: because that person chooses to do so. This application of **choice theory** to criminal law is not absolute; if a defendant can prove that she or he lacked the ability to make a rational choice, in certain circumstances the defendant will not be punished as harshly for a crime as would normally be the case. But such allowances are relatively recent. From the early days of this country, the general presumption in criminal law has been that behavior is a consequence of free will.

Theories of Classical Criminology An emphasis on free will and human rationality in the realm of criminal behavior has its roots in **classical criminology.** Classical theorists believed that crime was an expression of a person's rational decision-making process: before committing a crime, a person would weigh the benefits of the crime against the costs of being apprehended. Therefore, if punishments were stringent enough to outweigh the benefits of crime, they would dissuade people from committing the crime in the first place.

The earliest popular expression of classical theory came in 1764 when the Italian Cesare Beccaria (1738–1794) published his *Essays on Crime and Punishments.* Beccaria criticized existing systems of criminal law as irrational and argued that criminal procedures should be more consistent with human behavior. He believed that, to be just, criminal law should reflect three truths:

1 All decisions, including the decision to commit a crime, are the result of rational choice.

2 Fear of punishment can have a deterrent effect on the choice to commit crime.

3 The more swift and certain punishment is, the more effective it will be in controlling crime.[6]

Beccaria believed that any punishment that purported to do anything other than deter crime was cruel and arbitrary. This view was shared by his contemporary, Britain's Jeremy Bentham (1748–1832). In 1789, Bentham pronounced that "nature has placed man under the governance of two sovereign masters, *pain* and *pleasure.*" Bentham applied his theory of **utilitarianism** to the law by contending that punishment should use the threat of pain against criminal individuals to assure the pleasure of society as a whole.[7] As a result, Bentham felt that punishment should have four goals:

Utilitarianism

An approach to ethical reasoning in which the "correct" decision is the one that results in the greatest amount of good for the greatest number of people affected by that decision.

1 To prevent all crime.

2 When it cannot prevent crime, to assure that a criminal will commit a lesser crime to avoid a harsher punishment.

3 To give the criminal an incentive not to harm others in the pursuit of crime.

4 To prevent crime at the least possible cost to society.[8]

Positivism

A school of social science that sees criminal and delinquent behavior as the result of biological, psychological, and social forces. Because wrongdoers are driven to deviancy by external factors, they should not be punished but treated to lessen the influence of those factors.

Positivism and Modern Rational Theory By the end of the nineteenth century, the positivist school of criminologists had superseded classical criminology. According to **positivism,** criminal behavior is determined by biological, psychological, and social forces and is beyond the control of the individual. The Italian physician Cesare Lombroso (1835–1909), an early adherent of positivism who is known as the "Father of Criminology," believed that criminals were throwbacks to the savagery of early humankind and could therefore be identified by certain physical characteristics such as sharp teeth and large jaws. He also theorized that criminality was similar to mental illness and could be genetically passed down from generation to generation in families that had cases of insanity, syphilis, epilepsy, and even deafness. Such individuals, according to Lombroso and his followers, had no free choice when it came to wrongdoing—their criminality had been predetermined at birth.

Positivist theory lost credibility as crime rates began to climb in the 1970s. If crime was caused by external factors, critics asked, why had the proactive social programs of the 1960s not brought about a decrease in criminal activity? An updated version of classical criminology, known as *rational choice theory,* found renewed acceptance. James Q. Wilson, one of the most prominent critics of the positivist school, sums up rational choice theory as follows:

> At any given moment, a person can choose between committing a crime and not committing it. The consequences of committing a crime consist of rewards (what psychologists call "reinforcers") and punishments; the consequences of not committing the crime also entail gains and losses. The larger the ratio of the net rewards of crime to the net rewards of [not committing a crime], the greater the tendency to commit a crime.[9]

According to rational choice theory, we can hypothesize that criminal actions, including acts of violence and drug abuse, are committed *as if* individuals had this ratio in mind.

The Seduction of Crime In expanding on rational choice theory, sociologist Jack Katz has stated that the "rewards" of crime may be sensual as well as financial. The inherent danger of criminal activity, according to Katz, increases the "rush" a criminal experiences on successfully committing a crime. Katz labels the rewards of this "rush" the *seduction of crime.*[10] For example, a person may decide to rob a bank not just for the money, but because of the inherent excitement of the action itself. Katz believes that seemingly "senseless" crimes can be explained by rational choice theory only if the intrinsic reward of the crime itself is considered.

Choice Theory and Public Policy The theory that wrongdoers choose to commit crimes is a cornerstone of the American criminal justice system. Because crime is seen as the end result of a series of rational choices, policymakers have reasoned that severe punishment can deter criminal activity by adding another variable to the decision-making process. Supporters of the death penalty—now used by thirty-eight states and the federal government—emphasize its deterrent effects, and legislators are increasingly using harsh mandatory sentences to control illegal drug use and trafficking.

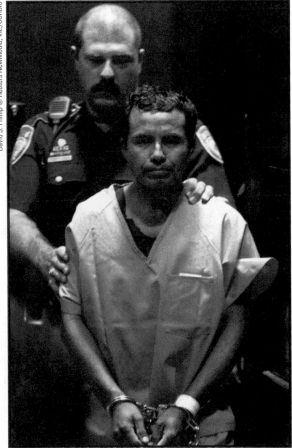

David J. Philip © Reuters NewMedia, Inc./CORBIS

Convicted serial murderer Angel Maturino Resendiz is escorted into the Harris County (Texas) Courthouse. Prosecutors claimed that Resendiz—linked to thirteen killings—had developed "a taste for murder and rape."

"BORN CRIMINAL": BIOLOGICAL
AND PSYCHOLOGICAL THEORIES OF CRIME

As we have seen, Cesare Lombroso believed in the "criminal born" man and woman and was confident that he could distinguish criminals by their apelike physical features. Such far-fetched notions have long been relegated to scientific oblivion. But many criminologists do believe that *trait theories* have validity. These theories suggest that certain biological or psychological traits in individuals could incline them toward criminal behavior given a certain set of circumstances.

The American Society of Criminology will keep you updated on the hot issues in criminology. Find this Web site by clicking on *Web Links* under *Chapter Resources* at www.cjinaction.com

Biochemical Conditions and Crime   One trait theory is that biochemical conditions can influence criminal behavior. These conditions can be genetic or brought about through environmental contacts. An example of the latter occurred in 1979, when Dan White was accused of murdering San Francisco Mayor George Moscone and Supervisor Harvey Milk. White successfully pleaded the "Twinkie defense"—that he should not be held accountable for his actions because he had suffered a major "mood disturbance" caused in part by an addiction to high-sugar junk food.[11]

Ann Green was found not guilty of the attempted murder of her infant child because of postpartum psychosis. This illness, believed to be partly caused by the hormonal changes that women experience after childbirth, causes abnormal behavior in a small percentage of recent mothers.[12] Criminal activity in males has also been linked to hormones—specifically *testosterone*, which controls secondary sexual characteristics (such as the growth of facial and pubic hair and the change of voice pitch) and has been linked to traits of aggression. Testing of inmate populations has shown that those incarcerated for violent crimes have higher testosterone levels than other prisoners.[13] High testosterone levels have also been used to explain the age-crime relationship, as the average testosterone level of men under the age of twenty-eight is double that of men between thirty-one and sixty-six years old.[14]

Genetics and Crime   Some criminologists might contend that Katz's "seduction of crime" provides more support for a modern, gene-based, evolutionary theory of crime than for rational choice theory. In other words, the seduction of crime represents an ancestral urge—which is stronger in some people than others—to commit acts that are considered crimes only in modern society.

Behavioral Genes   Recently, psychologist Leda Cosmides and anthropologist John Tooby have advocated a "Swiss army knife model" to explain how genetics influences brain activity. According to this model, humans have evolved special modules and networks in their brains that dispose them toward certain behavioral patterns.[15] Criminologists such as Lee Ellis and Anthony Walsh have suggested that some of these behavior patterns, which at one time were beneficial to human survival, have now become antisocial and have had sanctions imposed on them by society. In prehistoric eras, for example, extreme sexual aggressiveness in males toward a large number of females would have diversified a community's gene pool. Now laws against sexual assault and rape restrict such behavior.[16]

Another theory suggests that a person's genetic make-up may contribute to personality traits associated with criminal behavior. Researchers have hunted in vain for a "crime gene," or a genetic abnormality that could conclusively predict criminal behavior. In 2002, however, British criminologist Terrie Moffitt and several colleagues published results of a study that linked violent behavior to the absence of the gene for a protein called monoamine oxidase-A (MAOA).[17] This protein helps adjust a person's mood by regulating the molecules that carry "command signals" from one cell to another. Following more than five hundred men in New Zealand from birth to their late twenties, Moffitt and her team found that 12 percent of these males had *both* low levels of MAOA and had been abused as children. This group of 12 percent accounted for 85 percent of the entire sample who showed signs of overly aggressive behavior and 44 percent of those who had been convicted of violent crimes.

Because people who have been abused as children generally exhibit higher levels of antisocial behavior than those who have not—regardless of their MAOA supply—these findings are hardly decisive. Nor will they affect the consistent view of the courts that medical evidence has not been able to establish a causal relationship between genetic defects and criminal behavior.[18] Nevertheless, the efforts of Moffitt and her colleagues have spurred interest in the possibility that a "crime gene" does exist.

Twin Studies Because genes are inherited, some researchers have turned to *twin studies* to determine the relationship between genetics and criminal behavior. If the two are linked, then twins should exhibit similar antisocial tendencies. The problem with twin studies is that most twins grow up in the same environment, so it is difficult to determine whether their behavior is influenced by their genes or by their surroundings. To overcome this difficulty, criminologists compare identical twins, known as MZ twins, and fraternal twins of the same sex, known as DZ twins. Because MZ twins are genetically identical while DZ twins share only half of their genes, the latter should be less likely to have similar behavior patterns than the former.

Indeed, some studies seem to support this hypothesis. Researcher Karl Christiansen, for example, examined nearly four thousand male twin pairs and found that 52 percent of MZ pairs exhibited similar behavior patterns compared to only 22 percent for DZ pairs.[19] As is often the frustrating case in criminology, however, other studies seem to refute the idea that genetics is more important than environment in determining delinquent behavior. Research by criminologist David Rowe shows that nontwin siblings resemble each other in terms of delinquency to the same extent as twins do.[20] Consequently, though twin studies have contributed much to the discussion of trait theories, they have not proved conclusive in determining the effect of genetics on criminal behavior.[21]

Brain Activity and Crime The study of brain activity, or *neurophysiology*, has also found a niche in criminology. Some criminologists hypothesize that criminal behavior can be influenced by neurological defects that are acquired early in life. Neurophysiological studies of crime have relied on *electroencephalographic (EEG)* scans of brain activity. An EEG records the series of electric oscillations, or waves, given off by the part of the brain that controls functions such as learning and memory. These brain waves are measured according to their frequency and strength, and certain patterns of brain waves can be associated with criminal behavior. (For more information on "brain mapping" procedures, see the feature

"Crime is a fact of the human species, a fact of that species alone, but it is above all the secret aspect, impenetrable and hidden. Crime hides, and by far the most terrifying things are those which elude us."
—Georges Bataille, French novelist (1965)

GREAT DEBATES
Perhaps the most controversial trait theory holds that some persons are more genetically disposed to committing crimes than others. For more information on scientific research in the area of the "crime gene," as well as a discussion of the many political and ethical issues raised by these studies, click on *Great Debates* under *Book Resources* at www.cjinaction.com

On June 20, 2001, Andrea P. Yates methodically drowned her five children, aged six months to seven years, in the family bathtub. A state psychiatrist found that Yates, shown here in a Houston courtroom, suffered from severe depression with "psychotic features." After her arrest, Yates told doctors that she saw Satan in the walls of her jail cell. What if Yates's psychological problems could be successfully treated? Do you believe that she should still be severely punished for her crimes?

CJ and Technology—Mapping Crime in the Brain.) One study of a random sample of 333 subjects referred for an EEG found that those who exhibited lifelong patterns of violence had an incidence of EEG abnormality of 65 percent, three times higher than the same trait in those who had been charged with only one violent offense.[22]

Psychology and Crime   For all of his accomplishments in the field of psychology, Sigmund Freud (1856–1939) rarely turned his attention to the causes of crime. His followers, however, have proposed a *psychoanalytic theory* for criminal behavior. This theory rests on the belief that the human personality is made up of three parts:

1   The *id*, which controls sexual urges.
2   The *ego*, which controls behavior that leads to the fulfillment of the id.
3   The *superego*, which is directly related to the conscience and determines which actions are right and wrong, in the context of a person's environment.

Psychoanalytic theorists contend that people who exhibit criminal behavior have an overdeveloped ego or an underdeveloped superego. A strong ego leads to such feelings of guilt that a person commits a crime in order to be punished; alternatively, a weak superego means that a person cannot control his or her violent urges.

Because these theories are based on often untestable hypotheses rather than empirical data, psychological explanations for criminal behavior are quite controversial. During the middle of the twentieth century, the concept of the criminal as *psychopath* (used interchangeably with the term *sociopath*) gained a great deal of credence. The psychopath was seen as a person who had somehow lost her or his "humanity" and was unable to experience human emotions such as love or regret, to control criminal impulses, or to understand the consequences of her or his decisions.[23] Over the past few decades, the concept of psychopathy has lost standing, as criminologists have criticized the notion that emotions can be "measured."

The Role of Intelligence   Recently, psychological studies of crime have turned toward intelligence as a determinant of crime. In *The Bell Curve,* their best-selling treatment of the subject, Richard J. Herrnstein and Charles Murray contended that the lower a person's IQ, the higher the chance that that person will commit a crime. Gathering what they said was all available information, the authors made the "informed guess" that, on average, the IQs of criminals are ten points lower than those of noncriminals.[24] Many criminologists viewed *The Bell Curve* with mistrust, not the least because it made the highly contentious proclamation that African Americans were more likely to commit crimes because they were genetically disposed to be of lower intelligence than other races.[25] Furthermore, many experts argue, Herrnstein and Murray were unable to prove that low intelligence causes crime; at best, it is one of a number of factors that influence criminal behavior.[26]

Trait Theory and Public Policy   Whereas choice theory justifies punishing wrongdoers, biological and psychological views of criminality suggest that antisocial behavior should be identified and treated before it manifests itself in first-

> Mapping Crime in the Brain

During the trial of John Hinckley, Jr., who attempted to assassinate President Ronald Reagan in 1981, the defense offered the jury a black-and-white photo of Hinckley's brain. This picture, the defense claimed, showed that Hinckley was schizophrenic and not responsible for his actions. In a controversial decision, the defendant was found not guilty by reason of insanity.

Twenty years later, "brain mapping" techniques make the black-and-white photo of Hinckley's brain look like the drawing of a child. By placing electrodes on a subject's scalp, scientists can use computerized electroencephalography (CEEG) to measure the brain's spontaneous electrical activity, or its electrical response to visual and auditory stimuli. Using CEEG, scientists can present a color-coded display of brain activity. Other neuroimaging measures include positron emission computer tomography (PET scanning), which produces a computerized image of molecular variations in brain metabolism, and magnetic resonance imaging (MRI), which depicts the brain's form and structure by bombarding it with magnetic fields and radio waves.

Scans that measure brain activity can be particularly helpful in identifying *attention deficit/hyperactivity disorder (ADHD),* a condition most commonly found in children of elementary school age. The symptoms of ADHD include an inability to concentrate and a tendency to be impulsive and hyperactive. The condition—which is believed to affect between 3 and 5 percent of the children in the United States—is associated with substance abuse, learning disabilities, and delinquency. Observers believe that because those who suffer from ADHD perform poorly in school, they are at much greater risk of developing antisocial and delinquent behavioral patterns. Brain scans can identify ADHD in "problem" children and lead to treatment that lessens the risk of future criminality.

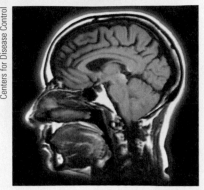

Centers for Disease Control

An MRI scan showing the human brain.

In the Future

The use of brain scanning to show a proclivity toward criminal behavior or as a defense strategy in criminal trials is dismissed as "junk science" by many criminologists. A number of studies, though, have established that certain brain patterns are associated with criminal behavior. As scientific methods improve, brain mapping may allow physicians to "predict" crime—with all the controversial implications that ability would bring.

 For more information on brain scans and other CJ technologies, click on Web Links under Chapter Resources at www.cjinaction.com

time or further criminal activity. Though the focus on treatment has diminished somewhat in the past three decades, it is still evident in the criminal justice system. Some offenders are treated with mood-altering drugs to control their antisocial behavior, and nearly all corrections facilities offer group or individual therapy to help prisoners address possible root causes of their criminal predilections.

SOCIOLOGICAL THEORIES OF CRIME

The problem with trait theory, many criminologists contend, is that it falters when confronted with certain crime patterns. Why is the crime rate in Detroit, Michigan, twenty-five times that of Sioux Falls, South Dakota? Do high levels of air pollution cause an increase in abnormal brain activity, or lower intelligence, or higher levels of testosterone? As no evidence has been found that would suggest that biological factors can be so easily influenced, several generations of criminologists have instead focused on social and physical environmental factors in their study of criminal behavior.

See Crime Times for an online publication dedicated to understanding the role brain dysfunction plays in criminal behavior. Find this Web site by clicking on *Web Links* under *Chapter Resources* at www.cjinaction.com

The Chicago School The importance of sociology in the study of criminal behavior was established by a group of scholars who were associated with the Sociology Department at the University of Chicago in the early 1900s. These sociologists, known collectively as the Chicago School, gathered empirical evidence from the slums of the city that showed a correlation between conditions of poverty, such as inadequate housing and poor sanitation, and high rates of crime. Chicago School members Ernest Burgess (1886–1966) and Robert Ezra Park (1864–1944) argued that neighborhood conditions, be they of wealth or poverty, had a much greater determinant effect on criminal behavior than ethnicity, race, or religion.[27] The methods and theories of the Chicago School, which stressed that humans are social creatures whose behavior reflects their environment, have had a profound effect on criminology over the past century.

The study of crime as correlated to social structure revolves around three specific theories: (1) social disorganization theory, (2) strain theory, and (3) cultural deviance theory.

Social Disorganization Theory Park and Burgess introduced an *ecological* analysis of crime to criminology. Just as ecology studies the relationships between animals and their environment, the two Chicago School members studied the relationship between inner-city residents and their environment. In addition, Clifford Shaw and Henry McKay, contemporaries of the Chicago School and researchers in juvenile crime, popularized the idea of ecology in criminology through **social disorganization theory.** This theory states that crime is largely a product of unfavorable conditions in certain communities.[28]

Studying juvenile delinquency in Chicago, Shaw and McKay discovered certain "zones" that exhibited high rates of crime. These zones were characterized by "disorganization," or a breakdown of the traditional institutions of social control such as family, school systems, and local businesses. By contrast, in the city's "organized" communities, residents had developed certain agreements about fundamental values and norms. Shaw and McKay found that residents in high-crime neighborhoods had to a large degree abandoned these fundamental values and norms. Also, a lack of social controls had led to increased levels of antisocial, or criminal, behavior.[29] According to social disorganization theory, ecological factors that lead to crime in these neighborhoods are perpetuated by continued elevated levels of high school dropouts, unemployment, deteriorating infrastructures, and single-parent families. (See Figure 2.1 to better understand social disorganization theory.)

Recently, some criminologists questioned the usefulness of conventional social disorganization theory. As Robert J. Sampson, a sociologist from Harvard University, has pointed out, the "ideal typical neighborhoods" characterized by close-knit ties between residents on which Shaw and McKay based their research are no longer common in the United States.[30] Social bonds between people who live in the same area are weakening, meaning that members of any given community have less influence on each other than in the past. Furthermore, the concept of the neighborhood as a distinct place, separate and different from other neighborhoods, is no longer helpful in most contemporary cities.[31] Sampson and those who agree with him do not think the ideas of the Chicago School should be abandoned, but rather feel that they should not be limited by reliance on traditional notions of neighborhood and community.

Social Disorganization Theory
The theory that deviant behavior is more likely in communities where social institutions such as the family, schools, and criminal justice system fail to exert control over the population.

The Problem: Poverty		The Problem: Social Disorganization		The Problem: Breakdown of Social Control
The Consequences: Formation of isolated impoverished areas, racial and ethnic discrimination, lack of legitimate economic opportunities.	Leads to	**The Consequences:** Breakdown of institutions such as school and the family.	Leads to	**The Consequences:** Peer groups replace family and educators as primary influences on youth; formation of gangs.

The Problem: Criminal Careers		The Problem: Cultural Transmission		The Problem: Criminal Areas
The Consequences: The majority of youths "age out" of crime, start families, and, if they can, leave the neighborhood. Those who remain still adhere to the values of the impoverished-area culture and become career criminals.	Leads to	**The Consequences:** The younger juveniles inherit the values of delinquency and crime from their older siblings and friends, establishing a deep-rooted impoverished-area culture.	Leads to	**The Consequences:** Rise of crime in poverty-stricken neighborhood; delinquent behavior becomes socially acceptable for youths; outside investment and support shun the area.

Strain Theory   Another self-perpetuating aspect of disorganized neighborhoods is that once residents gain the financial means to leave a high-crime community, they usually do so. This desire to escape the inner city is related to the second branch of social structure theory: **strain theory.** Most Americans have similar life goals, which include gaining a certain measure of wealth and financial freedom. The means of attaining these goals, however, are not universally available. Many citizens do not have access to the education or training necessary for financial success. This often results in frustration and anger, or *strain.*

Strain theory has its roots in the works of French sociologist Emile Durkheim (1858–1917) and his concept of ***anomie*** (derived from the Greek word for "without norms"). Durkheim believed that *anomie* resulted when social change threw behavioral norms into a flux, leading to a weakening of social controls and an increase in deviant behavior.[32] Another sociologist, American Robert K. Merton, expanded on Durkheim's ideas in his own theory of strain. Merton believed that *anomie* was caused by a social structure in which all citizens have similar goals without equal means to achieve them.[33] One way to alleviate this strain is to gain wealth by the means that are available to the residents of disorganized communities: drug trafficking, burglary, and other criminal activities.

In the 1990s, Robert Agnew of Emory University in Atlanta, Georgia, updated this line of criminology with his *general strain theory,* or GST.[34] Agnew reasoned that of all "strained" individuals, very few actually turn to crime to relieve the strain. GST tries to determine what factors, when combined with strain, actually lead to criminal activity. By the early 2000s, Agnew and other criminologists settled on the factor of *negative emotionality,* a term used to cover personality traits of those who are easily frustrated, quick to lose their tempers, and disposed to blame others for their own problems.[35] Thus, GST mixes strain theory with aspects of psychological theories of crime.

Cultural Deviance Theory   Combining, to a certain extent, social disorganization and strain theories, **cultural deviance theory** asserts that people adapt to the values of the subculture to which they belong. A **subculture** (a subdivision that exists within the dominant culture) has its own standards of behavior, or norms. By definition, a disorganized neighborhood is isolated from society at large, and

FIGURE 2.1 The Stages of Social Disorganization Theory

Social disorganization theory holds that crime is related to the environmental pressures that exist in certain communities or neighborhoods. These areas are marked by the desire of many of their inhabitants to "get out" at the first possible opportunity. Consequently, residents tend to ignore the important institutions in the community, such as business and education, causing further erosion and an increase in the conditions that lead to crime.

Source: Adapted from Larry J. Siegel, *Criminology,* 8th ed. (Belmont, CA: Thomson/Wadsworth, 2003), 183.

Strain Theory

The assumption that crime is the result of frustration felt by individuals who cannot reach their financial and personal goals through legitimate means.

Anomie

A condition in which the individual suffers from the breakdown or absence of social norms. According to this theory, this condition occurs when a person is disconnected from these norms or rejects them as inconsistent with his or her personal goals.

Cultural Deviance Theory

A branch of social structure theory based on the assumption that members of certain subcultures reject the values of the dominant culture through deviant behavior patterns.

Subculture

A group exhibiting certain values and behavior patterns that distinguish it from the dominant culture.

the strain of this isolation encourages the formation of subcultures within the slum. According to cultural deviance theory, members of low-income subcultures are more likely to conform to value systems that celebrate behavior, such as violence, that directly confronts the value system of society at large and therefore draws criminal sanctions.

Sociologist Walter Miller rejected the idea that these deviant value systems were formed in protest against prevailing social norms, an idea that had gained much currency among criminologists. Instead, Miller saw the formation of a number of "homegrown" concerns that were "natural" given the context and situation of lower-class life. He identified six of these *focal concerns* that dominate the day-to-day existence of the disorganized community:

1 *Trouble.* Trouble—in the form of drinking, fighting, sexual adventures, and the like—is a mainstay of lower-class community life. The ability to "get out of trouble" lends a certain amount of prestige to a person, whereas the inability to avoid punishment for trouble can be seen as a weakness.

2 *Toughness.* Physical strength is highly valued in lower-class communities, and such toughness is more highly prized when used to show prowess in criminal acts.

3 *Smartness.* The ability to "con," or outsmart other members of the community, and particularly representatives of the dominant culture such as the police, is also appreciated. In lower-class communities, "street smarts" are often more highly prized than a formal education.

4 *Fate.* Because they do not have the means to better their financial situations, many residents of lower-class neighborhoods feel that their lives are subject to forces beyond their control.

5 *Excitement.* "Living on the edge" can be a tonic for the boredom that characterizes lower-class neighborhoods with their high rates of unemployment.

6 *Autonomy.* A common goal of individuals in lower-class neighborhoods is not to be perceived as being under the control of authority figures, such as parents, teachers, or law enforcement officers.[36]

Miller's theory has been criticized on the ground that it does not account for the many law-abiding citizens who live in lower-class neighborhoods. It has also suffered from cultural stereotyping of minority groups. Many criminologists have felt the need to conduct studies reinforcing the class—as opposed to the racial—aspects of social structure theories of crime.[37]

Social Structure Theory and Public Policy   If criminal behavior can be explained by the conditions in which certain groups of people live, then it stands to reason that changing those conditions can prevent crime. Indeed, government programs to decrease unemployment, reduce poverty, and improve educational facilities in low-income neighborhoods have been partly justified as part of large-scale attempts at crime prevention.

FAMILY, FRIENDS, AND THE MEDIA: SOCIAL PROCESSES OF CRIME

Some criminologists find class theories of crime overly narrow. Surveys that ask people directly about their criminal behavior have shown that the criminal instinct is pervasive in middle- and upper-class communities, even if it is

> Robert Agnew Criminologist

I had no plans to become a criminologist when I began my Ph.D. program in sociology at the University of North Carolina. In fact, I never took a course in criminology during my undergraduate days. The turning point came when I had to pick my dissertation subject. I discovered a survey that had some excellent measures of the relationship between a person's social environment and later delinquent behavior. I had my topic: the impact of social environment on delinquency.

My research led to the "strain" or "anomie" theories that said when a person stumbles in achieving financial success or middle-class status due to social factors beyond their control, they may turn to crime. That is, if you don't have access to a good education because your local school was poor, or perhaps your parents just didn't have the money to send you to college, or you couldn't land a good job because of your background, you might respond to these kinds of frustrations by turning to crime. While strain theory made a lot of sense to me, I felt that the theory was incomplete.

When I looked around me, it was easy to spot other sources of frustration and anger, such as harassment by peers, conflict with parents or romantic partners, poor grades in school, or poor working conditions. In addition, strain theory did not explain why some people reacted to strain by turning to crime, while others did not.

My dissertation proposed additional sources of strain besides failure to achieve monetary success. I continued to research this topic after I joined the faculty at Emory University. I drew upon strain theory, social psychology, and my own experiences to develop a new "general strain theory."[34]

I outlined sources of strain as the loss of "positively valued stimuli" such as romantic relationships, or the threat of "negatively-valued stimuli" such as an insult or physical assault. I also pointed out that monetary success was just one among many "positively valued goals" that might cause strain when not achieved.

Finally, I noted that people who experience strain may turn to crime for several reasons—crime might allow them to achieve their monetary and status goals, protect positively-valued stimuli, escape negative stimuli, achieve revenge against wrongs, or simply to deal with the strain (such as taking drugs to forget problems).

Courtesy of Robert Agnew

Robert Agnew

I think that general strain theory is important because it significantly expands the scope of strain theory and — in doing so — it has helped generate new interest in strain theories of crime.

I've explored a number of factors that influence whether a person will respond to strain by turning to crime, including coping skills and resources, social support, and association with delinquent peers.[35]

If you are planning to do research on strain theory or on the causes of crime more generally, first familiarize yourself with relevant literature. Ask yourself whether a particular theory or argument makes sense— does it jibe with your experiences and your observations of others? If not, you may want to suggest an extension or revision in the theory.

Likewise, ask yourself whether the empirical tests of the theory make sense – are adequate samples employed, are all major concepts measured, etc. It is not as difficult to make an original contribution as you might think.

 Go to the Careers in Criminal Justice Interactive CD for more profiles in the field of criminal justice.

---

expressed differently. Anybody, these criminologists argue, has the potential to act out criminal behavior, regardless of class, race, or gender.

Psychologist Philip Zimbardo conducted a well-known, if rather unscientific, experiment to make this point. Zimbardo placed an abandoned automobile with its hood up on the campus of Stanford University. The car remained in place, untouched, for a week. Then, the psychologist smashed the car's window with a sledgehammer. Within minutes, passerbys had joined in the destruction of the automobile, eventually stripping its valuable parts.[38] **Social process theories**

Social Process Theories
A school of criminology that considers criminal behavior to be the predictable result of a person's interaction with his or her environment. According to these theories, everybody has the potential for wrongdoing. Those who act upon this potential are conditioned to do so by family or peer groups, or institutions such as the media.

function on the same basis as Zimbardo's "interdependence of decisions experiment": the potential for criminal behavior exists in everyone and will be realized depending on an individual's interaction with various institutions and processes of society. There are three main branches of social process theory: (1) learning theory, (2) control theory, and (3) labeling theory.

Learning Theory The hypothesis that delinquents and criminals must be taught both the practical and emotional skills necessary to partake in illegal activity.

Theory of Differential Association Sutherland's theory that criminality is the result of the values an individual is exposed to by family, friends, and other members of the community. When these values favor deviant behavior over conventional norms, criminal activity is more likely.

Learning Theory Popularized by Edwin Sutherland in the 1940s, **learning theory** contends that criminal activity is a learned behavior. In other words, a criminal is taught both the practical methods of crime (such as how to pick a lock) and the psychological aspects of crime (how to deal with the guilt of wrongdoing). Sutherland's **theory of differential association** held that individuals are exposed to values from family and peers such as school friends or co-workers. If the dominant values one is exposed to favor criminal behavior, then that person is more likely to mimic such behavior.[39] Sutherland concentrated particularly on familial relations, believing that a child was more likely to commit crimes if she or he saw an older sibling or a parent doing so.

Recently, learning theory has been expanded to include the growing influence of the media. In the latest in a long series of studies, psychologists at the University of Michigan's Institute for Social Research released data in 2003 showing that exposure to high levels of televised violence erodes a natural aversion to violence and increases aggressive behavior among young children.[40] Such findings have spurred a number of legislative attempts to curb violence on television.[41] (To see how another medium has come under scrutiny for its violent tendencies, see the feature *CJ and the Media*—The Matrix *Made Me Do It.*)

Control Theory A series of theories that assume that all individuals have the potential for criminal behavior, but are restrained by the damage that such actions would do to their relationships with family, friends, and members of the community. Criminality occurs when these bonds are broken or nonexistent.

Control Theory Criminologist Travis Hirschi focuses on the reasons why individuals *do not* engage in criminal acts, rather than why they do. According to Hirschi, social bonds promote conformity to social norms. The stronger these social bonds—which include attachment to, commitment to, involvement with, and belief in societal values—the less likely that any individual will commit a crime.[42] **Control theory** holds that although we all have the potential to commit crimes, most of us are dissuaded from doing so because we care about the opinions of our family and peers. James Q. Wilson and George Kelling describe control theory in terms of the "broken windows" effect. Neighborhoods in poor condition are filled with cues of lack of social control (for example, broken windows) that invite further vandalism and other deviant behavior.[43] If these cues are removed, according to Wilson and Kelling, so is the implied acceptance of crime within a community.

Labeling Theory The hypothesis that society creates crime and criminals by labeling certain behavior and certain people as deviant. The stigma that results from this social process excludes a person from the community, thereby increasing the chances that she or he will adopt the label as her or his identity and engage in a pattern of criminal behavior.

Labeling Theory A third social process theory, **labeling theory,** focuses on perceptions of criminal behavior rather than the behavior itself. Labeling theorists study how being labeled a criminal—a "whore," or a "junkie," or a "thief"—affects that person's future behavior. Sociologist Howard Becker contends that deviance is

> a consequence of the application by others of rules and sanctions to an offender. The deviant is one to whom that label has successfully been applied; deviant behavior is behavior that people so label.[44]

Such labeling, some criminologists believe, becomes a self-fulfilling prophecy. Someone labeled a "junkie" will begin to consider himself or herself a deviant and continue the criminal behavior for which he or she has been labeled. Following

> The *Matrix* Made Me Do It>

Much of the action in the Matrix trilogy of films (*The Matrix, Matrix Reloaded,* and *The Matrix Revolutions*) takes place in a hallucinatory world created by machines to keep the human race in a state of perpetual enslavement. Consequently, the violence perpetrated by Neo (played by Keanu Reeves) and his cohorts against a never-ending series of combatants is not "real," in the sense that it is taking place in the setting of an elaborate computer program.

Some of the films' fans, however, seem to have difficulty separating reality and fiction. Between 2000 and 2003, a number of disturbing crimes were linked to the *Matrix* films. In San Francisco, Vadim Mieseges killed and dismembered his landlord, saying that he had been "sucked into *The Matrix*" before committing the crime. A lawyer for Josh Cooke of Oakton, Virginia, who killed his parents, claimed that his client believed "he was in a virtual reality world similar to *The Matrix*." Tonda Ansey, who murdered a college professor at the University of Miami in Ohio, also felt she was living inside *The Matrix.* Finally, John Lee Malvo, a suspect in the sniper shootings in the Washington, D.C., area in 2002, wrote on the wall of his jail cell: "Free yourself of *The Matrix* control."

Very few criminologists believe that a movie or any other form of entertainment can *cause* a person to commit a crime unless some of the other factors that we have discussed in this chapter are present. John Murray, a child psychologist at Kansas State University, does believe, however, that there is a link among memory, learning, and violent images. Repeated viewings of violent films such as *The Matrix,* violent television programs, and violent video games may cause images of violence to be stored in memory to be recalled as a "hair-trigger" response to frustration or anger. Murray feels that repeated

CORBIS/Sygma

exposure to violence changes the values of children, making them more likely to "act out aggressively." In fact, research by Jacqueline Helfgott, a criminal justice professor at Seattle University, suggests that nearly 25 percent of juveniles arrested for crimes use films, video games, or songs to explain their criminal activity.

---

this line of reasoning, the criminal justice system is engaged in artificially creating a class of criminals by labeling victimless crimes such as drug use, prostitution, and gambling as "criminal."

Social Process Theory and Public Policy   Because adult criminals are seen as too "hardened" to unlearn their criminal behavior, crime prevention policies associated with social process theory focus on juvenile offenders. Many youths, for example, are diverted from the formal juvenile justice process to keep them from being labeled "delinquent." Furthermore, many schools have implemented programs that attempt to steer children away from crime by encouraging them to "just say no" to drugs and stay in school. As we shall see in Chapter 6, implementation of Wilson and Kelling's "broken windows" principles has been credited with lowering the violent crime rate in New York and a number of other major cities.

INFOTRAC KEYWORDS
labeling theory

For more information, use this search term with InfoTrac College Edition, your online library at www.infotrac-college.com

Social Conflict Theories
A school of criminology that views criminal behavior as the result of class conflict. Certain behavior is labeled illegal not because it is inherently criminal, but because the ruling class has an economic or social interest in restricting such behavior in order to protect the status quo.

Social Reality of Crime
The theory that criminal laws are designed by those in power (the rich) to help them keep power at the expense of those who do not have power (the poor). This would explain, for example, why the punishment for white-collar crime, mostly committed by members of the upper and middle classes, is less severe than the punishment for property and violent crimes, mostly committed by members of the lower class.

SOCIAL CONFLICT THEORIES

A more recent movement in criminology focuses not on psychology, biology, or sociology, but on *power*. Those who identify power—seen as the ability of one person or group of persons to control the economic and social positions of other people or groups—as the key component in explaining crime entered the mainstream of American criminology during the 1960s. These theorists saw social ills such as poverty, racism, sexism, and destruction of the environment as the "true crimes," perpetrated by the powerful, or ruling, classes. Burglary, robbery, and even violent crimes were considered reactions by the powerless against laws that were meant to repress, not protect, them. Supporters of these ideas aligned themselves with Marxist, radical, conflict, and feminist schools of criminology. Collectively, they have constructed the **social conflict theories** of crime causation.

Marxism versus Capitalism The genesis of social conflict theory can be found in the political philosophy of Karl Marx (1818–1883). Though he did not concentrate on crime in his writings, Marx's belief that a capitalist economic system necessarily produces income inequality and leads to exploitation of the working classes has been adopted by social conflict theorists.[45] These criminologists generally hold that crime is the natural result of class inequality as identified by Marx.

For this reason, social conflict theory is often associated with a critique of our capitalist economic system. Capitalism is seen as leading to high levels of violence and crime because of the disparity of income that results. The poor commit property crimes for reasons of need and because, as members of a capitalist society, they desire the same financial rewards as everybody else. They commit violent crimes because of the frustration and rage they feel when these rewards seem unattainable. Laws, instead of reflecting the values of society as a whole, reflect only the values of the segment of society that has achieved power and is willing to use the criminal justice system as a tool to keep that power.[46] Thus, the harsh penalties for "lower-class" crimes such as burglary can be seen as a means of protecting the privileges of the "haves" from the aspirations of the "have-nots."

The Social Reality of Crime It is important to note that, according to social conflict theory, power is not synonymous with wealth. Women and members of minority groups can be wealthy and yet still be disassociated from the benefits of power in our society. Richard Quinney, one of the most influential social conflict theorists of the past thirty years, encompasses issues of race, gender, power, and crime in a theory known as the **social reality of crime.**[47] For Quinney, along with many of his peers, criminal law does not reflect a universal moral code, but instead is a set of "rules" through which those who hold power can control and subdue those who do not. Any conflict between the "haves" and the "have-nots," therefore, is bound to be decided in favor of the "haves," who make the law and control the criminal justice system. Following this reasoning, Quinney sees violations of the law not as inherently criminal acts, but rather as political ones—as revolutionary acts against the power of the state.

Thinking along racial lines, many observers would assert that African Americans as a group have been "have-nots" since the colonial period. Today, the median income of an African American male is nearly $10,000 less than that of a white male. In 2003, only three of the nation's five hundred most profitable companies had a black chief executive.[48] Similarly, women have run up against what has been called the "glass ceiling" as they attempt to assume positions of power in corporations: only six major U.S. corporations have a female chief executive.[49] Furthermore, those women most likely to be arrested and imprisoned have exactly the characteristics—low income, often raising children without the aid of a partner—that social conflict theorists would predict.

Those who perceive the criminal justice system as an instrument of social control point to a number of historical studies and statistics to support their argument. In the nineteenth century, nearly three-quarters of female inmates had been incarcerated for sexual misconduct; they were sent to institutions such as New York's Western House of Refuge at Albion to be taught the virtues of "true" womanhood.[50] Today, approximately 90,000 women are arrested each year for prostitution. After the Civil War, many African Americans were driven from the South by "Jim Crow laws" designed to keep them from attaining power in the postwar period. Today, the criminal justice system performs a similar function. One out of every eleven adult black males is incarcerated on any given day, and one out of every three black males between the ages of eighteen and thirty-four is either in prison, in jail, or on probation or parole.[51]

Social Conflict Theory and Public Policy   Given its radical nature, social conflict theory has had a limited impact on public policy. Even in the aftermath of situations in which class conflict has had serious and obvious repercussions, such as the Los Angeles riots of 1991, few observers feel that enough has been accomplished to improve the conditions that led to the violence. Indeed, many believe that the best hope for a shift in the power structure is the employment of more women and minorities in the criminal justice system itself.

LOOKING BACK TO CHILDHOOD: LIFE COURSE THEORIES OF CRIME

Over the past decade, a number of criminologists have begun to fill a gaping hole in the study of the causes of crime. As Francis T. Cullen and Robert Agnew put it, "throughout much of the history of American criminology, scholars simply ignored the fact that humans have a childhood."[52] Instead, the bulk of research on youthful offending has focused on teen-agers.

This emphasis on adolescents has occurred for two very good reasons. First, because adolescents and young adults commit proportionally more crimes than any other age groups, criminologists have tended to focus on what happens during these years. Second, studying the behavior patterns of juveniles into adulthood is difficult enough. Extending these studies back to childhood is an even more daunting task.

Nevertheless, childhood may hold the key to many questions criminologists have been asking for years. The other theories we have studied in this chapter tend to attribute criminal behavior to factors—such as unemployment or poor educational performance—that take place long after an individual's personality has been established. Practitioners of **life course criminology** believe that lying, stealing, bullying, and other conduct problems that occur in childhood are the strongest predictors of future criminal behavior and have been seriously undervalued in the examination of why crime occurs.[53]

Life Course Criminology
The study of crime based on the belief that behavioral patterns developed in childhood can predict delinquent and criminal behavior later in life.

Self-Control Theory   Focusing on childhood behavior raises the question of whether conduct problems established at a young age can be changed as one grows toward adulthood. Michael Gottfredson and Travis Hirschi, whose 1990 publication *A General Theory of Crime* is one of the foundations of life course criminology, think not.[54] Gottfredson and Hirschi believe that criminal behavior is linked to "low self-control," a personality trait that is formed before a child reaches the age of ten and can usually be attributed to poor parenting.[55]

Someone with low self-control is generally impulsive, thrill-seeking, and likely to solve problems with violence rather than his or her mind. Gottfredson and Hirschi think that once low self-control has been established, it will persist; that is, childhood behavioral problems are not "solved" by positive developments later in life, such as healthy personal relationships or a good job.[56] Thus, these two criminologists ascribe to what has been called the *continuity theory of crime*, which essentially says that once negative behavior patterns have been established, they cannot be changed.

The Possibility of Change   Not all of those who practice life course criminology follow the continuity theory. Terrie Moffitt, for example, notes that youthful offenders can be divided into two groups. The first group are life-course-persistent offenders; they are biting playmates at age five, skipping school at ten, stealing cars at sixteen, committing violent crimes at twenty, and perpetrating fraud and child abuse at thirty.[57] The second group are adolescent-limited offenders; as the name suggests, their "life of crime" is limited to the teenage years.[58]

So, according to Moffitt, change is possible, if not for the life-course-persistent offenders (who are saddled with psychological problems that lead to continued social failure and misconduct), then for the adolescent-limited offenders. Robert Sampson and John Laub take this line of thinking one step further. While acknowledging that "antisocial behavior is relatively stable" from childhood to old age, Sampson and Laub have gathered a great deal of data showing, in their opinion, that offenders may experience "turning points" when they are able to veer off the road to a life of crime.[59]

Life Course Criminology and Public Policy   As we will see in Chapter 15, the American public often seems of two minds as to how to treat juvenile offenders. The American juvenile justice system was created with an eye toward rehabilitating wayward youths, but in recent years it has become more of an instrument to punish them. Though it is too early to determine how life course criminology will affect public policy in this area, certain patterns are rather predictable. On the one hand, politicians who want to continue to "get tough" with juvenile delinquents will point to continuity theories to promote the view that "once a criminal, always a criminal"—no matter what the age. On the other hand, those who favor rehabilitation will use research such as that done by Sampson and Laub to argue that the juvenile justice system's primary purpose should be to provide the "turning points" that these troubled youths so badly need. (See *Mastering Concepts*.)

↗ ONLINE REVIEW *Go to the book's Web site for an interactive review of this section*

Criminology and Crime Trends

At this point, it may be helpful to restate the obvious: there is no single answer to the question of why crime occurs. The theories presented in the previous section are just that: theories. They must constantly be tested against the relevant data and adjusted when they fail to match the data. As happens in any science, theories

> The Causes of Crime

CHOICE THEORIES

Crime is the result of rational choices made by those who want to engage in criminal activity for the rewards it offers. The rewards may be financial or they may be psychological—criminals enjoy the "rush" that comes with committing a crime. According to choice theorists, the proper response to crime is harsh penalties, which force potential criminals to weigh the benefits of wrongdoing against the costs of punishment if they are apprehended.

BIOLOGICAL AND PSYCHOLOGICAL TRAIT THEORIES

Criminal behavior is explained by biological and psychological attributes of the individual. Those who support biological theories of crime believe that the secret to crime is locked in the human body: in genes, brain disorders, reaction to improper diet or allergies, and so on. Psychological attempts to explain crime are based on the study of the personality and intelligence and the development of a person's behavioral patterns during infancy.

SOCIOLOGICAL THEORIES

Crime is not something a person is "born to do." Instead, it is the result of the social conditions under which a person finds himself or herself. Those who are socially disadvantaged—because of poverty or other factors such as racial discrimination—are more likely to commit crimes because other avenues to "success" have been closed off. High-crime areas will develop their own cultures that are in constant conflict with the dominant culture and create a cycle of crime that claims the youth who grow up in the area and go on to be career criminals.

SOCIAL PROCESS THEORIES

The major influence on any individual is not society in general, but the interactions that dominate everyday life.

Therefore, individuals are drawn to crime not by general factors such as "society" or "community," but by family, friends, and peer groups. Crime is "learned behavior"; the "teacher" is usually a family member or friend. Everybody has the potential to become a criminal. Those who form positive social relationships instead of destructive ones have a better chance of avoiding criminal activity. Furthermore, if a person is labeled "juvenile" or "criminal" by the authority figures or organizations in his or her life, there is a better chance he or she will create a personality and actions to fit that label.

SOCIAL CONFLICT THEORIES

Criminal laws are a form of social control. Through these laws, the dominant members of society control the minority members, using institutions such as the police, courts, and prisons as tools of oppression. Crime is caused by the conflict between the "haves" and "have-nots" of society. The poor commit crimes because of the anger and frustration they feel at being denied the benefits of society.

LIFE COURSE THEORIES

Even though criminal behavior usually begins after the age of fourteen, the factors that lead to that behavior start much earlier. To fully understand why crime occurs, then, criminologists must better understand conduct problems of early childhood and how those problems lead to or predict later wrongdoing. The most pressing question becomes whether early misbehavior necessarily leads to a life of crime, or whether it can be used as a warning signal to prevent such a future from taking place.

sometimes cannot survive in the face of advances in knowledge. Cesare Lombroso may be known as the "Father of Criminology," but his nineteenth-century hypothesis that criminal behavior can be predicted by the sharpness of a tooth or the shape of a jawbone would find little, if any, support among criminologists today.

Consequently, those who study crime have a basic need for information concerning crime rates and factors that could influence those rates. In this area, modern criminologists do have a significant advantage over Lombroso and his peers. More data on crime are available today than at any time in this nation's history, thanks to efforts by government law enforcement agencies (discussed in the following chapter), educational institutions, and private individuals. These figures provide a crucial litmus test for criminological theories and help us to establish a more detailed picture of criminal trends.

THE GEOGRAPHY OF CRIME

Data gathered annually by the Federal Bureau of Investigation (FBI) show that states in the South and West have higher rates of crime than do those in the Midwest and Northeast.[60] (See Figure 2.2.) Why? One could put forward the theory that, like most of the rest of us, criminals prefer to be outdoors (and are therefore more likely to commit a criminal act) where and when the weather is warm. This theory is strengthened by figures that show higher rates of crime in the warmer summer months than at any other time of the year.

Another geographic factor in crime concerns the concentration of people in any given area. According to the Bureau of Justice Statistics, nearly 20 percent of all households in urban areas in the United States were victimized by violent or property crimes in 2000, compared to only 13 percent of households in rural areas.[61] In fact, even as violent crime rates have dropped or stayed relatively constant over the past decade, rates in many cities have climbed sharply, especially recently. In Oakland, California, the murder rate jumped 28.6 percent from 2001 to 2002; Los Angeles saw an 11.1 percent rise over the same period.[62] Chicago's murder rate was running higher in 2003 than in 2002, a year when the city recorded the highest rate in the nation.[63] Smaller cities such as Cincinnati, Ohio, are also experiencing crime waves out of proportion with rates in the rest of the country.[64]

Law enforcement officials in each city have their own ideas about the deteriorating situations they face. In Los Angeles and Chicago, police report increased gang activity. In Oakland, city representatives point to a high unemployment rate, which has "forced" more citizens into the drug trade. In Cincinnati, the problem is identified as a backlash against the 2001 shooting of an African American teenager by a white police officer. As far as many criminologists are concerned, high crime rates in urban areas can be traced to the problems identified by social disorganization theory: a breakdown of community values (see page 46).

CRIME, RACE, AND POVERTY

Social disorganization theory is also used to explain crime trends *within* a city. In Los Angeles, for example, the Santa Monica area is plagued by very few violent crimes, while, several miles away, South-Central Los Angeles has a murder rate twice as high as the infamously dangerous Bogotá, Colombia.[65] Looking at the demographics of the two areas, the racial and economic differences are immediately

FIGURE 2.2 **2002 Violent and Property Crime Rates, by Region, per 100,000 Inhabitants**

Source: Federal Bureau of Investigation, *Crime in the United States, 2002* (Washington, D.C.: U.S. Department of Justice, 2003), figure 2.4, page 12.

evident: South-Central Los Angeles is more heavily populated by minority groups and has much lower income levels than does Santa Monica.

In general, poor people and members of minority groups commit more crimes—and are more often the victims of crimes—than wealthier people and whites. But the relationship among race, income level, and crime is much more complicated than any generalization. Studies have shown that, even in low-income neighborhoods, the rate of violent crime is associated much more strongly with family disorganization (lack of a father in the household, family members committing crimes) than with race.[66] Furthermore, even when income levels are similar, juveniles and young adults from households in which the father is absent are twice as likely to be incarcerated as those from two-parent families.[67]

Class and Crime According to social disorganization theory, loss or lack of employment has a devastating effect on individuals, families, and, by extension, communities. In fact, the highest crime rates in the United States are consistently recorded in the low-income, urban neighborhoods with the highest unemployment rates. Lack of education, another handicap most often faced by low-income citizens, also seems to correlate with criminal activity. Forty-one percent of all inmates in state and federal prisons failed to obtain a high school degree, compared to 18 percent in the population at large.[68]

It might seem logical that those who believe they lack a legal opportunity to gain the consumer goods and services that dominate American culture would turn to illegal methods to do so. But, logic aside, many criminologists are skeptical of such an obvious class-crime relationship. After all, poverty does not *cause* crime; the majority of residents in low-income neighborhoods are law-abiding. Furthermore, higher-income citizens are also involved in all sorts of criminal activities and are more likely to commit white-collar crimes, which are not included in statistics on violent crime.

In addition, self-reported surveys, which you will learn about in the next chapter and involve researchers asking people directly about their criminal activity, have shown that as far as less serious crimes are concerned, lower-, middle-, and upper-class criminal behavior differ very little.[69] These findings tend to support the theory that high crime rates in low-income communities are at least partly the result of a greater willingness of police to arrest poor citizens, and of the court system to convict them.

INFOTRAC KEYWORDS
race and crime

For more information, use these search terms with InfoTrac College Edition, your online library at www.infotrac-college.com

Race and Crime   The class-crime relationship and the class-race relationship are invariably linked. Official crime data seem to indicate a strong correlation between minority status and crime: African Americans—who make up 13 percent of the population—constitute 38 percent of those arrested for violent crimes and 30 percent of those arrested for property crimes.[70] Furthermore, African Americans are victims of violent crime at a rate of 31.2 per 1,000, compared to 24.5 per 1,000 for whites.[71]

The racial differences in the crime rate are one of the most controversial areas of the criminal justice system (see the feature *CJ in Focus—Myth versus Reality: Race Stereotyping and Crime*). At first glance, crime statistics seem to support the idea that the subculture of African Americans in the United States is disposed toward criminal behavior. Not all of the data, however, support that assertion. A number of crime-measuring surveys show consistent levels of crime and drug abuse across racial lines.[72] In addition, a study of nearly 900 African American children (400 boys and 467 girls) from neighborhoods with varying income levels showed that, regardless of the different factors often cited by criminologists, family income level had the only significant correlation with violent behavior. The authors of the study were so impressed by the results that they called on their colleagues to make greater efforts to include African American families living outside urban neighborhoods in future research in order to give a more complete—and perhaps less stereotypical—picture of race and crime in this country.[73]

Why, then, are proportionally more minorities arrested and incarcerated than whites? This discrepancy has been attributed to inherent racism in the criminal justice system, though criminologists are by no means of one mind regarding this possibility. A number of other factors, including poor economic and social conditions in the low-income neighborhoods where many minorities reside, have been offered to explain the complex problem of race and crime. We will address this issue throughout this textbook.

Another point to remember when reviewing statistical studies of minority offenders and victims is that they tend to focus on *race,* which distinguishes groups based on physical characteristics such as skin color, rather than *ethnicity,* which denotes national or cultural background. Thus, the bulk of criminological research in this area has focused on the differences between European Americans and African Americans, both because the latter have been the largest minority group in the United States for most of its history and because the racial differences between

> Race Sterotyping and Crime

In an effort to study the effect of race on perception, Birt Duncan gathered 104 white undergraduate students at the University of California and had them observe an argument between two people in which one person shoved the other. The undergraduates were randomly assigned to view one of four different conditions: (1) white shover/African American victim, (2) white shover/white victim, (3) African American shover/white victim, and (4) African American shover/African American victim. The students were then asked to rate the behavior of the person who did the shoving.

Duncan found that when the shover was African American and the victim was white, 75 percent of the students considered the shove to be "violent behavior" and 6 percent saw it as "playing around." In contrast, when the shover was white and the victim black, only 17 percent characterized the shove as violent while 42 percent saw it as playful.

The Myth

The results of Duncan's study are not, in the end, surprising. Racial stereotyping is not an aberration in our society. Negative stereotypes of minorities, especially African Americans, label them as prone to violence and more likely to be criminals or members of gangs than others.

The Reality

According to the University of Maryland's Katheryn K. Russell, the best-kept secret in criminology is that the United States has a "white crime" problem. Whites, Russell points out, are the subject of about two-thirds of the arrests in this country each year. Russell's point is that public and academic obsession with "black crime" has severely limited discussion of "white crime." This fascination can be explained, at least from a criminological standpoint, by the different *proportional* involvement of racial minorities in crime. As Figure 2.3 shows, although white involvement in crime is high, it is "relatively" low given the percentage of the American population that is of European descent. In contrast, minorities have a disproportionate involvement in crime—especially as a percentage of prison and jail inmates—based on their population statistics.

FOR CRITICAL ANALYSIS

According to Figure 2.3, although African Americans are arrested at less than half the rate of whites, they comprise almost 30 percent more of the prison population. How might this statistical anomaly be explained?

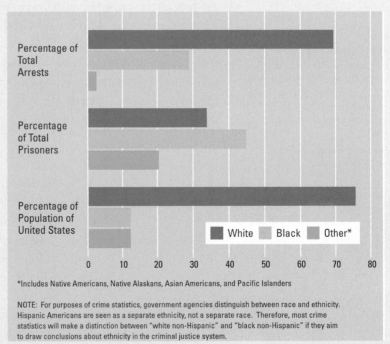

FIGURE 2.3
Crime and Race in the United States
Source: U.S. Census, U.S. Department of Justice, Federal Bureau of Investigation.

*Includes Native Americans, Native Alaskans, Asian Americans, and Pacific Islanders

NOTE: For purposes of crime statistics, government agencies distinguish between race and ethnicity. Hispanic Americans are seen as a separate ethnicity, not a separate race. Therefore, most crime statistics will make a distinction between "white non-Hispanic" and "black non-Hispanic" if they aim to draw conclusions about ethnicity in the criminal justice system.

the two groups are easily identifiable. Americans of Hispanic descent have either been excluded from many crime studies or been linked with whites or blacks based on racial characteristics.[74] Other minority groups, such as Asian Americans,

Native Americans, and immigrants from the South Pacific or Eastern Europe, have been similarly underreported in crime studies.

AGE AND CRIME: THE PEAK YEARS

The strongest statistical determinant of criminal behavior appears to be age. Criminal behavior peaks during the teen-age years; for most offenses, rates are at their highest around ages seventeen and eighteen (a few years later for violent crime).[75] As Figure 2.4 shows, criminal activity begins to decline as a person grows older; 85 percent of former delinquents are no longer involved in wrong-doing by the time they reach age twenty-eight.[76]

Why is the crime rate dramatically higher for young people? Once again, there is no single, simple answer. As already noted, biological theories of crime point to high testosterone levels in young males, which increase levels of aggression and violence. Adolescents are also more susceptible to peer pressure, and sociological and social process theories of crime in this area are backed by studies showing that juvenile delinquents tend to socialize with other juvenile delinquents.[77] A recent survey conducted by researchers from Columbia University found that juveniles who were frequently bored were 50 percent more likely than other teen-agers to abuse illegal drugs and alcohol, and those who received more than $25 a week in spending money were twice as likely to get high or drunk as those who received less than that amount.[78]

Criminologists call possible sources of juvenile delinquency such as boredom and too much pocket money *risk factors.* Common risk factors cited by those who study juvenile delinquency include poor parental supervision, poor academic achievement, weapon carrying, gang membership, and low intelligence. No single risk factor can predict delinquency, and the consensus seems to be that the more risk factors that are present in the life of any juvenile, the better chances he or she will have of offending.[79] As we saw earlier, life course theories of crime have convinced a number of criminologists to begin searching for risk factors in early childhood, without waiting until a person has reached adolescence and entered the juvenile justice system. We will take a comprehensive look at juvenile delinquency and crime in Chapter 15.

GUNS AND CRIME

Since at least the 1930s, young people have committed more violent crimes than have their elders. Starting nearly two decades ago, however, such rates have increased *significantly.* Between 1985 and 1992, homicide rates went up by 50 percent for white males aged fourteen to seventeen and tripled for African Americans of the same age.[80] This sharp increase has been linked to the role guns play in juvenile criminal behavior. The rise in gun ownership among gang members in high-crime urban areas has been well documented,[81] but these high rates of violence also reflect a growing pattern of gun ownership among suburban youths as well.[82]

According to government figures, 71 percent of all homicides in 2002 were committed with a firearm.

INFOTRAC KEYWORDS
crime and age

For more information, use these search terms with InfoTrac College Edition, your online library at www.infotrac-college.com

FIGURE 2.4
Percentage of Arrests by Age

As this graph shows, the majority of those persons arrested for property crimes in the United States are under twenty-five years old, and more violent crimes are committed by eighteen- to twenty-four-year-olds than by any other age group.

Source: Federal Bureau of Investigation, *Crime in the United States, 2002* (Washington, D.C.: U.S. Department of Justice, 2003), 244–245.

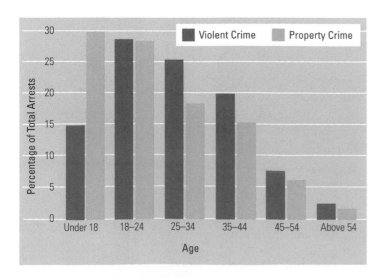

Jacqueline Castillo, aged thirteen, left, Jasmin Amaya, aged thirteen, top, and Jacquelyn Rodriguez, aged twenty, right, are members of Aspira, a national organization devoted to developing leadership skills and strengthening community ties among Latina youth. In 2002, Florida's Department of Juvenile Justice awarded Aspira and several other groups $7.5 million in grants to help prevent delinquency. According to learning theory (see page 50), how might organizations composed of young people such as Jacqueline, Jasmin, and Jacquelyn be able to affect levels of juvenile delinquency in areas with high concentrations of young offenders?

In addition, 42 percent of all robberies and 19 percent of all aggravated assaults were carried out by someone brandishing a gun.[83] Victims' rights groups and gun control advocates argue that America's high rates of violence reflect the ease with which firearms are available to its citizens; hence, they push for legislation to restrict the ability to sell and purchase such weapons. Criminologists have struggled to determine the actual impact of our firearm laws. Some argue that the relative ease with which most Americans can purchase firearms increases rates of gun violence, while others claim that gun ownership deters would-be criminals who are afraid of being shot in the act.[84] (To learn about a project that has been successful in reducing gun-related crimes, see *What Works—Project Exile* on p. 62. Then, for a discussion of gun policies and their possible impact on violent crimes, go to the feature *Criminal Justice in Action—The Link between Guns and Crime* at the end of the chapter.)

The issue of guns and crime is widely debated on the Internet. The `Coalition to Stop Gun Violence` offers the pro–gun control view, while the `National Rifle Association` provides arguments against gun control. Find these Web sites by clicking on *Web Links* under *Chapter Resources* at www.cjinaction.com

DRUGS AND ALCOHOL AND CRIME

As with firearms, strong statistical evidence links drugs and alcohol to criminal behavior. A report published by the National Center on Addiction and Substance Abuse at Columbia University concluded that eight out of every ten prisoners in the United States were involved with alcohol or others drugs at the time of their crimes. In other words, 80 percent were under the direct influence of alcohol or other drugs while committing the crime, had a history of drug abuse, or were arrested for violating drug or alcohol laws.[85] Indeed, many observers blame the virtual explosion of violent crime that shook this country in the late 1980s and early 1990s on the widespread sale and use of crack cocaine at that time.[86]

Given the large role alcohol and drugs play in our national crime picture, criminologists have devoted a great deal of time and energy to exploring the subject. One, M. Lyn Exum of the Department of Criminal Justice at the University of North Carolina, believes that significant alcohol use among criminals subverts the rational choice theory of crime (see page 41).[87] Exum has found that someone who is intoxicated—and overly aggressive as result—is unable to make any rational decision about acting violently. Because the drunken offender is not thinking clearly about the consequences of his or her criminal act, laws designed to deter the act often do not have the desired effect.

INFOTRAC KEYWORDS
drugs and alcohol and crime
For more information, use these search terms with InfoTrac College Edition, your online library at www.infotrac-college.com

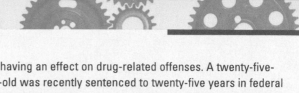

> Project Exile

Passing through Richmond, Virginia, drivers will notice an interesting message on some of the city's billboards: "AN ILLEGAL GUN GETS YOU FIVE YEARS IN PRISON." This advertising is sponsored by Project Exile, a crime control program designed to reduce gun violence in what used to be one of the most crime-ridden cities in the nation. In 1997, Richmond had the second highest murder rate in the United States—reporting 140 murders, 122 of which were committed with handguns. Home to only 3 percent of Virginia's population, the city accounted for 27 percent of the state's murders. "Guns were essentially a part of the uniform among criminals in Richmond, as much as your belt or your shoes," said one official.

The basic idea behind Project Exile is as simple as the billboards promoting it. A person convicted of illegally carrying a gun will be sentenced to five years in prison with no parole. The program, which began in 1997, achieves this through cooperation between federal and local law enforcement officials. When a person is arrested for a firearm-related crime, local authorities have the option of referring the case to the U.S. Attorney's Office. In general, punishment for gun crimes is harsher under federal law than state law. Also, conviction rates are significantly higher in federal courts than in state courts. In the end, the effect of the program is to "exile" local offenders from the Richmond community to distant federal prisons. The program is also having an effect on drug-related offenses. A twenty-five-year-old was recently sentenced to twenty-five years in federal prison for selling crack cocaine. Under normal circumstances, the case would have gone to state court, and the punishment would have been much less severe. But because the defendant was in possession of an illegal .380-caliber handgun, he was prosecuted under Project Exile.

From 1998 to 2003, Project Exile secured 194 convictions and was responsible for the removal of 457 guns from the streets of Richmond. The number of homicides in the city also dropped by a third. Although it is difficult to prove that Project Exile alone is responsible for making Richmond a safer place, the program has been adopted by a number of cities, including Indianapolis, Denver, and Detroit, and the Bush administration has decided to establish it in all ninety-four federal court districts.

FOR CRITICAL ANALYSIS
"People weigh the pros and cons and they take the risk they feel they have to," one Richmond official said of Project Exile. "And for some, when it comes to use of firearms, the reward, in their opinion, outweighs the risk." Which theory of crime that we have discussed in this chapter agrees with this line of thinking? How does that theory support the reasoning behind Project Exile?

The drug-crime relationship has also proved to be a rich field of study for social conflict theorists. The fact that a disproportionate number of those arrested and imprisoned for drug crimes in this country are low-income minorities supports the basic contention of these criminologists that crime is more a matter of who you are than what you have done. Furthermore, because members of this "underclass" are more likely to be unemployed and live in disorganized neighborhoods, both the sale (as an alternative to poverty) and use (as a means of escaping harsh reality) of illegal drugs are attractive options for them.[88] Issues concerning illegal drugs and the "war" to restrict their use will be addressed in Chapter 16.

Chronic Offender
A delinquent or criminal who commits multiple offenses and is considered part of a small group of wrongdoers who are responsible for a majority of the antisocial activity in any given community.

Cohort
A group of persons gathered for study because they share a certain characteristic, such as age, income, or criminal background.

CAREER CRIMINALS

Criminology has struggled with the enigma of the career criminal, or **chronic offender.** The idea of the chronic offender was established by the pioneering research of Marvin Wolfgang, Robert Figlio, and Thorsten Sellin. The trio used official records to follow a **cohort** of 9,945 males born in Philadelphia in 1945 until they turned eighteen years of age in 1963. Released in 1972, the resulting study showed that 6 percent of the cohort had committed five or more offenses. Furthermore, this "chronic 6 percent" were responsible for 71 percent of the murders attributed to the cohort, 82 percent of the robberies, 69 percent of the aggravated assaults, and 73 percent of the rapes.[89] The existence of chronic offenders has been corroborated by further research, such as that done by Lawrence Sherman in Kansas City. Sherman found that although only 2.7 percent of the city's roughly 500,000 inhabitants were arrested twice or more in 1990, these offenders accounted for over 60 percent of all arrests that year.[90]

Why do chronic offenders persist in their criminal behavior? Each of the theories that we have studied in this chapter offers a glimpse of an answer. Those that focus on the individual posit that chronic offenders continue to commit crimes because they choose to or because they are biologically or psychologically disposed in that direction. Other theories concentrate on the social context of the chronic offender. Whatever the reasons behind repeat offending, criminologists' work in this area has had a significant impact on the criminal justice system. Law enforcement agencies and district attorneys' offices have devised specific strategies to apprehend and prosecute repeat offenders, with dozens of local police agencies forming career criminal units to combat the problem. Legislators have also reacted to this research, and habitual offender laws—with harsher prison sentences for repeat offenders—have become very popular. We will discuss these statutes, including the controversial "three-strikes-and-you're-out" laws, in Chapter 11.

↗ONLINE REVIEW *Go to the book's Web site for an interactive review of this section*

AP Photo/Nick Ut

Actor Robert Downey, Jr., makes a plea to Municipal Court Judge Lawrence Mia in a Malibu, California, courtroom. Downey was eventually sentenced to prison for a prior drug conviction. Why do many observers believe there is a strong link between the use of illegal drugs and crime?

Criminology from Theory to Practice

You have almost completed the only chapter in this textbook that deals primarily with theory. What follows will concentrate on the more practical and legal aspects of the criminal justice system: how law enforcement agencies fight crime, how our court systems determine guilt or innocence, and how we punish those who are found guilty. As career criminal units and "three-strikes-and-you're-out" laws show, however, criminology plays a crucial role in controlling crime. To cite just one example of many, several years ago nearly 25 percent of Boston youth homicides, gun assaults, and drug offenses occurred in an area covering 4 percent of the city.[91] Due in part to the efforts of crime researchers such as Lawrence W. Sherman and David Weisburd,[92] law enforcement agencies in the city started to target these high-crime settings, known as "hot spots," with intensive prevention strategies. Using computer programs that "map" patterns of crime, police departments are increasingly able to divert resources to the areas that need them the most. (We will further discuss the use of this technology in police operations in Chapter 6.)

There is a sense, however, that criminology has not done enough to make our country a safer place. When investigators took nearly eight months to search the backyard of Ward Weaver III in the incident that opened this chapter, many Oregon City residents wondered what took so long. After all, as you recall, Weaver's father had committed a similar murder twenty years earlier. "I'm not a

INFOTRAC KEYWORDS
career criminals

For more information, use this search term with InfoTrac College Edition, your online library at www.infotrac-college.com

cop," said a local waitress, "but I think they should have been looking at that concrete slab."[93] To put it another way, if criminologists know that there is a link between family members and criminal activity, why didn't the law enforcement agents when searching for the two missing girls make use of this knowledge?

Many criminal justice practitioners would argue that too much of the research done by criminologists is inaccessible. As Sarah J. Hart, director of the National Institute of Justice, has noted, an overworked police chief simply does not have the time or the patience to wade through the many scientific journals in which crime research appears.[94] Hart urges researchers to recognize who their audience is and to present their material accordingly. The lines of communication between criminologists and practitioners are critical, especially because, in the opinion of many crime experts, researchers know more today about "what works" in criminology than at any time in our nation's history.[95]

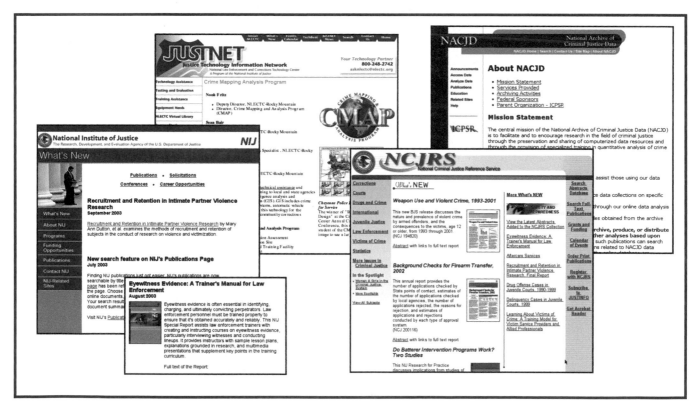

The Internet has become a very important resource for information on crime in the United States. Pictured above are just a few of the numerous Web sites devoted to the study of crime. Such sites provide statistics that criminologists and others interested in criminal behavior can use to support or criticize the various theories discussed in this chapter.

>The Link between Guns and Crime

Approximately 40,000 Americans are killed each year by guns in incidents ranging from suicide to homicide. As noted earlier, according to the most recent FBI statistics, firearms are used in 71 percent of murders and 42 percent of robberies in the United States.[96] Roughly speaking, there is one gun per person in this country, and half of our households own at least one firearm.[97] The link between guns and violent behavior seems obvious, but drawing conclusions from statistics is often problematic. As we will see in this *Criminal Justice in Action* feature, there is considerable debate as to whether there is, in fact, any causal relationship between the prevalence of firearms in our society and their use in criminal activity and, if so, whether gun control laws can affect this relationship.

Do Guns Mean More Crime?

Supporters of the theory that gun ownership promotes crime have a wealth of information at their fingertips, some of it reaching back more than one hundred years. Criminologist Gregory Weaver of Auburn University has suggested that a dramatic increase in homicides by gunfire in the final decades of the 1800s is directly related to a rise in the availability of guns following the Civil War (1861–1865).[98] The national supply of guns grew sharply after the end of the war, as the Union army sold its stockpile of weapons back to private manufacturers, which in turn sold the firearms to the public. Furthermore, soldiers on both sides were often allowed to keep their guns as they returned home.

Weaver also cites a significant increase in the size of gun sections in the Sears, Roebuck and Montgomery Ward mail-order catalogues between 1880 and 1900 to show that Americans were becoming more interested in gun ownership during that time period.[99] Mark Duggan of the University of Chicago

has used a similar technique in one of the latest studies to connect gun ownership with violent crime.[100] One of the problems of research on this subject is that it is very difficult to know exactly how many people own guns and how many guns they own. To tackle this problem, Duggan obtained information concerning state- and county-level sales of gun magazines, reasoning that readers of such publications were likely to be gun owners. Using data covering 1990 to 1998, Duggan found that a 10 percent average increase in a state's gun ownership (as measured by sales of the magazines) was associated with a 2 percent rise in its homicide rate.

Do Guns Mean More Crime? Part II

Figures that show violent crime rates increasing with gun ownership are often interpreted one of two ways: either crime rises when people have more guns, or people buy

Peggy Landry of New Orleans is pictured here proudly showing off her handgun and concealed-weapon license. Thanks to a law passed recently by the Louisiana legislature, Landry and other citizens of the state are allowed to open fire on a person "who is reasonably believed" to be using "unlawful force" or making an "unlawful entry" into a car they happen to be driving. What might some of the drawbacks of such a law be?

more guns to defend themselves when crime rises. Economist John Lott of the American Enterprise Institute supports a third, and controversial, point of view. Lott believes that gun ownership deters crime. By comparing crime rates in communities before and after they passed "right-to-carry" gun laws (which allow an adult applicant to be granted a concealed-weapon permit unless he or she is a felon or has a history of mental illness), Lott has estimated that such laws reduced homicide by 8 percent, sexual assault by 5 percent, aggravated assault by 7 percent, and robbery by 3 percent. In the more than thirty states that currently have right-to-carry laws on the books, violent crime is 13 percent lower than in those states that do not have such laws.[101] Though even Lott is not willing to say that right-to-carry laws directly cause a drop in violent crime—other contributing factors could include population density and sentencing lengths—he does believe that these reductions are partly attributable to the deterrent effect that weapons have on criminal behavior by reducing the number of "helpless victims" who are often targets of criminals.[102]

The Brady Bill

For government and law enforcement agencies, the important question is not "Do guns cause crime?" but rather, "How can we keep people from using guns to commit crimes?" Statistically, most guns will never be used to inflict harm on another human being; only 1.1 percent of all handguns and 0.1 percent of "long guns" (shotguns, rifles, and so on) in the United States are involved in criminal activity each year.[103] The challenge, therefore, is first to determine who might use a gun to commit a crime and then to keep the gun out of that person's hands.

In general, a criminal obtains a firearm in one of three ways: by stealing it, by purchasing it from a gun dealer, or by purchasing it from a private citizen.[104] As it is almost impossible to control the private gun market among law-abiding citizens, and law enforcement agencies already expend a great deal of energy trying to control traffic in stolen guns, most recent gun control laws focus on gun dealers.

To that end, Congress passed the Brady Handgun Violence Prevention Act in 1993.[105] Commonly known as the Brady Bill, this measure requires local law enforcement agencies to conduct background checks of potential handgun purchasers. From the effective date of the Brady Bill until 2002, approximately 40,000 gun-

purchase applications were rejected. Nearly 60 percent of the denials were based on felony convictions or indictments found during the background check, with another 15 percent due to domestic violence misdemeanors.[106] From 1993 to 1998, the Justice Department found that crimes committed with handguns fell 52 percent, or twice the rate that crimes fell overall.[107]

The Brady Bill has been criticized for not going far enough. The law requires background checks only for those who purchase guns from federally licensed firearms dealers. It does not cover purchases made at gun shows or from private citizens, which represent between 30 and 40 percent of the market.[108] Indeed, a number of states have enacted much more restrictive gun control laws than are required under the Brady Bill. In a reaction to the fatal shootings at Columbine High School, in 2001 Colorado became the twentieth state to require background checks for all public gun sales, including sales at gun shows. In Massachusetts, gun dealers may not sell a firearm unless it has a safety device that enables a user to know whether the gun is loaded and a "trigger lock" designed to prevent accidental shootings. That state also banned all sales of "Saturday night specials," cheap handguns that are often used in crimes.

Fingerprinting Firearms

Perhaps the most important development in this area is the ability of the federal government to "fingerprint" guns. Today, almost every gun is manufactured with a serial number, and firearm companies provide the Bureau of Alcohol, Tobacco, Firearms and Explosives (ATF) with detailed information concerning the marks made on shell casings by every weapon they produce. With this information, the ATF can "trace" a gun used in a crime to its original owner and the store where it was purchased. This technology, developed in Canada, is being used in twenty-seven countries, including Australia, Germany, Spain, and Sweden. Only two states, Maryland and New York, require that ballistics data be gathered on every handgun made and sold within state lines. Public pressure to require more firearm fingerprinting increased after the sniper shootings in the Washington, D.C., area in 2002. Supporters of the technology argue that a national database would have led law enforcement agents to the suspects much more quickly, perhaps even before all of their eighteen victims had been killed or injured.[109]

MAKING SENSE OF THE LINK BETWEEN GUNS AND CRIME

1 After reviewing the various theories concerning ownership of guns and crime in this feature, which one do you think is most likely to be correct? Why?

2 In a single year, guns are used to murder about 15 people in Japan, 30 people in Great Britain, 100 people in Canada, and about 11,500 in the United States. Are these figures relevant for the gun control debate in our country? Explain your answer.

3 With the "fingerprinting" system described above, law enforcement agents can now trace guns back to their dealers. Should a gun dealer be charged with a crime if he or she improperly sells a handgun that is later used to commit a homicide? Why or why not?

INFOTRAC KEYWORDS

crime and age; guns and crime; Brandy Handgun Violence Prevention Act

For more information, use these search terms with InfoTrac College Edition, your online library at www.infotrac-college.com

---

Chapter Summary

1 **Explain why classical criminology is based on choice theory.** Choice theory holds that those who commit crimes choose to do so. Classical criminology was based on a model of a person rationally making a choice before committing a crime—weighing the benefits against the costs.

2 **Contrast positivism with classical criminology.** Whereas classical theorists believe criminals make rational choices, those of the positivist school believe that criminal behavior is determined by psychological, biological, and social forces that the individual cannot control.

3 **List and describe the three theories of social structure that help explain crime.** Social disorganization theory states that crime is largely a product of unfavorable conditions in certain communities, or zones of disorganization. The strain theory argues that most people seek increased wealth and financial security and that the strain of not being able to achieve these goals legally leads to criminal behavior. Finally, cultural deviance theory asserts that people adapt to the values of the subculture—which has its own standards of behavior—to which they belong.

4 **List the six focal concerns that dominate disorganized community existence.** (a) Trouble, (b) toughness, (c) smartness, (d) fate, (e) excitement, and (f) autonomy.

5 **List and briefly explain the three branches of social process theory.** (a) Learning theory, which contends that people learn to be criminals from their family and peers. (b) Control theory, which holds that most of us are dissuaded from a life of crime because we place importance on the opinions of family and peers. (c) Labeling theory, which holds that a person labeled a "junkie" or a "thief" will respond by remaining whatever she or he is labeled.

6 **Explain some of the links between income level and crime.** Statistically, poor people commit more crimes, and are the victims of more crimes, than those in the middle- and upper-income levels. Evidence shows, however, that income is not as important as other factors such as family disorganization, lack of education, and lack of employment. Indeed, the majority of all residents in low-income neighborhoods are law abiding.

7 **Identify some of the reasons criminologists give to explain the high rate of delinquent and criminal behavior by adolescents and young adults.** (a) Young males have high levels of testosterone, which increases aggression; (b) adolescents are more susceptible to peer pressure and, therefore, can be convinced to misbehave by friends and peers; (c) teen-agers often seek the "thrill" of crime or delinquency to alleviate boredom; and (d) risk factors such as lack of parental supervision, poor academic achievement, weapon carrying, gang membership, and low intelligence increase the likelihood of criminal behavior.

STORIES FROM THE STREET

Go to the Stories from the Street feature at www.cjinaction.com to hear Larry Gaines tell insightful stories related to this chapter and his experiences in the field.

8 **Discuss how social conflict theory can be used to explain the disproportionate number of minority group members who are arrested for committing crimes involving illegal drugs.** Social conflict theory holds that criminal law is designed to protect whatever members of society are in power. Even though drug use is basically constant regardless of income level and race, the majority of Americans arrested for drug crimes are members of the "underclass." Therefore, some criminologists believe that our drug laws and the way they are enforced contribute to the repression of the poor and minorities.

9 **Identify the problem that criminal justice practitioners have with crime researchers, and discuss what can be done to resolve it.** Often, practitioners do not have the time or the patience to read about crime research in scientific journals. Consequently, the research does not reach those for whom it would be the most useful. Criminologists are urged to consider their audience when presenting their research; by making it more accessible, they will ensure that it has a greater impact on the criminal justice system.

Key Terms

anomie   47
choice theory   40
chronic offender   62
classical criminology   40
cohort   62
control theory   50
criminology   39
cultural deviance
   theory   47

labeling theory   50
learning theory   50
life course
   criminology   53
positivism   40
social conflict
   theories   52
social disorganization
   theory   46

social process
   theories   49
social reality of crime   52
strain theory   47
subculture   47
theory of differential
   association   50
utilitarianism   40

Questions for Critical Analysis

1 What is one possible reason for higher crime rates in lower-income communities?

2 If you believe that fear of punishment can have a deterrent effect on criminal activity, to what view of human behavior are you subscribing?

3 If you believe that criminals learn how to be criminals, to what theory are you subscribing?

4 Why have social conflict theories had a limited impact on public policy in the United States?

5 Why is it important for criminologists to study the behavior of preadolescents?

6 Why is it significant that two neighborhoods located near each other can have quite different crime rates?

7 What are some of the explanations for the high rate of arrests of minorities compared to whites?

8 What is a chronic offender, and why is this sort of person of interest to criminologists?

▶ TEST PREPARATION ONLINE

Go to www.cjinaction.com for tools to aid you in studying for your exams. Click on *Online Reviews* under *Chapter Resources* for an interactive review of each major section of this chapter. Under *Chapter Resources*, you will also find the *Chapter Outline*, *Chapter Summary*, *Flashcards*, *Glossary*, *Learning Objectives*, *Lecture Presentations*, *Concept Builder*, *Essay Questions*, and a *Tutorial Quiz*. You can also test yourself with a game of *Concentration* or the *Crossword Puzzle*.

Go to www.cjinaction.com for a wealth of online resources. Explore the *Internet Activities* and *Class Project*s under *Chapter Resources*. Check out the *Web Links* to access the Web sites mentioned in the text, as well as many others. You can also access recent perspectives by clicking on *CJ in the News* and *Terrorism Update* under *Course Resources*. If you'd like some mentoring, click on *Board of Mentors* under *Book Resources*.

For additional information, explore InfoTrac College Edition, your online library that offers complete full-length articles from thousands of scholarly and popular publications. Click on *InfoTrac College Edition* under *Chapter Resources* at www.cjinaction.com for a list of key words and InfoTrac exercises. Use the passcode that came with your book.

Cote, Suzette, ed., *Criminological Theories: Bridging the Past to the Future,* Thousand Oaks, CA: Sage Publications, 2002. This anthology covers all the major criminological theories, including articles on social, biological, and cultural causes of crime. It also offers a criminological perspective on white-collar crime and investigates feminist criminal theory. Though most of the thirty-six articles were originally published in scholarly journals, they have been edited in this edition to make them accessible to students interested in delving deeper into the various explanations of criminal behavior.

Lott, John R., *More Guns, Less Crime: Understanding Crime and Gun-Control Laws,* Chicago: University of Chicago Press, 2000. This controversial book contains the statistical results of an economist's research. He purports to show that those states that allow concealed weapons have less crime than other states. In other words, Lott argues that when citizens can legally carry guns, crime rates fall.

Notes

1. Fox Butterfield, "Father Steals Best: Crime in an American Family," *New York Times* (August 21, 2002), 1A.
2. National Center for Policy Analysis, "Is Crime Hereditary?" September 5, 2002, at http://www.ncpa.org/iss/cri/2002/pd090502a.html.
3. *Ibid.*
4. Richard Rosenfeld, "Book Review: The Limits of Crime Control," *Journal of Criminal Law and Criminology* (Fall 2002), 290.
5. Tim Cahill, *Buried Dreams: Inside the Mind of a Serial Killer* (New York: Bantam Books, 1986), 349.
6. James Q. Wilson and Richard J. Hernstein, *Crime and Human Nature: The Definitive Study of the Causes of Crime* (New York: Simon & Schuster, 1985), 515.
7. *Ibid.*
8. Jeremy Bentham, *An Introduction to the Principles of Morals and Legislation,* ed. W. Harrison (Oxford: Basil Blackwell, 1948).
9. Wilson and Hernstein, 44.
10. Jack Katz, *Seductions of Crime: Moral and Sensual Attractions of Doing Evil* (New York: Basic Books, 1988).
11. "Ex-Supervisor Held Unable to Tell Right from Wrong," *New York Times* (May 8, 1979), A16.
12. Laura Mansnerus, "The Darker Side Of the 'Baby Blues,'" *New York Times* (October 12, 1988), C1.
13. L. E. Kreuz and R. M. Rose, "Assessment of Aggressive Behavior and Plasma Testosterone in a Young Criminal Population," *Psychosomatic Medicine* 34 (1972), 321–332.
14. H. Persky, K. Smith, and G. Basu, "Relation of Psychological Measures of Aggression and Hostility to Testosterone Production in Men," *Psychosomatic Medicine* 33 (1971), 265, 276.
15. Leda Cosmides and John Tooby, "Cognitive Adaptations for Social Exchange," in *The Adapted Mind: Evolutionary Psychology and the Generation of Culture,* ed. Jerome H. Berkow, Leda Cosmides, and John Tooby (New York: Oxford University Press, 1992).
16. Lee Ellis and Anthony Walsh, "Gene-Based Evolutionary Theories in Criminology," *Criminology* 35 (May 1997), 229–276.
17. Avshalom Caspi, Joseph McClay, Terrie E. Moffitt, and Jonathan Mill, "Role of Genotype in the Cycle of Violence in Maltreated Children," *Science* (August 2, 2002), 851–854.
18. 14 Wash.App. 733–744, 544 P. 2d 758 (1976).
19. Sarnoff A. Mednick and Karl O. Christiansen, eds., *Biosocial Bases in Criminal Behavior* (New York: Gardner Press, 1977).
20. David C. Rowe, "Genetic and Environmental Components of Antisocial Behavior: A Study of 265 Twin Pairs," *Criminology* 24 (1986), 513–532.
21. Alison Pike and Robert Plomin, "Importance of Nonshared Environmental Factors for Childhood and Adolescent Psychopathology," *Journal of the American Academy of Child and Adolescent Psychopathology* 35 (May 1996), 560.

22. D. Williams, "Neural Factors Related to Habitual Aggression," *Brain* 92 (1969), 503.

23. Hervey M. Cleckley, *The Mask of Sanity,* 4th ed. (St. Louis: Mosby, 1964.)

24. Richard J. Herrnstein and Charles Murray, *The Bell Curve: Intelligence and Class Structure in American Life* (New York: Free Press, 1994), n. 19.

25. Claude S. Fischer, *Inequality by Design: Cracking the Bell Curve Myth* (Princeton, NJ: Princeton University Press, 1996), 185.

26. Francis T. Cullen, Paul Gendreau, G. Roger Jarjoura, and John P. Wright, "Crime and the Bell Curve: Lessons from Intelligent Criminology," *Crime and Delinquency* (October 1997), 387–411.

27. Robert Park, Ernest Burgess, and Roderic McKenzie, *The City* (Chicago: University of Chicago Press, 1929).

28. Clifford R. Shaw, Henry D. McKay, and Leonard S. Cottrell, *Delinquency Areas* (Chicago: University of Chicago Press, 1929).

29. Clifford R. Shaw and Henry D. McKay, *Report on the Causes of Crime, Vol. 2: Social Factors in Juvenile Delinquency* (Washington, D.C.: National Commission on Law Observance and Enforcement, 1931).

30. Robert. J. Sampson, "Transcending Tradition: New Directions in Community Research, Chicago Style," *Criminology* (May 2002), 216–217.

31. Jeffrey D. Morenoff, Robert J. Sampson, and Stephen W. Raudenbush, "Neighborhood Inequality, Collective Efficacy, and the Spatial Dynamics of Urban Violence," *Criminology* (August 2001), 517–560.

32. Emile Durkheim, *The Rules of Sociological Method,* trans. Sarah A. Solovay and John H. Mueller (New York: Free Press, 1964).

33. Robert K. Merton, *Social Theory and Social Structure* (New York: Free Press, 1957). See the chapter on "Social Structure and *Anomie*."

34. Robert Agnew, "Foundation for a General Strain Theory of Crime and Delinquency," *Criminology* 30 (1992), 47–87.

35. Robert Agnew, Timothy Brezina, John Paul Wright, and Francis T. Cullen, "Strain, Personality Traits, and Delinquency: Extending General Strain Theory," *Criminology* (February 2002), 43–71.

36. Walter B. Miller, "Lower Class Culture as a Generating Milieu of Gang Delinquency," *Journal of Social Issues* 14 (1958), 5–19.

37. Liqun Cao, Anthony Adams, and Vickie J. Jensen, "A Test of the Black Subculture of Violence Thesis," *Criminology* 35 (May 1997), 367–379.

38. Philip G. Zimbardo, "The Human Choice: Individuation, Reason, and Order versus Deindividuation, Impulse, and Chaos," in *Nebraska Symposium on Motivation,* ed. William J. Arnold and David Levie (Lincoln, Neb: University of Nebraska Press, 1969), 287–293.

39. Edwin H. Sutherland, *Criminology,* 4th ed. (Philadelphia: Lippincott, 1947).

40. L. Rowell Huesmann, Jessica Moise-Titus, Cheryl-Lynn Podolski, and Leonard D. Eron, "Longitudinal Relations between Children's Exposure to TV Violence and Their Aggressive and Violent Behavior in Young Adulthood: 1977–1992," *Developmental Psychology* (March 2003), 201.

41. Telecommunications Act of 1996, 47 U.S.C. Section 303 (1999). The act requires that televisions with a diagonal screen of thirteen inches or larger that are sold or manufactured in the United States contain a "V-chip" blocking device. This technology allows parents or other users to block television signals based on the sexual and violent content of the programs.

42. Travis Hirschi, *Causes of Delinquency* (Berkeley: University of California Press, 1969).

43. James Q. Wilson and George L. Kelling, "Broken Windows," *Atlantic Monthly* (March 1982), 29.

44. Howard S. Becker, *Outsiders: Studies in the Sociology of Deviance* (New York: Free Press, 1963).

45. Lawrence L. Shornack, "Conflict Theory and the Family," *International Social Science Review* 62 (1987), 154–157.

46. Robert Meier, "The New Criminology: Continuity in Criminology Theory," *Journal of Criminal Law and Criminology* 67 (1977), 461–469.

47. Richard Quinney, *The Social Reality of Crime* (Boston: Little, Brown, 1970).

48. "U.S. Census Bureau Special Edition Black History Month Daily Feature," *U.S. Newswire* (February 7, 2003).

49. Laura Session Stepp, "Young-Girl Network," *Washington Post* (August 9, 2003), C01.

50. Nicole Hahn Rafter, *Partial Justice: Women, Prisons, and Social Control* (New Brunswick, NJ: Transaction Publishers, 1990).

51. John A. Coleman, "Book Review: *Urban Injustice: How Ghettos Happen,*" *America* (December 1, 2002), 20.

52. Francis T. Cullen and Robert Agnew, *Criminological Theory, Past to Present: Essential Readings,* 2nd ed. (Los Angeles: Roxbury Publishing Co., 2003), 12.

53. *Ibid.,* 443.

54. Michael R. Gottfredson and Travis Hirschi, *A General Theory of Crime* (Stanford, CA: Stanford University Press, 1990).

55. *Ibid.,* 90.

56. *Ibid.*

57. Terrie Moffitt, "Adolescent-Limited and Life-Course-Persistent Antisocial Behavior: A Developmental Taxonomy," *Psychological Review* 100 (1993), 679–680.

58. *Ibid.,* 674.

59. Robert J. Sampson and John H. Laub, *Crime in the Making: Pathways and Turning Points through Life* (Cambridge, MA: Harvard University Press, 1993), 11.

60. Federal Bureau of Investigation, *Crime in the United States, 2002* (Washington, D.C.: U.S. Department of Justice, 2003), Figure 2.4, page 12.

61. Patsy A. Klaus, *Crime and the Nation's Households, 2000* (Washington, D.C.: Bureau of Justice Statistics, September 2002), 5.

62. "Homicide and Other Crimes Are on the Rise in California," *New York Times* (April 28, 2002), A20.

63. "Fighting Back," *Chicago Tribune* (June 25, 2003), 18.

64. Kevin Johnson, "Crime Keeps Cincinnati Reeling," *USA Today* (July 8, 2002), A03.

65. Jill Levoy, "The Untold Agony of Black-on-Black Murder," *Los Angeles Times* (January 26, 2003), A22.

66. James Q. Wilson, "The Family Way," *Wall Street Journal* (January 7, 2003), A12.

67. *Ibid.*

68. Caroline Wolf Harlow, *Education and Correctional Populations* (Washington, D.C.: Bureau of Justice Statistics, January 2003), 1.

69. Charles Tittle and Robert Meier, "Specifying the SES/Delinquency Relationship," *Criminology* 28 (1990), 270–301.

70. *Crime in the United States, 2002,* 252.

71. Bureau of Justice Statistics, *Criminal Victimization, 2001* (Washington, D.C.: U.S. Department of Justice, September 2002), Table 2, page 6.

72. Arthur H. Garrison, "Disproportionate Minority Arrests: A Note on What Has Been Said and How It Fits Together," *New England Journal on Criminal and Civil Confinement* (Winter 1997), 29.

73. Eric A. Stewart, Ronald L. Simons, and Rand D. Donger, "Assessing Neighborhood and Social Psychological Influences on Childhood Violence in an African American Sample," *Criminology* (November 2002), 801–829.

74. Margaret Farnworth, Raymond H. C. Teske, Jr., and Gina Thurman, "Ethnic, Racial, and Minority Disparity in Felony Court Processing," in *Race and Criminal Justice,* ed. Michael J. Lynch and E. Britt Patterson (New York: Harrow & Heston, 1991), 55–57.

75. Robert Agnew, *Juvenile Delinquency: Causes and Control* (Los Angeles: Roxbury Publishing Co., 2001), 1–3.

76. Avshalom Caspi and Terrie Moffitt, "The Continuity of Maladaptive Behavior: From Description to Under-standing in the Study of Antisocial Behavior," in Dante Cicchetti and Donald J. Cohen, eds., *Manual of Developmental Psychology* (New York: John Wiley, 1995), 493.

77. Delbert S. Elliot and Scott Menard, "Delinquent Friends and Delinquent Behavior: Temporal and Developmental Patterns," in Rolf Loeber and David P. Farrington, eds., *Delinquency and Crime: Current Theories* (Thousand Oaks, CA: Sage Publications, 1996), 47–66.

78. *National Survey of American Attitudes on Substance Abuse VIII: Teens and Parents* (New York: National Center on Addiction and Substance Abuse at Columbia University, August 2003), 2.

79. Rolf Loeber, David P. Farrington, and David Petechuk, *Child Delinquency: Early Intervention and Prevention* (Washington, D.C.: Office of Juvenile Justice and Delinquency Prevention, May 2003), 6–9.

80. James Q. Wilson, "What to Do about Crime," *Commentary* (September 1994), 25–35.

81. Beth Bjerregaard and Alan J. Lizotte, "Gun Ownership and Gang Membership," *Journal of Criminal Law and Criminology* (Fall 1995), 37–58.

82. Joseph F. Sheley and Victoria E. Brewer, *Public Health Reports* (January–February 1995), 18–27.

83. *Crime in the United States, 2002,* 22, 32, 38.

84. Scott H. Decker, Leanne Fiftal Alarid, and Charles M. Katz, *Controversies in Criminal Justice: Contemporary Readings* (Los Angeles: Roxbury Publishing Co., 2003), 36–37.

85. *Behind Bars: Substance Abuse and America's Prison Population* (New York: The National Center on Addiction and Substance Abuse at Columbia University, 1998), 6.

86. James Alan Fox and Jack Levin, *The Will to Kill: Making Sense of Senseless Murder* (Needham, MA: Allyn & Bacon, 2001), 33–37.

87. M. Lyn Exum, "The Application and Robustness of the Rational Choice Perspective in the Study of Intoxicated and Angry Intentions to Aggress," *Criminology* (November 2002), 933–966.

88. Celia C. Lo, "An Application of Social Conflict Theory to Arrestees' Use of Cocaine and Opiates," *Journal of Drug Issues* (January 1, 2003), 237.

89. Marvin Wolfgang, Robert Figlio, and Thorsten Sellin, *Delinquency in a Birth Cohort* (Chicago: University of Chicago Press, 1972).

90. Lawrence W. Sherman, "Attacking Crime: Police and Crime Control," in *Modern Policing,* ed. Michael Tonry and Norval Morris (Chicago: University of Chicago Press, 1992), 159.

91. David M. Kennedy, "Pulling Levers: Chronic Offenders, High Crime Settings, and a Theory of Prevention," *Valparaiso University Law Review* (Spring 1997), 449.

92. See Lawrence W. Sherman, Patrick R. Gartin, and Michael E. Buerger, "Hot Spots of Predatory Crime: Routine Activities and Criminology of Place," *Criminology* 27 (1989), 27–55; and John Eck and David Weisburd, "Crime Place in Crime Theory," in *Crime and Place,* ed. John Eck and David Weisburd (Monsey, NY: Criminal Justice Press, 1995).

93. John Ritter, "A Town Wonders: Does Crime Run in Families?" *USA Today* (September 5, 2002), 1A.

94. Sarah J. Hart, "A New Way of Doing Business at the NIJ," *Law Enforcement News* (January 15/31, 2002), 9.

95. Rosenfeld, 292.

96. *Crime in the United States, 2002,* 22, 32.

97. Gary Kleck, *Targeting Guns* (New York: Aldine de Gruyter, 1997), 8.

98. William Claiborne, "Decades of Murders Restored to Life," *Washington Post* (March 6, 2001), A3.

99. *Ibid.*

100. Mark Duggan, *More Guns, More Crime* (Cambridge, MA: National Bureau of Economic Research, October 2000).

101. John R. Lott, Jr., "Does Allowing Law-Abiding Citizens to Carry Concealed Handguns Save Lives?" *Valparaiso University Law Review* 31 (Spring 1997), 355.

102. John R. Lott, Jr., and David Muster, "Crime, Deterrence, and Right to Carry Concealed Handguns," *Journal of Legal Studies* 26 (1997), 1.

103. Kleck, 8.

104. Jerry J. Phillips, "The Relation of Constitutional and Tort Law to Gun Injuries and Deaths in the United States," *Connecticut Law Review* (Summer 2000), 1342.

105. Pub. L. No. 103-159, 107 Stat. 1536 (1993); codified as amended at 18 U.S.C. Sections 922(s)-(t) (1995).

106. Lee Davidson, "Is the Brady Bill Doing Enough?" *Deseret News* (September 23, 2002), A01.

107. Fox Butterfield, "Study Disputes Success of the Brady Law," *New York Times* (August 2, 2000), A12.

108. Jens Ludwig and Philip J. Cook, "Homicide and Suicide Rates Associated with Implementation of the Brady Handgun Violence Prevention Act," *Journal of the American Medical Association* 284 (August 2, 2000), 585–591.

109. Jonathan Alter, "Pull the Trigger on Fingerprints," *Newsweek* (October 28, 2002), 41.

STANDARD INDEX CRIME
1971 - 2002

9,000
8,000
7,000
6,000
5,000
4,000
3,000
2,000
1,000
0

>Chapter 3<

Defining and Measuring Crime

>chapter objectives<

After reading this chapter, you should be able to:

1 Explain the differences between crimes *mala in se* and *mala prohibita*.

2 List and explain the six basic elements of any crime.

3 Delineate the elements required to establish *mens rea* (a guilty mental state).

4 Explain how the doctrine of strict liability applies to criminal law.

5 Identify the publication in which the FBI reports crime data and list the three ways it does so.

6 Distinguish between Part I and Part II offenses as defined in the Uniform Crime Report (UCR).

7 Describe some of the shortcomings of the UCR as a crime-measuring tool.

8 Distinguish between the National Crime Victimization Survey and self-reported surveys.

9 Explain why criminologists pay particular attention to the age of crime victims in the United States.

10 List the arguments for and against a constitutional amendment to protect victims' rights.

Murder or a Terrorist Attack?

According to the Federal Bureau of Investigation (FBI), criminal homicide occurs when one human being willfully kills another. Using this definition, more than 3,480 criminal homicides took place in New York City during 2001—a 400 percent increase over the previous year's figures. When the federal government released its crime data for that year, however, the criminal homicide rate in New York had dropped by 12 percent. How was this possible?

Sometimes, homicide is not homicide. After months of deliberation, FBI officials decided not to include the 2,752 victims of the September 11, 2001, terrorist attacks on the World Trade Center in New York's final criminal homicide totals. This was not a snap decision. At various times over several months, the FBI had not only considered counting the dead as homicide victims, but also the thousands injured in the attacks as aggravated assaults and the destruction of the affected area as a property crime.

Finally, however, the bureau decided that the events of September 11 were not part of the "day-to-day crimes committed in this country" and that including them in official statistics would "create many difficulties in defining and analyzing crime as we know it." Instead, FBI statisticians are considering creating a new crime classification solely to measure the result of terrorism on American soil.

At a memorial service in Weston, Massachusetts, each rolled flag represents a victim of the September 11, 2001, terrorist attacks.

> **What difference** does it make whether those killed in the September 11 attacks were victims of criminal homicide or criminal terrorism? In fact, as we will see in this chapter, definitions and measurements of crimes are tools that help us fight crime. In the United States, including the victims of terrorist attacks in annual crime figures would "skew" those figures, limiting their usefulness.[1] German law enforcement officials, however, chose to label the September 11 suicide pilots "murderers" so that two Moroccan students living in Germany could be charged with 3,066 counts of "assisting in homicide" for providing aid to the terrorists.[2]

The collection of crime data is not an exact science. In 2001, after almost a decade of falling crime rates, data collected by one method—which relies on police reports—indicated that rates had begun to rise.[3] A year later, according to data collected by another method—which relies on victims' reports—crime rates were at

CONCEPT BUILDER
Crime patterns assist criminologists and criminal justice professionals in important decision-making tasks. Visit www.cjinaction.com for an interactive exploration of this key topic.

their lowest levels in thirty years.[4] Crime data also raise numerous questions. Could the dramatic drop in murders in the 1990s have been due not to better police work, but to improvements in emergency medical care that enabled those wounded by criminal acts to get to hospitals before they had a chance to die?[5] We will start our examination of these subjects with an overview of how crimes are classified, move on to the various methods of measuring crime, and end with a discussion of a group that crime statistics have helped bring to national attention—the victims.

Classification of Crimes

The huge body of the law may be broken down according to various classifications. Three of the most important distinctions can be made between (1) civil law and criminal law, (2) felonies and misdemeanors, and (3) crimes *mala in se* and *mala prohibita*.

CIVIL LAW AND CRIMINAL LAW

All law can be divided into two categories: civil law and criminal law. As U.S. criminal law has evolved, it has diverged from U.S. civil law. The two categories of law are distinguished by their primary goals. The criminal justice system is concerned with protecting society from harm by preventing and prosecuting crimes. A crime is an act so reprehensible that it is considered a wrong against society as a whole, as well as against the individual victim.[6] Therefore, the state prosecutes a person who commits a criminal act. If the state is able to prove that a person is guilty of a crime, the government will punish her or him with imprisonment or fines, or both.

Civil law, which includes all types of law other than criminal law, is concerned with disputes between private individuals and between entities. Proceedings in civil lawsuits are normally initiated by an individual or a corporation (in contrast to criminal proceedings, which are initiated by public prosecutors). Such disputes may involve, for example, the terms of a contract, the ownership of property, or an automobile accident. Under civil law, the government provides a forum for the resolution of torts, or private wrongs, in which the injured party, called the *plaintiff,* tries to prove that a wrong has been committed by the accused party, or the *defendant.* (Note that the accused party in both criminal and civil cases is known as the defendant.) Most civil cases involve a request for monetary damages in recognition that a wrong has been committed. If, for example, a driver runs a red light and hits a pedestrian, the pedestrian could file a civil suit asking for monetary compensation for the "pain and suffering" caused by his or her injuries. (See *Mastering Concepts* on the next page for a comparison of civil and criminal law.)

AP/Daniel Hulshizer

Former professional basketball player Jayson Williams, center, was charged with manslaughter in the shooting death of his limousine driver, Costas Christofi. In 2003, while the criminal trial was ongoing, Williams paid Christofi's family $2.75 million to settle a civil wrongful death lawsuit. How does this case highlight the differences between civil law and criminal law?

Civil Law
The branch of law dealing with the definition and enforcement of all private or public rights, as opposed to criminal matters.

> Civil Law versus Criminal Law

ISSUE	CIVIL LAW	CRIMINAL LAW
Area of concern	Rights and duties between individuals	Offenses against society as a whole
Wrongful act	Harm to a person or business entity	Violation of a statute that prohibits some type of activity
Party who brings suit	Person who suffered harm (plaintiff)	The state
Party who responds	Person who supposedly caused harm (defendant)	Person who allegedly committed crime (defendant)
Standard of proof	Preponderance of the evidence	Beyond a reasonable doubt
Remedy	Damages to compensate for the harm	Punishment (fine or incarceration)

Although criminal law proceedings are completely separate from civil law proceedings in the modern legal system, the two systems do have some similarities. Both attempt to control behavior by imposing sanctions on those who violate the law. Furthermore, criminal and civil law often supplement each other. In certain instances, a victim may file a civil suit against an individual who is also the target of a criminal prosecution by the government.

Because the burden of proof is much greater in criminal trials than civil ones, it is usually easier to win monetary damages than a criminal conviction.[7] After shooting sixteen-year-old exchange student Yoshihiro Hattori of Japan, for example, Rodney Pearis was acquitted of manslaughter charges by a Louisiana jury. Pearis claimed he thought Hattori—who mistook the defendant's home for the site of a Halloween party—was an intruder. After the criminal trial, however, Hattori's family brought a civil suit against Pearis and was awarded more than $650,000 in damages. While the government had been unable to prove *beyond a reasonable doubt* (the burden of proof in criminal cases) that Pearis had intended to kill Hattori, the civil trial established that a *preponderance of the evidence* (the burden of proof in civil cases) showed this to be the case.

FELONIES AND MISDEMEANORS

Depending on their degree of seriousness, crimes are classified as felonies or misdemeanors. Felonies are serious crimes punishable by death or by imprisonment in a federal or state penitentiary for one year or longer (though some states, such as North Carolina, consider felonies to be punishable by at least two years' incarceration). The Model Penal Code, a general guide for criminal law that you will learn more about in the next chapter, provides for four degrees of felony:

1 Capital offenses, for which the maximum penalty is death.

2 First degree felonies, punishable by a maximum penalty of life imprisonment.

3 Second degree felonies, punishable by a maximum of ten years' imprisonment.

4 Third degree felonies, punishable by a maximum of five years' imprisonment.[8]

Degrees of Murder   Though specifics vary from state to state, some general rules apply when grading crimes. For example, most jurisdictions punish a burglary that involves a nighttime forced entry into a home more seriously than one

"The good of the people is the greatest law."
—Cicero, Roman philosopher (106–43 B.C.E.)

that takes place during the day and involves a nonresidential building or structure. Murder in the first degree occurs under two circumstances:

1 When the crime is *premeditated,* or considered beforehand by the offender, instead of being a spontaneous act of violence.

2 When the crime is *deliberate,* meaning that it was planned and decided on after a process of decision making. Deliberation does not require a lengthy planning process; a person can be found guilty of first degree murder even if she or he made the decision to murder only seconds before committing the crime.

Second degree murder occurs when no premeditation or deliberation was present, but the offender did have *malice aforethought* toward the victim. In other words, the offender acted with wanton disregard of the consequences of his or her actions. The difference between first and second degree murder is clearly illustrated in a case involving a California man who beat a neighbor to death with a partially full brandy bottle. The crime took place after Ricky McDonald, the victim, complained to Kazi Cooksey, the offender, about the noise coming from a late-night barbecue Cooksey and his friends were holding. The jury could not find sufficient evidence that Cooksey's actions were premeditated, but he certainly acted with wanton disregard of his victim's safety. Therefore, the jury convicted Cooksey of second degree murder rather than first degree murder.

A homicide committed without malice toward the victim is known as *manslaughter* and is usually punishable by up to fifteen years in prison. V*oluntary manslaughter* occurs when the intent to kill may be present, but malice was lacking. Voluntary manslaughter covers crimes of passion, in which the emotion of an argument between two friends may lead to a homicide. Voluntary manslaughter can also occur when the victim provoked the offender to act violently. *Involuntary manslaughter* covers incidents in which the offender's acts were negligent, even though there was no intent to kill. In 2002, for example, Thomas Junta was convicted of involuntary manslaughter in the beating death of Michael Costin following an argument over their sons' rough play during a youth hockey practice in Reading, Massachusetts. Junta apparently struck Costin repeatedly while the latter lay on the ground, severing an artery near his brain. Though Junta undoubtedly intended to injure Costin, there was no evidence that he intended to kill him.

Degrees of Misdemeanor   Under federal law and in most states, any crime that is not a felony is considered a misdemeanor. Misdemeanors are crimes punishable by a fine or by confinement for up to a year. If imprisoned, the guilty party goes to a local jail instead of a penitentiary. Disorderly conduct and trespassing are common misdemeanors. Like felonies, misdemeanors are graded by level of seriousness. In Illinois, for

> "Crime, like virtue, has its degrees."
> —Jean Racine, French playwright (1639–1699)

In a Cambridge, Massachusetts, courtroom, Thomas Junta demonstrates "what happened" during his fight with Michael Costin during a youth hockey practice in which their sons were participating. In 2002, Junta was found guilty of involuntary manslaughter and sentenced to six to ten years imprisonment. Junta, a large man, had severely beaten Costin, a smaller man, and severed an artery in Costin's head during the fight, but the judge in the matter was unwilling to infer that Junta had intended to kill his opponent. What purpose is served by punishing people for what they *intended* to occur rather than for what *actually* occurred?

AP Photo/Steven Senne, Pool

example, misdemeanors are either Class A (confinement for up to a year), Class B (not more than six months), or Class C (not more than thirty days).

Most states similarly distinguish between *gross misdemeanors,* which are offenses punishable by thirty days to a year in jail, and *petty misdemeanors,* or offenses punishable by fewer than thirty days in jail. The least serious form of crime is a *violation* (such as a traffic offense), which is punishable only by a small fine and does not appear on the wrongdoer's criminal record. Whether a crime is a felony or a misdemeanor can also determine whether the case is tried in a magistrate's court (for example, by a justice of the peace) or in a general trial court (for example, superior court).

Probation and community service are often imposed on those who commit misdemeanors, especially juveniles.[9] Also, most states have decriminalized all but the most serious traffic offenses. These infractions are treated as civil proceedings, and civil fines are imposed. In many states, the violator has "points" assessed against her or his driving record.

MALA IN SE AND *MALA PROHIBITA*

Mala in Se
A descriptive term for acts that are inherently wrong, regardless of whether they are prohibited by law.

Mala Prohibita
A descriptive term for acts that are made illegal by criminal statute and are not necessarily wrong in and of themselves.

Criminologists often express the social function of criminal law in terms of *mala in se* or *mala prohibita* crimes. A criminal act is referred to as **mala in se** if it would be considered wrong even if there were no law prohibiting it. *Mala in se* crimes are said to go against "natural laws"; that is, against the "natural, moral, and public" principles of a society.[10] Murder, rape, and theft are examples of *mala in se* crimes. These crimes are generally the same from country to country or culture to culture. In contrast, the term **mala prohibita** refers to acts that are considered crimes only because they have been codified as such through statute—"human-made" laws. A *mala prohibita* crime is considered wrong only because it has been prohibited; it is not inherently a wrong, though it may reflect the moral standards of a society at a given time.[11] Thus, the definition of a *mala prohibita* crime can vary from country to country or even from state to state. Bigamy could be considered a *mala prohibita* crime.

Some observers believe that the distinction between *mala in se* and *mala prohibita* is problematic. First, it is difficult to define a "pure" *mala in se* crime; that is, it is difficult to separate a crime from the culture that has deemed it a crime.[12] Even murder, in certain cultural circumstances, is not considered a criminal act. In a number of poor, traditional areas of the Middle East and Asia, for example, the law excuses "honor killings" in which men kill female family members suspected of sexual indiscretion. Our own legal system excuses homicide in extreme situations, such as self-defense or when a law enforcement agent kills in the course of upholding the law. Therefore, all "natural" laws can be seen as culturally specific. Second, similar difficulties occur in trying to define a "pure" *mala prohibita* crime.[13]

↗ ONLINE REVIEW *Go to the book's Web site for an online interactive review of this section*

The Elements of a Crime

Corpus Delicti
The body of circumstances that must exist for a criminal act to have occurred.

In fictional accounts of police work, the admission of guilt is often portrayed as *the* crucial element of a criminal investigation. Although an admission is certainly useful to police and prosecutors, it alone cannot establish the innocence or guilt of a suspect. Criminal law normally requires that the ***corpus delicti,*** a Latin phrase for

> The Elements of a Crime

Carl Robert Winchell walked into the SunTrust Bank in Volusia County, Florida, and placed a bag containing a box on a counter. He announced that the box held a bomb, and demanded to be given an unspecified amount of money. After being provided with several thousand dollars in cash, Winchell fled, leaving the box behind. A Volusia County Sheriff's Office bomb squad subsequently determined that the box did not in fact contain any explosive device. Winchell was eventually arrested and charged with robbery.

Winchell's actions were criminal because they satisfy the three elements of a crime:

1 **Actus reus**—The physical act of a crime took place. In this case, Winchell committed bank robbery.
2 **Mens rea**—The offender must intentionally, knowingly, or willingly commit the criminal act. In this case, Winchell obviously planned to rob the SunTrust Bank using the false threat of a bomb.
3 A **concurrence** of *actus reus* and *mens rea*—The criminal act must be the result of the offender's intention to commit that particular criminal act. In this case, the robbery was the direct result of Winchell's intent to take property using the threat of the fake bomb. If, in addition, a bank customer had died of a heart attack during the robbery attempt, Winchell could not be charged with first degree murder, because he did not intend to harm anyone.

Note that the fact that there was no bomb in the box has no direct bearing on the three elements of the crime. It could, however, lead to Winchell receiving a lighter punishment than if he had used a real bomb.

"the body of the crime," be proved before a person can be convicted of wrong-doing.[14] *Corpus delicti* can be defined as "proof that a specific crime has actually been committed by someone."[15] It consists of the basic elements of any crime, which include (1) *actus reus,* or a guilty act; (2) *mens rea,* or a guilty intent; (3) concurrence, or the coming together of the criminal act and the guilty mind; (4) a link between the act and the legal definition of the crime; (5) any attendant circumstances; and (6) the harm done, or result of the criminal act. (See *Mastering Concepts* for an example showing some of the various elements of a crime.)

CRIMINAL ACT: *ACTUS REUS*

Suppose Mr. Smith walks into a police department and announces that he just killed his wife. In and of itself, the confession is insufficient for conviction unless the police find Mrs. Smith's corpse, for example, with a bullet in her brain and establish through evidence that Mr. Smith fired the gun. (This does not mean that an actual dead body has to be found in every homicide case. Rather, it is the fact of the death that must be established in such cases.)

Most crimes require an act of *commission;* that is, a person must *do* something in order to be accused of a crime. The prohibited act is referred to as the ***actus reus,*** or guilty act. Furthermore, the act of commission must be voluntary. For example, if Mr. Smith had an epileptic seizure while holding a hunting rifle and accidentally shot his wife, he would normally not be held criminally liable for her death. (See *You Be the Judge—A Voluntary Act?* on the following page.)

In some cases, an act of *omission* can be a crime, but only when a person has a legal duty to perform the omitted act. One such legal duty is assumed to exist

Actus Reus
(pronounced *ak*-tus *ray*-uhs). A guilty (prohibited) act. The commission of a prohibited act is one of the two essential elements required for criminal liability, the other element being the intent to commit a crime.

The Facts

On a bright, sunny afternoon, Emil was driving on Delaware Avenue in Buffalo, New York. As he was making a turn, Emil suffered an epileptic seizure and lost control of his automobile. The car careened onto the sidewalk and struck a group of six schoolgirls, killing four of them. Emil knew that he was subject to epileptic attacks that rendered him likely to lose consciousness.

The Law

An "act" committed while one is unconscious is in reality not an act at all. It is merely a physical event or occurrence over which the defendant has no control; that is, such an act is involuntary. If the defendant voluntarily causes the loss of consciousness by, for example, using drugs or alcohol, however, then he or she will usually be held criminally responsible for any consequences.

Your Decision

Emil was charged in the deaths of the four girls. He asked the court to dismiss the charges, as he was unconscious at the time of the accident and therefore had not committed a voluntary act. In your opinion, is there an *actus reus* in this situation, or should the charges against Emil be dismissed?

[To see how the appellate court in New York ruled in this case, go to Example 3.1 in Appendix B.]

based on a "special relationship" between two parties, such as a parent and child, adult children and their aged parents, and spouses.[16] Those persons involved in contractual relationships with others, such as physicians and lifeguards, must also perform legal duties to avoid criminal penalty. In 2003, for example, a Hawaiian home nurse was arrested on charges of second degree murder afer a 102-year-old woman in her care was found to have died due to lack of required medical treatment. Rhode Island, Vermont, Minnesota, and Wisconsin have even passed statutes requiring their citizens to report criminal conduct and to aid victims of such conduct if possible.[17] Another example of a criminal act of omission is failure to file a federal income tax return when required by law to do so.

The *guilty act* requirement is based on one of the premises of criminal law—that a person is punished for harm done to society. Planning to kill someone or to steal a car may be wrong, but the thoughts do no harm and are therefore not criminal until they are translated into action. Of course, a person can be punished for attempting murder or robbery, but normally only if he or she took substantial steps toward the criminal objective. Furthermore, the punishment for an *attempt* normally is less severe than if the act had succeeded.

MENTAL STATE: *MENS REA*

Mens Rea
(pronounced *mehns* ray-uh). Mental state, or intent. A wrongful mental state is as necessary as a wrongful act to establish criminal liability.

A wrongful mental state—**mens rea**—is as necessary as a wrongful act in establishing guilt. The mental state, or requisite *intent,* required to establish guilt of a crime is indicated in the applicable statute or law. For theft, the wrongful act is the taking of another person's property, and the required mental state involves both the awareness that the property belongs to another and the desire to deprive the owner of it.

The Categories of *Mens Rea*   A guilty mental state includes elements of purpose, knowledge, negligence, and recklessness.[18] A defendant is said to have *purposefully* committed a criminal act when he or she desires to engage in certain criminal conduct or to cause a certain criminal result. For a defendant to have *knowingly* committed an illegal act, he or she must be aware of the illegality, must believe that the illegality exists, or must correctly suspect that the illegality exists but fail to do anything to dispel (or confirm) his or her belief. Criminal **negligence** involves the mental state in which the defendant grossly deviates from the standard of care that a reasonable person would use under the same circumstances. The defendant is accused of taking an unjustified, substantial, and foreseeable risk that resulted in harm. In Texas, for example, a parent commits a felony if she or he fails to secure a loaded firearm or leaves it in such a manner that it could easily be accessed by a child.

A defendant who commits an act *recklessly* is more blameworthy than one who is criminally negligent. The Model Penal Code defines criminal recklessness as "consciously disregard[ing] a substantial and unjustifiable risk."[19] Some courts, particularly those adhering to the Model Penal Code, will not find criminal recklessness on the part of a defendant who was subjectively unaware of the risk when she or he acted.

Criminal Liability   Intent plays an important part in allowing the law to differentiate among varying degrees of criminal liability for similar, though not identical, guilty acts. The role of intent is clearly seen in the different classifications of homicide, defined generally as the willful killing of one human being by another. It is important to emphasize the word *willful*, as it precludes deaths caused by accident or negligence and those deemed justifiable. A death that results from negligence or accident normally is considered a private wrong and a matter for civil law, although some statutes allow for culpable negligence, which permits certain negligent homicides to be criminalized. As we saw earlier, when the act of killing is willful, deliberate, and premeditated (planned beforehand), it is considered first degree murder. When premeditation does not exist but intent does, the act is considered second degree murder. (See Figure 3.1 for an example of the different homicide statutes in Florida.)

Different degrees of criminal liability for various categories of homicide lead to different penalties. The distinction between murder and manslaughter was evident in the punishment given to Kevin Kelly, a resident of Manassas, Virginia, who left his twenty-one-month-old daughter buckled in the family van for more than seven hours. With the temperature inside the car rising to 140 degrees, the child eventually died of heat stroke. Local prosecutors had the option of charging Kelly with murder, but could find no indication that he had *intentionally* killed his daughter. Instead, the evidence showed that Kelly, who has twelve other children, forgot where he had

Negligence
A failure to exercise the standard of care that a reasonable person would exercise in similar circumstances.

FIGURE 3.1 **Florida Homicide Statutes (Excerpts)**

782.02 Justifiable use of deadly force.
The use of deadly force is justifiable when a person is resisting any attempt to murder such person or to commit any felony upon him or her or upon or in any dwelling house in which such person shall be.

782.03 Excusable homicide.
Homicide is excusable when committed by accident and misfortune in doing any lawful act by lawful means with usual ordinary caution, and without any unlawful intent, or by accident and misfortune in the heat of passion, upon any sudden and sufficient provocation, or upon a sudden combat, without any dangerous weapon being used and not done in a cruel or unusual manner.

782.04 Murder.
(1)(a) The unlawful killing of a human being:

  1. When perpetrated from a premeditated design to effect the death of the person killed or any human being;

  2. When committed by a person engaged in the perpetration of, or in the attempt to perpetrate, any: [such acts as arson, robbery, burglary, etc.]; . . .

is murder in the first degree and constitutes a capital felony, ...

(2) The unlawful killing of a human being, when perpetrated by any act imminently dangerous to another and evincing a depraved mind regardless of human life, although without any premeditated design to effect the death of any particular individual, is murder in the second degree and constitutes a felony of the first degree, punishable by imprisonment for a term of years not exceeding life . . . .

782.07 Manslaughter; aggravated manslaughter of an elderly person or disabled adult; aggravated manslaughter of a child.
(1) The killing of a human being by the act, procurement, or culpable negligence of another, without lawful justification according to the provisions of chapter 776 and in cases in which such killing shall not be excusable homicide or murder, according to the provisions of this chapter, is manslaughter, a felony of the second degree, ...

placed the girl. Kelly was charged with involuntary manslaughter; found guilty, he was sentenced to spend one day in jail each year for seven years. A murder conviction, in contrast, could have brought the death penalty.

Strict Liability   For certain crimes, criminal law holds the defendant to be guilty even if intent to commit the offense is lacking. These acts are known as **strict liability** crimes and generally involve endangering the public welfare in some way.[20] Drug control statutes, health and safety regulations, and traffic laws are all strict liability laws. To a certain extent, the concept of strict liability is inconsistent with the traditional principles of criminal law, which hold that *mens rea* is required for an act to be criminal. The goal of strict liability laws is to protect the public by eliminating the possibility that wrongdoers could claim ignorance or mistake to absolve themselves of criminal responsibility.[21] Thus, a person caught dumping waste in a protected pond or driving 70 miles per hour in a 55 miles-per-hour zone cannot plead a lack of intent in his or her defense.

One of the most controversial strict liability crimes is statutory rape, in which an adult engages in a sexual relationship with a minor. In most states, even if the minor consents to the sexual act, the crime still exists because, being underage, he or she is considered incapable of making a rational decision on the matter.[22] Therefore, statutory rape has been committed even if the adult was unaware of the minor's age or had been misled to believe that the minor was older.

Accomplice Liability   Under certain circumstances, a person can be charged with and convicted of a crime that he or she did not actually commit. This occurs when the suspect has acted as an *accomplice* to a crime; that is, he or she has helped another person commit the crime. Generally, to be found guilty as an accomplice a person must have the "dual intent" (1) to aid the person who committed the crime and (2) that such aid would lead to the commission of the crime.[23] As for the *actus reus,* the accomplice must have helped the primary actor in either a physical sense (e.g., providing the getaway car) or a psychological sense (e.g., encouraging her or him to commit the crime).[24]

Kevin Kelly with wife and daughter leaving a Prince William County courtroom in Manassas, Virginia. Kelly was convicted of involuntary manslaughter for accidentally forgetting his infant child in the family van, where she eventually died of heat stroke. Why did prosecutors charge Kelly with manslaughter and not murder?

AP/Tracy A. Woodward, Pool

In some states, a person can be convicted as an accomplice even without intent if the crime was a "natural and probable consequence" of his or her actions.[25] Suppose that Jim and Mary enter Frank's home with the goal of burglary. Frank walks in on them while they are carrying out his television, and Jim shoots and kills Frank with a shotgun. Mary could be charged as an accomplice to murder because it is reasonably foreseeable that if one illegally enters another's home with a dangerous weapon, a homicide could occur.

CONCURRENCE

According to criminal law, there must be *concurrence* between the guilty act and the guilty intent. In other words, the guilty act and the guilty intent must occur together.[26] Suppose, for example, that a woman intends to murder her husband with poison in order to collect his life insurance. Every evening, this woman drives her husband home from work. On the night she plans to poison him, however, she swerves to avoid a cat crossing the road and runs into a tree. She survives the accident, but her husband is killed. Even though her intent was realized, the incident would be considered an accidental death because she had not planned to kill him by driving the car into a tree.

CAUSATION

Criminal law also requires that the criminal act cause the harm suffered. In Michigan, for example, two defendants were convicted of murder even though their victim died several years after the initial crime. In the course of that robbery, the defendants had shot the victim in the heart and abdomen and abandoned him in a sewer. Though the victim survived, his heart remained very weak. Four years later, the victim collapsed during a basketball game and died. Medical examination established that his heart failed as a direct result of the earlier injury, and the Michigan Supreme Court ruled that, despite the passing of time, the defendants' criminal act had been the cause of the man's death.[27] (It is interesting to contrast this decision with the historical rule that a victim's death must occur within a year and a day from the date of the defendant's crime.)

ATTENDANT CIRCUMSTANCES

In certain crimes, attendant circumstances—also known as accompanying circumstances—are relevant to the *corpus delicti*. Most states, for example, differentiate between simple assault and the more serious offense of aggravated assault depending on whether the defendant used a weapon such as a gun or a knife while committing the crime. Criminal law also classifies degrees of property crimes based on the amount stolen. According to federal statutes, robbing a bank of less than $100 is a misdemeanor, while taking any amount over $100 results in a felony.[28]

In the late 1980s and early 1990s, a number of states used attendant circumstances to impose harsher penalties on hate crimes. In 2000, many of these state laws were invalidated by the United States Supreme Court's decision in *Apprendi v. New Jersey*.[29] In that case, a white man named Charles Apprendi had fired several shots at the home of an African American family that had just moved into an all-white neighborhood in Vineland, New Jersey. The defendant pled guilty to the second degree offense of possession of a firearm for unlawful purposes, a crime with a maximum penalty of ten years in prison. The trial judge, however, applied the state's ethnic intimidation law and sentenced Apprendi to twelve years' incarceration.[30] The law allowed the longer sentence when a defendant "in committing the crime acted with a purpose to intimidate an individual or group of individuals because of race, color, gender, handicap, religion, sexual orientation or ethnicity."[31]

The Supreme Court ruled that when racial bias increases the penalty for committing a crime, such bias is an element of the crime and must be proved beyond a reasonable doubt.[32] In the *Apprendi* case, it was not. Judges cannot, in sentencing a person, add additional time simply because they *believe* the act was

a hate crime. Rather, the "hate" element must come before the jury or judge during the trial itself. As we shall see in the *Criminal Justice in Action* feature at the end of this chapter, proving racist intent in court can be very difficult. When a state law is written so that this "intent" is part of the definition of the crime (and therefore must be proved beyond a reasonable doubt), however, the Court has been more willing to uphold the statutes. In 2003, for example, the Court upheld a state law that punishes a person who burns a cross for the express purpose of intimidation.[33] (See *CJ in Focus—Landmark Cases:* Virginia v. Black.)

HARM

For most crimes to occur, some harm must have been done to a person or to property. A certain number of crimes are actually categorized depending on the harm done to the victim, regardless of the intent behind the criminal act. Take two offenses, both of which involve one person hitting another in the back of the head with a tire iron. In the first instance, the victim dies, and the offender is charged with murder. In the second, the victim is only knocked unconscious, and the offender is charged with battery. Because the harm in the second instance was less severe, so was the crime with which the offender was charged, even though the act was exactly the same. Furthermore, most states have different degrees of battery depending on the extent of the injuries suffered by the victim. (See *You Be the Judge—Intent to Cause Injury?* on p. 86.)

Many acts are deemed criminal if they could do harm that the laws try to prevent. Such acts are called **inchoate offenses.** They exist when only an attempt at a criminal act was made. If Jenkins solicits Peterson to murder Jenkins's business partner, this is an inchoate offense on the part of Jenkins, even though Peterson fails to carry out the act. Conspiracies also fall into the category of inchoate offenses; in 2003, the Supreme Court ruled that a person could be convicted of criminal conspiracy even though police intervention made the completion of the illegal plan impossible.[34]

ONLINE REVIEW *Go to the book's Web site for an online interactive review of this section*

The Uniform Crime Report

Suppose that a firefighter dies while fighting a fire at an office building. Later, police discover that the building manager intentionally set the fire. All of the elements of the crime of arson are certainly met, but can the manager be charged with murder? In some jurisdictions, the act might be considered a form of manslaughter, but according to the U.S. Department of Justice, "arson-related deaths and injuries of police officers and firefighters due to the hazardous natures of their professions" are not murders.[35]

The distinction is important because the Department of Justice provides the most far-reaching and oft-cited set of national crime statistics. Each year, the department releases the **Uniform Crime Report (UCR).** Since its inception in 1930, the UCR has attempted to measure the overall rate of crime in the United States by compiling "crimes known to the police."[36] To produce the UCR, the FBI relies on the voluntary participation of local law enforcement agencies. These agencies—approximately 17,000 in total, covering 95 percent of the population—base their information on three measurements:

The concept of "harm" in criminal law does not apply only to property and violent crimes. Prostitution, for example, is illegal in almost all U.S. jurisdictions because of the perceived harm the practice causes society. This harm includes the spread of sexually transmitted diseases such as AIDS, the linkage of prostitution to illicit drug use (as many prostitutes sell their services to get the cash to buy drugs), and the violence done to prostitutes by customers and pimps. Under certain circumstances, however, the state of Nevada has legalized prostitution. How might legalized prostitution reduce some of the social harms attributed to the practice?

Inchoate Offenses
Conduct deemed criminal without actual harm being done, provided that the harm that would have occurred is one the law tries to prevent.

Uniform Crime Report (UCR)
An annual report compiled by the FBI to give an indication of criminal activity in the United States. The FBI collects data from local, state, and federal law enforcement agencies in preparing this report.

> Virginia v. Black

The *Black* case involved two separate cross-burning incidents. The first incident involved Barry Black, who organized a Ku Klux Klan rally in a privately owned field in Carroll County, Virginia. As part of the ceremony, the participants burned a large cross, which could be seen by some area residents. In the second incident, Jonathan O'Mara and Richard Elliot drove a truck onto the front lawn of the home of an African American family in Virginia Beach, Virginia, planted a cross about twenty feet from the front door, and set the cross on fire. Black, O'Mara, and Elliot were prosecuted under a Virginia statute that made it unlawful for any person "with the intent of intimidating any person or group of persons, to burn, or cause to be burned, a cross on the property of another, a highway, or other public place." The Virginia Supreme Court consolidated the cases and invalidated the state law, ruling that it improperly infringed on freedom of speech. The United States Supreme Court agreed with the state supreme court, but only to a certain extent.

Virginia v. Black
United States Supreme Court
123 S.Ct. 1536 (2003)
http://laws.findlaw.com/us/000/01-1107.html

> In the words of the court . . .

Justice O'Connor, majority opinion
* * * *

The First Amendment * * * provides that "Congress shall make no law . . . abridging the freedom of speech." The hallmark of the protection of free speech is to allow "free trade in ideas"—even ideas that the overwhelming majority of people might find distasteful or discomforting. * * * The First Amendment affords protection to symbolic or expressive conduct as well as to actual speech.

The protections afforded by the First Amendment, however, are not absolute, and we have long recognized that the government may regulate certain categories of expression consistent with the [United States] Constitution.* * * Thus, for example, a State may punish those words "which by their very utterance inflict injury or tend to incite an immediate breach of the peace." * * * And the First Amendment also permits a State to ban a

"true threat." "True threats" encompass those statements where the speaker means to communicate a serious expression of an intent to commit an act of unlawful violence to a particular individual or group of individuals. The speaker need not actually intend to carry out the threat. Rather, a prohibition on true threats "protect[s] individuals from the fear of violence" and "from the disruption that fear engenders," in addition to protecting people "from the possibility that the threatened violence will occur." Intimidation in the constitutionally proscribable sense of the word is a type of true threat, where a speaker directs a threat to a person or group of persons with the intent of placing the victim in fear of bodily harm or death. * * * [T]he history of cross burning in this country shows that cross burning is often intimidating, intended to create a pervasive fear in victims that they are a target of violence.
* * * *

As the history of cross burning indicates [however] a burning cross is not always intended to intimidate. Rather, sometimes the cross burning is a statement of ideology, a symbol of group solidarity. It is a ritual used at Klan gatherings, and it is used to represent the Klan itself. Thus, "[b]urning a cross at a political rally would almost certainly be protected expression."

> Decision

The Court overturned Black's conviction, but sent those of O'Mara and Elliot back to the state court where the state would have to prove beyond a reasonable doubt that the two men "intended" to intimidate with their actions. Thus, while a state can ban hateful speech and expressive conduct like cross burning, the burden is on the government to show that it was a "true threat" and not "a statement of ideology."

FOR CRITICAL ANALYSIS
Why do you think the Court ruled that Black's cross burning did not constitute a "true threat"? Can you make the argument that cross burning is always *intended to intimidate and therefore is a criminal act not protected by the Constitution?*

 For more information and activities related to this case, click on Landmark Cases *under* Book Resources *at* www.cjinaction.com

---

1 The number of persons arrested.
2 The number of crimes reported by victims, witnesses, or the police themselves.
3 The number of officers and support law enforcement specialists.[37]

Once this information has been sent to the FBI, the agency presents the crime data in three ways:

> Intent to Cause Injury?

The Facts

Sean and his friend Marty were leaving a party in Orland Township, Illinois, when they were approached by William. William demanded that Marty give him a beer from the six-pack that Marty was carrying. Marty refused. In retaliation, William struck Sean in the face with a wine bottle, breaking his upper and lower jaws, his nose, and his left cheek. As a result of these injuries, Sean suffered a permanent condition called "mucosal mouth" and had permanent numbness in one lip.

The Law

Illinois law holds that a person who "intentionally or knowingly" causes "permanent disability or disfigurement" has committed aggravated battery instead of simple battery.

Your Decision

William has been charged with aggravated battery. William does not dispute that he caused Sean's injuries or that he intended to strike Sean in the face. He does claim, however, that he had no intent to cause the permanent injuries and therefore should not be charged with the more serious crime of aggravated battery. Do you agree with William's argument?

[To see how the Illinois Appellate Court ruled in this case, go to Example 3.2 in Appendix B.]

The Federal Bureau of Investigation posts many of its statistical findings, including the Uniform Crime Report. Find this Web site by clicking on *Web Links* under *Chapter Resources* at www.cjinaction.com

1 As a *rate* per 100,000 people. In 2002, for example, the crime index rate was 4,119. In other words, for every 100,000 inhabitants of the United States, 4,119 *index crimes* (explained below) were reported to the FBI. This statistic is known as the *crime rate* and is often cited by media sources when discussing the level of crime in the United States.

2 As a *percentage* change from the previous year or other time periods. From 2001 to 2002, there was a 1.1 percent drop in the crime index rate.

3 As an *aggregate,* or total, number of crimes. In 2002, the FBI recorded 11,877,218 index crimes.[38]

The Department of Justice publishes these data annually in *Crime in the United States.* Along with the basic statistics, this publication offers an exhaustive array of crime information, including breakdowns of crimes committed by city, county, and other geographic designations and by the demographics (gender, race, age) of the individuals who have been arrested for crimes.

THE CRIME INDEX

Index Crimes
Those crimes reported annually by the FBI in its Uniform Crime Report. Index crimes include murder, rape, robbery, aggravated assault, burglary, larceny, motor vehicle theft, and arson. Also known as Part I offenses.

The UCR divides the criminal offenses it measures into two major categories: Part I and Part II offenses. Part I offenses, or **index crimes,** are those crimes that, due to their seriousness and frequency, are recorded by the FBI to give a general idea of the "crime picture" in the United States in any given year. For a description of the eight index crimes, see Figure 3.2.

The index crime rate is hardly constant. As you can see in Figure 3.3, the last two decades have seen "peaks" (the early and late 1980s) and "valleys" (the mid-1980s and late 1990s) in the index crime rate. As we have seen, the reasons for these fluctuations are a matter of great debate among those who study crime in the United States; some point to social conditions such as poverty and education,

FIGURE 3.2 Part I Index Crime Offenses

Every month local law enforcement agencies voluntarily provide information on serious offenses in their jurisdiction to the FBI. These serious offenses are known as Part I offenses, or index crimes, and are defined here. The FBI collects data on Part I offenses in order to present an accurate picture of criminal activity in the United States.

Criminal homicide. a. Murder and nonnegligent manslaughter: the willful (nonnegligent) killing of one human being by another. Deaths caused by negligence, attempts to kill, assaults to kill, suicides, accidental deaths, and justifiable homicides are excluded. Justifiable homicides are limited to: (1) the killing of a felon by a law enforcement officer in the line of duty; and (2) the killing of a felon, during the commission of a felony, by a private citizen. **b. Manslaughter by negligence:** the killing of another person through gross negligence. Traffic fatalities are excluded. While manslaughter by negligence is a Part I crime, it is not included in the Crime Index.

Forcible rape. The carnal knowledge of a female forcibly and against her will. Included are rapes by force and attempts or assaults to rape. Statutory offenses (no force used—victim under age of consent) are excluded.

Robbery. The taking or attempting to take anything of value from the care, custody, or control of a person or persons by force or threat of force or violence and/or by putting the victim in fear.

Aggravated assault. An unlawful attack by one person upon another for the purpose of inflicting severe or aggravated bodily injury. This type of assault usually is accompanied by the use of a weapon or by means likely to produce death or great bodily harm. Simple assaults are excluded.

Burglary—breaking or entering. The unlawful entry of a structure to commit a felony or a theft. Attempted forcible entry is included.

Larceny-theft (except motor vehicle theft). The unlawful taking, carrying, leading, or riding away of property from the possession or constructive possession of another. Examples are thefts of bicycles or automobile accessories, shoplifting, pocket-picking, or the stealing of any property or article that is not taken by force and violence or by fraud. Attempted larcenies are included. Embezzlement, "con" games, forgery, worthless checks, etc., are excluded.

Motor vehicle theft. The theft or attempted theft of a motor vehicle. A motor vehicle is self-propelled and runs on the surface and not on rails. Specifically excluded from this category are motorboats, construction equipment, airplanes, and farming equipment.

Arson. Any willful or malicious burning or attempt to burn, with or without intent to defraud, a dwelling house, public building, motor vehicle or aircraft, personal property of another, etc.

Source: "Appendix II: Offenses in Uniform Crime Reporting," in Federal Bureau of Investigation, *Crime in the United States, 2002* (Washington, D.C.: U.S. Department of Justice, 2003), 454.

---

while others see the rates as a reflection of criminal laws and the efforts of law enforcement agencies.

Index crimes are those most likely to be covered by the media and, consequently, inspire the most fear of crime in the population. These crimes have come to dominate crime coverage to such an extent that, for most Americans, the first image that comes to mind at the mention of "crime" is one person physically attacking another person or a robbery taking place with the use of threat or force.[39] Furthermore, the stereotype of crime usually involves a situation in which the offender and the victim do not know each other.

Given the trauma of violent crimes, this perception is understandable. It is not, however, accurate, according to UCR statistics. A friend or acquaintance of the victim commits about 43 percent of the homicides in the United States.[40] Furthermore, as is evident from Figure 3.4 on the next page, the majority of index

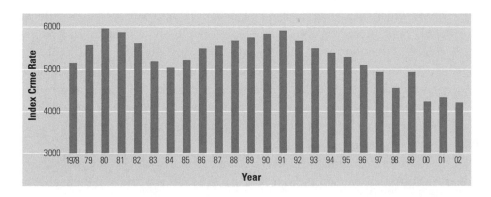

FIGURE 3.3 Index Crime Rates

These data chart the rate of index crime per 100,000 inhabitants in the United States from 1978 to 2002.

Source: Federal Bureau of Investigation, *Crime in the United States, 2002* (Washington, D.C.: U.S. Department of Justice, 2003), 9.

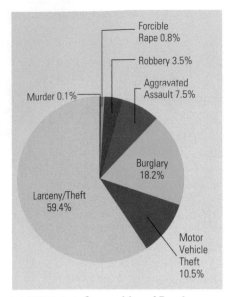

FIGURE 3.4 Composition of Part I Index Crimes

Source: Federal Bureau of Investigation, *Crime in the United States, 2002* (Washington, D.C.: U.S. Department of Justice, 2003), figure 2.3, page 11.

Part II Offenses

All crimes recorded by the FBI that do not fall into the category of Part I offenses. Include both misdemeanors and felonies.

INFOTRAC KEYWORDS

crime index, UCR

For more information, use these search terms with InfoTrac College Edition, your online library at www.infotrac-college.com

crimes committed are property crimes. Notice that 59 percent of all reported index crimes are larceny-thefts, and nearly another 18 percent are burglaries.[41]

PART II OFFENSES

Not only do violent crimes represent the minority of index crimes, but index crimes are far outweighed by **Part II offenses,** or those crimes that can be designated as either misdemeanors or felonies. While information gathered on index crimes reflects those offenses "known," or reported to the FBI by local agencies, Part II offenses are measured only by arrest data. In 2002, the FBI recorded slightly more than 2,234,000 arrests for index crimes in the United States. That same year, 11.5 million arrests for Part II offenses took place.[42] In other words, a Part II offense was about 5 times more common than an index crime (for a description of Part II offenses and their rates, see Figure 3.5). Such statistics have prompted Marcus Felson, a professor at Rutgers University School of Criminal Justice, to comment that "most crime is very ordinary."[43]

THE UCR: A FLAWED METHOD?

Even though the UCR is the predominant source of crime data in the country, there are numerous questions about the accuracy of its findings. These criticisms focus on the methods by which the UCR statistics are collected by local law enforcement agencies and reported to the FBI.

Discretionary Distortions   For the UCR to be accurate, citizens must report criminal activity to the police, and the police must then pass this information on to the FBI. Criminologists have long been aware that neither can be expected to perform these roles with consistency.[44] Citizens may not report a crime for any number of reasons, including fear of reprisal, embarrassment, or a personal bias in favor of the offender. Many also feel that police cannot do anything to help them in the aftermath of a crime, so they do not see the point of involving law enforcement agents in their lives. Surveys of crime victims show that only 49 percent of violent crimes and 40 percent of property crimes were reported to the police in 2002.[45] Studies have shown that police underreport crimes in certain instances, such as when the offense has occurred within a family or the victim does not want the offender to be charged.[46]

Furthermore, the FBI and local law enforcement agencies do not always interpret index crimes in the same manner. FBI guidelines, for example, define forcible rape as the "carnal knowledge" of a woman "forcibly and against her will." Although some local agencies may strictly adhere to this definition, others may define rape more loosely—listing any assault on a woman as a rape. Furthermore, different jurisdictions have different definitions of rape. In Alabama, rape occurs only in cases where the woman offers "earnest resistance" to sexual intercourse,[47] and in a number of other jurisdictions, the courts require proof that the victim physically opposed her attacker's advances. A number of jurisdictions have also expanded their definition of the crime to include the possibility that males can be raped.

These factors influence the arrest decision, as police officers are more likely to make arrests that can be cleared. An arrest is *cleared* when the suspect is

FIGURE 3.5 **Part II Crime Offenses**

OFFENSE	EST. ANNUAL ARRESTS	OFFENSE	EST. ANNUAL ARRESTS
Drug abuse violations	1,538,813	Offenses against family and children	140,286
Driving under the influence	1,461,746	Stolen property	126,422
Other assaults	1,288,682	Runaways	125,688
Disorderly conduct	669,938	Forgery and counterfeiting	115,735
Liquor laws	653,819	Sex offenses (except forcible rape and prostitution)	95,066
Drunkenness	572,735	Prostitution and commercialized vice	79,733
Fraud	337,404	Vagrancy	27,295
Vandalism	276,697	Embezzlement	18,552
Weapons	164,446	Gambling	10,506
Curfew and loitering law violations	141,252	Suspicion	8,899

Curfew and loitering laws (persons under age 18)—Offenses relating to violations of local curfew or loitering ordinances where such laws exist.

Disorderly conduct—Breach of the peace.

Driving under the influence—Driving or operating any vehicle or common carrier while drunk or under the influence of liquor or narcotics.

Drug abuse violations—State and/or local offenses relating to the unlawful possession, sale, use, growing, and manufacturing of narcotic drugs. The following drug categories are specified: opium or cocaine and their derivatives (morphine, heroin, codeine); marijuana; synthetic narcotics—manufactured narcotics that can cause true addiction (demerol, methadone); and dangerous nonnarcotic drugs (barbiturates, benzedrine).

Drunkenness—Offenses relating to drunkenness or intoxication. Excluded is "driving under the influence."

Embezzlement—Misappropriation or misapplication of money or property entrusted to one's care, custody, or control.

Forgery and counterfeiting—Making, altering, uttering, or possessing, with intent to defraud, anything false in the semblance of that which is true. Attempts are included.

Fraud—Fraudulent conversion and obtaining money or property by false pretenses. Included are confidence games and bad checks, except forgeries and counterfeiting.

Gambling—Promoting, permitting, or engaging in illegal gambling.

Liquor laws—State and/or local liquor law violations, except "drunkenness" and "driving under the influence." Federal violations are excluded.

Offenses against the family and children—Nonsupport, neglect, desertion, or abuse of family and children.

Other assaults (simple)—Assaults and attempted assaults where no weapon is used and that do not result in serious or aggravated injury to the victim.

Prostitution and commercialized vice—Sex offenses of a commercialized nature, such as prostitution, keeping a bawdy house, procuring, or transporting women for immoral purposes. Attempts are included.

Runaways (persons under age 18)—Limited to juveniles taken into protective custody under provisions of local statutes.

Sex offenses (except forcible rape, prostitution, and commercialized vice)—Statutory rape and offenses against chastity, common decency, morals, and the like. Attempts are included.

Stolen property; buying, receiving, possessing—Buying, receiving, and possessing stolen property, including attempts.

Suspicion—No specific offense; suspect released without formal charges being placed.

Vagrancy—Vagabondage, begging, loitering, etc.

Vandalism—Willful or malicious destruction, injury, disfigurement, or defacement of any public or private property, real or personal, without consent of the owner or persons having custody or control.

Weapons; carrying, possessing, etc.—All violations of regulations or statutes controlling the carrying, using, possessing, furnishing, and manufacturing of deadly weapons or silencers. Included are attempts.

Source: Federal Bureau of Investigation, *Crime in the United States, 2002* (Washington, D.C.: U.S. Department of Justice, 2003), table 29, pages 234; page 454–455.

charged with a particular crime and turned over to the court for trial. With law enforcement agents in different jurisdictions operating under different definitions of rape, or any other crime, their reports to the FBI for UCR purposes may be misleading. Indeed, when a police department in Alabama and a police department in Oregon both report a rape to the federal agency, they may not be describing the same act. Given that the UCR incorporates reports from 17,000 different local agencies, varying methods of defining offenses could have a significant effect on the overall outcome.

Overreporting Violent Crime   Many observers also believe that the UCR over-reports violent crime and underreports Part II offenses. This is partially due to human nature; a triple murder will certainly get more attention from a police department than the theft of a bicycle. There is evidence, however, that FBI instructions to local law enforcement agencies contribute to this situation as well. For example, if police cannot distinguish the aggressors from the victims in a multiparty physical dispute, the *Uniform Crime Reporting Handbook* advises that officers report the number of persons involved as the number of index crime offenses.[48] A barroom brawl involving five people, therefore, may be reported as five incidents of aggravated assault.

The manner of reporting multiple crimes committed by a single offender also skews results toward violent index crimes. Under the so-called hierarchy rule, the UCR handbook instructs local agencies to report only the most serious crime if an individual has committed a number of crimes in a single crime "spree." So, if a person steals an automobile, robs a convenience store, and then kills the store clerk, only the murder will be recorded for the UCR.[49]

THE NATIONAL INCIDENT-BASED REPORTING SYSTEM

INFOTRAC KEYWORDS

National Incident-Based Reporting System

For more information, use this search term with InfoTrac College Edition, your online library at www.infotrac-college.com

In the 1980s, well aware of the various criticisms of the UCR, the Department of Justice began seeking ways to revise its data-collecting system. The result was the National Incident-Based Reporting System (NIBRS). In the NIBRS, local agencies collect data on each single crime occurrence within twenty-two offense categories made up of forty-six specific crimes called Group A offenses (see Figure 3.6 for a list of NIBRS offense categories). These data are recorded on computerized record systems provided—though not completely financed—by the federal government.

Though the NIBRS became available to local agencies in 1989, fifteen years later only 24 states had been NIBRS certified, with 12 other states in the process of test-

FIGURE 3.6   NIBRS Offense Categories

The NIBRS collects data on each single incident and arrest within twenty-two offense categories made up of these forty-six specific crimes, called Group A offenses.

1. Arson
2. Assault Offenses—Aggravated Assault, Simple Assault, Intimidation
3. Bribery
4. Burglary/Breaking and Entering
5. Counterfeiting/Forgery
6. Destruction/Damage/Vandalism of Property
7. Drug/Narcotic Offenses—Drug/Narcotic Violations, Drug Equipment Violations
8. Embezzlement
9. Extortion/Blackmail
10. Fraud Offenses—False Pretenses/Swindle/Confidence Game, Credit Card/Automatic Teller Machine Fraud, Impersonation, Welfare Fraud, Wire Fraud
11. Gambling Offenses—Betting/Wagering, Operating/Promoting/Assisting Gambling, Gambling Equipment Violations, Sports Tampering
12. Homicide Offenses—Murder and Nonnegligent Manslaughter, Negligent Manslaughter, Justifiable Homicide
13. Kidnapping/Abduction
14. Larceny/Theft Offenses—Pocket-picking, Purse-snatching, Shoplifting, Theft from Building, Theft from Coin-Operated Machine or Device, Theft from Motor Vehicle, Theft of Motor Vehicle Parts or Accessories, All Other Larceny
15. Motor Vehicle Theft
16. Pornography/Obscene Material
17. Prostitution Offenses—Prostitution, Assisting or Promoting Prostitution
18. Robbery
19. Sex Offenses, Forcible—Forcible Rape, Forcible Sodomy, Sexual Assault with an Object, Forcible Fondling
20. Sex Offenses, Nonforcible—Incest, Statutory Rape
21. Stolen Property Offenses (Receiving, etc.)
22. Weapon Law Violations

Source: The Federal Bureau of Investigation.

ing the new process.[50] Even in states that are certified, only certain jurisdictions are collecting data for the NIBRS, and as yet no major cities are connected to the new measuring system. Many local agencies have been reluctant to switch to the NIBRS because of the costs and officer-training time involved.[51] Furthermore, the average difference between UCR and NIBRS estimates has been quite small. On average, the violent crime rate as measured by the NIBRS is less than 1 percent higher than that of the UCR, and the property crime rate is higher by slightly more than 2 percent.[52]

↗ONLINE REVIEW *Go to the book's Web site for an interactive review of this section*

Alternative Measuring Methods

The shortcomings of the UCR have led to other attempts to collect data that better measure crime in the United States. Two of the most highly regarded methods, along with their shortcomings, are discussed below.

VICTIM SURVEYS

One alternative source of data collecting attempts to avoid the distorting influence of the "intermediary," or the local police agencies. In **victim surveys**, criminologists or other researchers ask the victims of crime directly about their experiences, using techniques such as interviews or mail and phone surveys. The first large-scale victim survey took place in 1966, when members of 10,000 households answered questionnaires as part of the President's Commission on Law Enforcement and the Administration of Justice. The results indicated a much higher victimization rate than had been previously expected, and researchers felt the process gave them a better understanding of the **dark figure of crime,** or the actual amount of crime that occurs in the country.

Victim Surveys
A method of gathering crime data that directly surveys participants to determine their experiences as victims of crime.

The National Crime Victimization Survey   Criminologists were so encouraged by the results of the 1966 experiment that the federal government decided to institute an ongoing victim survey. The result was the National Crime Victimization Survey (NCVS), which started in 1972. Conducted by the U.S. Bureau of the Census in cooperation with the Bureau of Justice Statistics of the Justice Department, the NCVS conducts an annual survey of more than 40,000 households with nearly 75,000 occupants over twelve years of age. Participants are interviewed twice a year concerning their experiences with crimes in the prior six months. As you can see in Figure 3.7 on the next page, the questions cover a wide array of possible victimization.

Dark Figure of Crime
A term used to describe the actual amount of crime that takes place. The "figure" is "dark," or impossible to detect, because a great number of crimes are never reported to the police.

Supporters of the NCVS highlight a number of aspects in which the victim survey is superior to the UCR:

1 It measures both reported and unreported crime.
2 It is unaffected by police bias and distortions in reporting crime to the FBI.
3 It does not rely on victims directly reporting crime to the police.[53]

Most important, some supporters say, is that the NCVS gives victims a voice in the criminal justice process.

Reliability of the NCVS   Even supporters of the NCVS would not, however, claim that the process is infallible. For one thing, there is no guarantee that those who answer the questionnaire will do so accurately. For reasons of shame, forgetfulness,

INFOTRAC KEYWORDS

Naitonal Crime Victimization Survey

For more information, use these search terms with InfoTrac College Edition, your online library at www.infotrac-college.com

or fear of reprisal, a participant may not give a completely true picture of her or his recent history. Also, as with any survey research, the manner in which the questions are asked can have a distorting effect on the answers.[54] Consider the following two questions:

1 Have you ever been the victim of a rape?
2 Were you knifed, shot, or attacked with some other weapon? Did someone try to attack you in some other way?

The second question is, in fact, one of the methods the NCVS has used in the past to measure rape. Surveyors expected, or hoped, that someone who had been raped would answer accordingly, as they had been "attacked in some other way." On the one hand, the first question was more direct and may have elicited more "yes" answers. On the other hand, because of the stigma attached to the word *rape,* it may have discouraged participants from answering truthfully. As a result of complaints that the vagueness of the second question led rape to be seriously underreported in the NCVS (see the new version in Figure 3.7), in the early 1990s the surveyors altered their methods of gaining information concerning sexual assaults. (See *What Works—The Sexual Victimization of College Women Survey.*)

Victim surveys also present a number of other potential problems. Many citizens are not well versed in the terminology of criminal justice and may not know, for example, that a break-in that occurred at their home while they were at the movies is a burglary and not a robbery. (Remember that *burglary* refers to breaking into a structure with the intention to commit a felony, whereas *robbery* is the illegal taking of property using force or the threat of force.) There are also a number of crimes that victim surveys cannot record, such as drug use or gambling, for legal reasons, and murder, for more obvious ones.[55]

FIGURE 3.7 Sample Questions from the NCVS (*National Crime Victimization Survey*)

36a. Was something belonging to YOU stolen, such as:
a. Things that you carry, like luggage, a wallet, purse, briefcase, book—
b. Clothing, jewelry, or calculator—
c. Bicycle or sports equipment—
d. Things in your home—like a TV, stereo, or tools—
e. Things from a vehicle, such as a package, groceries, camera, or cassette tapes— OR
f. Did anyone ATTEMPT to steal anything belonging to you?

41a. Has anyone attacked or threatened you in any of these ways:
a. With any weapon, for instance, a gun or knife—
b. With anything like a baseball bat, frying pan, scissors, or stick—
c. By something thrown, such as a rock or bottle—
d. Include any grabbing, punching, or choking,
e. Any rape, attempted rape, or other type of sexual attack—
f. Any face-to-face threats— OR
g. Any attack or threat or use of force by anyone at all? Please mention it even if you are not certain it was a crime.

42a. People often don't think of incidents committed by someone they know. Other than the incidents already mentioned, did

you have something stolen from you OR were you attacked or threatened by:
a. Someone at work or school—
b. A neighbor or friend—
c. A relative or family member—
d. Any other person you've met or known?

43a. Incidents involving forced or unwanted sexual acts are often difficult to talk about. Have you been forced or coerced to engage in unwanted sexual activity by—
a. someone you didn't know before—
b. a casual acquaintance— OR
c. someone you know well—

44a. During the last 6 months (other than any incidents already mentioned), did you call the police to report something that happened to YOU which you thought was a crime?

45a. During the last 6 months (other than any incidents already mentioned), did anything which you thought was a crime happen to YOU, but you did NOT report to the police?

Source: U.S. Department of Justice, *National Crime Victimization Survey, 2003* (Washington, D.C.: Bureau of Justice Statistics, 2003).

> The Sexual Victimization of College Women Survey

R esearchers have long been aware that young women who live on college campuses are at greater risk for rape and other forms of sexual assault than are other women of a comparable age. Many of these same experts also believe that the National Crime Victimization Survey (NCVS), even with its improvements, does not adequately measure the problem. To test this hypothesis, the Department of Justice sponsored a survey called "The Sexual Victimization of College Women" (NCWSV) that varied the process used by the NCVS.

Both surveys follow a two-stage format that relies on responses to "screen questions" to determine victimization. If the respondent answers "yes" to one of these questions, then a more detailed incident report is filled out. As you can see in Figure 3.7, the NCVS "screen question" asks respondents if they have been "attacked or threatened" and then follows with a short list of cue responses that includes "rape, attempted rape, or other type of sexual attack." In contrast, the NCWSV uses much more specific screen questions, such as "Since the school year began . . . has anyone made you have sexual intercourse by using force or threatening to harm you? Just so there is no mistake, by intercourse I mean putting a penis in your vagina."

The results were dramatic. Female students were more than ten times more likely to tell a NCWSV researcher that they were raped than one utilizing the NCVS. The NCWSV found that 350 women—about 2 percent of all female college students—are raped every year on campuses with 10,000 or more students. The authors of the report believe that, because of the sensitive nature of sexual assault, "graphically descriptive screen questions are needed to prompt reluctant victims" to report being victims of sexual assault. Along the same lines, the survey also estimated that, because of embarrassment, self-blame, or other reasons, only about 5 percent of all rapes or attempted rapes of college women are reported to law enforcement officials.

FOR CRITICAL ANALYSIS
Why might someone be more likely to answer "yes" to the NCWSV screen question concerning rape than to the NCVS screen question? Do you think that more graphic descriptions of other crimes would also result in higher rates of positive responses?

Comparing the UCR and the NCVS   For most of the past twenty-five years, the NCVS and the UCR have been remarkably consistent in tracking American crime trends. Both showed crime rates peaking in the early 1980s, with relatively steady declines (interrupted by increases in the early 1990s) since. Then, in the first few years of the new century, the two surveys began to diverge, as two headlines on the front page of the *Washington Post* illustrate. The first appeared during the summer of 2002: "Major Crimes in U.S. Increase."[56] The second in the summer of 2003: "Crime Rate Continues to Drop."[57] The former headline reflected the 2001 UCR, which showed an increase in crime rates after nine years of declines. The latter told the dramatic tale of the 2002 NCVS, which boasted the lowest crime levels in thirty years.

The reasons behind this discrepancy are hard to pinpoint. Some statisticians believe that the NCVS is more accurate because it counts crimes that are not reported to the police and therefore not counted by the UCR. Others caution, however, that victim surveys can lead to distortions, and while the NCVS is based on statistical sampling, the UCR is based on numbers gathered from actual reports. Other differences also influence the data: unlike the UCR, the NCVS does not track victims under the age of twelve. Furthermore, the victim survey is heavily weighted toward simple assaults, including pushing and shoving, which are not covered in the UCR. One criminologist says that comparing the two methods is like comparing Fahrenheit and wind-chill factor: "These are two different ways of measuring crime, just like there are two ways of measuring the temperature."[58]

SELF-REPORTED SURVEYS

Self-Reported Surveys
A method of gathering crime data that relies on participants to reveal and detail their own criminal or delinquent behavior.

INFOTRAC KEYWORDS

self-report surveys

For more information, use this search term with InfoTrac College Edition, your online library at www.infotrac-college.com

Based on many of the same principles as victim surveys, but focusing instead on offenders, **self-reported surveys** are a third source of data for criminologists. In this form of data collection, persons are asked directly—through personal interviews or questionnaires, or over the telephone—about specific criminal activity to which they may have been a party. Though not implemented on the scale of the UCR or NCVS, self-reported surveys are most useful in situations in which the group to be studied is already gathered in an institutional setting, such as a juvenile facility or a prison. One of the most widespread self-reported surveys in the United States, the Drug Use Forecasting Program, collects information on narcotics use from arrestees who have been brought into booking facilities.

Such studies can also be particularly helpful in finding specific information about groups of subjects. When professors Peter B. Wood, Walter R. Grove, James A. Wilson, and John K. Cochran wanted to learn how criminals "felt" when committing crimes, for example, they used self-reported surveys. By comparing these results to those gathered from a group of male students at a state university, the researchers were able to draw conclusions on the "high" a criminal experiences during a crime.[59]

A "Giant" Dark Figure Because there is no penalty for admitting to criminal activity in a self-reported survey, subjects tend to be more forthcoming in discussing their behavior. The researchers mentioned above found that a significant number of the students interviewed admitted to committing minor crimes for which they had never been arrested. This fact points to the most striking finding of self-reported surveys: the dark figure of crime, referred to earlier in the chapter as the *actual* amount of crime that takes place, appears to be much larger than the UCR or NCVS would suggest.

The first major self-reported survey, conducted by James S. Wallerstein and Clement J. Wyle in 1947, queried 1,020 men and 678 women from a wide spectrum of different backgrounds on their participation in a number of crimes. Ninety-nine percent of the participants admitted to committing at least one of the crimes referenced by Wallerstein and Wyle.[60] When alcohol offenses, recreational drug use, truancy, and petty theft are factored in, self-reported surveys consistently show that almost everybody has committed at least one crime in their lifetime.[61]

Besides their usefulness in determining the criminal behavior of the average American, self-reported surveys are also valued for their ability to target specific criminological subjects. For example, to test a theory that drug use by parents leads to a greater possibility of drug use in their children, researchers can do a self-reported survey with a cross-section of drug users. Also, self-reported surveys allow researchers to control aspects of the data collection themselves, thereby assuring that race, class, and gender will not bias the results.

Reliability of Self-Reported Surveys Again, despite these advantages there are a number of perceived disadvantages with self-reported surveys. The manner in which a subject answers questions often relies on his or her personality or beliefs. If a person sees criminal behavior as something to be ashamed of, he or she may downplay such behavior. In contrast, a person who sees criminal behavior as positive may exaggerate the truth to impress the questioner.

For the same reason that a participant has nothing to lose by telling the truth, she or he has nothing to gain by telling the truth, either. The effects of lying on self-reported surveys can be dramatic. In a self-reported survey of juveniles, researchers Thomas Gray and Eric Walsh tested their subjects with urinalysis as well as asking them about their drug use. Less than 33 percent of the juveniles who tested positive for marijuana also admitted to using the drug, and only 15 percent of those who tested positive for cocaine were truthful about their habits.[62] These types of results have led many criminologists to conclude that self-reported surveys are skewed by many of the same inaccuracies that plague the other collection methods.[63]

⟋ONLINE REVIEW *Go to the book's Web site for an interactive review of this section*

The Growing Role of the Victim

As noted earlier, crime surveys, particularly the NCVS, have contributed to a greater awareness of the victims of criminal acts. Thanks to that survey, we know that, in the space of one year, approximately 17.5 million Americans are victims of property crimes such as burglary and theft, and 5.3 million Americans are the victims of violent crimes such as rape and assault.[64] The NCVS has also provided crime experts with a better understanding of who crime victims are (see Figure 3.8).

THE EXPERIENCE OF BEING A VICTIM

Crimes can be economically devastating to victims. Taking into account factors ranging from lost wages to medical costs to psychological trauma, Ross Macmillan of the University of Minnesota has estimated that an adolescent victim of a crime will lose nearly $240,000 over the course of his or her lifetime.[65] A number of studies have also shown that victimization results in mental health problems and

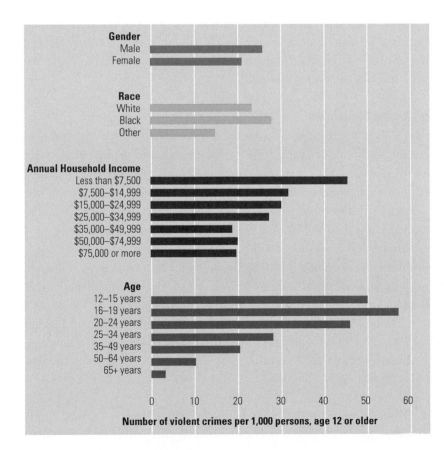

FIGURE 3.8

Crime Victims in the United States
According to the NCVS, men, African Americans, households with annual incomes of less than $7,500, and teen-agers between the ages of sixteen and nineteen are most likely to be victims of violent crime in this country.
Source: Bureau of Justice Statistics, *Criminal Victimization, 2002* (Washington, D.C.: U.S Department of Justice, 2003), 4, 6.

substance abuse, as crime victims struggle to deal with the emotional aftermath of the experience.[66] Furthermore, data show that the same persons tend to be both victims and offenders, suggesting that being a victim may lead to future criminal wrongdoing.[67]

Because of the long-term consequences of victimization, criminologists have paid particular attention to the effect of crime on children and adolescents. These studies paint a bleak picture. Juvenile victims of crime are more likely than adult victims to have mental health problems such as depression, to abuse alcohol and illegal drugs, and to become offenders themselves.[68] These findings are even more cause for concern given that, as Figure 3.8 shows, persons between the ages of sixteen and nineteen are the most common targets of violent crimes.

Criminalization rates also wave a red flag when it comes to matters of race and class. Once again referring to Figure 3.8, you can see that African American individuals and poor households are more likely to be the targets of crime than other demographic groups. As we learned in Chapter 2, this leads to a "vicious cycle" in which the social problems that make these groups most likely to be victims also contribute to their continued high rates of offending and incarceration.

See the National Organization for Victim Assistance, an advocacy organization for victims' rights. Find this Web site by clicking on *Web Links* under *Chapter Resources* at www.cjinaction.com

PROTECTING VICTIMS' RIGHTS

Other than their statistical importance, victims of crime have historically played only a small role in the criminal justice system. Once the crime had been committed, the victim's role in the process has generally been limited to appearing as a witness for the prosecution. Indeed, in criminal trials, the state brings charges against the defendant "in the name of the people," effectively reducing the victim to an afterthought. "[T]he purpose of the criminal trial is not to stand by the victim," says Stephen J. Schulhofer, a professor at the New York University School of Law. "The purpose of the trial is to determine whether the defendant is factually and legally responsible for an offense."[69]

The Victims' Rights Movement   A large number of Americans, particularly victims themselves, do not agree with Schulhofer. The modern victims' rights movement began with the opening of rape-crisis centers by feminist groups in the early 1970s. Since then, hundreds of grassroots organizations have been formed to deal with the needs of victims. Some, such as Parents of Murdered Children, are primarily concerned with the emotional state of victims. Others, such as Mothers Against Drunk Driving and the National Organization for Victim Assistance, concentrate on lobbying legislators for victims' rights laws.

Crime victims have become a politically powerful group, able to influence federal legislation.[70] The federal Victims of Crime Act of 1984 established a federal crime victims fund that can distribute $550 million a year.[71] The President's Task Force on Victims of Crime, which gathers data on victimization, was formed in the early 1980s. In 1994, Congress passed the Violence Against Women Act, which has authorized more than $4.3 billion to programs to combat domestic violence and other crimes against women.[72]

State Laws   Even more impressive has been the impact of the victims' rights movement on state laws. State legislators have passed nearly 30,000 victim-related laws over the past twenty years, and thirty-two state constitutions now include protections for the rights of crime victims.[73] Often these protections are contained in a state Victims' Bill of Rights. These rights focus on three areas:

> Enabling the victim to receive restitution from the person who committed the crime.

> Allowing the victim to participate in the criminal prosecution of the offender.

> Protecting the victim from harassment or abuse from the criminal justice process (such as intrusive interviews by the police).[74]

A state Victims' Bill of Rights gives the victim a legal ground on which to challenge actions taken by members of the criminal justice system. Several years ago, for example, an Arizona parole board granted a rapist parole without notifying his victim of his parole hearing. She challenged the decision, noting that the state constitution gave her the right to be present at any such hearing. Citing this failure to notify the victim, the Arizona Supreme Court ordered a new parole hearing at which she was given the chance to tell her "side of the story." The parole decision was reversed, and the offender was sent back to prison.[75]

EXPANDING VICTIMS' RIGHTS

Despite decisions such as the Arizona parole reversal, many observers feel that state laws do not go far enough in protecting victims' rights. A large-scale federal study found that these laws are not consistently observed. Fewer than 60 percent of victims were notified of the offender's sentencing hearing, and fewer than 40 percent were told that the offender was going to be released from jail before trial.[76]

Striving for a Constitutional Amendment   Many trial judges are antagonistic toward victims' rights laws and tend to ignore them.[77] This attitude is possible, according to many observers, because criminal defendants have numerous rights guaranteed by the U.S. Constitution, while crime victims have none. To lessen this disparity, Senators Dianne Feinstein (Democrat from California) and Jon Kyl (Republican from Arizona) have proposed a Victims' Rights Amendment to the Constitution that would give a victim the right:

> To notice of any public proceeding involving the crime and of any release or escape of the accused.

> To be included in any public proceedings and a "reasonable" opportunity to be heard at public release, plea, pardon, and sentencing hearings.

> To have the court consider his or her safety in any decisions made concerning the accused.[78]

Although the amendment has a great deal of support in Congress, adding it to the Constitution will be difficult. Realistically, to be passed, an amendment must be approved by a two-thirds vote in each chamber of Congress and then by three-fourths (thirty-eight) of the legislatures of the various states.

Nell Rankins, whose daughter was murdered, holds a candle at the Victims of Crime and Leniency vigil on the steps of the Public Safety Building in Montgomery, Alabama. What have been some of the results of these kinds of efforts to give victims and their families a greater voice in the criminal justice system?

> Victims in the Courtroom

The juries set to decide whether Timothy McVeigh and Terry Nichols, co-conspirators in the Oklahoma City bombing of 1995, deserved the death penalty were provided with a great deal of information during the defendants' respective sentencing hearings. Much of the information came from the mouths of those most affected by the crime—its victims. Thirty-nine people, including four police officers who had helped clear bodies from the wreckage, gave their opinions at the McVeigh hearing, and fifty-five spoke at Nichols's hearing.

Such victim impact statements allow friends and relatives of a homicide victim to describe the effect of the crime on their lives to jurors deciding whether to impose the death penalty. The United States Supreme Court upheld the use of such statements in this manner in 1991. Before then, although relatives of the defendant were allowed to speak on his or her behalf, families of the victims were effectively barred from sentencing hearings. Thanks to the efforts of victims' rights groups, however, today the federal government and every state provide eligible victims the opportunity to offer input, either orally or in writing, to the court regarding punishment.

Many observers feel that this trend compromises some of the most basic rights of defendants in our criminal justice system. Since the middle of the nineteenth century, American ideals of criminal justice have rejected the idea that a wrongdoer must pay a penalty or a debt directly to the victim of his or her wrongdoing. Instead, a public prosecution system has evolved, in which a public prosecutor, and not the victim, conducts the prosecution against the defendant on behalf of all citizens. Victim impact statements return the victim to a position of prominence in trial proceedings.

Furthermore, critics believe that victim impact statements risk introducing an element of emotionalism into a courtroom that our legal system is designed to eliminate. They fear that, instead of focusing only on the facts and the law, jurors will be influenced by the suffering of victims and therefore sentence the defendant to harsher penalties than they would otherwise. A juror who hears a family member of murder victims say, as happened in one case, "It's our prayer that this person who planned and maliciously traumatized and killed our loved ones . . . be [executed]," may find it difficult not to become personally involved in what is supposed to be an impersonal decision of life and death.

FOR CRITICAL ANALYSIS
Do you feel that victim impact statements should be allowed in a courtroom? Explain your answer.

Concern for the Rights of the Accused   Even those who believe in more rights for victims worry that such an amendment would impinge on the constitutional rights of the accused to a fair trial, a subject we will study in more detail in Chapter 10. Some believe that victims already have *too much* of a presence in criminal trials. The increased use of victim impact statements, which allow a victim—in person or through a written statement—to participate in the sentencing phase of a trial, is of particular concern. (See the feature *CJ in Focus—The Balancing Act: Victims in the Courtroom.*)

The Constitution, opponents of the proposed amendment point out, guarantees protections to defendants to make sure that the government does not infringe on their basic rights. In contrast, the government is not prosecuting victims and thus is not in a position to unfairly convict and detain them. By elevating the status of victims, the amendment would place "enormous new burdens" on law enforcement agencies and possibly make it more difficult for the criminal justice system to effectively punish wrongdoers.[79]

ONLINE REVIEW *Go to the book's Web site for an interactive review of this section*

>Punishing Hate

In this chapter, we have seen that a crime, as traditionally understood, has two basic elements: an *actus reus* and a *mens rea*. Criminal law, however, is not set in stone; it changes with the values of the society it is meant to protect. Under certain circumstances, many state penal codes have expanded to include a third element: motive. In most cases, a person's motive for committing a crime is irrelevant—a court will not try to read the accused's mind. But, as we will discuss in this *Criminal Justice in Action* feature, when the motive involves hate or bias, many jurisdictions have decided that the harm done by the crime is more serious, and therefore the punishment should be as well.

Two Brutal Crimes

Shortly after midnight on June 7, 1998, an African American named James Byrd was walking to his home in Jasper, Texas. Three white men in a pickup pulled over and offered Byrd a ride, which he accepted. The driver and his companions proceeded to take Byrd into the nearby woods and beat him unconscious. Then they chained him to the back of their truck and dragged him until he was dead.

Four months later, the body of twenty-one-year-old University of Wyoming freshman Matthew Shepard was found tied to a deer fence off Snowy Mountain View Road, one mile east of Laramie. Shepard's head and face had been brutally beaten, his arms were scorched with burn marks, and he had been left unconscious and bleeding on the fence for nearly eighteen hours. Five days later, he died in a local hospital. Investigators quickly learned that Shepard's two assailants had been aware that he was homosexual and had lured him to their truck by feigning romantic interest.

Byrd and Shepard were two of the approximately 7,500 Americans who are victims of violent crimes motivated by hate or bias each year.[80] At the time of these murders, Wyoming and Texas were two of only nine states that did not have a **hate crime law**—a fact mentioned numerous times in the wake of both deaths by those who felt that the lack of such a law created a climate in which verbal and physical attacks against minorities were subtly tolerated. (Texas has since passed such a law.) In general, hate crime laws provide for greater sanctions against those who commit crimes motivated by animosity against a person or group because of race, ethnicity, religion, gender, sexual orientation, disability, or age. (See Figure 3.9.)

Penalty Enhancement Statutes

The concept of a hate crime as a measurable, definable criminal act, separate from other criminal acts, is a relatively new one. The UCR did not start measuring hate

Hate Crime Law
A statute that provides for greater sanctions against those who commit crimes motivated by animosity against an individual or a group based on race, ethnicity, religion, gender, sexual orientation, disability, or age.

FIGURE 3.9
Offenses Motivated by Bias

In 2002, the Federal Bureau of Investigation reported 7,462 bias-motivated offenses. This chart shows the percentage distribution of the motivating factors.

Source: Adapted from Federal Bureau of Investigation, *Crime in the United States, 2002* (Washington, D.C.: U.S. Department of Justice, 2003), Figure 2.19 at page 61.

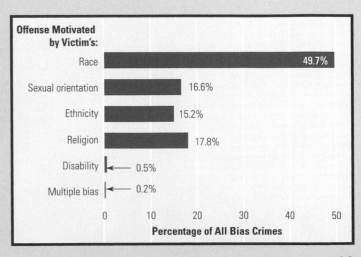

crimes until 1992, and the NCVS did not ask questions relating to crimes of "bigotry and prejudice" until 1997.[81] Due to the lack of a federal hate crime statute, the full weight of prosecuting these crimes has fallen on those states that have passed relevant laws. In general, these laws are based on a model created by the Anti-Defamation League (ADL) in 1981. The ADL model was centered around the concept of "penalty enhancement": just as someone who robs a convenience store using a gun will face a greater penalty than if he or she had been unarmed, so will someone who commits a crime because of prejudice against her or his victim or victims.[82]

The specifics of hate crime legislation vary from jurisdiction to jurisdiction. Not all states follow the penalty enhancement model, preferring instead to create new categories of crimes committed "because of" or "by reason of" the victim's characteristics. Some states do not specify which groups are protected by the legislation, while others list some aspects, such as race, but not others, such as mental or physical disability. Furthermore, some states establish training in dealing with hate crimes for law enforcement personnel. A number of police departments have created specialized bias units to prevent hate crimes and collect data on them. Despite the lack of federal hate crime legislation, in 2003 federal prosecutors decided to seek the death penalty for Darrell David Rice, who allegedly murdered two hikers in Shenandoah National Park because they were lesbians.[83]

Supreme Court Rulings

The legal basis for hate crime legislation was established by two cases heard by the Supreme Court in the early 1990s. In *R.A.V. v. St. Paul* (1992),[84] the Court reviewed a case involving a group of white teen-agers who burned a cross on the lawn of an African American family in St. Paul, Minnesota. One of the youths, who had been arrested and convicted under the city's Bias-Motivated Crime Ordinance, claimed that the law violated his right to free speech. The Minnesota Supreme Court upheld the conviction, ruling that the law was constitutional because it applied only to "fighting words," or speech that is likely to evoke a violent response. The United States Supreme Court, however, reversed the state court's decision, holding that the statute was too broad and therefore could be used to outlaw forms of expression that are protected under the First Amendment, as well as "fighting words."

Participants in the "Hike for Hope"—a seventy-mile trek to raise awareness of hate crimes—pause at the site where Matthew Shepard was beaten to death.

The following year, however, the Supreme Court upheld Wisconsin's penalty enhancement statute in *State of Wisconsin v. Todd Mitchell* (1993).[85] The case involved Todd Mitchell, a nineteen-year-old African American who incited his friends to attack a white teen-ager after viewing the film *Mississippi Burning*. The victim was left in a coma for two days, and Mitchell was convicted of felony aggravated battery and sentenced to two years in prison, plus an additional two years under the state's hate crime law. The Court upheld the statute, reasoning that the results of hate crime, such as community fear, justify harsher punishments. Furthermore, it ruled that speech could be used as evidence of motive, and because motive is an integral part of sentencing, hate speech could be used to augment sentences. (As we saw earlier in this chapter, the Court later clarified its ruling, requiring that the motive be an element of a hate crime and be proved beyond a reasonable doubt.)

Questioning Hate Laws

Many of those who question the validity of hate crime legislation do so on First Amendment grounds. Punish Todd Mitchell for his acts, they say, but not for his beliefs, which he has a constitutional right to hold. Some of these opponents also question laws that seem to indicate that some victims are worthy of more protection than others. They find it disturbing that Mitchell would have received a lesser sentence if he and his friends had beaten an African American youth instead of a white youth.[86]

In addition, James B. Jacobs, a professor of law at New York University, points out that it is difficult enough to establish the *mens rea* of someone who has committed a criminal act without trying to establish his or her motivation.[87] Jacobs envisions court cases becoming bogged down as prosecutors try to establish the defendant's levels of prejudice and bias, a difficult task considering the deep psychological and sociological roots of such feelings. Law enforcement officials are also wary of the demands of hate crime legislation. "I'm very fearful of the concept of thought police," said a commander in the Kenosha (Wisconsin) police department. "It makes me nervous."[88]

MAKING SENSE OF HATE CRIME LAWS

1 Review the last two paragraphs of this feature. Do you agree with any of the arguments presented there? Explain your answer.

2 Why do you suppose that motive is usually not considered in criminal law? Why might determining motive be difficult?

3 How does society suffer a greater "harm" from crimes motivated by bias than from those driven by greed, jealousy, or some other emotion?

Chapter Summary

1 **Explain the differences between crimes *mala in se* and *mala prohibita*.** A criminal act is *mala in se* if it is inherently wrong, while a criminal act *mala prohibita* is illegal only because it goes against the "natural, moral, and public" principles of society. It is sometimes difficult to distinguish between these two sorts of crimes because what may be considered a *mala in se* crime in one culture may not go against the "natural laws" of another.

2 **List and explain the six basic elements of any crime.** (a) The *actus reus,* or the guilty act; (b) the *mens rea,* or the proof of guilty intent by the alleged criminal; (c) a concurrence of act and intent; (d) a link between the act and the crime; (e) any attendant circumstances; and (f) the existence of harm done, or the result of a criminal act.

3 **Delineate the elements required to establish *mens rea* (a guilty mental state).** (a) Purpose, (b) knowledge, (c) negligence, or (d) recklessness.

4 **Explain how the doctrine of strict liability applies to criminal law.** Strict liability crimes do not allow the alleged wrongdoer to claim ignorance or mistake to avoid criminal responsibility; for example, exceeding the speed limit and statutory rape.

5 **Identify the publication in which the FBI reports crime data and list the three ways** it does so. Every year the FBI releases the Uniform Crime Report (UCR), in which it presents different crimes as (a) a rate per 100,000 people; (b) a percentage change from the previous year; and (c) an absolute, or aggregate, number.

6 **Distinguish between Part I and Part II offenses as defined in the Uniform Crime Report (UCR).** Part I offenses are always felonies and include the most violent crimes. They are called index crimes and yield the index crime rate. Part II offenses can be either misdemeanors or felonies and constitute the majority of crimes committed.

7 **Describe some of the shortcomings of the UCR as a crime-measuring tool.** To collect its data, the Uniform Crime Report (UCR) relies on citizens reporting crimes to the police and the police passing this information on to the FBI. If either fails to do so, the UCR will not accurately reflect criminal activity in the United States. Furthermore, the FBI and local law enforcement agencies do not always define crimes in the same manner, leading to inconsistencies in the data. Finally, the UCR tends to overreport violent crimes and underreport more common offenses.

8 **Distinguish between the National Crime Victimization Survey and self-reported**

 STORIES FROM THE STREET

Go to the Stories from the Street feature at www.cjinaction.com to hear Larry Gaines tell insightful stories related to this chapter and his experiences in the field.

Chapter Summary
continued

surveys. The NCVS involves an annual survey of more than 40,000 households conducted by the Bureau of the Census along with the Bureau of Justice Statistics. The survey queries citizens on crimes that have been committed against them. As such, the NCVS includes crimes not necessarily reported to police. Self-reported surveys, in contrast, involve asking individuals about criminal activity to which they may have been a party.

9 Explain why criminologists pay particular attention to the age of crime victims in the United States. Various studies have shown a number of negative consequences for crime victims, including mental health problems, substance abuse, and a greater likelihood of deviant behavior. Young people are more likely than adults to exhibit these "symptoms of victimization." Juveniles are also more likely to be victims of crime, contributing to their vulnerability as a demographic group.

10 List the arguments for and against a constitutional amendment to protect victims' rights. (a) Even though the majority of state constitutions contain provisions to protect victims' rights, these guarantees do not have the legal force of an amendment to the U.S. Constitution. Only through such an amendment would the rights of victims match the rights of the accused in our criminal justice system. (b) Victims are excluded from the trial process because that process is designed to determine the guilt or innocence of the accused. Because the defendant is in an adversarial relationship with the government, he or she needs the protections guaranteed by the Constitution. The victim is not "on trial," and therefore providing equal protection would only "bog down" the criminal justice system.

Key Terms

actus reus 79	index crimes 86	self-reported surveys 94
civil law 75	*mala in se* 78	strict liability 82
corpus delicti 78	*mala prohibita* 78	Uniform Crime Report
dark figure of crime 91	*mens rea* 80	(UCR) 84
hate crime law 99	negligence 81	victim surveys 91
inchoate offenses 84	Part II offenses 88	

Questions for Critical Analysis

1 Give an example of how one person could be involved in a civil lawsuit and a criminal lawsuit for the same action.

2 Many people are careless. At what point can such carelessness be deemed criminal negligence?

3 Assume you are planning to pay someone to set fire to an old barn (arson) for the insurance money. Before you get a chance to carry out your plan, you accidentally drop a tool on another metal object, creating a spark that ignites some dry hay and burns the barn down. What essential element of a crime is missing in your actions?

4 Why are accompanying, or attendant, circumstances sometimes important to alleged perpetrators of certain acts?

5 What is the distinction between the crime rate and crime in America?

6 Although Part II offenses constitute the bulk of crimes, Part I offenses get the most publicity. Is this necessarily irrational? Why or why not?

7 Why might self-reported surveys be the best method of learning the dark figure of crime?

8 What sort of protections do state laws offer victims of crime? Why are these protections sometimes insufficient?

Go to www.cjinaction.com for tools to aid you in studying for your exams. Click on *Online Reviews* under *Chapter Resources* for an interactive review of each major section of this chapter. Under *Chapter Resources,* you will also find the *Chapter Outline, Chapter Summary, Flashcards, Glossary, Learning Objectives, Lecture Presentations, Concept Builder, Essay Questions,* and a *Tutorial Quiz.* You can also test yourself with a game of *Concentration* or the *Crossword Puzzle.*

Go to www.cjinaction.com for a wealth of online resources. Explore the *Internet Activities* and *Class Project*s under *Chapter Resources.* Check out the *Web Links* to access the Web sites mentioned in the text, as well as many others. You can also access recent perspectives by clicking on *CJ in the News* and *Terrorism Update* under *Course Resources.* If you'd like some mentoring, click on *Board of Mentors* under *Book Resources.*

For additional information, explore InfoTrac College Edition, your online library that offers complete full-length articles from thousands of scholarly and popular publications. Click on *InfoTrac College Edition* under *Chapter Resources* at www.cjinaction.com for a list of key words and InfoTrac exercises. Use the passcode that came with your book.

Henry, Stuart, and Mark M. Lanier, eds., *What Is Crime? Controversies over the Nature of Crime and What to Do about It,* Blue Ridge Summit, PA: Rowman & Littlefield Publishers, 2001. This book raises a number of interesting questions. Is crime simply a violation of criminal law, or is it behavior that causes harm? Does it matter who the victims of this behavior are? What if the perpetrator of the harm happens to be the government? The articles gathered here attempt to determine exactly what we are talking about when we talk about "crime."

Temple-Raston, Dina, *A Death in Texas: A Story of Race, Murder, and a Small*

Town's Struggle for Redemption, New York: Henry Holt, 2002. On June 7, 1998, James Byrd was dragged to death behind a pickup truck. *A Death in Texas* explores this hate crime—one of the most infamous of the past decade in the United States—from various angles. The author, a former foreign correspondent, examines the lives of the three white men driving the truck, in the process revealing a great deal about the nature of racism and the gestation period of a hate crime. She also describes the reaction to the crime in the small town of Jasper, Texas, where it occurred, as residents tried to come to grips with the evil in their midst.

Notes

1. Federal Bureau of Investigation, *Crime in the United States, 2001* (Washington, D.C.: U.S. Department of Justice, 2002), 303.

2. Hugh Williamson, "New Strategy in Second Hamburg Terror Trial," *Financial Times* (August 23, 2003), 5.

3. *Crime in the United States, 2001,* 1.

4. Bureau of Justice Statistics, *Criminal Victimization, 2002* (Washington, D.C.: U.S. Department of Justice, 2003), 1.

5. Anthony R. Harris, Stephen H. Thomas, Gene A. Fisher, and David J. Hirsch, "Murder and Medicine: The Lethality of Criminal Assault 1960-1999," *Homicide Studies* (May 2002), 128–166.

6. Robert W. Drane and David J. Neal, "On Moral Justifications for the Tort/Crime Distinction," *California Law Review* 68 (1980), 398.

7. Gail Heriot, "An Essay on the Civil-Criminal Distinction with Special Reference to Punitive Damages," *Journal of Contemporary Legal Issues* 7 (1996), 43.

8. Model Penal Code Section 1.04 (2).

9. Advisory Task Force on the Juvenile Justice System, *Final Report* (Minneapolis, MN: Minnesota Supreme Court, 1994), 5–11.

10. *Black's Law Dictionary,* 6th ed. (St. Paul, MN: West Publishing Co., 1990), 959.

11. *Ibid.,* 960.

12. Johannes Andenaes, "The Moral or Educative Influence of Criminal Law," *Journal of Social Issues* 27 (Spring 1971), 17, 26.

13. Stuart P. Green, "Why It's a Crime to Tear the Tag Off a Mattress," *Emory Law Journal* 46 (Fall 1997), 1533–1614.

14. Thomas A. Mullen, "Rule without Reason: Requiring Independent Proof of the *Corpus Delicti* as a Condition of Admitting Extrajudicial Confession," *University of San Francisco Law Review* 27 (1993), 385.

15. *Hawkins v. State,* 219 Ind. 116, 129, 37 N.E.2d 79 (1941).

16. David C. Biggs, "'The Good Samaritan Is Packing': An Overview of the Broadened Duty to Aid Your Fellowman, with the Modern Desire to Possess Concealed Weapons," *University of Dayton Law Review* 22 (Winter 1997), 225.

17. Christopher H. White, "No Good Deed Goes Unpunished: The Case for Reform of the Rescue Doctrine," *Northwestern University Law Review* (Fall 2002), 511.

18. Model Penal Code Section 2.02.

19. Model Penal Code Section 2.02 (c).

20. *Black's Law Dictionary,* 1423.

21. *United States v. Dotterweich,* 320 U.S. 277 (1943).

22. *State v. Stiffler,* 763 P.2d 308, 311 (Idaho Ct. App. 1988).

23. *State v. Harrison,* 425 A.2d 111 (1979).

24. Richard G. Singer and John Q. LaFond, *Criminal Law: Examples and Explanations* (New York: Aspen Law & Business, 1997), 322.

25. *State v. Linscott,* 520 A.2d 1067 (1987).

26. *Morissette v. United States,* 342 U.S. 246, 251–252 (1952).

27. *People v. Harding,* 443 Mich. 699–703, 506 N.W.2d 486–487 (1994).

28. Federal Bank Robbery Act, 18 U.S.C.A. Section 2113.

29. 530 U.S. 466 (2000).

30. *Ibid.,* 471.

31. N.J. Stat. Ann. Section 2C:44-3(e) (West Supp. 1999–2000).

32. Erwin Chemerinsky, "Striking a Balance on Hate Speech," *Trial* (July 2003), 78.

33. *Virginia v. Black,* 123 S.Ct. 1536 (2003).

34. *United States v. Jimenez Recio,* __ S.Ct. __ (2003).

35. Federal Bureau of Investigation, *Uniform Crime Reporting Handbook* (Washington, D.C.: U.S. Department of Justice, 1992), 30.

36. Federal Bureau of Investigation, *Crime in the United States, 2002* (Washington, D.C.: U.S. Department of Justice, 2003).

37. *Ibid.*

38. *Ibid.,* 9.

39. Jeffrey Reiman, *The Rich Get Richer and the Poor Get Prison,* 4th ed. (Boston: Allyn & Bacon, 1995), 59–60.

40. *Crime in the United States, 2002,* 22.

41. *Ibid.,* 11.

42. *Ibid.,* 234.

43. Marcus Felson, *Crime in Everyday Life* (Thousand Oaks, CA: Pine Forge Press, 1994), 3.

44. Donald J. Black, "Production of Crime Rates," *American Sociological Review* 35 (1970), 733–748.

45. *Criminal Victimization, 2002,* 1.

46. Victoria W. Schneider and Brian Weirsma, "Limits and Use," in Doris Layton MacKenzie, Phyllis Jo Baunach, and Roy R. Robergs, eds., *Measuring Crime: Large Scale, Long Range Efforts* (Albany, NY: State University of New York Press, 1990), 21–27.

47. Alabama Code Sections 13A-6-60(8), 13A-6-61(a)(1) (1994).

48. William Chambliss, *Exporting Criminology* (New York: Macmillan, 1988), 30.

49. *Uniform Crime Reporting Handbook, 33.*

50. *Crime in the United States, 2002, 5.*

51. Domingo Ramirez, Jr., and Betsy Blaney, "FBI Revises Crime Log Categories," *Ft. Worth Star-Telegram* (December 1, 1996), 1.

52. Romana R. Rantala, *The Effect of the NIBRS on Crime Statistics* (Washington, D.C.: Bureau of Justice Statistics, 2000), 3.

53. Victor E. Kappeler, Mark Blumberg, and Gary W. Potter, *The Mythology of Crime and Criminal Justice,* 2d ed. (Prospect Heights, IL: Waveland Press, 1993), 31.

54. Alfred D. Biderman and James P. Lynch, *Understanding Crime Statistics: Why the UCR Diverges from the NCVS* (New York: Springer-Verlag, 1991).

55. L. Edward Vells and Joseph Rankin, "Juvenile Victimization: Convergent Validation of Alternative Measurement," *Journal of Research in Crime and Delinquency* 32 (1995), 287–307.

56. Dan Eggen, "Major Crimes in U.S. Increase," *Washington Post* (June 23, 2002), A1.

57. Curt Anderson, "Crime Rate Continues to Drop," *Washington Post* (August 25, 2003), A1.

58. Dan Eggen, "Survey Shows Continuing Drop in Violent Crime," *Washington Post* (June 14, 2001), A1.

59. Peter B. Wood, Walter R. Grove, James A. Wilson, and John K. Cochran, "Nonsocial Reinforcement and Criminal Conduct: An Extension of Learning Theory," *Criminology* 35 (May 1997), 335–366.

60. James S. Wallerstein and Clement J. Wyle, "Our Law-Abiding Law Breakers," *Probation* 35 (April 1947), 107–118.

61. Michael Hindelang, "Causes of Delinquency: A Partial Replication and Extension," *Social Problems* 20 (1973), 471–487.

62. Thomas Gray and Eric Walsh, *Maryland Youth at Risk: A Study of Drug Use in Juvenile Detainees* (College Park, MD: Center for Substance Abuse Research, 1993).

63. John Braithwaite, *Inequality, Crime, and Public Policy* (London: Routledge & Kegan Paul, 1979), 21.

64. *Criminal Victimization, 2002,* 1.

65. Ross Macmillan, "Adolescent Criminalization and Income Deficits in Adulthood," *Criminology* (May 2000), 574.

66. Scott Menard, *Short- and Long-Term Consequences of Adolescent Victimization* (Washington, D.C.: Office of Juvenile Justice and Delinquency Prevention, February 2002), 2.

67. Robert J. Sampson and Janet L. Lauritsen, "Deviant Lifestyles, Proximity to Crime, and the Offender-Victim Link in Personal Violence," *Journal of Research in Crime and Delinquency* 27 (1990), 110–139.

68. Menard, 1–16.

69. Stephen J. Schulhofer, "The Trouble with Trials; the Trouble with Us," *Yale Law Journal* 105 (1995), 840.

70. Office for Victims of Crime, *New Directions from the Field: Victims' Rights and Services for the 21st Century* (Washington, D.C.: U.S. Department of Justice, May 1998), 325.

71. Victims of Crime Act, Section 1402, 42 U.S.C. Sections 10601 *et seq.* (1984).

72. Violent Crime Control and Law Enforcement Act of 1994, Title IV, Pub. L. No. 103-222 (September 13, 1994), codified as amended at 42 U.S.C.A. Sections 13931–14040.

73. David Beatty and Trudy Gregorie, "Implementing Victims' Rights," *Corrections Today* (August 1, 2003), 81.

74. Gessner H. Harrison, "The Good, the Bad, and the Ugly: Arizona's Courts and the Crime Victims' Bill of Rights," *Arizona State Law Journal* (Summer 2002), 531.

75. *Ibid.*

76. Dean G. Kirkland, David Beatty, and Susan Smith Howley, *The Rights of Crime Victims—Does Legal Protection Make a Difference?* (Washington, D.C.: National Institute of Justice, December 1998).

77. *Ibid.*

78. Senate Joint Resolution 35, 107th Congress, Section 2 (2002).

79. Kelly McMurry, "Victims' Rights Movement Rises to Power," *Trial* (July 1, 1997), 12.

80. *Crime in the United States, 2002,* 61–62.

81. "Statement of the Anti-Defamation League on Bias-Motivated Crime and H.R. 1082—The Hate Crimes Prevention Act," *Chicago-Latino Law Review* (Spring 2000), 56.

82. Steve M. Freeman, "Hate Crime Laws: Punishment Which Fits the Crime," *Annual Survey of American Law* 4 (1992/93), 581–585.

83. Jen McCaffery, "Prosecutors Allowed to Seek Death Penalty in Park Slaying Case," *Roanoke Times & World News* (February 1, 2003), B4.

84. 505 U.S. 377 (1992).

85. 508 U.S. 476 (1993).

86. Nat Hentoff, "Letting Loose the Hate Crimes Police," *The Village Voice* (July 13, 1993).

87. James B. Jacobs, "Should Hate Be a Crime?" *The Public Interest* (Fall 1993), 3–14.

88. Quoted in Hentoff.

Inside Criminal Law

>chapter outline<

- The Development of American Criminal Law
- Written Sources of American Criminal Law
- The Purposes of Criminal Law
- Criminal Responsibility and the Law
- Justification Criminal Defenses and the Law
- Procedural Safeguards
- Criminal Justice in Action—The Consent Defense and Rape

>chapter objectives<

After reading this chapter, you should be able to:

1 Explain precedent and the importance of the doctrine of *stare decisis.*

2 List the four written sources of American criminal law.

3 Explain the two basic functions of criminal law.

4 List and briefly define the most important excuse defenses for crimes.

5 Describe the four most important justification criminal defenses.

6 Distinguish between substantive and procedural criminal law.

7 Determine where Americans find most of their criminal procedural safeguards.

8 Explain the importance of the due process clause in the criminal justice system.

9 Discuss how the United States Supreme Court has incorporated the due process clause.

The Vegan Baby Trial

Before starting on a vegan diet, Silva Swinton had weighed close to three hundred pounds. The regime, which forbids the eating of any animal products, worked so well for Silva that she decided to use the same diet for her infant daughter, Iice [pronounced ICE]. Silva and her husband, Joseph, spent hours preparing meat- and dairy-free meals for Iice. These efforts did not, however, produce the desired effect. When health authorities were finally summoned, fifteen-month-old Iice was severely malnourished (weighing only ten pounds, half the average for a girl that age) and toothless; she suffered from broken bones, rickets, and a number of internal problems.

The district attorney's office in Queens, New York, charged the Swintons with first degree assault. Prosecutors claimed that that the parents—by ignoring Iice's obviously deteriorating health—knowingly endangered their child's life. During the trial, doctors testified that Iice was at risk of heart failure or seizures as a result of being denied sufficient protein and calcium in a diet that consisted mostly of ground nuts, fruit juice, herb tea, cod liver oil and a liquid mixture of potatoes, plantains, and fresh vegetables. In 2003, a jury found the Swintons guilty of, essentially, nearly starving Iice to death. Queens County Supreme Court Judge Richard Buchter sentenced Silva to six years in prison and Joseph to a five-year term. (He was given a lighter punishment because of his below-average IQ, which the court felt made him less culpable than his wife.) While not denying that the Swintons loved their daughter, Judge Buchter said, "Love is no substitute for proper food and nutrition, nor for decent child care."

Michael Norcia/NYP/REX USA

Silva and Joseph Swinton, convicted of nearly starving their infant daughter to death by putting her on a strict vegan diet.

CONCEPT BUILDER
Mental state or intent (*Mens rea*) is essential in many criminal cases and can affect sentencing dispositions. Visit www.cjinaction.com for an interactive exploration of this key topic.

> **Was the law fair** to the Swintons? In Chapter 3, we learned that a defendant must have a guilty mental state, or *mens rea*, to have committed a crime. Arguably, the Swintons did not have such a mental state. Even the judge acknowledged that they loved Iice and probably did not intend to harm her in any way. Nonetheless, it is important to clearly understand the words in the statute under which the couple was charged. The criminal code of New York State defines first

degree assault as "recklessly" engaging in conduct "which creates a grave risk of death to another person, and thereby causes serious physical injury."[1]

Apparently, the jury at the Swintons' trial believed the couple acted recklessly; that is, they *should have* known that their actions—which did create a risk of death for their daughter and cause her serious physical injury—placed Iice in danger. Generally, of course, poor child care is not a criminal offense. As the Swintons' case suggests, however, criminal law must be flexible enough to encompass acts that are not obviously criminal, yet still pose a threat to society and therefore, in the eyes of some, deserve punishment. In this chapter, we will examine how these "threats to society" are identified and focus on the guidelines that determine how the criminal justice system resolves and punishes criminal guilt.

The Development of American Criminal Law

Given its various functions, a single definition of *law* is difficult to establish. To the Greek philosopher Aristotle (384–322 B.C.E.) law was a "pledge that citizens of a state will do justice to one another." Aristotle's mentor, Plato (427–347 B.C.E.), saw the law as primarily a form of social control. The British jurist Sir William Blackstone (1723–1780) described law as "a rule of civil conduct prescribed by the supreme power in a state, commanding what is right, and prohibiting what is wrong." In the United States, jurist Oliver Wendell Holmes, Jr. (1841–1935), contended that law was a set of rules that allowed one to predict how a court would resolve a particular dispute.

THE CONCEPTION OF LAW

Although these definitions vary in their particulars, they are all based on the following general observation: *law* consists of enforceable rules governing relationships among individuals and between individuals and their society.[2] Searching back into history, several sources for modern American law can be found in the rules laid out by ancient societies. One of the first known sets of written law was created during the reign of Hammurabi (1792–1750 B.C.E.), the sixth king of the ancient empire of Babylon. The Code of Hammurabi set out crimes and their punishments based on *lex Talionis,* or "an eye for an eye." This concept of retribution is still important and will be discussed in Chapter 11.

Another ancient source of law can be found in the Mosaic Code of the Israelites (1200 B.C.E.). According to tradition, Moses—acting as an intermediary for God—presented the code to the tribes of Israel. The two sides entered into a covenant, or contract, in which the Israelites agreed to follow the code and God agreed to protect them as the chosen people. Besides providing the basis for Judeo-Christian teachings, the Mosaic Code is also reflected in modern American law, as evident by similar prohibitions against murder, theft, adultery, and perjury.

Modern law also owes a debt to the Code of Justinian, promulgated throughout the Roman Empire in the sixth century. This code collected many of the laws that Western society had produced. It was influential in the development of the civil law systems of the European continent. To some extent, it influenced the common law of England.

"Justice?—You get justice in the next world, in this world you have the law."
—William Gaddis, American novelist (1994)

 See the Legal Information Institute for an overview of criminal law and links to an extensive number of documents relating to criminal justice. Find this Web site by clicking on *Web Links* under *Chapter Resources* at www.cjinaction.com

ENGLISH COMMON LAW

Common Law
The body of law developed from custom or judicial decisions in English and U.S. courts and not attributable to a legislature.

The English system of law as it stands today was solidified during the reign of Henry II (1154–1189). Henry sent judges on a specific route throughout the country known as a circuit. These circuit judges established a **common law** in England; that is, they solidified a national law in which legal principles applied to all citizens equally, no matter where they lived or what the local customs had dictated in the past. When confusion about any particular law arose, the circuit judges could draw on English traditions, or they could borrow from legal decisions made in other European countries. Once a circuit judge made a ruling, other circuit judges faced with similar cases generally followed that ruling. Each interpretation became part of the law on the subject and served as a legal **precedent**—a decision that furnished an example or authority for deciding subsequent cases involving similar legal principles or facts. Over time, a body of general rules that prescribed social conduct and that was applied throughout the entire English realm was established, and subsequently it was passed on to British colonies, including those in the New World that would eventually become the thirteen original states.

Precedent
A court decision that furnishes an example of authority for deciding subsequent cases involving similar facts.

What is important about the formation of the common law is that it developed from the customs of the people rather than simply the will of a ruler. As such, the common law came to reflect the social, religious, economic, and cultural values of the people. All the while, a system of sheriffs, courts, juries, and lawyers accompanied the development of the common law.

STARE DECISIS

Stare Decisis
(pronounced *ster*-ay dih-*si-ses*). A common law doctrine under which judges are obligated to follow the precedents established under prior decisions.

The practice of deciding new cases with reference to precedents is the basis for a doctrine called ***stare decisis*** ("to stand on decided cases"). Under this doctrine, judges are obligated to follow the precedents established within their jurisdictions.[3] For example, any decision of a particular state's highest court will control the outcome of future cases on that issue brought before all of the lower courts within that same state (unless preempted by the federal Constitution). All United States Supreme Court decisions on issues involving the U.S. Constitution are normally binding on *all* courts, because the U.S. Constitution is the supreme law of the land and the Court is its final interpreter.

George Washington, standing at right, presided over the Constitutional Convention of 1787. The convention resulted in the U.S. Constitution, the source of a number of laws that continue to form the basis of our criminal justice system today.

Controlling precedents in a jurisdiction are referred to as binding authorities, as are statutes or other laws that must be followed. In contrast, in civil law systems, which rely primarily on legislation and custom rather than case law, precedent is not binding. (To see the extent to which common law and the doctrine of *stare decisis* have been adopted in other countries, see Figure 4.1.)

The doctrine of *stare decisis* helps the courts to be more efficient, because if other courts have carefully examined a similar case, their legal reasoning and opinions can serve as a guide. This does not mean, however, that the system is rigid. The United States Supreme Court, for example, will sometimes rule against precedent set in a previous Court decision. It does so when there have been sufficient changes in society to warrant departing from the doctrine of *stare decisis*. In general, however, the judicial system is slow to change, and courts rarely alter major points of law. The doctrine of *stare decisis* leads to stability in the law, allowing people to predict how the law will be applied in given circumstances.

The Granger Collection

↑ ONLINE REVIEW *Go to the book's Web site for an interactive review of this section*

Written Sources of American Criminal Law

Originally, common law was *uncodified;* that is, it relied primarily on judges following precedents, and the body of the law was not written down in any single place. Uncodified law, however, presents a number of drawbacks, not the least being that citizens have difficulty learning which acts are illegal and understanding the procedures that must be followed to establish innocence or guilt. Consequently, U.S. history has seen the development of several written sources of American criminal law, also known as "substantive" criminal law. These sources include:

1 The U.S. Constitution and the constitutions of the various states.
2 Statutes, or laws, passed by Congress and by state legislatures, plus local ordinances.
3 Regulations, created by regulatory agencies, such as the federal Food and Drug Administration.
4 Case law (court decisions).

We describe each of these important written sources of law in the following pages (see Figure 4.2 on the next page).

FIGURE 4.1	Selected Countries with Civil and Common Law Systems
CIVIL LAW	**COMMON LAW**
Argentina	Australia
Austria	Bangladesh
Brazil	Canada
Chile	Ghana
China	India
Egypt	Israel
Finland	Jamaica
France	Kenya
Germany	Malaysia
Greece	New Zealand
Indonesia	Nigeria
Iran	Singapore
Italy	United Kingdom
Japan	United States
Mexico	Zambia
Poland	
South Korea	
Sweden	
Tunisia	
Venezuela	

↑The United States was not the only country to adopt the basics of English common law and *stare decisis.* Many of Britain's former colonies have assimilated elements of common law to complement their traditional legal practices. As this figure shows, however, a number of countries operate under civil legal systems (not be confused with the classification of civil versus criminal law, which was explained in Chapter 3). Civil law systems rely primarily on legislation and custom rather than case law and *stare decisis.* In a country with a civil law system, the courts normally refer only to legislation on the subject. The decisions of civil law judges do not necessarily set precedents for later cases.

CONSTITUTIONAL LAW

The federal government and the states have separate written constitutions that set forth the general organization and powers of, and the limits on, their respective governments. **Constitutional law** is the law as expressed in these constitutions.

The U.S. Constitution is the supreme law of the land. As such, it is the basis of all law in the United States. Any law that violates the Constitution, as ultimately determined by the United States Supreme Court, will be declared unconstitutional and will not be enforced. The Tenth Amendment, which defines the powers and limitations of the federal government, reserves to the states all powers not granted to the federal government. Under our system of federalism (see Chapter 1), each state also has its own constitution. Unless they conflict with the U.S. Constitution or a federal law, state constitutions are supreme within their respective borders. (You will learn more about how constitutional law applies to our criminal justice system in later chapters.)

Constitutional Law
Law based on the U.S. Constitution and the constitutions of the various states.

STATUTORY LAW

Statutes enacted by legislative bodies at any level of government make up another source of law, which is generally referred to as **statutory law.** *Federal statutes* are laws that are enacted by the U.S. Congress. *State statutes* are laws enacted by state legislatures, and statutory law also includes the ordinances passed by cities and counties. A federal statute, of course, applies to all states. A state statute, in contrast, applies only within that state's borders. City or county ordinances (statutes) apply only to those jurisdictions where they are enacted. As mentioned, statutory law found by the Supreme Court to violate the U.S. Constitution will be overturned.

Statutory Law
The body of law enacted by legislative bodies.

FIGURE 4.2   Sources of American Law

1   **Constitutional law**   The law as expressed in the U.S. Constitution and the various state constitutions. The U.S. Constitution is the supreme law of the land. State constitutions are supreme within state borders to the extent that they do not violate the U.S. Constitution or a federal law.

2   **Statutory law**   Laws or ordinances created by federal, state, and local legislatures and governing bodies. None of these laws can violate the U.S. Constitution or the relevant state constitution. Uniform laws, when adopted by a state legislature, become statutory law in that state.

3   **Administrative law**   The rules, orders, and decisions of federal or state government administrative agencies. Federal administrative agencies are created by enabling legislation enacted by the U.S. Congress. Agency functions include rulemaking, investigation and enforcement, and adjudication.

4   **Case law and common law doctrines**   Judge-made law, including interpretations of constitutional provisions, of statutes enacted by legislatures, and of regulations created by administrative agencies. The common law—the doctrines and principles embodied in case law—governs all areas not covered by statutory law (or agency regulations issued to implement various statutes).

In the late 1980s, for example, the Court ruled that any state laws banning the burning of the American flag were unconstitutional because they impinged on the individual's right to freedom of expression.[4]

Common Law and State Statutes   Even though the body of statutory law has expanded greatly since the beginning of this nation, thus narrowing the applicability of common law doctrines, there is significant overlap between statutory law and common law. For example, many statutes essentially codify existing common law rules. Therefore, the courts, when interpreting the statutes, often rely on the common law as a guide to what the legislators intended. In some instances, statutory law has brought common law principles more in line with modern criminal theory. Under common law, for example, the law of rape applied only when the victim was a female. Today, many states recognize that both sexes may be the targets of sexual assault. Under common law, burglary was defined as the breaking and entering of a dwelling during the nighttime. State legislatures, in contrast, generally have defined burglary as occurring at any time. They have extended it to apply to structures beyond dwellings and even to automobiles.

Model Penal Code   Until the mid–twentieth century, state statutes were disorganized, inconsistent, and generally inadequate for modern society. In 1952, the American Law Institute began to draft a uniform penal code in hopes of solving this problem. The first Model Penal Code was released ten years later and has had a broad effect on state statutes.[5] Though not a law itself, the code defines the general principles of criminal responsibility and codifies specific offenses; it is the source for many of the definitions of crime in this textbook. The majority of the states have adopted parts of the Model Penal Code into their statutes, and some states, such as New York, have adopted a large portion of the Code.[6]

It is important to keep in mind that there are essentially fifty-two different criminal codes in this country—one for each state, the District of Columbia, and the federal government. Even if a state has adopted a large portion of the Model Penal Code, there may be certain discrepancies. Indeed, a state's criminal code often reflects specific values of its citizens, which may not be in keeping with those of the majority of other states. New Mexico and Louisiana, for example, are the only states where cockfighting is still legal. Sometimes, old laws remain on the books even though they are clearly anachronistic and are rarely, if ever, enforced: in Oklahoma, a person can be sentenced to thirty days in jail for "injuring fruit," and a hundred counties in North Carolina prohibit swearing.[7]

Administrative Law
The body of law created by administrative agencies (in the form of rules, regulations, orders, and decisions) in order to carry out their duties and responsibilities.

ADMINISTRATIVE LAW

A third source of American criminal law consists of **administrative law**—the rules, orders, and decisions of regulatory agencies. A regulatory agency is a federal, state, or local government agency established to perform a specific function. The Occupational Safety and Health Administration (OSHA), for example, oversees the safety and health of American workers; the Environmental Protection Agency (EPA) is concerned with protecting the natural environment; and the Food and Drug Administration (FDA) regulates food and drugs produced in the United States. Disregarding certain laws created by regulatory agencies can be a criminal violation. Many modern federal statutes, such as the Clean Air Act, designate authority to a specific regulatory agency, such as the EPA, to promulgate regulations to which criminal sanctions are attached. The number of criminal investigators employed by the EPA has grown from six in 1982 to more than 150 at present. These investigators are involved in nearly 500 law enforcement cases each year.[8]

CASE LAW

As is evident from the earlier discussion of the common law tradition, another basic source of American law consists of the rules of law announced in court decisions. These rules of law include interpretations of constitutional provisions, of statutes enacted by legislatures, and of regulations created by administrative agencies. Today, this body of law is referred to variously as the common law, judge-made law, or **case law.**

Case law relies to a certain extent on how courts interpret a particular statute. If you wanted to learn about the coverage and applicability of a particular statute, for example, you would need to locate the statute and study it. You would also need to see how the courts in your jurisdiction have interpreted the statute—in other words, what precedents have been established in regard to that statute. The use of precedent means that judge-made law varies from jurisdiction to jurisdiction. (To learn about the sources of criminal law in many parts of the Muslim world, see *International CJ—Shari'a and Islamic Law* on the next page.)

↗ ONLINE REVIEW *Go to the book's Web site for an interactive review of this section*

Case Law
The rules of law announced in court decisions. Case law includes the aggregate of reported cases that interpret judicial precedents, statutes, regulations, and constitutional provisions.

The Purposes of Criminal Law

Why do societies need laws? Many criminologists believe that criminal law has two basic functions: one relates to the legal requirements of a society, and the other pertains to its need to maintain and promote social values.[9]

PROTECT AND PUNISH: THE LEGAL FUNCTION OF THE LAW

The primary legal function of the law is to maintain social order by protecting citizens from *criminal harm.* This term refers to a variety of harms that can be generalized to fit into two categories:

1 Harms to individual citizens' physical safety and property, such as the harm caused by murder, theft, or arson.

2 Harms to society's interests collectively, such as the harm caused by unsafe foods or consumer products, a polluted environment, or poorly constructed buildings.[10]

The first category is self-evident, although even murder has different degrees, or grades, of offense to which different punishments are assigned. The second, however, has proved more problematic, for it is difficult to measure society's

Shari'a and Islamic Law

Despite the influence of Judeo-Christian doctrine on our legal system, the U.S. Constitution, in the words of Thomas Jefferson, created a "wall of separation of Church and State." In contrast, Islamic law, one of the three major legal systems in the world along with civil law and common law, is primarily based on the Koran.

The Koran is the most important source of *Shari'a,* a term that can be translated as "path" and refers to the laws and way of life provided to Muhammad by Allah. For most Muslims, *Shari'a* is a guide to religious activities such as prayer and fasting. Many Muslim countries have also adopted *Shari'a* as their civil law, allowing it to govern marriages, inheritance, the formation of contracts, and other matters. A few countries also use *Shari'a* as the basis for criminal law, a practice that has drawn criticism from their own citizens and human rights activists in the West.

Zafran Bibi, after a Pakistani court overturned her sentence to death by stoning for adultery in 2002.

AP Photo/Tariq Aziz

Under the strictest interpretation of *Shari'a,* the penalty for a first theft is amputation of the right hand. After a second conviction for that crime, the offender loses the left foot. An unmarried person who has sexual intercourse is to receive one hundred lashes from a whip, while the punishment for adultery is burial to the waist and stoning to death. In Nigeria, a man and woman who were not married were sentenced to death for telling each other, "I like you."

Shari'a forms the basis for criminal law in Saudi Arabia and Iran and was widely used in Afghanistan under the Taliban before 2003. Recently, it has spread to countries such as Nigeria and Pakistan, where it has come into conflict with constitutional governments. In Pakistan, for example, a local *Shari'a* court convicted a woman who had been raped of adultery and sentenced her to death by stoning. Bowing to public outrage, an Islamic appeals court eventually overturned the decision.

FOR CRITICAL ANALYSIS
Depending on how it is interpreted, Shari'a *can be particularly harsh on women, and many women's rights groups from Western nations have worked to change these laws. What are the possible drawbacks when a person from one culture tries to change the traditions of another culture? Do you think that foreign governments should pressure countries that implement strict* Shari'a *to modify their criminal laws?*

"collective" interests. Often, laws passed to reduce such harms seem overly intrusive and marginally necessary. An extreme example would seem to be the Flammable Fabrics Act, which makes it a crime for a retailer to willfully remove a precautionary instruction label from a mattress that is protected with a chemical fire retardant.[11] Yet even in this example, a criminal harm is conceivable. Suppose a retailer removes the tags before selling a large number of mattresses to a hotel chain. Employees of the chain then unknowingly wash the mattresses with an agent that lessens their flame-resistant qualities. After the mattresses have been placed in rooms, a guest falls asleep while smoking a cigarette, starting a fire that burns down the entire hotel and causes several deaths.[12]

MAINTAIN AND TEACH: THE SOCIAL FUNCTION OF THE LAW

If criminal laws against acts that cause harm or injury to others are almost universally accepted, the same cannot be said for laws that criminalize "morally" wrongful activities that may do no obvious, physical harm outside the families of those involved. Why criminalize gambling or prostitution if the participants are consenting?

Expressing Public Morality The answer lies in the social function of criminal law. Many observers believe that the main purpose of criminal law is to reflect the values and norms of society, or at least of those segments of society that hold power. Legal scholar Henry Hart has stated that the only justification for criminal law and punishment is "the judgment of community condemnation."[13]

Take, for example, the misdemeanor of bigamy, which occurs when someone knowingly marries a second person without terminating her or his marriage to an original husband or wife. Apart from moral considerations, there would appear to be no victims in a bigamous relationship, and indeed many societies have allowed and continue to allow bigamy to exist. In the American social tradition, however, as John L. Diamond of the University of California's Hastings College of the Law points out:

> Marriage is an institution encouraged and supported by society. The structural importance of the integrity of the family and a monogamous marriage requires unflinching enforcement of the criminal laws against bigamy. The immorality is not in choosing to do wrong, but in transgressing, even innocently, a fundamental social boundary that lies at the core of social order.[14]

When discussing the social function of criminal law, it is important to remember that a society's views of morality change over time. Puritan New England society not only had strict laws against adultery, but also considered lying and idleness to be criminal acts.[15] Today, such acts may carry social stigmas, but only in certain extreme circumstances do they elicit legal sanctions. Furthermore, criminal laws aimed at minority groups, which were once widely accepted in the legal community as well as society at large, have increasingly come under question. (See the feature *CJ in Focus—Landmark Cases:* Lawrence v. Texas on the next page.)

Teaching Societal Boundaries Some scholars believe that criminal laws not only express the expectations of society, but "teach" them as well. Professor Lawrence M. Friedman of Stanford University thinks that just as parents teach children behavioral norms through punishment, criminal justice "'teaches a lesson' to the people it punishes, and to society at large." Making burglary a crime, arresting burglars, placing them in jail—each step in the criminal justice process reinforces the idea that burglary is unacceptable and is deserving of punishment.[16]

This teaching function can also be seen in traffic laws. There is nothing "natural" about most traffic laws; Americans drive on the right side of the street, the British on the left side, with no obvious difference in the results. These laws, such as stopping at intersections, using headlights at night, and following speed limits, do lead to a more orderly flow of traffic and fewer accidents—certainly socially desirable goals. Various forms of punishment for breaking traffic laws teach drivers the "social" order of the road.

ONLINE REVIEW Go to the book's Web site for an interactive review of this section

Criminal Responsibility and the Law

INFOTRAC KEYWORDS
civil law, criminal law
For more information, use these search terms with InfoTrac College Edition, your online library at www.infotrac-college.com

Tabitha Pollock was sound asleep when her boyfriend, Scott English, hit her three-year-old daughter twice in the head, killing the child. Agreeing with the prosecution's theory that Pollock should have known that English was capable of

olice officers in Houston arrested John Geddes Lawrence and Tyron Garner for violating a Texas law that prohibits individuals of the same sex from engaging in "deviate sexual intercourse." Lawrence and Garner challenged the law as unconstitutional because it banned sexual practices—in this case, sodomy—by homosexual couples that are lawful when performed by a man and a woman. The Texas Supreme Court upheld the statute, relying on the United States Supreme Court's decision in *Bowers v. Hardwick* (1986), which preserved a similar state law (since repealed) in Georgia. Lawrence and Garner appealed to the Supreme Court, in essence telling the highest court in the land that it had been mistaken when it ruled on the *Bowers* case and asking it to reconsider.

Lawrence v. Texas
United States Supreme Court
123 S.Ct. 2472
http://laws.findlaw.com/us/000/02-102.html

> **In the words of the court . . .**
Justice KENNEDY, majority opinion

* * * *

The laws involved in *Bowers* and here are, to be sure, statutes that purport to do no more than prohibit a particular sexual act. Their penalties and purposes, though, have more far-reaching consequences, touching upon the most private human conduct, sexual behavior, and in the most private of places, the home. The statutes do seek to control a personal relationship that, whether or not entitled to formal recognition in the law, is within the liberty of persons to choose without being punished as criminals.

This, as a general rule, should counsel against attempts by the State, or a court, to define the meaning of the relationship or to set its boundaries absent injury to a person or abuse of an institution the law protects. It suffices for us to acknowledge

that adults may choose to enter upon this relationship in the confines of their homes and their own private lives and still retain their dignity as free persons. * * * The liberty protected by the Constitution allows homosexual persons the right to make this choice.

* * * *

When homosexual conduct is made criminal by the law of the State, that declaration in and of itself is an invitation to subject homosexual persons to discrimination both in the public and in the private spheres. The central holding of *Bowers* has been brought in question by this case, and it should be addressed. Its continuance as precedent demeans the lives of homosexual persons.

* * * *

The petitioners are entitled to respect for their private lives. The State cannot demean their existence or control their destiny by making their private sexual conduct a crime.

> **Decision**

Overturning its earlier *Bowers* decision, the Court ruled that the Texas antisodomy law was unconstitutional, at the same time invalidating similar statutes in three other states—Kansas, Oklahoma, and Missouri.

FOR CRITICAL ANALYSIS
Nine states still have laws on the books that make sodomy illegal for both heterosexual and homosexual partners. How do you think one of these laws would fare if brought before the Supreme Court today? Have the morals of American society changed to the point where any law criminalizing consensual sexual conduct between adults is outdated?

For more information and activities related to this case, click on Landmark Cases *under* Book Resources *at www.cjinaction.com.*

---

such an act, an Illinois jury convicted her of first degree murder, and she was sentenced to thirty-six years in prison. In 2002, the Illinois Supreme Court freed Pollock after seven years' incarceration, holding that she could not be held responsible for a crime she did not commit.[17]

The idea of responsibility plays a significant role in criminal law. In certain circumstances, the law recognizes that a person is not responsible for wrongdoing because he or she does not meet certain mental conditions. In many jurisdictions, for example, children under a specific age are believed incapable of committing crimes because they are too young to understand the ramifications of their actions. Thus, *infancy* is an "excuse" defense, or a defense that argues that the accused's wrongdoing should be excused because he or she lacked the capacity to be held liable for the crime. Other important excuse defenses include insanity, intoxication, and mistake.

INSANITY

After Tonda Lynn Ansley killed her landlady with a .40 caliber Smith & Wesson in broad daylight, she told homicide detectives that she thought she was living in the "the Matrix," following the script of the movie by the same name. In 2003, a Butler County (Ohio) judge found that Ansley was so divorced from reality that she could not be found guilty of murder, even though the shooting occurred in front of nine eyewitnesses.[18] As a result, the defendant was sent to a mental hospital rather than to prison. Thus, **insanity** may be a defense to a criminal charge when the defendant's state of mind is such that she or he cannot claim legal responsibility for her or his actions.

Measuring Sanity Although criminal law has accepted the idea that an insane person cannot be held responsible for criminal acts, society has long debated what standards should be used to measure sanity for the purposes of a criminal trial. One of the oldest tests for insanity resulted from a case in 1843 in which Daniel M'Naughten shot and killed Edward Drummond in the belief that Drummond was Sir Robert Peel, the British prime minister. At trial, M'Naughten claimed that he was suffering from delusions at the time of the murder, and he was found not guilty by reason of insanity. In response to public outcry over the decision, the British court established the *M'Naughten* **rule.** Also known as the right-wrong test, the *M'Naughten* rule states that a person is legally insane and therefore not criminally responsible if, at the time of the offense, he or she was not able to distinguish between right and wrong.[19]

As Figure 4.3 on page 118 shows, twenty-two states still use a version of the *M'Naughten* rule. Several other jurisdictions, reacting to criticism of the *M'Naughten* rule as too narrow, have supplemented it with the less restrictive **irresistible impulse test.** Under this combined approach, a person may be found insane even if he or she was aware that a criminal act was "wrong," provided that some "irresistible impulse" resulting from a mental deficiency drove him or her to commit the crime.[20]

Another method of determining criminal sanity—the *Durham* **rule**—rejects the *M'Naughten* test by focusing on the many personality factors that lead to mental instability. Under the *Durham* test, mental illness may be viewed as a permanent defect in the defendant or as a disease that can be treated. Created in New Hampshire in the nineteenth century, the *Durham* rule was adopted by the Court of Appeals for the District of Columbia in the 1954 case *Durham v. United States.*[21] Judge David Bazelon, who presided over the case, placed the burden on prosecutors to prove beyond a reasonable doubt that the defendant was not insane. The jury is then expected to determine whether the criminal act was the product of a mental defect or disease; for this reason the rule is referred to as the *products test.*

Today, all federal courts and about two-thirds of the states use the **substantial capacity test** to determine sanity. Characterized as a modern improvement on the *M'Naughten* test, substantial capacity guidelines state that:

> A person is not responsible for criminal conduct if at the time of such conduct
> as a result of mental disease or defect he lacks substantial capacity either to

Insanity
A defense for criminal liability that asserts a lack of criminal responsibility. According to the law, a person cannot have the requisite state of mind to commit a crime if she or he did not know at the time of the act that it was wrong, or did not know the nature and quality of the act.

***M'Naughten* Rule**
A common law test of criminal responsibility derived from *M'Naughten's case* in 1843 that relies on the defendant's inability to distinguish right from wrong.

Irresistible Impulse Test
A test for the insanity defense under which a defendant who knew his or her action was wrong may still be found insane if he or she was nonetheless unable, as a result of a mental deficiency, to control the urge to complete it.

***Durham* Rule**
A test of criminal responsibility adopted in a 1954 case: "an accused is not criminally responsible if his unlawful act was the product of mental disease or mental defect."

Substantial Capacity Test
From the Model Penal Code, a test that states that a person is not responsible for criminal behavior if when committing the act "as a result of mental disease or defect he lacks substantial capacity either to appreciate the wrongfulness of his conduct or to conform his conduct to the requirements of the law."

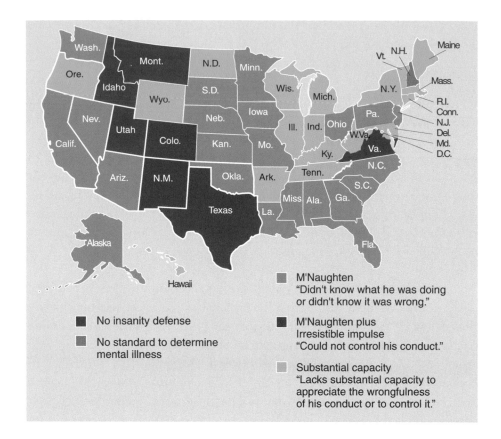

FIGURE 4.3 Insanity Defenses

Source: Bureau of Justice Statistics, *State Court Organization, 1998* (Washington, D.C.: U.S. Department of Justice, 2000), 257–259.

Map legend:

■ No insanity defense

■ No standard to determine mental illness

■ M'Naughten "Didn't know what he was doing or didn't know it was wrong."

■ M'Naughten plus Irresistible impulse "Could not control his conduct."

■ Substantial capacity "Lacks substantial capacity to appreciate the wrongfulness of his conduct or to control it."

appreciate the wrongfulness of his conduct or to conform his conduct to the requirements of the law.[22]

The key element of this rule is that it requires only a lack of "substantial capacity" to release a defendant from criminal responsibility. This standard is considerably easier to meet than the "right-wrong" requirements of the *M'Naughten* rule or the irresistible impulse test.

Use of the Insanity Defense   During a New Mexico legislative session, an amendment to a bill was offered to the effect that when a psychologist enters a courtroom, he or she "shall wear a cone-shaped hat that is not less than two feet tall" and the "surface of the hat shall be imprinted with stars and lightning bolts."[23] This sarcastic amendment (it did not pass) reflects the disdain with which many Americans view the insanity defense; it is seen as a method of inappropriately disguising *mens rea* as mental illness. Such perceptions are given credence by certain high-visibility cases, such as when John Hinckley was found not guilty of attempted murder of President Ronald Reagan in 1981 by reason of insanity.

In fact, the public perception is faulty. The insanity defense is rarely entered and is even less likely to result in an acquittal, as it is difficult to prove.[24] (See the feature *CJ in Focus—Myth versus Reality: Are Too Many Criminals Found Not Guilty by Reason of Insanity?*) Psychiatry is far more commonly used in the courtroom in determining the "competency" of a defendant to stand trial. If a judge believes that the defendant is unable to understand the nature of the proceedings or to assist in his or her own defense, the trial will not take place. When competency hearings (which may also take place after the initial arrest and before sentencing) reveal that the defendant is in fact incompetent, the court may decide to

> Are Too Many Criminals Found Not Guilty by Reason of Insanity?

To many Americans, it seems likely that any person who commits a gruesome murder or any other sort of violent crime has psychological problems. The question, then, is, how do we balance the need to punish such a person with the possibility that he or she may be seriously ill?

> The Myth

The American system of criminal justice answers this question by stating that a person may not be tried for an offense if that person cannot be held legally responsible for her or his actions. Because of the publicity surrounding the insanity defense, many people are under the impression that it is a major loophole in our system, allowing criminals to be "let off" no matter how heinous their crimes.

> The Reality

In fact, the insanity defense is raised in only about 1 percent of felony trials, and is successful only one out of every four times it is raised. The reason: it is extremely difficult to prove insanity

under the law. For example, after drowning her five children in a bathtub, Andrea Pia Yates entered a plea of not guilty by reason of insanity. The success of this strategy seemed inevitable to many observers, who felt that only an insane woman could systematically kill her children as Yates had done. Indeed, Yates was on antipsychotic medication throughout her trial. Nonetheless, the prosecutors were able to convince a Houston jury that Yates understood her actions were "wrong," and she was found guilty of murder and sentenced to life in prison. Even if Yates had succeeded with the insanity defense, she would not have been "let off" in the sense that she would have been set free. Many defendants found not guilty by reason of insanity spend more time in mental hospitals than criminals who are convicted of similar acts spend in prison.

FOR CRITICAL ANALYSIS
What do the relatively limited use and success rate of the insanity defense indicate about the impact of public opinion on criminal law?

place the defendant under treatment. Once competency has been restored to the defendant, the proceedings may recommence.[25]

Guilty but Mentally Ill   Partly as a response to public backlash against the insanity defense, some state legislatures have passed "guilty but mentally ill" statutes. Under these laws, a defendant is guilty but mentally ill if

> at the time of the commission of the act constituting the offense, he had the capacity to distinguish right from wrong . . . but because of mental disease or defect he lacked sufficient capacity to conform his conduct to the requirements of the law.[26]

In other words, the laws allow a jury to determine that a defendant is "mentally ill," though not insane, and therefore criminally responsible for his or her actions. Defendants found guilty but mentally ill generally spend the early years of their sentences in a psychiatric hospital and the rest of the time in prison, or they receive treatment while in prison.

Proponents of guilty but mentally ill statutes say the laws protect the public by assuring the incarceration of those who may be found not guilty by reason of insanity but still pose a threat to society.[27] Critics counter that there is virtually no difference between a guilty but mentally ill verdict and a guilty verdict, given that many "mentally ill" convicts do not receive any treatment while incarcerated. The real purpose of the laws, they say, is to provide an alternative for jurors who feel that a defendant is legally insane but would like to see her or him punished anyway.[28] Indeed, juries have embraced these statutes; between 1981 and 2001 in Illinois, 230 persons were convicted and sentenced under the state's guilty but mentally ill law.[29]

INTOXICATION

The law recognizes two types of **intoxication,** whether from drugs or from alcohol: *voluntary* and *involuntary.* Involuntary intoxication occurs when a person is physically forced to ingest or is injected with an intoxicating substance, or is unaware that a substance contains drugs or alcohol. Involuntary intoxication is a viable defense to a crime if the substance leaves the person unable to form the mental state necessary to understand that the act committed while under the influence was wrong.[30] In Colorado, for example, the murder conviction of a man who shot a neighbor was overturned on the basis that the jury in the initial trial was not informed of the possibility of involuntary intoxication. At the time of the crime, the man had been taking a prescription decongestant that contained phenylpropanolamine, which has been known to cause psychotic episodes.

Voluntary drug or alcohol intoxication is also used to excuse a defendant's actions, though it is not a defense in itself. Rather, it is used when the defense attorney wants to show that the defendant was so intoxicated that *mens rea* was negated. In other words, the defendant could not possibly have had the state of mind that a crime requires. Many courts are reluctant to allow voluntary intoxication arguments to be presented to juries, however. After all, the defendant, by definition, voluntarily chose to enter an intoxicated state.

Twelve states have eliminated voluntary intoxication as a possible defense, a step that has been criticized by many legal scholars but was upheld by the United States Supreme Court in *Montana v. Egelhoff* (1996).[31] The case concerned a double murder committed by James Allen Egelhoff, who was extremely drunk at the time of the crime. Egelhoff was convicted on two counts of deliberate homicide, which is defined by Montana law as "knowingly" or "purposefully" causing the death of another human being.[32] Egelhoff appealed his conviction, arguing that the state statute prohibiting evidence of voluntary intoxication kept his attorneys from showing the jury that he was too inebriated to "knowingly" or "purposefully" commit the murders.[33] The Court allowed Egelhoff's conviction, ruling that states were constitutionally within their rights to abolish the voluntary intoxication defense.

MISTAKE

Everyone has heard the saying, "Ignorance of the law is no excuse." Ordinarily, ignorance of the law or a *mistaken idea* about what the law requires is not a valid defense.[34] A few years ago, for example, Gilbert A. Robinson appealed his conviction for possession of sexually explicit photographs of teen-age boys, claiming he did not know that such an act had become illegal. Chief Judge Juan R. Torruella del Valle of the Fifth Circuit Court of Appeas upheld Robinson's conviction, stating that child pornography is "inherently deleterious" and that the "probability of regulation is so great that anyone who is aware that he is in possession of [it] . . . must be presumed to be aware of the regulation."[35]

In some states, however, that rule has been modified. People who claim that they honestly did not know that they were breaking a law may have a valid defense if (1) the law was not published or reasonably known to the public or (2) the person relied on an official statement of the law that was erroneous.[36]

A *mistake of fact,* as opposed to a *mistake of law,* operates as a defense if it negates the mental state necessary to commit a crime. If, for example, Oliver mistakenly walks off with Julie's briefcase because he thinks it is his, there is no theft. Theft requires knowledge that the property belongs to another. The mistake of fact defense has proved very controversial in rape and sexual assault cases, where the accused claims that the sex was consensual while the alleged victim claims it was coerced. (See the *Criminal Justice in Action* feature at the end of this chapter for further discussion of this issue.)

⬆ ONLINE REVIEW *Go to the book's Web site for an interactive review of this section*

Justification Criminal Defenses and the Law

In certain instances, a defendant will accept responsibility for committing an illegal act, but contend that—given the circumstances—the act was justified. In other words, even though the guilty act and the guilty intent are present, the particulars of the case relieve the defendant of criminal liability. In 2002, for example, there were 564 "justified" killings of felons who were in the process of committing a felony: 339 were killed by law enforcement officers, and 225 by private citizens.[37] Four of the most important justification defenses are duress, self-defense, necessity, and entrapment.

Duress
Unlawful pressure brought to bear upon a person, causing the person to perform an act that he or she would not otherwise perform.

DURESS

Duress exists when the *wrongful* threat of one person induces another person to perform an act that she or he would otherwise not perform. In such a situation, duress is said to negate the *mens rea* necessary to commit a crime. For duress to qualify as a defense, the following requirements must be met:

1　The threat must be of serious bodily harm or death.

2　The harm threatened must be greater than the harm caused by the crime.

3　The threat must be immediate and inescapable.

4　The defendant must have become involved in the situation through no fault of his or her own.[38]

Special agents examine the body of Brian Douglas Wells, who was killed after robbing a bank in Summit Township, Pennsylvania, when a bomb attached to his neck detonated. Before his death, Wells told state troopers that the explosive device was used to force him to commit the crime. If this is true, and he had survived, would Wells have been able to claim duress as a defense?

When ruling on the duress defense, courts often examine whether the defendant had the opportunity to avoid the threat in question. Two narcotics cases illustrate this point. In the first, the defendant claimed that an associate threatened to kill him and his wife unless he participated in a marijuana deal. Although this contention was proved true during the course of the trial, the court rejected the duress defense because the defendant made no apparent effort to escape, nor did he report his dilemma to the police. In sum, the drug deal was avoidable—the defendant could have made an effort to extricate himself, but he did not, thereby surrendering the protection of the duress defense.[39]

Reprinted with permission of Times Publishing Company, Erie, PA, copyright 2003

In the second case, a taxi driver in Bogotá, Colombia, was ordered by a passenger to swallow cocaine-filled balloons and take them to the United States. The taxi driver was warned that if he refused, his wife and three-year-old daughter would be killed. After a series of similar threats, the taxi driver agreed to transport the drugs. On arriving at customs at the Los Angeles airport, the defendant consented to have his stomach X-rayed, which led to discovery of the contraband and his arrest. During trial, the defendant told the court that he was afraid to notify the police in Colombia because he believed them to be corrupt. The court accepted his duress defense, on the grounds that it met the four requirements listed above and the defendant had notified American authorities when given the opportunity to do so.[40]

JUSTIFIABLE USE OF FORCE—SELF-DEFENSE

A person who believes he or she is in danger of being harmed by another is justified in defending himself or herself with the use of force, and any criminal act committed in such circumstances can be justified as **self-defense.** Other situations that also justify the use of force include the defense of one's dwelling, the defense of other property, and the prevention of a crime. In all these situations, it is important to distinguish between deadly and nondeadly force. Deadly force is likely to result in death or serious bodily harm.

Generally speaking, people can use the amount of nondeadly force that seems necessary to protect themselves, their dwellings, or other property or to prevent the commission of a crime. Deadly force can be used in self-defense if there is a *reasonable belief* that imminent death or bodily harm will otherwise result, if the attacker is using unlawful force (an example of lawful force is that exerted by a police officer), if the defender has not initiated or provoked the attack, and if there is no other possible response or alternative way out of the life-threatening situation.[41]

In the past several years, for example, a number of states have enacted so-called battered woman self-defense statutes. These laws allow defendants charged with murder or manslaughter to present evidence that they had been the victims of repeated acts of violence by the deceased. This evidence may then be used to establish that any violent action taken by the woman against her abuser was done in self-defense.[42] In contrast, deadly force normally can be used to defend a dwelling only if the unlawful entry is violent and the person believes deadly force is necessary to prevent imminent death or great bodily harm or—in some jurisdictions—if the person believes deadly force is necessary to prevent the commission of a felony (such as arson) in the dwelling. (See the feature *You Be the Judge—Justifying a Shooting.*)

NECESSITY

After a New Orleans (Louisiana) man, standing on his balcony, shot and killed a nineteen-year-old who was breaking into his car, he told police that he had to do it to prevent auto theft. Unimpressed by this claim, the local district attorney's office charged him with manslaughter. The **necessity** defense is valid under other circumstances, however. According to the Model Penal Code, the necessity defense is justifiable if "the harm or evil sought to be avoided by such conduct is greater than that sought to be prevented by the law defining the offense charged."[43]

Self-Defense
The legally recognized privilege to protect one's self or property from injury by another. The privilege of self-defense protects only acts that are reasonably necessary to protect one's self or property.

GREAT DEBATES
The "battered woman defense" goes to the heart of the debate over the justifiable use of force. Does an abused woman who strikes against her abuser without provocation deserve the law's protection? Or, is deadly self-defense justified only if the threat of danger is immediate? For an in-depth discussion of the issues that inform this debate, click on *Great Debates* under *Book Resources* at www.cjinaction.com

Necessity
A defense against criminal liability in which the defendant asserts that circumstances required her or him to commit an illegal act.

For example, in one case a convicted felon was threatened by an acquaintance with a gun. The felon grabbed the gun and fled the scene, but subsequently he was arrested under a statute that prohibits convicted felons from possessing firearms. In this situation, the necessity defense was valid because the defendant's crime avoided a "greater evil."[44] The one crime for which the necessity defense is not viable is murder.[45]

ENTRAPMENT

Entrapment is a justification defense that criminal law allows when a police officer or government agent deceives a defendant into wrongdoing. Although law enforcement agents can legitimately use various forms of subterfuge—such as informants or undercover agents—to gain information or apprehend a suspect in a criminal act, the law places limits on these strategies. Police cannot persuade an innocent person to commit a crime, nor can they coerce a suspect into doing so, even if they are certain she or he is a criminal.

The guidelines for determining entrapment were established in the 1932 case of *Sorrells v. United States*.[46] The case, which took place during Prohibition when the sale of alcoholic beverages was illegal, involved a federal prohibition agent who repeatedly urged the defendant to sell him bootleg whiskey. The defendant initially rejected the agent's overtures, stating that he "did not fool with whiskey." Eventually, however, he sold the agent a half-gallon of the substance and was summarily convicted of violating the law. The Supreme Court held that the agent had improperly induced the defendant to break the law and reversed his conviction.

In *Sorrells,* the Supreme Court set the precedent for taking a "subjective" view of entrapment. In other words, the Court decided that entrapment occurs if

Entrapment
A defense in which the defendant claims that he or she was induced by a public official—usually an undercover agent or police officer—to commit a crime that he or she would otherwise not have committed.

a defendant who is not predisposed to commit a crime is enticed to do so by an agent of the government.[47] In the 1992 case of *Jacobson v. United States*,[48] for example, the U.S. Postal Inspection Service targeted the defendant as a potential purchaser of child pornography. Over a period of more than two years, postal agents sent the defendant seven letters inquiring about his sexual preferences, two sex catalogues, and two sexual-attitude surveys, all from fictitious persons and organizations. Eventually, the defendant ordered a publication called "Boys Who Love Boys," and was arrested and convicted for breaking child pornography laws.[49] The Court overturned the conviction, ruling that entrapment had taken place because the defendant had shown no predisposition to order the illicit publication in the absence of the government's efforts. (For an overview of justification and excuse defenses, see Figure 4.4.)

ONLINE REVIEW Go to the book's Web site for an interactive review of this section

The American Civil Liberties Union defines its mission with the slogan, "Defending the Bill of Rights." To find its Web site, click on *Web Links* under *Chapter Resources* at www.cjinaction.com

Substantive Criminal Law
Law that defines the rights and duties of individuals with respect to each other.

Procedural Criminal Law
Rules that define the manner in which the rights and duties of individuals may be enforced.

Procedural Safeguards

To this point, we have focused on **substantive criminal law,** which defines the acts that the government will punish. We will now turn our attention to **procedural criminal law.** (The section that follows will provide only a short overview of criminal procedure. In later chapters, many other constitutional issues will be examined in more detail.) Criminal law brings the force of the state, with all its resources, to bear against the individual. Criminal procedures, drawn from the ideals stated in the Bill of Rights, are designed to protect the constitutional rights of individuals and to prevent the arbitrary use of power by the government.

THE BILL OF RIGHTS

For various reasons, proposals related to the rights of individuals were rejected during the framing of the U.S. Constitution in 1787. In fact, the original constitution contained only three provisions that referred to criminal procedure. Article I, Section 9, Clause 2 states that the "Privilege of the Writ of Habeas Corpus shall not be suspended." As you will see in Chapter 10, a writ of *habeas corpus* is an

As part of heightened airport security following the September 11, 2001, terrorist attacks, a police officer leads a bomb-sniffing dog through Boston's Logan Airport. Other new measures included increased scrutiny of luggage, a ban on customer parking within three hundred feet of a terminal, and not allowing anyone without a ticket past airline checkpoints. Do any of these measures appear to infringe on the due process clause of the U.S. Constitution? Would they if they were applied only, or mostly, to passengers of Middle Eastern descent?

AP Photo/Bizuayehu Tesfaye

FIGURE 4.4 **Justification and Excuse Defenses**

Justification Defenses: Based on a defendant admitting that he or she committed the particular criminal act, but asserting that, under the circumstances, the criminal act was justified.

DURESS

The Defendant Must Prove That: He or she performed the criminal act under the use or threat of use of unlawful force against his or her person that a reasonable person would have been unable to resist.

Situation in Which the Defense Has Been Offered: A mother assists her boyfriend in committing a burglary after he threatens to kill her children if she refuses to do so.

SELF-DEFENSE

The Defendant Must Prove That: He or she acted in a manner to defend him- or herself, others, or property, or to prevent the commission of a crime.

Situation in Which the Defense Has Been Offered: A husband awakes to find his wife standing over him, pointing a shotgun at his chest. In the ensuing struggle, the firearm goes off, killing the wife.

NECESSITY

The Defendant Must Prove That: The criminal act he or she committed was necessary in order to avoid a harm to himself or herself or another that was greater than the harm caused by the act itself.

Situation in Which the Defense Has Been Attempted: Four people physically remove a friend from her residence on the property of a religious cult, arguing that the crime of kidnapping was justified in order to remove the victim from the damaging influence of cult leaders.

ENTRAPMENT

The Defendant Must Prove That: She or he was encouraged by agents of the state to engage in a criminal act she or he would not have engaged in otherwise.

Situation in Which the Defense Has Been Attempted: The owner of a boat marina agrees to allow three federal drug enforcement agents, posing as drug dealers, to use his dock to unload shipments of marijuana from Colombia.

Excuse Defenses: Based on a defendant admitting that she or he committed the criminal act, but asserting that she or he cannot be held criminally responsible for the act due to lack of criminal intent.

AGE

The Defendant Must Prove That: Because he or she was under a statutorily determined age, he or she did not have the maturity to make the decisions necessary to commit a criminal act.

Situation in Which the Defense Has Been Attempted: A fourteen-year-old takes a handgun from his backpack at school and begins shooting at fellow students, killing three. (In such cases, the offender is often processed by the juvenile justice system rather than the criminal justice system.)

INSANITY

The Defendant Must Prove That: At the time of the criminal act, he or she did not have the necessary mental capacity to be held responsible for his or her actions.

Situation in Which the Defense Has Been Attempted: A man with a history of mental illness pushes a woman in front of an oncoming subway train, which kills her instantly.

INTOXICATION

The Defendant Must Prove That: She or he had diminished control over her or his actions due to the influence of alcohol or drugs.

Situation in Which the Defense Has Been Attempted: A woman who had been drinking malt liquor and vodka stabs her boyfriend to death after a domestic argument. She claims to have been so drunk as to not remember the incident.

MISTAKE

The Defendant Must Prove That: He or she did not know that his or her actions violated a law (this defense is very rarely even attempted), or that he or she violated the law believing a relevant fact to be true when, in fact, it was not.

Situation in Which the Defense Has Been Attempted: A woman, thinking that her divorce in another state has been finalized when it was not, marries for a second time, placing herself in a situation in which she has committed bigamy.

order that requires jailers to bring a person before a court or judge and explain why the person is being held in prison. Article I, Section 9, Clause 3 holds that no "Bill of Attainder or ex post facto Law shall be passed." A bill of attainder is a legislative act that targets a particular person or group for punishment without a trial, while an *ex post facto* law operates retroactively, making an event or action illegal though it took place before the law was passed. Finally, Article III, Section 2, Clause 3 maintains that the "Trial of all Crimes" will be by jury and "such Trial shall be held in the State where the said crimes shall have been committed."

Amending the Constitution   The need for a written declaration of rights of individuals eventually caused the first Congress to draft ten amendments to the Constitution and submit them for approval by the states. These amendments, commonly known as the **Bill of Rights,** were adopted in 1791. Since then, seventeen more amendments have been added.

The Bill of Rights, as interpreted by the United States Supreme Court, has served as the basis for procedural safeguards of the accused in this country. These safeguards include the following:

Bill of Rights
The first ten amendments to the U.S. Constitution.

1 The Fourth Amendment protection from unreasonable searches and seizures.

2 The Fourth Amendment requirement that no warrants for a search or an arrest can be issued without probable cause.

3 The Fifth Amendment requirement that no one can be deprived of life, liberty, or property without the "due process" of law.

4 The Fifth Amendment prohibition against *double jeopardy* (trying someone twice for the same criminal offense).

5 The Fifth Amendment guarantee that no person can be required to be a witness against (incriminate) himself or herself.

6 The Sixth Amendment guarantees of a speedy trial, a trial by jury, a public trial, the right to confront witnesses, and the right to a lawyer at various stages of criminal proceedings.

7 The Eighth Amendment prohibitions against excessive bails and fines and cruel and unusual punishments. (For a full text, see Appendix A.)

Expanding the Constitution   The Bill of Rights offered citizens protection only against the federal government. Shortly after the end of the Civil War, in 1868, three-fourths of the states ratified the Fourteenth Amendment to expand the protections of the Bill of Rights. For our purposes, the most important part of the amendment reads:

> No State shall make or enforce any law which shall abridge the privileges or immunities of citizens of the United States, nor shall any State deprive any person of life, liberty, or property, without due process of the law; nor deny to any person within its jurisdiction the equal protection of the laws.

The United States Supreme Court did not immediately interpret the Fourteenth Amendment as extending the procedural protections of the Bill of Rights to people who had been charged with breaking state criminal law. Indeed, it would be nearly a hundred years before those accused of crimes on the state level would enjoy all the same protections as those accused of breaking federal law.[50] As these protections are crucial to criminal justice procedures in the United States, they will be afforded much more attention in Chapter 6, with regard to police action, and in Chapter 10, with regard to the criminal trial.

DUE PROCESS

Due Process Clause
The provisions of the Fifth and Fourteenth Amendments to the Constitution that guarantee that no person shall be deprived of life, liberty, or property without due process of law. Similar clauses are found in most state constitutions.

Both the Fifth and Fourteenth Amendments provide that no person should be deprived of "life, liberty, or property without due process of the law." This **due process clause** basically requires that the government not act unfairly or arbitrarily. In other words, the government cannot rely on individual judgment and impulse when making decisions, but must stay within the boundaries of reason and the law. Of course, disagreements as to the meaning of these provisions have plagued courts, politicians, and citizens since this nation was founded, and will undoubtedly continue to do so.

To understand due process, it is important to consider its two types: procedural due process and substantive due process.

Procedural Due Process
A provision in the Constitution that states that the law must be carried out in a fair and orderly manner.

Procedural Due Process   According to **procedural due process**, the law must be carried out by a *method* that is fair and orderly. It requires that certain procedures bc followed in administering and executing a law so that an individual's basic freedoms are never violated.

For example, the United States Supreme Court requires that schools follow certain procedures before suspending students for misconduct. The Court has held that a student facing a suspension of ten days or less must be given oral or written notice of the charges against him or her. Furthermore, if the student denies the charges, he or she must be given an explanation of the evidence of misconduct and an opportunity to present his or her side of the story.[51] In criminal law, procedural due process prevents a host of unfair practices, such as forced confessions, denial of counsel, and unreasonable searches.

Substantive Due Process   Fair procedures would obviously be of little use if they were used to administer unfair laws. For example, suppose a law requires everyone to wear a red shirt on Mondays. You wear a blue shirt on Monday, and you are arrested, convicted, and sentenced to one year in prison. The fact that all proper procedures were followed and your rights were given their proper protections would mean very little because the law that you broke was unfair and arbitrary.

Thus, **substantive due process** requires that the laws themselves be reasonable. The idea is that if a law is unfair or arbitrary, even if properly passed by a legislature, it must be declared unconstitutional. In the 1930s, for example, Oklahoma instituted the Habitual Criminal Sterilization Act. Under this statute, a person who had been convicted of three felonies could be "rendered sexually sterile" by the state (that is, the person would no longer be able to produce children). The United States Supreme Court held that the law was unconstitutional, as there are "limits to the extent which a legislatively represented majority may conduct biological experiments at the expense of the dignity and personality and natural powers of a minority."[52]

The Supreme Court's Role in Due Process   As the last example suggests, the United States Supreme Court often plays the important role of ultimately deciding when due process has been violated and when it has not. (See Figure 4.5 on page 128 for a list of important Supreme Court due process cases.) This is not a role that the Court has always embraced. As noted earlier, for most of its history the Court did not apply the Bill of Rights to criminal procedures in state trials. Until relatively recently most justices have felt that due process rights were not violated if state procedures were fair and, therefore, there was no need to burden the states with the Bill of Rights.[53]

This line of thinking changed in the early 1960s, when the Court—presided over by Chief Justice Earl Warren—began to *incorporate* the procedural safeguards in the Bill of Rights, meaning that they were now applicable to the states. Between 1961 and 1968, the Warren Court incorporated the right to a jury trial,[54] the right of the accused to confront witnesses at trial,[55] the right against self-incrimination,[56] the right to counsel,[57] and the right to be free from cruel and unusual punishment, among others.[58]

Substantive Due Process
The constitutional requirement that laws used in accusing and convicting persons of crimes must be fair.

Nashala "Tallah" Hearn, shown in this October 8, 2003 photo, wears a head scarf, known as a hijab, that she was told violated the Muskogee Public School dress code. Civil rights experts say the suspension of the eleven-year-old Muslim student for wearing a religious head scarf to class is illegal.

AP Photo/Muskogee Daily Phoenix, Jennifer Lyles

FIGURE 4.5 Important United States Supreme Court Due Process Decisions

YEAR	ISSUE	AMENDMENT INVOLVED	COURT CASE
1948	Right to a public trial	VI	*In re Oliver,* 333 U.S. 257
1949	No unreasonable searches and seizures	IV	*Wolf v. Colorado,* 338 U.S. 25
1961	Exclusionary rule	IV	*Mapp v. Ohio,* 367 U.S. 643
1963	Right to a lawyer in all criminal felony cases	VI	*Gideon v. Wainwright,* 372 U.S. 335
1964	No compulsory self-incrimination	V	*Malloy v. Hogan,* 378 U.S. 1
1964	Right to have counsel when taken into police custody and subject to questioning	VI	*Escobedo v. Illinois,* 378 U.S. 478
1965	Right to confront and cross-examine witnesses	VI	*Pointer v. Texas,* 380 U.S. 400
1966	Right to an impartial jury	VI	*Parker v. Gladden,* 385 U.S. 363
1966	Confessions of suspects not notified of due process rights ruled invalid	V	*Miranda v. Arizona,* 384 U.S. 436
1967	Right to a speedy trial	VI	*Klopfer v. North Carolina,* 386 U.S. 21
1967	Juveniles have due process rights, too	V	*In re Gault,* 387 U.S. 1
1968	Right to a jury trial ruled a fundamental right	VI	*Duncan v. Louisiana,* 391 U.S.145
1969	No double jeopardy	V	*Benton v. Maryland,* 395 U.S. 784

Challenges to Due Process   The due process clause does not, however, automatically doom laws that may infringe on procedural or substantive rights. In certain circumstances, the lawmaking body may be able to prove that its interests are greater than the due process rights of the individual, and in those cases the statute may be upheld. In 2003, for example, a U.S. appeals court upheld the immediate suspension of a kindergarten student who said, "I'm going to shoot you," to classmates during recess. Although, as we saw earlier, in most cases a school must follow certain steps before suspending a student, the court in this instance felt that the kindergarten's interest in limiting this kind of violent speech was more important than the student's due process rights.[59]

The U.S. court system, including the Supreme Court, is more likely to defer to the government in times of national crisis. The Court was powerless in 1861, when President Abraham Lincoln suspended constitutional guarantees of *habeas corpus.*[60] During World War II, in perhaps its most widely criticized decision of the twentieth century, the Court gave its approval to the federal government's rounding up of Japanese American citizens and confining them in "relocation" camps.[61] Finally, since the September 11, 2001, terrorist attacks, the U.S. Department of Justice has moved to limit the due process rights of suspected terrorists and certain types of immigrants. (See the feature *CJ in Focus—The Balancing Act: Due Process for Terrorists?*) Although many of the lawsuits arising out of this strategy have yet to reach the Court, some observers feel that the federal government is overstepping the bounds of the Constitution by limiting access

> Due Process for Terrorists?

About two months after the terrorist attacks on September 11, 2001, Attorney General John Ashcroft announced that suspected terrorists would be prosecuted in U.S. military tribunals. Although many people immediately insisted that this process would violate constitutional safeguards, President George W. Bush called military tribunals "absolutely the right thing to do."

Because the U.S. Constitution guarantees a jury trial, these military tribunals can be used only to try noncitizens suspected of terrorist activities. Defendants in such trials do not enjoy the same protections as those in standard criminal trials—prosecutors can use evidence that would not be allowed in a criminal court, and there is no civilian review of the military judges' decision.

The Bush administration has also limited other due process rights in its "war against terrorism." Immigrants have been held in custody for more than a month without being notified of the charges against them. Numerous suspects, including several Americans, have been denied access to a lawyer. In 2003, a U.S. appeals court ruled that none of those suspects held at the U.S. naval base at Cuba's Guantanamo Bay have the right to due process protections because they are not American citizens and are not incarcerated within the borders of the United States.

Government officials argue that in view of the "extraordinary times," such steps are necessary to safeguard evidence that could be used to prevent future terrorist attacks against the United States. Vice President Dick Cheney has stated that foreign terrorist suspects do not "deserve the same guarantees and safeguards that would be used for an American citizen."

FOR CRITICAL ANALYSIS
Do you agree with Vice President Cheney? Under what circumstances should foreign terrorist suspects have the same constitutional rights that ordinary criminal suspects have in our criminal justice system?

to counsel, the right to confront hostile witnesses, and a number of other due process rights. These issues will be explored in more detail in Chapter 17.

◢ ONLINE REVIEW *Go to the book's Web site for an interactive review of this section*

>The Consent Defense and Rape

In general, criminal law is uninterested in the state of mind of a violent-crime victim. Except in very limited circumstances (mostly involving sports such as boxing or football), one cannot agree to be violently assaulted. For one felony, however, the *mens rea* of the alleged victim is crucial: sexual assault. In this chapter, we discussed a number of defenses to crimes. Here, we will look at the consent defense and its role in the evolving law surrounding rape, an issue that returned to the spotlight in 2003 when sexual-assault charges were brought against professional basketball player Kobe Bryant.

Defining Rape

Although jurisdictions vary, most criminal codes define rape as sexual intercourse without consent accomplished by force or fear.[62] Historically, this classification has proved problematic when it comes to actually prosecuting those suspected of rape. Until the 1970s, a marital rape exemption made it virtually impossible for a wife to

Professional basketball player Kobe Bryant, left, is reassured by defense attorney Pamela Mackey during a hearing in Eagle, Colorado. Bryant was charged with felony sexual assault against a nineteen-year-old; she claimed he forced her to have sex, while Bryant insisted that the sex was consensual.

bring sexual-assault charges against her husband; wedding vows were seen as automatic "consent to sex, no matter what the actual circumstances surrounding the incident."[63] Furthermore, to prove that the sex act was "accomplished by force or fear," the victim needed physical evidence (such as bruises and scratches) to show that she had resisted. "I told him 'no,'" was insufficient.[64]

Another difficulty is that there are no witnesses to most sexual encounters. Because, in the oft-quoted words of a seventeenth-century English jurist, rape was, and is, seen as "an accusation easily to be made and hard to be proved," for most of this nation's history a woman could not be the sole witness to her own rape.[65] Because sexual acts, consensual or not, usually take place in private, the lack of corroborative witnesses severely hampered prosecutors' attempts to press charges against rapists. More often than not, they never bothered to try.[66]

The Chastity Requirement

Often, rapes were never reported. Perhaps the strongest disincentive for rape victims to report the crime was what Professor Michelle Anderson of the Villanova University School of Law calls the "chastity requirement."[67] According to Anderson and numerous other experts, rape victims who were perceived by juries to be sexually virtuous were much more likely to be believed than those who had been sexually active. If a woman had consented to sex before, so the line of thought went, she was more likely to do so again. According to a 1911 ruling by the Iowa Supreme Court, "voluntary sexual relations . . . may and should have been considered as substantive proof of the fact that, whatever the act done it was with the consent of" the accuser.[68]

The message was clear: if a woman had been sexually active, she "assumed the risk" that she would be sexually assaulted and did not deserve the protection of the law.

Consequently, defense attorneys inevitably and successfully focused on the accuser's sexual history, convincing juries that consent had been given in the present instance by establishing a pattern of consent in past ones. Rather than expose their private lives to this kind of scrutiny, many women decided not to bring charges against their attackers.[69]

Rape Shield Laws

In an attempt to keep sexual assault judicial proceedings from being little more than morality trials of the accuser, in 1974 Michigan passed the first **rape shield law** in the United States. The statute kept specific evidence, reputation evidence, or opinion evidence of the victim's sexual conduct out of the courtroom, except under certain circumstances.[70] Today, such evidence is inadmissible in every state but Arizona. In 1978, the U.S. Congress also imposed a rape shield law in federal courts with Federal Rule of Evidence 412.[71] These laws have severely restricted the ability of the defense to use prior sexual conduct in an attempt to undermine the credibility of the victim's testimony.

Not surprisingly, defense lawyers complain that rape shield laws have "swung the pendulum" too far in favor of the accused. Sometimes, they argue, the victim's past sexual history has a great deal of bearing on the question of whether she would consent to sex—for example, if the accuser is known to be a prostitute. Despite these complaints, however, the consensus seems to be that rape victims continue to face a number of hurdles in proving that the crime has taken place. The highest of these hurdles may be the consent defense, which lies at the heart of the matter because if the alleged victim consented to the sex, then no crime has taken place.

Defining Consent

Because of DNA evidence that uses traces of sperm, blood, hair, and other "clues" to link sexual partners, those accused of sexual assault often find it difficult to

Rape Shield Law

A state or federal law that disallows any evidence of an alleged sexual-assault victim's prior sexual conduct to be used against her or him in a criminal trial. These laws are designed to spare the victim the humiliation of irrelevant references to past sexual behavior that may improperly influence the jury.

insist that no sex took place. Consequently, according to Anne Munch, the director of Ending Violence Against Women, "consent is the defense all of the time."[72] Such was the case with Kobe Bryant of the Los Angeles Lakers, who admitted to committing adultery with an employee of the Lodge & Spa resort in Cordillera, Colorado, on June 30, 2003, but claimed that the sex was consensual. The employee insisted that she did not want to have sex with Bryant in his room, and the basketball star was charged with Class 3 felony sexual assault—the use of threats or physical violence to force someone into sex. From preliminary evidence, it appeared that the case would rest on whether state prosecutors could prove that the employee was telling the truth about the lack of consent.

Under Colorado law, consent is defined as "cooperation in act or attitude pursuant to an exercise of free will and with knowledge of the nature of the act." Consent is not present if the "exercise of free will" is made "under the submission of fear."[73] Rape victim activists applaud the Colorado law because it holds that mere agreement to have sex is not enough, if that agreement is made under pressure.

Other states go even further. A 2003 Illinois law emphasizes that a person can withdraw consent at any time during the sex act, even if she (or he) initially agreed. In other words, the moment someone says "no," the other person must stop or rape has occurred.[74] The Illinois legislature decided to clarify its definition of consent after watching California's courts struggle for several years over a case in which a teen-age girl withdrew consent in the middle of the sex act and was ignored by her partner. The California Supreme Court finally decided that he did commit rape.[75]

Incriminating Evidence?

Defense attorney Roy Black, who successfully defended William Kennedy Smith (nephew of Senator Edward Kennedy of Massachusetts) on rape charges in 1991, says that the jury's decision in these cases hinges almost entirely on whether the jurors believe that the alleged victim consented to sex. Although rape shield laws have cut off several means of proving that consent was given, a number of avenues still exist. In the Kennedy Smith case, Black was able to obtain the accuser's medical records—which raised the possibility that she was mentally disturbed—and present them to the jury. Such records are admissible in court because they do not touch on the victim's sexual history.

Kobe Bryant's legal team indicated that they would use the same strategy. Several months before the alleged sexual assault, Bryant's accuser was taken to the hospital because University of Northern Colorado campus police determined she was "a danger to herself." There were also published reports that she had overdosed on pills. Bryant's lawyers could use these facts to suggest that the accuser was not a reliable witness, thereby tainting her testimony.[76]

Constitutional Concerns

The exceptions to rape shield laws, noted earlier, also allow evidence of past sexual history before the jury in certain circumstances. First, all rape shield laws admit evidence of sexual relations between the accuser and the defendant. Second, these laws also allow physical evidence to show that a person other than the accused was the source of any semen or injury (which can establish that, for example, a woman had sex with more than one person on the night in question). Finally, judges have the discretion to allow evidence in order to protect the constitutional rights of the defendant.[77]

The constitutional exception brings us back to the topic of due process, discussed earlier in this chapter. The Sixth Amendment provides that in all criminal matters, the accused has the right "to be confronted with the witnesses against him" and "to have compulsory process." As the argument goes, rape shield laws impair a defendant's constitutional right to present a defense based on all the relevant evidence and to confront those who made the charge that he is a criminal.[78]

People v. Jovanovic

The constitutional argument was used successfully, and to much criticism, in a trial in New York. In 1996, Oliver Jovanovic invited a student who shared his interest in sadomasochism to his apartment, had her undress, tied her to a bed, poured hot wax on her body, and had sexual intercourse with her. Jovanovic, who was arrested and initially convicted of kidnapping and sexual abuse, claimed that these actions were consensual, even though the victim said she had told him to stop and a neighbor testified that the woman's screams made it seem like "someone was undergoing a root canal" in the apartment.[79]

Jovanovic appealed his conviction, arguing that the trial judge's decision, based on the state's rape shield law, to keep several of the victim's e-mails from the jury violated his Sixth Amendment rights. His lawyers insisted that these e-mails—which evinced a strong interest in sadomasochism on the victim's part but also revealed her sexual history—could have persuaded the jury that she had indeed consented to take part in the violent sexual acts. (In one such e-mail, in describing another relationship, she wrote, "[H]e was a sadomasochist and now I'm his slave, but the fun of telling my friend, 'hey I'm a sadomasochist' more than outweighs the torment.") In "the interests of justice," a New York appeals court agreed and overturned Jovanovic's conviction.[80]

MAKING SENSE OF THE CONSENT DEFENSE AND RAPE

1 What is your opinion of the new Illinois law that allows a person to withdraw consent at any time during the sex act? Do you think there is some point at which it is "too late" to say "no"?

2 Consider the following hypothetical situation. John and Trudy are recently divorced and living apart. John shows up at Trudy's new apartment in an agitated state, believing that she is living with another man. To calm John down, and in an attempt to avoid physical abuse that she has good reason to fear from past experience, Trudy coaxes John into the bedroom and has sex with him. Did John rape Trudy? Explain your answer, using the definitions of rape and consent described in this feature and your own beliefs concerning the matter.

3 On page 120, we learned that sometimes mistake is a valid defense against criminal conviction. Under what circumstances, if any, do you think that a defendant in a rape trial could successfully argue that he mistakenly believed that his victim had consented to sexual relations? Should we require sexual partners to explicitly give each other permission before continuing to the act itself?

1 **Explain precedent and the importance of the doctrine of _stare decisis_.** Precedent is a common law concept in which one decision becomes the example or authority for deciding future cases with similar facts. Under the doctrine of _stare decisis_, judges in a particular jurisdiction are bound to follow precedents of that same jurisdiction. The doctrine of _stare decisis_ leads to efficiency in the judicial system.

2 **List the four written sources of American criminal law.** (a) The U.S. Constitution and state constitutions; (b) statutes passed by Congress and state legislatures (plus local ordinances); (c) administrative agency regulations; and (d) case law.

3 **Explain the two basic functions of criminal law.** The primary function is to protect citizens from harms to their safety and property and from harms to society's interest collectively. The second function is to maintain and teach social values as well as social boundaries; for example, laws against bigamy and speed limits.

4 **List and briefly define the most important excuse defenses for crimes.** Insanity— different tests of insanity can be used including (a) the _M'Naughten_ rule (right-wrong test); (b) the irresistible impulse test; (c) the _Durham_ rule, also called the products test, where the criminal act was the product of a mental defect or disease; and (d) the substantial capacity test. **Intoxication**—voluntary and involuntary, the latter being a possible criminal defense. **Mistake**—sometimes valid if the law was not published or reasonably known or if the alleged offender relied on an official statement of the law that was erroneous. Also, a mistake of fact may negate the mental state necessary to commit a crime.

5 **Describe the four most important justification criminal defenses. Duress**— requires that (a) the threat is of serious bodily harm or death, (b) the harm is greater than that caused by the crime; (c) the threat is immediate and inescapable; and (d) the defendant became involved in the situation through no fault of his or her own.

Justifiable use of force—the defense of one's person, dwelling, or property, or the prevention of a crime. **Necessity**— justifiable if the harm sought to be avoided is greater than that sought to be prevented by the law defining the offense charged. **Entrapment**—if the criminal action was induced by certain governmental persuasion or trickery.

6 **Distinguish between substantive and procedural criminal law.** The former concerns questions about what acts are actually criminal. The latter concerns procedures designed to protect the constitutional rights of individuals and to prevent the arbitrary use of power by the government.

7 **Determine where Americans find most of their criminal procedural safeguards.** Basic safeguards for the accused are found in the Bill of Rights; for example, Fourth Amendment protections from unreasonable searches and seizures, as well as the requirements that no warrants for a search or an arrest can be issued without probable cause, and the Fifth Amendment's due process requirement, prohibition against double jeopardy, and rule against self-incrimination.

8 **Explain the importance of the due process clause in the criminal justice system.** The due process clause acts to limit the power of government. In the criminal justice system, the due process clause requires that certain procedures be followed to ensure the fairness of criminal proceedings and that all criminal laws be reasonable and in the interest of the public good.

9 **Discuss how the United States Supreme Court has incorporated the due process clause.** Even though the Fourteenth Amendment requires states to respect the "life, liberty, and property" of their citizens, the United States Supreme Court did not initially believe that those charged with breaking state criminal laws were protected by the U.S. Constitution. Not until the 1960s did the Supreme Court begin to incorporate the due process clause by applying the Bill of Rights to criminal procedures in state trials.

STORIES FROM THE STREET

Go to the Stories from the Street feature at www.cjinaction.com to hear Larry Gaines tell insightful stories related to this chapter and his experiences in the field.

Key Terms

administrative law 112	intoxication 120	rape shield law 131
Bill of Rights 125	irresistible impulse	self-defense 122
case law 113	test 117	*stare decisis* 110
common law 110	*M'Naughten* rule 117	statutory law 111
constitutional law 111	necessity 122	substantial capacity
due process clause 126	precedent 110	test 117
duress 121	procedural criminal	substantive criminal
Durham rule 117	law 124	law 124
entrapment 123	procedural due	substantive due
insanity 117	process 126	process 127

Questions for Critical Analysis

1 Why is the common law said to be uncodified?

2 How does *stare decisis* contribute to the efficiency of a court system?

3 What is the Model Penal Code, and how has it contributed to criminal law in the United States?

4 Give an example of how the criminal justice system teaches societal boundaries.

5 What is the most often used test for insanity, and how does it differ from other tests?

6 Why would a defense attorney admit that a client had voluntarily gotten drunk before an accident in which she hit and killed a pedestrian?

7 Under what circumstances is the use of deadly force a justified criminal defense?

8 What is the difference between procedural due process and substantive due process?

9 What are some of the circumstances that led states and the federal government to pass rape shield laws?

TEST PREPARATION ONLINE

Go to www.cjinaction.com for tools to aid you in studying for your exams. Click on *Online Reviews* under *Chapter Resources* for an interactive review of each major section of this chapter. Under *Chapter Resources*, you will also find the *Chapter Outline*, *Chapter Summary*, *Flashcards*, *Glossary*, *Learning Objectives*, *Lecture Presentations*, *Concept Builder*, *Essay Questions*, and a *Tutorial Quiz*. You can also test yourself with a game of *Concentration* or the *Crossword Puzzle*.

Web Resources

Go to www.cjinaction.com for a wealth of online resources. Explore the *Internet Activities* and *Class Project*s under *Chapter Resources*. Check out the *Web Links* to access the Web sites mentioned in the text, as well as many others. You can also access recent perspectives by clicking on *CJ in the News* and *Terrorism Update* under *Course Resources*. If you'd like some mentoring, click on the *Board of Mentors* under *Book Resources*.

Search Online with InfoTrac College Edition

For additional information, explore InfoTrac College Edition, your online library that offers complete full-length articles from thousands of scholarly and popular publications. Click on *InfoTrac College Edition* under *Chapter Resources* at www.cjinaction.com for a list of key words and InfoTrac exercises. Use the passcode that came with your book.

Suggested Readings

Bonnie, Richard J., *A Case Study in the Insanity Defense: The Trial of John W. Hinckley, Jr.*, 2d ed., New York: Foundation Press, 2000. On March 30, 1981, John W. Hinckley shot President Ronald Reagan at pointblank range, nearly killing him. Hinckley was eventually acquitted of attempted murder by reason of insanity, a verdict that aroused widespread outrage among the public. This casebook takes an in-depth look at what many observers call the starting point for the modern insanity defense. Bonnie explores the reasons why the jury felt obliged to hand down this controversial verdict and explains how it changed the way many courts handle the insanity defense. The book also discusses Hinckley's hospitalization and treatment and tries to answer the question so many Americans asked in the early 1980s: Did he get away with (attempted) murder?

Duhl, Robert Alan, *How Democratic Is the American Constitution?* New Haven, CT: Yale University Press, 2002. In this thin volume, Yale University professor Duhl challenges the democratic credentials of the U.S. Constitution. From its inception, Duhl notes, the Constitution was stained by several "undemocratic elements," including the acceptance of slavery and limitation of voting rights to white males. While these elements have been removed, Duhl points out that some of the most sacred aspects of our modern political system—federalism, the bicameral legislature, judicial review, and the electoral college—often contradict "the will of the people." Most disturbing, Duhl suggests that the framers "rigged" the Constitution to discourage democratic reform.

Notes

1. New York Penal Law, Section 120.10 (McKinney 1996).
2. Roger LeRoy Miller and Gaylord A. Jentz, *Business Law Today, Comprehensive Edition,* 5th ed. (St. Paul, MN: West Publishing Co., 2000), 2–3.
3. *Neff v. George,* 364 Ill. 306, 4 N.E.2d 388, 390, 391 (1936).
4. *Texas v. Johnson,* 491 U.S. 397 (1989).
5. Joshua Dressler, *Understanding Criminal Law,* 2d ed. (New York: Richard D. Irwin, 1995), 22–23.
6. *Ibid.,* 23.
7. Jim Yardley, "Unmarried and Living Together, Till the Sheriff Do Us Part," *New York Times* (March 25, 2000), A7.
8. Chris Bowman, "EPA Pumps Up Its Record," *Sacramento Bee* (July 7, 2003), 1A.
9. *State v. Saunders,* 75 N.J. 200, 381 A.2d 333 (1977).
10. Joel Feinberg, *The Moral Limits of the Criminal Law: Harm to Others* (New York: Oxford University Press, 1984), 221–232.
11. Flammable Fabrics Act, 15 U.S.C. Section 1196 (1994).
12. Stuart P. Green, "Why It's a Crime to Tear the Tag Off a Mattress," *Emory Law Journal* 16 (Fall 1997), 1533–1614.
13. Henry M. Hart, Jr., "The Aims of the Criminal Law," *Law & Contemporary Problems* 23 (1958), 405–406.
14. John L. Diamond, "The Myth of Morality and Fault in Criminal Law Doctrine," *American Criminal Law Review* 34 (Fall 1996), 111.
15. Lawrence M. Friedman, *Crime and Punishments in American History* (New York: Basic Books, 1993), 34.
16. *Ibid.,* 10.
17. Bryan Smith, "Conviction for Killing Girl 'Never Made Sense' to Mom," *Chicago Sun-Times* (December 15, 2002), 26.
18. Janice Morse, "Shooter Ruled Insane," *Cincinnati Enquirer* (May 14, 2003), 1.
19. *M'Naughten's Case,* 10 Cl.&F. 200, Eng.Rep. 718 (1843). Note that the name of the rule is also spelled M'Naghten and McNaughten.
20. Joshua Dressler, *Cases and Materials on Criminal Law,* 2d ed. (St. Paul, MN: West Group, 1999), 599.
21. 214 F.2d 862 (D.C. Cir. 1954).
22. Model Penal Code Section 401 (1952).
23. Bruce Wiseman, "Confronting the Breakdown of Law and Order," *USA Today Magazine* (January 1, 1997), 32.
24. Stephen Lally, "Making Sense of the Insanity Plea," *Washington Post Weekly Edition* (December 1, 1997), 23.
25. Bruce J. Winick, "Presumptions and Burdens of Proof in Determining Competency to Stand Trial: An Analysis of *Medina v. California* and the Supreme Court's New Due Process Methodology in Criminal Cases," *University of Miami Law Review* 47 (1993), 817.
26. South Carolina Code Ann. Section 17-24-20(A) (Law. Co-op. Supp. 1997).
27. Rene J. Leblanc-Allman, "Guilty but Mentally Ill: A Poor Prognosis," *South Carolina Law Review* 49 (Summer 1998), 1095.
28. Steve Mills and Bob Kemper, "Court Rules Mentally Ill Law Unconstitutional," *Chicago Tribune* (June 24, 1997), 1.
29. Ted Gregory and Flynn McRoberts, "Lemak's Defense to Use Experts, Kin," *Chicago Tribune* (December 2, 2001), 1.
30. Lawrence P. Tiffany and Mary Tiffany, "Nosologic Objections to the Criminal Defense of Pathological Intoxication: What Do the Doubters Doubt?" *International Journal of Law and Psychiatry* 13 (1990), 49.
31. 518 U.S. 37 (1996).
32. Mont. Code Ann. Section 45-5-102 (1997).
33. Mont. Code Ann. Section 45-2-203 (1997).
34. Kenneth W. Simons, "Mistake and Impossibility, Law and Fact, and Culpability: A Speculative Essay," *Journal of Criminal Law and Criminology* 81 (1990), 447.
35. *United States v. Robinson,* 119 F.3rd 1205 (5th Cir. 1997).
36. *Lambert v. California,* 355 U.S. 225 (1957).
37. Federal Bureau of Investigation, *Crime in the United States, 2002* (Washington, D.C.: U.S. Department of Justice, 2003), 28.
38. Craig L. Carr, "Duress and Criminal Responsibility," *Law and Philosophy* 10 (1990), 161.
39. *United States v. May,* 727 F.2d 764 (1984).
40. *United States v. Contento-Pachon,* 723 F.2d 691 (1984).
41. *People v. Murillo,* 587 N.E.2d 1199, 1204 (Ill. App. Ct. 1992).
42. Michael K. Molitor, "The 'Battered Child Syndrome' as Self-Defense," *Wayne Law Review* 40 (Fall 1993), 237.
43. Model Penal Code Section 3.02.
44. *United States v. Paolello,* 951 F.2d 537 (3rd Cir. 1991).
45. *People v. Petro,* 56 P.2d 984 (Cal. Ct. App. 1936); and *Regina v. Dudley and Stephens,* 14 Q.B.D. 173 (1884).
46. 287 U.S. 435 (1932).
47. Kenneth M. Lord, "Entrapment and Due Process: Moving toward a Dual System of Defenses," *Florida State University Law Review* 25 (Spring 1998), 463.
48. 503 U.S. 540 (1992).
49. Fred Warren Bennett, "From *Sorrells* to *Jacobson:* Reflections on Six Decades of Entrapment Law and Related Defenses in Federal Court," *Wake Forest Law Review* 27 (1992), 829.
50. Henry J. Abraham, *Freedom and the Court: Civil Liberties in the United States,* 7th ed. (New York: Oxford University Press, 1998), 38–41.
51. *Goss v. Lopez,* 419 U.S. 565 (1975).
52. *Skinner v. Oklahoma,* 316 U.S. 535, 546–547 (1942).
53. William J. Stuntz, "The Substantive Origins of Criminal Procedure," *Yale Law Journal* 105 (1995), 440.
54. *Duncan v. Louisiana,* 391 U.S. 145 (1968).
55. *Pointer v. Texas,* 380 U.S. 400 (1965).
56. *Malloy v. Hogan,* 387 U.S. 1 (1964).
57. *Gideon v. Wainwright,* 372 U.S. 335 (1963).
58. *Robinson v. California,* 370 U.S. 660 (1962).
59. *"S.G.V. Sayreville Board of Education et al.,"* No. 02-2384," *New Jersey Law Journal* (July 14, 2003), 139.
60. Alfred H. Kelley and Winfred A. Harbison, *The American Constitution: Its Origins and Developments,* 7th ed. (New York: Norton, 1991), 441–448.
61. *Korematsu v. United States,* 323 U.S. 214 (1944).
62. David P. Bryden, "Redefining Rape," *Buffalo Criminal Law Review* 3 (2000), 320–321.
63. Laleyna Weintraub Siegel, "The Marital Rape Exemption: Evolution to Extinction," *Cleveland State Law Review* 43 (1995), 364–369.
64. Susan Estrich, *Real Rape* (Cambridge, MA: Harvard University Press, 1987), 40.
65. Jeffrey Toobin, "The Consent Defense," *New Yorker* (September 1, 2003), 41.
66. *Ibid.*
67. Michelle J. Anderson, "From Chastity Requirement to Sexuality License: Sexual Consent and a New Rape Shield Law," *George Washington Law Review* (February 2002), 51.
68. *State v. Johnson,* 133 N.W. 115 (Iowa 1911).
69. Anderson, 60.
70. Michigan Comp. Laws Ann. Section 750.520j (West 1991).
71. *Federal Rules of Evidence,* 412(a)(1)-(2).
72. Quoted in Toobin, 43.
73. Colorado Rev. Stat. Section 18-3-401(1.5) (1997).
74. "New Illinois Rape Law Tries to Clarify Consent Issue," *Deseret News* (July 30, 2003), A5.
75. Harriet Chiang, "Court Says Sex after Rescinded Consent Is Rape," *San Francisco Chronicle* (January 7, 2003), A17.
76. Charlie Brennan and Jeff Kass, "Bryant Team Seeks ER Files," *Rocky Mountain News* (September 3, 2003), 5A.
77. Anderson, 58–59.
78. Shawn J. Wallach, "Rape Shield Laws: Protecting the Victim at the Expense of the Defendant's Constitutional Rights," *New York Law School Journal of Human Rights* 13 (1997), 521.
79. *Jovanovic I,* 700 N.Y.S.2d 174 (N.Y. App. Div. 1999).
80. *Ibid.,* 156.

>Chapter 5<

Law
Enforcement Today

>chapter objectives<

After reading this chapter, you should be able to:

1 Describe the first systems of law enforcement in colonial America.

2 Tell how the patronage system affected policing.

3 Indicate the results of the Wickersham Commission.

4 List five main types of law enforcement agencies.

5 List some of the most important law enforcement agencies under the control of the new Department of Homeland Security.

6 Identify the five investigative priorities of the FBI.

7 Analyze the importance of private security today.

8 List the four basic responsibilities of the police.

9 Indicate why patrol officers are allowed discretionary powers.

10 Explain how some states have reacted to perceived leniency to perpetrators of domestic violence.

Just Doing His Job

At first, Murphy (North Carolina) Police Officer Jeffrey Postell thought he had interrupted a break-in. It was 3:30 in the morning on June 1, 2003, and Postell was on patrol when he saw a man rummaging in a garbage dumpster behind the local Sav-A-Lot supermarket. As Postell approached, the man tried to hide behind some milk crates. Postell, thinking he had a potential breaking-and-entering or a prowler, arrested the man, who said his name was Jerry Wilson, and took him to the police station.

A few hours later, Postell found out that he had succeeded where a $24 million, five-year manhunt had failed. The man's name was not Jerry Wilson but Eric Robert Rudolph, and he was a suspected serial bomber who had spent time at the top of the FBI's 10 Most Wanted List. Rudolph had disappeared in 1998 after federal law enforcement officials named him the official suspect in a number of incidents, including an explosion in Atlanta, Georgia, during the 1996 Summer Olympics and bombings of several abortion clinics and a gay nightclub. In total, he is believed to be responsible for injuring more than one hundred people and killing two, including a police officer in Birmingham, Alabama.

Hundreds of federal, state, and local law enforcement officers had searched for Rudolph in the hills and forests of North Carolina. Postell, a twenty-one-year-old rookie who had been on the job for less than a year (following a stint as a security guard at Wal-Mart), realized that he was in the right place at the right time. He did not seem bothered that his status as a police officer made him ineligible for the $1 million bounty that had been placed on Rudolph's head. "I was doing what I was supposed to be doing," he told reporters. "That's just in a day's work. I don't deserve any credit."

Alan Mothner © Reuters NewMedia Inc./CORBIS

Jeffrey Postell

> **Law enforcement holds** endless surprises. Officer Jeffrey Postell, through a combination of luck and just doing what he "was supposed to be doing," became an overnight hero; his face was plastered on newspapers and magazines, and his story dominated local and national television news shows. Police officers are the most visible representatives of our criminal justice system; indeed, they symbolize the system for many Americans who may never see the inside of a courtroom or a prison cell. The police are entrusted with immense power to serve and protect the public good: the power to use weapons and the power to arrest.

CONCEPT BUILDER

Is policing considered a profession or a trade? Visit www.cjinaction.com for an interactive exploration of this key topic.

But that same power alarms many citizens, who fear that it may be turned arbitrarily against them. The role of the police is constantly debated as well. Is their primary mission to fight crime, or should they also be concerned with the social conditions that presumably lead to crime?

This chapter will lay the foundation for our study of law enforcement agents and the work that they do. A short history of policing will be followed by an examination of the many different agencies that make up the American law enforcement system. We will also look at the various responsibilities of police officers and discuss the crucial role of discretion in law enforcement.

A History of the American Police

Although modern society relies on law enforcement officers to control and prevent crime, in the early days of this country police services had little to do with crime control. The policing efforts in the first American cities were directed toward controlling certain groups of people (mostly slaves and Native Americans), delivering goods, regulating activities such as buying and selling in the town market, maintaining health and sanitation, controlling gambling and vice, and managing livestock and other animals.[1] Furthermore, these police services were for the most part performed by volunteers, as a police force was an expensive proposition. Most communities simply could not afford to pay a group of law enforcement officers.[2]

Eventually, of course, as the populations of American cities grew, so did the need for public order and the willingness to devote resources to the establishment of formal police forces. Policing in the United States and in England evolved along similar lines, and many of our policing institutions have their roots in English tradition. Consequently, we will begin our discussion of the history of American police with a look back at its English beginnings.

ENGLISH ROOTS

Before William the Conqueror invaded the island in 1066, the dominant system of law enforcement in Anglo-Saxon England was the **tithing system.** Every male was enrolled in a group of ten families, which was called a *tithing.* If one person in the tithing committed a crime, then every person in the group was responsible for paying the fine. The theory was that this obligation would be an incentive for the tithing to engage in collective community policing. Later, ten tithings were joined together to form a *hundred,* whose top law official was the *reeve.* Finally, the hundreds were consolidated into *shires* (the equivalent of modern counties), and the law enforcement official became known as the **shire-reeve.** As the phonetics suggest, this official is the earliest example of what is now the county sheriff.

The Role of the Constable In 1326, the office of the **justice of the peace** was established to replace the shire-reeve. Over the next centuries, in most English cities the justice of the peace, with the help of a constable, came to oversee various law enforcement activities, including organizing the night watch, investigating crimes, and securing criminals for trial. In the countryside, the hundred was replaced by the parish, which corresponded to the territory served by a particular church and included its members. Under the *parish constable system,* the parish hired a person to oversee criminal justice for its parishioners.

"Every society gets the kind of criminal it deserves. What is equally true is that every community gets the kind of law enforcement it insists on."
—Robert Kennedy, U.S. attorney general (1964)

Tithing System
In Anglo-Saxon England, a system of law enforcement in which groups of ten families, known as tithings, were collectively responsible for law and order within their groups.

Shire-Reeve
The chief law enforcement officer in an early English shire, or county. The forerunner of the modern sheriff.

Justice of the Peace
Established in fourteenth-century England, a government official who oversaw various aspects of local law enforcement. The post eventually became strictly identified with judicial matters.

The London Experiments   By the mid-1700s, London, England—one of the largest cities in the Western world—still did not have an organized system of law enforcement. Crime was endemic to city life, and the government's only recourse was to *read the riot act* (call in the military when the lawbreaking became unbearable). Such actions were widely unpopular, as the townspeople did not appreciate being disciplined (and fired on) by soldiers whose salaries they were paying. Furthermore, the soldiers proved unreliable peacemakers, as they were hesitant to use force against their fellow London citizens. Despite rampant crime in the city, most Londoners were not in favor of a police force under the control of the city government. English history is rife with instances in which the king or some other government official abused military power by turning it against the citizens. Therefore, the citizenry were wary of any formal, armed organization that could restrict their individual liberties.

This mistrust began to ebb in 1829, when British Home Secretary Sir Robert "Bobbie" Peel pushed the Metropolitan Police Act through Parliament. This legislation has had a lasting impact, as many of its operating goals were similar to those of modern police forces (see Figure 5.1 for a summary of the act). Under the terms of this act, the London Metropolitan Police was formed. One thousand members strong at first, the members of this police force were easily recognizable in their uniforms that included blue coats and top hats. Under Peel's direction, the "bobbies," as the police were called in honor of their founder, had four specific operating philosophies:

1   To reduce tension and conflict between law enforcement officers and the public.

2   To use nonviolent means (they did not carry firearms) in keeping the peace, with violence to be used only as a last resort. This point was crucial, because, as mentioned earlier, the English were suspicious of armed government military organizations. Being unarmed, the bobbies could hardly be confused with soldiers.

3   To relieve the military from certain duties, such as controlling urban violence. (Peel specifically hoped that his police would be less inclined to use excessive force than the military had been.)

4   To be judged on the absence of crime rather than through high-visibility police action.[3]

London's police operation was so successful that it was soon imitated in smaller towns throughout England and, eventually, in the United States.

THE EARLY AMERICAN POLICE EXPERIENCE

In colonial America and immediately following the American Revolution, law enforcement virtually mirrored the English

FIGURE 5.1   **Fundamental Principles of the Metropolitan Police Act of 1829**

The first modern police force was established in London by the Metropolitan Police Act of 1829. Sir Robert Peel, the politician who pushed through the legislation, wanted a police force that would provide citizens with "the full and complete protection of the law" and "check the increase of crime." To fulfill these objectives, Peel's early police were guided by the basic principles listed here.

1   The police force must be organized along military lines.

2   Police administrators and officers must be under government control.

3   Emphasis must be placed on hiring qualified persons and training them properly.

4   New police officers must complete a probationary period; if they fail to meet standards during this time, they will not be hired as permanent officers.

5   Police personnel should be assigned to specific areas of the city for a specific time period.

6   Police headquarters must be centrally located in the city.

7   Police officers must maintain proper appearances at all times in order to gain and keep the respect of citizens.

8   Individual police officers should be able to control their temper and refrain from violence whenever possible.

9   Police records must be kept in order to measure police effectiveness.

system. Constables and night watchmen were taken from the ranks of ordinary citizens. The governor of each colony hired a sheriff in each county to oversee the formal aspects of law enforcement, such as selecting juries and managing jails and prisons.[4] These colonial appointees were not always of the highest moral character. In 1730, the Pennsylvania colony felt the need to pass laws specifically prohibiting sheriffs from extorting money from prisoners or selling "strong liquors" to "any person under arrest."[5]

The First Police Department In 1801, Boston became the first American city to acquire a formal night watch; the watchmen were paid 50 cents a night. For the next three decades, most major cities went no further than the watch system. Finally, facing the same pressures as London, major American metropolitan areas began to form "reactive patrol units" geared toward enforcing the law and preventing crime.[6] In 1833, Philadelphia became the first city to employ both day and night watchmen. Five years later, working from Sir Robert Peel's model, Boston formed the first organized police department, consisting of six full-time officers. In 1844, New York City set the foundation for the modern police department by combining its day and night watches under the control of a single police chief. By the onset of the Civil War in 1861, a number of American cities, including Baltimore, Boston, Chicago, Cincinnati, New Orleans, and Philadelphia, had similarly consolidated police departments, modeled on the Metropolitan Police of London.

Like their modern counterparts, many early police officers were hard working, honest, and devoted to serving and protecting the public. On the whole, however, in the words of historian Samuel Walker, "The quality of American police service in the nineteenth century could hardly have been worse."[7] This poor quality can be attributed to the fact that the recruitment and promotion of police officers were intricately tied into the politics of the day. Police officers received their jobs as a result of political connections, not because of any particular skills or knowledge. Whichever political party was in power in a given city would hire its own cronies to run the police department; consequently, the police were often more concerned with serving the interests of the political powers than with protecting the citizens.[8]

The Spoils System Corruption was rampant during this *political era* of policing, which lasted roughly from 1840 to 1930. (See Figure 5.2 on the following page for an overview of the three eras of policing, which are discussed in this chapter and referred to throughout the book.) Police salaries were relatively low; thus, many police officers saw their positions as opportunities to make extra income through any number of illegal activities. Bribery was common, as police would use their close proximity to the people to request "favors," which went into the police officers' own pockets or into the coffers of the local political party as "contributions."[9] This was known as the **patronage system,** or the "spoils system," because to the political victors went the spoils.

CORBIS/Bettmann

A horse-drawn police wagon used by the New York City Police Department, circa 1886. In the 1880s a number of American cities introduced patrol wagon services, which included transporting prisoners and drunks as well as performing ambulance duties. Along with signal service, or "call boxes," the police wagon represented a "revolution" in police methods. If a patrol officer made an arrest far from headquarters, he could now call the station and request a police wagon to pick up and deliver the arrested person (instead of having to deliver the arrestee himself).

Patronage System
A form of corruption in which the political party in power hires and promotes police officers, receiving job-related "favors" in return.

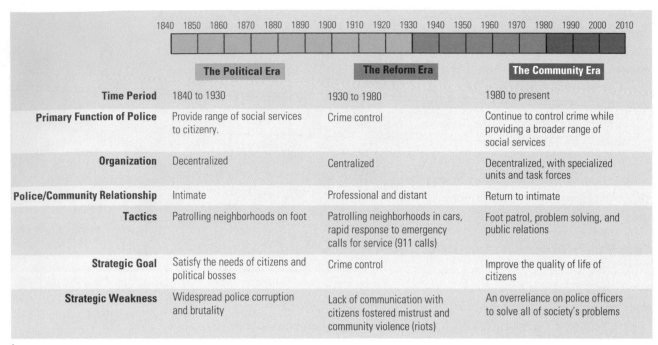

	The Political Era	The Reform Era	The Community Era
Time Period	1840 to 1930	1930 to 1980	1980 to present
Primary Function of Police	Provide range of social services to citizenry.	Crime control	Continue to control crime while providing a broader range of social services
Organization	Decentralized	Centralized	Decentralized, with specialized units and task forces
Police/Community Relationship	Intimate	Professional and distant	Return to intimate
Tactics	Patrolling neighborhoods on foot	Patrolling neighborhoods in cars, rapid response to emergency calls for service (911 calls)	Foot patrol, problem solving, and public relations
Strategic Goal	Satisfy the needs of citizens and political bosses	Crime control	Improve the quality of life of citizens
Strategic Weakness	Widespread police corruption and brutality	Lack of communication with citizens fostered mistrust and community violence (riots)	An overreliance on police officers to solve all of society's problems

↑ **FIGURE 5.2 The Three Eras of American Policing**

George L. Kelling and Mark H. Moore have separated the history of policing in the United States into three distinct periods. Above is a brief summarization of these three eras.

Source: Adapted from George L. Kelling and Mark H. Moore, "From Political to Reform to Community: The Evolving Strategy of Police," in *Community Policing: Rhetoric or Reality,* ed. Jack R. Greene and Stephen D. Mastrofski (New York: Praeger Publishers, 1991), 14–15, 22–23; plus authors' updates. Reproduced with permission of Greenwood Publishing Group, Inc., Westport, Connecticut.

The political era also saw police officers take an active role in providing social services for their bosses' constituents. In many instances, this role even took precedence over law enforcement duties. Politicians realized that they could attract more votes by offering social services to citizens than by arresting them, and they required the police departments under their control to act accordingly.

THE MODERNIZATION OF THE AMERICAN POLICE

The abuses of the political era of policing did not go unnoticed. But it was not until 1929 that President Herbert Hoover appointed the national Commission on Law Observance and Enforcement to assess the American criminal justice system. The Wickersham Commission, named after its chairman, George Wickersham, focused on two areas of American policing that were in need of reform: (1) police brutality and (2) "the corrupting influence of politics." According to the commission, this reform should come about through higher personnel standards, centralized police administrations, and the increased use of technology.[10] Reformers of the time took the commission's findings as a call for the professionalization of American police and initiated the progressive (or *reform*) era in American policing.

Professionalism In truth, the Wickersham Commission was not ground breaking. Many of its recommendations echoed the opinions of one of its contributors—August Vollmer, the police chief of Berkeley, California, from 1905 until 1932. Known as "the father of modern police administration," Vollmer pioneered the training of potential police officers in institutions of higher learning. The first program to grant a degree in law enforcement, at San Jose State College (now a university), was developed under Vollmer.

Along with increased training, Vollmer also championed the use of technology in police work. His Berkeley police department became the first in the nation to use automobiles to patrol city streets and to hire a scientist to assist in solving crimes.[11] Furthermore, Vollmer believed that police could prevent crime by involving themselves in the lives of *potential* criminals, which led to his establishing the first juvenile crime unit in the nation.

Vollmer's devotion to modernism was also apparent in the career of his most successful protégé, police reformer O. W. Wilson, who promoted a style of policing known as the **professional model.** In an attempt to remove politics from police work, Wilson stressed the need for efficiency through bureaucracy and technology.

Administrative Reforms   Under the professional model police chiefs, who had been little more than figureheads during the political era, took more control over their departments. A key to these efforts was the reorganization of police departments in many major cities. To improve their control over operations, police chiefs began to add midlevel positions to the force. These new officers, known as majors or assistant chiefs, could develop and implement crime-fighting strategies and more closely supervise individual officers. Police chiefs also tried to consolidate their power by bringing large areas of a city under their control so that no local ward, neighborhood, or politician could easily influence a single police department.

Finally, police chiefs set up special units such as criminal investigation, vice, and traffic squads with jurisdiction-wide power. Previously, all police powers within a precinct were controlled by the politicians in that precinct. By creating specialized units that worked across all precincts, the police chiefs increased their own power at the expense of the political bosses.

Technological innovations on all fronts—including patrol cars, radio communications, public records systems, fingerprinting, toxicology (the study of poisons), and forensics (the application of chemistry to the examination of physical evidence)—allowed police operations to move even more quickly toward O. W. Wilson's professional model. By the 1950s, America prided itself on having the most modern and professional police force in the world. (The pace of technological innovation continues to this day, as you can see in the feature *CJ and Technology—Going Wireless.*) As efficiency became the goal of the reform era police chief, however, relations with the community suffered. Instead of being members of the community, police officers were now seen almost as intruders, patrolling the streets in the anonymity of their automobiles. The drawbacks of this perception—and the professional model in general—would soon become evident.

Turmoil in the 1960s   The 1960s was one of the most turbulent decades in American history. The civil rights movement, though not inherently violent, intensified feelings of helplessness and impoverishment in African American communities. These frustrations resulted in civil unrest, and many major American cities experienced race riots in the middle years of the decade.

Even though police brutality often provided the spark for riots—and there is little question that police departments often overreacted to antiwar demonstrations during the Vietnam era (1963–1975)—it would be simplistic to blame the strife of the 1960s on the police. The rioters were reacting to social circumstances that they found unacceptable. Their clashes with the police were the result rather than the cause of these problems. Many observers, however, believed that the police *contributed* to the disorder. The National Advisory Commission on Civil Disorders stated bluntly that poor relations between the police and African American communities were partly to blame for the violence that plagued many

Professional Model
A style of policing advocated by August Vollmer and O. W. Wilson that emphasizes centralized police organizations, increased use of technology, and a limitation of police discretion through regulations and guidelines.

"He may be a very nice man. But I haven't got the time to figure that out. All I know is, he's got a uniform and a gun and I have to relate to him that way."
—James Baldwin, American author (1971)

> Going Wireless

Yes

No

Remote Data Terminal

PREV
0123

NEXT
456

SPECIAL
789

AP Photo/Nick Ut

Despite the many technological advances that have transformed police work since August Vollmer sent out the first patrol cars in the early 1900s, law enforcement agents have always faced one important limitation. Any information taken down on paper by a police officer in the field—such as speeding tickets or arrest warrants—would have to be refiled when he or she returned to the station. Time that could be better spent on providing services to citizens was taken up with paperwork that, essentially, had already been done.

Thanks to a new technology known as wireless-fidelity, or Wi-Fi, police departments can set up wide-area networks (WANs) that connect computer systems via directional antennas. Each of these antennas has a radius of fifteen to thirty miles, and they can be chained together to create large areas of coverage. Any police officer with a laptop or dashboard computer that has the proper network card (and an antenna on the roof of the patrol car) can use this wireless technology to link up not only with local police headquarters, but also with other law enforcement agencies, courtrooms, and government departments. The potential for Wi-Fi as an information transmitter goes well beyond saving police officers from having to fill out an arrest report twice. Jail authorities could, for example, use Wi-Fi to send a mug shot of an escaped convict to all law enforcement agencies in the immediate vicinity.

> In the Future

Today, Wi-Fi systems are often limited by the range of the antennae or "access points." Thus, if a patrol car moves out of range of an access point, the police officer will enter a "dead zone" with no wireless access. Some systems have developed a backup plan in which the connection is immediately reestablished through a cellular WAN (using the same technology as a cellular phone), but many experts worry that any information transferred in this manner can easily be intercepted by someone with the proper tools. The scope of this problem may be reduced, however, as more WANs use satellite links, which both increases their range and protects against information theft. Furthermore, until 2002 the Federal Communications Commission required all WANs to be licensed. Now that the networks are unregulated, it will be much easier for law enforcement agencies to create and use them.

The "ISBS" is a wireless device that can record a fingerprint at the scene of an investigation and then send the image to be checked against a database.

For more information on wireless-fidelity and other CJ technologies, click on Web Links under Chapter Resources at www.cjinaction.com

of those communities.[12] In striving for professionalism, the police appeared to have lost touch with the citizens they were supposed to be serving. To repair their damaged relations with a large segment of the population, police would have to rediscover their community roots.

RETURNING TO THE COMMUNITY

The beginning of the third era in American policing, the *community era,* may have started with several government initiatives that took place in 1968. Of primary importance was the Omnibus Crime Control and Safe Streets Act, which was passed that year.[13] Under this act, the federal government provided state and local police departments with funds to create a wide variety of police-community programs. Most large-city police departments established entire units devoted to community relations, implementing programs that ranged from summer recreation activities for inner-city youths to "officer-friendly" referral operations that encouraged citizens to come to the police with their crime concerns.

In the 1970s, as this vital rethinking of the role of the police was taking place, the country was hit by a crime wave. Thus, police administrators were forced to combine efforts to improve community relations with aggressive and innovative crime-fighting strategies. At first, these strategies were *reactive;* that is, they focused on reducing the amount of time the police took to react to crime—how quickly they were able to reach the scene of a crime, for example. Eventually, police departments began to focus on *proactive* strategies –that is, strategies aimed at stopping crimes before they are committed. A dedication to proactive strategies led to widespread acceptance of community policing in the 1980s. Community policing is based on the notion that meaningful interaction between officers and citizens will lead to a partnership in preventing and fighting crime.[14] Though the idea of involving members of the community in this manner is hardly new—a similar principle was set forth by Sir Robert Peel—innovative tactics in community policing, many of which will be discussed in Chapter 6, have had a significant impact on modern police work.

↗ ONLINE REVIEW *Go to the book's Web site for an interactive review of this section*

Law Enforcement Agencies

Another aspect of modern police work is the "multilayering" of law enforcement. For example, a wide network of local, state, and federal law enforcement agencies was involved in the extensive hunt for Eric Robert Rudolph across the Southeast United States, mentioned in the introduction to this chapter. The Federal Bureau of Investigation (FBI), acting as lead agency, coordinated the search efforts of dozens of local police and sheriffs' departments, as well as the Georgia Bureau of Investigation, the Alabama Bureau of Investigation, the North Carolina Bureau of Investigation, the North Carolina Highway Patrol, the U.S. Forest Service, and the Bureau of Alcohol, Tobacco, Firearms and Explosives.

The manhunt illustrates how many agencies can become involved in a single incident. There are over 13,900 law enforcement agencies in the United States, employing over 950,000 people.[15] The various agencies include:

> 3,088 sheriffs' departments.

> 1,332 special police agencies, limited to policing parks, schools, airports, and so on.

> 49 state police departments, with Hawaii being the one exception.

> 50 federal law enforcement agencies.

Each level has its own set of responsibilities, which we shall discuss starting with local police departments.

Irving (Texas) Police Department Public Information Officer David Tull posts artists' renditions of seven inmates who escaped a South Texas prison in late 2000. After committing several robberies and killing a Dallas police officer, the fugitives were finally apprehended in Colorado thanks to a tip prompted by the television show *America's Most Wanted.* Why would local law enforcement agencies seek the aid of state and federal law enforcement agencies in a situation such as this one?

AP Photo/Jerry W. Hoefer

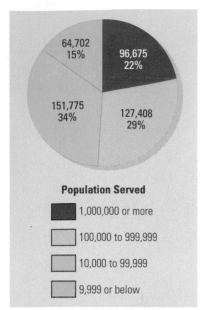

↑ FIGURE 5.3 **Full-Time Police Personnel, by Size of Population Served**

Source: Bureau of Justice Statistics, *Local Police Departments, 2000* (Washington, D.C.: U.S. Department of Justice, January 2003), Table 3, p. 3.

Sheriff

The primary law enforcement officer in a county, usually elected to the post by a popular vote.

MUNICIPAL LAW ENFORCEMENT AGENCIES

According to the FBI, there are 3.5 state and local police officers for every 1,000 citizens in the United States.[16] This average somewhat masks the discrepancies between the police forces in urban and rural America. As noted in Chapter 1, the vast majority of all police officers work in small and medium-sized police departments (see Figure 5.3). While the New York City Police Department has more than 40,000 employees, almost 680 small towns have only one police officer.[17]

Of the three levels of law enforcement, municipal agencies have the broadest authority to apprehend criminal suspects, maintain order, and provide services to the community. Whether the local officer is part of a large force or the only law enforcement officer in the community, he or she is usually responsible for a wide spectrum of duties, from responding to noise complaints to investigating homicides. Much of the criticism of local police departments is based on the belief that local police are too underpaid or poorly trained to handle these various responsibilities. Reformers have suggested that residents of smaller American towns would benefit from greater statewide coordination of local police departments.[18]

SHERIFFS AND COUNTY LAW ENFORCEMENT

A vestige of the English shire-reeve discussed earlier in the chapter, the **sheriff** is still an important figure in American law enforcement. Almost every one of the more than three thousand counties in the United States (except those in Alaska) has a sheriff. In every state except Rhode Island and Hawaii, sheriffs are elected by members of the community for two- or four-year terms and are paid a salary set by the state legislature or county board. As elected officials who do not necessarily need a background in law enforcement, modern sheriffs resemble their counterparts from the political era of policing in many ways. Simply stated, the sheriff is also a politician. When a new sheriff is elected, she or he will sometimes repay political debts by appointing new deputies or promoting those who have given her or him support. This high degree of instability and personnel turnover in many states is seen as one of the weaknesses of county law enforcement.[19]

Size and Responsibility of Sheriffs' Departments Like municipal police forces, sheriffs' departments vary in size. The largest is the Los Angeles County Sheriffs' Department, with more than 8,400 full-time employees. Of the 3,088 sheriffs' departments in the country, twelve employ more than 1,000 officers, while eleven have only one.[20]

The image of the sheriff as a powerful figure patrolling vast expanses is not entirely misleading. Most sheriffs' departments are assigned their duties by state law. Almost 90 percent of all sheriffs' departments have the primary responsibility for investigating violent crimes in their jurisdictions. Other common responsibilities of a sheriff's department include:

> Protecting the public.

> Maintaining the county jail.

> Carrying out civil and criminal processes within county lines, such as serving eviction notices and court summonses.

> Keeping order in the county courthouse.

> Collecting taxes.

> Enforcing orders of the court, such as overseeing the sequestration of a jury during a trial.[21]

It is easy to confuse sheriffs' departments and local police departments. As Figure 5.4 shows, both law enforcement agencies are responsible for many of the same tasks, including crime investigation and routine patrol. There are differences, however, also evident in Figure 5.4: sheriffs' departments are more likely to be involved in county court and jail operations and to perform certain services such as search and rescue. Local police departments, for their part, are more likely to perform traffic-related functions than are sheriffs' departments.

The County Coroner   Another elected official on the county level is the **coroner,** or medical examiner. Duties vary from county to county, but the coroner has a general mandate to investigate "all sudden, unexplained, unnatural, or suspicious deaths" reported to the office. The coroner is ultimately responsible for determining the cause of death in these cases. Coroners also perform autopsies and assist other law enforcement agencies in homicide investigations.[22] In certain rare circumstances, such as when the sheriff is arrested or otherwise forced to leave his or her post, the coroner becomes the leading law enforcement officer of the county.

Coroner
The medical examiner of a county, usually elected by popular vote.

STATE POLICE AND HIGHWAY PATROLS

The most visible state law enforcement agency is the state police or highway patrol agency. Historically, state police agencies were created for four reasons:

1 To assist local police agencies, which often did not have adequate resources or training to handle their law enforcement tasks.

2 To investigate criminal activities that crossed jurisdictional boundaries (such as when bank robbers committed a crime in one county and then fled to another part of the state).

3 To provide law enforcement in rural and other areas that did not have local or county police agencies.

4 To break strikes and control labor movements.

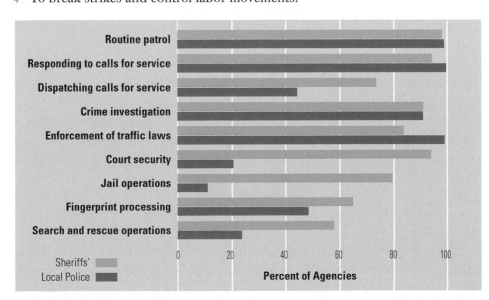

FIGURE 5.4 The Functions of Sheriffs' and Local Police Departments
Sheriffs' and local police departments perform many of the same functions. As you see here, however, the emphasis is often different. Sheriffs' departments are much more involved in operating local jails, while police departments are more likely to deal with traffic control.

Source: Bureau of Justice Statistics, *Sheriffs' Departments, 1997* (Washington, D.C.: U.S. Department of Justice, February 2000), 14.

The first statewide police organization was the Texas Rangers. When this organization was initially created in 1835, the Rangers' primary purpose was to patrol the border with Mexico as scouts for the Republic of Texas Army. The Rangers evolved into a more general-purpose law enforcement agency, and in 1874 they were commissioned as police officers and given law enforcement duties. The Arizona Rangers (created in 1901) and the New Mexico Mounted Police (1905) were formed in a similar manner.

The Difference between the State Police and Highway Patrols   Today, there are twenty-three state police agencies and twenty-six highway patrols in the United States. State police agencies have statewide jurisdiction and are authorized to perform a wide variety of law enforcement tasks. Thus, they provide the same services as city or county police departments and are limited only by the boundaries of the state. Such full-service state police agencies exist in Virginia, Michigan, Texas, New Mexico, Louisiana, Oregon, New York, Kentucky, Pennsylvania, and Rhode Island.

In contrast, highway patrols have limited authority. They are limited either by their jurisdiction or by the specific types of offenses they have the authority to control. As their name suggests, most highway patrols concentrate primarily on regulating traffic; specifically, they enforce traffic laws and investigate traffic accidents. Furthermore, they usually limit their activity to patrolling state and federal highways. States such as Florida, Georgia, Ohio, Nevada, and North Carolina have highway patrols.

Trying to determine what state agency has which duties can be confusing. The Washington State Highway Patrol, despite its name, also has state police powers. In addition, thirty-five states have investigative agencies that are independent of the state police or highway patrol. Such agencies are usually found in states with highway patrols, and they have the primary responsibility of investigating criminal activities. For example, in addition to its highway patrol, Oklahoma runs a State Bureau of Investigation and a State Bureau of Narcotics and Dangerous Drugs. Each state has its own methods of determining the jurisdictions of these various organizations.

For the most part, however, state police are complementary to local law enforcement agencies. They maintain crime labs to assist in local investigations and also keep statewide intelligence files. State officers in some cases also provide training to local police and will assist local forces when needed.[23]

Limited-Purpose Law Enforcement Agencies   Even with the agencies just discussed, a number of states have found that certain law enforcement areas need more specific attention. As a result, a wide variety of limited-purpose law enforcement agencies have sprung up in the fifty states. For example, most states have an alcoholic beverage control commission (ABC), or a similarly named organization, which monitors the sale and distribution of alcoholic beverages. The ABC monitors alcohol distributors to assure that all taxes are paid on the beverages and is responsible for revoking or suspending the liquor licenses of establishments that have broken relevant laws.

Many states have fish and game warden organizations that enforce all laws relating to hunting and fishing. Motor vehicle compliance (MVC) agencies monitor interstate carriers or trucks to make sure that they are in compliance with state

Nearly every law enforcement agency hosts a Web site. To find the home pages of the Pennsylvania State Police and the Washington State Highway Patrol, click on *Web Links* under *Chapter Resources* at www.cjinaction.com

and federal laws. MVC officers generally operate the weigh stations that are commonly found on interstate highways. Other limited-purpose law enforcement agencies deal with white-collar and computer crime, regulate nursing homes, and provide training to local police departments.

FEDERAL LAW ENFORCEMENT AGENCIES

Statistically, employees of federal agencies do not make up a large part of the nation's law enforcement force. In fact, the New York City Police Department has nearly half as many employees as all of the federal law enforcement agencies combined.[24] The influence of these federal agencies, however, is substantial. Unlike local police departments, which must deal with all forms of crime, federal agencies have been authorized, usually by Congress, to enforce specific laws or attend to specific situations. The U.S. Coast Guard, for example, patrols the nation's waterways, while U.S. Postal Inspectors investigate and prosecute crimes perpetrated through the use of the U.S. mails. In response to the terrorist attacks of September 11, 2001, the Federal Aviation Administration has resurrected a program that places law enforcement agents on passenger aircraft. (See the feature *International CJ—Sky Marshals Fly Again* on the following page.)

As mentioned in Chapter 1, the most far-reaching reorganization of the federal government since World War II took place in 2002 and 2003. These changes, particularly the formation of the Department of Homeland Security, have had a profound effect on federal law enforcement. (See Figure 5.5 for the new federal law enforcement "lineup.") We will address the most important agencies in this section, grouping them according to the federal department or bureau to which they report.

The Department of Homeland Security   On November 25, 2002, President George W. Bush signed the Homeland Security Act.[25] This legislation created the Department of Homeland Security (DHS), a new cabinet-level department designed to coordinate federal efforts to protect the United States against international and

See the U.S. Department of Homeland Security for information on how this new branch of federal law enforcement will fight terrorism. Find the Web site by clicking on *Web Links* under *Chapter Resources* at www.cjinaction.com

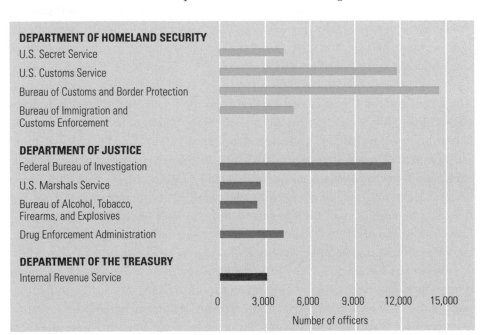

FIGURE 5.5 **Federal Law Enforcement Agencies**
A number of federal agencies employ law enforcement officers who are authorized to carry firearms and make arrests. The most prominent ones are under the control of the U.S. Department of Homeland Security, the U.S. Department of Justice, or the U.S. Department of the Treasury.

Source: Bureau of Justice Statistics, *Federal Law Enforcement Officers, 2002* (Washington, D.C.: U.S. Department of Justice, August 2003), 1–2, 5.

Sky Marshals Fly Again

I n 1970, more than thirty years before terrorists commandeered four commercial aircraft and used them as weapons against American citizens in New York and Washington, D.C., hijackers in Europe carried out a somewhat similar plot. A coordinated group of terrorists took over four commercial airplanes, managing to divert three of the jets to the Middle Eastern country of Jordan. The fourth plane, operated by El Al, Israel's national airline, did not reach Jordan, however. One hijacker was killed and another apprehended as security guards regained control of the aircraft, allowing it to land safely in London. The presence of a law enforcement agent on the El Al flight was no accident. Operating in one of the most volatile areas of the world, the airline (which is operated by Israel's government) incorporates a number of security measures into its day-to-day operations. One of these measures is that every El Al flight has at least one plainclothes sky marshal on board.

In the wake of the September 11, 2001, terrorist attacks in the United States, many politicians seized on the idea of duplicating Israel's sky marshal program on American air carriers as a "new" way to combat hijackings. In fact, the U.S. Federal Aviation Administration (FAA) formed its own sky marshal pro-

gram in the 1970s, in response to a series of airplane hijackings to Cuba. As the perceived threat lessened over the past three decades, though, many of the specially trained agents were allowed to leave the program.

At the time of the terrorist attacks, only thirty-two sky marshals were still employed. In 2003, the Bush administration announced a plan to combine a revamped air marshals program with the new immigration security bureau under the Department of Homeland Security. The reorganization is designed to make 5,000 armed federal agents available to protect commercial flights. In particular, government officials would like to be able to quickly deploy a large number of sky marshals when intelligence reports indicate a hijacking may be imminent.

FOR CRITICAL ANALYSIS

Even when intelligence reports indicate a heightened risk of hijacking, with only 5,000 sky marshals, the FAA will not be able to place a law enforcement agent on each of the 35,000 domestic commercial flights that originate in this country each day. What criteria do you think FAA officials should consider in deciding which flights will be policed in this manner?

domestic terrorism. The new department has no new agencies; rather, twenty-two existing agencies were shifted under the control of Secretary of Homeland Security Tom Ridge. For example, the Transportation Security Administration, which was formed in 2001 to revive the Federal Air Marshals program placing undercover federal agents on commercial flights, was moved from the Department of Transportation to the DHS. The Directorate of Customs and Border Security, the U.S. Customs Service, and the U.S. Secret Service are the three most visible agencies under the direction of the DHS.

The Directorate of Customs and Border Security One of the most significant effects of the Homeland Security Act was the termination of the Immigration and Naturalization Service (INS), which had monitored and policed the flow of immigrants into the United States since 1933. The INS faced particular criticism in the aftermath of the terrorist attacks on Washington, D.C., and New York City after it became clear that several of the hijackers were in the country illegally at the time.[26] The architects of the Homeland Security Act hope that separating the functions of the old INS into several new bureaus will cure some of the inefficiency problems that had plagued the INS since its inception.

Before the formation of the DHS, the INS was responsible for enforcing our immigration laws and for providing immigration benefits. According to the dictates of the Homeland Security Act, the Bureau of Citizenship and Immigration Services will process applications for immigration benefits, and the new

President George W. Bush promotes the Department of Homeland Security, a large federal agency designed to protect the United States against terrorist attacks. Considering that the United States already has a federal crime-fighting agency—the FBI—why might a Department of Homeland Security be necessary?

Directorate of Customs and Border Security will oversee the two bureaus now responsible for immigration law enforcement:

1 The *Bureau of Customs and Border Protection (CBP)* will concentrate on policing the flow of goods and people across the United States' international borders with Mexico and Canada.

2 The *Bureau of Immigration and Customs Enforcement (BICE)* will implement laws concerning customs and immigration inside the United States.[27]

Even before September 11, 2001, a large number of illegal immigrants and huge amounts of illicit drugs entered the United States via Mexico and Canada. Government officials hope that the reorganization of the INS will help control these traditional concerns of immigration services and protect against terrorist attacks.

U.S. Border Patrol Much of the burden for policing both the Mexican and Canadian borders will fall on the U.S. Border Patrol, now a part of the CBP. In 2001, the Border Patrol caught nearly 1.2 million people entering the country illegally. The agency also seized 18,500 pounds of cocaine and more than 1.1 million pounds of marijuana, worth more than $1.4 billion.[28] In 2003, the Bush administration proposed increasing the number of Border Patrol agents by nearly 600, which would bring the total to 11,000—more than double the number of ten years earlier.

Particular attention is being paid to the Canadian border. As recently as 2001, the 4,200-mile border was policed by only 300 Border Patrol agents. One of the first moves made by the CBP after its inception was to raise that number to well over 1,000.

The flash point of immigration enforcement, however, remains the line between Mexico and the United States. Under the CBP, the Border Patrol hopes not only to restrict the flow of contraband and illegal aliens across the Rio Grande, but also to limit the human tragedy that is a side effect of this traffic. In 2002, 145 people died while trying to enter the United States illegally from Mexico; 85 of

Border Patrol agents frisk illegal aliens captured in Nogales, Arizona. Starting in 1994, Operation Gatekeeper increased the number of Border Patrol agents in the southwestern United States from 800 to 2,300, resulting in a dramatic increase in the number of illegal aliens captured and returned to Mexico. The increase in agents also appears to have led to an increase in violent confrontations between agents and aliens. Do you believe society benefits from efforts to keep illegal aliens out of the country? Is the use of force to carry out these efforts justifiable?

them perished from heat exposure. In response, the federal government added hundreds of new agents and three surveillance helicopters, as well as solar-power rescue beacons that send a radio distress signal when activated, to an area on the Arizona border known as the "devil's corridor" because of its high death rate.[29]

U.S. Customs Service The U.S. Customs Services, which stations agents at every port of entry and exit to the United States, moved from the Department of the Treasury to the Directorate of Customs and Border Security. Customs agents have widespread authority to investigate and search all international passengers, including those arriving on airplanes, ships, or other forms of transportation. Furthermore, the Customs Service is responsible for ensuring that proper tariffs and taxes have been paid on all goods imported into the United States. It collects about $22 billion a year in these duties and fees.

Before September 11, 2001, the primary goal of the Customs Service was to prevent the smuggling of contraband (anything that is unlawful to produce or possess), while allowing the free flow of goods to encourage commerce between the United States and its trading partners. Today, the bureau is asked to balance these economic concerns against the need for security. This has placed a particular burden on the agents at the Mexican and Canadian borders, who have been on continual "high alert" since the terrorist attacks. Around 1.3 million people in 350,000 cars, trucks, and buses cross at border posts each day, and at the more popular routes Customs agents have between thirty seconds and two minutes to decide whether a vehicle and its passengers are suspicious. If they take any longer, the resulting lines at the border stops would make travel between the United States and either Canada or Mexico nearly impossible.[30]

The U.S. Secret Service When created in 1865, the Secret Service was primarily responsible for combating currency counterfeiters. In 1901, the agency was given the added responsibility of protecting the president of the United States, the president's family, the vice president, the president-elect, and ex-presidents. These duties have remained the cornerstone of the agency, with several expansions. After a number of threats against presidential candidates in the 1960s and early 1970s, including the shootings of Robert Kennedy and Governor George Wallace of Alabama, in 1976 Secret Service agents became responsible for protecting those political figures as well.

In addition to its special plainclothes agents, the agency also directs two uniformed groups of law enforcement officers. The Secret Service Uniformed Division protects the grounds of the White House and its inhabitants, and the Treasury Police Force polices the Treasury Building in Washington, D.C. This responsibility includes investigating threats against presidents and those running for presidential office.

To aid its battle against counterfeiters and forgers of government bonds, the agency has the use of a laboratory at the Bureau of Engraving and Printing in the nation's capital.

The Department of Justice   The U.S. Department of Justice, created in 1870, is still the primary federal law enforcement agency in the country. With the responsibility of enforcing criminal law and supervising the federal prisons, the Justice Department plays a leading role in the American criminal justice system. To carry out its responsibilities to prevent and control crime, the department has a number of law enforcement agencies, including the Federal Bureau of Investigation, the federal Drug Enforcement Administration, the Bureau of Alcohol, Tobacco, Firearms and Explosives, and the U.S. Marshals Service.

The Federal Bureau of Investigation (FBI)   Initially created in 1908 as the Bureau of Investigation, this agency was renamed the **Federal Bureau of Investigation (FBI)** in 1935. One of the primary investigative agencies of the federal government, the FBI has jurisdiction over nearly two hundred federal crimes, including sabotage, espionage (spying), kidnapping, extortion, interstate transportation of stolen property, bank robbery, interstate gambling, and civil rights violations. Note that the FBI is not considered a "national" police force. In general, law enforcement is seen as the responsibility of state and local governments. There is no doubt, however, that the agency plays a crucial role in today's law enforcement landscape. With its network of agents across the country and the globe, the FBI is uniquely positioned to combat worldwide criminal activity such as terrorism and drug trafficking. Furthermore, in times of national emergency the FBI is the primary arm of federal law enforcement. Within hours after the terrorist attacks on September 11, 2001, more than 7,000 FBI employees in 57 different countries had begun an intense search for those responsible.

Today, the FBI has nearly 26,000 employees and an annual budget of over $3.6 billion. The agency has five investigative priorities: (1) terrorism, (2) organized crime, (3) foreign intelligence operations in the United States, (4) federal drug offenses, and (5) white-collar crime.[31] The agency also offers valuable assistance to local and state law enforcement agencies. The FBI's Identification Division maintains a huge database of fingerprint information and offers assistance in finding missing persons and identifying the victims of fires, airplane crashes, and other disfiguring disasters. The services of the FBI Laboratory, the largest crime laboratory in the world, are available at no charge to other agencies. Finally, the FBI's National Crime Information Center (NCIC) provides lists of stolen vehicles and firearms, missing license plates, vehicles used to commit crimes, and other information to local and state law enforcement officers who may access the NCIC database. (See the feature *Careers in CJ* on the next page.)

The Drug Enforcement Administration (DEA)   With a $1.8 billion budget and more than 4,000 special agents, the Drug Enforcement Administration (DEA) is one of the fastest-growing law enforcement agencies in the country. The mission of the DEA is to enforce domestic drug laws and regulations and to assist other federal and foreign agencies in combating illegal drug manufacture and trade on an international level. The agency also enforces the provisions of the Controlled Substances Act, which controls the manufacture, distribution, and dispensing of legal drugs, such as prescription drugs.

Federal Bureau of Investigation (FBI)
The branch of the Department of Justice responsible for investigating violations of federal law. The bureau also collects national crime statistics and provides training and other forms of aid to local law enforcement agencies.

INFOTRAC KEYWORD
FBI
For more information, use this search term with InfoTrac College Edition, your online library at www.infotrac-college.com

> Jim Rice Federal Bureau of Investigation (FBI)

Growing up in a small town in rural West Virginia, I always knew that I wanted to be an FBI agent. There were probably a lot of other kids in America who shared this dream, but the murder of a woman who at one time was my baby-sitter convinced me to do everything that I could to make my dream of becoming a law enforcement officer come true.

I received a B.S. in biology from John Marshall University in West Virginia and subsequently earned a master's degree in biochemistry from there as well. During college, I worked at several part-time jobs, loading trucks and bagging groceries, and also served in the Coast Guard as a reservist.

Following college, I went to work for the West Virginia State Police (WVSP) as a forensic toxicologist, a job that prepared me well for my current position with the FBI. These four years were well spent, because it was an interesting and challenging job and also because the FBI seeks to attract candidates who are competitive and who bring a speciality or work experience to the job.

I joined the FBI as a Special Agent in 1988 and spent the first sixteen weeks of my Bureau career at the FBI Academy in Quantico, Virginia, as do all new agents. The FBI Academy is similar to a small college campus, with classrooms, dormitories, a cafeteria, and a gymnasium, with hundreds of students in residence at any given time, including new agents, experienced agents who are back for a week or two of specialized training, and police officers from all over the country and the world.

Following graduation from the FBI Academy, agents are subject to transfer to one of the fifty-six field offices in the United States for their first assignment. I was sent to the Indianapolis (Indiana) Office, where I was assigned to a "reactive squad," which handled violent criminal violations, such as bank robberies, fugitives, kidnappings, and extortions.

It was during my time in Indianapolis that I worked on a case that had a major impact on me and reaffirmed that the FBI was the right career choice for me. A young boy was kidnapped by an adult family friend and driven cross-country in the subject's

truck. The FBI had surveillances on a number of locations in the Midwest, including the home of the subject's relatives in Indianapolis. After many long hours of surveillance in the cold and rain, our team found a truck that matched the description of the subject's truck, parked beside a house in a desolate part of the city. We continued the surveillance on the truck and finally, the subject and the victim emerged from the house. As they drove off in the truck, our team followed discreetly at a distance until the order came from the lead agent to move in and conduct a tactical car stop. The subject was arrested and the boy was rescued, frightened but unharmed, and reunited with his parents.

Courtesy Jim Rice

Jim Rice

A rotational transfer brought me to the Washington, D.C., field office in 1992, where I joined the SWAT team and worked on a "Safe Streets Gang Task Force" and then on a Cold Case Homicide Squad. Soon thereafter, a Joint Terrorism Task Force was formed to address domestic terrorism matters in the nation's capital, an area filled with symbolic targets for would-be terroristic activities.

I volunteered to be part of this task force in late 1992 and was promoted to the position of Supervisory Special Agent of the squad in 1998. My duties include the operational and emergency response to incidents of domestic terrorism; bombings and bomb threats; chemical, biological, and nuclear incidents; and the security for special events, like presidential inaugurations and the fiftieth anniversary celebration of NATO, which brought dozens of heads of state to Washington in 1999 without incident.

 Go to the Careers in Criminal Justice Interactive CD *for more profiles in the field of criminal justice.*

As we shall see in Chapter 16, the federal government has had a role in policing the manufacture and sale of illicit drugs since 1914. The first federal drug agency, the Federal Bureau of Narcotics (FBN), was established in 1930 under President Herbert Hoover. The FBN's main priorities were cocaine and opiates such as heroin. As the level of illegal drug use expanded over the decades, and international trafficking became a more pressing problem, several additional agencies were formed to deal with drug enforcement. Then, in 1970 Congress passed the comprehensive Drug Abuse Prevention and Control Act,[32] which gave Congress the authority to regulate interstate commerce of legal drugs. With the Bureau of Narcotics and Dangerous Drugs (a successor to the FBN), the U.S.

Customs Service, the FBI, and hundreds of state and local law enforcement agencies all working to enforce drug laws—as well as the government's new responsibility with regard to legal drugs—it was evident that a new "superagency" was needed. In 1973, by order of President Richard Nixon, the DEA was formed.

Today, DEA agents often work in conjunction with local and state authorities to prevent illicit drugs from reaching communities. The agency also conducts extensive operations with law enforcement entities in other drug-producing countries. The DEA's "Operation Double Trouble," for example, saw American agents join with their counterparts in Colombia to reduce the role of Colombian banks in providing cash for drug dealers in that country. The operation culminated in 2003 with the seizure of $12.8 million in cash, 161 pounds of cocaine, and 10 pounds of heroin, along with the dismantling of a system in which the banks had hidden more than $30 million in profits from the drug trade.[33] Like the FBI, the DEA operates a network of six regional laboratories used to test and categorize seized drugs. Local law enforcement agencies have access to the DEA labs and often use them to ensure that information about particular drugs that will be presented in court is accurate and up to date. In recent years Congress has given the FBI more authority to enforce drug laws, and the two agencies now share a number of administrative controls.

INFOTRAC KEYWORD
DEA

For more information, use this search term with InfoTrac College Edition, your online library at www.infotrac-college.com

The Bureau of Alcohol, Tobacco, Firearms and Explosives (ATF)   As its name suggests, the Bureau of Alcohol, Tobacco, Firearms and Explosives (ATF) is primarily concerned with the illegal sale, possession, and use of firearms and the control of untaxed tobacco and liquor products. The Firearms Division of the agency has the responsibility of enforcing the Gun Control Act of 1968, which sets the circumstances under which firearms may be sold and used in this country. The bureau also regulates all gun trade between the United States and foreign countries and collects taxes on all firearm importers, manufacturers, and dealers. In keeping with these duties, the ATF is also responsible for policing the illegal use and possession of explosives. Furthermore, the ATF is charged with enforcing federal gambling laws.

Because it has jurisdiction over such a wide variety of crimes, especially those involving firearms and explosives, the ATF is a constant presence in federal criminal investigations. Since 1982, for example, the agency has been working in conjunction with the FBI to prevent the bombing of abortion clinics. Recently, the agency, along with the FBI, has begun to place undercover informants inside antiabortion groups to gain information about proposed bombings. Furthermore, the ATF has been active in forming multijurisdictional drug task forces with other federal and local law enforcement agencies to investigate drug crimes involving firearms.

The U.S. Marshals Service   The oldest federal law enforcement agency is the U.S. Marshals Service. In 1789, President George Washington assigned thirteen U.S. Marshals to protect his attorney general. That same year, Congress created the office of the U.S. Marshals and Deputy Marshals. Originally, the U.S. Marshals acted as the main law enforcement officers in the western territories. Following the Civil War, when most of these territories had become states, these agents were assigned to work for the U.S. district courts, where federal crimes are tried. The relationship between the U.S. Marshals Service and the federal courts continues today and forms the basis for the officers' main duties, which include:

1 Providing security at federal courts for judges, jurors, and other courtroom participants.

2 Controlling property that has been ordered seized by federal courts.

3 Protecting government witnesses who place themselves in danger by testifying against the targets of federal criminal investigations. This protection is sometimes accomplished by relocating the witnesses and providing them with different identities.

4 Transporting federal prisoners to detention institutions.

5 Investigating violations of federal fugitive laws.[34]

The Department of the Treasury The Department of the Treasury, formed in 1789, is mainly responsible for all financial matters of the federal government. It pays all the federal government's bills, borrows money, collects taxes, mints coins, and prints paper currency. The largest bureau of the Treasury Department, the Internal Revenue Service (IRS), is concerned with violations of tax laws and regulations. The bureau has three divisions, only one of which is involved in criminal investigations. The examination branch of the IRS audits the tax returns of corporations and individuals. The collection division attempts to collect taxes from corporations or citizens who have failed to pay the taxes they owe. Finally, the criminal investigation division investigates cases of tax evasion and tax fraud. Criminal investigation agents can make arrests. The IRS has long played a role in policing criminal activities such as gambling and selling drugs for one simple reason: those who engage in such activities almost never report any illegally gained income on their tax returns. Therefore, the IRS is able to apprehend them for tax evasion. The most famous instance of this took place in the 1920s, when the IRS finally arrested crime boss Al Capone—responsible for numerous violent crimes—for not paying his taxes.

↗ ONLINE REVIEW *Go to the book's Web site for an interactive review of this section*

Private Security

Even with increasing numbers of local, state, and federal law enforcement officers, the police do not have the ability to prevent every crime. Recognizing this, many businesses and citizens have decided to hire private guards for their properties and homes. In fact, over $100 billion a year is spent on **private security** in the United States, about double the amount spent on public, taxpayer-financed law enforcement. More than 60,000 private security firms employ around 2 million people.[35]

PRIVATIZING LAW ENFORCEMENT

In the eyes of the law, a private security guard is the same as any other private person when it comes to police powers such as being able to arrest or interrogate a person suspected of committing a crime. Ideally, a security guard—lacking the training of a law enforcement agent—should only observe and report criminal activity unless use of force is needed to prevent a felony.[36]

Citizens' Arrests Any private citizen, however, may perform a "citizen's arrest" under certain circumstances. The California Penal Code, for example, allows a private person to arrest another:

Private Security
The practice of private corporations or individuals offering services traditionally performed by police officers.

> For a public offense committed in his or her presence.

> When the person arrested has committed a felony, even if it was not in the arrester's presence, if he or she has reasonable cause to believe that the person committed the felony.[37]

Obviously, these are not very exacting standards, and, in reality, private security guards have many, if not most, of the same powers to prevent crime that a police officer does.

The Deterrence Factor As a rule, however, private security is not designed to "replace" law enforcement. It is intended to deter crime rather than stop it.[38] A uniformed security guard patrolling a shopping mall parking lot or a bank lobby has one primary function—to convince a potential criminal to search out a shopping mall or bank that does not have private security. For the same reason, many citizens hire security personnel to drive marked cars through their neighborhoods, making them a less attractive target for burglaries, robberies, vandalism, and other crimes.

Sometimes, private security is a necessity because public law enforcement agencies are shorthanded or do not have the budgetary resources required. For example, following the September 11, 2001, terrorist attacks, National Guard troops were stationed at each of the nation's 429 commercial airports. According to a plan drawn up by the Transportation Security Administration, these troops were to be replaced by federal law enforcement agents by the spring of 2002. When the new officers were not available by that time, many small airports were allowed to hire private security guards to protect their operations until the federal replacements were properly trained for the job.[39]

PROBLEMS WITH PRIVATE SECURITY

Despite the proliferation of private security, many questions remain about this largely unregulated industry. In 2003, twenty-one people were trampled to death in a Chicago nightclub after a private security guard unwisely used pepper spray to break up a fight, causing hundreds of guests to stampede toward a narrow exit staircase.[40] The only requirement for becoming a security guard in Illinois is three days of training, to be completed within a month of being hired.[41]

Lack of Standards As there are no federal regulations regarding private security, each state has its own rules for employment as a security guard. In several states, including California and Florida, prospective guards must have at least forty hours of training. Thirty states, however, have no specific training requirements. By comparison, Spain mandates 160 hours of theoretical training, 20 hours of practical training, and 20 hours of annual continuing education for anybody hoping to find employment as a security guard.[42]

The quality of employees is also a problem in the United States. Save for those who work in the largest firms, for many guards private security is a second job, and turnover rates are high. Furthermore, given the low pay (an average of $17,570) and lack of benefits such as health care, paid vacation time, and sick days, the industry does not always attract highly qualified and motivated recruits.[43] In 2003, forty-five foreign-born security guards scheduled to work the

Super Bowl in San Diego, California, were arrested for immigration violations and past criminal convictions—a disturbing development, given that the championship football game is considered a potential terrorist target.[44]

A number of security firms want the ability to run FBI background checks on possible employees to improve the overall quality of private security. In 2003, supporters in Congress introduced the Private Security Officer Employment Authorization Act, which would allow such checks for criminal records.[45]

Continued Growth in the Industry   Issues surrounding private security promise to gain even greater prominence in the criminal justice system, as indicators point to higher rates of growth for the industry (see Figure 5.6). The Hallcrest Report II, a far-reaching overview of private security trends funded by the National Institute of Justice, identifies four factors driving this growth:

1   An increase in fear on the part of the public triggered by the growing rate of crime, either real or perceived.

2   The problem of crime in the workplace.

3   Budget cuts in states and municipalities that have forced reductions in the number of public police, thereby raising the demand for private ones.

4   A rising awareness of private security products (such as home burglar alarms) and service as cost-effective protective measures.[46]

Another reason is fear of terrorism. The U.S. Bureau of Labor Statistics reported that nearly 15,000 new security guards were hired between September 11, 2001, and October 11, 2001.[47] The Bureau predicts that private security will expand by 21 to 35 percent by 2008.[48]

↗ ONLINE REVIEW *Go to the book's Web site for an interactive review of this section*

The Responsibilities of the Police

Some law enforcement officials welcome the massive influx of private security. Private firms, they believe, may be able to relieve the constant budget and staffing pressures that public police forces face.[49] The problem with this theory, however, is that public and private police have different basic functions. For a private security firm, the primary goal is to protect property. As noted earlier, that often means persuading a criminal to choose an alternative target for a burglary or some other crime. As a manager at one private security company noted, "We're a business, not a law enforcement agency."[50]

The goal of public law enforcement, in contrast, is to stop crimes, not simply shift them from one location to another—which is not to say that preventing crime is the only duty of a police officer. For the most part, the incidents that make up a police officer's daily routine would not make it onto television dramas such as *Law and Order*. Besides catching criminals, police spend a great deal of time on

---

FIGURE 5.6	**The Demand for Private Secutiry**

Concern about both violent and property crime has spurred the growth in private security spending. As these figures show, the demand for various private security services increased over the five-year period from 1996 to 2001, and by all indications it will continue to grow.

Service	Amount spent, 2001*	% increase from 1996
Private guards	$ 11.65	3.1
Alarm monitoring	11.05	9.9
Private investigations	2.13	1.4
Management of private prisons	2.06	24.2
Security consulting	.91	11.6
	*in billions	

Source: "Private Security Services," The Freedonia Group (April 1, 2003).

such mundane tasks as responding to noise complaints, confiscating firecrackers, and poring over paperwork. Sociologist Egon Bittner warned against the tendency to see the police primarily as agents of law enforcement and crime control. A more inclusive accounting of "what the police do," Bittner believed, would recognize that they provide "situationally justified force in society."[51] In other words, the function of the police is to solve any problem that may *possibly*, though not *necessarily*, require the use of force.

Within Bittner's rather broad definition of "what the police do," we can pinpoint four basic responsibilities of the police:

1 To enforce laws.

2 To provide services.

3 To prevent crime.

4 To preserve the peace.

As will become evident over the next two chapters, there is a great deal of debate among legal and other scholars and law enforcement officers over which responsibilities deserve the most police attention and what methods should be employed by the police in meeting those responsibilities.

ENFORCING LAWS

In the public mind, the primary role of the police is to enforce society's laws—hence, the term *law enforcement officer*. In their role as "crime fighters," police officers have a clear mandate to seek out and apprehend those who have violated the law. The crime-fighting responsibility is so dominant that all police activity—from the purchase of new automobiles to a plan to hire more minority officers—must often be justified in terms of its law enforcement value.[52]

Police officers also primarily see themselves as crime fighters, or "crook catchers," a perception that often leads people into what they believe will be an exciting career in law enforcement. Although the job certainly offers challenges unlike any other, police officers normally do not spend the majority of their time in law enforcement duties. Several studies from the 1970s suggested that police officers spent a very small percentage of their workday on law enforcement matters. Both Thomas Bercal, who examined police calls in St. Louis and Detroit, and John A. Webster, who made a similar study on a wider basis, estimated that only 16 percent of those calls were related to law enforcement.[53]

More recently, police experts have come to the conclusion that these early studies of police activities were flawed in several ways, not the least of which was that they tended to focus only on general patrol officers while discounting criminal investigation units or special response units, which have heavier law enforcement duties. Researchers Jack Greene and Carl Klockars revisited questions of police workload in Wilmington, Delaware, with the goal of improving on the earlier research.[54] Using a more methodical set of data, they found that police officers spend about half of their time enforcing the law or dealing with crimes.

PROVIDING SERVICES

If Greene and Klockars are correct, what are police officers doing the other half of working hours? The emphasis on crime fighting and law enforcement tends to overshadow the fact that a great deal of a police officer's time is spent providing services for the community. The motto "To Serve and Protect" has been adopted

A New York City police officer directs traffic through Times Square following a massive blackout on August 14, 2003. Law enforcement agents provide a number of services to the community that have little to do with fighting crime.

by thousands of local police departments, and the *Law Enforcement Code of Ethics* recognizes the duty "to serve the community" in its first sentence.[55] The services that police provide are numerous—a partial list would include directing traffic, performing emergency medical procedures, counseling those involved in domestic disputes, providing directions to tourists, and finding lost children. Along with firefighters, police officers are among the first public servants to arrive at disaster scenes to conduct search and rescue operations. This particular duty adds considerably to the dangers faced by law enforcement agents (discussed in more detail in Chapter 6). When the World Trade Center collapsed in September 2001 following the terrorist attack, for example, seventy-one New York City police officers lost their lives. As mentioned earlier, a number of police departments have adopted the strategy of community policing, and as a consequence, many officers find themselves providing assistance in areas that have not until recently been their domain.[56] For example, police are required to deal with the problems of the homeless and the mentally ill to a greater extent than in past decades.

PREVENTING CRIME

Perhaps the most controversial responsibility of the police is to *prevent* crime. According to Jerome Skolnick of the University of California at Berkeley, there are two predictable public responses when crime rates begin to rise in a community. The first is to punish convicted criminals with stricter laws and more severe penalties. The second is to demand that the police "do something" to prevent crimes from occurring in the first place. Is it, in fact, possible for the police to "prevent" crimes? The strongest response that Professor Skolnick is willing to give to this question is "maybe."[57]

On a limited basis, police can certainly prevent some crimes. If a rapist is dissuaded from attacking a solitary woman because a patrol car is cruising the area, then the police officer behind the wheel has prevented a crime. In general, however, the deterrent effects of police presence are unclear. Carl Klockars has written that the "war on crime" is a war that the police cannot win because they cannot control the factors—such as unemployment, poverty, immorality, inequality, political change, and lack of educational opportunities—that lead to criminal behavior in the first place.[58] As we shall see in the next chapter, many police stations have adopted the idea of community policing in an attempt to better prevent crime.

"That's the only thing that made me feel safe last night when I came home from work."
—Penny Baily, resident of Indianapolis, commenting on the police car patrolling her neighborhood (1996)

PRESERVING THE PEACE

To a certain extent, the fourth responsibility of the police, that of preserving the peace, is related to preventing crime. Police have the legal authority to use the power of arrest, or even force, in situations in which no crime has yet occurred, but might occur in the immediate future.

In the words of James Q. Wilson, the police's peacekeeping role (which Wilson believes is the most important role of law enforcement officers) often takes on a pattern of simply "handling the situation."[59] For example, when police officers arrive on the scene of a loud late-night house party, they may feel the need to disperse the party and even arrest some of the party goers for disorderly conduct. By their actions, the officers have lessened the chances of serious and violent crimes taking place later in the evening. The same principle is often used when dealing with domestic disputes, which, if escalated, can lead to homicide. Such situations are in need of, to use Wilson's terminology again, "fixing up," and police can use the power of arrest, or threat, or coercion, or sympathy, to do just that.

The basis of Wilson and George Kelling's zero-tolerance theory is similar: street disorder—such as public drunkenness, urination, and loitering—signals to both law-abiding citizens and criminals that the law is not being enforced and therefore leads to more violent crime. Hence, if police preserve the peace and "crack down" on the minor crimes that make up street disorder, they will in fact be preventing serious crimes that would otherwise occur in the future.[60]

ONLINE REVIEW Go to the book's Web site for an interactive review of this section

The Role of Discretion in Policing

Though the responsibilities just discussed provide a helpful overview of "what police do," they also highlight the ambiguity of a police officer's duties. To say, for example, that highway patrol officers have a responsibility to enforce speed laws is to oversimplify their "real" job. In fact, most highway patrol officers would not find it feasible to hand out speeding tickets to every driver who exceeds the posted speed limit. Furthermore, depending on the circumstances, a patrol officer may decide not to issue a ticket to a driver who has been pulled over. Rather, most officers selectively enforce speed laws, ticketing only those who significantly exceed the limit or drive so recklessly that they endanger other drivers. As noted in Chapter 1, when police officers use their judgment in deciding which offenses to punish and which to ignore, they are said to be using *discretion*. Whether this discretion applies to speed limits or any other area of the law, it is a crucial aspect of policing.

INFOTRAC KEYWORDS

police discretion

For more information, use this search term with InfoTrac College Edition, your online library at www.infotrac-college.com

JUSTIFICATION FOR POLICE DISCRETION

One of the ironies of law enforcement is that patrol officers—often the lowest-paid members of an agency with the least amount of authority—have the greatest amount of discretionary power. Part of the explanation for this is practical. Patrol officers spend most of the day on the streets, beyond the control of their supervisors. Usually, only two people are present when a patrol officer must make a decision: the officer and the possible wrongdoer. In all cases, the law enforcement officer has a great deal of freedom to take the action that he or she feels best corresponds to the situation.[61] (For a circumstance in which this discretion is being taken away from many police officers, see the feature *CJ in Focus: The Balancing Act—To Pursue or Not to Pursue?*)

This is not to say that police discretion is misplaced. In general, courts have recognized that a patrol officer is in a unique position to be allowed discretionary powers:

> Police officers are considered trustworthy and are therefore assumed to make honest decisions, regardless of contradictory testimony by a suspect.

> Experience and training give officers the ability to determine whether certain activity poses a threat to society, and to take any reasonable action necessary to investigate or prevent such activity.

> Due to the nature of their jobs, police officers are extremely knowledgeable in human, and by extension criminal, behavior.

> Police officers may find themselves in danger of personal, physical harm and must be allowed to take reasonable and necessary steps to protect themselves.[62]

MAKING THE DECISION

In deciding how to apply the law to any particular situation, police officers generally consider three factors. First, and most important, is the nature of the criminal act. The less serious a crime, the more likely a police officer is to ignore it. A person driving 60 miles per hour in a 55 miles-per-hour zone, for example, is much less likely to be ticketed than someone doing 80 miles per hour. A second factor often considered is the attitude of the wrongdoer toward the officer. A motorist who is belligerent toward a highway patrol officer is much more likely to be ticketed than one who is contrite and apologetic. Third, departmental policy can place limits on discretion.[63] If a police chief decides that all motorists who exceed the speed limit by 10 miles will be ticketed, that policy will influence the patrol officer's decisions. (For a discussion of one area where police discretion has been limited, see the chapter-ending feature *Criminal Justice in Action—The Police and Domestic Violence.*)

ONLINE REVIEW *Go to the book's Web site for an interactive review of this section*

> To Pursue or Not to Pursue?

The chase began when Los Angeles police officers ran a check on a silver BMW sedan that nearly struck a patrol car and found that it had been stolen two days earlier. The pursuit ended five minutes later, when the driver of the BMW, attempting to escape the police, ran a red light and hit a minivan. The minivan slammed into a light post, sending it crashing down onto a busy sidewalk, where it struck and killed a four-year-old girl named Evelyn Vargas.

According to the National Highway Traffic Safety Administration, Evelyn was one of the nearly four hundred people killed in high-speed police pursuits in 2002. As Figure 5.7 shows, the potential for injury and death is quite high; the study cited shows more than four out of every ten high-speed police pursuits ending with an accident. Many observers question whether the risk created by such pursuit is greater than the need to enforce the law, especially when the initial infraction is not a serious one, as was the case in Los Angeles. (Figure 5.7 also shows that nearly half of all pursuits are initiated by traffic offenses.) Those who believe the risk is too great favor policies to limit police discretion in deciding when to engage in a high-speed chase.

Many police departments have instituted guidelines that take the decision out of the officer's hands. The Virginia Beach (Virginia) Police Department, for example, recently established guidelines that allow chases only when the initial crime is a violent felony or involves guns or explosives. Consequently, Virginia Beach police may no longer pursue drunk drivers, car thieves, burglars, or other nonviolent suspects. According to the U.S. Department of Justice, more than 90 percent of the nation's local police departments have implemented pursuit driving policies, with 57 percent of those placing greater restrictions on their officers.

FOR CRITICAL ANALYSIS

Given that the police's primary duty is to protect the public, what might be some of the drawbacks of restrictions such as those imposed in Virginia Beach? What steps might be taken to reduce the risk of third party deaths other than limiting police discretion?

FIGURE 5.7 The Causes and Consequences of High-Speed Pursuits

Over a five-year period, Metro-Dade County (Florida) police officers engaged in 994 high-speed pursuits. As you can see, most of the chases were the result of traffic violations and lasted between five and ten minutes. Furthermore, one out of every five police chases in Metro-Dade County resulted in an injury.

Source: Geoffrey P. Alpert, "Pursuit Driving: Planning Policies and Action from Agency, Officer, and Public Information," *Police Forum* 7 (January 1997), 3.

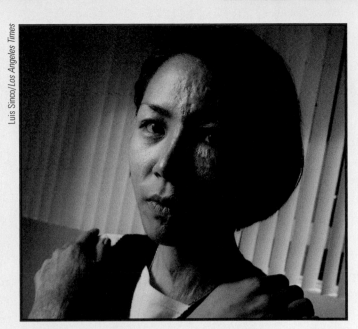

Luis Sinco/Los Angeles Times

Jung Won Ko suffered serious burns when her car was hit by a drunken driver trying to outrun Los Angeles police officers.

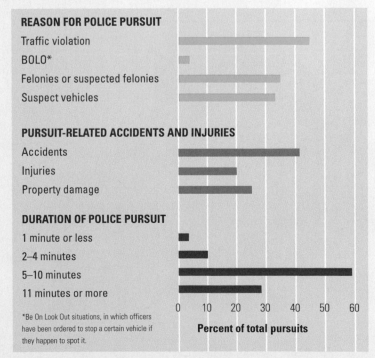

REASON FOR POLICE PURSUIT

Traffic violation
BOLO*
Felonies or suspected felonies
Suspect vehicles

PURSUIT-RELATED ACCIDENTS AND INJURIES

Accidents
Injuries
Property damage

DURATION OF POLICE PURSUIT

1 minute or less
2–4 minutes
5–10 minutes
11 minutes or more

0   10   20   30   40   50   60

*Be On Look Out situations, in which officers have been ordered to stop a certain vehicle if they happen to spot it.

Percent of total pursuits

> The Police and Domestic Violence

A factor that often influences police discretion is the relationship between the person committing the criminal act and the victim. The closer this relationship, the less likely many police officers are to respond to the victim's complaints and arrest the wrongdoer.[64] This tendency is often evident in police action (or lack thereof) concerning *domestic violence*. The statistics surrounding this crime speak volumes as to the extent of the problem in the United States. According to the National Violence Against Women Survey, of the estimated 5.9 million physical assaults against women that occur each year, current or former husbands, cohabiting partners, or dates commit 76 percent.[65] The U.S. Department of Justice has found that about one-third of all female homicide victims are killed by a husband, former husband, or boyfriend.[66] In all, intimate partner violence causes more than 2 million injuries each year to American women aged eighteen and over.[67] For most of this nation's history, the police role in domestic violence was limited to "calming" the situation, a short-term response that did little to prevent future violence. Today, as we shall see in this feature, more is expected.

The Problem: Lack of Police Involvement in "Family Matters"

As we will discuss in more detail in Chapter 7, police have a great deal of discretion in deciding whether to make an arrest. Basically, if a police officer has good reason (known as "probable cause") to believe that a person has committed a crime or is about to commit a crime, that officer can arrest the suspect.

Historically, police officers have been hesitant to make arrests when the dispute involves a "family matter," even when faced with strong evidence that domestic violence has taken place. This hesitancy has been obvious in studies such as the one conducted by James J. Fyfe of Temple University, David Klinger of the University of Houston, and Jeanne Flavin of Fordham University with regard to the Chester (Pennsylvania) Police Department.[68] The researchers found that Chester police were less likely to arrest male felony assailants who had attacked former or present female partners than other males who had committed similarly violent acts against strangers. Among the cases that did not lead to arrests were 4 attacks on domestic partners with guns, 38 attacks involving cutting instruments (including one with an ax), and 27 attacks with blunt instruments such as baseball bats or hammers. In one incident that did not result in arrest, a woman was held by her feet over a second floor landing and dropped on her head.

A number of factors have been considered to explain this leniency. Many police officers see domestic violence cases as the responsibility of social-service providers, not law enforcement officers. Furthermore, officers are often uncomfortable with the intensely private nature of domestic disputes.[69] Finally, even when a police officer does arrest the abuser, the victim often chooses to drop the charges.

AP Photo/*The Charlotte Observer*, Patrick Schneider

Women in Charlotte, North Carolina, take part in a silent march to mark the start of Domestic Violence Awareness Week. Pressure from activist citizens played a large role in the passage of state mandatory arrest laws for those who commit domestic violence.

The Response: Mandatory Arrest Laws

Whatever the reasons for this reluctance to arrest domestic abusers, many jurisdictions have responded by severely limiting police discretion in domestic violence cases.[70] Today, twenty-three states and the District of Columbia have passed *mandatory arrest laws.*[71] Under these laws, a police officer *must* arrest a person who has battered a spouse or domestic partner. No discretion is involved.

Several early studies encouraged the passage of these laws. In the landmark Minneapolis Domestic Violence Experiment of 1983, the Minneapolis Police Department and Professors Lawrence Sherman and Richard Berk attempted to determine the consequences of police inaction in domestic violence cases. The researchers found that the most effective deterrent to repeat incidents of battering was the arrest of the batterer.[72] A similar project in Duluth, Minnesota, had similar results, with rates of rearrest of domestic abusers dropping to levels as low as 16 percent seven to twelve months after the initial arrest.[73]

The theory behind mandatory arrest laws is relatively straightforward: they act as a deterrent to criminal behavior. Costs are imposed on a person who is arrested. He or she must go to court and face the possibility of time in jail. Arrest may also lead to humiliation, loss of job, and separation from family and friends. To avoid these unpleasant consequences, the argument goes, potential abusers will not act in a manner that increases the risk that they will be arrested.

Questioning Mandatory Arrests

Despite the popularity of mandatory arrest statutes, not all of the evidence supports limiting police discretion in this manner. The National Institute of Justice commissioned studies in six other cities to verify the findings of the Minneapolis experiment. In only one of the sites—Miami, Florida—were researchers able to match the Minneapolis results.[74]

More troubling are recent findings by Professor Sherman that led him to conclude that "mandatory arrests in domestic violence cases may cause more violence against women in the long run."[75] After completing a research project in Milwaukee, Wisconsin, Sherman found that while arrest deterred employed men from committing domestic violence, being arrested increased repeat violence by 44 percent in unemployed men.[76] Thus, it seems that only those who have "more to lose" by being arrested (such as their jobs, standing in the community, and so on) are likely to be deterred by arrest. As Sherman noted, "Mandatory arrest puts us in the moral dilemma of reducing violence against women who are relatively well off [living with or married to an employed assailant], at the price of increasing violence against women whose abusers are unemployed."[77]

A Return to Discretion?

Mandatory arrest statutes raise other questions. For the most part, the police rely on the victim to report incidents of domestic abuse. Under certain circumstances, the risk that the abuser will be arrested may actually keep the victim from calling the police. A victim in a low-income family might not want to lose the wages that the abuser provides. Similarly, immigrant victims might not want to run the risk that they or their abuser will be deported.[78]

Furthermore, what should the police consider evidence of abuse? A few years ago, professional hockey player Patrick Roy was taken into custody under Colorado's mandatory arrest law even though he did not physically harm his wife. Instead, during an argument, he had torn a door off its hinges, and under state law destruction of property is considered a form of domestic violence.

Finally, what if a victim uses force to protect himself or herself against an abuser? Statistics show that in jurisdictions with mandatory arrest laws, arrests of women under domestic abuse charges have increased dramatically. These women may be less willing to report domestic violence in the future, fearing that they themselves will be arrested again for "abusing" their attackers in self-defense.[79]

To reduce some of the harsher effects of mandatory arrest laws and resolve some of these inconsistencies, Professors Sherman and Berk favor a policy of "presumption of arrest." In other words, after finding evidence of domestic violence, police should make an arrest unless there are "good, clear reasons why an arrest would be counterproductive."[80] Of course, it would be up to the police officers to determine whether these "good, clear reasons" exist, in effect returning to them the ability and the responsibility of using discretion to make the final decision.

1 What reasons can be given to support widespread police discretion in general? What reasons can be given to limit police discretion in general?

2 Why might police officers welcome mandatory arrest laws or any other limitation on their discretionary abilities?

3 Can you think of any other reasons why a victim might *not* call the police if she or he was sure that it would result in the arrest of the abuser?

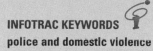

INFOTRAC KEYWORDS

police and domestic violence

For more information, use these search terms with InfoTrac College Edition, your online library at www.infotrac-college.com

Chapter Summary

1 **Describe the first systems of law enforcement in colonial America.** Constables and night watchmen were drawn from the ranks of ordinary citizens. Each colony had a sheriff in each county who selected juries and managed incarcerations. Local citizens assisted sheriffs in peacekeeping duties.

2 **Tell how the patronage system affected policing.** During the political era of policing (1840–1930), bribes paid by citizens and business owners often went into the coffers of the local political party. This became known as the patronage system.

3 **Indicate the results of the Wickersham Commission.** The Wickersham Commission of 1929 called for reform to eliminate police brutality and the corrupting influence of politics. The result was the professionalization of American police, sometimes called the progressive era in American policing. Potential police officers began to be trained in institutes of higher learning. Another result was the increased use of technology in police work.

4 **List five main types of law enforcement agencies.** (a) Municipal police departments; (b) sheriffs' departments; (c) special police agencies, such as those limited to school protection or airport security; (d) state police departments (in all states except Hawaii); and (e) federal law enforcement agencies.

5 **List some of the most important law enforcement agencies under the control of the new Department of Homeland Security.** (a) The Directorate of Customs and Border Security, which oversees the Bureau of Customs and Border Protection, the Bureau of Immigration and Customs Enforcement, the U.S. Border Patrol, and the U.S. Customs Service; and (b) the U.S. Secret Service.

6 **Identify the five investigative priorities of the FBI.** (a) Terrorism, (b) organized crime, (c) foreign intelligence operations in the United States, (d) federal drug offenses, and (e) white-collar crime.

7 **Analyze the importance of private security today.** Businesses and citizens spend $100 billion a year on private security, more than double the amount spent on public law enforcement. Heightened fear of crime and increased crime in the workplace have fueled the growth in spending on private security.

8 **List the four basic responsibilities of the police.** (a) To enforce laws, (b) to provide services, (c) to prevent crime, and (d) to preserve the peace.

9 **Indicate why patrol officers are allowed discretionary powers.** Police officers are considered trustworthy and able to make honest decisions. They have experience and training. They are knowledgeable in criminal behavior. Finally, they must be able to have the discretion to reasonably protect themselves.

 STORIES FROM THE STREET

Go to the Stories from the Street feature at www.cjinaction.com to hear Larry Gaines tell insightful stories related to this chapter and his experiences in the field.

10 Explain how some states have reacted to perceived leniency to perpetrators of domestic violence. Some states have passed mandatory arrest laws, requiring a police officer to arrest a person who has battered a spouse or domestic partner. Such laws eliminate police officers' discretion.

Key Terms

coroner 147
Federal Bureau of
   Investigation (FBI) 153
justice of the peace 139

patronage system 141
private security 156
professional model 143
sheriff 146

shire-reeve 139
tithing system 139

Questions for Critical Analysis

1 What was the major problem faced by the earliest formal American police departments? Why did it occur?

2 Increased professionalism in police forces has been made possible by two-way radios, telephones, and automobiles. In what way has society *not* benefited from this increased professionalism? Explain your answer.

3 The latest era in policing has been called the community era and dates from the 1980s. How does this "new" era differ from the era of professionalism?

4 To what extent are state police complementary to, rather than substitutes for, local law enforcement agencies?

5 What economic and security concerns does the U.S. Customs Service need to balance, and how does it do so?

6 Besides the FBI's five principal investigative priorities, how does that agency benefit local policing units?

7 Why do experts believe that the private security industry will continue to grow for the foreseeable future?

8 Which of the four basic responsibilities of the police do you think is most important? Why?

9 Is it ever possible to completely eliminate discretion in policing? Explain.

TEST PREPARATION ONLINE

Go to www.cjinaction.com for tools to aid you in studying for your exams. Click on *Online Reviews* under *Chapter Resources* for an interactive review of each major section of this chapter. Under *Chapter Resources*, you will also find the *Chapter Outline*, *Chapter Summary*, *Flashcards*, *Glossary*, *Learning Objectives*, *Lecture Presentations*, *Concept Builder*, *Essay Questions*, and a *Tutorial Quiz*. You can also test yourself with a game of *Concentration* or the *Crossword Puzzle*.

Web Resources

Go to www.cjinaction.com for a wealth of online resources. Explore the *Internet Activities* and *Class Projects* under *Chapter Resources*. Check out the *Web Links* to access the Web sites mentioned in the text, as well as many others. You can also access recent perspectives by clicking on *CJ in the News* and *Terrorism Update* under *Course Resources*. If you'd like some mentoring, click on the *Board of Mentors* under *Book Resources*.

Search Online with InfoTrac College Edition

For additional information, explore InfoTrac College Edition, your online library that offers complete full-length articles from thousands of scholarly and popular publications. Click on *InfoTrac College Edition* under *Chapter Resources* at www.cjinaction.com for a list of key words and InfoTrac exercises. Use the passcode that came with your book.

Suggested Readings

DeLong, Candice, and Elisa Petrini, *Special Agent: My Life on the Front Lines as a Woman in the FBI,* New York: Hyperion Press, 2001. DeLong describes her twenty-year career in the FBI, especially the grueling training process at the Quantico training academy. She tells the stories of numerous dangerous arrests that she made. She also refers to the initial hostility to female agents in the 1980s.

Wadman, Robert C., and William Thomas Allison, *To Protect and Serve: A History of Police in America,* Upper Saddle River,

NJ: Prentice Hall, 2003. This book offers a comprehensive and readable look at the development of law enforcement in the United States. In particular, it focuses on the challenge of maintaining law and order in a democratic society, a task that American law enforcement agencies have been dealing with since the earliest days of the nation. The authors also provide a strong survey of the recent history of our police forces, from the increased emphasis on professionalism, to police and technology, to the main issues facing law enforcement in the twenty-first century.

Notes

1. M. K. Nalla and G. R. Newman, "Is White Collar Crime Policing, Policing?" *Policing and Society* 3 (1994), 304.
2. Richard Maxwell Brown, "Vigilante Policing," in *Thinking about Police,* ed. Carl Klockars and Stephen Mastrofski (New York: McGraw-Hill, 1990), 66.
3. Peter K. Manning, *Police Work* (Cambridge, MA: MIT Press, 1977), 82.
4. Carol S. Steiker, "Second Thoughts about First Principles," *Harvard Law Review* 107 (1994), 820.
5. Lawrence M. Friedman, *Crime and Punishment in American History* (New York: Basic Books, 1993), 29.
6. Mark H. Moore and George L. Kelling, "'To Serve and Protect': Learning from Police History," *Public Interest* 70 (1983), 53.
7. Samuel Walker, *The Police in America: An Introduction* (New York: McGraw-Hill, 1983), 7.
8. Moore and Kelling, 54.
9. Mark H. Haller, "Chicago Cops, 1890–1925," in *Thinking about Police,* ed. Carl Klockars and Stephen Mastrofski (New York: McGraw-Hill, 1990), 90.
10. William J. Bopp and Donald O. Shultz, *A Short History of American Law Enforcement* (Springfield, IL: Charles C Thomas, 1977), 109–110.
11. Roger G. Dunham and Geoffrey P. Alpert, *Critical Issues in Policing: Contemporary Issues* (Prospect Heights, IL: Waveland Press, 1989).
12. National Advisory Commission on Civil Disorders, *Report* (Washington, D.C.: U.S. Government Printing Office, 1968), 157–160.
13. 18 U.S.C.A. Sections 2510–2521.
14. Jayne Seagrave, "Defining Community Policing," *American Journal of Police* 1 (1996), 1–22.
15. Federal Bureau of Investigation, *Crime in the United Staes, 2002* (Washington, D.C.: U.S. Department of Justice, 2003), 322.
16. *Ibid.*
17. Matthew J. Hickman and Brian A. Reaves, *Local Police Departments, 2000* (Washington, D.C.: U.S. Department of Justice, January 2003), 2.

18. G. Robert Blakey, "Federal Criminal Law," *Hastings Law Journal* 46 (April 1995), 1175.
19. Vern L. Folley, *American Law Enforcement* (Boston: Allyn & Bacon, 1980), 228.
20. Matthew J. Hickman and Brian A. Reaves, *Sheriffs' Offices, 2000* (Washington, D.C.: U.S. Department of Justice, January 2003), 2.
21. *Ibid.,* 10–14.
22. *Black's Law Dictionary,* 982.
23. Robert Borkenstein, "Police: State Police," *Encyclopedia of Crime and Justice,* ed. Sanford H. Kadish (New York: Free Press, 1983), 1131.
24. Brian A. Reaves and Lynn M. Bauer, *Federal Law Enforcement Officers, 2002* (Washington, D.C.: U.S. Department of Justice, August 2003), 1.
25. Pub. L. No. 107-296, 116 Stat. 2135.
26. "A New Look at USA's Porous Borders," *Law Enforcement News* (December 15–31, 2001), 8.
27. Reaves and Bauer, 5.
28. U.S. Border Patrol Web site at http://www.immigration.gov/graphics/shared/lawenfor/bpatrol/overview.htm#Staffing.
29. "Border Patrol Heats Up Efforts to Curb Desert Deaths," *Law Enforcement News* (April 30, 2003), 8.
30. Tim Weiner, "Border Customs Agents Are Pushed to the Limit," *New York Times* (July 25, 2002), A14.
31. "Feds Have a Plan if Terrorists Strike," *UPI Online* (February 19, 1998).
32. Pub. L. No. 91-513, 84 Stat. 1242 (1970), codified as amended at 21 U.S.C. Section 801 (1994).
33. Jerry Seper, "Federal Agents Clean Up Money-Laundering Operation," *Washington Times* (August 30, 2003), A2.
34. http://www.usdoj.gov/marshals/factsheets/general.htm.
35. William C. Cunningham, "U.S. Security Private Trends," at http://www.lcc.gc.ca/en/ress/conf/conf_flyer/speakers_abstract/cunningham.asp.
36. John B. Owens, "Westec Story: Gated Communities and the Fourth Amendment," *American Criminal Law Review* (Spring 1997), 1138.

37. Cal. Penal Code Section 837 (West 1995).
38. Bruce L. Benson, "Guns, Crime, and Safety," *Journal of Law and Economics* (October 2001), 725.
39. "Private Security Forces Can Replace National Guard at Smaller Airports, Government Says," *Associated Press Newswires* (May 9, 2002).
40. Carlos Sadovi, "Grand Jury Targets E2 Owners," *Chicago Tribune* (July 19, 2003), 12.
41. Jeremy Bagott, "Security Standards Putting Public at Risk," *Chicago Tribune* (February 24, 2003), 15.
42. *Ibid.*
43. Mimi Hall, "Private Security Guards: Homeland Defense's Weak Link," *USA Today* (January 23, 2003), A1.
44. Bruce Madelblit, "A Sorry State of Security?" *Security* (April 1, 2003), 54.
45. 108th Congress, S. 769 (April 2, 2003).
46. William C. Cunningham, John J. Strauchs, and Clifford W. Van Meter, *The Hallcrest Report II: Private Security Trends, 1970 to 2000* (Boston: Butterworth-Heinemann, 1990), 236.
47. Cameron Conant, "Private Security Firms See Improved Status, Job Growth in Recent Months," *Grand Rapids Press* (December 15, 2001), D4.
48. Bagott, 15.
49. Ronnie L. Paynter, "Privatization: Something to Think About?" *Law Enforcement Technology* (September 2000), 6.
50. Ronald L. Soble, "Private Firms on Patrol: Security Is Big Business," *Los Angeles Times* (May 21, 1985), section 1, page 1.
51. Egon Bittner, *The Functions of the Police in a Modern Society,* Public Health Service Publication No. 2059 (Chevy Chase, MD: National Institute of Mental Health, 1970), 38–44.
52. Carl Klockars, "The Rhetoric of Community Policing," in *Community Policing: Rhetoric or Reality,* ed. Jack Greene and Stephen Mastrofski (New York: Praeger Publishers, 1991), 244.
53. Thomas Bercal, "Calls for Police Assistance," *American Behavioral Scientist* 13 (1970), 681–91; and John A.

Webster, "Police Task and Time Study," *Journal of Criminal Law, Criminology, and Police Science* 61 (1970), 94–100.

54. Jack R. Greene and Carl B. Klockars, "What Do Police Do?" in *Thinking about Police,* 2d ed., ed. Carl B. Klockars and Stephen B. Mastrofski (New York: McGraw-Hill, 1991), 273–284.

55. Reprinted in *Police Chief* (January 1990), 18.

56. Eric J. Scott, *Calls for Service: Citizen Demand and Initial Police Response* (Washington, D.C.: U.S. Government Printing Office, 1981), 28–30.

57. Jerome H. Skolnick, "Police: The New Professionals," *New Society* (September 5, 1986), 9–11.

58. Klockars, 250.

59. James Q. Wilson, *Varieties of Police Behavior: The Management of Law and Order in Eight Communities* (Cambridge, MA: Harvard University Press, 1968).

60. James Q. Wilson and George L. Kelling, "Broken Windows," *Atlantic Monthly* (March 1982), 29.

61. A. J. Reiss, Jr., "Police Organization in the Twentieth Century," in *Modern Policing,* ed. Michael Tonry and Norval Morris (Chicago: University of Chicago Press, 1992), 51–98.

62. C. E. Pratt, "Police Discretion," *Law and Order* (March 1992), 99–100.

63. Herbert Jacob, *Urban Justice* (Boston: Little, Brown, 1973), 27.

64. Stephen D. Mastrofski, Jeffrey B. Snipes, Roger B. Parks, and Christopher D. Maxwell, "The Helping Hand of the Law: Police Control of Citizens on Request," *Criminology* 38 (May 2000), 307.

65. "Intimate Partner Violence Fact Sheet," Centers for Disease Control and Prevention Web site, at http://www.cdc.gov/ncipc/factsheets/ipvfacts.htm.

66. Callie Marie Rennison, *Intimate Partner Violence, 1993–2001* (Washington, D.C.: U.S. Department of Justice, February 2003), 1.

67. Patricia Tjaden and Nancy Thoennes, *Prevalence, Incidence, and Consequences of Violence Against Women: Findings from the National Violence Against Women Survey* (Washington, D.C.: National Institute for Justice and Centers for Disease Control and Prevention, 1998), 1.

68. James J. Fyfe, David A. Klinger, and Jeanne M. Flavin, "Differential Police Treatment of Male-on-Female Spousal Violence," *Criminology* 35 (August 1997), 455–473.

69. L. Craig Parker, Robert D. Meier, and Lynn Hunt Monahan, *Interpersonal Psychology for Criminal Justice* (St. Paul, MN: West Publishing Co., 1989), 113.

70. Douglas R. Marvin, "The Dynamics of Domestic Abuse," *FBI Law Enforcement Bulletin* (July 1997), 13–19.

71. David Hirschel and Eve Buzawa, "Understanding the Context of Dual Arrest with Directions for Future Research," *Violence Against Women* 8 (2002), 1451.

72. Lawrence W. Sherman and Ellen G. Cohn, "The Impact of Research on Legal Policy: The Minneapolis Domestic Violence Experiment," *Law and Society Review* 23 (1989), 261.

73. Ellen Pence, "The Duluth Domestic Abuse Intervention Project," *Hamline Law Review* 6 (1983), 258.

74. J. David Hirschel and Ira W. Hutchison, "Realities and Implications of the Charlotte Spousal Abuse Experiment," in *Do Arrests and Restraining Orders Work?* ed. Eve S. Buzawa and Carl G. Buzawa (Thousand Oaks, CA: Sage Publications, 1996), 54–55.

75. Franklyn W. Dunford *et al.,* "The Role of Arrest in Domestic Assault: The Omaha Police Experiment," *Criminology* 28 (1990), 167.

76. *Ibid.*

77. Quoted in Roger Worthington, "Value of Mandatory Arrest for Women Beaters Questioned," *Chicago Tribune* (November 19, 1991), C5.

78. Donna Coker, "Shifting Power for Battered Women: Law, Material Resources, and Poor Women of Color," *University of California at Davis Law Review* (Summer 2000), 1042.

79. Cecelia M. Expenoza, "No Relief for the Weary: VAWA Relief Denied for Battered Immigrants," *Marquette Law Review* 83 (1999), 163.

80. Lawrence W. Sherman and Richard A. Berk, "The Specific Deterrence Effects of Arrest for Domestic Assault," *American Society Review* 49 (1984), 270.

>Chapter 6<

Challenges to Effective Policing

># chapter outline <

- Recruitment and Training: Becoming a Police Officer
- Police Organization
- Refocusing on the Community
- Law Enforcement in the Field
- "Us versus Them": Issues in Modern Policing
- Police Ethics
- Criminal Justice in Action—The Globalization of Law Enforcement

># chapter objectives <

After reading this chapter, you should be able to:

1 Explain some of the benefits of a culturally diverse police force.

2 List three criticisms of standard bureaucratic police organizations.

3 Describe the theory behind a differential response strategy of responding to calls for service.

4 Explain community policing and its strategies.

5 Describe two types of problem-solving policing.

6 List the three primary purposes of police patrol.

7 Indicate some investigation strategies that are considered aggressive.

8 Determine when police officers are justified in using deadly force.

9 Identify the three traditional forms of police corruption.

10 Explain what an ethical dilemma is and name four categories of ethical dilemmas typically facing a police officer.

The Final Straw

African American residents of Benton Harbor, Michigan, do not trust the police, and they have not trusted the police for a long time. Too many fellow blacks have died over the past fifteen years, they believe, because of racist police action. In 1991, a teen-ager named Eric McGinnis drowned under mysterious circumstances. Law enforcement officials said McGinnis fell into the St. Joseph River while fleeing the police after breaking into a car. Members of the African American community insist that he was murdered for dating a white girl. A few years later, seven-year-old Trent Patterson was killed when he was struck by the car of a man fleeing police officers.

Then, in the spring of 2003, Arthur Partee was choked to death during a struggle with the police at his home. Two months later, Terrance Shurn died after crashing his motorcycle into an abandoned building while being chased by the highway patrol. Reaction to Shurn's death was swift and violent— three nights of rioting that destroyed several dozen buildings and caused hundreds of thousands of dollars in damage. "We're just tired," remarked one Benton Harbor local, trying to explain the violence. "We're sick of them killing us."

AP Photo/*The Herald-Palladium*, Neal Vaughan

Police officers move toward a building set on fire during a series of riots in Benton Harbor, Michigan, following the death of an African American motorist.

> **A community is in trouble** when people start referring to themselves as "us" and law enforcement agents as "them." Ideally, police would like to be seen as an integral part of society, with the same goals of crime prevention and public safety as everybody else. When the relationship between police officers and those they serve is marked by ill will and distrust, those goals will be very difficult to reach. In Benton Harbor, Terrance Shurn was wearing a full-face helmet and gloves, making it impossible for Wesley Koza, the police officer in pursuit, to know the color of his skin. Because of past incidents, however, the city's African Americans were absolutely unwilling to give Koza the benefit of the doubt. (Officials eventually cleared Koza of any racial motivation in the chase.)

Most Americans cannot imagine the on-the-job situations that the average law enforcement agent faces daily. As James Fyfe of Temple University explains, by telling police officers that we expect them to eradicate crime, we are putting them in a "no win war." Like some soldiers in such combat, Fyfe adds, "they commit atrocities."[1] In this chapter, we will examine some of these "atrocities," such as police brutality and corruption. We will also consider the possible causes of police misconduct and review the steps that are being taken to limit these problems. Our discussion begins with a look at how a person becomes a police officer—a process that can have a significant impact on the quality of law enforcement in small communities such as Benton Harbor and in the United States as a whole.

CONCEPT BUILDER

Ethical considerations are relevant to any occupation, but especially so for police who are public figures sworn to uphold the law. Visit www.cjinaction.com for an interactive exploration of this key topic.

Recruitment and Training: Becoming a Police Officer

In 1961, police expert James H. Chenoweth commented that the methods used to hire police officers had changed little since 1829 when the Metropolitan Police of London was created.[2] The past forty years, however, have seen a number of improvements on the original model. Efforts have been made to diversify police rolls, and recruits in most police departments undergo a substantial array of tests and screens—discussed below—to determine their aptitude. Furthermore, annual starting salaries of up to $50,000, along with the opportunities offered by an interesting profession in the public service field, have attracted a wide variety of applicants to police work. (To learn what a police officer can expect to earn in his or her first year on the job, see Figure 6.1.)

BASIC REQUIREMENTS

The selection process involves a number of steps, and each police department has a different method of choosing candidates. Most agencies, however, require at a minimum that a police officer:

> Be a U.S. citizen.

> Not have been convicted of a felony.

> Have or be eligible to have a driver's license in the state where the department is located.

> Be at least twenty-one years of age.

Beyond these minimum requirements, police departments usually engage in extensive background checks, including drug tests; a review of the applicant's educational, military, and driving records; credit checks; interviews with spouses, acquaintances, and previous employers; and a Federal Bureau of Investigation (FBI)

FIGURE 6.1 Average Annual Salary for Entry-Level Officers by Size of Population Served

Source: Matthew J. Hickman and Brian A. Reaves, *Local Police Departments 2000* (Washington, D.C.: U.S. Department of Justice, January 2003), Table 14, page 8.

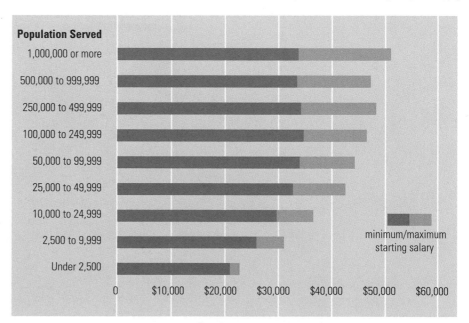

search to determine whether the applicant has been convicted of any criminal acts.[3] Police agencies generally require certain physical attributes in applicants: normally, they must be able to pass a physical agility or fitness test. (For an example of one such test, see Figure 6.2.)

Age is also a factor, as few departments will accept candidates younger than twenty-one years of age or older than forty-five. In some departments, the applicant must take a polygraph (lie-detector) exam in conjunction with the background check. The results of the polygraph exam are often compared to the information from the background check to ensure that the applicant has not been deceptive. According to one study, around 20 percent of the nearly 70,000 persons who apply for police jobs annually are rejected because they lied during the screening process.[4]

The Oakland Police Academy, located in Auburn Hills, Michigan, is a full-service police training facility. To visit its Web site, click on *Web Links* under *Chapter Resources* at www.cjinaction.com

Educational Requirements   One of the most dramatic differences between today's police recruits and those of several generations ago is their level of education. In the 1920s, when August Vollmer began promoting the need for higher education in police officers, few had attended college. By the 1990s, 65 percent of police officers had some college credits and 25 percent were college graduates.[5] Today, 83 percent of all local police departments require at least a high school diploma, and 8 percent require a degree from a two-year college.[6] Recruits with college or university experience are generally seen as having an advantage in hiring and promotion.[7]

Not all police observers believe, however, that education is a necessity for police officers. In the words of one police officer, "effective street cops learn their skills on the job, not in a classroom."[8] By emphasizing a college degree, say some, police departments discourage those who would make solid officers but lack the education necessary to apply for positions in law enforcement.

Training   Almost every state requires that police recruits pass through a training period during which they are taught the basics of police work and are under con-

---

FIGURE 6.2   **Physical Agility Exam for the Henrico County (Virginia) Division of Police**

Those applying for the position of police officer must finish this physical agility exam within 3 minutes, 30 seconds. During the test, applicants are required to wear the equipment (with a total weight of between 9 and 13 pounds) worn by patrol officers, which includes: the police uniform; leather gun belt; firearm; baton; portable radio; and ballistics vest.

1   Applicant begins test seated in a police vehicle, door closed, seat belt fastened.

2   Applicant must exit vehicle and jump or climb a six-foot barrier.

3   Applicant then completes a one-quarter mile run or walk, making various turns along the way (to simulate a pursuit run).

4   Applicant must jump a simulated five-foot culvert/ditch.

5   Applicant must drag a "human simulator" (dummy) weighing 175 pounds a distance of 50 feet (to simulate a situation in which an officer is required to pull or carry an injured person to safety).

6   Applicant must draw his or her weapon and fire five rounds with the strong hand and five rounds with the weak hand.

Source: Henrico County Division of Police.

stant observation by superiors. The training period usually has two components: the police academy and field training. On average, local police departments require 1,054 hours of training—637 hours in the classroom and 417 hours in the field.[9]

The *police academy,* run by either the state or a police agency, provides recruits with a controlled, militarized environment in which they receive their introduction to the world of the police officer. They are taught the laws of search, seizure, arrest, and interrogation; how and when to use weapons; the procedures of securing a crime scene and interviewing witnesses; first aid; self-defense; and other essentials of police work. Academy instructors evaluate the recruits' performance and send intermittent progress reports to police administrators.

Field training takes place outside the confines of the police academy. A recruit is paired with an experienced police officer known as a field training officer (FTO). The goal of field training is to help rookies apply the concepts they have learned in the academy "to the streets," with the FTO playing a supervisory role to make sure that nothing goes awry. According to many, the academy introduces recruits to the formal rules of police work, but field training gives the rookies their first taste of the informal rules. In fact, the initial advice to recruits from some FTOs is along the lines of "O.K., kid. Forget everything you learned in the academy. You're in the real world now." Nonetheless, the academy is a critical component in the learning process, as it provides rookies with a road map to the job.

RECRUITING MEMBERS OF MINORITY GROUPS AND WOMEN

For many years, the typical American police officer was white and male. As recently as 1968, African Americans represented only 5 percent of all sworn officers in the United States, and the percentage of "women in blue" was even less.[10] Only within the past twenty-five years has this situation been addressed, and only within the past decade have many police departments actively tried to recruit women, African Americans, Hispanics, Asian Americans, and other members of minority groups.

Discrimination and the Law   Initially, external pressures drove law enforcement agencies to take these steps. The 1964 Civil Rights Act and its 1972 amendments guaranteed minorities and women equal access to jobs in law enforcement, and the Equal Employment Opportunity Act of 1972 set the stage for affirmative action in hiring and promotion. Court decisions also played a role: in several cases in the 1970s, the United States Supreme Court ruled that police departments could be held in violation of federal law if their hiring and promotion policies were tainted by racial discrimination.[11]

The Benefits of a Culturally Diverse Police Force   Not all of the efforts to increase minority representation in law enforcement are simply the

Field Training
The segment of a police recruit's training in which he or she is removed from the classroom and placed on the beat, under the supervision of a senior officer.

Adam Kasanof at Columbia University, where he studied Latin before becoming a New York City police officer. Although police work is still not considered an intellectual activity, the ranks of departments across the country are more highly educated than at any time in this nation's history. Many officers such as Kasanof are graduates from "elite" schools. They are sometimes considered "eggheads with a shield" by fellow officers. Members of academia also question the life of a cop for an Ivy Leaguer; one of Kasanof's professors called him a "saintly madman." What stereotypes of the police profession do these attitudes reflect?

NYT Pictures/Edward Keating

result of orders from the Congress and the Supreme Court. (See Figure 6.3 for information on how this representation has improved in recent years.) Many departments, particularly those in urban areas, have realized that a culturally diverse police force can offer a number of benefits, including improved community relations and higher levels of service.[12]

For example, after a series of racially motivated riots in 1967, Detroit decided to institute quotas to increase its percentage of black police officers—which had been 5 percent in a city that was more than 50 percent African American. In defending itself during a court case that challenged the constitutionality of these quotas, the city argued that it needed a representative police force to fulfill its duties to the citizens of Detroit. The Sixth Circuit Court of Appeals agreed, noting that the presence of a "mostly white police force in minority communities can be a 'dangerous irritant' which can trigger" a destructive response.[13] In 1986, United States Supreme Court Justice John Paul Stevens agreed, stating that police administrators "might reasonably conclude that an integrated police force could develop a better relationship and thereby do a more effective job of maintaining law and order than a force composed of white officers."[14]

Police Diversity in Boston and New York   Efforts to recruit African Americans, Hispanics, and other minorities are generally hampered by a lack of aggressiveness on the part of police recruiters and the continuing negative view of law enforcement in minority communities.[15] The different experiences of Boston and New York show, however, that a well-designed recruitment strategy can aid in integrating the police.

In the 1970s, both cities had similarly low percentages of African Americans on their police forces. Today, 24 percent of the police officers in Boston are black—a percentage that is actually higher than black representation in the city. In New York, by contrast, only 14 percent of the police force is African American—about half the percentage of the city's black population.[16]

What accounts for the difference? First, Boston's hiring standards are more conducive to minority representation. The city accepts high school graduates, while New York requires two years of college, a condition that disproportionately disqualifies minorities. Furthermore, about a decade ago Boston enacted an ordinance that requires all municipal employees to be city residents, making it more likely that the racial and ethnic composition of the police will mirror that of the city. New York has no such residency requirement. Lastly and perhaps most importantly, the starting salary for a beginning Boston police officer is about $10,000 more than for a counterpart in New York. Becoming a police officer is, in the words of one observer, "the best job in Boston for someone with a high school diploma."[17]

Women in Policing   If anything, the barriers against women in law enforcement have been greater than those facing racial and ethnic minorities. As of 1946, only 141 out of 417 American cities had any policewomen at

FIGURE 6.3 Female and Minority Police Officers, 1990 and 2000

Source: Matthew J. Hickman and Brian A. Reaves, *Local Police Departments 2000* (Washington, D.C.: U.S. Department of Justice, January 2003), Figure 2, page 4.

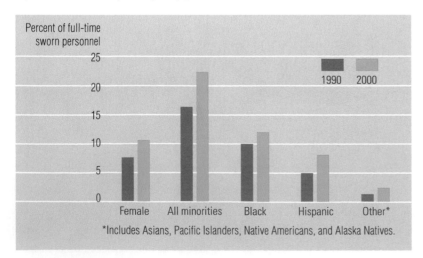

> Women Make Bad Cops

S ince the formation of the earliest police departments in the nineteenth century, policing has been seen as "man's work." Only men were considered to have the physical strength necessary to deal with the dangers of the street.

> The Myth

The perception that women are not physically strong enough to be effective law enforcement officers prevails both in the public mind and within police forces themselves. Criminologist Susan Martin has found that policewomen are under "constant pressure to demonstrate their competence and effectiveness vis-à-vis their male counterparts." One female police officer describes her experience:

> I got a call. They send another male officer and then another male officer. The attitude is—get a guy. I'm there with the one male officer and when the other guy shows up, the first male officer says to the second, this is right in front of me—"I'm glad you came."

> The Reality

A number of studies have shown, however, that policewomen can be as effective as men in most situations, and often more so. Citizens appear to prefer dealing with a female police officer rather than a male during service calls—especially those that involve domestic violence. In general, policewomen are less aggressive and more likely to reduce the potential for a violent situation by relying on verbal skills rather than their authority as law enforcement agents. According to a study conducted by the

Copyright © Dwayne Newton/PhotoEdit

Two members of the San Francisco (California) Police Department.

National Center for Women & Policing, payouts in lawsuits for cases of brutality and misconduct involving male officers exceed those involving females by a ratio of 43 to 1.

FOR CRITICAL ANALYSIS
Anecdotal evidence tells us that policewomen still face a great deal of bias from male police officers and that sexual harassment still occurs in many departments. What effect might a "male-dominated" police department have on attempts to recruit and keep women as law enforcement officers? What steps can the heads of police departments take to improve the situation?

all, and it was not until 1968 that a city—Indianapolis—had two female patrol officers on the force.[18] During the 1990s, the number of women in law enforcement grew by only 5.3 percent.[19] (See the feature *CJ in Focus—Myth versus Reality: Women Make Bad Cops*.)

Unlike with members of minority groups, a law enforcement agency can legally discriminate against women in recruitment and hiring. Often, the instrument of this discrimination is the physical fitness test. In California, for example, by state law all applicants must scale a six-foot wall to be considered for a police job. Officials estimate that this requirement eliminates half the women who apply because they do not possess the physical strength to get over the wall.[20]

In 2002, the Third Circuit Court of Appeals upheld a similar Pennsylvania law that requires transit police officers to run 1.5 miles in twelve minutes. Even though the effect of this test is to discriminate against female applicants, 93 percent of whom fail the test, the court ruled that the requirement is legal because it represents a reasonable "minimum qualification" that any applicant, regardless of gender, needs to be able to meet to serve the citizens of Pennsylvania.[21] Of course, police departments that value a diverse force may adjust their physical fitness tests to level the playing field. The Champaign (Illinois) Police Department, for example, requires male applicants to run 1.5 miles in thirteen minutes and female applicants to complete the course in sixteen minutes.[22]

↗ ONLINE REVIEW *Go to the book's Web site for an interactive review of this section*

Police Organization

Studies have shown that female police officers are particularly effective in the area of community relations.[23] Consequently, police administrators have an incentive to recruit more women, because "connecting" with the public has become an important organizational objective for law enforcement agencies. Police departments are indeed organizations, and like most organizations, they have missions, goals, structures, managers, workers, and clients.[24]

The ultimate goal for any police department is to reach its maximum efficiency—to provide the best service to the community with limited resources such as staff and budget. Although some police departments are experimenting with alternative structures based on a partnership between management and the officers in the field,[25] most continue to rely on the hierarchical structure described below.

THE STRUCTURE OF THE POLICE DEPARTMENT

Each police department is organized according to its environment: the size of its jurisdiction, the type of crimes it must deal with, and the demographics of the population it must police. A police department in a racially diverse city often faces different challenges than a department in a homogeneous one. Geographic location also influences police organization. The make-up of the police department in Miami, Florida, for example, is partially determined by the fact that the city is a gateway for illegal drugs from Central and South America. The department directs a high percentage of its resources to special drug-fighting units and has formed cooperative partnerships with federal agencies such as the FBI and the U.S. Customs Service in an effort to stop the flow of narcotics and weapons into the South Florida area.

Hierarchal Structure Whatever the size or location of a police department, it needs a clear rank structure and strict accountability to function properly.[26] One of the goals of the police reformers, especially beginning in the 1950s, was to lessen the corrupting influence of politicians. The result was a move toward a militaristic organization of police.[27] As you can see in Figure 6.4, a typical police department is based on a chain of command that leads from the police chief down through the various levels of the department. In this formalized structure, all persons are aware of their place in the chain and of their duties and responsibilities within the organization.

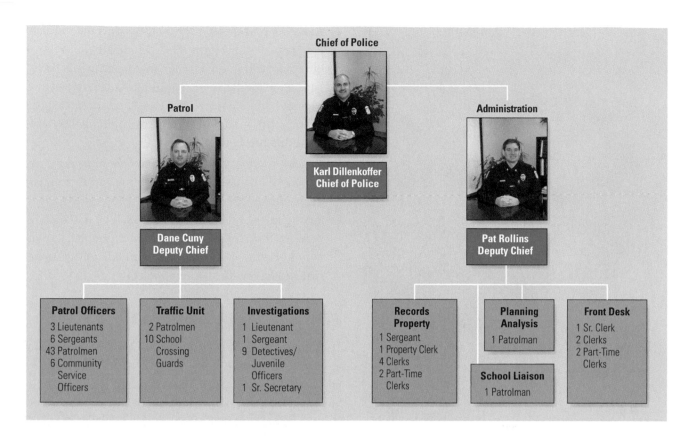

Chief of Police

Karl Dillenkoffer
Chief of Police

Patrol

Dane Cuny
Deputy Chief

Administration

Pat Rollins
Deputy Chief

Patrol Officers	**Traffic Unit**	**Investigations**	**Records Property**	**Planning Analysis**	**Front Desk**
3 Lieutenants 6 Sergeants 43 Patrolmen 6 Community Service Officers	2 Patrolmen 10 School Crossing Guards	1 Lieutenant 1 Sergeant 9 Detectives/ Juvenile Officers 1 Sr. Secretary	1 Sergeant 1 Property Clerk 4 Clerks 2 Part-Time Clerks	1 Patrolman	1 Sr. Clerk 2 Clerks 2 Part-Time Clerks

School Liaison

1 Patrolman

Delegation of authority is a critical component of the chain of command, especially in larger departments. The chief of police delegates authority to division chiefs, who delegate authority to commanders, and so on down through the organization. This structure creates a situation in which nearly every member of a police department is directly accountable to a superior. As was the original goal of police reformers, these links encourage discipline and control and lessen the possibility that any individual police employee will have the unsupervised freedom to abuse her or his position.[28] In keeping with the need to delegate authority, police departments in large cities divide their jurisdictions into *precincts*. The precinct commander is then held responsible by his or her superiors at police headquarters for the performance of the officers in the precinct.

Criticisms of Police Organization   The model of the modern police department is bureaucratic. In a **bureaucracy,** formal rules govern an individual's actions and relationships with co-employees. Today, the word *bureaucracy* often has a negative connotation. For some, it conjures up visions of depersonalized automatons performing their chores without any sensitivity to the needs of those they serve. This stigma has not bypassed police organizations, which have been criticized for:

1 *Limiting personal ingenuity.* The more rules that are placed on individuals, the less ability they have to use their particular skills in solving a problem. Many people choose police work as a career because they see it as an alternative to the deskbound, "9 to 5" routine that seems to characterize many other occupations. Regulations add a measure of drudgery to the job that many officers find personally and professionally limiting. In some instances, *groupthink* can take over, as members of the police force blindly follow rules and suppress tendencies toward individual initiative.

FIGURE 6.4
The Command Chain of the Lombard (Illinois) Police Department
The Lombard (Illinois) Police Department is made up of seventy-three sworn law enforcement officers and thirty-three civilians. As you can see, the chain of command runs from the chief of police down to crossing guards and part-time secretaries.

Source: Lombard Police Department.

Delegation of Authority
The principles of command on which most police departments are based; personnel take orders from and are responsible to those in positions of power directly above them.

Bureaucracy
A hierarchically structured administrative organization that carries out specific functions.

A lieutenant (in the white shirt) gives instructions to two sergeants. To the extreme left, a patrol officer appears to be awaiting instructions. How do the delegation of authority and the chain of command contribute to police efficiency?

Incident-Driven Policing
A reactive approach to policing that emphasizes a speedy response to calls for service.

Response Time
A measurement of police efficiency based on the rapidity with which calls for service are answered.

2 *Limiting contact with the community.* One of the initial purposes of reform was to eradicate police abuse of citizens. Now, however, many departments seem to have gone too far in promoting distance between officers and "the people."[29] (As we shall see later in the chapter, the spread of community policing has lessened this problem.)

3 *Limiting contact among members of the police department.* By sharply delineating relationships within a department, the delegation of authority can limit contact among members at different ranks. The distance between a patrol officer and the police chief, as evident in Figure 6.4 on page 179, practically assures the two will have little, if any, contact.

STRIVING FOR EFFICIENCY

If the ultimate goal of a bureaucratic organization is efficiency, have police bureaucracies made departments more efficient? This question is difficult to answer. On the whole, any bureaucracy responds best to statistical measures. In the era of professional policing, the double yardsticks of statistical efficiency for police have been (1) response time and (2) arrest rates.

Response Time and Efficiency   Though police do not like to think of themselves as being at "the beck and call" of citizens, that is essentially the *modus operandi* of many law enforcement officers. All departments practice **incident-driven policing,** in which calls for service are the primary instigators of action. Between 40 and 60 percent of police activity is the result of 911 calls or other citizen requests, which means that only about half of such activity is initiated by a police officer in the field.[30]

The speed with which the police respond to calls for service has traditionally been seen as a crucial aspect of crime fighting and crime prevention. The ideal scenario in incident-driven policing is as follows: a citizen sees a person committing a crime and calls 911; the police arrive quickly and catch the perpetrator in the act. Or, a citizen who is the victim of a crime, such as a mugging, calls 911 as soon as possible, and the police arrive to catch the mugger before she or he can flee the immediate area of the crime. Although, as we shall see, such scenarios are quite rare in real life, **response time,** or the time elapsed between the instant a call for service is received and the instant the police arrive on the scene, has become a benchmark for police efficiency.

Differential Response   Many police departments have come to realize that overall response time is not as critical as response time for the most important calls. In Dallas, Texas, the overall response time rose from 10 minutes in 1986 to 23 minutes in 1996, drawing criticism from local politicians. The Dallas Police Department, however, pointed out that the response time for calls involving shootings, knifings, and robberies had actually dropped—from 9.7 minutes in 1986 to 7.3 minutes in 1996.[31]

The Dallas police had instituted a **differential response** strategy, in which the department distinguishes among different calls for service so that it can respond more quickly to the most serious incidents. Suppose, for example, that a police department receives two calls for service at the same time. The first caller reports that her house is in the process of being robbed, and the second says that he has returned home to find his automobile missing. If the department has instituted a differential response strategy, the robbery in progress—a "hot" crime—will receive immediate attention. The missing automobile—a "cold" crime that could have been committed several hours earlier—will receive attention "as time permits," and the caller may even be asked to make an appointment to come to the station. (See Figure 6.5 for possible responses to calls to a 911 operator.)

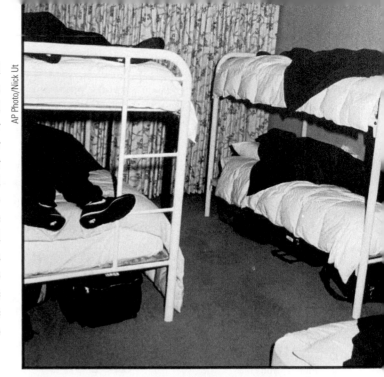

AP Photo/Nick Ut

Arrest Rates and Efficiency   The other measure of police efficiency, arrest rates, also seems logical. The more arrests a police department makes, the fewer the number of criminals there should be on the streets of the community.

Again, practice does not necessarily follow theory. The amount of crime is not a function of arrest rates; self-reported surveys show that many, if not most, criminal acts do not lead to arrests. To make a generalization, police will never be able to make an arrest for *every* crime that is committed. Observers have offered other, more specific reasons for a possible disconnect between arrest rates and crime

Police discovery of the mass suicide of thirty-nine members of the Heaven's Gate cult in Rancho Santa Fe, California, provided an example of both the strengths and the weaknesses of calls for service. Former cult member Rio DiAngelo, the first person to discover the bodies, called 911 and told the emergency dispatcher what he had found. For some undetermined reason, however, San Diego County sheriff's deputies did not respond to DiAngelo's call until two hours later. What factors might contribute to police not quickly responding to a call under such circumstances?

FIGURE 6.5   **Putting the Theory of Differential Response into Action**

Differential response strategies are based on a simple concept: treat emergencies like emergencies and nonemergencies like nonemergencies. As you see, calls for service that involve "hot crimes" will be dealt with immediately, while those that report "cold crimes" will be dealt with at some point in the future.

"HOT" CALLS FOR SERVICE—IMMEDIATE RESPONSE

Complaint to 911 Officer	Rationale
"I just got home from work, and I can see someone in my bedroom through the window."	Possibility that the intruder is committing a crime.
"My husband has a baseball bat, and he's says he's going to kill me."	Crime in progress.
"A woman in a green jacket just grabbed my purse and ran away."	Chances of catching the suspect are increased with immediate action.

"COLD" CALLS FOR SERVICE—ALTERNATIVE RESPONSE

Complaint to 911 Officer	Rationale
"I got to my office about two hours ago, but I just noticed that the fax machine was stolen at some point during the night."	The crime occurred at least two hours earlier.
"The guy in the apartment above me has been selling pot for years, and I'm sick and tired of it."	Not an emergency situation.
"My husband came home late two nights ago with a black eye, and I finally got him to admit that he didn't run into a doorknob. Larry Smith smacked him."	Past crime with a known suspect who is unlikely to flee.

Source: Adapted from John S. Dempsey, *An Introduction to Policing*, 2d ed. (Belmont, CA: West/Wadsworth Company, 1999), Table 8.1, page 175.

Differential Response
A strategy for answering calls for service in which response time is adapted to the seriousness of the call.

rates. One explanation is that, given the amount of paperwork each arrest forces upon a police officer, more arrests mean less time for crime prevention.[32] Perhaps arrest rates and crime rates would prove more consistent if all arrests were made for serious crimes. But, as we have discussed, this is not the case. Most arrests are for misdemeanors, not felonies. Furthermore, arrests are poor predictors of incarceration: one study found that nearly sixty times more Americans are arrested than are sent to prison each year.[33]

In sum, it is difficult to measure the effectiveness of the police. Even crime rates are at least partially determined by elements beyond police control, such as the sociological, biological, and psychological factors discussed in Chapter 2. Hence, crime rates cannot be relied on as definitive indicators of the job a police department is doing.

↗ ONLINE REVIEW *Go to the book's Web site for an interactive review of this section*

INFOTRAC KEYWORDS

community policing

For more information, use this search term with InfoTrac College Edition, your online library at www.infotrac-college.com

Redlands (California) police officer Stephen Crane takes part in a one-legged jumping race with neighborhood children. The race was sponsored by Redlands's Risked Focus Policing Program, which works to reduce juvenile delinquency in the community. How can establishing friendly relations with citizens help law enforcement agencies reduce crime?

Refocusing on the Community

An additional measure of police effectiveness, which has only recently been recognized, is *citizen satisfaction*. As all businesspersons know, the customers are the most important people in any service industry (which includes police work), and the greater the effort to listen to customers' concerns, the greater their level of satisfaction will be. In analyzing the results of a foot patrol experiment in Flint, Michigan, in which the police department made a concerted effort to forge bonds with citizens, Robert Trojanowicz of Michigan State University found a significant increase in citizen confidence in police performance.[34]

This strategy of increasing police presence in the community has been part of, in the words of George Kelling, a "quiet revolution" in American law enforcement over the past two decades.[35] This revolution has been fueled by the emergence of two theories of police strategy, now combined under the umbrella term of *community policing:* community-oriented policing and problem-oriented policing. Though conceptually different, both theories are based on the philosophy that to prevent and control crime effectively, police need to form partnerships with members of the community.

AP Photo/Damian Dovarganes

COMMUNITY POLICING

For all its negative associations, the political era of policing (discussed in Chapter 5) did have characteristics that many observers have come to see as advantageous. During the nineteenth century, police were much more involved in the community than they were after the reforms. Police officers performed many duties that today are associated with social services, such as operating soup kitchens and providing lodging for homeless people. They also played a more direct role in keeping public order by "running in" drunks and intervening in minor disturbances.[36]

Return to the Community To a certain extent, **community policing** advocates a return to this understanding of the police mission. In general, community policing can be defined as an approach that promotes community-police partnerships, proactive problem solving, and community engagement to address issues such as fear of crime and the causes of crime in a particular area.[37] In the reform era, the police were, in a sense, detached from the community. They did their jobs to the best of their ability, but were more concerned with making arrests or speedily answering calls for service than learning about the problems or concerns of the citizenry. In their efforts to eliminate police corruption, administrators put more emphasis on segregating the police from the public than on cooperatively working with citizens to resolve community problems. Under community policing, patrol officers have much more freedom to improvise. They are expected to develop personal relationships with residents and to encourage those residents to become involved in making the community a safer place. (See *Mastering Concepts—The Professional Model of Policing versus Community Policing*.)

Thinking Locally Local initiatives have played a significant role in the community era of policing. When the Bridgeport (Connecticut) Police Department

Community Policing
A policing philosophy that emphasizes community support for and cooperation with the police in preventing crime. Community policing stresses a police role that is less centralized and more proactive than reform era policing strategies.

MASTERING CONCEPTS

> **The** Professional **Model of Policing versus Community Policing**

The past sixty years have seen two dominant trends in the style of American policing. The first was the professional model, designed to reduce corruption and improve performance by emphasizing efficiency. The second, community policing, was a reaction against the professional model, which many thought went too far in relying on statistics and technology. The main characteristics of these two trends are summarized below.

PROFESSIONAL MODEL OF POLICING

- The separation of policing from politics.
- Reduced emphasis on the social-service function of police, with resources and strategies directed toward crime control.
- Limits placed on police discretion; emphasis placed on following guidelines and respecting the authority of the law.
- Centralized, bureaucratic police departments.
- The promotion of a certain distance between police officers and citizens, also the result of increased use of automobile patrols as opposed to foot patrols.
- Main strategies:
  1. Rapid response to calls for service, made possible by technological innovations such as the two-way radio.
  2. Preventive patrol, which attempts to use police presence to deter criminal activity.

COMMUNITY POLICING

- Although professionalism is still valued, it is tempered by recognition that police serve the community and its citizens, as well as the ideal of the law.
- Decentralized, less bureaucratic police departments, allowing more authority and discretion to rest in the hands of police officers.
- Recognition that crime control is only one function of law enforcement, to be included with crime prevention and the provision of social services.
- A more intimate relationship between police and citizens, which comes from an understanding that police officers can do only so much to fight crime; ultimately, they need the cooperation of the community to be successful.
- Main strategies:
  1. Return to foot patrol to "reconnect" with the community.
  2. Problem solving, which treats crimes not just as isolated incidents but as "problems" that can be "solved" with innovative, long-term approaches.

decided to target a high-crime neighborhood known as the "Beirut of Bridgeport," it adopted community policing methodology. The department opened a Strategic Interventions for High-Risk Youth office in the neighborhood and invited citizens to attend meetings there to discuss their crime problems. A Neighborhood Watch Council was founded, and both police and citizens worked to improve the appearance of the area. Within four years, overall crime rates in the neighborhood dropped 75 percent.[38]

The Columbia (South Carolina) Police Department has taken the idea of community involvement to the extreme with its adoption of the Japanese *koban* system. A *koban* is a mini–police station where police officers live as well as work. The initial *koban* in Columbia was set up on Lady Street, which runs through one of the city's high-crime neighborhoods. Two volunteer police officers stay rent free in the upper floor of the building, while the lower floor is a police station/ community center. Residents are encouraged to come to the *koban* to report crimes, and it also serves as a work station for social and educational services. According to Charles Austin, Columbia's police chief, the *koban* is a sign to residents that the police have "a vested stake in the community."[39]

These programs and others across the country typify the essence of community policing. First, they show how the police can engage in problem solving as opposed to only responding to calls for service. Second, they are examples of how the police are attempting to forge partnerships with neighborhoods or community groups. Finally, the programs illustrate how the police can engage the community by encouraging citizens' active involvement in crime and disorder problems.

PROBLEM-SOLVING POLICING

Problem solving, a key component of community policing, has its roots in **problem-solving policing,** which was introduced by Herman Goldstein of the Police Executive Research Forum in the late 1970s. Goldstein's basic premise was that police departments were devoting too many of their resources to reacting to calls for service and too few to "acting on their own initiative to prevent or reduce community problems."[40] To rectify this situation, problem-solving policing moves beyond simply responding to incidents and attempts instead to control or even solve the root causes of criminal behavior.

Goldstein's theory was in direct contrast to the reform era theories of policing, discussed in the previous chapter.[41] Goldstein was suggesting that patrol officers must become intimately involved with citizens. For example, instead of responding to a call concerning illegal drug use by simply arresting the offender— a short-term response—the patrol officers should also look at the long-term implications of the situation. They should analyze the pattern of similar arrests in the area and interview the arrestee to determine the reasons, if any, that the site had been selected for drug activity.[42] Then additional police actions should be taken to prevent further drug sales at the identified location.

Hot Spots   According to the tenets of reform era policing, patrol officers should be spread evenly throughout a precinct, giving each citizen the same level of service. Many observers find this shortsighted, at best. Professor Lawrence Sherman compares it to giving every citizen an equal dose of penicillin—whether that person is sick or not.[43]

Some say a more practical response is for police to concentrate on **hot spots,** or areas of high criminal activity. Minneapolis police discovered, for example, that 100 percent of the robberies in a certain year occurred in only 2 percent of the city's zip codes.[44] Similarly, law enforcement officials in Jersey City, New Jersey, found that fifty-six hot spots of drug activity (occupying 4.4 percent of the city's street sections) accounted for 45 percent of the city's narcotics sales arrests and 46 percent of emergency calls for service.[45]

In both cases, the city's police department took part in experiments in which extra patrol coverage—in brief bursts of activity—was directed to a select number of the hot spots. In Minneapolis, robbery rates in the targeted hot spots fell by more than 20 percent, and in both cities, calls for service reporting public disorder also decreased. Neither police department, however, concluded that the hot spots experiment had decreased overall crime. Criminals had simply moved to other areas, or "scattered like cockroaches in the light," as one observer put it.[46]

Crime Mapping   Many police departments are using *crime mapping* technology to locate and identify hot spots. A new generation of geographic information systems (GISs) provides departments with colored maps that allow them to easily spot patterns of crime and determine where increased coverage is needed. (See Figure 6.6.) With the press of a button, GIS software can find and predict crime patterns by matching variables such as time of day, type of crime, and type of weapon used. When Fontana, California, experienced a spate of burglaries, for example, the police department's GIS was able to direct officers to virtually the exact spot where the next attempt would take place. Deputies were able to follow the burglars into a target house, where they were arrested and confessed to more than thirty other similar crimes.[47]

Hot Spots
Concentrated areas of high criminal activity that draw a directed police response.

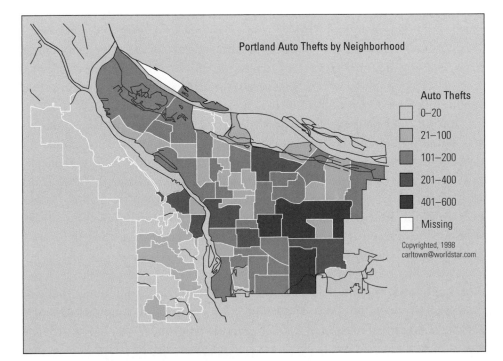

FIGURE 6.6
Geographic Information Systems and Auto Theft in Portland, Oregon

A geographic information system (GIS) uses digital maps to highlight areas in which crime occurs. As you can see, the Portland (Oregon) Police Department has taken advantage of GIS technology to pinpoint the incidence of auto theft in the city.

Source: City of Portland Police Bureau.

BROKEN WINDOWS: POPULARIZING COMMUNITY POLICING

If Herman Goldstein introduced the idea of problem-solving policing, James Q. Wilson and George L. Kelling brought it widespread attention. Many observers believe that Wilson and Kelling set the modern wave of community policing in motion with their 1982 article in *Atlantic Monthly* entitled "Broken Windows."[48]

The Broken Windows Theory   In "Broken Windows," Wilson and Kelling argued that reform era police strategies focused on violent crime to the detriment of the vital police role of promoting the quality of life in neighborhoods. As a result, many American communities, particularly in large cities, had fallen into a state of disorder and disrepute, with two very important consequences. First, these neighborhoods—with their broken windows, dilapidated buildings, and lawless behavior by citizens—send out "signals" that criminal activity is tolerated. Second, this disorder promotes fear among law-abiding citizens, dissuading them from leaving their homes or attempting to improve their surroundings.

The **broken windows theory,** therefore, is based on "order maintenance" of neighborhoods by cracking down on "quality-of-life" crimes such as panhandling, public drinking and urinating, loitering, and graffiti painting. Only by encouraging police diligence with regard to these quality-of-life crimes, the two professors argued, could American cities be rescued from rising crime rates.

Community policing played a prominent role in Wilson and Kelling's article. To reduce fear and crime, they insisted, police had to rely on the cooperation of the citizens. Many cities have found that a crucial step in "reconnecting" with the community has been the reintroduction of foot patrols in high-crime neighborhoods. Studies have shown that foot patrol officers pay more attention to "order maintenance crimes" such as drunkenness, vagrancy, and panhandling than do patrol officers in police cars. Although these crimes are not serious, they do increase fear of crime in a community.

Crackdowns   In many American cities, the implementation of the broken windows theory has been accompanied by aggressive patrol tactics known as "crackdowns." When police intensely focus their energies on a particular crime or set of crimes in a given area, they are said to be conducting a "crackdown." Crackdowns, which are related to the "hot spot" tactics discussed earlier, are typically used to solve a significant crime or disorder problem in an area.

In 2002, for example, officials in Seattle, Washington, announced that the city was setting up an Alcohol Impact Area (AIA) in its downtown to combat the problem of homeless alcoholics. Within the boundaries of the AIA, the sale and possession of certain types of (mostly cheap) alcohol are banned.[49] New York City, which experienced a dramatic drop in violent crime in the 1990s, is often held up as the ultimate example of what can be accomplished when the broken windows theory and aggressive police actions are combined. (See the feature *What Works—Compstat.*)

The Continued Impact of Community Policing   The community policing "revolution" shows no signs of abating. The Office of Community Oriented Policing Services, a branch of the U.S. Department of Justice, has distributed close to $9 billion in grants to law enforcement agencies in the past decade to pro-

Broken Windows Theory
Wilson and Kelling's theory that a neighborhood in disrepair signals that criminal activity is tolerated in the area. Thus, by cracking down on quality-of-life crimes, police can reclaim the neighborhood and encourage law-abiding citizens to live and work there.

INFOTRAC KEYWORDS

crime and hot spots; crime mapping; broken windows theory

For more information, use these search terms with InfoTrac College Edition, your online library at www.infotrac-college.com

> Compstat

What makes crime rates drop and rise? According to Lawrence M. Friedman, Stanford University professor of law, "the honest answer is that no one knows." Many law enforcement experts, however, credit a system instituted in New York City in the mid-1990s for much of the success police departments have had fighting crime in recent years. The system is known as Compstat, and it starts with beat officers reporting the exact location of crimes and other crime-related information—such as crack houses and abandoned cars—to department officials. These reports are then fed into a database, which prepares grids of a particular city or neighborhood that highlight areas with a high incidence of violent crime, drug dealing, and so on.

William Bratton, New York's police commissioner from 1994 to 1996, and his deputy commissioner Jack Maple modeled the earliest version of Compstat after England's use of radar to target and shoot down German Luftwaffe bombers in World War II. Twice a week, Maple would hold a meeting of all precinct chiefs and place pressure on those who presided over high-crime neighborhoods by showing them exactly where the problems were the worst. Compstat allowed these officers to apply "zero-tolerance" strategies to these "hot spots," cracking down on minor offenses such as loitering and aggressively searching for illegal weapons.

The results—in 1997, New York registered its lowest homicide rate since 1987—spurred other areas to adopt similar methods. Minneapolis, for example, which modeled its CODEFOR system on Compstat, enjoyed dramatic decreases in homicides, aggravated assaults, robberies, burglaries, and auto thefts from 1998 to 1999. In New Orleans, where Jack Maple consulted with city officials to create a version of Compstat, homicides dropped 55 percent between 1994 and 1999. In 2003, law enforcement agencies in Hernando County, Florida, and Mount Pleasant, South Carolina, launched crime prevention programs based on the Compstat model.

FOR CRITICAL ANALYSIS

Along with community policing, computer-run systems such as Compstat are considered the two pillars of "The New Policing." How do you think that the two approaches can be combined for greatest effect? Note that the New York Police Department has been criticized for ignoring many of the practices of community policing in its aggressive crime fighting strategies.

mote the strategy.[50] About two-thirds of all local police departments, employing 86 percent of all police officers in the country, have full-time community policing officers.[51] The "broken windows" theory now has proponents all over the globe and has influenced public policy in places such as Mexico and Honduras.

Some law enforcement officials worry that community policing has become so widespread that it has lost any coherence as a useful policing philosophy. More than half of the police chiefs and sheriffs in a survey conducted by the National Institute of Justice were unclear about the actual meaning of "community policing,"[52] leading one observer to joke that Professor Kelling's revolution is even quieter than had been expected.[53] Generally, however, the trend toward community policing is regarded as having a positive impact—if for no other reason than that it forces police departments to consider the complex relationship between law enforcement agents and the community.

ONLINE REVIEW *Go to the book's Web site for an interactive review of this section*

Law Enforcement in the Field

Community policing is one of the *field services* that police officers perform. Also known as "operations" or "line services," field services include patrol activities, investigations, and special operations. According to Henry M. Wrobleski and Karen M. Hess, most police departments are "generalists;" that is, police officers are assigned to general areas and perform all field service functions within the boundaries of their beats. Larger departments may be more specialized, with personnel assigned to specific types of crime, such as drugs or white-collar crime, rather than geographic locations. Smaller departments, which make up the bulk of local law enforcement agencies, rely almost exclusively on general patrol.[54]

POLICE ON PATROL: THE BACKBONE OF THE DEPARTMENT

One of the great ironies of the police organization is that the people lowest on the hierarchical "stepladder"—the patrol officers—are considered the most valuable members of the force. (Many patrol officers, considering their pay and work hours, would call the situation unjust, not ironic.) As many as two-thirds of the *sworn officers,* or those officers authorized to make arrests and use force, in some large police departments are patrol officers, and every department has a patrol unit.

"Life on the street" is not easy. Patrol officers must be able to handle any number of difficult situations, and experience is often the best, and, despite training programs, the only, teacher. As one patrol officer commented:

> You never stop learning. You never get your street degree. The person who says . . . they've learned it all is the person that's going to wind up dead or in a very compromising position. They've closed their minds.[55]

It may take a patrol officer years to learn when a gang is "false flagging" (trying to trick rival gang members into the open) or what to look for in a suspect's eyes to sense if he or she is concealing a weapon. This learning process is the backdrop to a number of different general functions that a patrol officer must perform on a daily basis.

The Purpose of Patrol   As was mentioned earlier, patrol officers do not spend a great deal of time chasing, catching, and handcuffing suspected criminals. The vast majority of patrol shifts are completed without a single arrest.[56] Officers spend a great deal of time meeting with other officers, taking breaks, and patrolling with the goal of preventing crime in general rather than any specific crime or criminal activity.

As Samuel Walker noted, the basic purposes of the police patrol have changed very little since 1829, when Sir Robert Peel founded the modern police department. These purposes include:

1 The deterrence of crime by maintaining a visible police presence.

2 The maintenance of public order and a sense of security in the community.

3 The twenty-four-hour provision of services that are not crime related.[57]

The first two goals—deterring crime and keeping order—are generally accepted as legitimate police functions. The third, however, has been more controversial.

As noted in Chapter 5, the community era has seen a resurgence of the patrol officer as a provider of community services, many of which

Police Scanner allows you to listen in on radio reports from police officers in the field over the Internet. To find this Web site, click on *Web Links* under *Chapter Resources* at www.cjinaction.com

Police officers spend a great deal of time performing community services such as visiting classrooms and interacting with students. Do you think that the time police officers dedicate to community services is well spent, or should they concentrate on fighting and preventing crime?

Paul Conklin/PhotoEdit

have little to do with crime. The extent to which noncrime incidents dominate patrol officers' time is evident in the Police Services Study, a survey of 26,000 calls to police in sixty different neighborhoods. The study found that only one out of every five calls involved the report of criminal activity.[58] (See Figure 6.7.)

There is some debate over whether community services should be allowed to dominate patrol officers' duties. The question, however, remains: If the police do not handle these problems, who will? Few cities have the financial resources to hire public servants to deal specifically with, for example, finding shelter for homeless persons. Furthermore, the police are the only public servants on call twenty-four hours a day, seven days a week, making them uniquely accessible to citizen needs. (See the *Careers in CJ* feature on the next page.)

Patrol Activities   To recap, the purposes of police patrols are to prevent and deter crime and also to provide social services. How can the police best accomplish these goals? Of course, each department has its own methods and strategies, but William Gay, Theodore Schell, and Stephen Schack are able to divide routine patrol activity into four general categories:

1 *Preventive patrol.* By maintaining a presence in a community, either in a car or on foot, patrol officers attempt to prevent crime from occurring. This strategy, which O. W. Wilson called "omnipresence," was a cornerstone of policing philosophy and still takes up roughly 40 percent of patrol time.

2 *Calls for service.* Patrol officers spend nearly a quarter of their time responding to 911 calls for emergency service or other citizen problems and complaints.

3 *Administrative duties.* Paperwork takes up nearly 20 percent of patrol time.

FIGURE 6.7   **Calls for Service**

Over a period of two years, the Project on Policing Neighborhoods gathered information on calls for service in Indianapolis, Indiana, and St. Petersburg, Florida. As you can see, the largest portion of these calls involved disputes where no violence or threat of violence existed. Be aware also that nearly two-thirds of the nonviolent dispute calls and nearly half of the assault calls answered by police dealt with domestic confrontations.

Description of Violation	Percentage of Total Calls
NONSERIOUS CRIME CALLS	
Nonviolent disputes	41.7
Public disorder (drunk, disorderly, begging, prostitution, etc.)	11.1
Assistance (missing persons, traffic accident, damaged property, etc.)	9.8
Minor violations (shoplifting, trespassing, traffic/parking offense, refusal to pay, etc.)	4.5
SERIOUS CRIME CALLS	
Assaults (using violence against a person, kidnaping, child abuse, etc.)	26.0
Serious theft (motor vehicle theft, burglary, purse snatching, etc.)	5.1
General disorder (illicit drugs, fleeing police, leaving the scene of of an accident, etc.)	1.8

Source: Stephen D. Mastrofski, Jeffrey B. Snipes, Roger B. Parks, and Christopher D. Maxwell, "The Helping Hand of the Law: Police Control of Citizens on Request," *Criminology* 38 (May 2000), Table 5, page 328.

> Lois Perillo Bicycle Community Policing Officer

I did not always want to be a police officer. I wanted to be an astronaut. So I graduated with a B.S. in aeronautics and promptly went to work as an accountant for the City of New York. Loving the Broadway theater and my Italian/Ukrainian family, yet knowing there was something more, I emptied my bank account of its $700, bought a bike rack, packed my '76 Datsun B-210 hatchback. and drove across the country to join my college roommate in San Francisco. Seventeen years later, I still live in the Bay Area, working as a police officer for fourteen of those years.

A career in law enforcement first entered my mind when I saw a recruitment poster hanging in a very bohemian San Francisco restaurant. It depicted a United Nations of women in uniform and encouraged that I join them. I did. However, the hiring process, inclusive of background checks and written, oral, physical, and polygraph testing, took two years. Concerned with my ability to scale the six-foot wall, I talked my way into a specialized physical prep class designed for female firefighter candidates.To stay motivated, I enrolled in a preacademy study class and I hunkered down for the wait.

In late June 1994, I received a letter from the San Francisco Police Department: my academy class was to begin in four weeks. By July, my hair was significantly shorter, and I was starching a gray rookie uniform weekly and polishing my brass and shoes daily. Those of us who could write easily were forced to do pushups, and those whose pushup style was one hand behind their backs were compelled to write. After three months, my star was pinned to my navy blue wool uniform by the chief of police, and I was off to four years of midnights before falling into the daylight and community policing.

I credit my fall to Valerie, one of the very first San Francisco community officers, who was about to move to another department when she recruited me to join the Community Police Officer Program, or C.P.O.P, as her replacement. I left the darkness of Mission Police Station's midnight watch, bought a very good pair of sunglasses, and began my adjustment to days. Soon, I was investigating a stalking incident on my beat. The suspect kept eluding us until I went undercover, riding a bicycle. We caught the guy, found he was affected by dementia, and placed him in mental-health treatment. My career as S.F.P.D.'s first bicycle community officer had begun.

At first we rode our personal bicycles with rubber bands around pant legs to protect ourselves from chain snags. After

ten years of bicycles on the beat, we are now fully funded with departmental supplies, equipment, and uniforms.

As a bicycle community officer, I don't just lock 'em up and go to court to testify. I am charged to be a problem solver and to stem repeat calls to dispatch. For example, after catching graffiti vandals in the act, I contracted with the teens and their parents that they remove their markings in lieu of facing arrest. I managed a crime alert system that the merchants use to share information and hopefully avert criminal activity. I helped organize the community to encourage a judge to compel a once ever present, panhandling heroin addict to choose drug treatment over jail time. And when Headquarters called me into action, I've switched into cop and robber mode to chase and catch bike thieves, shoplifters, burglars, and drug dealers on my bike.

Lois Perillo

Though it doesn't fit on my gun belt like the other tools I carry, the bicycle is an asset to my job and helps me expand my potential; it is a barrier breaker. Children and adults approach me easily, making my duties flow smoothly. My responsibilities include daily bicycle patrol, ongoing contact with the residents and merchants, and liaison with other city departments. I frequent community meetings and crime prevention talks. I listen to neighborhood concerns and prioritize my response according to their issues, assisting in their empowerment. I maintain voice mail at the station, shortcutting community calls to dispatch for issues that are not time sensitive, yet require a police response. I share information with the community by writing the Police Beat column for the local paper, *The Noe Valley Voice,* which posts to the Web. As with all police officers, I answer radio calls for service, take reports, comfort the aggrieved, bandage wounds, collect evidence, and arrest suspects. I think of myself as an old-fashioned beat officer (with the plus of my bicycle) who was fortunate enough to fall into my life's work. And while off duty, I still keep a watchful eye on the space program and the stars.

 Go to the Careers in Criminal Justice Interactive CD *for more profiles in the field of criminal justice.*

4   *Officer-initiated activities.* Incidents in which the patrol officer initiates contact with citizens, such as stopping motorists and pedestrians and questioning them, account for 15 percent of patrol time.[59]

The category estimates made by Gay, Schell, and Schack are not universally accepted. Professor of law enforcement Gary W. Cordner argues that administrative duties account for the largest percentage of patrol officers' time and that when these officers are not consumed with paperwork and meetings, they are either answering calls for service (which takes up 67 percent of the officers' time on the street) or initiating activities themselves (the remaining 33 percent).[60]

Indeed, there are dozens of academic studies that purport to answer the question of how patrol officers spend their days and nights. Perhaps it is only fair, then, to give a police officer the chance to describe the duties patrol officers perform. In the words of Anthony Bouza, a former police chief:

> [Patrol officers] hurry from call to call, bound to their crackling radios, which offer no relief—especially on summer weekend nights. . . . The cops jump from crisis to crisis, rarely having time to do more than tamp one down sufficiently and leave for the next. Gaps of boredom and inactivity fill the interims, although there aren't many of these in the hot months. Periods of boredom get increasingly longer as the nights wear on and the weather gets colder.[61]

Bouza paints a picture of a routine beat as filled with "noise, booze, violence, drugs, illness, blaring TVs, and human misery." This may describe the situation in high-crime neighborhoods, but it certainly does not represent the reality for the majority of patrol officers in the United States. Duties that all patrol officers have in common, whether they work in Bouza's rather nightmarish city streets or in the quieter environment of rural America, include controlling traffic, conducting preliminary investigations, making arrests, and patrolling public events.

Preventive Patrol and the Kansas City Experiment

On the night of May 2, 2003, nearly one hundred uniformed and plainclothes New Orleans police officers flooded a seven-square-mile area of the city that had been plagued by violent crime. Within several hours, the officers made eighty-two arrests, a quarter of them on felony charges. This type of activity is a **directed patrol.** Such patrols are specifically designed to deal with crimes that commonly occur in certain locations and under circumstances that provide police with opportunity for preparation.

Most police work, in contrast, is done on **general patrol,** during which officers make the rounds of a specific area with the purpose of carrying out the various patrol functions. Every police department in the United States patrols its jurisdiction using automobiles; in addition, 62 percent utilize foot patrols, 43 percent bicycle patrols, 12 percent motorcycle patrols, 3 percent boat patrols, and 2 percent horse patrols.[62] In a sense, general patrols are random because the officers spend a substantial amount of their shifts hoping to notice any crimes that may be occurring.

Testing Preventive Patrol Theories in Kansas City

Some observers have compared a patrol officer to a scarecrow because of the hope that the officer's presence alone will deter any would-be criminals from attempting a crime.[63] The theory of *preventive patrol* was tested by the Kansas City Preventive Patrol Experiment, conducted in 1972 and 1973.[64] With the cooperation of the local police department, a team of researchers chose three areas, comprised of five beats each, with similar crime statistics. Over the course of twelve months, the police applied different patrol strategies to each designated area:

"One night . . . it was so slow that three patrol cars showed up for a dispute between two crackheads over a shopping cart."
—Marcus Laffey, New York police officer (2000)

Directed Patrol
Patrol strategies that are designed to respond to a specific criminal activity at a specific time.

General Patrol
Patrol strategies that rely on police officers monitoring a certain area with the goal of detecting crimes in progress or preventing crime due to their presence. Also known as random or preventive patrol.

> On the *control* beats, normal preventive measures were taken, meaning that a single automobile drove the streets when not answering a call for service.

> On the *proactive* beats, the level of preventive measures was increased, with automobile patrols being doubled and tripled.

> On the *reactive* beats, preventive patrol was eliminated entirely, and patrol cars only answered calls for service.

Before, during, and after the experiments, the researchers also interviewed residents of the three designated areas to determine their opinion of police service and fear of crime.

The results of the Kansas City experiment were somewhat shocking. Researchers found that increasing or decreasing preventive patrol had little or no impact on crimes, public opinion of the effectiveness of police, police response time, traffic accidents, or reports of crime to police.[65]

Interpreting the Kansas City Experiment   Criminologists were, and continue to be, somewhat divided on how to interpret these results. For some, the Kansas City experiment and other similar data proved that patrol officers, after a certain threshold, were not effective in preventing crime, and therefore scarce law enforcement resources should be diverted to other areas. "It makes about as much sense to have police patrol routinely in cars to fight crime as it does to have firemen patrol routinely in fire trucks to fight fire," noted University of Delaware professor Carl Klockars.[66]

Others saw the experiment as proving only one conclusion in a very specific set of circumstances and were unwilling to accept the results as universal. Professor James Q. Wilson, for example, said that the study showed only that random patrols in marked automobiles were of questionable value and that it proved nothing about other types of police presence such as foot patrols or patrols in unmarked automobiles.[67]

Indeed, despite the Kansas City Preventive Patrol Experiment, most modern police departments continue to assign officers to random, preventive patrols. Such patrols bring local governments revenue through traffic tickets and also are believed to reassure citizens. The lasting benefit of the Kansas City study, according to researchers Robert Sheehan and Gary Cordner, seems to be that it has freed police departments from their reliance on the random patrol.[68] In light of the study, police departments realized that they could divert patrol officers from their traditional patrol duties without setting off an increase in crime. Therefore, administrators felt free to experiment with alternative strategies and tactics.

POLICE INVESTIGATIONS

Investigation is the second main function of police, along with patrol. Whereas patrol is primarily preventive, investigation is reactive. After a crime has been committed and the patrol officer has gathered the preliminary information from the crime scene, the responsibility of finding "who dunnit" is delegated to the investigator, most commonly known as the **detective.** Today detectives make up about 15 percent of the personnel in the average midsized and large-city police department.[69] Detectives have not been the focus of nearly as much reform attention as their patrol counterparts, mainly because the scope of the detective's job is

Detective
The primary police investigator of crimes.

limited to law enforcement, with less emphasis given to social services or order maintenance.

The job is not a glamorous one, however. Detectives spend much of their time investigating common crimes such as burglaries and are more likely to be tracking down stolen property than a murderer. They must also prepare cases for trial, which involves a great deal of time-consuming paperwork. Furthermore, a landmark Rand Corporation study estimated that more than 97 percent of cases that are "solved" can be attributed to a patrol officer making an arrest at the scene, witnesses or victims identifying the perpetrator, or detectives undertaking routine investigative procedures that could easily be performed by clerical personnel.[70] "There is no Sherlock Holmes," said one investigator. "The good detective on the street is the one who knows all the weasels and one of the weasels will tell him who did it."[71]

The Detection Function   A detective division in the larger police departments usually has a number of sections. These sections often include crimes against persons, such as homicide or sexual assault, and crimes against property, such as burglary and robbery. Many departments have separate detective divisions that deal exclusively with *vice,* a broad term that covers a number of public order crimes such as prostitution, gambling, and pornography. In the past, vice officers have also been primarily responsible for narcotics violations, but many departments now devote entire units to that growing social and legal problem.

The ideal case for any detective, of course, is one in which the criminal stays on the scene of the crime, has the weapon in his or her hands when apprehended, and, driven by an overriding sense of guilt, confesses immediately. Such cases are, needless to say, rare. University of Cincinnati criminal justice professor John E. Eck, in attempting to improve the understanding of the investigative process, concluded that investigators face three categories of cases:

> *Unsolvable cases,* or weak cases that cannot be solved regardless of investigative effort.

> *Solvable cases,* or cases with moderate evidence that can be solved with considerable investigative effort.

> *Already solved cases,* or cases with strong evidence that can be solved with minimum investigative effort.[72]

Eck found that the "unsolvable cases," once identified as such, should not be investigated because the effort would be wasted, and that the "already solved cases" require little additional effort or time on the part of detectives. Therefore, Eck concluded, the investigation resources of a law enforcement agency should primarily be aimed at "solvable cases." Further research by Steven G. Brandl and James Frank found that detectives had relatively high success rates in investigating burglary and robbery cases for which a moderate level of evidence was available.[73] Thus, the Rand study cited above may be somewhat misleading, in that investigators can routinely produce positive results as long as they concentrate on those cases that potentially can be solved.

Aggressive Investigation Strategies   Detective bureaus also have the option of implementing more aggressive strategies. For example, if detectives

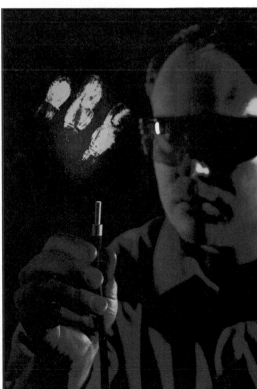

A special light designed to illuminate fingerprints is tested at Sandia National Laboratories in Livermore, California. Fingerprints—the result of sweat and grease from the pores of the skin—bloodstains, footprints, tire impressions, fiber from clothing, hair and skin samples, and weapons are important types of physical evidence that help police officers investigate crimes and convict offenders.

AP Photo/Sandia National Laboratories

suspect that a person was involved in the robbery of a Mercedes-Benz parts warehouse, one of them might pose as a "fence"—or purchaser of stolen goods. In what is known as a "sting" operation, the suspect is deceived into thinking that the detective (fence) wants to buy stolen car parts; after the transaction takes place, the suspect can be arrested.

Perhaps the most dangerous and controversial operation a detective can undertake is to go *undercover,* or to assume a different identity in order to obtain information concerning illegal activities. Though each department has its own guidelines on when undercover operations are necessary, all that is generally required is the suspicion that illegal activity is taking place. (As you may recall from the discussion of entrapment in Chapter 4, police officers are limited in what they can do to convince the target of an undercover operation to participate in the illegal activity.) Today, undercover officers are most commonly used to infiltrate large-scale narcotics operations or those run by organized crime.

In some cases, a detective bureau may not want to take the risk of exposing an officer to undercover work or may believe that an outsider cannot infiltrate an organized crime network. When the police need access and information, sometimes they turn to a **confidential informant (CI).** A CI is a person who is involved in criminal activity and gives information about the activity and those who engage in it to the police. The United States Supreme Court, in *Rovario v. United States* (1957),[74] held that the state has a confidential informant privilege, which means that it is not required to disclose the identity of an informant unless a court finds that such information is needed to determine the guilt or innocence of a suspect.

Confidential Informant (CI)
A human source for police who provides information concerning illegal activity in which he or she is involved.

THE MILITARY AND LAW ENFORCEMENT

With high-profile cases, the pressure on detective and patrol officers to solve and prevent crimes can be intense. That was certainly the case during the sniper attacks in the Washington, D.C., area in the fall of 2002. As the number of victims grew, the various police departments involved in the investigation turned to a source outside the traditional sphere of law enforcement for help: the U.S. military. The Pentagon agreed to provide the services of the RC-7, an Army surveillance jet with a high-resolution, zoom-lens camera that can take pictures for miles in all directions.[75]

While the idea that a spy plane was patrolling the skies may have comforted those living in the area, the strategy raised some eyebrows in the criminal justice community. The U.S. military and law enforcement have traditionally been separate entities, though the "wall" dividing them has been showing more and more cracks in recent years.

The Posse Comitatus Act By law, the U.S. military cannot participate in domestic law enforcement.

New York detective Mary Glatzke, wearing a gray wig and the nonthreatening clothes of a civilian, sits on a park bench. By posing as a "Muggable Mary," Detective Glatzke is using herself as bait to lure would-be robbers. This sort of undercover strategy hopes to deter crime as well as catch criminals in the act. What might be some of the deterrent effects of Detective Glatzke's assignment?

CORBIS/Bettmann

According to the Posse Comitatus Act (PCA) of 1878, anyone who uses a branch of the military to carry out the law may be punished by a fine or two years' imprisonment.[76] The statute reflects the wish of lawmakers, both at the time it was passed and today, that armed soldiers could never be used by the federal government to oppress the citizenry. The act does, however, allow the use of the military in law enforcement when so authorized by the U.S. Congress. To fight the "war on drugs," for example, in 1981 Congress created an exception to the PCA and encouraged the military to share equipment and information with law enforcement agencies fighting the illegal drug trade in Central and South America and Southeast Asia.[77]

The U.S. Army also provides Blackhawk helicopters to aid the U.S. Customs Service's efforts against the smuggling of goods and illegal immigrants between the Bahamas and the United States. Indeed, as the long arm of domestic law enforcement stretches beyond our borders to combat criminal activity such as the illicit drug trade and terrorism, the duties of police officers and soldiers will dovetail more often, leading to an inevitable overlap of operations. (For a discussion of the globalization of law enforcement, see the *Criminal Justice in Action* feature at the end of this chapter.)

A Military Culture in Law Enforcement   Some believe that American law enforcement has already adopted a "culture of paramilitarism."[78] As mentioned earlier in the chapter, most police departments in the United States are organized according to a military structure of command. Police officers who operate near military bases often train with soldiers, and military equipment is becoming more widely available to law enforcement agencies. In the early 2000s, nine different police departments began using Forward Looking Infrared Technology, a viewer mounted within the police car that allows officers to "see in the dark" by noting differences in heat as small as one-tenth of one degree Fahrenheit.[79]

In addition, many police departments, particularly in large cities, operate Special Weapons and Tactics (SWAT) teams. These special operations units are more heavily armed than regular police officers and use military tactics to respond to particularly dangerous circumstances such as hostage situations, barricaded suspects, and drug raids. The most significant challenge to the separation of military and police, however, will come as law enforcement reorganizes to combat terrorism. In 2002, President George W. Bush called on Congress to effectively eliminate the PCA by allowing military personnel to arrest, search, and seize terrorism suspects on American soil.[80]

◢ONLINE REVIEW *Go to the book's Web site for an interactive review of this section*

AP Photo/Lisa Poole

Dean Julien, a U.S. Army military policeman, stands guard at the entrance to a security checkpoint at Boston's Logan Airport. The "war against terrorism" often requires military forces to provide services that have traditionally been the responsibility of local law enforcement.

GREAT **DEBATES**
Many observers insist that the threat of terrorism is the greatest danger ever faced by this nation and that the military should be given greater powers, including the power to engage in law enforcement, in the interests of national security. For a closer look at this argument, as well as an explanation of the role the military has played in American law enforcement, click on *Great Debates* under *Book Resources* at www.cjinaction.com

"Us versus Them": Issues in Modern Policing

In the days following his death, the question on the minds of the law enforcement community in Seattle was, "Why didn't Richard Herzog draw his gun?" The answer, for many, came down to fear. Herzog, a King's County sheriff's deputy,

"The police subculture permits and sometimes demands deception of courts, prosecutors, defense attorneys, and defendants."
—Jerome Skolnick, professor of law, University of California at Berkeley (1966)

was killed trying to restrain a man who had been running naked in traffic. When the man, named Ronald Matthews, turned and attacked, Herzog pulled out pepper spray instead of his firearm. Matthews knocked the sheriff's deputy to the ground, grabbed his holstered handgun, and shot him several times.

County Executive Ron Sims, the highest-ranking African American in the city, had no doubt that Herzog had been inhibited in using his weapon because he was white and Matthews was black. Several killings of black suspects by white police officers in the months before Herzog's death—and the ensuing criticism—had, Sims said, made police officers afraid to protect themselves in situations involving African Americans.[81] Racial tension is one of the many on-the-job issues that make law enforcement such a challenging and often difficult career. When faced with these issues, sometimes police officers make the right decisions, and sometimes they make the wrong ones. In the worst-case scenario, as with Deputy Herzog, even a seemingly "right" decision may have an unexpected outcome.

POLICE SUBCULTURE

At a press conference after Richard Herzog's death, King's County Sheriff Dave Reichert vented his frustrations. "We are sick and tired of being nitpicked about decisions we make every day," said Reichert.[82] His words encapsulate the bitterness toward civilians that often marks **police subculture,** a broad term used to describe the basic assumptions and values that permeate law enforcement agencies and are taught to new members of a law enforcement agency as the proper way to think, perceive, and act.[83] Every organization has a subculture, with values shaped by the particular aspects and pressures of that organization. In the police subculture, those values are formed in an environment characterized by danger, stress, boredom, and violence.

Police Subculture
The values and perceptions that are shared by members of a police department and, to a certain extent, by all law enforcement agents. These values and perceptions are shaped by the unique and isolated existence of the police officer.

The Core Values of Police Subculture   From the first day on the job, rookies begin the process of **socialization,** in which they are taught the values and rules of police work. This process is aided by a number of rituals that are common to the law enforcement experience. Police theorist Harry J. Mullins believes that the following rituals are critical to the police officer's acceptance, and even embrace, of police subculture:

> Attending a recruit academy.

> Working with a senior officer, who passes on the "lessons" of police work and life to the younger officer.

> Making the initial felony arrest.

> Using force to make an arrest for the first time.

> Using or witnessing deadly force for the first time.

> Witnessing major traumatic incidents for the first time.[84]

Socialization
The process through which a police officer is taught the values and expected behavior of the police subculture.

Each of these rituals makes it clear to the police officer that this is not a "normal" job. The only other people who can understand the stresses of police work are fellow officers, and consequently law enforcement officers tend to insulate themselves from civilians. Eventually, the insulation breeds mistrust, and the police officer develops an "us versus them" outlook toward those outside the force.[85]

In turn, this outlook creates what sociologist William Westly called the **blue curtain,** also known as the "blue wall of silence" or simply "the code."[86] This curtain separates the police from the civilians they are meant to protect.

Police Cynicism   A cynic is someone who universally distrusts human motives and expects nothing but the worst from human behavior. **Police cynicism** is characterized by a rejection of the ideals of truth and justice—the very values that an officer is sworn to uphold.[87] As cynical police officers lose respect for the law, they replace legal rules with those learned in the police subculture, which are believed to be more reflective of "reality." The implications for society can be an increase in police misconduct, corruption, and brutality.[88]

Police cynicism is exacerbated by a feeling of helplessness—to report another officer's wrongdoing is a severe breach of the blue wall of silence. As one officer said:

> If you were to challenge somebody for something that was going on, they would say: "Listen, if the supervisor isn't saying anything, what the hell are you interjecting for? What are you, a rat?" You've gotta work with a lot of these guys. You go on a gun job, the next thing you know, you got nobody following you up the stairs.[89]

The officer's statement highlights one of the reasons why police subculture resonates beyond department walls—he has basically admitted that he will not report wrongdoing by his peers. In this manner, police subculture influences the actions of police officers, sometimes to the detriment of society. In the next two sections, we will examine two areas of the law enforcement work environment that help create police subculture and must be fully understood if the cynical nature of police subculture is ever to be changed: (1) the danger of police work and (2) the need for police officers to establish and maintain authority.[90]

THE PHYSICAL AND MENTAL DANGERS OF POLICE WORK

Police officers face the threat of physical harm every day. According to the U.S. Department of Justice, police have the most dangerous job in the United States, with 261 of every 1,000 officers targets of nonfatal violence each year.[91] In 2002–2003, almost 300 police officers were killed in the line of duty.

In addition to physical dangers, police work entails considerable mental pressure and stress. According to the U.S. Bureau of Labor Statistics, policing is one of the ten most stressful occupations in the country, along with firefighting, driving a taxi, and being a surgeon.[92] The social isolation police officers must deal with also leads to one of the highest divorce rates of

Blue Curtain
A metaphorical term used to refer to the value placed on secrecy and the general mistrust of the outside world shared by many police officers.

Police Cynicism
The suspicion that citizens are weak, corrupt, and dangerous. This outlook is the result of a police officer being constantly exposed to civilians at their worst and can negatively affect the officer's performance.

New York Port Authority Police carry the casket of fellow officer Dominick Pezzulo, who was one of the nearly eighty law enforcement agents killed in the September 11, 2001, terrorist attacks on the World Trade Center. Why were so many police officers in a position of danger when the two towers collapsed shortly after being struck by hijacked commercial airplanes? What are some of the occupational threats that police officers face on a daily basis?

AP Photo/Beth A. Keiser

any job, which adds to stress. Stress, in turn, contributes to other problems. Law enforcement officers are 300 percent more likely to suffer from alcoholism than the average American.[93] The average life expectancy of a police officer is fifty-seven years, compared to seventy-one for the general public—a statistic that can be attributed to police officers' top ranking among professions in rates of heart disease, hypertension, and diabetes.[94]

AUTHORITY AND THE USE OF FORCE

If the police subculture is shaped by the dangers of the job, it often finds expression through authority. The various symbols of authority that decorate a police officer—including the uniform, badge, nightstick, and firearm—establish the power she or he holds over civilians. For better or for worse, both police officers and civilians tend to equate terms such as *authority* and *respect* with the ability to use force. Near the turn of the twentieth century, a police officer stated that his job was to "protect the good people and treat the crooks rough."[95] Implicit in the officer's statement is the idea that to do the protecting, he had to do some roughing up as well. This attitude toward the use of force is still with us today. Indeed, it is generally accepted that not only is police use of force inevitable, but that police officers who are unwilling to use force in certain circumstances cannot do their job effectively.

The "Misuse" of Force   The Department of Justice estimates that law enforcement officers threatened to use force or used force in encounters with more than 421,000 Americans in 1999.[96] (See Figure 6.8.) Of course, police officers are often justified in using force to protect themselves or other citizens. At the same time, few observers would be naïve enough to believe that police are *always* justified in the use of force. How, then, is "misuse" of force to be defined?

One attempt to qualify excessive force that has been lauded by legal scholars, if not necessarily by police officers, was offered by the Christopher Commission. Established in Los Angeles in 1992 after the beating of African American motorist Rodney King, the commission advised that "an officer may resort to force only where he or she faces a credible threat, and then may only use the minimum amount necessary to control the subject."[97]

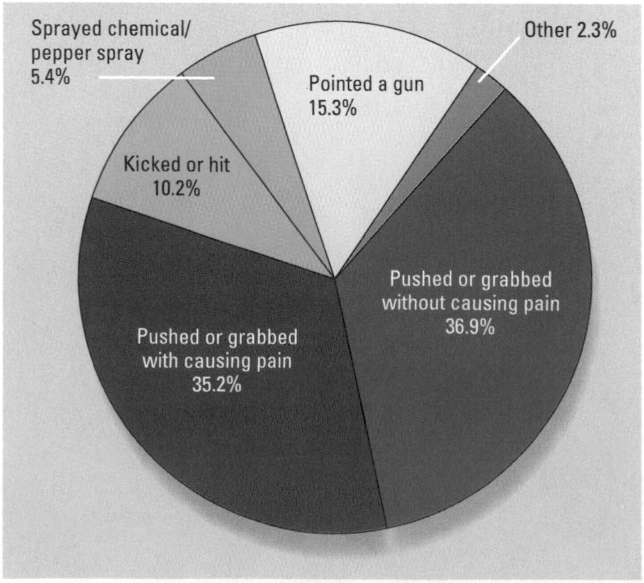

The Phoenix Study   Terms such as *credible* and *necessary* are, of course, quite subjective, rendering these definitions too vague to be practical. To better understand the subject, the Phoenix (Arizona) Police Department, in a partnership with Rutgers University and Arizona State University, implemented a study to measure how often police officers used force. The results showed that police used some form of "physical force"—defined as any "weaponless tactic" (such as kicking or shoving) or the threatened or actual use of any weapon—in 22 percent of the surveyed arrests.[98] The study also examined the predictors of force; that is, the factors that were present in the situations where force was used. As one might expect, the study found that the best predictor of police use of force was the suspect's use of force.[99]

FIGURE 6.8 The Use of Force by Police against Suspects

Of the 421,714 people who reported forceful behavior on the part of the police in 1999, about 22.5 percent said that force was threatened but not actually used. When force was used, as you can see, about 72 percent of the time it involved pushing and grabbing.

Source: Bureau of Justice Statistics, *Contacts between Police and the Public* (Washington, D.C.: U.S. Department of Justice, February 2001), 25.

Sprayed chemical/pepper spray 5.4%

Other 2.3%

Pointed a gun 15.3%

Kicked or hit 10.2%

Pushed or grabbed without causing pain 36.9%

Pushed or grabbed with causing pain 35.2%

Types of Force   To comply with the various, and not always consistent, laws concerning the use of force, a police officer must understand that there are two kinds of force: *nondeadly force* and *deadly force*. Most force used by law enforcement is nondeadly force. In most states, the use of nondeadly force is regulated by the concept of **reasonable force,** which allows the use of nondeadly force when a reasonable person would assume that such force was necessary. In contrast, **deadly force** is force that an objective police officer realizes will place the subject in direct threat of serious injury or death.

The United States Supreme Court and Use of Force   The United States Supreme Court set the limits for the use of deadly force by law enforcement officers in *Tennessee v. Garner* (1985).[100] The case involved an incident in which Memphis police officer Elton Hymon shot and killed a suspect who was trying to climb over a fence after stealing ten dollars from a residence. Hymon testified that he had been trained to shoot to keep a suspect from escaping, and indeed Tennessee law at the time allowed police officers to apprehend fleeing suspects in this manner.

In reviewing the case, the Court focused not on Hymon's action but on the Tennessee statute itself, ultimately finding it unconstitutional:

> When the suspect poses no immediate threat to the officer and no threat to others, the use of deadly force is unjustified.... It is not better that all felony suspects die than that they escape.[101]

The Court's ruling forced twenty-three states to change their fleeing felon rules. It did not, however, completely eliminate police discretion in such situations; police officers may use deadly force if they have probable cause to believe that the fleeing suspect poses a threat of serious injury or death to the officers or others. (We will discuss the concept of probable cause in the next chapter.) In essence, the Court recognized that police officers must be able to make split-second decisions without worrying about the legal ramifications. Four years after the *Garner* case, the Court tried to clarify this concept in *Graham v. Connor* (1989), stating that the use of any force should be judged by the "reasonableness of the moment."[102] (See *You Be the Judge—Justified Force?* on the next page.)

Reasonable Force
The degree of force that is appropriate to protect the police officer or other citizens and is not excessive.

Deadly Force
Force applied by a police officer that is likely or intended to cause death.

AP Photo/Brad Graverson, Pool

Los Angeles County Sheriff's Department commander Charles Heal testifies during the trial of Jeremy Morse, a former Inglewood (California) police officer. Morse, shown on the video screen as he slams teen-ager Donovan Jackson against a police car, was charged with felony assault under the color of authority. Under what circumstances can a law enforcement agent use nondeadly force?

> Justified Force?

The Facts

Just after midnight, New York City police officers Sean, Ken, Rich, and Ed were riding through a high-crime area in an unmarked car when they saw African immigrant Amadou acting "suspiciously" in front of a building (which turned out to be his home). Sean and Ed, in street clothes, got out of the car and walked toward Amadou. They identified themselves as police officers and told Amadou to keep his hands where they could see them. According to their testimony, instead Amadou "darted into" the building, then reached into his pocket and produced a dark object. Sean shouted "Gun!" and the four officers began firing at Amadou, who fell to the ground almost immediately. Sean walked up to the prone body and searched for the weapon, but found only a wallet in Amadou's hand. Sean tried to revive Amadou with CPR, but he had already died of nineteen bullet wounds.

The Law

The United States Supreme Court has ruled that cases involving the use of police force should be decided by observing all the circumstances surrounding the incident and then determining whether the police officer was "reasonable" in the use of force. In other words, would a reasonable police officer in this officer's shoes have been justified in using force?

Your Decision

Sean, Ken, Rich, and Ed have been charged with Amadou's murder. Are they guilty, or, under the circumstances, were they justified in firing at Amadou?

[To see how a jury in Albany, New York, decided this case, go to Example 6.1 in Appendix B.]

Nonlethal Weapons   Regardless of any legal restrictions, violent confrontations between officers and suspects are inevitable. To decrease the likelihood that such confrontations will result in death or serious injury, many police departments use *nonlethal weapons,* which are designed to subdue but not seriously harm suspects. More than 90 percent of local police departments authorize the use of Oleoresin capsicum, or OC pepper spray.[103] An organic substance that combines ingredients such as resin and cayenne pepper, OC causes a sensation "similar to having sand or needles" in the eyes when sprayed into a suspect's face. Other common nonlethal weapons include tear gas; water cannons; 37-mm pistols that fire wood, rubber, beanbags, or polyurethane bullets; and hand-held electronic "stun guns." (See the feature *CJ and Technology—The "Glock on Steroids" Approach.*)

A number of problems have sprung up with the use of these nonlethal weapons. First, some of them have proved to be not so nonlethal. From 2001 to 2003, for example, twelve people were killed or seriously injured by beanbag guns.[104] Second, as we saw with Deputy Richard Herzog on page 196, sometimes nonlethal weapons do not provide police officers with the protection they need.

RACIAL AND ETHNIC BIASES IN POLICING

In its guidelines for the use of deadly force by undercover officers, the New York Police Department warns its officers not to be victims of symbolic opponent syndrome, defined as a "preconceived notion that places suspects into a 'BAD GUY' category because of race, nationality, grooming, or mode of dress."[105] The warn-

> The "Glock on Steroids" Approach

According to the FBI, police are involved in about four hundred justifiable homicides each year. Even though these killings occur only when the officer is required to use force to protect himself or herself or a third party, law enforcement officials realize that each such incident can damage relations with the community. Furthermore, police officers may hesitate to use deadly force even when justified, for fear of the repercussions.

In an attempt to alleviate these worries, more than 1,500 law enforcement agencies now use the Advanced Taser M26, a form of nonlethal stun gun that police call a "Glock on Steroids." When an officer pulls the trigger on an M26, which looks like a regular handgun, two quarter-inch darts attached to electrical wires are propelled up to twenty-one feet. Once the darts snag the target's clothes or become embedded in his or her skin, a five-second jolt of electricity is automatically discharged. The current attacks the target's central nervous system, paralyzing him or her for up to ninety seconds.

Some human rights groups have called for a ban on these types of weapons, wanting more research to be conducted on how the weapon's electrical charge affects the human body. These groups point out that since 1996, six people have died after being shot with a stun gun. Supporters of the nonlethal weapon counter that drug use by the target was the main cause of death in each of these cases, and point to an overwhelming success of the guns in most jurisdictions. The Los Angeles Police Department, for example, has used various types of stun guns approximately 5,600 times over the past three decades, and no serious injuries have been linked to these weapons.

In the Future

A research company in San Diego, California, is in the process of perfecting the latest line of nonlethal stun guns. Called the Anti-Personnel Beam Weapon (APBW), the device uses ultraviolet radiation to send an electrical current through the air toward the target. Like the electrical charge of the M26, this current freezes muscle contraction, causing paralysis. The APBW has a range of about one hundred feet, and the same company is working on a similar device that would disable automobile engines.

Clay Winn, of TASER International, demonstrates the company's Advanced M26 nonlethal "stun gun."

AP Photo/Joe Cavaretta

 For more information on stun guns and other CJ technologies, click on Web Links under Chapter Resources at www.cjinaction.com

ing may seem self-evident, but it addresses a clear problem in law enforcement today. The Department of Justice study cited earlier reports that police officers are almost three times more likely to use force when coming into contact with African Americans than with whites and more than twice as likely with Hispanics as with whites.[106] Furthermore, Malcolm D. Holmes of the University of Wyoming has determined that in some of the nation's largest cities blacks and Hispanics are significantly more likely than whites to file civil rights complaints alleging police brutality.[107]

The "Just Us" System These experiences have led some to believe that the United States has, in practice, not a justice system but a "just us" system. In the next chapter's discussion of racial profiling, we will see that many African Americans believe that they are often targeted for a particular "offense"—DWB, or "driving while black." This perception is supported by empirical evidence gathered in the 1990s in Florida, New Jersey, and Maryland showing that African American drivers were stopped more often for traffic violations than other racial or ethnic groups.[108]

Since the September 11, 2001 terrorist attacks, Muslims living in the United States have also felt that they are being singled out for law enforcement attention. This perception is strengthened by such actions as the FBI directive in 2003 ordering field supervisors to count the mosques and Muslim populations in their areas as part of their antiterrorism duties.

Police Attitudes and Discretion   Such attitudes, say critics, lead to unnecessary harassment of members of minority groups by police and arouse ill will toward law enforcement in many minority neighborhoods. A greater police presence in these neighborhoods is not automatic evidence of law enforcement bias, however. As we learned earlier in the chapter, the primary operational tactic of all metropolitan police forces is responding to calls for service. According to research by law enforcement expert Richard J. Ludman, the greater police presence in these communities is mainly the result of calls for service from residents, which, in turn, are caused by higher local crime rates. Indeed, Randall Kennedy believes that such "selective law enforcement" should be, and for the most part is, welcomed by those who live in high-crime areas and appreciate the added protection.[109]

Furthermore, as several experts point out, cultural differences often exist between police officers and the residents of the neighborhoods they patrol. One survey found that police working in minority areas perceived higher levels of abuse and less respect from those citizens than from those in nonminority areas.[110] In looking at police abuse in Inglewood, California, the *Los Angeles Times* found that most of the victims claimed they were assaulted after "contempt of cop" incidents, such as not immediately following orders or verbally challenging the officer.[111] Judging someone's demeanor is often a subjective task and can be influenced by a lack of communication between two people of different backgrounds—another reason why it is so important for police departments to attract members of minority groups, as noted in our discussion of recruiting strategies.

POLICE CORRUPTION

Police corruption has been a concern since the first organized American police departments. As you recall from Chapter 4, a desire to eradicate, or at least limit, corruption was one of the motivating factors behind the reform movement of policing. For general purposes, **police corruption** can be defined as the misuse of authority by a law enforcement officer "in a manner designed to produce personal gain." Corrupt police officers fall into two categories: "grass eaters" and "meat eaters." "Grass eaters" are involved in passive corruption; they simply accept the payoffs and opportunities that police work can provide. As the name implies, "meat eaters" are more aggressive in their quest for personal gain, initiating and going to great lengths to carry out corrupt schemes.

Types of Corruption   Certain forms of corruption have been endemic to police work since its inception. These traditional forms of corruption include:

Police Corruption
The abuse of authority by a law enforcement officer for personal gain.

1   *Bribery,* in which the police officer accepts money or other forms of payment in exchange for "favors," which may include allowing a certain criminal activity to continue or misplacing a key piece of evidence before a trial. Related to bribery are *payoffs,* in which an officer demands payment from an individual or a business in return for certain services.

2   *Shakedowns,* in which an officer attempts to coerce money or goods from a citizen or criminal.

3   *Mooching,* in which the police officer accepts free "gifts" such as cigarettes, liquor, or services in return for favorable treatment of the gift giver.

Perhaps the most visible corruption scandal of the last decade was touched off when Rafael Perez, an officer in a Los Angeles Police Department (LAPD) antigang unit, was arrested for stealing cocaine from an evidence locker. Perez proceeded to admit to a number of other crimes and implicated others members of the unit. Eventually, in 2000, the evidence of widespread corruption forced the LAPD to accept a federal consent degree, placing part of its operations under the watch of the U.S. Department of Justice.

Corruption in Police Subculture   There is no single reason that police corruption occurs. In covering corrupt behavior by a group of Miami police officers known as the Miami River Cops, journalist John Dorschner highlighted some of the factors that lead to unethical behavior, including a lack of proper training, a lack of supervision, and the fact that most officers can double or triple their salaries through corrupt activities.[112]

Lawrence Sherman identifies several stages in the moral decline of police officers.[113] In the first stage, the officers accept minor gratuities, such the occasional free meal from a restaurant on their beats. These gratuities gradually evolve into outright bribes, in which the officers receive the gratuity for overlooking some violation. For example, a law officer may accept pay from a bar owner to ensure that the establishment is not investigated for serving alcohol to minors. In the final stage, officers no longer passively accept bribes, but actively seek them out, to the point where the officers may even force the other party to pay for unwanted police services. This stage often involves large amounts of money and may entail protection of or involvement in drug, gambling, or prostitution organizations.

The insulating effects of police subculture also contribute to corruption by making it difficult to uncover. The Knapp Commission, which investigated police corruption in New York City in the 1970s, highlighted the "code of silence" that exists in police departments, a code that brands anybody within the department who exposes corrupt behavior as a traitor. "The rookie who comes into the department," it was noted, "is faced with the situation where it is easier for him to become corrupt than to remain honest."[114]

POLICE ACCOUNTABILITY

Even in a police department with excellent recruiting methods, state-of-the-art ethics and discretionary training programs, and a culturally diverse work force that nearly matches the make-up of the community, the problems discussed earlier in this chapter are bound to occur. The question then becomes—given the inevitability of excessive force, corruption, and other misconduct—*who shall police the police?*

Samuel Walker, Professor of Criminal Justice at the University of Nebraska, is one of the nation's leading experts on the Best Practices in Police Accountability. Click on *Web Links* under *Chapter Resources* at www.cjinaction.com for access to his Web site.

INFOTRAC KEYWORDS
police corruption
For more information, use this search term with InfoTrac College Edition, your online library at www.infotrac-college.com

Internal Investigations "The minute the public feels that the police department is not investigating its own alleged wrongdoing well, the police department will not be able to function credibly in even the most routine of matters" says Sheldon Greenberg, a professor of police management at Johns Hopkins University.[115] The mechanism for these investigations within a police department is the **internal affairs unit (IAU).** In many smaller police departments, the police chief conducts internal affairs investigations, while midsized and large departments will have a team of internal affairs officers.

As much as police officers may resent internal affairs units, most realize that it is preferable to settle disciplinary matters in house. The alternatives may be worse. Police officers are criminally liable for any crimes they might commit, and city and state governments can be held civilly liable for wrongdoing by their police officers. In 2003, for example, three members of the Oakland (California) police department were accused of beating a handcuffed suspect and tried on charges that included kidnapping, falsifying arrest reports, and assault. The city of Oakland paid the victim of the beating $10.9 million to settle a police brutality lawsuit. By 2004, the city of Los Angeles had paid $42 million to settle lawsuits springing from its most recent scandals, and city officials expected to disburse tens of millions more.

Michael Cox successfully sued the city of Boston following an incident in which he was mistaken for a suspect and severely beaten by members of the city's police force.

Internal Affairs Unit (IAU)
A division within a police department that receives and investigates complaints of wrongdoing by police officers.

Citizen Oversight
The process by which citizens review complaints brought against individual police officers or police departments. The citizens often do not have the power to discipline misconduct, but can recommend that action be taken by police administrators.

Citizen Oversight After Portland (Oregon) police officer Scott McCollister shot and killed a woman when she tried to drive away following a traffic stop in 2003, many community activists were unimpressed with internal department efforts to investigate and discipline the officer. They called for the formation of an external procedure for handling citizens' complaints known as **citizen oversight.** In this process, citizens—people who are not sworn officers and, by inference, not biased in favor of law enforcement officers—review allegations of police misconduct or brutality. According to Samuel Walker, nearly one hundred cities now operate some kind of review procedure by an independent body.[116] For the most part, citizen review boards can only recommend action to the police chief or other executive. They do not have the power to discipline officers directly. Police officers generally resent this intrusion of civilians and most studies have shown that civilian review boards are not widely successful in their efforts to convince police chiefs to take action against their subordinate officers.[117]

ONLINE REVIEW *Go to the book's Web site for an interactive review of this section*

Police Ethics

Ethics
The rules or standards of behavior governing a profession; aimed at ensuring the fairness and rightness of actions.

Police corruption is intricately connected with the ethics of law enforcement officers. **Ethics** has to do with fundamental questions of the fairness, justice, rightness, or wrongness of any action. Given the significant power that police officers hold, society expects very high standards of ethical behavior from them. These expectations are summed up in the *Police Code of Conduct,* which was developed by the International Association of Chiefs of Police in 1989.

To some extent, the *Police Code of Conduct* is self-evident: "A police officer will not engage in acts of corruption or bribery." In other aspects, it is idealistic, perhaps unreasonably so: "Officers will never allow personal feelings, animosities, or friendships to influence official conduct." The police working environment—rife with lying, cheating, lawbreaking, and violence—often does not allow for such ethical absolutes.[118]

ETHICAL DILEMMAS

Some police actions are obviously unethical, such as the behavior of a Pennsylvania officer who paid a woman he was dating $500 to pretend to be an eyewitness in a murder trial. The majority of ethical dilemmas that a police officer will face are not so clear-cut. Joycelyn M. Pollock and Ronald F. Becker, both members of the Criminal Justice Department at Southwest Texas State University, define an ethical dilemma as a situation in which law enforcement officers:

> Do not know the right course of action;

> Have difficulty doing what they consider to be right; and/or

> Find the wrong choice very tempting.[119]

These ethical dilemmas can occur often in police work, and it is how an officer deals with them that determines to what extent he or she is behaving ethically. (For further discussion of the difficult ethical situations that police officers face, see the feature *CJ in Focus—A Question of Ethics: The Dirty Harry Problem* on page 206.)

ELEMENTS OF ETHICS

Pollock and Becker, both of whom have extensive experience as ethics instructors for police departments, further identify four categories of ethical dilemmas, involving discretion, duty, honesty, and loyalty.[120]

> *Discretion.* The law provides rigid guidelines for how police officers must act and how they cannot act, but it does not offer guidelines for how officers *should* act in many circumstances.[121] As mentioned in Chapter 5, police officers often use discretion to determine how they should act, and ethics play an important role in guiding discretionary actions.

> *Duty.* The concept of discretion is linked with **duty,** or the obligation to act in a certain manner. Society, by passing laws, can make a police officer's duty more clear and, in the process, help eliminate discretion from the decision-making process. But an officer's duty will not always be obvious, and ethical considerations can often supplement "the rules" of being a law enforcement agent.

> *Honesty.* Of course, honesty is a critical attribute for an ethical police officer. A law enforcement agent must make hundreds of decisions in a day, and most of them require him or her to be honest in order to properly do the job.

> *Loyalty.* What should a police officer do if he or she witnesses a partner using excessive force on a suspect? The choice often sets loyalty against ethics, especially if the officer does not condone the violence.

Although there is no easy "formula" to guide police officers through ethical challenges, Linda S. Miller of the Midwest Regional Community Policing Institute

INFOTRAC KEYWORDS
police ethics

For more information, use this search term with InfoTrac College Edition, your online library at www.infotrac-college.com

Duty
The moral sense of a police officer that she or he should apply authority in a certain manner.

> The Dirty Harry Problem

Do the ends justify the means? This is one of the most difficult and complex questions of ethics, and one that is particularly crucial for police officers. Should they take steps that they know to be illegal in order to achieve a positive goal?

In addressing this moral dilemma, the University of Delaware's Carl B. Klockars turns to one of the most popular police dramas of all time, the 1971 film *Dirty Harry*. In this movie, Detective Harry Callahan, played by Clint Eastwood, faces a situation in which a young girl has been kidnapped by a psychotic killer named Scorpio. Demanding $200,000 in ransom, Scorpio has buried the girl alive, leaving her just a few hours' worth of oxygen. Callahan manages to find Scorpio, and in his efforts to learn the location of the girl, he shoots and then tortures the kidnapper. Although Callahan eventually gets the information out of Scorpio, it is too late. By the time he finds the girl, she has suffocated.

Assuming for argument's sake that Callahan was able to save the girl, would he have been justified in taking such drastic measures? After all, Callahan, like all officers, took an oath to obey the U.S. Constitution, which certainly does not permit the torture of suspects. Following proper procedure, Callahan should have arrested Scorpio and advised him of his right to an attorney. If Scorpio had exercised his right, the attorney would certainly have reminded him of his right to remain silent, and Callahan would have had no chance to save the little girl. In fact, Callahan committed a crime himself by assaulting Scorpio. Given all these factors, was the detective justified in doing what he did in order to save a life?

According to Klockars:

[The] core scene in *Dirty Harry* should only be understood as a dramatic example of a far more common problem: real, everyday, routine situations in which police officers know they can only achieve good ends by employing dirty means. Each time a police officer considers deceiving a suspect into confessing by telling him that his fingerprints were found at the scene or that a conspirator has already confessed, each time a police officer considers adding some untrue details to his account of probable cause to legitimate a crucial stop or search [he or she] faces a Dirty Harry Problem.

Klockars calls the effects of the Dirty Harry problem on police officers "devastating." On the one hand, if the officers decide not to use dirty means, they must face the consequences: perhaps a suspect the officers know is guilty will be set free to commit further crimes. On the other hand, if the officers do abandon rules and procedures to serve the law, they are essentially breaking the very laws that they took an oath to uphold. The Dirty Harry problem, Klockars says, makes policing the most "morally corrosive occupation."

FOR CRITICAL ANALYSIS
Are police ever justified in using unlawful methods, whatever good may be ultimately achieved? What do you believe is the proper solution to the Dirty Harry problem?

---

and Karen M. Hess of Normandale Community College have come up with three questions that can act as personal "checks" for police officers. Miller and Hess suggest that officers, when considering a particular action, ask themselves:

1 Is it legal?

2 Is it balanced?

3 How does it make me feel about myself?[122]

ONLINE REVIEW Go to the book's Web site for an interactive review of this section

>The Globalization of Law Enforcement

Our criminal justice system was not designed for exportation. Historically, American criminal law has been based on the premise that where a crime took place was the single most important factor determining which law applied to that crime. Today, of course, law limited by such territorial concerns is as outdated as it is impractical. How could it apply to, say, the case of Ludwig Feinberg, an American citizen living in Russia who arranged to sell a diesel submarine to drug runners so that they could deliver illegal narcotics from Panama to the West Coast of the United States? Crimes and criminals are not limited to American soil, and neither are criminal investigations. In this *Criminal Justice in Action* feature, we will explore how the globalization of crime had led to the globalization of law enforcement.

Crossing Borders with Crime

A banker hides money in Austria for drug lords in Colombia. A heroin dealer in downtown Detroit is linked to poppy growers in Turkey. China-based organized crime bosses control gambling operations in San Francisco and fraudulent credit-card rings in Singapore.[123] The United Nations estimates that annual profits in the global illegal drug market reach $600 billion. There is a worldwide trade in chemical, biological, bacteriological, and nuclear weapons. Without a passport, a person sitting in front of the computer in his or her bedroom can cause billions of dollars in damage across the world with a computer worm or virus.

As these examples show, advances in transportation and communication technology, computer networks, and money transfer systems have erased national borders when it comes to criminal activity. The international law enforcement community has had to adjust to these new realities, and it has taken a number of steps to do so.

In 2000, eighty-one countries signed a protocol laying the groundwork for combating the illegal smuggling of persons for purposes of slavery, prostitution, and other forms of forced labor. Over the past three decades, numerous countries have joined together in mutual legal assistance treaties (MLATs) to combat a specific type of crime. Interpol, the world's largest international police organization, has 181 member countries that share information on crime. In 2003, a tip passed along through Interpol enabled South African police in Cape Town to arrest two U.S. citizens wanted for bank robbery.

Matters of Jurisdiction

Despite signs of international cooperation, law enforcement agents from the United States or any other country cannot simply go where they please to apprehend criminal suspects. As you may recall from our discussion in Chapter 4, a law enforcement agency must have jurisdiction in a certain area in order to uphold the law (make arrests and so on) there. In the example cited above, because they did not have jurisdiction in South Africa, American police officers could not go to Cape Town and arrest the bank robbers unless the South African government gave its permission.

This does not mean that jurisdiction is completely limited by territory. U.S. courts, and those in other countries, recognize several bases for extraterritorial jurisdiction, including:

> *Objective territorial jurisdiction.* Acts done outside a jurisdiction but intended to produce detrimental effects within that jurisdiction are treated as if they were committed within national boundaries.[124] Thus, for example, the U.S. Coast Guard had jurisdiction to board a shrimping vessel carrying a load of marijuana in Mexican territorial waters. The boat was headed toward North America, and the captain had maps of Alabama and Florida signifying that the contraband would be sold in the United States.[125]

> *Nationality principle of jurisdiction.* This holds that a nation can require its citizens to follow its laws outside its boundaries. So, if a U.S. citizen commits murder on an island in the Caribbean, he can be charged with homicide under American law.[126]

> *Universal jurisdiction.* International law considers some crimes so heinous that any country may have jurisdiction if one of its citizens is the target or perpetrator of such a crime, or if she or he has committed the crime and is afterward found within that country's borders.[127] In general, the U.S. government believes that war crimes, crimes against humanity (such as genocide), torture, and hijacking fall under universal jurisdiction.[128]

Combating Illegal Drugs

Besides these legal and theoretical bases for international jurisdiction, governments can enter into agreements providing law enforcement agents with powers outside their

AP Photo/Khaled Tanveer

Women in Multan, Pakistan, protest FBI activity in their country. The Pakistani government has allowed the agency to conduct raids of terrorist cells and detain suspects within its borders. Even without permission, under what theory of jurisdiction would the FBI have the right to conduct these sorts of antiterrorism operations?

own borders. The incentive for many of these agreements has been the continuing battle against illegal drugs. In 2000, the United States and China signed an MLAT establishing the guidelines for cooperative efforts to fight the "common threat" of heroin and methamphetamine use.[129] Other agreements arrange for **extradition,** in which one jurisdiction surrenders a person charged with a crime to another jurisdiction. Usually, the country requesting extradition has charged the person with a

crime and requests his or her return to face the charges. In 2003, in accordance with an extradition treaty, Argentina sent four suspected heroin traffickers to the United States for trial.

Cooperation against Terrorism

In recent years, the most impressive instances of international cooperation to fight global crime have come, as might be expected, in the field of antiterrorism. In August 2003, law enforcement agents from three countries—the United States, Great Britain, and Russia—were involved in an intricate "sting" operation that lasted five months. The operation began when the Russian government passed a tip to the FBI that a British arms dealer named Hemant Lakhani was looking to sell the same type of surface-to-air missile that had recently been fired by terrorists at an Israeli passenger jet in Kenya. With help from MI5, Britain's domestic intelligence agency, an FBI agent posed as someone interested in purchasing the Russian SA-18 Igla missile. When Lakhani met with the FBI agent in New Jersey to close the deal, he was arrested for providing material support to terrorists and selling arms without a license.

The same week as the Lakhani arrest, American law enforcement agents monitoring an Indonesian al Qaeda operative named Riduan Isamuddin tracked him to an apartment building in Ayutthaya, Thailand. The American agents informed Thai police of Isamuddin's whereabouts, and he was quickly arrested. A year earlier, information from law enforcement officials in Yemen helped the Central Intelligence Agency pinpoint and kill six other al Qaeda agents in that Muslim country. "There is a tremendous amount of law enforcement and intelligence cooperation from countries that wouldn't previously be expected to provide it," noted one terrorism expert.[130]

Extradition

The surrender of a fugitive offender by one jurisdiction to another in which the offender has been convicted or is liable for punishment.

Extradition Trouble with Mexico

Despite these examples of cooperation, territory is still an important concept in international criminal law. If there is no extradition treaty and no government permission, American law enforcement agents cannot carry out operations on foreign soil or exercise any power over suspects outside the United States. For example, although Mexican police arrest more than one hundred fugitives wanted in the United States each year, the government will not extradite a captured criminal suspect if that person faces the death penalty or life in prison without parole in this country.

Thus, extradition is routinely denied for persons suspected of the most serious crimes, such as Miguel Loza, who is wanted in California for murdering a woman by slashing her throat and then raping her friend. Loza remains in a Mexico City jail, as prosecutors in the United States will not assure the Mexican government that a California jury will not sentence him to death or life imprisonment. "We will wait until he comes back and arrest him in the U.S.," says the Santa Cruz County chief deputy district attorney. "It's not much of a plan, but it's all we've got."[131]

MAKING SENSE OF THE GLOBALIZATION OF LAW ENFORCEMENT

1 Is Mexico justified in holding suspects wanted for crimes committed in the United States because of its stance against the death penalty? Would American agents be justified in kidnapping suspects such as Miguel Loza and bringing them back to the United States?

2 Why do you think that countries generally do not want foreign law enforcement agents operating on their soil?

3 Reread the situation of Ludwig Feinberg, described in the introduction to this feature. Under what theory, or theories, of extraterritorial jurisdiction would the United States have jurisdiction to capture and prosecute him for his crimes?

Chapter Summary

1 **Explain some of the benefits of a culturally diverse police force.** Members of an integrated police force are more likely to develop strong relationships with the community, which may allow them to do a more effective job of maintaining law and order. Specifically, a predominantly white department can be a "dangerous irritant" in minority neighborhoods during times of crisis.

2 **List three criticisms of standard bureaucratic police organizations.** (a) They limit personal ingenuity and sometimes result in groupthink; (b) they limit contact with the community; and (c) they limit contact among members of the police department.

3 **Describe the theory behind a differential response strategy of responding to calls for service.** A differential response strategy allows a police department to distinguish among calls for service so that officers may respond to important calls more quickly. Therefore, a "hot" crime, such as a burglary in progress, will receive more immediate attention than a "cold" crime, such as a missing automobile that disappeared several days earlier.

4 **Explain community policing and its strategies.** Community policing involves proactive problem solving and a community-police partnership in which the community engages itself along with the police to address crime and the fear of crime in a particular geographic area. Strategies include sending police officers to schools, opening community intervention offices for high-risk youths, and encouraging police officers to live in high-crime neighborhoods.

5 **Describe two types of problem-solving policing.** (a) By concentrating on *hot spots,* or areas of high criminal activity, police can prepare specific strategies for combating those crimes; and (b) *crime mapping* allows law enforcement officials to identify geographic areas that are likely to be

STORIES FROM THE STREET
Go to the Stories from the Street feature at www.cjinaction.com to hear Larry Gaines tell insightful stories related to this chapter and his experiences in the field.

susceptible to certain types of crimes, and deploy personnel to those areas accordingly.

6 **List the three primary purposes of police patrol.** (a) The deterrence of crime, (b) the maintenance of public order, and (c) the provision of services that are not related to crime.

7 **Indicate some investigation strategies that are considered aggressive.** Using undercover officers is considered an aggressive (and often dangerous) investigative technique. The use of informants is also aggressive, but involves danger for those who inform.

8 **Determine when police officers are justified in using deadly force.** Police officers must make a reasonable judgment in determining when to use force that will place the suspect in threat of injury or death; that is, given the circumstances, the officer must reasonably assume that the use of such force is necessary to avoid serious injury or death to the officer or someone else.

9 **Identify the three traditional forms of police corruption.** The three traditional forms are bribery, shakedowns, and mooching.

10 **Explain what an ethical dilemma is and name four categories of ethical dilemmas typically facing a police officer.** An ethical dilemma is a situation in which police officers (a) do not know the right course of action; (b) have difficulty doing what they consider to be right; and/or (c) find the wrong choice very tempting. The four types of ethical dilemmas involve (a) discretion, (b) duty, (c) honesty, and (d) loyalty.

Key Terms

blue curtain 197
broken windows
   theory 186
bureaucracy 179
citizen oversight 204
community policing 183
confidential informant
   (CI) 194
delegation of
   authority 179
deadly force 199

detective 192
differential response 181
directed patrol 191
duty 205
ethics 204
extradition 208
field training 175
general patrol 191
hot spots 185
incident-driven
   policing 180

internal affairs unit
   (IAU) 204
police corruption 202
police cynicism 197
police subculture 196
problem-solving
   policing 184
reasonable force 199
response time 180
socialization 196

Questions for Critical Analysis

1 In what sense have police departments' physical standards been used to discriminate against women?

2 Contrast the community policing model with the professional policing model.

3 The Kansas City Preventive Patrol Experiment involved control beats, proactive beats, and reactive beats. Did the results of that experiment show any benefits to increasing preventive police patrol? If yes, how? If not, why not?

4 Relate the concept of "broken windows" to high-crime neighborhoods and potential ways to combat crime in such neighborhoods.

5 What are the various experiences that rookie police officers undergo that make them aware they are not in a "normal" job?

6 How does the police subculture affect police officers?

7 Under what circumstances can a police officer legally shoot a suspect who is trying to escape a crime scene?

8 How does the police subculture contribute to police corruption?

Go to www.cjinaction.com for tools to aid you in studying for your exams. Click on *Online Reviews* under *Chapter Resources* for an interactive review of each major section of this chapter. Under *Chapter Resources,* you will also find the *Chapter Outline, Chapter Summary, Flashcards, Glossary, Learning Objectives, Lecture Presentations, Concept Builder, Essay Questions,* and a *Tutorial Quiz.* You can also test yourself with a game of *Concentration* or the *Crossword Puzzle.*

Go to www.cjinaction.com for a wealth of online resources. Explore the *Internet Activities* and *Class Projects* under *Chapter Resources.* Check out the *Web Links* to access the Web sites mentioned in the text, as well as many others. You can also access recent perspectives by clicking on *CJ in the News* and *Terrorism Update* under *Course Resources.* If you'd like some mentoring, click on *Board of Mentors* under *Book Resources.*

For additional information, explore InfoTrac College Edition, your online library that offers complete full-length articles from thousands of scholarly and popular publications. Click on *InfoTrac College Edition* under *Chapter Resources* at www.cjinaction.com for a list of key words and InfoTrac exercises. Use the passcode that came with your book.

TEST PREPARATION ONLINE

Web Resources

Search Online with InfoTrac College Edition

Suggested Readings

Delattre, Edwin J., *Character and Cops: Ethics in Policing,* Washington, D.C.: AIE Press, 2002. This far-reaching study looks at ethical and unethical police behavior and asks, "Why?" Why do some cops exhibit incredible heroism while others seem to personify the worst in human nature? Why is a good cop a good cop and why is a bad cop a bad cop? The author explores the numerous factors that seem to affect ethics in the criminal justice system, including the many conflicting pressures placed on police officers by the society they are sworn to serve.

Lee, Henry, and Thomas W. O'Neil, *Cracking Cases: The Science of Solving Crimes,* Amherst, NY: Prometheus Books, 2002. In this book, wrongdoers go to great lengths to avoid capture. One destroys the body of his victim in a wood chipper. Another cranks up the air-conditioning to mask the victim's time of death, while a third tries to turn a shooting into a suicide. The reader is guided through a step-by-step tour of the investigative processes that were used to solve these crimes, along with several others. The authors also revisit the O. J. Simpson murder trial (Lee worked for the defense), and explain how the Los Angeles Police Department's bumbled investigations in that case helped Simpson go free.

Notes

1. Quoted in Gordon Witkin, "When the Bad Guys Are Cops," *U.S. News and World Report* (September 11, 1995), 22.
2. James H. Chenoweth, "Situational Tests: A New Attempt at Assessing Police Candidates," *Journal of Criminal Law, Criminology and Police Science* 52 (1961), 232.
3. Matthew J. Hickman and Brian A. Reaves, *Local Police Departments 2000* (Washington, D.C.: U.S. Department of Justice, January 2003), 10.
4. Frank Horvath, "Polygraphic Screening Candidates for Police Work in Large Police Agencies in the United States: A Survey of Practices, Policies, and Evaluative Comments," *American Journal of Police* 12 (1993), 67–86.
5. David L. Carter and Allen D. Sapp, "College Education and Policing: Coming of Age," *FBI Law Enforcement Bulletin* 61 (1992), 8.
6. Hickman and Reaves, 11.
7. Alan Vodicka, "Educational Requirements for Police Recruits," *Law and Order* 42 (1994), 91.
8. D. P. Hinkle, "College Degree: An Impractical Prerequisite for Police Work," *Law and Order* (July 1991), 105.
9. Hickman and Reaves, 11.
10. National Advisory Commission on Civil Disorder, *Report* (Washington, D.C.: U.S. Government Printing Office, 1968), Chapter 11.
11. *Griggs v. Duke Power Co.,* 401 U.S. 424 (1971); and *Abermarle Paper Co. v. Moody,* 422 U.S. 405 (1975).
12. Corrine Streit, "Recruiting Minority Officers," *Law Enforcement Technology* (February 2001), 70–75.
13. *Detroit Police Officers' Association v. Young,* 608 F.2d 671, 675 (1979).
14. *Wygant v. Jackson Board of Education,* 476 U.S. 314 (1986).
15. George F. Cole, *The American System of Criminal Justice,* 5th ed. (Pacific Grove, CA: Brooks/Cole, 1998), 291.
16. C. J. Chivers, "From Court Order to Reality: A Diverse Boston Police Force," *New York Times* (April 4, 2001), A1.
17. *Ibid.*
18. Lawrence M. Friedman, *Crime and Punishment in American History* (New York: Basic Books, 1993), 364–365.

19. Marion E. Gold, "The Progress of Women in Policing," *Law and Order* (June 2000), 159.

20. Liz Tascio, "Women Recruits Meet High Standard," *Contra Costa Times* (March 16, 2003), 4.

21. *Lanning v. SEPTA*, No. 01-1040 (3d Cir. 2002).

22. "DOJ Decides Suit Is a Bad Fit," *Law Enforcement News* (October 31, 2001), 1.

23. Penny E. Harrington, *Recruiting and Retaining Women: A Self-Assessment Guide for Law Enforcement* (Los Angeles: National Center for Women & Policing, 2001), 22–27.

24. Larry K. Gaines and Gary W. Cordner, *Policing Perspectives: An Anthology* (Los Angeles: Roxbury Publishing Co., 1999), 351.

25. H. Nees, "Policing 2001," *Law and Order* (January 1990), 257–264.

26. Peter K. Manning, *Police Work: The Social Organization of Policing*, 2d ed. (Prospect Heights, IL: Waveland Press, 1997), 96.

27. Samuel Walker, *The Police in America: An Introduction*, 2d ed. (New York: McGraw-Hill, 1992), 16.

28. George L. Kelling and Mark H. Moore, "From Political to Reform to Community: The Evolving Strategy of Police," in *Community Policing: Rhetoric or Reality*, ed. Jack Greene and Stephen Mastrofski (New York: Praeger Publishers, 1988), 13.

29. Mark H. Moore and Robert C. Trojanowicz, *Corporate Strategies for Policing* (Washington, D.C.: National Institute of Justice, November 1988), 6.

30. Henry M. Wrobleski and Karen M. Hess, *Introduction to Law Enforcement and Criminal Justice*, 7th ed. (Belmont, CA: Wadsworth/Thomson Learning, 2003), 173.

31. Lori Stahl and Stephen Power, "Response Slows on 911 Calls," *Dallas Morning News* (September 28, 1997), 1A.

32. Lawrence W. Sherman, "Attacking Crime: Police and Crime Patrol," in *Modern Policing*, ed. Michael H. Tonry and Norval Morris, vol. 16 of *Crime and Justice: A Review of Research* (Chicago: University of Chicago Press, 1992), 335.

33. Ibid., 338.

34. Robert Trojanowicz, *An Evaluation of the Neighborhood Foot Patrol Program in Flint, Michigan* (East Lansing, MI: Michigan State University, 1982), 85–87.

35. George Kelling, "Police and Community: The Quiet Revolution," in *Perspectives on Policing* (Washington, D.C.: National Institute of Justice, 1988).

36. Mark H. Moore and George L. Kelling, "'To Serve and Protect': Learning from Police History," *Public Interest* (Winter 1983), 54–57.

37. A. Steven Dietz, "Evaluating Community Policing: Quality Police Service and Fear of Crime," *Policing: An International Journal of Police Strategies and Management* 20 (1997), 83–100.

38. Bureau of Justice Assistance, *Crime Prevention and Community Policing: A Vital Partnership* (Washington, D.C.: Office of Justice Programs, September 1997), 7–8.

39. "Fighting Crime, Japanese Style," *Economist* (August 7, 1999), 24.

40. Herman Goldstein, "Improving Policing: A Problem-Oriented Approach," *Crime and Delinquency* 25 (1979), 236–258.

41. Kelling and Moore, 12.

42. Bureau of Justice Assistance, *Problem-Oriented Drug Enforcement: A Community-Based Approach for Effective Policing* (Washington, D.C.: Office of Justice Programs, 1993), 5.

43. Sherman, 331–332.

44. Lawrence W. Sherman, Patrick R. Gartin, and Michael E. Buerger, "Hot Spots of Predatory Crime: Routine Activities and the Criminology of Place," *Criminology* 27 (1989), 27–55.

45. *National Institute of Justice Research Preview: Policing Drug Hot Spots* (Washington, D.C.: Office of Justice Programs, January 1996).

46. Brian J. Taylor, "The Screening of America," *Reason* (May 1, 1997), 44.

47. Elizabeth Douglass, "Crime Mapping Software Helps Officers Put Pieces Together," *Los Angeles Times* (February 16, 1998), D3.

48. James Q. Wilson and George L. Kelling, "Broken Windows," *Atlantic Monthly* (March 1982), 29–38.

49. Angel Gonzales, "Board Restricts Alcohol Sales in Pioneer Square," *Seattle Times* (July 24, 2003), B1.

50. Office of Community Oriented Policing Services, *Promising Strategies from the Field: A National Overview* (Washington, D.C.: U.S. Department of Justice, 2002), 1.

51. Hickman and Reaves, 15.

52. National Institute of Justice Research Preview, *Community Policing Strategies* (Washington, D.C.: Office of Justice Programs, November 1995).

53. Jihong Zhao and Quint C. Thurman, "Community Policing: Where Are We Now?" *Crime and Delinquency* (July 1997), 345–357.

54. Wrobleski and Hess, 119.

55. Connie Fletcher, "What Cops Know," *On Patrol* (Summer 1996), 44–45.

56. David H. Bayley, *Police for the Future* (New York: Oxford University Press, 1994), 20.

57. Walker, 103.

58. Eric J. Scott, *Calls for Service: Citizens Demand an Initial Police Response* (Washington, D.C.: National Institute of Justice, 1981), 28–30.

59. William G. Gay, Theordore H. Schell, and Stephen Schack, *Routine Patrol: Improving Patrol Productivity*, vol. 1 (Washington, D.C.: National Institute of Justice, 1977), 3–6.

60. Gary W. Cordner, "The Police on Patrol," in *Police and Policing: Contemporary Issues*, ed. Dennis Jay Kenney (New York: Praeger Publishers, 1989), 60–71.

61. Anthony V. Bouza, *The Police Mystique: An Insider's Look at Cops, Crime, and the Criminal Justice System* (New York: Plenum Press, 1990), 27.

62. Hickman and Reaves, 10.

63. Dale O. Cloninger, "Enforcement Risks and Deterrence: A Reexamination," *Journal of Socio-Economics* 23 (1994), 273.

64. George L. Kelling, Tony Pate, Duane Dieckman, and Charles Brown, *The Kansas City Preventive Patrol Experiment: A Summary Report* (Washington, D.C.: The Police Foundation, 1974), 3–4.

65. Ibid.

66. Carl B. Klockars and Stephen D. Mastrofski, "The Police and Serious Crime," in *Thinking about Police*, ed. Carl Klockars and Stephen Mastrofski (New York: McGraw-Hill, 1990), 130.

67. James Q. Wilson, *Thinking about Crime* (New York: Basic Books, 1983), 65–66.

68. Robert Sheehan and Gary W. Cordner, *Introduction to Police Administration*, 2d ed. (Cincinnati, OH: Anderson, 1989), 367–368.

69. U.S. Bureau of Labor Statistics, "Police and Detectives," in *Occupational Outlook Handbook*, at http://www.bls.gov/oco/ocos160.htm.

70. Peter W. Greenwood and Joan Petersilia, *The Criminal Investigation Process: Summary and Policy Implications* (Santa Monica, CA: Rand Corporation, 1975).

71. Fletcher, 46.

72. John E. Eck, *Solving Crimes: The Investigation of Burglary and Robbery* (Washington, D.C.: Police Executive Research Forum, 1983).

73. Steven G. Brandl and James Frank, "The Relationship between Evidence, Detective Effort, and the Disposition of Burglary and Robbery Investigations," *American Journal of Police* 1, 149–168.

74. 353 U.S. 53 (1957).

75. Fred Kaplan and Lyle Denniston, "Army Plane Joins Sniper Hunt," *Boston Globe* (October 17, 2002), A1.

76. Army Appropriations Act, ch. 263, Section 15, 20 Stat. 145 (1878), codified as amended at 18 U.S.C. Section 1385 (2000).

77. Military Cooperation with Law Enforcement Officials Act of 1981, Pub. L. No. 97-86, Section 905, 95 Stat. 1115, codified as amended at 10 U.S.C. Sections 371–378 (1998).

78. Diane Cecilia Weber, *Warrior Cops: The Ominous Growth of Paramilitarism in American Police Departments*, Cato Institute Briefing Paper No. 50 (1999), at http://www.cato.org/pubs/briefs/bp-050es.html.

79. Raytheon Corporation, *NightSight Field Assessment: Creative Technology Solutions to Law Enforcement Problems* (Rockville, MD: National Criminal Justice Reference Service, 2002), 2.

80. Scott Lindlaw, "U.S. Mulls Military's Domestic Role," *Associated Press* (July 22, 2002).

81. Timothy Egan, "Killing of White Deputy Quiets Protests over Police Shootings of 2 Blacks," *New York Times* (July 13, 2002), A7.

82. Ibid.

83. Edgar H. Schein, *Organizational Culture and Leadership* (San Francisco: Jossey-Bass, 1985), 9.

84. Harry J. Mullins, "Myth, Tradition, and Ritual," *Law and Order* (September 1995), 197.

85. John Van Maanen, "Observations on the Making of a Policeman," *Human Organization* 32 (1973), 407–418.

86. William Westly, *Violence and the Police: A Sociological Study of Law, Custom, and Morality* (Cambridge, MA: MIT Press, 1970).

87. Wallace Graves, "Police Cynicism: Causes and Cures," *FBI Law Enforcement Bulletin* (June 1996), 16–21.

88. Robert Regoli, *Police in America* (Washington, D.C.: R. F. Publishing, 1977).

89. Bob Herbert, "A Cop's View," *New York Times* (March 15, 1998), 17.

90. Jerome H. Skolnick, *Justice without Trial: Law Enforcement in a Democratic Society* (New York: Wiley, 1966), 44.

91. Detis T. Duhart, *Violence in the Workplace, 1993–99* (Washington, D.C.: U.S. Department of Justice, December 2001), 1.

92. Les Krantz, *Job-Related Almanac* (New York: World Almanac, 1998).

93. James Hibberd, "Police Psychology," *On Patrol* (Fall 1996), 26.

94. "Dispatches," *On Patrol* (Summer 1996), 25.

95. Friedman, 362.

96. Bureau of Justice Statistics, *Contacts between Police and the Public* (Washington, D.C.: U.S. Department of Justice, February 2001), 25.

97. Independent Commission on the Los Angeles Police Department, *Report of the Independent Commission on the Los Angeles Police Department* (1991), ix.

98. Joel Garner, John Buchanan, Tom Schade, and John Hepburn, *Research in Brief: Understanding the Use of Force by and against the Police* (Washington, D.C.: Office of Justice Programs, November 1996), 5.

99. Ibid., 1.

100. 471 U.S. 1 (1985).

101. 471 U.S. 1, 11 (1985).

102. 490 U.S. 386 (1989).

103. Hickman and Reaves, 22.

104. "Reducing the Death Toll from Non-Lethal Weapons," *Law Enforcement News* (March 15–31, 2003), 8.

105. Cited in Peter Noel, "I Thought He Had a Gun," *Village Voice* (July 13, 1998), 41.

106. Bureau of Justice Statistics, *Contacts between Police and the Public*, 24.

107. Malcolm D. Holmes, "Minority Threat and Police Brutality: Determinants of Civil Rights Criminal Complaints in U.S. Municipalities," *Criminology* 38 (May 2000), 361.

108. Sean Hecker, "Race and Pretextual Traffic Stops: An Expanded Role for Civilian Review," *Columbia Human Rights Law Review* 28 (Spring 1997), 551.

109. Randall L. Kennedy, "*McCleskey v. Kemp*, Race, Capital Punishment, and the Supreme Court," *Harvard Law Review* 101 (1988), 1436–1438.

110. Douglas A. Smith, "Minorities and the Police: Attitudinal and Behavioral Questions," *Race and Criminal Justice*, ed. Michael J. Lynch and E. Britt Patterson (New York: Harrow & Heston, 1991), 28–30.

111. Matt Lait and Scott Glover, "Inglewood Police Accused of Abuse in Other Cases," *Los Angeles Times* (July 15, 2002), A1.

112. J. Dorschner, "Police Deviance: Corruption and Controls," in *Critical Issues in Policing, Contemporary Readings*, ed. Roger G. Dunham and Geoffrey P. Albert (Prospect Heights, IL: Waveland Press, 1989), 249–285.

113. Lawrence W. Sherman, "Becoming Bent: Moral Careers of Corrupt Policemen," in *Police Corruption: A Sociological Perspective*, ed. Lawrence W. Sherman (Garden City, NY: Doubleday, 1974), 191–208.

114. Knapp Commission, *Report on Police Corruption* (New York: Brazilier, 1973).

115. Quoted in Jennifer Dukes and Loren Keller, "Can Police Be Police to Selves?" *Omaha World-Herald* (February 22, 1998), 1A.

116. "Roster of Civilian Oversight Agencies in the U.S.," National Association for Civilian Oversight of Law Enforcement, at http://www.nacole.org.

117. Hazel Glenn Beh, "Municipal Liability for Failure to Investigate Citizen Complaints against Police," *Fordham Urban Law Journal* 23 (Winter 1998), 209.

118. Jocelyn M. Pollock-Byrne, *Ethics in Crime and Justice: Dilemmas and Decisions* (Pacific Grove, CA: Brooks/Cole Publishing Co., 1989), 84–86.

119. Jocelyn M. Pollock and Ronald F. Becker, "Ethics Training Using Officers' Dilemmas," *FBI Law Enforcement Bulletin* (November 1996), 20–28.

120. *Ibid.*

121. Peter K. Manning, *Police Work: The Social Organization of Policing* (Cambridge, MA: MIT Press, 1977), 100–101.

122. Linda S. Miller and Karen M. Hess, *Police in the Community: Strategies for the 21st Century*, 2d ed. (Belmont, CA: Wadsworth Publishing, 1998), 81.

123. John Kerry, *The New War: The Web of Crime That Threatens America's Security* (New York: Simon & Schuster, 1997), 24.

124. *Strassheim v. Daily*, 221 U.S. 280 (1911).

125. *United States v. DeWeese*, 632 F.2d 1267 (5th Cir. 1980).

126. *Jones v. United States*, 137 U.S. 202 (1890).

127. 49 U.S.C. Section 46502(b) (2001).

128. Frank Turkheimer, "Globalization of U.S. Law Enforcement: Does the Constitution Come Along?" *Houston Law Review* (Summer 2002), 324.

129. Agreement on Mutual Legal Assistance in Criminal Matters, June 19, 2000, United States–People's Republic of China (on file with the U.S. Department of State, Office of Treaty Affairs).

130. Jules Crittenden, "In Terrorism Fight, U.S. Begins to Reap Rewards," *Boston Herald* (November 10, 2002), 8.

131. Maria Alicia Guara, "How Killers in State Stay Untouchable," *San Francisco Chronicle* (August 10, 2003), A1.

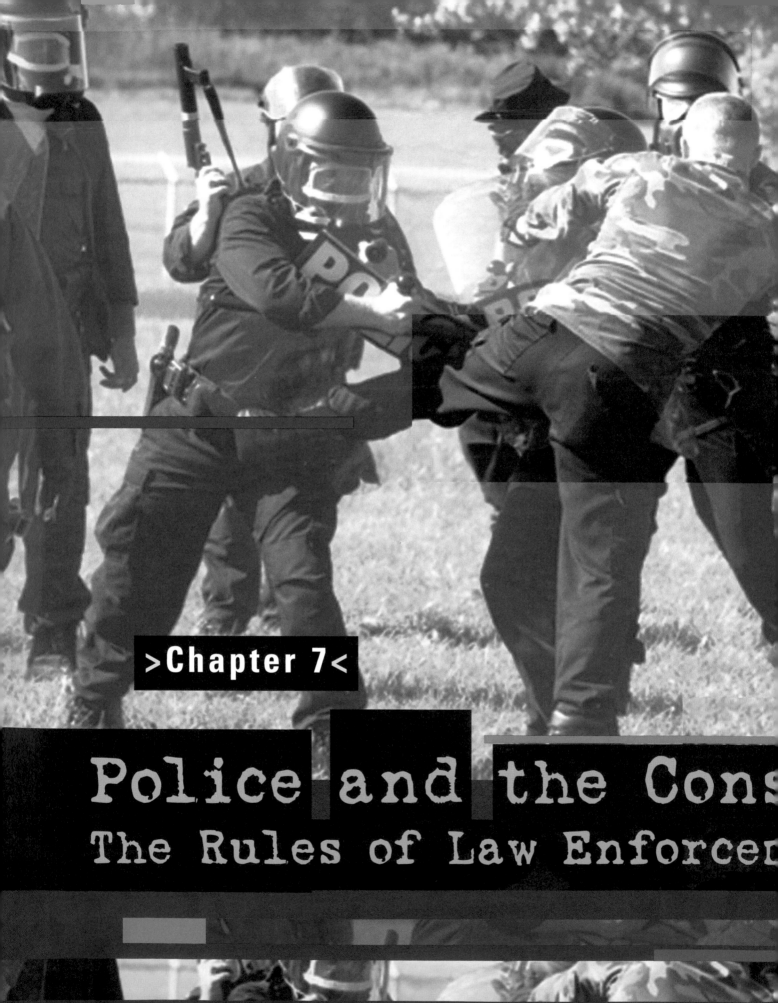

>Chapter 7<

Police and the Cons
The Rules of Law Enforcer

>chapter objectives<

After reading this chapter, you should be able to:

1 Outline the four major sources that may provide probable cause.

2 Explain the exclusionary rule and the exceptions to it.

3 Distinguish between a stop and a frisk, and indicate the importance of the case *Terry v. Ohio.*

4 List the four elements that must be present for an arrest to take place.

5 List the four categories of items that can be seized by use of a search warrant.

6 Explain when searches can be made without a warrant.

7 Describe how the USA Patriot Act of 2001 changed the guidelines for electronic surveillance of suspected terrorists.

8 Recite the *Miranda* warning.

9 Indicate situations in which a *Miranda* warning is unnecessary.

10 List the three basic types of police identification.

The Seat Belt Case

When Gail Atwater was pulled over by a police officer on a local street in Lago Vista, Texas, she did not appear to be engaged in any serious wrongdoing. She was driving her two children home from soccer practice at fifteen miles per hour. There was no contraband in her pickup truck—rather, it was filled with two tricycles, a bag of charcoal, a cooler, toys, food, and two pairs of children's shoes. In fact, Atwater had been stopped because neither she nor her children were wearing a seat belt. Under Texas law, this offense is a misdemeanor, punishable by a maximum fine of $50.

While the police officer's stop was unremarkable, his actions following the stop led Atwater and the city of Lago Vista to the United States Supreme Court. Instead of writing a ticket, he ordered Atwater out of her car, placed her in handcuffs, and informed her that she would be taken to jail. He threatened to take Atwater's children into custody as well, but a neighbor happened onto the scene of the incident and took them home.

Atwater's lawyers argued that the police officer had overstepped his discretion, and asked the Supreme Court to rule that it is unreasonable for an officer to arrest someone for a minor traffic offense that carries only a fine. The Court refused this request. Justice David Souter, while agreeing that Atwater had been subjected to "gratuitous humiliations," said that the Court was not willing to limit an officer's ability to make an arrest as long as he or she believes that a law—any law—has been broken.

Gail Atwater, left, with her children Anya and Mac at their home in Lago Vista, Texas.

AP Photo/Pat Sullivan

> **Note that this** was not an easy case for the Supreme Court. Four of the nine justices agreed with Atwater that the police officer had acted unreasonably. In effect, each member of the Court was forced to weigh Atwater's personal freedoms against the ability of the local police department to do its job. This balance between the need for effective law enforcement and the rights of American citizens under the U.S. Constitution has been, and remains, a controversial issue. Many observers feel that courts go too far in protecting the rights of the accused, but others believe that police have been given a dangerous amount of leeway in using their powers. In this chapter we will examine the extent to which police behavior is controlled by the law, starting with a discussion of the constitutional principles on which such control is grounded.

The Fourth Amendment

In *Atwater v. City of Lago Vista*,[1] the Supreme Court did not address the defendant's illegal activity. (In fact, Atwater pleaded no contest to the seat belt charge.) Rather, it ruled that the police officer had not overstepped the boundaries of his authority in making the arrest. To understand these boundaries, law enforcement officers must understand the Fourth Amendment, which reads as follows:

> The right of the people to be secure in their persons, houses, papers, and effects, against unreasonable searches and seizures, shall not be violated, and no Warrants shall issue, but upon probable cause, supported by Oath or affirmation, and particularly describing the place to be searched, and the persons or things to be seized.

This amendment contains two critical legal concepts: a prohibition against *unreasonable* **searches and seizures** and the requirement of *probable cause* to issue a warrant (see Figure 7.1).

REASONABLENESS

Law enforcement personnel use searches and seizures to look for and collect the evidence they need to convict individuals suspected of crimes. As you have just read, when police are conducting a search or seizure, they must be *reasonable*. Though courts have spent innumerable hours scrutinizing the word, no specific meaning for "reasonable" exists. A thesaurus can provide useful synonyms—logical, practical, sensible, intelligent, plausible—but because each case is different, those terms are relative.

In the *Atwater* case, the Court rejected the argument that the arrest had been so unreasonable as to violate the Fourth Amendment's prohibition against unreasonable searches and seizures. That does not mean that the officer's actions would have been unreasonable under any circumstances. What if Atwater could have proved that there was no way the officer could have known whether she was wearing a seat belt and that he had pulled her over in retaliation for contesting a speeding ticket that he had written her two months earlier? The officer's conduct would almost certainly have been considered unreasonable.

CONCEPT BUILDER
Probable cause is often misunderstood by the general public, and is even difficult at times for law enforcement officials to establish. Visit www.cjinaction.com for an interactive exploration of this key topic.

Searches and Seizures
The legal term, as found in the Fourth Amendment of the U.S. Constitution, that generally refers to the searching for and the confiscating of evidence by law enforcement agents.

INFOTRAC KEYWORDS
Fourth Amendment
For more information, use this search term with InfoTrac College Edition, your online library at www.infotrac-college.com

FIGURE 7.1 The Meaning of Unreasonable Searches and Seizures and Probable Cause

UNREASONABLE SEARCHES AND SEIZURES

The Fourth Amendment provides that individuals have the right to be "secure in their persons" against "unreasonable searches and seizures" conducted by government agents. In practice, this means that law enforcement officers are required to obtain a search warrant prior to any search and seizure. Basically, the search warrant is the acknowledgment by a judge that probable cause exists for law enforcement officers to search for or take a person or property. In other words, the search and seizure must be "reasonable."

PROBABLE CAUSE

Before a search can take place or an individual can be arrested, the requirement of probable cause must be met. Probable cause exists if there is a substantial likelihood that (1) a crime was committed and (2) the individual committed the crime. Note that probable cause involves a *likelihood*—not just a possibility—that the suspect committed the crime. Probable cause must exist before police can get an arrest warrant or a search warrant from a judge.

Probable Cause
Reasonable grounds to believe the existence of facts warranting certain actions, such as the search or arrest of a person.

The concept of reasonableness is linked to **probable cause.** The Supreme Court has ruled, for example, that any arrest or seizure is unreasonable unless it is supported by probable cause.[2] The burden of probable cause requires more than mere suspicion on a police officer's part; that officer must know of facts and circumstances that would reasonably lead to "the belief that an offense has been or is being committed."[3]

Sources of Probable Cause   If no probable cause existed when a police officer took a certain action, it cannot be retroactively applied. If, for example, a police officer stops a person for jaywalking and then finds several ounces of marijuana in that person's pocket, the arrest for marijuana possession would probably be disallowed. Remember, suspicion does not equal probable cause. If, however, an informant had tipped the officer off that the person was a drug dealer, probable cause might exist and the arrest could be valid. Informants are one of several sources that may provide probable cause. Others include:

1 *Personal observation.* Police officers may use their personal training, experience, and expertise to infer probable cause from situations that may not be obviously criminal. If, for example, a police officer observes several people in a car slowly circling a certain building in a high-crime area, that officer may infer that the people are "casing" the building in preparation for a robbery. Probable cause could be established for detaining the suspects.

2 *Information.* Law enforcement officers receive information from victims, eyewitnesses, informants, and official sources such as police bulletins or broadcasts. Such information, as long as it is believed to be reliable, is a basis for probable cause.

3 *Evidence.* In certain circumstances, which will be examined later in this chapter, police have probable cause for a search or seizure based on evidence—such as a shotgun—in plain view.

4 *Association.* In some circumstances, if the police see a person with a known criminal background in a place where criminal activity is openly taking place, they have probable cause to stop that person. Generally, however, association is not adequate to establish probable cause.[4]

Michigan state and federal law enforcement officers take part in a predawn raid of a Detroit residence. Before taking such action, the officers must receive permission from a judge or magistrate in the form of a search warrant. Ideally, the judicial official will issue such a warrant only if the law enforcement agency involved can provide probable cause that an illegal activity is taking place in the dwelling. How does the need to provide probable cause in such instances limit police power?

AP Photo, *Detroit News*/Charles V. Tines

The Probable Cause Framework   In a sense, the concept of probable cause allows police officers to do their job effectively. Most arrests are made without a warrant because most arrests are the result of quick police reaction to the commission of a crime. Indeed, it would not be practical to expect a police officer to obtain a warrant before making an arrest on the street. Thus, probable cause provides a framework that limits the situations in which police officers can make arrests, but also gives officers the freedom to act within that framework. Once an arrest is made, however, the arresting officer must prove to a judge that probable cause existed. In *County of Riverside v. McLaughlin* (1991),[5] the Supreme Court ruled that this judicial determination of probable cause must be made within forty-eight hours after the arrest, even if this two-day period includes a weekend or holiday.

THE EXCLUSIONARY RULE

Historically, the courts have looked to the Fourth Amendment for guidance in regulating the activity of law enforcement officers, as the language of the Constitution does not expressly do so. The courts' most potent legal tool in this endeavor is the **exclusionary rule,** which prohibits the use of illegally seized evidence. According to this rule, any evidence obtained by an unreasonable search or seizure is inadmissible (may not be used) against a defendant in a criminal trial.[6] Even highly incriminating evidence, such as a knife stained with the victim's blood, usually cannot be introduced at a trial if illegally obtained. Furthermore, any physical or verbal evidence police are able to acquire by using illegally obtained evidence is known as the **fruit of the poisoned tree** and is also inadmissible. For example, if the police use the existence of the bloodstained knife to get a confession out of a suspect, that confession will be excluded as well.

One of the implications of the exclusionary rule is that it forces police to gather evidence properly. If they follow appropriate procedures, they are more likely to be rewarded with a conviction. If they are careless or abuse the rights of the suspect, they are unlikely to get a conviction. Critics of the exclusionary rule, however, argue that its strict application may permit guilty people to go free because of police carelessness or innocent errors (for an example, see the feature *CJ in Focus—The Balancing Act: Excluding Justice?* on the next page).

Establishing the Exclusionary Rule   The exclusionary rule is applied to all evidence presented in federal courts as a result of the decision in *Weeks v. United States.*[7] For almost fifty years after this 1914 case, however, state courts continued to allow illegally obtained evidence, and federal courts could do so if the evidence had been obtained by state officers. This practice was known rather sarcastically as the *silver platter doctrine,* because such evidence handed the prosecution a conviction "on a silver platter." The only exception to the silver platter doctrine was when police actions were so extreme that they "shocked the conscience" of the court.

The "shocks the conscience" standard was established in *Rochin v. California* (1952).[8] In this case, police officers entered Rochin's home without a warrant and saw him place what they thought were narcotics in his mouth. The police tried to forcibly expel the items from Rochin. When this failed, they took him to the hospital and had his stomach pumped. This action produced two tablets of morphine. Rochin was convicted of possession of illegal drugs and sentenced to sixty days in jail. The Supreme Court overturned his conviction on the ground that the police officers' actions violated Rochin's Fourth Amendment due process rights; Justice Felix Frankfurter compared the police's methods to the "rack and screw."

Rochin did not make the exclusionary rule applicable to all state cases. Instead, the Supreme Court ruled that it applied only in cases that involved serious police misconduct. The silver platter doctrine was finally eliminated nine

Exclusionary Rule
A rule under which any evidence that is obtained in violation of the accused's rights under the Fourth, Fifth, and Sixth Amendments, as well as any evidence derived from illegally obtained evidence, will not be admissible in criminal court.

Fruit of the Poisoned Tree
Evidence that is acquired through the use of illegally obtained evidence and is therefore inadmissible in court.

INFOTRAC KEYWORDS
exclusionary rule
For more information, use this search term with InfoTrac College Edition, your online library at www.infotrac-college.com

> Excluding Justice?

Early on a spring morning in Washington Heights, a drug-infested area of New York City, two detectives watched four men load a duffel bag into the trunk of a Chevrolet. When the men saw the officers, they ran, leaving only the woman who was driving the car. The detectives proceeded to find seventy-five pounds of cocaine and five pounds of heroin in the automobile. The woman admitted to being a drug courier and to making similar deliveries from Detroit twenty times for her son, a dealer.

During the woman's pretrial hearing, U.S. District Judge Harold Baer, Jr., of Manhattan ruled that the evidence the detectives had found was inadmissible. Baer's reasoning was that the officers did not have reasonable cause to stop the car and that the actions of the other four men were understandable because "residents in that neighborhood tended to regard police officers as corrupt, abusive, and violent."

The judge's decision highlighted the conflicts inherent in the exclusionary rule. On the one hand, the rule does deter police from violating an individual's constitutional rights and acts as a clear demonstration that law enforcement officers are not above the law. On the other hand, the exclusionary rule imposes costs on society. There was little doubt that the woman in this case was guilty. A number of admittedly guilty defendants have been placed back on the streets because of this rule. Furthermore, the rule weakens public confidence in American courts by giving victims and other members of society the perception that "the truth" is less important than procedure in the criminal justice system.

In this particular case, the general uproar over Baer's decision from victims' rights groups and many prominent politicians forced the judge to reconsider. Three months after his initial ruling, he reversed himself and allowed the drug evidence and a videotaped confession to be admitted at trial.

FOR CRITICAL ANALYSIS
Do you think there are other means of ensuring proper police behavior that would be more effective than the exclusionary rule? What if police officers were subject to criminal sanctions for improperly gathering evidence? What if the victim of an unlawful search and seizure or arrest could sue a police officer in civil court?

---

years later by the Court's decision in *Mapp v. Ohio* (1961).[9] This case involved an illegal search and seizure conducted by Cleveland (Ohio) police officers. Whereas the Court had previously been hesitant to apply the exclusionary rule to a decision made in state courts, the *Mapp* case signaled a new willingness to apply the Fourth Amendment to both federal and state law enforcement officers.[10]

Exceptions to the Exclusionary Rule   Critics of the exclusionary rule have long maintained that the costs to society of losing critical evidence were higher than the benefits of deterring police misconduct. In recent years, a number of Supreme Court decisions have mirrored this view and provided exceptions to the exclusionary rule. The **"inevitable discovery" exception** was established in the wake of the disappearance of ten-year-old Pamela Powers of Des Moines, Iowa, on Christmas Eve, 1968. The police's primary suspect in the case, a religious fanatic named Robert Williams, was tricked by a detective into leading police to the site where he had buried Powers. Specifically, the detective convinced Williams that if he did not lead police to the body, he would soon forget where it was buried. This would deny his victim a "Christian burial." Initially, in *Brewer v. Williams* (1977),[11] the Court ruled that the evidence (Powers's body) had been obtained illegally because Williams's attorney had not been present during the interrogation that led to his admission. The state of Iowa appealed this decision. In *Nix v. Williams* (1984),[12] the Court reversed itself, ruling that the evidence was admissible because the body would have eventually ("inevitably") been found by lawful means.

"Inevitable Discovery" Exception
The legal principle that illegally obtained evidence can be admitted in court if police using lawful means would have "inevitably" discovered it.

The scope of the exclusionary rule was further diminished in the wake of the Supreme Court's ruling in *United States v. Leon* (1984).[13] The case involved evidence that had been seized by police on the authority of a search warrant that had been improperly issued by a magistrate. In allowing the evidence, the Court created a **"good faith" exception** to the exclusionary rule. Under this exception, evidence acquired by a police officer using a technically incorrect search warrant is admissible if the officer was unaware of the error. In this situation, the officer is said to have acted in "good faith." By the same token, if police officers use a search warrant that they know to be technically incorrect, the good faith exception does not apply and the evidence can be suppressed.

"Good Faith" Exception
The legal principle, established through court decisions, that evidence obtained with the use of a technically faulty search warrant is admissible during trial if the police acted in good faith when they sought the warrant from a judge.

↗ONLINE REVIEW *Go to the book's Web site for an interactive review of this section*

Stops and Frisks

Several years ago, an off-duty Miami–Dade County police officer named Aaron Campbell was driving on the Florida turnpike when he was pulled over by two Orange County deputies, allegedly for changing lanes without properly signaling. A fistfight ensued. At the resulting trial, Campbell claimed that he was stopped because he fit a drug courier profile in use by the deputies; he was an African American and had South Florida license plates. A circuit judge agreed, ruling that Campbell had been stopped illegally.[14]

The problem was not that the deputies had stopped Campbell. Law enforcement officers are expected to stop and question people if there is a suspicion of illegal behavior. The problem was that the Orange County deputies did not have a "reasonable" suspicion that Campbell was breaking the law. Instead, they had only a "mere" suspicion based on the drug courier profile—without any other specific facts. (See the feature *Criminal Justice in Action—Racial Profiling and the Constitution* at the end of the chapter.) When reasonable suspicion exists, police officers are well within their rights to *stop and frisk* a suspect. In a stop and frisk, law enforcement officers (1) briefly detain a person they reasonably believe to be suspicious, and (2) if they believe the person to be armed, proceed to pat down, or "frisk," that person's outer clothing.[15]

THE ELUSIVE DEFINITION OF REASONABLE SUSPICION

Like so many elements of police work, the decision of whether to stop a suspect is based on the balancing of conflicting priorities. On the one hand, a police officer feels a sense of urgency to act when he or she believes that criminal activity is occurring or is about to occur. On the other hand, law enforcement agents do not want to harass innocent individuals, especially if doing so runs afoul of the U.S. Constitution. In stop-and-frisk law, this balancing act rests on the fulcrum of reasonable suspicion.

Terry v. Ohio The precedent for the ever-elusive definition of a "reasonable" suspicion in stop-and-frisk situations was established in *Terry v. Ohio* (1968).[16] In that case, a detective named McFadden

John Boykin/PhotoEdit

A police officer frisks a suspect in Lockhart, Texas. What is the main purpose behind a frisk? When are police justified in frisking someone who has been detained?

FindLaw has a handy summary of the many laws regarding police procedure that can be traced to the Fourth Amendment. Find this Web site by clicking on *Web Links* under *Chapter Resources* at www.cjinaction.com

observed two men (one of whom was Terry) acting strangely in downtown Cleveland. The men would walk past a certain store, peer into the window, and then stop at a street corner and confer. While they were talking, another man joined the conversation and then left quickly. Several minutes later the three men met again at another corner a few blocks away. Detective McFadden believed the trio was planning to break into the store. He approached them, told them who he was, and asked for identification. After receiving a mumbled response, the detective frisked the three men and found handguns on two of them, who were tried and convicted of carrying concealed weapons.

The Supreme Court upheld the conviction, ruling that Detective McFadden had reasonable cause to believe that the men were armed and dangerous and that swift action was necessary to protect himself and other citizens in the area.[17] The Court accepted McFadden's interpretation of the unfolding scene as based on objective facts and practical conclusions. It therefore concluded that his suspicion was reasonable. In the Florida case described above, the deputies' reasons for stopping Campbell—his race and place of car registration—were not seen as reasonable.

The "Totality of the Circumstances" Test   For the most part, the judicial system has refrained from placing restrictions on police officers' ability to make stops. In the *Terry* case, the Supreme Court did say that an officer must have "specific and arguable facts" to support the decision to make a stop, but added that the facts may be "taken together with rational inferences."[18] The Court has consistently ruled that because of their practical experience, law enforcement agents are in a unique position to make such references and should be given a good deal of freedom in doing so.

In the years since the *Terry* case was decided, the Court has settled on a "totality of the circumstances" test to determine whether a stop is based on reasonable suspicion.[19] In 2002, for example, the Court ruled that a U.S. Border Patrol agent's stop of a minivan in Arizona was reasonable.[20] On being approached by the Border Patrol car, the driver had stiffened, slowed down his van, and avoided making eye contact with the agent. Furthermore, the children in the van waved at the officer in a mechanical manner, as if ordered to do so. The agent pulled over the van and found 128 pounds of marijuana. In his opinion, Chief Justice William Rehnquist pointed out that such conduct might have been unremarkable on a busy city highway, but on an unpaved road thirty miles from the Mexico border it was enough to reasonably arouse the agent's suspicion.[21] The justices also made clear that the need to prevent terrorist attacks is part of the "totality of the circumstances" and, therefore, law enforcement agents will have more leeway to make stops near U.S. borders.

Informants and Reasonable Suspicion   A "bare-bones" anonymous tip is at the opposite end of the reasonable suspicion spectrum from a situation that meets the "totality of the circumstances" test. In 2000, the Supreme Court overturned a conviction based on such a "bare-bones" tip. An anonymous caller had told the Miami–Dade County (Florida) police that a young African American male standing at a bus stop was illegally carrying a handgun. Even though the information was correct, the police officer who made the stop and subsequent arrest had no reason other than the anonymous tip to suspect criminal activity.[22]

This restriction does not prevent tips from informants from being valuable resources for police officers. The Court has held that a tip from a *known* informant who had provided reliable information in the past is sufficient to justify a *Terry* stop, even if there is no other supporting evidence to make the stop.[23] Furthermore, an anonymous tip can pass the "totality of the circumstances" test if it is specific enough and the police verify it with their own observations.[24] (See the feature *CJ and the Media—America's Newest Crime Fighter: The Tipster* on page 224 for information on how widespread the "help" of anonymous callers has become.)

A STOP

The terms *stop* and *frisk* are often used in concert, but they describe two separate acts. A **stop** takes place when a law enforcement officer has reasonable suspicion that a criminal activity is about to take place. Because an investigatory stop is not an arrest, there are limits to the extent police can detain someone who has been stopped. For example, in one situation an airline traveler and his luggage were detained for ninety minutes while the police waited for a drug-sniffing dog to arrive. The Court ruled that the initial stop of the passenger was constitutional, but that the ninety-minute wait was excessive.[25]

Stop
A brief detention of a person by law enforcement agents for questioning. The agents must have a reasonable suspicion of the person before making a stop.

A FRISK

The Supreme Court has stated that a **frisk** should be a protective measure. Police officers cannot conduct a frisk as a "fishing expedition" simply to try to find items besides weapons, such as illegal narcotics, on a suspect.[26] A frisk does not necessarily follow a stop and in fact may occur only when the officer is justified in thinking that the safety of police officers or other citizens may be endangered.

Frisk
A pat-down or minimal search by police to discover weapons; conducted for the express purpose of protecting the officer or other citizens, and not to find evidence of illegal substances for use in a trial.

Again, the question of reasonable suspicion is at the heart of determining the legality of frisks. In the *Terry* case, the Court accepted that Detective McFadden reasonably believed that the three suspects posed a threat. The suspects' refusal to answer McFadden's questions, though within their rights because they had not been arrested, provided him with sufficient motive for the frisk.

↗ ONLINE REVIEW *Go to the book's Web site for an interactive review of this section*

Arrests

As in the *Terry* case, a stop and frisk may lead to an **arrest.** An arrest is the taking into custody of a citizen for the purpose of detaining him or her on a criminal charge. It is important to understand the difference between a stop and an arrest. In the eyes of the law, a stop is a relatively brief intrusion on a citizen's rights, whereas an arrest—which involves a deprivation of liberty—is deserving of a full range of constitutional protections, which we shall discuss throughout the chapter (see *Mastering Concepts—The Difference between a Stop and an Arrest* on page 225). Consequently, while a stop can be made based on a reasonable suspicion, a law enforcement officer needs a probable cause, as defined earlier, to make an arrest.[27]

Arrest
To take into custody a person suspected of criminal activity. Police may use only reasonable levels of force in making an arrest.

ELEMENTS OF AN ARREST

When is somebody under arrest? The easy—and incorrect—answer would be whenever the police officer says so. In fact, the state of being under arrest is dependent not only on the actions of the law enforcement officers but also on the

> America's Newest Crime Fighter: The Tipster

When law enforcement agents in northern Utah wanted to find a gang member nicknamed "Popcorn" in connection with a murder, they turned to the media for help. Popcorn's picture was sent to local television stations, along with a phone number to call if viewers had any information on his whereabouts. "Right now, we have four or five detectives looking for a person," said Officer James Gent. "But if we put the information in the [media], then we get 4,000 to 5,000 looking for him."

This strategy has proved popular and effective. Tips provided by callers to *America's Most Wanted,* a national television show, have led to the capture of nearly eight hundred fugitives. Bank robber Leslie Rogge, who had fled to Guatemala, was apprehended when a neighbor recognized his photo on the FBI's Web site and alerted officials at the U.S. embassy in Guatemala City. Law enforcement agents relied on two anonymous tips—one pointing to a liquor store robbery-murder in Montgomery, Alabama, and the other describing a trigger-happy neighbor in Tacoma, Washington—to track down the two snipers who terrorized the Washington, D.C., area in October 2002.

Anonymous phone calls do have their drawbacks, however. In the Washington, D.C., sniper hunt, law enforcement officials used television, radio, print media, and the Internet to urge people to report any relevant information they might possess. The result was an avalanche of tips, many regarding a nonexistent white van that was initially (and wrongly) thought to be the suspects' vehicle. As a result of these tips, agents wasted thousands of hours following false leads and dozens of innocent people were stopped for questioning. In another case, the California Highway Patrol closed a freeway and dispatched two police cars, two motorcycles, and a helicopter because an anonymous motorist on a cell phone erroneously identified a man on a trip to Las Vegas with his wife as a murder suspect featured on *America's Most Wanted.*

According to the United States Supreme Court, the use of anonymous tips is within the bounds of the Fourth Amendment as long as an independent police investigation shows that the tip might be valid. Although this requires more work by police officers and cannot always protect against mistakes, the Court believes that it allows law enforcement agents to meet the reasonable suspicion standard when conducting a stop based on an anonymous tip.

perception of the suspect. Suppose Mr. Jones is stopped by plainclothes detectives, driven to the police station, and detained for three hours for questioning. During this time, the police never tell Mr. Jones he is under arrest, and in fact, he is free to leave at any time. But if Mr. Jones or any other reasonable person *believes* he is not free to leave, then, according to the Supreme Court, that person is in fact under arrest and should receive the necessary constitutional protections.[28]

Criminal justice professor Rolando V. del Carmen of Sam Houston State University has identified four elements that must be present for an arrest to take place:

1 The *intent* to arrest. In a stop, though it may entail slight inconvenience and a short detention period, there is no intent on the part of the law enforcement officer to take the person into custody. Therefore, there is no arrest. As intent is a subjective term, it is sometimes difficult to determine whether the police officer intended to arrest. In situations when the intent is unclear, courts often rely—as in our hypothetical case of Mr. Jones—on the perception of the arrestee.[29]

2 The *authority* to arrest. State laws give police officers the authority to place citizens under custodial arrest, or take them into custody. Like other state laws, the authorization to arrest varies among the fifty states. Some states, for example, allow off-duty police officers to make arrests, while others do not.

> The Difference between a Stop and an Arrest

Both stops and arrests are considered seizures because both police actions involve the restriction of an individual's freedom to "walk away." Both must be justified by a showing of reasonableness as well. You should be aware, however, of the differences between a stop and an arrest.

The stop is an important part of police activity. Police officers therefore have the right to stop and frisk a person if they suspect that a crime is about to be committed. Police may stop those who are acting strangely, do not "fit" the time or place, are knwn to associate with criminals, or are loitering. They may also stop a person who reasonably fits a description of a person who is wanted in conjunction with a crime. During a stop, police can interrogate the person and make a limited search of his or her outer clothing. If anything occurs during the stop, such as the discovery of an illegal weapon, then officers may arrest the person. If an arrest is made, the suspect is now in police custody and is protected by the U.S. Constitution in a number of ways that will be discussed later in the chapter.

	STOP	ARREST
Justification	Reasonable suspicion	Probable cause
Warrant	None	Required in some, though not all, situations
Intent of Officer	The investigation of suspicious activity	To make a formal charge against the suspect
Search	May frisk, or "pat down," for weapons	Full search for weapons and evidence
Scope of Search	Outer clothing only	Area within the suspect's immediate control, or "reach"

3 *Seizure or detention.* A necessary part of an arrest is the detention of the subject. Detention is considered to have occurred as soon as the arrested individual submits to the control of the officer, whether peacefully or under the threat or use of force.

4 The *understanding* of the person that she or he has been arrested. Through either words—such as "you are now under arrest"—or actions, the person taken into custody must understand that an arrest has taken place. If a subject has been forcibly subdued by the police, handcuffed, and placed in a patrol car, that subject is believed to understand that an arrest has been made. This understanding may be lacking if the person is intoxicated, insane, or unconscious.[30]

ARRESTS WITH A WARRANT

When law enforcement officers have established a probable cause to arrest an individual who is not in police custody, they obtain an **arrest warrant** for that person. An arrest warrant contains information such as the name of the person suspected and the crime he or she is suspected of having committed. (See Figure 7.2 on the following page for an example of an arrest warrant.) Judges or magistrates issue arrest warrants after first determining that the law enforcement officers have indeed established probable cause.

Arrest Warrant
A written order, based on probable cause and issued by a judge or magistrate, commanding that the person named on the warrant be arrested by the police.

FIGURE 7.2 Example of an Arrest Warrant

United States District Court

DISTRICT OF

UNITED STATES OF AMERICA
V.

WARRANT FOR ARREST

CASE NUMBER:

To: The United States Marshal
and any Authorized United States Officer

YOU ARE HEREBY COMMANDED to arrest ______________________
Name

and bring him or her forthwith to the nearest magistrate to answer a(n)

☐ Indictment ☐ Information ☐ Complaint ☐ Order of Court ☐ Violation Notice ☐ Probation Violation Petition

charging him or her with (brief description of offense)

in violation of Title ____________ United States Code, Section(s) ______________

Name of Issuing Officer — Title of Issuing Officer

Signature of Issuing Officer — Date and Location

Bail fixed at $ — by ____________________
Name of Judicial Officer

RETURN

This warrant was received and executed with the arrest of the above-named defendant at ______________

DATE RECEIVED	NAME AND TITLE OF ARRESTING OFFICER	SIGNATURE OF ARRESTING OFFICER
DATE OF ARREST		

There is a perception that an arrest warrant gives law enforcement officers the authority to enter a dwelling without first announcing themselves. This is not accurate. In *Wilson v. Arkansas* (1995),[31] the Supreme Court reiterated the common law requirement that police officers must knock and announce their identity and purpose before entering a dwelling. Under certain conditions, known as **exigent circumstances,** law enforcement officers need not announce themselves. These circumstances include situations in which the officers have a reasonable belief of any of the following:

Exigent Circumstances
Situations that require extralegal or exceptional actions by the police. In these circumstances, police officers are justified in not following procedural rules, such as those pertaining to search and arrest warrants.

> The suspect is armed and poses a strong threat of violence to the officers or others inside the dwelling.

> Persons inside the dwelling are in the process of destroying evidence or escaping because of the presence of the police.

> A felony is being committed at the time the officers enter.[32]

For example, in *Minnesota v. Olson* (1990),[33] the Court ruled that officers acted legally when they forcibly entered the home of an armed robber who had been fleeing arrest.

ARRESTS WITHOUT A WARRANT

Arrest warrants are not always required, and in fact, most arrests are made on the scene without a warrant.[34] A law enforcement officer may make a **warrantless arrest** if:

1 The offense is committed in the presence of the officer; or

2 The officer has knowledge that a crime has been committed and a probable cause to believe the crime was committed by a particular suspect.[35]

The type of crime also comes to bear in questions of arrests without a warrant. As a general rule, officers can make a warrantless arrest for a crime they did not see if they have probable cause to believe that a felony has been committed. For misdemeanors, the crime must have been committed in the presence of the officer for a warrantless arrest to be valid.

In certain situations, warrantless arrests are unlawful even though a police officer can establish probable cause. In *Payton v. New York* (1980),[36] for example, the Supreme Court held that when exigent circumstances do not exist and the suspect does not give consent to enter a dwelling, law enforcement officers cannot force themselves in for the purpose of making a warrantless arrest. The *Payton* ruling was expanded to cover the homes of third parties when, in *Steagald v. United States* (1981),[37] the Court ruled that if the police wish to arrest a criminal suspect in another person's home, they cannot enter that home to arrest the suspect without first obtaining a search warrant, a process we will discuss in the following section.

ONLINE REVIEW Go to the book's Web site for an interactive review of this section

Lawful Searches and Seizures

How far can law enforcement agents go in searching and seizing private property? Consider the steps taken by Jenny Stracner, an investigator with the Laguna Beach (California) Police Department. After receiving information that a suspect, Greenwood, was engaged in drug trafficking, Stracner enlisted the aid of the local trash collector in procuring evidence. Instead of taking Greenwood's trash bags to be incinerated, the collector agreed to give them to Stracner. The officer found enough drug paraphernalia in the garbage to obtain a warrant to search Greenwood's home. Subsequently, he was arrested and convicted on narcotics charges.[38]

Remember, the Fourth Amendment is quite specific in forbidding unreasonable searches and seizures. Were Stracner's search of Greenwood's garbage and her seizure of its contents "reasonable"? The Supreme Court thought so, holding that Greenwood's garbage was not protected by the Fourth Amendment.[39]

THE ROLE OF PRIVACY IN SEARCHES

A crucial concept in understanding search and seizure law is *privacy*. By definition, a **search** is a governmental intrusion on a citizen's reasonable expectation of privacy. The recognized standard for a "reasonable expectation of privacy" was established in *Katz v. United States* (1967).[40] The case dealt with the question of whether the defendant was justified in his expectation of privacy in the calls he

Warrantless Arrest
An arrest made without first seeking a warrant for the action; permitted under certain circumstances, such as when the arresting officer has witnessed the crime or has a reasonable belief that the suspect has committed a felony.

Search
The process by which police examine a person or property to find evidence that will be used to prove guilt in a criminal trial.

made from a public phone booth. The Supreme Court held that "the Fourth Amendment protects people, not places." Katz prevailed.

In his concurring opinion, Justice John Harlan, Jr., set a two-pronged test for a person's expectation of privacy:

1 The individual must prove that she or he expected privacy, and
2 Society must recognize that expectation as reasonable.[41]

Accordingly, the Court agreed with Katz's claim that he had a reasonable right to privacy in a public phone booth. (Remember, however, that the *Terry* case allows for conditions under which a person's privacy rights are superseded by a reasonable suspicion on the part of a law enforcement officer that a threat to public safety is present.)

In contrast, in *California v. Greenwood* (1988),[42] described on the previous page, the Court did not believe that the suspect had a reasonable expectation of privacy when it came to his garbage bags. The Court noted that when we place our trash on a curb, we expose it to any number of intrusions by "animals, children, scavengers, snoops, and other members of the public."[43] In other words, if Greenwood had truly intended for the contents of his garbage bags to remain private, he would not have left them on the side of the road. "Reasonable" expectations of privacy can, and do, change. For a discussion of one possible change following the September 11, 2001, terrorist attacks on New York and Washington, D.C., see the feature *CJ and Technology—Biometrics*.

SEARCH AND SEIZURE WARRANTS

To protect against charges that they have unreasonably infringed on privacy rights during a search, law enforcement officers can obtain a **search warrant.** (See Figure 7.3 on page 230 for an example of a search warrant.) Similar to an arrest warrant, a search warrant is a court order that authorizes police to search a certain area. Before a judge or magistrate will issue a search warrant, law enforcement officers must generally provide:

> Information showing probable cause that a crime has been or will be committed.

> Specific information on the premises to be searched, the suspects to be found and the illegal activities taking place at those premises, and the items to be seized.

The purpose of a search warrant is to establish, before the search takes place, that a *probable cause to search* justifies infringing on the suspect's reasonable expectation of privacy.

Particularity of Search Warrants   The members of the First Congress specifically did not want law enforcement officers to have the freedom to make "general, exploratory" searches through a person's belongings.[44] Consequently, the Fourth Amendment requires that a warrant describe with "particularity" the place to be searched and the things—either people or objects—to be seized.

This "particularity" requirement places a heavy burden on law enforcement officers. Before going to a judge to ask for a search warrant, they must prepare an

Search Warrant
A written order, based on probable cause and issued by a judge or magistrate, commanding that police officers or criminal investigators search a specific person, place, or property to obtain evidence.

> Biometrics

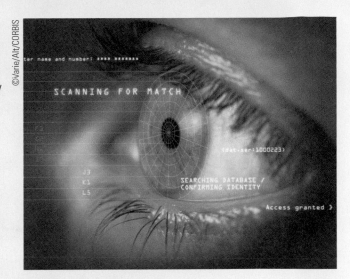

Americans have become accustomed to being watched. Surveillance cameras are commonplace in banks, malls, lobbies of office buildings, and other private and public places. But these cameras are only recorders; they do not "recognize" us or send information about us to a third party. The technology does exist, however, that would let these cameras do just this, and much more.

Broadly known as "biometrics," this technology allows a camera to identify anyone who comes into view by scanning her or his physical characteristics and matching the results of the scan with information in a database. Airports in Iceland and Great Britain, for example, utilize face recognition biometrics to protect against terrorism. A computer linked to surveillance cameras in these airports profiles individuals based on as many as eighty different facial structures, such as cheekbone formation, the width of the nose bridge, and the space between the eyes. These facial "signatures," once noted, are compared to facial structures of known criminals or terrorists.

In the United States, privacy concerns have limited the use of biometrics. Facial recognition cameras, after all, would circumvent the anonymity that is important to many Americans. But as security concerns have become paramount after the terrorist attacks of September 11, 2001, resistance to biometrics seems to have weakened.

Biometric systems that scan and match fingerprints are already being used in banks, hospitals, schools, and apartment complexes. Several American airports have tested iris scanning devices on employees, and the International Biometrics Group estimates that annual spending on biometrics will rise from over $900 million in 2004 to $4 billion in 2007. The possibilities of biometrics in fighting terrorism are intriguing. A video taken at a terrorist training camp, for example, could be fed into a computer, which would log the features of the faces. This informa-

tion would then be distributed to airports, embassies, and other locations for use in their own systems.

In the Future

In 2003, the U.S. Department of Homeland Security announced that biometric technology will be eventually used to check the fingerprints of all foreign visitors to the United States. The program will require travelers from abroad to be fingerprinted as a condition for obtaining an entrance visa so that U.S. Customs officials can verify their identities when they arrive in the country. The strategy is intended to stop suspected terrorists at U.S. borders and keep them from entering the United States.

 For more information on biometrics and other CJ technologies, click on Crime and Technology *under* Book Resources *at www.cjinaction.com*

---

affidavit in which they provide specific, written information on the property that they wish to search and seize. They must know the specific address of any place they wish to search; general addresses of apartment buildings or office complexes are not sufficient. Furthermore, courts generally frown upon vague descriptions of goods to be seized. "Stolen goods" would most likely be considered unacceptably imprecise, while "1 Lexmark E321 Laser Printer" would be preferred.

A **seizure** is the act of taking possession of a person or property by the government because of a (suspected) violation of the law. In general, four categories of items can be seized by use of a search warrant:

Affidavit
A written statement of facts, confirmed by the oath or affirmation of the party making it and made before a person having the authority to administer the oath or affirmation.

Seizure
The forcible taking of a person or property in response to a violation of the law.

FIGURE 7.3 **Example of a Search Warrant**

United States District Court

DISTRICT OF_____

In the Matter of the Search of
(Name, address or brief description of person or property to be searched)

SEARCH WARRANT

CASE NUMBER:

TO:_____ and any Authorized Officer of the United States

Affidavit(s) having been made before me by_____ who has reason to
                                                    Affiant

believe that ☐ on the person of or ☐ on the premises known as (name, description and/or location)

in the_____District of_____there is now
concealed a certain person or property, namely (describe the person or property)

I am satisfied that the affidavit(s) and any recorded testimony establish probable cause to believe that the person
or property so described is now concealed on the person or premises above-described and establish grounds for
the issuance of this warrant.

YOU ARE HEREBY COMMANDED to search on or before_____
                                                                    Date

(not to exceed 10 days) the person or place named above for the person or property specified, serving this warrant
and making the search (in the daytime — 6:00 A.M. to 10:00 P.M.) (at any time in the day or night as I find
reasonable cause has been established) and if the person or property be found there to seize same, leaving a copy
of this warrant and receipt for the person or property taken, and prepare a written inventory of the person or property seized and promptly return this warrant to_____
as required by law.   U.S. Judge or Magistrate

_____ at _____
Date and Time Issued   City and State

_____   _____
Name and Title of Judicial Officer   Signature of Judicial Officer

INFOTRAC KEYWORDS

search and seizure

For more information, use these search
terms with InfoTrac College Edition, your
online library at www.infotrac-college.com

1 Items that resulted from the crime, such as stolen goods.

2 Items that are inherently illegal for anybody to possess (with certain exceptions), such as narcotics and counterfeit currency.

3 Items that can be called "evidence" of the crime, such as a bloodstained
   sneaker or a ski mask.

4 Items used in committing the crime, such as an ice pick or a printing press
   used to make counterfeit bills.[45]

Reasonableness during a Search and Seizure   No matter how "particular" a
warrant is, it cannot provide for all the conditions that are bound to come up during its service. Consequently, the law gives law enforcement officers the ability to
act "reasonably" during a search and seizure in the event of unforeseeable circumstances. For example, if a police officer is searching an apartment for a stolen
Lexmark E321 laser printer and notices a vial of crack cocaine sitting on the suspect's bed, that contraband is considered to be in "plain view" and can be seized.
(See the feature *You Be the Judge—A Valid Search?*)

Note that if law enforcement officers have a search warrant that authorizes
them to search for a stolen laser printer, they would *not* be justified in opening
small drawers. Because a printer could not fit in a small drawer, an officer would

not have a basis for reasonably searching one. Officers are restricted in terms of where they can look by the items they are searching for.

SEARCHES AND SEIZURES WITHOUT A WARRANT

Although the Court has established the principle that searches conducted without warrants are *per se* (by definition) unreasonable, it has set "specifically established" exceptions to the rule.[46] In fact, most searches, like most arrests, take place in the absence of a judicial order. Warrantless searches and seizures can be lawful when police are in "hot pursuit" of a subject or when they search bags of trash left at the curb for regular collection. Because of the magnitude of smuggling activities in "border areas" such as airports, seaports, and international boundaries, a warrant is normally not needed to search property in those places. The two most important circumstances in which a warrant is not needed, though, are (1) searches incidental to an arrest and (2) consensual searches.

Searches Incidental to an Arrest   The most frequent exception to the warrant requirement involves **searches incidental to arrests,** so called because nearly every time police officers make an arrest, they also search the suspect. As long as the original arrest was based on probable cause, these searches are valid for two reasons, established by the Supreme Court in *United States v. Robinson* (1973):[47]

1   The need for a police officer to find and confiscate any weapons a suspect may be carrying.

2   The need to protect any evidence on the suspect's person from being destroyed.

Law enforcement officers are, however, limited in the searches they may make during an arrest. These limits were established by the Supreme Court in *Chimel v.*

Searches Incidental to Arrests
Searches for weapons and evidence of persons who have just been arrested. The fruit of such searches is admissible if any items found are within the immediate vicinity or control of the suspect.

NYT Pictures/William Lopez

In 1999, New York City implemented a plan that allows police officers to seize the cars of people arrested for driving with blood alcohol levels of .10 or higher. As "specifically established" exceptions to search and seizure law, such seizures are considered constitutional. Are you in favor of this method of controlling drunk drivers? What might be some of the practical problems that New York police officers will encounter while enforcing this policy?

Consent Searches
Searches by police that are made after the subject of the search has agreed to the action. In these situations, consent, if given of free will, validates a warrantless search.

California (1969).[48] In that case, police arrived at Chimel's home with an arrest warrant but not a search warrant. Even though Chimel refused their request to "look around," the officers searched the entire three-bedroom house for nearly an hour, finding stolen coins in the process. Chimel was convicted of burglary and appealed, arguing that the evidence of the coins should have been suppressed.

The Supreme Court held that the search was unreasonable. In doing so, the Court established guidelines as to the acceptable extent of searches incidental to an arrest. Primarily, the Court ruled that police may search any area within the suspect's "immediate control" to confiscate any weapons or evidence that the suspect could destroy. The Court found, however, that there was no justification:

> for routinely searching rooms other than that in which the arrest occurs—or, for that matter, for searching through all desk drawers or other closed or concealed areas in that room itself. Such searches, in the absence of well-recognized exceptions, may be made only under the authority of a search warrant.

The exact interpretation of the "area within immediate control" has been left to individual courts, but in general it has been taken to mean the area within the reach of the arrested person. Thus, the Court is said to have established the "arm's reach doctrine" in its *Chimel* decision.

Searches with Consent   **Consent searches,** the second most common type of warrantless searches, take place when individuals give law enforcement officers permission to search their persons, homes, or belongings. (For an overview of the circumstances under which warrantless searches are allowed, see *Mastering Concepts—Exceptions to the Requirement That Officers Have a Search Warrant.*) The consent must, however, be *voluntary.* If a person has been physically threatened or otherwise coerced into giving consent, the search is invalid.[49] The standard for consent searches was set in *Schneckcloth v. Bustamonte* (1973),[50] in which, after being asked, the defendant told police officers to "go ahead" and search his car. A packet of stolen checks found in the trunk was ruled valid evidence because the driver consented to the search.

Critics of consent searches hold that such searches are rarely voluntary because most citizens are intimidated by police and will react to a request for permission to make a search as if it were an order.[51] Furthermore, most citizens are unaware that they have the option *not* to comply with a request for a search. Thus, if a police officer asks to search a citizen's car after issuing a speeding ticket, the citizen is well within her or his rights to refuse. According to the United States Supreme Court in *Florida v. Bostick* (1991),[52] as long as police officers do not improperly coerce a suspect to cooperate, they are not *required* to inform the person that he or she has a choice in the matter.

> Exceptions to the Requirement
That Officers Have a Search Warrant

In many circumstances, it would be impractical for police officers to leave a crime scene, go to a judge, and obtain a search warrant before conducting a search. Therefore, under a number of circumstances a search warrant is not required.

EXCEPTION	CIRCUMSTANCE NOT REQUIRING A WARRANT
Incident to Lawful Arrest	Police officers may search the area within immediate control of a person after they have arrested him or her.
Consent	Police officers may search a person without a warrant if that person voluntarily agrees to be searched and has the legal authority to authorize the search.
Stop and Frisk	Police officers may frisk, or "pat down," a person if they suspect that the person may be involved in criminal activity or pose a danger to those in the immediate area.
Hot Pursuit	If police officers are in "hot pursuit" or chasing a person they have probable cause to believe committed a crime, and that person enters a building, the officers may search the building without a warrant.
Automobile Exception	If police officers have probable cause that an automobile contains evidence of a crime, they may, in most instances, search the vehicle without a warrant.
Plain View	If police officers are legally engaged in police work and happen to see evidence of a crime in "plain view," they may seize it without a search warrant.
Abandoned Property	Any property, such as a hotel room that has been vacated or contraband that has been discarded, may be searched and seized by police officers without a warrant.
Border Searches	Law enforcement officers on border patrol do not need a warrant to search vehicles crossing the border.
Inevitable Discovery	Evidence that has been illegally obtained (without the necessary warrant) may be admitted as evidence if the prosecution can prove that it would have "inevitably" been found by lawful means.

Consequently, in *Ohio v. Robinette* (1996),[53] the Court held that police officers do *not* need to notify citizens that they are "free to go" after an initial stop when no arrest is involved. Similarly, in 2002, the Court ruled that the inside of a bus is not an inherently coercive environment and thus officers do not need to advise passengers that they can refuse to be searched.[54] The significance of this line of cases is underscored by data presented in connection with the *Robinette* ruling: in the two years leading up to that case, four hundred Ohio drivers were convicted of narcotics offenses that resulted directly from search requests that could have been denied but were not.[55]

SEARCHES OF AUTOMOBILES

Though the *Chimel* case limited the scope of searches and seizures incident to an arrest in most circumstances, the Supreme Court has not been as restrictive concerning searches in arrests involving automobile passengers. In *New York v. Belton* (1981),[56] the Court held that when police officers lawfully arrested a person driving a car, they could legally make a warrantless search of the car's entire front and back compartments. This expansive interpretation of "the area within immediate control" is indicative of the Supreme Court's lenient view of automobile searches.

The "Movable Vehicle Exception" In *Carroll v. United States* (1925),[57] the Supreme Court ruled that the law would distinguish among automobiles, homes,

A police officer searches a car in front of the Capitol building in Washington, D.C. According to the United States Supreme Court, under some circumstances the Fourth Amendment to the U.S. Constitution does not require police officers to obtain a warrant before searching an automobile. What is the reasoning behind this "movable vehicle exception"?

and persons in questions involving police searches. In the years since *Carroll,* the Court has established that the Fourth Amendment docs not require police to obtain a warrant to search automobiles or other movable vehicles when they have probable cause that a vehicle contains contraband or evidence of criminal activity.[58] The reasoning behind such leniency is straightforward: requiring a warrant to search an automobile places too heavy a burden on police officers. By the time the officers could communicate with a judge and obtain the warrant, the suspects could drive away and destroy any evidence. Consequently, the Supreme Court has consistently held that someone in a vehicle does not have the same reasonable expectation of privacy as someone at home or even in a phone booth.

A number of rulings have increased police powers in these situations. In *Whren v. United States* (1996),[59] the Supreme Court ruled that the "true" motivation of police officers in making traffic stops was irrelevant as long as they had probable cause to believe that a traffic law had been broken. In other words, police may stop a car they believe to be transporting drugs in order to issue a speeding citation. The fact that the officers are using the speeding ticket as a pretext to search for drugs (and would not have stopped the driver otherwise) does not matter, as long as the driver actually was speeding. One year later, in *Maryland v. Wilson* (1997),[60] the Court further expanded police power by ruling that an officer may order passengers as well as the driver out of a car during a traffic stop; the Court reasoned that the danger to an officer is increased when there is a passenger in the automobile.

"Individualized Suspicion" Nevertheless, the "movable vehicle exception" has not provided police officers with complete freedom in searching automobiles. Recently, the Supreme Court overturned a roadblock system in Indianapolis, Indiana, that was designed to discover illegal drugs in automobiles. At the roadblocks, a police officer would check a driver's license and registration and then subject the automobile to a "sniff search" by a dog specially trained to find narcotics.[61] Because the Court had, in prior cases, upheld checkpoints designed to apprehend drunk drivers[62] and illegal aliens,[63] the city of Indianapolis felt that its practice was constitutionally acceptable.

But, in *City of Indianapolis v. Edmond* (2000),[64] the Court distinguished the behavior being regulated in the earlier cases from the illegal behavior the city sought to uncover. Governments, the Court noted, have a special interest in protecting citizens from the dangers of drunks on the road and in controlling the flow of illegal immigrants across their borders. General searches for drugs, however, do not serve any specific purpose beyond general crime control. Therefore, the Fourth Amendment does not allow the police to stop drivers without any "individualized suspicion" that they have broken the law, in this case by possessing drugs.[65]

Searches of Luggage in Automobiles Note that the rules governing searches incidental to an arrest apply to automobile searches. So, if a police officer has not made a custodial arrest and does not have reasonable suspicion that a crime has been or is about to be committed, that officer cannot search a car she or he has stopped.[66] In practice, however, this is rarely a problem for law enforcement agents. As mentioned earlier, the Supreme Court's *Belton* ruling allows the arresting officer to make a complete search of the passenger compartment of an automobile as long as he or she had probable cause to make the arrest.[67]

THE PLAIN VIEW DOCTRINE

Though police must have probable cause to search luggage in an automobile's trunk, no such protection applies to contraband in *plain view*. For example, suppose a traffic officer pulls over a person for speeding, looks in the driver-side window, and clearly sees what appears to be a bag of heroin resting on the passenger seat. In this instance, under the **plain view doctrine,** the officer would be justified in seizing the drugs without a warrant.

The plain view doctrine was first enunciated by the Supreme Court in *Coolidge v. New Hampshire* (1971).[68] The Court ruled that law enforcement officers may make a warrantless seizure of an item if four criteria are met:

1 The item is positioned so as to be detected easily by an officer's sight or some other sense.

2 The officer is legally in a position to notice the item in question.

3 The discovery of the item is inadvertent; that is, the officer had not intended to find the item.

4 The officer immediately recognizes the illegal nature of the item. No interrogation or further investigation is allowed under the plain view doctrine.

(For a discussion of how the plain view doctrine is being tested by new technology, see *CJ and Technology—X-Ray Eyes and the Fourth Amendment* on p. 236.)

Plain View Doctrine
The legal principle that objects in plain view of a law enforcement agent who has the right to be in a position to have that view may be seized without a warrant and introduced as evidence.

INFOTRAC KEYWORDS
plain view doctrine
For more information, use this search term with InfoTrac College Edition, your online library at www.infotrac-college.com

ELECTRONIC SURVEILLANCE AND THE FIGHT AGAINST TERRORISM

During the course of a criminal investigation, law enforcement officers may decide to use *electronic surveillance,* or electronic devices such as wiretaps or hidden microphones ("bugs"), to monitor and record conversations, observe movements, and trace or record telephone calls.

Basic Rules: Consent and Probable Cause Given the invasiveness of electronic surveillance, the Supreme Court has generally held that the practice is prohibited by the Fourth Amendment. In *Burger v. New York* (1967),[69] however, the Court ruled that it was permissible under certain circumstances. That same year, *Katz v. United States* (discussed earlier) established that recorded conversations are inadmissible as evidence unless certain procedures are followed.

In general, law enforcement officers can use electronic surveillance only if:

1 Consent is given by one of the parties to be monitored; or

2 There is a warrant authorizing the use of the devices.[70]

> X-Ray Eyes and the Fourth Amendment

Suppose a detective enters a room with a warrant to search for a handgun used in a murder. The weapon is resting on a table and is immediately seized. Hidden in a closed drawer, however, is a packet of heroin. Under the plain view doctrine, the detective would most likely not have the right to search the drawer and seize the heroin. What if that detective could somehow see into the drawer without opening it? How would the plain view doctrine then apply?

A cop with X-ray eyes sounds like something out of a science fiction novel, but in fact courts around the country are already struggling with such situations. Thanks to thermal imagers, also known as forward-looking infrared devices (FLIR), law enforcement agencies now have the ability to look through walls.

The Thermal Imager at Work

Every object with a temperature above absolute zero emits infrared radiation, which cannot be seen by the naked eye. A thermal imager, however, can detect this radiation and project its reading onto a screen. The devices have been most commonly used in missing person searches—with our high body temperature, humans are easy targets for thermal imagers. Only recently have the devices been put to use by law enforcement agencies. Thermal imagers can be particularly effective in detecting marijuana grown indoors because marijuana plants require considerable heat to survive.

The question for the courts has been whether, in the absence of a warrant, an infrared search of a dwelling is in violation of Fourth Amendment protections of privacy. In one marijuana case, where police used a helicopter fitted with FLIR devices, a Hawaii court ruled that no reasonable expectation of privacy was involved. The court held that the FLIR device measured only heat emanating from the defendant's house and that this "abandoned heat" was not subject to privacy laws because the defendants had not tried to prevent its escape. A Pennsylvania court, ruling on a similar case, rejected the "abandoned heat" justification because thermal imaging allowed the police to see what otherwise would have been hidden to them. The Pennsylvania court warned that thermal imaging "can extract information from within a person's home, the place most deserving of protection from government intrusion."

In the Future

In 2001, the Supreme Court settled the issue by ruling that the use of a thermal imaging device by police was a search and was therefore subject to the Fourth Amendment. The Court's ruling covered not only these devices but also *any* technology that allows police to gain knowledge that would otherwise be impossible to obtain without entering the home. This does not mean that this technology is lost to law enforcement agents, but it does require them to obtain a warrant before using it.

 For more information on thermal imaging and other CJ technologies, click on Crime and Technology *under* Book Resources *at* www.cjinaction.com

Note that the consent of only one of the parties being monitored is needed to waive the reasonable expectation of privacy. The Court has ruled that people whose conversations have been recorded by supposed friends who turn out to be police informers have not been subjected to an unreasonable search.[71] Therefore, at least theoretically, a person always assumes the risk that whatever he or she says to someone else may be monitored by the police. A number of states do, however, have statutes that forbid private citizens from tape-recording another person's conversation without her or his knowledge. In Maryland, for example, such an act is a felony.

If consent exists, then law enforcement officers are not required to obtain a warrant before engaging in electronic surveillance. In most other instances, however, a warrant is required. For the warrant to be valid, it must:

1 Detail with "particularity" the conversations that are to be overheard.

2 Name the suspects and the places that will be under surveillance.

3 Show with probable cause that a specific crime has been or will be committed.[72]

Once the specific information has been gathered, the law enforcement officers must end the electronic surveillance immediately.[73] In any case, the surveillance cannot last more than thirty days without a judicial extension.

New Rules: The USA Patriot Act   The federal government has long struggled with how to apply these basic rules to the area of national security. In the late 1970s, responding to concerns that the FBI had too much power to "spy" on domestic religious and political groups, Congress passed legislation restricting this power. Under the Foreign Intelligence Surveillance Act (FISA), government agents could wiretap or otherwise bug a target only if there was probable cause that the target was a foreign infiltrator.[74]

The USA Patriot Act of 2001 amended the FISA. This new legislation, as noted earlier in this textbook, was a legislative response to the terrorist attacks of September 11, 2001. It effectively did away with the probable cause requirements of the FISA, allowing agents to procure a warrant for electronic surveillance as long as the surveillance serves a "significant purpose" in gathering foreign intelligence.[75] Under the old rules, for example, an FBI agent could not randomly surf the Internet looking for signs of wrongdoing because there was no "particularity" to support a showing of probable cause that terrorist activity was taking place. Under the new guidelines, the agent can search Web sites and chat rooms randomly because this activity might serve the significant purpose of providing leads to future terrorist attacks.[76]

⬆ ONLINE REVIEW *Go to the book's Web site for an interactive review of this section*

The Interrogation Process and *Miranda*

After the Pledge of Allegiance, there is perhaps no recitation that comes more readily to the American mind than the *Miranda* warning:

> You have the right to remain silent. If you give up that right, anything you say can and will be used against you in a court of law. You have the right to speak with an attorney and to have the attorney present during questioning. If you so desire and cannot afford one, an attorney will be appointed for you without charge before questioning.

The *Miranda* warning is not a mere prop. It strongly affects one of the most important aspects of any criminal investigation—the **interrogation,** or questioning of a suspect from whom the police want to get information concerning a crime and perhaps a confession.

Interrogation
The direct questioning of a suspect to gather evidence of criminal activity and try to gain a confession.

THE LEGAL BASIS FOR *MIRANDA*

The Fifth Amendment guarantees protection against self-incrimination. A defendant's choice not to incriminate himself or herself cannot be interpreted as a sign of guilt by a jury in a criminal trial. A confession, or admission of guilt, is by definition a statement of self-incrimination. How, then, to reconcile the Fifth Amendment with the critical need of law enforcement officers to gain confessions? The answer lies in the concept of *coercion*. When torture or brutality is

INFOTRAC KEYWORDS
Miranda rule
For more information, use this search term with InfoTrac College Edition, your online library at www.infotrac-college.com

A Los Angeles police officer reads a handcuffed "suspect" his *Miranda* rights during a training exercise. Does a police officer need to take this action every time he or she arrests a suspect? If not, under what circumstances must an officer present the *Miranda* warning?

involved, it is relatively easy to determine that a confession was improperly coerced and is therefore invalid.

Setting the Stage for *Miranda* The Supreme Court first recognized that a confession could not be physically coerced in a 1936 case concerning a defendant who was beaten and whipped until confessing to a murder.[77] It was not until 1964, however, that the Court specifically recognized that the accused's due process rights should be protected during interrogation. That year, the Court heard the case of *Escobedo v. Illinois,*[78] concerning a convicted murderer who claimed that police had forced incriminating statements from him during interrogation and that this evidence had been portrayed as voluntary during his trial. In *Escobedo,* the Court ruled that the defendant had been denied his Sixth Amendment right to counsel during the interrogation. He therefore had also been denied his Fifth Amendment right against self-incrimination.

The *Miranda* Case Two years later, the Supreme Court expanded on *Escobedo* in its *Miranda* decision,[79] establishing the ***Miranda* rights** and introducing the concept of what University of Columbia law professor H. Richard Uviller called *inherent coercion;* that is, even if a police officer does not lay a hand on a suspect, the general atmosphere of an interrogation is in and of itself coercive.[80]

Though the *Miranda* case is best remembered for the procedural requirement it spurred, at the time the Supreme Court was more concerned about the treatment of suspects during interrogation. (See the feature *CJ in Focus— Landmark Cases:* Miranda v. Arizona.) The Court found that routine police interrogation strategies, such as leaving suspects alone in a room for several hours before questioning them, were inherently coercive. Therefore, the Court reasoned, every suspect needed protection from coercion, not just those who had been physically abused. The *Miranda* warning is a result of this need. In theory, if the warning is not given to a suspect before an interrogation, the fruits of that interrogation, including a confession, are invalid.

WHEN A *MIRANDA* WARNING IS REQUIRED

As we shall see, a *Miranda* warning is not necessary under several conditions, such as when no questions are asked of the suspect. Generally, *Miranda* requirements apply only when a suspect is in **custody.** In a series of rulings since *Miranda,* the Supreme Court has defined custody as an arrest or a situation in which a reasonable person would not feel free to leave.[81] Consequently, a **custodial interrogation** occurs when a suspect is under arrest or is deprived of her or his freedom in a significant manner. Remember, a *Miranda* warning is only required before a custodial interrogation takes place.

Miranda Rights
The constitutional rights of accused persons taken into custody by law enforcement officials. Following the United States Supreme Court's decision in *Miranda v. Arizona,* on taking an accused person into custody, the arresting officer must inform the person of certain constitutional rights, such as the right to remain silent and the right to counsel.

Custody
The forceful detention of a person, or the perception that a person is not free to leave the immediate vicinity.

Custodial Interrogation
The questioning of a suspect after that person has been taken in custody. In this situation, the suspect must be read his or her *Miranda* rights before interrogation can begin.

> *Miranda v. Arizona*

Ernesto Miranda, a produce worker, was arrested in Phoenix, Arizona, in 1963 and charged with kidnapping and rape. After being identified by the victim in a lineup, Miranda was taken into an interrogation room and questioned for two hours by detectives. At no time was Miranda informed that he had a right to have an attorney present. When the police emerged from the session, they had a signed statement by Miranda confessing to the crimes. He was subsequently convicted and sentenced to twenty to thirty years in prison. After the conviction was confirmed by the Arizona Supreme Court, Miranda appealed to the United States Supreme Court, claiming that he had not been warned that any statement he made could be used against him, and that he had a right to counsel during the interrogation. The *Miranda* case was one of four examined by the Court that dealt with the question of coercive questioning.

AP/Wide World

Ernesto Miranda

Miranda v. Arizona
United States Supreme Court
384 U.S. 436 (1966)
http://laws.findlaw.com/US/384/436.html

> **In the words of the court . . .**
Chief Justice WARREN, majority opinion
* * * *

The cases before us raise questions which go to the roots of our concepts of American criminal jurisprudence: the restraints society must observe consistent with the Federal Constitution in prosecuting individuals for crime. More specifically, we deal with the admissibility of statements obtained from an individual who is subjected to custodial police interrogation and the necessity for procedures which assure that the individual is accorded his privilege under the Fifth Amendment to the Constitution not to be compelled to incriminate himself.
* * * *

As for the procedural safeguards to be employed, unless other fully effective means are devised to inform accused persons of their right of silence and to assure a continuous opportunity to exercise it, the following measures are required. Prior to any questioning, the person must be warned that he has a right to remain silent, that any statement he does make may be used as evidence against him, and that he has a right to the presence of an attorney, either retained or appointed. The defendant may waive effectuation of these rights, provided the waiver is made voluntarily, knowingly and intelligently. * * * The mere fact that he may have answered some questions or volunteered some statements on his own does not deprive him of the right to refrain from answering any further inquiries until he has consulted with an attorney and thereafter consents to be questioned.
* * * *

It is obvious that such an interrogation environment is created for no purpose other than to subjugate the individual to the will of his examiner. This atmosphere carries its own badge of intimidation. To be sure, this is not physical intimidation, but it is equally destructive of human dignity. The current practice of incommunicado interrogation is at odds with one of our Nation's most cherished principles—that the individual may not be compelled to incriminate himself. Unless adequate protective devices are employed to dispel the compulsion inherent in custodial surroundings, no statement obtained from the defendant can truly be the product of his free choice.

> **Decision**
The Court overturned Miranda's conviction, stating that police interrogations are, by their very nature, coercive and therefore deny suspects their constitutional right against self-incrimination by "forcing" them to confess. Consequently, any person who has been arrested and placed in custody must be informed of his or her right to be free from self-incrimination and to be represented by counsel during any interrogation. In other words, suspects must be told that they *do not have to* answer police questions. To accomplish this, the Court established the *Miranda* warning, which must be read prior to questioning of a suspect in custody.

FOR CRITICAL ANALYSIS
What is meant by the phrase "coercion can be mental as well as physical"? What role does the concept of "mental coercion" play in Chief Justice Warren's opinion?

For more information and activities related to this case, click on Landmark Cases *under* Book Resources *at www.cjinaction.com*

WHEN A *MIRANDA* WARNING IS NOT REQUIRED

A *Miranda* warning is not necessary in a number of situations:

1 When the police do not ask the suspect any questions that are *testimonial* in nature. Such questions are designed to elicit information that may be used against the suspect in court. "Routine booking questions," such as the suspect's name, address, height, and eye color, however, are an exception to this rule. Even though answering these questions may provide incriminating evidence (especially if the person answering is a prime suspect), the Supreme Court has held that they are absolutely necessary if the police are to do their jobs.[82] (Imagine the officer not being able to ask a suspect her or his name.)

2 When the police have not focused on a suspect and are questioning witnesses at the scene of a crime.

3 When a person volunteers information before the police have asked a question.

4 When the suspect has given a private statement to a friend or some other acquaintance. *Miranda* does not apply to these statements as long as the government did not orchestrate the situation.

5 During a stop and frisk, when no arrest has been made.

6 During a traffic stop.[83]

Furthermore, suspects can *waive* their Fifth Amendment rights and speak to a police officer, but only if the waiver is made voluntarily. Silence on the part of a suspect does not mean that his or her *Miranda* protections have been relinquished. To waive their rights, suspects must state—either in writing or orally—that they understand those rights and that they will voluntarily answer questions without the presence of counsel.

To ensure that the suspect's rights are upheld, prosecutors are required to prove by a preponderance of the evidence that the suspect "knowing and intelligently" waived his or her *Miranda* rights.[84] To make the waiver perfectly clear, police will ask suspects two questions in addition to giving the *Miranda* warning:

1 Do you understand your rights as I have read them to you?

2 Knowing your rights, are you willing to talk to another law enforcement officer or me?

If the suspect indicates that she or he does not want to speak to the officer, thereby invoking her or his right to silence, the officer must *immediately* stop any questioning.[85] Similarly, if the suspect requests a lawyer, the police can ask no further questions until an attorney is present.[86] The suspect must be clear about this intention, however. In *Davis v. United States* (1994),[87] the Supreme Court upheld the interrogation of a suspect after he said, "Maybe I should talk to a lawyer." The Court found that this statement was too ambiguous, stating that it did not want to force police officers to "read the minds" of suspects who make vague declarations.

THE LAW ENFORCEMENT RESPONSE TO *MIRANDA*

When the *Miranda* decision was first handed down, many people, particularly police officials, complained that it distorted the Constitution by placing the rights of criminal suspects above the rights of society as a whole.[88] In the nearly four decades since the ruling, however, law enforcement agents have adapted to the *Miranda* restrictions, and strategies to work within their boundaries have become a standard part of police training.

Policing around *Miranda*   After an extensive on-site study of police interrogation tactics, Richard A. Leo, a criminologist from the University of California at Irvine, noted a pattern of maneuvers that officers would use to convince suspects to voluntarily waive their *Miranda* rights. Leo identifies three such strategies:

> The *conditioning* strategy is geared toward creating an environment in which the suspect is encouraged to think positively of the interrogator and thus is conditioned to cooperate. The interrogator will offer the suspect coffee or a cigarette and make pleasant small talk. These steps are intended to lower the suspect's anxiety level and generate a sense of trust that is conducive to a *Miranda* waiver and confession.

> The *deemphasizing* strategy tries to downplay the importance of *Miranda* protections, giving the impression that the rights are unimportant and can be easily waived. For example, one officer told a suspect, "I need to advise you of your rights. It's a formality. I'm sure you've watched television with the cop shows and you hear them say their rights so you can probably recite this better than I can, but it's something I need to do and we can get this out of the way before we talk about what happened."

> When using the *persuasion* strategy, an officer will explicitly try to convince the suspect to waive her or his rights. Commonly, the detective will tell suspects that waiving the rights is the only way they will be able to get their side of the story out. Otherwise, the detective continues, only the victim's side of the story will be considered during the trial.[89]

(To learn how these interrogation tactics are being spread abroad, see *International CJ—Building a Police Force for Iraq* on the following page.)

The Problem of False Confessions   In a number of instances, the police appear to have become *too* skilled at gaining confessions. In 2002, the reopening of the Central Park jogger case focused national attention on the phenomenon of false confessions. Thirteen years after an investment banker was raped and severely beaten while jogging in New York City, a judge overturned the convictions of four young men who had confessed to attacking the woman. DNA evidence showed that another person was responsible for the crime.

About 20 percent of wrongful convictions in recent years can be attributed to false confessions.[90] Experts point to a number of reasons why people admit to a crime they did not commit. Saul Kassin, a professor of psychology at Williams College, suggests that the police tactics described above amount to a form of legal coercion, with some suspects more susceptible than others. Many times, a person will confess in the absence of any wrongdoing because he or she is hungry, frightened, or exhausted.[91] In the Central Park jogger case, several "risk factors" for a false confession were present, including the age of the subjects (the five defendants were between fourteen and sixteen years old) and the interrogation methods (they had been in custody for between fourteen and thirty hours).

GREAT DEBATES
In 2003, the United States took custody of Khalid Shaikh Mohammed, a senior official in the al Qaeda terrorist network. Should government agents have been allowed to use "any means necessary," including torture, to get information out of Mohammed? Or, does the U.S. Constitution protect him just as it would any other arrested criminal? To better understand the debate surrounding the interrogation of suspected terrorists, click on *Great Debates* under *Book Resources* at www.cjinaction.com

> Building a Police Force for Iraq

Lieutenant Hussein al-Saedi of the Nasr police station in a poor section of Baghdad, Iraq, remembers the good old days. "Before, we used to bring the guy, we beat him, hung him by a hook on the ceiling, and he would confess to every single criminal act he committed since he was a toddler," he says. "Before, it was much better. Before, we used to solve these cases in one night."

"Before," in al-Saedi's words, refers to the time prior to the fall of Saddam Hussein in the spring of 2003 and the establishment of a provisional government in Iraq. Under the leadership of the United States, one of the main goals of this temporary government is to create a modern police force for the country. To that end, the U.S. government has spent hundreds of millions of dollars and recruited former New York City Police Commissioner Bernard Kerik to help organize Baghdad's police departments on the American model.

The fledgling security forces face a number of challenges: lack of equipment, lack of training, and lack of recruits. Six months after the end of the war, for example, the sixty police officers at the Nasr police station had forty-four guns, two cars,

and three radios that could be used only every other day because of weak batteries. The Iraqi concept of the rule of law was also somewhat different from that which Americans are used to, as is evident in al-Saedi's view of the best way to gain a confession.

In an attempt to remove torture from the Iraqi police's list of interrogation tactics, American officials set up a police academy in Baghdad with the goal of training 5,500 officers in the "human rights" approach to policing. Corporal Zuhair Mudthafir came away from the three-week course with a favorable impression of police methods in the United States. "You know, the Americans have genius officers who find ways to extract confessions from defendants without beating them," he said.

FOR CRITICAL ANALYSIS
Why is it important to train Iraqi police officers in "human rights" as well as other policing strategies? Why should the United States impose its idea of what constitutes a fair interrogation on Iraq's police force?

"Torture Lite" Obviously, police officers cannot physically abuse a suspect in order to get a confession. The courts will, nonetheless, sanction other methods that have been referred to as "torture lite." Maryland law enforcement agents, for example, questioned a suspect named Keith Longtin for thirty-eight hours about the death of his wife. During that time, he was allowed only fifty minutes' sleep before confessing (falsely, as it turned out) to committing murder. Officers may also use outright lies in the interrogation process; for example, they might tell a suspect that they have proof, such as eyewitness reports, a collaborator's confession, or fingerprints at the crime scene, of her or his guilt when they have no such evidence.[92]

The interrogation of terrorist suspects has also raised questions about what kind of "pain and suffering" can be inflicted in the process. John Walker Lindh, an American citizen who trained with terrorist organizations in Afghanistan, was reportedly stripped naked, blindfolded, and strapped to a chair with heavy tape while being questioned by U.S. Marines.[93] While techniques such as sleep and light deprivation and the withholding of food, water, and medical attention are generally accepted, some observers believe that, given the potential damage of terrorist attacks, law enforcement and military personnel should be able to do "more" to force these suspects to talk.

THE FUTURE OF *MIRANDA*

The Supreme Court recently made a strong ruling in favor of the continued importance of *Miranda*. In *Dickerson v. United States* (2001),[94] the Court rejected the application of a little-known law passed by Congress in 1968 that allowed police in federal cases to use incriminatory statements even if the suspect had not been read the warning. "*Miranda* has become embedded in routine police practice to the point where the warnings have become part of our national culture," wrote Chief Justice William Rehnquist in his opinion. The chief justice added that *Miranda* was a "constitutional rule" that Congress could not overturn by passing a law.[95]

INFOTRAC KEYWORDS

United States v. Dickerson

For more information, use this search term with InfoTrac College Edition, your online library at www.infotrac-college.com

The Erosion of *Miranda*   Despite these strong words, many legal scholars believe that a series of Supreme Court rulings have slowly eroded *Miranda*'s protections. According to legal scholar Alan M. Dershowitz, the Court has carved "out so many exceptions that [*Miranda*] is falling of its own weight."[96] (See Figure 7.4 for a run-down of the Court rulings that have weakened *Miranda* over the past several decades.) The Court will again consider its *Miranda* decision in 2004, when it looks at a Colorado case in which a suspect told police the location of his gun without being read his rights. The Court will decide whether physical evidence—the gun, in this case—is admissible in court under circumstances in which any incriminating remarks would be inadmissible because no *Miranda* warning was given.[97]

FIGURE 7.4   **Supreme Court Decisions Eroding *Miranda* Rights**

Rhode Island v. Innis (446 U.S. 291 [1980]). In this case the Supreme Court clarified its definition of an interrogation, which it said could extend only to "actions or words" that the police "should have known were reasonably likely to elicit an incriminating response." In making this ruling, the Court allowed as evidence an admission made by a suspect as to where a shotgun he had used in a crime was hidden. The suspect confessed after police mentioned that there was a possibility that a handicapped child might find the firearm, given that a home for such children was nearby. This was not, the Court ruled, an interrogation and therefore *Miranda* rights were not necessary.

New York v. Quarles (467 U.S. 649 [1984]). This case established the "public-safety" exception to the *Miranda* rule. It concerned a police officer who, after feeling an empty shoulder holster on a man he had just arrested, asked the suspect the location of the gun without informing him of his *Miranda* rights. The Court ruled that the gun was admissible as evidence and that the need for police officers to protect the public is more important than a suspect's *Miranda* rights.

Moran v. Burbine (475 U.S. 412 [1986]). This case established that police officers are not required to tell suspects undergoing custodial interrogation that their attorney is trying to reach them. The Court ruled that events that the suspect could have no way of knowing about have no bearing on his ability to waive his *Miranda* rights.

Illinois v. Perkins (496 U.S. 292) [1990]). Perkins was a suspected murderer in prison on an unrelated drug charge who admitted to the murder in order to impress his cellmate, who happened to be an undercover police officer. The Court ruled that even though the undercover officer goaded Perkins into making the admission, the defendant was not being subjected to a custodial interrogation; indeed, he eagerly bragged to his cellmate, describing the murder in detail in order to impress. *Miranda* does not protect suspects from their own foolishness.

Arizona v. Fulminante (499 U.S. 279 [1991]). In this very important ruling, the Court held that a conviction is not automatically overturned if the suspect was coerced into making a confession. If the other evidence introduced at the trial is strong enough to justify a conviction without the confession, then the fact that the confession was illegally gained can be, for all intents and purposes, ignored.

Davis v. United States (512 U.S. 452 [1994]). This case involved a suspect who, instead of demanding that he be provided with his *Miranda* right to an attorney, said, "Maybe I should talk to a lawyer" during his custodial interrogation. The Court ruled that a suspect must unequivocally and assertively state his right to counsel in order to stop police questioning. Furthermore, police officers are not required to try and decipher the suspect's intentions in such cases.

Texas v. Cobb (532 U.S. 162 [2001]). When a suspect refuses to waive his or her *Miranda* rights, a police officer cannot lawfully continue the interrogation until the suspect's attorney arrives on the scene. In this case, however, the Court held that a suspect may be questioned without the presence of a lawyer if the interrogation does not focus on the crime for which he or she was arrested, but does touch on another, closely related, offense.

Videotaping Confessions   *Miranda* may eventually find itself obsolete regardless of any decisions made in the courts. A relatively new trend in law enforcement has been for agencies to record interrogations and confessions on videotape, making it more difficult for defense attorneys to claim that their clients were illegally coerced. In New Mexico, officers now carry tape recorders on their waist belts. State laws in Alaska and Minnesota require interrogations to be recorded.

Videotaping can have unexpected bonuses: in Hennepin County, Minnesota, the camera recorded a suspect who claimed to be blind reading a newspaper. Many police departments, however, do not want to assume the costs associated with videotaped interrogations. The police commissioner of New York City said the logistics of videotaping would be "mind boggling" for an agency that handles as many as 250,000 arrests in one year.[98] Nonetheless, some scholars have suggested that the videotaping of all custodial interrogations would satisfy the Fifth Amendment's prohibition against coercion and in the process render the *Miranda* warning unnecessary.[99]

ONLINE REVIEW   *Go to the book's Web site for an interactive review of this section*

The Identification Process

A confession is a form of self-identification; the suspect has identified herself or himself as the guilty party. If police officers are unable to gain a confession, they must use other methods to link the suspect with the crime. In fact, to protect against false admissions, police must do so even if the suspect confesses.

ESSENTIAL PROCEDURES

Unless police officers witness the commission of the crime themselves, they must establish the identity of the suspect using three basic types of identification procedures:

1   *Showups,* which occur when a suspect who matches the description given by witnesses is apprehended near the scene of the crime within a reasonable amount of time after the crime has been committed. The suspect is usually returned to the crime scene for possible identification by witnesses.

2   *Photo arrays,* which occur when no suspect is in custody but the police have a general description of the person. Witnesses and victims are shown "mug shots" of people with police records that match the description. Police will also present witnesses and victims with pictures of people they believe might have committed the crime.

3   *Lineups,* which entail lining up several physically similar people, one of whom is the suspect, in front of a witness or victim. The police may have each member of the lineup wear clothing similar to that worn by the criminal and say a phrase that was used during the crime. These visual and oral cues are designed to help the witness identify the suspect.

As with the other procedures discussed in this chapter, constitutional law governs the identification process, though some aspects are more tightly restricted than others. The Sixth Amendment right to counsel, for example, does not apply during showups or photo arrays. In showups, the police often need to establish a suspect quickly, and it would be unreasonable to expect them to wait for an attorney to arrive. According to the Supreme Court in *United States v. Ash* (1973),[100] however,

Lineups are one of the primary means police have of identifying suspects. As you can see, in a lineup several people with similar appearances are placed so that a victim or witness can study them. The victim or witness is then asked to point out the one that most closely resembles the person who committed the crime. Lineup identifications are generally considered most valuable if they take place within several hours after the crime has been committed. Why is timing so important with regard to a lineup?

the police must be able to prove this need for immediate identification, perhaps by showing that it was necessary to keep the suspect from fleeing the state. As for photo arrays, courts have found that any procedure that does not require the suspect's presence does not require the presence of his or her attorney.[101] The lack of an attorney does not mean that police can "steer" a witness toward a positive identification with statements such as "Are you sure this isn't the person you saw robbing the grocery store?" Such actions would violate the suspect's due process rights.

NONTESTIMONIAL EVIDENCE

Some observers feel that the standard **booking** procedure—the process of recording information about the suspect immediately after arrest—infringes on a suspect's Fifth Amendment rights. During booking, the suspect is photographed and fingerprinted, and blood samples may be taken. If these samples lead to the suspect's eventual identification, according to some, they amount to self-incrimination. In *Schmerber v. California* (1966),[102] however, the Supreme Court held that such tests are not the equivalent of *testimonial* self-incrimination (where the suspect testifies verbally against himself or herself) and therefore do not violate the Fifth Amendment.

Using similar legal reasoning, the Court has also determined that voice and handwriting samples gathered by police may be used to identify a suspect.[103] The Court has, however, set some limits on the use of nontestimonial evidence. In the early 1980s, Ralph Watkinson of Richmond, Virginia, shot a man who had assaulted him and then fled the scene of the crime. Police found Rudolph Lee a few blocks away bleeding from a bullet wound beneath his collarbone. Watkinson identified Lee as the assailant, and the local prosecutor tried to get a court order to remove the bullet from Lee's body to match it with Watkinson's gun. In *Winston v. Lee* (1985),[104] the Court ruled that the surgery required was "highly intrusive" and was offensive to Lee's "human dignity." Therefore, the bullet was not allowed as nontestimonial evidence in the trial.

ONLINE REVIEW *Go to the book's Web site for an interactive review of this section*

See Officer.com for a wealth of information on the identification process and other law enforcement issues. Find this Web site by clicking on *Web Links* under *Chapter Resources* at www.cjinaction.com

Booking
The process of entering a suspect's name, offense, and arrival time into the police log following her or his arrest.

> Racial Profiling and the Constitution

As noted earlier in this chapter, the Fourth Amendment protects persons against "unreasonable searches and seizures." Nowhere in the Constitution, however, did the framers explain the term *unreasonable.* Thus, the participants in the criminal justice system have been left to find their own coherent and useful definition. Initially, as you will recall, the burden is on the police officer to decide whether his or her actions are reasonable, a decision that—in the absence of a warrant—will be reviewed in a court. In recent years, the question of reasonableness in the context of police stops and counterterrorism strategies has become intertwined with the troubling specter of racism in our nation's law enforcement agencies. In this *Criminal Justice in Action* feature, we will explore the question of whether it is possible for law enforcement to do its job without taking into account observable features of people such as race or ethnicity. The Supreme Court has essentially left this question unanswered, creating a vacuum that has been filled by lawsuits, controversy, and frustration.

patterns of police behavior can provide a clearer picture. Statistics gathered for two groundbreaking lawsuits concerning police activity on Interstate 95 seem to point to a serious problem.[105] On a particular stretch of the highway in New Jersey, where 13.5 percent of the vehicles carried an African American occupant, 46.2 percent of the stops were of black motorists.[106] Further south in Maryland, although only 17.5 percent of those violating traffic laws were African American, 72.9 percent of the motorists actually stopped and searched were black.[107]

In both cases, the statistics were seen as proof that the local police were using *racial profiling* in deciding which motorists to stop. Racial profiling occurs when a police action is initiated by the race, ethnicity, or national origin of the suspect, rather than by any evidence or information that the suspect has broken the law. Although it is rare to find a law enforcement agency that has an official policy of racial profiling, many observers feel that the practice is widespread.

By the Numbers

Though it is often difficult to determine whether an individual officer acted reasonably in a particular situation,

Demonstrators in front of Dearborn, Michigan city hall protest racial profiling against Arab Americans in the "war on terrorism." Following the September 11, 2001, attacks, the U.S. government requested interviews with nearly six hundred Middle Eastern men in eastern Michigan.

The "Rational Discrimination" Argument

This belief is only encouraged by statements such as the one made by Colonel Carl. A. Williams, superintendent of the New Jersey State Police. In answering charges that his officers targeted nonwhite motorists, Williams replied, "Two weeks ago, the president of the United States went to Mexico to talk ... about drugs. He didn't go to Ireland. He didn't go to England."[108]

In other words, Williams (who subsequently resigned) felt that his officers were justified in stopping nonwhite motorists because they were more likely to be breaking the law. This line of thinking, known as "rational discrimination," relies on statistics that show a correlation between race and crime. Because minorities, the argument goes, are more likely to commit crimes, police are justified in making group distinctions.[109]

David Cole, a professor at Georgetown University Law Center, and John Lamberth, an associate professor of psychology at Temple University, refute the idea of "rational discrimination." If blacks are more likely to be carrying drugs than whites, Cole and Lamberth say, then police should find drugs more often on the African Americans that they stop than on the whites that they stop. This is not the case. In Maryland, for example, the percentages of black and white drivers stopped who actually were in possession of drugs or other contraband were almost equal. Furthermore, in New Jersey, police found contraband on 25 percent of the white drivers, 13 percent of blacks, and only 5 percent of Hispanics.[110]

Does Profiling "Work"?

Given the mistrust of law enforcement agents that racial profiling arouses in minority communities, it would seem in society's best interest to eradicate the practice. This may prove difficult, however. As Jerome H. Skolnick has explained, stereotyping is integral to the world of law enforcement. A police officer's job is essentially to investigate behavior that appears to her or him to be out of the ordinary or "different." Race is a very strong cue toward indicating "differences." Consequently, police officers may believe that they are acting "reasonably" in relying on race as an indication of criminal behavior.[111]

Some observers also argue that, under certain circumstances, racial profiling "works." In the late 1990s, the Street Crimes Unit, a branch of the New York Police Department known for its aggressive tactics, came under a great deal of criticism. Over a two-year period, the unit made 45,000 stop and frisks. Only 22 percent of the stops led to arrests, and 90 percent of them involved members of a minority group.[112] In response to these figures and the 2002 shooting death of an immigrant from West Africa named Amadou Diallo, the Street Crimes Unit was disbanded.

Criminologists James Q. Wilson and Heather Mac Donald argue that the Street Crimes Unit's strategy actually made New York City a safer place. Those 45,000 stop and frisks, they point out, resulted in the seizure of 2,500 illegal guns, a ratio of one firearm confiscated for every eighteen stops. "No doubt some people regarded the stop as worse than an inconvenience and some stops may have been hard to justify," Wilson and Mac Donald write. "But the hassle factor has to be evaluated in the light of the great gains: 2,500 fewer dangerous weapons in dangerous hands."[113]

Terrorist Profiling

While the term *racial profiling* initially referred primarily to police stops of African Americans and Hispanics, in the past few years it has also come to be associated with counterterrorism efforts and their effects on the Muslim community. In the weeks following the September 11, 2001, terrorist attacks, federal law enforcement agents apprehended more than 1,000 males of Islamic background for questioning. Very few of these suspects were ever charged with any crime. The U.S. Department of Justice targeted nearly 8,000 young Muslim men visiting the United States for interviews, and the U.S. Treasury Department raided a number of homes and offices of Arab Americans believed to be associating with terrorist groups.

Again, though civil liberties groups and Muslim organizations have denounced these tactics, many observers support them as a "common-sense" approach to fighting terrorism. Just as detectives gather information on suspects most likely to have committed a particular crime, they argue, counterterrorist agents must "detail profile" to determine the most likely terrorists. These details include race, gender, and national origin, as well as behavioral traits such as enrollment at a flying school or participation in anti-American activities abroad or in the United States. No single detail would label someone a terrorist suspect, but a combination could be enough to meet reasonable suspicion standards.[114]

The *Whren* Effect

Those looking to the United States Supreme Court for answers to the questions raised by racial profiling have been disappointed. In 2001, the Court refused to hear an appeal of a case brought by a group of African American students in Oneonta, New York, who were "rounded up" and questioned following an assault in the area.[115] The best clues to the Court's view of racial profiling come from its decision in *Whren v. United States* (1996),[116] a case discussed on page 234.

In the *Whren* case, the Court ruled that the subjective intentions of the police, including any motives based on racial stereotyping or bias, are irrelevant under Fourth

Amendment analysis.[117] As long as there is objective probable cause of a traffic violation or other wrongdoing, any other reasons for the stop will not be considered. Thus, if a suspect was driving over the speed limit or was not wearing a seat belt, then a police officer's decision to stop that driver is constitutional, even if there is proof that the "real" reason for the stop was the driver's race. The Court reasoned that it is already very difficult to define such terms as *reasonable* and *probable cause*. To try to measure the motivation of a law enforcement agent would be more difficult still.[118]

Protecting Minorities (Sometimes)

In the absence of guidance from the Supreme Court, jurisdictions have had to make their own decisions on what steps to take to combat possible racial stereotyping. In 2003, for example, the California Highway Patrol announced that its officers would no longer use minor traffic violations as a pretext for searching automobiles for illegal drugs. Statistics showed that in certain parts of the state African Americans and Hispanics were three times more likely than whites to be the targets of such stops and searches.[119]

That same year, the administration of President George W. Bush issued guidelines designed to eradicate racial profiling in the seventy federal law enforcement agencies. Under the guidelines, a Drug Enforcement Administration officer cannot focus on a certain neighborhood simply because of its racial make-up. The guidelines do provide, however, an exception in "narrow" cases when race and ethnicity help "identify terrorist threats and stop potential catastrophic attacks."[120]

MAKING SENSE OF RACIAL PROFILING

1 Do you agree with the Supreme Court's reasoning in the *Whren* decision? What might be some of the practical consequences of allowing the suspect's race to be a factor in the "reasonableness" test of the Fourth Amendment?

2 Recall the "soccer mom" case discussed in the introduction to this chapter. How does Gail Atwater's experience relate to the racial profiling debate?

3 Revisit the arguments made in this feature in favor of some level of racial profiling. Do you agree with these positions? Are there any circumstances in which stereotyping—racial or otherwise—might be useful in fighting crime or terrorism?

Chapter Summary

STORIES FROM THE STREET

Go to the Stories from the Street feature at www.cjinaction.com to hear Larry Gaines tell insightful stories related to this chapter and his experiences in the field.

1 **Outline the four major sources that may provide probable cause.** (a) Personal observation, usually due to an officer's personal training, experience, and expertise; (b) information, gathered from informants, eyewitnesses, victims, police bulletins, and other sources; (c) evidence, which often has to be in plain view; and (d) association, which generally must concern a person with a known criminal background who is seen in a place where criminal activity is openly taking place.

2 **Explain the exclusionary rule and the exceptions to it.** This rule, established federally in *Weeks v. United States* and at the state level in *Mapp v. Ohio*, prohibits the use of illegally seized evidence, or evidence obtained by an unreasonable search and seizure in an inadmissible way. Exceptions to the exclusionary rule are the "inevitable

discovery" exception established in *Nix v. Williams* and the "good faith" exception established in *United States v. Leon.*

3 **Distinguish between a stop and a frisk, and indicate the importance of the case *Terry v. Ohio.*** Though the terms *stop* and *frisk* are often used in concert, a stop is the separate act of detaining a suspect when an officer reasonably believes that a criminal activity is about to take place. A frisk is the physical "pat-down" of a suspect. In *Terry v. Ohio,* the Supreme Court ruled that an officer must have "specific and articulable" facts before making a stop, but those facts may be "taken together with rational inferences."

4 **List the four elements that must be present for an arrest to take place.** (a) Intent, (b) authority, (c) seizure or

detention, and (d) the understanding of the person that he or she has been arrested.

5 **List the four categories of items that can be seized by use of a search warrant.** (a) Items resulting from a crime, such as stolen goods; (b) inherently illegal items; (c) evidence of the crime; and (d) items used in committing crimes.

6 **Explain when searches can be made without a warrant.** Searches and seizures can be made without a warrant if they are incidental to an arrest (but they must be reasonable); when they are made with voluntary consent; when they involve the "movable vehicle exception"; when property has been abandoned; and when items are in plain view, under certain restricted circumstances (see *Coolidge v. New Hampshire*).

7 **Describe how the USA Patriot Act of 2001 changed the guidelines for electronic surveillance of suspected terrorists.** Under the old surveillance guidelines, law enforcement agents needed probable cause of a crime to engage in counterterrorism. Under the USA Patriot Act of 2001, agents are free to search for leads or clues to terrorist activities if such surveillance serves a "significant purpose." The

"significant purpose" standard is much easier to meet than "probable cause."

8 **Recite the *Miranda* warning.** You have the right to remain silent. If you give up that right, anything you say can and will be used against you in a court of law. You have the right to speak with an attorney and to have the attorney present during questioning. If you so desire and cannot afford one, an attorney will be appointed for you without charge before questioning.

9 **Indicate situations in which a *Miranda* warning is unnecessary.** (a) When no questions that are testimonial in nature are asked of the suspect; (b) when there is no suspect and witnesses in general are being questioned at the scene of a crime; (c) when a person volunteers information before the police ask anything; (d) when a suspect has given a private statement to a friend without the government orchestrating it; (e) during a stop and frisk when no arrests have been made; and (f) during a traffic stop.

10 **List the three basic types of police identification.** (a) Showups, (b) photo arrays, and (c) lineups.

affidavit 229
arrest 223
arrest warrant 225
booking 245
consent searches 232
custodial interrogation 238
custody 238
exclusionary rule 219
exigent circumstances 226

frisk 223
fruit of the poisoned tree 219
"good faith" exception 221
"inevitable discovery" exception 220
interrogation 237
Miranda rights 238
plain view doctrine 235

probable cause 218
search 227
search warrant 228
searches and seizures 217
searches incidental to arrests 231
seizure 229
stop 223
warrantless arrest 227

Questions for Critical Analysis

1 What are the two most significant legal concepts contained in the Fourth Amendment, and why are they important?

2 Suppose that a police officer stops a person who "looks funny." The person acts strangely, so the police officer decides to frisk him. The officer feels a bulge in the suspect's coat pocket, which turns out to be a bag of cocaine. Would the arrest for cocaine possession hold up in court? Why or why not?

3 What continues to be the best indicator of probable cause in the face of no hard and fast definitions?

4 How does the expression "fruit of the poisoned tree" relate to the issue of searches and seizures?

5 Is it possible for a person legally to be under arrest without an officer indicating to that person that she or he is in fact under arrest? Explain.

6 Are there any circumstances in which an officer can make a warrantless arrest for a crime that is a misdemeanor? Explain.

7 What is the difference between an arrest warrant and a search warrant?

8 "A person always assumes the risk that her or his conversation may be monitored by the police." Is there any truth to this statement? Why or why not?

9 Describe some of the interrogation strategies that police officers use to gain confessions within the guidelines set down by the Supreme Court's *Miranda* decision.

10 What circumstances have led some states to videotape interrogations, and why have some jurisdictions decided not to do so?

TEST PREPARATION ONLINE

Go to www.cjinaction.com for tools to aid you in studying for your exams. Click on *Online Reviews* under *Chapter Resources* for an interactive review of each major section of this chapter. Under *Chapter Resources,* you will also find the *Chapter Outline, Chapter Summary, Flashcards, Glossary, Learning Objectives, Lecture Presentations, Concept Builder, Essay Questions,* and a *Tutorial Quiz.* You can also test yourself with a game of *Concentration* or the *Crossword Puzzle.*

Web Resources

Go to www.cjinaction.com for a wealth of online resources. Explore the *Internet Activities* and *Class Projects* under *Chapter Resources.* Check out the *Web Links* to access the Web sites mentioned in the text, as well as many others. You can also access recent perspectives by clicking on *CJ in the News* and *Terrorism Update* under *Course Resources.* If you'd like some mentoring, click on *Board of Mentors* under *Book Resources.*

Search Online with InfoTrac College Edition

For additional information, explore InfoTrac College Edition, your online library that offers complete full-length articles from thousands of scholarly and popular publications. Click on *InfoTrac College Edition* under *Chapter Resources* at www.cjinaction.com for a list of key words and InfoTrac exercises. Use the passcode that came with your book.

Suggested Readings

Mac Donald, Heather, *Are Cops Racist?* Chicago: Ivan R. Dee, 2003. The author uses extensive fieldwork in an attempt to debunk the theory that racial profiling is an endemic problem among American law enforcement officers. Mac Donald argues that, far from being evidence of racism among the police, statistics showing higher rates of stops and arrests in minority neighborhoods reflect a positive attempt to fight crime where it is most prevalent. She also claims that the past decade "should have been a time of triumph for law enforcement, not an occasion for frenzied cop-bashing."

Parenti, Christian, *Soft Cage: Surveillance in America from Slavery to the War on Terror,* New York: Basic Books, 2003. For most of this nation's history, government surveillance of American citizens has been justified in the name of national security. In this book, Parenti explores the political and sociological underpinnings for "Big Brother" in the United States. He contends that an eighteenth-century slave pass, designed to keep track of the movement of slaves, and modern Social Security cards perform the same function of population control. Not surprisingly, the author strongly believes that although surveillance is justified as a means of crime control, its actual purpose is to limit civil liberties and other freedoms guaranteed to American citizens under the U.S. Constitution.

Notes

1. 532 U.S. 318 (2001).
2. *Michigan v. Summers,* 452 U.S. 692 (1981).
3. *Brinegar v. United States,* 338 U.S. 160 (1949).
4. Rolando V. del Carmen, *Criminal Procedure for Law Enforcement Personnel* (Monterey, CA: Brooks/Cole Publishing Co., 1987), 63–64.
5. 500 U.S. 44 (1991).
6. *United States v. Leon,* 468 U.S. 897 (1984).
7. 232 U.S. 383 (1914).
8. 342 U.S. 165 (1952).
9. 367 U.S. 643 (1961).
10. Potter Stewart, "The Road to *Mapp v. Ohio* and Beyond: The Origins, Development, and Future of the Exclusionary Rule in Search-and-Seizure Cases," *Columbia Law Review* 83 (October 1983), 1365.
11. 430 U.S. 387 (1977).
12. 467 U.S. 431 (1984).
13. 468 U.S. 897 (1984).
14. "Jury's Mixed Verdict in Cop Trial," *UPI Online* (April 3, 1998).
15. Karen M. Hess and Henry M. Wrobleski, *Police Operation: Theory and Practice* (St. Paul, MN: West Publishing Co., 1997), 122.
16. 392 U.S. 1 (1968).
17. *Ibid.,* 20.
18. *Ibid.,* 21.
19. See *United States v. Cortez,* 449 U.S. 411 (1981); and *United States v. Sokolow,* 490 U.S. 1 (1989).
20. *United States v. Arvizu,* 534 U.S. 266 (2002).
21. *Ibid.,* 270.
22. *Florida v. J.L.,* 529 U.S. 266, 274 (2000).
23. *Adams v. Williams,* 407 U.S. 143 (1972).
24. *Alabama v. White,* 496 U.S. 325 (1990).
25. *United States v. Place,* 462 U.S. 696 (1983).
26. *Minnesota v. Dickerson,* 508 U.S. 366 (1993).
27. Rolando V. del Carmen and Jeffrey T. Walker, *Briefs of Leading Cases in Law Enforcement,* 2d ed. (Cincinnati, OH: Anderson, 1995), 38–40.
28. *Florida v. Royer,* 460 U.S. 491 (1983).
29. See also *United States v. Mendenhall,* 446 U.S. 544 (1980).
30. del Carmen, *Criminal Procedure,* 97–98.
31. 514 U.S. 927 (1995).
32. Linda J. Collier and Deborah D. Rosenbloom, *American Jurisprudence,* 2d ed. (Rochester, NY: Lawyers Cooperative Publishing, 1995), 122.
33. 495 U.S. 91 (1990).
34. Wayne R. LeFave and Jerold H. Israel, *Criminal Procedure* (St. Paul, MN: West Publishing Co., 1985), 141–144.
35. David Orlin, Jacob Thiessen, Kelli C. McTaggart, Lisa Toporek, and James Pearl, "Warrantless Searches and Seizures," in "Twenty-sixth Annual Review of Criminal Procedure," *Georgetown Law Journal* 85 (April 1997), 847.
36. 445 U.S. 573 (1980).
37. 451 U.S. 204 (1981).
38. *California v. Greenwood,* 486 U.S. 35 (1988).
39. *Ibid.*
40. 389 U.S. 347 (1967).
41. *Ibid.,* 361.
42. 486 U.S. 35 (1988).
43. *Ibid.*
44. *Coolidge v. New Hampshire,* 403 U.S. 443, 467 (1971).
45. del Carmen, *Criminal Procedure,* 158.
46. *Katz v. United States,* 389 U.S. 347, 357 (1967).
47. 414 U.S. 234–235 (1973).

48. 395 U.S. 752 (1969).
49. *Bumper v. North Carolina,* 391 U.S. 543 (1960).
50. 412 U.S. 218 (1973).
51. Ian D. Midgley, "Just One Question before We Get to *Ohio v. Robinette:* 'Are You Carrying Any Contraband . . . Weapons, Drugs, Constitutional Protections . . . Anything Like That?'" *Case Western Reserve Law Review* 48 (Fall 1997), 173.
52. 501 U.S. 429 (1991).
53. 519 U.S. 33 (1996).
54. *United States v. Drayton,* 536 U.S. 194 (2002).
55. Linda Greenhouse, "Supreme Court Upholds Police Methods in Vehicle Drug Searches," *New York Times* (November 19, 1996), A23.
56. 435 U.S. 454 (1981).
57. 267 U.S. 132 (1925).
58. *United States v. Ross,* 456 U.S. 798, 804–809 (1982); and *Chambers v. Maroney,* 399 U.S. 42, 44, 52 (1970).
59. 517 U.S. 806 (1996).
60. 519 U.S. 408 (1997).
61. Linda Greenhouse, "Supreme Court Bars Traffic Stops That Are Intended as Drug Checks," *New York Times* (November 29, 2000), A1.
62. *Michigan Department of State Police v. Sitz,* 496 U.S. 455 (1990).
63. *United States v. Martinez-Fuerte,* 428 U.S. 556 (1976).
64. 531 U.S. 32 (2000).
65. *Ibid.*
66. *Knowles v. Iowa,* 525 U.S. 113 (1998).
67. *New York v. Belton,* 435 U.S. 454 (1981).
68. 403 U.S. 443 (1971).
69. 388 U.S. 42 (1967).
70. 18 U.S.C. Sections 2510(7), 2518(1)(a), 2516 (1994).
71. *Lee v. United States,* 343 U.S. 747 (1952).
72. Christopher K. Murphy, "Electronic Surveillance," in "Twenty-Sixth Annual Review of Criminal Procedure," *Georgetown Law Journal* (April 1997), 920.
73. *United States v. Nguyen,* 46 F.3d 781, 783 (8th Cir. 1995).
74. Foreign Intelligence Surveillance Act of 1978, Pub. L. No. 95-511, 92 Stat. 1783, codified at 50 U.S.C. Sections 1801–1811 (2000).
75. Uniting and Strengthening America by Providing Appropriate Tools Required to Interrupt and Obstruct Terrorism Act of 2001, Pub. L. No. 107-56, 115 Stat. 272, codified as amended at 50 U.S.C.A. Sections 1801–1811 (West 2000 & Supp. 2002).
76. David Hardin, "The Fuss over Two Small Words: The Unconstitutionality of the USA Patriot Act Amendments to FISA under the Fourth Amendment," *George Washington Law Review* (April 2003), 291.
77. *Brown v. Mississippi,* 297 U.S. 278 (1936).
78. 378 U.S. 478 (1964).
79. *Miranda v. Arizona,* 384 U.S. 436 (1966).
80. H. Richard Uviller, *Tempered Zeal* (Chicago: Contemporary Books, 1988), 188–198.
81. *Orozco v. Texas,* 394 U.S. 324 (1969); *Oregon v. Mathiason,* 429 U.S. 492 (1977); *California v. Beheler,* 463 U.S. 1121 (1983).
82. *Pennsylvania v. Muniz,* 496 U.S. 582 (1990).
83. del Carmen, *Criminal Procedure,* 267–268.
84. *Moran v. Burbine,* 475 U.S. 412 (1986).
85. *Michigan v. Mosley,* 423 U.S. 96 (1975).
86. *Fare v. Michael C.,* 442 U.S. 707, 723–724 (1979).
87. 512 U.S. 452 (1994).
88. Patrick Malone, "You Have the Right to Remain Silent: *Miranda* after Twenty Years," *American Scholar* 55 (1986), 367.

89. Richard A. Leo, "The Impact of *Miranda* Revisited," *Journal of Criminal Law and Criminology* 86 (Spring 1996), 621–692.
90. Shaila K. Dewan, "New York Police Resist Videotaping Interrogations," *New York Times* (September 2, 2002), A21.
91. Saul Kassin, "False Confessions and the Jogger Case," *New York Times* (November 1, 2002), A31.
92. Margot Talbot, "True Confessions," *Atlantic Monthly* (July/August 2002), 25.
93. Edwin Dobb, "Should John Walker Lindh Go Free?" *Harper's Magazine* (May 2002), 31–41.
94. 530 U.S. 428 (2000).
95. *Ibid.,* 443.
96. Alan M. Dershowitz, "A Requiem for the Exclusionary Rule," in *Taking Liberties: A Decade of Hard Cases, Bad Laws, and Bum Raps* (Chicago: Contemporary Books, 1988), 10.
97. *United States v. Patane,* No. 02-1183.
98. Dewan, 21.
99. Paul G. Cassell, "The Grand Illusion of *Miranda's* Defenders," *Northwestern University Law Review* 90 (1996), 1118–1124.
100. 413 U.S. 300 (1973).
101. *United States v. Barker,* 988 F.2d 77, 78 (9th Cir. 1993).
102. 384 U.S. 757 (1966).
103. *United States v. Dionisio,* 410 U.S. 1 (1973); and *United States v. Mara,* 410 U.S. 19 (1973).
104. 470 U.S. 753 (1985).
105. *State v. Soto,* 734 A.2d 350 (1996); and *Wilkins v. Maryland State Police* (available at www.aclu.org/court/mspet.html).
106. Tracey Maclin, "Race and the Fourth Amendment," *Vanderbilt Law Review* 51 (March 1998), 347.
107. *Ibid.,* 349.
108. Quoted in Jackson Toby, "'Racial Profiling' Doesn't Prove Cops Are Racist," *Wall Street Journal* (March 11, 1999), A22.
109. Dinesh D'Souza, *The End of Racism: Principles for a Multiracial Society* (New York: Free Press, 1995), 284.
110. David Cole and John Lamberth, "The Fallacy of Racial Profiling," *New York Times* (May 13, 2001), 13.
111. Jerome H. Skolnick, *Justice without Trial: Law Enforcement in Democratic Society,* 3d ed. (New York: Macmillan, 1994), 80.
112. Melanie Lefkowitz, "Policy Set on the Street," *Newsday* (March 14, 2002), A3.
113. James Q. Wilson and Heather Mac Donald, "Profiles in Courage," *Wall Street Journal* (January 10, 2002), A12.
114. Siobhan Gorman, "Profiling Terror," *National Journal* (April 13, 2002), 1058–1061.
115. "High Court Doesn't Want to Face Up to Profiling Appeal," *Law Enforcement News* (October 31, 2001), 7.
116. 517 U.S. 806 (1996).
117. *Ibid.,* 813.
118. Maclin, 377.
119. Maura Dolan and John M. Glionna, "CHP Settles Lawsuit over Claims of Racial Profiling," *Los Angeles Times* (February 28, 2003), A1.
120. Eric Lichtblau, "Bush Issues Racial Profiling Ban but Exempts Security Inquiries," *New York Times* (June 18, 2003), A1.

Courts and the Quest for Justi

>Chapter 8<

Courts and the
Quest for Justice

>chapter objectives<

After reading this chapter, you should be able to:

1 Define and contrast the four functions of the courts.

2 Define jurisdiction and contrast geographical and subject-matter jurisdiction.

3 Explain the difference between trial and appellate courts.

4 Outline the several levels of a typical state court system.

5 Outline the federal court system.

6 Explain briefly how a case is brought to the Supreme Court.

7 List the actions that a judge might take prior to an actual trial.

8 Explain the difference between the selection of judges at the state level and at the federal level.

9 List and describe the members of the courtroom work group.

10 Explain the consequences of excessive caseloads.

Bad Days in Court

Tiny Tulia, Texas (population 5,000), hardly seemed the ideal target for a drug sting. Nonetheless, for eighteen months Officer Thomas Coleman of the Panhandle Regional Narcotics Trafficking Task Force lived in Tulia, pretending to be T. J. Dawson, a field worker whose girlfriend required cocaine before she would have sex with him. Based on Coleman's testimony, thirty-eight people, thirty-five of them African American, were convicted of selling small amounts of cocaine and sentenced to prison.

Thirteen defendants on drug charges sit in a jury box of the Swisher County courthouse during a hearing in Tulia, Texas. These defendants, along with twenty-five others, were convicted based on the testimony of undercover agent Tom Coleman. Authorities never found any drugs or money during the arrests, and Coleman was later charged with perjury for his role in the convictions. Coleman was also condemned as a racist for his documented use of racial epithets and the fact that thirty-five of the thirty-eight Tulia citizens arrested on his word were African American.

Observing that those arrested represented 10 percent of Tulia's entire black population, several volunteer lawyers began to take a closer look at the convictions. As it turned out, the only evidence that any wrongdoing had taken place was Coleman's uncorroborated testimony. The undercover narcotics agent had no written records or videotapes of the numerous drug deals he supposedly made with Tulia's citizens. No witnesses to any of these buys were to be found, and, most remarkably, no actual illegal drugs or drug paraphernalia were ever presented as evidence. Furthermore, defense attorneys and the jury were not informed that Coleman had been arrested for stealing more than $7,000 worth of gasoline in the middle of his "investigation."

Eventually, the Texas Court of Criminal Appeals ordered new hearings. During these hearings, state District Judge Ron Chapman, local prosecutors, and defense attorneys agreed that Thomas Coleman was, in essence, a racist, a liar, and a thief. By the fall of 2003, all of those convicted on the basis of his testimony were set free.

> **Looking back** at the Tulia debacle, some of the convictions were so ridiculous as to strain belief. The supposed "drug kingpin" of Tulia was a hog farmer named Joe Welton Moore who lived in a shack with red dirt for a front yard. Moore was sentenced to ninety years in prison for his alleged cocaine-related activities. During the special hearings, Judge Ron Chapman called Thomas Coleman "the most devious . . . law enforcement officer this court has witnessed

in twenty-five years on the bench in Texas."[1] In short, the Tulia matter showcased the worst of the American judicial system: manufactured evidence, a perjuring witness, a gullible (at best) jury, misleading prosecutors, and ineffective defense attorneys. By the same token, this system, for all its evident flaws, did eventually see justice done.

Famed jurist Roscoe Pound characterized "justice" as society's demand "that serious offenders be convicted and punished," while at the same time "the innocent and unfortunate are not oppressed."[2] We can expand on this noble, if idealistic, definition. Citizens expect their courts to discipline the guilty, provide deterrents for illegal activities, protect civil liberties, and rehabilitate criminals—all simultaneously. Over the course of the next four chapters, we shall examine these lofty goals and the extent to which they can be reached. We start with a discussion of how courts in the United States work.

Functions of the Courts

Simply stated, a court is a place where arguments are settled. The argument may be between the federal government and a corporation accused of violating environmental regulations, between business partners, between a criminal and the state, or between any other number of parties. The court provides an environment in which the basis of the argument can be settled through the application of the law.

Courts have extensive powers in our criminal justice system: they can bring the authority of the state to seize property and to restrict individual liberty. Given that the rights to own property and to enjoy personal freedom are enshrined in the U.S. Constitution, a court's *legitimacy* in taking such measures must be unquestioned by society. This legitimacy is based on two factors: impartiality and independence.[3] In theory, each party involved in a courtroom dispute must have an equal chance to present its case and must be secure in the belief that no outside factors are going to influence the decision rendered by the court. In reality, it does not always work that way. The defendants in the Tulia drug stings would probably never have been convicted if they had been able to afford better legal representation, an issue we will address in the *Criminal Justice in Action* feature at the end of this chapter. Everyone, from a poor pig farmer in the Texas panhandle to mass murderers such as terrorists, must receive a fair and impartial hearing if the court system as a whole is to retain the confidence of the public.

DUE PROCESS AND CRIME CONTROL IN THE COURTS

As mentioned in Chapter 1, the criminal justice system has two sets of underlying values: due process and crime control. Due process values focus on protecting the rights of the individual; crime control values stress the punishment and repression of criminal conduct.[4] The competing nature of these two value systems is often most evident in the nation's courts.

The Due Process Function The primary concern of early American courts was to protect the rights of the individual against the power of the state. Memories of

CONCEPT BUILDER
Justice is an elusive ideal, yet central to how society deals with law violators. What exactly is justice? Visit www.cjinaction.com for an interactive exploration of this key topic.

" The judge is condemned when the criminal is acquitted."
—Publius Syrus, Roman philosopher (42 B.C.E.)

AP Photo/The Denver Post/Hyoung Chang

Eagle County (Colorado) Judge Frederick Gannett listens to oral arguments at a preliminary hearing in professional basketball player Kobe Bryant's sexual assault case. Gannett decided that the prosecution presented enough evidence to have Bryant stand trial—just one of the many decisions judges make as "gatekeepers" of the criminal justice system.

INFOTRAC KEYWORDS

due process and courts

For more information, use these search terms with InfoTrac College Edition, your online library at www.infotrac-college.com

injustices suffered at the hands of the British monarchy were still strong, and most of the procedural rules that we have discussed in this textbook were created with the express purpose of giving the individual a "fair chance" against the government in any courtroom proceedings. Therefore, the due process function of the courts is to protect individuals from the unfair advantages that the government—with its immense resources—automatically enjoys in legal battles. Seen in this light, constitutional guarantees such as the right to counsel, the right to a jury trial, and protection from self-incrimination are equalizers in the "contest" between the state and the individual. The idea that the two sides in a courtroom dispute are adversaries is, as we shall see in the next chapter, fundamental in American courts.

The Crime Control Function Advocates of crime control distinguish between the court's obligation to be fair to the accused and its obligation to be fair to society.[5] The crime control function of the courts emphasizes punishment and retribution—criminals must suffer for the harm done to society, and it is the courts' responsibility to see that they do so. Given this responsibility to protect the public, deter criminal behavior, and "get criminals off the streets," the courts should not be concerned solely with giving the accused a fair chance. Rather than using due process rules as "equalizers," the courts should use them as protection against blatantly unconstitutional acts. For example, a detective who beats a suspect with a tire iron to get a confession has obviously infringed on the suspect's constitutional rights. If, however, the detective uses trickery to gain a confession, the court should allow the confession to stand because it is not in society's interest that law enforcement agents be deterred from outwitting criminals.

THE REHABILITATION FUNCTION

A third view of the court's responsibility is based on the "medical model" of the criminal justice system. In this model, criminals are analogous to patients, and the courts perform the role of doctors who dispense "treatment."[6] The criminal is seen as sick, not evil, and therefore treatment is morally justified. Of course, treatment varies from case to case, and some criminals require harsh penalties such as incarceration. In other cases, however, it may not be in society's best interest for the criminal to be punished according to the formal rules of the justice system. Perhaps the criminal can be rehabilitated to become a productive member of society and thus save taxpayers the costs of incarceration or other punishment.

THE BUREAUCRATIC FUNCTION

To a certain extent, the crime control, due process, and rehabilitation functions of a court are secondary to its bureaucratic function. In general, a court may have the goal of protecting society or protecting the rights of the individual, but on a day-to-day basis that court has the more pressing task of dealing with the cases brought before it. Like any bureaucracy, a court is concerned with speed and efficiency, and loftier concepts such as justice can be secondary to a judge's need to wrap up a particular case before six o'clock so that administrative deadlines can be met. Indeed, many observers feel that the primary adversarial relationship in the courts is not between the two parties involved but between the ideal of justice and the reality of bureaucratic limitations.[7]

↗ ONLINE REVIEW *Go to the book's Web site for an interactive review of this section*

The Basic Principles of the American Judicial System

One of the most often cited limitations of the American judicial system is its complex nature. In truth, the United States does not have a single judicial system, but fifty-two different systems—one for each state, the District of Columbia, and the federal government. As each state has its own unique judiciary with its own set of rules, some of which may be in conflict with the federal judiciary, it is helpful at this point to discuss the basics—jurisdiction, trial and appellate courts, and the dual court system.

JURISDICTION

In Latin, *juris* means "law," and *diction* means "to speak." Thus, **jurisdiction** literally refers to the power "to speak the law." Before any court can hear a case, it must have jurisdiction over the persons involved in the case or its subject matter. The jurisdiction of every court, even the United States Supreme Court, is limited in some way.

Geographical Jurisdiction   One limitation is geographical. Generally, a court can exercise its authority over residents of a certain area. A state trial court, for example, normally has jurisdictional authority over crimes committed in a particular area of the state, such as a county or a district. A state's highest court (often called the state supreme court) has jurisdictional authority over the entire state, and the United States Supreme Court has jurisdiction over the entire country. (For a global perspective on this issue, see the feature *International CJ— Jurisdiction and the International Criminal Court* on the next page.)

Domestic Jurisdiction   Determining which court has geographical jurisdiction can sometimes be complicated. Take the cases of John Allen Muhammad and John Lee Malvo. Although media attention focused on their sniper activities in the Washington, D.C., area in the fall of 2002, the two were charged with killing fourteen people and injuring several others in Washington State, Alabama, Georgia, and Louisiana, as well as in Virginia, Maryland, and the District of Columbia.

Almost immediately after Muhammad and Malvo were arrested, the question became: Where would they stand trial? Technically, each jurisdiction in which they had committed a crime had jurisdiction. The entity in the best position to give an answer was the federal government, which had custody over the pair and therefore the power to decide where their first trials would take place. Maryland authorities argued that because more people were killed in their state—six—than in any other jurisdiction, they should have "first crack" at the alleged snipers. The U.S. Department of Justice, however, wanted Muhammad and Malvo to receive the death penalty if found guilty, and felt that Virginia had, in the words of Attorney General John Ashcroft, "the best law, the best facts, and the best range of available penalties."[8] Therefore, Malvo's initial trial was in Chesapeake, Virginia, and Muhammad's was in Virginia Beach, Virginia.

Jurisdiction
The authority of a court to hear and decide cases within an area of the law or a geographical territory.

> Jurisdiction and the International Criminal Court

The United States has a long history of supporting international prosecution of the most heinous of crimes. In 1946, the United States was the guiding force behind the Nuremberg Trials, which established that individuals could be convicted for war crimes and crimes against humanity. (The trials resulted in Nazi leaders being found guilty of the extermination of millions of Jews.) Over the past decade, the United States has provided funds and information to international tribunals set up to punish the instigators of genocide in Rwanda and the Balkans. Yet, when the International Criminal Court (ICC)—the world's first permanent court for the prosecution of war criminals—was created on April 11, 2002, the United States refused to take part.

This decision earned the United States a great deal of international criticism, especially from the nations of the European Union. For the Bush administration, however, it was a matter of jurisdiction. The ICC assumes jurisdiction over acts of genocide, crimes against humanity, and war crimes committed by individuals regardless of nationality. In theory, this means that any American, from a high-ranking government official to soldiers in the field, could be accused of committing a crime against humanity by the court's chief prosecutor. Because the United States is currently the world's only superpower, with military operations in dozens of countries at any one time, the administration worries that Americans will be easy targets for frivolous accusations. Furthermore, as some constitutional scholars have pointed out, the ICC does not provide for a trial by jury, as guaranteed to any American charged with committing a crime by the Bill of Rights.

Supporters of the ICC counter that the United States overestimates the risks of seeing its citizens hauled before the court, as the court's jurisdiction is only "secondary"; that is, the court will prosecute only in situations in which the home country of the accused is unable or unwilling to do so. Regardless of this argument, the United States has insisted that it will not cooperate with the ICC unless Americans are given immunity from its

The United States chair remains empty during the first meeting of the International Criminal Court at United Nations headquarters in New York City on September 3, 2002.

jurisdiction, a request that has been rejected by most participating nations.

FOR CRITICAL ANALYSIS
Do you agree with the Bush administration's position against the ICC? Which is more important—protecting the rights of Americans (to trial by jury, for example), or cooperating with the international community in fighting the crimes over which the ICC has jurisdiction?

International Jurisdiction Policy concerns also play a large role in questions of international geographical jurisdiction. Although many countries have agreed to extradite suspects when asked to do so, the decision is fraught with extralegal concerns. Many European countries, for example, will not extradite suspects to the United States if the accused could face the death penalty at trial. In 2003, for example, Germany refused to send two suspected supporters of the al Qaeda terrorist organization to the United States until it received assurances that they would not be executed if found guilty.

Similarly, a country may face internal pressure not to hand over a suspect. The government of Pakistan refused repeated requests from U.S. officials to extra-

Ahmed Omar Saeed, who is presumed to have planned the kidnapping and murder of American journalist Daniel Pearl in 2002, is escorted into the provincial high court in Karachi, Pakistan. The United States sought Saeed's extradition, but Pakistani government officials refused, insisting that the suspect stand trial in the country where his crime took place. (Saeed was eventually convicted and sentenced to death.) What reasons might a country have for refusing an extradition request?

dite Ahmed Omar Saeed to this country. To do so, many Pakistanis believed, would be to somehow "taint" Pakistan's criminal justice system by insinuating that it was inferior to that of the United States. Consequently, Saeed was convicted and sentenced to death by a Pakistani court for the role he played in the murder of American journalist Daniel Pearl.

Subject-Matter Jurisdiction   Jurisdiction over subject matter also acts as a limitation on the types of cases a court can hear. State court systems include courts of *general* (unlimited) *jurisdiction* and courts of *limited jurisdiction.* Courts of general jurisdiction have no restrictions on the subject matter they may address, and therefore deal with the most serious felonies and civil cases. Courts of limited jurisdiction, also known as lower courts, handle misdemeanors and civil matters under a certain amount, usually $1,000. To alleviate caseload pressures in lower courts, many states have created special subject-matter courts that only dispose of cases involving a specific crime. For example, a number of jurisdictions have established drug courts to handle an overload of illicit narcotics arrests, and California has created twelve courts that deal specifically with domestic violence offenders.

TRIAL AND APPELLATE COURTS

Another distinction is between courts of original jurisdiction and courts of appellate, or review, jurisdiction. Courts having *original jurisdiction* are courts of the first instance, or **trial courts.** Almost every case begins in a trial court. It is in this court that a trial (or a guilty plea) takes place, and the judge imposes a sentence if the defendant is found guilty. Trial courts are primarily concerned with *questions of fact;* that is, they are designed to determine exactly what events occurred that are relevant to questions of the defendant's guilt or innocence.

Courts having *appellate jurisdiction* act as reviewing courts, or **appellate courts.** In general, cases can be brought before appellate courts only on appeal by

Trial Courts
Courts in which most cases usually begin and in which questions of fact are examined.

Appellate Courts
Courts that review decisions made by lower courts, such as trial courts. Also known as courts of appeals.

one of the parties in the trial court. Note that because of constitutional protections against being tried twice for the same crime, prosecutors who lose in criminal trial court *cannot* appeal the verdict. An appellate court does not use juries or witnesses to reach its decision. Instead, its judges make a decision on whether the case should be *reversed* and *remanded,* or sent back to the court of original jurisdiction for a new trial. Appellate judges present written explanations for their decisions, and these **opinions** of the court are the basis for a great deal of the precedent in the criminal justice system.

It is important to understand that appellate courts do not determine the defendant's guilt or innocence—they only make judgments on questions of procedure. In other words, they are concerned with *questions of law* and normally accept the facts as established by the trial court. An appeals court will rarely question a jury's decision. Instead, the appellate judges will review the manner in which the facts and evidence were provided to the jury and rule on whether errors were made in the process.

THE DUAL COURT SYSTEM

Like many other aspects of American government, the structure of the judicial system was the result of a compromise. During the framing of the U.S. Constitution, two camps emerged with different views on the courts. The Anti-Federalists, interested in limiting the power of the federal government, wanted the Supreme Court to be the only *national* court, with the states handling the majority of judicial work. The Federalists, dedicated to ensuring that the states did not have too much power, wanted all cases to be heard in federal courts. Both sides eventually made concessions, and the outcome is reflected in the **dual court system** that we have today (see Figure 8.1).[9]

Federal and state courts both have limited jurisdiction. Generally stated, federal courts deal with acts that violate federal law, and state courts deal with acts that violate state law. The distinction is not, however, always clear. A number of crimes—such as kidnapping and transportation of narcotics—are deemed illegal by both federal and state statutes, and persons accused of such crimes can be tried

Opinion
A statement by the court expressing the reasons for its decision in a case.

Dual Court System
The separate but interrelated court system of the United States, made up of the courts on the national level and the courts on the state level.

FIGURE 8.1 **The Dual Court System**

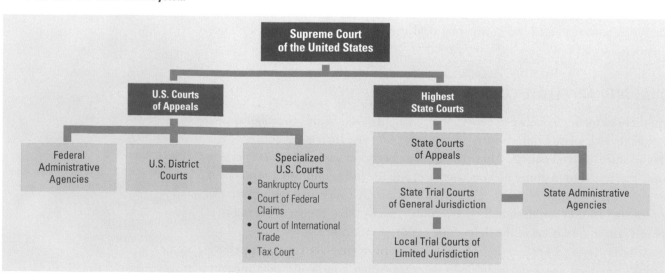

in either court system. In these instances, federal and state prosecutors must decide among themselves who will handle the case—a decision based on a number of factors, including the notoriety of the crime and the relative caseloads of the respective court systems. Often, the prosecutors will "steer" a suspect toward the harsher penalty. Thus, if the punishment for a particular crime is more severe under federal law than state law, then law enforcement officials may decide to try the defendant in federal court (and vice versa).

◢ ONLINE REVIEW *Go to the book's Web site for an interactive review of this section*

State Court Systems

Typically, a state court system includes several levels, or tiers, of courts. State courts may include (1) lower courts, or courts of limited jurisdiction; (2) trial courts of general jurisdiction; (3) appellate courts; and (4) the state's highest court. As previously mentioned, each state has a different judicial structure, in which different courts have different jurisdictions, but there are enough similarities to allow for a general discussion. Figure 8.2 shows a typical state court system.

FIGURE 8.2
A Typical State Court System

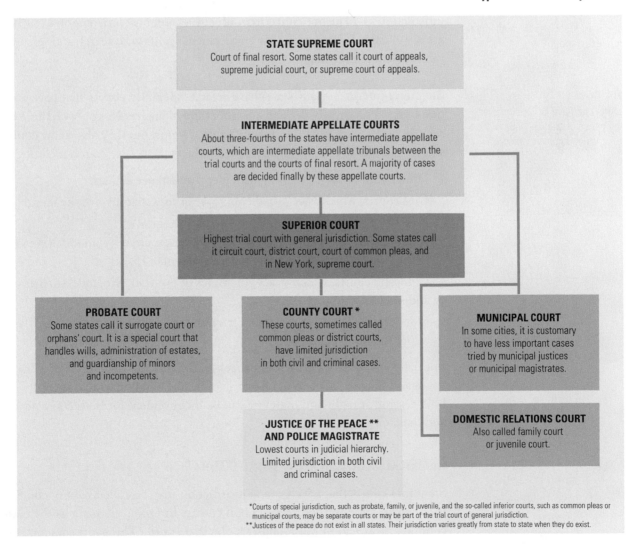

STATE SUPREME COURT
Court of final resort. Some states call it court of appeals, supreme judicial court, or supreme court of appeals.

INTERMEDIATE APPELLATE COURTS
About three-fourths of the states have intermediate appellate courts, which are intermediate appellate tribunals between the trial courts and the courts of final resort. A majority of cases are decided finally by these appellate courts.

SUPERIOR COURT
Highest trial court with general jurisdiction. Some states call it circuit court, district court, court of common pleas, and in New York, supreme court.

PROBATE COURT
Some states call it surrogate court or orphans' court. It is a special court that handles wills, administration of estates, and guardianship of minors and incompetents.

COUNTY COURT *
These courts, sometimes called common pleas or district courts, have limited jurisdiction in both civil and criminal cases.

MUNICIPAL COURT
In some cities, it is customary to have less important cases tried by municipal justices or municipal magistrates.

JUSTICE OF THE PEACE **
AND POLICE MAGISTRATE
Lowest courts in judicial hierarchy. Limited jurisdiction in both civil and criminal cases.

DOMESTIC RELATIONS COURT
Also called family court or juvenile court.

*Courts of special jurisdiction, such as probate, family, or juvenile, and the so-called inferior courts, such as common pleas or municipal courts, may be separate courts or may be part of the trial court of general jurisdiction.
**Justices of the peace do not exist in all states. Their jurisdiction varies greatly from state to state when they do exist.

LIMITED-JURISDICTION COURTS

Most states have local trial courts that are limited to trying cases involving minor criminal matters, such as traffic violations, prostitution, and drunk and disorderly conduct. Although these minor courts usually keep no written record of the trial proceedings and cases are decided by a judge rather than a jury, defendants have the same rights as those in other trial courts. The majority of all minor criminal cases are decided in these lower courts. Limited-jurisdiction courts can also be responsible for the preliminary stages of felony cases. Arraignments, bail hearings, and preliminary hearings often take place in these lower courts.

Magistrate Courts   One of the earliest courts of limited jurisdiction was the *justice court,* presided over by a *justice of the peace,* or JP. In the early days of this nation, JPs were found everywhere in the country. One of the most famous JPs was Judge Roy Bean, the "hanging judge" of Langtry, Texas, who presided over his court at the turn of the twentieth century. Today, more than half the states have abolished justice courts, though JPs still serve a useful function in some cities and rural areas, notably in Texas. The jurisdiction of justice courts is limited to minor disputes between private individuals and to crimes punishable by small fines or short jail terms. The equivalent of a county JP in a city is known as a **magistrate** or, in some states, a municipal court judge. Magistrate courts have the same limited jurisdiction as do justice courts in rural settings. In most jurisdictions, magistrates are responsible for providing law enforcement agents with search and seizure warrants, discussed in Chapter 7.

Magistrate
A public civil officer or official with limited judicial authority within a particular geographical area, such as the authority to issue an arrest warrant.

Specialty Courts   Many states have created **specialty courts** that have jurisdiction over very narrowly defined areas of criminal justice. Not only do these courts remove many cases from the existing court systems, but they also allow court personnel to become experts in a particular subject. Specialty courts include:

Specialty Courts
Lower courts that have jurisdiction over one specific area of criminal activity, such as illegal drugs or domestic violence.

1 Drug courts, which deal only with illegal substance crimes.
2 Gun courts, which have jurisdiction over crimes that involve the illegal use of firearms.
3 Juvenile courts, which specialize in crimes committed by minors. (We will discuss juvenile courts in more detail in Chapter 15.)
4 Domestic courts, which deal with crimes of domestic violence, such as child and spousal abuse.
5 Elder courts, which focus primarily on the special needs of the elderly victims rather than the offenders.

Specialty courts do have their drawbacks, primarily the difficulty of finding court space and time to set them up. Because of these limitations, most specialty courts hold session at night and therefore can be inconvenient for both court personnel and the community.

GENERAL-JURISDICTION TRIAL COURTS

State trial courts that have general jurisdiction may be called county courts, district courts, superior courts, or circuit courts. In Ohio, the name is the court of common pleas and in Massachusetts, the trial court. (The name sometimes does not correspond with the court's functions. For example, in New York the trial court is called the supreme court, whereas in most states the supreme court is the state's highest court.) General-jurisdiction courts have the authority to hear and decide cases involving many types of subject matter, and they are the setting for criminal trials (discussed in Chapter 10).

STATE COURTS OF APPEALS

Every state has at least one court of appeals (known as an appellate, or reviewing, court), which may be an intermediate appellate court or the state's highest court. About three-fourths have intermediate appellate courts. The highest appellate court in a state is usually called the supreme court, but in both New York and Maryland, the highest state court is called the court of appeals. The decisions of each state's highest court on all questions of state law are final. Only when issues of federal law or constitutional procedure are involved can the United States Supreme Court overrule a decision made by a state's highest court.

ONLINE REVIEW *Go to the book's Web site for an interactive review of this section*

The Supreme Court of the United States provides an up-to-date record of its decisions and the most important issues that it considers. Visit the Court's Web site by clicking on *Web Links* under *Chapter Resources* at www.cjinaction.com

The Federal Court System

The federal court system is basically a three-tiered model consisting of (1) U.S. district courts (trial courts of general jurisdiction) and various courts of limited jurisdiction, (2) U.S. courts of appeals (intermediate courts of appeals), and (3) the United States Supreme Court.

Unlike state court judges, who are usually elected, federal court judges—including the justices of the Supreme Court—are appointed by the president of the United States, subject to the approval of the Senate. All federal judges receive lifetime appointments (because under Article III of the Constitution they "hold their offices during Good Behavior").

U.S. DISTRICT COURTS

On the lowest tier of the federal court system are the U.S. district courts, or federal trial courts. These are the courts in which cases involving federal laws begin, and a judge or jury decides the case (if it is a jury trial). Every state has at least one federal district court, and there is one in the District of Columbia. The number of judicial districts varies over time, primarily owing to population changes and corresponding caseloads. Currently, there are ninety-four judicial districts. The federal system also includes other limited-jurisdiction trial courts, such as the tax court and the court of international trade.

U.S. COURTS OF APPEALS

In the federal court system, there are thirteen U.S. courts of appeals—also referred to as U.S. circuit courts of appeals. The federal courts of appeals for twelve of the circuits hear appeals from the district courts located within their respective judicial circuits (see Figure 8.3 on the following page). The Court of Appeals for the Thirteenth Circuit, called the Federal Circuit, has national appellate jurisdiction over certain types of cases, such as cases involving patent law and cases in which

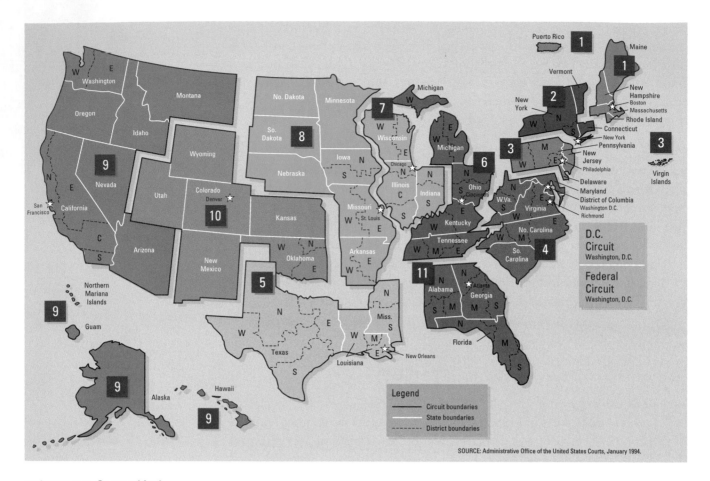

FIGURE 8.3 **Geographical Boundaries of the Federal Circuit Courts of Appeals**

the U.S. government is a defendant. The decisions of the circuit courts of appeals are final unless a further appeal is pursued and granted; in that case, the matter is brought before the Supreme Court.

THE UNITED STATES SUPREME COURT

Alexander Hamilton, writing in *Federalist Paper* No. 78, believed that the United States Supreme Court would be the "least dangerous branch" of the federal government because it had neither the power of the purse nor the power of the sword (that is, it could not raise any money, nor did it have an enforcement agency).[10] The other two branches of the government—the president and Congress—would have to accept its decisions, or the Court would be superfluous.

In the Supreme Court's earliest years, it appeared that Hamilton's prediction would come true. The first chief justice of the Supreme Court, John Jay, resigned to become governor of New York because he thought the Court would never play an important role in American society. The next chief justice, Oliver Ellsworth, quit to become an envoy to France. In 1801, when the federal capital was moved to Washington, no one remembered to include the Supreme Court in the plans. It did not have its own meeting space until 1835.[11]

Interpreting and Applying the Law   Despite these early bouts of inconsequence, the Supreme Court has come to dominate the country's legal culture.

Although it reviews fewer than 0.5 percent of the cases decided in the United States each year, the decisions of the Supreme Court profoundly affect our lives. The impact of Court decisions on the criminal justice system is equally far reaching: *Gideon v. Wainwright* (1963)[12] established every American's right to be represented by counsel in a criminal trial; *Miranda v. Arizona* (1966)[13] transformed pretrial interrogations; *Furman v. Georgia* (1972)[14] ruled that the death penalty was unconstitutional; and *Gregg v. Georgia* (1976)[15] spelled out the conditions under which it could be allowed. As you have no doubt noticed from references in this textbook, the Court has addressed nearly every important facet of criminal law.

The Supreme Court "makes" criminal justice policy in two important ways: through judicial review and through its authority to interpret the law. *Judicial review* refers to the power of the Court to determine whether a law or action by the other branches of the government is constitutional. For example, in the late 1980s Congress and several state legislatures passed laws criminalizing the act of burning the U.S. flag. In two separate decisions—*Texas v. Johnson* (1989)[16] and *United States v. Eichman* (1990)[17]—the Court invalidated these laws as unconstitutional on the ground that they violated First Amendment protections of freedom of expression.

The United States Supreme Court tends to be associated with the philosophy of its chief justice. Accordingly, since William Rehnquist (see above) took over the position in 1986, the "Rehnquist Court" is seen as adopting his conservative views. Examine the record of the Rehnquist Court on criminal matters to determine whether it has followed a crime control or due process philosophy.

As the final interpreter of the Constitution, the Court must also determine the meaning of certain statutory provisions when applied to specific situations. Deciding what the framers of the Constitution or a legislative body meant by a certain phrase or provision is never easy, and inevitably, at least to some extent, the personal attributes of the justices come into play during the process. For example, those justices who oppose the death penalty for ideological reasons have tended to interpret the Eighth Amendment prohibition against "cruel and unusual punishment" as sufficient constitutional justification to outlaw the execution of criminals by the state.[18]

Jurisdiction of the Supreme Court   The United States Supreme Court consists of nine justices—a chief justice and eight associate justices. The Court has original, or trial, jurisdiction only in rare instances (set forth in Article III, Section 2, of the Constitution). In other words, only rarely does a case originate at the Supreme Court level. Most of the Court's work is as an appellate court. The Supreme Court has appellate authority over cases decided by the U.S. courts of appeals, as well as over some cases decided in the state courts when federal questions are at issue.

Which Cases Reach the Supreme Court?   There is no absolute right to appeal to the United States Supreme Court. Although thousands of cases are filed with the Supreme Court each year, on average the Court hears fewer than one hundred. With a **writ of *certiorari*** (pronounced sur-shee-uh-*rah*-ree), the Supreme Court orders a lower court to send it the record of a case for review. A party can petition the Supreme Court to issue a writ of *certiorari,* but whether the Court will do so is entirely within its discretion.

Writ of *Certiorari*
A request from a higher court asking a lower court for the record of a case. In essence, the request signals the higher court's willingness to review the case.

More than 90 percent of the petitions for writs of *certiorari* (or "certs," as they are popularly called) are denied. A denial is not a decision on the merits of a case, nor does it indicate agreement with the lower court's opinion. Therefore, the denial of the writ has no value as a precedent.[19] The Court will not issue a writ unless at least four justices approve of it. This is called the **rule of four.** Although the justices are not required to give their reasons for not hearing a case, most often the discretionary decision is based on whether the legal issue involves a "substantial federal question." Political considerations aside, if the justices do not feel the case addresses an important federal law or constitutional issue, they will vote to deny the writ of *certiorari.*

Supreme Court Decisions   Like all appellate courts, the Supreme Court normally does not hear any evidence. The Court's decision in a particular case is based on the written record of the case and the written arguments (briefs) that the attorneys submit. The attorneys also present **oral arguments**—arguments presented in person rather than on paper—to the Court, after which the justices discuss the case in *conference.* The conference is strictly private—only the justices are allowed in the room.

When the Court has reached a decision, the chief justice, if in the majority, assigns the task of writing the Court's opinion to one of the justices. When the chief justice is not in the majority, the most senior justice voting with the majority assigns the writing of the Court's opinion. The opinion outlines the reasons for the Court's decision, the rules of law that apply, and the decision.

Often, one or more justices who agree with the Court's decision may do so for different reasons than those outlined in the majority opinion. These justices may write **concurring opinions** setting forth their own legal reasoning on the issue. Frequently, one or more justices disagree with the Court's conclusion. These justices may write **dissenting opinions** outlining the reasons why they feel the majority erred. Although a dissenting opinion does not affect the outcome of the case before the Court, it may be important later. In a subsequent case concerning the same issue, a justice or attorney may use the legal reasoning in the dissenting opinion as the basis for an argument to reverse the previous decision and establish a new precedent.

↗ ONLINE REVIEW *Go to the book's Web site for an interactive review of this section*

Judges in the Court System

Supreme Court justices are the most visible and best-known American jurists, but in many ways they are unrepresentative of the profession as a whole. Few judges enjoy three-room office suites fitted with a fireplace and a private bath, as do the Supreme Court justices. Few judges have four clerks to assist them. Few judges get a yearly vacation that stretches from July to September. Most judges, in fact, work at the lowest level of the system, in criminal trial courts, where they are burdened with overflowing caseloads and must deal daily with the detritus of society.

One thing a Supreme Court justice and a criminal trial judge in any small American city do have in common is the expectation that they will be just. Of all the participants in the criminal justice system, no single person is held to the same high standards as the judge. From her or his lofty perch in the courtroom, the

Rule of Four
A rule of the United States Supreme Court that the Court will not issue a writ of *certiorari* unless at least four justices approve of the decision to hear the case.

Oral Arguments
The verbal arguments presented in person by attorneys to an appellate court. Each attorney presents reasons why the court should rule in his or her client's favor.

Concurring Opinions
Separate opinions prepared by judges who support the decision of the majority of the court but who want to make or clarify a particular point or to voice disapproval of the grounds on which the decision was made.

Dissenting Opinions
Separate opinions in which judges disagree with the conclusion reached by the majority of the court and expand on their own views about the case.

judge is counted on to be "above the fray" of the bickering defense attorneys and prosecutors. When the other courtroom contestants rise at the entrance of the judge, they are placing the burden of justice squarely on the judge's shoulders.

THE ROLES AND RESPONSIBILITIES OF TRIAL JUDGES

One of the reasons that judicial integrity is considered so important is the amount of discretionary power a judge has over the court proceedings. As you can see in Figure 8.4, nearly every stage of the trial process includes a decision or action to be taken by the presiding judge. (See *Careers in CJ* on page 268.)

Before the Trial   A great deal of the work done by a judge takes place before the trial even starts, free from public scrutiny. These duties, some of which you have seen from a different point of view in the section on law enforcement agents, include determining the following:

1   Whether there is sufficient probable cause to issue a search or arrest warrant.

2   Whether there is sufficient probable cause to authorize electronic surveillance of a suspect.

3   Whether enough evidence exists to justify the temporary incarceration of a suspect.

4   Whether a defendant should be released on bail, and if so, the amount of the bail.

5   Whether to accept pretrial motions by prosecutors and defense attorneys.

6   Whether to accept a plea bargain.

FIGURE 8.4 The Role of the Judge in the Criminal Trial Process

In the various stages of a felony case, judges must undertake the actions described here.

1. Before an Arrest
• Decide whether law enforcement officers have provided sufficient probable cause to justify a search or arrest warrant.

2. Initial Appearance
• Inform the suspect of the charges against him or her and of his or her rights.
• Review the charges to see if probable cause exists that the suspect committed the crime; if not, the judge will dismiss the case.
• Set the amount of bail (or deny bail) and determine any other conditions of pretrial release.

3. Preliminary Hearing
• Based on evidence provided by the prosecution and defense, decide whether there is probable cause that the suspect committed the crime.
• Continue to make sure that the defendant's constitutional rights are not being violated.

4. Arraignment
• Ensure that the defendant has been informed of the charges against him or her.
• Ensure that the defendant understands the plea choices before him or her (to plead guilty, not guilty, or *nolo contendere*).

5. Plea Bargain
• Assist with the plea bargaining process, if both sides are willing to "make a deal."
• If the defendant decides to plead guilty in return for charges being lessened, ensure that the defendant understands the nature of the plea bargain and has not been pressured into pleading guilty by his or her attorney.

6. Pretrial Motions
• Rule on pretrial motions presented by the defense.
• Decide whether to grant continuances (the postponement of the trial to allow more time for gathering evidence).

7. Trial
• Ensure that proper procedure is followed in jury selection.
• "Officiate" the trial, making sure that both the prosecutor and the defense follow procedural rules in presenting evidence and questioning witnesses.
• Explain points of law that affect the case to the jury.
• Provide jury instructions, or instruction to jurors on the meaning of the laws applicable to the case.
• Receive the jury's final verdict of guilty or not guilty.

8. Sentencing
• If the verdict is "guilty," impose the sentence on the convict.

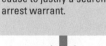

> Richard S. Gebelein Superior Court Judge

When I began my undergraduate studies, I was very much interested in sciences. Indeed, I ultimately obtained a B.S. in mathematics, with minors in chemistry and physics. During college, however, I began to think that I would like to work in a career where I was directly involved with people. Thus, I decided that I would attend law school. I obtained my J.D. from Villanova but was really unsure of what type of law I wanted to practice.

I began my legal career as a law clerk in the Delaware Court of Chancery. Observing many good trial lawyers that year, I decided I would like to do trial practice, or litigation as it's called. My first position was as a deputy attorney general in Delaware's Department of Justice. There I prosecuted criminal cases as well as defending the state in civil actions. I left the Justice Department and became Delaware's chief deputy public defender. In that role, I defended serious criminal charges including murder. After a short time in private law practice I was elected Delaware attorney general in 1978. After returning to private practice, I was appointed by the governor to my current position as a superior court judge. I was reappointed to a second twelve-year term in 1996.

As a superior court judge, I try both civil and criminal cases as well as hear appeals from administrative boards and agencies. I am currently assigned to do primarily criminal work. The large majority of all criminal cases are resolved by pleas so a large part of my work is taking those pleas, assuring that the defendant knows what he or she is doing, and then sentencing the defendant. In superior court these are usually serious felony charges. In those cases where there is no plea, it is my job to ensure that the defendant receives a fair trial. That means I rule on evidence issues and instruct the jury as to the law to be applied in the case. In some cases the jury will be waived, and then I must decide the facts as well as the law.

Our criminal justice system depends on the lawyers and the judge performing their different functions fairly and effectively. Thus, the responsibilities on each participant are great. Our system only works if each participant actively and aggressively fulfills the duties of his or her office.

The seriousness and reality of those duties came home to me several years ago when I was assigned to try the case of

Delaware's first serial killer. The case was an extremely "high profile" case that resulted in almost daily headlines. It was not an easy case in that there were many difficult evidence issues. These included the attempt to use DNA identification for the first time in Delaware as well as an evidence suppression issue involving the key evidence that broke the case. Luckily, both the prosecutors and the defense lawyers were excellent and did their jobs professionally. After a long trial and lengthy jury deliberations, the defendant was convicted of two counts of first degree murder. The jury could not reach a verdict on the third count of murder. A penalty trial was held, and the jury could not reach a unanimous recommendation of death, thereby causing a life sentence to be imposed by law.

Courtesy RS Gebelein

Richard S. Gebelein

But this was not the end of the case as evidence was developed during the trial to link the defendant directly to a fourth murder. He was reindicted for that murder as well as the undecided murder from the first trial. The defendant waived a jury trial for this second case, and I had to try the case as to both facts and law. After conviction, I then had to hear the penalty phase. Nothing in my training prepared me to make the solitary decision that his crimes demanded the death penalty. Nothing really can prepare you to announce in front of the defendant's family, mother, wife, and child that he is to die by lethal injection.

This one hard decision, this one hard act makes it crystal clear why it is absolutely essential that good, bright, and ethical people participate as lawyers and judges in our criminal justice system. It is critical that every defendant be assured a fair trial, and that means a good, energetic effective defense lawyer, an ethical, effective prosector, and a fair judge. These are not easy jobs, but if they are done right, you can feel satisfaction that you are doing your part to ensure justice in America.

 Go to the Careers in Criminal Justice Interactive CD *for more profiles in the field of criminal justice.*

During these pretrial activities, the judge takes on the role of the *negotiator.*[20] As most cases are decided through plea bargains rather than through trial proceedings, the judge often offers his or her services as a negotiator to help the prosecution and the defense "make a deal." The amount at which bail is set is often negotiated as well. Throughout the trial process, the judge usually spends a great of time in his or her *chambers,* or office, negotiating with the prosecutors and defense attorneys.

During the Trial   When the trial starts, the judge takes on the role of *referee.* In this role, she or he is responsible for seeing that the trial unfolds according to the dictates of the law and that the participants in the trial do not overstep any legal or ethical bounds. In this role, the judge is expected to be neutral, determining the admissibility of testimony and evidence on a completely objective basis. The judge also acts as a *teacher* during the trial, explaining points of law to the jury. If the trial is not a jury trial, then the judge must also make decisions concerning the guilt or innocence of the defendant. If the defendant is found guilty, the judge must decide on the length of the sentence and the type of sentence. (Different types of sentences, such as incarceration, probation, and other forms of community-based corrections, will be discussed in Chapters 12 through 15.)

The Administrative Role   Judges are also *administrators;* that is, they are responsible for the day-to-day functioning of their courts. A primary administrative task of a judge is scheduling. Each courtroom has a **docket,** or calendar of cases, and it is the judge's responsibility to keep the docket current. This entails not only scheduling the trial, but also setting pretrial motion dates and deciding whether to grant attorneys' requests for *continuances,* or additional time to prepare for a case. Judges must also keep track of the immense paperwork generated by each case and manage the various employees of the court. In some instances, judges are even responsible for the budgets of their courtrooms.[21] In 1939, Congress, recognizing the burden of such tasks, created the Administrative Office of the United States Courts to provide administrative assistance for federal court judges.[22] Most state court judges, however, do not have the luxury of similar aid, though they are supported by a court staff.

Docket
The list of cases entered on a court's calendar and thus scheduled to be heard by the court.

SELECTION OF JUDGES

In the federal court system, all judges are appointed by the president and confirmed by the Senate. It is difficult to make a general statement about how judges are selected in the state court system, however, because the procedure varies widely from state to state. In some states, such as Delaware, all judges are appointed by the governor and confirmed by the upper chamber of the state legislature. In other states, such as Arkansas, all judges are elected on a partisan ballot, meaning they must be affiliated with a political party and that affiliation is noted on the ballot. In still other states, such as Kentucky, all judges are elected on a nonpartisan ballot, where no party affiliation is required. Finally, some states, such as Missouri, select judges based on a subjective definition of merit. Figure 8.5 on page 270 shows the variety in the procedures for selecting judges.

The two key concepts in discussing methods of selecting judges are *independence* and *accountability.*[23] Those who feel that judicial fairness is dependent on the judges' belief that they will not be removed from office as the result of an unpopular ruling support methods of selection that include appointment.[24] In contrast, some observers feel that judges are "politicians in robes" who make policy decisions every time they step to the bench. Following this line of thought, judges should be held accountable to those who are affected by their decisions and therefore should be chosen through elections, as legislators are.[25] The most independent, and therefore least accountable, judges are those who hold lifetime appointments. They are influenced neither by the temptation to make popular

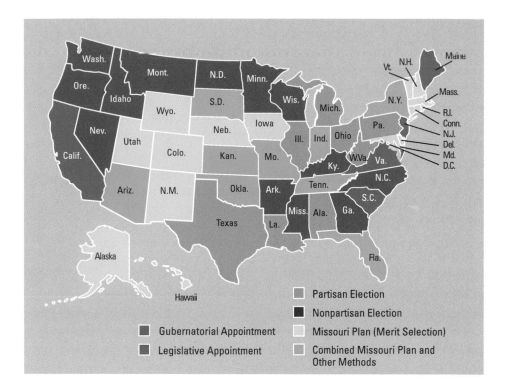

FIGURE 8.5 Methods of Judicial Selection in the Fifty States

Most states use a variety of methods to select their judges, with different procedures in different jurisdictions. The information presented here, therefore, identifies the predominant method in each state.

Source: American Judicature Society.

Map legend:
- Partisan Election
- Nonpartisan Election
- Gubernatorial Appointment
- Missouri Plan (Merit Selection)
- Legislative Appointment
- Combined Missouri Plan and Other Methods

decisions to impress voters nor by the need to follow the ideological or party line of the political bosses who provided them with their posts.

Appointment of Judges   Article II, Section 2, of the Constitution authorizes the president to appoint the justices of the Supreme Court with the advice and consent of the Senate. Subsequent laws enacted by Congress provide that the same procedure is used for appointing judges to the lower federal courts as well.

On paper, the appointment process is relatively simple. After selecting a nominee, the president submits the name to the Senate for approval. The Senate Judiciary Committee then holds hearings and makes its recommendation to the Senate, where a majority vote is needed to confirm the nomination. In practice, the process does not always proceed smoothly. In fact, almost 20 percent of presidential nominations to the federal courts have been either rejected or not acted on by the Senate. Many bitter battles over federal judicial appointments have ensued when the Senate and the president have disagreed on political issues. In 2003, after a two-year struggle, Miguel Estrada withdrew his nomination by President George W. Bush for a spot on the U.S. Circuit Court of Appeals for the District of Columbia. Democrats in the Senate had criticized Estrada's conservative political views and used that body's rules to block his appointment.

Three states, as well as Puerto Rico, employ similar selection methods, with the governor offering nominees for the approval of the state legislature. Judges in these states, as would be expected, serve longer terms than their counterparts in nonappointment judicial systems.[26] They are also regarded as products of *patronage,* as are judges appointed to federal positions by the president. In other words, appointed judges often obtain their positions because they belong to the same political party as the president (or governor, at the state level) and have been active in supporting the candidates and ideology of the party in power. One of the most prevalent criticisms of appointing judges is that the system is based on "having friends in high places" rather than on merit.[27]

Election of Judges Most states moved from an appointive to an elective system for judges in the mid–nineteenth century. The reasoning behind the move was to make judges more representative of the communities in which they served. Today, elections are the dominant method of selecting judges in twenty-one states.[28] Of these, eight states rely primarily on **partisan elections,** in which the judicial candidate is openly supported and endorsed by a political party. The other thirteen states conduct mostly **nonpartisan elections,** in which the candidate is not affiliated with a political party.

Proponents of elections insist that unless judges are regularly forced to submit themselves to the will of the electorate, there is no way to hold them accountable for their actions. Critics, such as Judge Hans A. Linde of the Oregon Supreme Court, counter:

> "Judicial accountability" has a virtuous ring to it, until one asks, accountability for what? For judging fairly and impartially, for conscientious attention to law and facts, for staying awake, sober, and courteous to the parties, witnesses, and court personnel—in short, for performing according to the classic model of judging? Or does it mean accountability for decisions in controversial cases?[29]

The answer to Judge Linde's rhetorical question, at least in his mind, is that the public will hold a judge accountable for making popular rulings, not "correct" ones. In recent years, many elected judges have felt pressure to hand out harsher sentences to convicted criminals in order to appear "tough on crime." (See the feature *CJ in Focus—A Question of Ethics: Judging Judicial Elections* on page 272.)

Merit Selection In 1940, Missouri became the first state to combine appointment and election in a single merit selection. When all jurisdiction levels are counted, twenty-four states and the District of Columbia now utilize the **Missouri Plan,** as merit selection has been labeled. The Missouri Plan consists of three basic steps:

> When a vacancy on the bench arises, candidates are nominated by a nonpartisan committee of citizens.

> The names of the three most qualified candidates are sent to the governor or executive of the state judicial system, and that person chooses who will be the judge.

> A year after the new judge has been installed, a "retention election" is held so that voters can decide whether the judge deserves to keep the post.[30]

The goal of the Missouri Plan is to eliminate partisan politics from the selection procedure, while at the same time giving the citizens a voice in the process. One noted drawback of the merit system—and indeed of any elective method of selecting judges—is that voters may lack knowledge not only of the issues of a judicial election, but of who the candidates are in the first place. A poll in Michigan found that nine out of ten voters could not identify any sitting state supreme court justice, and an equal number did not know how many justices served on the state's highest court or the length of their term in office.[31] (For a review of the different

Partisan Elections
Elections in which candidates are affiliated with and receive support from political parties; the candidates are listed in conjunction with their party on the ballot.

Nonpartisan Elections
Elections in which candidates are presented on the ballot without any party affiliation.

Missouri Plan
A method of selecting judges that combines appointment and election. Under the plan, the state governor or another government official selects judges from a group of nominees chosen by a nonpartisan committee. After a year on the bench, the judges face a popular election to determine whether the public wishes to keep them in office.

> Judging Judicial Elections

Several years ago, a North Carolina judge made a ruling that resulted in a group of retirees receiving nearly $800 million in tax refunds. When that judge ran for reelection several months later, he sent out a fund-raising letter to the same retirees asking them to "look back and recall what [the judge's] wisdom and demeanor have meant to each of us" and contribute to his campaign.

Did the North Carolina judge cross an ethical line? Ideally, we would like our judges to decide impartially the cases before them, relying only on the facts and the law, and not on the hope of future campaign contributions. In reality, however, nearly nine out of every ten state judges will face some form of popular election to win or keep their seats on the bench. The costs of these elections have skyrocketed. State supreme court justices raise more than $50 million for their election campaigns each year, a jump of more than 65 percent since 1998. So, even if the North Carolina judge did not make the ruling with the intent of later "hitting up" its beneficiaries, he did create that perception.

In the criminal justice arena, the worry is that judges will make decisions based not on the law but on the need to win votes. A judge who does not consistently hand down the harshest possible sentences or who frees convicts on technicalities runs the risk of being labeled "soft on crime" by an opponent in a future election. Consequently, judges may act with a motive of convincing voters that they are indeed "tough on crime." In Alabama, for example, a judge running for reelection complained that because of his job he would never have the opportunity to go to death row "and actually pull the switch and fry someone and watch them die."

FOR CRITICAL ANALYSIS

The solution to these problems, whether real or perceived, would be to do away with the election of judges. What is your position on the election of local and state judges? Should citizens have the right to vote for judicial positions? Should a judge reflect the will of the people or the will of the law?

---

selection processes, see *Mastering Concepts—The Selection of State and Federal Judges*.)

DIVERSITY ON THE BENCH

Another criticism of the Missouri Plan is that the members of the selection committees, who are mostly white, upper-class attorneys, nominate mostly white, upper-class attorneys.[32] Similar criticisms, however, have been leveled at the federal judiciary and at judges in states that do not use the Missouri Plan. Indeed, of the nearly 1,600 federal judges, only about 7 percent are African American, 4 percent are Hispanic, and 1 percent are Asian American.[33] Of the 108 justices who have served on the United States Supreme Court, only two have been African American: Thurgood Marshall (1970–1991) and Clarence Thomas (1991–present). State judiciaries show similar patterns. The discrepancy is particularly striking in areas with diverse populations. In California, where minority groups make up a majority of the population (54 percent), only 17 percent of state court judges are African American, Hispanic, or Asian American.[34] Women are also underrepresented on the bench. Only one in five federal judges is a woman.[35] Only two women have been appointed to the Supreme Court: Sandra Day O'Connor (1981–present) and Ruth Bader Ginsburg (1993–present).

The Impact of Past Discrimination Edward Chen, a federal magistrate judge for the Northern District of California, identifies a number of reasons for the low minority representation on the bench. Past discrimination in law schools has limited the pool of experienced minority attorneys who have the political ties, access

Justice at Stake is an organization dedicated to fair and impartial courts in the United States. Find its Web site by clicking on *Web Links* under *Chapter Resources* at www.cjinaction.com

> The Selection of State and Federal Judges

Federal Judges

The president nominates a candidate to the U.S. Senate.

↓

The Senate Judiciary Committee holds hearings concerning the qualifications of the candidate and makes its recommendation to the full Senate.

↓

The full Senate votes to confirm or reject the president's nomination.

State Judges

Partisan Elections
Judicial candidates, supported by and affiliated with political parties, place their names before the voters for consideration for a particular judicial seat.

↓

The electorate votes to decide who will retain or gain the seat.

Executive Appointment
The governor nominates a candidate to the state legislature.

↓

The legislature votes to confirm or reject the governor's nomination.

Nonpartisan Elections
Judicial candidates, not supported by or affiliated with political parties, place their names before the voters for consideration for a particular judicial seat.

↓

The electorate votes to decide who will retain or gain the seat.

Missouri Plan
A nominating commission provides a list of worthy candidates.

↓

An elected official (usually the governor) chooses from the list submitted by the commission.

↓

A year later, a "retention election" is held to allow voters to decide whether the judge will stay on the bench.

to "old boy" networks, and career opportunities that lead to judgeships.[36] Only recently, as increased numbers of minorities have graduated from law schools, have rates of minority judges begun to creep slowly upward.

The Benefits of Diversity   Traditionally, efforts to diversify American judges by race, ethnicity, and gender have been met with resistance from those who argue that because judges must be impartial, it makes no difference whether a judge is black, Asian, Hispanic, or white.[37]

Sherrilyn A. Ifill of the University of Maryland School of Law rejects this argument. She believes that "diversity on the bench" can only enrich our judiciary by introducing a variety of voices and perspectives into what are perhaps the most powerful positions in the criminal justice system. By the same token, Ifill credits the lack of diversity in many trial and appeals courts with a number of harmful consequences, such as more severe sentences for minority youths than for white youths who have committed similar crimes, disproportionate denial of bail to minority defendants, and the disproportionate imposition of the death penalty on minority defendants accused of killing white victims.[38]

Statistics and Stereotypes   There is some basis for Ifill's contentions, at least to the extent that different backgrounds do lead to measurably different patterns in judicial practice. In a study of verdicts in gender discrimination lawsuits, political scientist Nancy Crowe found that white, male judges who identified themselves as

AP Photo/Kelley McCall

Ronnie L. White became the first African American to hold the post of chief justice of the Missouri Supreme Court in 2003. "I truly believe that within the judicial department, we need to work a little bit harder to try and place people of color within our organization," said Judge White upon taking his post. What are some of the benefits of diversity on the bench?

Judicial Misconduct
A general term describing behavior that diminishes public confidence in the judiciary. This behavior includes obviously illegal acts, such as bribery, and conduct that gives the appearance of impropriety, such as consorting with known felons.

Republicans ruled in favor of the plaintiff (the person claiming to have been discriminated against) only 28 percent of the time, while African American, male judges found for the plaintiff 61 percent of the time.[39]

It should be noted, however, that expectations of how a particular group will act do not always match reality. Many people believe, for example, that female judges are more compassionate than their male counterparts. The evidence coming from the Harris County (Texas) courthouse, one of the few in the country where a majority of the judges—twelve of twenty-one—are women, does not support this stereotype. Between 1976 and 2000, Harris County was responsible for sixty-three executions, more than the entire state of Florida, which ranked third among states in total executions over that time period.[40]

JUDICIAL CONDUCT

The question of judicial accountability is further complicated by the gulf between what the public expects of judges and what the law expects of judges. The public wants judges to administer justice, while the law demands that they make sure proper legal procedures and rules have been followed. Sometimes, such as when a judge must overturn a conviction he or she knows to be justified because tainted evidence contributed to the jury's finding, proper judicial conduct leads to what we would call injustice—setting a guilty person free. In other words, for judges, proper behavior does not necessarily lead to justice, a concept many citizens have a difficult time accepting.

Judicial Ethics   During the nineteenth century, the American public showed little enthusiasm for formal regulation of judicial conduct—as long as judges were competent, their ethics and honesty were of secondary concern.[41] It was not until the 1920s, when the entire criminal justice system was being reformed, that the American Bar Association (ABA) created the first code to regulate judicial behavior. The ABA's Canons of Judicial Ethics was updated in 1972 and 1990, and today the Model Code of Judicial Conduct forms the basis for judicial conduct codes in forty-seven states and the District of Columbia.[42]

The essence of the Code of Judicial Conduct is to prevent conduct that would "tend to reduce public confidence in the integrity and impartiality of the judiciary."[43] Consequently, the judicial ethics codes disfavor not only obviously illegal and corrupt activities such as bribery but also personal conduct that is lawful yet gives the appearance of impropriety. Rhode Island, for example, saw two successive state supreme court chief justices resign because of **judicial misconduct.** The first, Chief Justice Thomas Fay, stepped down because of allegations that he used his position to help a relative and friends, and the second, Chief Justice Joseph Bevilacqua, was under investigation for associating with organized crime figures.

Some believe that judicial ethics codes overstep the boundaries of the Constitution in their efforts to limit misconduct. Washington Supreme Court Justice Richard Sanders, for example, faced disciplinary charges from a state commission for making comments against abortion at a political rally. Canon 7 of the Code of Judicial Conduct states that judges should not announce their views on disputed political issues because doing so could give the impression that a judge's biases would affect courtroom decisions.[44] In a decision that many observers hailed for its freedom of speech implications, Sanders was eventually cleared by a special panel of judges, who ruled that his statements did not lessen public confidence in the judiciary.[45]

The Removal of Judges The ABA's Code of Judicial Conduct is not a binding document; it merely offers a model of judicial ethics. As the states adopted aspects of the code, however, they also developed procedures for removing those guilty of judicial misconduct from office. Nearly every state has a *judicial conduct commission,* which consists of lawyers, judges, and other prominent citizens and is often a branch of the state's highest court. This commission investigates charges of judicial misconduct and may recommend removal if warranted by the circumstances. The final decision to discipline a judge must generally be made by the state supreme court.[46]

On average, about ten state judges are removed from office each year. Recent examples include Montgomery County (New York) family court judge Robert N. Going, who lost his seat after the end of a romantic liaison with his law clerk led to unseemly behavior, including sleeping during the workday and drinking beer in the courtroom basement. Such transgressions, however deplorable, would be unlikely to result in a similar outcome if committed by a federal judge. Appointed under Article II of the U.S. Constitution, federal judges can be removed from office only if found guilty of "Treason, Bribery, or other high Crimes and Misdemeanors." Before a federal judge can be **impeached,** the U.S. House of Representatives must be presented with specific charges of misconduct and vote on whether these charges merit further action. If the vote passes in the House, the U.S. Senate—presided over by the chief justice of the United States Supreme Court—holds a trial on the matter. At the conclusion of this trial, a two-thirds majority vote is required in the Senate for the removal of a federal judge.

This disciplinary action is extremely rare; only eleven federal judges have been impeached and convicted in the nation's history. Most recently, in 1989, federal judges Alcee Hastings and Walter Nixon were both removed from office—Hastings for accepting a $150,000 bribe and lying to a grand jury and Nixon for lying to a grand jury. In 1993, Judge Robert Collins resigned before he could be impeached for receiving a $100,000 bribe from a marijuana smuggler.

ONLINE REVIEW *Go to the book's Web site for an interactive review of this section*

Impeached
As authorized by Article I of the Constitution, impeachment is voted on by the House of Representatives and then sent to the Senate for a vote to remove the president, vice president, or civil officers (such as federal judges) of the United States.

The Courtroom Work Group

Television dramas often depict the courtroom as a battlefield, with prosecutors and defense attorneys spitting fire at each other over the loud and insistent protestations of a frustrated judge. Consequently, many people are somewhat disappointed when they witness a real courtroom at work. Rarely does anyone raise his or her voice, and the courtroom professionals appear—to a great extent—to be cooperating with each other. In Chapter 6, we discussed the existence of a police subculture, based on the shared values of law enforcement agents. A courtroom subculture exists as well, centered on the **courtroom work group.** The most

Courtroom Work Group
The social organization consisting of the judge, prosecutor, defense attorney, and other court workers. The relationships among these persons have a far-reaching impact on the day-to-day operations of any court.

important feature of any work group is that it is a *cooperative* unit, whose members establish shared values and methods that help the group efficiently reach its goals. Though cooperation is not a concept usually associated with criminal courts, it is in fact crucial to the adjudication process.[47]

MEMBERS OF THE COURTROOM WORK GROUP

The courtroom work group is made up of those individuals who are involved with the defendant from the time she or he is arrested until sentencing. The most prominent members are the judge, the prosecutor, and the defense attorney (the latter two will be discussed in detail in the next chapter). Three other court participants complete the work group:

1. The *bailiff of the court* is responsible for maintaining security and order in the judge's chambers and the courtroom. Bailiffs lead the defendant in and out of the courtroom and attend to the needs of the jurors during the trial. A bailiff, often a member of the local sheriff's department but sometimes an employee of the court, also delivers summonses in some jurisdictions.

2. The *clerk of the court* has an exhausting list of responsibilities. Any plea, motion, or other matter to be acted on by the judge must go through the clerk. The large amount of paperwork generated during a trial, including transcripts, photographs, evidence, and any other records, is maintained by the clerk. The clerk also issues subpoenas for jury duty and coordinates the jury selection process. In the federal court system, judges select clerks, while state clerks are either appointed or, in nearly a third of the states, elected.

3. *Court reporters* record every word that is said during the course of the trial. They also record any *depositions,* or pretrial question-and-answer sessions in which a party or a witness answers an attorney's questions under oath.

FORMATION OF THE COURTROOM WORK GROUP

The premise of the work group is based on constant interaction that fosters relationships among the members. As legal scholar David W. Neubauer describes:

> Every day, the same group of courthouse regulars assembles in the same courtroom, sits or stands in the same places, and performs the same tasks as the day before. The types of defendants and the nature of the crimes they are accused of committing also remain constant. Only the names of the victim, witnesses, and defendants are different.[48]

After a period of time, the members of a courtroom work group learn how the others operate. The work group establishes patterns of behavior and norms, and cooperation allows the adjudication process to function informally and smoothly.[49] In some cases, the members of the work group may even form personal relationships, which only strengthen the courtroom culture.

One way in which the courtroom work group differs from a traditional work group at a company such as Microsoft Corporation is that each member answers to a different sponsoring organization. Although the judge has ultimate authority over a courtroom, he or she is not the "boss" of the attorneys. The prosecutor is hired by the district attorney's office; the defense attorney by a private individual or the public defender's office; the judge by the court system itself.

Each member of the work group is under pressure from his or her sponsoring organization to carry out certain tasks.[50] A judge, for example, needs to take care of the cases on her or his docket, or else a backlog will accumulate. A defense attorney—under constant pressure to attain the best results—usually has many clients and often cannot afford to spend too much time on a single case. A prosecutor must win convictions. Within the courtroom work group, each member relies on the others to help alleviate these pressures. If a defense attorney disrupts the trial routine with unnecessary motions or unreasonably rejects sentence bargains for his or her client, all members of the work group become less efficient in performing their roles. (See Figure 8.6 for an overview of the relationships among the main participants in the courtroom work group.)

THE JUDGE IN THE COURTROOM WORK GROUP

The judge is the dominant figure in the courtroom and therefore exerts the most influence over the values and norms of the work group. A judge who runs a "tight ship" follows procedure and restricts the freedom of attorneys to deviate from regulations, while a *"laissez-faire"* judge allows more leeway to members of the work group. A judge's personal philosophy also affects the court proceedings. If a judge has a reputation for being "tough on crime," both prosecutors and defense attorneys

FIGURE 8.6 The Courtroom Work Group and Incentives to Cooperate
Ideally, we like to think of the courtroom as a place where justice is served. In reality, however, the courtroom is a workplace, and each of its workers has her or his own goals, which may or may not include the accepted definition of "doing justice." Like any workplace, the courtroom functions more smoothly when workers cooperate with one another by sharing information, avoiding conflict, and reducing uncertainty. The major figures of the courtroom work group—judges, prosecutors, and defense attorneys—benefit from a certain degree of cooperation. As you can see, one of the primary considerations of each of the three principals is to dispose of cases as quickly as possible.

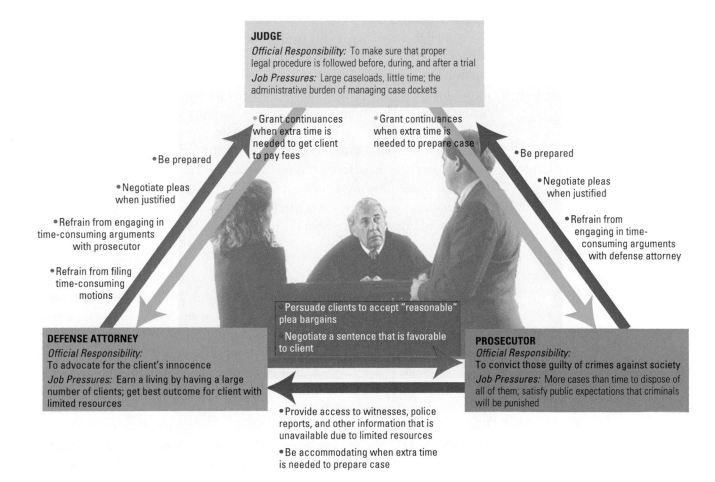

JUDGE
Official Responsibility: To make sure that proper legal procedure is followed before, during, and after a trial
Job Pressures: Large caseloads, little time; the administrative burden of managing case dockets

• Grant continuances when extra time is needed to get client to pay fees

• Grant continuances when extra time is needed to prepare case

• Be prepared

• Negotiate pleas when justified

• Refrain from engaging in time-consuming arguments with prosecutor

• Refrain from filing time-consuming motions

• Be prepared

• Negotiate pleas when justified

• Refrain from engaging in time-consuming arguments with defense attorney

• Persuade clients to accept "reasonable" plea bargains

• Negotiate a sentence that is favorable to client

DEFENSE ATTORNEY
Official Responsibility: To advocate for the client's innocence
Job Pressures: Earn a living by having a large number of clients; get best outcome for client with limited resources

PROSECUTOR
Official Responsibility: To convict those guilty of crimes against society
Job Pressures: More cases than time to dispose of all of them; satisfy public expectations that criminals will be punished

• Provide access to witnesses, police reports, and other information that is unavailable due to limited resources

• Be accommodating when extra time is needed to prepare case

Over the past fifteen years, thousands of new police officers were placed on the nation's streets, increasing arrest rates. A corresponding increase in district prosecuting attorneys has not followed. The result: a backlog of cases in courthouses across the nation. Some jurisdictions have tried to lessen the pressure on criminal courts by operating specialty courts, such as the Juvenile and Family Court of Orange, California, the entrance of which is shown here. But even these courts have become overcrowded. Why do you think that federal, state, and local governments have provided the necessary tax dollars to beef up law enforcement but have been unwilling to put significantly more money into American courts?

will alter their strategies accordingly. In fact, a lawyer may be able to manipulate the system to "shop" for a judge whose philosophy best fits the attorney's goals in a particular case.[51] If a lawyer is caught trying to influence the assignment of judges, she or he is said to be "corrupting judicial independence" and may face legal proceedings.

Although preeminent in the work group, a judge must still rely on other members of the group. To a certain extent, the judge is the least informed member of the trio; like a juror, the judge learns the facts of the case as they are presented by the attorneys. If the attorneys do not properly present the facts, then the judge is hampered in making rulings. Furthermore, if a judge deviates from the norms of the work group—by, for example, refusing to grant continuances—the other members of the work group can "discipline" the judge. Defense attorneys and prosecutors can request further continuances, fail to produce witnesses in a timely matter, and slow down the proceeding through a general lack of preparedness. The delays caused by such acts can ruin a judge's calendar—especially in large courts—and bring pressure from the judge's superiors.

"A judge is not supposed to know anything about the facts . . . until they have been presented in evidence and explained to him at least three times."
—Lord Chief Justice Parker, British judge (1961)

ASSEMBLY-LINE JUSTICE

In discussing the goals of the courtroom work group, several general concepts figure prominently—efficiency, cooperation, rapidity, and socialization. One aim of the work group, however, is glaring in its absence: justice. One of the main criticisms of the American court system is that it has sacrificed the goal of justice for efficiency. Some observers claim that only the wealthiest can afford to receive justice as promised by the Constitution, while the rest of society is left with a watered-down version of *assembly-line justice.*

The Impact of Excessive Caseloads   Given the caseloads that most courts face, some degree of assembly-line justice seems inevitable. A quick survey of the nation's court system provides clear examples of the extent of the problem and its consequences. Approximately two out of every three states are consistently behind on their dockets. In Tennessee, each criminal court judge handles between 2,300 and 4,800 cases a year.[52] Murder cases in Boston, Massachusetts, commonly take between fifteen months and two years to reach trial, thanks to overcrowded courts.[53] In Tacoma, Washington, a felony conviction that would have sent one Bruce Eric Smith to prison for life was overturned because prosecutors took too long to start his trial. The problem: no available courtrooms. As a result of the delay, Smith was set free, only to be rearrested when, in an attempt to flee police after an alleged rape, he rammed his vehicle into another car, killing the driver.[54]

The federal court system faces many of the same problems. Caseloads in federal criminal courts have grown by almost a third since 1993, spurred by tougher illegal narcotics laws.[55] The lack of resources to deal with excessive caseloads is generally recognized as one of the most critical issues facing both federal and state law enforcement agencies and courtrooms.[56]

The Courtroom Work Group and Overloaded Courts   Because a judge's worth is increasingly measured by her or his ability to keep the "assembly line" of cases moving, rather than by the quality of her or his judicial work, the judicial process is accused of being "careless and haphazard" and of routinely making decisions on the basis of incomplete information. Though definitive statistics on the subject have never been adequately gathered, many observers feel that assembly-line justice affects the actions of others in the criminal justice system as well:

> Beyond filling out a crime report, police officers often do not investigate misdemeanors and less serious felonies unless the offender was caught in the act.

> Police officers often are encouraged to obtain confessions—using whatever means necessary—from defendants, rather than find incriminating evidence, because a confession is more likely to lead to conviction.

> Prosecutors often press charges for misdemeanors and nonviolent felonies only when the case is a "slam dunk"—that is, when conviction is certain.

> To wrap up cases quickly, prosecutors generally bargain reduced sentences for guilty verdicts; as a result, criminals spend less time in prison than is in society's best interests.[57]

If the public is under the impression that police, judges, and lawyers are more interested in speed than in justice, the pressure of caseloads may also lead to loss of respect for the criminal justice system as a whole.

↗ ONLINE REVIEW *Go to the book's Web site for an interactive review of this section*

INFOTRAC KEYWORDS 🜨
court congestion
For more information, use this search term with InfoTrac College Edition, your online library at www.infotrac-college.com

>Is Justice for Sale?

By connotation, "assembly-line justice" implies injustice. The term suggests that defendants are being hurried through the process, losing the safeguards built into our criminal justice system in the blur. For many observers, however, justice in the American courts is related more closely to *money* than to *speed*. As we close this chapter, we will examine the contention that, despite the stated intention of the United States Supreme Court, defendants get not the justice they deserve, but the justice they can afford.

Gideon v. Wainwright

In the landmark case of *Gideon v. Wainwright* (1963),[58] the Supreme Court unanimously held that "any person haled into court, who is too poor to hire a lawyer, cannot be assured a fair trial unless counsel is provided for him." It seems to be "an obvious truth," wrote Justice Hugo Black, that "lawyers in criminal cases are necessities, not luxuries."[59] For the most part, the letter of the *Gideon* case has been followed in the forty years since Justice Black wrote those words. Many observers claim, however, that the spirit of the decision has been abandoned in America's courts—that, in fact, a person's ability to receive justice is directly related to how much money he or she is able to spend. "If you're the average poor person, you are going to be herded through the criminal justice system about like an animal is herded through the stockyards," says Stephen Bright, the director of the Southern Center for Human Rights in Atlanta, Georgia.[60]

Working for the Minimum Wage

The Sixth Amendment to the U.S. Constitution provides that all criminal defendants have a right to the assistance of counsel for their defense. The *Gideon* decision assured that right for indigent defendants who could not afford to hire a lawyer. Today, more than eight out of every ten Americans accused of a felony use a publicly appointed defense attorney. As spending for new prisons

and law enforcement personnel has increased over the last decade, however, the budgets for public defenders are being slashed. Although Congress approved a pay hike for defense attorneys in federal courts in 1986, most of the country's ninety-four federal districts have yet to implement the raise due to Congress's refusal to appropriate the necessary funds. Therefore, defense lawyers in those districts are still paid an hourly rate of $65 for courtroom time and $45 for out-of-court time—barely enough to cover the costs of maintaining a law office. Even in the districts that have provided the extra wages, defense attorneys still receive less than half the $200 rate charged by private lawyers.

The contrast is even more pronounced in some states. Alabama, for example, limits compensation to court-appointed attorneys to $40 an hour for out-of-court preparation and $60 an hour for time in court.[61] Considering the wages from private clients that these lawyers lose every hour they work for the state, an Alabama defense attorney who spends an average amount of time preparing for a death penalty case is being paid less than the national minimum wage. In Virginia, the most a court-appointed attorney can be paid to work on a noncapital charge with a punishment of more than twenty years in prison is $1,235. Even if the lawyer spends only eighty hours on such a case, a very small amount of time in the legal business, he or she would be making less than $16 an hour.[62] A report by the Texas state bar commission pointed out that the fees provided for public defenders in that state barely cover a lawyer's overhead, and this low level of compensation "often translates into a disincentive to provide maximum performance."[63]

Public defenders are often overworked as well. In the Florida counties of Orange and Osceola, public defenders handle about 750 cases a year, about five times their recommended caseload. Sometimes, there simply are not enough lawyers to meet the needs of poor defendants. Twelve thousand indigent defendants a year in Riverside

County, California, plead guilty without ever speaking to a lawyer, while in Oregon thousands of nonviolent misdemeanor and low-level felony cases are dismissed due to lack of available court-appointed attorneys.[64]

Under pressure of continued budget cuts, some regions are contracting out their defense work. In this "low-bid contracting," one or more attorneys agree to represent all or a portion of a jurisdiction's caseload for a fixed price. For example, McDuffie County (Georgia) officials recently decided that the $46,000 the county was spending annually on indigent defense was too much. They allowed local attorneys to bid on the service and awarded a contract to Bill Wheeler, whose $25,000 was the lowest bid submitted. Wheeler continued to maintain a private practice as he took on the county's caseload.[65]

"You Get What You Pay For"

Critics of low-bid contracting argue that by emphasizing price over quality, officials are sacrificing the constitutional guarantees of indigent defendants.[66] In the first three years that he held McDuffie County's contract, for example, Wheeler tried one felony case and entered 213 guilty pleas. In that time span, he entered only three pretrial motions for his defendants. This is remarkable, considering that pretrial motions are one of the primary weapons defense attorneys have to protect their clients. Furthermore, the quality of some public defenders is unacceptable. In a Florida murder trial, the presiding judge ordered that the defense attorney's breath be checked for alcohol each morning. During trial recesses, the defense attorney was spotted using speed, Quaaludes, alcohol, morphine, and marijuana. The defendant was eventually executed.[67]

Such behavior raises a crucial question: When a lawyer does such a poor job, has she or he essentially denied her or his client the Sixth Amendment right to assistance of counsel? In *Strickland v. Washington* (1984),[68] the Supreme Court set up a two-pronged test to determine whether constitutional requirements have been met. To prove that prior counsel was not sufficient, a defendant must show (1) that counsel's performance was deficient, *and* (2) that this deficiency *more likely than not* caused the defendant to lose the case. In practice, it has been very difficult to prove the second prong, because the prosecution can always argue that the defen-

AP Photo/Brett Coomer

Calvin Jerold Burdine, age forty-six, was freed in 2000 after spending sixteen years on death row in Texas for murder. U.S. District Judge David Hittner overturned Burdine's conviction because his lawyer allegedly slept through long portions of his 1984 trial.

dant would have lost the case even if his or her lawyer had not been asleep, drunk, or otherwise incapacitated.[69]

Some observers have called for the Supreme Court to abandon the *Strickland* test under certain circumstances where the lawyer's behavior is so reprehensible that there is no possibility of a "fair trial." Some lower courts seem to be moving in this direction. In 2000, a federal judge in Texas ruled that Calvin Burdine, who had spent sixteen years on death row for a murder conviction, did not receive a fair hearing because his defense lawyer slept for periods as long as ten minutes during the trial.[70] Several years earlier, a judge decided that defense counsel was automatically ineffective because he called his client a "stupid nigger son of a bitch" and promised to be "very ineffective" if his client insisted on going to trial.[71] In both cases, the defendants had been appointed counsel.

Paying to Defend the Poor

Attempts are being made to improve the situation. In 2003, Quitman County, located in rural Mississippi, sued the state to improve the level of legal service for its indigent defendants. The lawsuit claims that while the state pays upwards of $13 billion a year to prosecute criminal cases, in Quitman County two attorneys are paid $1,350 a month to represent every person who cannot afford his or her own defense.[72] In a sworn statement, Quitman County resident Diane Brown described how, on the same day she was facing charges for assault, drunken driving, and leaving the scene of an accident, she met her court-appointed lawyer for five minutes. This was the amount of time he gave her to accept a deal to spend ten years in prison, an offer she felt she had no choice but to accept.[73]

Similar suits have been filed in Connecticut, Illinois, Indiana, and Louisiana, based on the idea that poor defendants are not being provided with the effective assistance of counsel as required by the Constitution. A number of states are taking steps to increase the flow of funds to public defender systems. Georgia will spend an estimated $60 million a year on court-appointed attorneys starting in 2005. For the most part, however, legal scholars believe the promise of "equal justice for all" inherent in the Constitution and the *Gideon* ruling is not being fulfilled. Few would dispute the assertion of one observer, who stated, "If O. J. Simpson [who spent nearly $6 million on his defense] had been a poor black man in a different part of Los Angeles County, he would be on death row now."[74]

MAKING SENSE OF THE SIXTH AMENDMENT RIGHT TO COUNSEL

1 Why is it important for indigent defendants to have counsel that is as effective as if they had paid for it themselves? Is this a reasonable goal for state, local, and federal governments?

2 Do you think that criminal defense counsel should *automatically* be deemed ineffective if the attorney does not show up for trial? What if the attorney is under the influence of drugs or alcohol during the trial? What if the attorney is asleep for portions of the trial? Should it matter if he or she sleeps for only a few seconds?

3 What if the defense lawyer makes an honest mistake, such as failing to challenge evidence that should not be allowed in court because of the exclusionary rule (see Chapter 7)? Is that evidence of "deficient" counsel?

Chapter Summary

STORIES FROM THE STREET

Go to the Stories from the Street feature at www.cjinaction.com to hear Larry Gaines tell insightful stories related to this chapter and his experiences in the field.

1 **Define and contrast the four functions of the courts.** The four functions are (a) due process, (b) crime control, (c) rehabilitation, and (d) bureaucratic. The most obvious contrast is between the due process and crime control functions. The former is mainly concerned with the procedural rules that allow each accused individual to have a "fair chance" against the government in a criminal proceeding. For crime control, the courts are supposed to impose enough "pain" on convicted criminals to deter criminal behavior. For the rehabilitation function, the courts serve as "doctors" who dispense "treatment." In their bureaucratic function, courts are more concerned with speed and efficiency.

2 **Define jurisdiction and contrast geographical and subject-matter jurisdiction.** Jurisdiction relates to the power of a court to hear a particular case. Courts are typically limited in geographical jurisdiction; for example, to a particular state. Some courts are restricted in subject matter, such as a small claims court, which can hear only cases involving civil matters under a certain amount.

3 **Explain the difference between trial and appellate courts.** Trial courts are courts of the first instance, where a case is first heard. Appellate courts review the proceedings of a lower

court. Appellate courts do not have juries.

4 **Outline the several levels of a typical state court system.** (a) At the lowest level are courts of limited jurisdiction, (b) next are trial courts of general jurisdiction, (c) then appellate courts, and (d) finally, the state's highest court.

5 **Outline the federal court system.** (a) At the lowest level are the U.S. district courts in which trials are held, as well as various minor federal courts of limited jurisdiction; (b) next are the U.S. courts of appeals, otherwise known as circuit courts of appeal; and (c) finally, the United States Supreme Court.

6 **Explain briefly how a case is brought to the Supreme Court.** Cases decided in U.S. courts of appeals, as well as cases decided in the highest state courts (when federal questions arise), can be appealed to the Supreme Court. If at least four justices approve of a case filed with the Supreme Court, the Court will issue a writ of *certiorari,* ordering the lower court to send the Supreme Court the record of the case for review.

7 **List the actions that a judge might take prior to an actual trial.** Trial judges may do the following before an actual trial: (a) issue search or arrest warrants, (b) authorize electronic surveillance of a suspect, (c) order the temporary incarceration of a suspect, (d) decide whether a suspect should be released on bail and the amount of that bail, (e) accept or reject pretrial motions by prosecutors and defense attorneys, and (f) accept or reject a plea bargain.

8 **Explain the difference between the selection of judges at the state level and at the federal level.** The president nominates all judges at the federal level, and the Senate must approve the nominations. A similar procedure is used in some states. In other states, all judges are elected on a partisan ballot or on a nonpartisan ballot. Some states use merit selection, or the Missouri Plan, in which a citizen committee nominates judicial candidates, the governor or executive of the state judicial system chooses among the top three nominees, and a year later a "retention election" is held.

9 **List and describe the members of the courtroom work group.** (a) The judge; (b) the prosecutor, who brings charges in the name of the people (the state) against the accused; (c) the defense attorney; (d) the bailiff, who is responsible for maintaining security and order in the judge's chambers and the courtroom; (e) the clerk, who accepts all pleas, motions, and other matters to be acted on by the judge; and (f) court reporters, who record what is said during a trial as well as at depositions.

10 **Explain the consequences of excessive caseloads.** Excessive caseloads have led to assembly-line justice. Such a criminal justice system increases the possibility that (a) police officers will not investigate crimes unless the offender was caught in the act; (b) officers will seek only confessions, rather than spending time finding incriminating evidence; (c) prosecutors will press charges in criminal cases only when conviction is certain; and (d) plea bargaining will be common.

Key Terms

Questions for Critical Analysis

1 "The primary adversarial relationship in the courts is not between the plaintiff (prosecutor, or state) and defendant, but rather between the ideal of justice and the reality of bureaucratic limitations." Explain why you agree or disagree with this statement.

2 Which court has virtually unlimited geographical and subject-matter jurisdiction? Why is this so?

3 How did we end up with a dual court system?

4 Federal judges and justices typically hold office for many years. Why is this so?

5 What effect does the Supreme Court's refusal to issue a writ of *certiorari* have on lower courts' decisions?

6 What are some of the various functions that a judge undertakes during a trial? What function does a judge assume when presiding over a trial that is not a jury trial?

7 Many states, even those using the merit system, elect their judges. What is the main drawback of using elections to select or maintain judges in office?

8 How does a courtroom work group differ from the management of a corporation?

9 *Gideon v. Wainwright* guarantees that everyone has counsel in a criminal proceeding. Is this any guarantee that "justice will be served for all"?

TEST PREPARATION ONLINE

Go to www.cjinaction.com for tools to aid you in studying for your exams. Click on *Online Reviews* under *Chapter Resources* for an interactive review of each major section of this chapter. Under *Chapter Resources*, you will also find the *Chapter Outline, Chapter Summary, Flashcards, Glossary, Learning Objectives, Lecture Presentations, Concept Builder, Essay Questions,* and a *Tutorial Quiz.* You can also test yourself with a game of *Concentration* or the *Crossword Puzzle.*

Web Resources

Go to www.cjinaction.com for a wealth of online resources. Explore the *Internet Activities* and *Class Projects* under *Chapter Resources.* Check out the *Web Links* to access the Web sites mentioned in the text, as well as many others. You can also access recent perspectives by clicking on *CJ in the News* and *Terrorism Update* under *Course Resources.* If you'd like some mentoring, click on *Board of Mentors* under *Book Resources.*

Search Online with InfoTrac College Edition

For additional information, explore InfoTrac College Edition, your online library that offers complete full-length articles from thousands of scholarly and popular publications. Click on *InfoTrac College Edition* under *Chapter Resources* at www.cjinaction.com for a list of key words and InfoTrac exercises. Use the passcode that came with your book.

Suggested Readings

O'Connor, Sandra Day, and Craig Joyce, *The Majesty of the Law: Reflections of a Supreme Court Justice,* New York: Random House, 2003. O'Connor, the first female Supreme Court justice, offers an insider's view of the nation's highest court. O'Connor also profiles the justices that she feels had the greatest impact on the modern Court, including John Marshall, Warren Burger, and Thurgood Marshall. As might be expected, hot-button issues such as the death penalty, abortion rights, and affirmative action are discussed in a way to avoid controversy for this sitting justice, but this book does provide an interesting perspective on the evolution of the Court and those who have sat on its bench.

Stolzenberg, Lisa, and Stewart J. D'Alessio, *Criminal Courts for the 21st Century,* 2nd ed., Englewood Cliffs, NJ: Prentice Hall, 2001. In this book, Stolzenberg and D'Alessio provide a "best of" collection that includes twenty articles on all aspects of our criminal courts as well as issues surrounding criminal justice in general. Topics addressed include the use of DNA evidence in felony prosecutions, incompetent lawyers, jury misconduct, and the prosecution of pregnant drug users. Although the articles have been taken from scholarly journals, the editors tried to choose those pieces that would hold the most interest for a general audience.

Notes

1. David Pasztor, "In Infamous Tulia, 13 to Walk Free Today," *Austin American-Statesman* (June 16, 2003), A1.

2. Roscoe Pound, "The Administration of Justice in American Cities," *Harvard Law Review* 12 (1912).

3. Russell Wheeler and Howard Whitcomb, *Judicial Administration: Text and Readings* (Englewood Cliffs, NJ: Prentice-Hall, 1977), 3.

4. Herbert Packer, *The Limits of the Criminal Sanction* (Stanford, CA: Stanford University Press, 1968), 154–173.

5. Herbert Packer, "The Courts, the Police and the Rest of Us," *Criminal Law, Criminology & Political Science* 57 (1966), 238–239.

6. Larry J. Siegal, *Criminology: Instructor's Manual,* 6th ed. (Belmont, CA: West/Wadsworth Publishing Co., 1998), 440.

7. Gerald F. Velman, "Federal Sentencing Guidelines: A Cure Worse than the Disease," *American Criminal Law Review* 29 (Spring 1992), 904.

8. "State, Feds Should Help Pay Costs of Sniper Trials," *Virginian-Pilot & Ledger Star* (September 30, 2003), B8.

9. David W. Neubauer, *America's Courts and the Criminal Justice System,* 5th ed. (Belmont, CA: Wadsworth Publishing Co., 1996), 41.

10. Alexander Hamilton, *The Federalist,* No. 78 in Clinton Rossiter, ed., *The Federalist Papers* (New York: New American Library, 1961), 467–470.

11. G. Edward White, *History of the Supreme Court, Volumes III–IV: The Marshall Court and Cultural Change* (New York: Oxford University Press, 1988), 157–200.

12. 372 U.S. 335 (1963).

13. 384 U.S. 436 (1966).

14. 408 U.S. 238 (1972).

15. 428 U.S. 153 (1976).

16. 491 U.S. 397 (1989).

17. 496 U.S. 310 (1990).

18. Mark Alan Ozimek, "The Case for a More Workable Standard in Death Penalty Jurisprudence: *Atkins v. Virginia* and Categorical Exemptions under the Imprudent 'Evolving Standards of Decency' Doctrine," *University of Toledo Law Review* (Spring 2003), 651.

19. *Singleton v. Commissioner of Internal Revenue,* 439 U.S. 940 (1978).

20. Barry R. Schaller, *A Vision of American Law: Judging Law, Literature, and the Stories We Tell* (Westport, CT: Praeger, 1997).

21. Harlington Wood, Jr., "Judiciary Reform: Recent Improvements in Federal Judicial Administration," *American University Law Review* 44 (June 1995), 1557.

22. Pub. L. No. 76-299, 53 Stat. 1223, codified as amended at 28 U.S.C. Sections 601–610 (1988 & Supp. V 1993).

23. Peter D. Webster, "Selection and Retention of Judges: Is There One 'Best' Method?" *Florida State Law Review* 23 (Summer 1995), 1.

24. Irving R. Kaufman, *Chilling Judicial Independence* (New York: Association of the Bar of the City of New York, 1979).

25. Ray M. Harding, "The Case for Partisan Election of Judges," *ABA Journal* 55 (1969), 1162–1163.

26. Daniel R. Deja, "How Judges Are Selected: A Survey of the Judicial Selection Process in the United States," *Michigan Bar Journal* 75 (September 1996), 904.

27. Edmund V. Ludwig, "Another Case against the Election of Trial Judges," *Pennsylvania Lawyer* 19 (May/June 1997), 33.

28. *Judicial Selection in the States* (Des Moines, IA: American Judicature Society, 2003), 1–2.

29. Quoted in Daniel Burke, "Code of Judicial Conduct Canon 7B(1)(c): Toward the Proper Regulation of Speech in Judicial Campaigns," *Georgetown Journal of Legal Ethics* 81 (Summer 1993), 181.

30. James E. Lozier, "The Missouri Plan a.k.a. Merit Selection Is the Best Solution for Selecting Michigan's Judges," *Michigan Bar Journal* 75 (September 1996), 918.

31. William Ballenger, "In Judicial Wilderness, Even Brickley's Not Safe," *Michigan Politics* 28 (1996), 1–3.

32. Richard A. Watson and Rondal G. Downing, *The Politics of the Bench and Bar: Judicial Selection under the Missouri Nonpartisan Court Plan* (New York: John Wiley & Sons, 1969).

33. Employee Relations Office, *Judiciary Fair Employment Practices, Fiscal Year 2001* (Washington, D.C.: Administrative Office of the U.S. Courts, 2002), page 32, table B-1.

34. "Survey Finds Bar Makeup Is Shifting, but Slowly," *California State Bar Journal* (November 2001), 1.

35. *Judiciary Fair Employment Practices, Fiscal Year 2001,* page 32, table B-1.

36. Edward M. Chen, "The Judiciary, Diversity, and Justice for All," *California Law Review* (July 2003), 1109.

37. Theresa B. Beiner, "The Elusive (but Worthwhile) Quest for a Diverse Bench in the New Millennium," *University of California at Davis Law Review* (February 2003), 599.

38. Sherrilyn A. Ifill, "Racial Diversity on the Bench: Beyond Role Models and Public Confidence," *Washington and Lee Law Review* (Spring 2000), 405.

39. Nancy E. Crowe, "The Effects of Judges' Sex and Race on Judicial Decision Making on the U.S. Courts of Appeals, 1981–1996," dissertation, Department of Political Science, University of Chicago (1999), 80.

40. Jeffrey Toobin, "Women in Black," *New Yorker* (October 30, 2000), 54.

41. Shirley S. Abrahamson, *Foreword to Judicial Conduct and Ethics* (Charlottesville, VA: Michie Co., 1990), vi–vii.

42. American Bar Association, *Model Code of Judicial Conduct* (Chicago: ABA, August 1990).

43. ABA Commission on Ethics and Professional Responsibility, Informal Opinion 1468 (1981).

44. Canon 7B(1) (c), Model Code of Judicial Conduct.

45. Hunter T. George, "Panel Clears Washington Justice of Misconduct," *Portland Oregonian* (April 29, 1998), B7.

46. John Gardiner, "Preventing Judicial Misconduct: Defining the Role of Conduct Organizations," *Judicature* 70 (1986), 113–121.

47. Roy B. Fleming, Peter F. Nardulli, and James Eisenstein, *The Craft of Justice: Politics and Work in Criminal Court Communities* (Philadelphia: University of Pennsylvania Press, 1992).

48. Neubauer, 41.

49. Alissa P. Worden, "The Judge's Role in Plea Bargaining: An Analysis of Judges' Agreement with Prosecutors' Sentencing Recommendations," *Justice Quarterly* 10 (1995), 257–278.

50. Neubauer, 72.

51. Kimberly Jade Norwood, "Shopping for Venue: The Need for More Limits," *University of Miami Law Review* 50 (1996), 295–298.

52. "Overcrowded Courts Are Threat to City and Justice," *Tennessean-Nashville* (May 1, 2003), 16.

53. Jeff Lemberg, "A Year Later, Facing Life after Death," *Boston Globe* (November 17, 2002), 1.

54. Stacey Burns, "Free Felon in Fatal Car Chase," *Morning News Tribune* (January 12, 2002), A1.

55. Administrative Office of the United States Courts, *Annual Report to the Director, 2002* (Washington, D.C.: Administrative Office of the U.S. Courts, 2003), 6.

56. Special Committee on Criminal Justice in a Free Society, *Criminal Justice in Crisis* (Washington, D.C.: American Bar Association, Criminal Justice Section 1988), 39.

57. Malcolm Feeley, *Felony Arrests: Their Prosecution and Disposition in New York Courts* (New York: Vera Institute, 1981), xii.

58. 372 U.S. 335, 344 (1963).

59. *Ibid.*

60. Quoted in Bob Herbert, "Cheap Justice," *New York Times* (March 1, 1998), 15.

61. "Dallas County Attorneys Consider Strike on Indigent Cases," *Associated Press Newswires* (February 26, 2002).

62. "No Hollywood Ending in Defending the Indigent," *Virginian-Pilot & Ledger Star* (March 28, 2003), B10.

63. Allen K. Butcher and Michael K. Moore, *Muting Gideon's Trumpet: The Crisis in Indigent Criminal Defense in Texas* (2000), available at www.uta.edu/pols/moore/indigent/last.pdf.

64. Bill Rankin, "Right to a Lawyer Still Not a Given for Poor Defendants," *Atlanta Journal-Constitution* (March 24, 2003), B1.

65. Adele Bernhard, "Take Courage: What the Courts Can Do to Improve the Delivery of Criminal Defense Services," *University of Pittsburgh Law Review* (Winter 2002), 293.

66. *American Bar Association Standards for Criminal Justice,* 3d ed. (Boston: Little, Brown, 1992), 46.

67. Jeffrey L. Kirchmeier, "Drink, Drugs, and Drowsiness: The Constitutional Right to Effective Assistance of Counsel and the *Strickland* Prejudice Requirement," *Nebraska Law Review* 75 (1996), 425.

68. 466 U.S. 668 (1984).

69. *Burnett v. Collins,* 982 F.2d 922, 930 (5th Cir. 1993).

70. Ross E. Milloy, "Judge Frees Texas Inmate Whose Lawyer Slept at Trial," *New York Times* (March 2, 2000), A19.

71. *Frazer v. United States,* 18 F.3d 778 (9th Cir. 1994).

72. Reed Branson, "Poor County Sues Miss., Says Indigent Get Unequal Defense," *Commercial Appeal* (April 28, 2003), A1.

73. Adam Liptak, "County Says It's Too Poor to Defend the Poor," *New York Times* (April 15, 2003), A1.

74. M. A. Stapleton, "Crisis Seen in Privatizing Public Defender Work," *Chicago Daily Law Bulletin* (October 15, 1997), 1.

> Chapter 9 <

Pretrial Procedures

The Adversary System in A

>chapteroutline<

- The Prosecution
- The Defense Attorney
- Truth, Victory, and the Adversary System
- Pretrial Detention
- Establishing Probable Cause
- The Prosecutorial Screening Process
- Pleading Guilty
- Going to Trial
- Criminal Justice in Action—The DNA Revolution

>chapterobjectives<

After reading this chapter, you should be able to:

1 List the different names given to public prosecutors and the general powers that they have.

2 Contrast the prosecutor's roles as an elected official and as a crime fighter.

3 Delineate the responsibilities of defense attorneys.

4 Indicate the three types of defense allocation programs.

5 List the three basic features of an adversary system of justice.

6 Identify the steps involved in the pretrial criminal process.

7 Indicate the three influences on a judge's decision to set bail.

8 Explain how a prosecutor screens potential cases.

9 List and briefly explain the different forms of plea bargaining agreements.

10 Indicate the ways that both defense attorneys and prosecutors can induce plea bargaining.

The American Taliban Makes a Deal

"**A**re you in fact guilty?" Judge T. S. Ellis III asked the young man standing before him. "Yes, sir," answered John Walker Lindh, a twenty-year-old U.S. citizen known as the "American Taliban."

Lindh had just admitted that he had committed two felonies: providing services to the Taliban, the extremist Muslim group that had ruled Afghanistan, and carrying two grenades while doing so. Each charge carried a punishment of ten years in prison; Lindh was facing two decades behind bars.

John Walker Lindh

Yet Lindh, his family, and his defense attorneys were happy with the outcome. Initially, he had been charged with ten crimes, some of which—conspiracy to murder American citizens and provide material support to a terrorist organization—carry a penalty of life in prison. The government's case against him appeared strong. Lindh had admitted on national television that he had fought for the Taliban's army as part of a "religious experience." Furthermore, if his trial had gone ahead, Lindh faced the probable wrath of a jury composed of citizens from Alexandria, Virginia, located just miles from Washington, D.C., where terrorists had crashed a hijacked airplane into the Pentagon several months earlier. "Our goal," said James Brosnahan, Lindh's defense attorney, "was to give him some kind of future."

> **To the surprise** of many, the federal government also seemed pleased with the result. Attorney General John Ashcroft, who had earlier labeled John Walker Lindh a fanatic who "sided with tyrants" against his own people, called the plea agreement an "important victory in America's war on terrorism." Why had prosecutors let Lindh "off easy" when a conviction on more serious charges seemed likely? Some observers suggest that a highly publicized trial could have been embarrassing for the government. Lindh's attorneys planned to highlight how their client had been denied adequate medical care and access to a lawyer and to argue that his confessions may have been coerced by his interrogators: he was blindfolded, strapped to a stretcher with heavy tape, and placed in a steel container.[1] U.S. Attorney Paul McNulty said the deal would enable the government to avoid a long and costly trial, allowing it to save staff and resources for other cases against more important terrorist suspects.[2]

In fact, prosecutors and defendants are constantly "making deals" just like the one between Lindh and the federal government. The *formal* adversary process of the trial is the exception rather than the rule in American courts. About 90 percent of those charged with a felony in this country opt, as Lindh did, for the *informal* process; that is, they plead guilty, thereby avoiding a trial and serving, in almost all instances, a lighter sentence.[3] Indeed, most prosecutors, defense attorneys, and judges could not imagine a system in which plea bargaining was not the predominant means of resolving cases. Given, then, that the vast majority of cases never go to trial, is it realistic to claim that the United States even has an adversary system? In this chapter, we will attempt to answer these questions by examining the actions of the courtroom work group with regard to plea bargaining, bail, and other pretrial procedures. We will start with a discussion of the two main combatants of the adversary system: the prosecutor and the defense attorney.

CONCEPT BUILDER

Having the power or authority to make decisions and to have latitude in choices is an integral aspect of the criminal justice system. Visit www.cjinaction.com for an interactive exploration of this key topic.

The Prosecution

Criminal cases are tried by **public prosecutors,** who are employed by the government. The public prosecutor in federal criminal cases is called a U.S. attorney. In cases tried in state or local courts, the public prosecutor may be referred to as a *prosecuting attorney, state prosecutor, district attorney, county attorney,* or *city attorney.* Given their great autonomy, prosecutors are generally considered the most dominant figures in the American criminal justice system. In some jurisdictions, the district attorney is the chief law enforcement officer, with broad powers over police operations. Prosecutors have the power to bring the resources of the state against the individual and hold the legal keys to meting out or withholding punishment.[4] Ideally, this power is balanced by a duty of fairness and a recognition that the prosecutor's ultimate goal is not to win cases, but to see that justice is done. In *Berger v. United States* (1935), Justice George Sutherland called the prosecutor

> in a peculiar and very definite sense the servant of the law, the twofold aim of which is that guilt shall not escape or innocence suffer. He may prosecute with earnestness and vigor—indeed, he should do so. But, while he may strike hard blows, he is not at liberty to strike foul ones. It is as much his duty to refrain from improper methods calculated to produce a wrongful conviction as it is to use every legitimate means to bring about a just one.[5]

Public Prosecutors

Individuals, acting as trial lawyers, who initiate and conduct cases in the government's name and on behalf of the people.

THE OFFICE OF THE PROSECUTOR

When he or she is acting as an *officer of the law* during a criminal trial, there are limits on the prosecutor's conduct, as we shall see in the next chapter. During the pretrial process, however, prosecutors hold a great deal of discretion in deciding the following:

1 Whether an individual who has been arrested by the police will be charged with a crime.

2 The level of the charges to be brought against the suspect.

3 If and when to stop the prosecution.[6]

INFOTRAC KEYWORDS
prosecutor

For more information, use this search term with InfoTrac College Edition, your online library at www.infotrac-college.com

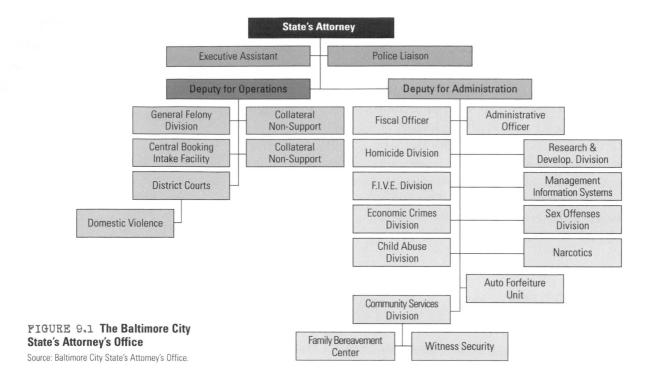

FIGURE 9.1 The Baltimore City State's Attorney's Office

Source: Baltimore City State's Attorney's Office.

Attorney General

The chief law officer of a state; also, the chief law officer of the nation.

There are more than eight thousand prosecutor's offices around the country—serving state, county, and municipal jurisdictions. Even though the **attorney general** is the chief law enforcement officer in any state, she or he has limited (and in some states, no) control of prosecutors within the state's boundaries.

Each jurisdiction has a chief prosecutor who is sometimes appointed but more often elected. As an elected official, he or she typically serves a four-year term, though in some states, such as Alabama, the term is six years. In smaller jurisdictions, the chief prosecutor has several assistants, and they work closely together. In larger ones, the chief prosecutor may administer numerous *assistant prosecutors,* many of whom he or she will rarely meet. (See the feature *Careers in CJ.*) Assistant prosecutors—for the most part young attorneys recently graduated from law school—may be assigned to particular sections of the organization, such as criminal prosecutions in general or areas of *special prosecution,* such as narcotics or gang crimes. (See Figure 9.1 for a typical prosecutor's office.)

THE PROSECUTOR AS ELECTED OFFICIAL

The chief prosecutor's autonomy is not complete: as an elected official, she or he must answer to the voters. (There are exceptions: U.S. attorneys are nominated by the president and approved by the Senate, and chief prosecutors in Alaska, Connecticut, New Jersey, Rhode Island, and the District of Columbia are either appointed or hired as members of the attorney general's office.) The prosecutor may be part of the political machine; in many jurisdictions the prosecutor must declare a party affiliation and is expected to reward fellow party members with positions in the district attorney's office if elected. The post is often seen as a "stepping stone" to higher political office, and many prosecutors have gone on to serve in legislatures or as judges. Arlen Specter, a Republican senator from Pennsylvania; Ron Castille, who sits on the state's supreme court; and Ed

> John Esmerado Assistant Prosecutor

Courtesy John Esmerado

John Esmerado

My name is John G. Esmerado. I am an assistant prosecutor in Elizabeth, New Jersey, for the county of Union. Union County is comprised of twenty-one independent townships with a population of approximately one-half million. Our county lies across the river from New York City. In my office there is the prosecutor, the chief law enforcement officer of the county, and fifty-five assistant prosecutors.

I first became interested in the field of prosecution when I was in high school. In ninth grade I read Harper Lee's *To Kill a Mockingbird*. After reading the book, I wanted to be like Atticus Finch. I wanted to be a lawyer who helped people. In eleventh grade, I participated in a high school mock trial program. Our attorney adviser was a former assistant prosecutor. From her I learned for the first time the role of a prosecutor. I was intrigued. I applied to a nearby Catholic university, Seton Hall, and majored in American history. I sought to learn everything I could about the world. I took courses on a variety of liberal arts and business topics. More and more I felt drawn to being a prosecutor, to pursue the truth and to aid people in crisis. I graduated college with honors and applied to Seton Hall University Law School. After receiving early acceptance, I took all the criminal law courses offered by the school. By my third year, I secured a part-time position as a law clerk in the Union County Prosecutor's Office appellate section. I wrote and argued numerous motions.

On graduation and the day after I sat for the New Jersey bar exam, I started full-time at the prosecutor's office. In March of 1993, I was sworn in as a full-time assistant prosecutor. Since then I have tried fifty-six jury trials and worked in the appellate section, the juvenile and family court section, and pre-indictment plea screening and now work full-time on a trial team. Twice a month, I try a case. I have litigated everything from murder to robbery, sexual assault, police misconduct, drug distribution, prostitution, and aggravated assault.

My current responsibilities are twofold. Primarily, I represent the state of New Jersey at trial. With a detective staff, I investigate crime by interviewing witnesses, searching out evidence, and asking people questions in court to establish beyond a reasonable doubt that a defendant committed a crime. Trial work is incredibly fun. It requires vast amounts of pretrial preparation. Once it starts, however, it moves at lightning speed. Trials are strategic chess games of facts and law as well as all-out mental combat, a blitzkrieg of sorts, to find the truth. My secondary responsibility is to act as legal adviser to the police. Many times during the week and periodically in the early morning hours while the world sleeps, detectives call to discuss problematic cases. They arrest someone and are not clear what the appropriate charges are. I listen to the facts and authorize certain complaints and ask the detectives to pursue additional facts to help make the case stronger for trial.

Recently, I was confronted with a moral dilemma. I was asked to participate as the second prosecutor in a death penalty trial. As a Catholic, I was ambivalent at best about the use of the death penalty by the state. I consulted the *Gospel of Life* and other Church teachings on the topic as well as my own conscience. The defendant was charged with hiring a hit man to kill his long-time girlfriend. The defendant had served a previous state prison sentence for threatening the same woman in the past. The defendant was no angel and had a lengthy criminal record. After much soul searching, I consented to work on the case with the premier assistant prosecutor in the office, Regina Caulfield. After a three-week trial, we secured a conviction for first degree murder for hire. The guilt phase of the trial was over. We had one week off to prepare for the penalty phase. I began to have doubts about the whole process. Was this really fair to both the defendant and the victim's family? Is death a legitimate tool in the prosecutor's arsenal of justice? After a four-day hearing and a day and a half of deliberation, the jury returned a verdict for life and not for death. The victim's family was disappointed. I was relieved.

As a prosecutor, I have always sought to do what is right and just. Incoming data support the conclusion that the current system with all its Byzantine rules cannot function properly. Jurors disregard legal instructions, while defense attorneys engender emotional sympathy for the defendant's upbringing, and victims are offered little if any opportunity to place their loss before the jury. Death must be reevaluated by the entire criminal justice community.

Immediately after this trial, I took some time off, grew a beard, and gained weight. I was depressed. For the first time in my career I had participated in something I did not wholly believe in. Since that time, I found my razor, exercise consistently, and have firmly resolved not to participate in another capital case.

In summary, I am glad to have a job that provides an outlet for my desire to do good. Sometimes, when I am working late at night, for free, on a case, I say to myself, "This is the greatest job in the world." I receive a salary to find the truth. I help people in crisis, people subject to violence, confront their attackers and ultimately bring some form of closure. Truth, justice, and the American way, a job far too important to leave to Superman cartoons, is the job of the prosecutor every day in and out of court.

 Go to the Careers in Criminal Justice Interactive CD *for more profiles in the field of criminal justice.*

U.S. Senator Patrick Leahy, a Democrat from Vermont, was a local prosecutor in Chittenden County, Vermont, for eight years before being elected to his present post in 1974. Give several reasons why ex-prosecutors are often attractive candidates for positions in state or federal government.

Rendell, a former mayor of Philadelphia and now governor of the state, all served as Philadelphia district attorneys early in their careers.

Prosecutors are also subject to community pressures. As antidrug sentiment becomes more prevalent around the country, for example, many prosecutors feel obliged to aggressively prosecute and charge narcotics law offenders.[7] In 2003, voters in Lake County (Michigan) went so far as to recall David Woodruff, their local prosecutor. Woodruff had come under intense criticism for negotiating a plea bargain with Daryl Dwayne Henderson, who had murdered his ex-girlfriend and shot her three-year-old son in the eye. Community members, particularly the victims' family, were outraged that Woodruff's deal had given Henderson a chance to spend only twenty-five years in prison.

THE PROSECUTOR AS CRIME FIGHTER

One of the reasons the prosecutor's post is a useful first step in a political career is that it is linked to crime fighting. Thanks to savvy public relations efforts and television police dramas such as *Law and Order*—with its opening line "In the criminal justice system, the people are represented by two separate yet equally important groups: the police who investigate crime and the district attorneys who prosecute the offenders"—prosecutors are generally seen as law enforcement agents. Indeed, the prosecutors and the police do have a symbiotic relationship. Prosecutors rely on police to arrest suspects and gather sufficient evidence, and police rely on prosecutors to convict those who have been apprehended.

Police-Prosecutor Conflict Despite, or perhaps because of, this mutual dependency, the relationship between the two branches of law enforcement is often strained. Part of this can be attributed to different backgrounds. Most prosecutors come from middle- or upper-class families, while police are often recruited from the working class. Furthermore, prosecutors are required to have a level of education that is not attained by most police officers.

More important, however, is a basic divergence in the concept of guilt. For a police officer, a suspect is guilty if he or she has in fact committed a crime. For a prosecutor, a suspect is guilty if enough evidence can be legally gathered to prove such guilt in a court of law.[8] In other words, police officers often focus on *factual guilt,* whereas prosecutors are ultimately concerned with *legal guilt.*[9] Thus, police officers will feel a great deal of frustration when a suspect they "know" to be guilty is set free. Similarly, a prosecutor may become annoyed when police officers do not follow the letter of the law in gathering evidence, thereby effectively ruining the chances of conviction.

Attempts at Cooperation   Tension arising from these grievances can hamper crime control efforts. As a result, a number of jurisdictions are trying to achieve better police-prosecutor relations. A key step in the process seems to be improving communications between the two groups. In San Diego, for example, the district attorney has a permanent office in the police department for the express purpose of counseling officers on legal questions. From the office, a deputy district attorney (DDA) acts as a human legal reference book, advising the police on how to write a search warrant, what steps they can take to help solidify a prosecutor's case, and other issues. The DDA will even sit in on morning briefings, giving updates on how changes in the law may affect police work.

ONLINE REVIEW *Go to the book's Web site for an interactive review of this section*

The Defense Attorney

The media provide most people's perception of defense counsel: the idealistic public defender who nobly serves the poor, the "ambulance chaser," or the celebrity attorney in the $3,000 suit. These stereotypes, though not entirely fictional, tend to obscure the crucial role that the **defense attorney** plays in the criminal justice system. Most persons charged with crimes have little or no knowledge of criminal procedure. Without assistance, they would be helpless against a government prosecutor. By acting as a staunch advocate for her or his client, the defense attorney (ideally) assures that the government proves every point against that client beyond a reasonable doubt, even for cases that do not go to trial. In sum, the defense attorney provides a counterweight against the state in our adversary system. (See the feature *CJ and Technology—The Myth of Fingerprints* on p. 294.)

Defense Attorney
The lawyer representing the defendant.

"Look at the stakes. In civil law, if you screw up, it's just money. Here, it's the client—his life, his time in jail—and you never know how much time people have in their life."
—Criminal defense attorney Stacey Richman (2001)

THE RESPONSIBILITIES OF THE DEFENSE ATTORNEY

The Sixth Amendment right to counsel is not limited to the actual criminal trial. In a number of instances, the United States Supreme Court has held that defendants are entitled to representation as soon as their rights may be denied, which, as we have seen, includes the custodial interrogation and lineup identification procedures.[10] Therefore, the primary responsibility of the defense attorney is to represent the defendant at the various stages of the custodial process, such as arrest, interrogation, lineup, and arraignment. Other responsibilities include:

> Investigating the incident for which the defendant has been charged.

> Communicating with the prosecutor, which includes negotiating plea bargains.

> Preparing the case for trial.

> Submitting defense motions, including motions to suppress evidence.

> Representing the defendant at trial.

> Negotiating a sentence, if the client has been convicted.

> Determining whether to appeal a guilty verdict.[11]

> **The Myth of Fingerprints**

For nearly a century, police and prosecutors have relied on fingerprints as a powerful tool to link suspects to crimes. Today, however, defense attorneys are challenging this traditional weapon of forensic science, saying that it is not really "scientific" at all.

When forensic scientists compare a fingerprint lifted from a crime scene and one taken from a suspect, they are looking for "points of similarity." Today, these experts will usually declare a match if there are between eight and sixteen points of similarity between the two samples. Many defense attorneys claim that this method is flawed. First, prints found at crime scenes tend to be incomplete, which means that examiners do not compare whole fingerprints but rather fragments of fingerprints. So, while it may be true that no two fingerprints are alike, it also may *not* be true that fragments of fingerprints are always similar or identical. Second, fingerprint evidence found at crime scenes requires treatment with chemicals or illumination with ultraviolet light to make it clear enough to work with. Is it scientifically acceptable to compare this "altered" print with a "clean" one obtained from a suspect in controlled circumstances?

Fingerprint misidentifications are rare, but not unheard of. In 1999, Richard Jackson was cleared of a murder conviction when it was found that three examiners had erroneously matched his fingerprints to those taken from the crime scene. Three years later, Louis H. Pollak, who presides over the U.S. District Court in Philadelphia, became the first judge to rule that fingerprint experts cannot testify that a suspect's prints "definitely" match those found at a crime scene. Although Pollak later reversed this decision, it provided the first hint that judges may begin to instruct

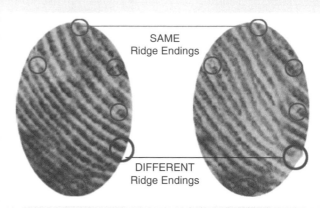

These two fingerprints were taken from different people. Still, they have five common points of similarity.

juries that fingerprint analysts are not scientists offering exact matches but expert witnesses giving opinions. This would give defense attorneys an opportunity to challenge these opinions.

In the Future

DNA testing, as we will see at the end of this chapter, may eventually do to fingerprinting what fingerprinting did to the Bertillon system, a nineteenth-century identification process that matched eleven bodily measurements, facial features, scars, tattoos, and birthmarks. In other words, DNA testing may make fingerprinting obsolete.

 For more information on fingerprinting and other CJ technologies, click on Web Links *under* Chapter Resources *at* www.cjinaction.com

THE PUBLIC DEFENDER

Public Defenders
Court-appointed attorneys who are paid by the state to represent defendants who are unable to hire private counsel.

Generally speaking, there are two different types of defense attorneys: (1) private attorneys, who are hired by individuals, and (2) **public defenders,** who work for the government. The distinction is not absolute, as many private attorneys hire out as public defenders, too. The modern role of the public defender was established by the Supreme Court's interpretation of the Sixth Amendment in *Gideon v. Wainwright* (1963).[12] As discussed in the previous chapter, the Court ruled that no defendant can be "assured a fair trial unless counsel is provided for him," and therefore the state must provide a public defender to those who cannot afford to hire one for themselves. Subsequently, the Court extended this protection to juveniles in *In re Gault* (1967)[13] and those faced with imprisonment for committing misdemeanors in *Argersinger v. Hamlin* (1972).[14] The impact of these decisions has been substantial: approximately three out of every four inmates in state prisons and jails were represented by publicly paid counsel.[15]

Defense Counsel Programs   In most areas, the county government is responsible for providing indigent defendants with attorneys. Three basic types of programs are used to allocate defense counsel:

1 *Assigned counsel programs,* in which local private attorneys are assigned clients on a case-by-case basis by the county.
2 *Contracting attorney programs,* in which a particular law firm or group of attorneys is hired to regularly assume the representative and administrative tasks of indigent defense (see Chapter 8).
3 *Public defender programs,* in which the county assembles a salaried staff of full-time or part-time attorneys and creates a public (taxpayer-funded) agency to provide the service.[16]

Jurisdictions can use several of these programs concurrently. In the most recent published survey, 63 percent of state court prosecutors' offices used assigned counsel, 29 percent contracted out their defense counsel, and 68 percent had public defender programs.[17]

Effectiveness of Public Defenders   As we saw in the last chapter, many observers believe that public defenders, assigned counsel, and contracted lawyers do not provide an acceptable level of defense to indigents. (When is a defendant indigent? See the feature *You Be the Judge—Indigent or Not?* on page 296.) Although there is certainly a great deal of anecdotal evidence to support this contention, statistics gathered by the U.S. Department of Justice seem to indicate that the outcome of a trial is not greatly affected by the private or public nature of the defense attorney. In federal courts, 92 percent of the defendants with public counsel and 91 percent of those with private counsel were found guilty either through a plea or at trial. Furthermore, if found guilty, those with private counsel were about 10 percent more likely to be sent to prison than those represented by public counsel, but defendants whose attorneys were provided by the state received sentences that were on average about four months less than their counterparts with private attorneys.[18]

THE ATTORNEY-CLIENT RELATIONSHIP

To defend a client effectively, a defense attorney must have access to all the facts concerning the case, including those that may be harmful to the defense. To promote the unrestrained flow of information between the two parties, laws of **attorney-client privilege** have been constructed. These laws require that communications between a client and his or her attorney be kept confidential, unless the client consents to disclosure. The scope of this privilege is not all encompassing, however. In *United States v. Zolin* (1989),[19] the Supreme Court ruled that attorneys may disclose the contents of a conversation with a client if the client has provided information concerning a crime that has yet to be committed.

The implied trust between an attorney and her or his client is not usually in question when the attorney has been hired directly by the defendant—as an "employee," the attorney well understands her or his duties. Relationships between public defenders and their clients, however, are often marred by suspicion on both sides. As Northwestern University's Jonathan D. Casper discovered while interviewing indigent defendants, many of them feel a certain amount of respect for the prosecutor. Like police officers, prosecutors are just "doing their

The National Association of Criminal Defense Lawyers represents more than ten thousand lawyers and advocates on a number of issues relating to the criminal justice system. To find its Web site, click on *Web Links* under *Chapter Resources* at www.cjinaction.com

Attorney-Client Privilege
A rule of evidence requiring that communications between a client and his or her attorney be kept confidential, unless the client consents to disclosure.

> Indigent or Not?

The Facts

Noel, a student at the University of Hawaii, was charged with driving under the influence of alcohol (DUI). Noel claimed that he did not have the resources to hire an attorney and asked the state to provide him with one. At the time he was arrested, Noel had $32 in his bank account and $1.50 in pocket money. He also had a 1971 Volkswagen sedan with a value of $1,000.

The Law

Hawaii law provided that an "indigent" person was entitled to free counsel if charged with an offense punishable by imprisonment for thirty days or more. (DUI in Hawaii carried a maximum penalty of one year in jail.)

Your Decision

The trial judge ruled that because Noel could have sold his car to get money for an attorney, he was not indigent under Hawaii's law. Do you agree?

[To see how the Hawaii Supreme Court ruled in this case, go to Example 9.1 in Appendix B.]

---

job" by trying to convict the defendant. In contrast, the defendants' view of their own attorneys can be summed up in the following exchange between Casper and a defendant:

> Did you have a lawyer when you went to court the next morning?
> No, I had a public defender.[20]

This attitude is somewhat understandable. Given the caseloads that most public defenders carry, they may have as little as five or ten minutes to spend with a client before appearing in front of a judge. How much, realistically, can a public defender learn about the defendant in that time?[21] Furthermore, the defendant is well aware that the public defender is being paid by the same source as the prosecutor and the judge. In 1998, "Unabomber" Ted Kaczynski acted on impulses felt by many defendants when he requested the right to defend himself, complaining that his public counsel was "supping from the same trough" as the prosecution.[22]

The situation handcuffs the public defenders as well. With so little time to spend on each case, they cannot validate the information provided by their clients. If the defendant says he or she has no prior offenses, the public defender often has no choice but to believe the client. Consequently, many public defenders later find that their clients have deceived them. In addition to the low pay and high pressures of the job, a client's lack of cooperation and disrespect can limit whatever satisfaction a public defender may find in the profession.[23]

ONLINE REVIEW *Go to the book's Web site for an interactive review of this section*

Truth, Victory, and the Adversary System

In strictly legal terms, three basic features characterize the **adversary system:**

1 A neutral and passive decision maker, either the judge or the jury.

2 The presentation of evidence from both parties.

3 A highly structured set of procedures (in the form of constitutional safeguards) that must be followed in the presentation of that evidence.[24]

GREAT **DEBATES**
One question that has troubled defense attorneys and legal ethicists is whether a lawyer has a duty to defend a client he or she knows to be guilty. To better understand the issues in this debate, click on *Great Debates* under *Book Resources* at www.cjinaction.com

Adversary System
A legal system in which the prosecution and defense are opponents, or adversaries, and present their cases in the light most favorable to themselves. The court arrives at a just solution based on the evidence presented by the contestants and determines who wins and who loses.

Some critics of the American court system believe that it has been tainted by overzealous prosecutors and defense attorneys. Gordon Van Kessel, a professor at Hastings College of Law in California, complains that American lawyers see themselves as "prize fighters, gladiators, or, more accurately, semantic warriors in a verbal battle," and bemoans the atmosphere of "ritualized aggression" that is endemic to the courts.[25]

Our discussion of the courtroom work group in the last chapter, however, seems to belie this image of "ritualized aggression." As political scientists Herbert Jacob and James Eisenstein have written, "pervasive conflict is not only unpleasant; it also makes work more difficult."[26] The image of the courtroom work group as "negotiators" rather than "prize fighters" seems to be supported by the fact that nine out of every ten cases conclude with negotiated "deals" rather than trials. Jerome Skolnick of the University of California at Berkeley has found that work group members grade each other according to "reasonableness"[27]—a concept criminal justice scholar Abraham S. Blumberg has embellished by labeling the defense attorney a "double agent." Because a defense attorney's main object is, Blumberg believes, to finish the case quickly so as to collect the fee and move on, these lawyers are likely to cooperate with the prosecutor in convincing a client to accept a negotiated plea of guilty.[28]

Perhaps, then, the most useful definition of the adversary process tempers Professor Van Kessel's criticism with the realities of the courtroom work group. University of California at Berkeley law professor Malcolm Feeley observes:

> In the adversary system the goal of the advocate is not to determine truth but to win, to maximize the interests of his or her side within the confines of the norms governing the proceedings. This is not to imply that the theory of the adversary process has no concern for the truth. Rather, the underlying assumption of the adversary process is that truth is most likely to emerge as a by-product of vigorous conflict between intensely partisan advocates, each of whose goal is to win.[29]

Blumberg takes a more cynical view when he calls the court process a "confidence game" in which "victory" is achieved when a defense attorney—with the implicit aid of the prosecutor and judge—is able to persuade the defendant to plead guilty.[30] As you read the rest of the chapter, which deals with pretrial procedures, keep in mind Feeley's and Blumberg's contentions concerning "truth" and "victory" in the American courts.

Pretrial Detention

After an arrest has been made, the first step toward determining the suspect's guilt or innocence is the **initial appearance** (for an overview of the entire process, see Figure 9.2 on the next page). During this brief proceeding, a magistrate (see Chapter 8) informs the defendant of the charges that have been brought against him or her and explains his or her constitutional rights—particularly, the right to remain silent (under the Fifth Amendment) and the right to be represented by counsel (under the Sixth Amendment). At this point, if the defendant cannot afford to hire a private attorney, a public defender may be appointed, or private counsel may be hired by the state to represent the defendant. As the U.S. Constitution does not specify how soon a defendant must be brought before a magistrate after arrest, it has been left to the judicial branch to determine the timing

Initial Appearance
An accused's first appearance before a judge or magistrate following arrest; during the appearance, the defendant is informed of the charges, advised of the right to counsel, told the amount of bail, and given a date for the preliminary hearing.

High-profile defense attorney Johnnie Cochran has represented a number of celebrities, including O. J. Simpson, Michael Jackson, and Sean "Puffy" Combs, and hosted a television show on CourtTV. What are some of the responsibilities of the defense attorney?

FIGURE 9.2
The Steps Leading to a Trial

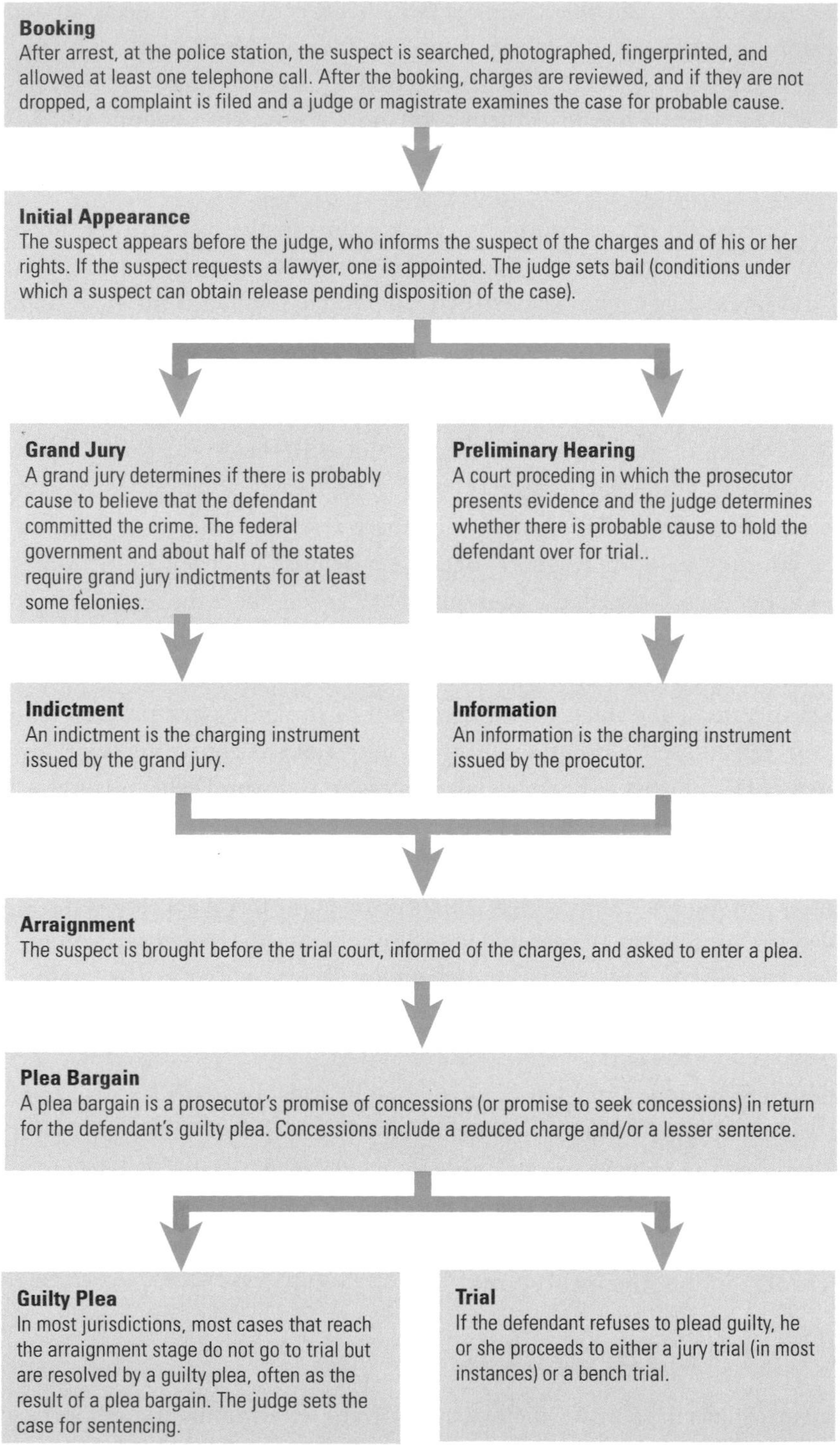

Booking
After arrest, at the police station, the suspect is searched, photographed, fingerprinted, and allowed at least one telephone call. After the booking, charges are reviewed, and if they are not dropped, a complaint is filed and a judge or magistrate examines the case for probable cause.

Initial Appearance
The suspect appears before the judge, who informs the suspect of the charges and of his or her rights. If the suspect requests a lawyer, one is appointed. The judge sets bail (conditions under which a suspect can obtain release pending disposition of the case).

Grand Jury
A grand jury determines if there is probably cause to believe that the defendant committed the crime. The federal government and about half of the states require grand jury indictments for at least some felonies.

Preliminary Hearing
A court proceeding in which the prosecutor presents evidence and the judge determines whether there is probable cause to hold the defendant over for trial..

Indictment
An indictment is the charging instrument issued by the grand jury.

Information
An information is the charging instrument issued by the proecutor.

Arraignment
The suspect is brought before the trial court, informed of the charges, and asked to enter a plea.

Plea Bargain
A plea bargain is a prosecutor's promise of concessions (or promise to seek concessions) in return for the defendant's guilty plea. Concessions include a reduced charge and/or a lesser sentence.

Guilty Plea
In most jurisdictions, most cases that reach the arraignment stage do not go to trial but are resolved by a guilty plea, often as the result of a plea bargain. The judge sets the case for sentencing.

Trial
If the defendant refuses to plead guilty, he or she proceeds to either a jury trial (in most instances) or a bench trial.

of the initial appearance. The Supreme Court has held that the initial appearance must occur "promptly," which in most cases means within forty-eight hours of booking.[31]

In misdemeanor cases, a defendant may decide to plead guilty and be sentenced during the initial appearance. Otherwise, the magistrate will usually release those charged with misdemeanors on their promise to return at a later date for further proceedings. For felony cases, however, the defendant is not permitted to make a plea at the initial appearance, because a magistrate's court does not have jurisdiction to decide felonies. Furthermore, in most cases the defendant will be released only if she or he posts **bail**—an amount of money paid by the defendant to the court and retained by the court until the defendant returns for further proceedings. Defendants who cannot afford bail are generally kept in a local jail or lockup until the date of their trial, though many jurisdictions are searching for alternatives to this practice because of overcrowded incarceration facilities.

THE PURPOSE OF BAIL

Bail is provided for under the Eighth Amendment. The amendment does not, however, guarantee the right to bail. Instead, it states that "excessive bail shall not be required." This has come to mean that in all cases except those involving a capital crime (where bail is prohibited), the amount of bail required must be reasonable compared with the seriousness of the wrongdoing. It *does not* mean that the amount of bail must be within the defendant's ability to pay.

The vagueness of the Eighth Amendment has encouraged a second purpose of bail: to protect the community from a defendant's committing another crime before trial. To achieve this purpose, a judge can simply set bail at a level the suspect cannot possibly afford. As we shall see, several states and the federal government have passed laws that allow judges to detain suspects deemed a threat to the community without going through the motions of setting relatively high bail.

SETTING BAIL

There is no uniform system for pretrial detention; each jurisdiction has its own *bail tariffs,* or general guidelines concerning the proper amount of bail. For misdemeanors, the police usually follow a preapproved bail schedule created by local judicial authorities. In felony cases, the primary responsibility to set bail lies with the judge. Figure 9.3 shows typical bail amounts for various offenses.

The Judge and Bail Setting Bail tariffs can be quite extensive. In Illinois, for example, a judge is required to take thirty-eight different factors into account when setting bail: fourteen involve the crime itself, two refer to the evidence gathered, four to the defendant's record, nine to the defendant's flight risk and immigration status, and nine to the defendant's general character.[32] For the most part, however, judges are free to use such tariffs as loose guidelines, and they have a great deal of discretion in setting bail according to the circumstances in each case.

Extralegal factors may also play a part in bail setting. University of New Orleans political scientist David W. Neubauer has identified three contexts that may influence a judge's decision-making process:[33]

1 *Uncertainty.* To a certain extent, predetermined bail tariffs are unrealistic, given that judges are required to set bail within forty-eight hours of arrest. It is often difficult to get information on the defendant in that period of time, and even if a judge can obtain a "rap sheet," or list of prior arrests ("priors"), she or he will probably not have an opportunity to verify its accuracy. Due to this uncertainty, most judges have no choice but to focus primarily on the seriousness of the crime in setting bail.

2 *Risk.* There is no way of knowing for certain whether a defendant released on bail will return for his or her court date, or whether he or she will commit a

Bail
The amount or conditions set by the court to ensure that an individual accused of a crime will appear for further criminal proceedings. If the accused person provides bail, whether in cash or by means of a bail bond, then she or he is released from jail.

FIGURE 9.3 Average Bail Amounts for Various Misdemeanors and Felonies
These figures represent the median bail figures for the seventy-five largest counties in the nation.

Offense	Median Bail Amount
Murder	$250,000
Rape	$30,000
Robbery	$25,000
Assault	$10,000
Weapons offense	$10,000
Burglary	$8,000
Drug offense	$7,500
Theft	$3,500

Source: Adapted from Bureau of Justice Statistics, *Federal Defendants In Large Urban Counties* (Washington, D.C.: U.S. Department of Justice, November 2001), Table 16, page 18.

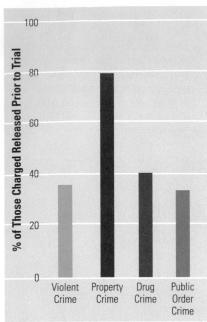

FIGURE 9.4
The Likelihood of Pretrial Release

Source: Adapted from Bureau of Justice Statistics, *Compendium of Federal Justice Statistics, 2000* (Washington, D.C.: U.S. Department of Justice, 2002), 41, 43.

See the `Professional Bail Agents of the United States` for a wealth of information about how bail bondspersons operate. Find its Web site by clicking on *Web Links* under *Chapter Resources* at www.cjinaction.com

crime while free. Judges are aware of the criticism they will come under from police groups, prosecutors, the press, and the public if a crime is committed during that time. Consequently, especially if she or he is up for reelection, a judge may prefer to "play it safe" and set a high bail to detain a suspect or refuse outright to offer bail when legally able to do so. In general, risk aversion also dictates why those who have committed violent crimes are less likely to be released prior to trial than those who have committed property crimes (see Figure 9.4). In the minds of many judges, someone who is under suspicion of stealing a television is much less of a risk than someone who is under suspicion of murder.

3 *Overcrowded jails.* As we will discuss in detail in Chapter 13, many of the nation's jails are overcrowded. This may force a judge to make a difficult distinction between those suspects she or he believes must be detained and those who might need to be detained. To save jail space, a judge might be more lenient in setting bail for members of the latter group.[34]

Prosecutors, Defense Attorneys, and Bail Setting   Though the judge has ultimate discretion in setting bail, the prosecutor and, to a lesser extent, the defense attorney can influence his or her decision. If the two sides disagree on the question of bail, a judge will usually side with the prosecutor. In many cases, given the uncertainty mentioned above, a trusted prosecutor can be a useful source of information for the judge. A hearing in Brigham City, Utah, provides a fairly typical example of the extent of the adversary process in determining pretrial detention. The defense attorney for a man charged with rape and sexual abuse asserted that his client was not a risk to the community. The prosecutor countered that the defendant had been accused of an average of one sexual offense every ten days over a three-month period. Not surprisingly, the judge denied bail.

Defense attorneys have a number of incentives for wanting their clients to be free on bail before a trial. A defendant who shows that she or he can function in the community without committing any further crimes may reduce the chances of conviction or at least impress on the judge the feasibility of a lighter sentence. Furthermore, a defendant on bail is able to assist in the preparation for her or his defense by helping to gather evidence and personally steering the defense attorney toward favorable witnesses. Finally, a client free on bail is more likely to be able to earn income to pay legal bills.

The Benefits of Bail   In a classic study of Philadelphia conviction rates, legal scholar Caleb Foote found that 67 percent of those suspected of violent crimes who had been released on bail were acquitted, compared to 25 percent of those who had been jailed before their trials.[35] Additional research in Philadelphia by Temple University professor of criminal justice John Goldkamp showed that convicted offenders who had been denied bail were more likely to go to prison than to receive a less severe sentence.[36] (Critics of these studies point out, though, that none of them controlled completely for the fact that those not released on bail were likely to be more violent and to have more extensive prior criminal records than those granted bail.)

Given these benefits, one would think that defense attorneys would fight vigorously for low bail for their clients. This is not the case, however. Most courtroom work groups establish "rules of the game" that determine the levels at which bail will be set for particular crimes, and judges, prosecutors, and defense attorneys do not spend a great deal of time contesting the matter.[37]

GAINING PRETRIAL RELEASE

Earlier, we mentioned that many jurisdictions are looking for alternatives to the bail system. One of the most popular options is **release on recognizance (ROR).** This is used when the judge, based on the advice of trained personnel, decides that the defendant is not at risk to "jump" bail and does not pose a threat to the community. The defendant is then released at no cost with the understanding that he or she will return at the time of the trial. The Vera Institute, a nonprofit organization in New York City, introduced the concept of ROR as part of the Manhattan Bail Project in the 1960s, and such programs are now found in nearly every jurisdiction. When properly administered, ROR programs seem to be successful, with less than 5 percent of the participants failing to show for trial.[38]

Posting Bail   Those suspected of committing a felony are, however, rarely released on recognizance. These defendants may post, or pay, the full amount of the bail in cash to the court. The money will be returned when the suspect appears for trial. Given the large sums involved, and the relative lack of wealth of many criminal defendants, a defendant can rarely post bail in cash. Another option is to use personal property as collateral. These *property bonds* are also rare because most courts require property valued at double the bail amount. Thus, if bail is set at $5,000, the defendant (or the defendant's family and friends) will have to produce a piece of property valued at $10,000.

Bail Bondspersons   If unable to post bail with cash or property, a defendant may arrange for a **bail bondsperson** to post a bail bond on the defendant's behalf. The bondsperson, in effect, promises the court that he or she will turn over to the court the full amount of bail if the defendant fails to return for further proceedings. The defendant usually must give the bondsperson a certain percentage of the bail (often 10 percent) in cash. This amount, which is often not returned to the defendant later, is considered payment for the bondsperson's assistance and assumption of risk. Depending on the amount of the bail bond, the defendant may also be required to sign over to the bondsperson rights to certain property (such as a car, a valuable watch, or other asset) as security for the bond.

Although bail bondspersons obviously provide a service for which there is demand, several states have abolished bail bonding for profit. The rationale for such reform focuses on two perceived problems with the practice.[39]

1 Bail bondspersons provide opportunities for corruption, as they may bribe officials who set bail (police, and so on) to inflate the bail.

2 Because they can refuse to post a bail bond, bail bondspersons are, in essence, making a business decision concerning a suspect's pretrial release. This is considered the responsibility of a judge, not a private individual with a profit motive.[40]

The states that have banned bail bondspersons have established an alternative known as **ten percent cash bail.** This process, pioneered in Chicago in the

Release on Recognizance (ROR)
A judge's order that releases an accused from jail with the understanding that he or she will return for further proceedings of his or her own will; used instead of setting a monetary bond.

Bail Bondsperson
A businessperson who agrees, for a fee, to pay the bail amount if the accused fails to appear in court as ordered.

Ten Percent Cash Bail
An alternative to traditional bail in which defendants may gain pretrial release by posting 10 percent of their bond amount to the court instead of seeking a bail bondsperson.

Beau Cabell, The Macon Telegraph

In Macon, Georgia, bounty hunter Cedric Miller takes aim at Stan Bernard Rouse. Miller, a former Macon narcotics cop, is often paid substantial sums by bail bondspeople to capture bond-jumping clients.

INFOTRAC KEYWORDS

bail bondsmen, bounty hunters

For more information, use these search terms with InfoTrac College Edition, your online library at www.infotrac-college.com

early 1960s, requires the court, in effect, to take the place of the bonds-person. An officer of the court will accept a deposit of 10 percent of the bail amount, refundable when the defendant appears at the assigned time.[41] A number of jurisdictions allow for both bail bondspersons and ten percent cash bail, with the judge deciding whether a defendant is eligible for the latter.

Bounty Hunters Supreme Court Justice Robert Jackson once called the possibility that an accused person would not return to face trial "a calculated risk which the law takes as the price of our system of justice."[42] This risk is often taken by bail bondspersons, who suffer a monetary loss if a suspect skips bail. To protect their financial interests, bail bondspersons sometimes hire a *bounty hunter* to retrieve a client who has skipped bail. Under a Supreme Court decision issued in 1873, bounty hunters have almost unlimited power to apprehend someone who has signed a bail contract, including imprisoning the fugitive and breaking and entering into his or her house.[43]

Despite the police powers involved, bounty hunting is essentially unregulated in most of the United States. In Virginia, for example, of the 34,233 registered bounty hunters, 464 have criminal records. This became an issue in 2002 when ex-felon bounty hunter James Howard Dickerson broke down the wrong door and wound up killing the wrong man.[44] Because a bondsperson can recover a bond by providing the court with the defendant's death certificate, bounty hunters would seem to have an incentive to use any means necessary, including violent ones, to catch fugitives.

BAIL REFORM AND PREVENTIVE DETENTION

Release on recognizance programs and ten percent cash bail were the result of a movement in the 1960s to reform the bail system. As various researchers produced empirical proof that pretrial detention increased the odds of conviction and led to longer sentences, reformers began to point out that this created an imbalance of justice between the wealthy and the poor.[45] Those who could afford to post bail were convicted less frequently and spent less time in jail than those who could not. Furthermore, the conditions in pretrial detention centers were considerably worse than the conditions in prison, and the cost of maintaining these centers was becoming prohibitive.

The Bail Reform Acts In response to these concerns, Congress passed the Bail Reform Act of 1966.[46] Though the new law did not place statutory restrictions on the discretionary powers of federal judges, it did strongly suggest that judges implement a wide range of "conditions of release" for suspects who qualified.[47]

The Bail Reform Act of 1966 was criticized for concentrating on ways of increasing pretrial release, while failing to give judges the ability to detain suspects who posed a danger to the community.[48] Although judges have always had the *de*

> Innocent on Bail?

Sylvia Hernandez was stabbed to death in Austin, Texas, by Leonard Saldana, her common law husband. Saldana, it turned out, had been arrested a month earlier for violating a court order to keep away from Hernandez. He had been jailed nineteen times in ten years, including four times for assaults involving domestic violence and once for violating a protective court order concerning a different woman. When he murdered Hernandez, Saldana was free on $4,000 bail.

In retrospect, Saldana should not have been released for such a small amount, given his background. Concern over such situations has convinced three-fifths of the states and the federal government to pass laws that allow judges to confine suspects before trial without bail if there is a threat of harm to the community. Civil libertarians, however, believe such preventive detention laws unjustly sacrifice the individual's right to be presumed innocent to a generally unsubstantiated government interest in pretrial detention. Supreme Court Justice Thurgood Marshall, in his dissent in the case in which the Bail Reform Act of 1984 was upheld, wrote that the denial of due process in such judicial decisions was "consistent with the usage of tyranny and the excesses of what bitter experience teaches us to call the police state."

The main criticism of preventive detention is that it presumes a certain ability to predict future criminal activity on the basis of past activity (a presumption that is usually not allowed in criminal trials). Criminologist Charles Ewing has concluded that statistical predictions about violent criminal behavior are "much more likely to be wrong than right." Some observers believe preventive detention will be used indiscriminately by judges who do not want to risk being criticized for freeing a suspect who goes on to commit a crime while out on bail. Furthermore, though it is possible to measure how many suspects eligible to be detained under these laws committed violent crimes after being released, it is not possible to determine how many of those who *were* detained would *not* have committed crimes if freed.

FOR CRITICAL ANALYSIS
Given the relatively low rate of criminal activity by suspects who have been released pending trial, are preventive detention laws justified?

---

facto power to do just that by setting prohibitively high bails for dangerous defendants, thirty states have passed **preventive detention** laws that allow judges to deny bail to suspects with prior records of violence or nonappearance for trial. The Bail Reform Act of 1984 similarly states that federal offenders can be held without bail to assure "the safety of any other person and the community."[49]

The Constitutionality of Bail Critics of the 1984 act believe that it violates the U.S. Constitution by allowing the freedom of a citizen to be restricted before he or she has been proved guilty in a court of law. For many, the act also brings up the troubling issue of *false positives*—erroneous predictions that defendants, if given pretrial release, would commit a crime, when in fact they would not. (See the feature *CJ in Focus—The Balancing Act: Innocent on Bail?*.) In *United States v. Salerno* (1987),[50] however, the Supreme Court upheld the act's premise. Chief Justice William Rehnquist wrote that preventive detention was not a "punishment for dangerous individuals" but a "potential solution to a pressing social problem." Therefore, "there is no doubt that preventing danger to the community is a legitimate . . . goal." In fact, about 16 percent of released defendants are rearrested before their trials begin, 3 percent for violent felonies.[51]

Preventive Detention
The retention of an accused person in custody due to fears that she or he will commit a crime if released before trial.

ONLINE REVIEW *Go to the book's Web site for an interactive review of this section*

Establishing Probable Cause

Once the initial appearance has been completed and bail has been set, the prosecutor must establish *probable cause;* that is, the prosecutor must prove that a crime was committed and link the defendant to that crime. There are two formal

INFOTRAC KEYWORDS
probable cause
For more information, use this search term with InfoTrac College Edition, your online library at www.infotrac-college.com

procedures for establishing probable cause at this stage of the pretrial process: preliminary hearings and grand juries.

THE PRELIMINARY HEARING

During the **preliminary hearing,** the defendant appears before a judge or magistrate who decides whether the evidence presented is sufficient for the case to proceed to trial. Normally, every person charged by warrant has a right to this hearing within a reasonable amount of time after his or her initial arrest[52]—typically, no later than ten days if the defendant is in custody or within thirty days if he or she has gained pretrial release.

The Preliminary Hearing Process The preliminary hearing is conducted in the manner of a mini-trial. Typically, a police report of the arrest is presented by a law enforcement officer, supplemented with evidence provided by the prosecutor. Because the burden of proving probable cause is relatively light (compared to proving guilt beyond a reasonable doubt), prosecutors rarely call witnesses during the preliminary hearing, saving them for the trial. During this hearing, the defendant has a right to be represented by counsel, who may cross-examine witnesses and challenge any evidence offered by the prosecutor. In most states, defense attorneys can take advantage of the preliminary hearing to begin the process of **discovery,** in which they are entitled to have access to any evidence in the possession of the prosecution relating to the case. Discovery is considered a keystone in the adversary process, as it allows the defense to see the evidence against the defendant prior to making a plea.

Waiving the Hearing The preliminary hearing often seems rather perfunctory, although in some jurisdictions it replaces grand jury proceedings. It usually lasts no longer than five minutes, and the judge or magistrate rarely finds that probable cause does not exist. In one study, only 2 percent of the cases were dismissed by the judicial official at this stage in the process.[53] For this reason, defense attorneys commonly advise their clients to waive their right to a preliminary hearing. Once a judge has ruled affirmatively on probable cause, the defendant is bound over to the grand jury in many jurisdictions. If the grand jury believes there are grounds for a trial, it issues an *indictment.* In other jurisdictions, the government prosecutor issues an **information,** which replaces the police complaint as the formal charge against the defendant for the purposes of a trial.

THE GRAND JURY

The federal government and about half of the states require a grand jury to make the decision as to whether a case should go to trial. A **grand jury** is a group of citizens called to decide whether probable cause exists. Grand juries are *impaneled,* or created, for a period of time usually not exceeding three months. During that time, the grand jury sits in closed (secret) session and hears only evidence presented by the prosecutor—the defendant cannot present evidence at this hearing. The prosecutor presents to the grand jury whatever evidence the state has against the defendant, including photographs, documents, tangible objects, the testimony of witnesses, and other items. If the grand jury finds that probable cause exists, it issues an **indictment** against the defendant. Like an information in a preliminary hearing, the indictment becomes the formal charge against the defendant. As Figure 9.5 shows, some states require a grand jury to indict for certain crimes, while in other states a grand jury indictment is optional.

The "Shield" and the "Sword"   The grand jury has a long history in the United States, having been brought over from England by the colonists and codified in the Fifth Amendment to the U.S. Constitution. Historically, it has been seen to act as both a "shield" and a "sword" in the criminal justice process. By giving citizens the chance to review government charges of wrongdoing, it "shields" the individual from the power of the state. At the same time, the grand jury offers the government a "sword"—the opportunity to provide evidence against the accused—in its efforts to fight crime and protect society.[54]

A "Rubber Stamp"   Today, the protective function of the grand jury is in doubt—critics say that the "sword" aspect works too well and the "shield" aspect not at all. Statistically, the grand jury is even more prosecutor friendly than the preliminary hearing. Defendants are indicted at a rate of more than 99 percent,[55] leading to the common characterization of the grand jury as little more than a "rubber stamp" for the prosecution. Certainly, the procedural rules of the grand jury favor prosecutors. The exclusionary rule (see Chapter 7) does not apply in grand jury investigations, so prosecutors can present evidence that would be disallowed at any subsequent trial. Furthermore, because the grand jury is given only one version of the facts—the prosecution's—it is likely to find probable cause. In the words of one observer, a grand jury would indict a "ham sandwich" if the government asked it to do so.[56] As a result of these concerns, more than half of the jurisdictions have abolished grand juries.

ONLINE REVIEW *Go to the book's Web site for an interactive review of this section*

FIGURE 9.5
State Grand Jury Requirements

As you can see, in some states a grand jury indictment is required to charge an individual with a crime, while in others it is either optional or prohibited. When a grand jury is not used, the discretion of whether to charge or not is left to the prosecutor, who must then present his or her argument at the preliminary hearing (discussed earlier in the chapter).

Source: Bureau of Justice Statistics, *State Court Organization 1998* (Washington, D.C.: U.S. Department of Justice, June 2000), 283–285.

The Prosecutorial Screening Process

Some observers see the high government success rates in pretrial proceedings as proof that prosecutors successfully screen out weak cases before they get to a grand jury or preliminary hearing. If, however, grand juries have indeed abandoned their traditional duties in favor of "rubber stamping" most cases set in front of them, and preliminary hearings are little better, what is to keep prosecutors from using their charging powers indiscriminately?

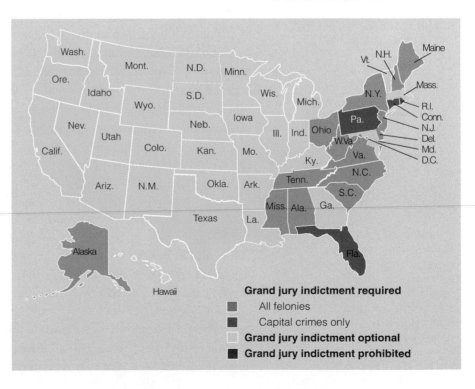

Grand jury indictment required
All felonies
Capital crimes only
Grand jury indictment optional
Grand jury indictment prohibited

> Japan's All-Powerful Prosecutors

Prosecutors in the United States are generally believed to have a great deal of charging discretion. The discretionary power of American prosecutors, however, does not equal that of their Japanese counterparts. With the ability to "cherry pick" their cases, prosecutors in Japan routinely have annual conviction rates of over 99.9 percent.

The "Confession Mill"

One observer described the Japanese courts as a "confession mill." Unlike the American system, Japan has no arraignment procedure during which the accused can plead guilty or innocent. Instead, the focus of the Japanese criminal justice system is on extracting confessions of guilt: police can hold and question suspects for up to twenty-three days without pressing charges. Furthermore, the suspect has no absolute right to counsel during the interrogation, and police are often able to get confessions that make for open-and-shut convictions. The prosecutor also has the "benevolent" discretion to drop the case altogether if the suspect expresses remorse.

The extraordinarily high conviction rate is also a product of Japanese culture. To fail in an attempt to convict results in a loss of face, not only for the individual prosecutor but also for the court system as a whole. The Japanese Justice Ministry

estimates that, to avoid the risk of losing, prosecutors decline to press charges against 35 percent of indictable suspects each year. Japanese judges—there are no juries—contribute to the high conviction rate by rarely questioning the manner in which prosecutors obtain confessions.

No Plea Bargaining

Interestingly, given the amount of prosecutorial discretion, the Japanese criminal justice system does not allow for plea bargaining. The Japanese see the practice of "trading" a guilty plea for a lesser sentence as counterproductive, as a defendant may be tempted to confess to crimes she or he did not commit if the prosecution has a strong case. For the Japanese, a confession extracted after twenty-three days of interrogation may be "voluntary," but a confession gained through a promise of leniency is "forced" and therefore in conflict with the system's goals of truth seeking and accuracy.

FOR CRITICAL ANALYSIS

Explain the fundamental differences between the American and Japanese criminal justice systems. Do you think the lack of a comparable adversarial system weakens or strengthens the Japanese system in comparison with the American one?

Nothing, say many observers. Once the police have initially charged a defendant with committing a crime, the prosecutor can prosecute the case as it stands, reduce or increase the initial charge, file additional charges, or dismiss the case. In a system of government and law that relies on checks and balances, asked legal expert Kenneth Culp Davis, why should the prosecutor be "immune to review by other officials and immune to review by the courts?"[57] (For even more powerful prosecutors, see the feature *International CJ—Japan's All-Powerful Prosecutors.*)

Though American prosecutors have far-ranging discretionary charging powers, it is not entirely correct to say that they are unrestricted. Controls are indirect and informal, but they do exist.

CASE ATTRITION

Case Attrition
The process through which prosecutors, by deciding whether or not to prosecute each person arrested, effect an overall reduction in the number of persons prosecuted. As a result, the number of persons convicted and sentenced is much smaller than the number of persons arrested.

Prosecutorial discretion includes the power *not* to prosecute cases. Figure 9.6 depicts the average outcomes of one hundred felony arrests in the United States. As you can see, of the sixty-five adult arrestees brought before the district attorney, only thirty-five were prosecuted, and only eighteen of these prosecutions led to incarceration. Consequently, only one in three and a half adults arrested for a felony sees the inside of a prison or jail cell. This phenomenon is known as **case attrition,** and it is explained in part by prosecutorial discretion.

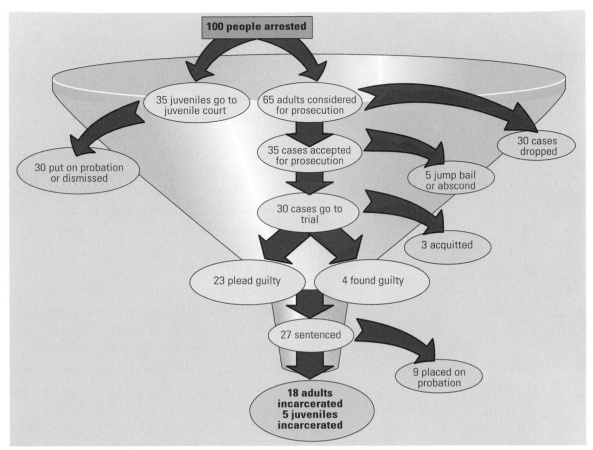

FIGURE 9.6
Following One Hundred Felony Arrests: The Criminal Justice Funnel
Source: Brian Reaves and Pheny Smith, *Felony Defendants in Large Urban Counties, 1992* (Washington D.C.: Bureau of Justice Statistics, 1995).

About half of those adult felony cases brought to prosecutors by police are dismissed through a *nolle prosequi*. Why are these cases "nolled," or not prosecuted by the district attorney? In the section on law enforcement, you learned that the police do not have the resources to arrest every lawbreaker in the nation. Similarly, district attorneys do not have the resources to prosecute every arrest. They must choose how to distribute their scarce resources. In some cases, the decision is made for them, such as when police break procedural law and negate important evidence. This happens rarely—less than 1 percent of felony arrests are dropped because of the exclusionary rule, and almost all of these are the result of illegal drug searches.[58]

The Screening Process   Most prosecutors have a *screening process* for deciding when to prosecute and when to "noll." This process varies a bit from jurisdiction to jurisdiction, but most prosecutors consider several factors in making the decision:

> The most important factor in deciding whether to prosecute is not the prosecutor's belief in the guilt of the suspect, but whether there is *sufficient evidence for conviction*.[59] If prosecutors have strong physical evidence and a number of reliable and believable witnesses, they are quite likely to prosecute.

> Prosecutors also tend to establish *case priorities*. In other words, everything else being equal, a district attorney will prosecute a rapist instead of a jaywalker because the former presents a greater threat to society than does the latter. A prosecutor will also be more likely to prosecute someone with an extensive record of wrongdoing than a first-time offender. Often, in coordination with the

"Let me tell you, you can paint pictures and get people indicted for just about anything."
—Alfonse D'Amato, former U.S. senator from New York (1996)

Jimmy "Spunk" Williams, pictured here at his attorney's office in Akron, Ohio, with his girlfriend and stepson, spent ten years in prison after being convicted of raping a twelve-year-old girl. In 2001, however, the girl admitted that she had never seen her attacker's face and recanted her identification of Williams. Following his release in 2003, Williams agreed to a $750,000 settlement—the largest wrongful conviction award ever paid by the state of Ohio.

police, a district attorney's office will target a single area of crime, such as drug use or drunk driving.

> Sometimes a case is dropped even when it involves a serious crime and a wealth of evidence exists against the suspect. These situations usually involve *uncooperative victims.* For example, violent offenses committed by one member of a family against another member are difficult to prosecute because the victim is often unwilling to cooperate. Despite legislative and law enforcement attempts to protect victims of domestic violence (discussed at more length in Chapter 5), prosecutors are three times more likely to drop charges after arrests for intrafamily violence than for violence between strangers.[60]

> *Unreliability of victims* can also affect a charging decision. If the victim in a rape case is a crack addict and a prostitute, while the defendant is the chief executive officer of a large corporation, prosecutors may be hesitant to have a jury decide which one is more trustworthy.

> A prosecutor may be willing to drop a case, or reduce the charges, against a *defendant who is willing to testify against other offenders.* In New Jersey, for example, prosecutors are allowed to waive mandatory sentencing laws for low-level drug traffickers who agree to "snitch," or give the police information on major narcotics suppliers.[61]

In some circumstances, a prosecutor's most difficult task is finding a law under which to bring charges. In 2002, Herbert E. Franklin, the district attorney in Walker County, Georgia, had to decide what to do about Ray Brent Marsh, the operator of the Tri-State Crematory. Over a span of two decades, Marsh had dumped more than 330 bodies on the grounds of his property rather than cremating them as he had been paid to do. As the law does not provide a serious penalty for "desecration of corpses," Franklin had no choice but to file 787 lesser fraud charges against Marsh, hoping that the accumulated weight of these actions would satisfy public anger.[62]

Postconviction Prosecutorial Action   Occasionally, prosecutors will reopen a case in which they won a guilty verdict if new evidence indicates that the initial ruling was incorrect. In most instances, a district attorney's office is pressured to review a case by defense attorneys who have found new evidence such as a new witness or mistakes by the police officers who investigated the crime. In the past five years, DNA evidence has been used to correct a number of wrongful convictions. In 2002, the Ramsey County (Minnesota) district attorney's office vacated a rape conviction after DNA testing showed that the wrong man had been convicted. This was the first time that the initial action to review a case based on DNA evidence came from the prosecution rather than the defense.63 (For more information on how DNA testing has changed the criminal justice system, see the *Criminal Justice in Action* feature at the end of this chapter.)

PROSECUTORIAL CHARGING AND THE DEFENSE ATTORNEY

For the most part, there is little the defense attorney can do when the prosecutor decides to charge a client. If a defense attorney feels strongly that the charge has been made in violation of the defendant's rights, he or she can, however, submit *pretrial motions* to the court requesting that a particular action be taken to protect his or her client. Pretrial motions include the following:

1 Motions to suppress evidence gained illegally.

2 Motions for a change of venue because the defendant cannot receive a fair trial in the original jurisdiction.

3 Motions to invalidate a search warrant.

4 Motions to dismiss the case because of a delay in bringing it to trial.

5 Motions to obtain evidence that the prosecution may be withholding.

As we shall soon see, defense attorneys sometimes use these pretrial motions to pressure the prosecution into offering a favorable deal for their client.

↗ ONLINE REVIEW *Go to the book's Web site for an interactive review of this section*

Arraignment
A court proceeding in which the suspect is formally charged with the criminal offense stated in the indictment. The suspect enters a plea (guilty, not guilty, *nolo contendere*) in response.

Nolo Contendere
Latin for "I will not contest it." A criminal defendant's plea, in which he or she chooses not to challenge, or contest, the charges brought by the government. Although the defendant may still be sentenced or fined, the plea neither admits nor denies guilt.

Pleading Guilty

Based on the information (delivered during the preliminary hearing) or indictment (handed down by the grand jury), the prosecutor submits a motion to the court to order the defendant to appear before the trial court for an **arraignment.** Due process of law, as guaranteed by the Fifth Amendment, requires that a criminal defendant be informed of the charges brought against her or him and be offered an opportunity to respond to those charges. The arraignment is one of the ways in which due process requirements are satisfied by criminal procedure law.

At the arraignment, the defendant is informed of the charges and must respond by pleading not guilty or guilty. In some but not all states, the defendant may also enter a plea of ***nolo contendere,*** which is Latin for "I will not contest it." The plea of *nolo contendere* is neither an admission nor a denial of guilt. (The con-

Sara Jane Olson, left, in a Sacramento, California, courtroom. In 2003, Olson, a former member of the Symbionese Liberation Army, was sentenced to six years in prison after pleading guilty to being involved in a 1975 murder carried out by other members of the group. Olson later told reporters that she was innocent of the charges but had made "a deal" to avoid a possible life sentence if found guilty at trial.

sequences for someone who pleads guilty and for someone who pleads *nolo contendere* are the same in a criminal trial, but the latter plea cannot be used in a subsequent civil trial as an admission of guilt.) Most frequently, the defendant pleads guilty to the initial charge or to a lesser charge that has been agreed on through *plea bargaining* between the prosecutor and defendant. If the defendant pleads guilty, no trial is necessary, and the defendant is sentenced based on the crime he or she has admitted committing.

Photo by Justin Sullivan/Getty Images

PLEA BARGAINING IN THE CRIMINAL JUSTICE SYSTEM

Plea Bargaining
The process by which the accused and the prosecutor work out a mutually satisfactory conclusion to the case, subject to court approval. Usually, plea bargaining involves the defendant's pleading guilty to a lesser offense in return for a lighter sentence.

Plea bargaining usually takes place after the arraignment and before the beginning of the trial. In its simplest terms, it is a process by which the accused, represented by the defense counsel, and the prosecutor work out a mutually satisfactory disposition of the case, subject to court approval. Plea bargaining agreements can have several different forms:

> *Charge bargaining.* In charge bargaining, the defendant pleads guilty in exchange for a reduction of the charges. A felony burglary charge, for example, could be reduced to the lesser offense of breaking and entering. The more serious the initial charge, the more an accused has to gain by bargaining: pleading guilty to second degree murder can save the defendant from the risk of being convicted of first degree murder, which carries the death penalty in some states.

> *Sentence bargaining.* In sentence bargaining, the defendant pleads guilty in exchange for a lighter sentence, which may include a shorter prison term or probation. In most jurisdictions, the judge makes the final decision on whether to accept this agreement; the prosecutor can only recommend a lighter sentence. The prosecutor may also suggest that the defendant be placed in a counseling program, such as a drug rehabilitation center, in return for the guilty plea.

> *Count bargaining.* A person can be charged with multiple counts, either for committing multiple crimes or for different aspects of a single incident. A person who goes on a killing spree that results in seven deaths, for example, would be charged with seven counts of first degree murder. A person who breaks into a home, sexually assaults the inhabitants, and then takes their credit cards could be charged with counts of rape, aggravated burglary, misdemeanor theft, felony theft, and criminal use of a credit card. In count bargaining, a defendant pleads guilty in exchange for a reduction in the counts against him or her.

In a sense, count bargaining is a form of sentence bargaining. If a person is convicted of multiple counts, her or his prison time is calculated by combining the attendant sentence of each count (which is why some criminals are sentenced to a seemingly ridiculously long prison term, well past their life expectancy). If a count is dropped, so is the prison time that goes with it.

In *Santobello v. New York* (1971),[64] the Supreme Court held that plea bargaining "is not only an essential part of the process but a highly desirable part for many reasons." Many observers would agree, but with ambivalence. They understand that plea bargaining offers the practical benefit of saving court resources, but question whether it is the best way to achieve justice.[65] Given the pressures placed on the court system, many participants conclude that plea bargaining is, in fact, an ethically acceptable means of determining the defendant's fate.

INFOTRAC KEYWORDS
plea bargaining
For more information, use this search term with InfoTrac College Edition, your online library at www.infotrac-college.com

MOTIVATIONS FOR PLEA BARGAINING

Given the high rate of plea bargaining—see Figure 9.7 on the following page—it follows that the prosecutor, defense attorney, and defendant each have strong reasons to engage in the practice.

Prosecutors and Plea Bargaining In most cases, a prosecutor has a single goal after charging a defendant with a crime: conviction. If a case goes to trial, no matter how certain a prosecutor may be that a defendant is guilty, there is always a chance that a jury or judge will disagree. Plea

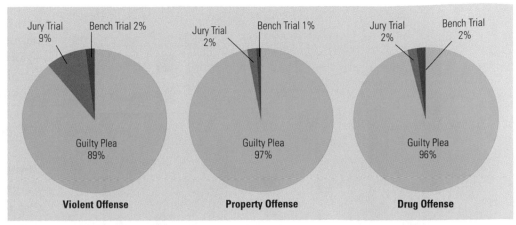

FIGURE 9.7
Rates of Plea Bargaining
As you can see, most convictions are gained when the defendant pleads guilty. The numbers used here refer to convictions in cases terminating in federal courts between October 1, 1999, and September 30, 2000.
Source: Bureau of Justice Statistics, *State Court Sentencing of Convicted Felons, 2000* (Washington, D.C.: U.S. Department of Justice, June 2003), Table 4.2, page 43.

bargaining removes this risk. Furthermore, the prosecutorial screening process described earlier in the chapter is not infallible. Sometimes, a prosecutor will find that the evidence against the accused is weaker than first thought or will uncover new information that changes the complexion of the case. In these situations, the prosecutor may decide to drop the charges or, if he or she still feels that the defendant is guilty, turn to plea bargaining to "save" a questionable case.

The prosecutor's role as an administrator also comes into play. She or he may be interested in the quickest, most efficient manner to dispose of caseloads, and plea bargains reduce the time and money spent on each case. Personal philosophy can affect the proceedings as well. A prosecutor who feels that a mandatory minimum sentence for a particular crime, such as marijuana possession, is too strict may plea bargain in order to lessen the penalty. Similarly, some prosecutors will consider plea bargaining only in certain instances—for burglary and theft, for example, but not for more serious felonies such as rape and murder.[66]

Defense Attorneys and Plea Bargaining Political scientist Milton Heumann has said that the most important thing that a defense attorney learns is that "most of his clients are guilty."[67] Given this stark reality, favorable plea bargains are often the best a defense attorney can do for clients, aside from helping them to gain acquittals. Some have suggested that defense attorneys have other, less savory motives for convincing a client to plead guilty, such as a desire to increase profit margins by quickly disposing of cases[68] or a wish to ingratiate themselves with the other members of the courtroom work group by showing their "reasonableness."[69] In other cases, a defense attorney may want to go to trial, even though it is *not* in the client's best interest, to win publicity or gain work experience.[70]

Defendants and Plea Bargaining The plea bargain allows the defendant a measure of control over his or her fate. When John Walker Lindh accepted the deal offered by the federal government, as discussed in the introduction to this chapter, he guaranteed that he would be a free man at the relatively young age of forty years, rather than risking a life in prison. The benefits of plea bargaining are tangible. As Figure 9.8 on p. 312 shows, defendants who plea bargain receive significantly lighter sentences on average than those who are found guilty at trial.

PLEA BARGAINING AND THE ADVERSARY SYSTEM

One criticism of plea bargaining is that it subverts the adversary system, the goal of which is to determine innocence or guilt. Although plea bargaining does value

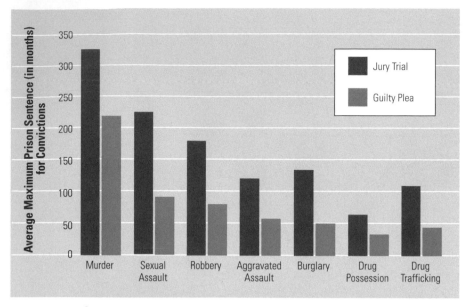

FIGURE 9.8 Sentencing Outcomes for Guilty Pleas

Source: Adapted from Bureau of Justice Statistics, *State Court Sentencing of Convicted Felons, 2000* (Washington, D.C.: U.S. Department of Justice, June 2003), Table 4.5.

negotiation over conflict, it is important to remember that it does so in a context in which legal guilt has already been established. Even within this context, plea bargaining is not completely divorced from the adversary process.

Strategies to Induce a Plea Bargain Earlier, we pointed out that the most likely reason why a prosecutor does not bring charges is the lack of a strong case. This is also the most common reason why a prosecutor agrees to a plea bargain once charges have been brought. Defense attorneys are well aware of this fact and often file numerous pretrial motions in an effort to weaken the state's case. Even if the judge does not accept the motions, the defense may hope that the time required to process them will wear on the prosecutor's patience. As one district attorney has said, "the usual defense strategy today is to bring in a stack of motions as thick as a Sunday newspaper; defense attorneys hope that we won't have the patience to ride them out."[71]

Prosecutors have their own methods of inducing a plea bargain. The most common is the ethically questionable practice of *overcharging;* that is, charging the defendant with more counts than may be appropriate. There are two types of overcharging:

1 In *horizontal overcharging,* the prosecutor brings a number of different counts for a single criminal incident.

2 In *vertical overcharging,* the prosecutor raises the level of a charge above its proper place. For example, the facts of the case warrant a charge of battery, but the prosecutor charges the defendant with attempted murder.

After overcharging, prosecutors allow themselves to be "bargained down" to the correct charge, giving the defense attorney and the defendant the impression that they have achieved victory.

Protecting the Defendant Watching the defense attorney and the prosecutor maneuver in this manner, the defendant often comes to the conclusion that the plea bargaining process is a sort of game with sometimes incomprehensible rules.[72] The Supreme Court is also aware of the potential for taking advantage of the defendant in plea bargaining and has taken steps to protect the accused. Until *Boykin v. Alabama* (1969),[73] judges would often accept the defense counsel's word that the defendant wanted to plead guilty. In that case, the Court held that the defendant must make a clear statement that he or she accepts the plea bargain. As a result, many jurisdictions now ask the accused to sign a **Boykin form** waiving his or her right to a trial. A statement in which the defendant admits exactly what crime he or she committed must accompany this guilty plea. (For other important cases protecting the defendant during plea bargaining, see Figure 9.9.)

Boykin **Form**

A form that must be completed by a defendant who pleads guilty; the defendant states that she or he has done so voluntarily and with full comprehension of the consequences.

The constitutional justification of the plea bargain as an accepted part of the criminal justice process has been fortified by these Supreme Court rulings.

Boykin v. Alabama (395 U.S. 238 [1969]). This case established the formal procedures that must be followed when a plea bargain is agreed on, with the goal of ensuring that the defendant has voluntarily agreed to the plea bargain and understands the consequences of entering a guilty plea.

Brady v. United States (397 U.S. 742 [1970]). In this case, the defendant entered a guilty plea in order to avoid the death penalty. In allowing this action, the Court ruled that plea bargains are a legitimate part of the adjudication process as long as they are entered into voluntarily and the defendant has full knowledge of the consequences of pleading guilty.

North Carolina v. Alford (400 U.S. 25 [1970]). Although maintaining he was innocent of the first degree murder for which he was charged, Alford pleaded guilty to second degree murder in order to avoid the possibility of the death penalty that came with the original charges. After being sentenced to thirty years in prison, Alford argued that he was forced to plea bargain because of the threat of the death penalty. The Court refused to invalidate Alford's guilty plea, stating that plea bargains are valid even if the defendant claims innocence, as long as the plea was entered into voluntarily.

Santobello v. New York (404 U.S. 257 [1971]). This case focused on the prosecutor's role in the plea bargain process. The Court ruled that if a prosecutor promises a more lenient sentence in return for the defendant's guilty plea, the promise must be kept.

Bordenkircher v. Hayes (434 U.S. 357 [1978]). A Kentucky prosecutor told Hayes that if he entered a guilty plea, the prosecutor would recommend a light sentence. If not, he would indict Hayes under the state's habitual offender act, which carried the possibility of life imprisonment. The Court ruled that prosecutors are within their rights to threaten defendants with harsher sentences in order to induce a guilty plea.

Ricketts v. Adamson (483 U.S. 1 [1987]). In return for a reduction of charges, Ricketts agreed to plead guilty and to testify against a co-defendant in a murder case. When the co-defendant's conviction was reversed on appeal, Ricketts refused to testify a second time. Therefore, the prosecutor rescinded his offer of leniency. The Court ruled that the prosecutor's action was justified, and that defendants must uphold their side of the plea bargain in order to receive its benefits.

United States v. Mezzanatto (513 U.S. 196 [1995]). The Court ruled that a prosecutor can refuse to plea bargain with a defendant unless the defendant agrees that any statements made by him or her during the bargaining process can be used against him or her in a possible trial. In other words, if the defendant admits to committing the crime during plea bargain negotiations, and then decides to plead not guilty, the prosecution can use the admission as evidence during the trial.

IS PLEA BARGAINING INEVITABLE?

Observers on both sides of the criminal justice "fence" feel that the compromises inherent in plea bargaining make the process unjust. Those interested in protecting due process believe that negotiated pleas deny defendants the stricter procedural protections of a criminal trial.[74] Furthermore, the practice gives innocent people an incentive to plead guilty if they feel that the evidence is against them. For their part, those committed to crime control believe that plea bargaining allows dangerous criminals to "beat the system" by negotiating for lighter sentences than they deserve; consequently, these observers feel that it undermines the deterrent effects of punishment.[75]

The Best Available Solution   It is not easy to combat these criticisms. Instead, proponents of plea bargaining argue that although it may not be the ideal solution to problems such as overwhelming caseloads, it is the best one available under the circumstances. In a 1970 speech to the American Bar Association, then Supreme Court Chief Justice Warren Burger said:

> The consequences of what might seem on its face a small percentage change in the rate of guilty pleas can be tremendous. A reduction from 90 percent to 80 percent in guilty pleas requires the assignment of twice the judicial manpower and facilities—judges, court reporters, bailiffs, clerks, jurors and courtrooms. A reduction to 70 percent trebles this demand.[76]

Was Chief Justice Burger correct in stating, essentially, that the court system could not function without plea bargaining? Skeptics point out that rates of guilty pleas in felony cases vary from jurisdiction to jurisdiction, implying that some court systems have managed to reduce the practice without collapsing.[77] The main body of research, however, implies the opposite: that, regardless of regulations governing plea bargaining from jurisdiction to jurisdiction, the rate of guilty pleas remains stable.

Limiting Plea Bargaining Perhaps more to the point, certain jurisdictions have provided case studies for Chief Justice Burger's assumption by abolishing plea bargaining. In 1975, prosecutors and defense attorneys in El Paso, Texas, were prohibited from negotiating the sentencing of a guilty party. Instead, punishment was determined by a "point system" that would base probation or imprisonment on a set of guidelines. This removed the incentive for either side to plea bargain, and most cases went to trial. Within three years, the county's caseload increased by 250 percent, and the prohibition was eventually rescinded.[78]

U.S. Attorney General John Ashcroft showed his adherence to crime control notions of criminal justice in 2003 when he issued a directive ordering all federal prosecutors to charge all defendants "with the most serious, readily provable offense" and not to engage in plea bargaining, with some exceptions. Critics charged Ashcroft with getting on "a political soapbox" to appear tough on crime and warned that "the courts [would] be overrun in no time" if prosecutors followed his instructions. Several loopholes in the directive, which would allow plea bargaining if prosecutors are "particularly overburdened" or if the duration of the trial would be "exceptionally long," seemed to ensure, however, that the practice will continue to be a "necessary thing" in this nation's federal courts.[79]

ONLINE REVIEW *Go to the book's Web site for an interactive review of this section*

Going to Trial

The pretrial process does not inexorably lead to a guilty plea. Just as prosecutors, defense attorneys, and defendants have reasons to negotiate, they may also be motivated to take a case to trial. If either side is confident in the strength of its arguments and evidence, it will obviously be less likely to accept a plea bargain. Both prosecutors and defense attorneys may favor a trial to gain publicity, and sometimes public pressure after an extremely violent or high-profile crime will force a chief prosecutor (who is, remember, normally an elected official) to take a weak case to trial. Also, some defendants may insist on their right to a trial, regardless of their attorney's advice. In the next chapter, we will examine what happens to the 10 percent of indictments that do lead to the courtroom.

>The DNA Revolution

The use of deoxyribonucleic acid (DNA) finger-printing has affected the entire criminal justice system, but nowhere has the impact been as revolutionary as in the courtroom. Since 1989, more than 140 persons have been cleared of wrongdoing by the postconviction use of DNA. During that same time period, prosecutors and police have used DNA evidence to put thousands of criminals behind bars. In this *Criminal Justice in Action* feature, we will see, however, that DNA has done little to reduce the adversarial nature of the adversary system.

The DNA "Miracle at Work"

In 1979, Diane Gregory was stabbed to death in her apartment in Mount Vernon, New York. A good deal of physical evidence was found at the site of the crime, including a pillowcase, a jagged piece of glass, and a sheet, all covered with blood. At the time, police officers were certain that some of the blood belonged to Walter Gill, the main suspect. But, as there was no proof, investigators lacked evidence to charge Gill with the crime.[80]

Twenty-one years later, local police finally obtained the evidence they needed. A new state law allowed them to take a DNA sample from Gill, who was serving a prison term for robbery. Investigators retrieved the pillowcase, glass shard, and sheet from a storage bin and were able to analyze the DNA in the decades-old blood. The samples matched those taken from Gill, placing him at the scene of the crime. In March 2001, a jury convicted him of first degree manslaughter in the death of Diane Gregory. It was, said the prosecuting district attorney, "like the finger of God pointing 21 years later, saying 'You can't get away with it.'"[81]

DNA, which is the same in each cell of a person's body, provides a "genetic blueprint" or "code" for every living organism. DNA "profiling" is useful in criminal investigations because no two people, save for identical twins, have the same genetic code. Therefore, lab technicians, using the process described in Figure 9.10, can compare the DNA sample of a suspect such as Gill to the evidence found at the crime scene. If the match is negative, it is certain that the two samples did not come from the same source. If the match is positive, the lab will

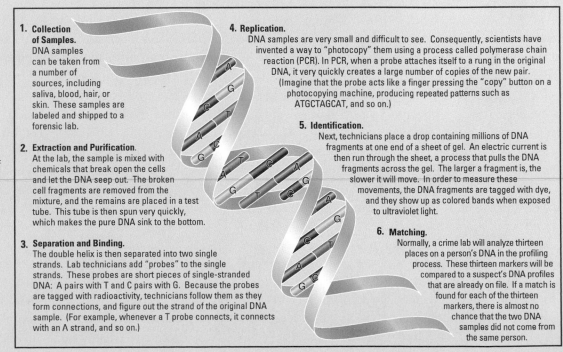

FIGURE 9.10
Unlocking Evidence in DNA

Deoxyribonucleic acid, or DNA, is the genetic material that carries the code for all living cells. DNA is useful to crime solvers thanks to the discovery that the DNA of one person is different from the DNA of all other persons (except identical twins). Through DNA profiling, a process explained here, forensic scientists test DNA samples to see if they match with the DNA profile of a known criminal or other test subject.

1. Collection of Samples.
DNA samples can be taken from a number of sources, including saliva, blood, hair, or skin. These samples are labeled and shipped to a forensic lab.

2. Extraction and Purification.
At the lab, the sample is mixed with chemicals that break open the cells and let the DNA seep out. The broken cell fragments are removed from the mixture, and the remains are placed in a test tube. This tube is then spun very quickly, which makes the pure DNA sink to the bottom.

3. Separation and Binding.
The double helix is then separated into two single strands. Lab technicians add "probes" to the single strands. These probes are short pieces of single-stranded DNA: A pairs with T and C pairs with G. Because the probes are tagged with radioactivity, technicians follow them as they form connections, and figure out the strand of the original DNA sample. (For example, whenever a T probe connects, it connects with an A strand, and so on.)

4. Replication.
DNA samples are very small and difficult to see. Consequently, scientists have invented a way to "photocopy" them using a process called polymerase chain reaction (PCR). In PCR, when a probe attaches itself to a rung in the original DNA, it very quickly creates a large number of copies of the new pair. (Imagine that the probe acts like a finger pressing the "copy" button on a photocopying machine, producing repeated patterns such as ATGCTAGCAT, and so on.)

5. Identification.
Next, technicians place a drop containing millions of DNA fragments at one end of a sheet of gel. An electric current is then run through the sheet, a process that pulls the DNA fragments across the gel. The larger a fragment is, the slower it will move. In order to measure these movements, the DNA fragments are tagged with dye, and they show up as colored bands when exposed to ultraviolet light.

6. Matching.
Normally, a crime lab will analyze thirteen places on a person's DNA in the profiling process. These thirteen markers will be compared to a suspect's DNA profiles that are already on file. If a match is found for each of the thirteen markers, there is almost no chance that the two DNA samples did not come from the same person.

determine the odds that the DNA sample could have come from somebody other than the subject. These odds are so high—sometimes reaching 30 billion to one—that juries often see the match as conclusive.[82]

Proving Guilt or Innocence

The initial use of DNA to establish criminal guilt took place in Britain in 1986; the Federal Bureau of Investigation (FBI) used it for the first time in the United States two years later. The process begins when forensic technicians gather blood, semen, skin, saliva, or hair from the scene of the crime. Blood cells and sperm are rich in DNA, making the practice particularly useful in murder and rape cases. Once a suspect is identified, her or his DNA can be tested to determine whether she or he can be placed at the crime scene. In cases of murder or when the victim is unable to provide a suspect, police rely on DNA databases.

"Dusting" for genetic information on a wide variety of evidence has helped clear those convicted of crimes. In 2002, Detroit native Eddie Joe Lloyd was exonerated because of tests done on two pieces of evidence—a green bottle and a pair of long underwear—prosecutors said he had used to sexually assault and strangle a woman in 1984. Paul B. Ferrera, the Virginia state director of forensic science, has cracked cases using DNA traces found on a partially eaten chicken sandwich, urine in the snow, and a lipprint on a glass.[83]

A Double Standard?

Such forensic accomplishments do not impress all prosecutors, many of whom believe that too much emphasis has been placed on DNA testing. Although the procedure is reliable, they say, it does not automatically prove innocence when there is other evidence of guilt.[84] Consequently, in a number of instances prosecutors have fought to keep a suspect incarcerated even after evidence used in the initial conviction has been proved untrustworthy.

In Florida, for example, Wilton Dredge was convicted of rape in 1981 based on two light brown hairs found on the victim's bed sheet. The hairs were the only physical evidence presented at the trial, and the prosecutor told the jury that they were "microscopically identical" to those found on Dredge's head. Dredge had to sue the state to use DNA technology on the hairs, and recent tests concluded that the hairs were not his. Prosecutors, however, insisted that Dredge had not proved his inno-

cence, citing three other pieces of evidence against him: victim identification, the testimony of a prison informant, and a "scent test" done on the sheet by a police dog. "They used it against me," complained Dredge of the hair evidence, "and now they say it doesn't matter."[85]

The Embarrassment Factor

Peter J. Neufeld, who co-directs the Innocence Project at the Benjamin N. Cardozo School of Law in New York City, gives two reasons why prosecutors may resist DNA testing in these situations. First, it can be embarrassing to find out that the wrong person has been convicted. Second, an investigation into the cause of the wrongful conviction may lead to negative publicity and perhaps disciplinary action.[86]

Not all prosecutors have been unwilling to risk embarrassment or worse. District attorneys in San Diego and Ramsey County, Minnesota, have reviewed hundreds of old cases using DNA fingerprinting. In Minnesota, the effort led to the exoneration of a man convicted of rape. "I'm not proud we goofed, but I'm proud that we welcome the light to be shown on our prior cases," said Susan Gaertner, an attorney for Ramsey County.[87] After revelations that the city of Houston's crime laboratory had been so mismanaged that evidence that passed through its doors was unreliable, Harris County (Texas) prosecutors ordered a DNA review of 525 case files.

Databases and Cold Hits

Prosecutors also realize that DNA testing is a powerful tool for solving crimes and will become even more effective as state and national DNA databases become more inclusive and efficient. Today, every state allows law enforcement agencies to collect DNA samples from certain types of criminals for inclusion in state databases. At the least, these state laws require DNA samples to be taken from convicted sex offenders. Six states allow such samples to be taken from anybody convicted of any felony, and Wisconsin goes so far as to require samples from everyone who is incarcerated, on probation, paroled, or found not guilty by reason of mental disease.[88] In addition to these state databases, there is also a national information retrieval service. Operated by the FBI since 1998, the Combined DNA Index System (CODIS) gives local and state law enforcement agencies access to the DNA profiles of a wide variety of felons who have been convicted of homicide and sexual assault.

These databases can lead to what police call a *cold hit,* or the solving of a case where there are no suspects. For example, the first cold hit using CODIS occurred when Leon Dundas was found dead after being shot in the back in Jacksonville, Florida. An investigator with the local sheriff's office took a blood sample from Dundas, who had a history of drug arrests, and ran it through CODIS. The sample matched DNA evidence at the scene of eleven different unsolved rape cases, three in Jacksonville and eight in Washington, D.C. The Virginia DNA bank, the largest state database in the nation, produces more than 300 cold hits a year. In 2002, the federal government announced plans to set up a database of DNA collected from suspected terrorists captured in Afghanistan and Iraq. A year later, the Bush administration pledged $1 billion to help states work through a backlog of 350,000 untested DNA samples gathered in rape and homicide cases.

Privacy Concerns

There is not much doubt that in little more than a decade, DNA testing has transformed many aspects of crime investigation. One government official has gone so far as to call the process a "scientific miracle for human justice" that "shines the light of irrefutable truth into our courtrooms for our juries."[89] But many observers are wary of DNA's ability to give the government agencies information about citizens that goes beyond the scope of their criminal liability.

The main issue concerns personal privacy, which the United States Supreme Court has identified as a "fundamental right" guaranteed by our Constitution.[90] Having been found guilty of a crime by a jury, convicted felons are said to have relinquished their right to privacy. But what of those who have only been arrested and have not been convicted? Do they have a right to keep certain information that DNA testing can reveal—such as a genetic predisposition to disease—private? Observers such as Barry Steinhardt, associate director of the American Civil Liberties Union, are troubled by laws such as the one recently passed in California that allow DNA searches before conviction for those arrested for violent crimes such as murder, sexual assault of a child, and kidnapping.[91] Steinhardt points out that about half of those charged with such violent crimes ultimately have their cases dismissed, and therefore California's law imposes a heavy burden on possibly innocent people. Further, he is worried that the law will encourage police officers to make "pretextual" arrests solely for the purpose of collecting DNA from suspects whom the officers do not have enough evidence to arrest.[92]

The issue of privacy was at the heart of a lawsuit brought by a convicted sex offender against the state of Connecticut.[93] The convict argued that the state did not have reasonable cause to store his DNA in its database because it could not be sure that he would commit another crime. Therefore, he argued, the DNA collection was an illegal search.[94] The U.S. Court of Appeals for the Second Circuit rejected this argument, holding that Connecticut's interest in protecting its citizens from possible sex offenders was greater than an individual convict's interest in keeping his or her blood from being tested.[95]

MAKING SENSE OF DNA PROFILING

1 Do you agree that the positive impact of DNA profiling on crime-fighting efforts outweighs an individual's interest in privacy? Why or why not?

2 How far should the government be allowed to go in collecting DNA samples from citizens? Should such methods be limited to felons convicted of violent crimes? To anybody convicted of any felony? To those who have only been arrested?

3 Considering how successful DNA is in identifying criminals, should those accused or convicted of crimes automatically be given access to DNA material in preparing their defense? What might be the pros and cons of such a policy? In making your answer, be aware that only three states—New York, Illinois, and Minnesota—have laws that require courts to honor such a request. In most other states, judges can deny such a request under most circumstances.

INFOTRAC KEYWORDS
crime and DNA; CODIS

For more information, use these search terms with InfoTrac College Edition, your online library at www.infotrac-college.com

Chapter Summary

1 **List the different names given to public prosecutors and the general powers that they have.** At the federal level, the prosecutor is called the U.S. attorney. In state and local courts, the prosecutor may be referred to as the prosecuting attorney, state prosecutor, district attorney, county attorney, or city attorney. Prosecutors in general have the power to decide when and how the state will pursue an individual suspected of criminal wrongdoing. In some jurisdictions, the district attorney is also the chief law enforcement officer, holding broad powers over police operations.

2 **Contrast the prosecutor's roles as an elected official and as a crime fighter.** In most instances, the prosecutor is elected and therefore may feel obliged to reward members of her or his party with jobs. To win reelection or higher political office, the prosecutor may feel a need to bow to community pressures. As a crime fighter, the prosecutor is dependent on the police, and indeed prosecutors are generally seen as law enforcement agents. Prosecutors, however, generally pursue cases only when they believe there is sufficient legal guilt to obtain a conviction.

3 **Delineate the responsibilities of defense attorneys.** (a) Representation of the defendant during the custodial process; (b) investigation of the supposed criminal incident; (c) communication with the prosecutor (including plea bargaining); (d) preparation of the case for trial; (e) submission of defense motions; (f) representation of the defendant at trial; (g) negotiation of a sentence after conviction; and (h) appeal of a guilty verdict.

4 **Indicate the three types of defense allocation programs.** (a) Assigned counsel programs, which use local private attorneys; (b) contracting attorney programs; and (c) public defender programs.

5 **List the three basic features of an adversary system of justice.** (a) A neutral decision maker (judge or jury); (b) presentation of evidence from both parties; and (c) a highly structured set of procedures that must be used when evidence is presented.

6 **Identify the steps involved in the pretrial criminal process.** (a) Suspect taken into custody or arrested; (b) initial appearance before a magistrate, at which time the defendant is informed of his or her constitutional rights and a public defender may be appointed or private counsel may be hired by the state to represent the defendant; (c) the posting of bail or release on recognizance; (d) preventive detention, if deemed necessary to ensure the safety of other persons or the community, or regular detention, if the defendant is unable to post bail; (e) preliminary hearing (mini-trial), at which the judge rules on whether there is probable cause and the prosecutor issues an information; or in the alternative (f) grand jury hearings, after which an indictment is issued against the defendant if the grand jury finds probable cause; (g) arraignment, in which the defendant is informed of the charges and must respond by pleading not guilty or guilty (or in some cases *nolo contendere*); and (h) plea bargaining.

7 **Indicate the three influences on a judge's decision to set bail.** (a) Uncertainty about the character and past criminal history of the defendant; (b) the risk that the defendant will commit another crime if out on bail; and (c) overcrowded jails, which may influence a judge to release a defendant on bail.

8 **Explain how a prosecutor screens potential cases.** (a) Is there sufficient evidence for conviction? (b) What is the priority of the case? The more serious the alleged crime, the higher the priority. The more extensive the defendant's criminal record, the higher the priority. (c) Are the victims cooperative? Violence against family members often yields uncooperative victims; therefore, these cases are rarely prosecuted. (d) Are the victims reliable? (e) Might the defendant be willing to testify against other offenders?

🎧 **STORIES FROM THE STREET**

Go to the Stories from the Street feature at www.cjinaction.com to hear Larry Gaines tell insightful stories related to this chapter and his experiences in the field.

9 List and briefly explain the different forms of plea bargaining agreements. (a) Charge bargaining, in which the charge is reduced to a lesser crime; (b) sentence bargaining, in which a lighter sentence is obtained; (c) count bargaining, in which a certain number or most of the multiple counts are eliminated.

10 Indicate the ways that both defense attorneys and prosecutors can induce plea bargaining. Defense attorneys can file numerous pretrial motions in an effort to weaken the state's case. Prosecutors can engage in horizontal or vertical overcharging, so they can be "bargained down" in the process of plea bargaining.

Questions for Critical Analysis

1 Why are public prosecutors considered the most dominant figures in the American criminal justice system?

2 Which of the three basic types of programs used to allocate defense counsel in criminal cases has aroused the most criticism recently?

3 Is it true that there is no concern for truth in our adversary system of justice? Explain your answer.

4 During an initial appearance, can defendants plead guilty of having committed a felony? Why or why not?

5 What are the arguments against preventive detention?

6 What is the distinction between a preliminary hearing and an initial appearance?

7 If grand juries indict almost all criminal defendants brought before them, why do we use grand juries?

8 What is case attrition, and why does it occur?

9 Is plea bargaining inevitable?

10 How can DNA testing help both prosecutors and defense attorneys?

TEST PREPARATION ONLINE

Go to www.cjinaction.com for tools to aid you in studying for your exams. Click on *Online Reviews* under *Chapter Resources* for an interactive review of each major section of this chapter. Under *Chapter Resources*, you will also find the *Chapter Outline*, *Chapter Summary*, *Flashcards*, *Glossary*, *Learning Objectives*, *Lecture Presentations*, *Concept Builder*, *Essay Questions*, and a *Tutorial Quiz*. You can also test yourself with a game of *Concentration* or the *Crossword Puzzle*.

Web Resources

Go to www.cjinaction.com for a wealth of online resources. Explore the *Internet Activities* and *Class Projects* under *Chapter Resources*. Check out the *Web Links* to access the Web sites mentioned in the text, as well as many others. You can also access recent perspectives by clicking on *CJ in the News* and *Terrorism Update* under *Course Resources*. If you'd like some mentoring, click on *Board of Mentors* under *Book Resources*.

Search Online with InfoTrac College Edition

For additional information, explore InfoTrac College Edition, your online library that offers complete full-length articles from thousands of scholarly and popular publications. Click on *InfoTrac College Edition* under *Chapter Resources* at www.cjinaction.com for a list of key words and InfoTrac exercises. Use the passcode that came with your book.

Suggested Readings

Delsohn, Gary, *The Prosecutors: A Year in the Life of a District Attorney's Office,* New York: Dutton, 2003. A reporter for the *Sacramento Bee,* the author spent a year following assistant district attorneys in that city. Delsohn shows how life in a district attorney's office is dominated by statistics: number of trials completed, number of trials won, and number of trials lost. Not surprisingly, sometimes "justice" gets lost in the mix. The author follows six specific cases, including those of a Ukrainian immigrant who murdered his family and a doctor who killed his young daughter by throwing her out a window. The book is particularly strong in detailing the struggles between prosecutors and defense attorneys, the "foot soldiers" of the American adversary system.

Dwyer, Jim, Peter Neufeld, and Barry Scheck, *Actual Innocence: When Justice Goes Wrong and How to Make It Right,* New York: New American Library, 2001. Neufeld and Scheck run the Innocence Project, an organization that provides free legal aid for felons who believe that DNA testing can prove their innocence. In this book, the two lawyers—with the aid of journalist Dwyer—tell the stories of some of the convicts the Innocence Project has helped to free. In many ways, the book is an indictment of the criminal justice system, full of sloppy and unethical police work, vindictive prosecutors, and incompetent defense attorneys. The authors also look at the difficulty those who have been wrongly convicted encounter when trying to restore their lives "on the outside" after release from prison.

Notes

1. Timothy Roche, "A Short Course in Miracles: The Inside Story of How Accused Terrorist John Walker Lindh Cut a Deal to Avoid Life in Prison—And Why the Government Went Along," *Time* (July 29, 2002), 34.

2. David Johnston, "Lindh: An Insignificant Case," *South Florida Sun-Sentinel* (July 16, 2002), 4A.

3. Bureau of Justice Statistics, *Federal Criminal Case Processing, 2001* (Washington, D.C.: U.S. Department of Justice, January 2003), 11.

4. Bennett L. Gershman, "Abuse of Power in the Prosecutor's Office," in *Criminal Justice 92/93,* ed. John J. Sullivan and Joseph L. Victor (Guilford, CT: The Dushkin Publishing Group, 1991), 117–123.

5. 295 U.S. 78 (1935).

6. Celesta Albonetti, "Prosecutorial Discretion: The Effects of Uncertainty," *Law and Society Review* 21 (1987), 291–313.

7. Eric Blumenson and Eva Nilson, "Policing for Profit: The Drug War's Hidden Economic Agenda," *University of Chicago Law Review* 35 (1998), 65.

8. Malcolm M. Feeley and Mark H. Lazerson, "Police-Prosecutor Relationships: An Interorganizational Perspective," in *Empirical Theories about Court,* ed. Keith O. Boyum and Lynn Mather (New York: Longman, 1983), 229–232.

9. Herbert Packer, *Limits of the Criminal Sanction* (Stanford, CA: Stanford University Press, 1968), 166–167.

10. *Gideon v. Wainwright,* 372 U.S. 335 (1963); *Massiah v. United States,* 377 U.S. 201 (1964); *United States v. Wade,* 388 U.S. 218 (1967); *Argersinger v. Hamlin,* 407 U.S. 25 (1972); and *Brewer v. Williams,* 430 U.S. 387 (1977).

11. Larry Siegel, *Criminology,* 6th ed. (Belmont, CA: West/Wadsworth Publishing Co., 1998), 487–488.

12. 372 U.S. 335 (1963).

13. 387 U.S. 1 (1967).

14. 407 U.S. 25 (1972).

15. Bureau of Justice Statistics, *Indigent Defense* (Washington, D.C.: U.S. Department of Justice, 1996), 3.

16. "Criminal Justice for the Poor, 1986," *Bureau of Justice Statistics Bulletin* (Washington, D.C.: U.S. Department of Justice, 1988).

17. Caroline Wolf Harlow, *Defense Counsel in Criminal Cases* (Washington, D.C.: U.S. Department of Justice, November 2000), 4.

18. *Ibid.,* 3–4.

19. 491 U.S. 554 (1989).

20. Jonathan D. Casper, *American Criminal Justice: The Defendant's Perspective* (Englewood Cliffs, NJ: Prentice-Hall, 1972), 101.

21. *Ibid.,* 106.

22. William Finnegan, "Defending the Unabomber," *New Yorker* (March 16, 1998), 61.

23. Anthony Platt and Randi Pollock, "Channeling Lawyers: The Careers of Public Defenders," in *The Potential for Reform in Criminal Justice,* ed. Herbert Jacob (Newbury Park, CA: Sage, 1974).

24. Johannes F. Nijboer, "The American Adversary System in Criminal Cases: Between Ideology and Reality," *Cardozo Journal of International and Comparative Law* 5 (Spring 1997), 79.

25. Gordon Van Kessel, "Adversary Excesses in the American Criminal Trial," *Notre Dame Law Review* 67 (1992), 403.

26. James Eisenstein and Herbert Jacob, *Felony Justice* (Boston: Little, Brown, 1977), 24.

27. Jerome Skolnick, "Social Control in the Adversary System," *Journal of Conflict Resolution* 11 (1967), 52–70.

28. Abraham S. Blumberg, "The Practice of Law as Confidence Game: Organizational Cooption of a Profession," *Law and Society Review* 4 (June 1967), 115–139.

29. Malcolm Feeley, "The Adversary System," in *Encyclopedia of the American Judicial System,* ed. Robert J. Janosik (New York: Scribners, 1987), 753.

30. Blumberg, 115.

31. *Riverside County, California v. McLaughlin,* 500 U.S. 44 (1991).

32. Illinois Ann. Stat. ch. 725, para. 5/110-5.

33. David W. Neubauer, *America's Courts and the Criminal Justice System,* 5th ed. (Belmont, CA: Wadsworth Publishing Co., 1996), 179–181.

34. Roy Flemming, C. Kohfeld, and Thomas Uhlman, "The Limits of Bail Reform: A Quasi Experimental Analysis," *Law and Society Review* 14 (1980), 947–976.

35. Caleb Foote, "Compelling Appearance in Court: Administration of Bail in Philadelphia," *University of Pennsylvania Law Review* 102 (1954), 1031–1052.

36. John Goldkamp, *Two Classes of Accused* (Cambridge, MA: Ballinger, 1979).

37. Frederic Suffet, "Bail Setting: A Study of Courtroom Interaction," *Crime and Delinquency* 12 (1966), 318.

38. Wayne H. Thomas, Jr., *Bail Reform in America* (Berkeley, CA: University of California Press, 1976), 4.

39. Andrew D. Patrick, "Running from the Law," *Vanderbilt Law Review* (January 1999), 172.

40. John S. Goldkamp and Michael R. Gottfredson, *Policy Guidelines for Bail: An Experiment in Court Reform* (Philadelphia: Temple University Press, 1985), 18.

41. Thomas, 7.

42. *Stack v. Boyle,* 342 U.S. 1, 7–8 (1951).

43. *Taylor v. Taintor,* 83 U.S. (16 Wall.) 366 (1873).

44. "Virginia Moves to Control Actions of Bounty Hunters," *New York Times* (January 15, 2003), A14.

45. Esmond Harmsworth, "Bail and Detention: An Assessment and Critique of the Federal and Massachusetts Systems," *New England Journal on Criminal and Civil Confinement* 22 (Spring 1996), 213.

46. 18 U.S.C. Section 3146(b) (1966).

47. Harmsworth, 213.

48. Thomas C. French, "Is It Punitive or Is It Regulatory?" *University of Toledo Law Review* 20 (Fall 1988), 189.

49. 18 U.S.C. Sections 3141–3150 (Supp. III 1985).

50. 481 U.S. 739 (1987).

51. Bureau of Justice Statistics, *Felony Defendants in Large Urban Counties, 1998* (Washington, D.C.: U.S. Department of Justice, November 2001), page 22, Table 21.

52. *Gerstein v. Pugh,* 420 U.S. 103 (1975).

53. David W. Neubauer, *Criminal Justice in Middle America* (Morristown, NJ: General Learning Press, 1974).

54. Andrew D. Leipold, "Why Grand Juries Do Not (and Cannot) Protect the Accused," *Cornell Law Review* 80 (January 1995), 260.

55. Robert L. Misner, "In Partial Praise of Boyd: The Grand Jury as Catalyst for the Fourth Amendment Change," *Arizona State Law Review* (Fall 1997), 805.

56. New York Court of Appeals Judge Sol Wachtler, quoted in David Margolik, "Law Professor to Administer Courts in State," *New York Times* (February 1, 1985), B2.

57. Kenneth C. Davis, *Discretionary Justice: A Preliminary Inquiry* (Baton Rouge, LA: Louisiana State University Press, 1969), 189.

58. Barbara Boland, Paul Mahanna, and Ronald Scones, *The Prosecution of Felony Arrests, 1988* (Washington, D.C.: Bureau of Justice Statistics, 1992).

59. *Ibid.*

60. Brian Forst, Frank Leahy, Jean Shirhall, Herbert Tyson, Eric Wish, and John Bartolemo, *Arrest Convictability as a Measure of Police Performance* (Washington, D.C.: Institute for Law and Social Research, 1981).

61. Kathy B. Carter, "Court Orders Statewide Drug Penalties, Ending County Disparities," *Newark Star-Ledger* (February 20, 1998), 46.

62. David Firestone, "Cremation Case Calls for Creative Prosecution," *New York Times* (February 28, 2002), A14.

63. Paul Gustafson, "DNA Exonerates Man Convicted of '85 Rape," *Minneapolis-St. Paul Star Tribune* (November 14, 2002), 1A.

64. 404 U.S. 257 (1971).

65. Fred C. Zacharias, "Justice in Plea Bargaining," *William and Mary Law Review* 39 (March 1998), 1121.

66. Albert W. Alschuler, "The Prosecutor's Role in Plea Bargaining," *University of Chicago Law Review* 36 (1968), 52.

67. Milton Heumann, *Plea Bargaining: The Experiences of Prosecutors, Judges, and Defense Attorneys* (Chicago: University of Chicago Press, 1978), 58.

68. Albert W. Alschuler, "The Defense Attorney's Role in Plea Bargaining," *Yale Law Journal* 84 (1975), 1200.

69. Stephen J. Schulhofer, "Plea Bargaining as Disaster," *Yale Law Journal* 101 (1992), 1987.

70. Kevin Cole and Fred C. Zacharias, "The Agony of Victory and the Ethics of Lawyer Speech," *Southern California Law Review* 69 (1996), 1660–1663.

71. Alschuler, "The Prosecutor's Role in Plea Bargaining," 53.

72. Casper, 77–81.

73. 395 U.S. 238 (1969).

74. Stephen A. Saltzburg, "Lawyers, Clients, and the Adversary System," *Mercer Law Review* 37 (1986), 651–655.

75. Douglas A. Smith, "The Plea Bargaining Controversy," *Journal of Criminal Law and Criminology* 77 (1986), 949.

76. Warren Burger, "Address to the American Bar Association Annual Convention," *New York Times* (August 11, 1970), 24.

77. Stephen J. Schulhofer, "Is Plea Bargaining Inevitable?" *Harvard Law Review* 97 (March 1984), 1037.

78. Robert A. Weninger, "The Abolition of Plea Bargaining: A Case Study of El Paso County, Texas," *UCLA Law Review* 35 (December 1987), 265.

79. Adam Liptak and Eric Lichtblau, "New Plea Bargain Limits Could Swamp Courts, Experts Say," *New York Times* (September 24, 2003), A23.

80. C. J. Chivers, "Larger DNA Database Links an Inmate to a 1979 Murder, Officials Say," *New York Times* (March 13, 2000), A21.

81. *Ibid.*

82. Judith E. Lewter, "The Use of Forensic DNA in Criminal Cases in Kentucky as Compared with Other Selected States," *Kentucky Law Journal* 86 (1997–1998), 223.

83. Francis X. Clines, "Virginia May Get DNA from Felony Suspects," *New York Times* (February 17, 2002), 16.

84. James Dao, "In Same Case, DNA Clears Convict and Finds Suspect," *New York Times* (September 6, 2003), A7.

85. Adam Liptak, "Prosecutors Fight DNA Use for Exoneration," *New York Times* (August 29, 2003), A1.

86. Jodi Wilgoren, "Prosecutors Use DNA Test to Clear Man in '85 Rape," *New York Times* (November 14, 2002), A20.

87. *Ibid.*

88. Deborah F. Barfield, "DNA Fingerprinting—Justifying the Special Need for the Fourth Amendment's Intrusion into the Zone of Privacy," *Richmond Journal of Law and Technology* (Spring 2000), 4.

89. George Pataki, quoted in DeWayne Wickham, "Don't Use DNA Test to Excuse Bad Idea," *USA Today* (February 29, 2000), 15A.

90. *Katz v. United States,* 389 U.S. 347 (1967).

91. Barry Steinhardt, "Law Opens Door to Abuse," *USA Today* (January 2, 2001), 10A.

92. *Ibid.*

93. *Roe v. Marcotte,* 193 F.3d 76 (2d Cir. 1999).

94. *Ibid.*

95. *Ibid.,* 82.

>Chapter 10<

The Criminal Trial

>chapter objectives<

After reading this chapter, you should be able to:

1 Identify the basic protections enjoyed by criminal defendants in the United States.

2 List the three requirements of the Speedy Trial Act of 1974.

3 Explain what "taking the Fifth" really means.

4 List the requirements normally imposed on potential jurors.

5 Contrast challenges for cause and peremptory challenges during *voir dire*.

6 List the standard steps in a criminal jury trial.

7 Explain the difference between testimony and real evidence; between lay witnesses and expert witnesses; and between direct and circumstantial evidence.

8 List possible affirmative defenses.

9 Delineate circumstances in which a criminal defendant may in fact be tried a second time for the same act.

10 List the six basic steps of an appeal.

Story Time

One death. Two stories. Kathleen Peterson was found dead in her home in Durham, North Carolina. Attorneys for her husband Michael said that she died from an accidental fall down a flight of stairs. Prosecutors claimed that Michael killed his wife because the couple was under severe financial pressure and Kathleen had just found out about his sexual interest in men.

At the murder trial, defense attorneys dismissed the possibility that Michael would have murdered his wife because the two had a "storybook" marriage. Prosecutors countered by trying to paint the relationship as something less than a fairy tale. They showed the jury hundreds of pornographic photos taken from Michael's computer. They called as a witness an Army reservist, identified only as "Brad," who had offered his services to Michael as a "male escort."

Michael Peterson, center, during his 2003 trial in Durham, North Carolina. Peterson, who was eventually found guilty of murdering his wife, Kathleen, listens to arguments over whether his gay pornography collection and e-mails soliciting sex with another man should be presented to the jury. The judge ruled that the materials would be allowed in court because they could provide a motive for the murder.

They produced records showing that the Petersons carried more than $145,000 in credit-card debt at the time of Kathleen's death.

Defense attorneys accounted for the pornography with the explanation that Michael—a novelist—was doing research for a book on gay men in the military. They said that Kathleen knew about and accepted her husband's bisexuality, and pointed out that the couple had more than enough equity to cover their debts. The prosecution, in turn, revealed the results of Kathleen's autopsy: seven deep, long lacerations with ragged edges on the back of her head that came from "multiple blunt force impacts" inconsistent with a fall downstairs. In closing arguments, Assistant District Attorney Freda Black told the jury that Michael had staged Kathleen's death to look like an accident. "We're dealing with a fictional writer," she said. "He is a person who knows how to create a fictional plot."

> **The jury believed** the prosecution's story and convicted Michael Peterson of first degree murder on October 10, 2003. Vowing to appeal, Michael's lawyers claimed that the judge had erred by allowing "Brad" to take the witness stand. His presence in the courtroom had no bearing on Michael's guilt or innocence, said defense attorney Thomas Maher, and was arranged solely to provoke an "emotional reaction" against the defendant. "If even one juror looks at Mr.

Peterson and says, 'Oh, my God. This guy's gay,' Mr. Peterson has been denied a fair trial," Maher argued.[1]

Fairness is, of course, a crucial component of the criminal trial. Protection against the arbitrary abuse of power is at the heart of the U.S. Constitution, and the right to a criminal trial before a jury is one means of assuring this protection. In this chapter, we will examine the fairness of the criminal trial in the context of the current legal environment. Because "fairness" can only be defined subjectively, we will also make an effort to look into the effect human nature has on the adversary process. Trials may be based on fact finding, but as Judge Jerome Frank once sardonically asserted, when it comes to a jury, "facts are guesses."[2]

Special Features of Criminal Trials

Civil trials (see Chapter 4) and criminal trials have many similar features. In both types of trials, attorneys from each side select a jury, make their opening statements to the court, examine and cross-examine witnesses, and summarize their positions in closing arguments. The jury is charged (instructed), and if it reaches a verdict, the trial comes to an end.

The principal difference is that in civil trials, the adversaries are persons (including corporations, which are legal persons, and businesses), one of whom often is seeking a remedy in the form of damages from the other. In a criminal trial, it is the state, not the victim of the crime, that brings the action against an alleged wrongdoer.[3] Criminal trial procedures reflect the need to protect criminal defendants against the power of the state by providing them with a number of rights. Many of the significant rights of the accused are spelled out in the Sixth Amendment, which reads, in part, as follows:

> In all criminal prosecutions, the accused shall enjoy the right to a speedy and public trial, by an impartial jury of the State and the district wherein the crime shall have been committed, . . . and to be informed of the nature and cause of the accusation; to be confronted with the witnesses against him; to have compulsory process for obtaining witnesses in his favor; and to have the Assistance of Counsel for his defense.

In this section, we will examine the aspects of the criminal trial that make it unique, beginning with two protections explicitly stated in the Sixth Amendment: the right to a speedy trial by an impartial jury. (For a discussion of how televising trials might affect a defendant's Sixth Amendment rights, see the feature *Criminal Justice in Action—Cameras in the Courtroom: Is Justice Served?* at the end of this chapter.)

A "SPEEDY" TRIAL

As you have just read, the Sixth Amendment requires a speedy trial for those accused of a criminal act. The reason for this requirement is obvious: depending on various factors, the defendant may lose his or her right to move freely and may be incarcerated prior to trial. Also, the accusation that a person has committed a crime jeopardizes that person's reputation in the community. If the defendant is innocent, the sooner the trial is held, the sooner his or her innocence can be established in the eyes of the court and the public.

CONCEPT BUILDER

Did you know that the words "presumption of innocence" are not found in the Constitution of the United States? How did this concept come about in the American legal system? Visit www.cjinaction.com for an interactive exploration of this key topic.

INFOTRAC KEYWORDS

speedy, trial

For more information, use these search terms with InfoTrac College Edition, your online library at www.infotrac-college.com

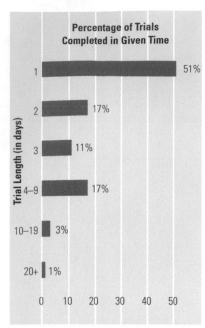

Percentage of Trials Completed in Given Time

Trial Length (in days)

Trial Length	Percentage
1	51%
2	17%
3	11%
4–9	17%
10–19	3%
20+	1%

0 10 20 30 40 50

FIGURE 10.1 The Length of Criminal Trials in U.S. District Courts

Because many of the trials in the public eye last for weeks, one could easily get the impression that trials are lengthy undertakings. As you can see here, that is not true in most cases.

Source: Administrative Office of the United States Courts, *Judicial Business of the United States Courts: 2002 Annual Report of the Director* (Washington, D.C.: United States Government Printing Office, 2003), 165.

Jury Trial
A trial before a judge and a jury.

Bench Trial
A trial conducted without a jury, in which a judge makes the determination of the defendant's guilt or innocence.

Reasons for Delay   As the preceding chapter made clear, there are numerous reasons for delay in bringing a defendant to trial. In defending the rights of the accused, a defense attorney may use a number of legal tactics, including pretrial motions and plea negotiations. Court congestion also contributes to the problem; many jurisdictions do not have enough judges and courtroom space to meet the needs of the system. This situation has been aggravated by the recent increase in drug-related arrests, which threatens to create judicial "gridlock" in certain metropolitan courthouses.[4]

The Definition of a Speedy Trial   The Sixth Amendment does not specify what is meant by the term *speedy*. The Supreme Court has refused to quantify "speedy" as well, ruling instead in *Barker v. Wingo* (1972)[5] that only in situations in which the delay is unwarranted and proved to be prejudicial can the accused claim a violation of Sixth Amendment rights.

As a result, all fifty states have their own speedy-trial statutes.[6] For example, the Illinois Speedy Trial Act states that a defendant must be tried within 120 days of arrest unless both the prosecution and the defense agree otherwise. States can also decide what constitutes the "go point" of a particular case. The Tennessee Supreme Court, for example, ruled that a five-year period between the issuance of an arrest warrant and the actual arrest of the defendant did not deny the accused his right to a speedy trial. The decision was based on the court's belief that the clock does not begin to run until the defendant is arrested or is indicted by a grand jury.[7]

At the national level, the Speedy Trial Act of 1974[8] (amended in 1979) specifies time limits for those in the federal court system. This act requires:

1 No more than thirty days between arrest and indictment.
2 No more than ten days between indictment and arraignment.
3 No more than sixty days between arraignment and trial.

Federal law allows extra time for hearings on pretrial motions, mental competency examinations, and other procedural actions.

Note that when discussing issues of a "speedy trial," the primary issue is the time period between the arrest and the beginning of the actual trial, not the length of the trial itself. Indeed, most trials are completed relatively quickly, as you can see in Figure 10.1.

THE ROLE OF THE JURY

The Sixth Amendment also states that anyone accused of a crime shall be judged by "an impartial jury." In *Duncan v. Louisiana* (1968),[9] the Supreme Court solidified this right by ruling that in all felony cases, the defendant is entitled to a **jury trial.** The Court has, however, left it to the individual states to decide whether juries are required for misdemeanor cases.[10] If the defendant waives her or his right to trial by jury, a **bench trial** takes place in which a judge decides questions of legality and fact, and no jury is involved.

Jury Size   The predominant American twelve-person jury is not the result of any one law—the Constitution does not require that the jury be a particular size. Historically, the number was inherited from the size of English juries, which was fixed at twelve during the fourteenth century.

In 1970, responding to a case that challenged Florida's practice of using a six-person jury in all but capital cases, the Supreme Court ruled that the accused did not have the right to be heard by a twelve-person jury. Indeed, the Court labeled the number twelve "a historical accident, wholly without significance except to mystics."[11] In *Ballew v. Georgia* (1978),[12] however, the Court did strike down attempts to use juries with fewer than six members, stating that a jury's effectiveness was severely hampered below that limit. About half the states allow fewer than twelve persons on criminal juries, though only for misdemeanor cases. In federal courts, defendants are entitled to have the case heard by a twelve-member jury unless both parties agree in writing to a smaller jury.

Unanimity In most jurisdictions, jury verdicts in criminal cases must be *unanimous* for **acquittal** or conviction. As will be explained in more detail later, if the jury cannot reach unanimous agreement on whether to acquit or convict the defendant, the result is a hung jury, and the judge may order a new trial.

Again, the Supreme Court has not held unanimity to be a rigid requirement. It has declared that jury verdicts must be unanimous in federal criminal trials, but has given states leeway to set their own rules.[13] Five states—Louisiana, Montana, Oklahoma, Oregon, and Texas—permit nonunanimous trial verdicts, though none allow more than three dissenting votes for convictions by twelve-person juries.

> **Acquittal**
> A declaration following a trial that the individual accused of the crime is innocent in the eyes of the law and thus absolved from the charges.

THE PRIVILEGE AGAINST SELF-INCRIMINATION

In addition to the Sixth Amendment, which specifies the protections we have just discussed, the Fifth Amendment to the Constitution also provides important safeguards for the defendant. The Fifth Amendment states that no person "shall be compelled in any criminal case to be a witness against himself." Therefore, a defendant has the right *not* to testify at a trial if to do so would implicate him or her in the crime. Witnesses may also refuse to testify on this ground. For example, if a witness, while testifying, is asked a question and the answer would reveal her or his own criminal wrongdoing, the witness may "take the Fifth." In other words, she or he can refuse to testify on the ground that such testimony may be self-incriminating. This rarely occurs, however, as witnesses are often granted immunity before testifying, meaning that no information they disclose can be used to bring criminal charges against them. Witnesses who have been granted immunity cannot refuse to answer questions on the basis of self-incrimination.

It is important to note that not only does the defendant have the right to "take the Fifth," but also that the decision to do so should not prejudice the jury in the prosecution's favor. The Supreme Court came to this controversial decision while reviewing *Adamson v. California* (1947),[14] a case involving the convictions of two defendants who had declined to testify in their own defense against charges of robbery, kidnapping, and murder. The prosecutor in *Adamson* frequently and insistently brought this silence to the notice of the jury in his closing argument, insinuating that if the pair had been innocent, they would not have been afraid to testify. The Court ruled that such tactics effectively invalidated the Fifth Amendment by using the defendants' refusal to testify against them. Now judges are required to inform the jury that an accused's decision to remain silent cannot be held against him or her.

>
> **INFOTRAC KEYWORDS**
> **Fifth Amendment**
> For more information, use this search term with InfoTrac College Edition, your online library at www.infotrac-college.com

THE PRESUMPTION OF A DEFENDANT'S INNOCENCE

A presumption in criminal law is that a defendant is innocent until proved guilty. The burden of proving guilt falls on the state (the public prosecutor). Even if a defendant did in fact commit the crime, she or he will be "innocent" in the eyes of the law unless the prosecutor can substantiate the charge with sufficient evidence to convince a jury (or judge in a bench trial) of the defendant's guilt.[15] (To see how this right may be compromised when it comes to high-profile suspects, see the feature *CJ and the Media: Presumed Guilty*.)

A STRICT STANDARD OF PROOF

In a criminal trial, the defendant is not required to prove his or her innocence. As mentioned, the burden of proving the defendant's guilt lies entirely with the state. Furthermore, the state must prove the defendant's guilt **beyond a reasonable doubt;** that is, the prosecution must show that, based on all the evidence, the defendant's guilt is clear and unquestionable. In *In re Winship* (1970),[16] a case involving the due process rights of juveniles, the Supreme Court ruled that the Constitution requires the reasonable doubt standard because it reduces the risk of convicting innocent people and therefore reassures Americans of the law's moral force and legitimacy.

This high standard of proof in criminal cases reflects a fundamental social value—the belief that it is worse to convict an innocent individual than to let a guilty one go free. The consequences to the life, liberty, and reputation of an accused person from an erroneous conviction for a crime are enormous, and this has been factored into the process. Placing a high standard of proof on the prosecutor reduces the margin of error in criminal cases (at least in one direction).

ONLINE REVIEW *Go to the book's Web site for an interactive review of this section*

Jury Selection

The initial step in a criminal trial involves choosing the jury. The framers of the Constitution ensured that the importance of the jury would not be easily overlooked. The right to a trial by jury is explicitly mentioned no fewer than three times in the Constitution: in Article III, Section 2; in the Sixth Amendment; and again in the Seventh Amendment. The use of a peer jury not only provided safeguards against the abuses of state power that the framers feared, but also gave Americans a chance—and a duty—to participate in the criminal justice system.

In the early years of the country, a jury "of one's peers" meant a jury limited to white, landowning males. Now, as the process has become fully democratized, there are still questions about what "a jury of one's peers" actually means and how effective the system has been in providing the necessary diversity in juries.

INITIAL STEPS: THE MASTER JURY LIST AND *VENIRE*

The main goal of jury selection is to produce a cross section of the population in the jurisdiction where the crime was committed. Sometimes, a defense attorney

Beyond a Reasonable Doubt
The standard used to determine the guilt or innocence of a person charged with a crime. To be guilty of a crime, a suspect must be proved guilty "beyond and to the exclusion of a reasonable doubt."

The photo below was shown as an exhibit in the murder trial of John William King, who was charged with dragging an African American named James Byrd, Jr., to his death behind a pickup truck. Jurors were shown a number of photos of images tattooed on King's body, including one that showed a black man hanging from a tree. Do you agree with prosecutors that the intricate racist, satanic, and neo-Nazi tattoos covering King's body helped prove motive, intent, and state of mind? Or do you agree with the defense attorney who said that the tattoos do not necessarily make King a racist?

© Jasper County District Attorney's Office, AP/Wide World Photos

> Presumed Guilty>

According to prosecutors in Modesto, California, fertilizer salesman Scott Peterson killed his pregnant wife Laci at their home on Christmas Eve, 2002. From initial accounts, the case against Scott looked strong. Laci's body washed up on the shore of San Francisco Bay, just miles from where Scott claimed he was fishing when his wife vanished. He had also taken out a $250,000 life insurance policy on Laci, had traded in her car for a new pickup truck following her disappearance, and allegedly had been involved in an extramarital affair.

A "Slam Dunk"?

For many observers, however, Scott Peterson's Fifth Amendment guarantee of presumption of innocence was rendered meaningless by the rabid media coverage of Laci's murder. Months before the trial began, California Attorney General Bill Lockyer called the case against Peterson a "slam dunk," a claim widely repeated on television and radio. Fox News Channel correspondent Geraldo Rivera told viewers that Peterson's alibi "stunk as badly as the [fertilizer] he sells" and called the suspect a "rat now caught in the trap." When asked by Larry King if Peterson could have killed Laci by accident, Nancy Grace of CourtTV responded, "Why would you attach her feet to a concrete block and throw her into the bay?" even though there was no evidence that the victim had been killed in that manner. Grace went on to say, "In my mind, he seems guilty beyond a reasonable doubt."

The Risk of Unfair Prejudice

Similar media "feeding frenzies" have been misguided in the past. In 1996, Atlanta security guard Richard Jewell was falsely suspected of bombing Centennial Olympic Park, and the Ramseys of Boulder, Colorado, were hounded for years con-

AP Photo/Ann Johansson

Reporters surround Scott Peterson during a news conference. Media speculation over Peterson's role in the death of his pregnant wife, Laci, was widespread long before the start of his murder trial in 2004.

cerning the death of their daughter JonBenet although no charges were ever filed against them. Besides the hardship for those involved, what is the impact of intense media scrutiny and speculation in these cases? One of Peterson's lawyers argued that the coverage "obviously prejudices" members of the community—twelve of whom will act as jurors—against his client.

A judge has the authority to change the venue of a trial if he or she believes undue publicity will affect the ability of local jurors to make a reasoned judgment. Much of the coverage of the Peterson case, however, was broadcast nationally on cable television. As one professor of journalism commented, "Where could you find an untainted jury? In Tasmania?"

may argue that his or her client's trial should be moved to another community to protect against undue prejudice. Judges, mindful of the intent of the Constitution, are hesitant to grant such pretrial motions.

This belief that trials should take place in the community where the crime was committed is central to the purpose of selecting a jury of the defendant's "peers." The United States is a large, diverse nation, and the outlook of its citizens varies accordingly. Two very different cases, one tried in rural Maine and the other in San Francisco, illustrate this point.[17] In Maine, the defendant had accidentally shot and killed a woman standing in her back yard; he had mistaken her white mittens for a deer's tail. His attorney argued that it was the responsibility of the victim to wear bright-colored clothing in the vicinity of hunters during hunting season. The jury agreed, and the defendant was acquitted of manslaughter. In the San Francisco case, two people were charged with distributing sterile needles to intravenous drug users. Rather than denying that the defendants had distributed the needles, the defense admitted the act but insisted that it was necessary to stem the transmission of AIDS and, thus, to save lives. The jury voted 11–1 to acquit, causing a mistrial.

These two outcomes may surprise or even anger people in other parts of the country, but they reflect the values of the regions where the alleged crimes were committed. Thus, a primary goal of the jury selection process is to ensure that the defendant is judged by members of her or his community—peers in the true sense of the word.

The Master Jury List   Besides having to live in the jurisdiction where the case is being tried, there are very few restrictions on eligibility to serve on a jury. State legislatures generally set the requirements, and they are similar in most states. For the most part, jurors must be

1 Citizens of the United States.
2 Over eighteen years of age.
3 Free of felony convictions.
4 Of the necessary good health to function in a jury setting.
5 Sufficiently intelligent to understand the issues of a trial.
6 Able to read, write, and comprehend the English language.

Master Jury List
The list of citizens in a court's district from which a jury can be selected; often compiled from voter-registration lists, driver's license lists, and other sources.

The **master jury list,** sometimes called the *jury pool,* is made up of all the eligible jurors in a community. This list is usually drawn from voter-registration lists or driver's license rolls, which have the benefit of being easily available and timely.

Increasing Jury List Diversity   The drawback of tying master jury lists to voter registration lists is that the practice has tended historically to exclude the poor, racial minorities, the young, and the uneducated (in other words, the same groups who are less likely to vote). Also, it has been surmised that some people don't vote for the express reason of keeping their names off the master jury list. These people may not be able to afford to miss work at the low pay offered jurors—less than $30 per day on average—or simply may not want to deal with the inconvenience.

A number of states have taken steps to increase the diversity of the master jury list. Both Arizona and New York access welfare and unemployment rolls to find potential jurors, and Arizona also canvasses phone books and water service customer lists for that purpose. California uses Social Security rolls and tax returns as sources of names. In Florida and elsewhere, lists of persons with driver's licenses are also consulted. According to New Mexico's constitution, non-English-speaking citizens cannot be eliminated from jury lists simply because of their lack of language skills.[18] (In every other state, however, potential jurors may be automatically removed if they cannot speak or understand English.)

Venire
The group of citizens from which the jury is selected.

Venire   The next step in gathering a jury is to draw together the **venire** (Latin for "to come"). The *venire* is composed of all those people who are notified by the clerk of the court that they have been selected for jury duty. Those selected to be part of the *venire* are ordered to report to the courthouse on the date specified by the notice.

Some people are excused from answering this summons. Persons who do not meet the qualifications listed earlier in this section either need not appear in court or, in some states, must appear only in order to be officially dismissed. Also, people in some professions, including teachers, physicians, and judges, can receive exemptions due to the nature of their work. Each court sets its own guidelines for the circumstances under which it will excuse jurors from service, and these guidelines can be as strict or as lenient as the court desires.

See NJcourtsonline.com for information provided to potential jurors by the state of New Jersey. Find this Web site by clicking on *Web Links* under *Chapter Resources* at www.cjinaction.com

VOIR DIRE

At the courthouse, prospective jurors are gathered, and the process of selecting those who will actually hear the case begins. This selection process is not haphazard. The court ultimately seeks jurors who are free of any biases that may affect their willingness to listen to the facts of the case impartially. To this end, both the prosecutor and the defense attorney have some input into the ultimate make-up of the jury. Each attorney questions prospective jurors in a proceeding known as **voir dire** (French for "to speak the truth"). During *voir dire,* jurors are required to provide the court with a significant amount of personal information, including home address, marital status, employment status, arrest record, and life experiences.

Voir Dire
The preliminary questions that the trial attorneys ask prospective jurors to determine whether they are biased or have any connection with the defendant or a witness.

The *voir dire* process involves both written and oral questioning of potential jurors. Attorneys fashion their inquiries in such a manner as to uncover any biases on the parts of prospective jurors and to find persons who might identify with the plights of their respective sides. As one attorney noted, though a lawyer will have many chances to talk to a jury as a whole, *voir dire* is his only chance to talk with the individual jurors.

Challenging Potential Jurors   During *voir dire,* the attorney for each side may exercise a certain number of challenges to prevent particular persons from serving on the jury. Both sides can exercise two types of challenges: challenges "for cause" and peremptory challenges.

If a defense attorney or prosecutor concludes that a prospective juror is unfit to serve, the attorney may exercise a **challenge for cause** and request that that person not be included on the jury. Attorneys must provide the court with a sound, legally justifiable reason for why potential jurors are "unfit" to serve. For example, jurors can be challenged for cause if they are mentally incompetent, do not speak English, or are proved to have a prior link—be it personal or financial— with the defendant or victim.

Challenge for Cause
A *voir dire* challenge for which an attorney states the reason why a prospective juror should not be included on the jury.

Jurors can also be challenged if they are outwardly biased in some way that would prejudice them for or against the defendant. In the 2003 case of Clara Harris, who drove over and killed her husband after catching him in an extramarital affair in Houston, for example, one potential juror was dismissed because she announced she could "emotionally relate" to Harris's action. Another was turned away after admitting that she had hit her own husband with a car after discovering that he had a mistress. A third was disallowed because he had assaulted his unfaithful wife.[19] The Supreme Court has ruled that individuals may also be legally excluded from a jury in a capital case if they would under no circumstances vote for a guilty verdict if it carried the death penalty.[20] At the same time, potential jurors cannot be challenged for cause if they have "general objections" or have "expressed conscientious or religious scruples" against capital punishment.[21] The final responsibility for deciding whether a potential juror should be excluded rests with the judge, who may choose not to act on an attorney's request.

Peremptory Challenges

Voir dire challenges to exclude potential jurors from serving on the jury without any supporting reason or cause.

Peremptory Challenges   Each attorney may also exercise a limited number of **peremptory challenges.** These challenges are based *solely* on an attorney's subjective reasoning; that is, the attorney is usually not required to give any legally justifiable reason for wanting to exclude a particular person from the jury. Because of the rather random nature of peremptory challenges, each state limits the number that an attorney may utilize: between five and ten for felony trials (depending on the state) and ten and twenty for capital trials (also depending on the state). Once an attorney's peremptory challenges are used up, he or she must accept forthcoming jurors, unless a challenge for cause can be used.

An attorney's decision to exclude a juror may sometimes seem whimsical. One state prosecutor who litigated drug cases was known to use a peremptory challenge whenever he saw a potential juror with a coffee mug or backpack bearing the insignia of the local public broadcasting station. The attorney presumed that this was evidence that the potential juror had donated money to the public station, and that anybody who would do so would be too "liberal" to give the government's case against a drug offender a favorable hearing.[22] Lawyers have been known to similarly reject potential jurors for reasons of demeanor, dress, and posture. (See the feature *You Be the Judge—The Sympathetic Juror*.)

RACE AND GENDER ISSUES IN JURY SELECTION

The Sixth Amendment guarantees the right to an *impartial* jury. But, as researcher Jeremy W. Barber notes, it is in the best interests of neither the defense nor the prosecution to seek an impartial jury.[23] In fact, the goal of the attorneys' peremptory challenges is to create a *partial* jury—partial, that is, toward or against

---

> The Sympathetic Juror

YOU BE THE JUDGE

The Facts
Alan is a prosecutor in West Palm Beach, Florida. During *voir dire* for the trial of Jason, who was indicted for assaulting a police officer, Alan used one of his peremptory challenges to dismiss Robert. Alan said that he reasoned that because Robert was a pastor, he was more likely to be sympathetic to defendants. Therefore, Alan did not want Robert on the jury, and a trial judge allowed the challenge to stand. Jason was convicted, and on appeal he argued that Robert had in fact been denied a seat on the jury because, like Jason, he was African American.

The Law
Generally, an attorney is not required to give any reason for dismissing a juror

through a peremptory challenge. The United States Supreme Court has ruled, however, that the rationale for a peremptory challenge cannot be the juror's race. According to Florida law, a "trial judge's ruling on the 'genuineness' of a peremptory challenge will be affirmed on appeal unless clearly erroneous."

Your Decision
Does the law allow an attorney to use a peremptory challenge when he or she believes the juror may be "too sympathetic"? Can religious leaders as a group be excluded on these grounds? Was the trial judge's decision "clearly erroneous"?

[To see how the District Court ruled in this case, go to Example 10.1 in Appendix B.]

the defendant. If the jury turns out to be impartial, it may be that the efforts of the two sides have balanced each other out.

For many years, prosecutors used their peremptory challenges as an instrument of *de facto* segregation in juries. Prosecutors were able to keep African Americans off juries in cases in which an African American was the defendant. The argument that African Americans—or members of any other minority group— would be partial toward one of their own was tacitly supported by the Supreme Court. Despite its own assertion, made in *Swain v. Alabama* (1965),[24] that blacks have the same right to appear on a jury as whites, the Court mirrored the apparent racism of society as a whole by protecting the actions of many prosecutors.

The *Batson* Reversal   The Supreme Court reversed this policy in 1986 with *Batson v. Kentucky*.[25] In this case, the Court declared that the equal protection clause prohibits prosecutors from using peremptory challenges to strike possible jurors on the basis of race. Under *Batson,* the defendant must prove that the prosecution's use of a peremptory challenge was racially motivated. Doing so requires a number of legal steps.[26]

1 First, the defendant must make a *prima facie* case that there has been discrimination during *venire.* (*Prima facie* is Latin for "at first sight"; legally, it refers to a fact that is presumed to be true unless contradicted by evidence.)

2 To do so, the defendant must show that he or she is a member of a recognizable racial group and that the prosecutor has used peremptory challenges to remove members of this group from the jury pool.

3 Then, the defendant must show that these facts and other relevant circumstances raise the possibility that the prosecutor removed the prospective jurors solely because of their race.

4 If the court accepts the defendant's charges, the burden shifts to the prosecution to prove that its peremptory challenges were race neutral. If the court finds against the prosecution, it rules that a *Batson* violation has occurred. (For a closer look at the *Batson* decision, see *CJ in Focus—Landmark Cases: Batson v. Kentucky* on the next page.)

The Court has revisited the issue of race a number of times in the years since *Batson.* In *Powers v. Ohio* (1991),[27] it ruled that a defendant may contest race-based peremptory challenges even if the defendant is not of the same race as the excluded jurors. In *Georgia v. McCollum* (1992),[28] the Court placed defense attorneys under the same restrictions as prosecutors when making race-based peremptory challenges.

Then, in 2003, the Court stayed the execution of Thomas Miller-El by the state of Texas, giving Miller-El the chance to argue that prosecutors had violated his rights by striking ten of eleven potential black jurors because of their race.[29] (The only African American juror approved by the prosecution had stated that, in his opinion, the correct punishment for murderers was to "pour some honey on them and stake them out over an ant bed.") Many observers hope that the Court will use Miller-El's case to answer an important question: Can a decision to remove jurors because they will not impose the death penalty be "race neutral" when there is other evidence that the decision was actually based on the color of the jurors' skin?

INFOTRAC KEYWORDS
Batson v. Kentucky
For more information, use this search term with InfoTrac College Edition, your online library at www.infotrac-college.com

"A jury consists of twelve persons chosen to decide who has the better lawyer."
—Robert Frost, American poet (1874–1963)

> *Batson v. Kentucky*

James Kirkland Batson, an African American, had been charged with second degree burglary and receipt of stolen goods. In the jury selection process for Batson's trial, the prosecutor used his peremptory challenges to strike the only four African Americans in the *venire,* resulting in an all-white jury. Batson was convicted. In appealing his conviction, Batson claimed that by removing the potential jurors on the basis of their race, the prosecution had denied him his right to a jury drawn from a cross section of the community. Previously, the Supreme Court had ruled that racially discriminatory peremptory challenges could not be proved in a single case, but had to be shown as a pattern over a period of time. With *Batson,* however, the Court would reject this ruling.

Batson v. Kentucky
United States Supreme Court
476 U.S. 79 (1986)
http://laws.findlaw.com/US/476/79.html

> **In the words of the court . . .**

Justice Powell, majority opinion

* * * *

More than a century ago, the Court decided that the State denies a black defendant equal protection of the laws when it puts him on trial before a jury from which members of his race have been purposefully excluded. [*Strauder v. West Virginia,* 100 U.S. 303 (1880).] That decision laid the foundation for the Court's unceasing efforts to eradicate racial discrimination in the procedures used to select the venire from which individual jurors are drawn.

* * * *

Purposeful racial discrimination in selection of the venire violates a defendant's right to equal protection because it denies him the protection that a trial by jury is intended to secure. "The very idea of a jury is a body . . . composed of the peers or equals of the person whose rights it is selected or summoned to determine; that is, of his neighbors, fellows, associates, persons having the same legal status in society as that which he holds."

* * * *

The harm from discriminatory jury selection extends beyond that inflicted on the defendant and the excluded juror to touch the entire community. Selection procedures that purposefully exclude black persons from juries undermine public confidence in the fairness of our system of justice.

* * * *

The reality of [peremptory challenges], amply reflected in many state- and federal-court opinions, shows that the challenge may be, and unfortunately at times has been, used to discriminate against black jurors. By requiring trial courts to be sensitive to the racially discriminatory use of peremptory challenges, our decision enforces the mandate of equal protection and furthers the ends of justice. In view of the heterogeneous population of our Nation, public respect for our criminal justice system and the rule of law will be strengthened if we ensure that no citizen is disqualified from jury service because of his race.

> **Decision**

The Court overturned Batson's conviction and remanded the case, holding that prosecutors could not constitutionally use peremptory challenges to strike potential jurors based solely on their race. It also rejected the notion that African American jurors, as a whole, are unable to impartially consider a case against an African American defendant. To protect against discrimination, the Court set standards by which a defendant could prove that the jury in his or her trial had been tainted by racially motivated peremptory challenges.

FOR CRITICAL ANALYSIS
In this ruling, the Court (a) states a belief that diverse juries are necessary to ensure fair trials and (b) rejects the notion that a juror's race will influence his or her judgment. Some observers, while noting the obvious drawbacks of discrimination in jury selection, have labeled this the "Batson Paradox." How could these two opinions contradict each other when applied to a potential Batson *violation?*

 For more information and activities related to this case, click on Landmark Cases *under Book Resources at* www.cjinaction.com

Women on the Jury   Given the *Batson* precedent, it seemed inevitable that the Supreme Court would eventually address another issue: whether women were constitutionally protected from peremptory challenges based on their gender.[30] The exclusion of women has been more codified than the exclusion of racial groups. At the end of World War II, twenty-one states still prohibited female jurors, and the last state to end this practice—Alabama—did not do so until 1966.

In *J.E.B. v. Alabama* (1994),[31] the Supreme Court extended *Batson* to cover gender bias in jury selection. The case was a civil suit for paternity and child support brought by the state of Alabama. Prosecutors used nine of their ten challenges to remove men from the jury, while the defense made similar efforts to remove women. When challenged, the state defended its actions on what it called the rational belief that men and women might have different views on the issues of paternity and child support. The Court held this to be unconstitutional under the equal protection clause.

ALTERNATE JURORS

Because unforeseeable circumstances or illness may necessitate that one or more of the sitting jurors be dismissed, the court may also seat several *alternate jurors* who will hear the entire trial. Depending on the rules of the particular jurisdiction, two or three alternate jurors may be present throughout the trial. If a juror has to be excused in the middle of the trial, an alternate may take his or her place without disrupting the proceedings.

ONLINE REVIEW *Go to the book's Web site for an interactive review of this section*

The Trial

Once the jury members are seated, the judge swears in the jury and the trial itself can begin. A rather pessimistic truism among attorneys is that every case "has been won or lost when the jury is sworn." This reflects the belief that a juror's values are the major, if not dominant, factor in the decision of guilt or innocence.[32]

In actuality, it is difficult to predict how a jury will go about reaching a decision. Despite a number of studies on the question, researchers have not been able to provide any definitive answers. Sometimes, jurors in a criminal trial will follow instructions to find a defendant guilty unless there is a reasonable doubt, and sometimes they seem to follow instinct or prejudice and apply the law any way they choose.[33]

OPENING STATEMENTS

Attorneys may choose to open the trial with a statement to the jury, though they are not required to do so. In these **opening statements,** the attorneys give a brief version of the facts and the supporting evidence that they will present during the trial. Because some trials can drag on for weeks or even months, it is extremely helpful for jurors to hear a summary of what will unfold. In short, the opening statement is a kind of "road map" that describes the destination that each attorney hopes to reach and outlines how she or he plans to reach it. The danger for attorneys is that they will offer evidence during the trial that might contradict an assertion made during the opening statement. This may cause jurors to disregard the evidence or shift their own narrative further away from the narrative being offered by the attorney.[34] In *United States v. Dinitz* (1976),[35] the Supreme Court ruled that attorneys are limited in the opening statements to subjects they believe will be presented in the trial itself.

Opening Statements
The attorneys' statements to the jury at the beginning of the trial. Each side briefly outlines the evidence that will be offered during the trial and the legal theory that will be pursued.

The opening statement is also the first opportunity for the prosecution and defense to put their "spin" on the events being addressed in the trial. As you can see in Figure 10.2, the attorneys will often employ dramatic language in an immediate attempt to win the jury over to their side.

THE ROLE OF EVIDENCE

Once the opening statements have been made, the prosecutor begins the trial proceedings by presenting the state's evidence against the defendant. Courts have complex rules about what types of evidence may be presented and how the evidence may be brought out during the trial. **Evidence** is anything that is used to prove the existence or nonexistence of a fact. For the most part, evidence can be broken down into two categories: testimony and real evidence. **Testimony** consists of statements by competent witnesses. **Real evidence,** presented to the court in the form of exhibits, includes any physical items—such as the murder weapon or a bloodstained piece of clothing—that affect the case.

Rules of evidence are designed to ensure that testimony and exhibits presented to the jury are relevant, reliable, and not unfairly prejudicial against the defendant. One of the tasks of the defense attorney is to challenge evidence presented by the prosecution by establishing that the evidence is not reliable. Of course, the prosecutor also tries to demonstrate the irrelevance or unreliability of evidence presented by the defense. The final decision on whether evidence is allowed before the jury rests with the judge, in keeping with his or her role as the "referee" of the adversary system.

Testimonial Evidence A person who is called to testify on factual matters that would be understood by the average citizen is referred to as a **lay witness.** If asked about the condition of a victim of an assault, for example, a lay witness could relate certain facts, such as "she was bleeding from her forehead" or "she lay uncon-

Evidence
Anything that is used to prove the existence or nonexistence of a fact.

Testimony
Verbal evidence given by witnesses under oath.

Real Evidence
Evidence that is brought into court and seen by the jury, as opposed to evidence that is described for a jury.

Lay Witness
A witness who can truthfully and accurately testify on a fact in question without having specialized training or knowledge; an ordinary witness.

FIGURE 10.2 **The Opening Statement**

Sherri Dally of Ventura, California, was kidnapped from a parking lot and later killed. Prosecutors charged Diana Haun with the murder, alleging that she was in love with Dally's husband and wanted to "replace" her. In his opening statements, Deputy District Attorney Michael Frawley immediately attempts to humanize Dally for the jury, with the ultimate purpose of making her murder all the more worthy of harsh punishment.

Mr. FRAWLEY: *I would like to start by showing you a photograph so that you can have a face to go with some of the names that you're going to be hearing throughout this trial.*

> This photograph is of Sherri Dally and her family. That's Michael Dally, the other adult in the picture, and Max and Devon. Max is the younger one. On the date that Sherri was killed, . . . Max was six. And Devon, he had just turned eight a couple months before.

> You will learn that children were Sherri's life.

> Aside from her own, she ran a day-care center out of her home.

> And beyond that, the other focus of Sherri's life was Michael Dally. They had been married for fourteen years.

> Michael Dally was the only male that Sherri had ever dated.

> And what the evidence is going to show is that the defendant, Diana Haun, wanted to take Sherri Dally's place.

scious on the ground for several minutes." A lay witness could not, however, give information about the medical extent of the victim's injuries, such as whether she suffered from a fractured skull or internal bleeding. Coming from a lay witness, such testimony would be inadmissible. When the matter in question requires scientific, medical, or technical skill beyond the scope of the average person, prosecutors and defense attorneys may call an **expert witness** to the stand. The expert witness is an individual who has professional training, advanced knowledge, or substantial experience in a specialized area, such as medicine, computer technology, or ballistics. The rules of evidence state that expert witnesses may base their opinions on three types of information:

1 Facts or data of which they have personal knowledge.
2 Material presented at trial.
3 Secondhand information given to the expert outside the courtroom.[36]

Expert witnesses are considered somewhat problematic for two reasons. First, they may be chosen for their "court presence"—whether they speak well or will appear sympathetic to the jury—rather than their expertise. Second, attorneys pay expert witnesses for their services. Given human nature, the attorneys expect a certain measure of cooperation from an expert they have hired, and an expert witness has an interest in satisfying the attorneys so that he or she will be hired again.[37] Under these circumstances, some have questioned whether the courts can rely on the professional nonpartisanship of expert witnesses.[38]

Direct versus Circumstantial Evidence   Two types of testimonial evidence may be brought into court: direct evidence and circumstantial evidence. **Direct evidence** is evidence that has been witnessed by the person giving testimony. "I saw Bill shoot Chris" is an example of direct evidence. **Circumstantial evidence** is indirect evidence that, even if believed, does not establish the fact in question but only the degree of likelihood of the fact. In other words, circumstantial evidence can create an inference that a fact exists.

Suppose, for example, that the defendant owns a gun that shoots bullets of the type found in the victim's body. This circumstantial evidence, by itself, does not establish that the defendant committed the crime. Combined with other circumstantial evidence, however, it may do just that. For instance, if other circumstantial evidence indicates that the defendant had a motive for harming the victim and was at the scene of the crime when the shooting occurred, the jury might conclude that the defendant committed the crime.

Prosecutors take a risk if the *only* evidence they present is circumstantial. In charging Zacarias Moussaoui with conspiring in the September 11, 2001, terrorist attacks on New York City and Washington, D.C., federal prosecutors pointed to several pieces of "proof": Moussaoui received a $14,000 wire transfer from a former roommate of one of the leaders of that attack and operated a guest house used by members of the al Qaeda terrorist organization. Moussaoui was in prison on September 11, however, and the government has not produced

Expert Witness

A witness with professional training or substantial experience qualifying her or him to testify on a certain subject.

Direct Evidence

Evidence that establishes the existence of a fact that is in question without relying on inference.

Circumstantial Evidence

Indirect evidence that is offered to establish, by inference, the likelihood of a fact that is in question.

The job of the prosecution is to remove any traces of doubt concerning the defendant's guilt. This task can prove more difficult when the alleged crime took place many years earlier, as was the case in the 2002 trial of Kenneth K. Behrel, the long-time chaplain of the St. James School near Hagerstown, Maryland. Behrel was eventually found guilty of sexually molesting a male student in the early 1980s. A key piece of evidence in Behrel's trial was a black footlocker containing pornography that his victim had described to police officers. Is this footlocker direct evidence or circumstantial evidence of any wrongdoing?

AP Photo/Dennis Grundman

direct evidence of any contact between him and the nineteen hijackers. Consequently, it may be difficult to convince a jury of Moussaoui's guilt.[39]

Relevant Evidence
Evidence tending to make a fact in question more or less probable than it would be without the evidence. Only relevant evidence is admissible in court.

Relevance   Evidence will not be admitted in court unless it is relevant to the case being considered. **Relevant evidence** is evidence that tends to prove or disprove a fact in question. Forensic proof that the bullets found in a victim's body were fired from a gun discovered in the suspect's pocket at the time of arrest, for example, is certainly relevant. The suspect's prior record, showing a conviction for armed robbery ten years earlier, is, as we shall see in the next section, irrelevant to the case at hand and in most instances will be ruled inadmissible by the judge.

Prejudicial Evidence   Evidence may be excluded if it would tend to distract the jury from the main issues of the case, mislead the jury, or cause jurors to decide the issue on an emotional basis. In American trial courts, this rule precludes prosecutors from using prior purported criminal activities or actual convictions to show that the defendant has criminal propensities or an "evil character."[40]

This concept is codified in the Federal Rules of Evidence, which state that evidence of "other crimes, wrongs, or acts is not admissible to prove the character of a person in order to show action in conformity therewith." Such evidence is allowed only when it does not apply to character construction and focuses instead on "motive, opportunity, intent, preparation, plan, knowledge, identity, or absence of mistake or accident."[41]

Though this legal concept has come under a great deal of criticism, it is consistent with the presumption-of-innocence standards discussed earlier. Presumably, if a prosecutor is allowed to establish that the defendant has shown antisocial or even violent character traits, this will prejudice the jury against the defendant. (For a discussion of similar rules that protect the victim, see the feature *CJ in Focus—The Balancing Act: Rape Shield Laws.*) While discussing a 1930 murder case, New York Court of Appeals Chief Judge Benjamin Cardozo addressed the issue thusly:

> With only the rough and ready tests supplied by their experience of life, the jurors were to look into the workings of another's mind, and discover its capacities and disabilities, its urges and inhibitions, in moments of intense excitement. Delicate enough and subtle is the inquiry, even in the most favorable conditions, with every warping influence excluded. There must be no blurring of the issues by evidence illegally admitted and carrying with it in its admission an appeal to prejudice and passion.[42]

Authentication
Establishing the genuineness of an item that is to be introduced as evidence in a trial.

Authentication of Evidence   At trial, an attorney must lay the proper foundation for the introduction of certain evidence, such as documents, exhibits, and other objects, and must demonstrate to the court that the evidence is competent; that is, the evidence is what the attorney claims. The process by which this is accomplished is referred to as **authentication.** The authentication requirement relates to relevance because something offered in evidence is relevant to the case only if it is authentic, or genuine.

Commonly, evidence is authenticated by the testimony of witnesses. For example, if an attorney wants to introduce an autopsy report as evidence in a case, he or she can have the report authenticated by the testimony of the medical examiner who signed it. By the same token, before drugs taken from a crime scene can

> Rape Shield Laws

During the rape trial of University of Akron freshman Nathaniel Lewis, the defense offered as evidence a passage from the accuser's diary. "I think I pounced on Nate because he was the last straw," the diary read. "I'm sick of men taking advantage of me and I'm sick of myself for giving in to them. I'm not a nympho like all of those guys think. I'm just not strong enough to say no to them."

The defense wanted to present the diary passage as evidence that the accuser had engaged in sex willingly with the defendant and may have fabricated the rape charge because she was ashamed of her behavior. The Summit County (Ohio) Court, however, ruled that the diary was inadmissible as evidence because it introduced prejudicial information about the accuser's past sexual history.

Protecting the Victim

Ohio, like many other states, has enacted so-called rape shield laws in the past decade to right what had been seen as a social wrong—a woman who brought a rape charge was likely to have her sexual history dragged into the courtroom. The defense used such evidence to place doubt in the jurors' minds, insinuating that the alleged victim could have "asked for it" because she might have been promiscuous in the past. Rape shield laws specifically protect rape victims from having their prior sexual history used against them in court. These laws make the presumption that past history generally has no relevance to whether the woman consented to have sex with the accused rapist in the situation under question.

Protecting the Accused

The law protects those charged with sexual assault in a similar manner. The Federal Rules of Evidence permit testimony of prior sexual assault "on any matter for which it is relevant," but impose the condition that the value of the evidence not be "substantially outweighed by the danger of unfair prejudice." Similar language is written into many state laws.

FOR CRITICAL ANALYSIS
Do rape shield laws infringe on the rights of the accused? When would past sexual history be "relevant" in a courtroom?

---

be admitted as evidence, the law enforcement agent who collected them will be required to testify that they are in fact the same drugs.

The rules of evidence require authentication because certain types of evidence, such as exhibits and objects, cannot be cross-examined by opposing counsel, as witnesses can, yet such evidence may have a significant effect on the jury. (The cross-examination process will be examined later in the chapter.) The authentication requirement provides a safeguard against the introduction of non-verified evidence that may strongly influence the outcome of the case.

THE PROSECUTION'S CASE

Because the burden of proof is on the state, the prosecution is generally considered to have a more difficult task than the defense. The prosecutor attempts to establish guilt beyond a reasonable doubt by presenting the *corpus delicti* ("body of the offense" in Latin) of the crime to the jury. The *corpus delicti* is simply a legal term that refers to the substantial facts that show a crime has been committed. By establishing such facts through the presentation of evidence, the prosecutor hopes to convince the jury of the defendant's guilt.

Sometimes, poor strategy decisions can cost prosecutors a case. In 2002, Derek King, shown here, and his brother Alex were convicted of murdering their parents with a baseball bat. A Florida judge overturned the boys' convictions on learning that prosecutors had presented evidence showing that another man had committed the crime in a different trial.

AP Photo/Phil Coale

As was mentioned earlier, this evidence must be relevant and nonprejudicial. For example, a prosecutor might not be allowed to show the jury graphic photographs of a victim in a murder trial. Such photographs could elicit emotional responses from jurors and prejudice them against a defendant who is to be presumed innocent.[43] This is not to say, however, that evidence is never used for emotional effect. A prosecutor may, for example, place the murder weapon on a table in plain view of the jury, forcing the jurors to consider that a violent crime has in fact taken place and focus on their duty to ensure that the guilty party is punished.

Direct Examination of Witnesses   Witnesses are crucial to establishing the prosecutor's case against the defendant. The prosecutor will call witnesses to the stand and ask them questions pertaining to the sequence of events that the trial is addressing. This form of questioning is known as **direct examination.** During direct examination, the prosecutor will usually not be allowed to ask *leading questions*—questions that might suggest to the witness a particular desired response. A leading question might be something like "So, Mrs. Williams, you noticed the defendant threatening the victim with a broken beer bottle?" If Mrs. Williams answers "yes" to this question, she has, in effect, been "led" to the conclusion that the defendant was, in fact, threatening with a broken beer bottle. (A properly worded query would be, "Mrs. Williams, please describe the defendant's manner toward the victim during the incident.") The fundamental purpose behind testimony is to establish what actually happened, not what the trial attorneys would like the jury to believe happened.

Hearsay   When interviewing a witness, both the prosecutor and the defense attorney will make sure that the witness's statements are based on the witness's own knowledge and not hearsay. **Hearsay** can be defined as any testimony given in court about a statement made by someone else. Literally, it is what someone heard someone else say. For the most part, hearsay is not admissible as evidence. It is excluded because the listener may have misunderstood what the other person said, and without the opportunity of cross-examining the originator of the statement, the misconception cannot be challenged.

There are a number of exceptions to the hearsay rule, and as a result, a good deal of hearsay evidence is allowed before the jury. For example, a hearsay statement is usually admissible if there seems to be little risk of a lie. Therefore, a statement made by someone who believes that his or her death is imminent—a "dying declaration"—is allowed in court even though it is hearsay.[44] The rules of most courts also allow hearsay when the person who made the statement is unavailable to be questioned in court or when the statement is particularly important to the argument being made by one side. Consequently, an admission of guilt by the defendant is often permitted even when it falls under the strict definition of hearsay.[45]

Competence and Reliability of Witnesses   The rules of evidence include certain restrictions and qualifications pertaining to witnesses. Witnesses must have sufficient mental competence to understand the significance of testifying under oath. They must also be reliable in the sense that they are able to give a clear and unadulterated description of the events in question. For example, attorneys for Mir Aimal Kasi, who was convicted of murdering two CIA agents, challenged his conviction on the basis that prosecution witness Judy Becker-Darling was under

Direct Examination
The examination of a witness by the attorney who calls the witness to the stand to testify.

Hearsay
An oral or written statement made by an out-of-court declarant that is later offered in court by a witness (not the declarant) concerning a matter before the court. Hearsay usually is not admissible as evidence.

medical treatment for traumatic stress disorder during her testimony. Becker-Darling's medical condition, the defense argued, made her an unreliable witness.[46] (The judge denied the motion.)

CROSS-EXAMINATION

After the prosecutor has directly examined her or his witnesses, the defense attorney is given the chance to question the same witnesses. The Sixth Amendment states that "In all criminal prosecutions, the accused shall enjoy the right . . . to be confronted with witnesses against him." In practical terms, this gives the accused, through his or her attorneys, the right to cross-examine witnesses. **Cross-examination** refers to the questioning of an opposing witness during trial, and both sides of a case are allowed to do so (see Figure 10.3).

Cross-examination allows the attorneys to test the truthfulness of opposing witnesses and usually entails efforts to create doubt in the jurors' minds that the witness is reliable. Cross-examination is also linked to the problems presented by hearsay evidence. When a witness offers hearsay, the person making the original remarks is not in the court and therefore cannot be cross-examined. If such testimony were allowed, the defendant's Sixth Amendment right to confront witnesses against him or her would be violated.

Cross-Examination
The questioning of an opposing witness during trial.

FIGURE 10.3 **The Cross-Examination**

In the so-called Boston Nanny case, nineteen-year-old British *au pair* Louise Woodward was charged with second degree murder of an infant left in her care. Prosecutors tried to convince the jury that Woodward was a temperamental teen-ager who became frustrated with caring for a sick child and "snapped." The defense claimed that the brain hemorrhage that killed the child was actually the delayed result of another accident that had occurred several weeks earlier.

  Detective Sergeant William Byrne, who interviewed Woodward following the boy's death, testified that she claimed to have dropped the infant on a towel on the bathroom floor, and that the infant "may have banged his head on the floor where it meets the tub." On cross-examination, defense counsel tried to clarify exactly what Woodward, who denied making such statements, had told the police officer.

  DEFENSE: You asked her, "What do you mean by 'drop him on the floor,'" and her answer was, "I was angry."

  DETECTIVE SERGEANT BYRNE: Yes, sir.

  DEFENSE: So she wasn't telling you, according to your testimony, that "I dropped him by accident."

  DETECTIVE SERGEANT BYRNE: No, sir.

  DEFENSE: She wasn't saying, "I tripped and he fell."

  DETECTIVE SERGEANT BYRNE: No, sir.

  DEFENSE: She wasn't saying, "He slipped out of my hands."

  DETECTIVE SERGEANT BYRNE: No, sir.

  DEFENSE: You're saying that she told you that she did this on purpose.

  DETECTIVE SERGEANT BYRNE: She was angry, sir.

  DEFENSE: Okay. That's what she meant by "angry," according to you, right, that she did this on purpose.

  DETECTIVE SERGEANT BYRNE: She didn't say that she did it on purpose.

  DEFENSE: But you understood that to mean that she did it on purpose.

  DETECTIVE SERGEANT BYRNE: That was my feeling.

In this case, the cross-examination may have hurt the defendant, as Detective Sergeant Byrne was able to reassert his belief that Woodward was responsible for the death. In fact, the Boston jury did convict Woodward, though the trial judge later overturned the conviction.

After the defense has cross-examined a prosecution witness, the prosecutor may want to reestablish any reliability that might have been lost. The prosecutor can do so by again questioning the witness, a process known as *redirect examination.* Following the redirect examination, the defense attorney will be given the opportunity for *recross-examination,* or to ask further questions of prosecution witnesses. Thus, each side has two opportunities to question a witness. The attorneys need not do so, but only after each side has been offered the opportunity will the trial move on to the next witness or the next stage.

MOTION FOR A DIRECTED VERDICT

After the prosecutor has finished presenting evidence against the defendant, the government will inform the court that it has rested the people's case. At this point, the defense may make a **motion for a directed verdict** (now also known as a *motion for judgment as a matter of law* in federal courts). Through this motion, the defense is basically saying that the prosecution has not offered enough evidence to prove that the accused is guilty beyond a reasonable doubt. If the judge grants this motion, which rarely occurs, then a judgment will be entered in favor of the defendant, and the trial is over.

THE DEFENDANT'S CASE

Assuming that the motion for a directed verdict is denied, the defense attorney may offer the defendant's case. Because the burden is on the state to prove the accused's guilt, the defense is not required to offer any case at all. It can simply "rest" without calling any witnesses or producing any real evidence and ask the jury to judge the merits of the case on what it has seen and heard from the prosecution.

Placing the Defendant on the Stand   If the defense does present a case, its first—and often most important—decision is whether the defendant will take the stand in her or his own defense. Because of the Fifth Amendment protection against self-incrimination, the defendant is not required to testify. Therefore, the defense attorney must make a judgment call. He or she may want to place the defendant on the stand if the defendant is likely to appear sympathetic to the jury or is well spoken and able to aid the defense's case. With a less sympathetic or less effective defendant, the defense attorney may decide that exposing the defendant before the jury presents too large a risk. Also, if the defendant testifies, she or he is open to cross-examination under oath from the prosecutor. In any case, remember that the prosecution cannot comment on a defendant's refusal to testify.[47]

It is not uncommon for a defendant to take the stand against the advice of his or her attorney. Sometimes, defendants feel frustrated by the enforced silence of the courtroom and relish the chance to give their "side of the story." In other instances, they may simply want to vent anger—one murder suspect took advantage of his time before the court to call the jurors "scumbags."[48] Given that all Americans have a constitutional right to testify in their own defense, lawyers can do little when a client insists on taking the stand. When this does occur, the defense attorney is best served by notifying the court that the defendant is testifying against the advice of counsel—a step that protects the attorney from facing charges of ineffective representation later in the appeals process.

Creating a Reasonable Doubt   Defense lawyers most commonly defend their clients by attempting to expose weaknesses in the prosecutor's case. Remember that if the defense attorney can create reasonable doubt concerning the client's guilt in the mind of just a single juror, the defendant has a good chance of gaining an acquittal or at least a *hung jury,* a circumstance explained later in the chapter.

Even if the prosecution can present seemingly strong evidence, a defense attorney may succeed by creating reasonable doubt. In an illustrative case, Jason Korey bragged to his friends that he had shot and killed Joseph Brucker in Pittsburgh, Pennsylvania, and a great deal of circumstantial evidence linked Korey to the killing. The police, however, could find no direct evidence: they could not link Korey to the murder weapon, nor could they match his footprints to those found at the crime scene. Michael Foglia, Korey's defense attorney, explained his client's bragging as a ploy to gain attention from his friends. Though this explanation may strike some as unlikely, in the absence of physical evidence it did create doubt in the jurors' minds, and Korey was acquitted.

This strategy is also very effective in cases that essentially rely on the word of the defendant against the word of the victim. In sexual assault cases, for example, if the defense attorneys can create doubt about the victim's credibility—in other words, raise the possibility that he or she is lying—then they may prevail at trial. According to the Alcohol and Rape Study, carried out by researchers at Rutgers University and the University of New Hampshire, juries acquit about 90 percent of the time when the defendant says the sex was consensual and there is evidence that the alleged victim was drinking alcohol before the incident in question.[49]

Other Defense Strategies   The defense can choose among a number of strategies to generate reasonable doubt in the jurors' minds. It can present an *alibi defense,* by submitting evidence that the accused was not at or near the scene of the crime at the time the crime was committed. Another option is to attempt an *affirmative defense,* by presenting additional facts to the ones offered by the prosecution. Possible affirmative defenses, which we discussed in detail in Chapter 4, include the following:

1 Self-defense   2 Insanity   3 Duress   4 Entrapment

With an affirmative defense strategy, the defense attempts to prove that the defendant should be found not guilty because of extenuating circumstances surrounding the crime. An affirmative strategy can be difficult to carry out because it forces the defense to prove the veracity of its own evidence, not simply disprove the evidence offered by the prosecution.

The defense is often willing to admit that a certain criminal act took place, especially if the defendant has already confessed. In this case, the primary question of the trial becomes not whether the defendant is guilty, but what the defendant is guilty of. In these situations, the defense strategy focuses on obtaining the lightest possible penalty for the defendant. As we saw in the last chapter, this strategy is responsible for the high percentage of proceedings that end in plea bargains.

REBUTTAL AND SURREBUTTAL

After the defense closes its case, the prosecution is permitted to bring new evidence forward that was not used during its initial presentation to the jury. This is called the **rebuttal** stage of the trial. When the rebuttal stage is finished, the

CourtTV is a cable television channel that offers continuous coverage of the most important criminal trials of the day. Find its Web site, which offers news on current and classic trials, by clicking on *Web Links* under *Chapter Resources* at www.cjinaction.com

Rebuttal
Evidence given to counteract or disprove evidence presented by the opposing party.

defense is given the opportunity to cross-examine the prosecution's new witnesses and introduce new witnesses of its own. This final act is part of the *surrebuttal*. After these stages have been completed, the defense may offer another motion for a directed verdict, asking the judge summarily to find in the defendant's favor. If this motion is rejected, and it almost always is, the case is closed, and the opposing sides offer their closing arguments.

CLOSING ARGUMENTS

Closing Arguments
Arguments made by each side's attorney after the cases for the plaintiff and defendant have been presented.

In their **closing arguments,** the attorneys summarize their presentations and argue one final time for their respective cases. In most states, the defense attorney goes first, and then the prosecutor. (In Colorado, Kentucky, and Missouri, the order is reversed.) An effective closing argument includes all of the major points that support the government's or the defense's case. It also emphasizes the shortcomings of the opposing party's case. Jurors will view a closing argument with some skepticism if it merely recites the central points of a party's claim or defense without also responding to the unfavorable facts or issues raised by the other side. Of course, neither attorney wants to focus too much on the other side's position, but the elements of the opposing position do need to be acknowledged and their flaws highlighted.

One danger in the closing arguments is that an attorney will become too emotional and make remarks that are later deemed by appellate courts to be prejudicial. Once both attorneys have completed their remarks, the case is submitted to the jury, and the attorneys' role in the trial is, for the moment, complete.

↗ ONLINE REVIEW *Go to the book's Web site for an interactive review of this section*

The Final Steps of the Trial and Postconviction Procedures

After closing arguments, the outcome of the trial is in the hands of the jury. In this section, we examine the efforts to give jurors the means necessary to make informed decisions about the guilt or innocence of the accused. We will also look at the posttrial motions that can occur when the defense feels that the jurors, prosecution, or trial judge made errors that necessitate remedial legal action.

JURY INSTRUCTIONS

Charge
The judge's instructions to the jury following the attorneys' closing arguments; the charge sets forth the rules of law that the jury must apply in reaching its decision, or verdict.

Before the jurors begin their deliberations, the judge gives the jury a **charge,** summing up the case and instructing the jurors on the rules of law that apply to the issues in the case. These charges, also called jury instructions, are usually prepared during a special *charging conference* involving the judge and the trial attorneys. In this conference, the attorneys suggest the instructions they would like to see be sent to the jurors, but the judge makes the final decision as to the charges submitted.[50] If the defense attorney disagrees with the charges sent to the jury, he or she can enter an objection, thereby setting the stage for a possible appeal.

The Judge's Role   The judge usually begins by explaining basic legal principles, such as the need to find the defendant guilty beyond a reasonable doubt. Then the jury instructions narrow to the specifics of the case at hand, and the judge explains to the jurors what facts the prosecution must have proved in order to convict. (See Figure 10.4.) If the defense strategy centers on an affirmative defense such as insanity or entrapment, the judge will discuss the relevant legal principles that the defense must have proved to obtain an acquittal. The final segment of the charges discusses possible verdicts. These always include "guilty" and "not guilty," but some cases also allow for the jury to find "guilt by reason of insanity" or "guilty but mentally ill." Juries are often charged with determining the seriousness of the crime as well, such as deciding whether a homicide is murder in the first degree, murder in the second degree, or manslaughter.

Understanding the Instructions   A serious problem with jury instructions is that jurors often do not seem to understand them.[51] This is hardly surprising, as most average Americans do not have the education or legal background to understand the somewhat unfathomable jargon of the law. One study came to the unfortunate conclusion that juries that received no instructions whatsoever were basically as well equipped—or poorly equipped, as the case may be—as juries that did receive instructions.[52]

One solution is to simplify the language of the jury instructions. This idea, however, has met resistance among legal professionals, who are accustomed to "legal speak" and do not wish to change. Another suggestion is for the judge to give the jury its instructions before and after the trial. In this way, some of the legal concepts would be introduced before the evidence and narratives are established, giving jurors a chance to comprehend the issues involved before they are overwhelmed by the evidence in a complicated case.

JURY DELIBERATION

After receiving the charge, the jury begins its deliberations. Jury deliberation is a somewhat mysterious process, as it takes place in complete seclusion. In extreme cases, the judge will order that the jury be *sequestered,* or isolated from the public, during the trial and deliberation stages of the proceedings. Sequestration is used when deliberations are expected to be lengthy, or the trial is attracting a high amount of interest and the judge wants to keep the jury from being unduly influenced. Juries are usually sequestered in hotels and kept under the watch and

Terry Nichols was convicted of conspiracy and eight counts of involuntary manslaughter in the 1995 bombing of the Oklahoma City federal building. When the twelve jurors began deliberating Nichols's fate, however, their first vote was 10–2 for acquittal. "I couldn't believe it," recalled juror Tim Burge, who initially voted to convict. "I was like, man, did I miss something here or what." It took six days of heated arguments, which left some of the jurors in tears, before a compromise verdict was worked out in which the defendant was acquitted of more serious murder and weapons-related counts. How does this case show the strengths and/or weaknesses of the jury system?

FIGURE 10.4   **Jury Instructions**

These are model jury instructions for cases where the charge is involuntary manslaughter.

The defendant is charged in [Count _____ of] the indictment with involuntary manslaughter in violation of Section 1112 of Title 18 of the United States Code. [Involuntary manslaughter is the unlawful killing of a human being without malice aforethought and without an intent to kill.] In order for the defendant to be found guilty of that charge, the government must prove each of the following elements beyond a reasonable doubt.

> FIRST, the defendant committed an unlawful act not amounting to a felony, or a lawful act, done either in an unlawful manner or with wanton or reckless disregard for human life, which might produce death;

> SECOND, the defendant's act was the proximate cause of the death of the victim. A proximate cause is one which played a substantial part in bringing about the death so that the death was the direct result or a reasonably probable consequence of the defendant's act;

> THIRD, the killing was unlawful; and

> FOURTH, the defendant either knew that such conduct was a threat to the lives of others or knew of circumstances that would reasonably cause the defendant to foresee that such conduct might be a threat to the lives of others.

Source: Office of the Circuit Executive, Ninth Circuit.

INFOTRAC KEYWORDS

jury deliberation

For more information, use this search term with InfoTrac College Edition, your online library at www.infotrac-college.com

guard of officers of the court. (For information on a courtroom participant who oversees sequestering and many other aspects of the trial, see this chapter's *Careers in CJ* feature.)

Most of what is known about how a jury deliberates comes from mock trials or interviews with jurors after the verdict has been reached. A general picture of the deliberation process can be constructed from this research. It shows that the romantic notion of jurors with high-minded ideals of justice making eloquent speeches is, for the most part, not the reality. In approximately three out of every ten cases, the initial vote by the jury led to a unanimous decision. In 90 percent of the remaining cases, the majority eventually dictated the decision.[53] Furthermore, the peer pressure inherent in small-group situations is usually too great for dissenters to resist.[54] After a jury found hip-hop artist Sean ("P. Diddy") Combs not guilty on weapons possession charges in 2001, one juror told the press that he had not agreed with the verdict. "For two nights [following the end of the trial], I cried like a baby," said the juror, who was guilt-ridden at the thought that he may have violated his duty as a member of the jury.[55]

THE VERDICT

Verdict

A formal decision made by the jury.

Once it has reached a decision, the jury issues a **verdict.** The most common verdicts are guilty and not guilty, though as we have seen, juries may signify different degrees of guilt if instructed to do so. Following the announcement of a guilty or not guilty verdict, the jurors are discharged, and the jury trial proceedings are finished. (See Figure 10.5 for a review of the steps of a jury trial.)

The Hung Jury When a jury in a criminal trial is unable to agree on a unanimous verdict—or a majority in certain states—it returns with no decision. This is known as a **hung jury.** After the trauma of a trial, a hung jury is often unsatisfactory to the participants of the trial. After a hung jury was announced in the 2003 trial of Jeremy Morse, a white Inglewood (California) police officer who had been caught on videotape beating a black teenager, someone in the courtroom shouted out, "There's no justice here."[56]

Hung Jury

A jury whose members are so irreconcilably divided in their opinions that they cannot reach a verdict.

A judge can do little to reverse a hung jury, considering that "no decision" is just as legitimate a verdict as guilty or not guilty. In some states, if there are only a

FIGURE 10.5
The Steps of a Jury Trial

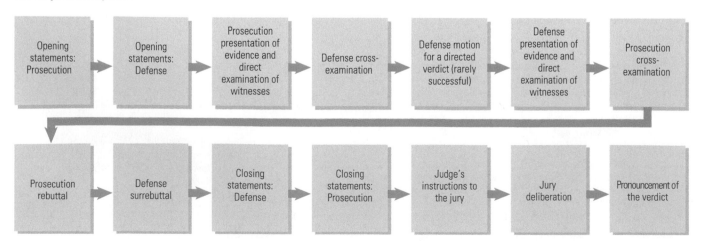

> Collins E. Ijoma Trial Court Administrator

I moved to the United States from Nigeria in 1976 to complete my college education, majoring in accounting and business administration. I earned a master's degree in public administration from Seton Hall University in 1982 with a concentration in public budgeting and finance. I was immensely interested in public service but was not particularly aware of the judiciary as a potential employer. My first job in the court system was by accident rather than design. After completing a graduate internship with the Essex County government, I had the opportunity to seek permanent employment with the county-funded judiciary. I was first employed in the Trial Court Administrator's Office in Newark, New Jersey, as the court finance officer in 1983. Much of my education in court administration was gained through the Institute for Court Management of the National Center for State Courts. I pursued this program of professional development from 1984 through 1991 when I graduated as a fellow of ICM.

My initial position offered many opportunities to learn about court management and the workings of a large urban court system. My primary concentration was in human resources, budget, and finance. As a state court, funded by the county, we had to continually justify and fight for positions, space, and equipment. Our court was growing rapidly, and we needed additional resources to allow for an effective and efficient operation. In 1985, I was promoted to Director of Personnel. I had direct responsibility for all personnel programs, policies, and practices. My association with professional organizations, including the National Association for Court Administration, the American Judicature Society, the Mid-Atlantic Association for Court Administration, and the American Society for Public Administration was critical to my professional development. The knowledge gained combined with experience helped me to successfully seek the position of assistant trial court administrator and my present position as trial court administrator.

As the trial court administrator, I serve principally as the chief administrative officer for the largest trial and municipal court system in New Jersey. We provide technical and manage-rial support to the court (over sixty superior court judges and thirty-six municipal court judges) on such matters as personnel, program development, case flow, resources, and facilities management. This description may sound highfalutin considering that most people can only describe a court in terms of a judge, one or two courtroom staff, and a few other employees associated with the visible activities in the courthouse. Obviously, there is a lot more going on behind the scenes of which the average citizen is not aware. For example, besides directing case flow for the four major divisions (criminal, civil, family, and probation) the work involved in managing personnel programs for more than 1,200 employees, information systems and technology infrastructure, maintaining records of proceedings,

Courtesy Collins E. Ijoma

Collins E. Ijoma

coordination of transcription, grand and petit jury operations, and court interpreting, to mention but a few examples, is enormous. The modern court needs dedicated professionals in each of these areas.

One thing that keeps me going and enthused about this profession is the resolve and dedication of our judges and staff. The family division embraces a host of issues, and in some cases those who seek help are hurting and desperate. The court may be their only hope. We are also actively engaged in pursuing new ways to offer and manage dispute resolution. Some of these include drug courts to give nonviolent drug offenders a chance at rehabilitation rather than going to jail, complimentary dispute resolution to reach more satisfactory conclusions in less time and at a lower cost to litigants, and creative uses of volunteers to assist in the work of the court and create a positive connection to the community.

 Go to the Careers in Criminal Justice Interactive CD *for more profiles in the field of criminal justice.*

few dissenters to the majority view, a judge can send the jury back to the jury room under a set of rules set forth more than a century ago by the Supreme Court in *Allen v. United States* (1896).[57] The **Allen Charge,** as this instruction is called, asks the jurors in the minority to reconsider the majority opinion. Many jurisdictions do not allow *Allen* Charges on the ground that they improperly coerce jurors with the minority opinion to change their minds.[58]

For all of the attention they receive, hung juries are relatively rare. Juries are unable to come to a decision in only about 6 percent of all cases.[59] Furthermore, juries may be more lenient (or easy to "trick") than is generally perceived; one

Allen Charge

An instruction by a judge to a deadlocked jury with only a few dissenters that asks the jurors in the minority to reconsider the majority opinion.

study found that juries were six times more likely than judges (in bench trials) to acquit a person who turns out to be guilty.[60]

Jury Nullification   The last statistic points to a growing concern of a number of criminal justice observers: the question of whether the jury's verdict is always based on the proper legal principles. This question deals with the controversial subject of **jury nullification,** which occurs when jurors "nullify" the law by acquitting a defendant who may be guilty according to the instruction given to them by the court. In other words, the jury acquits *in spite of* the evidence, rather than *because of* the evidence.[61] The specter of jury nullification is most often raised in cases that involve issues on which jurors may have strong ideological opinions, such as race, the death penalty, assisted suicide, or drug offenses. The not guilty verdict in O. J. Simpson's 1995 criminal trial was widely seen as an example of jury nullification, with jurors swayed by the racially based arguments of the defense rather than the facts of the case.

Many observers believe jury nullification is counter to the principles of American law because it allows a jury to "play by its own rules." Others, however, feel that jurors are within their rights when they question not only the facts in the case before them, but also the merits of the laws that the court is asking them to enforce. This argument has been made since the earliest days of the American legal system, when John Adams (1735–1826) said that a juror has not only a right, but a duty, "to find the verdict according to his own best understanding, judgment, and conscience, though in direct opposition to the direction of the court."[62] By this reasoning, jurors who feel that a particular law is unjust, or that the penalty for a law is too severe, are justified in nullifying a guilty verdict. (See the feature *CJ in Focus—A Question of Ethics: The Nullifying Juror* for other arguments in favor of jury nullification.)

APPEALS

Even if a defendant is found guilty, the trial process is not necessarily over. In our criminal justice system, a person convicted of a crime has a right to appeal. An **appeal** is the process of seeking a higher court's review of a lower court's decision for the purpose of correcting or changing the lower court's judgment. Any defendant who loses a case in a trial court cannot automatically appeal the conviction. The defendant normally must first be able to show that the trial court acted improperly on a question of law. Common reasons for appeals include the introduction of tainted evidence by the prosecution or faulty jury instructions delivered by the trial judge. In federal courts, about 16 percent of criminal convictions are appealed.[63]

Double Jeopardy   The appeals process is available only to the defense. If a jury finds the accused not guilty, the prosecution cannot appeal to have the decision reversed. To do so would infringe on the defendant's Fifth Amendment rights against multiple trials for the same offense. This guarantee against being tried a second time for the same crime is known as protection from **double jeopardy.**

The Limits of Double Jeopardy   The prohibition against double jeopardy means that once a criminal defendant is found not guilty of a particular crime, the government may not reindict the person and retry him or her for the same crime. The basic idea behind the double jeopardy clause, in the words of Supreme Court Justice Hugo Black, is that the state should not be allowed to

Jury Nullification
An acquittal of a defendant by a jury even though the evidence presented and the judge's instructions indicate that the defendant is guilty.

INFOTRAC KEYWORDS
jury nullification
For more information, use this search term with InfoTrac College Edition, your online library at www.infotrac-college.com

Appeal
The process of seeking a higher court's review of a lower court's decision for the purpose of correcting or changing the lower court's judgment or decision.

Double Jeopardy
To twice place at risk (jeopardize) a person's life or liberty. The Fifth Amendment to the U.S. Constitution prohibits a second prosecution for the same criminal offense.

> The Nullifying Juror

I magine that you are a juror in the following case. The victim, the Reverend Maurice J. Blackwell, is a priest who was suspended in the early 2000s after complaints that he sexually abused several of his parishioners. The defendant, Dontee Stokes, is one of those who claimed to have been molested by Blackwell as a teen-ager. Stokes, frustrated that Baltimore police refused to press charges in the case, confronted Blackwell in the street and shot him in the left hand and hip. The facts are clear: Stokes tried to kill his victim, and he was charged with attempted murder.

Even if you believe that Stokes had justification for his actions, would you be willing to vote for his acquittal? In 2002, a Baltimore jury did just that, exonerating Stokes from any felony charges related to the incident. Many in Baltimore were satisfied that the verdict was just. "[Here] is a young man that was abused as a child," said one community leader, who added that she was "happy that this young man did not have to pay the price for a broken system."

Paul Butler, an associate professor at George Washington Law School, takes the idea of jury nullification a step further, suggesting that it should be common practice for all African American jurors in cases involving African American defendants. Butler's "framework for criminal justice in the black community" includes the following points:

> In cases involving violent crimes, jurors should consider the evidence and acquit when they have reasonable doubt about the guilt of the African American defendant.

> In cases involving nonviolent crimes (such as theft), jury nullification is an option to be used at the juror's discretion. If, for example, a poor African American is on trial for stealing from a wealthy person, the juror should acquit, but if the victim is also poor, the juror should convict.

> In cases involving victimless crimes such as prostitution or drug violations, the juror should nullify as a matter of course. An African American charged with cocaine possession, for example, should be automatically acquitted.

Butler believes that he is calling on African American jurors to, in his words, "serve a higher calling than the law: justice." His critics point out that different people have different concepts of what "justice" is, and that such broad-based jury nullification has its own dangers. These dangers were shown in a very clear and dramatic way in the South, where, until the 1960s, white juries virtually never found another white person guilty of a crime committed against an African American.

FOR CRITICAL ANALYSIS
Do you agree with the stand taken by Stokes's jury and Butler? Should laws be held accountable to the people that they serve? How might widespread jury nullification affect the criminal justice system?

make repeated attempts to convict an individual for an alleged offense, thereby subjecting him to embarrassment, expense and ordeal and compelling him to live in a continuing state of anxiety and insecurity, as well as enhancing the possibility that though innocent he may be found guilty.[64]

The bar against double jeopardy does not preclude a *civil* suit's being brought against the same person by the crime victim to recover damages. For example, in 2003, after a criminal trial in which he was found guilty of kidnapping and murdering seven-year-old Danielle van Dam (and sentenced to be executed), David Westerfield agreed to pay the van Dam family between $400,000 and $1 million to settle a wrongful death suit. This was not considered double jeopardy because the second suit involved a civil claim, not a criminal one. Therefore, Westerfield was not charged with committing the same *crime* twice.

The Possibility and Risk of Retrial   Additionally, a state's prosecution of a crime will not prevent a separate federal prosecution of the same crime, and vice versa; that is, a defendant found not guilty of violating a state law can be tried in federal court for the same act, if the act is also defined as a crime under federal law. Furthermore, different states can prosecute the same person. After John Allen

On May 6, 2002, Court of Appeals Chief Judge Judith S. Kaye and Judge Howard A. Levine enter the New York State Court of Appeals to hear arguments as to whether Darrel K. Harris should be executed by the state. The Court of Appeals eventually overturned Harris's death sentence. Six of the seven judges found that he had been unfairly forced to choose between exercising his constitutional rights under the Fifth and Sixth Amendments, or pleading guilty to a lesser charge that was not punishable by execution. How does Harris's case show the important role that appeals courts play in the criminal justice system?

Muhammad was convicted in Virginia for murder for his sniper attacks on residents of that state, for example, he may still be tried in Maryland, Georgia, Alabama, and Louisiana for his crimes in those jurisdictions. Even though a Virginia court sentenced Muhammad to be executed, the other states may theoretically prosecute him for crimes against their citizens.

Note that a hung jury is *not* an acquittal for purposes of double jeopardy. So, if a jury is deadlocked, the government is free to seek a new trial. The United States Supreme Court reiterated this principle in *Sattazahn v. Pennsylvania* (2003),[65] a case involving a defendant who was convicted of murder but then had a hung jury in the penalty phase of his trial—resulting in an automatic sentence of life in prison rather than execution. The defendant appealed the initial conviction and won a new trial. When he was convicted a second time, the state once again sought the death penalty and succeeded. The Court held that as no acquittal had taken place in the sentencing phase of the first trial, double jeopardy protections were irrelevant.

> "Appeal: In law, to put the dice into the box for another throw."
>
> —Ambrose Bierce, American author (c. 1900)

The Appeal Process There are two basic reasons for the appeal process. The first is to correct an error made during the initial trial. The second is to review policy. Because of this second function, the appellate courts are an important part of the flexible nature of the criminal justice system. When existing law has ceased to be effective or no longer reflects the values of society, an appellate court can effectively change the law through its decisions and the precedents that it sets.[66] A classic example was the *Miranda v. Arizona* decision, which, although it failed to change the fate of the defendant (he was found guilty on retrial), had a far-reaching impact on custodial interrogation of suspects.

It is also important to understand that once the appeal process begins, the defendant is no longer presumed innocent. The burden of proof has shifted, and the defendant is obligated to prove that her or his conviction should be overturned. The method of filing an appeal differs slightly among the fifty states and the federal government, but the six basic steps are similar enough for summarization in Figure 10.6.

For the most part, defendants are not required to exercise their right to appeal. The one exception is in the case of the death sentence. Given the seriousness of capital punishment, the defendant is required to appeal the case, regardless of his or her wishes.

FIGURE 10.6 **The Steps of an Appeal**

FIGURE 10.6 **The Steps of an Appeal**

1. Within a specific period of time—usually between thirty and ninety days—the defendant must file a *notice of appeal*. This is a short written statement outlining the basis of the appeal.

2. The appellant, or losing party in the lower court, must then transfer the trial court record to the appellate court. This record contains items of the case file, including exhibits, and a transcript of the testimony.

3. Next, the briefs must be filed. A *brief* is a written argument that presents the party's legal arguments and precedents to support these arguments. Both the appellant and the winning prosecutorial team must submit briefs to the appellate court.

4. The briefs are followed by *oral arguments,* in which attorneys from both sides appear before the appellate court panel to state their positions. In oral arguments, the judge or judges ask questions of the attorneys to clarify certain points or voice a particular disagreement.

5. After the oral arguments, the judges retire to deliberate the case. After a decision has been made, one or more of the judges prepare the *written opinion.* (This process is described in Chapter 8 in more detail.) A judge who disagrees with the majority opinion may write a *dissenting opinion.*

6. Finally, the court holds a disposition in which it announces the next step for the case. The court can *uphold* the decision of the lower court, or it can *modify* the lower court decision by changing a part of it but not the whole. The lower court's decision can be *reversed,* or set aside, or the appellate court can *reverse* and *remand* the case, meaning that the lower court's decision is overturned and the matter is sent back for further proceedings. Or, the appellate court may simply *remand* the case without overturning it.

HABEAS CORPUS

The 1980s and early 1990s saw a rise in a postconviction process known as ***habeas corpus*** (Latin for "you have the body"). *Habeas corpus* is a judicial order that literally commands a corrections official to bring a prisoner before a federal court so that the court can hear the person's claim that he or she is being illegally. A writ of *habeas corpus* differs from an appeal in several respects. First, it can be filed only by someone who is imprisoned. Second, it can address only constitutional issues, not technical errors. Thus, an inmate can file a *habeas corpus* petition claiming that the conditions of her or his imprisonment constitute cruel and unusual punishment, but not that the judge provided the jury with improper instructions during the trial.

The most aggressive move to limit *habeas corpus* review in recent years has come from Congress. In 1996, motivated by the politically popular goal of shortening the time between conviction and execution in death penalty cases, Congress passed the Antiterrorism and Effective Death Penalty Act, which placed a one-year time limit on filing a *habeas corpus* petition and restricted a federal court's ability to overturn a state court's criminal conviction.[67] Many observers felt that the United States Supreme Court would not uphold this legislation in the event that it was challenged on the basis that Article I of the Constitution limits Congress's ability to suspend *habeas corpus.*[68]

The Court was given the chance to do so almost immediately when Georgia inmate Ellis Wayne Felker challenged the new law, claiming it unconstitutionally limited the appeals of convicted murderers. Felker had been found guilty of rape and murder in 1983 and sentenced to die, but he had managed to elude the death penalty through *habeas corpus* petitions. In a unanimous decision, the Court rejected Felker's claim and upheld the act,[69] setting the stage for further erosion of *habeas corpus* in the future.

ONLINE REVIEW Go to the book's Web site for an interactive review of this section

Habeas Corpus
An order that requires correctional officials to bring an inmate before a court or a judge and explain why he or she is being held in prison.

> Cameras in the Courtroom: Is Justice Served?

German physicist Werner Heisenberg once commented that the act of observation changes the thing that is being observed. Heisenberg was referring to Albert Einstein's theories of space and time, but this principle may also be applied to the criminal trial. In this chapter, we have discussed many of the guidelines to the trial process contained in the U.S. Constitution. The framers, however, would have been hard pressed to envision CourtTV and the modern media storm that surrounds high-profile cases. Consequently, the decision to televise or not to televise rests with individual judges. As we close this chapter, we will examine two crucial questions: (1) Does the act of televising trials change them? (2) Even if it does, should the practice continue to be allowed?

A Right or a Wrong?

The issue of media in the courtroom has been debated since the 1935 trial of Bruno Hauptman, who was charged with kidnapping and murdering the baby of aeronautic pioneer Charles Lindbergh. After the disruption caused by 120 photographers at the trial, the presiding judge banned all cameras from the courtroom, and the American Bar Association moved to remove journalists permanently from court proceedings. In the 1981 case of *Chandler v. Florida*,[70] the Supreme Court ruled that states have free rein to set their own regulations concerning cameras in the courtroom.

Those who favor cameras in the courtroom point to the First Amendment's guarantee of freedom of the press. They argue that viewers have a right of access to the trial process and that this scrutiny will make the system more accountable to the public. Also, a televised trial is, in the words of one proponent, "the ultimate civics lesson" and contributes to Americans' overall understanding of the criminal justice system.[71]

Opponents of televised trials counter that the presence of cameras infringes on the defendant's right to a fair trial. The participants in a trial, they claim, will mod-

AP Photo/Cliff McBride, Pool

The 2003 trial of Paula Gutierrez for her role in the murder of a Tampa, Florida, police officer (her boyfriend actually fired the fatal shots) was watched by millions of Americans on television.

ify their behavior if they are aware that they are on television. These opponents insist that even the slightest change in behavior by a judge, attorney, witness, or juror damages the entire process of justice.[72]

The Simpson Shadow

As in so many areas of the criminal justice system, the example of the 1995 O. J. Simpson trial has come to dominate the debate on televised trials. Attorneys from both sides came under criticism for grandstanding before the cameras, as did Los Angeles Superior Court Judge Lance Ito. In banning cameras from a South Carolina courtroom during the trial of Susan Smith, who was accused of murdering her two children, Judge William Howard said the Simpson trial earlier that year was a key component in his decision.[73]

Other members of the courtroom work group are also suspicious of the influence of the camera's eye in court. In 2002, Paul Ebert of Prince William County, Virginia, the chief prosecutor in the trial of sniper John Muhammad, drew on personal experience when he opposed televising those proceedings. Almost a decade earlier, Ebert prosecuted Lorena Bobbit, who had mutilated her husband in one of the most widely followed cases of the 1990s. Local television stations and CourtTV were allowed to cover the trial. "At one point in time, I had no objection to live coverage," remembers Ebert. But, after the Bobbit trial, he changed his mind. "Witnesses, for a lack of a better word, tend to ham it up" when they know they are being filmed, he said.[74] Circuit Judge LeRoy F. Millette, Jr., agreed and denied the request to televise Muhammad's trial.

The public is also uneasy about the influence of cameras in the courtroom, at least in certain situations. Fifty-five percent of those polled felt that the trial of alleged terrorist Zacarias Moussaoui should not be televised, mostly on the grounds of national security.[75] There is little doubt, however, that if a high-profile trial is on television, people will watch it. It is estimated that 62 percent of the public tuned in to some part of the Lorena Bobbit trial, and similar ratings were garnered for the Menendez brothers' trial for killing their parents (53 percent), the Rodney King police brutality trial (81 percent), and the William Kennedy Smith rape trial (55 percent).[76]

Levels of Access

The level of access to the courtroom varies across the country and in different jurisdictions. Although all states have passed legislation that allows televised trials, some states limit that access to the appellate level, keeping the cameras out of trial courts. In 1996, federal district courts were given the discretion to decide whether to provide electronic coverage of their proceedings.[77] Only two of the thirteen federal district courts have chosen to do so, and opposition to any form of coverage is still strong. Some federal courts are starting to ban cell phones and other small electronic devices because of concerns that they will be used to transmit voices and images of the trial. The United States Supreme Court has staunchly resisted the idea of televising its proceedings. Testifying before Congress on the subject, Justice David Souter said, "The day you see a camera come into our courtroom, it's going to roll over my dead body."[78]

Possible Benefits of Televising Trials

In jurisdictions that allow for the practice, the decision of whether a trial will be televised is the domain of the presiding judge. Consequently, the question often comes down to personal preferences. In allowing cameras to record the Massachusetts murder trial of British *au pair* Louise Woodward, Judge Hiller B. Zobel asked, "Who are we to say that we can work in an isolated little courtroom with a select few people who can stand in line to get in?" Zobel added, "If one hundred people can see it, then why can't the rest of the world see it? The public should have access, simple as that."[79]

Other judges feel that there are practical benefits to broadcasting trials of great interest to the community. In 2000, New York Justice Joseph Teresi struck down that state's ban on the televising of trials as unconstitutional under the First Amendment. In his ruling, Teresi said that televising the trial of four white police officers accused of shooting African immigrant Amadou Diallo would contribute to public understanding of the judicial system and enhance public confidence in the courts.[80] Given the highly emotional nature of the case, many observers credited the televising of the proceedings for keeping community anger to a minimum when the officers were acquitted.[81]

Support for a "Camera-Free Zone"

Many in the judicial community remain skeptical about the televising of trials, however. When Los Angeles Superior Court Judge James Ideman declared his courtroom a "camera-free zone" for the trial of Symbionese Liberation Army fugitive Sara Jane Olson in 2000, he cited worries that the nearly two hundred witnesses set to appear would become targets of harassment if their faces were to appear on television. (During jury selection in 2001, Olson pleaded guilty to two charges of attempted murder.) A few months earlier, the Oklahoma Court of Criminal Appeals blocked the televising of hearings for convicted Oklahoma bombing co-conspirator Terry Nichols on the ground that the cameras would violate Nichols's due process rights.

Many critics of televised trials share the Oklahoma court's concern that televised trials may be unfair to the defendant. A study conducted by the Federal Judicial

Center found that the presence of cameras makes witnesses more nervous than they would be otherwise and, in many cases, makes witnesses less willing to appear in court.[82] The study also found that attorneys and witnesses often feel obligated to "play to the camera," thereby changing their behavior. Supreme Court Justice David H. Souter, in arguing against the presence of cameras in the Court, attested to television's effect on the judge. As a state judge in New Hampshire, Souter admitted, he altered his behavior when he knew he was going to appear on the evening news.[83]

Others believe that, by its nature, television is not the proper medium for trials. After all, the purpose of television is to entertain, while the purpose of a criminal trial is to determine the guilt or innocence of the accused. Indeed, viewers may actually lose confidence in the court system if the particular trial they are watching does not have the "happy ending" they have come to expect from most television shows.[84]

Two Rights in Conflict?

Many see the issue of televised trials as a conflict between the media's right to freedom of the press and the defendant's right to a fair trial. In 1941, Justice Hugo Black commented that "free speech and fair trials are two of the most cherished policies of our civilization, and it would be a trying task to choose between them."[85]

If such a choice must be made, argues legal scholar Taffiny L. Smith, the right to a fair trial must carry more weight.[86] Smith points out that the Supreme Court, in *Richmond Newspapers, Inc. v. Virginia* (1980),[87] ruled that the media's right of access to trials is not absolute and may be subject to reasonable limitations. These limitations come in the form of judicial discretion. Furthermore, though a judge has an inherent right to set the courtroom off-limits to television cameras, she or he may not exclude the print media from the proceedings. That *would* deny the media freedom of the press.

Proponents of televised trials argue that it is precisely this judicial discretion that allows the rights of the press and the trial to coexist. If a judge sees media coverage contaminating the trial, he or she can take several steps to remedy it, including the following:

> Sequestering the jurors, or isolating them from contact with the public or the media during the course of the trial. Officers of the court control the flow of information to jurors while they are sequestered, keeping them from being unduly influenced by media reports on the trial.

> Ordering a *change of venue,* in which the trial is transferred to a new location. A judge will take this step if the publicity and interest in a case in its original jurisdiction are so intense that the judge believes the defendant cannot receive a fair trial in that area.

> Placing a *gag order* on the participants in the trial.

If a judge believes any of these efforts to secure a fair trial has been compromised, she or he can take dramatic action. For example, in DeKalb County, Georgia, a judge declared a mistrial after one of the witnesses violated a direct order by watching testimony on television.[88]

MAKING SENSE OF CAMERAS IN THE COURTROOM

1 What steps could courts take to prevent judges, attorneys, and jurors from changing their behavior because of the camera's presence?

2 Do you think certain types of trials should never be broadcast; for example, those involving sex crimes or children?

3 In 2002, a trial judge in Houston decided to allow the videotaping of jury deliberations in a death penalty case. What are the arguments for and against the televising of jury deliberations? How does the nature of jury deliberations differ from other aspects of the criminal trial when it comes to questions of public access? (An appeals court eventually reversed the trial judge's decision and did not allow the jury proceedings to be videotaped.)

Chapter Summary

1 Identify the basic protections enjoyed by criminal defendants in the United States. According to the Sixth Amendment, a criminal defendant has the right to a speedy and public trial by an impartial jury in the physical location where the crime was committed. Additionally, a person accused of a crime must be informed of the nature of the crime and be confronted with the witnesses against him or her. Further, the accused must be able to summon witnesses in her or his favor and have the assistance of counsel.

2 List the three requirements of the Speedy Trial Act of 1974. In federal court, those accused of crimes must experience (a) no more than thirty days between arrest and indictment; (b) no more than ten days between indictment and arraignment; and (c) no more than sixty days between arraignment and trial. Of course, extra time is allowed for hearings on pretrial motions, mental competency examinations, and other procedural actions.

3 Explain what "taking the Fifth" really means. The Fifth Amendment states that no person "shall be compelled in any criminal case to be a witness against himself." Thus, defendants do not have to testify if their testimony would implicate them in the crime. Witnesses may refuse to testify on this same ground. (Witnesses, though, are often granted immunity and thereafter can no longer take the Fifth.) In the United States, silence on the part of a defendant cannot be used by the jury in forming its opinion about guilt or innocence.

4 List the requirements normally imposed on potential jurors. They must be (a) citizens of the United States; (b) over eighteen years of age; (c) free of felony convictions; (d) of the necessary health to function on a jury; (e) sufficiently intelligent to understand the issues at trial; and (f) able to read, write, and comprehend the English language.

5 Contrast challenges for cause and peremptory challenges during *voir dire*. A challenge for cause occurs when an attorney provides the court with a legally justifiable reason why a potential juror should be excluded; for example, because the juror does not speak English. In contrast, peremptory challenges do not require any justification by the attorney and are usually limited to a small number. They cannot, however, be based, even implicitly, on race or gender.

6 List the standard steps in a criminal jury trial. (a) Opening statements by the prosecutor and the defense attorney; (b) presentation of evidence, usually in the form of questioning by the prosecutor, known as direct examination; (c) cross-examination by the defense attorney of the same witnesses; (d) at the end of the prosecutor's presentation of evidence, motion for a directed verdict by the defense (also called a motion for judgment as a matter of law in the federal courts), which is normally denied by the judge; (e) presentation of the defendant's case, which may include placing the defendant on the stand and direct examination of the defense's witnesses; (f) cross-examination by the prosecutor; (g) after the defense closes its case, rebuttal by the prosecution, which may involve new evidence that was not used initially by the prosecution; (h) cross-examination of the prosecution's new witnesses by the defense and introduction of new witnesses of its own, called the surrebuttal; (i) closing arguments by both the defense and the prosecution; (j) the charging of the jury by the judge, during which the judge sums up the case and instructs the jurors on the rules of law that apply; (k) jury deliberations; and (l) presentation of the verdict.

7 Explain the difference between testimony and real evidence; between lay witnesses and expert witnesses; and between direct and circumstantial evidence. Testimony consists of statements by competent witnesses, whereas real evidence includes physical items that affect the case; a lay

STORIES FROM THE STREET

Go to the Stories from the Street feature at www.cjinaction.com to hear Larry Gaines tell insightful stories related to this chapter and his experiences in the field.

witness is an "average person," whereas an expert witness speaks with the authority of one who has professional training, advanced knowledge, or substantial experience in a specialized area; direct evidence is evidence presented by witnesses as opposed to circumstantial evidence, which can create an inference that a fact exists, but does not directly establish the fact.

8 List possible affirmative defenses. (a) Self-defense, (b) insanity, (c) duress, and (d) entrapment.

9 Delineate circumstances in which a criminal defendant may in fact be tried a second time for the same act. A defendant who is acquitted in a criminal trial may be sued in a civil case for essentially the same act. When an act is a crime under both state and federal law, a defendant who is acquitted in state court may be tried in federal court for the same act, and vice versa.

10 List the six basic steps of an appeal. (a) The filing of a notice of appeal; (b) the transfer of the trial court records to the appellate court; (c) the filing of briefs; (d) the presentation of oral arguments; (e) the deliberation of the appellate judges who then prepare a written opinion; and (f) the announcement of the judges— upholding the decision of the lower court, modifying part of the decision, reversing the decision, or reversing and remanding the decision to the trial court.

Key Terms

acquittal 327
Allen Charge 347
appeal 348
authentication 338
bench trial 326
beyond a reasonable
  doubt 328
challenge for cause 331
charge 344
circumstantial
  evidence 337
closing arguments 344
cross-examination 341

direct evidence 337
direct examination 340
double jeopardy 348
evidence 336
expert witness 337
habeas corpus 351
hearsay 340
hung jury 346
jury nullification 348
jury trial 326
lay witness 336
master jury list 330

motion for a directed
  verdict 342
opening statements 335
peremptory
  challenges 332
real evidence 336
rebuttal 343
relevant evidence 338
testimony 336
venire 330
verdict 346
voir dire 331

Questions for Critical Analysis

1 If a defendant waives his or her right to a jury trial, what type of trial then takes place?

2 Why is there a higher standard of proof in criminal cases than in civil cases?

3 What danger lies in a defense attorney's or prosecutor's decision to present an opening statement to the jury?

4 Under what circumstances may evidence be excluded?

5 How does an attorney authenticate evidence presented?

6 Are there exceptions to the hearsay rule, and if so, what are they?

7 Why might a defense attorney not want to call the defendant to the stand to testify?

8 What is the major problem with the jury instructions that judges usually present prior to jury deliberations?

9 What are the arguments for and against televising criminal trials?

Go to www.cjinaction.com for tools to aid you in studying for your exams. Click on *Online Reviews* under *Chapter Resources* for an interactive review of each major section of this chapter. Under *Chapter Resources,* you will also find the *Chapter Outline, Chapter Summary, Flashcards, Glossary, Learning Objectives, Lecture Presentations, Concept Builder, Essay Questions,* and a *Tutorial Quiz.* You can also test yourself with a game of *Concentration* or the *Crossword Puzzle.*

Go to www.cjinaction.com for a wealth of online resources. Explore the *Internet Activities* and *Class Projects* under *Chapter Resources.* Check out the *Web Links* to access the Web sites mentioned in the text, as well as many others. You can also access recent perspectives by clicking on *CJ in the News* and *Terrorism Update* under *Course Resources.* If you'd like some mentoring, click on *Board of Mentors* under *Book Resources.*

For additional information, explore InfoTrac College Edition, your online library that offers complete full-length articles from thousands of scholarly and popular publications. Click on *InfoTrac College Edition* under *Chapter Resources* at www.cjinaction.com for a list of key words and InfoTrac exercises. Use the passcode that came with your book.

Dwyer, William, *In the Hands of the People: The Trial Jury's Origins, Triumphs, Troubles, and Future in American Democracy,* New York: Thomas Dunne Books, 2002. The author, a federal district court judge, is an ardent admirer and historian of the U.S. jury system. He sees it as a crucial component of our democratic form of government and offers a number of "war stories" to prove his point. This does not mean, however, that he does not acknowledge its weaknesses. Indeed, Dwyer worries that the jury system is in danger from neglect and incompetence, and he offers his solutions to keep "trial by jury" an American institution that works.

Spence, Gerry, *The Smoking Gun: Day by Day through a Shocking Murder Trial* with Gerry Spence, New York: Scribner, 2003. Spence, one of the nation's best-known defense attorneys, takes his readers on a detailed voyage through a criminal trial. The defendants are Sandy Jones and her son, who have been charged with murdering a real estate developer on their Oregon farm. The trial develops into a classic battle between Jones, a poor woman, and the "powers that be" in the community who seem convinced of her guilt regardless of any evidence to the contrary. Spence jumps into his role as a voluntary member of Jones's defense team, and this book follows his efforts as he struggles with two different judges and lead prosecutors. The author is particularly insightful as he describes how he selects the jury and the reasoning behind his questioning of witnesses.

Notes

1. John Springer, "Jurors Will See Novelist's Computer Porn, E-mails with Male Prostitute" (October 5, 2003), at http://www.courttv.com/trials/novelist/080703_ctv.html.
2. Jerome Frank, *Courts on Trial: Myth and Reality in American Justice* (New York: Atheneum, 1969), 14–33.
3. William L. Prosser, *Handbook of the Law of Torts,* 2d ed. (St. Paul, MN: West Publishing Co., 1955), 7.
4. David L. Cook, Steven R. Schlesinger, Thomas J. Bak, and William T. Rule II, "Criminal Caseload in U.S. District Courts: More than Meets the Eye," *American University Law Review* 44 (June 1995), 44.
5. 407 U.S. 514 (1972).
6. Roger Misner, *Speedy Trials: Federal and State Practice* (Charlottesville, VA: The Michie Co., 1983).
7. *State v. Utley,* 956 S.W.2d 489 (Tenn. 1997).
8. 18 U.S.C. Section 3161.
9. 391 U.S. 145 (1968).
10. *Blanton v. Las Vegas,* 489 U.S. 538 (1989).
11. *Williams v. Florida,* 399 U.S. 102 (1970).
12. 435 U.S. 223 (1978).
13. *Johnson v. Louisiana,* 406 U.S. 356 (1972); and *Apodaca v. Oregon,* 406 U.S. 404 (1972).
14. 332 U.S. 46 (1947).
15. Barton L. Ingraham, "The Right of Silence, the Presumption of Innocence, the Burden of Proof, and a Modest Proposal," *Journal of Criminal Law and Criminology* 85 (1994), 559–595.
16. 397 U.S. 358 (1970).

17. James P. Levine, "The Impact of Local Political Cultures on Jury Verdicts," *Criminal Justice Journal* 14 (1992), 163–164.

18. *State v. Gonzales,* No. CR-99-139 (N.M. January 19, 2000).

19. Kate Zernike, "Trial Will Weigh Matters of Intent of Betrayed Wife Who Killed Her Husband," *New York Times* (January 24, 2003), A16.

20. *Lockhart v. McCree,* 476 U.S. 162 (1986).

21. *Witherspoon v. Illinois,* 391 U.S. 510 (1968).

22. John Kaplan and Jon R. Waltz, *The Trial of Jack Ruby* (New York: Macmillan, 1965), 91–94.

23. Jeremy W. Barber, "The Jury Is Still Out," *American Criminal Law Review* 31 (Summer 1994) 1225–1252.

24. 380 U.S. 224 (1965).

25. 476 U.S. 79 (1986).

26. Eric L. Muller, "Solving the *Batson* Paradox: Harmless Error, Jury Representation, and the Sixth Amendment," *Yale Law Journal* 106 (October 1996), 93.

27. 499 U.S. 400 (1991).

28. 502 U.S. 1056 (1992).

29. *Miller-El v. Cockrell,* 123 S.Ct. 1029 (2003).

30. Karen L. Cipriani, "The Numbers Don't Add Up: Challenging the Premise of *J.E.B. v. Alabama,*" *American Criminal Law Review* 31 (Summer 1994) 1253–1277.

31. *J.E.B. v. Alabama ex rel T.B.,* 511 U.S. 127 (1994).

32. Harry Kalven and Hans Zeisel, *The American Jury* (Boston: Little, Brown, 1966), 163–167.

33. Douglas D. Koski, "Testing the Story Model of Juror Decision Making," *Sex Offender Law* (June/July 2003), 53–58.

34. Nancy Pennington and Reid Hastie, "The Story Model for Juror Decision Making," in *Inside the Juror: The Psychology of Juror Decision Making* (Cambridge, MA: Harvard University Press, 1983), 192, 194–195.

35. 424 U.S. 600 (1976).

36. Federal Rule of Evidence 703.

37. Richard A. Epstein, "Judicial Control over Expert Testimony: Of Deference and Education," *Northwestern University Law Review* 87 (1993), 1156.

38. L. Timothy Perrin, "Expert Witnesses under Rules 703 and 803(4) of the Federal Rules of Evidence: Separating the Wheat from the Chaff," *Indiana Law Journal* 72 (Fall 1997), 939.

39. Jeffrey Rosen, "The Need to Test Evidence," *New York Times* (October 13, 2002), section 6, page 4.

40. Thomas J. Reed, "Trial by Propensity: Admission of Other Criminal Acts Evidenced in Federal Criminal Trials," *University of Cincinnati Law Review* 50 (1981), 713.

41. *Ibid.*

42. *People v. Zackowitz,* 254 N.Y. 192 (1930).

43. Charles McCormick, *Handbook on Evidence* (St. Paul, MN: West Publishing Co., 1987), Chapter 1.

44. Federal Rules of Procedure, Rule 804(b)(2).

45. Arthur Best, *Evidence: Examples and Explanations,* 4th ed. (New York: Aspen Law & Business, 2001), 89–90.

46. Wendy Melillo, "Judge Rejects Kasi's Request for a New Trial," *Washington Post* (February 5, 1998), D1.

47. *Griffin v. California,* 380 U.S. 609 (1965).

48. Hilary E. MacGregor, "Shopper's Murderer Receives Life Term," *Los Angeles Times* (March 20, 1998), B1.

49. Douglas D. Koski, "Alcohol and Rape Study," *Criminal Law Bulletin* 38 (2002), 21–159.

50. Roger LeRoy Miller and Mary S. Urisko, *West's Paralegal Today* (St. Paul, MN: West Publishing Co., 1995), 443.

51. Firoz Dattu, "Illustrated Jury Instructions," *Judicature* 82 (September/October 1998), 79.

52. Walter J. Steele, Jr., and Elizabeth Thornburg, "Jury Instructions: A Persistent Failure to Communicate," *Judicature* 74 (1991), 249–254.

53. David W. Broeder, "The University of Chicago Jury Project," *Nebraska Law Review* 38 (1959), 744–760.

54. Harold J. Rothwax, *Guilty: The Collapse of the Criminal Justice System* (New York: Random House, 1996), 214.

55. Katherine E. Finkelstein and Dan Barry, "Jurors in Rapper Trial Recall 3 Days of Heated Exchanges," *New York Times* (April 12, 2001), A1.

56. Robert Jablon, "Hung Jury Declared in Police Brutality Trial," *San Diego Union-Tribune* (July 30, 2003), A3.

57. 164 U.S. 492 (1896).

58. *United States v. Fioravanti,* 412 F.2d 407 (3d Cir. 1969).

59. National Center for State Courts, *Are Hung Juries a Problem?* (Washington, D.C.: U.S. Department of Justice, 2002), 1.

60. Joseph L. Gastwirth and Michael D. Sinclair, "Diagnostic Test Methodology in the Design and Analysis of Judge-Jury Agreement Studies," *Jurimetrics Journal* 39 (Fall 1998), 59.

61. Peter Western, "The Three Faces of Double Jeopardy: Reflections on Government Appeals of Criminal Sentences," *Michigan Law Review* 78 (1980), 1001–1002.

62. Quoted in Jeffrey Abramson, *We, the Jury: The Jury System and the Ideal of Democracy* (New York: Basic Books, 1994), 250.

63. Bureau of Justice Statistics, *Federal Criminal Appeals, 1999 with Trends 1985–1999* (Washington, D.C.: U.S. Department of Justice, April 2001), 1.

64. *Green v. United States,* 355 U.S. 184 (1957).

65. Slip Opinion No. 01-7574 (2003).

66. David W. Neubauer, *America's Courts and the Criminal Justice System,* 5th ed. (Belmont, CA: Wadsworth Publishing Co. 1996), 254.

67. 28 U.S.C. Section 2254(d)(1).

68. F. Martin Tieber, "Federal *Habeas Corpus* Law and Practice—The Antiterrorism and Effective Death Penalty Act of 1996," *Michigan Bar Journal* 77 (January 1998), 50.

69. *Felker v. Turpin,* 518 U.S. 1051 (1996).

70. 949 U.S. 560 (1981).

71. Claire Papanastasiou, "Cameras in the Courtroom," *The Massachusetts Lawyer* (December 15, 1997), B1.

72. Taffiny L. Smith, "The Distortion of Criminal Trials through Televised Proceedings," *Law and Psychology Review* 21 (Spring 1997), 257.

73. Jennifer J. Miller, "Cameras in the Courtroom: The Lens of the Public Eye on Our System of Justice," *South Carolina Lawyer* (March/April 2002), 27.

74. Jayson Blair, "Judge Bars Cameras from Trial in Sniper Case," *New York Times* (December 13, 2002), A27.

75. Miller, 25.

76. Dan Trigoboff, "Court Coverage Hindered by O. J. Backlash?" *Broadcasting & Cable* (June 23, 1997), 24.

77. Marcia Coyle, "Federal Judges OK Cameras for Appeals," *National Law Journal* (March 25, 1996), A14.

78. Miller, 27.

79. Papanastasiou, B1.

80. Dan Trigoboff, "Judge Affirms Cameras in New York Courtroom," *Broadcast & Cable* (January 31, 2000), 37.

81. Henry Schleiff, "Cameras in the Courtroom: A View in Support of More Access," *Human Rights* (Fall 2001), 14.

82. Statement of Chief Judge Edward R. Becker on Behalf of the Judicial Conference of the United States before the Senate Judiciary Subcommittee on Administrative Oversight and the Courts, September 6, 2000.

83. Jim Gordon, "No Camera Fans Here," *News Photographer* (May 1, 1996), 4.

84. Neil Postman, *Amusing Ourselves to Death: Public Discourse in an Age of Show Business* (New York: Viking Press, 1985), 87.

85. *Bridges v. California,* 314 U.S. 252 (1941).

86. Smith, 257.

87. 448 U.S. 555 (1980).

88. Celia Sibley, "Sandlin Ruling: Eye Is on Courtroom Cameras," *Atlanta Journal and Atlanta Constitution* (July 19, 1997), B2.

Punishment and Sentencing

>chapter objectives<

After reading this chapter, you should be able to:

1 List and contrast the four basic philosophical reasons for sentencing criminals.

2 Contrast indeterminate with determinate sentencing.

3 Explain why there is a difference between a sentence imposed by a judge and the actual sentence carried out by the prisoner.

4 List the six forms of punishment.

5 State who has input into the sentencing decision and list the factors that determine a sentence.

6 Explain some of the reasons why sentencing reform has occurred.

7 Contrast sentencing guidelines with mandatory sentencing guidelines.

8 Outline the Supreme Court rulings on capital punishment.

Dealing with Drunk Driving

By the time Daniel Lanzaro left Giants Stadium in East Rutherford, New Jersey, he had downed fourteen beers. Despite his drunken state, Lanzaro got behind the wheel of his pickup truck and headed

home. On the way, he swerved across a double yellow line and struck the car of the Verni family. As a result of the accident, two-year-old Antonio Verni was paralyzed from the neck down for life. On August 9, 2003, a superior court judge in Hackensack, New Jersey, sentenced Lanzaro to five years in prison.

Three days earlier and fifty miles to the east, in Central Islip, New York, Michele April also faced a sentencing hearing. She had killed one man and badly hurt another when driving while intoxicated. Unlike Lanzaro, however, April did not receive any prison or jail time. Instead, she was sentenced to 280 hours of community service.

Given that drunk driving accidents are the leading cause of death in the United States for people under the age of thirty-one and account for nearly 40 percent of all traffic fatalities, one might ask why April got off with the proverbial "slap on the wrist." Furthermore, how could she and Lanzaro, who committed similar crimes, be given such disparate punishments?

The wreck of a car that had been carrying one of the more than 17,000 people killed each year in this country by drunk drivers.

> **Because each state** has the authority to pass its own drunk driving laws, there are at least fifty different answers to the question of how we should punish intoxicated drivers. In New Jersey, prosecutors were able to charge Daniel Lanzaro with aggravated assault—a felony. In New York, because Michele April was not speeding or driving outside her lane when she hit her victims, she had not engaged in criminally negligent or reckless conduct and thus could be found guilty only of a misdemeanor.

Is it possible to argue that either New York or New Jersey is "better" at penalizing drunk drivers? Punishment and sentencing present some of the most complex issues of the criminal justice system. One scholar has even asserted that:

> There is no such thing as "accurate" sentencing; there are only sentences that are more or less just, more or less effective. Nothing in the recent or distant history of sentencing reform suggests that anything approaching perfection is attainable.[1]

In this chapter, we will discuss the various attempts to "perfect" the practice of sentencing over the past century and explore the ramifications of these efforts for the American criminal justice system. Whereas previous chapters have concentrated on the prosecutor and defense attorney, this one will spotlight the judge and his or her role in making the sentencing decision. We will particularly focus on recent national and state efforts to limit judicial discretion in this area, a trend that has had the overall effect of producing harsher sentences for many offenders. Finally, we will examine the issues surrounding the death penalty, a controversial subject that forces us to confront the basic truth of sentencing: the way we punish criminals says a great deal about the kind of people we are.[2]

CONCEPT BUILDER
Deterrence is a common justification for many crime policies and a main goal of sentencing. Does deterrence work? Visit www.cjinaction.com for an interactive exploration of this key topic.

The Purpose of Sentencing

Professor Herbert Packer has said that punishing criminals serves two ultimate purposes: the "deserved infliction of suffering on evil doers" and "the prevention of crime."[3] Even this straightforward assessment raises several questions. How does one determine the sort of punishment that is "deserved"? How can we be sure that certain penalties "prevent" crime? Should criminals be punished solely for the good of society, or should their well-being also be taken into consideration? Sentencing laws indicate how any given group of people has answered these questions, but do not tell us why they were answered in that manner. To understand why, we must first consider the four basic philosophical reasons for sentencing—retribution, deterrence, incapacitation, and rehabilitation.

Retribution
The philosophy that those who commit criminal acts should be punished based on the severity of the crime and that no other factors need be considered.

Just Deserts
A sanctioning philosophy based on the assertion that criminals deserve to be punished for breaking society's rules. The severity of the punishment should be determined by no other factor than the severity of the crime.

RETRIBUTION

The oldest and most common justification for punishing someone is that he or she "deserved it"—as the Old Testament states, "an eye for an eye and a tooth for a tooth." Under a system of justice that favors **retribution,** a wrongdoer who has freely chosen to violate society's rules must be punished for the infraction. Retribution relies on the principle of **just deserts,** which holds that the severity of the punishment must be in proportion to the severity of the crime. Retributive justice is not the same as *revenge*. Whereas revenge implies that the wrongdoer is punished only with the aim of satisfying a victim or victims, retribution is more concerned with the needs of society as a whole.

The *principle of willful wrongdoing* is central to the idea of retribution; that is, society is morally justified in punishing someone only if that person was aware that he or she had committed a crime. Therefore, animals, children, and the mentally incapacitated are not responsible for criminal action, even though they may be a threat to the community.[4] Furthermore, the principles of retribution reject any wide-reaching social benefit as a goal of punishment. The philosopher Immanuel Kant, an early proponent of retributivism, believed that punishment by a court:

> can never be inflicted merely as a means to promote some other good for the criminal himself or for civil society. It must always be inflicted upon him only because he has committed a crime. For a man can never be treated merely as a means to the purposes of another.[5]

In other words, punishment is an end in itself and cannot be justified by any future good that may result from a criminal's suffering.

One problem with retributive ideas of justice lies in proportionality. Whether or not one agrees with the death penalty, the principle behind it is easy to fathom:

In 2003, Clara Harris was sentenced to twenty years in prison for murder. She could have received a life term, but a Houston jury decided on the lesser punishment, finding her to have been in an anguished mental state when she repeatedly ran over her husband—who had been committing adultery—with a car.

AP Photo/Buster Dean, Pool

the punishment (death) fits the crime (death). But what about the theft of an automobile? How does one fairly determine the amount of time the thief must spend in prison? Should the type of car or the wealth of the car owner matter? Theories of retribution often have a difficult time providing answers to such questions.[6]

DETERRENCE

Deterrence
The strategy of preventing crime through the threat of punishment. Assumes that potential criminals will weigh the costs of punishments versus the benefits of the criminal act; therefore, punishments should be severe.

The concept of **deterrence** (as well as incapacitation and rehabilitation) takes the opposite approach: rather than seeking only to punish the wrongdoer, the goal of sentencing should be to prevent future crimes. By "setting an example," society is sending a message to potential criminals that certain actions will not be tolerated. Jeremy Bentham, a nineteenth-century British reformer who first articulated the principles of deterrence, felt that retribution was counterproductive because it does not serve the community. (See Chapter 2 to review Bentham's utilitarian theories.) He believed that a person should be punished only when doing so was in society's best interests and that the severity of the punishment should be based on its deterrent value, not on the severity of the crime.[7] (See *International CJ—Singapore: A Utilitarian Oasis*.)

Deterrence can take two forms: general and specific. The basic idea of *general deterrence* is that by punishing one person, others will be dissuaded from committing a similar crime. *Specific deterrence* assumes that an individual, after being punished once for a certain act, will be less likely to repeat that act because she or he does not want to be punished again.[8] Both forms of deterrence have proved prob-

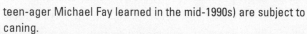

INTERNATIONAL CJ

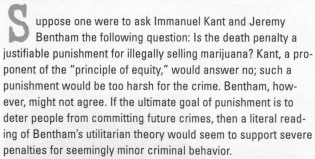

> Singapore—A Utilitarian Oasis

Suppose one were to ask Immanuel Kant and Jeremy Bentham the following question: Is the death penalty a justifiable punishment for illegally selling marijuana? Kant, a proponent of the "principle of equity," would answer no; such a punishment would be too harsh for the crime. Bentham, however, might not agree. If the ultimate goal of punishment is to deter people from committing future crimes, then a literal reading of Bentham's utilitarian theory would seem to support severe penalties for seemingly minor criminal behavior.

Singapore, a nation-city of three million people in Southeast Asia, leans toward Bentham rather than Kant in its sentencing theories. According to Singapore law, the selling of any drug—including marijuana—carries a mandatory death sentence by hanging, as do murder and the use of a firearm in committing or attempting to commit a crime. Someone caught smoking marijuana is sentenced to a ten-year prison term. Citizens who litter are fined the equivalent of $1,000, with similar penalties imposed for chewing gum and failing to flush a public toilet. Vandals are sentenced to up to three years in prison and (as American

teen-ager Michael Fay learned in the mid-1990s) are subject to caning.

Many observers criticize Singapore, claiming its strict laws violate human rights. But Singaporeans point to one of the world's lowest crime rates as justification for their system. The year after robbery with a firearm was deemed punishable by death, for example, not one such incident took place in the city. Singapore officials also point out that the United States—which consistently criticizes human rights abuses in other nations—has the highest violent crime rate and the most citizens in prison of any country in the West.

FOR CRITICAL ANALYSIS
It is important to note that Singapore is a democracy, and many, if not most, of its citizens support its law enforcement principles. How do you think the American public would react if given the chance to vote on implementing similarly harsh punishments for crime in this country?

lematic in practice. General deterrence assumes that a person commits a crime only after a rational decision-making process, in which he or she implicitly weighs the benefits of the crime against the possible costs of the punishment. This is not necessarily the case, especially for young offenders who tend to value the immediate rewards of crime over the possible future consequences.[9] Specific deterrence, for its part, seems to be contradicted by the fact that a relatively small number of habitual offenders are responsible for the majority of certain criminal acts.[10]

Another criticism of deterrence is that for most crimes, wrongdoers are unlikely to be caught, sentenced, and imprisoned. As Figure 11.1 shows, the majority of all crimes go unpunished. A study by Texas A&M economist Morgan Reynolds found that, after factoring in the low likelihood of capture and imprisonment, the average statistically expected stay in prison is only 4.8 days for an act of burglary, 60.5 days for rape, and 1.8 years for murder.[11] Thus, in general, potential criminals have less to fear from the criminal justice system than one might expect. Professors Paul H. Robinson of Northwestern University School of Law and John M. Darley of Princeton University note that this low probability of punishment could be offset by making the punishment so severe that even the slightest chance of apprehension could act as a deterrent—for example, an eighty-five-year-prison term for shoplifting or the loss of a hand for burglary.[12] Our society is, however, unwilling to allow for this possibility.

INCAPACITATION

"Wicked people exist," said James Q. Wilson. "Nothing avails except to set them apart from innocent people."[13] Wilson's blunt statement summarizes the justification for **incapacitation** as a form of punishment. As a purely practical matter, incarcerating criminals guarantees that they will not be a danger to society, at least for the length of their prison terms. To a certain extent, the death penalty is justified in terms of incapacitation, as it prevents the offender from committing any future crimes.

U.S. Attorney General John Ashcroft is a proponent of public policies that focus on taking "criminals off the street and keeping them off the street" as a method of reducing criminal activity.[14] Indeed, several studies support incapacitation's efficacy as a crime-fighting tool. Criminologist Isaac Ehrlich of the University of Chicago estimated that a 1 percent increase in sentence length will produce a 1 percent decrease in crime rates.[15] Another Chicago professor, Steve Levitt, has noticed a trend that further supports incapacitation: violent crime rates rise in communities where inmate litigation over prison overcrowding has forced the early release of some inmates and a subsequent drop in the prison population.[16]

Incapacitation as a theory of punishment suffers from several weaknesses, however. Unlike retribution, it offers no proportionality with regard to a particular crime. Giving a burglar a life sentence would certainly assure that she or he would not commit another burglary; does that justify such a severe penalty? Furthermore, incarceration protects society only until the criminal is freed. Many studies have shown that, on

"Men are not hanged for stealing horses, but that horses may not be stolen."
—Marquis de Halifax, *Political Thoughts and Reflections* (1750)

Incapacitation
A strategy for preventing crime by detaining wrongdoers in prison, thereby separating them from the community and reducing criminal opportunities.

FIGURE 11.1 Risk of Punishment
Source: Paul H. Robinson and John M. Darley, "The Utility of Desert," *Northwestern University Law Review* 91 (Winter 1997), Table 1, p. 453.

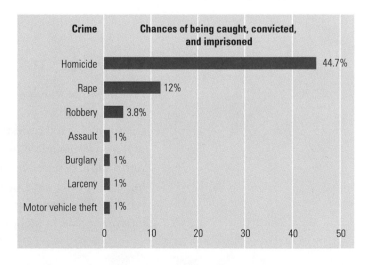

Crime	Chances of being caught, convicted, and imprisoned
Homicide	44.7%
Rape	12%
Robbery	3.8%
Assault	1%
Burglary	1%
Larceny	1%
Motor vehicle theft	1%

release, offenders may actually be more likely to commit crimes than before they were imprisoned.[17] In that case, incapacitation may increase the likelihood of crime, rather than diminish it.

Some observers believe that strategies of *selective incapacitation* should be favored over strategies of *collective incapacitation* to solve this problem. With collective incapacitation, all offenders who have committed a similar crime are imprisoned for the same time period, whereas selective incapacitation provides longer sentences for individuals, such as career criminals, who are judged more likely to commit further crimes if and when they are released.[18] The problem with selective incapacitation, however, lies in the difficulty of predicting just who is at the greatest risk to commit future crimes. Studies have shown that with even the most effective methods the predictions are correct less than half of the time.[19]

REHABILITATION

Rehabilitation
The philosophy that society is best served when wrongdoers are not simply punished, but provided the resources needed to eliminate criminality from their behavioral pattern.

For most of the past century, **rehabilitation** has been seen as the most "humane" goal of punishment. This line of thinking reflects the view that crime is a "social phenomenon" caused not by the inherent criminality of a person, but by factors in that person's surroundings. By removing wrongdoers from their environment and intervening to change their values and personalities, the rehabilitative model suggests, criminals can be "treated" and possibly even "cured" of their proclivities toward crime.

As will become clear over the course of this chapter, the American criminal justice system is currently in the process of rejecting many of the precepts of rehabilitation in favor of "get tough" retributive, deterrent, and incapacitating sentencing strategies. The American public, however, does not seem as ready to dismiss rehabilitation as elected officials may think. A survey by the Public Policy Forum found that only 46 percent of those polled favored spending more money on punishment than rehabilitation, while 65 percent wanted to create alternatives to prison for nonviolent offenders and 63 percent wanted better drug and alcohol treatment for lawbreakers.[20]

Nevertheless, it would be a mistake to separate these four philosophies. For the most part, a society's overall sentencing direction is influenced by all four theories, with political and social factors determining which one is predominant at any given time.

↗ ONLINE REVIEW *Go to the book's Web site for an interactive review of this section*

The Structure of Sentencing

Philosophy not only is integral to explaining *why* we punish criminals, but also influences *how* we do so. The history of criminal sentencing in the United States has been characterized by shifts in institutional power among the three branches of the government. When public opinion moves toward more severe strategies of retribution, deterrence, and incapacitation, *legislatures* have responded by asserting their power over determining sentencing guidelines. In contrast, periods of rehabilitative justice are marked by a transfer of this power to the *judicial* and *administrative* branches.

LEGISLATIVE SENTENCING AUTHORITY

Because legislatures are responsible for making law, these bodies are also initially responsible for passing the criminal codes that determine the length of sentences.

Indeterminate Sentencing   For most of the twentieth century, goals of rehabilitation dominated the criminal justice system, and legislatures were more likely to enact **indeterminate sentencing** policies. Penal codes with indeterminate sentences set a minimum and maximum amount of time that a person must spend in prison. For example, the indeterminate sentence for aggravated assault could be three to nine years, or six to twelve years, or twenty years to life. Within these parameters, a judge can prescribe a particular term, after which an administrative body known as the *parole board* decides at what point the offender is to be released. A prisoner is aware that he or she is eligible for *parole* as soon as the minimum time has been served and that good behavior can further shorten the sentence.

> **Indeterminate Sentencing**
> An indeterminate term of incarceration in which a judge determines the minimum and maximum terms of imprisonment. When the minimum term is reached, the prisoner becomes eligible to be paroled.

Determinate Sentencing   Disillusionment with the ideals of rehabilitation has led to **determinate sentencing**, or fixed sentencing. As the name implies, in determinate sentencing an offender serves exactly the amount of time to which she or he is sentenced (minus "good time," described below). For example, if the legislature deems that the punishment for a first-time armed robber is ten years, then the judge has no choice but to impose a sentence of ten years, and the criminal will serve ten years minus good time before being freed.

> **Determinate Sentencing**
> A period of incarceration that is fixed by a sentencing authority and cannot be reduced by judges or other corrections officials.

"Good Time" and Truth in Sentencing   Often, the amount of time prescribed by a judge bears little relation to the amount of time the offender actually spends behind bars. In states with indeterminate sentencing, parole boards have broad powers to release prisoners once they have served the minimum portion of their sentence. Furthermore, all but four states offer prisoners the opportunity to reduce their sentences by doing **"good time"**—or behaving well—as determined by prison administrators. (See Figure 11.2 on the next page for an idea of the effects of good-time regulations and other early-release programs.)

> **"Good Time"**
> A reduction in time served by prisoners based on good behavior, conformity to rules, and other positive actions.

Sentence-reduction programs promote discipline within a correctional institution and reduce overcrowding; therefore, many prison officials welcome them. The public, however, may react negatively to news that a violent criminal has served a shorter term than ordered by a judge and pressure elected officials to "do something." In Illinois, for example, some inmates were serving less than half their sentences by receiving a one-day reduction in their term for each day of "good time." Under pressure from victims' groups, the state legislature passed a **truth-in-sentencing law** that requires murderers and others convicted of serious crimes to complete at least 85 percent of their sentences with no time off for good behavior.[21] Today, forty states have instituted some form of truth-in-sentencing laws, though the future of such statutes is in doubt due to numerous challenges on constitutional grounds and the pressure of overflowing prisons.

> **Truth-in-Sentencing Laws**
> Legislative attempts to assure that convicts will serve approximately the terms to which they were initially sentenced.

JUDICIAL SENTENCING AUTHORITY

Determinate sentencing is a direct encroachment on the long-recognized power of judges to make the final decision on sentencing. Historically, the judge bore most of the responsibility for choosing the proper sentence within the guidelines

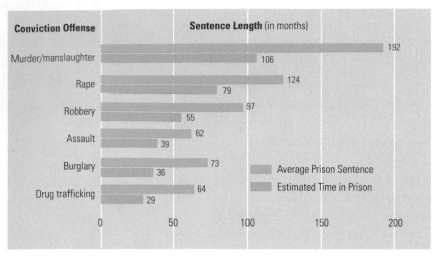

Conviction Offense	Sentence Length (in months)
Murder/manslaughter	192 / 106
Rape	124 / 79
Robbery	97 / 55
Assault	62 / 39
Burglary	73 / 36
Drug trafficking	64 / 29

Average Prison Sentence
Estimated Time in Prison

FIGURE 11.2 Average Sentence Length and Estimated Time to Be Served in State Prison

Source: Bureau of Justice Statistics, *Sourcebook of Criminal Justice Statistics 2001* (Washington, D.C., 2002), Table 6.40, page 505.

INFOTRAC KEYWORDS

sentencing

For more information, use this search term with InfoTrac College Edition, your online library at www.infotrac-college.com

set by the legislature.[22] In the twentieth century, this power was reinforced by the rehabilitative ethic. Each offender, it was believed, has a different set of problems and should therefore receive a sentence tailored to her or his particular circumstances. Legislators have generally accepted a judge as the most qualified person to choose the proper punishment.

Between 1880 and 1899, seven states passed indeterminate sentencing laws, and in the next dozen years, another twenty-one followed suit. By the 1960s, every state in the nation allowed its judges the freedom of operating under an indeterminate sentencing system.[23] In the 1970s, however, criticism of indeterminate sentencing began to grow. Marvin E. Frankel, a former federal district judge in New York, gained a great deal of attention when he described sentencing authority as "unchecked" and "terrifying and intolerable for a society that professes devotion to a rule of law."[24] As we shall see, the 1980s and 1990s saw numerous attempts on both the state and federal levels to limit this judicial discretion.

ADMINISTRATIVE SENTENCING AUTHORITY

Parole is a condition of early release in which a prisoner is released from a correctional facility but is not freed from the legal custody and supervision of the state. Generally, after an inmate has been released on parole, he or she is supervised by a parole officer for a specified amount of time. The decision of whether to parole an inmate lies with the parole board. Parole is a crucial aspect of the criminal justice system and will be discussed in detail in Chapter 14.

For now, it is important to understand the role rehabilitation theories play in *administrative sentencing authority*. The formation in 1910 of the U.S. Parole Commission and similar commissions in the fifty states implied that the judge, though a legal expert, was not trained to determine when an inmate had been rehabilitated. Therefore, the sentencing power should be given to experts in human behavior, who were qualified to determine whether a convict was fit to return to society.[25] The recent repudiation of rehabilitation principles has not spared these administrative bodies; since 1976, fourteen states and the federal government have abolished traditional parole for their prisoners.[26] (See *Mastering Concepts—Who Has the Responsibility to Determine Sentences?*)

↗ ONLINE REVIEW *Go to the book's Web site for an interactive review of this section*

Individualized Justice and the Judge

During the pretrial procedures and the trial itself, the judge's role is somewhat passive and reactive. She or he is a primarily a "procedural watchdog," assuring that the rights of the defendant are not infringed on while the prosecutor and defense attorney dictate the course of action.

At a traditional sentencing hearing, however, the judge is no longer an arbiter between parties; she or he is now called on to exercise the ultimate authority of the state in determining the defendant's fate.

From the 1930s to the 1970s, when theories of rehabilitation held sway over the criminal justice system, indeterminate sentencing practices were guided by the theory of "individualized justice." Just as a physician gives specific treatment to individual patients depending on their particular health needs, the hypothesis goes, a judge needs to consider the specific circumstances of each individual offender in choosing the best form of punishment. Taking the analogy one step further, just as the diagnosis of a qualified physician should not be questioned, a qualified judge should have absolute discretion in making the sentencing decision. *Judicial discretion* rests on the assumption that a judge should be given

> Who Has the Responsibility to Determine Sentences?

Three different sentencing authorities determine the amount of time a person who has been convicted of a felony will spend in prison: legislatures, judges, and officials of the executive branch (governor's office). The process through which these three groups influence the sentencing process is summarized below.

FIRST STEP: LEGISLATORS PASS LAWS

Federal and state legislators are responsible for creating and updating the criminal codes that define how the law will punish those who commit crimes. Legislatures specify the terms of imprisonment in two different ways:

> By passing *indeterminate sentencing laws*. These laws designate a maximum and minimum amount of time that a person who commits a specific crime must spend in prison—one to three years, five to ten years, and so on.

> By passing *determinate sentencing laws*. These laws designate a fixed amount of time that a person who commits a specific crime must spend in prison—seven years, for example, instead of five to ten.

If lawmakers feel that the other two bodies—judges and officials of the executive branch—are being too lenient in their sentencing decisions, they can pass truth-in-sentencing laws that require convicts to serve the amount of time indicated in criminal codes.

SECOND STEP: JUDGES IMPOSE SENTENCES

Judges have the authority to choose among the sentencing options provided by legislatures. They are expected to consider all of the circumstances that surround a case and decide the length of the sentence based on these circumstances. (There are a few exceptions to this judicial authority. Only a jury, for example, can decide whether to impose the death penalty.)

THIRD STEP: EXECUTIVE OFFICIALS SET THE DATE OF RELEASE

Although judges impose the sentence, officials of the executive branch are responsible for deciding the extent to which a prisoner will serve his or her entire sentence. Most prisoners do not serve their maximum possible terms of imprisonment. Parole boards, appointed in most states by the governor, decide whether an inmate is eligible for *parole*—the conditional release of a prisoner before his or her sentence has been served. Executive officials also determine whether an inmate will have his or her sentence reduced because of *"good time,"* which is awarded for good behavior and participation in various treatment, vocational, and educational programs. (Remember, however, that legislatures can restrict parole and good-time provisions.)

ample leeway in determining punishments that fit both the crime and the criminal.[27] As we shall see later in the chapter, the growth of determinate sentencing has severely restricted judicial discretion in many jurisdictions.

FORMS OF PUNISHMENT

Within whatever legislative restrictions apply, the sentencing judge has a number of options when it comes to choosing the proper form of punishment. These sentences, or *dispositions,* include:

1 *Capital punishment.* Reserved normally for those who commit first degree murder under aggravated circumstances, capital punishment, or the death penalty, is a sentencing option in thirty-eight states and in federal courts.

2 *Imprisonment.* Whether for the purpose of retribution, deterrence, incapacitation, or rehabilitation, a common form of punishment in American history has been imprisonment. In fact, it is currently so common that judges—and legislators—are having to take factors such as prison overcrowding into consideration when making sentencing decisions. The issues surrounding imprisonment will be discussed in Chapters 13 and 14.

3 *Probation.* One of the effects of prison overcrowding has been a sharp rise in the use of probation, in which an offender is permitted to live in the community under supervision and is not incarcerated. Probation is covered in Chapter 12. *Alternative sanctions* (also discussed in Chapter 12) combine probation with other dispositions such as electronic monitoring, house arrests, boot camps, and shock incarceration.

4 *Fines.* Fines can be levied by judges in addition to incarceration and probation or independently of other forms of punishment. When a fine is the full extent of the punishment, it usually reflects the judge's belief that the offender is not a threat to the community and does not need to be imprisoned or supervised. In some instances, mostly involving drug offenders, a judge can order the seizure of an offender's property, such as his or her home.

5 *Restitution and community service.* Whereas fines are payable to the government, restitution and community service are seen as reparations to the injured party. Restitution is a direct payment to the victim or victims of a crime; community service consists of "good works"—such as cleaning up highway litter or tutoring disadvantaged youths—that benefit the entire community.

6 *Restorative justice.* Where the offender has committed a less serious crime, many judges are turning to restorative justice to provide a remedy. At the heart of restorative justice is the apology. So, for example, a judge in Texas required a teenager who had vandalized thirteen schools to go to each school and apologize to the students and faculty. In many such cases, victims appreciate the expression of remorse, and offenders are

Judges can have a profound impact on the sentencing process. U.S. District Judge Charles Pickering of Mississippi, pictured here, showed this power in the case of Daniel Swan, who had been sentenced to seven years in prison for burning a cross on the front lawn of a bi-racial couple in Walthall County, Mississippi. Pickering believed that the punishment was too harsh, and went to great lengths to convince prosecutors to reduce the sentence to twenty-seven months. When Pickering was announced as a candidate for promotion to the Fifth U.S. Circuit Court of Appeals in 2002, his efforts to reduce the sentence came under intensive scrutiny and criticism. Congress eventually blocked Pickering's nomination.

AP Photo/Hattiesburg American, George Clark

thankful for a chance to "set things right."[28] Restorative justice focuses more on "healing" the harm that a crime does to individual relationships and the community than on punishing the offender. (For information on a form of restorative justice practiced in Native American jurisdictions in the United States, see the feature *What Works—Navajo Peacemaker Courts* on the following page.)

In some jurisdictions, judges have a great deal of discretionary power and can impose sentences that do not fall into any of these categories. In California, for example, El Dorado County Superior Court Judge Jerald Lasarow ordered a man with AIDS who was convicted of sexually assaulting a four-year-old boy to undergo chemical castration for his crime.[29] Though a number of state legislatures are considering making this punishment mandatory for certain sex offenders, it is still considered cruel and unusual punishment in most jurisdictions.

THE SENTENCING PROCESS

The decision of how to punish a wrongdoer is the end result of what Yale Law School professor Kate Stith and federal appeals court judge José A. Cabranes call the "sentencing ritual."[30] The two main participants in this ritual are the judge and the defendant, but prosecutors, defense attorneys, and probation officers also play a role in the proceedings. Individualized justice requires that the judge consider all the relevant circumstances in making sentencing decisions. Therefore, judicial discretion is often tantamount to *informed* discretion—without the aid of the other members of the courtroom work group, the judge would not have sufficient information to make the proper sentencing choice.

The Presentence Investigative Report   For judges operating under various states' indeterminate sentencing guidelines, information in the **presentence investigative report** is a valuable component of the sentencing ritual. Compiled by a probation officer, the report describes the crime in question, notes the suffering of any victims, and lists the defendant's prior offenses (as well as any alleged but uncharged criminal activity). The report also contains a range of personal data such as family background, work history, education, and community activities—information that is not admissible as evidence during trial. In putting together the presentence investigative report, the probation officer is supposed to gain a "feel" for the defendant and communicate these impressions of the offender to the judge.

The report also includes a sentencing recommendation. In the past, this aspect has been criticized as giving probation officers too much power in the sentencing process, because lazy judges would simply rely on the recommendation in determining punishment.[31] Consequently, as we shall see, many jurisdictions have moved to limit the influence of the presentence investigative report.

The Prosecutor and Defense Attorney   To a certain extent, the adversary process does not end when the guilt of the defendant has been established. Both the prosecutor and the defense attorney are interviewed in the process of preparing the presentence investigative report, and both will try to present a version of the facts consistent with their own sentencing goals. The defense attorney in

Presentence Investigative Report
An investigative report on an offender's background that assists a judge in determining the proper sentence.

> Navajo Peacemaker Courts

When the Navajo returned to their native lands in 1892 after being forcibly relocated to Fort Sumner, New Mexico, by the U.S. Army during the "Long Walk" twenty-eight years earlier, the federal government operated the criminal courts on tribal property. In 1959, the Navajo Nation, which extends across several southwestern states, took control of its court system, which was still patterned after the American model and, in the words of one Navajo, had "little meaning for us in the Navajo way." Now, the tribe's judicial system is returning to the "Navajo way" in the form of Peacemaker courts. These courts reflect the traditional function of Navajo criminal law, which strives not so much to punish wrongdoers as to use community participation to resolve the issues behind the wrongdoing.

Restoring Harmony

The American concept of "crime" is referred to in Navajo culture as "disharmony." Disharmony is caused by *nayee,* which can be translated as "anything that gets in the way of a person living her or his life," such as depression, poverty, illness, or problems in a personal relationship. Therefore, the goal of Peacemaker courts is to restore harmony by bringing the offender back into the proper relationship with other members of the family and community who have been harmed by his or her actions. In contrast, as we have seen, American courts operate under an adversarial system that encourages conflict between the parties involved.

A Peacemaker court is "resided" over by a *naat'aani,* a respected member of the community. The *naat'aani* gathers the parties to the dispute and their relatives in a room and facilitates a process of "talking out." During the conversation, the group discusses the episode and decides what steps should be taken to resolve the problem. The *naat'aani* then gives a kind of lecture that spells out the community values that relate to the dispute. Next, the victim can request restitution or reparation. Rather than punishing the individual, a successful resolution aims at achieving *hozho nahasadli,* or a return to good relations and harmony for those involved.

In 1992, its first year, the Peacemaker court heard only forty-two cases. Today, there are more than three hundred Peacemaker courts in the seven districts of the Navajo Nation, and they hear more than two thousand cases a year. Most of these cases involve crimes such as domestic violence, property damage, and child abuse that are alcohol-related, and are referred to the Peacemaker court by a Navajo district court.

FOR CRITICAL ANALYSIS
Under the umbrella term community justice, *a number of American courts—mostly dealing with low-level drug crimes and misdemeanors—have adopted some of the methods of the Peacemaker courts. What aspects, if any, of the Navajo criminal justice system do you think could be usefully integrated into the "mainstream" criminal justice system?*

---

particular has a duty to make sure that the information contained in the report is accurate and not prejudicial toward his or her client. Depending on the norms of any particular courtroom work group, prosecutors and defense attorneys may petition the judge directly for certain sentences. Note that this process is not always adversarial. As we saw in Chapter 9, in some instances the prosecutor will advocate leniency and may join the defense attorney in requesting a short term of imprisonment, probation, or some form of intermediate sanction.[32]

FACTORS OF SENTENCING

The sentencing ritual strongly lends itself to the concept of individualized justice. With inputs—sometimes conflicting—from the prosecutor, attorney, and probation officer, the judge can be reasonably sure of getting the "full picture" of the crime and the criminal. In making the final decision, however, most judges consider two factors above all others: the seriousness of the crime and any mitigating or aggravating circumstances.

The Seriousness of the Crime   As would be expected, the seriousness of the crime is the primary factor in a judge's sentencing decisions. The more serious the crime, the harsher the punishment, for society demands no less. (See Figure

11.3.) Each judge has his or her own methods of determining the seriousness of the offense. Many judges simply consider the "conviction offense"; that is, they base their sentence on the crime for which the defendant was convicted.

Other judges—some mandated by statute—focus instead on the **"real offense"** in determining the punishment. The "real offense" is based on the actual behavior of the defendant, regardless of the official conviction. For example, through a plea bargain, a defendant may plead guilty to simple assault when in fact he hit his victim in the face with a baseball bat. A judge, after reading the presentence investigative report, could decide to sentence the defendant as if he had committed aggravated assault, which is the "real" offense. Though many prosecutors and defense attorneys are opposed to "real offense" procedures, which can render a plea bargain meaningless, there is a growing belief in criminal justice circles that they bring a measure of fairness to the sentencing decision.[33]

"Real Offense"
The actual offense committed, as opposed to the charge levied by a prosecutor as the result of a plea bargain. Judges who make sentencing decisions based on the real offense are often seen as undermining the plea bargain process.

Mitigating and Aggravating Circumstances   Consider the case of Marcos Mascarenas of Questa, New Mexico, who was responsible for the death of his six-month-old son by "shaken baby syndrome." Mascarenas had an intelligence quotient (IQ) of 90 and purportedly was not aware of the harm he was doing when he shook the baby. The judge in his case, Peggy Nelson, expressed frustration that she was forced to sentence the defendant to prison for a minimum of twelve years under state law. Because of his lack of mental capacity, the judge felt that Mascarenas did not deserve the punishment he received. In many situations, circumstances surrounding the crime may prompt a judge to adjust a sentence so that it more accurately reflects the totality of the crime. Judge Nelson considered Mascarenas's lack of mental capacity a *mitigating circumstance,* and given the opportunity, she would have given him a lesser punishment. There are other **mitigating circumstances,** or those circumstances that allow a lighter sentence to be handed down. They can include a defendant's youth or the fact that the defendant was coerced into committing the crime. In contrast, **aggravating circumstances** such as a prior record, blatant disregard for safety, or the use of a weapon can lead a judge to inflict a harsher penalty than might otherwise be the case (see Figure 11.4 on the following page).

Mitigating Circumstances
Any circumstances accompanying the commission of a crime that may justify a lighter sentence.

Aggravating Circumstances
Any circumstances accompanying the commission of a crime that may justify a harsher sentence.

FIGURE 11.3 Average Maximum Sentences for Selected Crimes in State and Federal Courts
Source: Bureau of Justice Statistics, *Felony Sentences in State Courts, 2000* (Washington, D.C., U.S. Department of Justice, June 2003), 3.

Judicial Philosophy   Most states spell out mitigating and aggravating circumstances in statutes, but there is room for judicial discretion in applying the law to particular cases. Judges are not uniform, or even consistent, in their opinions concerning which circumstances are mitigating or aggravating. One judge may believe a fourteen-year-old is not fully responsible for his or her actions, while another may believe teen-agers should be treated as adults. Those judges who support rehabilitative theories of criminal justice have been found to give more lenient sentences than those who are governed by goals of

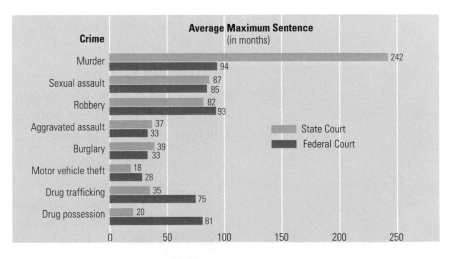

FIGURE 11.4 Aggravating and Mitigating Circumstances

FIGURE 11.4 Aggravating and Mitigating Circumstances

AGGRAVATING CIRCUMSTANCES

- An offense involved multiple participants and the offender was the leader of the group.

- A victim was particularly vulnerable.

- A victim was treated with particular cruelty for which an offender should be held responsible.

- The offense involved injury or threatened violence to others and was committed to gratify an offender's desire for pleasure or excitement.

- The degree of bodily harm caused, attempted, threatened, or foreseen by an offender was substantially greater than average for the given offense.

- The degree of economic harm caused, attempted, threatened, or foreseen by an offender was substantially greater than average for the given offense.

- The amount of contraband materials possessed by the offender or under the offender's control was substantially greater than average for the given offense.

MITIGATING CIRCUMSTANCES

- An offender acted under strong provocation, or other circumstances in the relationship between the offender and the victim make the offender's behavior less serious and therefore less deserving of punishment.

- An offender played a minor or passive role in the offense or participated under circumstances of coercion or duress.

- An offender, because of youth or physical or mental impairment, lacked substantial capacity for judgment when the offense was committed.

Source: *ABA Standards for Criminal Justice Sentencing* (Washington, D.C.: American Bar Association, 1994), 47, 52–53.

deterrence and incapacitation.[34] Furthermore, judges can have different philosophies with regard to different crimes, handing down, for example, harsh penalties for domestic abusers while showing leniency toward drug offenders.

ONLINE REVIEW Go to the book's Web site for an interactive review of this section

Inconsistencies in Sentencing

For some, the natural differences in judicial philosophies, when combined with a lack of institutional control, raise important questions. Why should a bank robber in South Carolina receive a different sentence than a bank robber in Michigan? Even federal indeterminate sentencing guidelines seem overly vague: a bank robber can receive a prison term from one day to twenty years, depending almost entirely on the judge.[35] Furthermore, if judges have freedom to use their discretion, do they not also have the freedom to misuse it?

Purported improper judicial discretion is often the first reason given for two phenomena that plague the criminal justice system: *sentencing disparity* and *sentencing discrimination*. Though the two terms are often used interchangeably, they describe different statistical occurrences—the causes of which are debatable.

SENTENCING DISPARITY

Justice would seem to demand that those who commit similar crimes should receive similar punishments. **Sentencing disparity** occurs when this expectation is not met in one of three ways:

1 Criminals receive similar sentences for different crimes of unequal seriousness.

2 Criminals receive different sentences for similar crimes.

3 Mitigating or aggravating circumstances have a disproportionate effect on sentences. Prosecutors, for example, reward drug dealers who inform on their associates with lesser sentences. As a result, low-level drug sellers, who have

INFOTRAC KEYWORDS

sentencing disparity

For more information, use this search term with InfoTrac College Edition, your online library at www.infotrac-college.com

Sentencing Disparity

A situation in which those convicted of similar crimes do not receive similar sentences.

no information to trade for reduced sentences, often spend more time in prison than their better-informed bosses.[36]

A number of different explanations have been offered to explain sentencing disparity. Two of these involve geography and courtroom norms.

Geographic Disparities   For wrongdoers, the amount of time spent in prison often depends as much on where the crime was committed as on the crime itself. A comparison of the sentences for simple possession of drugs reveals that someone convicted of the crime in the Northern District of California faces an average of seventy-one months in prison, whereas a similar offender in Alaska can expect an average of thirty-one months.[37] The average sentences imposed in the South are considerably harsher than those in the country as a whole: forty months longer for rape, thirty-four months longer for robbery, and twenty-nine months longer for burglary.[38] Such disparities can be attributed to a number of different factors, including local attitudes toward crime and available financial resources to cover the expenses of incarceration.

Courthouse Norms   The norms established by individual courtroom work groups can also lead to sentencing disparities. For nearly a century, scholars have been producing studies that point to different sentencing tendencies of different judges for similar crimes. A Department of Justice survey concluded that more than 20 percent of sentencing disparities can be directly attributed to the propensity of a particular judge to give harsh or lenient sentences.[39]

SENTENCING DISCRIMINATION

Sentencing discrimination occurs when disparities can be attributed to extralegal variables such as the defendant's gender, race, or economic standing.

The "Punishment Penalty"   At first glance, racial discrimination would seem to be rampant in sentencing practices. Research by Cassia Spohn and David Holleran of the University of Nebraska at Omaha suggests that minorities pay a "punishment penalty" when it comes to sentencing.[40] In Chicago, Spohn and Holleran found that convicted African Americans were 12.1 percent more likely to go to prison than convicted whites, and convicted Hispanics were 15.3 percent more likely. In Miami, Hispanics were 10.3 percent more likely to be imprisoned than either blacks or whites.[41] Nationwide, in 2002 nearly half of all inmates in state and federal prisons were African American, even though that minority group makes up only about 13 percent of the country's population.[42]

Interestingly, Spohn and Holleran found that the rate of imprisonment rose significantly for minorities who were young and unemployed. This led them to conclude that the disparities between races were not the result of "conscious" discrimination on the part of the sentencing judges. Rather, faced with limited time to make decisions and limited information about the offenders, the judges would resort to stereotypes, considering not just race, but age and unemployment as well.[43] (This research addresses the need for diversity among judges, discussed in Chapter 8.)

Furthermore, Spohn and Holleran found that none of the offender characteristics (race, age, employment) had an effect on the *length* of the prison sentence,[44] a result that is corroborated by national statistics. According to the Bureau of

Sentencing Discrimination
A situation in which the length of a sentence appears to be influenced by a defendant's race, gender, economic status, or other factor not directly related to the crime he or she committed.

This police photograph shows Brian Stewart, who was charged with injecting his son with blood infected with the AIDS virus because Stewart allegedly wanted to avoid paying child support. To make the punishment fit the crime, Circuit Judge Ellsworth Cundiff imposed the maximum sentence that he could: life in prison. The judge then told Stewart that such a sentence was "far too lenient." Will Stewart necessarily spend his entire life behind bars?

Reuters/HO/Getty Images

INFOTRAC KEYWORDS

sentence discrimination

For more information, use this search term with InfoTrac College Edition, your online library at www.infotrac.college.com

Justice Statistics, the average prison sentence handed out to blacks and whites in state courts was virtually the same. Indeed, with some crimes, such as murder, whites on average received longer sentences.[45]

Hispanics and Sentencing   Unfortunately, the federal data did not include Hispanics. Other studies, such as one conducted in Pennsylvania by Darrell Steffensmeier of Pennsylvania State University and Stephen DeMuth of Bowling Green State University, suggest that Hispanics receive harsher penalties than either whites or blacks.[46] Explanations for this finding vary. Some believe that the harsher sentences result from the "threat" posed by Hispanics as the most recent large immigrant group to change the ethnic outlook of the United States.[47] Steffensmeier and DeMuth suggest several other possibilities, including language barriers that put Hispanics at a disadvantage in court proceedings, for example, by making it difficult for them to understand what is offered in a plea bargain. A cultural emphasis on loyalty among Hispanics may also limit the number of sentencing "breaks" they get by informing on criminal associates.[48] (For a discussion of trends in sentencing women, see the feature *Criminal Justice in Action—The Gender Factor* at the end of this chapter.)

ONLINE REVIEW Go to the book's Web site for an interactive review of this section

Sentencing Reform

Judicial discretion, then, appears to be a double-edged sword. Although it allows judges to impose a wide variety of sentences to fit specific criminal situations, it appears to fail to rein in a judge's subjective biases, which leads to disparity and perhaps discrimination. Critics of judicial discretion believe that its costs (the lack of equality) outweigh its benefits (providing individualized justice). As Columbia law professor John C. Coffee noted:

> If we wish the sentencing judge to treat "like cases alike," a more inappropriate technique for the presentation could hardly be found than one that stresses a novelistic portrayal of each offender and thereby overloads the decisionmaker in a welter of detail.[49]

In other words, Professor Coffee feels that judges are given too much information in the sentencing process, making it impossible for them to be consistent in their decisions. It follows that limiting judicial discretion would not only simplify the process but lessen the opportunity for disparity or discrimination. Since the 1970s, this attitude has spread through state and federal legislatures, causing more extensive changes in sentencing procedures than in any other area of the American criminal justice system over that time period.

BEGINNINGS OF REFORM

Presumptive Sentencing
A sentencing strategy in which legislators set the average sentence that should be served for any particular crime, leaving judges with the ability to shorten or lengthen the sentence based on the circumstances of each case.

Research efforts in the mid-1970s laid the groundwork for sentencing reform. Particularly influential was the Twentieth Century Fund report developed by a task force of twelve criminal justice experts. The task force introduced the idea of **presumptive sentencing.** Revising ideas of determinate sentencing, the report urged lawmakers to legislate sentences that were "presumed" to be fair for any given crime category, restricting the court's discretion to finding aggravating or mitigating circumstances.[50]

Around the same time, Dr. Robert Martinson and several colleagues released an exhaustive study that seemed to prove that efforts to rehabilitate prisoners were generally unsuccessful.[51] Politicians on both sides seized on Martinson's report as an excuse to reject the idea of rehabilitating criminals and reestablish the ideals of determinate sentencing. Conservatives, believing judges, on the whole, to be too lenient, wished to limit their discretionary powers. Liberals—led by Senator Edward Kennedy (D-Mass.), who called sentencing a "national scandal" that leads to "massive injustice"[52]—felt the only way to eliminate the evils of sentencing disparity was to remove judicial bias from the process. Supported by a public alarmed by dramatic increases in violent crime, politicians moved sharply away from the notion of "treating" prisoners and toward the goal of punishing them.

SENTENCING GUIDELINES

As the rehabilitative model came under criticism, so did its manifestations; indeterminate sentencing discretion, parole, probation, and "good-time" credit became scapegoats for a failed system.[53] In an effort to reinstate determinacy into the sentencing process, many states and the federal government turned to **sentencing guidelines,** which require judges to dispense legislatively determined sentences based on factors such as the seriousness of the crime and the offender's prior record.

State Sentencing Guidelines   In 1978, Minnesota became the first state to create a Sentencing Guidelines Commission with a mandate to construct and monitor the use of a determinate sentencing structure. The Minnesota Commission left no doubt as to the philosophical justification for the new sentencing statutes, stating unconditionally that retribution was its primary goal.[54] Today, seventeen states employ some form of sentencing guidelines with similar goals.

In general, these guidelines remove discretionary power from state judges by turning sentencing into a mathematical exercise. Members of the courtroom work group are guided by a *grid*, which helps them determine the proper sentence. Figure 11.5 on page 379 shows the grid established by the Oregon Sentencing Commission. As with the grids used by most states, one axis ranks the type of crime, while the other refers to the offender's criminal history. In Oregon, each of roughly fifty felonies is ranked in seriousness for use with the grid.

For example, Burglary I is assigned a crime seriousness level of 9 if it involves the use of a deadly weapon, level 8 if the dwelling was occupied at the time of the crime, and so on. The state's crime history grid ranks the offender based on prior felonies and misdemeanors, with various points accrued on the basis of the seriousness of the prior crime. Of the ninety-nine cells in Oregon's grid, fifty-three "presume" prison terms and forty-six "presume" probationary sentences. The judge cannot deviate from these guidelines except under certain circumstances, which we will explore shortly.

Federal Sentencing Guidelines   In 1984, Congress passed the Sentencing Reform Act (SRA),[55] paving the way for federal sentencing guidelines that went into effect in 1987. Similar in many respects to the state guidelines, the SRA also eliminated parole for federal prisoners and severely limited early release from prison due to good behavior.[56] Furthermore, the act changed the sentencing role

AP Photo/Jeff Roberson

Daniel Leroy Crocker is shown here at his sentencing at the Johnson County Court House in Olathe, Kansas. Crocker had confessed to smothering nineteen-year-old Tracy Fesquez in 1979 after sexually assaulting the sleeping woman. Crocker was sentenced to only twenty years in prison with eligibility for parole in just ten years. This lenient sentence was based on the fact that he was never a suspect in the case. Rather, he eventually admitted to the murder, based on his religious faith. Three members of the victim's family urged in court that Crocker be given a life sentence. Should the reason Crocker voluntarily confessed affect his sentence?

Sentencing Guidelines
Legislatively determined guidelines that judges are required to follow when sentencing those convicted of specific crimes. These guidelines limit judicial discretion.

The United States Sentencing Commission is an independent agency in the judicial branch that establishes sentencing policies for federal courts. To visit its Web site, click on *Web Links* under *Chapter Resources* at www.cjinaction.com

Departure
A stipulation in many federal and state sentencing guidelines that allows a judge to adjust his or her sentencing decision based on the special circumstances of a particular case.

Mandatory Sentencing Guidelines
Statutorily determined punishments that must be applied to those who are convicted of specific crimes.

of U.S. probation officers. No longer would they be allowed to "suggest" the terms of punishment in presentence investigative reports. Instead, they are simply called on to calculate the presumptive sentence based on the federal sentencing guidelines grid.[57] The impact of the new law was dramatic: between 1986 and 1997, the average sentence for federal criminal offenses increased from thirty-six months to fifty-four months.[58]

Judicial Departures   Even in their haste to limit a judge's power, legislators realized that sentencing guidelines could not be expected to cover every possible criminal situation. Therefore, both state and federal sentencing guidelines allow an "escape hatch" of limited judicial discretion known as a **departure.** The SRA has a proviso that a judge may "depart" from the presumptive sentencing range if there are aggravating or mitigating circumstances present that are not adequately covered in the guidelines. For example, suppose two men are involved in the robbery of a liquor store, and during court proceedings it becomes clear that one of them forced his partner to take part in the crime by threatening physical harm. In this case, a federal judge could reduce the accomplice's sentence because he committed the crime under "duress," a factor that is not accounted for in the sentencing guidelines.

Judges do not, however, have unlimited access to departures. Any such decision must be justified in writing, and both the prosecution and the defense may appeal a judicial departure. In 1989, the Court of Appeals for the First Circuit ruled that departures must be measured on the basis of the circumstances and facts of the case and the reasonableness of the judge's decision.[59] (See the feature *You Be the Judge—What's the Sentence?* on page 382.)

Sentencing Guidelines Examined   Although guidelines have diminished the ability of judges to use unbridled discretion in their sentencing decisions, ample evidence shows that the guidelines have not eliminated disparities to the extent that reformers may have hoped. According to the U.S. Sentencing Commission, fifteen years after passage of the SRA, a person convicted in southern California or eastern Washington was twenty-five times more likely to have his or her sentence reduced by a federal judge than a person convicted in South Carolina.[60] The results have been similar with regard to racial disparities in sentencing: one study found that African Americans received 28 percent higher sentences for similar crimes than whites in federal courts.[61]

Observers say that these continuing disparities reflect a lack of willingness among judges to accept the guidelines' restrictions. Not only can judges use departure to circumvent the guidelines, they can also engage in "hidden" plea bargaining by allowing defendants to plead to lesser charges that the judge (and the prosecutor) believe to be more fair.

MANDATORY SENTENCING GUIDELINES

In response, politicians (urged on by their constituents) have passed sentencing laws even more contrary to the idea of individualized justice. These **mandatory (minimum) sentencing guidelines** further limit a judge's power to deviate from determinate sentencing laws by setting firm standards for certain crimes. Forty-six states have mandatory sentencing laws for crimes such as selling drugs, driving

FIGURE 11.5 Oregon's Sentencing Guidelines

Post-Prison Supervision	Crime	#	A — Multiple (3+) felony person offender (Three or more person felonies)	B — Repeat (2) felony person offender (Two person felonies, adult or juvenile)	C — Single (1) felony person with felony non-person offender (One person felony, plus one or more adult or juvenile non-person felony)	D — Single (1) felony person offender (One person felony and no other felony)	E — Multiple (4+) felony non-person offender (Four or more adult non-person felonies)	F — Repeat (2-3) felony non-person offender (Two or three adult non-person felonies)	G — Significant minor criminal record (4 or more adult A misdo's, or 1 adult non-person felony, or 3 or more juvenile non-person felonies)	H — Minor criminal record (No more than 3 adult A misdo's, or no more than 2 juvenile non-person felonies)	I — Minor misdemeanor or no criminal record (No juvenile felony or adult A misdemeanors)	Probation Term
3 years	Murder	11	225–269	196–224	178–194	149–177	149–177	135–148	129–134	122–128	120–121	5 years
	Manslaughter I, Assault I, Rape I, Arson I	10	121–130	116–120	111–115	91–110	81–90	71–80	66–70	61–65	58–60	5 years
	Rape I, Assault I, Kidnapping II, Arson I, Burglary I, Robbery I	9	66–72	61–65	56–60	51–55	46–50	41–45	39–40	37–38	34–36	
	Manslaughter II, Sexual Abuse I, Assault II, Rape II, Using Child in Display of Sexual Conduct, Drugs-Minors, Cult/Mftr/Delivery, Compelling Prostitution, Negligent Homicide	8	41–45	35–40	29–34	27–28	25–26	23–24	21–22	19–20	16–18	Opt probation
	Extortion, Coercion, Supplying Contraband, Escape I	7	31–36	25–30	21–24	19–20	16–18	180 / 90	180 / 90	180 / 90	180 / 90	3 years
2 years	Robbery II, Assault III, Rape III, Bribe Receiving, Intimidation, Property Crimes (more than $50,000), Drug Possession	6	25–30	19–24	15–18	13–14	10–12	180 / 90	180 / 90	180 / 90	180 / 90	3 years
	Robbery II, Theft by Receiving, Trafficking Stolen Vehicles, Property Crimes ($10,000–$49,999)	5	15–16	13–14	11–12	9–10	6–8	180 / 90	120 / 60	120 / 60	120 / 60	2 years
	FTA I, Custodial Interference II, Property Crimes ($5,000–$9,999), Drugs-Cult/Mftr/Delivery	4	10 / 10	8 / 9	120 / 60	120 / 60	120 / 60	120 / 60	120 / 60	120 / 60	120 / 60	2 years
1 year	Abandon Child, Abuse of Corpse, Criminal Nonsupport, Property Crimes, ($1,000–$4,999)	3	120 / 60	120 / 60	120 / 60	120 / 60	120 / 60	120 / 60	90 / 30	90 / 30	90 / 30	18 mos.
	Dealing Child Pornography, Violation of Wildlife Laws, Welfare Fraud, Property Crimes (less than $1,000)	2	90 / 30	90 / 30	90 / 30	90 / 30	90 / 30	90 / 30	90 / 30	90 / 30	90 / 30	18 mos.
	Altering Research, Habitual Offender Violation, Bigamy, Paramilitary Activity, Drugs–Possession	1	90 / 30	90 / 30	90 / 30	90 / 30	90 / 30	90 / 30	90 / 30	90 / 30	90 / 30	18 mos.

- In green blocks, numbers are presumptive prison sentences expressed as a range of months.
- In blue blocks, upper number is the maximum number of custody units, including all time spent in custody following the initial arrest, which may be imposed; lower number is the maximum number of jail days which may be imposed.

under the influence of alcohol, and committing any crime with a dangerous weapon. In Alabama, for example, any person caught selling drugs must spend at least two years in prison, with five years added to the sentence if the sale takes place within three miles of a school or housing project.[62] Similarly, Congress has set mandatory minimum sentences for more than one hundred crimes, mostly drug offenses.

The Facts
Twenty-three-year-old law school student Angela attended the rehearsal dinner for a friend's wedding. At the event, she took part in a series of toasts. Driving back to her home in Seattle, Washington, in her Porsche, Angela ran a red light and collided with another vehicle. The occupant of the other car suffered a broken neck. Angela had a blood alcohol level of 0.16 percent (the legal limit was 0.10 percent at the time and has since been lowered to 0.08 percent) and pled guilty to vehicular assault.

The Law
Under Washington State's Sentencing Reform Act (SRA), vehicular assault is considered a "violent offense" and categorized as a "most serious" Level IV felony. Under the SRA presumptive sentencing guidelines, Angela, who had no previous offense, could be sentenced to between three and nine months in jail.

Your Decision
Angela's lawyer presented the trial court with a number of arguments aimed at lowering her sentence, including her lack of a prior record, her history of charitable work, her sincere sense of regret, and her family background, which made it unlikely she would commit any further crimes. What sentence would you give Angela?

[To see how the Washington trial court ruled in this case, go to Example 11.1 in Appendix B.]

Habitual Offender Laws
Statutes that require lengthy prison sentences for those who are convicted of multiple felonies.

Habitual Offender Laws   **Habitual offender laws** are a form of mandatory sentencing that has proved increasingly popular over the past decade. Also known as "three-strikes-and-you're-out" laws, these statutes require that any person convicted of a third felony must serve a lengthy prison sentence. The crime does not have to be of a violent or dangerous nature. Under Washington's habitual offender law, for example, a "persistent offender" is automatically sentenced to life if the third felony offense happens to be "vehicular assault" (an automobile accident that causes injury), unarmed robbery, or attempted arson, among other lesser felonies.[63] Today, twenty-two states and the federal government employ "three-strikes" statutes, with varying degrees of severity.

The Supreme Court paved the way for these "three-strikes" laws when it ruled in *Rummel v. Estelle* (1980)[64] that Texas's habitual offender statute did not constitute "cruel and unusual punishment." Basically, the Court gave each state the freedom to legislate such laws in the manner that it deems proper. Twenty-three years later, in *Lockyer v. Andrade* (2003),[65] the Court upheld California's "three-strikes" law. The California statute allows prosecutors to seek penalties up to life imprisonment without parole on conviction of any third felony, including for nonviolent crimes. Leandro Andrade received fifty years in prison for stealing $153 of videotapes, his fourth felony conviction. A federal appeals court overturned the sentence, agreeing with Andrade's attorneys that it violated Eighth Amendment protections against cruel and unusual punishment.[66]

In a bitterly divided 5–4 decision, the Court reversed. Justice Sandra Day O'Connor, writing for the majority, stated that the sentence was not so "objectively" unreasonable that it violated the Constitution.[67] In his dissent, Justice David H. Souter countered that "[i]f Andrade's sentence is not grossly disproportionate, the principle has no meaning."[68] Basically, the justices who upheld the law said that if the California legislature—and by extension the California voters—felt that the law was reasonable, then the judicial branch was in no position to disagree.

Mandatory Sentences Reexamined   Despite the proliferation of "three-strikes" laws, California is the only state where prosecutors make much use of the statute. As of 2001, more than 50,000 offenders in California had been sentenced under its law; the next closest state—Georgia—had barely 1,000 convicts serving terms under "three-strikes" legislation.[69]

A study by the Sentencing Project, an organization that opposes these laws, highlights several reasons why the legislation may be more popular in theory than in practice. First, such laws increase the average age of prison populations by sending older convicts to prison for longer periods of time. As we saw in Chapter 2, the more a person ages, the less likely he or she is to commit crimes; thus, it makes less sense from a crime control perspective to focus on older wrongdoers. Furthermore, elderly prisoners cost more to imprison because they require greater expenditures for health care and other needs. One estimate places the bill for a prisoner given the minimum twenty-five-year penalty under California's "three-strikes" law at $1.5 million.[70]

Second, the impact on crime rates may not be worth the price. Although violent and property crime dropped about 40 percent in California in the six years after its "three-strikes" law was passed, other jurisdictions experienced similar declines without a comparable law: New York, 41 percent; Massachusetts, 33 percent; and Washington, D.C., 31 percent.[71] Finally, although the public strongly supports the tougher penalties for violent felons, that backing subsides dramatically when it comes to lesser crimes. In fact, only 13 percent of Californians support "three-strikes" penalties for less serious property offenses such as stealing videotapes.[72]

Outside a federal building in Los Angeles, activist Corey Nasario sits inside a makeshift cell to protest the thousands of California prisoners who have been jailed under the state's "three-strikes" law. The vast majority of these prisoners have never committed a violent crime, yet they will spend from twenty-five years to life behind bars. What are the arguments for and against the contention that such "three-strikes" laws violate the Eighth Amendment's prohibition of cruel and unusual punishment?

OPPOSITION TO DETERMINATE SENTENCING

Just as indeterminate sentencing produced outrageous examples of judicial discretion, so determinate sentencing has given its opponents fodder for criticism. Examples of mandatory sentencing "gone wild" usually involve situations such as the one in which a teen-ager was sentenced to life in prison for stealing a cell phone. Determinate sentencing, complained one observer, has "shown that there are things worse than disparity: rigidity, extreme severity, irrationality."[73] Among the staunchest opponents of the new sentencing measures have been members of the courtroom work group, who have seen the laws transform their well-established procedural norms.

Judges and Determinate Sentencing   As might be expected, judges, for the most part, have not welcomed the reduction in their discretionary powers. University of Minnesota law professor Michael Tonry has written that sentencing guidelines are the most "disliked sentencing reform initiative in the history of the United States" among judges.[74] Federal judges have called the guidelines "a farce," a "dismal failure," and "out of whack."[75] According to the U.S. Sentencing Commission, judges have shown their displeasure with the rules by "downward departing" in nearly 20 percent of all the sentences they hand out.[76] Indeed, U.S. Attorney General John Ashcroft became so frustrated with the high incidence of departures that in 2003 he ordered the U.S. Department of Justice to keep track of federal judges who give more lenient sentences than those provided for in the sentencing guidelines. Although such an action can have little practical effect on

Leandro Andrade, pictured here, unsuccessfully challenged California's "three-strikes" law. Under the state law, Andrade was sentenced to fifty years in prison without possibility of parole for stealing $153 worth of videocassettes—the lengthy sentence coming because of previous convictions for the "serious" felony of residential burglary. In 2003, the United States Supreme Court upheld California's law and Andrade's sentence, ruling that even though the punishment may be disproportionate, it is not unconstitutional. What effect do you think the knowledge that a third felony conviction will lead to a long sentence has on those people already found guilty of two such crimes?

federal judges, who, as we learned in Chapter 8, are appointed for life, it was criticized in many judicial quarters as an attempt to intimidate them into compliance.[77]

A Transfer of Power   Determinate sentencing has also led to a transfer of power in the sentencing process from the judge to another member of the courtroom work group. Prosecutors can evade mandatory minimums by plea bargaining or charging offenders with lesser crimes than the "real offense." If a person with a limited criminal history commits aggravated robbery, for example, and the prosecutor decides to charge him or her with simple robbery, the prosecutor has effectively reduced the offender's presumptive prison sentence. Evidence from Minnesota shows that nearly half of all defendants with no prior record who had been alleged to commit aggravated robbery were convicted of charges that did not carry presumptive prison terms.[78] Federal law also allows prosecutors to request sentences below the mandatory minimum for defendants who have cooperated by giving evidence against other wrongdoers.[79]

Prosecutors use their own form of "downward departing" for the same reason they make other charging decisions: to best allocate scarce resources. Frank Zimring, a law professor at the University of California at Berkeley, estimates that prosecutors in his state use the "three-strikes" law in only 10 percent of eligible cases; most consider it a "nuclear weapon" to be reserved for the most violent criminals.[80]

SENTENCING AND THE JURY

At the end of the nineteenth century, in almost half the states juries decided the sentence in cases that did not involve the death penalty, and as late as 1960 thirteen states still allowed the practice. Today, only six states (Arkansas, Kentucky, Missouri, Oklahoma, Texas, and Virginia) allow juries, rather than the judge, to make sentencing decisions in noncapital cases. The jury's declining role in sentencing is the result of concern that jurors' lack of experience and legal expertise may lead to improper verdicts and sentencing disparity.[81]

Proponents of a larger jury role in sentencing disagree that juries are incapable of handling the responsibility of sentencing. A study of sentences of robbers in Alabama before and after that state abolished jury sentencing found no discernible difference in sentencing between jurors and judges.[82] Furthermore, many observers note the inconsistency of prohibiting juries from choosing between, say, a five-year sentence and a seven-year sentence while requiring them to have the final word on whether a convict will be executed.[83] In fact, as we will see in the next section, the United States Supreme Court recently gave juries *more* responsibility in determining the sentence of death.

ONLINE REVIEW *Go to the book's Web site for an interactive review of this section*

Capital Punishment-- The Ultimate Sentence

"You do not know how hard it is to let a human being die," Abraham Lincoln (1809–1865) once said, "when you feel that a stroke of your pen will save him." Despite these misgivings, during his four years in office Lincoln approved the execution of 267 soldiers, including those who had slept at their post.[84] Our sixteenth president's ambivalence toward **capital punishment** is reflected in America's continuing struggle to reconcile the penalty of death with the morals and values of society. Capital punishment has played a role in sentencing since the earliest days of the Republic and—having survived a brief period of abolition between 1972 and 1976—continues to enjoy public support.

Still, few topics in the criminal justice system inspire such heated debate. Death penalty opponents such as legal expert Stephen Bright wonder, does "there comes a time when a society gets beyond some of the more primitive forms of punishment?"[85] They point out that two dozen countries have abolished the death penalty since 1985, and the United States is the only Western democracy that continues the practice. Critics also claim that a process whose subjects are chosen by "luck and money and race" cannot serve the interests of justice.[86] Proponents believe that the death penalty serves as the ultimate deterrent for violent criminal behavior and that the criminals who are put to death are the "worst of the worst" and deserve their fate.

Today, more than 3,500 convicts are living on "death row" in American prisons, meaning they have been sentenced to death and are awaiting execution. In the 1940s, as many as two hundred people were put to death in the United States in one year; as Figure 11.6 shows, the most recent high-water mark was ninety-eight in 1999. Despite declines since then, states and the federal government are currently executing convicts at a rate not seen in five decades. Consequently, the questions that surround the death penalty—Is it fair? Is it humane? Does it deter crime?—will continue to inflame both its supporters and its detractors.

THE AMERICAN TRADITION OF CAPITAL PUNISHMENT

"Before there were prisons" in the American tradition, points out social psychologist Mark Costanzo, "there was the penalty of death."[87] The first person executed by an American colonial government—taking its cue from the homeland of England, where capital punishment was widespread—was George Kendall, who was executed by a firing squad in Virginia for spying for Spain in 1608.[88] Since Kendall, more than 18,000 Americans have been legally executed as punishment for their crimes.

Capital Punishment
The use of the death penalty to punish wrongdoers for certain crimes.

INFOTRAC KEYWORDS
death penalty
For more information, use this search term with InfoTrac College Edition, your online library at www.infotrac-college.com

FIGURE 11.6 Executions in the United States, 1976 to Present
Source: Death Penalty Information Center.

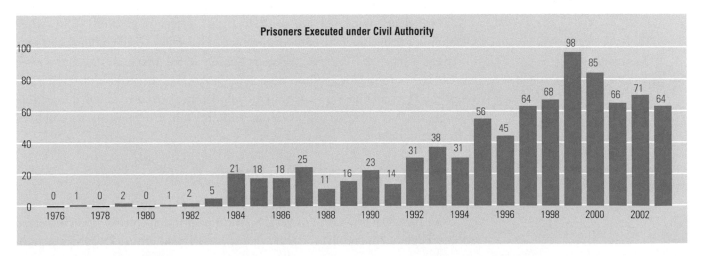

Capital Punishment in the Seventeenth and Eighteenth Centuries   In studying capital punishment in the colonies and the early days of the United States, one is struck by two aspects of the practice: the variety of crimes that were punished by death, and the public nature of the executions. During the 1600s, colonists were put to death for the crime of murder, but also for witchcraft, blasphemy, sodomy, and adultery. In the 1700s, citizens were executed for robbery, forgery, and illegally cutting down a tree.[89] These executions by hanging, beheading, or firing squad regularly took place in the town square or common area and were attended by the public. In fact, by modern standards the death penalty was often carried out in an overly gruesome manner in an attempt to deter criminal behavior by members of the audience. In 1710, a Virginia court ordered the bodies of two slaves who had been hanged for inciting rebellion to be cut up and displayed in various parts of the colony to keep "other Slaves from entering into such dangerous Conspiracys."[90]

The practice of public executions continued unabated until the 1830s, when reformers instigated the first widespread movement to abolish capital punishment. Government officials in northeastern states, aware that public executions provided death penalty opponents with opportunities to protest, passed a number of laws limiting the number of witnesses at an execution and requiring law enforcement officers to set up enclosures for the event. Furthermore, a desire to "civilize" the execution process moved it indoors, transforming it from a public spectacle to a sober action of the state.[91] The last public execution in the United States took place in Missouri in 1937. (See the feature *CJ and the Media—To See or Not to See?*)

Methods of Execution   The desire to civilize executions can also be seen in the evolution of the methods used to carry out the death sentence. Hanging was considered a more humane form of execution than other methods adopted from England, which including drawing and quartering and boiling the subject alive, and was the primary means of carrying out the death sentence in the United States until the end of the nineteenth century. (Indeed, the "long drop" method, in which the subject was hung from a greater height to ensure that death came from breaking the neck rather than strangulation, resulted from the reform movement in the 1830s and 1840s.) The 1890s saw the introduction of electrocution as a less painful method of execution than hanging, and in 1890 in Auburn Prison, New York, William Kemmler became the first American to die in an electric chair.

The "chair" remained the primary form of execution until 1977, when Oklahoma became the first state to adopt lethal injection. Today, almost all of the thirty-eight states that execute prisoners employ lethal injection; the condemned convict is given a sedative, followed by a combination of drugs administered intravenously. Ten states allow the prisoner to choose an alternative to lethal injection, meaning that the electric chair, hanging, and, in Utah, firing squads are still used from time to time.

THE DEATH PENALTY AND THE SUPREME COURT

See the `Death Penalty Information Center` and `Pro-Death Penalty.com` for opposing views on capital punishment. Find these Web sites by clicking on *Web Links* under *Chapter Resources* at www.cjinaction.com

In 1890, William Kemmler challenged his sentence to die in New York's new electric chair (for murdering his mistress) on the grounds that electrocution infringed on his Eighth Amendment rights against cruel and unusual punishment.[92]

> To See or Not to See?

When Timothy McVeigh, the Oklahoma City bomber, requested that his execution be televised, many Americans treated the idea with scorn and derision. Television programming, they argued, is easily oversaturated with both fictional and, increasingly, real violence. Furthermore, images of such events are already easily available in our culture. *The Green Mile*, a 1999 film starring Tom Hanks that was nominated for an Academy Award, graphically depicts three executions. In 2001, Georgia officials released an eleven-minute audiotape of actual executions in their state. Furthermore, high-profile capital punishment cases such as McVeigh's receive intense media coverage, which seems to show everything but the convict's death.

There is, however, a good deal of support for televising executions from both supporters and critics of the death penalty. Proponents believe that public viewing of executions adds to their deterrent value. Opponents believe that by "hiding" executions, the government prevents people from seeing how gruesome they really are. These critics are convinced that if the public were allowed to witness these events, support for the death penalty would drop dramatically.

Evidence to uphold such a theory is hard to find, however. In fact, human curiosity seems to drive large numbers of people to horrific events, whether they are televised or not. In 1837, when support for capital punishment was as high as it is today, 20,000 spectators gathered in Philadelphia to watch the hanging of pirate James Moran. More than 160 years later, in 1999, Florida Supreme Court Justice Leander J. Shaw, Jr., placed photos of the electrocution of Allen Lee "Tiny" Davis on the court's Web site to highlight the brutality of the electric chair. (The photos showed Davis hemorrhaging blood from his nose onto his white prison shirt.) The site received so many hits in such a short period of time that it crashed.

AP Photo/Florida Department of Corrections

The electric chair was the sole method of capital punishment in Florida from 1922 until July 8, 1999. On that day, the execution of convicted murderer Allen Lee Davis, shown above, turned grisly when the chair's current caused a significant amount of blood to flow from his nose during the electrocution. Critics of the electric chair hoped that Davis's macabre death would finally convince the United States Supreme Court that the method ran counter to the U.S. Constitution's prohibition of "cruel and unusual punishment." To head off any possible legal problems, in January 2000, Florida Governor Jeb Bush signed a bill that gave the state's death-row inmates the choice between dying by lethal injection or in the electric chair. Why might Davis's extensive nosebleeding have signified to the Court that execution by electric chair is unconstitutional?

Kemmler's challenge is historically significant in that it did not challenge the death penalty itself as being cruel and unusual, but only the method by which it was carried out. Many constitutional scholars believe that the framers never questioned the necessity of capital punishment, as long as due process is followed in determining the guilt of the suspect.[93] Accordingly, the Supreme Court rejected Kemmler's challenge, stating that:

> Punishments are cruel when they involve torture or a lingering death; but the punishment of death is not cruel, within the meaning of that word as used in the Constitution. It implies there something inhuman and barbarous, something more than the mere extinguishment of life.[94]

Thus, the Court set a standard that it has followed to this day. No *method* of execution has ever been found to be unconstitutional by the Supreme Court.

Weems v. United States   For nearly eight decades following its decision regarding Kemmler, the Supreme Court was silent on the question of whether capital punishment was constitutional. In *Weems v. United States* (1910),[95] however, the Court did make a ruling that would significantly affect debate on the death penalty. *Weems* concerned a defendant who had been sentenced to fifteen years of hard labor, a heavy fine, and a number of other penalties for the relatively minor crime of falsifying official records. The Court overturned the sentence, ruling that the penalty was too harsh considering the nature of the offense. Ultimately, in the *Weems* decision, the Court set three important precedents concerning sentencing:

1 Cruel and unusual punishment is defined by the changing norms and standards of society and therefore is not based on historical interpretations.

2 Courts may decide whether a punishment is unnecessarily cruel with regard to physical pain.

3 Courts may decide whether a punishment is unnecessarily cruel with regard to psychological pain.[96]

Furman v. Georgia   In 1971, three cases challenging the death penalty as "cruel and unusual" were brought before the Supreme Court. Again, these cases did not question the death penalty itself as cruel and unusual. Instead, they raised the argument that capital punishment was imposed arbitrarily; that is, the death penalty was unconstitutional because there were no recognizable standards under which it could or could not be imposed.

In *Furman v. Georgia* (1972),[97] the lead case, the Supreme Court issued a very complex ruling on this issue. By a 5–4 margin, the Court essentially agreed that the death penalty violated the Eighth Amendment. Only two of those in the majority (Justices Marshall and Brennan), however, were willing to state that capital punishment was blatantly unconstitutional. The other three (Justices Douglas, Stewart, and White) took the narrower view that the sentence was unconstitutional as practiced by the states. Justice Potter Stewart was particularly eloquent on the subject, stating that the sentence of death was so arbitrary as to be comparable to "being struck by lightning."[98] In its decision, therefore, the Court did not rule that the death penalty inherently violated the Eighth Amendment's protection against cruel and unusual punishment or the Fourteenth Amendment's guarantee of due process, only that it did so as practiced by the states. So, although *Furman* invalidated the death penalty for over six hundred offenders on death row at the time, it also provided the states with a window of opportunity to bring their death penalty statutes up to constitutional standards.

The Bifurcated Process   By 1976, thirty-five states had done just that, attempting to comply with *Furman* by either making the death penalty mandatory for certain offenses or adopting elaborate procedures to ensure that standards of due process were upheld during the sentencing process. The ten states that attempted the mandatory route found their statutes invalidated for a second time in 1976, when, in *Woodson v. North Carolina*,[99] the Supreme Court ruled that such laws failed to allow for different circumstances in different cases.

The remaining twenty-five states adopted an alternate means of satisfying the questions raised in *Furman* by establishing a two-stage, or *bifurcated*, procedure for capital cases. In the first stage, a jury determines the guilt or innocence of the

Gary Gilmore is led to a Provo, Utah, court on December 1, 1976. Less than two months later, Gilmore became the first American executed under a new bifurcated system adopted by a number of states in the mid-1970s. Why did the United States Supreme Court put a halt to executions in this country in 1972?

AP Photo/Ron Barker

> **The Bifurcated Death Penalty Process**

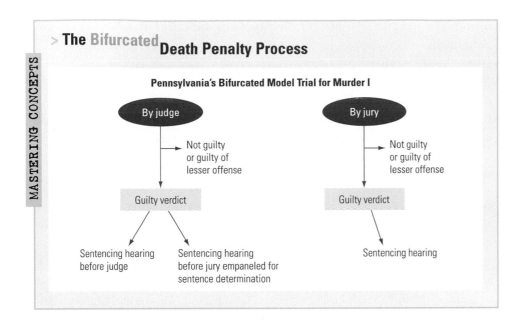

Pennsylvania's Bifurcated Model Trial for Murder I

defendant for a crime that has statutorily been determined to be punishable by death. If the defendant is found guilty, the jury reconvenes in the second stage and considers all relevant evidence to decide whether the death sentence is in fact warranted. Therefore, even if a jury were to find the defendant guilty of a crime, such as first degree murder, that *may be* punishable by death, in the second stage it could decide that the circumstances surrounding the crime justified only a punishment of life in prison. (See *Mastering Concepts—The Bifurcated Death Penalty Process* above.)

Gregg v. Georgia   In *Gregg v. Georgia* (1976),[100] the Supreme Court ruled in favor of Georgia's new bifurcated process, stating that the state's legislative guidelines removed the ability of a jury to "wantonly and freakishly impose the death penalty." The Court upheld similar procedures in Texas and Florida, establishing a "road map" for all states to follow that would assure them protection from lawsuits based on Eighth Amendment grounds. On January 17, 1977, Gary Mark Gilmore became the first American executed (by Utah) under the new laws, and today thirty-eight states and the federal government have capital punishment laws based on the guidelines established by *Gregg*. (Note that state governments are responsible for almost all executions in this country. When the federal government executed Timothy McVeigh and Juan Raul Garza in 2001, this marked the first death sentences carried out by the federal government since 1963.)

The Court reaffirmed the important role of the jury in death penalties in *Ring v. Arizona* (2002).[101] The case involved Arizona's bifurcated process: after the jury determined a defendant's guilt or innocence, it would be dismissed, and the judge would decide whether execution was warranted. The Court found that this procedure violated the defendant's Sixth Amendment right to a jury trial; juries must be involved in *both* stages of the bifurcated process. The decision invalidated death penalty laws in Arizona, Colorado, Idaho, Montana, and Nebraska, forcing legislatures in those states to hastily revamp their procedures.

Mitigating Circumstances   Several mitigating circumstances will prevent a defendant found guilty of first degree murder from receiving the death penalty.

Insanity   In 1986, the United States Supreme Court held that the Constitution prohibits the execution of a person who is insane. The Court failed to provide a test for insanity other than Justice Lewis F. Powell's statement that the Eighth Amendment "forbids the execution only of those who are unaware of the punishment they are about to suffer and why they are to suffer it."[102] Consequently, each state must come up with its own definition of "insanity" for death penalty purposes. A state may also force convicts on death row to take medication that will make them sane enough to be aware of the punishment they are about to suffer and why they are about to suffer it.[103]

Mentally Handicapped   The Supreme Court's recent change of mind on the question of whether a mentally handicapped convict may be put to death underscores the continuing importance of the *Weems* test. In 1989, the Court rejected the argument that execution of a mentally handicapped person was "cruel and unusual" under the Eighth Amendment.[104] At that time, only two states barred execution of the mentally handicapped. Today, eighteen states have such laws, and the Court has apparently decided that this increased number reflects "changing norms and standards of society." In *Atkins v. Virginia* (2002),[105] the Court used the *Weems* test as the main rationale for barring the execution of the mentally handicapped. (See the feature *CJ in Focus—Landmark Cases:* Atkins v. Virginia.)

Age   Following the *Atkins* case, many observers, including four Supreme Court justices, hoped that the same reasoning would be applied to the question of whether convicts who committed the relevant crime when they were juveniles may be executed. In sixteen states and federal courts, defendants must have been at least eighteen years old when they committed the crime to be eligible for death. Five states set the minimum age at seventeen, while the seventeen other states that employ the death penalty will execute offenders who were sixteen or older. Today, about eighty people who committed their crimes as juveniles are on death row.

The Court set the age "floor" for these state laws in 1988, when it halted the execution of fifteen-year-old William Wayne Thompson.[106] Within a year, however, it upheld death sentences for a sixteen-year-old and a seventeen-year-old,[107] and as recently as 2003 it refused to hear an appeal on the issue.[108] For the foreseeable future, then, states will be able to set their own age limits for capital punishment.

DEBATING THE SENTENCE OF DEATH

Of the topics covered in this textbook, few inspire the passion of argument that can be found concerning the death penalty. Many advocates believe that execution is "just deserts" for those who commit heinous crimes. In the words of Ernest van den Haag, death is the "only fitting retribution for murder that I can think of."[109] Opponents worry that retribution is simply another word for vengeance and that "the use of the death penalty by the state will increase the acceptance of revenge in our society and will give official sanction to a climate of violence."[110] As the debate over capital punishment continues, it tends to focus on several key issues: deterrence, incapacitation, fallibility, arbitrariness, constitutionality, and discrimination.

Deterrence   Those advocates of the death penalty who wish to show that the practice benefits society often turn to the idea of deterrence. In other words, they believe that by executing convicted criminals, the criminal justice system discour-

"We didn't feel she should get the death penalty. When you're on Death Row, you're there so long with nothing to bother you. In jail, she'll be with murderers and rapists. We thought the death penalty would be too easy for her."
—Jodi Dotts, explaining her decision to ask the prosecutor not to seek capital punishment for her daughter's killer (1999)

> *Atkins v. Virginia*

A trial court convicted Daryl Renard Atkins of abduction, armed robbery, and capital murder. During the penalty phase of the trial, the defense relied heavily on testimony from a forensic psychologist that Atkins was "mildly mentally retarded" and on tests showing the defendant to have an IQ of 59. (The generally accepted definition of mental retardation is an IQ of 70 or less.) After the jury sentenced Atkins to death, the case was appealed to the Virginia Supreme Court. That court upheld the sentence based on a 1989 decision in which the United States Supreme Court declined to create an exemption from the death penalty for the mentally retarded. In accepting Atkins's appeal, the United States Supreme Court focused on changing attitudes toward the death penalty between 1989 and 2002, especially the fact that sixteen states had adopted laws preventing the execution of the mentally retarded during that time period.

Atkins v. Virginia
United States Supreme Court
536 U.S. 304 (2002)
http://laws.findlaw.com/us/000/00-8452.htm

> In the words of the court . . .

Justice STEVENS, majority opinion
* * * *

Those mentally retarded persons who meet the law's requirements for criminal responsibility should be tried and punished when they commit crimes. Because of their disabilities in areas of reasoning, judgment, and control of their impulses, however, they do not act with the level of moral culpability that characterizes the most serious adult criminal conduct. Moreover, their impairments can jeopardize the reliability and fairness of capital proceedings against mentally retarded defendants. Presumably for these reasons, in the 13 years since we decided *Penry v. Lynaugh* (1989) the American public, legislators, scholars, and judges have deliberated over the question whether the death penalty should ever be imposed on a mentally retarded criminal. The consensus reflected in those deliberations informs our answer to the question presented by this case: whether such executions are "cruel and unusual punishments" prohibited by the Eighth Amendment to the Federal Constitution.
* * * *

We have pinpointed that the "clearest and most reliable objective evidence of contemporary values is the legislation enacted by the country's legislatures." [Justice Stevens then lists and describes acts taken by sixteen states to ban execution of the mentally retarded.] * * * It is not so much the number of these States that is significant, but the consistency of the direction of change. Given the well-known fact that anticrime legislation is far more popular than legislation providing protections for persons guilty of violent crime, the large number of States prohibiting the execution of mentally retarded persons (and the complete absence of States passing legislation reinstating the power to conduct such executions) provides powerful evidence that today our society views mentally retarded offenders as categorically less culpable than the average criminal.
* * * *

This consensus unquestionably reflects widespread judgment about the relative culpability of mentally retarded offenders, and the relationship between mental retardation and the penological purposes served by the death penalty. Additionally, it suggests that some characteristics of mental retardation undermine the strength of the procedural protections that our capital jurisprudence steadfastly guards.

> Decision

The Court found that, applying the Eighth Amendment in light of "evolving standards of decency" criteria, the execution of Atkins and other mentally retarded convicts was cruel and unusual punishment and therefore would violate the U.S. Constitution. The Virginia Supreme Court's ruling was, therefore, reversed and remanded.

FOR CRITICAL ANALYSIS
At the time of the Atkins *decision, twenty states, including Virginia, allowed the execution of the mentally retarded. What impact should these state laws have on "evolving standards of decency"?*

For more information and activities related to this case, click on Landmark Cases *under* Book Resources *at* www.cjinaction.com

ages potential criminals from committing similar violent acts. (When people speak of "deterrence" with regard to the death penalty, they are usually referring to general deterrence rather than specific deterrence.) Deterrence was the primary justification for the frequent public executions carried out in this country before the 1830s and for the brutality of those events. Many social scientists claim that there is little valid statistical proof of the deterrent effect of capital punishment.

> GREAT **DEBATES**

Does the death penalty deter murder? For many, this is the central question of the capital punishment debate. To better understand the issues of deterrence and the death penalty, click on *Great Debates* under *Book Resources* at www. cjinaction.com

Nonetheless, in 1975, Isaac Ehrlich, an economist at the University of Chicago, attempted to find some by focusing on the relationship between different jurisdictions' homicide rates and the percentage of those convicted of murder who were actually executed. According to Ehrlich, each additional execution that would have taken place between 1933 and 1967 could have saved the lives of as many as eight murder victims.[111] Ehrlich's results, though widely hailed at the time of their release, remain controversial; they have not been duplicated to the satisfaction of some scholars, and numerous subsequent studies have found that execution rates appear to have little effect on homicide rates. In fact, the latest major study on the issue, conducted in 2000 by the *New York Times,* showed that those states without the death penalty have had *lower* homicide rates since 1976 than those states that do allow capital punishment.[112]

In the end, the deterrence debate follows a familiar pattern. Opponents of the death penalty claim that murderers rarely consider the consequences of their act, and therefore it makes no difference whether capital punishment exists or not. Proponents counter that this proves the death penalty's deterrent value, because if the murderers *had* considered the possibility of execution, they would *not* have committed the crime.

Incapacitation   In one sense, capital punishment acts as the ultimate deterrent by rendering those executed incapable of committing further crimes. A study done by Paul Cassell and Stephen Markman analyzed the records of 52,000 state inmates doing time for murder and found that 810 of them had been previously convicted for the same crime. These 810 recidivists had killed 821 people after being released from prison the first time.[113] If, hypothetically, the death penalty was mandatory for those convicted of murder, then 821 innocent lives would have been saved in Cassell and Markman's example, and thousands of others among the general population. Such projections seem to show that by incapacitating dangerous criminals, capital punishment could provide society with measurable benefits.

Fallibility   The incapacitation justification for capital punishment, however, rests on two questionable assumptions: (1) every convicted murderer is likely to recidivate; and (2) the criminal justice system is *infallible.* In other words, the system never convicts someone who is actually not guilty. In fact, between 1976, when the Supreme Court reinstated capital punishment, and October 2003, 107 American men and women who had been convicted of capital crimes and sentenced to death were later found to be innocent. Over that same time period, 877 executions took place, meaning that for every eight convicts put to death since *Gregg,* one death-row inmate has been found innocent.

There are several explanations for this relatively high ratio of error in capital cases. First, police and prosecutors are often under a great deal of public pressure to solve violent crimes and may be overzealous in arresting and prosecuting suspects. Such was the case with Rolando Cruz, who spent a decade on Illinois's death row for the rape and murder of a ten-year-old girl. Even after another man named Brian Dugan confessed to the crime and DNA testing linked Dugan to the crime scene, prosecutors still insisted that Cruz

Prizefighter Rubin "Hurricane" Carter was convicted in 1966 of a triple murder in New Jersey and sentenced to life. In 1985, he was exonerated. Today, he heads the Association in Defense of the Wrongly Convicted. At one conference he stated, "There is no separation between being on death row or being held unjustly for the rest of your life. Prison is death." What might be the cost to society if no sentences of life imprisonment were ever handed out?

AP Photo/Barry Thumma

was the culprit. Only after a police officer admitted that he lied under oath concerning Cruz's "confession" was Cruz declared not guilty.[114]

Outright lying by persons involved in capital cases contributes to false convictions. Professors Hugo Bedau of Tufts University and Michael Radelet of the University of Florida found that one-third of wrongful capital convictions resulted from "jailhouse snitches" who perjured themselves by telling the court that they overhead a confession by the defendant. In addition, false confessions and faulty eyewitness identifications were found to be responsible for two of every seven wrongful convictions.[115] The single factor that contributes the most to the criminal justice system's fallibility, however, is widely believed to be unsatisfactory legal representation. Many states and counties cannot or will not allocate adequate funds for death penalty cases, meaning that poor capital defendants are often provided with a less-than-vigorous defense. During a double homicide trial in Vinton County, Ohio, for example, public defenders for Gregory McKnight presented one witness on their client's behalf while prosecutors called forty against him. After a relatively short—two and a half weeks—trial, McKnight was convicted and sentenced to death.[116]

Arbitrariness   One of the reasons it is so difficult to determine the deterrent effect of the death penalty is that it is rarely meted out. Despite the bifurcated process required by *Furman,* a certain amount of arbitrariness appears to remain in the system. Comparing the number of murders known by police to the number of executions, the chances of a murderer being executed are approximately 1,000 to 1.[117]

The chances of a defendant in a capital trial being sentenced to death seem to depend heavily on, as we have just seen, the quality of the defense counsel and the jurisdiction where the crime was committed. A recent Columbia University study, headed by Professor James Liebman, reported that of the 4,578 death sentences handed down between 1973 and 1995, two-thirds were reversed on appeal. About

FIGURE 11.7 **Number of Executions by State, 1976–2003**

37 percent of the reversals occurred because of incompetent lawyering.[118] Furthermore, as Figure 11.7 shows, a convict's chances of being executed are strongly influenced by geography. Six states (Texas, Virginia, Florida, Missouri, Oklahoma, and Louisiana) account for nearly two-thirds of all executions, while twelve states and the District of Columbia do not provide for capital punishment within their borders. Therefore, a person on trial for first degree murder in New Mexico has a much better chance of avoiding execution than someone who has committed the same crime in Texas. Dramatic differences can even exist within the same state. Further research by Professor Liebman and his associates showed that the death sentence was handed down in 93 of 1,000

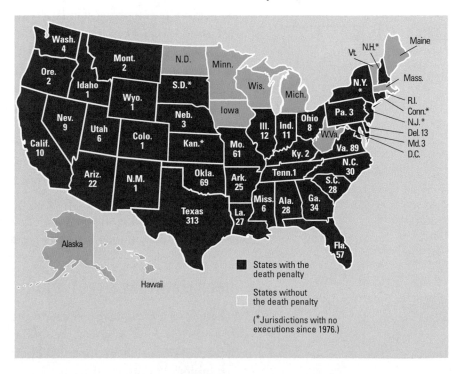

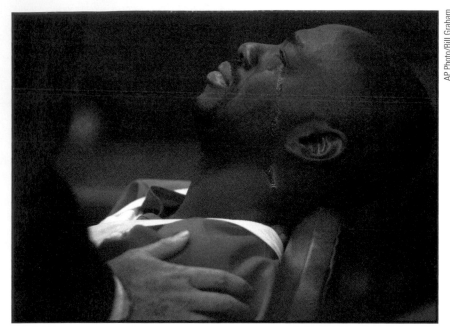

Gregory McKnight is comforted by his attorney in a Vinton County (Ohio) Common Pleas Court. Even though McKnight was convicted of aggravated murder, which is punishable by execution, the judge in his case initially ruled that McKnight was not eligible for the death penalty because Vinton County did not have the funds to provide him with an adequate defense. The judge later rescinded this ruling, and McKnight was sentenced to death in 2002. What role, if any, should the level of representation by the defense attorney play in a court's decision to execute a convict?

homicides in Lexington County, South Carolina. Richland County, South Carolina, only a few miles away, had a rate of 9 per 1,000.[119] Accordingly, Profesor Hugo Bedau compares those who arc cxccuted to "losers in an arbitrary lottery."[120]

Not all observers of the criminal justice system agree with Professor Bedau's assessment. In responding to the first Columbia University study mentioned above, James Q. Wilson points out that its authors do not claim that any innocent people have actually been executed.[121] Instead, Wilson suggests, the system is designed to give convicted murderers every chance to prove their innocence. In the *Gregg* case, the Supreme Court interpreted the Fourteenth Amendment as requiring "meaningful appellate review" for anybody found guilty of a capital crime.[122] In other words, the case of any defendant sentenced to death must automatically be reviewed by a higher court. To decrease the chances that the death sentence will be imposed "in a freakish manner," to use the Court's phrase, the appeals process in capital cases usually lasts twelve years. Thus, Wilson notes, the death penalty is actually quite rare: of the 4,578 death sentences considered in the Columbia University study, only 313 led to executions.[123]

Still Cruel and Unusual   Finally, many observers believe that the Supreme Court should revisit the idea of the death penalty as cruel and unusual punishment, given the changing standards of society provided for in the *Weems* decision discussed earlier. Even lethal injection, critics point out, may cause undue suffering. Some medical experts believe that pancuronium bromide, one of the chemicals used in the process, only paralyzes its subjects, rendering them unable to speak or cry out in pain as they suffocate to death.[124] (In 2001, Tennessee made it a crime to use the chemical to euthanize pets.)

Developments in Louisiana may cause the Supreme Court to revisit another Eighth Amendment issue. In 1977, the Court held that the death penalty could not be imposed for rape, labeling as "cruel and unusual" a punishment that is not proportionate to the crime.[125] In 2003, however, a Louisiana court sentenced Patrick O. Kennedy to be executed for raping an eight-year-old girl. If the state supreme court upholds the sentence, the question of whether the death penalty can be applied to crimes other than murder may once again come before the highest court in the land.

DISCRIMINATORY EFFECT AND THE DEATH PENALTY

Whether or not capital punishment is imposed arbitrarily, some observers claim that it is not done without bias. Of the 4,220 prisoners executed in the United States between 1930 and 1996, 53 percent were African American, even though that minority group made up between 10 and 15 percent of the national popula-

Andy Hulette testifies at the 2002 trial of his former roommate Shane Ragland in a Lexington, Kentucky, courtroom. Ragland was eventually convicted of first degree murder in the 1994 sniper death of Trent DiGiuro, a University of Kentucky football player. Prosecutors had asked that Ragland receive the death penalty. What impact did the fact that Ragland was tried and convicted in Kentucky have on his chances of being executed? In what states is it most likely that a person convicted of murder will receive the death penalty?

tion during that time span.[126] Today, 42 percent of all inmates on death row are black; thus, the black proportion of the death-row population is more than triple the black proportion of the population.

The Race of the Victim   Another set of statistics also continues to be problematic. African Americans are approximately four times more likely to receive the death penalty if their victim is white than if he or she is black.[127] A study of death penalty cases in North Carolina found that the odds of getting a death sentence for convicts of any race increased three and a half times if the victim was white rather than black.[128] In fact, although less than half of murder victims are white, four out of every five executions involve white victims (see Figure 11.8).

In *McCleskey v. Kemp* (1987),[129] the defense attorney for an African American sentenced to death for killing a white police officer used similar statistics to challenge Georgia's death penalty law. A study of two thousand Georgia murder cases showed that although African Americans were the victims of six out of every ten murders in the state, over 80 percent of the cases in which death was imposed involved murders of whites.[130] In a 5–4 decision, the United States Supreme Court rejected the defense's claims, ruling that statistical evidence did not prove discriminatory intent on the part of Georgia's lawmakers.

The Income of the Victim   One of the reasons the study was unpersuasive in the *McKleskey* case is that statistics, as we noted in Chapter 3, are often imperfect tools to measure trends. Even though the studies mentioned above show that race has an effect on the probability of receiving the death penalty, to prove discrimination, from a legal standpoint, race must be the *only* determinant. Thus, a study must show that race, and not other factors, such as the severity of the

FIGURE 11.8 Race and the Death Penalty

As these two graphs show, a disproportionate percentage of executed murders had white victims.

Source: U.S. Bureau of Justice Statistics.

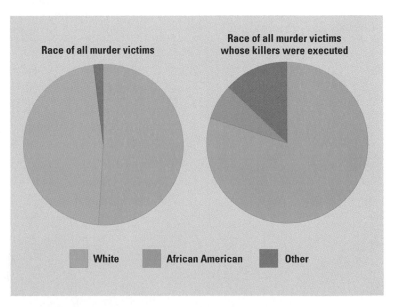

Race of all murder victims

Race of all murder victims whose killers were executed

White   African American   Other

crime, the criminal history of the defendant, and the quality of the defense attorney was the determining factor.[131]

Furthermore, some experts contend that the wealth, and not the race, of the defendant is the most important factor in death penalty cases. This hypothesis is based on the truism that adequate representation lessens the probability of being sentenced to death, and adequate representation is expensive.[132] Research by William M. Holmes of the Criminal Justice Center at the University of Massachusetts in Boston found that race did not account for wrongful convictions in capital cases. A much more important factor, according to Holmes, was education level, which correlates strongly with income.[133]

THE IMMEDIATE FUTURE OF THE DEATH PENALTY

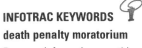

INFOTRAC KEYWORDS

death penalty moratorium

For more information, use this search term with InfoTrac College Edition, your online library at www.infotrac-college.com

Perhaps the most significant event in the recent history of the capital punishment debate took place in January 2000, when Governor George Ryan of Illinois halted all executions in his state. Ryan, a death penalty supporter, put the moratorium into effect after Anthony Porter, who had spent nearly sixteen years on the state's death row for a double murder, was found innocent and released two days before his scheduled execution. Porter was the thirteenth death-row convict to be exonerated in Illinois since 1977. "People are starting to understand that there's a possibility that innocent people are going to be put to death," said Ryan of his decision. "I don't think anyone wants that on their hands or their consciences."[134] On January 11, 2003, just two days before the end of his term, Ryan commuted all of Illinois's 167 death sentences to terms of life or less, the largest emptying of a state death row in the history of the United States.

A Decline in Executions Other indicators also show a recent downturn in the use of the death penalty. Between 1998 and 2003, the number of executions in this country declined by approximately 30 percent. In 2001, the death-row population decreased for the first time since 1976 (albeit by only eight inmates). Thirty-five of the thirty-eight states (the exceptions being Kansas, New Mexico, and Texas) that allow for the death penalty now allow juries to impose a sentence of life in prison without parole as an alternative to death. In response, more juries seem to be choosing the life sentence; the number of death sentences imposed dropped by 50 percent between 1998 and 2001.[135] In 2003, fifteen out of sixteen federal juries refused to impose the death penalty on convicted murderers.[136]

Fairness Concerns Does this mean society's "standards of decency" are changing to the point that the death sentence is in danger of being abolished? Probably not. Although public support for the death penalty has been steadily dropping since the mid-1990s, a Gallup poll taken in 2002 showed that 72 percent of Americans still favor the practice. Other surveys have found a different worry: that the death penalty be administered fairly. A number of steps have been taken to allay these concerns. Some states have begun to put aside funds for more effective defense counsel in capital cases. The U.S. Congress is considering legislation that would make DNA testing available to more individuals on death row. Indeed, the tenor of the death penalty debate seems to have shifted. The main focus is no longer on the morality of executions, but rather on how the sentence of death can be made fairer.

ONLINE REVIEW *Go to the book's Web site for an interactive review of this section*

>The Gender Factor

As has been noted throughout this chapter, many observers believe that race plays a large role in the criminal justice system's decisions concerning who gets punished and for how long. Statistically, however, the most important characteristic when it comes to sentencing is gender. Women, on the whole, are not punished as harshly as men, and in many instances the differences are striking. In this *Criminal Justice in Action* feature, we will examine the "gender gap" and discuss some of the reasons why it exists.

The Drastic Rise in Female Offenders

As was noted in Chapter 1, women account for a small fraction of this country's criminal offenders. Only 11 percent of the national jail population and 6 percent of the national prison population are female, and in 2002 only 23 percent of all arrests involved women.[137] These statistics, however, fail to convey the startling rate at which the female presence in the criminal justice system has been increasing. In 1970, there were about 6,000 women in federal and state prisons; today, there are nearly 100,000. During the 1990s, the number of women incarcerated in this country doubled,[138] and the number of women arrested increased by 30 percent.

There is little support in the academic community for any idea that the basic nature of American women has changed over the past thirty years. Freda Adler, a professor of criminal justice at Rutgers University, uses the "liberation hypothesis" to partially explain the increase in female arrestees and inmates.[139] This theory holds that as women become more and more equal in society as a whole, their opportunities to commit crimes will increase as well. "You can't embezzle if you're not near funds," Professor Adler notes. "You can't get involved in a fight at the bar if you're not allowed in the bar."[140] Criminologist Meda Chesney-Lind believes that the "get tough" attitude among politicians and law enforcement agencies has been the main contributor to increased rates

of female criminality. "Simply put," she says, "it appears that the criminal justice system is now more willing to incarcerate women."[141]

Women and the "War on Drugs"

A closer look at the offenses for which women are sent to prison and jail supports Chesney-Lind's thesis. The vast majority of women are prosecuted for nonviolent crimes, usually drug-related offenses. In fact, drug offenses account for nearly two-thirds of the women sent to federal prison each year (violent crimes account for only about 2 percent).[142] The habitual offender statutes and mandatory sentences for drug crimes that have accompanied the "war on drugs" have been particularly influential. In the 1980s, many of the women now in prison would not have been arrested or would have received light sentences for their drug-related wrongdoing.

When women do commit violent crimes, the patterns are distinct as well. Research conducted by social psychologists Angela Browne and Kirk R. Williams shows that when women do kill, the victim is usually an intimate male partner. Moreover, a woman is likely to kill in response to physical aggression or threats of physical aggression by her partner.[143]

The "New Female Criminal"

As the last sentence suggests, not only are the criminal patterns of women distinct from those of their male counterparts, but the reasons behind the crime are different as well. According to Jane Roberts Chapman, the "new female criminal" is a single mother with children, who commits property crimes out of need or abuses drugs as an avenue of escape from her difficult situation.[144] Four-fifths of all female prisoners are mothers, and nearly 30 percent describe themselves as the "primary care giver" of their children (meaning they do not have a partner to share the responsibility).[145] Chapman predicts that if the number of single mothers below the poverty line increases, female crime rates will rise accordingly.

Using information found in presentencing investigative reports, feminist criminologist Kathleen Daly has identified several distinct pathways to crime that women follow.[146] The *harmed-and-harming woman,* for example, suffered from abuse and neglect as a child, which in turn led her to "act out" and be labeled a "problem child." As an adult, this woman reacts to difficult situations with violence. The *battered woman,* in contrast, does not necessarily have a history of childhood abuse, but uses violence to defend herself against an abusive partner. Similarly, the *drug-connected woman* does not have a criminal past, but has become involved in a relationship—either with a partner or with a child—characterized by drug use. A drug-connected woman might, for example, let her son use their home as a place to sell drugs or turn to street crime to support a boyfriend or husband's drug habit.

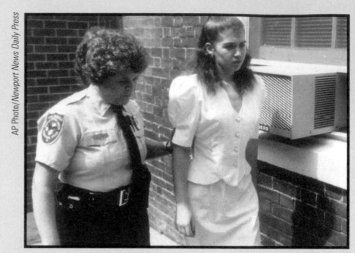

In 1990, teen-age lovers Douglas Christopher Thomas and Jessica Wiseman (right) shot and killed her parents. Wiseman was sent to a juvenile detention center and released in 1997. Thomas, in contrast, wound up in an adult prison and was executed by the state of Virginia in 2000. Is this necessarily evidence of a gender disparity in sentencing? Does it matter that Wiseman was fourteen years old and Thomas was seventeen at the time of the crime?

The Chivalry Effect

Few people would argue that race or ethnicity should be a factor in sentencing decisions. The system should be "colorblind." But what about women—should the system be "genderblind" as well? On a policy level, at least, Congress answered that question in the Sentencing Reform Act of 1984, which emphasized the ideal of gender-neutral sentencing.[147] In practice, however, this is not the case. Women who are convicted of crimes are less-

likely to go to prison than men, and those who are incarcerated serve shorter sentences (see Figure 11.9). One study attributes these differences to the elements of female criminality: in property crimes, women are usually accessories, and in violent crimes, women are usually reacting to physical abuse. In both cases, the mitigating circumstances would lead to lesser punishment.[148] Wider evidence suggests, however, that the *chivalry effect,* a theory that women are treated more leniently

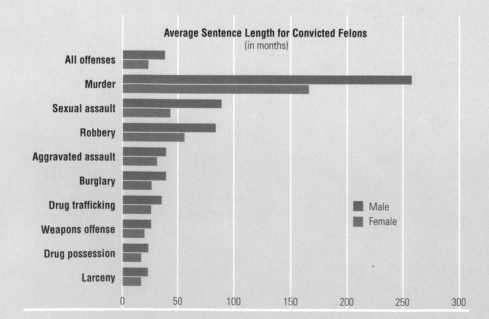

FIGURE 11.9 Sentence Length by Gender

Source: Bureau of Justice Statistics, *State Court Sentencing of Convicted Felons, 2000* (Washington, D.C.: U.S. Department of Justice, 2003), Table 2.6.

than men, plays a large part in the decisions of prosecutors, judges, and juries.

Data compiled by the U.S. Sentencing Commission show that prosecutors are more likely to offer women beneficial plea bargains.[149] Several self-reported studies have shown that judges may treat female defendants more "gently" than male ones and that judges are influenced by mitigating factors such as marital status and family background with women that they would ignore with men.[150] As for juries, their leniency toward women can be most clearly seen in death penalty cases. Though women account for 13 percent of all murder arrests, they represent only 1.5 percent of those prisoners on death row. According to Karen Jo Koonan, an Oakland (California) jury consultant, jurors do not want to believe that a woman, in her role as nurturer, could also be a cold-blooded killer.[151]

Is Chivalry Dead?

There are signs, however, that some of these attitudes are changing. Overall, chivalry appears to be dying. Twenty-five years ago, almost two-thirds of all women sentenced in federal court were given probation, and, as mentioned before, the female presence in prison was negligible.[152] Between 1976 and 1997, only one woman was executed in the United States; since 1998, nine have been put to death. And, it must be noted, the chivalry effect was never in effect for African American women. In Florida, for example, black women are nine times more likely to be sentenced as habitual offenders for drug-related offenses than white women.[153]

Is there an argument to be made in favor of the chivalry effect? In fact, some observers are now supporting judicial leniency for women and claim that gender-neutral sentencing exacts a heavy price on society. By separating increasing numbers of nonviolent female offenders from their children, the sentencing guidelines often shift the cost of caring for these children to the taxpayer through social service programs.[154] Furthermore, by increasing the chances that the children themselves will have emotional problems due to lack of an active parent, such laws increase the probability that these children will become delinquent. Instead of sending nonviolent offenders who are pregnant or have children to jail or prison, the argument goes, the correctional system should place them in community-based programs where they can continue to care for their offspring.

MAKING SENSE OF THE GENDER GAP IN PUNISHMENT AND SENTENCING

1 Do you believe that sentencing should be gender neutral? What are the arguments for and against giving women more lenient sentences for nonviolent crimes?

2 To what extent should a judge consider the motivation behind a crime committed by a woman (self-defense, did it for boyfriend, and so on) as a mitigating circumstance? What might be the result if judges did this more often?

3 Give some reasons to explain why so few women are on death row. Why do you think society seems to be uncomfortable with the idea of sentencing a woman to be executed? Do you think that there are some crimes a woman could commit that a judge or jury might be *more* likely to punish with the death sentence?

Chapter Summary

1 **List and contrast the four basic philosophical reasons for sentencing criminals.** (a) Retribution, (b) deterrence, (c) incapacitation, and (d) rehabilitation. Under the principle of retributive justice, the severity of the punishment is in proportion to the severity of the crime. Punishment is an end in itself. In contrast, the deterrence approach seeks to prevent future crimes by setting an example. Such punishment is based on its deterrent value and not necessarily on the severity of the crime. The incapacitation theory of punishment simply argues that a criminal in jail cannot impose further harm on society. In contrast, the rehabilitation theory believes that criminals can be rehabilitated in the appropriate prison environment.

2 **Contrast indeterminate with determinate sentencing.** Indeterminate sentencing follows from legislative penal codes that set minimum and maximum amounts of incarceration time; determinate sentencing carries a fixed amount of time,

STORIES FROM THE STREET
Go to the Stories from the Street feature at www.cjinaction.com to hear Larry Gaines tell insightful stories related to this chapter and his experiences in the field.

although this may be reduced for "good time."

3 **Explain why there is a difference between a sentence imposed by a judge and the actual sentence carried out by the prisoner.** Although judges may decide on indeterminate sentencing, thereafter it is parole boards that decide when prisoners will be released after the minimum sentence is served.

4 **List the six forms of punishment.** (a) Capital (death sentence), (b) imprisonment, (c) probation, (d) fines, (e) restitution and community service, and (f) restorative justice.

5 **State who has input into the sentencing decision and list the factors that determine a sentence.** The prosecutor, defense attorney, probation officer, and judge provide inputs. The factors considered in sentencing are (a) the seriousness of the crime, (b) mitigating circumstances, (c) aggravating circumstances, and (d) judicial philosophy.

6 **Explain some of the reasons why sentencing reform has occurred.** One reason is sentencing disparity, which has been seen on a geographic basis and on a courtroom basis (due to a particular judge's philosophy). Sentencing discrimination has also occurred on the basis of defendants' gender, race, or economic standing. An additional reason for sentencing reform has been a general desire to "get tough on crime."

7 **Contrast sentencing guidelines with mandatory sentencing guidelines.** At the state level, courtroom work groups are guided by a grid, which determines the proper sentence. The grid uses the type of crime, the seriousness of the crime, and other factors to generate a "presumed" prison term. Starting in 1987, a similar grid system was put into place at the federal level. In response to judges' continued departures from such sentencing guidelines, federal and state legislatures have instituted mandatory (minimum) sentencing guidelines, which limit a judge's discretion for certain classes of crimes, such as selling drugs. The most stringent guideline is represented by "three-strikes-and-you're-out" laws, which require any person convicted of a third felony to serve a lengthy prison sentence without the possibility of parole.

8 **Outline the Supreme Court rulings on capital punishment.** In 1967, the Supreme Court placed a hold on all scheduled executions. In 1972, the Court invalidated the death penalty in states that imposed it because the way it was practiced violated the Eighth and Fourteenth Amendments. By 1976, thirty-five states had changed their death penalty statutes to comply with the Supreme Court ruling. The Supreme Court then declared mandatory death penalty statutes invalid, but established a bifurcated process that involved two steps. Today, thirty-eight states have adopted this process and provide for legally acceptable capital punishment.

Key Terms

aggravating circumstances 373
capital punishment 383
departure 378
determinate sentencing 367
deterrence 364
"good time" 367
habitual offender laws 380
incapacitation 365

indeterminate sentencing 367
just deserts 363
mandatory sentencing guidelines 378
mitigating circumstances 373
presentence investigative report 371
presumptive sentencing 376

"real offense" 373
rehabilitation 366
retribution 363
sentencing discrimination 375
sentencing disparity 374
sentencing guidelines 377
truth-in-sentencing laws 367

1 How can punishing a wrongdoer be reconciled with the concept of rehabilitation?

2 How does the limitation of "good time" along with fixed sentencing make a prison warden's job more difficult?

3 What single fact will probably lead to a reduction in truth-in-sentencing laws as well as a reduction in mandatory minimum sentencing laws?

4 What restricts judicial discretion in sentencing in many jurisdictions?

5 What has caused the gradual disappearance of presentence investigative reports in some jurisdictions?

6 How do "real offense" procedures effectively render plea bargains almost meaningless?

7 What happens to the concept of parole under a system of mandatory sentencing guidelines?

8 How do mandatory sentences lead to a disproportionate number of persons from minority groups in prison?

9 What are some of the arguments that proponents of the death penalty offer in its favor? What are some of the arguments that opponents offer against it?

Go to www.cjinaction.com for tools to aid you in studying for your exams. Click on *Online Reviews* under *Chapter Resources* for an interactive review of each major section of this chapter. Under *Chapter Resources*, you will also find the *Chapter Outline*, *Chapter Summary*, *Flashcards*, *Glossary*, *Learning Objectives*, *Lecture Presentations*, *Concept Builder*, *Essay Questions*, and a *Tutorial Quiz*. You can also test yourself with a game of *Concentration* or the *Crossword Puzzle*.

Go to www.cjinaction.com for a wealth of online resources. Explore the *Internet Activities* and *Class Project*s under *Chapter Resources*. Check out the *Web Links* to access the Web sites mentioned in the text, as well as many others. You can also access recent perspectives by clicking on *CJ in the News* and *Terrorism Update* under *Course Resources*. If you'd like some mentoring, click on *Board of Mentors* under *Book Resources*.

For additional information, explore InfoTrac College Edition, your online library that offers complete full-length articles from thousands of scholarly and popular publications. Click on *InfoTrac College Edition* under *Chapter Resources* at www.cjinaction.com for a list of key words and InfoTrac exercises. Use the passcode that came with your book.

Pickett, Carroll, and Carlton Stowers, *Within These Walls: Memoirs of a Death House Chaplain*, New York: St. Martin's Press, 2002. Rev. Carroll Pickett spent fifteen years as chaplain for the Huntsville Unit of the Texas prison system. During that time, he ministered to ninety-five men before they were executed, giving him a unique perspective on the inner thoughts of the condemned in the final hours before their deaths. Co-author Stowers gives this book the feel of a "true crime" novel, as he and Pickett describe not only the disturb-ing process of the death penalty but the horrible crimes committed by the men who have ended up on death row.

Zimring, Franklin E., *The Contradictions of American Capital Punishment*, New York: Oxford University Press, 2003. One of the country's leading criminologists examines why Americans are so determined to keep the death penalty, even though nearly every other developed nation in the world has decried the practice as barbaric. Zimring's conclusions are, to say the least, unsettling. He shows that while public support for capital punishment is fairly uniform across the United States, almost all executions take place in a few states in the South and Southwest. These same states, Zimring notes, are where the lynching of African Americans and other forms of vigilante violence were most prevalent in our nation's history. The author also explores how these vigilante values have clashed with another American tradition—mistrust of government—to create the lengthy appeals process that ensures that more inmates on death row die of old age than by execution.

Notes

1. David Yellen, "Just Deserts and Lenient Prosecutors: The Flawed Case for Real Offense Sentencing," *Northwestern University Law Review* 91 (Summer 1997), 1434.

2. Brian Forst, "Prosecution and Sentencing," in *Crime,* ed. James Q. Wilson and Joan Petersilia (San Francisco: ICS Press, 1995), 386.

3. Herbert L. Packer, "Justification for Criminal Punishment," in *The Limits of Criminal Sanction* (Palo Alto, CA: Stanford University Press, 1968), 36–37.

4. Jami L. Anderson, "Reciprocity as a Justification for Retributivism," *Criminal Justice Ethics* (Winter/ Spring 1997), 13–14.

5. Immanuel Kant, *Metaphysical First Principles of the Doctrine of Right,* trans. by Mary Gregor (Cambridge, UK: Cambridge University Press, 1991), 331.

6. Harold Pepinsky and Paul Jesilow, *Myths That Cause Crime* (Cabin John, MD: Seven Locks Press, 1984).

7. Jeremy Bentham, *An Introduction to the Principles of Morals and Legislation 1789* (New York: Hafner Publishing Corp., 1961).

8. Forst, 376.

9. John J. DiIulio, Jr., "Help Wanted: Economists, Crime, and Public Policy," *Journal of Economic Perspectives* 10 (1996), 3, 16–17.

10. Sue T. Reid, *Crime and Criminology,* 7th ed. (New York: Holt, Rinehart, and Winston, 1995), 352.

11. Morgan O. Reynolds, *Why Does Crime Pay?* (Dallas, TX: National Center for Policy Analysis Backgrounder #110, 1990), 5.

12. Paul H. Robinson and John M. Darley, "The Utility of Desert," *Northwestern University Law Review* 91 (Winter 1997), 453.

13. James Q. Wilson, *Thinking about Crime* (New York: Basic Books, 1975), 235.

14. Joe Gyan, Jr., "Ashcroft Seeks End to 'Revolving Door' for Violent Criminals," *Baton Rouge Advocate* (September 25, 2003), 9B.

15. Isaac Ehrlich, "Participation in Illegitimate Activities: A Theoretical and Empirical Investigation," *Journal of Political Economy* 81 (May/June 1973), 521–564.

16. Steve Levitt, "The Effect of Prison Population Size on Crime Rates," *Quarterly Journal of Economics* 111 (May 1996), 319.

17. Todd Clear, *Harm in Punishment* (Boston: Northeastern University Press, 1980).

18. Franklin E. Zimring and Gordon Hawkins, *Incapacitation: Penal Confinement and Restraint of Crime* (New York: Oxford University Press, 1995), 60–70.

19. Jan Chaiken, Marcia Chaiken, and William Rhodes, "Predicting Violent Behavior and Classifying Violent Offenders," in *Understanding and Preventing Violence,* ed. Albert J. Reiss, Jr., and Jeffrey A. Roth (Washington, D.C.: National Academy Press, 1994).

20. Public Policy Forum, "Prevention Advocated More Than Punishment in PPF Survey," *Research Brief* (February 12, 2001), 7.

21. Gregory W. O'Reilly, "Truth-in-Sentencing, Illinois Adds Yet Another Layer of 'Reform' to Its Complicated Code of Corrections," *Loyola University of Chicago Law Journal* (Summer 1996), 986, 999–1000.

22. Arthur W. Campbell, *Law of Sentencing* (Rochester, NY: Lawyers Cooperative Publishing Co., 1978), 9.

23. Marvin Zalman, "The Rise and Fall of the Indeterminate Sentence," *Wayne Law Review* 24 (1977), 45, 52.

24. Marvin E. Frankel, *Criminal Sentences: Law without Order* (New York: Hill & Wang, 1972), 5.

25. Jessica Mitford, *Kind and Usual Punishment* (New York: Alfred A. Knopf, 1973), 80–83.

26. Bureau of Justice Statistics, *Truth in Sentencing in State Prisons* (Washington, D.C.: Department of Justice, 1999).

27. Paul W. Keve, *Crime Control and Justice in America: Searching for Facts and Answers* (Chicago: American Library Association, 1995), 77.

28. Mark S. Umbreit, *Victim Meets Offender: The Impact of Restorative Justice and Mediation* (Monsey, N.Y.: Criminal Justice Press, 1994), 2.

29. "Tahoe Man with AIDS Ordered Castrated for Child Sexual Assault," *Associated Press Newswires* (June 20, 2003).

30. Kate Stith and José A. Cabranes, "Judging under the Federal Sentencing Guidelines," *Northwestern University Law Review* 91 (Summer 1997), 1247.

31. Mark M. Lanier and Claud H. Miller III, "Attitudes and Practices of Federal Probation Officers towards Pre-Plea/Trial Investigative Report Policy," *Crime & Delinquency* 41 (July 1995), 365–366.

32. Stith and Cabranes, 1247.

33. Julie R. O'Sullivan, "In Defense of the U.S. Sentencing Guidelines Modified Real-Offense System," *Northwestern University Law Review* 91 (1997), 1342.

34. Brian Forst and Charles Wellford, "Punishment and Sentencing: Developing Sentencing Guidelines Empirically from Principles of Punishment," *Rutgers Law Review* 33 (1981).

35. 18 U.S.C. Section 2113(a) (1994).

36. Bob Barr and Eric Sterling, "The War on Drugs: Fighting Crime or Wasting Time?" *American Criminal Law Review* (Fall 2001), 1545.

37. Office of Policy Analysis, United States Sentencing Commission, 2001.

38. Bureau of Justice Statistics, *State Court Sentencing of Convicted Felons, 1996* (Washington, D.C.: U.S. Department of Justice, 2000), Tables 5.2 and 5.3, pages 56–57.

39. U.S.C.C.A.N. 3182, 3228 (1984).

40. Cassia Spohn and David Holleran, "The Imprisonment Penalty Paid by Young, Unemployed Black and Hispanic Male Offenders," *Criminology* 35 (2000), 281.

41. *Ibid.,* 297.

42. Bureau of Justice Statistics, *Prisoners in 2002* (Washington, D.C.: U.S. Department of Justice, July 2003), 9.

43. Spohn and Holleran, 301.

44. *Ibid.,* 291.

45. Bureau of Justice Statistics, *State Court Sentencing of Convicted Felons,* 15.

46. Darrell Steffensmeier and Stephen DeMuth, "Ethnicity and Judges' Sentencing Decisions: Hispanic-Black-White Comparisons," *Criminology* 39 (2001), 145.

47. *Ibid.*

48. *Ibid.,* 167.

49. John C. Coffee, "Repressed Issues of Sentencing," *Georgetown Law Journal* 66 (1978), 987.

50. *Twentieth Century Fund Task Force on Criminal Sentencing, Fair and Certain Punishment* (New York: McGraw-Hill, 1976).

51. Robert Martinson, "What Works?—Questions and Answers about Prison Reform," *Public Interest* 35 (Spring 1974), 22.

52. Edward Kennedy, "Introduction to Symposium on Sentencing," *Hofstra Law Review* 1 (1978), 1.

53. Francis A. Allen, *The Decline of the Rehabilitative Ideal* (New Haven, CT: Yale University Press, 1981), 8.

54. J. S. Bainbridge Jr., "The Return of Retribution," *ABA Journal* (May 1985), 63.

55. Pub. L. No. 98–473, 98 Stat. 1987, codified as amended at 18 U.S.C. Sections 3551–3742 and 28 U.S.C. Sections 991–998 (1988).

56. Julia L. Black, "The Constitutionality of Federal Sentences Imposed under the Sentencing Reform Act of 1984 after *Mistretta v. United States,*" *Iowa Law Review* 75 (March 1990), 767.

57. Roger Haines, Kevin Cole, and Jennifer Wole, *Federal Sentencing Guidelines Handbook* (New York: McGraw-Hill, 1994), 3.

58. Bureau of Justice Statistics, *Time Served in Prison by Federal Offenders, 1986–97* (Washington, D.C.: U.S. Department of Justice, 1999), 1.

59. *United States v. Diaz-Villafane,* 874 F.2d 43, 49 (1st Cir. 1989).

60. *2001 Annual Report* (Washington, D.C.: United States Sentencing Commission, 2002).

61. Barbara S. Meierhoefer, *The General Effect of Mandatory Minimum Prison Terms: A Longitudinal Study of Federal Sentences Imposed* (Washington, D.C.: Federal Judicial Center, 1992), 20.

62. Alabama Code 1975 Section 20-2-79.

63. Washington Rev. Code Ann. Sections 9.94A.030.

64. 445 U.S. 263 (1980).

65. 123 S.Ct. 1166 (2003).

66. *Lockyer v. Andrade,* 270 F.3d 743 (2001).

67. 123. S.Ct. 1174–1175.

68. *Ibid.,* 1179.

69. Ryan S. King and Marc Mauer, *Aging behind Bars: "Three Strikes" Seven Years Later* (Washington, D.C.: The Sentencing Project, August 2001), 3.

70. *Ibid.,* 12.

71. *Ibid.,* 8.

72. Press Release, "UCR Study Sheds Light on 'Three Strikes' Law," www.ucr.edu/SubPages/2CurNewsFold/UnivRelat/strikes.html.

73. Yellen, 1434.

74. Michael Tonry, "The Failure of the U.S. Sentencing Commission's Guidelines," *Crime & Delinquency* 39 (1993), 131–149.

75. Erik Luna, *Misguided Guidelines: A Critique of Federal Sentencing* (Washington, D.C.: Cato Institute, 2002), 3.

76. Richard Willing, "Judges Go Soft on Sentences More Often," *USA Today* (August 28, 2003), 1A.

77. *Ibid.*

78. Kay A. Knapp, "Impact of Minnesota Sentencing Guidelines on Sentencing Practices," *Hamline Law Review* 5 (1982), 255.

79. 18 U.S.C. Section 3553(e) (1991).

80. Quoted in Martin Kasindorf, "Three Strikes Laws Fall Out of Favor," *USA Today* (February 28, 2002), 3A.

81. Jenia Iontcheva, "Jury Sentencing as Democratic Practice," *Virginia Law Review* (April 2003), 325.

82. Brent L. Smith and Edward H. Stevens, "Sentence Disparity and the Judge-Jury Sentencing Debate: An Analysis of Robbery Sentences in Six Southern States," *Criminal Justice Review* 9 (1984), 1.

83. Iontcheva, 313.

84. Walter Berns, "Abraham Lincoln (book review)," *Commentary* (January 1, 1996), 70.

85. Comments made at the Georgetown Law Center, "The Modern View of Capital Punishment," *American Criminal Law Review* 34 (Summer 1997), 1353.

86. David Bruck, quoted in Bill Rankin, "Fairness of the Death Penalty Is Still on Trial," *Atlanta Constitution & Journal* (July 29, 1997), A13.

87. Mark Costanzo, *Just Revenge: Costs and Consequences of the Death Penalty* (New York: St. Martin's Press, 1997), 11.

88. Randall Coyne and Lyn Entzeroth, *Capital Punishment and the Judicial Process* (Durham, NC: Carolina Academic Press, 1994), 2.

89. Jeffrey C. Matura, "When Will It Stop? The Use of the Death Penalty for Non-Homicide Crimes," *Journal of Legislation* 24 (1998), 249.

90. Thorsten Sellin, "The Philadelphia Gibbet Iron," *Journal of Criminal Law, Criminology, and Police Science* 46 (1955), 19.

91. G. Mark Mamantov, "The Executioner's Song: Is There a Right to Listen?" *Virginia Law Review* 69 (March 1983), 373.

92. Larry C. Berkson, *The Concept of Cruel and Unusual Punishment* (Lexington, MA: Lexington Books, 1975), 43.

93. John P. Cunningham, "Death in the Federal Courts: Expectations and Realities of the Federal Death Penalty Act of 1994," *University of Richmond Law Review* 32 (May 1998), 939.

94. *In re Kemmler*, 136 U.S. 447 (1890).

95. 217 U.S. 349 (1910).

96. Pamela S. Nagy, "Hang by the Neck until Dead: The Resurgence of Cruel and Unusual Punishment in the 1990s," *Pacific Law Journal* 26 (October 1994), 85.

97. 408 U.S. 238 (1972).

98. 408 U.S. 309 (1972), (Stewart, concurring).

99. 428 U.S. 280 (1976).

100. 428 U.S. 153 (1976).

101. 536 U.S. 584 (2002).

102. *Ford v. Wainwright,* 477 U.S. 399, 422 (1986).

103. Neil A. Lewis, "Judges Let Stand Ruling That Allows Forcibly Drugging an Inmate before Execution," *New York Times* (October 7, 2003), A14.

104. *Penry v. Lynaugh,* 492 U.S. 302 (1989).

105. 536 U.S. 304 (2002).

106. 487 U.S. 815 (1988).

107. *Stanford v. Kentucky,* 492 U.S. 361 (1989); *Wilkins v. Missouri,* 492 U.S. 361 (1989).

108. Linda Greenhouse, "Justices Deny Inmate Appeal in Execution of Juveniles," *New York Times* (January 28, 2003), A19.

109. Ernest van den Haag, "The Ultimate Punishment: A Defense," *Harvard Law Review* 99 (1986), 1669.

110. *The Death Penalty: The Religious Community Calls for Abolition* (pamphlet published by the National Coalition to Abolish the Death Penalty and the National Interreligious Task Force on Criminal Justice, 1988), 48.

111. Isaac Ehrlich, "The Deterrent Effect of Capital Punishment: A Question of Life and Death," *American Economic Review* 65 (June 1975), 397–417.

112. Raymond Bonner and Ford Fessenden, "States with No Death Penalty Share Lower Homicide Rates," *New York Times* (September 22, 2000), A1.

113. Stephen Markman and Paul Cassell, "Protecting the Innocent: A Response to the Bedau-Radelet Study," *Stanford Law Review* 41 (1988), 153.

114. Joseph F. Shapiro, "The Wrong Men on Death Row," *U.S. News & World Report* (November 9, 1998), 26.

115. Hugo Adam Bedau and Michael L. Radelet, "Miscarriages of Justice in Potentially Capital Cases," *Stanford Law Review* 40 (1987), 21–23.

116. Frank Hinchey, "McKnight Gets Death Penalty," *Columbus Dispatch* (October 26, 2002), A1.

117. John J. DiIulio, "Abolish the Death Penalty, Officially," *Wall Street Journal* (December 15, 1997), A23.

118. James S. Liebman, Jeffrey Fagan, and Valeria West, "A Broken System: Error Rates in Capital Cases, 1973–1995," (2000), www.justice.policy.net/jpreport.

119. James S. Liebman, Andrew Gelman, Garth Davies, Jeffrey Fagan, Valerie West, and Alexandra Kiss, *A Broken System, Part II: Why There Is So Much Error in Capital Cases, and What Can Be Done about It* (Washington, D.C.: Criminal Justice Reform Education Fund, 2002), 348.

120. Quoted in Walter Berns and Joseph Bessette, "Why the Death Penalty Is Fair," *Wall Street Journal* (January 9, 1998), A16.

121. James Q. Wilson, "What Death-Penalty Errors?" *New York Times* (July 10, 2000), A19.

122. *Gregg v. Georgia,* 428 U.S. 153, 195 (1976).

123. Wilson, "What Death-Penalty Errors?"

124. "Chemical Used in Executions Is Questioned," *Chicago Tribune* (October 7, 2003), 9.

125. *Coker v. Georgia,* 433 U.S. 584 (1977).

126. Scott Shepherd, "More Blacks Agreeing with Death Penalty," *Fresno Bee* (April 18, 1998), A6.

127. Janice Joseph, "Young, Black, and Sentenced to Die: Black Males and the Death Penalty," *Challenge: A Journal of Research on African American Men* 7 (December 1996), 68.

128. Isaac Utah and John Charles Boger, *Race and the Death Penalty in North Carolina* (Raleigh, NC: The Common Sense Foundation, 2001).

129. 481 U.S. 279 (1987).

130. David C. Baldus, George Woodworth, and Charles A. Pulaski, *Equal Justice and the Death Penalty: A Legal and Empirical Analysis* (Boston: Northeastern University Press, 1990), 140–197, 306.

131. Laura Argys and Naci Mocan, *Who Shall Live and Who Shall Die? An Analysis of Prisoners on Death Row in the United States* (Cambridge, MA: National Bureau of Economic Research, February 2003), 22.

132. *Ibid.,* 8.

133. William M. Holmes, "Who Are the Wrongly Convicted on Death Row?" in *Wrongly Convicted: When Justice Fails,* ed. Saundra Westervelt and John Humphrey (Piscataway, NJ: Rutgers University Press, 2001).

134. Toni Locy, "Push to Reform Death Penalty Growing," *USA Today* (February 20, 2001), 5A.

135. "The Needle Paused," *The Economist* (March 22, 2003), 29.

136. Adam Liptak, "Juries Reject Death Penalty in Nearly All Federal Trials," *New York Times* (July 15, 2003), section A, page 12.

137. *FBI, Crime in the United States 2002,* 232.

138. Bureau of Justice Statistics, *Prisoners in 2000* (Washington, D.C.: U.S. Department of Justice, 2000), 6.

139. Freda Adler, *Sisters in Crime: The Rise of the New Female Criminal* (New York: McGraw–Hill, 1975), 95.

140. Barry Yoeman, "Violent Tendencies: Crime by Women Has Skyrocketed in Recent Years," *Chicago Tribune* (March 15, 2000), 3.

141. Meda Chesney-Lind, "Patriarchy, Prisons, and Jails: A Critical Look at Trends in Women's Incarceration," *Prison Journal* (Spring/Summer 1991), 57.

142. Bureau of Justice Statistics, *Sourcebook of Criminal Justice Statistics* (Washington, D.C.: U.S. Department of Justice, 1998), 505.

143. Angela Browne and Kirk R. Williams, "Exploring the Effect of Resource Availability and the Likelihood of Female-Perpetrated Homicides," *Law and Society Review* 23 (1989), 75–94.

144. Jane Roberts Chapman, *Economic Realities and Female Crimes* (Lexington, MA: Lexington Books, 1980).

145. Stefanie Fleischer Seldin, "A Strategy for Advocacy on Behalf of Women Offenders," *Columbia Journal of Gender and Law* 1 (1995), 1.

146. Kathleen Daly, "Women's Pathways to Felony Court: Feminist Theory of Lawbreaking and Problems of Representation," *Review of Law and Women's Studies* 2 (1992), 11–52.

147. 28 U.S.C. Section 991 (1994).

148. Clarice Feinmen, *Women in the Criminal Justice System,* 3d ed. (Westport, CT: Praeger, 1994), 35.

149. Ilene H. Nagel and Barry L. Johnson, "The Role of Gender in a Structured Sentencing System: Equal Treatment, Policy Choices, and the Sentencing of Female Offenders under the United States Sentencing Guidelines," *Journal of Criminal Law and Criminology* 85 (1994), 181–190.

150. Darrell Steffensmeir, John Kramer, and Cathy Streifel, "Gender and Imprisonment Decisions," *Criminology* 31 (1993), 411.

151. Quoted in Raymond Smith, "Death Penalty Rare for Women," *Press-Enterprise* (Riverside, California) (July 30, 1998), A12.

152. Elizabeth F. Moulds, "Chivalry and Paternalism: Disparities of Treatment in the Criminal Justice System," in *Women, Crime, and Justice,* ed. Susan Datesman and Frank Scarpitti (New York: Oxford University Press, 1980), 286–287.

153. Charles Crawford, "Sentencing in Florida," *Criminology* 38 (February 2000), 277.

154. Myrna S. Raeder, "Gender and Sentencing: Single Moms, Battered Women, and Other Sex-Based Anomalies in the Gender-Free World of the Federal Sentencing Guidelines," *Pepperdine Law Review* 20 (1993), 14.

> **Chapter 12**

Probation and
Community Correctio

>chapter objectives<

After reading this chapter, you should be able to:

1 Explain the justifications for community-based corrections programs.

2 Indicate when probation started to fall out of favor and explain why.

3 Explain several alternative sentencing arrangements.

4 Specify the conditions under which an offender is most likely to be denied probation.

5 Describe the three general categories of conditions placed on a probationer.

6 Explain why probation officers' work has become more dangerous.

7 Explain the three stages of probation revocation.

8 List the five sentencing options for a judge besides imprisonment and probation.

9 Contrast day reporting centers with intensive supervision probation.

10 List the three levels of home monitoring.

The Wages of Shoplifting

On November 7, 2002, actress Winona Ryder was found guilty of grand theft and vandalism. The charge arose from an incident a year earlier in which Ryder walked out of a Saks Fifth Avenue department

Actress Winona Ryder during her 2002 trial for felony grand theft and vandalism in Beverly Hills (California) Municipal Court. She was eventually found guilty and sentenced to three years' probation, as well as ordered to pay restitution, perform community service, and undergo counseling.

store in Beverly Hills, California, without paying for $5,560 worth of merchandise. She also cut sensor tags off some of the items.

Although Ryder could have been incarcerated for three years and eight months under California law, Judge Elden S. Fox of Los Angeles Superior Court sentenced the actress to three years' probation, ordered her to perform 480 hours of community service, fined her $3,700, and required her to pay $6,355 in restitution to the Saks store. The judge also commanded her to participate in a court–approved drug and psychological counseling program. "It is not my intention to make an example of you," Judge Fox told Ryder. "I am going to hold you accountable for what happened. If you steal again, you will go to jail."

> **Ryder's sentence** sparked skepticism, as many felt she had been "let off easy" because of her fame and high-priced defense attorney. In fact, Judge Fox was hardly breaking new ground. Defendants found guilty of crimes far more serious than grand theft and vandalism are routinely given probation in this country. A system that initially gave judges the discretion to show leniency to first-time, minor offenders increasingly allows those who have committed serious crimes to serve their time in the community rather than prison or jail. Nearly one out of every four probationers has been convicted of a violent felony such as assault or rape.[1]

Ironically, the trend toward probation can be partly attributed to the "get tough" approach to crime that has emerged in public policy. Campaigns to crack down on drunk drivers, the "war on drugs," harsher sentencing statutes, and limitations on judicial discretion have placed intense pressure on the American corrections infrastructure. Even with unprecedented rates of prison and jail construction, there is simply not enough space to incarcerate all the new criminals. The result: nearly 4 million adults are under the supervision of state and federal probation organizations—a figure growing at a rate of 3 percent each year.[2]

In this chapter, we will discuss the strengths and weaknesses of probation and other community sanctions such as intensive probation, fines, boot camps, electronic monitoring, and home confinement. Given the scarcity of prison resources, decisions made today concerning community-based punishment will affect the criminal justice system for decades to come.

The Justification for Community Corrections

In the court of popular opinion, retribution and crime control take precedence over community-based correctional programs. America, says University of Minnesota law professor Michael Tonry, is preoccupied with the "absolute severity of punishment" and the "widespread view that only imprisonment counts."[3] Mandatory sentencing guidelines and "three-strikes" laws are theoretically opposed to community-based corrections.[4] To a certain degree, correctional programs that are administered in the community are considered a less severe, and therefore less worthy, alternative to imprisonment.

REINTEGRATION

Supporters of probation and intermediate sanctions reject such views as not only shortsighted, but also contradictory to the aims of the corrections system. A very small percentage of all convicted offenders have committed crimes that warrant capital punishment or life imprisonment—most, at some point, will return to the community. Consequently, according to one group of experts, the task of the corrections system

> includes building or rebuilding solid ties between the offender and the community, integrating or reintegrating the offender into community life—restoring family ties, obtaining employment and an education, securing in the larger sense a place for the offender in the routine functioning of society.[5]

Considering that some studies have shown higher recidivism rates for offenders who are subjected to prison culture, a frequent justification of community-based corrections is that they attempt to reintegrate the offender into society.

Reintegration has a strong theoretical basis in rehabilitative theories of punishment. An offender is generally considered to be "rehabilitated" when he or she no longer represents a threat to other members of the community and therefore is believed to be fit to live in that community. In the context of this chapter and the two that follow, it will also be helpful to see reintegration as a process through which corrections officials such as probation and parole officers provide the offender with incentives to follow the rules of society. In doing so, the corrections system must constantly balance the rights of the individual offender against the rights of law-abiding members of the community. (See *CJ in Focus—The Balancing Act: "Jason's Law" and Compromised Justice* on the next page.)

DIVERSION

Another justification for community-based corrections, based on practical considerations, is **diversion.** As you are already aware, most criminal offenses fall into the category of "petty," and it is practically impossible, as well as unnecessary, to

CONCEPT BUILDER
Reintegration of offenders into the community is a common strategy for rehabilitative programs utilized by community corrections. Visit www.cjinaction.com for an interactive exploration of this key topic.

The Sentencing Project is a nonprofit organization that promotes reduced reliance on incarceration and alternative forms of sentencing. To visit its Web site, click on *Web Links* under *Chapter Resources* at www.cjinaction.com

Reintegration
A goal of corrections that focuses on preparing the offender for a return to the community unmarred by further criminal behavior.

Diversion
In the context of corrections, a strategy to divert those offenders who qualify away from prison and jail and toward community-based and intermediate sanctions.

When the Roberts family learned that a man named Callahan had been released from a Massachusetts county jail after only three months, under the condition that he wear an electronic monitoring bracelet, they were outraged. A year earlier, a drunk Callahan had killed twenty-one-year-old Jason Roberts in an automobile accident. Callahan had been sentenced to thirty months in jail, with eighteen months suspended. The Roberts family felt that Sheriff John Flood, who made the decision to release Callahan, had betrayed their trust and the trust of the community.

Community-based corrections represent a compromise society makes with certain wrongdoers. Theoretically, society benefits by saving scarce incarceration space for truly dangerous criminals and by giving supposedly low-risk offenders the opportunity to reintegrate into the community. These utilitarian justifications, however, often fail to counterbalance the cold, hard facts of an incident such as Jason Roberts's death. Given that we cannot predict criminal activity, inevitably some convicts being supervised outside prison or jail will commit crimes, and some of those crimes will be violent. In any given year, offenders in community corrections programs are responsible for more

than 10,000 murders and nearly 40,000 robberies, along with tens of thousands of other crimes. For the victims of these acts, the scales of justice appear to be heavily weighted in favor of the individual offender and against the best interests of society.

In response to the Callahan incident, the Massachusetts legislature considered passing "Jason's Law," which would have prohibited sheriffs from transferring inmates sentenced to prisons or jails into programs such as house arrest and electronic monitoring. The Massachusetts Sheriff's Association strongly protested the bill, arguing that its members use an objective classification system to determine who is eligible for community supervision. Furthermore, noted critics of the bill, existing local corrections facilities were already overcrowded, and the county in question did not have the financial resources to incarcerate all convicts: the cost of keeping an inmate in jail for a year is $35,000, compared to only $6,000 for electronic monitoring.

FOR CRITICAL ANALYSIS
Should victims and victims' families such as the Roberts family have a say in whether criminals are sentenced to community-based corrections?

imprison every offender for every offense. Community-based corrections are an important means of diverting criminals to alternative modes of punishment so that scarce incarceration resources are consumed by only the most dangerous criminals. In his "strainer" analogy, corrections expert Paul H. Hahn likens this process to the workings of a kitchen strainer. With each "shake" of the corrections "strainer," the less serious offenders are diverted from incarceration. At the end, only the most serious convicts remain to be sent to prison.[6] (The concept of diversion is closely linked to that of selective incapacitation, mentioned in Chapter 11.)

The diversionary role of community-based punishments has become more pronounced as prisons and jails have filled up over the past three decades. In fact, probationers now account for nearly two-thirds of all adults in the American corrections systems (see Figure 12.1). According to the U.S. Department of Justice, on any single day, nearly 2 percent of all adult citizens are under probation supervision.[7]

ONLINE REVIEW Go to the book's Web site for an interactive review of this section

Probation: Doing Time in the Community

Probation
A criminal sanction in which a convict is allowed to remain in the community rather than be imprisoned as long as she or he follows certain conditions set by the court.

As Figure 12.1 shows, **probation** is the most common form of punishment in the United States. Although it is administered differently in various jurisdictions, probation can be generally defined as the legal status of an offender who, after being convicted of a crime, has been directed by the sentencing court to remain in the community under the supervision of a probation service for a designated period of time and subject to certain conditions imposed by the court or by law.[8]

The theory behind probation is that certain offenders, having been found guilty of a crime, can be more economically and humanely treated by placing them under controls while still allowing them to live in the community. One of the advantages of probation has been that it provides for the rehabilitation of the offender while saving society the costs of incarceration. Despite probation's widespread use, certain participants in the criminal justice system question its ability to reach its rehabilitative goals. Critics point to the immense number of probationers and the fact that many of them are violent felons as evidence that the system is "out of control." Supporters contend that nothing is wrong with probation in principle, but admit that its execution must be adjusted to meet the goals of modern corrections.[9]

THE ROOTS OF PROBATION

In its earliest forms, probation was based on a desire to inject leniency into an often harsh criminal justice system. Nineteenth-century English judges had the power to issue **judicial reprieves,** or to suspend sentences for a certain amount of time, on the condition of continued good behavior on the part of the defendant. This practice was adopted in the United States, albeit in a different form. American judges used their reprieve power to suspend the imposition of a penalty indefinitely, so long as the offender committed no second crime. If another crime was committed, the offender could be punished for both crimes.

In *Ex parte United States* (1916),[10] the Supreme Court ruled that such indefinite reprieves were unconstitutional because they limited the ability of the legislative and administrative branches to make and enforce sentencing laws. With this diversion option removed, judges increasingly turned to the model of probation first established in Massachusetts eighty years earlier.

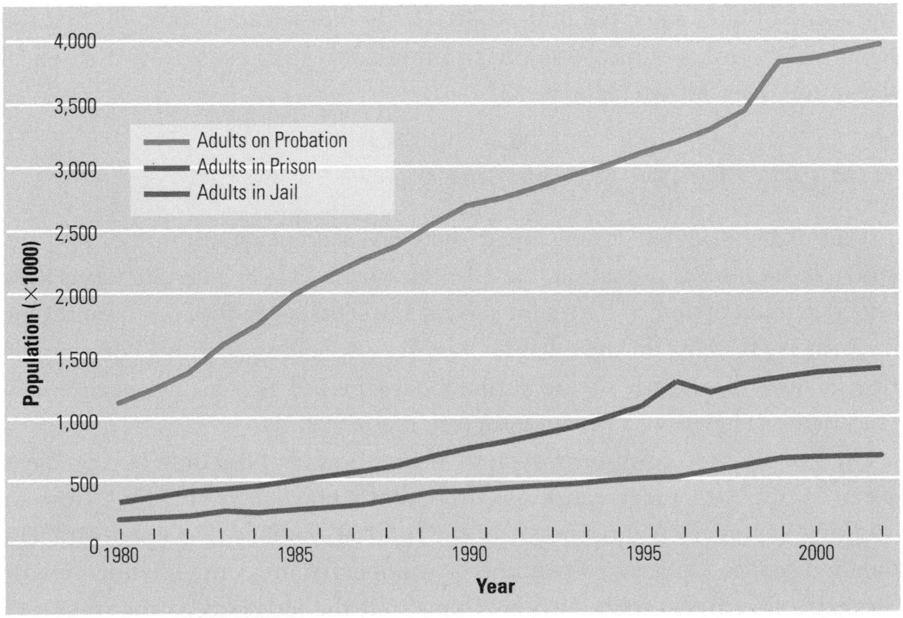

INFOTRAC KEYWORDS

probation

For more information, use this search term with InfoTrac College Edition, your online library at www.infotrac-college.com

Judicial Reprieve

Temporary relief or the postponement of a sentence on the authority of a judge. In the United States, the judicial power to offer a reprieve has been limited by the Supreme Court.

FIGURE 12.1 Probation in American Corrections

As you can see, the number of Americans on probation more than tripled between 1980 and 2002 (matching the growth rate of prison and jail populations).

Source: Department of Justice Statistics, *Probation and Parole in the United States, 2002* (Washington, D.C.: U.S. Department of Justice, 2003), 1.

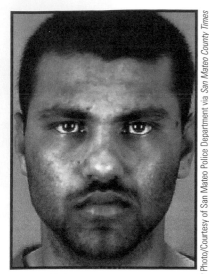

In 2001, Mohammed Haroon Ali, pictured here, was sentenced to sixty-four years in prison for the first degree murder of his girlfriend, Tracey Biletnikoff. Three years before the killing, Ali pleaded guilty to felony kidnapping and threatening bodily injury in an incident involving a former girlfriend. Instead of being sent to prison for these crimes, however, Ali was sentenced to probation. How does a case such as Ali's leave the probation system open to criticism?

John Augustus and the Origins of Probation   The roots of probation can be directly traced to a Boston shoemaker named John Augustus. In 1841, Augustus, a religious person with considerable wealth, offered to post bail for a man charged with drunkenness. Augustus persuaded the judge to defer sentencing for three weeks, during which time the offender would be in his custody. At the end of this probationary period, the offender was able to convince the judge that he had been reformed and received a fine instead of incarceration.

During the next eighteen years until his death, Augustus bailed out and supervised nearly 1,800 persons in lieu of confinement in the Boston House of Corrections. He carefully screened potential probationers, researching their personal backgrounds before deciding whether to include them in his caseload. Generally, Augustus accepted only first offenders of otherwise good character. During the probationary period, he helped his charges find employment and lodging and aided them in obtaining an education.[11] Augustus can be credited with nearly every aspect of modern probation, from the name itself (from the Latin term *probatio*, or a "period of governing or trial"), to presentence investigations, to supervision, to revocation.

Augustus's work was continued by a group of volunteer "probation officers" who worked to rescue youths from the dangers of imprisonment. In 1869, the state of Massachusetts passed a law that allowed for probation of juveniles and, nine years later, provided for paid probation officers to be hired by Boston's criminal courts. The law limited probation to "such persons as may reasonably be expected to be reformed without punishment." By 1891, Massachusetts had established the first statewide probation program.[12]

The Evolution of Probation   Even as probation systems have been adopted in each of the fifty states and the federal government, the basic conflict between "help" and "punishment" has dominated the context of probation. When both criminal justice practitioners and the public hold the rehabilitative model in favor, as was the case for most of the first half of the twentieth century, probation is generally considered a valuable aspect of treatment. When, however, retributive goals come to the fore, probation is seen as being in need of reform, as has been the case in the United States since the mid-1970s. (It should be noted, though, that the number of Americans on probation has continued to grow even as its theoretical underpinnings are being challenged.)

SENTENCING CHOICES AND PROBATION

Probation is basically an "arrangement" between sentencing authorities and the offender. In traditional probation, the offender agrees to follow certain terms for a specified amount of time in return for serving the sentence in the community. One of the primary benefits for the offender, besides not getting sent to a correctional facility, is that the length of the probationary period is usually considerably shorter than the length of a prison term (see Figure 12.2).

The "traditional" form of probation is not, however, the only arrangement that can be made. A judge can forgo probation altogether by handing down a **suspended sentence.** A descendant of the judicial reprieve discussed earlier, a suspended sentence places no conditions or supervision on the offender. He or she remains free for a certain length of time, but the judge keeps the option of

Suspended Sentence
A judicially imposed condition in which an offender is sentenced after being convicted of a crime, but is not required to begin the sentence immediately. The judge may revoke the suspended sentence and remit the offender to prison or jail if he or she does not follow certain conditions.

AP Photo/Courtesy of San Mateo Police Department via *San Mateo County Times*

revoking the suspended sentence and remanding the offender to prison or jail if circumstances call for such action.

Alternative Sentencing Arrangements   Judges can also combine probation with incarceration. Such sentencing arrangements include:

> *Split sentences.* In **split sentence probation,** also known as *shock probation,* the offender is sentenced to a specific amount of time in prison or jail, to be followed by a period of probation.

> *Shock incarceration.* In this arrangement, an offender is sentenced to prison or jail with the understanding that after a period of time, she or he may petition the court to be released on probation. Shock incarceration is discussed more fully later in the chapter.

> *Intermittent incarceration.* Intermittent incarceration requires that the offender spend a certain amount of time each week, usually during the weekend, in a jail, workhouse, or other government institution.

All three arrangements have become more popular with judges, as they combine the "treatment" aspects of probation with the "punishment" aspects of incarceration. For example, according to the Department of Justice, nearly 30 percent of all convicted felons receive split sentences.[13]

> **Split Sentence Probation**
> A sentence that consists of incarceration in a prison or jail, followed by a probationary period in the community.

Eligibility for Probation   Not every offender is eligible for probation. In Bell County, Texas, for example, juries can recommend probation only for assessed prison sentences of ten years or less. Generally, research has shown that offenders are most likely to be denied probation if they:

> Are convicted on multiple charges.

> Were on probation or parole at the time of the arrest.

> Have two or more prior convictions.

> Are addicted to narcotics.

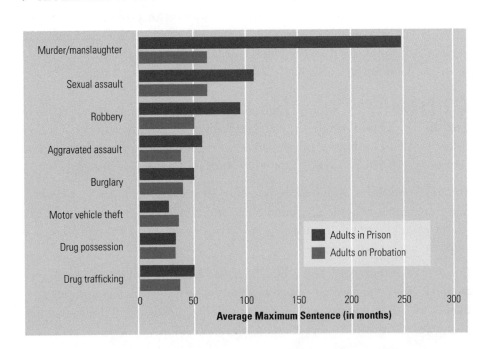

FIGURE 12.2 Average Length of Sentence: Prison versus Probation

As you can see, the average probation sentence is much shorter than the average prison sentence for most crimes.

Source: Adapted from Bureau of Justice Statistics, *Felony Sentences in the United States, 2000* (Washington, D.C.: U.S. Department of Justice, 2003), 4.

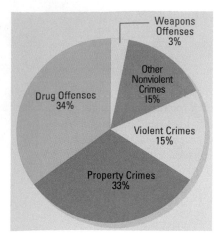

FIGURE 12.3 Adults on Probation by Felony Conviction Type

As you see here, the majority of adults on probation were convicted of property crimes or drug offenses.

Source: Adapted from Bureau of Justice Statistics, *State Court Sentencing of Convicted Felons, 2000* (Washington, D.C.: U.S. Department of Justice, 2003), Table 3.6.

> Seriously injured the victim of the crime.

> Used a weapon during the commission of the crime.[14]

As might be expected, the chances of a felon being sentenced to probation are highly dependent on the seriousness of the crime he or she has committed (see Figure 12.3).

CONDITIONS OF PROBATION

As part of the decision to sentence an offender to probation, a judge may also set conditions of probation. These conditions represent a "contract" between the judge and the offender, in which the latter agrees that if she or he does not follow certain rules, probation may be revoked (see Figure 12.4). The probation officer usually recommends the conditions of probation, but judges also have the power to set any terms they believe to be necessary.

Principles of Probation   This power is far-reaching, and a judge's personal philosophy is often reflected in the probation conditions that are set. In *In re Quirk* (1998),[15] for example, the Supreme Court upheld the ability of a Louisiana trial judge to impose church attendance as a condition of probation. Though judges have a great deal of discretion in setting the conditions of probation, they do operate under several guiding principles. First, the conditions must be related to the dual purposes of probation, which most federal and state courts define as (1) the rehabilitation of the probationer and (2) the protection of the community. Second, the conditions must not violate the U.S. Constitution; that is, probationers are generally entitled to the same constitutional rights as other prisoners.[16]

Of course, probationers do give up certain constitutional rights when they consent to the terms of probation; most probationers, for example, agree to spot checks of their homes for contraband such as drugs or weapons, and they therefore have a diminished expectation of privacy. In *United States v. Knights* (2001),[17] the Supreme Court upheld the actions of deputy sheriffs in Napa County, California, who searched a probationer's home without a warrant or probable cause. The decision, which was unanimous, reasoned that because those on probation are more likely to commit crimes, law enforcement agents "may therefore justifiably focus on probationers in a way that [they do] not on the ordinary citizen."[18]

Types of Conditions   Obviously, probationers who break the law are very likely to have their probation revoked. Other, less serious infractions may also result in revocation. The conditions placed on a probationer fall into three general categories:

> *Standard conditions,* which are imposed on all probationers. These include reporting regularly to the probation office, notifying the agency of any change of address, not leaving the jurisdiction without permission, and remaining employed.

> *Punitive conditions,* which usually reflect the seriousness of the offense and are intended to increase the punishment of the offender. Such conditions include fines, community service, restitution, drug testing, and home confinement (discussed later).

FIGURE 12.4 Conditions of Probation

**CONDITIONS OF PROBATION
UNITED STATES DISTRICT COURT
FOR THE DISTRICT OF COLUMBIA**

To _____ No. 84-417

Address: 1440 N St., N.W., #10, Wash., D.C.

In accordance With authority conferred by the United States Probation Law, you have been placed on probation this date, January 25, 2004 for a period of one year by the Hon. Louis F. Oberdorfer United States District Judge, sitting in and for this District Court at Washington, D.C.

CONDITIONS OF PROBATION

It is the order of the Court that you shall comply with the following conditions of probation:

(1) You shall refrain from violation of any law (federal, state, and local). You shall get in touch immediately with your probation officer if arrested or questioned by a law-enforcement officer.

(2) You shall associate only with law-abiding persons and maintain reasonable hours.

(3) You shall work regularly at a lawful occupation and support your legal dependents, if any, to the best of your ability. When out of work you shall notify your probation officer at once. You shall consult him prior to job changes.

(4) You shall not leave the judicial district without permission of the probation officer.

(5) You shall notify your probation officer immediately of any change in your place of residence.

(6) You shall follow the probation officer's instructions.

(7) You shall report to the probation officer as directed.

(8) You shall not possess a firearm (handgun or rifle) for any reason.

The special conditions ordered by the Court are as follows:

Imposition of sentence suspended, one year probation, Fine of $75 on each count.

I understand that the Court may change the conditions of probation, reduce or extend the period of probation, and at any time during the probation period or within the maximum probation period of 5 years permitted by law, may issue a warrant and revoke probation for a violation occurring during the probation period.

I have read or had read to me the above conditions of probation. I fully understand them and I will abide by them.

(Signed)   1/25/04

You will report as follows: Probationer Date

As directed by your Probation Officer

(Signed)   2/5/04

U.S. Probation Officer Date

> *Treatment conditions,* which are imposed with the goal of helping the offender with a condition that may contribute to his or her criminal activity. Data show that more than 40 percent of probationers were required to undergo drug or alcohol treatment as part of their sentences, and an additional 18 percent were ordered to seek other kinds of treatment such as anger-control therapy.[19] (Figure 12.5 on the following page shows the most common conditions for adult felony probationers.)

Some observers feel that judges have too much discretion in imposing overly restrictive conditions that no person, much less one who has exhibited antisocial tendencies, could meet. Citing prohibitions on drinking liquor, gambling, and associating with "undesirables," as well as requirements such as meeting early curfews, University of Delaware professor Carl B. Klockars claims that if probation rules were taken seriously, "very few probationers would complete their terms without violation."[20] As more than eight out of ten federal probationers do complete their terms successfully, Klockars's statement suggests that either probation

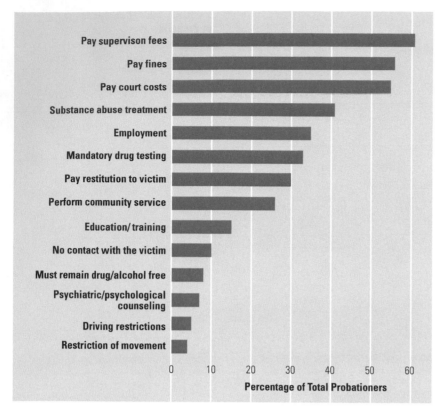

FIGURE 12.5 Special Conditions Imposed on Probationers

Source: Bureau of Justice Statistics, *Characteristics of Adults on Probation, 1995* (Washington, D.C.: U.S. Department of Justice, December 1997), 7.

officers are unable to determine that violations are taking place, or many of them are exercising a great deal of discretion in reporting minor probation violations. Or, perhaps, the officers realize that violating probationers for every single "slip-up" is unrealistic and would add to the already immense problem of jail and prison overcrowding.

THE SUPERVISORY ROLE OF THE PROBATION OFFICER

The probation officer has two basic roles. The first is investigative and consists of conducting the presentence investigation (PSI), which was discussed in Chapter 11. The second is supervisory and begins as soon as the offender has been sentenced to probation. In smaller probation agencies, individual officers perform both tasks. In larger jurisdictions, the trend has been toward separating the responsibilities, with *investigating officers* handling the PSI and *line officers* concentrating on supervision. (For insight into this role, see this chapter's *Careers in CJ* feature.)

Supervisory policies vary and are often a reflection of whether the authority to administer probation services is *decentralized* (under local, judicial control) or *centralized* (under state, administrative control). In any circumstance, however, certain basic principles of supervision apply. Starting with a preliminary interview, the probation officer establishes a relationship with the offender. This relationship is based on the mutual goal of both parties: the successful completion of the probationary period. Just because the line officer and the offender have the same goal, however, does not mean that probation is necessarily marked by excessive cooperation.

The Use of Authority   The ideal probation officer–offender relationship is based on trust. In reality, this trust does not often exist. Any incentive an offender might have to be completely truthful with a line officer is marred by one simple fact: self-reported wrongdoing can be used to revoke probation. Even probation officers whose primary mission is to rehabilitate are under institutional pressure to punish their clients for violating conditions of probation. One officer deals with this situation by telling his clients

> that I'm here to help them, to get them a job, and whatever else I can do. But I tell them too that I have a family to support and that if they get too far off track, I can't afford to put my job on the line for them. I'm going to have to violate them.[21]

In the absence of trust, most probation officers rely on their **authority** to guide an offender successfully through the sentence. An officer's authority, or

Authority
The power designated to an agent of the law over a person who has broken the law.

> Scott T. Ballock U.S. Probation Officer

Uncertain about my future at the beginning of my sophomore year, I stumbled into an Introduction to Criminal Justice course at Indiana University and quickly became fascinated with the work of professionals in this field. The only difficulty was deciding which route to go; there were so many possibilities and they all seemed fun and interesting. Throughout the rest of my undergraduate and graduate programs, I set out to get a closer look at each career path and volunteered variously at the local jail, probation office, police department, courthouse, and different social services agencies. I rode along with police officers, interviewed prison administrators, and met with attorneys and judges. My time spent with these people provided me with a more realistic picture of each profession than I had received through my education. Ultimately, the field of probation and parole appeared to provide the best fit for my interests and goals.

As a federal probation officer, I work for the United States District Court in the District of Nevada (Las Vegas Office). U.S. probation officers serve as officers of the court and as agents of the U.S. Parole Commission. We are responsible for the supervision of all persons conditionally released to the community by the courts, the Parole Commission, the Federal Bureau of Prisons, and military authorities. Being released "conditionally" to the community means that in exchange for allowing an offender to remain in the community, the court expects him or her to meet certain standards and goals. These include remaining law-abiding and drug free, working, supporting family members, repaying victims, perhaps performing volunteer work for the community, and making other improvements in his or her life.

Supervising offenders in the community, our mission is to execute the court's sentence, control risk, and promote law-abiding behavior. In order to meet these goals, probation officers must become very knowledgeable about an offender's activities and lifestyle. We do so by meeting with him or her on a regular basis in the community, conducting unannounced home inspections, speaking regularly with his or her family, friends, neighbors, and employers, and—when necessary—conducting surveillance or warrantless searches of his or her home and vehicle.

I am often asked whether probation officers are law enforcement officers or social workers. We are both. Responsible for protecting the public, we are also charged with promoting positive change among our probationers and parolees. Half of our day may be spent following an offender through the city to learn if he is engaged in illegal activities, while the second half is spent counseling offenders, helping them prepare résumés, or referring them to local social service agencies for further assistance. Our dual role is an especially challenging aspect of the job.

Fortunately, we have the guidance of our boss, the sentencing judge. I used to think that justice was dispensed routinely and methodically with little consideration given to the impact of a sentence. Having worked for several judges, however, I have learned that sentences are carefully crafted and well thought out. Probation officers and judges are genuinely concerned about the welfare of the people who appear before them. If offenders have a substance abuse problem, they'll be offered treatment. If they are lacking in job skills, a judge may order successful completion of a vocational training program.

Courtesy Scott T. Ballock

Scott T. Ballock

We recognize that a prison sentence is a very costly proposition, to both the offender and the community. A decision to send or return a person to a prison setting is a serious matter, and great lengths are taken to first effect positive change. I think even those we supervise come to realize this. It's not infrequent that a person I've spent months trying to help, and who ultimately fails and is sent back to prison, extends his hand to thank me for trying—even as he's being led away by the U.S. marshals.

Probation officers come from a variety of fields and bring wide-ranging experiences to the job. Such diversity is necessary for the type of work we do. We have so many responsibilities, ranging from conducting financial investigations to investigating evidence of new criminal activity, and this requires that we develop a working knowledge of many different areas of criminal justice. Probation offices are filled with officers who have backgrounds in financial matters, counseling, law enforcement, and social service work. I would strongly recommend students consider probation and parole as an option for employment. It's a good feeling to know that each day, simply by going to work, you've made a difference for the community.

 Go to the Careers in Criminal Justice Interactive CD *for more profiles in the field of criminal justice.*

In 2003, musician Bobby Brown, shown here in a DeKalb County (Georgia) courtroom, was arrested for violating his probation from an earlier drunk driving conviction. Police apprehended Brown because he failed to show up for community service and drug treatment, as required by the terms of his probation. The singer spent seven days in jail for his transgression.

ability to influence a person's actions without resorting to force, is based not only on her or his power to revoke probation, but also on a number of lesser sanctions. For example, if a probationer fails to attend a required alcohol treatment program, the officer can place him or her in a "lockup," or detention center, overnight. To be successful, a probation officer must establish this authority early in the relationship; it is the primary tool in persuading the probationer to behave in a manner acceptable to the community.[22]

The Offender's Perspective   The public perception of probationers is that they are lucky not to be in prison or jail and should be grateful for receiving a "second chance." Although they may not describe their situation in that way, many probationers are willing to comply with the terms of their sentences, if for no other reason than to avoid any further punishments. Such offenders can make a line officer's supervision duties relatively simple.

By the same token, as we discussed in Chapter 2, criminal behavior is often predicated on a lack of respect for authority. This outlook does not coincide with the supervisory aspects of probation. According to the Department of Justice, in any given month, 61 percent of offenders have a face-to-face meeting with their supervisors in a probation office, at home, at work, or in another setting. Another 25 percent were in contact through the mail or over the phone.[23] Furthermore, to follow the conditions of probation, convicts may have to discontinue activity that they find enjoyable, such as going to a bar for a drink on Saturday night. Consequently, some probationers consider supervision as akin to "baby-sitting" and resist the strict controls placed on them by the government.

The Changing Environment of the Probation Officer   To some extent, today's probation officers function similarly to John Augustus's volunteers. They spend a great deal of time in the community, working with businesses, churches, schools, and neighborhood groups on behalf of their charges.

Nevertheless, the profession has seen considerable changes over the past two decades. As noted earlier, probation is being offered to more offenders with violent criminal histories than in the past. Inevitably, this has changed the job description of the probation officer, who must increasingly act as a law enforcement agent rather than concentrating on the rehabilitation of clients. Probation officers now conduct surveillance and search and seizure operations, administer drug tests, and accompany police officers on high-risk law enforcement assignments.[24] Consequently, the work has become more dangerous. According to the National Institute of Corrections, about twenty probation officers have been killed since 1974.[25]

As a result, many probation officers are seeking permission to carry guns on the job. In 2002, for example, the Arizona Probation Officer Association convinced state authorities that probation officers should be able to wield firearms if they so desire. Making a similar argument, Los Angeles probation officer Janis

Jones said, "We're not in the '70s anymore. We're not dealing with little dope dealers on the corner selling nickel bags of marijuana." Jones, whose unit collects about a dozen guns a week, added, "These guys are into hard-core, heavy firepower to protect their interests. You feel totally vulnerable [without a gun]."[26] In the federal probation system, eighty-three of the ninety-four federal judicial districts permit their probation officers to carry firearms.

REVOCATION OF PROBATION

The probation period can end in one of two ways. Either the probationer successfully fulfills the conditions of the sentence, or the probationer misbehaves and probation is revoked, resulting in a prison or jail term. The decision of whether to revoke after a **technical violation**—such as failing to report a change of address or testing positive for drug use—is often a "judgment call" by the probation officer and therefore the focus of controversy.

Revocation Trends In the past, a technical violation almost always led to revocation. Today, many probation officers will take that step only if they believe the technical violation in question represents a danger to the community. At the same time, the public's more punitive attitude, along with improved drug-testing methods, has increased the number of conditions under which probationers are placed and, consequently, the odds that they will violate one of those conditions.

In the 1980s and 1990s, to a certain extent, these two trends negated each other: between 1987 and 1996, there was almost no change in the percentage (between 75 and 80 percent) of offenders who successfully completed their probation terms.[27] In the past few years, however, this rate has dropped. In 2002, only 62 percent of probationers completed their terms without revocation.[28] Because revocation results in incarceration, it can make a significant contribution to prison and jail overcrowding. In Texas, for example, about one-third of prison admissions are for probation revocations.[29]

The Revocation Process Probationers do not enjoy the same rights as other members of society. In *Griffin v. Wisconsin* (1987),[30] the Supreme Court ruled that probationers have only "conditional liberty" that is dependent "on observance of special restrictions." As long as the restrictions assure that a probationer works toward rehabilitation and does not harm the community, the Court allows the probationer's privacy to be restricted in a manner it would not accept otherwise.

The Supreme Court has not stripped probationers of all due process rights. In *Mempa v. Rhay* (1967),[31] the Court ruled that probationers were entitled to an attorney during the revocation process. Then, in *Morrissey v. Brewer* (1972) and *Gagnon v. Scarpelli* (1973),[32] the Court established a three-stage procedure by which the "limited" due process rights of probationers must be protected in potential revocation situations:

See the Corrections Connection for information on the corrections industry, including community corrections. Find this Web site by clicking on *Web Links* under *Chapter Resources* at www.cjinaction.com

Technical Violation

An action taken by a probationer that, although not criminal, breaks the terms of probation as designated by the court; can result in the revocation of probation and a return to prison or jail.

Juvenile Court Probation Officer Michael J. Manteria, left, consults with a probationer at the Hampden County Hall of Justice in Springfield, Massachusetts. The ideal probation officer–probationer relationship is based on trust, but often probation officers must rely on their authority to do their jobs correctly. Why is trust often so difficult to achieve between probation officers and offenders?

AP Photo/*Springfield Union-News*, Michael Gordon

INFOTRAC KEYWORDS

probation revocation

For more information, use this search term with InfoTrac College Edition, your online library at www.infotrac-college.com

> *The preliminary hearing.* In this appearance before a "disinterested person" (often a judge), the facts of the violation or arrest are presented, and it is determined whether probable cause for revoking probation exists. This hearing can be waived by the probationer.

> *The revocation hearing.* During this hearing, the probation agency presents evidence to support its claim of violation, and the probationer can attempt to refute this evidence. The probationer has the right to know the charges being brought against him or her. Furthermore, probationers can testify on their own behalf and present witnesses in their favor, as well as confront and cross-examine adverse witnesses. A "neutral and detached" body must hear the evidence and rule in favor of the probation agency or the offender.

> *Revocation sentencing.* If the presiding body rules against the probationer, then the judge must decide whether to impose incarceration and for what length of time. In a revocation hearing dealing with technical violations, the judge will often reimpose probation with stricter terms or intermediate sanctions.

In effect, this is a "bare-bones" approach to due process. Most of the rules of evidence that govern regular trials do not play a role in revocation hearings. Probation officers are not, for example, required to read offenders *Miranda* rights when questioning them about crimes that may have been committed during probation. In *Minnesota v. Murphy* (1984),[33] the Supreme Court ruled that a meeting between probation officer and client does not equal custody and, therefore, the Fifth Amendment protection against self-incrimination does not apply.

DOES PROBATION WORK?

To address the question of whether probation is effective, one must first establish its purpose. Should the probation system be designed to rehabilitate offenders? Is it primarily a method of surveillance and control? Should probation's role in the criminal justice system be to reduce pressure on prison and jail populations? Each of these aspects of probation has its supporters and critics. Indeed, the only consensus among supporters of probation is that the system is severely underfunded. As many states face growing budget deficits, spending for probation agencies has at best remained stagnant and, in many cases, has been reduced despite increasing probation populations.

"I try to get in the field two to three nights a week to see my offenders. It's really the only way to stop trouble before it happens. Otherwise, it's a free-for-all."

—Kevin Dudley, Salt Lake City probation officer (1997)

The Caseload Dilemma   As a result of these low budgets, say observers, probation agencies do not have the resources to provide full services to all offenders. Patrick A. Langan of the U.S. Department of Justice estimates that fully half of this country's probationers do not comply with the conditions of their sentences. The problem, contends Langan and many of his colleagues, is that probation officers have such large caseloads that they cannot rigorously enforce the conditions imposed on many of their clients.[34]

Unlike a prison cell, a probation officer can always take on "just one more" offender/client. As there is no accepted standard for determining optimal case loads, probation officers can find themselves responsible for supervising an extremely large number of convicts. One official interviewed by Professors Charles Linder and Robert L. Bonn at John Jay College of Criminal Justice admitted to having 6,500 clients supervised by four probation officers.[35] Though data vary from state to state, Professor Joan Petersilia of the University of California at Irvine estimates that, on average, each probation officer in the United States has a caseload of 175 offenders.[36] Another study found that 20 percent of adult *felony* probationers had no personal contact with their probation officers whatsoever.[37]

Recidivism and Probation   Such statistics fuel the popular belief that probation allows dangerous felons to roam the streets and commit new crimes at will. This perception is not entirely accurate. In fact, the majority of probationers complete their terms without being arrested (which does not necessarily mean that they did not commit a new offense). Low rearrest rates are not surprising, given that many of those on probation are first-time, low-risk offenders. Furthermore, a controlled comparison of the recidivism rates of 511 probationers and 511 offenders released from prison found that probation can be at least as effective as incarceration, if not more so. Seventy-two percent of the prisoners were rearrested and 47 percent were imprisoned, while only 38 percent of the probationers were rearrested and 31 percent incarcerated.[38]

By the same token, there is no question that probationers do commit numerous crimes. Researchers John DiIulio, John Walters, and William Bennett have written that convicted offenders living in the community "do tremendous numbers of serious crimes, including a frightening fraction of all murders."[39] They found that, in one year, probation violators were convicted of nearly 6,500 homicides, more than 7,000 rapes, about 10,000 assaults, and 17,000 robberies.[40]

Not surprisingly, there seems to be a positive correlation between probationary success and the completion of treatment and education programs. In Arizona, for example, the state supreme court ordered adult education programs for its county probation departments.[41] The results, exhibited in Figure 12.6, have been encouraging.

Risk Assessment Management   Many reformers reject the notion that large caseloads are to blame for the inadequacies of the supervision system. These critics believe that probation agencies have failed to direct their limited resources efficiently. In other words, they have failed to devote more supervisory controls to the relatively small percentage of offenders who run the highest risk of recidivism and pose the greatest threat to the community.

In 1981, the National Institute of Corrections developed a "model system" of case management to address these concerns. Based on the notion that some offenders require more attention than others, the model provides probation officers with statistical methods—based on the type of crime committed—to identify these offenders.[42] Within a decade, nearly every probation system in the nation was using similar classification devices to determine the level of supervision based on *risk assessment*.[43]

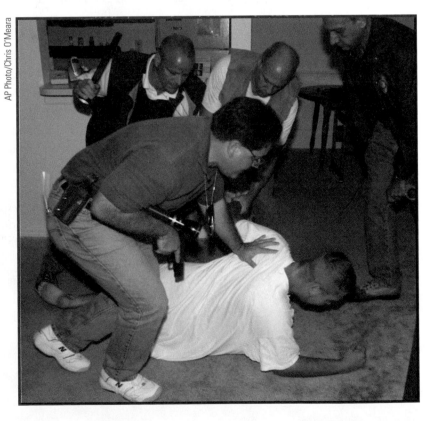

AP Photo/Chris O'Meara

Three probation officers and a sheriff's deputy take down a probation violator during a roundup in Tampa, Florida. When an offender violates the terms of probation, his or her status can be revoked, and he or she can be sent to jail or prison. This is often a "judgment call" by the probation officer. What might be some reasons that a probation officer would not revoke an offender's probation even though that person has committed a violation?

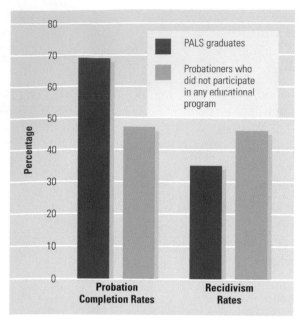

FIGURE 12.6 Literacy Programs, Successful Probation Completion, and Recidivism

The Principle of Alphabet Literacy System (PALS) is a part of Pima County, Arizona's, Adult Probation Department's Literacy, Education, and Reading Network. PALS targets those probationers who read below a sixth-grade level and have difficulty writing complete sentences. On finishing 80 to 100 hours of instruction, PALS graduates are able to write complete sentences and fill out job applications. In a study comparing those probationers who completed PALS to those who did not, Arizona correctional officials found a correlation between literacy and positive results. As you can see, PALS graduates are more likely to complete their probation period without revocation and less likely to recidivate.

Source: Adapted from Gayle R. Seigel and Joanne Basta, "The Effect of Adult Education Programs on Probationers," *Perspectives* (Spring 1998), 42–44.

Intermediate Sanctions

Sanctions that are more restrictive than probation and less restrictive than imprisonment. Intended to alleviate pressure on overcrowded corrections facilities and understaffed probation departments.

Basically, risk assessment management strategies determine the offender's threat to the community and the level of supervision required to lessen that threat.[44] In doing so, the probation officer or other officer of the court considers several factors, such as the offender's record of committing violent crimes; previous performance in probation, parole, or other community-based corrections programs; previous experience in jail or prison; and substance abuse or anger-management problems. In general, those offenders who are believed to pose the greatest threat to the community are labeled "maximum" risk and subjected to the highest level of supervision. Offenders who have not committed violent crimes or are deemed "medium" or "minimum" risks for other reasons are subjected to less supervision, thus freeing probation officers to deal with their most dangerous clients. This risk assessment model has two benefits: (1) in keeping with "just deserts," those who have committed more serious crimes are subject to more restrictive probationary terms, and (2) it prioritizes community protection.

↗ONLINE REVIEW *Go to the book's Web site for an interactive review of this section*

Intermediate Sanctions

During the 1960s and 1970s, many probation departments experimented with smaller caseloads under a management program known as *intensive supervision probation (ISP)*. These programs were discontinued when research showed that offenders in ISP had similar rearrest rates and more technical violations than those under regular supervision.[45] ISP was resurrected by the state of Georgia in 1982, however, with a different mandate. The state, experiencing prison crowding and a limited corrections budget, saw ISP as an alternative sanction for offenders who would have otherwise gone to prison. Georgia's version of ISP has been adopted in some measure by all fifty states, and it is at the vanguard of a movement to use **intermediate sanctions** to a greater degree in the American corrections system.

Many observers feel that the most widely used sentencing options—imprisonment or probation—fail to reflect the immense diversity of crimes and criminals. Intermediate sanctions provide a number of additional sentencing options for those wrongdoers who require stricter supervision than that supplied by probation, but for whom imprisonment would be unduly harsh and counterproductive.[46] The intermediate sanctions discussed in this section are designed to match the specific punishment and treatment of an individual offender with a corrections program that reflects that offender's situation.

Dozens of different variations of intermediate sanctions are handed down each year. To cover the spectrum succinctly, two general categories of such sanctions will be discussed in this section: those administered primarily by the courts and those administered primarily by probation departments, including day reporting centers, ISP programs, shock incarceration, and home confinement. Remember that none of these sanctions are exclusive; they are often combined with imprisonment and probation, and with each other.

JUDICIALLY ADMINISTERED INTERMEDIATE SANCTIONS

The lack of sentencing options is most frustrating for the person who, in the majority of cases, does the sentencing: the judge. Consequently, when judges are given the discretion to "color" a punishment with intermediate sanctions, they will often do so. Besides imprisonment and probation (and, to a lesser extent, other intermediate sanctions), a judge has five sentencing options:

1 Fines
2 Community service
3 Restitution
4 Forfeiture
5 Pretrial diversion programs

Fines, community service, and restitution were discussed in Chapter 11. In the context of intermediate sanctions, it is important to remember that these punishments are generally combined with incarceration or probation. For that reason, some critics feel the retributive or deterrent impact of such punishments is severely limited. Many European countries, in contrast, rely heavily on fines as the sole sanctions for a variety of crimes. (See *International CJ—Swedish Day-Fines* on p. 420.)

Forfeiture   In 1970, Congress passed the Racketeer Influenced and Corrupt Organizations Act (RICO) in an attempt to prevent the use of legitimate business enterprises as shields for organized crime.[47] As amended, RICO and other statutes give judges the ability to implement forfeiture proceedings in certain criminal cases. **Forfeiture** refers to a process by which the government seizes property gained from or used in criminal activity. For example, if a person is convicted for smuggling cocaine into the United States from South America, a judge can order the seizure of not only the narcotics, but also the speedboat the offender used to deliver the drugs to a pickup point off the coast of South Florida. In *Bennis v. Michigan* (1996),[48] the Supreme Court ruled that a person's home or car could be forfeited even if the owner was unaware that it was connected to illegal activity.

Once property is forfeited, the government has several options. It can sell the property, with the proceeds going to the state and/or federal government law enforcement agencies involved in the seizure. Alternatively, the government agency can use the property directly in further crime-fighting efforts or award it to a third party, such as an informant. Forfeiture has proved highly profitable: federal law enforcement agencies impound close to $1 billion worth of contraband and property from alleged criminals each year.

Forfeiture
The process by which the government seizes private property attached to criminal activity.

Two gang members perform their court-ordered community service under the watchful eye of a supervisor. Community service is one of a number of intermediate sanctions used to punish offenders instead of probation or incarceration. Why might corrections officials support the increased use of intermediate sanctions?

PhotoEdit/Phil McCarten

> Swedish Day-Fines

ew ideals are cherished as highly in our criminal justice system as equality. Most Americans take it for granted that individuals guilty of identical crimes should face identical punishments. From an economic perspective, however, this emphasis on equality renders our system decidedly *unequal*. Take two citizens, one a millionaire investment banker and the other a check-out clerk earning the minimum wage. Driving home from work one afternoon, each is caught by a traffic officer doing 80 miles per hour in a 55-mile-per-hour zone. The fine for this offense is $150. This amount, though equal for both, has different consequences: it represents mere pocket change for the investment banker, but a significant chunk out of the check-out clerk's weekly paycheck.

Restricted by a "tariff system" that sets specific amounts for specific crimes, regardless of the financial situation of the convict, American judges often refrain from using fines as a primary sanction. They either assume that poor offenders cannot afford the fine or worry that a fine will allow wealthier offenders to "buy" their way out of a punishment.

Paying for Crime

In searching for a way to make fines more effective sanctions, many reformers have seized on the concept of the "day-fine," as practiced in Sweden and several other European countries. In this system, which was established in the 1920s and 1930s, the fine amount is linked to the monetary value of the offender's daily income. Depending on the seriousness of the crime, a Swedish wrongdoer will be sentenced to between 30 and 150 days or, as combined punishment for multiple crimes, up to 200 days. Each day, the offender is required to pay the equivalent of one-third of her or his daily discretionary income (as established by the Prosecutor General's Office) to the court. Consequently, the day-fine system not only reflects the degree of the crime, but ensures that the economic burden will be equal for those with different means.

Swedish police and prosecutors can levy day-fines without court involvement. Consequently, plea bargaining is nonexistent, and more than 80 percent of all offenders are sentenced to intermediate sanctions without a trial. The remaining cases receive full trials, with an acquittal rate of only 6 percent, compared to roughly 30 percent in the United States.

FOR CRITICAL ANALYSIS

Do you think a "day-fine" system would be feasible in the United States? Why might it be difficult to implement in this country?

Pretrial Diversion Programs Not every criminal violation requires the courtroom process. Consequently, some judges have the discretion to order an offender into a **pretrial diversion program** during the preliminary hearing. (Prosecutors can also offer an offender the opportunity to join such a program in return for reducing or dropping the initial charges.) These programs represent an "interruption" of the criminal proceedings and are generally reserved for young or first-time offenders who have been arrested on charges of illegal drug use, child or spousal abuse, or sexual misconduct. Pretrial diversion programs usually include extensive counseling, often in a treatment center. If the offender successfully follows the conditions of the program, the criminal charges are dropped.

Pretrial Diversion Program
An alternative to trial offered by a judge or prosecutor, in which the offender agrees to participate in a specified counseling or treatment program in return for withdrawal of the charges.

Like other intermediate sanctions, pretrial diversion programs are not risk free. In Jacksonville, Florida, for example, those arrested for sexually assaulting children were indiscriminately placed in counseling programs. The practice led to a public scandal when a man who had already completed two diversion programs for molesting children murdered a third victim. He was eventually sentenced to die in the state's electric chair.[49]

DAY REPORTING CENTERS

Day Reporting Center
A community-based corrections center to which offenders report on a daily basis for purposes of treatment, education, and incapacitation.

First used in Great Britain, **day reporting centers** are mainly tools to reduce jail and prison overcrowding. Although the offenders are allowed to remain in the community, they must spend all or part of each day at a reporting center. To a certain extent, being sentenced to a day reporting center is an extreme form of supervision. With offenders under a single roof, they are much more easily controlled and supervised.

Day reporting centers are also instruments of rehabilitation. Many house treatment programs for drug and alcohol abusers and provide counseling for a number of psychological problems, such as depression and anger management. Many of those found guilty in the Roanoke (Virginia) Drug Court, for example, are ordered to participate in a year-long day reporting program. At the center, offenders meet with probation officers, submit to urine tests, and attend counseling and education programs, such as parenting and life-skills classes. After the year has passed, if the offender has completed the program to the satisfaction of the judge and found employment, the charges will be dropped.[50]

Judges and prosecutors may, in certain cases, give offenders the chance to attend pretrial diversion programs. Offered by care-giving facilities such as the community substance abuse center pictured here, these programs provide a chance to treat the causes behind criminal behavior without sending the offender to prison or jail. Do pretrial diversion programs "punish" offenders? If not, can they be justified as part of the corrections system?

Given that each day reporting center is unique, it is difficult to evaluate the success of this particular intermediate sanction. One survey of six Massachusetts day reporting centers, however, did find that nearly 80 percent of the participants completed the programs successfully, with only 5 percent being returned to jail or prison for having committing further crimes over a five-year period.[51] More recent studies have not been as encouraging, however. One review of intensive supervision programs (see below) in North Carolina found no effect on recidivism when participants were sent to day reporting centers.[52] In West Virginia, day reporting centers have a 15 percent recidivism rate, only slightly lower than the 18 percent rate for probationers.[53]

INTENSIVE SUPERVISION PROBATION

As stated previously, **intensive supervision probation (ISP)** offers a more restrictive alternative to regular probation, with higher levels of face-to-face contact between offenders and officers, drug testing, and electronic surveillance. Different jurisdictions have different methods of determining who is eligible for ISP. In New Jersey, for example, violent offenders may not be placed in the program, while a majority of states limit ISP to those who do not have prior probation violations. The frequency of officer-client contact also varies widely. A Rand study of fourteen ISP sites found that offenders in Contra Costa County, California, had 2.7 contacts per month, compared to 22.8 contacts per month in Waycross, Georgia.[54]

Intensive supervision has two primary functions: (1) to *divert* offenders from overcrowded prisons or jails, and (2) to place these offenders under higher levels of *control*, as befits the risk they pose to the community. Researchers have had difficulty, however, in determining whether ISP is succeeding in these two areas. Any diversion benefits of ISP programs have tended to be offset by the stricter sentencing guidelines discussed in Chapter 11.[55] Furthermore, a number of studies have found that ISP clients have higher violation rates than traditional probationers.[56]

Intensive Supervision Probation (ISP)
A punishment-oriented form of probation in which the offender is placed under stricter and more frequent surveillance and control by probation officers with limited caseloads.

One theory is that ISP "causes" these high failure rates—greater supervision increases the chances that an offender will be caught breaking conditions of probation. Despite its questionable performance, ISP is viable in today's political landscape because it satisfies the public's desire for stricter controls on convicts, while providing intermediate sanctions options for judges, prosecutors, and corrections administrators.

SHOCK INCARCERATION

Before the concept of intermediate sanctions was widely recognized in the criminal justice community, "Scared Straight" programs were used by some jurisdictions with the express purpose of deterring further criminal activity by juveniles and first-time offenders. The original Scared Straight was developed by the Lifers Group at Rahway State Prison (now East Jersey State Prison) in New Jersey in the mid-1970s. Consisting of about forty inmates serving sentences from twenty-five years to life, the Lifers Group would oversee juvenile offenders who had not yet been incarcerated but were considered "at risk" during a short stint (between 30 and 120 days) in the prison. The hope, as the program's name indicates, was that by getting a taste of the brutalities of daily prison life, the offender would be shocked into a crime-free existence.

Shock Incarceration
A short period of incarceration that is designed to deter further criminal activity by "shocking" the offender with the hardships of imprisonment.

A form of **shock incarceration,** Scared Straight programs generally fell out of favor in the 1980s, though several states, including Nevada, still employ them. Critics contended that the programs seemed to have no discernible effect on recidivism rates and thus needlessly exposed minor offenders to mental and physical cruelties from hardened criminals.[57]

Today, corrections officials are turning toward programs such as Colorado's "Shape-Up" and Idaho's DETOUR. These programs assign a juvenile offender to an adult "partner" who is serving a prison term. The juvenile spends a day in prison with the partner; then, the adult offender, the juvenile offender, and the juvenile's family meet together. A coordinator of DETOUR believes that these programs are more effective because they are not merely trying to scare already hardened juvenile offenders. Instead, he sees DETOUR as an educational program.[58] The concept appears to work; Colorado's juvenile corrections department reports an 86 percent success rate for Shape-Up.[59]

The precepts of shock incarceration have not disappeared, however. In fact, this particular form of intermediate sanctioning has prospered with the rapid, and controversial, proliferation of boot camps. (For an in-depth discussion of the controversy surrounding this form of shock incarceration, see the feature *Criminal Justice in Action—Boot Camps: Do They Work?* at the end of the chapter.)

HOME CONFINEMENT AND ELECTRONIC MONITORING

Home Confinement
A community-based sanction in which offenders serve their terms of incarceration in their homes.

Various forms of **home confinement**—in which offenders serve their sentences not in a government institution but at home—have existed for centuries. It has often served, and continues to do so, as a method of political control, used by totalitarian regimes to isolate and silence dissidents. For example, the military government of Myanmar (Burma) has confined Nobel Peace laureate Aung San Suu Kyi to her home for years at a time since she won an election for leadership of that country in 1990.

For purposes of general law enforcement, home confinement was impractical until relatively recently. After all, one could not expect offenders to "promise" to stay at home, and the personnel costs of guarding them were prohibitive. In the 1980s, however, with the advent of **electronic monitoring,** or using technology to "guard" the prisoner, home confinement became more viable. Today, all fifty states and the federal government have home monitoring programs.

The Levels of Home Monitoring and Their Benefits   Home monitoring has three general levels of restriction:

1 *Curfew,* which requires offenders to be in their homes at specific hours each day, usually at night.

2 *Home detention,* which requires that offenders remain home at all times, with exceptions being made for education, employment, counseling, or other specified activities such as the purchase of food or, in some instances, attendance at religious ceremonies.

3 *Home incarceration,* which requires the offender to remain home at all times, save for medical emergencies.

Under ideal circumstances, home confinement serves many of the goals of intermediate sanctions. It protects the community. It saves public funds and space in correctional facilities by keeping convicts out of institutional incarceration. It meets public expectations of punishment for criminals. Uniquely, home confinement also recognizes that convicts, despite their crimes, play important roles in the community, and allows them to continue in those roles. An offender, for example, may be given permission to leave confinement to care for elderly parents.

Home confinement is also lauded for giving sentencing officials the freedom to match the punishment with the needs of the offender. In Missouri, for instance, the conditions of detention for a musician required him to remain at home during the day, but allowed him to continue his career at night. In addition, he was obliged to make antidrug statements before each performance, to be verified by the manager at whichever club he appeared.

Offenders who are confined to their homes are often monitored by an electronic device that fits around the ankle. A transmitter in the device sends a continuous signal to a receiver, also located within the home. If this signal is broken—that is, the offender moves outside the range of the device—the police are automatically notified. What are some of the drawbacks of this form of electronic monitoring?

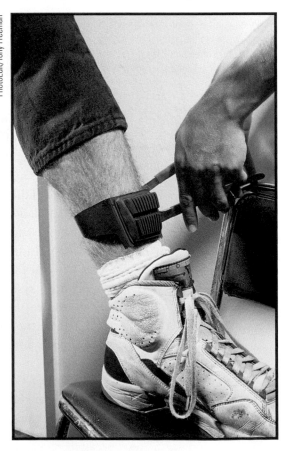

PhotoEdit/Tony Freeman

Types of Electronic Monitoring   According to some reports, the inspiration for electronic monitoring was a *Spiderman* comic book in which the hero was trailed by the use of an electronic device on his arm. In 1979, a New Mexico judge named Jack Love, having read the comic, convinced an executive at Honeywell, Inc., to begin developing similar technology to supervise convicts.[60]

Two major types of electronic monitoring have grown out of Love's initial concept. The first is a "programmed contact" program, in which the offender is contacted periodically by telephone or beeper to verify his or her whereabouts. Verification is obtained via a computer that uses voice or visual identification techniques or by requiring the offender to enter a code in an electronic box when called. The second is a "continuously signaling" device, worn around the convict's wrist, ankle, or neck. A transmitter in the device sends out a continuous signal to a "receiver-dialer" device located in the offender's dwelling. If the receiver device does not detect a signal from the transmitter, it informs a central computer, and the police are notified.[61] (For advances in this field, see *CJ and Technology—Satellite Tracking: The Next Step in Electronic Monitoring*.)

Effectiveness of Home Confinement   As might be expected, technical problems can limit the effectiveness of an electronic monitoring device. So can tampering by the offender. In Washington, D.C., for example, a participant in a home monitoring program was caught on the street holding eighty small bags of cocaine. His continuous signal device was still at his home, transmitting the "all is well" signal. The possibility of such problems will decrease as tamper-resistant monitoring devices are perfected. One such device reacts to the application of heat, which normally loosens some transmitters, by contracting; if enough heat is applied, the offender's circulation will be cut off.[62]

Because most participants in home confinement programs are low-risk offenders, their recidivism rates are quite low. Joan Petersilia found that most home confinement programs report rearrest rates of less than 5 percent.[63] The data are less supportive when measuring how many offenders broke the conditions of confinement. In Indiana, over 40 percent of participants had at least one violation, and between one-third and one-half failed to complete the program.[64]

One concern about home confinement is that offenders are often required to defray program costs, which can be as high as $100 per week (see Figure 12.7). Consequently, those who cannot afford to pay for electronic monitoring may not be eligible. Furthermore, families of offenders confined to the home can experience high levels of stress and a loss of privacy.[65] In general, however, those who successfully complete a home confinement term seem to benefit in areas such as obtaining and holding employment.[66]

WIDENING THE NET

As mentioned above, most of the convicts chosen for intermediate sanctions are low-risk offenders. From the point of view of the corrections official doing the choosing, this makes sense. Such offenders are less likely to commit crimes and attract negative publicity. This selection strategy, however, appears to invalidate one of the primary reasons intermediate sanctions exist: to reduce prison and jail populations. If most of the offenders in intermediate sanctions programs would otherwise have received probation, then the effect on these populations is nullified. Indeed, studies have shown this to be the case.[67]

At the same time, such selection processes broaden the reach of the corrections system. In other words, they increase rather than decrease the amount of control the state exerts over the individual. Suppose a person is arrested for a misdemeanor such as shoplifting and, under normal circumstances, would receive probation. With access to intermediate sanctions, the judge may add a period of home confinement to the sentence. Critics contend that such practices **widen the net** of the corrections system by augmenting the number of citizens who are under the control and surveillance of the state and also *strengthen the net* by increasing the government's power to intervene in the lives of its citizens.[68]

↱ ONLINE REVIEW *Go to the book's Web site for an interactive review of this section*

Widen the Net
The criticism that intermediate sanctions designed to divert offenders from prison actually increase the number of citizens who are under the control and surveillance of the American corrections system.

FIGURE 12.7   Supervision Fees
One of the most popular aspects of intermediate sanctions is that convicts must often pay for the programs themselves. Here you can see listed the fees for various forms of court-ordered community supervision in Marin County, California.

Form of Supervision	Fee
Community service	$27.00
House arrest	$13/day
Anger management	$50.00
Domestic violence program	$20/visit
Drug education	$410
First-offender DUI counseling program	$516

Source: Marin County Probation Department.

> Satellite Tracking: The Next Step in Electronic Monitoring

As we have already discussed, all intermediate sanctions entail a certain amount of risk. In electronic monitoring, as with other sanctions, this risk is compounded by the fact that the success of the program depends on the offender's commitment to "play by the rules." If the offender decides to leave the area of confinement, the signaling device will emit an alarm, alerting the police of the infraction but giving them no clues as to where the person is going.

A new breakthrough in electronic monitoring may provide the solution to this problem. Pro Tech Monitoring, Inc., a Palm Harbor (Florida) company, has developed a system that uses federal government satellites to monitor an offender's movements from above. Under this system, each subject will carry a "smart box" along with an ankle bracelet. The "smart box" contains a tracking device and is programmed with information about the offender's geographic restrictions. A Global Positioning System (GPS) satellite monitors the offender's movements and notifies the police if she or he violates conditional boundaries. So, for example, if a pedophile approaches an "off-limits" junior high school, the satellite warning system would alert police of the person's present location.

This system is particularly alluring for economic reasons. In Florida, where almost 600 probationers and parolees are "on the box," it costs $45 a day to house someone in a state prison, compared with $10 a day for surveillance using the GPS device. Offenders may prefer this form of punishment as well. "You know you are being monitored, you know you are being watched," said one. "But if I had to choose prison or the box, I choose the box."

In the Future

As satellite tracking technology becomes more advanced, corrections agencies will have the ability to keep an "electronic eye" on convicts at all times, calling up a visual image whenever necessary.

For more information on satellite tracking and other CJ technologies, click on Web Links *under* Book Resources *at* www.cjinaction.com

The Future of Community Corrections

It should be noted that although the theoretical basis for intermediate sanctions is widely recognized, relatively few offenders have been sentenced to such programs. Researchers Norval Morris and Michael Tonry believe that this is attributable to the prominence of retribution and incapacitation in our corrections system. Regardless of the scope of the crime, imprisonment is regarded as "just deserts" for criminal behavior. Furthermore, even if a judge believes that a crime is not serious enough to warrant imprisonment, he or she can be certain of one thing: an incarcerated offender, being locked up, is in no position to harm the general community (and the judge is not at risk of being blamed for releasing a repeat offender). Morris and Tonry believe these two modes of thinking will have to be overcome if intermediate sanctions are to play a more prominent role in criminal justice.[69]

NEW STRATEGIES

As in other areas of the corrections system, efforts to reform community-based corrections have concentrated on making sentencing procedures more standardized. **Continuum-of-sanctions** strategies envision a corrections system in which an offender is not sentenced to a single sanction, but moves from different levels of punishment depending on behavior. Each crime is assigned an "accountability

INFOTRAC KEYWORDS

community corrections

For more information, use this search term with InfoTrac College Edition, your online library at www.infotrac-college.com

Continuum of Sanctions
A corrections strategy in which offenders are not assigned a single punishment, but rather are initially sentenced based on their criminal acts and then moved toward harsher or more lenient forms of sanction depending on their behavior within the corrections system.

rating" that determines the initial sanction; the convict's compliance with the conditions of that sanction then determine whether she or he will move to more or less restrictive punishment. Continuum-of-sanctions strategies are attractive because they can be codified, reducing the discretion of sentencing officials. (See Figure 12.8 for an example of how a continuum-of-sanctions strategy might be carried out.)

Another innovation is the idea of *exchange rates*, where a certain number of days of community supervision would be equated to a single day of incarceration in a prison or jail. For example, authorities might determine that five days of house detention equal one day in prison or jail and structure the length of community-based supervision accordingly. Such exchanges would be made after the offender has been sentenced to prison or jail, hopefully reducing the net-widening effect of intermediate sanctions.[70]

FIGURE 12.8 Continuum of Sanctions: From Theory to Action

John X. has been convicted of forging checks. It is his second conviction for this crime in a two-year period, and he is sentenced to three years under correctional supervision. He will start his term in a medium-security prison, but, under a continuum-of-sanctions strategy employed by the county, he will not necessarily stay there.

Initial Accountability Level: 850
Status: Incarcerated in medium-security prison
Mobility in the Community: 0%
Amount of Supervision: 24 hours/day

After one year of good behavior:

New Accountability Level: 550
Status: Work-release program, spends nights and weekends at minimum-security prison
Mobility in the Community: 30% (restricted 40–50 hours/week)
Amount of Supervision: Daily phone contact, daily face-to-face

After one year, no further violations:

New Accountability Level: 250
Status: On probation, weekly community service, no drinking allowed
Mobility in Community: 90% (restricted 0–10 hours/week)
Amount of Supervision: 1–2 face-to-face/month, 1–2 phone contact/week

Two months later, misses scheduled meeting with probation officer following a night of drinking with friends:

New Accountability Level: 450
Status: Mandatory alcohol treatment program, confined to home at nights and on weekends
Mobility in the Community: 60% (restricted 30–40 hours/week)
Amount of Supervision: 2–6 face-to-face/week, daily phone contact

After four months without any further violations, John X. is returned to Accountability Level 250. Three more months of good behavior follow, and John X. is reclassified at Level 50 for the remainder of his term.

New Accountability Level: 50
Status: Unsupervised probation
Mobility in the Community: 100%
Amount of Supervision: None

Such a system benefits both John X. and the correctional system. John X. has an incentive to behave because he knows that if he does, the circumstances of his sentence will be more pleasant. The correctional system is able to move John X.—a nonviolent felon—out of a crowded prison into less restrictive options.

Source: Adapted from Norval Morris and Michael Tonry, *Between Prison and Probation: Intermediate Punishments in a Rational Sentencing System* (New York: Oxford University Press, 1990), 66–67.

THE PARADOX OF COMMUNITY CORRECTIONS

The problem with such strategies, say some observers, is that they fail to address the basic paradox of community-based corrections: the more effectively offenders are controlled, the more likely they are to be caught violating the terms of their conditional release. As you may have noticed, the community supervision programs discussed in this chapter are "graded" according to rates of recidivism and revocation, with low levels of each reflecting a successful program. Increased control and surveillance, however, will necessarily raise the level of violations, thus increasing the probability that any single violation will be discovered. Therefore, as factors such as the number of conditions placed on probationers and the technological proficiency of electronic monitoring devices increase, so, too, will the number of offenders who fail to meet the conditions of their community-based punishment.

One observer calls this the "quicksand" effect of increased surveillance. Instead of helping offenders leave the corrections system, increased surveillance pulls them more deeply into it.[71] The quicksand effect can be quite strong, according to researchers Barbara Sims of Sam Houston State University and Mark Jones of East Carolina University. In a study of North Carolina corrections data, Sims and Jones found that 26 percent of the probationers whose probation terms were revoked had been guilty of violations such as failing a single drug test. The researchers believe this strategy is overly punitive—anybody who has tried to quit smoking is aware of the difficulties of breaking an addiction.[72]

>Boot Camps: Do They Work?

One might say that the American corrections system is "between a rock and a hard place." On the one hand, prisons and jails do not have enough space for all the offenders being arrested by law enforcement agencies. On the other hand, as noted throughout this chapter, community corrections and intermediate sanctions, while lessening the pressure on prisons and jails, are regarded as insufficiently "tough" by many citizens and public officials. In this *Criminal Justice in Action* feature, we will examine what would seem to be the perfect corrections option—a "tough" intermediate sanction known as the **boot camp.**

Boot camps rely on tough, militaristic discipline to steer young and first-time offenders away from a criminal lifestyle.

AP Photo/Las Cruces Sun-News, Vladimir Chaloupka

Beyond Punishment

You are nothing and nobody, fools, maggots, dummies, mothers, and you have just walked into the worst nightmare you ever dreamed. I don't like you. I have no use for you, and I don't give a f*** who you are on the street. This is my acre, hell's half acre, and it matters not one damn to me whether you make it here or get tossed out into the general prison population, where, I promise you, you won't last three minutes before you're somebody's wife. Do you know what that means, tough guys?[73]

Such was the welcome a group of inmates received on arriving at boot camp. A form of shock incarceration, boot camp programs are modeled after military basic training, emphasizing strict discipline, manual labor, and physical training. Boot camps provide a short term of incarceration—usually between three and six months—for young, first-time offenders. The idea is that the program's intense nature makes it as punitive as a longer prison term. But boot camps promise more than punishment. They are designed to instill self-discipline, self-responsibility, and self-respect, thereby lessening the chances that the offender will return to crime on release. The first boot camp program appeared in Georgia in 1983. Within ten years, fifty-nine similar programs were operating in twenty-nine states. An important reason for this rapid growth has been public acceptance of boot camps.[74] In contrast to generally negative feelings about probation, a recent survey found that 78 percent of the respondents had a positive impression of boot camps as a form of alternative sanctioning. Boot camps seem to reflect commonly held beliefs that offenders should receive strict punishment, while also offering the chance of rehabilitation within a confined space. Politicians, not wanting to appear soft on crime, have reacted to this

Boot Camp

A correctional facility based on militaristic principles of discipline and physical conditioning; reserved primarily for juvenile and first-time offenders serving terms of less than six months, with the ultimate goal of deterring further criminal behavior.

support by earmarking funds to construct new camps. After a two-decade-long honeymoon period, however, many criminal justice participants are questioning whether boot camps deliver on all of their promises.

The Benefits of Boot Camp

Offenders are sent to boot camps either by the sentencing judge or by an official within the corrections agency. (In four states, the decision is made by a probation or parole officer.)[75] Though eligibility varies across jurisdictions (see Figure 12.9), most boot camps are restricted to young (though not necessarily juvenile) first-time offenders. In most cases, attending a boot camp is a voluntary decision, and the offender can leave at any time and finish the sentence in a jail or prison.

The McNeil Island camp in Washington State is typical of such programs. Approximately 125 inmates, aged eighteen to twenty-eight, spend eight hours a day doing menial labor such as pulling weeds and painting the ferries that travel to and from the island. This work is supplemented by a number of seminars, including adult education, anger management, planning for life after the program, and victim awareness. Inmates also receive

drug-abuse counseling and other treatments. The dropout rate from McNeil Island is 30 percent, even though completion of the four-month program can reduce a prison term by as much as a year.[76]

Besides the benefits for individual inmates, supporters of boot camps believe the programs are advantageous to society in three ways:

1 By reducing prison and jail overcrowding.
2 By saving costs associated with prison and jail terms.
3 By lowering recidivism rates among offenders.

The explanations behind these three supposed benefits are fairly straightforward. First, inmates placed in boot camps do not take up space in prisons and jails. Second, even though the average yearly costs of housing an inmate in a boot camp and in a prison are comparable, the term of a boot camp is much shorter and therefore less costly. Third, through improved self-discipline and treatment programs, inmates will change their behavior and therefore be less likely to commit further crimes on release from the camp.

Evidence to the Contrary

Few observers doubt that the boot camp experience is a positive one for those who complete it—inmates learn valuable life skills and receive treatment, options often not available in prisons and jails.[77] Statistical benefits have also been reported: the state of Illinois estimates that boot camp graduates have a recidivism rate of 21 percent, as compared to 34 percent for those on probation or those who have served time behind bars.[78]

Criminologists, however, are wary of claims that boot camps are fulfilling their mandates. A number of long-term studies seem to show that although boot camps do not have a negative impact, they are not a panacea for the ills of the corrections system. One of the earliest surveys of boot camp graduates, compiled in Louisiana, found no difference in recidivism rates between boot campers and convicts who were confined in traditional correctional facilities.[79] A national study by the Koch Crime Institute showed that recidivism among those who attended boot camp ranged from 64 to 75 percent, slightly higher than for those juveniles who were sentenced to adult prisons.[80] A more extensive study of boot camps, evaluating programs from 1992 to 2002, concluded that the overall effect of boot camps on recidivism was negligible.[81]

FIGURE 12.9 **Eligibility Requirements of Boot Camps**

1. Offender Status

Boot camps are for the most part limited to first-time, nonviolent offenders.

2. Age

States differ in their age requirements, as these examples show:

> Oklahoma: Under 25 years
> Illinois: Ages 17 to 29
> New York: Age 30 or under
> Kansas: Ages 18 to 25
> Maryland: Under 32 years
> California: Age 40 or under
> Tennessee: Ages 17 to 29

3. Sentence Length

As one of the primary goals of boot camps is to reduce prison overcrowding, those who are sent to boot camps are generally diverted from prison. Consequently, many states have specific requirements concerning the prison sentences that boot "campers" must have received. In Maryland, for example, boot camps are restricted to offenders who have been sentenced for no longer than 10 years and who have at least 9 months remaining on their sentences. Illinois requires offenders to have been sentenced for up to 5 years and Tennessee for up to 6 years.

Source: John K. Zachariah, "Correctional Boot Camps: A Tough Intermediate Sanction—Chapter 2," in *An Overview of Boot Camp Goals, Components, and Results* (Washington, D.C.: National Institute of Justice, 1996).

Common Criticisms

Similar doubts are raised concerning boot camps' ability to reduce costs and prison overcrowding. Researcher Dale G. Parent notes that when calculating the amount saved by sending inmates to boot camps instead of to prison, officials tend to account only for the goods consumed by offenders, such as food, clothing, and health care. These short-term savings amount to only a few dollars a day. To achieve substantial, long-term savings, prison populations must be reduced to the point where a cell block or even an entire facility can be closed.[82] This has yet to occur.

Parent uses similar arguments to counteract claims that boot camps reduce prison and jail overcrowding. First of all, boot camps suffer from the net-widening effect discussed earlier in the chapter; that is, the offenders sent to boot camps would most likely have been given probation if intermediate sanctions did not exist. Even when specific steps are taken to avoid "net widening," the results are negligible. When the New York State Department of Correctional Services designed its boot camps, all inmates were chosen from incoming prison populations—no net widening was possible. In its first five years, the department estimated that it had reduced the state's prison rolls by 1,540 inmates. During that same period, however, the prison rolls grew from 41,000 to 58,000, overwhelming the small gains made by the boot camps. To have an effect on either costs or overcrowding, Parent concludes, boot camp populations would have to be increased significantly, which would lessen their ability to treat individual offenders.[83]

The Future of Boot Camps

Boot camps have raised other concerns. Working in a boot camp can be a demanding task, and some observers believe staff stress and burnout lead to verbal and physical intimidation of offenders. Sometimes, these intimidation tactics break the bounds of legality. In Houston, for example, five drill instructors were indicted on felony charges after choking and beating inmates with their fists, feet, and broomsticks. When fourteen-year-old Anthony Hayes died after being exposed to 111-degree temperatures for five hours at an Arizona boot camp on July 1, 2001, it was the thirtieth "camper" death at such a program in the past two decades.[84] A lawsuit filed by five girls against South Dakota's now-closed State Training School in 2003 claimed, among a number of disturbing allegations, that they were sexually and physically assaulted by staff members, "hogtied" (forced to run in hand and leg restraints), and placed in hygienically unclean conditions of solitary confinement.[85] After her daughter died of dehydration in a Florida boot camp, one woman echoed the thoughts of many observers: "either regulate this industry or abolish it."[86]

Given the continued popular support for boot camps, it seems highly unlikely that they will be abolished. As long as the media portray these programs as "tough on prisoners," the political appeal of boot camps will continue to be high.[87] Unfortunately for supporters of this form of intermediate sanction, budgetary problems in a number of states, including Georgia, Illinois, and Pennsylvania, have forced officials to either postpone plans to build new boot camps or shut down existing ones.

MAKING SENSE OF BOOT CAMPS

1. Recall the four basic philosophical reasons for sentencing from Chapter 11—retribution, deterrence, incapacitation, and rehabilitation. How does each one apply to boot camps? In practice, which one seems to receive the most emphasis? Why?

2. What are the strengths of boot camps when compared to probation? What are the weaknesses of boot camps when compared to probation?

3. Some observers believe correctional boot camps can never be as effective as military boot camps because a person at a military boot camp is usually there voluntarily. Do you agree? What difference should that make?

INFOTRAC KEYWORDS
boot camps

For more information, use this search term with InfoTrac College Edition, your online library at www.infotrac-college.com

Chapter Summary

1 **Explain the justifications for community-based corrections programs.** The first justification involves reintegration of the offender into society. Reintegration restores family ties, encourages employment and education, and secures a place for the offender in the routine functioning of society. The other justification involves diversion; by diverting criminals to alternative modes of punishment, further overcrowding of jail and prison facilities can be avoided.

2 **Indicate when probation started to fall out of favor and explain why.** When both criminal justice practitioners and the public held the rehabilitative model in favor, probation was generally considered a valuable aspect of this treatment. Since about the 1950s and more seriously since the mid-1970s, retributive goals have become more important, and probation has fallen out of favor in some criminal justice circles. Nonetheless, two-thirds of those involved in the American corrections system are on probation at any given time.

3 **Explain several alternative sentencing arrangements.** In addition to a suspended sentence, which is in fact a judicial reprieve, there are three general types of sentencing arrangements: (a) split sentence probation, in which the judge specifies a certain time in jail or prison followed by a certain time on probation; (b) shock incarceration, in which a judge sentences an offender to be incarcerated, but allows that person to petition the court to be released on probation; and (c) intermittent incarceration, in which an offender spends a certain amount of time each week in jail or in a halfway house or another government institution.

4 **Specify the conditions under which an offender is most likely to be denied probation.** The offender (a) has been convicted of multiple charges, (b) was on probation or parole when arrested, (c) has two or more prior convictions, (d) is addicted to narcotics, (e) seriously injured the victim of the crime, or (f) used a weapon while committing the crime.

5 **Describe the three general categories of conditions placed on a probationer.** (a) Standard conditions, such as requiring that the probationer notify the agency of a change of address, not leave the jurisdiction without permission, and remain employed; (b) punitive conditions, such as restitution, community service, and home confinement; and (c) treatment conditions, such as required drug or alcohol treatment.

6 **Explain why probation officers' work has become more dangerous.** One reason is that probation is increasingly offered to felons, even those who have committed violent crimes. Additionally, because there are more guns on the streets, a probationer is more likely to be armed.

7 **Explain the three stages of probation revocation.** (a) The preliminary hearing, which usually takes place before a judge, during which the facts of the probation violation are presented; (b) the revocation hearing, during which the claims of the violation are presented as well as any refutation by the probationer; and (c) revocation sentencing, during which a judge decides what to do with the probationer convicted of violating the terms of probation.

8 **List the five sentencing options for a judge besides imprisonment and probation.** (a) Fines, (b) community service, (c) restitution, (d) forfeiture, and (e) pretrial diversion programs.

9 **Contrast day reporting centers with intensive supervision probation.** In a day reporting center, the offender is allowed to remain in the community, but must spend all or part of each day at the reporting center. While at the center, offenders meet with probation officers, submit to drug tests, and attend counseling and education programs. In contrast, with intensive supervision probation (ISP), more restrictions are imposed, and there is more face-to-face contact between offenders and probation officers.

ISP may also include electronic surveillance.

10 List the three levels of home monitoring. (a) Curfew, which requires that the offender be at home during specified hours; (b) home detention, which requires that the offender be at home except for education, employment, and counseling; and (c) home incarceration, which requires that the offender be at home at all times except for medical emergencies.

Key Terms

Questions for Critical Analysis

1 What is the major reason that probationers account for nearly two-thirds of all adults in the American corrections system?

2 Why did the Supreme Court rule against indefinite reprieves?

3 What benefit might arise from more coordination between police and probation officers?

4 Why don't probationers have all constitutionally defined due process rights during revocation procedures?

5 Is the small number of probation officers a reason that recidivism is high?

6 What happens to property that is forfeited by a convicted criminal?

7 What is the purpose of day reporting centers?

8 "Home confinement is only for rich criminals." Comment.

9 What does the term *widening the net* mean, and why is it important today?

10 What benefits are attributed to boot camps, and what is the evidence to support these proposed benefits?

TEST PREPARATION ONLINE

Go to www.cjinaction.com for tools to aid you in studying for your exams. Click on *Online Reviews* under *Chapter Resources* for an interactive review of each major section of this chapter. Under *Chapter Resources*, you will also find the *Chapter Outline*, *Chapter Summary*, *Flashcards*, *Glossary*, *Learning Objectives*, *Lecture Presentations*, *Concept Builder*, *Essay Questions*, and a *Tutorial Quiz*. You can also test yourself with a game of *Concentration* or the *Crossword Puzzle*.

Web Resources

Go to www.cjinaction.com for a wealth of online resources. Explore the *Internet Activities* and *Class Projects* under *Chapter Resources*. Check out the *Web Links* to access the Web sites mentioned in the text, as well as many others. You can also access recent perspectives by clicking on *CJ in the News* and *Terrorism Update* under *Course Resources*. If you'd like some mentoring, click on *Board of Mentors* under *Book Resources*.

For additional information, explore InfoTrac College Edition, your online library that offers complete full-length articles from thousands of scholarly and popular publications. Click on *InfoTrac College Edition* under *Chapter Resources* at www.cjinaction.com for a list of key words and InfoTrac exercises. Use the passcode that came with your book.

Suggested Readings

Clear, Todd R., Harry R. Dammer, and V. R. Cardozier, *The Offender in the Community,* 2d ed., Belmont, CA: Wadsworth Publishing, 2002. An everything-you-wanted-to-know book on community-based corrections. The authors survey the alternatives to incarceration, including boot camps, fines, house arrest, and electronic monitoring. They also focus on how to keep juveniles out of detention and in the community, an increasingly important question that the criminal justice system has struggled to answer. This is an especially useful resource for anybody interested in a career in community-based corrections.

Festervan, Earlene, *Survival Guide for New Probation Officers,* Lanham, MD:

American Correctional Association, 2000. This no-nonsense guide for new—or potential—probation officers is sponsored by the American Correctional Association. It addresses the pressing issues in a profession that has undergone dramatic changes over the past few decades: the ethics of probation, maintaining a relationship with clients, officer safety, court work, and the perils of paperwork. With the number of Americans on probation and parole surpassing four million, the demand for officers in this field is growing; this publication offers a "leg up" into the world of probation.

Notes

1. Bureau of Justice Statistics, *Probation and Parole in the United States, 2002* (Washington, D.C.: U.S. Department of Justice, August 2003), Table 7, page 6.
2. *Ibid.,* 1.
3. Michael Tonry, *Sentencing Matters* (New York: Oxford Press, 1996), 28.
4. Todd Clear and Anthony Braga, "Community Corrections," in *Crime,* ed. James Q. Wilson and Joan Petersilia (San Francisco: ICS Press, 1995), 444.
5. Corrections Task Force of the President's Commission on Law Enforcement and Administration of Justice (1967).
6. Paul H. Hahn, *Emerging Criminal Justice: Three Pillars for a Proactive Justice System* (Thousand Oaks, CA: Sage Publications, 1998), 106–108.
7. *Probation and Parole in the United States, 2002,* 1.
8. Paul W. Keve, *Crime Control and Justice in America* (Chicago: American Library Association, 1995), 183.
9. Andrew R. Klein, *Alternative Sentencing, Intermediate Sanctions and Probation,* 2d ed. (Cincinnati: Anderson Publishing Co., 1997), 72.
10. 242 U.S. 27 (1916).
11. Joan Petersilia, "Probation in the United States," *Perspectives* (Spring 1998), 32–33.
12. Barry A. Krisberg and James F. Austin, "The Unmet Promise of Alternatives to Incarceration," in John Kaplan, Jerome H. Skolnick, and Malcolm M. Feeley, *Criminal Justice,* 5th ed. (Westbury, NY: The Foundation Press, 1991), 537.
13. "National Report on Probationers Says Half Got Split Sentences," *Corrections Journal* (December 22, 1997), 7.
14. Joan Petersilia and Susan Turner, *Prison versus Probation in California: Implications for Crime and Offender Recidivism* (Santa Monica, CA: Rand Corporation, 1986).
15. 97 U.S. 1143 (1998).
16. Neil P. Cohen and James J. Gobert, *The Law of Probation and Parole* (Colorado Springs, CO: Shepard's/McGraw-Hill, 1983), Section 5.01, 183–184; Section 5.03, 191–192.
17. 534 U.S. 112 (2001).
18. *Ibid.,* 113.
19. Bureau of Justice Statistics, *Substance Abuse and Treatment for Adults on Probation, 1995* (Washington, D.C.: U.S. Department of Justice, March 1998), 11.

20. Carl B. Klockars, Jr., "A Theory of Probation Supervision," *Journal of Criminal Law, Criminology, and Police Science* 63 (1972), 550–557.
21. *Ibid.,* 551.
22. Hahn, 116–118.
23. "Most Probationers Have Contact with Probation Officers," *Crime and Justice International* (March 1998), 23.
24. Shawn E. Small, "Arming Probation Officers: Enhancing Public Confidence and Officer Safety," *Federal Probation* (December 2001), 25.
25. Patty Machelor, "Juvenile Probation Officer to Be Armed," *Arizona Daily Star* (September 23, 2002), B1.
26. Nicholas Riccardi, "Probation Dept. Divided over Rule Prohibiting Guns," *Los Angeles Times* (January 2, 1999), B1.
27. Bureau of Justice Statistics, *Special Report, Federal Offenders under Community Supervisions, 1987–1996* (Washington, D.C.: U.S. Department of Justice, August 1998), Table 6, page 5.
28. *Probation and Parole in the United States, 2002,* Table 4, page 4.
29. "Put the Prison Bed Idea to Rest," *Dallas Morning News* (January 19, 2001), A28.
30. 483 U.S. 868, 874 (1987).
31. 389 U.S. 128 (1967).
32. *Morrissey v. Brewer,* 408 U.S. 471 (1972); *Gagnon v. Scarpelli,* 411 U.S. 778 (1973).
33. 465 U.S. 420 (1984).
34. Quoted in John J. DiIulio, Jr., "Reinventing Parole and Probation," *Brookings Review* 5 (Spring 1997), 43.
35. Charles Linder and Robert L. Bonn, "Probation Officer Victimization and Fieldwork Practices: Results of a National Study," *Federal Probation* (June 1996), 16.
36. Joan Petersilia, "Community Corrections," in *Crime: Public Policies for Crime Control,* ed. James Q. Wilson and Joan Petersilia (Oakland, CA: ICS Press, 2002) 483–508.
37. Patrick Langan and M. Cunniff, "Recidivism of Felons on Probation, 1986–89," *Special Report* (Washington, D.C.: U.S. Department of Justice, 1992).
38. Petersilia and Turner, vii.
39. William J. Bennett, John J. DiIulio, and John P. Walters, *Body Count: Moral Poverty and How to Win America's*

War against Crime and Drugs (New York: Simon & Schuster, 1996), 105.
40. *Ibid.*
41. Gayle R. Seigel and Joanne Basta, "The Effect of Adult Education Programs on Probationers," *Perspectives* (Spring 1998), 42–44.
42. James M. Byrne and Linda M. Kelly, *Restructuring Probation as an Intermediate Sanction: An Evaluation of the Massachusetts Intensive Probation Supervision Program* (Washington, D.C.: National Institute of Justice, 1989).
43. Todd R. Clear and George F. Cole, *American Corrections,* 4th ed. (Belmont, CA: Wadsworth Publishing Co., 1997), 179.
44. John P. Storm, "What United States Probation Officers Do," *Federal Probation* (March 1997), 13.
45. Robert M. Carter and Leslie T. Wilkins, "Caseloads: Some Conceptual Models," in *Probation, Parole, and Community Corrections,* ed. Robert M. Carter and Leslie T. Wilkins (New York: Wiley & Sons, 1976), 391–401.
46. Norval Morris and Michael Tonry, *Between Prison and Probation: Intermediate Punishments in a Rational Sentencing System* (Oxford, UK: Oxford University Press, 1990).
47. 18 U.S.C. Sections 1961–1968.
48. 516 U.S. 442 (1996).
49. "Duval's Counseling Program for Sex Offenders under Attack," *Tampa Tribune* (June 24, 1996), 2.
50. Laurence Hammck, "Drug Court to Recognize Those Who've Stayed Clean," *Roanoke Times & World News* (May 31, 1998), B1.
51. Jack McDevitt and Robin Miliano, "Day Reporting: An Innovative Concept in Intermediate Sanctions," in *Smart Sentencing: The Emergence of Intermediate Sanctions,* ed. James M. Byrne, Arthur Lurigio, and Joan Petersilia (Newbury Park, CA: Sage, 1992), 160.
52. Liz Marie Marcinak, "The Addition of Day Reporting to Intensive Supervision Probation: A Comparison of Recidivism Rates," *Federal Probation* (June 2000), 34.

53. Vada Mossavat, "Alternative to Area Jails Considerd," *Charleston Gazette & Daily Mail* (May 21, 2002), P1A.

54. Joan Petersilia and Susan Turner, *Intensive Supervision for High-Risk Probationers: Findings from Three California Experiments* (Santa Monica, CA: Rand Corporation, 1990).

55. Betsy Fulton, Edward J. Latessa, Amy Stichman, and Lawrence F. Travis, "The State of ISP: Research and Policy Implications," *Federal Probation* (December 1997), 65.

56. See Peter Jones, "Expanding the Use of Non-Custodial Sentencing Options: An Evaluation of the Kansas Community Corrections Act," *Howard Journal* 29 (1990), 114–129.

57. Dale Parent, *Shock Incarceration: An Overview of Existing Programs* (Washington, D.C.: U.S. Department of Justice, 1989).

58. Candice Chung, "Cigarette Money Will Fund Juvenile Program," *Idaho Statesman* (May 9, 1997), 2B.

59. *Ibid.*

60. Josh Kurtz, "New Growth in a Captive Market," *New York Times* (December 31, 1989), 12.

61. Jennifer Lee, "Putting Parolees on a Tighter Leash," *New York Times* (January 31, 2002), section 6, page 7.

62. Russell Carlisle, "Electronic Monitoring as an Alternative Sentencing Tool," *Georgia State Bar Journal* 24 (1988), 132.

63. Joan Petersilia, *Expanding Options for Criminal Sentencing* (Santa Monica, CA: Rand Corporation, 1987).

64. Terry Baumer and Robert Mendelsohn, "Electronically Monitored Home Confinement: Does It Work?" in *Smart Sentencing: The Emergence of Intermediate Sanctions,* ed. James M. Byrne, Arthur Lurigio, and Joan Petersilia (Newbury Park, CA: Sage, 1992).

65. Joseph B. Vaughn, "Planning for Change: The Use of Electronic Monitoring as a Correctional Alternative," in *Intermediate Punishments: Intensive Supervision, Home Confinement, and Electronic Surveillance,* ed. Belinda R. McCarthy (Monsey, NY: Criminal Justice Press, 1987), 158.

66. Terry Baumer and Robert Mendelsohn, *The Electronic Monitoring of Nonviolent Convicted Felons* (Washington, D.C.: National Institute of Justice, 1992).

67. Michael Tonry and Mary Lynch, "Intermediate Sanctions" in *Crime and Justice,* vol. 20, ed. Michael Tonry (Chicago: University of Chicago Press, 1996), 99.

68. Dennis Palumbo, Mary Clifford, and Zoann K. Snyder-Joy, "From Net Widening to Intermediate Sanctions: The Transformation of Alternatives to Incarceration from Benevolence to Malevolence," in *Smart Sentencing: The Emergence of Intermediate Sanctions,* ed. James M. Byrne, Arthur Lurigio, and Joan Petersilia (Newbury Park, CA: Sage, 1992), 231.

69. Morris and Tonry.

70. James M. Byrne and Mary Brewster, "Choosing the Future of American Corrections: Punishment or Reform," *Federal Probation* 57 (1993), 3–9.

71. Keve, 207.

72. Barbara Sims and Mark Jones, "Predicting Success or Failure on Probation: Factors Associated with Felony Probation Outcomes," *Crime & Delinquency* 43 (July 1997), 314–327.

73. Quoted in Doris L. Mackenzie and Claire Souryal, "A 'Machiavellian' Perspective on the Development of Boot-Camp Prison: A Debate," *University of Chicago Roundtable* 2 (1995), 435.

74. Teressa E. Ravenell, "Left, Left, Left, Right, Left: The Search for Rights and Remedies in Juvenile Boot Camps," *Columbia Journal of Law and Social Problems* (Summer 2002), 348.

75. United States General Accounting Office, *Prison Boot Camps: Short-Term Prison Costs Reduced, but Long-Term Impact Uncertain* (Washington, D.C.: U.S. General Accounting Office, 1993), 16.

76. Deborah Sharp, "Boot Camps—Punishment and Treatment," *Corrections Today* (June 1, 1995), 81.

77. Doris MacKenzie, *A National Study Comparing Boot Camps with Traditional Facilities for Juvenile Offenders* (Washington, D.C.: National Institute of Justice, August 2001), 3.

78. Sharp, 81.

79. Doris L. MacKenzie and Dale Parent, "Shock Incarceration and Prison Crowding in Louisiana," *Journal of Criminal Justice* 19 (1991), 231.

80. Brent Zaehringer, *Juvenile Boot Camps: Cost and Effectiveness vs. Residential Facilities* (Topeka, KS: Koch Crime Institute, 1998).

81. National Institute of Justice, *Correctional Boot Camps: Lessons from a Decade of Research* (Washington, D.C.: U.S. Department of Justice, June 2003), ii.

82. Dale G. Parent, "Boot Camps and Prison Crowding," in *Correctional Boot Camps: A Tough Intermediate Sanction,* ed. Doris L. MacKenzie and Eugeme E. Hebert (Washington, D.C.: National Institute for Justice, 1996).

83. *Ibid.*

84. Michael Janofsky, "Arizona Boot Camp Where Boy Died Re-opens," *New York Times* (September 7, 2001), A10.

85. Carson Walker, "One Girl Settles Boot Camp Case, Five Other Girls Head for Trial," *Associated Press Newswires* (October 7, 2003).

86. Mareva Brown, "4 Moms Rip Youth Boot Camps," *Sacramento Bee* (March 18, 1998), A1.

87. Adam Nossiter, "As Boot Camps for Criminals Multiply, Skepticism Grows," *New York Times* (December 18, 1993), 37.

Prisons and Jails

>chapter objectives<

After reading this chapter, you should be able to:

1 Contrast the Pennsylvania and the New York penitentiary theories of the 1800s.

2 List the factors that have caused the prison population to grow dramatically in the last several decades.

3 Explain the three general models of prisons.

4 List and briefly explain the four types of prisons.

5 Contrast formal with informal prison management systems.

6 List the reasons why private prisons can be run more cheaply than public ones.

7 Summarize the distinction between jails and prisons, and indicate the importance of jails in the American correctional system.

8 Explain how jails are administered.

9 Indicate the difference between traditional jail design and new-generation jail design.

10 Indicate some of the consequences of our high rates of incarceration.

The Largest Corrections System in the World

Sir Henry Alfred McCardie, the famed English jurist, once said, "Trying a man is easy, as easy as falling off a log, compared with deciding what to do with him when he has been found guilty." In the

American criminal justice system, to a certain extent, the decision has been simplified: many of the guilty go behind bars. The United States has the largest corrections system in the world. One out of every 143 Americans is in a federal or state prison or in a local jail. On June 30, 2002, the number of inmates in American prisons and jails passed the two million mark for the first time. The United States now locks up six times as many of its citizens as Canada does, and seven times as many as most European democracies. In fact, recent years have seen this country move past Russia to lay claim to the title of "the world's leading incarcerator."

For the most part, this high rate of imprisonment is a product of the past thirty years. From the 1920s until 1970, America's incarceration rates remained fairly stable at 110 per 100,000. Over the past three decades, the jail and prison population of the United States increased by nearly 700 percent. There is, it must be noted, some evidence that the growth rate of the nation's incarcerated population is beginning to slow down. The average annual growth of the nation's prison population dropped from 6.7 percent in 1995 to 2.6 percent in 2002; the 1.1 percent growth rate in 2001 was the lowest in three decades. Some corrections experts believe that this slowed growth is a result of the decline in crime rates in the 1990s: with fewer people committing crimes, fewer people will go to prison. Others point to a number of new state laws under which those convicted of drug possession are sent to treatment programs rather than prison or jail.

AP Photo/Kevin Glackmeyer

Inside Tutwiler Women's Prison in Wetumpka, Alabama, a handful of the two million inmates incarcerated in the United States pass time.

> **A few years of** slower growth cannot reverse a decades-long trend, however. The American corrections system remains a massive institution.[1] Throughout the course of this textbook, we have discussed many of the social and political factors that help explain the prison population "boom" of the past thirty years.

In this chapter and the next, we turn our attention to the incarceration system itself. This chapter focuses on the history and organizational structures of prisons (which generally hold those who have committed serious felonies for long periods of time) and jails (which generally hold those who have committed less serious felonies and misdemeanors, and those awaiting trial, for short periods of time). Though the two terms are often used interchangeably, they refer to two very different institutions, each with its own responsibilities and its own set of seemingly unsolvable problems.

▶ CONCEPT BUILDER

The medical model of "treating" criminals is the foundation of various alternatives to incarceration. Visit www.cjinaction.com for an interactive exploration of this key topic.

A Short History of American Prisons

Today, we view prisons as instruments of punishment; the loss of freedom imposed on inmates is society's retribution for the crimes they have committed. This has not always been the function of incarceration. The prisons of eighteenth-century England, known as "bridewells" after London's Bridewell Palace, actually had little to do with punishment. These facilities were mainly used to hold debtors or those awaiting trial, execution, or banishment from the community. (In many ways, as shall be made clear, these facilities resemble the modern jail.) English courts generally imposed one of two sanctions on convicted felons: they turned them loose, or they executed them.[2] To be sure, most felons were released, pardoned either by the court or the clergy after receiving a whipping or a branding.

The correctional system in the American colonies differed very little from that of their motherland. If anything, colonial administrators were more likely to use corporal punishment than their English counterparts, and the death penalty was not uncommon in early America. The one dissenter was William Penn, who adopted the "Great Law" in Pennsylvania in 1682. Based on Quaker ideals of humanity and rehabilitation, this criminal code forbade the use of torture and mutilation as forms of punishment; instead, felons were ordered to pay restitution of property or goods to their victims. If the felons did not have sufficient property to make restitution, they were placed in a prison, which was primarily a "workhouse."[3] The death penalty was still allowed under the "Great Law," but only in cases of premeditated murder. Penn proved to be an exception, however, and the path to reform was much slower in the colonies than in England.

WALNUT STREET PRISON: THE FIRST PENITENTIARY

On Penn's death in 1718, the "Great Law" was rescinded in favor of a harsher criminal code, similar to those of the other colonies. At the time of the American Revolution, however, the Quakers were instrumental in the first wide swing of the incarceration pendulum from punishment to rehabilitation. In 1776, Pennsylvania passed legislation ordering that offenders be reformed through treatment and discipline rather than simply beaten or executed.[4] Several states, including Massachusetts and New York, quickly followed Pennsylvania's example.

Pennsylvania continued its reformist ways by opening the country's first **penitentiary** in a wing of Philadelphia's Walnut Street Jail in 1790. The penitentiary operated on the assumption that silence and labor provided the best hope of rehabilitating the criminal spirit. Remaining silent would force the prisoners to think about their crimes, and eventually the weight of conscience would lead to

Penitentiary
An early form of correctional facility that emphasized separating inmates from society and from each other so that they would have an environment in which to reflect on their wrongdoing and ponder their reformation.

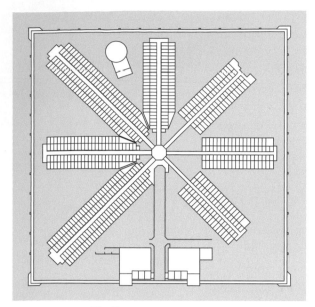

FIGURE 13.1 The Eastern Penitentiary

The Eastern Penitentiary opened in 1829 with the controversial goal of changing the behavior of inmates instead of merely punishing them. An important component of this goal was the layout of the facility. As you can see, the Eastern Penitentiary was designed in the form of a "wagon wheel," known today as the radial style. The back-to-back cells in each "spoke" of the wheel faced outward from the center to limit contact between inmates. About three hundred prisons worldwide have been built based on this design.

Separate Confinement

A nineteenth-century penitentiary system developed in Pennsylvania in which inmates were kept separate from each other at all times, with daily activities taking place in individual cells.

Congregate System

A nineteenth-century penitentiary system developed in New York in which inmates were kept in separate cells during the night but worked together in the daytime under a code of enforced silence.

repentance. At the same time, enforced labor would attack the problem of idleness—regarded as the main cause of crime by penologists of the time.[5] Consequently, inmates at Walnut Street were isolated from one another in solitary rooms and kept busy with constant menial chores.

Eventually, the penitentiary at Walnut Street succumbed to the same problems that continue to plague institutions of confinement: overcrowding and excessive costs. As an influx of inmates forced more than one person to be housed in a room, silence became a nearly impossible condition. By the early 1800s, officials could not find work for all of the convicts, so many were left idle.

THE GREAT PENITENTIARY RIVALRY: PENNSYLVANIA VERSUS NEW YORK

The apparent lack of success at Walnut Street did little to dampen enthusiasm for the penitentiary concept. Throughout the first half of the nineteenth century, a number of states reacted to prison overcrowding by constructing new penitentiaries. Each state tended to have its own peculiar twist on the roles of silence and labor, and two such systems—those of Pennsylvania and New York—emerged to shape the debate over the most effective way to run a prison.

The Pennsylvania System   After the failure of Walnut Street, Pennsylvania constructed two new prisons: the Western Penitentiary near Pittsburgh (opened in 1826) and the Eastern Penitentiary in Cherry Hill, near Philadelphia (1829). The Pennsylvania system took the concept of silence as a virtue to new extremes. Based on the idea of **separate confinement,** these penitentiaries were constructed with back-to-back cells facing both outward and inward. (See Figure 13.1 for the layout of the original Eastern Penitentiary.) To spare each inmate from the corrupting influence of the others, prisoners worked, slept, and ate alone in their cells. Their only contact with other human beings came in the form of religious instruction from a visiting clergyman or prison official.[6]

The New York System   If Pennsylvania's prisons were designed to transform wrongdoers into honest citizens, those in New York focused on obedience. When New York's Newgate Prison (built in 1791) became overcrowded, the state authorized the construction of Auburn Prison, which opened in 1816. Auburn initially operated under many of the same assumptions that guided the penitentiary at Walnut Street. Solitary confinement, however, seemed to lead to an inordinate amount of sickness, insanity, and even suicide among inmates, and it was abandoned in 1822. Nine years later, Elam Lynds became warden at Auburn and instilled the **congregate system,** also known as the Auburn system. Like Pennsylvania's separate confinement system, the congregate system was based on silence and labor. At Auburn, however, inmates worked and ate together, with silence enforced by prison guards.[7]

If either state can be said to have "won" the debate, it was New York. The Auburn system proved more popular, and a majority of the new prisons built during the first half of the nineteenth century followed New York's lead, though mainly for economic reasons rather than philosophical ones. New York's penitentiaries were cheaper to build because they did not require so much space. Furthermore, inmates in New York were employed in workshops, whereas those in Pennsylvania toiled alone in their cells. Consequently, the Auburn system was better positioned to exploit prison labor in the early years of widespread factory production.

INFOTRAC KEYWORDS

prisons, prison construction

For more information, use these search terms with InfoTrac College Edition, your online library at www.infotrac-college.com

THE REFORMERS AND THE PROGRESSIVES

The Auburn system did not go unchallenged. In the 1870s, a group of reformers argued that fixed sentences, imposed silence, and isolation did nothing to improve prisoners; they proposed that penal institutions should offer the promise of early release as a prime tool for rehabilitation. Echoing the views of the Quakers a century earlier, the reformers presented an ideology that would heavily influence American corrections for the next century.

This "new penology" was put into practice at New York's Elmira Reformatory in 1876. At Elmira, good behavior was rewarded by early release, and misbehavior was punished with extended time under a three-grade system of classification. On entering the institution, the offender was assigned a grade of 2. If the inmate followed the rules and completed work and school assignments, after six months he was moved up to grade 1, the necessary grade for release. If, however, the inmate broke institutional rules, he was lowered to grade 3. A grade 3 inmate needed to behave properly for three months before he could return to grade 2 and begin to work back toward grade 1 and eventual release.[8]

Although other penal institutions did not adopt the Elmira model, its theories came into prominence in the first two decades of the twentieth century thanks to the Progressive movement in criminal justice. The Progressives—linked to the positivist school of criminology discussed in Chapter 2—believed that criminal behavior was caused by social, economic, and biological reasons and, therefore, a corrections system should have a goal of treatment, not punishment. Consequently, they trumpeted a **medical model** for prisons, which held that institutions should offer a variety of programs and therapies to cure inmates of their "ills," whatever the root causes. The Progressives were greatly responsible for the spread of indeterminate sentences (Chapter 11), probation (Chapter 12), community sanctions (Chapter 12), and parole (Chapter 14) in the first half of the twentieth century.

Medical Model

A model of corrections in which the psychological and biological roots of an inmate's criminal behavior are identified and treated.

Inmates of Elmira State Prison in New York attend a presentation at the prison auditorium. Zebulon Brockway, the superintendent at Elmira, believed that criminals were an "inferior class" of human being and should be treated as society's defectives. Thus, mental exercises designed to improve the inmates' minds were part of the prison routine at Elmira. To what extent do you believe that treatment should be a part of the incarceration of criminals?

THE REASSERTION OF PUNISHMENT

Even though the Progressives had a great influence on the corrections system as a whole, their theories had little impact on the prisons themselves, many of which had been constructed in the nineteenth century and were impervious to change. More important, prison administrators usually did not agree with the Progressives and their followers, so the day-to-day lives of most inmates varied little from the congregate system of Auburn Prison.

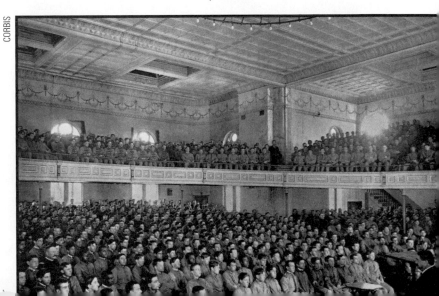
CORBIS

Academic attitudes began to shift toward the prison administrators in the mid-1960s. Then, in 1974, the publication of Robert Martinson's famous "What Works?" essay provided critics of the medical model with statistical evidence that rehabilitation efforts did nothing to lower recidivism rates.[9] This is not to say that Martinson's findings went unchallenged. A number of rebuttals arguing that rehabilitative programs could be successful appeared immediately after the publication of "What Works?"[10] In fact, Martinson himself retracted most of his claims in a little-noticed article published five years after his initial report.[11] Attempts by Martinson and others to "set the record straight" went largely unnoticed, however, as a sharp rise in crime in the early 1970s led many criminologists and politicians to champion "get tough" measures to deal with criminals they now considered "incurable." By the end of the 1980s, the legislative, judicial, and administrative strategies that we have discussed throughout this text had positioned the United States for an explosion in inmate populations and prison construction unparalleled in the nation's history.

✦ ONLINE REVIEW *Go to the book's Web site for an interactive review of this section*

The Prison Population Bomb

The number of Americans in prison or jail has almost tripled since 1985 and is continuing to rise, though at a slower rate, as mentioned earlier (see Figure 13.2). These numbers are not only dramatic, but also, say some observers, inexplicable, given the overall crime picture in the United States. In the 1990s, violent and property crime rates dropped; yet the number of inmates continued to rise. According to accepted theory, rising incarceration rates should be the result of a rise in crime, leaving one expert to comment that America's prison population is "defying gravity."[12] (See the feature *CJ in Focus—Myth versus Reality: Does Placing Criminals in Prison Reduce Crime?*)

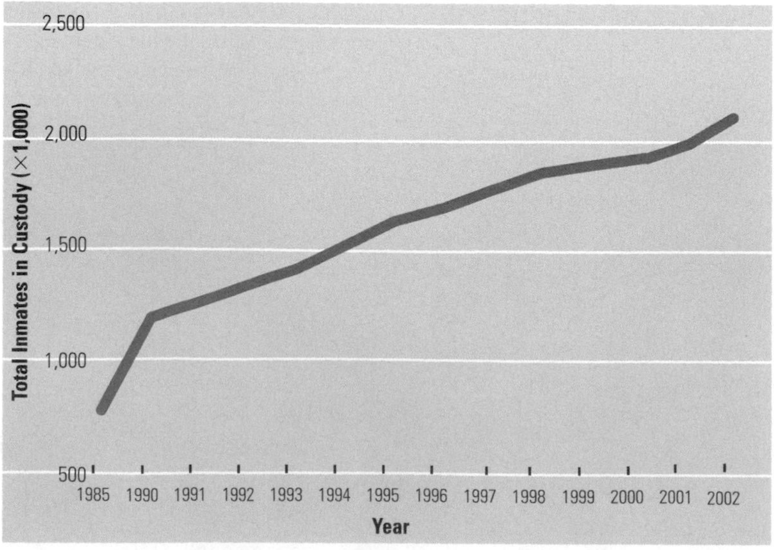

FACTORS IN PRISON POPULATION GROWTH

Alfred Blumstein of Carnegie Mellon University attributes much of the growth in the number of Americans behind bars to the enhancement and stricter enforcement of the nation's drug laws. Since 1980, he points out, the rate of incarceration for drug arrests in the United States has risen 1,000 percent, and there are more Americans in prison or jail for drug offenses today than there were for all offenses in the early 1970s.[13] In 1980, drug offenders accounted for 25 percent of the inmates in federal prison; today, they account for almost 60 percent.[14]

Other reasons for the growth in incarcerated populations include:

> *Increased probability of incarceration.* Simply stated, the chance of someone who is arrested going to prison today is much

FIGURE 13.2 The Inmate Population of the United States

The total number of inmates in custody in the United States has risen from 744,208 in 1985 to 2,019,234 in 2002.

Source: Adapted from Bureau of Justice Statistics, *Prison and Jail Inmates at Midyear 2002* (Washington, D.C.: U.S. Department of Justice, 2003), Table 1, page 2.

> Does Placing Criminals in Prison Reduce Crime?

Violent crime rates in the United States have been stable or declining in recent years. At the same time, as Figure 13.3 shows, the rate at which Americans have been imprisoned has climbed precipitously. The correlation between these two trends has become a subject of much discussion among crime experts.

The Myth

A popular view of incarceration is that "a thug in jail can't shoot your sister." Obviously, a prison inmate is incapable of doing any further harm to the community. By extension, then, as the number of criminals behind bars increases, the crime rate should drop accordingly.

The Reality

Numerous studies have shown that this is not always the case. Between 1985 and 1995, the prison population in the United States almost doubled, yet the number of all major violent crimes also increased. A study released in 2000 by the Sentencing Project, a research group in Washington, found that states that increased the number of prison inmates the most in the 1990s actually had less reduction in crime than those states with below-average increases in incarceration over the same time period. Louisiana has had the highest incarceration rates in the nation and also one of the highest rates of violent crime. At the other extreme, North Dakota has had both the lowest incar-

ceration rates and the lowest crime rates. Such statistics may show that other factors (particularly the social factors discussed in Chapter 2) play a more significant role in crime rates than the number of criminals who are incapacitated.

One theory offered to explain the apparent lack of positive correlation between rates of imprisonment and crime in general is the "replacement" hypothesis. Most crimes, especially those related to drug sales, are committed by groups of co-offenders, not by a single criminal. Consequently, when one member of the group is arrested, the criminal activity does not stop. Instead, the group merely recruits somebody else to take his or her place. Furthermore, there is widespread support for the idea that some inmates become hard-core criminals only after being exposed to prison culture and commit more crimes after being released from prison than they would have if they had never gone there in the first place.

Few observers would suggest that imprisonment rates have *no* effect on crime rates. Instead, criminologists seem to be cautioning that the relationship between the prison population and crime rates is not fully understood, and that public policymakers should not make laws on the assumption that more prisoners equals less crime.

FOR CRITICAL ANALYSIS
What other factors could explain the lack of positive correlation between incarceration rates and crime rates?

FIGURE 13.3 Comparing Crime Rates and Incarceration Rates
Source: Federal Bureau of Investigation and Bureau of Justice Statistics.

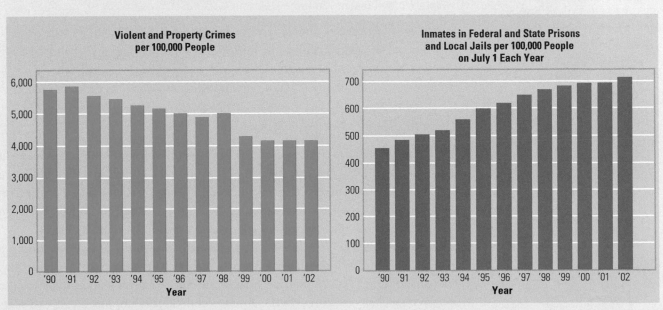

The `Federal Bureau of Prisons` is the largest incarceration system in the United States. Find its Web site by clicking on *Web Links* under *Chapter Resources* at www.cjinaction.com

greater than it was twenty years ago. Most of this growth took place in the 1980s, when the likelihood of incarceration after arrest increased fivefold for drug offenses, threefold for weapons offenses, and twofold for crimes such as sexual assault, burglary, auto theft, and larceny. These trends leveled off in the 1990s, though those arrested for murder, sexual assault, and weapons offenses still have a greater chance of going to prison or jail today than they did two decades ago.[15]

> *Inmates serving more time for each crime.* After the Sentencing Reform Act of 1984 (see Chapter 11), the length of time served by federal convicts for their crimes rose significantly. As noted in Chapter 11, in the twelve years after the law went into effect, the average time served by inmates in federal prisons climbed from thirty-nine months to fifty-four months—nearly a 40 percent increase.[16] Furthermore, six out of every ten defendants convicted of a federal drug offense receive a mandatory minimum prison term, with more than half of those sentenced to at least five years in prison.[17] State sentencing reform statutes and "truth-in-sentencing" laws have had similar consequences. In the thirty-two states that require their inmates to serve at least 85 percent of their sentence, for example, violent offenders are expected to spend an average of fifteen months more in prison than violent offenders in states without such laws.[18]

> *Federal prison growth.* Thanks in part to federal sentencing policy, the federal prison system is now the largest in the country with more than 150,000 inmates. In fact, since 1995 the federal prison population has been rising at a rate more than double that of state prisons (7.8 percent to 2.9 percent).[19] Besides the increase in federal drug offenders already mentioned, this growth can be attributed to efforts by Presidents Bill Clinton and George W. Bush to federalize gun possession crimes: from 1995 to 2001, the number of inmates sent to federal prisons for such crimes jumped by 68 percent.[20] Over that same time period, immigration law offenders increased by 133 percent; by 2002, they represented more than 10 percent of all federal inmates,[21] a situation we will discuss in more detail in Chapter 17.

As the name implies, `PrisonSucks.com` is highly critical of what it calls the "crime control industry." Find its Web site by clicking on *Web Links* under *Chapter Resources* at www.cjinaction.com

> *Rising incarceration rates of women.* In 1981, 14,000 women were prisoners in federal and state institutions; by 2002, the number had grown to 97,491. Women still account for only 6.8 percent of all prisoners nationwide, but their rates of imprisonment are growing twice as rapidly as those of men.[22]

THE PRISON CONSTRUCTION BOOM

The escalation in the prisoner population has brought with it an increased demand for new prisons. In 1980, the U.S. Bureau of Prisons had a budget of $330 million and operated forty-four prisons. Today, its budget is nearly $5 billion and there are 102 federal prisons. In the past two decades, nearly 1,000 new state prisons have been constructed.[23] In 1971, total corrections construction spending was $2.3 billion; today, it is nearly $50 billion.[24] These costs have pushed corrections' budgets to unprecedented levels. Eight states spend in excess of $1 billion each year on corrections-related services.[25] Indeed, for many states, the single largest item in their budgets is correctional expenditures. In the absence of politically unpopular tax increases, legislators are thereby forced to find another revenue source to pay for the new prisons. Thus, the opportunity cost of prison construction can be great—every dollar that goes to build a prison is a dollar that cannot be used to fund education programs, health care, and other social programs.

Legislative efforts have kept prison construction well financed. The 1994 Crime Bill allocated $10 billion in grants for the construction of new incarceration facilities through 2000.[26] Forty-five states are required by law and/or court order to keep crowding in prisons and jails below a certain level; therefore, as the number of inmates continues to increase, state corrections agencies are forced to build new facilities or find alternative forms of punishment such as the community-based sanctions discussed in Chapter 12.

AP Photo/Danny Johnston

The Ouachita River Correctional Unit in Malvern, Arkansas, opened in August 2003. The facility's 361 beds were filled immediately, but state corrections officials say more prison construction is needed to accommodate an inmate population that grows by fifteen to twenty people a day.

⬆ ONLINE REVIEW *Go to the book's Web site for an interactive review of this section*

The Role of Prisons in Society

The demands placed on penal institutions are hardly limited to providing tax and job benefits for the communities in which they are located. As University of Connecticut sociologist Charles Logan once noted, Americans expect prisons to "correct the incorrigible, rehabilitate the wretched . . . restrain the dangerous, and punish the wicked."[27] Basically, prisons exist to make society a safer place. Whether this is to be achieved through retribution, deterrence, incapacitation, or rehabilitation—the four justifications of corrections introduced in Chapter 11—depends on the operating philosophy of the individual penal institution.

Three general models of prisons have emerged to describe the different schools of thought behind prison organization:

> The *custodial model* is based on the assumption that prisoners are incarcerated for reasons of incapacitation, deterrence, and retribution. All decisions within the prison—such as what form of recreation to provide the inmates—are made with an eye toward security and discipline, and the daily routine of the inmates is highly controlled. The custodial model has dominated the most restrictive prisons in the United States since the 1930s.

> The *rehabilitation model* stresses the ideals of individualized treatment that we discussed in Chapter 11. Security concerns are often secondary to the well-being of the individual inmate, and a number of treatment programs are offered to aid prisoners in changing their criminal and antisocial behavior. The rehabilitation model came into prominence during the 1950s and enjoyed widespread popularity until it began to lose general acceptance in the 1970s and 1980s.

> In the *reintegration model,* the correctional institution serves as a training ground for the inmate to prepare for existence in the community. Prisons that

"To assert in any case that a man must be absolutely cut off from society because he is absolutely evil amounts to saying that society is absolutely good, and no one in his right mind will believe this today."

—Albert Camus, French author (1961)

have adopted this model give the prisoners more responsibility during incarceration and offer halfway houses and work programs (both discussed in Chapter 14) to help them reintegrate into society. This model is becoming more influential, as corrections officials react to problems such as prison overcrowding.[28]

Competing views of the prison's role in society are at odds with these three "ideal" perspectives. Professor Alfred Blumstein argues that prisons create new criminals, especially with regard to nonviolent drug offenders. Not only do these nonviolent felons become socialized to the criminal lifestyle while in prison, but the stigma of incarceration makes it more difficult for them to obtain employment on release. Their only means of sustenance "on the outside" is to apply the criminal methods they learned in prison.[29] A study by criminal justice professors Cassia Spohn of the University of Nebraska and David Holleran of East Tennessee State University found that convicted drug offenders who were sentenced to prison were 2.2 times more likely to be incarcerated for a new offense than those sentenced to probation.[30]

Maximum-Security Prison
A correctional institution designed and organized to control and discipline dangerous felons, as well as prevent escape, with intense supervision, cement walls, and electronic, barbed wire fences.

Types of Prisons

Prison administrators have long been aware of the need to separate different kinds of offenders. In federal prisons, this led to a system with six levels based on the security needs of the inmates, from level 1 facilities with the lowest amount of security to level 6 with the harshest security measures. (Many states also use the six-level system, an example of which can be seen in Figure 13.4.) To simplify matters, most observers refer to correctional facilities as being one of three levels—minimum, medium, or maximum. A fourth level—the supermaximum-security prison, known as the "supermax"—is relatively rare and extremely controversial due to its hyperharsh methods of punishing and controlling the most dangerous prisoners. (See the feature *Criminal Justice in Action—The End of the Line: Supermax Prisons* at the end of the chapter.)

MAXIMUM-SECURITY PRISONS

In a certain sense, the classification of prisoners today owes a debt to the three-grade system developed at the Elmira Penitentiary, discussed earlier in the chapter. Once wrongdoers enter a corrections facility, they are constantly graded on behavior. Those who serve good time, as we have seen, are often rewarded with early release. Those who compile extensive misconduct records are usually housed, along with violent and repeat offenders, in **maximum-security prisons.** The names of these institutions—Folsom, San Quentin, Sing Sing, Attica—conjure up foreboding images of concrete and steel jungles, with good reason.

FIGURE 13.4 Security Levels in Virginia

The security levels of correctional facilities in Virginia are graded from level 1 to level 6. As you can see, level 1 facilities are for those inmates who pose the least amount of risk to fellow inmates, staff members, and themselves. Level 6 facilities are for those who are considered the most dangerous by the Virginia Department of Corrections.

LEVEL	RESTRICTIONS
Level 1-Low	No Murder I or II, Robbery, Sex-Related crime, Kidnapping/abduction, Felonious Assault (current or prior), Flight/Escape, Carjacking, Malicious Wounding, No Escape Risk, No Disruptive Behavior
Level 1-High	No Murder I or II, Sex offense, Kidnap/Abduction, Escape history. No Disruptive Behavior for at least past 24 months.
Level 2	For initial assignment only. No escape history for past 5 years. No disruptive behavior for at least past 24 months prior to transfer to any less secure facility.
Level 3	Single, Multiple and Life + sentences. Must have served 20 consecutive years on sentence. No disruptive behavior for past 24 months for a transfer to any less secure facility.
Level 4	Single, Multiple and Life + sentences. No disruptive behavior for past 24 months for a transfer to any less secure facility.
Level 5	Same as level 4.
Level 6	Single, Multiple and Life + sentences. PROFILE OF INMATES: Disruptive, Assaultive, Severe Behavior Problems; Predatory-type behavior; Escape Risks; No disruptive behavior for past 24 months for a transfer to any less secure facility.

Source: Virginia Department of Corrections.

Maximum-security prisons are designed with full attention to security and surveillance. In these institutions, inmates' lives are programmed in a militaristic fashion to keep them from escaping or from harming themselves or the prison staff. About a quarter of the prisons in the United States are classified as maximum security, and these institutions house about 16 percent of the country's prisoners.

The Design Maximum-security prisons tend to be large—holding more than a thousand inmates—and they have similar features. The entire operation is usually surrounded by concrete walls that stand twenty to thirty feet high and have also been sunk deep into the ground to deter tunnel escapes; fences reinforced with razor-ribbon barbed wire that can be electrically charged may supplement or replace the walls. The prison walls are studded with watchtowers, from which guards armed with shotguns and rifles survey the movement of prisoners below. The designs of these facilities, though similar, are not uniform. Though correctional facilities built using the radial design pioneered by the Eastern State Penitentiary still exist, several other designs have become prominent in more recently constructed institutions. For an overview of these designs, including the radial design, see Figure 13.5 on the next page.

Inmates live in cells, most of them with similar dimensions to those found in the I-Max maximum-security prison for women in Topeka, Kansas: eight feet by fourteen feet with cinder block walls.[31] The space contains bunks, a toilet, a sink, and possibly a cabinet or closet. Cells are located in rows of *cell blocks,* each of which forms its own security unit, set off by a series of gates and bars. A maximum-security institution is essentially a collection of numerous cell blocks, each constituting its own prison within a prison.

Inmates' lives are dominated by security measures. Whenever they move from one area of the prison to another, they do so in groups and under the watchful eye of armed correctional guards. Television surveillance cameras may be used to monitor their every move, even when sleeping, showering, or using the toilet. They are subject to frequent pat-downs or strip searches at the guards' discretion. Constant "head counts" assure that every inmate is where he or she should be. Tower guards—many of whom have orders to shoot to kill in the case of a disturbance or escape attempt—constantly look down on the inmates as they move around outdoor areas of the facility.

Technology has added significantly to the power an institution holds over the individual prisoner. Walk-through metal detectors and X-ray body scanners can detect weapons or other contraband hidden on the body of an inmate. Ground-penetrating radar allows the correctional staff to search courtyards for buried items. Prison officials expect that within the next decade, electronic eye scans and non-invasive skin patches will be available to determine whether a prisoner has been using drugs.

Aging Foundations The advancing age of many maximum-security prisons is a major

INFOTRAC KEYWORDS
prison design

For more information, use this search term with InfoTrac College Edition, your online library at www.infotrac-college.com

This photograph shows the stark and austere quality of the Condemned Inmates Housing Adjustment Center (death row) at California's San Quentin Prison. Maximum-security prisons such as San Quentin are designed with one overriding concern in mind: control of inmates. Examine the photo and identify the various features of this area of San Quentin that show the facility's emphasis on security.

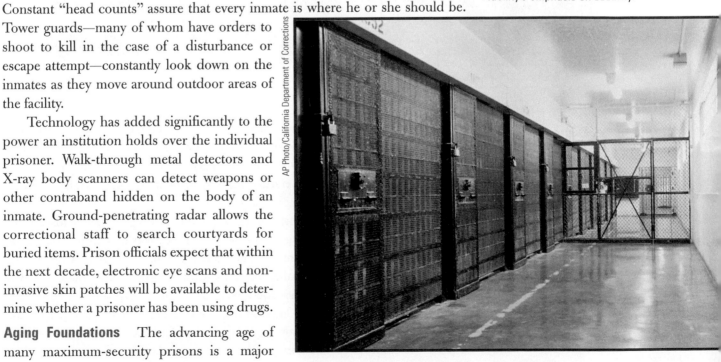

AP Photo/California Department of Corrections

FIGURE 13.5 **Prison Designs**

THE RADIAL DESIGN

The radial design has been utilized since the early nineteenth century. The "wagon wheel"–like form of the structure was created with the dual goals of separation and control. Inmates are separated from each other in their cells on the "spokes" of the wheel, and prison officials can control the activities of the inmates from the control center in the "hub" of the wheel.

THE COURTYARD STYLE

In the courtyard-style prison, a courtyard replaces the transportation function of the "pole" in the telephone-pole prison. The prison buildings form a square around the courtyard, and to get from one part of the facility to another, the inmates go across the courtyard. In a number of these facilities, the recreational area, mess hall, and school are located in the courtyard.

THE TELEPHONE-POLE DESIGN

The main feature of the telephone-pole design is a long central corridor that serves as a means for transporting inmates from one part of the facility to another. Branching off from this main corridor are the functional areas of the facility: housing, food services, workshops, treatment program rooms, etc. Prison officials survey the entire facility from the central "pole" and can shut off the various "arms" when necessary for security reasons. The majority of maximum-security prisons in the United States were constructed using this design blueprint.

THE CAMPUS STYLE

Some of the newer minimum-security prisons have adopted the campus style, a style that had previously been used in correctional facilities for women and juveniles. Like a college campus, housing units are scattered among functional units such as the dining room, recreation area, and treatment centers. The benefit of the campus style is that individual buildings can be used for different functions, making the operation more flexible. Due to concerns that the campus style provides less security than the other designs discussed, it is used for the most part only for medium- and minimum-security prisons.

Source: Text adapted from Todd R. Clear and George F. Cole, *American Corrections*, 4th ed. (Belmont, CA: Wadsworth Publishing Company, 1997), 255–256.

concern today. Given their size and the expense involved in their construction, these institutions were built to last, and many have achieved that goal. Fifty-four prisons constructed before 1900 are still in use. Illinois's Menard Correctional Center, for example, began operating in 1878 and experiences constant difficulties with outdated electric and plumbing systems.

Besides being inconvenient for staff and inmates, aging penal institutions increase the possibility of the most dangerous of all security situations: the escape. Six prisoners were able to tunnel out of the century-old State Correctional Institution near Pittsburgh, Pennsylvania, by drilling through the prison wall with a hydraulic jack. Though the escapees were eventually recaptured, state officials immediately budgeted $135.5 million for a new maximum-security prison that would have better sight lines from guard towers and enable corrections officers to exact more control over the inmates.[32]

MEDIUM- AND MINIMUM-SECURITY PRISONS

Medium-security prisons hold about 35 percent of the prison population and minimum-security prisons 49 percent. Inmates at **medium-security prisons** have for the most part committed less serious crimes than those housed in maximum-security prisons and are not considered high risks for escaping or causing harm. Consequently, medium-security institutions are not designed for control to the same extent as maximum-security prisons and have a more relaxed atmosphere. These facilities also offer more educational and treatment programs and allow for more contact between inmates. Medium-security prisons are rarely walled, relying instead on high fences. Prisoners have more freedom of movement within the structures, and the levels of surveillance are much lower. Living quarters are less restrictive as well—many of the newer medium-security prisons provide dormitory housing.

A **minimum-security prison** seems at first glance to be more like a college campus than an incarceration facility. Most of the inmates at these institutions are first-time offenders, nonviolent, and well behaved and include a high percentage of white-collar criminals. Indeed, inmates are often transferred to minimum-security prisons as a reward for good behavior in other facilities. Therefore, security measures are lax compared even to medium-security prisons. Unlike medium-security institutions, minimum-security prisons do not have armed guards. Prisoners are allowed amenities such as television sets and computers in their rooms, they enjoy freedom of movement, and they are allowed off prison grounds for educational or employment purposes to a much greater extent than those held in more restrictive facilities. Some critics have likened minimum-security prisons to "country clubs," but in the corrections system, everything is relative. A minimum-security prison may seem like a vacation spot when compared to the horrors of Sing Sing, but it still represents a restriction of personal freedom and separates the inmate from the outside world.

ONLINE REVIEW *Go to the book's Web site for an interactive review of this section*

PhotoEdit/A. Ramsey

Security measures—including television surveillance, pat-downs, and the constant attention of correctional officers in towers (pictured above)—dominate the lives of inmates in maximum-security prisons. How do guard towers contribute to the overall security of a prison facility? What might be some of the limitations of the guard tower as a security device?

Prison Administration

The security level of the institution generally determines the specific methods by which a prison is managed. There are, however, general goals of prison administration, summarized by Charles Logan as follows:

> The mission of a prison is to keep prisoners—to keep them in, keep them safe, keep them in line, keep them healthy, and keep them busy—and to do it with fairness, without undue suffering and as efficiently as possible.[33]

Considering the environment of a prison—an enclosed world inhabited by people who are generally violent and angry, and would rather be anywhere else—Logan's mission statement may be highly Utopian. A prison staff must supervise the daily routines of hundreds or thousands of inmates, a duty that includes providing them with meals, education, vocational programs, and different forms of leisure. The smooth operation of this supervision is made more difficult—if not, at times, impossible—by budgetary restrictions, overcrowding, and continual inmate turnover.

The implications of mismanagement are severe. While studying a series of prison riots, sociologists Bert Useem and Peter Kimball found that breakdowns in

Medium-Security Prison
A correctional institution that houses less dangerous inmates and therefore uses less restrictive measures to avoid violence and escapes.

Minimum-Security Prison
A correctional institution designed to allow inmates, most of whom pose low security risks, a great deal of freedom of movement and contact with the outside world.

INFOTRAC KEYWORDS

medium-security prisons, minimum-security prisons

For more information, use these search terms with InfoTrac College Edition, your online library at www.infotrac-college.com

managerial control commonly preceded such acts of mass violence.[34] During the 1970s, for example, conditions in the State Penitentiary in New Mexico deteriorated significantly; inmates who had become well organized and comfortable with their daily routines increasingly became the targets of harsh treatment from the prison staff, while at the same time a reduction in structured activities left prison life "painfully boring."[35] The result, in 1980, was one of the most violent prison riots in the nation's history. (To learn how new monitoring systems are helping prison administrators manage and control prison populations, see the feature *CJ and Technology—The Electronic Head Count*.)

FORMAL PRISON MANAGEMENT

In some respects, the management structure of a prison is similar to that of a police department, as discussed in Chapter 5. Both systems rely on a hierarchical (top-down) *chain of command* to increase personal responsibility. Both assign different employees to specific tasks, though prison managers have much more direct control over their subordinates than do police managers. The main difference is that police departments have a *continuity of purpose* that is sometimes lacking in prison organizations. All members of a police force are, at least theoretically, working to reduce crime and apprehend criminals. In a prison, this continuity is less evident. An employee in the prison laundry service and one who works in the visiting center have little in common. In some cases, employees may even have cross-purposes: a prison guard may want to punish an inmate, while a counselor in the treatment center may want to rehabilitate her or him.

Consequently, a strong hierarchy is crucial for any prison management team that hopes to meet Charles Logan's expectations. As Figure 13.6 shows, the **warden** (also known as a superintendent) is ultimately responsible for the operation of a prison. He or she oversees deputy wardens, who in turn manage the various organizational lines of the institution. The custodial employees, who deal directly with the inmates and make up more than half of a prison's staff, operate under a militaristic hierarchy, with a line of command passing from the deputy warden to the captain to the corrections officer.

Warden
The prison official who is ultimately responsible for the organization and performance of a correctional facility.

FIGURE 13.6 Organizational Chart for a Typical Correctional Facility

> The Electronic Head Count

I n Chapter 12, we saw how monitoring devices have changed the face of community corrections. Similar technology, though not as widespread, is beginning to have an equally dramatic effect on prison management. Called TSI PRISM, the monitoring equipment acts as a high-tech head count: inmates wear bracelets, while corrections officers wear small, pagerlike devices. Guided by a series of radio transmitters and receivers, the system is able to pinpoint the location of inmates and guards within twenty feet. Every two seconds, radio signals "search out" where each inmate and guard is, and relay this information to a central computer. On-screen, the inmate shows up as a yellow dot and the corrections officer as a blue dot on a grid of the prison. Administrators can quickly determine which inmates and officers are represented by each dot, and all movements are stored in a database for future reference, if necessary. "It completely revolutionizes a prison because you know where everyone is—not approximately but exactly where they are," says an official at the National institute of Justice.

In 2002, a new maximum-security juvenile prison in Michigan was outfitted with PRISM. The hope is that PRISM will end the "guessing games" that inevitably follow charges of assault—either physical or sexual—by one juvenile against another. With its tracing abilities, the system will allow corrections officials to immediately determine whether the accuser is telling the truth. "It's almost like having a videotape" of the attack, noted one official, "because you can track who was there." The bracelet is also tamper resistant, so if an inmate tries to remove it or damage it in any way, an alarm is immediately sent to the central computer system.

In the Future

Electronic monitoring experts predict that systems such as PRISM will soon be "customized" to fit the needs of any specific

AP Photo/Fred Greaves

Vincent Campos (above), a correctional officer at Calipatria State Prison in California, monitors inmates using the TSI PRISM system. Inmates wear electronic wrist bands so their movements can be tracked at all times.

prison population. So, for example, if officials are aware that two rival gangs exist, PRISM can be programmed to trigger an alarm when individual gang members come in close contact with each other. The bracelets could also be linked to satellite tracking systems, helping locate escaped convicts who manage to get outside the boundaries of the prison's radio transmitters.

 For more information on electronic monitoring of inmates and other CJ technologies, click on Crime and Technology *under* Book Resources *at* www.cjinaction.com

INFORMAL PRISON MANAGEMENT

Within the confines of the management structure, the personal philosophy of an administrator plays a significant role in prison management. Tara Gray and Jon'a F. Meyer of New Mexico State University illustrate this point by contrasting two influential prison administrators of the 1960s and 1970s.[36] George Beto, director of corrections in Texas for ten years, espoused the *control model* of administration, and Tom Murton, an Arkansas warden depicted in the 1980 film *Brubaker,* preferred the *participation model.*

Beto felt that by forcing inmates to abide by stringent prison rules, he was preparing them to follow the rules of society when they were released.

In the 1980 film *Brubaker,* Robert Redford, right, played Henry Brubaker, the new warden at an Arkansas prison. To get a first-hand view of how the prison is run, Brubaker disguises himself as an inmate. Brubaker tries to put an end to the corruption and violence he witnessed on the inside, only to be thwarted by the deep-seated resistance of prison officials and the local business community. Brubaker was loosely based on the real-life experiences of Tom Murton.

Consequently, Texas prisons under Beto were tightly controlled. Infractions such as talking in a loud voice were summarily—and, some said, cruelly—punished. Because Texas had only about half as many prison guards per convict as other states, Beto made widespread use of a practice in which selected inmates known as "building tenders" were given the status of guards or overseers in return for certain privileges. Building tenders had been employed in the South for nearly fifty years, and in many cases these inmate guards were more brutal than their state-employed counterparts.

In contrast, Murton felt that

Inmates cannot learn to dance by having their legs tied together. The only way to prepare them for life in a democracy is to expose them to democracy while they are incarcerated.[37]

In keeping with this philosophy, Murton allowed the inmates to govern some aspects of their prison lives. For example, he established inmate councils whose leaders were elected by the prisoners themselves. These councils were responsible for controlling inmate violence and making decisions such as who would be allowed to leave the prison on furlough. One criminologist, after visiting Murton's prison, stated that his theories would lead to a "renaissance in corrections."

The prediction failed to come true, not necessarily because Murton's ideas were invalid, but because the philosophy was rejected. Contemporary management practices frown on giving such power to inmates. As for Beto's system, building tenders were discontinued following the Texas prison reform lawsuit *Ruiz v. Estelle* (1977).[38] The fact that neither Beto's inmate guards nor Murton's inmate councils have survived suggests that prison management is an inherently conservative field. Most wardens have their hands full simply trying to run the prison, without attempting to "change the system"—even if the courts would let them. (See the feature *Careers in CJ.*)

ONLINE REVIEW *Go to the book's Web site for an interactive review of this section*

The Emergence of Private Prisons

In addition to all the other pressures placed on wardens and other prison administrators, they must operate within a budget assigned to them by an overseeing governmental agency. The great majority of all prisons are under the control of federal and state governments. The Federal Bureau of Prisons (BOP), part of the U.S. Department of Justice, operates more than one hundred prisons. The executive branch of each state is responsible for state prisons and, in some instances, jails. In the nineteenth century, not all correctional facilities were under the control of the state. In fact, the entire Texas prison system was privately operated from 1872 to the late 1880s. For most of the twentieth century, however, **private prisons,** or prisons run by private business firms to make a profit, could not be found in the United States.

Private Prisons
Correctional facilities operated by private corporations instead of the government and, therefore, reliant on profit for survival.

> Penny Lucero Warden

As warden of the New Mexico Women's Correctional Facility, I have executive oversight of the management and operation of the nation's first privately managed, multi-custody state prison. I became interested in corrections as a result of the employment opportunities made available with the state. When I entered the job market, I had received my undergraduate degree in psychology and completed work toward my graduate degree from New Mexico State University.

My corrections career began in 1981 with the New Mexico Department of Corrections, where I held a series of progressively more responsible positions, including training officer, ACA accreditation manager, and chief classification officer. In 1985, I became the first woman to be promoted to the rank of assistant warden at a male prison in New Mexico. In order to expand my experience to include juvenile corrections, I took the position of deputy superintendent at the Youth Diagnostic Center and New Mexico Girls' School.

Although I left corrections for a while to manage my own business, I realized that my true career had become corrections. Being my own boss had its "pros," but the "cons" had won my heart; I wanted to dedicate my energy, expertise, and leadership to corrections. Fortunately, Corrections Corporation of America was opening the new women's prison in Grants, and I was quickly recruited as a member of the management team. Joining this team of experienced corrections professionals is what I claim to be the catalyst that propelled me to the highest executive level of institutional leadership. The management team included three well-established professionals: two retired wardens from the New Mexico system and one nationally recognized warden of a female prison. All three became friends and mentors, always encouraging me to excel.

Working with adult female offenders and for a private company were both new experiences for me. The opening of the New Mexico Women's Correctional Facility was the first time the state had provided a purpose-built staffed and programmed facility specifically for female offenders. As program director, I had the opportunity to develop a wide array of state-of-the-art programs and services that would help prepare the women for a successful return to their communities.

As warden, I consider my major responsibilities to be maintaining a healthful, positive, safe, and mutually respectful environment for staff and inmates; establishing a working relationship with outside communities in order to assist with public education about offenders and the mutual benefit of working with them on release; participating in civic and professional organizations and encouraging the staff to do so; ensuring that the New Mexico Women's Correctional Facility meets established national correctional standards; and staying current on new management, program, and technology trends that can assist me in maintaining the standards of excellence established at the facility.

Penny Lucero

Prisons have changed dramatically over the past two decades. No longer "closed" communities where "outsiders" are unwelcome, they have become an extension of society, welcoming daily interaction with local citizens, elected officials, researchers, student interns, and volunteers in order to create a more normalized environment. Equally important is the commitment to assist offenders in preparing for a lawful return to society. To that end, correctional administrators are eager to recruit and retain creative, thoughtful, and industrious employees for rewarding careers in a lifetime of service to society.

 Go to the Careers in Criminal Justice Interactive CD *for more profiles in the field of criminal justice.*

That is certainly not the case today. With corrections exhibiting all appearances of, in the words of one observer, "a recession-proof industry," the American business community eagerly entered the market in the late 1980s and 1990s.[39] Fourteen private corrections firms operate nearly two hundred facilities across the United States. The two largest corrections companies, Corrections Corporation of America (CCA) and Wackenhut Corrections Corporation, are contracted to supervise nearly 85,000 inmates. In 1997, the BOP awarded the first contract paying a private company to operate one of its prisons—Wackenhut received $88 million to run the Taft Correctional Institution in Taft, California. By 2003, private penal institutions housed almost 94,000 inmates, representing 6.5 percent of all state prisoners and 12.4 percent of all federal prisoners.[40]

WHY PRIVATIZE?

It would be a mistake to automatically assume that private prisons are less expensive to run than public ones.[41] The incentive to privatize is, however, primarily financial. In the 1980s and 1990s, a number of states and cities saved operating costs by converting government-run services such as garbage collection and road maintenance to the private sector. Similarly, private prisons can be run more cheaply and efficiently than public ones for the following reasons:

> *Labor costs.* The wages of public employees account for nearly two-thirds of a prison's operating expenses. Although private corrections firms pay base salaries comparable to those enjoyed by public prison employees, their nonunionized staffs receive lower levels of overtime payments, workers' compensation claims, sick leave, and health-care insurance.

> *Competitive bidding.* Because of the profit motive, private corrections firms have an incentive to buy goods and services at the lowest possible price.

> *Less red tape.* Private corrections firms are not part of the government bureaucracy and therefore do not have to contend with the massive amount of paperwork that can clog government organizations.[42]

When the Arizona Department of Corrections compared three private prisons with fifteen public ones in the state, researchers found that the cost per day of incarcerating one person was $40.88 at a private facility and $45.85 at a public institution, a savings of 10.8 percent for private institutions.[43] A similar survey in Florida revealed not only that housing inmates in private prisons reduced the daily price tag by 10.5 percent, but that construction costs were 24 percent lower for private prisons than public ones.[44]

Executives at corrections firms claim that, because their contracts can be canceled for poor performance, private prisons have a greater incentive to provide higher-quality service than their public counterparts. At least one study, conducted by Charles Logan, supports this contention. Logan found that, according to statistical data and staff surveys, a private women's prison in New Mexico outperformed a state prison and a federal prison in a number of areas such as security, safety, living conditions, and management.[45] One reason a private prison might be expected to perform better than a public one is that the latter enjoys some immunity from civil liability suits. In other words, an aggrieved inmate can more easily sue a private prison in a civil court.[46]

THE ARGUMENT AGAINST PRIVATE PRISONS

Significantly, in Logan's study mentioned above, the inmates themselves gave the private prison lower scores than did the staff members. Opponents of private prisons worry that, despite the assurances of corporate executives, private corrections companies will "cut corners" to save costs, denying inmates important security guarantees in the process.

Financial Concerns   These criticisms find some support in the anecdotal evidence. U.S. District Judge Sam Bell of the Northern District of Ohio, for example, ordered CCA to devise a classification system to divert dangerous offenders after two inmates were killed and eleven others injured in a spate of stabbings at

INFOTRAC KEYWORDS

private prisons

For more information, use this search term with InfoTrac College Edition, your online library at www.infotrac-college.com

the company's medium-security facility in Youngstown, Ohio.[47] In 2001, two prison guards at Correctional System, Inc.'s Seal Beach City Jail in California were indicted and later fired for beating a drunken inmate who had been singing loudly in the jail's detoxification cell.[48] Wackenhut has also had problems with its facilities. Several years ago, the U.S. Department of Justice forced the company to relinquish one of its juvenile centers to the state of Louisiana after allegations that guards were physically and mentally abusing the young inmates, as well as using gas grenades to keep discipline. State police also had to be called to a Wackenhut facility in New Mexico after three hundred inmates rioted.[49]

An inmate is handcuffed prior to being removed from his cell at the Guadalupe County Correctional Facility in Santa Rosa, New Mexico. From 1998 to 2002, a corrections officer and four inmates were killed in New Mexico's private prisons, and several riots broke out at the facilities. What are some of the arguments against sending inmates to a privately run prison?

Furthermore, some observers note, if a private corrections firm receives a fee from the state for each inmate housed in its facility, would that not give management an incentive to increase the amount of time each prisoner serves? Though government parole boards make the final decision on an inmate's release from private prisons, the company could manipulate misconduct and good behavior reports to maximize time served and, by extension, profits.[50]

Philosophical Concerns   Other critics see private prisons as inherently unjust, even if they do save tax dollars or provide enhanced services. These observers believe that corrections is not simply another industry, like garbage collection or road maintenance, and that only the government has the authority to punish. In the words of University of Pennsylvania criminologist John DiIulio:

> It is precisely because corrections involves the deprivation of liberty, precisely because it involves the legally sanctioned exercise of coercion by some citizens over others, that it must remain wholly within public hands.[51]

THE FUTURE OF PRIVATIZATION IN THE CORRECTIONS INDUSTRY

Critics of private correctional facilities still hope to slow, and eventually stop, their growth. They believe that private prisons are constitutional contradictions and offer Article I of the U.S. Constitution as support. That passage states that "legislative powers herein granted shall be vested in a Congress of the United States." These powers include the authority to define penal codes and to determine the punishments that will be handed out for breaking the law. Therefore, a strict interpretation of the Constitution appears to prohibit the passing of this authority from the government to a private company.[52]

If the growth of private prisons and jails does slow, however, it appears that the motivation will be economic, not constitutional. For most of the past two decades, the primary clients for the private corrections industry have been state governments. In fact, five states (Alaska, Montana, New Mexico, Oklahoma, and Wyoming) house more than a quarter of their inmates in private facilities.[53] In the past few years, however, state budget problems have severely affected this relationship. In fact, since

GREAT DEBATES
Why privatize prisons? Does privatization of corrections provide taxpayers with a better service for a better price, or do private prisons deny inmates important guarantees of safety and general well-being? For more information on the issues in this debate, click on *Great Debates* under *Book Resources* at www.cjinaction.com

2000 no states have negotiated new contracts with private corrections firms, and several, including California, North Carolina, and Arkansas, have reduced their reliance on private incarceration.[54]

Although these developments have caused financial hardship for the private corrections industry (especially CCA, which almost went bankrupt in the early 2000s), it has found "a source of salvation" in the federal government.[55] As noted earlier, tougher drug and immigration laws have increased the number of federal prisoners dramatically, and the U.S. Bureau of Prisons has turned to private prisons to expand its capacity. New federal contracts valued at more than $100 million seem likely to ensure the health of the private prison industry for the foreseeable future.[56]

ONLINE REVIEW *Go to the book's Web site for an interactive review of this section*

Jails

Although prisons and prison issues dominate the public discourse on corrections, there is an argument to be made that jails are the dominant penal institutions in the United States. In general, a prison is a facility designed to house people convicted of felonies for lengthy periods of time, while a **jail** is authorized to hold pretrial detainees and offenders who have committed misdemeanors. On any given day, more than 668,000 inmates are in jail in this country, and approximately 7 million Americans spend at least a day in jail each year. Furthermore, the jail population has increased by more than 40 percent since 1990.[57] Yet jail funding is often the lowest priority for the tight budgets of local governments, leading to severe overcrowding and other dismal conditions.

Many observers see this negligence as having far-reaching consequences for criminal justice. Jail is often the first contact that citizens have with the corrections system. It is at this point that treatment and counseling have the best chance to deter future criminal behavior.[58] By failing to take advantage of this opportunity, says Professor Frank Zimring of the Earl Warren Legal Institute at the University of California at Berkeley, corrections officials have created a situation in which "today's jail folk are tomorrow's prisoners."[59]

THE FUNCTION OF JAILS

Until the eighteenth century, all penal institutions existed primarily to hold those charged with a crime until their trial. Although jails still serve this purpose, they have evolved to play a number of different roles in the corrections system. According to the Department of Justice, these roles include the following:

> Holding those convicted of misdemeanors.

> Receiving individuals pending arraignment and holding them while awaiting trial (if they cannot post bail), conviction, or sentencing.

> Temporarily detaining juveniles pending transfer to juvenile authorities.

> Holding the mentally ill pending transfer to health facilities.

> Detaining those who have violated conditions of probation or parole and those who have "jumped" bail.

Jail

A facility, usually operated by county government, used to hold persons awaiting trial or those who have been found guilty of misdemeanors.

> Housing inmates awaiting transfer to federal or state prisons.

> Operating community-based corrections programs such as home confinement and electronic monitoring.

Increasingly, jails are also called on to handle the overflow from saturated state and federal prisons. In Texas, for example, corrections officials were forced to rent a thousand county jail cells to house inmates for whom no space was available in state prisons.[60]

According to sociologist John Irwin, the unofficial purpose of the jail is to manage society's "rabble," so-called because

> [they] are not well integrated into conventional society, they are not members of conventional social organizations, they have few ties to conventional social networks, and they are carriers of unconventional values and beliefs.[61]

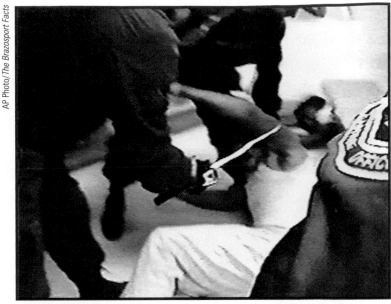

Local sheriffs' deputies strike an inmate of the Brazoria County Detention Center in Clute, Texas, with a baton. After viewing the video from which this scene was taken, the FBI began an investigation into possible civil rights violations at the jail. Guard-on-inmate violence is only one of the problems plaguing the nation's jails, others being inmate-on-inmate violence, poor living conditions, and inadequate health-care facilities. Yet jail issues do not receive nearly the same attention as prison issues. Why might this be the case?

In Irwin's opinion, "rabble" who act violently are arrested and sent to prison. The jail is reserved for merely offensive rabble, whose primary threat to society lies in their failure to conform to its behavioral norms. This concept has been used by some critics of American corrections to explain the disproportionate number of poor and minority groups who may be found in the nation's jails at any time.

THE JAIL POPULATION

Almost 90 percent of jail inmates in the United States are male. As in other areas of corrections, however, women are becoming more numerous. Since 1995, the adult female jail population has grown at an annual rate of 5.9 percent, compared to 3.8 percent for males.[62] Jails also follow the general corrections pattern in that a disproportionate number of their inmates are members of minority groups. (For an overview of the characteristics of the jail population, see Figure 13.7 on the next page.)

Pretrial Detainees As you can see in Figure 13.7, a significant number of those detained in jails technically are not prisoners. They are **pretrial detainees** who have been arrested by the police and, for a variety of reasons that we discussed in Chapter 9, are unable to post bail. Pretrial detainees are, in many ways, walking legal contradictions. According to the U.S. Constitution, they are innocent until proven guilty. At the same time, by being incarcerated while awaiting trial, they are denied a number of personal freedoms and are subjected to the poor conditions of many jails. In 1979, the Supreme Court rejected the notion that this situation is inherently unfair by refusing to give pretrial detainees greater legal protections than sentenced jail inmates have.[63] (See the feature *CJ in Focus—Landmark Cases: Bell v. Wolfish* on page 457.)

Pretrial Detainees
Individuals who cannot post bail after arrest and are therefore forced to spend the time prior to their trial incarcerated in jail.

Sentenced Jail Inmates According to the Department of Justice, 40 percent of those in jail have been convicted of their current charge.[64] In other words, they have been found guilty of a crime, usually a misdemeanor, and sentenced to time in jail.

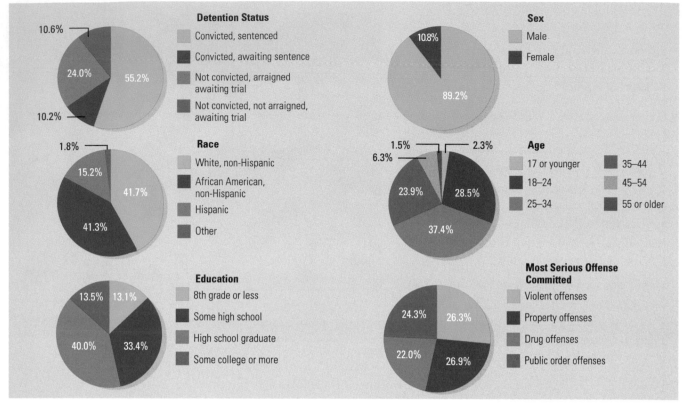

Detention Status
- Convicted, sentenced
- Convicted, awaiting sentence
- Not convicted, arraigned awaiting trial
- Not convicted, not arraigned, awaiting trial

10.6%
24.0%
55.2%
10.2%

Sex
- Male
- Female

10.8%
89.2%

Race
- White, non-Hispanic
- African American, non-Hispanic
- Hispanic
- Other

1.8%
15.2%
41.7%
41.3%

Age
- 17 or younger
- 18–24
- 25–34
- 35–44
- 45–54
- 55 or older

1.5%
2.3%
6.3%
23.9%
28.5%
37.4%

Education
- 8th grade or less
- Some high school
- High school graduate
- Some college or more

13.5%
13.1%
40.0%
33.4%

Most Serious Offense Committed
- Violent offenses
- Property offenses
- Drug offenses
- Public order offenses

24.3%
26.3%
22.0%
26.9%

FIGURE 13.7 The Characteristics of America's Jail Population

Source: Bureau of Justice Statistics, *Profile of Jail Inmates 1996* (Washington, D.C.: U.S. Department of Justice, April 1998), 1–4; and Bureau of Justice Statistics, *Census of Jails, 1999* (Washington, D.C.: U.S. Department of Justice, 2001), 22.

Time Served

The period of time a person denied bail has spent in jail prior to his or her trial. If the suspect is found guilty and sentenced to a jail or prison term, the judge will often lessen the duration of the sentence based on the amount of time served as a pretrial detainee.

The typical jail term lasts between thirty and ninety days, and rarely does a prisoner spend more than one year in jail for any single crime. Often, a judge will credit the length of time the convict has spent in detention waiting for trial—known as **time served**—toward his or her sentence. This practice acknowledges two realities of jails:

1 Terms are generally too short to allow the prisoner to gain any benefit (that is, rehabilitation) from the jail's often limited or nonexistent treatment facilities. Therefore, the jail term can serve no other purpose than to punish the wrong-doer. (Judges who believe jail time can serve purposes of deterrence and incapacitation may not agree with this line of reasoning.)

2 Jails are chronically overcrowded, and judges need to clear space for new offenders.

Other Jail Inmates Pretrial detainees and misdemeanants make up the vast majority of the jail population. As mentioned earlier, jail inmates also include felons either waiting for transfer or assigned to jails because of prison overcrowding, probation and parole violators, the mentally ill, and juveniles. In addition, jails can hold those who require incarceration but do not "fit" anywhere else. A material witness or an attorney in a trial who refuses to follow the judge's instructions may, for example, be held in contempt of court and sent to jail.

JAIL ADMINISTRATION

Of the nearly 3,300 jails in the United States, more than 2,700 are operated on a county level by an elected sheriff. Most of the remaining 600 are under the control of municipalities, although eight state governments (Alaska, Connecticut,

> *Bell v. Wolfish*

In a class-action suit, several pretrial detainees in the Metropolitan Corrections Center in New York City challenged the constitutionality of the conditions under which they were being held. The practices under dispute included placing two inmates in cells designed for one ("double-bunking"), restricting books and magazines, and intrusive body searches. The basis of the plaintiffs' argument was that, as pretrial detainees, they should not be subjected to the same terms of confinement as those persons in the jail who had been convicted of crimes. Both the district court and the court of appeals agreed with the plaintiffs. In addressing the case, the Supreme Court focused on whether the Constitution indeed could be seen to require different treatment of those who were awaiting trial and those who had been convicted.

Bell v. Wolfish
United States Supreme Court
441 U.S. 520 (1979)
http://laws.findlaw.com/US/441/520.html

> **In the words of the court . . .**

Justice Rehnquist, majority opinion

* * * *

The presumption of innocence is a doctrine that allocates the burden of proof in criminal trials; * * *. But it has no application to a determination of the rights of a pretrial detainee during confinement before his trial has even begun.

* * * *

[T]he Government concededly may detain [a person] to ensure his presence at trial and may subject him to the restrictions and conditions of the detention facility so long as those conditions and restrictions do not amount to punishment, or otherwise violate the Constitution.* * * Whether it be called a jail, a prison, or a custodial center, the purpose of the facility is to detain. Loss of freedom of choice and privacy are inherent incidents of confinement in such a facility. And the fact that such detention interferes with the detainee's understandable desire to live as comfortably as possible and with as little restraint as possible during confinement does not convert the conditions or restrictions of detention into "punishment."

* * * *

[M]aintaining institutional security and preserving internal order and discipline are essential goals that may require limitation or retraction of the retained constitutional rights of both convicted prisoners and pretrial detainees. * * * Prison officials must be free to take appropriate action to ensure the safety of inmates and corrections personnel and to prevent escape or unauthorized entry. Accordingly, we have held that even when an institutional restriction infringes a specific constitutional guarantee, such as the First Amendment, the practice must be evaluated in the light of the central objective of prison administration, safeguarding institutional security.

* * * *

Judges, after all, are human. They, no less than others in our society, have a natural tendency to believe that their individual solutions to often intractable problems are better and more workable than those of the persons who are actually charged with and trained in the running of the particular institution under examination. But under the Constitution, the first question to be answered is not whose plan is best, but in what branch of the Government is lodged the authority to initially devise the plan. This does not mean that constitutional rights are not to be scrupulously observed. It does mean, however, that the inquiry of federal courts into prison management must be limited to the issue of whether a particular system violates any prohibition of the Constitution or, in the case of a federal prison, a statute. The wide range of "judgment calls" that meet constitutional and statutory requirements are confided to officials outside of the Judicial Branch of Government.

> **Decision**

The Court reversed the court of appeals's ruling, holding that the possible innocence of pretrial detainees does not prevent corrections officials from taking any steps necessary to manage jails and maintain security. In a larger sense, the *Bell* decision is seen as giving corrections officials a great deal of freedom in making decisions without interference from the courts.

FOR CRITICAL ANALYSIS

Which constitutional principles apply to the arguments being made in Bell v. Wolfish*? How much weight does the Court give these principles in light of the need to maintain security in correctional facilities?*

 For more information and activities related to this case, click on Landmark Cases under Book Resources at www.cjinaction.com

The linear design is similar to that of a hospital in which long rows of rooms are placed along a corridor. To carry out her or his surveillance duties, the custodial officer must either look down the corridor, or walk down it and peer into the windows of the individual cells. What sorts of risks are inherent in this type of jail design?

Delaware, Hawaii, Maine, Rhode Island, Texas, and Vermont) manage jails.

The "Burden" of Jail Administration Given that the public's opinion of jails ranges from negative to indifferent, some sheriffs neglect their jail management duties.[65] Instead, they focus on high-visibility issues such as placing more law enforcement officers on the streets and improving security in schools. In fact, a jail usually receives publicity only after an escape or an incident in which inmates are abused by jailers.

Despite some sheriffs' general apathy toward jails, few would be willing to give up their management duties. As troublesome as they may be, jails can be useful in other ways. The sheriff appoints a jail administrator, or deputy sheriff, to oversee the day-to-day operations of the facility. The sheriff also has the power to hire other staff members, such as deputy jailers. The sheriff may award these jobs to people who helped her or him get elected, and, in return, jail staffers can prove helpful to the sheriff in future elections.

The Challenges of Overcrowding In many ways, the sheriff is placed in an untenable position when it comes to jail overcrowding. He or she has little control over the number of people who are sent to jail; that power resides with prosecutors and judges. Yet the jail is expected to find space to hold all comers, regardless of its capacity. A sheriff from Kane County, Utah, describes the situation:

> We have people who should get sixty or ninety days, and they just do a weekend and we kick them out. Unless we get a real habitual abuser, we have no choice but to set them free. Most of the time we're pretty sure they will be back in a couple of days with a new offense.[66]

One way to alleviate overcrowding is to build more jails. Currently, the United States is adding about 25,000 new jail beds each year in an effort to keep pace with demand. The problem, however, is what economists call supply creating its own demand; that is, the number of jail inmates seems to expand to meet the number of available beds. Today, the nation's jails are filled to 93 percent of their capacity, and seventeen of the nation's fifty largest jails have an occupancy rate of greater than 100 percent.[67]

NEW-GENERATION JAILS

The boom in jail construction has been accompanied by a growing realization that simply adding bed space is not sufficient to deal with the problems endemic to the facilities. These problems include high suicide rates, an influx of mentally ill inmates, high drug use, and violence and rape. In other words, *how* the jail is built is just as important as *why* it is built. Over the past thirty years, the trend in jail construction has moved away from a traditional design toward a structure known as the new-generation jail.

The Traditional Design For most of the nation's history, the architecture of a jail was secondary to its purpose of keeping inmates safely locked away. Consequently, most jails in the United States continue to resemble those from the days of the Walnut Street Jail in Philadelphia. In this *traditional,* or *linear, design,* jail cells are located along a corridor (see the photo above). To supervise the inmates while they are in their cells, correctional staff members must walk up and down the corridor; thus, the number of prisoners they can see at any one time is severely limited. With this limited supervision, inmates can more easily misbehave.

The harsh environment and lack of supervision inherent in the traditional design have been found to contribute to inmates' antisocial behavior. The prisoners spend most of their free time isolated and devoid of social control, and they have a tendency to respond with hostility.[68] Given that most jail inmates are released after a short period of confinement, many observers feel that the traditional design can pose a threat to the community by "creating" citizens who are more disposed toward violence on release than when they entered the jail.

Podular Design In the 1970s, the Federal Bureau of Prisons (BOP) decided to upgrade the traditional design based on the motto "If you can't rehabilitate, at least do no harm."[69] The BOP implemented a new management philosophy in designing three Metropolitan Correctional Centers in Chicago, New York, and San Diego. The National Institute of Corrections designated these three facilities **new-generation jails** to distinguish them from the older models.[70]

The new-generation jails differ significantly from their predecessors. The layout of the new facilities makes it easier for the staff to monitor cell-confined inmates. The basic structure of the new-generation jail is based on a **podular design.** Each "pod" contains "living units" for individual prisoners. These units, instead of lining up along a straight corridor, are often situated in a triangle so that a staff member in the center of the triangle has visual access to nearly all the cells. Daily activities such as eating and showering take place in the pod, which also has an outdoor exercise area. Treatment facilities are also located in the pod, allowing greater access for the inmates. Furthermore, the surroundings are not as harsh as in the older jails. Cells have comfortable furniture, rugs, and windows, and a communal "day-room" has televisions, radios, and telephones.[71]

Direct Supervision Approach The podular design also enables a new-generation jail to be managed using a **direct supervision approach.**[72] One or more jail officers are stationed in the living area of the pod and are therefore in constant interaction with all prisoners in that particular pod (see the photo on this page). Some new-generation jails even provide a desk in the center of the living area, which sends a very different message to the prisoners than the traditional control booth. Theoretically, jail officials who have constant contact with inmates will be able to stem misconduct quickly and efficiently and will also be able to recognize "danger signs" of individual inmates and stop outbursts before they occur.

Overcoming Initial Apprehension At first, the new-generation jails provoked a great deal of skepticism,

New-Generation Jail
A type of jail that is distinguished architecturally from its predecessors by a design that encourages interaction between inmates and jailers and that offers greater opportunities for treatment.

Podular Design
The architectural style of the new-generation jail. Each "pod" consists of between twelve and twenty-four one-person cells and a communal "day-room" to allow for social interaction.

Direct Supervision Approach
A process of prison and jail administration in which correctional officers are in continuous physical contact with inmates during the day.

In a direct supervision jail, the custodial officer is stationed at an in-pod control terminal. From this point, he or she has visual contact with all inmates and can communicate with inmates quickly and easily. During the day, inmates stay in the open area and are allowed in their cells only when given permission. The officer locks the door to the cells from his or her control terminal. How would the behavior of inmates in a direct supervision jail differ from that of inmates in a traditional, linear jail?

Courtesy National Corrections Corporation

About half a million children in the United States, including the three pictured above, can see their mothers only by visiting them in prison or jail. What are some of the possible consequences of this separation?

as they were seen as inherently "soft" on criminals. A number of empirical results, however, seem to speak to the success of podular design and direct supervision. One study measured inmate behavior in an adult detention facility before and after it was converted to a direct supervision jail. The researchers found a "dramatic reduction" in the number of assaults, batteries, attempted suicides, sex offenses, possession of weapons, and escapees.[73] Today, nearly two hundred new-generation jails are in operation or under construction.

↗ ONLINE REVIEW *Go to the book's Web site for an interactive review of this section*

The Consequences of Our High Rates of Incarceration

For many observers, especially those who support the crime control theory of criminal justice, America's high rate of incarceration has contributed significantly to the drop in the country's crime rates.[74] At the heart of this belief is the fact, which we covered in Chapter 2, that most crimes are committed by a relatively small group of repeat offenders. Several studies have tried to corroborate this viewpoint, with varying results—estimates of the number of crimes committed each year by habitual offenders range from three to 187.[75] If one accepts the higher estimate, each year a repeat offender spends in prison prevents a significant number of criminal acts.

Criminologists, however, note the negative consequences of America's growing prison and jail population. For one, incarceration can have severe social consequences for communities and the families that make up those communities. When a parent is imprisoned, her or his children will often suffer financial hardships, reduced supervision and discipline, and a general deterioration of the family structure.[76] These factors are used to explain the fact that children of convicts are more likely to become involved in delinquent behavior. Our high rates of incarceration also deny one of the basic rights of American democracy—the right to vote—to a large segment of the citizenry. (A number of states and the federal government disenfranchise, or take away the ability to vote, from those convicted of felonies. Some states do not, however.) This has a disproportionate impact on minority groups, weakening their voice in the democratic debate. Today, 10.4 percent of African American men between the ages of twenty-five and twenty-nine are in prison, compared to 2.4 percent of Hispanic men and 1.2 percent of white men in the same age group.[77] With more black men behind bars than enrolled in the nation's colleges and universities, Marc Mauer of the Sentencing Project believes that the "ripple effect on their communities and on the next generation of kids, growing up with their fathers in prison, will certainly be with us for at least a generation."[78]

Whether the American incarceration situation is "good" or "bad" depends to a large extent on one's personal philosophy. In the end, it is difficult to do a definitive cost-benefit analysis for each person incarcerated, weighing the benefits of preventing crimes that might (or might not) have been committed by an inmate against the costs to the convict's family and society. One thing that can be stated with some certainty is that, given the present political and social atmosphere, the increase in prison and jail populations will continue in the foreseeable future.

>The End of the Line:
Supermax Prisons

On Easter Sunday 1993, inmates at a maximum-security prison in Lucasville, Ohio, seized control of an entire cell block and held it for eleven days. During the extended rioting, one correctional officer and nine inmates were killed; afterward the state spent nearly $80 million on prison repairs, investigations, and lawsuits. The Easter riot had a profound effect on the state's prison system. Within five years, Ohio had added seven new penal institutions and doubled the budget of the Department of Rehabilitation and Corrections. The centerpiece of the new efforts was the Ohio State Penitentiary in Youngstown. At its opening in the spring of 1998, the Youngstown facility was celebrated by officials as the nation's latest **supermax** (short for supermaximum-security) **prison.** In this *Criminal Justice in Action* feature, we will examine these "intense" corrections facilities, condemned by critics as inhuman and lauded by supporters as the ultimate in "get tough" incarceration.

"The Worst of the Worst"

Supermax prisons are reserved for the "worst of the worst." Inmates generally are not sent to such facilities by a court; instead, commitment to a supermax prison is usually the result of misbehavior within a penal institution. As Figure 13.8 shows, the murder or attempted murder of a fellow inmate was the most common reason for commitment to the BOP's U.S. Penitentiary Administrative Maximum (ADX) in Florence, Colorado.

The main purpose of a supermax prison is to strictly control the inmates' movement, thereby limiting (or eliminating) situations that could lead to breakdowns in discipline. The conditions in California's Security

Supermax Prison

A correctional facility reserved for those inmates who have extensive records of misconduct in maximum-security prisons; characterized by extremely strict control and supervision over the inmates, including extensive use of solitary confinement.

Housing Unit (SHU) at Pelican Bay State Prison are representative of most supermax institutions. Prisoners are confined to their one-person cells for twenty-two and a half hours each day under video camera surveillance; they receive meals through a slot in the door. The cells measure eight by ten feet in size and are windowless. No decorations of any kind are permitted on the white walls.[79]

For the ninety minutes each day the inmates are allowed out of their cells (compared to twelve to sixteen hours in regular maximum-security prisons), they may either shower or exercise in an enclosed, concrete "yard" covered by plastic mesh. Prisoners are strip-searched before and after leaving their cells, and placed in waist restraints and handcuffs on their way to and from the "yard" and showers. They can have a limited number of books or magazines in their cells and, if they can afford it, a television or radio.[80]

Removing the most violent and problematic inmates from the general prison population is seen as a key to

FIGURE 13.8 Reasons for Transfer to a Supermax Prison

Rarely are offenders sent directly to a supermax facility by a court. For the most part, they are transferred there because of misbehavior in another correctional facility. This figure shows the reason inmates were transferred to the most secure facility operated by the Federal Bureau of Prisons: the U.S. Penitentiary Administrative Maximum (ADX) in Florence, Colorado.

REASON FOR TRANSFER	PERCENT
Murder or attempted murder of a fellow inmate	20
Assault of a fellow inmate with a weapon	18
Assault of a staff member	16
Escape attempt	10
Involved in riot	5
Judicial order	3
Other*	28

*Includes attempted murder of a staff member, involvement in a work or food strike, taking a staff member hostage, introducing drugs into a correctional facility, involvement in gang activity.

Source: Gregory L. Hershberger, "To the Max: Supermax Facilities Provide Prison Administrators with More Security Options," *Corrections Today* 60 (February 1, 1998), 54.

modern prison management. Because those inmates transferred to supermax facilities are more likely to be impulsive and unpredictable and to have a gang affiliation, their absence is believed to create a safer environment for other inmates and the correctional staff. Furthermore, prison administrators use the supermax as a disciplinary tool—problematic inmates may change their behavior if they fear being transferred.[81]

Marion--The First Supermax

The precursor of today's supermax was San Francisco's Alcatraz Prison. Opening in 1932 on Alcatraz Island in San Francisco Bay, the maximum-security prison was populated by the most dangerous and disruptive federal convicts. Alcatraz was closed in 1963—mainly due to the expense of operating an island prison. For most of the next two decades, the BOP used the **dispersion** model for placing the most hazardous inmates. In other words, the department dispersed its "hard-core" offenders to various federal prisons around the country, hoping the general inmate population would assimilate them.[82]

By the late 1970s, it became apparent that this strategy was not functioning as planned. The "hard cores" continued to act violently, endangering other inmates and correctional employees. Then, in October 1983, two staff members and an inmate were murdered within a week at the federal prison in Marion, Illinois. Prison officials instituted a **lockdown,** in which all inmates are confined to their cells, and social activities such as meals, recreational sports, and treatment programs are canceled. Lockdowns are considered temporary, "cooling-off" measures, but officials at Marion decided to leave the conditions in effect indefinitely, creating the first supermax prison. The supermax is based on the model

A typical supermax prison cell at the ADX outside Florence, Colorado. The cell is 8 ft. 8 in. × 12 ft. 3 in., and contains a stainless steel mirror and a 12-inch black-and-white television set, as well as a concrete desk, stool, and bed that are permanently fixed to the floor. The small window has no view.

of **consolidation:** all high-risk inmates are placed in a single institution, which is administered with a focus on complete control.[83]

The New-Generation Supermax

At first, the consolidation model led federal and state officials to construct supermax facilities on existing prison grounds. Over the past decade, however, the trend has been toward building new penal institutions, expressly designed with the goals of the supermax in mind. The Closed Maximum Security Correctional Center (CMAX) in Tamms, Illinois, for example, is designed around inmate housing pods (much like the new-generation jails mentioned earlier in the chapter). Each pod contains sixty cells on two levels, arranged around a control station with complete visual access. CMAX is designed so that an inmate never leaves his pod; medical facilities, library cells, and recreational areas are located within its boundaries.

All inmate movement in the pod takes place on the lower level, while armed security staff patrol the upper level. These guards can see through the upper-level flooring grid, allowing them to closely monitor any activity

Dispersion

A corrections model in which high-risk inmates are spread throughout the general prison population, in the hopes that they will be absorbed without causing misconduct problems.

Lockdown

A disciplinary action taken by prison officials in which all inmates are ordered to their quarters and nonessential prison activities are suspended.

Consolidation

A corrections model in which the inmates who pose the highest security risk are housed in a single facility to separate them from the general prison population.

below. Furthermore, officials can control circulation by sealing off portions of the facility at will.[84] These new-generation supermax prisons also strive to limit contact between staff and inmates through technology. Automatic doors, intercoms, and electronic surveillance cameras have reduced the exposure of guards to inmates at most of the new facilities.

Senseless Suffering?

Many prison officials support the proliferation of supermax prisons because they provide increased security for the most dangerous inmates. Observers believe that as the inmate population becomes aware of these new facilities, their harsh reputation will deter convicts from misbehaving for fear of transfer to a supermax.

The supermax has aroused a number of criticisms, however. Amnesty International and other human rights groups assert that the facilities violate international standards of proper treatment for prisoners. Other opponents point out that inmates are provided minimal due process protections during the transfer process. An inmate has no right to an attorney while being considered for a transfer, and the decision to send someone to a supermax cannot be appealed. Because this decision is made by an administrative—and not a judicial or legislative—body, in *Sandin v. Conner* (1995),[85] the Supreme Court ruled only that such a move must not impose an "atypical and significant hardship on the inmate in relation to the ordinary incidents of prison life." As yet, no court has found that the conditions in a supermax constitute such a hardship.[86]

Other observers believe not only that those conditions are atypical and significant, but that they violate Eighth Amendment protections against cruel and unusual punishment. The negative effects of solitary confinement on a prisoner's psyche are considerable, and supermax facilities are structured to keep their inmates isolated at all times. After studying inmates at California's

Pelican Bay, a Harvard University psychiatrist found that 80 percent suffered from what he called "SHU [security housing unit] syndrome"; after spending a certain amount of time at the facility, the inmates either exhibited new signs of mental instability, or their existing conditions were exacerbated.[87] In *Madrid v. Gomez* (1995),[88] U.S. District Judge Thelton Henderson found that Pelican Bay violated its inmates' Eighth Amendment rights, writing that "dry words on paper cannot adequately capture the senseless suffering" of the convicts.

Despite his harsh sentiments, Judge Henderson's ruling only forced the supermax to improve medical care and had no discernible effect on the operation of the facility. Indeed, it does not appear that the American courts will pose a threat to the operation of these institutions. According to the National Institute of Corrections, supermax prisons are the fasting-growing type of prison in the United States, and house more than 25,000 inmates.[89]

MAKING SENSE OF SUPERMAX PRISONS

1 Explain the thinking behind the dispersion and consolidation models of dealing with highly dangerous inmates. Why is the supermax prison considered to be an example of the consolidation model?

2 Summarize the arguments for and against the supermax prison. Which side do you fall on, and why?

3 Do you feel that supermax prisons infringe on inmates' Eighth Amendment right to be free from "cruel and unusual punishment"? What other information about how supermax prisons are operated might you need to know before you answer?

---

1 **Contrast the Pennsylvania and the New York penitentiary theories of the 1800s.** Basically, the Pennsylvania system imposed total silence on its prisoners. Based on the concept of separate confinement, penitentiaries were constructed with back-to-back cells facing both outward and inward.

Prisoners worked, slept, and ate alone in their cells. In contrast, New York used the congregate system; silence was imposed, but inmates worked and ate together.

2 **List the factors that have caused the prison population to grow dramatically in the last several decades.** (a) The

Chapter Summary

enhancement and stricter enforcement of the nation's drug laws; (b) increased probability of incarceration; (c) inmates serving more time for each crime; (d) federal prison growth; and (e) rising incarceration rates for women.

3 **Explain the three general models of prisons.** (a) The custodial model assumes the prisoner is incarcerated for reasons of incapacitation, deterrence, and retribution. (b) The rehabilitation model puts security concerns second and the well-being of the individual inmate first. As a consequence, treatment programs are offered to prisoners. (c) The reintegration model sees the correctional institution as a training ground for preparing convicts to reenter society.

4 **List and briefly explain the four types of prisons.** (a) Maximum-security prisons, which are designed mainly with security and surveillance in mind. Such prisons are usually large and consist of cell blocks, each of which is set off by a series of gates and bars. (b) Medium-security prisons, which offer considerably more educational and treatment programs and allow more contact between inmates. Such prisons are rarely walled, but rather are surrounded by high fences. (c) Minimum-security prisons, which permit prisoners to have television sets and computers and often allow them to leave the grounds for educational and employment purposes. (d) Supermaximum-security (supermax) prisons, in which prisoners are confined to one-person cells for up to twenty-two and a half hours per day under constant video camera surveillance.

5 **Contrast formal with informal prison management systems.** A formal system is militaristic with a hierarchical (top-down) chain of command; the warden (or superintendent) is on top, then deputy wardens, and last, custodial employees. The informal prison management system depends on the philosophy of the warden, or superintendent, and may even allow for inmate councils and inmate "guards."

6 **List the reasons why private prisons can be run more cheaply than public ones.** (a) Labor costs are lower because private prison employees are nonunionized and receive lower levels of overtime payments, sick leave, and health care. (b) Competitive bidding requires the operators of private prisons to buy goods and services at the lowest possible prices. (c) There is less red tape in a private prison facility.

7 **Summarize the distinction between jails and prisons, and indicate the importance of jails in the American correctional system.** Generally, a prison is for those convicted of felonies who will serve lengthy periods of incarceration, whereas a jail is for those who have been convicted of misdemeanors and will serve less than a year of incarceration. A jail also (a) receives individuals pending arraignment and holds them while awaiting trial, conviction, or sentencing; (b) temporarily holds juveniles pending transfer to juvenile authorities; (c) holds the mentally ill pending transfer to health facilities; (d) detains those who have violated probation or parole and those who have "jumped" bail; and (e) houses those awaiting transfer to federal or state prisons. Approximately 7 million Americans spend time in jail each year.

8 **Explain how jails are administered.** Most jails are operated at the county level by an elected sheriff, although about 20 percent are under the control of municipalities and eight states manage jails themselves. Sheriffs appoint jail administrators (deputy sheriffs) as well as deputy jailers.

9 **Indicate the difference between traditional jail design and new-generation jail design.** A traditional design is linear, with jail cells located along a corridor. Such a physical structure is rather cold with an emphasis on iron and steel fixtures that are not easily broken. New-generation jails, in contrast, use a podular design, with the "pods" often arranged in a triangle. Each cell has furniture, rugs, and windows, and

STORIES FROM THE STREET

Go to the Stories from the Street feature at www.cjinaction.com to hear Larry Gaines tell insightful stories related to this chapter and his experiences in the field.

there are communal "day-rooms" with televisions, radios, and telephones.

10 Indicate some of the consequences of our high rates of incarceration.
(a) Some people believe that the reduction in the country's crime rate is a direct result of increased incarceration rates; (b) others believe that high incarceration rates are having increasing negative social consequences, such as financial hardships, reduced supervision and discipline of children, and a general deterioration of the family structure when one parent is in prison; and (c) more money spent on prisons has taken away money for other public services, such as education.

Key Terms

congregate system 438
consolidation 462
direct supervision approach 459
dispersion 462
jail 454
lockdown 462
maximum-security prison 444
medical model 439
medium-security prison 447
minimum-security prison 447
new-generation jails 459
penitentiary 437
podular design 459
pretrial detainees 455
private prisons 450
separate confinement 438
supermax prison 461
time served 456
warden 448

Questions for Critical Analysis

1 Explain the benefit of nonfixed sentences coupled with the possibility of early release.

2 How did the Elmira Reformatory classify prisoners? How did the system work?

3 Crime rates are falling, yet prison rates are rising. Why?

4 What are several reasons why prison construction continues to increase?

5 The chain of command in prisons and police departments appears quite similar, yet there is a big difference. What is it?

6 Why have private prisons grown over the last decade?

7 Why are jails so important in the American corrections system?

8 Most sheriffs are quite apathetic toward the job of running jails, yet they do not want to give up their management duties. Why not?

9 In the first two decades after the closing of Alcatraz, what method did the Bureau of Prisons use in dealing with its most dangerous inmates? Was the method successful?

▸ TEST PREPARATION ONLINE

Go to www.cjinaction.com for tools to aid you in studying for your exams. Click on *Online Reviews* under *Chapter Resources* for an interactive review of each major section of this chapter. Under *Chapter Resources,* you will also find the *Chapter Outline, Chapter Summary, Flashcards, Glossary, Learning Objectives, Lecture Presentations, Concept Builder, Essay Questions,* and a *Tutorial Quiz.* You can also test yourself with a game of *Concentration* or the *Crossword Puzzle.*

▸ Web Resources

Go to www.cjinaction.com for a wealth of online resources. Explore the *Internet Activities* and *Class Project*s under *Chapter Resources.* Check out the *Web Links* to access the Web sites mentioned in the text, as well as many others. You can also access recent perspectives by clicking on *CJ in the News* and *Terrorism Update* under *Course Resources.* If you'd like some mentoring, click on *Board of Mentors* under *Book Resources.*

⚐ Search Online with InfoTrac College Edition

For additional information, explore InfoTrac College Edition, your online library that offers complete full-length articles from thousands of scholarly and popular publications. Click on *InfoTrac College Edition* under *Chapter Resources* at www.cjinaction.com for a list of key words and InfoTrac exercises. Use the passcode that came with your book.

Suggested Readings

Applebaum, Anne, *Gulag: A History*, New York: Doubleday, 2003. As the U.S. incarceration rate has risen to historic levels, many comparisons have been made to the Gulag system that operated under the Communist dictatorship of the Soviet Union. This book should dispel the notion that the American corrections system, whatever its problems, is comparable to that wide network of prison labor camps. From 1928 to the death of Soviet leader Joseph Stalin in 1953, Applebaum estimates that 18 million people passed through the Gulag camps, with about 4.5 million perishing there. Through painstaking research and interviews with survivors, the author provides a vivid look at how the prisoners lived, worked, slept, ate, and died.

Glenn, Lon, *The Largest Hotel Chain in Texas: Texas Prisons*, Burnet, TX: Eakin Publications, 2001. In 1966, at the age of twenty-one, Lon Glenn began his career in the Texas prison system as a corrections officer. Over the next three-plus decades, he advanced to the position of warden. During that time, Glenn watched the system change dramatically, and, in his opinion, for the worse. In this book, Glenn details how a massive expenditure of taxpayer dollars has built one of the largest corrections structures in the world, but has failed to advance one of the main purposes of incarceration: to make life safe for those inside and outside prisons. Though the author focuses primarily on Texas, the issues he raises apply to the criminal justice system as a whole.

Notes

1. Bureau of Justice Statistics, *Prisoners in 2002* (Washington, D.C.: U.S. Department of Justice, July 2003), 1.
2. James M. Beattie, *Crime and the Courts in England, 1660–1800* (Princeton, NJ: Princeton University Press, 1986), 506–507.
3. Samuel Walker, *Popular Justice* (New York: Oxford University Press, 1980), 11.
4. Michael Meranze, *Laboratories of Virtue: Punishment, Revolution, and Authority in Philadelphia, 1760–1835* (Chapel Hill, NC: University of North Carolina Press, 1996), 55.
5. Negley K. Teeters, *The Cradle of the Penitentiary: The Walnut Street Jail at Philadelphia, 1773–1835* (Philadelphia: 1955), 30.
6. Negley K. Teeters and John D. Shearer, *The Prison at Philadelphia's Cherry Hill* (New York: Columbia University Press, 1957), 142–143.
7. Henry Calvin Mohler, "Convict Labor Policies," *Journal of the American Institute of Criminal Law and Criminology* 15 (1925), 556–557.
8. Zebulon Brockway, *Fifty Years of Prison Service* (Montclair, NJ: Patterson Smith, 1969), 400–401.
9. Robert Martinson, "What Works? Questions and Answers about Prison Reform," *Public Interest* 35 (Spring 1974), 22.
10. See Ted Palmer, "Martinson Revisited," *Journal of Research on Crime and Delinquency* (1975), 133; and Paul Gendreau and Bob Ross, "Effective Correctional Treatment: Bibliotherapy for Cynics," *Crime & Delinquency* 25 (1979), 499.
11. Robert Martinson, "New Findings, New Views: A Note of Caution Regarding Sentencing Reform," *Hofstra Law Review* 7 (1979), 243.

12. Fox Butterfield, "'Defying Gravity,' Inmate Population Climbs," *New York Times* (January 19, 1998), A10.
13. *Ibid.*
14. Bureau of Justice Statistics, *Sourcebook of Criminal Justice Statistics, 2000* (Washington, D.C.: U.S. Department of Justice, 2001), Table 6.51, page 526.
15. Allen J. Beck, "Growth, Change, and Stability in the U.S. Prison Population, 1980–1995," *Corrections Management Quarterly* (Spring 1997), 9–10.
16. Bureau of Justice Statistics, *Time Served in Prison by Federal Offenders, 1986–97* (Washington, D.C.: U.S. Department of Justice, June 1999), 1.
17. Bureau of Justice Statistics, *Federal Drug Offenders, 1999, with Trends 1984–99* (Washington, D.C.: U.S. Department of Justice, August 2001), 1.
18. Bureau of Justice Statistics, *Truth in Sentencing in State Prisons* (Washington, D.C.: U.S. Department of Justice, 1999), 7.
19. *Prisoners in 2002*, Table 1, page 2.
20. *Ibid.*, 11.
21. *Ibid.*
22. *Ibid.*, 4.
23. J. C. Oleson, "The Punitive Coma," *California Law Review* (May 2002), 829.
24. Bureau of Justice Statistics, *Sourcebook of Criminal Justice Statistics 2001* (Washington, D.C.: U.S. Department of Justice, 2002), Table 1.5.
25. *Ibid.*, Table 1.9.
26. Holly Idelson, "Republican Crime Bills Take a 'Get Tougher' Approach," *Congressional Quarterly Weekly Report* 53 (1995), 211.

27. Charles H. Logan, *Criminal Justice Performance Measures in Prisons* (Washington, D.C.: U.S. Department of Justice, 1993), 5.
28. Todd R. Clear and George F. Cole, *American Corrections*, 4th ed. (Belmont, CA: Wadsworth Publishing Co., 1997), 245–246.
29. Alfred Blumstein, "Prisons," in *Crime*, ed. James Q. Wilson and Joan Petersilia (San Francisco: ICS Press, 1995), 392.
30. Cassia Spohn and David Holleran, "The Effect of Imprisonment on Recidivism Rates of Felony Offenders: A Focus on Drug Offenders," *Criminology* (May 1, 2002), 329–357.
31. Tony Izzo, "I-Max Awaits Green," *Kansas City Star* (May 26, 1996), A1.
32. "Pennsylvania Plans New Prison to Replace Site of Tunnel Escape," *Corrections Journal* (February 9, 1998), 6.
33. Charles H. Logan, "Well Kept: Comparing Quality of Confinement in a Public and Private Prison," *Journal of Criminal Law and Criminology* 83 (1992), 580.
34. Bert Useem and Peter Kimball, *Stages of Siege: U.S. Prison Riots, 1971–1986* (New York: Oxford University Press, 1989).
35. Bert Useem, "Disorganization and the New Mexico Prison Riot of 1980," *American Sociology Review* 50 (1985), 685.
36. Tara Gray and Jon'a F. Meyer, "Prison Administration: Inmate Participation versus the Control Model," in *Correction Contexts: Contemporary and Classical Readings*, ed. James W. Marquart and Jonathan R. Sorenson (Los Angeles: Roxbury Publishing Co., 1997), 203–211.
37. *Ibid.*, 208.

38. 550 F.2d 238 (5th Cir. 1977); *cert.* denied, 460 U.S. 1042 (1983).

39. "A Recession-Proof Industry," *Economist* (November 15, 1997), 28.

40. *Prisoners in 2002*, 6.

41. James Austin and Garry Coventry, *Emerging Issues on Privatized Prisons* (Washington, D.C.: Bureau of Justice Assistance, 2001), iii.

42. "A Tale of Two Systems: Cost, Quality, and Accountability in Private Prisons," *Harvard Law Review* (May 2002), 1872.

43. *Public-Private Prisons Comparison* (Phoenix, AZ: Arizona Department of Corrections, 2000), 47.

44. *Private Prison Review* (Tallahassee, FL: Office of Program Policy Analysis and Government Accountability, 2000), 5.

45. Charles Logan, "Well Kept: Comparing Quality of Confinement in Private and Public Prisons," *Journal of Criminal Law and Criminology* 83 (1992), 577.

46. Richard C. Brister, "Changing of the Guard: A Case for Privatization of Texas Prisons," *The Prison Journal* 76 (September 1996), 322–323.

47. "Private Prison Is Ordered to Screen Dangerous Inmates," *Corrections Journal* (March 9, 1998), 5.

48. Monte Morin and Stuart Pfeifer, "2 Jail Officers Indicted Over Inmates' Fight," *Los Angeles Times* (August 30, 2001), B8.

49. Mark Tatge, "Boys Will be Boys," *Fortune* (August 7, 2000), 70.

50. Richard L. Lippke, "Thinking about Private Prisons," *Criminal Justice Ethics* (Winter/Spring 1997), 32.

51. John Dilulio, "Prisons, Profits, and the Public Good: The Privatization of Corrections," in *Criminal Justice Center Bulletin* (Huntsville, TX: Sam Houston State University, 1986).

52. Ira P. Robbins, "Privatization of Prisons, Privatization of Corrections: Defining the Issues," *Vanderbilt Law Review* 40 (1987), 823.

53. *Prisoners in 2002*, 6.

54. Amy Cheung, *Prison Privatization and the Use of Incarceration* (Washington, D.C.: The Sentencing Project, 2002), 3.

55. *Ibid.*

56. Joseph T. Hallihan, "Bailed Out: Shaky Private Prisons Find Vital Customer in Federal Government," *Wall Street Journal* (November 6, 2001), A1.

57. Bureau of Justice Statistics, *Prison and Jail Inmates at Midyear 2002* (Washington, D.C.: U.S. Department of Justice, April 2003), 1.

58. Arthur Wallenstein, "Jail Crowding: Bringing the Issue to the Corrections Center Stage," *Corrections Today* (December 1996), 76–81.

59. Quoted in Butterfield, "Defying Gravity."

60. "State to Rent County Jails for Inmates," *UPI Online* (February 5, 1998).

61. John Irwin, *The Jail: Managing the Underclass in American Society* (Berkeley, CA: University of California Press, 1985), 2.

62. *Prison and Jail Inmates at Midyear 2002*, 6.

63. 441 U.S. 520 (1979).

64. *Prison and Jail Inmates at Midyear 2002*, 9.

65. G. Larry Mays and Joel A. Thompson, "The Political and Organizational Context of American Jails," in *American Jails: Public Policy Issues*, ed. Joel A. Thompson and G. Larry Mays (Chicago: Nelson-Hall, 1991), 10.

66. Quoted in Greg Burton, "Jail Builders Race to Keep Up with Demand," *Salt Lake City Tribune* (May 6, 1998), N31.

67. *Prison and Jail Inmates at Midyear 2002*, 9.

68. John J. Gibbs, "Environmental Congruence and Symptoms of Psychopathology: A Further Exploration of the Effects of Exposure to the Jail Environment," *Criminal Justice and Behavior* 18 (1991), 351–374.

69. Richard Weiner, William Frazier, and Jay Farbstein, "Building Better Jails," *Psychology Today* (June 1987), 40.

70. R. L. Miller, "New Generation Justice Facilities: The Case for Direct Supervision," *Architectural Technology* 12 (1985), 6–7.

71. Gerald J. Bayens, Jimmy J. Williams, and John Ortiz Smyka, "Jail Type and Inmate Behavior: A Longitudinal Analysis," *Federal Probation* (September 1997), 54.

72. Linda L. Zupan, *Jails: Reform and the New Generation Philosophy* (Cincinnati, OH: Anderson Publishing Co., 1991).

73. Gerald J. Bayens, Jimmy J. Williams, and John Ortiz Smykla, "Jail Type and Inmate Behavior: A Longitudinal Analysis," *Federal Probation* 61 (September, 1997), 54.

74. John Dilulio and Charles Logan, "Ten Deadly Myths about Crime and Punishment," in *Restoring Responsibility in Criminal Justice*, 2d ed., ed. Robert J. Bidinotto (Irvington-on-Hudson, NY: Foundation for Economic Education, 1996).

75. Franklin E. Zimring and Gordon Hawkins, *Incapacitation: Penal Confinement and the Restraint of Crime* (New York: Oxford University Press, 1995), 38, 40, 145.

76. Todd R. Clear and Dina R. Rose, "A Thug in Jail Can't Shoot Your Sister: The Unintended Consequences of Incarceration," paper presented to the American Sociological Association (August 18, 1996).

77. *Prisoners in 2002*, 9.

78. Quoted in Fox Butterfield, "Study Finds 2.6% Increase in U.S. Prison Population," *New York Times* (July 28, 2003), A8.

79. Charles A. Pettigrew, "Technology and the Eighth Amendment: The Problem of Supermax Prisons," *North Carolina Journal of Law and Technology* (Fall 2002), 195.

80. "Facts about Pelican Bay's SHU," *California Prisoner* (December 1991).

81. Jeffrey Endicott, Jerry Berge, and Gary McCaughtry, "Prison Wardens Push for 'Supermax' Prison," *Wisconsin State Journal* (February 12, 1996), 5A.

82. Gregory L. Hershberger, "To the Max," *Corrections Today* (February 1998), 55.

83. *Ibid.*, 55–56.

84. Robert A. Sheppard, Jeffrey G. Geiger, and George Welborn, "Closed Maximum Security: The Illinois Supermax," *Corrections Today* (July 1996), 4.

85. 515 U.S. 472 (1995).

86. "Supermax Placement Raises New Concerns about Due Process," *Correctional Law Reporter* (October/November 1997), 1–2, 45–46.

87. Robert Perkinson, "Shackled Justice: Florence Federal Penitentiary and the New Politics of Punishment," *Social Justice* 21 (Fall 1994), 117–123.

88. 889 F.Supp. 1146 (1995).

89. Claire Schaeffer-Duffy, "Long Term Lockdowns: Psychological Effects of Solitary Confinement and Stun Devices," *National Catholic Reporter* (December 8, 2000), 1.

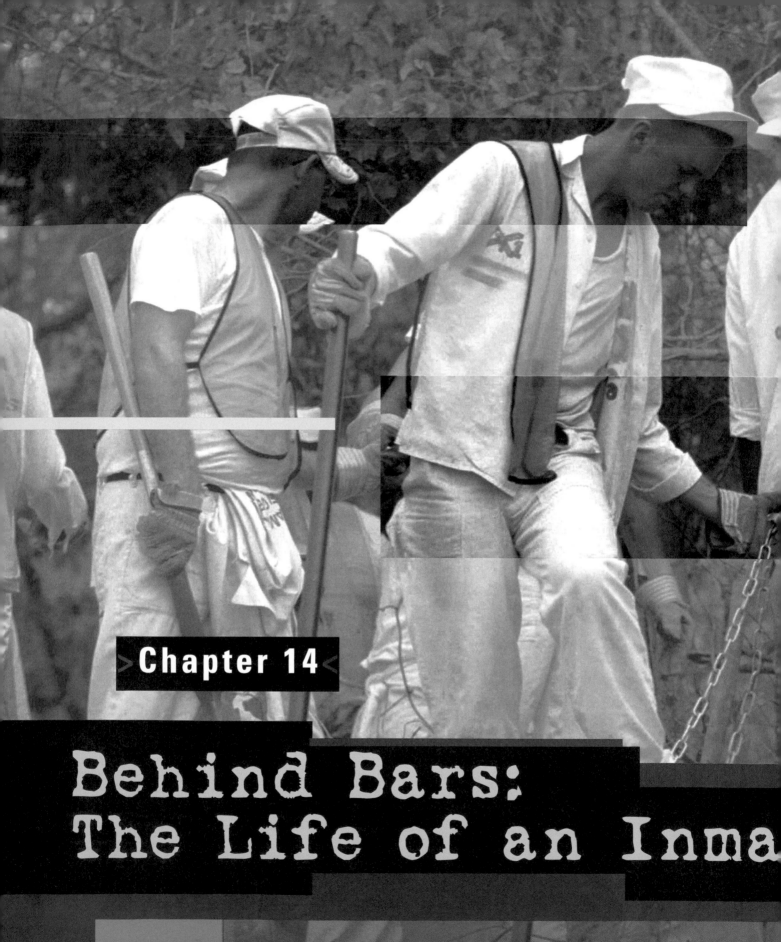

Chapter 14

Behind Bars:
The Life of an Inma

>chapter objectives<

After reading this chapter, you should be able to:

1 Explain the concept of prison as a total institution.

2 Describe the possible patterns of inmate behavior, which are driven by the inmate's personality and values.

3 Indicate some of the reasons for violent behavior in prisons.

4 List and briefly explain the six general job categories among correctional officers.

5 Contrast the hands-off doctrine of prisoner law with the hands-on approach.

6 List the concepts on which parole is based.

7 Contrast probation, parole, mandatory release, pardon, and furlough.

8 Describe truth-in-sentencing laws and their goals.

9 Describe typical conditions of parole.

10 Indicate typical conditions for release for a paroled child molester.

The "No Frills" Movement

In the autumn of 2003, about three hundred inmates rioted at Pleasant Valley State Prison in Coalinga, California, leaving dozens injured and one shot to death by a correctional officer. The riot took place in a maximum-security housing unit designed to hold about 2,500 inmates. When the disturbance broke out, nearly 5,000 were living in the unit, forcing prison officials to use gyms as dormitories. Under such circumstances, said one corrections expert investigating the incident, "the anger level increases and the potential of violence is there."

Members of a Correctional Emergency Response Team practice riot control in a federal prison.

© Lichtenstein Andrew/CORBIS Sygma

Today's penal institutions have been described as characterized by "grindingly dull routine interrupted by occasional flashes of violence and brutality." A "no frills" movement in political policy and prison management has moved to eliminate comforts from inmates' existence. Five states have banned weightlifting in their prisons, and others have barred televisions, radios, adult magazines, conjugal visits, and, to the chagrin of correctional officers, cigarettes. The pleasures, as they were, of food and dress are also under attack: Texas prisoners have dined on "vita-pro," a tasteless soybean-based meat substitute, while Mississippi inmates are required to wear color-coded, zebra-striped uniforms.

> **Life behind bars** has long been predicated on the principle of least eligibility, which holds that the least advantaged members of outside society should lead a better existence than any person living in prison or jail.[1] As the "no frills" movement shows, the idea that incarceration is not punishment enough, and that daily life itself must be an arduous trial for prisoners, is particularly popular at the moment. According to recent polls, as many as 82 percent of Americans believe life in prison is too easy. Many critics, however, feel that the treatment of prisoners has become increasingly inhumane and, indeed, unconstitutional. At one time or another over the past two decades, the federal government, nearly every state government, and countless local authorities have been under court order to improve living conditions in their penal institutions.[2]

In this chapter, we look at some of the factors that influence the quality of life in America's prisons and jails. To that end, we will discuss the ramifications of violence in prison, the role played by correctional officers, efforts by prisoners and prisoners' rights advocates to improve the conditions, and several other issues that are at the forefront of prison debate today. To start, we must understand the forces that shape prison culture and how those forces affect the overall operation of the correctional facility.

CONCEPT BUILDER
A different world exists behind prison walls, presenting unique challenges for those incarcerated. Visit www.cjinaction. com for an interactive exploration of the concept of prison culture.

Prison Culture

Any institution—whether a school, a bank, or a police department—has an organizational culture; that is, a set of values that help the people in the organization understand what actions are acceptable and what actions are unacceptable.[3] According to a theory put forth by the influential sociologist Erving Goffman, prison cultures are unique because prisons are **total institutions** that encompass every aspect of an inmate's life. Unlike a student or a bank teller, a prisoner cannot leave the institution or have any meaningful interaction with outside communities. Others arrange every aspect of daily life, and all prisoners are required to follow this schedule in exactly the same manner.[4]

Inmates develop their own argot, or language (see Figure 14.1). They create their own economy, which, in the absence of currency, is based on the barter of valued items such as food, contraband, and sexual favors. They establish methods of determining power, many of which, as we shall see, involve violence. Isolated

Total Institution
An institution, such as a prison, that provides all of the necessities for existence to those who live within its boundaries.

FIGURE 14.1 Prison Slang

Ace-duce. Best friend.

All day. Life sentence, as in "he's doing all day."

Big bitch. A felon who has been convicted under habitual criminal laws that carry a mandatory life sentence.

Catch a ride. To ask a friend with drugs to get you high, as in "Hey, man, can I catch a ride?"

Catch a square. To prepare to fight, as in "you'd better catch a square."

Chi-mo, also chester, baby-raper, short eyes. Child molester.

Click up. To join a gang.

Deck. Pack of cigarettes.

Ding. A term of derision for a mentally deranged prisoner.

Fish. A new arrival who does not yet know the rules of the prison culture.

Gangster, or monster. HIV/AIDS. As in "watch out for that guy, he's got the gangster."

Hacks, also hogs, snouts, pigs, cops, bulls, screws. Correctional officers.

Herb. Weak inmate.

The hole. Solitary confinement.

Jigger. An inmate who stands watch while an illegal act is taking place.

Luv, luv. Doing well, as in "living luv, luv."

Mule. A person who smuggles drugs into the correctional facility.

Nazi low rider. A member of a white prison gang.

Old school. A prisoner who is seen as having values from the "old days" in prisons, when more respect was given to fellow prisoners.

On the leg. A prisoner who is seen as being overly friendly with prison staff.

Pepsi generation. The newer, younger inmates who are seen as having no respect for the old school ways of the prison.

Pitcher. A sexually aggressive, dominant inmate.

Playing on ass. Gambling without having any cash, as in "if you lose, it's your ass."

Punk. A derogatory term referring to a homosexual or weak-willed person.

Rapo. Anyone imprisoned on a sex offense.

Riding leg. An inmate who is friendly with staff in order to receive preferential treatment.

Split your wig. A quick punch to the head.

Stick. A marijuana joint.

T-jones. An inmate's mother or parents, as in "I got a letter from my T-jones."

Wolf ticket. To "talk tough" without the will to back it up, as in, "he's selling wolf tickets," or "he's making a lot of noise but doesn't have the guts to stand up for himself."

Prisoners also use rhyming slang in order to make their conversations confusing to newcomers or outsiders. In rhyming slang, "bees and money" could mean "honey," "oh my dear" could mean "beer," and so on.

and heavily regulated, prisoners create a social world that is, out of both necessity and design, separate from the outside world.[5]

WHO IS IN PRISON?

The culture of any prison is heavily influenced by its inmates; their values, beliefs, and experiences in the outside world will be reflected in the social order that exists behind bars. In Chapter 2, we noted that a majority of Americans commit at least one crime that could technically send them to prison. In reality, slightly more than 5 percent will be confined in a state or federal prison during their lifetimes. That percentage is considerably higher for male members of minority groups: according to the U.S. Department of Justice, about one in three African American males and one in six Hispanic males, as compared to one in seventeen white males, are likely to go to prison during their lifetimes.[6]

The prison population is not static. The past two decades have seen the incarceration rates of women and minority groups rise sharply. Furthermore, the crimes of inmates have changed over that period. Figure 14.2 shows that inmates are increasingly likely to have been convicted on drug charges, and less likely to have been convicted of a violent or property crime.

Among age groups, persons aged twenty-five to thirty-four account for the highest percentage of inmates, approximately 40 percent.[7] The median age of the prison population is twenty-nine, though that number is expected to rise in the near future. In part, because of determinate sentences, longer terms, and more restrictive release policies, the number of persons between the ages of forty-five and fifty-four in prison has more than tripled since 1974; the inmate population of those fifty-five years and older has more than doubled over that time period.[8] Education also appears to be a determinant in who goes to prison. Nearly 70 percent of inmates have not earned a high school diploma, and only about one in ten has attended college.[9]

ADAPTING TO PRISON SOCIETY

On arriving at prison, each convict attends an orientation session and receives a "Resident's Handbook." The handbook provides information such as meal and official count times, disciplinary regulations, and visitation guidelines. The norms and values of the prison society, however, cannot be communicated by the staff or learned from a handbook. As first described by Donald Clemmer in his classic 1940 work, *The Prison Community*, the process of **prisonization**—or adaptation to the prison culture—advances as the inmate gradually understands what constitutes acceptable behavior in the institution, as defined not by the prison officials but by other inmates.[10]

In studying prisonization, criminologists have focused on two areas: how prisoners change

Prisonization
The socialization process through which a new inmate learns the accepted norms and values of the prison population.

FIGURE 14.2 Offenders in Prison
These figures show the changing proportion of inmates, based on crimes committed, in state correctional facilities in the United States between 1985 and 2001.

Sources: Bureau of Justice Statistics, *Correctional Population in the United States, 1995* (Washington, D.C.: U.S. Department of Justice, June 1997), Table 1.2, page 10; and Bureau of Justice Statistics, *Prisoners in 2002* (Washington, D.C.: U.S. Department of Justice, 2002), Table 15, page 10.

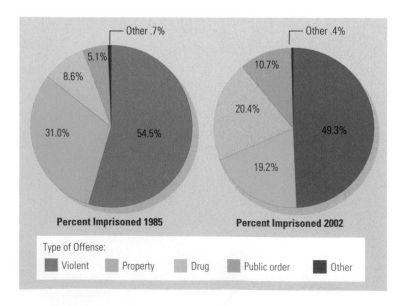

Other .7%
5.1%
8.6%
31.0%
54.5%

Percent Imprisoned 1985

Other .4%
10.7%
20.4%
19.2%
49.3%

Percent Imprisoned 2002

Type of Offense:
Violent   Property   Drug   Public order   Other

their behavior to adapt to life behind bars, and how life behind bars has changed because of inmate behavior. Sociologist John Irwin has identified several patterns of inmate behavior, each one driven by the inmate's personality and values:

1 Professional criminals adapt to prison by "doing time." In other words, they follow the rules and generally do whatever is necessary to speed up their release so they can continue their chosen careers.

2 Some convicts, mostly state-raised youths or those frequently incarcerated in juvenile detention centers, are more comfortable inside prison than outside. These inmates serve time by "jailing," or establishing themselves in the power structure of prison culture.

3 Other inmates take advantage of prison resources such as libraries or drug-treatment programs by "gleaning," or working to improve themselves to prepare for a return to society.

4 Finally, "disorganized" criminals exist on the fringes of prison society. These inmates may have mental impairments or low levels of intelligence and find it impossible to adapt to prison culture on any level.[11]

The process of categorizing prisoners has a theoretical basis, but it serves a practical purpose as well, allowing administrators to reasonably predict how different inmates will act in certain situations. An inmate who is "doing time" generally does not present the same security risk as one who is "jailing."

THE CHANGING PRISON CODE

The best evidence that prison culture has changed can be found in the shifts that have taken place in the traditional **prison code.** In the early studies of prisoner culture, researchers found that an unwritten set of rules guided inmate conduct. A prisoner's standing among his or her peers was determined by whether he or she followed the prison code; those who failed to do so were rejected by the institutional society. The two most important tenets of the code were "never rat on a con" and "do your own time"—in other words, never inform on another inmate and don't interfere in another inmate's affairs (see Figure 14.3).[12]

Prison Code

A system of social norms and values established by inmates to regulate behavior within the correctional institution.

During the era when the code dominated prison culture (generally encompassing the three decades following World War II), prisons were repressive but relatively safe. In contrast, one observer calls the modern institution an "unstable and violent social jungle."[13] There has been an influx of youthful inmates and drug offenders who are seen as being only "out for themselves" and unwilling to follow any code that preaches collective values. With the formation of racial gangs in prison, the traditional prison code has been replaced by one in which the shared values of gang loyalties are preeminent; as we shall see, inmate-on-inmate violence has risen accordingly.[14]

⬈ ONLINE REVIEW *Go to the book's Web site for an interactive review of this section*

FIGURE 14.3 **The Prison Code**

According to many studies of prison life done from the 1940s to the 1970s, inmates lived by an unwritten code. The tenets of the code, which are listed here, stressed reliability, toughness, and a social structure in which individual inmates avoided conflict with each other.

> **Never rat on a con.**
> **Do your own time.**
> **Don't interfere with the interests of other inmates.**
> **Mind your own business.**
> **Don't have a loose lip.**
> **Be tough.**

> **Be a man.**
> **Don't exploit inmates.**
> **Be sharp.**
> **Keep off a man's back.**
> **Don't put a guy on the spot.**
> **Be loyal to your class.**
> **Be cool.**

Source: Gresham Sykes and Sheldon Messinger, "The Inmate Social System," in *Theoretical Studies in the Social Organization of the Prison,* ed. R. Cloward *et al.* (New York: Social Science Research Council, 1960), 6–10.

Prison Violence

A prison is a dangerous place to live. Prison culture is predicated on violence. Prison guards use the threat of violence (and, at times, its reality) to control the inmate population. Among the prisoners, violence is used to establish power and dominance. Often, this violence leads to death. About one hundred inmates are murdered by fellow inmates each year, and about 26,000 inmate-on-inmate assaults take place annually. (See the feature *CJ and the Media—Reel Prison Violence*.)

VIOLENCE IN PRISON CULTURE

In the prison code era, with its emphasis on "noninterference," the prison culture did not support inmate-on-inmate violence. Prison "elders" would themselves punish any of their peers who showed a proclivity toward assaulting fellow inmates. Today, in contrast, violence is used to establish the prisoner hierarchy by separating the powerful from the weak. Humboldt State University's Lee H. Bowker has identified several other reasons for violent behavior:

> It provides a deterrent against being victimized, as a reputation for violence may eliminate an inmate as a target of assault.

> It enhances self-image in an environment that does not respect other attributes, such as intelligence.

> In the case of rape, it gives sexual relief.

> It serves as a means of acquiring material goods through extortion or outright robbery.[15]

The **deprivation model** can be used to explain the high level of prison violence. According to this model, the stressful and oppressive conditions of prison life lead to aggressive behavior on the part of inmates. When conditions such as overcrowding worsen, prison researcher Stephen C. Light found that inmate misconduct often increases.[16] In these circumstances, the violent behavior may not have any express purpose—it may just be a means of relieving tension.[17]

RIOTS

The deprivation model is helpful, though less convincing, in searching for the roots of collective violence. As far back as the 1930s, Frank Tannenbaum noted that harsh prison conditions can cause tension to build among inmates until it eventually explodes in the form of mass violence.[18] Living conditions in prisons are fairly constant, however, so how can the seemingly spontaneous outbreak of prison riots be explained?

Researchers have addressed these inconsistencies with the concept of **relative deprivation,** a theory that focuses on the gap between what is expected in a certain situation and what is achieved. Peter C. Kratcoski has argued that because prisoners enjoy such meager privileges to begin with, any further deprivation can spark disorder.[19] A number of criminologists, including Bert Useem in his studies made in the wake of a major riot at the Penitentiary of New Mexico in 1980, have noted that collective violence occurs in response to heightened measures of security at corrections facili-

Deprivation Model
A theory that inmate aggression is the result of the frustration inmates feel at being deprived of freedom, consumer goods, sex, and other staples of life outside the institution.

Relative Deprivation
The theory that inmate aggression is caused when freedoms and services that the inmate has come to accept as normal are decreased or eliminated.

Defrocked Catholic priest John Geoghan was strangled to death by another inmate at the maximum security Souza-Baranowski Correctional Center in Shirley, Massachusetts. At the time of his 2003 murder, Geoghan was serving a nine-to ten-year sentence for groping a ten-year-old boy. What are some of the reasons that violence is prevalent in prison culture?

AP Photo/Michael; Dwyer, Pool

> Reel Prison Violence

A homosexual prisoner is nearly beaten to death in the shower. A new inmate has a swastika branded onto his buttock. A prisoner is knocked unconscious by correctional officers and then set on fire by another inmate. A patient with AIDS is suffocated in the hospital ward.

Thus passes a day, or, more accurately, an episode, in Cell Block Five of the fictional Oswald Maximum Security Prison, the setting for Home Box Office's long-running program *Oz*. Prison has provided the setting for a number of television and film dramas, but few have been as graphically sadistic as the hell that is *Oz*. Certainly, prisons are violent places. By one calculation, the murder rate in prison is eight times that of "outside" society, and the assault rate is nearly twenty times greater. The worry among many observers is that images of inmate violence have become so commonplace in the media that Americans—especially judges—will come to see it as inevitable.

This line of thinking would practically absolve prison officials from responsibility to take measures to limit violent behavior. In fact, the United States Supreme Court has ruled that failure to

protect prison and jail inmates from harm violates the Eighth Amendment's prohibition against cruel and unusual punishment, as well as the due process clause (see Chapter 4). As a result, prison officials have been sued successfully for, in one instance, failing to protect an inmate against secondhand cigarette smoke and, in another, for placing a transsexual inmate in the general population of a maximum-security prison where he was raped and beaten by his cellmate.

If prison officials can prove that they were reasonably unaware of any potential danger to the inmate, however, they cannot be held responsible for harm that results from their inaction. Furthermore, an Indiana judge has upheld a decision by state correctional officers to charge an inmate with battery for striking, with a hot pot, another prisoner who had been attempting to sexually assault him. Similarly, in *Oz*, there is no right of self-defense for inmates. Even though the Supreme Court has stated that being exposed to violence is not "part of the penalty criminal offenders pay for their offense against society," the reality of prison life suggests otherwise.

ties.[20] Thus, the violence occurs in response to an additional reduction in freedom for inmates, who enjoy very little freedom to begin with.

Riots, which have been defined as situations in which a number of prisoners are beyond institutional control for a significant amount of time,[21] are relatively rare. Because of their explosive nature and potential for high casualties, however, riots have a unique ability to focus public attention on prison conditions. The collective violence at Attica Prison in upstate New York has been described as a turning point in the history of American corrections by alerting citizens to the situation in correctional facilities and spurring the prisoners' rights movement.[22]

Attica: Organized Violence   The Attica Prison riot lasted five days in September 1971. Nearly half of the institution's 2,500 inmates seized control of most of the prison. They took thirty-eight prison guards as hostages. The riot leaders, mostly members of the Black Muslims, presented prison administrators with a list of demands—modeled after the United Nations's Standards for Imprisoned Persons—that included better food, more programs, and due process for disciplinary action. In general, the riot appeared to be a reaction to the punitive atmosphere in Attica; one of its leaders complained to his lawyer that he had been beaten for walking with his hands in his pockets. During negotiations, another prisoner read the following statement:

> We are men, we are not beasts and we will not be beaten or driven as such. What has happened here is but the sound before the fury of those who are oppressed.[23]

INFOTRAC KEYWORDS

prison riots

For more information, use this search term with InfoTrac College Edition, your online library at www.infotrac-college.com

Officials at the Anderson County Sheriff's Department in Tennessee have provided a live "jail cam" that gives an inside look at the county jail. For access to this service through the department's Web site, click on *Web Links* under *Chapter Resources* at www.cjinaction.com

The negotiations ended abruptly when New York state troopers raided the prison grounds, killing thirty-nine inmates and wounding eighty-eight others. In the wake of the riot, however, New York Governor Nelson Rockefeller called for "radical reforms" in the state's corrections system, and twenty-four of the Attica prisoners' twenty-eight original demands were met. In 2000, declaring that they had been treated "like garbage," a federal judge awarded more than five hundred of the inmates involved in the violence and their relatives $8 million from the state for the abuse they had suffered.[24]

"I've seen seven stabbings, about six bashings, and three self-mutilations. Two hangings, one attempted hanging, any number of overdoses. And that's only me, in just seventy days."

—Anonymous jail inmate (1998)

INFOTRAC KEYWORDS

prison gangs

For more information, use this search term with InfoTrac College Edition, your online library at www.infotrac-college.com

Santa Fe: Disorganized Violence   The Attica riot has proved to be the exception rather than the rule. Most riots are disorganized and have no political agenda. They are marked by extreme levels of inmate-on-inmate violence. In a disturbance that broke out at the Penitentiary of New Mexico at Santa Fe in 1980, prisoners killed thirty-three of their fellow inmates, and nearly two hundred others were tortured, beaten, and raped. The riot was used as an excuse to take revenge for personal grievances, and the levels of violence—including the use of blowtorches on genitals—shocked the public.[25]

During the postriot investigations, prison administrators were strongly criticized for their lack of control over the Santa Fe institution. Two weeks before the riot, an outside consultant had warned that New Mexico prison officials were playing "Russian roulette with the lives of inmates" by failing to properly staff and train the personnel at the state's penal institutions.[26] Some observers see poor management, rather than levels of deprivation, as the primary cause of riots.[27]

Issues of Race and Ethnicity   The night before the Attica riot erupted, inmates yelled "[g]et a good night's sleep, whitey. Sleep tight, because tomorrow's the day." Officers in the prison were known to refer to their batons as "nigger sticks."[28] Race plays a major role in prison life, and prison violence is often an outlet for racial tension. As prison populations have changed over the past three decades, with African Americans and Hispanics becoming the majority in many penal institutions, issues of race and ethnicity have become increasingly important to prison administrators and researchers.

As early as the 1950s, researchers were noticing different group structures in inmate life. At that time, for example, prisoners at California's Soledad Prison informally segregated themselves according to geography as well as race: Tejanos (Mexicans raised in Texas), Chicanos, blacks from California, blacks from the South and Southwest, and the majority whites all formed separate social worlds.[29]

Leo Carroll, professor of sociology at the University of Rhode Island, has written extensively on how today's prisoners are "balkanized," with race determining nearly every aspect of an inmate's life, including friends, job assignments, and cell location.[30] Carroll's research has also shown how minority groups in prison have seized upon race to help form their prison identities.[31] In many instances, racial and ethnic identification is the primary focus of prison gangs, or cliques of inmates linked to illegal and violent activities such as prostitution, extortion, drug selling, gambling, and loan sharking. Though the stereotypical gang is composed of African Americans or Hispanics, in truth the array of different racial and ethnic prison groups is extensive. One of the most far-reaching and violent, for example, is the Aryan Brotherhood, whose members are dedicated to principles of white supremacy. Regardless of make-up, however, gangs share the same purpose:

> Their members have done in prison what many people do elsewhere when they feel personally powerless, threatened, and vulnerable: They align themselves with others, organize to fight back, and enhance their own status and control through their connection to a more powerful group.[32]

RAPE

In contrast to riots, the problem of sexual assault in prisons receives very little attention from media sources. This can be partly attributed to the ambiguity of the subject: that rape occurs in prisons and jails is undisputed, but determining exactly how widespread the problem is has proved difficult. Prison officials, aware that any sexual contact is prohibited in most penal institutions, are often unwilling to provide realistic figures for fear of negative publicity. Even when they are willing, they may be unable to do so. Most inmates are ashamed of being rape victims and refuse to report instances of sexual assault. Consequently, it has been difficult to come up with consistent statistics for sexual assault in prison. While research published in *The Prison Journal* found that about 21 percent of all inmates in four states had been sexually assaulted,[33] self-reported data gathered by the Human Rights Watch revealed that one in three inmates reported being raped.[34]

Whatever the figures, prison rape, like all rape, is considered primarily an act of violence rather than sex. Inmates subject to rape ("punks") are near the bottom of the prison power structure and, in some instances, may accept rape by one particularly powerful inmate in return for protection from others.[35] Raped inmates often suffer from rape trauma syndrome and a host of other psychological ailments, including suicidal tendencies. Many prisons do not offer sufficient medical treatment for rape victims, nor does the prison staff take the necessary measures to protect obvious targets of rape—young, slightly built, nonviolent offenders. Furthermore, corrections officials are rarely held liable for inmate-on-inmate violence.

ONLINE REVIEW *Go to the book's Web site for an interactive review of this section*

Inmates at a women's prison in Gatesville, Texas, prepare for work detail. Today, nearly 100,000 women are incarcerated in the United States, up from about 70,000 in 1995. Almost one hundred prisons in this country house only female inmates, compared to more than one thousand male correctional facilities.

Inside a Women's Prison

More than ten times as many research projects are conducted in men's prisons as in women's prisons.[36] This disparity is partly attributable to the small number of women's prisons: there are more than one thousand federal and state facilities for male inmates only, but fewer than one hundred women's institutions.[37] It is also, however, a result of the traditional lack of interest in women in the corrections system.

Andrew Lichtenstein/Corbis Sygma

CHALLENGES FACING FEMALE INMATES

Although women's prisons are not characterized by the levels of violence and oppression that occur in men's prisons, female inmates do not, by any stretch of the imagination, "have it easy."

Rape in Women's Prisons   Just as in men's institutions, sexual assault occurs in women's facilities, but the reported aggressor is much more likely to be a male correctional officer than another inmate. Recent lawsuits filed by female inmates in Georgia, Delaware, and the District of Columbia spotlight the problem,[38] as does a report by the human rights group Amnesty International, which revealed that forty prison staff members in California have been under investigation for sexual misconduct in the past few years.[39] Such assaults are almost certainly underreported, as victims fear reprisal.

Many experts believe the solution is to increase the number of female-only facilities and hire more female correctional officers.[40] Currently, 70 percent of the guards in federal women's prisons are male.[41] State and federal prison officials do not, however, have the resources to implement such changes to any large extent. Instead, all but six states have passed legislation prohibiting sexual misconduct by prison staff against inmates of either gender.

Female Inmates and Their Children   Criminologist Jocelyn Pollock-Bryne has suggested that the prison experience may be more difficult for women than men because of the family disintegration that often accompanies incarceration.[42] Nearly two-thirds of all female inmates lived with their children before being sentenced to prison or jail.[43] Either by their own choice or as a result of circumstances, nearly one in five of these women has no contact with her children or sees or speaks with them less than once a month.[44]

THE PSEUDO-FAMILY

As in male facilities, a system of prisonization is evident in women's prisons. The adaptation process in the female institution, however, relies on tightly knit cliques of prisoners that mimic the traditional family structure. The more experienced convicts adopt the role of the "father" or "mother" and act as parent-figures for younger, inexperienced "sons" or "daughters." Inmates choose their roles depending on appearance, personality, and background. As in "real" families, prison female families restrict sexual contact between members, relying on each other primarily for emotional support.[45]

Homosexuality often manifests itself in a women's prison through formation of another traditional family model: the monogamous couple. One member of the couple chooses the role of the husband, and the other becomes the wife.[46] In general, sex between inmates plays a different role in women's prisons than in men's prisons. In the latter, rape is considered an act of aggression and power rather than sex, and "true" homosexuals are related to the lowest rungs of the social hierarchy. By contrast, women who engage in sexual activity in prison are not automatically labeled homosexual, and lesbians are not hampered in their social-climbing efforts.[47]

Researchers have also found that female inmates share a great deal more than their male counterparts. In a men's prison, self-sufficiency and autonomy are valued, whereas in women's prisons members of cliques and families allocate cosmetics, foods, clothes, and other goods.[48] (One observer points out that this greater tendency to share may be attributed to the fact that women are allowed more personal belongings in prison than men are.[49])

✦ ONLINE REVIEW *Go to the book's Web site for an interactive review of this section*

Correctional Officers and Discipline

Under model circumstances, the presence of correctional officers—the standard term used to describe prison guards—would mitigate the levels of violence in American correctional institutions. To a large extent, this is indeed the case; without correctional officers, the prison would be a place of anarchy. But in the highly regulated, oppressive environment of the prison, correctional officers must use the threat of violence, if not actual violence, to instill discipline and keep order. Thus, the relationship between prison staff and inmates is marked by mutual distrust. Consider the two following statements, the first made by a correctional officer and the second by a prisoner:

> [My job is to] protect, feed, and try to educate scum who raped and brutalized women and children . . . who, if I turn my back, will go into their cell, wrap a blanket around their cellmate's legs, and threaten to beat or rape him if he doesn't give sex, carry contraband, or fork over radios, money, or other goods willingly. And they'll stick a shank in me tomorrow if they think they can get away with it.[50]
>
> The pigs in the state and federal prisons . . . treat me so violently, I cannot possibly imagine a time I could ever have anything but the deepest, aching, searing hatred for them. I can't begin to tell you what they do to me. If I were weaker by a hair, they would destroy me.[51]

INFOTRAC KEYWORDS
correctional officers
For more information, use this search term with InfoTrac College Edition, your online library at www.infotrac-college.com

It may be difficult for an outsider to understand the emotions that fuel such sentiments. French philosopher Michael Foucault points out that discipline, both in prison and in the general community, is a means of social organization as well as punishment.[52] Discipline is imposed when a person behaves in a manner that is contrary to the values of the dominant social group. Correctional officers and inmates have different concepts of the ideal structure of prison society, and, as the two quotations above demonstrate, this conflict generates intense feelings of fear and hatred, which often lead to violence.

RANK AND DUTIES OF CORRECTIONAL OFFICERS

After seven convicts escaped from the Connally Unit in Kenedy, Texas, several years ago, much of the blame fell on the custodial staff. Security at the facility had been extremely lax, with officers failing to properly identify individuals before opening gates, leaving prison vehicles unattended on the premises, and allowing unsupervised prisoners to work in a maintenance room. To avoid such problems and promote efficiency, in most prisons each correctional officer has a clearly delineated rank and duty. The custodial staff at most prisons is organized according to four general ranks—captain, lieutenant, sergeant, and officer. In keeping with the militaristic model, captains are primarily administrators who deal directly with the warden on custodial issues. Lieutenants are the disciplinarians of the prison, responsible for policing and transporting the inmates. Sergeants oversee platoons of officers in specific parts of the prison, such as various cell blocks or work spaces. (See the feature *Careers in CJ*.)

Lucien X. Lombardo, professor of sociology and criminal justice at Old Dominion University, has identified six general job categories among correctional officers.[53]

Block Officers   In Lombardo's opinion, the most demanding job assignment is that of the block officer. This employee may supervise the cell blocks of as many as four hundred inmates, as well as the correctional officers on block guard duty. During the day, the job is a hectic combination of security, housekeeping, and human services. At night, when the convicts are confined to their cells, block officers must maintain continuous inspections to assure that no self-destructive behavior is taking place.

In general, the block officer is responsible for the "well-being" of the inmates. In addition to making sure that inmates do not harm themselves or other prisoners, the block officer also acts as somewhat of a camp counselor, dispensing advice and seeing that inmates understand and follow the rules of the facility. Finally, because the block officer comes in daily close contact with prisoners, she or he is most likely to be the target of inmate violence when it erupts.

Work Detail Supervisors   In many penal institutions, the inmates work in the cafeteria, the prison store, the laundry, or other areas. Work detail supervisors oversee small groups of inmates as they perform their jobs. In general, the atmosphere in these work groups is more relaxed than in the cell blocks. The inmates and their supervisor are actively working toward the same goal—to complete the assignment—and therefore can develop a solidarity that does not exist in the cell blocks. If an inmate and work supervisor find themselves on the same detail for an extended period of time, they may even develop a friendly personal relationship, though it would be based on the parent-child model rather than a relationship of two equals.[54]

Industrial Shop and School Officers   These officers perform maintenance and security functions in educational and workshop programs. Their primary responsibility is to make sure that inmates are on time for these programs and that attendance requirements are followed. The officers must also make sure that the inmates are not disruptive during the sessions and that they do not steal items from the workshop or classroom.

The U.S. Department of Labor offers information about a career as a correctional officer. Find this Web site by clicking on *Web Links* under *Chapter Resources* at www.cjinaction.com

Yard Officers   Officers who work the prison yard usually have the least seniority, befitting the assignment's reputation as dangerous and stressful. Unlike the cell blocks, programs, and work details, which are strictly organized, the prison yard is a place of relative freedom for the inmates. Consequently, yard officers must be constantly on alert for breaches in prison discipline or regulations. If collective violence occurs, yard officers run the highest chance of being injured, taken hostage, or even killed.

Tower Guards   Previously, a wall post was considered the worst assignment in the prison. Tower guards spend their entire shifts, which usually last eight hours,

> Robert M. Lucas Corrections Facility Commander

My interest in the corrections field grew out of the need to be involved in solving problems associated with crime and punishment. I began my career as a law enforcement deputy. On completion of my undergraduate studies I sought experience in the counseling and programs aspects of detention. Ultimately I became interested in the management of jails and decided to become a sworn detention officer. My career path has given me a unique perspective from having experience in three major components of criminal justice: law enforcement, detention, and programs. Throughout my career I have continued my education as a corrections professional; my accomplishments include a master of arts degree in criminal justice from the University of South Florida, and I am a graduate of the Southern Police Institute's Administrative Officers Course.

I am currently assigned as a facility commander in a 1,714-bed direct supervision jail. The facility is divided into two factions: housing and central intake. Central intake encompasses all facets of booking as well as the classification and records bureau. There is a combined total of approximately 300 sworn and civilian employees assigned to this multidimensional command and responsible for the processing and booking of over 62,000 inmates in 1998. Additionally, my command must ensure that inmates make all required court appearances and that all transfers or releases are proper and within established releasing standards. My most important duties are ensuring that staff are properly trained; that staff are assigned to functions which guarantee security is maintained at the highest level; and that all inmates are treated in accordance with local, state, and federal standards.

A defining incident in my career was being involved in the mass arrest of 186 individuals as a result of a demonstration. As an assistant tactical commander, I was responsible for remote booking, security, crowd control, and the coordination of inmate transportation to the central jail facility. The incident was significant from two aspects: 1) the dynamics and logistics involved in the arrest, detainment, and booking of a large number of individuals in a short period of time; and 2) the awareness of the importance of a cooperative effort between law enforcement and detention. A number of problems were immediately evident in

the arrest and processing of this large number of inmates, including security, site location, feeding, sanitation, and medical care for those in need. As is typical with most agencies, the booking process was normally accomplished in a secure facility separate from any outside disruptive factors. The remote booking exposed the staff to dissidents and necessitated the initial processing of the inmates in a temporary booking area without normal security.

Courtesy Robert M. Lucas

Robert M. Lucas

This incident clearly displayed the talents and abilities of the detention staff assigned to the tactical unit. The members functioned as a disciplined team and demonstrated to law enforcement peers that the detention staff was capable and anxious to work together toward common goals. Subsequent to that mass arrest, the detention tactical unit has worked in tandem with law enforcement in training exercises, support for crowd control during a Super Bowl game, preparation for natural disasters, search for missing persons, and the development of a honor guard in which representatives from detention and law enforcement routinely perform together at funerals, civic events, dedications, and public demonstrations.

I feel the qualities essential to the corrections field are those common to most fields, such as a desire to perform at a high level of standards, a commitment to personal growth through change and development, and facing each task as a challenge as opposed to a problem. The management and operation of any detention facility is taxing, and it challenges the abilities, knowledge, and experience of those in supervisory roles. Staff are expected to fulfill a number of roles and encounter any number of problems or emergencies daily. The jail practitioner of today must be well versed in all aspects of the jail operation and applicable laws and standards, and be able to address problems associated with expanding inmate populations, construction needs, and specialized inmate categories.

 Go to the Careers in Criminal Justice Interactive CD *for more profiles in the field of criminal justice.*

in their isolated, silent posts high above the grounds of the facility. While keeping watch with a high-powered rifle, they communicate only through walkie-talkies. As prison violence has become more commonplace, however, the tower guard, being "above" any real danger, has become a more coveted position. Correctional officers now feel the benefits of safety outweigh the loneliness that comes with the job.

One benefit of the prison boom has been economic, as prisons infuse money and jobs into the regions where they are located. These regions are often rural and poor. In upstate New York's North County, for example, the average worker earns about $20,000 a year; the correctional officers at North County's Clinton Prison, shown above, earn an average of $40,000. Working as a correctional officer is one of the few ways that residents of North County who do not have a college degree can enjoy a middle-class life. Furthermore, as prisons are recession proof, job security among correctional officers is higher than in most other local industries. Why, despite these benefits, does the profession of correctional officer continue to have a negative image?

Administrative Building Assignments Officers who hold administrative building assignments are in even less personal danger than tower guards and therefore hold the most desired job assignments. These officers provide security at prison gates, oversee visitation procedures, act as liaisons for civilians, and handle administrative tasks such as processing the paperwork when an inmate is transferred from another institution. Because such assignments involve contact with the public, the officers are often chosen for their public relations skills as well as any other talents they may have.

DISCIPLINE

As Erving Goffman noted in his essay on the "total institution," in the general society adults are rarely placed in a position where they are "punished" as a child would be.[55] Therefore, the strict disciplinary measures imposed on prisoners come as something of a shock and can provoke strong defensive reactions. Correctional officers who must deal with these responses often find that disciplining inmates is the most difficult and stressful aspect of their job.

The Severity of Sanctions The prisoners' manual lists the types of behavior that can result in disciplinary action. An institutional disciplinary committee decides the sanctions for specific types of misconduct. These sanctions include loss of privileges such as visiting and recreational opportunities for minor infractions, as well as more serious punishments for major infractions. The most severe sanction is punitive segregation, also known as solitary confinement or sensory deprivation, in which the inmate is isolated in a cell known as "the hole." This punishment is considered so debilitating that most facilities—initially fearful that the courts would find long periods of total deprivation "cruel and unusual" under the Eighth Amendment— have placed a twenty-day limit on the length of the confinement. Prison officials can, if they so choose, remove the inmate for a short period of time and then return him or her to the hole, effectively sidestepping the restrictions.

Discipline and Discretion This is not to say that the judicial system has greatly restricted disciplinary actions in prison. For the most part, correctional officers are given the same discretionary powers as police officers (discussed in Chapter 5) to use their experience to determine when force is warranted. In *Whitley v. Albers* (1986),[56] the Supreme Court held that the use of force by prison officials violates an inmate's Eighth Amendment protections only if the force amounts to "the unnecessary and wanton infliction of pain." Excessive force can be considered "necessary" if the legitimate security interests of the penal institution are at stake. Consequently, an appeals court ruled that when officers at a Maryland prison formed an "extraction team" to remove the leader of a riot from his cell, beating him in the process, the use of force was justified given the situation.[57]

In contrast, in *Hudson v. McMillan* (1992)[58] the Supreme Court ruled that minor injuries suffered by a convict at the hands of a correctional officer following an argument did violate the inmate's rights, because there was no security concern at the time of the incident. To protect themselves from lawsuits, many corrections departments have developed codes to help guide correctional officers in the proper use of force.

↗ ONLINE REVIEW *Go to the book's Web site for an interactive review of this section*

Protecting Prisoners' Rights

The general attitude of the law toward inmates is summed up by the Thirteenth Amendment to the U.S. Constitution:

> Neither slavery nor involuntary servitude, except as a punishment for crime whereof the party shall have been duly convicted, shall exist within the United States.

In other words, inmates do not have the same guaranteed rights as other Americans. For most of the nation's history, courts have followed the spirit of this amendment by applying the **"hands-off" doctrine** of prisoner law. This (unwritten) doctrine assumes that the care of inmates should be left to prison officials and that it is not the place of judges to intervene in penal administrative matters.

The prison code flourished during the "hands-off" period; prisoners, unable to count on any outside forces to protect their rights, needed an internal social structure that would allow them to do so themselves. In the 1960s, as disenfranchised groups from all parts of society began to insist on their constitutional rights, prisoners did so as well. The prisoners' rights movement demanded, and received, fuller recognition of prisoners' rights and greater access to American courts. It would be difficult, however, to label the movement a complete success. As one observer notes, "conditions of confinement in many American prisons have deteriorated during the same time period in which judicial recognition and concern for prisoners' legal rights dramatically increased."[59]

THE "HANDS-ON" APPROACH

The end of the "hands-off" period can be dated to the Supreme Court's decision in *Cooper v. Pate* (1964).[60] In this case, Cooper, an inmate at the Illinois State Penitentiary, filed a petition for relief under the Civil Rights Act of 1871, stating that he had a First Amendment right to purchase reading material about the Black Muslim movement. The Court, overturning rulings of several lower courts, held that the act did protect the constitutional rights of prisoners. This decision effectively allowed inmates to file civil lawsuits under Title 42 of the United States Code, Section 1983—known simply as Section 1983—if they felt that a prison or jail was denying their civil rights. An inmate who has been beaten by a correctional officer, for example, can bring a Section 1983 suit against the penal institution for denial of Eighth Amendment protection from cruel and unusual punishment.

Symbolically, the Supreme Court's declaration in *Wolff v. McDonnell* (1974)[61] that "[t]here is no iron curtain drawn between the Constitution and the prisons of this country" was just as significant as the *Cooper* ruling. It signified to civil rights lawyers that the Court would no longer follow the "hands-off" doctrine. The case had practical overtones as well, establishing that prisoners have a right to the following basic due process procedures when being disciplined by a penal institution:

"Hands-Off" Doctrine
The unwritten judicial policy that favors noninterference by the courts in the administration of prisons and jails.

Michael Blucker filed a lawsuit, charging that prison officials at the Menard Correctional Center in Illinois failed to protect him from being sexually assaulted while he was an inmate at the facility. A jury found that five members of the prison staff were not liable for the pain and suffering of Blucker. How would the concepts of "simple negligence" and "deliberate indifference" apply to Blucker's case and its outcome?

Ted Dargan/*St. Louis Post-Dispatch*

> A fair hearing.

> Written notice at least twenty-four hours in advance of the hearing.

> An opportunity to speak at the hearing (though not to be represented by counsel during the hearing).

> An opportunity to call witnesses (unless doing so jeopardizes prison security).

> A written statement detailing the final decision and reasons for that decision.

Indeed, the prisoners' rights movement can count to its credit a number of legal decisions that have increased protection of inmates' constitutional rights. (See Figure 14.4 for a summary of the key Supreme Court decisions.)

LIMITING PRISONERS' RIGHTS

Despite these successes, not all proponents of prisoners' rights feel that the courts have entirely abandoned the "hands-off" doctrine. Instead, they believe that by establishing standards of "deliberate indifference" and "identifiable human needs," court rulings have merely provided penal institutions with legally acceptable methods of denying prisoners' constitutional protections.

"Deliberate Indifference"
A standard that must be met by inmates trying to prove that their Eighth Amendment rights were violated by a correctional facility. It occurs when prison officials are aware of harmful conditions of confinement but fail to take steps to remedy those conditions.

"Deliberate Indifference"   In the 1976 case *Estelle v. Gamble*,[62] the Supreme Court established the **"deliberate indifference"** standard. Specifically, Justice Thurgood Marshall wrote that prison officials violated a convict's Eighth Amendment rights if they deliberately failed to provide him or her with necessary medical care. At the time, the decision was hailed as a victory for prisoners' rights, and it continues to ensure that a certain level of health care is provided. (In 2002, for example, a California inmate received a heart transplant at a cost of nearly $1 million.) Defining "deliberate" has proved difficult, however. Does it mean that prison officials "should have known" that an inmate was placed in harm's way, or does it mean that prison officials purposefully placed the inmate in harm's way?

The "Purpose" Requirement   In subsequent decisions, the Supreme Court appears to have accepted the latter interpretation. In ruling on two separate 1986 cases, for example, the Court held that "simple negligence" was not acceptable grounds for a Section 1983 civil suit, and that a prison official's behavior was actionable only if it was done "maliciously or sadistically for the very purpose of causing harm."[63] Since it is quite difficult to prove in court a person's state of mind, the "deliberate negligence" standard has become a formidable one for prisoners to meet.

In *Wilson v. Seiter* (1991),[64] for example, Pearly L. Wilson filed a Section 1983 suit alleging that certain conditions of his confinement—including overcrowding; excessive noise; inadequate heating, cool-

FIGURE 14.4 **The United States Supreme Court in the 1970s: Expanding Prisoners' Rights**

In these cases, the Supreme Court recognized inmates' rights to freedom of religion, freedom of expression, due process, and protection from cruel and unusual punishment.

> *Cruz v. Beto* **(405 U.S. 319 [1972]).** Prisoners cannot be denied the right to practice their religion, even if that religion is not one of the "standard" belief systems in the United States. In this case, the inmate who had been denied the opportunity to practice was a Buddhist.

> *Procunier v. Martinez* **(416 U.S. 396 [1974]).** Correctional officials can censor an inmate's mail only when such censorship is necessary to maintain prison security.

> *Wolff v. McDonnell* **(418 U.S. 539 [1974]).** Prisoners have due process rights when they are faced with disciplinary action that may place them in segregation or add time to their sentences. The rights include the right to a hearing, an opportunity to speak at the hearing, and an opportunity to call witnesses (unless doing so would threaten prison security).

> *Hutto v. Finney* **(437 U.S. 678 [1978]).** Solitary confinement that lasts for more than thirty days is cruel and unusual punishment.

ing, and ventilation; and unsanitary bathroom and dining facilities—were cruel and unusual. The Supreme Court ruled against Wilson, stating that he had failed to prove that these conditions, even if they existed, were the result of "deliberate indifference" on the part of prison officials. Three years later, in a case concerning a transsexual inmate who was placed in the general population of a federal prison and subsequently beaten and raped, the Court narrowed the definition of "deliberate" even further. Though ruling in favor of the inmate, it held that the prison official must both be aware of the facts that create a potential for harm and also *draw the conclusion* that those facts will lead to harm.[65]

"Identifiable Human Needs"   The *Wilson* decision created another standard for determining Eighth Amendment violations that has drawn criticism from civil rights lawyers. It asserted that a prisoner must show that the institution has denied her or him a basic human need such as food, warmth, or exercise.[66] The Court failed, however, to mention any other needs besides these three, forcing other courts to interpret **"identifiable human needs"** for themselves. Taking a similar slant, in *Sandin v. Conner* (1995),[67] the Court ruled that inmates have rights to due process in disciplinary matters only when the punishment imposes "atypical or significant hardships in relation to ordinary incidents of prison life." Using this standard, inmates transferred to supermax prisons do not have the right to a hearing because the conditions in a supermax (discussed in Chapter 13) are not atypical. They are merely extreme.

ONLINE REVIEW *Go to the book's Web site for an interactive review of this section*

"Identifiable Human Needs"
The basic human necessities that correctional facilities are required by the Constitution to provide to inmates. Beyond food, warmth, and exercise, the court system has been unable to establish exactly what these needs are.

Parole and Release from Prison

An important fact to remember about inmates is that almost all of them will at some point be returned to the community. One of the great challenges facing prison administrators is to prepare their charges for "life on the outside." With that goal in mind, prisons offer a number of self-improvement programs for inmates. For many of these inmates, a successful adjustment following release is predicated on finding and keeping employment. Two main obstacles to achieving this goal are lack of education and a lack of employable skills. Consequently, many penal institutions offer programs in these areas. They also offer therapy programs to help inmates overcome emotional or psychological problems that may direct them toward criminal activity.

Though little empirical research exists to support the claim, many criminal justice experts suspect that inmates attend prison programs not for self-improvement but to secure an early release.[68] This can be accomplished in two ways. First, many penal institutions offer prisoners incentives to take part in the programs. Inmates in the Orange County (Florida) Jail, for example, earn eleven days of *good-time credit* for every month they successfully complete a program. As was discussed in Chapter 11, inmates receive these credits—which allow time to be subtracted from their terms—for obeying prison rules, working within the prison, and other laudable activities.

Second, inmates believe that by participating in prison programs, they can impress parole boards and increase their chances of early release by **parole,** or the *conditional* release of a prisoner after a portion of his or her sentence has been

Parole
The conditional release of an inmate before his or her sentence has expired. The remainder of the sentence is served in the community under the supervision of correctional (parole) officers, and the offender can be returned to incarceration if he or she breaks the conditions of parole, as determined by a parole board.

served. Parole allows the corrections system to continue to supervise an offender who is no longer incarcerated. As long as parolees follow the conditions of their parole, they are allowed to finish their terms outside the prison. If parolees break the terms of their early release, however, they face the risk of being returned to a penal institution.

According to Todd Clear and George F. Cole, parole is based on three concepts:

1 *Grace.* The prisoner has no right to be given an early release, but the government has granted her or him that privilege.

2 *Contract of consent.* The government and the parolee enter into an arrangement whereby the latter agrees to abide by certain conditions in return for continued freedom.

3 *Custody.* Technically, though no longer incarcerated, the parolee is still the responsibility of the state. Parole is an extension of corrections.[69] (The phonetic and administrative similarities between probation and parole can be confusing. See *Mastering Concepts—Probation versus Parole* for clarification.)

Because of good-time credits and parole, most prisoners do not serve their entire sentence in prison. In fact, the average felon serves only about half of the term handed down by the court.

OTHER TYPES OF PRISON RELEASE

Parole, a conditional release, is the most common form of release, but it is not the only one (see Figure 14.5). Prisoners receive an unconditional release when they have completed the terms of their sentence and no longer require incarceration or supervision. One form of unconditional release is **mandatory release** (also known as "maxing out"), which occurs when an inmate has served the maximum amount of time on the initial sentence, minus reductions for good-time credits.

Another, quite rare unconditional release is a **pardon,** a form of executive clemency. The president (on the federal level) and the governor (on the state level) can grant pardon, or forgive a convict's criminal punishment. Most states have a board of pardons—affiliated with the parole board—which makes recommendations to the governor in cases in which it believes a pardon is warranted. Most pardons involve obvious miscarriages of justice, though sometimes a governor will pardon an individual to remove the stain of conviction from his or her criminal record.

Certain *temporary releases* also exist. Some inmates, who qualify by exhibiting good behavior and generally proving that they do not represent a risk to society, are allowed to leave the prison on **furlough** for a certain amount of time, usually between a day and a week. At times, a furlough is granted because of a family emergency, such as a funeral. Furloughs can be particularly helpful for an inmate who is nearing release and can use them to ease the readjustment period.

Mandatory Release

Release from prison that occurs when an offender has served the length of his or her sentence, with time taken off for good behavior.

Pardon

An act of executive clemency that overturns a conviction and erases mention of the crime from the person's criminal record.

Furlough

Temporary release from a prison for purposes of vocational or educational training, to ease the shock of release, or for personal reasons.

FIGURE 14.5 Release from State and Federal Correctional Facilities

Source: Adapted from Bureau of Justice Statistics, *Correctional Populations in the United States, 1997* (Washington, D.C.: U.S. Department of Justice, 2000), Table 5.13.

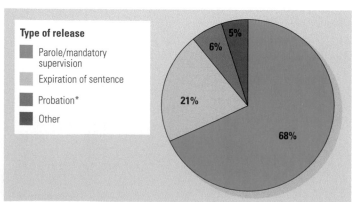

Type of release

- Parole/mandatory supervision
- Expiration of sentence
- Probation*
- Other

5%
6%
21%
68%

*As the second step in a split sentence.

> Probation versus Parole

Probation and parole have many aspects in common. In fact, probation and parole are so similar that many jurisdictions combine them into a single agency. There are, however, some important distinctions between the two systems, as noted below.

Because of these differences, many observers believe that probation and parole should not be combined in the same agency, though limited financial resources will assure that many jurisdictions will continue to do so.

	PROBATION	PAROLE
Basic Definition	An alternative to imprisonment in which a person who has been convicted of a crime is allowed to serve his or her sentence in the community subject to certain conditions and supervision by a probation officer.	An early release from a correctional facility as determined by an administrative body (the parole board), in which the convicted offender is given the chance to spend the remainder of his or her sentence under supervision in the community.
Timing	The offender is sentenced to a probationary term in place of a prison or jail term. If the offender breaks the conditions of probation, he or she is sent to prison or jail. Therefore, probation occurs *before* imprisonment.	Parole is a form of early release. Therefore, parole occurs *after* an offender has spent time behind bars.
Authority	Probation falls under the domain of the judiciary. In other words, judges make the decision whether to send a convicted offender to prison or jail or to give her or him a sentence of probation. If a person violates the terms of probation, a judge ultimately decides whether she or he should be sent to a correctional facility as punishment.	Parole falls under the domain of an administrative body (often appointed by an executive such as a state governor) known as the parole board. The parole board determines whether the prisoner is qualified for early release, and under which conditions he or she will be allowed to remain in the community. When a parolee violates the conditions of parole, the parole board must decide whether to send him or her back to prison. (Although they can be asked to make recommendations to the parole board, judges generally are *not* involved in the parole decision.)
Characteristics of Offenders	As a number of studies have shown, probationers are normally less involved in the criminal lifestyle. Most of them are first-time offenders who have committed nonviolent crimes.	Many parolees have spent months or even years in prison and, besides abiding by conditions of parole, must make the difficult transition to "life on the outside."

DISCRETIONARY RELEASE

As you may recall from Chapter 11, corrections systems are classified by sentencing procedure—indeterminate or determinate. Indeterminate sentencing occurs when the legislature sets a range of punishments for particular crimes, and the judge and the parole board exercise discretion in determining the actual length of the prison term. For that reason, states with indeterminate sentencing are said to have systems of **discretionary release.** Until the mid-1970s, all states and the federal government operated in this manner.

Discretionary Release
The release of an inmate into a community supervision program at the discretion of the parole board within limits set by state or federal law.

INFOTRAC KEYWORDS

parole

For more information, use this search term with InfoTrac College Edition, your online library at www.infotrac-college.com

Eligibility for Parole   Under indeterminate sentencing, parole is not a right but a privilege. This is a crucial point, as it establishes the terms of the relationship between the inmate and the corrections authorities during the parole process. In *Greenholtz v. Inmates of the Nebraska Penal and Correctional Complex* (1979),[70] the Supreme Court ruled that inmates did not have a constitutionally protected right to expect parole, thereby giving states the freedom to set their own standards for determining parole eligibility. In most states that have retained indeterminate sentencing, a prisoner is eligible to be considered for parole release after serving a legislatively determined percentage of the minimum sentence—usually one-half or two-thirds—less any good time or other credits.

Contrary to what is depicted in many films and television shows, a convict does not "apply" for parole. An inmate's case automatically comes up before the parole board a certain number of days—often ninety—before she or he is eligible for parole. The date of eligibility depends on statutory requirements, the terms of the sentence, and the behavior of the inmate in prison. The board has an eligibility report prepared, which provides information on the various factors that must be taken into consideration in making the decision. The board also reviews the case file to acquaint itself with the original crime and conducts an interview with the inmate. At some point before the eligibility date, the entire board, or a subcommittee of the board, votes on whether parole will be granted.

Not all convicts are eligible for parole. Many states have a sentencing system in which offenders who have committed the most serious crimes receive life terms without the possibility of early release. In general, life-without-parole is reserved for those offenders who have

> committed capital, or first degree, murder;

> committed serious offenses other than murder; or

> been defined by statute as habitual, or repeat, offenders, such as those sentenced under "three-strikes" laws.[71]

Besides murder, drug offenders and sex offenders are most commonly targeted for life-without-parole. The sentence is fraught with controversy, as many observers, including inmates, feel serving life-without-parole is a crueler punishment than the death penalty.[72] Furthermore, the Supreme Court has ruled that when a capital defendant who has been convicted of murder will be ineligible for parole, due process requires the jury to be told of this fact.[73] In other words, the jury must know that, in sentencing the defendant, it has a choice between execution and life-without-parole.

The Parole Board   The cumulated efforts of the police, the courtroom work group, and correctional officials lead to a single question in most cases: When should an offender be released?[74] This is a difficult question and is often left to the **parole board** to answer. When members of the parole board make what in retrospect was a mistake, they quickly draw the attention of the media, the public, and the courts.

According to the American Correctional Association, the parole board has four basic roles:

1 To decide which offenders should be placed on parole.

2 To determine the conditions of parole and aid in the continuing supervision of the parolee.

Parole Board

A body of appointed civilians that decides whether a convict should be granted conditional release before the end of his or her sentence.

3 To discharge the offender when the conditions of parole have been met.

4 If a violation occurs, to determine whether parole privileges should be revoked.[75]

Most parole boards are small, made up of five to seven members. In many jurisdictions, board members' terms are limited to between four and six years. The requirements for board members vary. Nearly half the states have no prerequisites, while others require a bachelor's degree or some expertise in the field of criminal justice.

AP Photo/Doral Chenoweth III, *Columbus Dispatch*

Peter "Commando Pedro" Langan, shown here as he is escorted by Franklin County (Ohio) sheriff's deputies from the county jail, was found guilty of participating in twenty-two bank robberies over a two-year period. Langan was the leader of the Midwestern Bank Bandits, a white separatist gang that declared itself in opposition to the government. U.S. District Judge John D. Holschuh sentenced Langan to a life sentence without possibility of parole. Do you agree with some observers who believe that life-without-parole is a harsher sentence than the death penalty? Or do you believe that life-without-parole is a humane alternative to the death penalty?

Parole boards are either affiliated with government agencies or act as independent bodies. In the first instance, board members are usually members of the correctional staff appointed by the state department of corrections. In contrast, independent parole boards are made up of citizens from the community who have been chosen for the post by a government official, usually the governor. Because most states with independent boards have no specific criteria for the members, critics believe that these boards tend to be "politicized" by the appointment of members—who have limited knowledge of the criminal justice system—as a return for political favors.[76]

The Parole Hearing In a system that uses discretionary parole, the actual release decision is made at a **parole grant hearing.** During this hearing, the entire board or a subcommittee reviews relevant information on the convict. Sometimes, but not always, the offender is interviewed. Because the board members have only limited knowledge of each offender, key players in the case are often notified in advance of the parole hearing and asked to provide comments and recommendations. These participants include the sentencing judge, the attorneys at the trial, the victims, and any law enforcement officers who may be involved.[77] After these preparations, the typical parole hearing itself is very short—usually lasting just a few minutes.

If parole is denied, the entire process is replayed at the next "action date," which depends on the nature of the offender's crimes and all relevant laws. In 2002, for example, Leslie Van Houten was denied parole for the fourteenth time. Van Houten was convicted of murder in 1969 for the role she played in the gruesome Beverly Hills, California, killing of pregnant actress Sharon Tate and six others under the direction of Charles Manson. While in prison, Van Houten—who claims that she played a minimal role in the murders—has earned bachelor's and master's degrees and has never had a disciplinary report filed against her. Families of the victims continue to petition the California Board of Prison Terms to keep her incarcerated, and although the board has said Van Houten's chances improve with each hearing, most observers believe she will never be released. (Manson himself has been denied parole nine times and stated during his last

Parole Grant Hearing
A hearing in which the entire parole board or a subcommittee reviews information, meets the offender, and hears testimony from relevant witnesses to determine whether to grant parole.

In August 2003, Kathy Boudin was released on parole after serving twenty-two years in prison for her role in an armored-car robbery and shootout that left three persons, including two police officers, dead. Despite opposition from the victims' families, the New York Parole Board decided that Boudin's work with AIDS sufferers and incarcerated mothers at the Bedford Hill Correctional Facility warranted her early release. What effect should such good works have on the parole decision when, as in this case, the initial crime was of a "serious and brutal nature"?

hearing in 1997 that he did not want to be released.) In some states, the parole board is required to give written reasons for denying parole, and some jurisdictions give the inmate, prosecution, or victims the option to appeal the board's decision.

THE EMERGENCE OF MANDATORY RELEASE

The legitimacy of discretionary release relies to a certain extent on the perception of parole decisions by offenders, victims, and the general public. Like judicial discretion (as we discussed in Chapter 11), parole board discretion is criticized when the decisions are seen as arbitrary and unfair and lead to rampant disparity in the release dates of similar offenders.[78] Proponents of discretionary release argue that parole boards must tailor their decisions to the individual case, but such protestations seem to be undermined by the raw data: research done by the Bureau of Justice Statistics has found that most offenders were serving less than a third of their sentences in the early 1990s.[79]

As Michael Tonry noted, such statistics gave the impression that parole board members "tossed darts at a dartboard" to determine who should be released, and when.[80] As a result of this criticism, twenty-seven states have now implemented determinate sentencing systems, which set minimum mandatory terms without possibility of parole. These systems provide for *mandatory release,* in which offenders leave incarceration when their sentences have expired, minus adjustments made for good time.

Truth in Sentencing　　The move toward mandatory release has come partly at the urging of the federal government. The federal sentencing guidelines that went into effect in 1987 required those who were convicted in federal courts to serve at least 85 percent of their terms.[81] Federal crime bills in 1994 and 1995 encouraged states to adopt this *truth-in-sentencing* (mentioned previously in Chapter 11) approach by making federal aid for prison construction conditional on the passage of such laws.[82] Many have done just that (see Figure 14.6).

"Truth in sentencing" is an umbrella term that covers a number of different state and federal statutes. In general, these laws have the following goals:

> To restore "truth" to the sentencing process by eliminating situations in which offenders are released by a parole board after serving less than the minimum term to which they were sentenced.

> To increase the percentage of the term that is actually served in prison, with the purpose of reducing crime by keeping convicts imprisoned for a longer period.

> To control the use of prison space by giving corrections officials the benefit of predictable terms and policymakers advance notice of the impact that sentencing statutes will have on prison populations.[83]

Note that fourteen states and the federal government have officially "abolished" parole. For the most part, however, these states simply emphasize prison terms that are "truthful," not necessarily "longer." Therefore, in Louisiana—noted for its

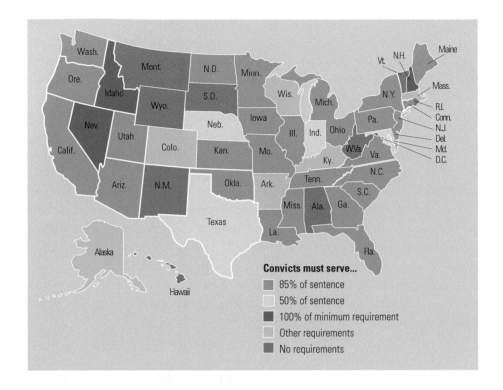

FIGURE 14.6 State Truth-in-Sentencing Requirements

Twenty-nine states and the District of Columbia have adopted federal truth-in-sentencing laws that require convicts to serve at least 85 percent of their sentences before being released.

Source: Adapted from Bureau of Justice Statistics, *Truth in Sentencing in State Prisons* (Washington, D.C.: U.S. Department of Justice, 1999), Table 1.

harsh sentencing practices—violent offenders who serve only 50 percent of their term spend more time in prison than do prisoners in many states that have "abolished" parole.[84]

Parole Guidelines   One of the most popular methods of ensuring truth in sentencing is the use of **parole guidelines.** Similar to sentencing guidelines (see Chapter 11), parole guidelines attempt to measure a potential parolee's risk of recidivism by considering factors such as the original offense, criminal history, behavior in prison, past employment, substance abuse, and performance under any previous periods of parole or probation. Inmates who score positively in these areas are considered less likely to pose a danger to society and have a better chance of obtaining an early release date.

Parole Guidelines

Employed to remove discretion from the parole process, these guidelines attempt to measure the risks of an offender recidivating, and then use these measurements to determine whether early release will be granted and under what conditions.

PAROLE SUPERVISION

The term *parole* has two meanings. The first, as we have seen, refers to the establishment of a release date. The second relates to the continuing supervision of convicted felons after they have been released from prison.

Conditions of Parole   Many of the procedures and issues of parole supervision are similar to those of probation supervision. Like probationers, when parolees are granted parole, they are placed under the supervision of correctional officers and required to follow certain conditions. Some of these conditions are fairly uniform. All parolees, for example, must comply with the law, and they are generally responsible for reporting to their parole officer at certain intervals. The frequency of these visits, along with the other terms of parole, are spelled out in the **parole contract,** which sets out the agreement between the state and the paroled

Parole Contract

An agreement between the state and the offender that establishes the conditions under which the latter will be allowed to serve the remainder of her or his prison term in the community.

"Johnny plus alcohol plus women equals trouble."
—Excerpt from 1976 parole report on Johnny Robert Eggers, who was released on parole five different times before stabbing a female teen-ager to death in 1994

Work Release Program
Temporary release of convicts from prison for purposes of employment. The offenders may spend their days on the job, but must return to the correctional facility at night and during the weekend.

Halfway House
A community-based form of early release that places inmates in residential centers and allows them to reintegrate with society.

offender. Under the terms of the contract, the state agrees to release the inmate under certain conditions, and the future parolee agrees to follow these conditions.

Each jurisdiction has its own standard parole contract, although the parole board can add specific provisions if it sees the need (see Figure 14.7). Besides common restrictions, such as no drug use, no association with known felons, and no change of address without notifying authorities, parolees have on occasion been ordered to lose weight and even to undergo chemical castration.

Recently, the U.S. Parole Commission began restricting high-risk federal parolees' ability to use the Internet. The new rules allow parole officers to make unannounced examinations of a parolee's computer and to check the required daily log of computer use. This move came as a result of the increase in online services that provide "how-to" instructions and other information in areas such as the illegal use of explosives, child pornography, and hate crimes.[85] Some precedents, however, suggest that parolees could argue that the restriction violates their constitutional rights. In 1971, a federal district court in New York struck down a condition that prohibited a parolee from making antiwar speeches, ruling that it impinged on his right to freedom of speech.[86]

Parole plans are not always so one sided. In some instances, prison authorities will agree to help the parolee find employment and a place to live during the supervision period. **Work release programs** are usually available for low-risk prisoners nearing the end of their sentences. Inmates on work release programs must either return to the correctional facility in the evening or live in community residential facilities, known as **halfway houses.** These facilities, also available to other parolees and those who have finished their sentences, are often remodeled hotels or private homes. They provide a less institutional living environment than a prison or jail for a small number of inmates (usually between ten and twenty-five).

Parole Officers   The correctional agent given the responsibility to supervise parolees is the parole officer. In many respects, the parole officer's relationship with the parolee mirrors that of the probation officer and the probationer (see

---

FIGURE 14.7   **Standard Conditions of Parole**

1. Upon my release I will report to my parole officer as directed and follow the parole officer's instructions.

2. I will report to my parole officer in person and in writing whenever and wherever the parole officer directs.

3. I agree that the parole officer has the right to visit my residence or place of employment at any reasonable time.

4. I will seek, obtain, and maintain employment throughout my parole term, or perform community service as directed by my parole officer.

5. I will notify my parole officer prior to any changes in my place of residence, in my place of employment, or of any change in my marital status.

6. I will notify my parole officer within 48 hours if at any time I am arrested for any offense.

7. I will not at any time have firearms, ammunition, or any other weapon in my possession or under my control.

8. I will obey all laws, and to the best of my ability, fulfill all my legal obligations, including payment of all applicable child support and alimony orders.

9. I will not leave the state of _____ without prior permission of my parole officer.

10. I will not at any time, use, or have in my possession or control, any illegal drug or narcotic.

11. I will not at any time have contact or affiliation with any street gangs or with any members thereof.

12. Your release on parole is based upon the conclusion of the parole panel that there is a reasonable probability that you will live and remain at liberty without violating the law and that your release is not incompatible with the welfare of society. In the event that you engage in conduct in the future which renders this conclusion no longer valid, then your parole will be revoked or modified accordingly.

Source: Connecticut Board of Parole.

Chapter 12); in fact, many municipal and state departments of corrections combine the two posts to create probation/parole officers. Parole officers are required to enforce the conditions of parole and initiate revocation hearings when these conditions are not met. Furthermore, a parole officer is expected to help the parolee readjust to life outside the correctional institution by helping her or him find a place to live and a job, and seeing that she or he receives any treatment or rehabilitation that may be necessary.

According to Todd Clear of Florida State University and Edward Latessa of the University of Cincinnati, the major role conflict for parole officers is whether to be a law enforcement officer or a social worker.[87] In other words, parole officers are constantly required to choose between the good of the community and the good of the paroled offender. In one study of parole officer stress and burnout, researchers found that more than 60 percent of the officers interviewed felt uncertain about how to balance these two requirements.[88] To be sure, some parole officers focus entirely on protecting the community and see the welfare of the client as a secondary concern. (For an example of this conflict, see the feature *CJ in Focus—The Balancing Act: Cop or Caretaker?* on the following page.)

A growing number of parole experts, however, believe that parole officers should act as agents of change, meaning that they should try not simply to control the offender's behavior but also to change it. This entails that the parole officer establish strong bonds of trust and commitment with the parolee by taking what could be called a parental attitude to the officer-client relationship.[89]

Parole Revocation   If convicts follow the conditions of their parole until the *maximum expiration date,* or the date on which their sentence ends, then they are discharged from supervision. A large number—about 40 percent, according to the latest research—return to incarceration before their maximum expiration date, most because they were convicted of a new offense or had their parole revoked (see Figure 14.8). **Parole revocation** is similar in many aspects to probation revocation. If the parolee commits a new crime, then a return to prison is very likely. If, however, the individual breaks a condition of parole, known as a technical violation, the parole authorities have discretion as to whether revocation proceedings should be initiated. An example of a technical violation would be failure to report a change in address to parole authorities. As with probation revocation, many observers believe that those who commit technical violations should not be imprisoned, as they have not committed a crime.

Until 1972, parole officers had the power to arbitrarily revoke parole status for technical violations. A parolee who was returned to prison had little or no recourse. In *Morrissey v. Brewer* (1972),[90] the Supreme Court changed this by deciding that a parolee has a "liberty interest" in remaining on parole. In other words, before parolees can be deprived of their liberty, they must be afforded a measure of due process at a parole revocation hearing.

Although this hearing does not provide the same due process protections as a criminal trial, the parolee does have the right to be notified of the charges, to present witnesses, to speak in his or her defense, and to

Parole Revocation
When a parolee breaks the conditions of parole, the process of withdrawing parole and returning the person to prison.

FIGURE 14.8 Terminating Parole
As you can see, nearly half of all parolees successfully complete their terms of parole. The rest are either returned to incarceration, transferred, die while on parole, or have successfully evaded parole officials.

Source: Adapted from Bureau of Justice Statistics, *Correctional Populations in the United States, 1998* (Washington, D.C.: U.S. Department of Justice, 2002), Table 6.5.

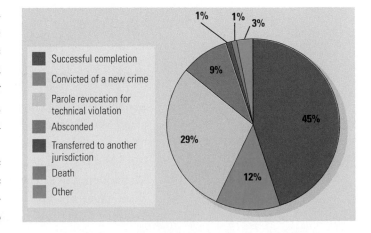

■ Successful completion
■ Convicted of a new crime
■ Parole revocation for technical violation
■ Absconded
■ Transferred to another jurisdiction
■ Death
■ Other

1% 1% 3%
9%
45%
29%
12%

> **Cop or Caretaker?**

When five parole officers burst into the residence in Noble, Oklahoma, they expected to find one Ned Snow, parolee. Snow was wanted for alleged parole violations. Even though Snow did not happen to be at the residence at the time of the "visit," the parole officers, who were accompanied by two local deputies, proceeded to search the house and seize prescription drugs from the women who lived there. Several days later, the parole officers returned to the dwelling, once again to find that Snow was not at home. Snow's wife and mother, to their misfortune, were present. The parole officers proceeded to handcuff the two women and place them in a state vehicle. At this point, Snow arrived in another car, but fled as soon as he saw what was taking place. One of the parole officers commandeered the women's pickup truck and chased Snow at a high speed until the truck's engine blew.

In the aftermath of these events, one of the parole officers involved lost her job and three others were suspended. This was not, however, an isolated incident. To the chagrin of many Oklahoma corrections and law enforcement officials, it represented an internal philosophical debate over the proper role of the state's parole officers. Was their primary purpose to act as surrogate police officers or as social workers concerned mainly with the well-being of their clients?

The parole officers involved in the Snow debacle, along with a number of their colleagues, leaned toward assuming the role of law enforcement officer. In the words of one insider, these officers felt that their job was "to take names and kick asses." According to another officer, "These few guys want to be 120 percent law enforcement and they don't want to do any of the social-work part of it."

A further worry was that this aggressive attitude was denying parolees their constitutional rights. Although parole officers are allowed to conduct unannounced "visits" at the homes and workplaces of parolees, they do not have the authority to conduct searches without a warrant. In the words of one parole officer, parolees "have a right to a search warrant just like everybody else does." In several Oklahoma counties, parole and probation officers have an understanding with local police agencies: if the police suspect a parolee of illegal activity but do not have a warrant to search his or her abode, they will call on the parolee's parole officer to make an unannounced visit and search.

Supporters of "John Wayne–style" parole officers argue that such tactics are needed to protect citizens. Senior Oklahoma probation and parole officer Kris Evans disagrees. "We do have a law enforcement component to our job, but we're not supposed to be out there playing detective," Evans says. "We supervise people on probation or parole, and that's the scope of our employment." He adds, "If you want to go kick in doors, go apply to the OSBI (Oklahoma State Bureau of Investigation) or a local law enforcement agency."

FOR CRITICAL ANALYSIS
What would be some of the consequences if all parole officers focused on the law enforcement aspects of their job rather than its social-service responsibilities?

question any hostile witnesses (so long as such questioning would not place them in danger). In the first stage of the hearing, the parole board determines whether there is probable cause that a violation occurred. Then, the board decides whether to return the parolee to prison.

ONLINE REVIEW *Go to the book's Web site for an interactive review of this section*

Too Dangerous for Release?

In a letter to the Pennsylvania Board of Pardons, Reginald McFadden asked for a chance to show that he could "function normally" among law-abiding citizens. "You have given me these years to reassess my life's values," McFadden wrote, "and as a result, I am a better person." Three months after being granted parole, McFadden was arrested on three charges of murder and suspected of a fourth. Such incidents not only lead to questions about the parole system, but also heighten fears of releasing any violent criminal.

CITIZENS IN LIMBO

This mistrust manifests itself in the legal restrictions faced by all convicts, even those who were model prisoners or parolees. Figure 14.9 provides a list of rights that are currently or have in the past been denied to convicts once they return to the community. Perhaps no statutory restrictions better represent society's feeling toward the "dangerous" ex-prisoner than sex offender notification laws, known as "Megan's Laws." (See the feature *Criminal Justice in Action—Protecting the Community from Sex Offenders* at the end of this chapter.)

For many released inmates, however, the inability to serve on a jury or other civil rights restrictions are the least of their worries. For all the hardships of incarceration, it does offer a haven from the day-to-day decisions that characterize life "on the outside." Furthermore, the prison environment insulates inmates; a convict released after a long prison term may find common acts such as using an ATM or pumping his or her gas completely alien.

In prison, according to one inmate, the "rules" of daily life followed by citizens on the outside are turned upside-down:

> An unexpected smile could mean trouble. A man in uniform was not a friend. Being kind was a weakness. Viciousness and recklessness were to be respected and admired.[91]

Consequently, inmates experience a shift in reality while behind bars. In other words, they live differently than do those on the outside. As another long-term inmate commented:

> For most, the prison experience is a one-way ride on a psychological roller coaster—downhill. And the easiest thing to do, in a world where almost everything is an assault against you, is to permit yourself to be defeated by the overwhelming indifference and sense of hopelessness that steals into your daily existence, slowly, almost unnoticeably sapping your drive, your dreams, your ambition, evoking cries from the soul to surrender.[92]

It is understandably difficult for many inmates to readjust to life on the outside after feeling such pressures. A friend of parolee Reginald McFadden's blamed his recidivism on the fact that he "could not handle any of the emotions that come with being set free."[93]

THE PROBLEM OF RECIDIVISM

Whatever its causes, recidivism has become one of the most pressing concerns in the criminal justice system. More than 1,500 men and women are released from state and federal prisons each day—around 600,000 every year. Disturbing numbers of these released prisoners are likely to find themselves back behind bars. An in-depth study of recidivism released by the U.S. Department of Justice in 2002 found that 67.5 percent of offenders are rearrested for a new crime within three years of release and just over half are returned to prison after being convicted of a felony or for parole violations.[94]

"Flooding" Communities   Although, as we have discussed numerous times in this textbook, there are many different reasons why an individual offender might commit a crime, some anecdotal evidence suggests that the prison experience can lead to recidivism. Northern Utah, for example, has been "flooded" with crimes

---

FIGURE 14.9

The Limited Rights of Convicts

In some states convicted offenders are denied the right to vote, the reasoning being that they do not have the required honesty and proper values to be allowed to participate in the voting process. Such restrictions have been lifted in most states, but other rights of convicted offenders are still limited in some jurisdictions.

In many jurisdictions, convicts do not have the right to:

> Hold public office
> Be employed in the public sector
> Live in public housing
> Own firearms
> Serve on a jury
> Have automobile and life insurance
> Adopt children
> Receive welfare or food stamps
> Be eligible for student loans
> Keep their children

GREAT DEBATES

"No frills" advocates do not believe that prisoners have the "right" to work, while those who support prison labor insist that the activity benefits both inmates and society. To better understand the issues of the "no frills" prison debate, click on *Great Debates* under the *Book Resources* at www.cjinaction.com

committed by men who joined supremacist gangs while in prison and use their gang connections to pursue criminal activity after release.[95]

Preventive Measures   Depending on the particular institution, prison officials implement a number of different approaches to combat recidivism. Educational programs are often cited for their ability to rehabilitate participants and reduce their chances of being reincarcerated. One Florida study found that the state correctional system saved $3.20 for every dollar it put into such programs, mostly because of reduced recidivism.[96] Drug treatment programs have shown similar results; consequently, their numbers skyrocketed from 23,700 in 1980 to 319,600 in 1999.[97] Some facilities have turned to alternative programs—such as gardening, horse care, and writing workshops—to instill inmates with a sense of responsibility that they may lack.

Most felons are poorly educated and, with a prison record, are unlikely to find a good-paying job when released. As a result, they have an incentive to return to crime. Many observers believe that prison employment programs can provide inmates with skills and a proper work ethic and can help them find a job that pays adequate wages. In the federal prison system, more than 20,000 well-behaved inmates earn up to $8 an hour in factories run by Federal Prison Industries, producing items from prescription eyeglasses to sofas to guided missile propulsion equipment. About 10 percent of state prisoners and 7 percent of those in local jails are working off the premises of the correctional facility in which they are housed.[98] (See the feature *What Works—Flame 'N' Go Hotshots*.)

WHAT WORKS

> Flame 'N' Go Hotshots

The Flame 'N' Go Hotshots are an elite firefighting crew; "hotshots" is slang for Type I firefighters, the highest rating given out by the federal government. During the summer of 2000, when a series of large and destructive fires crisscrossed the western United States, they were on almost constant duty. The most remarkable thing about the Flame 'N' Go Hotshots, however, is that they are all inmates from Bluffdale State Prison in Utah. Of the 25,000 firefighters who battled dozens of blazes that summer, about one in six was a state prisoner from California, Nevada, Wyoming, Utah, or Texas (though the Flame 'N' Go's were the only inmates to have achieved "hotshot" status).

Inmate firefighters, most of whom have stellar behavior records and are housed in minimum-security prisons, have provided much-needed relief to overworked U.S. Forest Service staff. In California, for example, the widespread use of inmates to deal with smaller fires freed civilian crews to focus on outbreaks in Idaho and Montana, which were hit particularly hard in 2000. The various programs also save taxpayer dollars. At $1 an hour, inmate firefighters receive only a fraction of the salary of their civilian counterparts. As a result, the convicts ease the annual firefighting costs in this country by nearly $1 billion.

The benefits are not one sided, however. In California, inmates earn a one-day credit in time served for every day that they are combating fires. This bonus is not available to the Flame 'N' Go Hotshots because of fixed sentencing in Utah, so instead they receive much higher wages of nearly $6 an hour. But, beyond the money, the inmates—many of whom are close to being paroled or released—relish the opportunity to live "on the outside." "All that time you're in prison, what's on your mind is to get out on the street," says Tommy Phong, who has served thirteen years for armed robbery. "And from my first years as a firefighter, I've seen what it's like."

FOR CRITICAL ANALYSIS

Several years ago, two inmates from Bluffdale State Prison were killed while training to become firefighters. Normally, the families of firefighters who die while on duty receive around $150,000 in federal benefits. Inmate firefighters, however, are not eligible for such benefits. Some prisoners' rights groups have lobbied for inmate firefighters to be subject to minimum-wage and other labor-protection laws. Do you think that inmate workers should receive the same benefits and protections as civilian workers? Why or why not?

The Economy of Release   A number of nonprofit organizations also help convicts find work after they have been released. America Works, based in New York City, places more than three hundred former prisoners in jobs each year; nearly half of them stay employed for at least six months.[99]

The need for such services is likely to grow. Each year, more inmates leave state and federal prisons than enter them—an astonishing figure given the size of the American corrections system. This development does not signal a change in public policy as much as it reflects economic reality: in 2003, state budgets faced a combined shortage of nearly $30 billion, and many states are finding prisoners too expensive to keep. Some states, such as Michigan, Texas, and Washington, have eased sentencing laws to reduce the number of prisoners. Others, including California and Kansas, are mandating drug treatment rather than prison for nonviolent drug offenders.

Some state officials are considering or taking a more dramatic step: releasing inmates outright. In 2003, Governor Gary Locke of Washington proposed to set free 1,200 inmates and eliminate parole supervision for another 25,000—measures that would save his state $90 million.[100] One year earlier, Governor Paul E. Patton of Kentucky ordered a mass commutation of the sentences of more than 550 jail inmates, some of whom had been convicted of violent felonies, in order to reduce his state's $500 million budget deficit. "A percentage of them are going to recommit a crime, and some of them are going to be worse than the crimes they are in for," admitted Governor Patton in the face of mounting criticism. But, he said, "I have to do what I have to do."[101]

↑ ONLINE REVIEW *Go to the book's Web site for an interactive review of this section*

>Protecting the Community from Sex Offenders

In the summer of 1994, seven-year-old Megan Kanka of Hamilton Township, New Jersey, was raped and murdered by a twice-convicted pedophile (an adult sexually attracted to children) who had moved into her neighborhood after being released from prison on parole. The next year, in response to public outrage, the state passed a series of laws known collectively as the New Jersey Sexual Offender Registration Act, or "Megan's Law."[102] Today, all fifty states and the federal government have passed their own versions of Megan's Law, which require local law authorities to alert the public when a sex offender has been released in the community. Hailed by victims' rights groups and reviled by civil libertarians, these laws—which are the focus of this *Criminal Justice in Action* feature—have been the topic of much controversy.

Active and Passive Notification

No two of these laws have exactly the same provisions, but all are designed with the goal of allowing the public to learn the identities of convicted sex offenders living in their midst. The incentive to institute such laws was enhanced in 1996 when Congress passed its own Megan's Law, which requires a state to provide communities with relevant information on sex offenders as a condition of receiving federal anticrime funds.[103] In 2000, Congress passed another law requiring sexual offenders to report their status to college administrations if they are enrolled at the school or if they have a job on campus.[104] By October 2002, all colleges had to give the public access to this information.

In general, these laws demand that a paroled sexual offender notify local law enforcement authorities on taking up residence in a state. This registration process must be renewed every time the parolee changes address. The process of community notification by the authorities has two models. The "active" model requires that they directly notify the community or community representatives. This often takes the form of bulletins or posters, distributed and posted within a certain distance from the

offender's home. In the "passive" model, information on sex offenders must be open and available for public scrutiny. In California, for example, the state has created a CD-ROM that provides the names, photos, and ZIP codes of tens of thousands of the state's released sex offenders.

In some instances, convicts must notify authorities themselves. Paroled sex offenders in Georgia are required to present themselves to both the sheriff and the superintendent of the public school district where they plan to reside.[105] Generally, sex offenders are supervised by parole officers and are subject to the same threat of revocation as other parolees. Paroled child molesters usually have the following conditions of release:

> Must have no contact with children under the age of sixteen.

> Must continue psychiatric treatment.

> Must receive permission from their parole officers to change residence.

> Must stay a certain distance from schools or parks where children are present.

Judge Manuel Banales ordered twenty-one registered sex offenders in Corpus Christi, Texas, to place signs similar to the one pictured here in their front yards. Do you think this unfairly infringes on the privacy rights of the sex offenders? Or, are such steps justified to protect children who live nearby?

AP Photo/*Corpus Christi Caller–Times*, Paul Iverson

> Cannot own toys that may be used to lure children.

> Cannot have a job or participate in any activity that involves children.

In some cases, after release from incarceration, sex offenders must return to the county where they committed their crimes. Nearly 400,000 convicted sex offenders have been required to register through one of these methods across the United States.

Legal Issues

In nearly every jurisdiction, Megan's Laws have been challenged as unconstitutional. The common theme among these court cases is that Megan's Laws represent a form of "punishment" and as such violate state and federal constitutional prohibitions against double jeopardy and cruel and unusual punishment. In other words, by forcing sex offenders to register in expectation of a crime they have yet to commit, these laws operate in opposition to the principle that persons are innocent until proven guilty. Furthermore, because of the scrutiny that is certain to fall on a pedophile whose past crimes have been broadcast to the community, offenders have filed suit claiming that the laws unconstitutionally invade their privacy.[106]

With two recent decisions, the United States Supreme Court signaled that it was going to give the states a great deal of leeway in managing sex offenders. In *Smith v. Doe* (2003),[107] the Court held that Alaska's sex offender law did not violate the *ex post facto* clause of the Constitution even though it required two men who had completed their prison sentences before its passage to register. (For a review of this clause, go to page 125.) The Court noted that even though some of the ramifications of Megan's Laws are punitive, their general purpose is remedial and, therefore, *ex post facto* protections do not apply.

The other case, *Connecticut Department of Public Safety v. Doe* (2003),[108] concerned a convicted sex offender's claim that he was denied his due process rights when the state posted his name and address on the Internet without first holding a hearing to determine whether he was still a threat to the community. The Court rejected this argument: because Connecticut requires *all* sex offenders to register and places information about *all* of them on the Web, the law is not unfair. In other words, the relative dangerousness of any individual offender is irrelevant.

Getting Tougher with Sex Offenders

Megan's Laws have increased community awareness of the danger of sex offenders—one in twelve of the 24,000 Californians who accessed the sex offender CD-ROM recognized a registrant. Furthermore, notification policies have no doubt forced some offenders to confront their psychological problems and driven them to participate more actively in their own rehabilitation.

Even some supporters are beginning to question the laws, however. Identified offenders often become targets of vigilante action, and sometimes that action is misguided. In New Jersey, for example, a man broke into an apartment and severely beat its occupant after finding the address on the state's sex offender computer bank. The convict had moved, however, and the beating victim was not a former criminal.

Such incidents are rare, but they have been more effective than the constitutional challenges in raising questions in the public mind about Megan's Laws. Why, observers are beginning to ask, is the government releasing people from prison when the state itself considers them so likely to reoffend that the community must be warned of their very presence? To address this problem, eighteen states have passed laws that say, in effect, Megan's Laws are not enough. In these states, sexual offenders can be sent to another, noncorrectional facility (such as a psychiatric hospital) after serving their prison or jail terms.

In 2001, the state of Washington's Community Protection Act—the model for many other such acts nationwide—withstood a challenge in the United States Supreme Court. The plaintiff, Andre Brigham Young, had been locked up in a health-care facility for twelve years after serving his prison term for rape. Young argued that he was being punished a second time for the same crime, which is unconstitutional under the Fifth Amendment. The Court rejected this argument, stating that Young's commitment to the health facility was a "civil" decision made by the state that did not involve criminal law. Therefore, the Fifth Amendment's prohibition of double jeopardy did not apply.[109] A year later, however, the Court did limit a state's ability to civilly confine sexual offenders, holding that there must "be proof of serious difficulty in controlling behavior" for such confinement to be constitutional.[110]

The Only Way?

The spread of sex offender laws reflects a dual need among citizens: notification and prevention. In the case of notification, it would appear that these laws can be effective; that is, they can help answer the question: Is my neighbor a sex offender? Whether the laws can prevent further sex offenses is more problematic, however.

Certainly, it would be simple if society could just send all sex offenders to an island and forget about them—simple, but unconstitutional and, ultimately, impossible. Megan's Law and similar legislation, for all the criticism they receive, may represent the best way to protect communities from sex offenders by providing citizens with the means to protect themselves.

MAKING SENSE OF SEX OFFENDER LAWS

1 What are the two "rights" that legislators must weigh in passing Megan's Laws? Do you agree that the rights of the community outweigh the rights of the individual offender? Explain your answer.

2 One of the primary justifications for Megan's Laws is that sex offenders have a high rate of recidivism. In other words, because they are unlikely to be "cured," these ex-convicts need to have greater restrictions placed on them than other criminals. Do you have any concerns about this reasoning? How do recent data released by the U.S. Department of Justice showing that sex offenders are less likely to be rearrested after release from prison than robbers, car thieves, and arsonists affect your opinion of Megan's Laws?

3 Some states and local communities post lists of convicted sex offenders, with photos, on the Internet. Is this a fair method of notification, or is it too intrusive on the privacy of the felon? Why?

Chapter Summary

1 **Explain the concept of prison as a total institution.** Though many people spend time in partial institutions—schools, companies where they work, and religious organizations—only in prison is every aspect of an inmate's life controlled, and that is why prisons are called total institutions. Every detail for every prisoner is fully prescribed and managed.

2 **Describe the possible patterns of inmate behavior, which are driven by the inmate's personality and values.** (a) Professional criminals adapt to prison by "doing time" and follow the rules in order to get out quickly. (b) Those who are "jailing" establish themselves within the power structure of prison culture. These are often veterans of juvenile detention centers and other prisons. (c) Those who are "gleaning" are working to improve themselves for return to society. (d) "Disorganized" criminals have mental impairments or low IQs and therefore are unable to adapt to prison culture.

3 **Indicate some of the reasons for violent behavior in prisons.** (a) To separate the powerful from the weak and to establish a prisoner hierarchy; (b) to minimize one's own probability of being a target of assault; (c) to enhance one's self-image; (d) to obtain sexual relief; and (e) to obtain material goods through extortion or robbery.

4 **List and briefly explain the six general job categories among correctional officers.** (a) Block officers, who supervise cell blocks or are on block guard duty; (b) work detail supervisors, who oversee the cafeteria, prison store, and laundry, for example; (c) industrial shop and school officers, who generally oversee workshop and educational programs; (d) yard officers, who patrol the prison yard when prisoners are allowed there; (e) tower guards, who work in isolation; and (f) those who hold administrative building assignments, such as prison gate guards, overseers of visitation procedures, and so on.

5 Contrast the hands-off doctrine of prisoner law with the hands-on approach. The hands-off doctrine assumes that the care of prisoners should be left entirely to prison officials and that it is not the place of judges to intervene. In contrast, the hands-on philosophy started in 1964 after the Supreme Court decision *Cooper v. Pate.* Prisoners have been able to file civil lawsuits, called Section 1983 petitions, when they feel their civil rights have been violated.

6 List the concepts on which parole is based. (a) Grace, (b) contract of consent, and (c) custody.

7 Contrast probation, parole, mandatory release, pardon, and furlough. Probation is an alternative to incarceration. Parole is an early release program for those incarcerated. Mandatory release occurs when the inmate has served the maximum time for her or his initial sentence minus good-time credits. A pardon can be given only by the president or one of the fifty governors. Furlough is a temporary release while in jail or prison.

8 Describe truth-in-sentencing laws and their goals. Such laws make more transparent the actual time that a con-victed criminal will serve in jail or prison. The goals are (a) to restore "truth" to the sentencing process; (b) to increase the percentage of the term that is actually served in prison in order to reduce crime by keeping convicts "off the streets" for a longer period; and (c) to better control the use of prison space by giving corrections officials predictable terms and policymakers advanced notice of potential overcrowding.

9 Describe typical conditions of parole. Parolees must not use drugs, not associate with known felons, not change their addresses without notifying authorities, and report to their parole officer at specified intervals. (The latter is usually specified in the parole contract.)

10 Indicate typical conditions for release for a paroled child molester. (a) Have no contact with children under the age of sixteen; (b) continue psychiatric treatment; (c) obtain permission from a parole officer to change residence; (d) keep away from schools or parks where children are present; (e) cannot own toys that may be used to lure children; and (f) cannot have a job or participate in any activity that involves children.

Key Terms

"deliberate indifference"   484
deprivation model   474
discretionary release   487
furlough   486
halfway house   492
"hands-off" doctrine   483
"identifiable human needs"   485
mandatory release   486
pardon   486
parole   485
parole board   488
parole contract   491
parole grant hearing   489
parole guidelines   491
parole revocation   493
prison code   473
prisonization   472
relative deprivation   474
total institution   471
work release program   492

Questions for Critical Analysis

1 Why is the principle of least eligibility relevant in today's political environment?
2 How does the deprivation model seek to explain prison violence?
3 How does the inmate culture differ in men's prisons and women's prisons?
4 What is the most demanding job assignment in the correctional institution hierarchy?
5 What has caused a reduction in the amount of discretion that parole boards have?
6 Who are some of the individuals who are asked to provide comments and recommendations for a parole grant hearing?

7 When a parolee is caught committing a crime, what typically tends to happen, and why?

8 Why have states been trying to reduce their prison populations, and what are some of the methods they have used to do so?

9 Why do civil libertarians criticize Megan's Laws?

TEST PREPARATION ONLINE

Go to www.cjinaction.com for tools to aid you in studying for your exams. Click on *Online Reviews* under *Chapter Resources* for an interactive review of each major section of this chapter. Under *Chapter Resources,* you will also find the *Chapter Outline, Chapter Summary, Flashcards, Glossary, Learning Objectives, Lecture Presentations, Concept Builder, Essay Questions,* and a *Tutorial Quiz.* You can also test yourself with a game of *Concentration* or the *Crossword Puzzle.*

Web Resources

Go to www.cjinaction.com for a wealth of online resources. Explore the *Internet Activities* and *Class Project*s under *Chapter Resources.* Check out the *Web Links* to access the Web sites mentioned in the text, as well as many others. You can also access recent perspectives by clicking on *CJ in the News* and *Terrorism Update* under *Course Resources.* If you'd like some mentoring, click on *Board of Mentors* under *Book Resources.*

Search Online with InfoTrac College Edition

For additional information, explore InfoTrac College Edition, your online library that offers complete full-length articles from thousands of scholarly and popular publications. Click on *InfoTrac College Edition* under *Chapter Resources* at www.cjinaction.com for a list of key words and InfoTrac exercises. Use the passcode that came with your book.

Suggested Readings

Conover, Ted, *Newjack,* New York: Random House, 2000. The author, a journalist, describes his experiences as an undercover "newjack," or rookie correctional officer, at Sing Sing prison in Ossining, New York. Early on, a supervisor tells Conover, "You're the zookeeper now.... Go run the zoo." This book explores the implications of this attitude for both correctional officers and prisoners.

Lerner, Jimmy, *You Got Nothing Coming: Notes from a Prison Fish,* New York: Broadway Books, 2002. The author killed a man in Las Vegas and was convicted of voluntary manslaughter. He is now serving time in the Nevada state prison system. A memoir of Lerner's first year behind bars, this book is a lively, graphic, and often funny recounting of what it's like to be a newcomer in prison.

Notes

1. Edward W. Sieh, "Less Eligibility: The Upper Limits of Penal Policy," *Criminal Justice Policy Review* 3 (1989), 159.

2. Edward L. Rubin and Malcolm M. Feeley, "Judicial Policy Making and Litigation against the Government," *University of Pennsylvania Journal of Constitutional Law* (April 2003), 617.

3. Gregory Moorhead and Ricky W. Griffin, *Organizational Behavior,* 2d ed. (Boston: Houghton Mifflin, 1989), 497.

4. Erving Goffman, "On the Characteristics of Total Institutions," in *Asylums: Essays on the Social Situation of Mental Patients and Other Inmates* (New York: Doubleday, 1961), 6.

5. Justin Brooks, "How Can We Sleep While the Beds Are Burning: The Tumultuous Prison Culture of Attica Flourishes in American Prisons Twenty-five Years Later," *Syracuse Law Journal* 47 (1996), 159.

6. Bureau of Justice Statistics, *Prevalence of Imprisonment in the U.S. Population, 1974–2001* (Washington, D.C.: U.S. Department of Justice, August 2003), 1.

7. Bureau of Justice Statistics, *Prisoners in 2002* (Washington, D.C.: U.S. Department of Justice, July 2003), Table 13, page 9.

8. *Prevalence of Imprisonment in the U.S. Population, 1974–2001,* Table 2, page 3.

9. Bureau of Justice Statistics, *Education and Correctional Trends* (Washington, D.C.: U.S. Department of Justice, January 2003), 1.

10. Donald Clemmer, *The Prison Community* (Boston: Christopher, 1940).

11. John Irwin, *Prisons in Turmoil* (Boston: Little, Brown, 1980), 67.

12. Gresham M. Sykes and Sheldon Messinger, "The Inmate Social System," in *Theoretical Studies in the Social Organization of the Prison,* ed. Richard A. Cloward *et al.* (New York: Social Science Research Council, 1960), 6–10.

13. Robert Johnson, *Hard Time: Understanding and Reforming the Prison,* 2d ed. (Belmont, CA: Wadsworth Publishing Company, 1996), 133.

14. Jocelyn Pollock, "The Social World of the Prisoner," in *Prisons: Today and Tomorrow,* ed. Jocelyn Pollock (Gaithersburg, MD: Aspen Publishers, 1997), 246–259.

15. Lee H. Bowker, *Prison Victimization* (New York: Elsevier, 1981), 31–33.

16. Stephen C. Light, "The Severity of Assaults on Prison Officers: A Contextual Analysis," *Social Science Quarterly* 71 (1990), 267–284.

17. Lee H. Bowker, "An Essay on Prison Violence," in *Prison Violence in America,* ed. Michael Braswell, Steven Dillingham, and Reid Montgomery, Jr. (Cincinnati, OH: Anderson Publishing Co., 1985), 7–18.

18. Frank Tannenbaum, *Crime and Community* (Boston: Ginn & Co., 1938).

19. Randy Martin and Sherwood Zimmerman, "A Typology of the Causes of Prison Riots and an Analytical Extension to the 1986 Virginia Riot," *Justice Quarterly* 7 (1990), 711–737.

20. Bert Useem, "Disorganization and the New Mexico Prison Riot of 1980," *American Sociological Review* 50 (1985), 677–688.

21. Bert Useem and Peter Kimball, *State of Siege: U.S. Prison Riots 1971–1984* (New York: Oxford University Press, 1989), 4.

22. Stuart B. Klein, "Prisoners' Rights to Physical and Mental Health Care: A Modern Expansion of the Eighth Amendment's Cruel and Unusual Punishment Clause," *Fordham University Law Journal* 7 (1978), 1.

23. Herman Badillo and Milton Haynes, *A Bill of No Rights: Attica and the American Prison System* (New York: Outerbridge & Lazard, 1972), 42.

24. David W. Chen, "Compensation Set on Attica Uprising," *New York Times* (August 29, 2000), A1.

25. Mark Colvin, *The Penitentiary in Crisis: From Accommodation to Crisis in New Mexico* (Albany, NY: SUNY Press, 1992).

26. Michael S. Serrill and Peter Katel, "New Mexico: The Anatomy of a Riot," *Corrections Magazine* (April 1980), 6–7.

27. Useem and Kimball; and John J. DiIulio, *Governing Prisons* (New York: Free Press, 1987).

28. Badillo and Haynes, 26.

29. Irwin, 47.

30. Leo Carroll, "Race, Ethnicity, and the Social Order of the Prison," in *The Pains of Imprisonment,* ed. R. Johnson and H. Toch (Beverly Hills, CA: Sage, 1982).

31. Leo Carroll, *Hacks, Blacks, and Cons: Race Relations in a Maximum-Security Prison* (Lexington, MA: Lexington Books, 1988), 78.

32. Craig Haney, "Psychology and the Limits to Prison Pain," *Psychology, Public Policy, and Law* 3 (December 1977), 499.

33. Robert W. Dumond, "Inmate Sexual Assault," *Prison Journal* 80 (December 2000), 407.

34. Human Rights Watch, "World Report 2000—United States."

35. Mary Dallao, "How to Make Your Facility Safer," *Corrections Today* (December 1996), 101.

36. Leanne F. Alarid, "Female Inmate Subcultures," in *Corrections Contexts: Contemporary and Classical Readings,* ed. James W. Marquart and Jonathan R. Sorenson (Los Angeles: Roxbury Publishing Co., 1997), 137.

37. Bureau of Justice Statistics, *Census of State and Federal Correctional Facilities, 2000* (Washington, D.C.: U.S. Department of Justice, October 2003), Table 10, page 6.

38. Brenda V. Smith, "Sexual Abuse against Women in Prison," *Criminal Justice* (Spring 2001), 30.

39. Amnesty International USA, "Not Part of My Sentence: Violations of the Human Rights of Women in Custody," available at http://www.amnestyusa.org/rightsforall/women/report/index.html.

40. Jennifer A. Segal, "Family Ties and Federal Sentencing: A Critique of the Literature," *Federal Sentencing Reporter* 13 (2001), 258.

41. Amnesty International USA.

42. Jocelyn Pollock-Byrne, *Women, Prison, and Crime* (Pacific Grove, CA: Brooks/Cole, 1990).

43. Bureau of Justice Statistics, *Incarcerated Parents and Their Children* (Washington, D.C.: U.S. Department of Justice, August 2000), 1.

44. *Ibid.,* Table 6, page 5.

45. Esther Heffermn, *Making It in Prison: The Square, the Cool, and the Life* (New York: Wiley, 1972), 91.

46. *Ibid.,* 88.

47. Alarid, 136–137.

48. James G. Fox, *Organizational and Racial Conflict in Maximum Security Prisons* (Lexington, MA: Lexington Books, 1982).

49. Lee H. Bowker, "Gender Differences in Prisoner Subcultures," in *Women and Crime in America,* ed. Lee H. Bowker (New York: Macmillan, 1981), 409–419.

50. Quoted in John J. Dilulio, Jr., *No Escape: The Future of American Corrections* (New York: Basic Books, 1991), 268.

51. Jack Henry Abbott, *In the Belly of the Beast* (New York: Vintage Books, 1991), 54.

52. Michael Foucault, *Discipline and Punish: The Birth of the Prison* (New York: Pantheon Books, 1977), 128.

53. Lucien X. Lombardo, *Guards Imprisoned: Correctional Officers at Work* (Cincinnati, OH: Anderson Publishing Co., 1989), 51–71.

54. Ben M. Crouch, "The Book vs. the Boot: Two Styles of Guarding in a Southern Prison," in *The Keepers,* ed. Ben M. Crouch (Springfield, IL: Thomas, 1980), 207–224.

55. Goffman, 7.

56. 475 U.S. 312 (1986).

57. *Stanley v. Hejirika* (U.S. Court of Appeals for the 4th Circuit, No. 97-62124, 1998).

58. 503 U.S. 1 (1992).

59. Haney, 499.

60. 378 U.S. 546 (1964).

61. 418 U.S. 539 (1974).

62. 429 U.S. 97 (1976).

63. *Daniels v. Williams,* 474 U.S. 327 (1986); and *Whitley v. Albers,* 475 U.S. 312 (1986).

64. 501 U.S. 296 (1991).

65. *Farmer v. Brennan,* 511 U.S. 825 (1994).

66. 501 U.S. 294, 304 (1991).

67. 515 U.S. 472 (1995).

68. Ted Palmer, "The Effectiveness of Intervention: Recent Trends and Current Issues," *Crime & Delinquency* 37 (1991), 34.

69. Todd R. Clear and George F. Cole, *American Corrections,* 4th ed. (Belmont, CA: Wadsworth Pubishing Co., 1997), 416.

70. 442 U.S. 1 (1979).

71. Danya W. Blair, "A Matter of Life and Death: Why Life without Parole Should Be a Sentencing Option in Texas," *American Journal of Criminal Law* 22 (Fall 1994), 191.

72. Julian H. Wright, Jr., "Life-without-Parole: An Alternative to Death or Not Much of a Life at All?" *Vanderbilt Law Review* 43 (March 1990), 529.

73. *Simmons v. South Carolina,* 512 U.S. 154 (1994).

74. Victoria J. Palacios, "Go and Sin No More: Rationality and Release Decisions by Parole Boards," *South Carolina Law Review* 45 (Spring 1994), 567.

75. William Parker, *Parole: Origins, Development, Current Practices, and Statutes* (College Park, MD: American Correctional Association, 1972), 26.

76. Susan Blaustein, "Witness to Another Execution," *Harper's Magazine* (May 1994), 57.

77. Mike A. Cable, "Limiting Parole: Required Consideration of Statements and Recommendations Received by the Parole Board," *Pacific Law Journal* 28 (Spring 1997), 778.

78. Andrew Von Hirsch and Kathleen J. Hanrahan, *The Question of Parole: Retention, Reform, or Abolition* (Cambridge, MA: Ballinger Publishing Company, 1979), 4.

79. Bureau of Justice Statistics, *Bulletin* (Washington, D.C.: U.S. Department of Justice, January 1995), 2.

80. Michael Tonry, "Twenty Years of Sentencing Reform: Steps Forward, Steps Backward," *Judicature* 78 (January/February 1995), 169.

81. Comprehensive Crime Control Act of 1984, Pub. L. No. 98-473, Section 217(a), 98 Stat. 1837, 2017 (1984), codified as amended at 28 U.S.C. Sections 991–998 (1988).

82. 42 U.S.C.A. Sections 13701–13709.

83. Marc Mauer, "The Truth about Truth in Sentencing," *Corrections Today* (February 1, 1996), S1.

84. *Ibid.*

85. "USPC Approves New Parole Conditions for Restricting Ex-Inmates' Computer Use," *M2 Presswire* (December 24, 1996).

86. *Sobell v. Reed,* 327 F.Supp. 1294 (S.D.N.Y., 1971).

87. Todd R. Clear and Edward Latessa, "Probation Officer Roles in Intensive Supervision: Surveillance versus Treatment," *Justice Quarterly* 10 (1993), 441–462.

88. J. T. Whitehead and C. A. Lindquist, "Job Stress and Burnout among Probation/Parole Officers: Perceptions and Causal Factors," *International Journal of Offender Therapy and Comparative Criminology* 29 (1985), 109–119.

89. Betsy Fulton, Amy Stichman, Lawrence Travis, and Edward Latessa, "Moderating Probation and Parole Officers' Attitudes to Achieve Desired Outcomes," *Prison Journal* (September 1, 1997), 295.

90. 408 U.S. 471 (1972).

91. Victor Hassine, *Life without Parole: Living in Prison Today,* ed. Thomas J. Bernard and Richard McCleary (Los Angeles: Roxbury Publishing Co., 1996), 12.

92. Wilbert Rideau and Ron Wikberg, *Life Sentences: Rage and Survival behind Bars* (New York: Times Books, 1992), 59–60.

93. "Deadly Spree Followed Vote to Give Killer '2nd Chance,'" *Buffalo News* (July 2, 1996), A12.

94. Bureau of Justice Statistics, *Recidivism of Prisoners Released in 1994* (Washington, D.C.: U.S. Department of Justice, June 2002), 1.

95. Nick Madigan, "North Utah Faces Influx of Racists," *New York Times* (April 4, 2003), A10.

96. Daniel L. Low, "Nonprofit Private Prisons: The Next Generation of Prison Management," *New England Journal on Criminal and Civil Confinement* (Winter 2003), 5.

97. The Sentencing Project, "U.S. Prison Populations—Trends and Implications," available at http://www.sentencingproject.org/pubs_02.cfm.

98. Peter T. Kilborn, "Towns with Odd Jobs Galore Turn to Inmates," *New York Times* (March 27, 2002), A1.

99. Steven Greenhouse, "Conservatives' New Cause: Jobs for Ex-Cons," *New York Times* (December 13, 2002), A29.

100. "Budget Gaps Lead to Early Prison Releases," *Law Enforcement News* (April 15, 2003), 10.

101. Fox Butterfield, "Inmates Go Free to Reduce Deficits," *New York Times* (December 19, 2002), A1.

102. NJ.REV.STAT. Section 2C:7-8(c) (1995).

103. Megan's Law, Pub. L. No. 104-145, 110 Stat. 1345 (1996).

104. 20 U.S.C. Section 1094(c)(3)(B) (2000).

105. Ga. Code Ann. Section 42-9-44.1(b)(1).

106. Tara L. Wayt, "Megan's Law: A Violation of the Right to Privacy?" *Temple Political and Civil Rights Law Review* 6 (Fall 1996/Spring 1997), 139.

107. 123 S.Ct. 1160 (2003).

108. 123 S.Ct. 1140 (2003).

109. *Seling v. Young,* 531 U.S. 250 (2001).

110. *Kansas v. Crane,* 534 U.S. 407, 415 (2002).

The Juvenile Justice System

>chapter objectives<

After reading this chapter, you should be able to:

1 Describe the child-saving movement and its relationship to the doctrine of *parens patriae*.

2 List the four major differences between juvenile courts and adult courts.

3 Identify and briefly describe the single most important Supreme Court case with respect to juvenile justice.

4 List the factors that normally determine what police do with juvenile offenders.

5 Describe the four primary stages of pretrial juvenile justice procedure.

6 Explain the distinction between an adjudicatory hearing and a disposition hearing.

7 List the four categories of residential treatment programs.

8 Describe the one variable that always correlates highly with juvenile crime rates.

9 Indicate some of the reasons why youths join gangs.

Old Enough to Do the Crime...

Nobody seemed to think that Lionel Tate deserved the punishment that he got. Tate was twelve years old when he killed his six-year-old playmate Tiffany Eunick, apparently while imitating the violent moves of a professional wrestler he had seen on television. The jurors at his trial found that although Tate did not mean to kill Tiffany, he did mean to hurt her and, therefore, he was guilty of first degree murder under Florida law. Even for someone of Tate's tender years, this conviction carried a mandatory sentence of life in prison without parole.

Three years after Tate was convicted, the prosecutor in the case stated that a sentence "without hope of rehabilitation" for such a young boy was too harsh. One of the jurors said that she would never have agreed to the conviction if she had known the consequences. "This is no solution," said another juror. "The problem is with the system." In 2003, a Florida appeals court ordered a new trial because of errors made by Tate's original defense attorneys. Before the trial could be held, Tate agreed to a plea bargain under which he pleaded guilty to second degree murder and was sentenced to three years in juvenile prison. Because he had already served almost this long, the sentence essentially amounted to "time served," allowing him to be freed early in 2004.

AP Photo/Lou Toman, Pool

Lionel Tate, right, is taken from the Fort Lauderdale, Florida, courtroom where, in 2001, he was sentenced to life in prison for killing a playmate.

> **The controversy over** Lionel Tate underscores a debate that goes to the heart of the American juvenile justice system, which has been both hailed as one of the "greatest social inventions of modern times" and criticized for "failing to protect either the legal rights of the juvenile offenders or the public on whom they prey."[1] The question: Should criminal acts by youths be given the same weight as those committed by adults or be seen as "mistakes" that can be "corrected" by the state?

For most of its century-long history, the system was dominated by the latter philosophy; only recently have opposing views summarized by the sound bite "old enough to do the crime, old enough to do the time" gained widespread acceptance—a change reflected in political trends. Since 1992, nearly every state has changed its laws to make it easier to try juveniles as adults, representing a shift toward harsher measures in a juvenile system that generally acts as a "compromise between rehabilitation and punishment, treatment and custody."[2]

In this chapter, we will discuss the successes and failures of this compromise and examine the aspects of the juvenile justice system that differentiate it from the criminal justice system. As you will see, observers on both sides of the "rehabilitation versus punishment" debate find many flaws with the present system; some have even begun to call for its dismantling. Others blame social problems such as racism, poverty, and a culture dominated by images of violence for creating a system that no government agency or policy can effectively control.[3]

CONCEPT BUILDER
The term *delinquency* is generally reserved for violators of the law who are below a certain age. Visit www.cjinaction.com for an interactive exploration of this key topic.

The Evolution of American Juvenile Justice

In a recent poll, 65 percent of Americans indicated that they favored trying violent youths in adult criminal court instead of juvenile courts, which were perceived as too lenient.[4] To a certain degree, such opinions reflect a desire to return the focus of the American juvenile justice system toward punishment and incapacitation, as was the case at the beginning of the nineteenth century. At that time, juvenile offenders were treated the same as adult offenders—they were judged by the same courts and sentenced to the same severe penalties. This situation began to change in the early 1800s, as urbanization and industrialization created an immigrant underclass that was, at least in the eyes of certain reformers, predisposed to deviant activity. Certain members of the Progressive movement, known as the child savers, began to take steps to "save" children from these circumstances, introducing the idea of rehabilitating delinquents in the process.

"This is a cultural virus. We have to ask ourselves what kind of children we are raising."
—Bill Owens, Colorado governor, following the massacre of fourteen classmates and one teacher by two students at Columbine High School in Littleton, Colorado (1999)

THE CHILD-SAVING MOVEMENT

In general, the child savers favored the doctrine of **parens patriae**, which holds that the state has not only a right but a duty to care for children who are neglected, delinquent, or in some other way disadvantaged. Juvenile offenders, the child savers believed, required treatment, not punishment, and they were horrified at the thought of placing children in prisons with hardened adult criminals. Supreme Court Justice Abe Fortas said of the child savers:

> They believed that society's role was not to ascertain whether the child was "guilty" or "innocent," but "What is he, how has he become what he is, and what had best be done in his interest and in the interest of the state to save him from a downward career." The child—essentially good, as they saw it—was made "to feel that he is the object of [the government's] care and solicitude," not that he was under arrest or on trial.[5]

Child-saving organizations convinced local legislatures to pass laws that allowed them to take control of children who exhibited criminal tendencies or had been neglected by their parents. To separate these children from the environment

Parens Patriae
A doctrine that holds that the state has a responsibility to look after the well-being of children and to assume the role of parent if necessary.

in which they were raised, the organizations created a number of institutions, the best known of which was New York's House of Refuge. Opening in 1825, the House of Refuge implemented many of the same reformist measures popular in the penitentiaries of the time, meaning that its charges were subjected to the healthful influences of hard study and labor. Although the House of Refuge was criticized for its harsh discipline (which caused many boys to run away), similar institutions sprang up throughout the Northeast during the middle of the nineteenth century.

An illustration detailing the daily activities in the New York House of Refuge that appeared in *Harper's Weekly* in 1868. The House of Refuge was created in 1825 as a result of reformers' outrage that children who broke the law were treated the same as adults. The purpose of the House was to receive "all such children as shall be taken up or committed as vagrants, or convicted of criminal offenses." As you can see, the children were put to work at a number of different tasks, such as making shoes and hoop skirts. They also attended four hours of school every day. Judging from this illustration, how would you characterize the philosophy behind the House of Refuge?

THE ILLINOIS JUVENILE COURT

The efforts of the child savers culminated with the passage of the Illinois Juvenile Court Act in 1899. The Illinois legislature created the first court specifically for juveniles, guided by the principles of *parens patriae* and based on the concepts that children are not fully responsible for criminal conduct and are capable of being rehabilitated.[6]

The Illinois Juvenile Court and those from other states that followed in its path were (and, in many cases, remain) drastically different from adult courts:

> *No juries.* The matter was decided by judges who wore regular clothes instead of black robes and sat at a table with the other participants rather than behind a bench. Because the primary focus of the court was on the child and not the crime, the judge had wide discretion in disposing of each case.

> *Different terminology.* To reduce the stigma of criminal proceedings, "petitions" were issued instead of "warrants"; the children were not "defendants," but "respondents"; they were not "found guilty" but "adjudicated delinquent."

> *No adversarial relationship.* Instead of trying to determine guilt or innocence, the parties involved in the juvenile court worked together in the best interests of the child, with the emphasis on rehabilitation rather than punishment.

> *Confidentiality.* To avoid "saddling" the child with a criminal past, juvenile court hearings and records were kept sealed, and the proceedings were closed to the public.

By 1945, every state had a juvenile court system modeled after the first Illinois court. For the most part, these courts were able to operate without interference until the 1960s and the onset of the juvenile rights movement.

After the first juvenile court was established in Illinois, the Chicago Bar Association described its purpose as, in part, to "exercise the same tender solicitude and care over its neglected wards that a wise and loving parent would exercise with reference to his [or her] own children under similar circumstances."[7] In other words, the state was given the responsibility of caring for those minors whose behavior seemed to show that they could not be controlled by their parents. As a result, many **status offenders** found themselves in the early houses of refuge and continue to be placed in state-run facilities today. Also known as "children (or minors, youths, and so on) in need of supervision," status offenders have exhibited behavior—such as violating curfew, truancy (skipping school), and alcohol consumption—that is considered illegal only if an offender is below a specified age (see Figure 15.1). In contrast, **juvenile delinquency** refers to conduct that would be criminal if committed by an adult.

CONSTITUTIONAL PROTECTIONS AND THE JUVENILE COURT

Though the ideal of the juvenile court seemed to offer the "best of both worlds" for juvenile offenders, in reality the lack of procedural protections led to many children being arbitrarily punished not only for crimes, but for status offenses. Juvenile judges were treating all violators similarly, which led to many status offenders being incarcerated in the same institutions as violent delinquents. In response to a wave of lawsuits demanding due process rights for juveniles, the Supreme Court issued several rulings in the 1960s and 1970s that significantly changed the juvenile justice system.

Kent v. United States   The first decision to extend due process rights to children in juvenile courts was *Kent v. United States* (1966).[8] The case concerned sixteen-year-old Morris Kent, who had been arrested for breaking into a woman's house, stealing her purse, and raping her. Because Kent was on juvenile probation, the state sought to transfer his trial for the crime to an adult court (a process to be discussed later in the chapter). Without giving any reasons for his decision, the juvenile judge consented to this judicial waiver, and Kent was sentenced in the adult court to a thirty- to ninety-year prison term. The Supreme Court overturned the sentence, ruling that juveniles have a right to counsel and a hearing in any instance in which the juvenile judge is considering sending the case to an adult court. The Court stated that, in jurisdiction waiver cases, a child receives "the worst of both worlds," getting neither the "protections accorded to adults" nor the "solicitous care and regenerative treatment" offered in the juvenile system.[9]

In re Gault   Kent provided the groundwork for *In re Gault* one year later. Considered by many the single most important case concerning juvenile justice, *In re Gault* involved a young offender who was arrested for allegedly making a lewd phone call while on probation.[10] (See the feature *CJ in Focus—Landmark Cases:* In re Gault on the next page.) In its decision, the Supreme Court held that juveniles are entitled to many of the same due process rights granted to adult offenders, including notice of charges, the right to counsel, the privilege against self-incrimination, and the right to confront and cross-examine witnesses.

Other Important Court Decisions   Over the next ten years, the Supreme Court handed down three more important rulings on juvenile court procedure. *In re Winship* (1970)[11] required the government to prove "beyond a reasonable doubt" that a juvenile had committed an act of delinquency, raising the burden of proof from a "preponderance of the evidence." In *Breed v. Jones* (1975),[12] the Court held that the Fifth Amendment's double jeopardy clause prevented a juvenile from being tried in an adult court for a crime that had already been adjudicated in juvenile court. In contrast, *McKeiver v. Pennsylvania* (1971)[13]

FIGURE 15.1 Status Offenses
A status offense is an act that, if committed by a juvenile, is considered grounds for apprehension and perhaps state custody. The same act, if committed by an adult, does not warrant law enforcement action.

1. **Smoking cigarettes**
2. **Drinking alcohol**
3. **Being truant (skipping school)**
4. **Disobeying teachers**
5. **Running away from home**
6. **Violating curfew**
7. **Participating in sexual activity**
8. **Using profane language**

Status Offender
A juvenile who has been found to have engaged in behavior deemed unacceptable for those under a certain, statutorily determined age.

Juvenile Delinquency
Behavior that is illegal under federal or state law that has been committed by a person who is under an age limit specified by statute.

> In re Gault

In 1964, fifteen-year-old Gerald Gault and a friend were arrested for making lewd telephone calls to a neighbor in Gila County, Arizona. Gault, who was on probation, was placed under custody with no notice given to his parents. The juvenile court in his district held a series of informal hearings to determine Gault's punishment. During these hearings, no records were kept, Gault was not afforded the right to counsel, and the complaining witness was never made available for questioning. At the close of the hearing, the judge sentenced Gault to remain in Arizona's State Industrial School until the age of twenty-one. The defendant filed a writ of *habeas corpus,* claiming that he had been denied due process rights at his hearing. The Arizona Supreme Court affirmed the dismissal of this writ, ruling that the proceedings did not infringe on Gault's due process rights, a matter eventually taken up by the United States Supreme Court.

In re Gault
United States Supreme Court
387 U.S. 1 (1967)
http://laws.findlaw.com/US/387/1.htm

> In the words of the court . . .

Justice FORTAS, majority opinion

* * * *

From the inception of the juvenile court system, wide differences have been tolerated—indeed insisted upon—between the procedural rights accorded to adults and those of juveniles. In practically all jurisdictions, there are rights granted to adults which are withheld from juveniles.

* * * *

Accordingly, the highest motives and most enlightened impulses led to a peculiar system for juveniles, unknown to our law in any comparable context. The constitutional and theoretical basis for this peculiar system is—to say the least—debatable. And in practice, as we remarked in the *Kent* case, the results have not been entirely satisfactory. * * * The absence of substantive standards has not necessarily meant that children receive careful, compassionate, individualized treatment. The absence of procedural rules based upon constitutional principle has not always produced fair, efficient, and effective procedures. Departures from established principles of due process have frequently resulted not in enlightened procedure, but in arbitrariness.

* * * *

Ultimately, however, we confront the reality of that portion of the Juvenile Court process with which we deal in this case. A boy is charged with misconduct. The boy is committed to an institution where he may be restrained of liberty for years. It is of no constitutional consequence—and of limited practical meaning—that the institution to which he is committed is called an Industrial School. The fact of the matter is that, however euphemistic the title, a "receiving home" or an "industrial school" for juveniles is an institution of confinement in which the child is incarcerated for a greater or lesser time. His world becomes "a building with whitewashed walls, regimented routine and institutional hours . . . ." Instead of mother and father and sisters and brothers and friends and classmates, his world is peopled by guards, custodians, state employees, and "delinquents" confined with him for anything from waywardness to rape and homicide. In view of this, it would be extraordinary if our Constitution did not require the procedural regularity and the exercise of care implied in the phrase "due process." Under our Constitution, the condition of being a boy does not justify a kangaroo court.

* * * *

> Decision

The Court held that juveniles were entitled to the basic procedural safeguards afforded by the Fourteenth Amendment, including the right to advance notice of charges, the right to counsel, the right to confront and cross-examine witnesses, and the privilege against self-incrimination. The decision marked a turning point in juvenile justice in this country: no longer would informality and paternalism be the guiding principles of juvenile courts. Instead, due process would dictate the adjudication process, much as in an adult court.

FOR CRITICAL ANALYSIS
What might be some of the negative consequences of the In re Gault *decision for juveniles charged with committing delinquent acts?*

For more information and activities related to this case, click on Landmark Cases *under* Book Resources *at www.cjinaction.com.*

represented the one instance in which the Court did not move the juvenile court further toward the adult model. It ruled that the Constitution did not give juveniles the right to a jury trial.

ONLINE REVIEW *Go to the book's Web site for an interactive review of this section*

Determining Delinquency Today

In the eyes of many observers, the net effect of the Supreme Court decisions during the 1966–1975 period was to move juvenile justice away from the ideals of the child savers and toward a formalized system that is often indistinguishable from its adult counterpart. But, though the Court has recognized that minors possess certain constitutional rights, it has failed to dictate at what age these rights should be granted and at what age minors are to be held criminally responsible for delinquent actions. Consequently, the legal status of children in the United States varies depending on where they live, with each state making its own policy decisions on the crucial questions of age and competency.

THE AGE QUESTION

When a six-year-old and a younger friend smothered her three-year-old brother to death with a pillow in Blythe, California, authorities refused to press charges. Under state law, they could have done so if they could prove that the girls knew the "wrongfulness" of their action. The local district attorney said that the system was "not prepared to do anything with kids five or six years old."[14]

Under common law, a child under the age of seven was considered to lack the requisite *mens rea* to commit a crime (that is, he or she did not possess the mental capacity to understand the consequences of his or her action). Also under common law, a child between the ages of seven and fourteen could use the defense of infancy (being a minor) to plead innocent. On attaining fourteen years of age, the youth was considered an adult and treated accordingly.[15]

Today, as Figure 15.2 shows, twenty-four states and the District of Columbia do not have age restrictions on prosecuting juveniles as adults. Indeed, many states require juveniles who commit violent felonies such as murder, rape, or armed robbery to be waived to adult courts. When juveniles in a state without such a requirement commit a serious crime, they are given a "limited" sentence,

INFOTRAC KEYWORDS

juvenile deinquency

For more information, use this search term with InfoTrac College Edition, your online library at www.infotrac-college.com

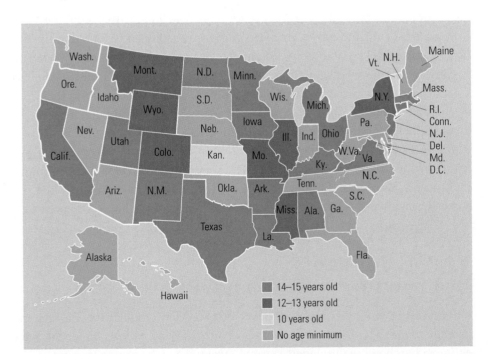

FIGURE 15.2
The Minimum Age at Which a Juvenile Can Be Tried as an Adult
Source: Office of Juvenile Justice and Delinquency Prevention.

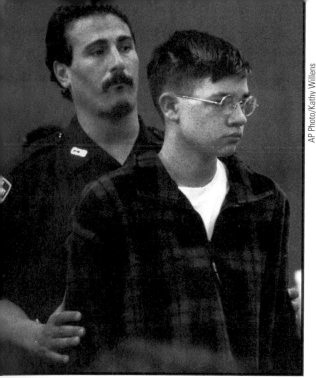

Fifteen-year-old Christopher Vasquez faced murder charges for stabbing Michael McMorrow, a forty-four-year-old man, in New York City's Central Park. The case attracted a great deal of interest because of Vasquez's age and the brutality of the crime—McMorrow was stabbed more than thirty times. Many observers felt that, despite his age, Vasquez should have received the same harsh punishment as would an adult who committed the same crime. In fact, the jury acquitted Vasquez of second degree murder, which would have carried a lifetime prison sentence. Instead he was found guilty of the less serious charge of manslaughter. Do you believe that a wrongdoer's age should be a consideration in determining punishment?

usually meaning they cannot remain incarcerated in juvenile detention centers past their eighteenth or twenty-first birthday.

THE COMPETENCY QUESTION

One of the precepts of *parens patriae* was the assumption that children are not legally competent and must, in the absence of parental care, be protected by the state. In today's juvenile justice environment, however, the question of a minor's competency to make informed decisions about criminal actions is far more complicated.

Psychological Competency   Most researchers believe that by the age of fourteen, an adolescent has the same ability to make a competent decision as does an adult.[16] Nevertheless, according to some observers, a juvenile's ability to theoretically understand the difference between "right" and "wrong" does not mean that she or he should be held to the same standards of competency as an adult. A study released in 2003 by the Research Network on Adolescent Development and Juvenile Justice found that 33 percent of juvenile defendants in criminal courts had the same low level of understanding of legal matters as mentally ill adults who had been found incompetent to stand trial.[17]

Legal psychologist Richard E. Redding believes that:

adolescents' lack of life experience may limit their real-world decision-making ability. Whether we call it wisdom, judgment, or common sense, adolescents may not have nearly enough.[18]

Juveniles are generally more impulsive, more likely to engage in risky behavior, and less likely to calculate the long-term consequences of any particular action. Furthermore, adolescents are far more likely to respond to peer pressure than are adults. The desire for acceptance and approval may drive them to commit crimes; juveniles are arrested as part of a group at much higher rates than adults.[19]

Legal Competency   In *Thompson v. Oklahoma* (1988),[20] the Supreme Court overturned the death penalty for a juvenile who was fifteen years old at the time he committed his capital crime. In ruling that such a punishment violated the Eighth Amendment's prohibition against "cruel and unusual punishment," the Court stated that a defendant that young "is not capable of acting with the degree of culpability that can justify the ultimate penalty."[21] One year later, however, the Court upheld the death penalty for sixteen- and seventeen-year-olds in *Stanford v. Kentucky* (1989).[22] Though the Court continued to hold that juveniles were less culpable than adults committing the same crime, it reversed its prior finding that capital punishment for juveniles *always* violates the Constitution. The Court basically gave states permission to determine their own age limits for executions.

↑ ONLINE REVIEW *Go to the book's Web site for an interactive review of this section*

First Contact: Delinquents and the Police

Until recently, most police departments allocated few resources to dealing with juvenile crime. The rise in violent crimes committed by citizens under the age of eighteen has, however, provided a strong incentive for departments to set up special services for children. The standard bearer for these operations is the *juvenile officer,* who operates either alone or as part of a juvenile unit within a department. The initial contact between a juvenile and the criminal justice system is usually handled by a regular police officer on patrol who either apprehends the juvenile while he or she is committing a crime or answers a call for service. (See Figure 15.3 for an overview of the juvenile justice process.) The youth is then passed on to a juvenile officer, who must decide how to handle the case.

POLICE DISCRETION AND JUVENILE CRIME

Police arrest about 1.6 million youths under the age of eighteen each year, 15 percent for violent crimes. In most states, police officers must have a probable cause to believe that the minor has committed an offense, as they would if the suspect was an adult. Police power with regard to juveniles is greater than with adults, however, because police can take youths into custody for status offenses such as possession of alcohol or truancy. In these cases, the officer is acting *in loco parentis,* or in the place of the parent. The officer's role is not necessarily to punish the youths, but to protect them from harmful behavior.

Low-Visibility Decision Making Police officers also have a great deal of discretion in deciding what to do with juveniles who have committed crimes or status offenses. Juvenile justice expert Joseph Goldstein labels this discretionary power **low-visibility decision making** because it relies on factors that the public is generally not in a position to understand or criticize. When a grave offense has taken place, a police officer may decide to formally arrest the juvenile, send him or her to juvenile court, or place the youth under the care of a social-service organization. About 85 percent of the cases in juvenile courts are referred by police.[23] In less serious situations, the officer may simply issue a warning or take the offender to the police station and release the child into the custody of her or his parents.

In making these discretionary decisions, police generally consider the following factors:

> The nature of the child's offense.

> The offender's past history of involvement with the juvenile justice system.

Low-Visibility Decision Making
A term used to describe the discretionary power police have in determining what to do with misbehaving juveniles. For the most part, this power goes unchallenged and unnoticed by citizens.

FIGURE 15.3
The Juvenile Justice Process
Source: Office of Juvenile Justice and Delinquency Prevention.

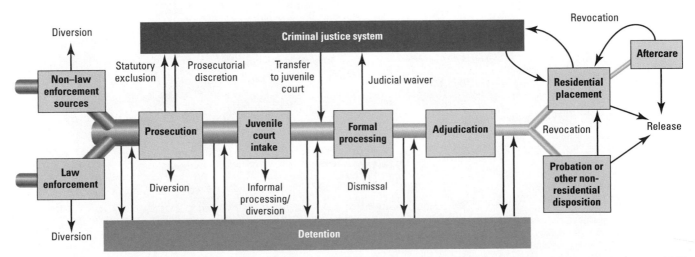

> The setting in which the offense took place.

> The ability and willingness of the child's parents to take disciplinary action.

> The attitude of the offender.

> The offender's race and gender.

Arrests and Minority Youths   As in other areas of the criminal justice system, members of minority groups are disproportionately represented in juvenile arrests. The violent crime arrest rate for African American juveniles is about four times that for white juveniles, and the property arrest crime rate for black juveniles is double that of whites. Furthermore, African American juveniles are referred to juvenile court twice as often as their white peers.[24]

A great deal of research, much of it contradictory, has been done to determine whether these statistics reflect inherent racism in the juvenile justice system or if social factors are to blame.[25] The latest large-scale study, performed by federal government crime researchers Carl E. Pope and Howard Snyder using the National Incident Based Reporting System (see page 90), found that nonwhite offenders were no more likely to be arrested for the same delinquent behavior than were white offenders.[26]

FIGURE 15.4 Juvenile Arrest Rates by Race, 1980–2000

Using the FBI's Uniform Crime Report, statisticians can determine the rates of arrest for persons aged ten to seventeen in the United States. As you can see, between 1980 and 2000 the rate of arrests per 100,000 juveniles was much higher for African Americans than for whites.

Source: Office of Juvenile Justice and Delinquency Prevention.

Failing the "Attitude Test"   In general, as Figure 15.4 shows, police officers do seem more likely to arrest members of minority groups. Although this may be partially attributed to the social factors discussed in Chapter 2, it also appears that minority youths fail the "attitude test" in interactions with police officers. After the seriousness of the offense and past history, the most important factor in the decision of whether to arrest or release appears to be the offender's attitude. An offender who is polite and apologetic generally has a better chance of being released. If the

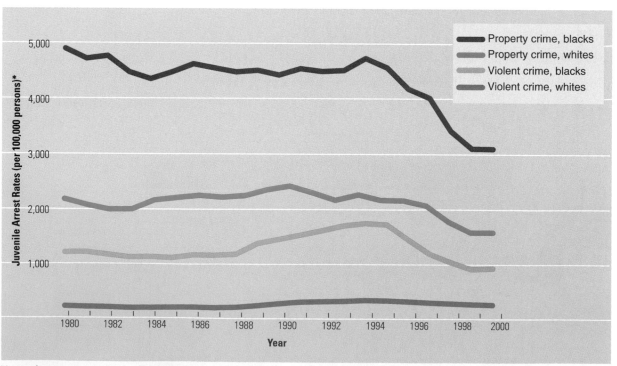

*Arrests of persons under age eighteen per 100,000 persons ages ten to seventeen in the population of the United States.

juvenile is hostile or unresponsive, the police are more likely to place him or her in custody for even a minor offense.[27]

Furthermore, police officers who do not live in the same community with minority youths may misinterpret normal behavior as disrespectful or delinquent and act accordingly.[28] This "culture gap" is of crucial importance to police-juvenile relations and underscores the community-oriented policing goal of having law enforcement agents be more involved in the communities they patrol (see Chapter 6).

JUVENILES AND THE CONSTITUTION

The privacy and *Miranda* rights of juveniles are protected during contact with law enforcement officers, though not to the same extent as for adults. In most jurisdictions, the Fourth Amendment ban against unreasonable searches and seizures and Fifth Amendment safeguards against custodial self-incrimination apply to juveniles. In other words, juvenile court judges cannot use illegally seized evidence in juvenile hearings, and police must read youths their *Miranda* rights after arrest.

Searches and Students   Such rights are not absolute, however. In *New Jersey v. T.L.O.* (1985),[29] the Supreme Court held that school officials may search a student on mere "reasonable suspicion" that he or she has violated school regulations or laws. The Court justified this lower standard—most searches require probable cause—on the grounds of maintaining school discipline and the *in loco parentis* doctrine.[30] In 1995, the Court further strengthened school officials' ability to search students by upholding a random drug-testing policy for high school athletes.[31] Seven years later, in *Board of Education v. Earls* (2002),[32] the Court allowed similar testing of students participating in any extracurricular activities.

***Miranda* Warnings**   In *Fare v. Michael C.* (1979),[33] the Supreme Court clarified law enforcement officials' responsibilities with regard to *Miranda* warnings and juveniles. The case involved a boy who had been arrested on suspicion of murder. After being read his rights, the youth asked to speak to his probation officer. The request was denied. The boy eventually confessed to the crime. The Court ruled that juveniles may waive their right to protection against self-incrimination and that admissions made to the police in the absence of counsel are admissible. The Court did, however, order juvenile courts to study the "totality of circumstances" to determine whether a child had been coerced into making a confession.

In other instances, the question is not whether the juvenile was coerced, but whether she or he can comprehend *Miranda* warnings or many other aspects of the interrogation process. As can be seen in the feature *CJ in Focus—A Question of Ethics: Interrogating Children* on the following page, police can be taking a chance by relying on the testimony of young suspects and witnesses.

Garry Moore/The Indianapolis Star

As second-grader Ejuanda Fields exits the school bus that takes her to Indianapolis Public School 84, Indianapolis Public Schools Police Sergeant Kelly Browning checks her backpack for weapons and drugs. Similar searches are being conducted with regularity at schools across the United States. The Supreme Court has upheld such searches based on two legal concepts. First, students on school grounds do not enjoy the same constitutional rights to privacy as does the general population. Second, the legality of a search of a student depends simply on the reasonableness, under all the circumstances, of the search. Do you believe that students should have the same privacy protections against searches as everybody else? What reasons can be given for denying them those protections?

↗ ONLINE REVIEW *Go to the book's Web site for an interactive review of this section*

The seven-year-old boy had been brought to the Wentworth Area police headquarters in Chicago for questioning in connection with the murder of Ryan Harris. Two weeks earlier, the beaten and sexually assaulted body of the eleven-year-old girl had been found lying in a lot behind an abandoned building. Two Chicago detectives took the boy into an empty room and asked him if he knew what a lie was. "You should never lie," he answered. Each detective took one of the boy's hands and then asked him about Harris. The seven-year-old admitted throwing a brick at the girl and knocking her off her bicycle, and then dragging her body into the weeds with the help of an eight-year-old friend. After checking the story with the friend, the police detained the boys and classified the case of Ryan Harris as "Cleared/Closed by Arrest."

Because of the age of the assailants and the brutality of the murder, the case immediately attracted the attention of the national media. Consequently, the spotlight was just as bright several weeks later, when the police abruptly released the two suspects. A forensic examination had found semen—that boys so young could not have produced—on the girl's torn underwear. Questions immediately arose concerning the Chicago police's interrogation techniques. Why had both boys been questioned at various times without the presence of counsel or even their parents? Both boys had waived their *Miranda* rights, but how could those so young understand the concept or conse-

quences of such an act? Why weren't obvious disparities between the two boys' stories given more attention, such as the contention by the eight-year-old that Harris was dead before she was hit in the head with the brick?

The Chicago police denied that they had bent any rules in gaining the confessions. In fact, a parent or guardian is not required by law to be present when police advise juvenile suspects of their constitutional rights—police must only make a "reasonable attempt" to contact parents, after which they can question the child. *Miranda* rights must be read only if the youth is "in custody," meaning that he or she does not feel free to leave. Finally, if a child "spontaneously confesses," as did the seven-year-old, *Miranda* warnings are not required.

To avoid situations such as occurred in Chicago, many police departments are considering digitally recording all interrogations of juveniles. Some observers are even suggesting that all interrogations of juveniles *must* take place in the presence of a parent or counsel.

FOR CRITICAL ANALYSIS

How reliable are the statements of juveniles, especially those as young as the boys in the Harris case? Regardless of the law, how should police approach the interrogation of children who may not fully understand the concept of constitutional rights?

Pretrial Procedures in Juvenile Justice

After arrest and before the start of the trial, various decision makers are provided the opportunity to determine how the juvenile justice system will dispose of each case. The offender may be diverted to a social-services program or detained in a juvenile lockup facility. In the most serious cases, the youth may even be transferred to adult court. To ensure due process during pretrial procedures, offenders and their families may retain an attorney or have one appointed by the court. The four primary stages of this critical period—intake, diversion, waiver, and detention—are discussed below.

INTAKE

If, following arrest, a police officer feels the offender warrants the attention of the juvenile justice process, the officer will refer the youth to juvenile court. As noted earlier, the juvenile court receives the majority of its respondents from the police, though parents, relatives, welfare agencies, and school officials may also refer juveniles. Once this step has been taken, a complaint is filed with a special division of the juvenile court, and the **intake** process begins. During intake, an official of the juvenile court—usually a probation officer, but sometimes a judge—must decide, in effect, what to do with the offender. The screening official has several options during intake.

1. Simply dismiss the case, releasing the offender without taking any further action.
2. Divert the offender to a social-services program, such as drug rehabilitation or anger management.
3. File a **petition** for a formal court hearing.
4. Transfer the case to an adult court where the offender will be tried as an adult.

The intake process is changing in several very important ways. In particular, the influence of prosecutors on the fate of the juvenile wrongdoer is growing significantly. In the past, the primary responsibility for providing a juvenile judge with a recommendation on how the case should be handled was left to probation personnel. Even though the judge handed down the final decision, in most cases she or he followed the recommendation of a probation officer as to whether the juvenile should take part in a formal court hearing. This approach, indicative of a system that favors rehabilitation, is being replaced in some jurisdictions.

PRETRIAL DIVERSION

To a certain extent, the juvenile justice system started as a diversionary program with the goal of diverting children from the punitive adult court to the more rehabilitative juvenile court.[34] By the 1960s, many observers felt that juvenile courts had lost sight of this early mandate and were badly in need of reform. One specific target for criticism was the growing number of status offenders—40 percent of all children in the system—who were being punished even though they had not committed a truly delinquent act.

The idea of diverting certain children, including status and first-time offenders, from the juvenile court system to nonjudicial community agencies was encouraged by the President's Commission on Law Enforcement and Administration of Justice in 1967.[35] Seven years later, Congress passed the Juvenile Justice and Delinquency Prevention (JJDP) Act, which ordered the development of methods "to divert juveniles from the traditional juvenile justice system."[36] Within a few years, hundreds of diversion programs had been put into effect. Today, **diversion** refers to the process of removing low-risk offenders from the formal juvenile justice system by placing them in community-based rehabilitation programs.

Diversion programs vary widely, but fall into three general categories:

1. *Probation.* In this program, the juvenile is returned to the community, but placed under the supervision of a juvenile probation officer. If the youth breaks the conditions of probation, he or she can be returned to the formal juvenile system.
2. *Treatment and aid.* Many juveniles have behavioral or medical conditions that contribute to their delinquent behavior, and many diversion programs offer remedial education, drug and alcohol treatment, and other forms of counseling to alleviate these problems.

Intake
Following referral of a juvenile to juvenile court by a police officer or other concerned party, the process by which an official of the court must decide whether to file a petition, release the juvenile, or place the juvenile under some other form of supervision.

Petition
The document filed with a juvenile court alleging that the juvenile is a delinquent or a status offender, and asking the court to either hear the case or transfer it to an adult court.

Diversion
The removal of an alleged juvenile delinquent from the formal criminal or juvenile justice system and the referral of that person to a treatment or rehabilitation program.

3   *Restitution.* In these programs, the offender "repays" her or his victim, either directly or, in the case of community service, symbolically.[37]

Proponents of diversion programs include many labeling theorists (see Chapter 2), who believe that contact with the formal juvenile justice system "labels" the youth a delinquent, which leads to further delinquent behavior.

TRANSFER TO ADULT COURT

One side effect of diversionary programs is that the youths who remain in the juvenile courts are more likely to be seen as "hardened" and less amenable to rehabilitation. This, in turn, increases the likelihood that the offender will be transferred to an adult court, a process in which the juvenile court waives jurisdiction over the youth. As the American juvenile justice system has shifted away from ideals of treatment and toward punishment, transfer to adult court has been one of the most popular means of "getting tough" on delinquents.

Methods of Transfer   Juveniles are most commonly transferred to adult court through **judicial waiver.** In forty-eight states (excluding New York and Nebraska), the juvenile judge is the official who determines whether jurisdiction over a minor offender should be waived to adult court. The judge formulates this ruling by taking into consideration the offender's age, the nature of the offense, and any criminal history.

Thirty-four states have taken the waiver responsibility out of judicial hands through **automatic transfer,** also known as legislative waiver. In these states, the legislatures have designated certain conditions—usually involving serious crimes such as murder and rape—under which a juvenile case is automatically "kicked up" to adult court. In Rhode Island, for example, a juvenile aged sixteen or older with two prior felony adjudications will automatically be transferred on being accused of a third felony.[38] Ten states allow for **prosecutorial waiver,** in which juvenile court judges are allowed to waive jurisdiction when certain age and offense conditions are met. In general, no matter what the process, those juveniles who commit violent felonies are most likely to be transferred to an adult court (see Figure 15.5).

In twenty-four states, criminal court judges also have the freedom to send juveniles who were transferred to adult court back to juvenile court. Known as *reverse transfer* statutes, these laws are designed to provide judges with a measure of discretion even when automatic transfer takes place.[39]

Consequences of Transfer   When transfer laws were first enacted, observers worried that judges in adult courts would tend to give juveniles more lenient sentences than adults who had committed the same crime. This "leniency gap" does not appear to exist. Indeed, critics of transfer laws insist that adult courts are *too* severe on juveniles. According to Donna Bishop of Northeastern University and Charles Frazier of the University of Florida, "transferred youths are sentenced more harshly, both in terms of the probability of receiving a prison sentence and the length of the sentences they receive."[40]

FIGURE 15.5 Felony Arrest Charge for Juveniles Transferred to Adult Criminal Courts

Two out of every three juveniles transferred to adult criminal court under suspicion of committing a felony were charged with a violent offense. The data shown here were collected in criminal courts located in forty of the largest urban counties in the United States.

Source: Bureau of Justice Statistics, *Juvenile Felony Defendants in Criminal Courts* (Washington, D.C.: U.S. Department of Justice, May 2003), Table 2, page 2.

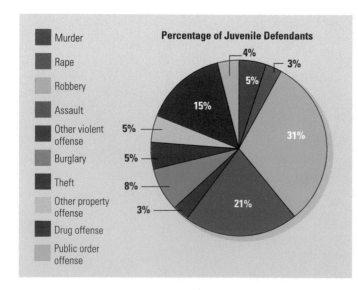

Murder
Rape
Robbery
Assault
Other violent offense
Burglary
Theft
Other property offense
Drug offense
Public order offense

Percentage of Juvenile Defendants

4%
3%
5%
15%
5%
5%
31%
8%
3%
21%

Furthermore, a number of observers believe that juveniles tried in adults courts have higher recidivism rates than those who are tried in juvenile courts. Comparing transferred and non-transferred juvenile offenders in Florida, Bishop and Frazier found that, over the short term, 30 percent of the transferred offenders were rearrested after release, compared to 19 percent of those processed in the juvenile court system.[41] Doing similar research in New York and New Jersey, Jeffrey Fagan of Columbia University found that 56 percent of the "criminal court group" were

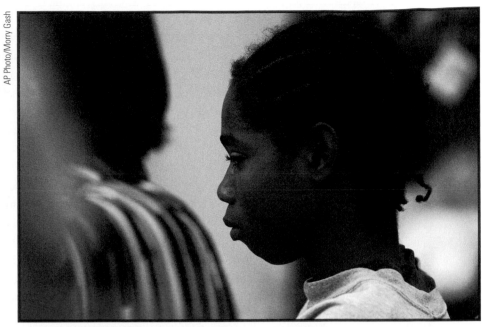

Thirteen-year-old Artieas Shanks, pictured here, was originally charged as an adult for his part in the beating death of Charlie Young, Jr., in Milwaukee, Wisconsin. Eventually, however, he reached a plea bargain with prosecutors allowing him to be found delinquent rather than pleading guilty to a felony. In 2003 his case was sent to Children's Court, and he was sentenced as a juvenile to two years in the custody of the Wisconsin Department of Youth Services. How might this "reverse transfer" benefit Shanks?

reincarcerated, while only 41 percent of the "juvenile court group" were returned to prison, jail, or a juvenile institution.[42]

DETENTION

Once the decision has been made that the offender will face adjudication in a juvenile court, the intake official must decide what to do with him or her until the start of the trial. Generally, the juvenile is released into the custody of parents or a guardian—most jurisdictions favor this practice in lieu of setting money bail for youths. The intake officer may also place the offender in **detention,** or temporary custody in a secure facility, until the disposition process begins. Once a juvenile has been detained, most jurisdictions require that a **detention hearing** be held within twenty-four hours. During this hearing, the offender has several due process safeguards, including the right to counsel, the right against self-incrimination, and the right to cross-examine and confront witnesses.

In justifying its decision to detain, the court will usually address one of three issues:

1 Whether the child poses a danger to the community.

2 Whether the child will return for the adjudication process.

3 Whether detention will provide protection for the child.

The Supreme Court upheld the practice of preventive detention (see Chapter 9) for juveniles in *Schall v. Martin* (1984)[43] by ruling that youths can be detained if they are deemed a "risk" to the safety of the community or to their own welfare.

↗ ONLINE REVIEW *Go to the book's Web site for an interactive review of this section*

Detention
The temporary custody of a juvenile in a state facility after a petition has been filed and before the adjudicatory process begins.

Detention Hearing
A hearing to determine whether a juvenile should be detained, or remain detained, while waiting for the adjudicatory process to begin.

Juveniles on Trial

Over the past thirty-five years, the one constant in the juvenile justice system has been change. Supreme Court rulings in the wake of *In re Gault* (1967) have increased the procedural formality and the overriding punitive philosophy of the

INFOTRAC KEYWORDS 🔍

juvenile courts

For more information, use this search term with InfoTrac College Edition, your online library at www.infotrac-college.com

juvenile court. Diversion policies have worked to remove many status offenders from the juvenile court's jurisdiction, and waiver policies assure that the most violent juveniles are tried as adults. Some observers feel these adjustments have "criminalized" the juvenile court, effectively rendering it indistinguishable both theoretically and practically from adult courts.[44]

Along with a number of his colleagues, law professor Barry C. Feld thinks that the juvenile court has become obsolete and should be abolished. Feld believes the changes noted above have "transformed the juvenile court from its original model as a social service agency into a deficient second-rate criminal court that provides young people with neither positive treatment nor criminal procedural justice."[45] Indeed, juvenile hearings do proceed along many of the same lines as the adult criminal court, with similar due process protections and rules of evidence (though minors do not enjoy the right to a jury trial). As the *Mastering Concepts* feature alongside explains, however, juvenile justice proceedings may still be distinguished from the adult system of criminal justice, and these differences are evident in the adjudication and disposition of the juvenile trial.

ADJUDICATION

Adjudicatory Hearing
The process through which a juvenile court determines whether there is sufficient evidence to support the initial petition.

During the adjudication stage of the juvenile justice process, a hearing is held to determine whether the offender is delinquent or in need of some form of court supervision. Most state juvenile codes dictate a specific set of procedures that must be followed during the **adjudicatory hearing,** with the goal of providing the respondent with "the essentials of due process and fair treatment." Consequently, the respondent in an adjudicatory hearing has the right to notice of charges, counsel, confrontation and cross-examination, and the privilege against self-incrimination. Furthermore, "proof beyond a reasonable doubt" must be established to find the child delinquent. When the child admits guilt—that is, admits to the charges of the initial petition—the judge must ensure that the admission was voluntary.

The increased presence of defense attorneys in juvenile courts has had a significant impact on juvenile adjudication. (See the feature *Careers in CJ* on page 522.) Aspects of the adversarial system have become increasingly apparent in juvenile courts, as has the practice of plea bargaining. To a certain extent, however, juvenile trials have retained the informal atmosphere that characterized pre–*In re Gault* proceedings. Respondents and their families often waive the due process rights provided by the Supreme Court at the suggestion of a juvenile probation officer or judge. One study of Minnesota juvenile courts found that no counsel was present in 50 percent of that state's adjudicatory hearings.[46]

At the close of the adjudicatory hearing, the judge is generally required to rule on the legal issues and evidence that have been presented. Based on this ruling, the judge determines whether the respondent is delinquent or in need of court supervision. Alternatively, the judge can dismiss the case based on a lack of evidence. It is important to remember that finding a child to be delinquent is *not* the same as convicting an adult of a crime. A delinquent does not face the same restrictions, such as those concerning the right to vote and to run for political office, as do adult convicts in some states (discussed in Chapter 14).

> The Juvenile Justice System versus the Criminal Justice System

When the juvenile justice system first began in the United States, its participants saw it as being separate from the adult criminal justice system. Indeed, the two systems remain separate in many ways. There are, however, a number of similarities between juvenile and adult justice. Here, we summarize both the similarities and the differences.

SIMILARITIES

> The right to receive the *Miranda* warning

> Procedural protections when making an admission of guilt

> Prosecutors and defense attorneys play equally important roles

> The right to be represented by counsel at the crucial stages of the trial process

> Access to plea bargains

> The right to a hearing and an appeal

> The standard of evidence is proof beyond a reasonable doubt

> Both can be placed on probation by the judge

> Both can be held before adjudication if the judge believes them to be a threat to the community

> Following trial, both can be sentenced to community supervision

DIFFERENCES

	Juvenile System	Adult System
Purpose	Rehabilitation of the offender	Punishment
Arrest	Juveniles can be arrested for acts (status offenses) that are not criminal for adults	Adults can only be arrested for acts made illegal by the relevant criminal code
Wrongdoing	Considered a "delinquent act"	A crime
Proceedings	Informal, closed to public	Formal and regimented; open to public
Information	Courts may NOT release information to the press	Courts MUST release information to the press
Parents	Play significant role	Play no role
Release	Into parent/guardian custody	May post bail when justified
Jury trial	In most, but not all states, juveniles do NOT have this right	All adults have this right
Searches	Juveniles can be searched in school without probable cause	No adult can be searched without probable cause
Records	Juvenile's record is sealed at age of majority	Adult's criminal record is permanent
Sentencing	Juveniles are placed in separate facilities from adults	Adults are placed in county jails or state prisons
Death penalty	No death penalty	When tried as an adult, juveniles over age sixteen can be punished with execution

DISPOSITION

Once a juvenile has been adjudicated delinquent, the judge must decide what steps will be taken toward treatment and/or punishment. Most states provide for a *bifurcated process* in which a separate **disposition hearing** follows the adjudicatory hearing. Depending on state law, the juvenile may be entitled to counsel at the disposition hearing.

Sentencing Juveniles In an adult trial, the sentencing phase is primarily concerned with the "needs" of the community to be protected from the convict. In contrast, a juvenile judge uses the disposition hearing to determine a sentence that will serve the "needs" of the child. For assistance in this crucial process, the judge will order the probation department to gather information on the juvenile and present it in the form of a **predisposition report.** The report usually contains information concerning the respondent's family background, the facts surrounding the delinquent act, and interviews with social workers, teachers, and other important figures in the child's life.

Disposition Hearing
Similar to the sentencing hearing for adults, a hearing in which the juvenile judge or officer decides the appropriate punishment for a youth found to be delinquent or a status offender.

Predisposition Report
A report prepared during the disposition process that provides the judge with relevant background material to aid in the disposition decision.

> Cathy Wasserman Public Defender: Juvenile Courts

Grandpa had always said I could talk my way out of the electric chair. So when a friend in college suggested applying to law school, I thought, yes, why not? I attended Seton Hall Law In Newark, New Jersey, where I participated in the Juvenile Justice Clinic for two and a half semesters. This experience representing delinquents, coupled with a childhood of being raised on *Perry Mason,* as well as a law clerkship with a Superior Court judge, helped me to recognize my strong interest in criminal law. The forum of pleading my case in open court seemed like the only place to be.

Following my clerkship, I was hired by the Office of the Public Defender. Working for the P.D. is the fastest way to be in command of your own cases and to appear in court on all kinds of matters, particularly trials. My case load consisted of clients charged with everything from fourth degree theft to armed robbery. The first year and a half, I represented adults. Then I went to the Appellate Section, where I wrote briefs for two and a half years. I enjoyed the treasure hunt of looking for the cases to support my arguments. I also enjoyed presenting those arguments to the Appellate Division panels. However, I found I missed being in court on a daily basis and dealing with clients in person. Thus, when the opportunity to transfer to another trial region arose, I grabbed it and began representing juveniles once again.

Every day I enter court prepared to do battle for a youngster who in all likelihood is not cognizant of how at risk his or her freedom is. Initially, my most important responsibility is to interview my client and his family to gain their trust, obtain information about the child, and learn their version of the facts in the case. I gather all the evidence provided by the State, review it carefully, and conduct my own investigations. Following a careful review of all the evidence available, weighing all the strengths and weaknesses in the case, and considering whether any trial would be before a judge rather than a jury, I discuss the options, risks, and penalties with my client. Whether we go to trial or negotiate a plea agreement, my duties are to be an effective attorney for the child. However, once we face a sentence, I must also become a social worker as I attempt to fashion the least restrictive disposition from the myriad of sentencing alternatives. It is this array of options and the court's discretion to

impose them which most clearly distinguishes the juvenile system from its adult counterpart.

Some of the most challenging cases of my career have involved representing children the State is seeking to have referred to adult court. In New Jersey, there is a presumption of referral where a juvenile is charged with the most serious offenses and is fourteen years or older. The discretion to file for referral lies solely in the hands of the prosecutor. There are few tasks more difficult than having to tell a fourteen-year-old, who had a fight in which someone died, that he could be spending the next thirty years of his life in an adult jail. I faced this very scenario a number of years ago. In that particular case, H. T. had no prior involvement with the system and did not inflict the fatal

Courtesy Cathy Wasserman

Cathy Wasserman

wound. Worse, the confession he gave to the police to "help" himself was the main evidence against him. Although the State's psychiatrist agreed with the defense expert that the boy could be rehabilitated in the juvenile system, the State pressed on. The pressure and emotional toll on me as counsel was enormous. I struggled to construct arguments out of the jigsaw puzzle of facts and the kid's life. I was confidante, commander, and advisor to not only my client in custody but also to his family. Contrary to the norm in waiver cases, H. T. prevailed. This case helped me to recognize how important my role can be in the life of a child.

I am an impassioned advocate for children because I believe most offenders should be allowed to survive childhood and adolescence without permanently damaging their prospects for a positive future. My skills as an attorney and negotiator give my clients the opportunity to rise above their acts, often committed through poor judgment, due to inexperience, or by succumbing to peer pressure. Occasionally, I make a significant difference in the life of a youngster.

 Go to the Careers in Criminal Justice Interactive CD *for more profiles in the field of criminal justice.*

Judicial Discretion In keeping with the rehabilitative tradition of the juvenile justice system, many judges have a great deal of discretion in choosing one of several disposition possibilities. Generally, the choice is among incarceration in a juvenile correctional facility, probation, or community treatment. In most cases, seriousness of the offense is the primary factor used in determining whether to incarcerate a juvenile, though history of delinquency, family situation, and the offender's attitude are all relevant. Some research suggests that race plays a significant role in disposition—that minority delinquents are more likely to be incarcerated than their white counterparts.[47]

Further indication of the treatment goals of juvenile courts can be found in the indeterminate sentencing practices that, until recently, dominated disposition. Under indeterminate sentencing, correctional administrators were given the freedom to decide when a delinquent had been sufficiently rehabilitated and could be released. In a clear indication of the shift toward the crime control model, today nearly half of the states have enacted determinate or minimum mandatory sentencing laws that cover convicted juvenile offenders. Such statutes shift the focus of disposition from the treatment needs of the delinquent to society's desire to punish and incapacitate.[48]

↗ ONLINE REVIEW *Go to the book's Web site for an interactive review of this section*

Juvenile Corrections

In general, juvenile corrections are based on the concept of **graduated sanctions**—that is, the severity of the punishment should fit the crime. Consequently, status and first-time offenders are diverted or placed on probation, repeat offenders find themselves in intensive community supervision or treatment programs, and serious and violent offenders are placed in correctional facilities.[49] As society's expectations of the juvenile justice system have changed, so have the characteristics of its corrections programs. In some cities, for example, juvenile probation officers join police officers on the beat. Because the former are not bound by the same search and seizure restrictions as other law enforcement officials, this interdepartmental teamwork provides more opportunities to fight youth crime aggressively. Juvenile correctional facilities are also changing their operations to reflect public mandates that they both reform and punish. Keep in mind as well that as of 2002, more than three thousand juveniles were serving time in state adult prisons—twice as many as a decade earlier.[50]

PROBATION AND RESIDENTIAL TREATMENT PROGRAMS

The most common form of juvenile corrections is probation—35 percent of all delinquency cases disposed of by juvenile courts result in conditional diversion. The majority of all adjudicated delinquents (nearly 58 percent) will never receive a disposition more severe than being placed on probation.[51] These statistics reflect a general understanding among juvenile court judges and other officials that removing a child from her or his home should be considered primarily as a last resort.

The organization of juvenile probation is very similar to adult probation (see Chapter 12), and juvenile probationers are increasingly subjected to electronic monitoring and other supervisory tactics. The main difference between the two programs lies in the attitude toward the offender. Adult probation officers have an overriding responsibility to protect the community from the probationer, while juvenile probation officers are expected to take the role of a mentor or a concerned relative in looking after the needs of the child.

When intensive supervision must be instituted, youths can be placed in **residential treatment programs.** These programs, run by either probation departments or social-service organizations, provide treatment in a nonsecure living

Graduated Sanctions
The practical theory in juvenile corrections that a delinquent or status offender should receive a punishment that matches in seriousness the severity of the wrongdoing.

Residential Treatment Programs
Government-run facilities for juveniles whose offenses are not deemed serious enough to warrant incarceration in a training school.

The State Correctional Institution at Pine Grove, Pennsylvania, offers a juvenile delinquency discussion program while at the same time providing for large numbers of newly admitted violent youth offenders. Here a prison counselor "tells it like it is" to young visitors while in the presence of current inmates. Under what circumstances might such a program work?

facility. Residential treatment programs can be divided into four categories:

1 *Foster care programs,* in which the juvenile lives with a couple who act as surrogate parents.

2 *Group homes,* which generally house between twelve and fifteen youths and provide treatment, counseling, and educational services by a professional staff.

3 *Family group homes,* which combine aspects of foster care and group homes, meaning that a single family, rather than a group of professionals, looks after the needs of the offenders.

4 *Rural programs,* which include wilderness camps, farms, and ranches where between thirty and fifty children are placed in an environment that provides recreational activities and treatment programs.[52]

INSTITUTIONALIZING JUVENILES

More than 110,000 American youths (up from 30,000 at the end of the 1970s) are incarcerated in public and private juvenile correctional facilities in the United States.[53] Most of these juveniles have committed crimes against people or property, but a significant number (about 16 percent) have been incarcerated because of other factors, such as familial neglect or mental incapacity.

The most restrictive of these facilities—referred to as **training schools**—are similar in many aspects to adult prisons and jails. In theory, training schools differ from adult prisons and jails in their efforts to treat and rehabilitate young offenders. In practice, although many juvenile facilities do uphold this traditional justification for incarcerating children, a number do not.

Most juveniles leave corrections facilities through an early release program or because they have served the length of their sentences. Juvenile corrections officials recognize that many of these children, like adults, need assistance readjusting to the outside world. Consequently, released juveniles are often placed in *aftercare* programs. Similar to adult parole, an aftercare program is designed to offer services for the juvenile, while at the same time supervising him or her to reduce the chances of recidivism. The ideal aftercare program includes community support groups, aid in finding and keeping employment, and continued monitoring to assure that the juvenile is able to deal with the demands of freedom.[54] (See the feature *What Works—Young Women's Support Project.*)

⬈ ONLINE REVIEW *Go to the book's Web site for an interactive review of this section*

Training Schools
Correctional institutions for juveniles found to be delinquent or status offenders.

The National Center for Juvenile Justice is a valuable source for juvenile delinquency information and data. Find its Web site by clicking on *Web Links* under *Chapter Resources* at www.cjinaction.com

Recent Trends in Juvenile Delinquency

When asked, juveniles will admit to a wide range of illegal or dangerous behavior, including carrying weapons, getting involved in physical fights, driving after drinking alcohol, and stealing or deliberately damaging school property.[55] Have juvenile law enforcement efforts, juvenile courts, and juvenile corrections been

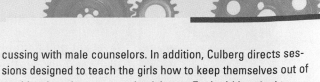

> Young Women's Support Project

On probation for a drug charge, sixteen-year-old Joy was returned to the King County Youth Detention Center in Seattle, Washington, after a fight at home. According to Laura Culberg, that may have been the best thing that could have happened to her. "They keep coming back to detention because they don't have anyone to support them," says Culberg. In juvenile detention (or "juvie"), however, Joy and about three hundred other girls have access to the Young Women's Support Project, a series of workshops run by Culberg that address a number of issues facing delinquent girls.

Culberg's ultimate goal is to change the defeatist perspective of girls who come through the juvenile justice system. The workshops are not unlike pep talks, in that Culberg and her female volunteer assistants try to improve the girls' self-esteem. The sessions also concentrate on sensitive subjects—such as birth control, rape, sexually transmitted diseases, and eating disorders—that many young women do not feel comfortable dis-

cussing with male counselors. In addition, Culberg directs sessions designed to teach the girls how to keep themselves out of trouble when they are sent back home. Each girl is asked to create a "stay out of juvie map" with a detailed plan on how she plans to achieve her goals once released.

The Young Women's Support Project is one of the few programs in the country that focuses on female delinquents. Many observers hope it becomes a model for similar programs in other areas, considering that young women are committing an increasing amount of juvenile crime. Over the past two decades, the arrest rate for girls has increased at twice the rate for boys, and girls now comprise almost 30 percent of the juvenile justice system's population.

FOR CRITICAL ANALYSIS
Why do you think that programs such as the Young Women's Support Project are so rare?

effective in controlling and preventing this kind of misbehavior, as well as more serious acts?

To answer this question, many observers turn to the Federal Bureau of Investigation's Uniform Crime Report (UCR), initially covered in Chapter 3. Because the UCR breaks down arrest statistics by age of the arrestee, it has been considered the primary source of information on the presence of juveniles in America's justice system. This does not mean, however, that the UCR is completely reliable when it comes to measuring juvenile delinquency. The process measures only those juveniles who were caught and therefore does not accurately reflect all delinquent acts in any given year. Furthermore, it measures the number of arrests but not the number of arrestees, meaning that—due to repeat offenders—the number of juveniles actually in the system could be below the number of juvenile arrests.

DELINQUENCY BY THE NUMBERS

With these cautions in mind, UCR findings are quite clear as to the extent of the juvenile delinquency problem in the United States today. In 2002, juveniles accounted for 14.9 percent of violent crime arrests and 16.5 percent of criminal activity arrests in general.[56] According to the 2002 UCR, juveniles were responsible for

> 9.6 percent of all murder arrests;

> 13 percent of all aggravated assault arrests;

> 16.7 percent of all forcible rapes;

> 21.4 percent of all weapons arrests;

> 23.1 percent of all robbery arrests;

James Edward Bates/The New York Times

> 29.8 percent of all property crimes; and
> 12.1 percent of all drug offenses.

IS JUVENILE CRIME LEVELING OFF?

A recent poll found that more than 70 percent of parents felt that a shooting was likely at their child's school.[57] Although, as we will see in the *Criminal Justice in Action* feature at the end of this chapter, school crime is a serious problem, the high visibility of violence on campus tends to skew public perceptions of juvenile offending. In fact, as Figure 15.6 shows, after a dramatic rise in the mid-1990s, juvenile arrest rates have been steadily dropping for nearly a decade.

Violent Crime Trends   Between 1994 and 2000, the juvenile arrest rate for violent crimes dropped 41 percent. The juvenile murder rate fell 74 percent in the 1990s, settling at levels not seen since the 1960s.[58] Incidences of juvenile robbery, burglary, and motor vehicle theft have seen similar downturns. Although juvenile arrest rates for some crimes, such as fraud, embezzlement, and driving under the influence, are still rising, the overall situation is not as bleak as it was at the height of the youth crime wave in the mid-1990s.

Reasons for the Decline   Although the theory is not universally accepted, many observers see the rise and decline of juvenile arrests as mirroring the rise and decline of crack cocaine.[59] When inner-city youths took advantage of the economic opportunities offered by the crack trade in the 1980s, they found they needed to protect themselves against rival dealers. This led to the proliferation of firearms among juveniles, as well as the formation of violent youth gangs. As the crack "epidemic" has slowed in recent years, so have arrest and violent crime rates for juveniles.

Other theories have been put forth as well. Some observers point to the increase in police action against "quality-of-life" crimes such as loitering, which they believe stops juveniles before they have a chance to commit more serious crimes. Furthermore, many schools have adopted "zero-tolerance" policies that punish students harshly for bringing weapons or drugs onto school grounds. (To see other steps schools are taking to make themselves safer, see the feature *CJ and Technology—The Electronic Hall Monitor*.) Richard Curtis, a professor of anthropology at John Jay College of Criminal Justice in New York, thinks young Americans have learned from the examples of

FIGURE 15.6 Arrest Rates of Juveniles, 1981–2000

After rising dramatically from 1985 to 1994, arrest rates for juveniles began to fall.

Source: Office of Juvenile Justice and Delinquency Prevention.

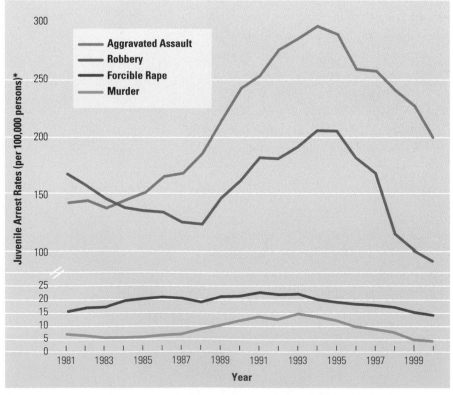

*Arrests of persons under age eighteen per 100,000 persons ages ten to seventeen in the population of the United States.

> The Electronic Hall Monitor

Americans are accustomed to being watched. Surveillance cameras are commonplace in banks, stores, office lobbies, and airports. But how about schools? Increasingly, the student hall monitor is being replaced by the electronic eye—or even better, dozens of electronic eyes.

Following the lead of colleagues across the United States, officials at Mansfield High, located just outside Boston, recently installed fourteen cameras in the school's halls and entryways. A video feed is piped into two television monitors in the school office, allowing administrators to watch and record a great deal of student activity. During their first year of operation, the devices were mainly successful in recording and consequently preventing acts of petty vandalism. Their main purpose, however, is to "create an atmosphere of safety," says principal Peter Deftos. In other words, Deftos and other proponents of using cameras in schools believe they will protect against acts of violence such as occurred in Columbine High School in Colorado in 1999, when two students shot and killed fourteen fellow students and a teacher.

Not everyone is convinced that the cameras can be effective in deterring such shootings. First, because of privacy concerns schools will generally not place cameras in bathrooms or classrooms, thereby severely limiting their scope and effectiveness. Second, just because school officials may be able to see a student with a gun walking down the hall, there is no guarantee that the official will be able to stop that student from committing a crime. In fact, Columbine High was equipped with hall cameras at the time of the tragedy.

In the Future

What if law enforcement officers, as well as school officials, could monitor the hallways? *Safewatch* is a real-time video monitoring system that allows the police to view the images from as many as ten cameras at one time on a Web browser. To protect student and teacher privacy, systems such as *Safewatch* remain dormant until activated by a trigger such as a

AP Photo/Jefferson County Sheriff's Department

Surveillance cameras in Columbine High School in Littleton, Colorado, show Eric Harris, left, and Dylan Klebold during their April 20, 1999, shooting spree in which they killed fourteen students and one teacher.

911 call, somewhat limiting their effectiveness in preventing a student or intruder from initiating a violent event. Because almost all police stations, as well as many police cars, are equipped with computer screens, however, officers responding to a crisis at a school would have the invaluable advantage of an electronic eye on the events within. "We could use the cameras to see inside the building before we sent in officers," said one police official. "It could save lives."

 For more information on school surveillance systems and other CJ technologies, click on Crime and Technology *under* Book Resources *at* www.cjinaction.com

friends and relatives. "They saw the toll that the whole epidemic of drugs . . . had taken on their families and peers, and they didn't want to go there," says Curtis.[60]

GIRLS IN THE JUVENILE JUSTICE SYSTEM

Though overall rates of juvenile offending have been dropping, one particular group of juveniles has become more involved in the juvenile justice system than ever before. Just as we saw earlier in this textbook that women are the fasting-growing segment of the adult prison population, girls are becoming more and more visible in the institutions that punish juvenile delinquency and crime.

A Growing Presence   Although girls have for the most part been treated more harshly than boys for status offenses,[61] a "chivalry effect" (see page 399) has traditionally existed in other areas of the juvenile justice system. In the past, police were likely to arrest offending boys while allowing girls to go home to the care of their families for similar behavior. This is no longer the case. Between 1992 and 2002, arrests of juvenile boys dropped 16.4 percent while arrests of juvenile girls rose 6.4 percent.[62] More young females are also being brought into juvenile court. From 1989 to 1998, drug cases involving girls increased 145 percent; violence cases, 124 percent; property cases, 35 percent; and public order cases, 79 percent.[63]

Family-Based Delinquency   Criminologists disagree on whether increasing arrest rates for female juveniles reflect a change in behavior or a change in law enforcement practices. A significant amount of data support the latter proposal, especially research showing that police are much more likely to make arrests in situations involving domestic violence than they were even a decade ago. Experts have found that girls are four times more apt to fight with parents or siblings than are boys, who usually engage in violent encounters with strangers. Consequently, a large percentage of female juvenile arrests for assault arise out of family disputes—arrests that until relatively recently would not have been made.[64]

Evidence also shows that law enforcement agents continue to treat girls more harshly for status offenses. More girls than boys are arrested for the status offense of running away from home, for example, even though studies show that male and female juveniles run away from home with equal frequency.[65] Criminologists who focus on issues of gender hypothesize that such behavior is considered normal for boys, but is seen as deviant for girls and therefore more deserving of punishment.[66]

↖ ONLINE REVIEW *Go to the book's Web site for an interactive review of this section*

Factors in Juvenile Delinquency

In one of the most influential studies in the field of criminology, Professor Marvin Wolfgang found that 6 percent of all boys in any given cohort (group of persons who share similar characteristics) will become chronic offenders, defined as someone who is arrested five or more times before his eighteenth birthday. Furthermore, Wolfgang found that these chronic offenders were responsible for half of all crimes and two-thirds of all violent crimes within the cohort.[67] Does this "6 percent rule" mean that no matter what steps society takes, six out of every hundred juveniles are "bad seeds" and will act delinquently? Or does it point to a situation in which a small percentage of children may be more likely to commit crimes under certain circumstances?

Most criminologists favor the second interpretation. It is generally believed that a number of "risk factors" are linked to delinquent activity (see Figure 15.7). Researchers have found a number of statistical trends that show certain youths to be at higher risk for antisocial behavior. For example, juvenile delinquency appears to be somewhat site specific—youths in certain geographic areas have a higher chance of being perpetrators or victims of murder. High school dropouts

↖ GREAT **DEBATES**
  Some observers feel that popular culture is another "risk factor," and bears some of the blame for delinquent behavior in juveniles. To better understand this controversial issue, click on *Great Debates* under *Book Resources* at www.cjinaction.com

also seem to be at greater risk of becoming part of Wolfgang's 6 percent; as we pointed out in Chapter 14, 70 percent of all adults in prison in the United States failed to complete the twelfth grade.[68] In this section, we will discuss the four factors that are most commonly used to explain juvenile criminal behavior and violent crime rates: age, substance abuse, family problems, and gangs.

THE AGE-CRIME RELATIONSHIP

Crime statistics are fairly conclusive on one point: the older a person is, the less likely he or she will exhibit criminal behavior. According to many criminologists, particularly Travis Hirschi and Michael Gottfredson, age is the one constant factor in criminal behavior, more important than gender, race, intelligence, or class.[69] Any group of at-risk persons—whether they be high school dropouts or (as we shall see) the children of abusive parents—will commit fewer crimes as they grow older. This process is known as **aging out.**

Another view sees the **age of onset,** or the age at which the youth begins delinquent behavior, as a consistent predictor of future criminal behavior. One study compared recidivism rates between juveniles first judged to be delinquent before the age of fifteen and those first adjudicated delinquent after the age of fifteen. Of the seventy-one subjects who made up the first group, 32 percent became chronic offenders. Of the sixty-five who made up the second group, none became chronic offenders.[70] Furthermore, according to the Office of Juvenile Justice and Delinquency Prevention, the earlier a youth enters the juvenile justice system, the more likely he or she will become a violent offender.[71] This research suggests that juvenile justice resources should be concentrated on the youngest offenders, with the goal of preventing crime and reducing the long-term risks for society.

SUBSTANCE ABUSE

As we have seen throughout this textbook and will see again in the next chapter, substance abuse plays a strong role in criminal behavior for adults. The same can certainly be said for juveniles. According to the Office of National Drug Control Policy, nearly 10 million Americans under the age of twenty consume alcohol each year, increasing the probability that they will experience academic problems, drop out of school, or commit acts of *vandalism* (the willful destruction of property).[72] The health consequences of this level of underage drinking are staggering: alcohol is a factor in between 50 and 65 percent of all teen-age suicides, and nearly 2,500 youths are killed each year in alcohol-related automobile crashes. Furthermore, the 2003 National Household Survey on Drug Abuse showed that nearly 11 percent of those between the ages of twelve and seventeen are current drug users, placing them at risk for delinquency.[73]

There are some signs, however, that use of illegal drugs and alcohol is declining. The Monitoring the Future survey, carried out annually by the University of Michigan's Institute for Social Research, found that cigarette smoking, alcohol intake, and use

Aging Out
A term used to explain the fact that criminal activity declines with age.

Age of Onset
The age at which a juvenile first exhibits delinquent behavior. The earlier the age of onset, according to some observers, the greater the chance a person will become a career offender.

FIGURE 15.7 Risk Factors for Juvenile Delinquency
The characteristics listed here are generally accepted as "risk factors" for juvenile delinquency. In other words, if one or more of these factors are present in a juvenile's life, he or she has a greater chance of exhibiting delinquent behavior—though such behavior is by no means a certainty.

Family
> Broken home/lack of parental role model
> Parental or sibling drug/alcohol abuse
> Extreme economic deprivation
> Family members in a gang

School
> Academic frustration/failure
> Learning disability
> Negative labeling by teachers
> Disciplinary problems

Community
> Social disorganization (refer to Chapter 2)
> Presence of gangs in the community
> Presence of obvious drug use in the community
> Availability of firearms
> High crime/constant feeling of danger
> Lack of social and economic opportunities

Peers
> Delinquent friends
> Friends who use drugs or are members of gangs
> Lack of "positive" peer pressure

Individual
> Tendency toward aggressive behavior
> Inability to concentrate or focus/easily bored/hyperactive
> Alcohol or drug use
> Fatalistic/pessimistic viewpoint

of illegal drugs by teen-agers all decreased in 2002, the first time this had happened in the survey's twenty-seven-year history.[74] A similar trend can be found in drug- and alcohol-related arrests. From 1993 to 2002, for example, juvenile arrests for drunkenness decreased 2.2 percent.[75] And, although arrests for drug abuse violations continued to increase until 1997, they fell 10 percent between 1998 and 2002.[76]

There is little doubt, however, that substance abuse plays a major role in juvenile delinquency and crime. Thirteen percent of all juvenile arrests involve a drug-related crime. About 60 percent of juveniles in correctional facilities admit to regular drug use, and 50 percent say that they were under the influence of drugs or alcohol at the time they committed the offense that led to their incarceration.[77] The impact seems even greater on female juveniles: 75 percent of young women incarcerated in juvenile facilities report regular drug and alcohol use—starting at the age of fourteen—and one study found that 87 percent of female teen-age offenders need substance abuse treatment.[78]

CHILD ABUSE AND NEGLECT

Abuse by parents also plays a substantial role in juvenile delinquency. **Child abuse** can be broadly defined as the infliction of physical or emotional damage on a child, while **child neglect** refers to deprivations—of love, shelter, food, proper care—children undergo by their parents. A significant portion (estimates can range from 40 percent[79] to 88 percent[80]) of parents who mistreat their children are believed to be under the influence of illegal drugs or alcohol.

Children in homes characterized by violence or neglect suffer from a variety of physical, emotional, and mental health problems at a much greater rate than their peers.[81] This, in turn, increases their chances of engaging in delinquent behavior. Research done for the Office of Juvenile Justice and Delinquency Prevention by David Huizinga, Rolf Loeber, and Terence Thornberry, for example, found that a history of maltreatment increases the chances of a youth being violent by 24 percent.[82] Another survey of violent juveniles showed that 75 percent had suffered severe abuse by a family member, 80 percent had witnessed violence in their home, 33 percent had a sibling with a criminal record, and 25 percent had at least one parent who abused drugs or alcohol.[83]

Cathy Spatz Widom, a professor of criminal justice and psychology at the State University of New York at Albany, compared the arrest records of two groups of subjects—one made up of 908 cases of substantiated parental abuse and neglect and the other made up of 667 children who had not been abused or neglected.

Child Abuse
Mistreatment of children by causing physical, emotional, or sexual damage without any plausible explanation, such as an accident.

Child Neglect
A form of child abuse in which the child is denied certain necessities such as shelter, food, care, and love. Neglect is justification for a government agency to assume responsibility for a child in place of the parents or legal guardian.

Two female juvenile offenders make their beds in their room at the Orange County Youth Guidance Center in Orange, California. According to data gathered by the National Council of Crime and Delinquency, 75 percent of all girls institutionalized by the California juvenile justice system reported regular use of drugs, including alcohol, starting around the age of fourteen.

Widom found that those who had been abused or neglected were 53 percent more likely to be arrested as juveniles than those who had not.[84]

GANGS

When youths cannot find the stability and support they require in the family structure, they will often turn to their peers. This is just one explanation for why juveniles join **youth gangs.** Although jurisdictions may have varying definitions, for general purposes a youth gang is viewed as a group of three or more persons who (1) self-identify themselves as an entity separate from the community by special clothing, vocabulary, hand signals, and names and (2) engage in criminal activity. Although the first gangs may have appeared at the time of the American Revolution in the 1780s, there have been four periods of major gang activity in American history: the late 1800s, the 1920s, the 1960s, and the present. According to an exhaustive survey of law enforcement agencies, there are probably around 29,000 gangs with more than 780,000 members in the United States.[85]

Who Joins Gangs?   The average gang member is seventeen to eighteen years old, though members tend to be older in cities with longer traditions of gang activity such as Chicago and Los Angeles.[86] Although it is difficult to determine with any certainty the make-up of gangs as a whole, one recent self-reported survey found that 47 percent of all gang members in the United States are Hispanic, 31 percent are African American, 13 percent are white, and 7 percent are Asian, with the remaining 2 percent belonging to other racial or ethnic backgrounds.[87] Though gangs tend to have racial or ethnic characteristics—that is, one group predominates in each gang—many researchers do not believe that race or ethnicity is the dominant factor in gang membership. Instead, gang members seem to come from lower-class or working-class communities, mostly in urban areas but with an increasing number from the suburbs and rural counties.

Why Do Youths Join Gangs?   Gang membership often appears to be linked with status in the community. This tends to be true of both males and females. Many teen-agers, feeling alienated from their families and communities, join gangs for the social relationships and the sense of identity a gang can provide.[88]

Gang membership is seen as a necessity for a number of youths, especially those who live in high-crime neighborhoods—joining a gang is a form of protection against violence from other gangs. Excitement is another attraction of the gang life, as is the economic incentive of enjoying the profits from illegal gang activities such as dealing drugs or robbery.[89] Finally, some teen-agers are literally forced to join gangs by the threat of violence from gang members.

Gangs and Crime   To a certain extent, the violent and criminal behavior of youths has been exaggerated by information sources such as the media. In proportion to all gang activities, violence is a rare event; gang members spend most of their time "hanging out" and taking part in other normal adolescent behavior.[90] That having been said, gang members are responsible for a disproportionate amount of violent and nonviolent criminal acts by juveniles. Traditional gang activities such as using and trafficking drugs, protecting their territory in "turf battles," and graffiti/vandalism all contribute to high crime rates among members.

Youth Gangs
Self-formed groups of youths with several identifiable characteristics, including a gang name and other recognizable symbols, a geographic territory, a leadership structure, a meeting pattern, and participation in illegal activities.

INFOTRAC KEYWORDS
youth gangs
For more information, use this search term with InfoTrac College Edition, your online library at www.infotrac-college.com

The National Youth Gang Center is a government-sponsored organization that researches the problems caused by gangs and proposes methods of solving them. Find its Web site by clicking on *Web Links* under *Chapter Resources* at www.cjinaction.com

In 2001, 698 murders in Chicago and Los Angeles—more than half of all murders in those cities—were gang related.[91] Statistics also show high levels of gang involvement in aggravated assault, larceny, and motor vehicle theft, while 42 percent of all youth gangs are believed to be involved in drug sales.[92] Furthermore, a recent study of criminal behavior among juveniles in Seattle found that gang members were considerably more likely to commit crimes than at-risk youths who shared many characteristics with gang members but were not affiliated with any gang (see Figure 15.8).[93] The gang members in Seattle were also much more likely to own firearms or to have friends who owned firearms.

GUNS

It is hardly surprising that the gang members in Seattle were much more likely to own firearms or to have friends who did. Studies have shown that youths who are members of gangs are three times as likely to own a handgun as those who are not.[94] Gang members are also much more likely to believe that they need a gun for protection and to be involved in gun-related crimes.[95]

The harmful link between juveniles and guns is hardly limited to gang members, however. Indeed, one explanation for the increase in youth violence in the late 1980s and early 1990s points to the unprecedented access minors had to illegal weapons during that time. According to Carnegie Mellon's Alfred Blumstein:

> [Y]outh have always fought with each other. But when it's a battle with fists, the dynamics run much more slowly. With a gun, it evolves very rapidly, too fast for a third party to intervene. That also raises the stakes and encourages others to arm themselves, thereby triggering a preemptive strike: "I better get him before he gets me."[96]

In fact, the correlation between access to guns and juvenile homicide rates is striking. The juvenile arrest rate for weapons violations doubled between 1987 and 1993. By 1994, 82 percent of all homicides committed by juveniles involved a handgun. Then, as the homicide rate began to drop, so did the arrest rate for weapons offenses, and many experts believe that the downward trend in juvenile homicide arrests can be traced largely to a decline in firearm usage.[97]

Despite these encouraging trends, guns are still widespread in youth culture. A recent survey by the Josephson Institute of Ethics found that 47 percent of high school and 22 percent of middle school students said they could obtain a gun if they felt the need.[98] More than 25,000 juveniles were arrested for gun-related crimes in 2002.[99]

↑ONLINE REVIEW *Go to the book's Web site for an interactive review of this section*

Keeping Juvenile Delinquency under Control

Though the decrease in juvenile crime over the past few years has been welcome, many criminologists and law enforcement officials have expressed concern that this recent drop in youth crime will lead to a sense of com-

> "My homeboys became my family—the older ones were father figures. Each time I shot someone, each time I put another gun on the set, each time I successfully recruited a combat soldier, I was congratulated by my older homeboys."
>
> —Sanyka Shakur, former gang member (1993)

Along with wearing "colors," speaking in code, and marking their turf with graffiti, gangs use hand signals to differentiate themselves from other gangs and to strengthen the social bonds among gang members, such as the Crips of the San Fernando Valley (California), pictured here. A number of communities have tried to limit gang activity by forbidding such expressions of unity, including barring gang members from appearing in public together.

PhotoEdit/A. Ramsey

placency among their colleagues. Any such decline, they believe, should be seen in the context of the immense growth in delinquency since 1985. Furthermore, the factors we have just discussed—substance abuse by adults and adolescents, child abuse and neglect, guns, and gang membership—continue to plague juveniles.

The Office of the Surgeon General, which produced a far-reaching report on juvenile violence in 2001, also cautions that the "war against youth crime" has not been won. Even as crime statistics have shown a decrease

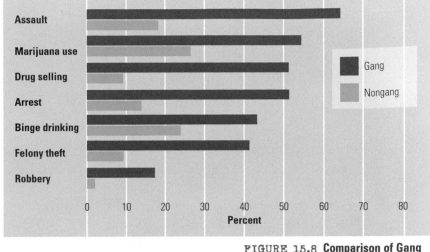

FIGURE 15.8 Comparison of Gang and Nongang Delinquent Behavior

Taking self-reported surveys of subjects aged thirteen to eighteen in the Seattle area, researchers for the Office of Juvenile Justice and Delinquency Prevention found that gang members were much more likely to exhibit delinquent behavior.

Source: Karl G. Hill, Christina Lui, and J. David Hawkins, *Early Precursors of Gang Membership: A Study of Seattle Youth* (Washington, D.C.: Office of Juvenile Justice and Delinquency Prevention, December 2001), Figure 1, page 2.

since 1994, self-reports of violent offending show no decline at all. In other words, when researchers ask juveniles about their violent behavior, the answers suggest that delinquency and youth crime are still quite high, leading the report to conclude that "the rise and fall in arrest rates are set against a backdrop of ongoing violent behavior."[100]

Three general strategies are being put in place to deal with juvenile delinquency—and its possible increase—in the near future. The first, transfer to adult court, was discussed earlier in the chapter and is based on the notion that harsher punishments will deter juvenile crime. The second, known as *social-control regulation,* aims to prevent crime by changing behavior without addressing underlying causes. Examples of social-control regulation would be

> *Juvenile curfews,* which restrict the movements of minors during certain hours, usually after dark. Juvenile arrests for curfew violations and loitering increased 35 percent between 1990 and 1999.[101]

> *Parental responsibility statutes,* which make parents responsible in some way for the offenses of their children. At present, forty-four states have enacted these statutes; seventeen of these states hold the parents *criminally* liable for their child's actions, punishing them with fines, community service, and even jail time.

The third method of juvenile prevention can be found in community-based programs that attempt to improve the chances that at-risk youth will not turn to crime. These programs may try to educate children about the dangers of drugs and crime, or they may counsel parents who abuse their children. Today, nearly a thousand private and public groups hold after-school workshops to prevent youth violence. Though the results of community-based efforts are difficult, if not impossible, to measure—it cannot be assumed that children would have become delinquent if they did not participate—they are generally considered a crucial element in keeping youth crime under control.

> The Bully Problem

From 1999 through 2003, juveniles wielding firearms were responsible for forty-five murders on school grounds in the United States. Although, as noted earlier in the chapter, these figures represent only a small percentage of all youth violence, shootings at schools have focused public attention on the problems surrounding juvenile delinquency and crime. As we will discuss in this feature, this attention has led to intense scrutiny of behavior that is as common on school grounds as homicides are rare.

"Typical Issues"

On September 25, 2003, according to eyewitnesses, fifteen-year-old Jason John McLaughlin took a .22 caliber semiautomatic handgun out of his gym bag. The freshman at Rocori High School in Cold Spring, Minnesota, then walked out of the school locker room and fired two shots down the hallway, hitting fellow students Aaron Rollins and Seth Bartell. Rollins was killed almost immediately, but Bartell tried to flee up a stairway. McLaughlin followed the wounded boy and shot him between the eyes. Bartell would die several days later in a local hospital.

As investigators looked into McLaughlin's background, a picture of an intensely shy, quiet boy emerged. School superintendent Scott Staska said, "There were some typical issues in the past, but nothing that would lead us to something like this."[102] These "typical issues" included a pattern of taunting by his schoolmates. In particular, friends said that McLaughlin's mood had darkened considerably since he developed a severe case of acne, which had brought with it a constant barrage of unkind comments, including—perhaps—some from Seth Bartell.[103] The reports of bullying brought back memories of the fatal shootings four years earlier at Columbine High School near Littleton, Colorado. There,

two students who claimed to have been mistreated by peers killed fourteen classmates and a teacher.

Other incidents also seem to point to a connection between bullying and violent, retaliatory behavior. Michael Carneal, who killed three students and injured five others at his high school in West Paducah, Kentucky, in 1997, had been called a "faggot" by his classmates. After Charles Williams killed two students and wounded thirteen others in a 2001 shooting at Santana High School in Santee, California, his father said that other students had burned his son with cigarette lighters, snapped him with wet towels, and twice slammed him against a tree. In a study of school shootings from 1974 to 2000 conducted by the U.S. Secret Service, revenge was cited as a motive more than half the time.[104]

Students from Rocori High School in Cold Spring, Minnesota, lay flowers as a memorial to Aaron Rollins and Seth Bartell, who were shot and killed by classmate Jason John McLaughlin in 2003.

AP Photo/St. Cloud Times, Kimm Anderson

Taking on Bullies

The first large-scale national study of bullying in American schools was released in 2001, about six weeks after the killings at Santana High. Of nearly 16,000 students interviewed, 10.6 percent reported being bullied "sometimes" or "weekly," and 13 percent admitted to having bullied others. About 6 percent said they had been both the targets of and the perpetrators of bullying. The bullying seemed to be most intense among the younger students: the researchers found that about a quarter of all middle school children had been involved in behavior that included threats, ridicule, name calling, punching, slapping, and taunting.[105]

These figures came as no surprise to many observers, who see bullying as a normal, if unfortunate, aspect of growing up. In the wake of the Columbine High tragedy, however, both schools and legislators have taken measures to, if not eliminate the behavior, at least keep it from leading to violence. Hundreds of schools have instituted "zero-tolerance" policies that impose harsh penalties on what in the past might have been seen as unthreatening behavior. A third grader in Hudson, Ohio, for example, was suspended from school for writing the words "You will die an honorable death" during a fortune-cookie writing project, while a seven-year-old Cincinnati elementary student was suspended for bringing a cap gun on the school bus. Many school authorities have banned the game of dodgeball, which experts say fosters overly aggressive behavior and stigmatizes less athletic students.[106]

In 2001, lawmakers in Colorado passed a law—similar to measures already on the books in several other states, including Georgia and New Hampshire—requiring every school district in the state to draw up a policy aimed at stopping student bullying.[107] That same year, the Washington State Senate passed a bill that would not only prohibit harassment and intimidating behavior at schools but would direct schools to notify the parents of the "bulliers" of their children's behavior.[108]

Warning Signs

Some experts criticize such policies and laws as an oversimplification of the problem of school violence. One clinical psychologist pointed out that if bullying were the actual cause of such incidents, "we would have millions of school shootings each year."[109] Instead, bullying appears to be only one piece of the puzzle, which includes violence and instability in the home, depression, violence in the culture at large, and the availability of firearms.

In fact, the best way to stem school violence seems to be to convince students to take threats of violence by their peers seriously. The morning before he shot Bartell and Rollins, McLaughlin sent a friend an e-mail hinting that some violent incident might take place and asking her not to tell her parents or the police. This is apparently typical behavior in such cases. The U.S. Secret Service found that in almost three-quarters of the school shootings that have taken place in this country since 1974, the shooters told someone what they were going to do.[110] Within three days after the killings at Santana High, eight other juveniles in southern California were arrested when students alerted law enforcement authorities of their plans for "copycat" violence.[111]

The Illusion of Safety?

Why did the student to whom McLaughlin had sent the e-mail keep silent about his scheme? The answer may lie in a government study that measured fear of crime in schools. The report found that twice as many African American and Hispanic students as white students are afraid of school violence.[112] In particular, the death of Aaron Rollins was only the third homicide ever in a Minnesota school, and violent crime is almost nonexistent in the small community of Cold Spring. Thus, McLaughlin's classmate may have found it hard to imagine that "it could happen here."

This lack of fear points to a crucial fact concerning school violence: even though minority youths living in low-income, urban areas have much higher rates of victimization, the majority of all school shootings take place in rural or suburban areas and are perpetrated by white students. Since the mid-1990s, when crime at inner-city schools reached its peak, many such schools have hired security guards and adopted other safety measures such as metal detectors. It is highly unlikely, for example, that McLaughlin could have easily carried his gun into Ballou High School, which is located in a high-crime area of Washington, D.C. At Ballou High, students must pass through a metal detector each time they enter the school and are constantly under observation by security guards.

Another explanation is that guns are not considered as dangerous in rural areas as in metropolitan ones. Whereas a teen-ager carrying a gun near Ballou High would set off a certain number of warning bells, it is relatively common for rural youths to have firearms for hunting and target practice. Indeed, McLaughlin appeared to have easy access to his father's gun collection, where he obtained the firearm that he eventually used on his classmates.

MAKING SENSE OF THE BULLY PROBLEM AND SCHOOL VIOLENCE

1 Why might schools in low-crime areas be reluctant to take safety measures such as setting up metal detectors or hiring security guards? Is this reluctance justified?

2 What would be your main concerns if you were to set up a policy against bullying at schools? Do you think any policy or plan could effectively stop such behavior?

3 Do you favor "zero-tolerance" plans that punish any hint of violent or illegal behavior at schools? What are the advantages and drawbacks of such plans?

Chapter Summary

1 **Describe the child-saving movement and its relationship to the doctrine of *parens patriae*.** Under the doctrine of *parens patriae*, the state has a right and a duty to care for neglected, delinquent, or disadvantaged children. The child-saving movement, based on the doctrine of *parens patriae*, started in the 1800s. Its followers believed that juvenile offenders require treatment rather than punishment.

2 **List the four major differences between juvenile courts and adult courts.** (a) No juries, (b) different terminology, (c) limited adversarial relationship, and (d) confidentiality.

3 **Identify and briefly describe the single most important Supreme Court case with respect to juvenile justice.** The case was *In re Gault,* decided by the Supreme Court in 1967. In this case a minor was arrested for allegedly making an obscene phone call. His parents were not notified. They were not present during the juvenile court judge's decision-making process. In this case, the Supreme Court held that juveniles are entitled to many of the same due process rights granted to adult offenders, including notice of charges, the right to counsel, the privilege against self-incrimination, and the right to confront and cross-examine witnesses.

4 **List the factors that normally determine what police do with juvenile offenders.** The arresting police officers consider (a) the nature of the offense, (b) the youthful offender's past criminal history, (c) the setting in which the offense took place, (d) whether the parents can take disciplinary action, (e) the attitude of the offender, and (f) the offender's race and gender.

5 **Describe the four primary stages of pretrial juvenile justice procedure.** (a) Intake, in which an official of the juvenile court engages in a screening process to determine what to do with the youthful offender; (b) pretrial diversion, which may consist of probation, treatment and aid, and/or restitution; (c) jurisdictional waiver to an adult court, in which case the youth leaves the juvenile justice system; and (d) some type of detention, in which the youth is held until the disposition process begins.

6 **Explain the distinction between an adjudicatory hearing and a disposition hearing.** An adjudicatory hearing is essentially the "trial." Defense attorneys may be present during the adjudicatory hearing in juvenile courts. In many states, once adjudication has occurred, there is a separate disposition hearing that is similar to the sentencing phase in an adult court. At this point, the court, often aided by a predisposition report, determines the sentence that serves the "needs" of the child.

7 **List the four categories of residential treatment programs.** Foster care, group homes, family group homes, and rural programs such as wilderness camps, farms, and ranches.

8 **Describe the one variable that always correlates highly with juvenile crime rates.** The older a person is, the less likely he or she will exhibit criminal behavior. This process is known as aging out. Thus, persons in any at-risk group will commit fewer crimes as they get older.

9 **Indicate some of the reasons why youths join gangs.** Some alienated teen-agers join gangs for the social relationships and the sense of identity that gangs can provide. Youths living in high-crime neighborhoods join gangs as a form of protection. The excitement of belonging to a gang is another reason to join.

Questions for Critical Analysis

1 In spite of the constitutional safeguards given to juvenile defendants by the Supreme Court decision *In re Gault,* only 50 percent of juvenile defendants have lawyers. Why?

2 Why is the discretion given to police officers over juveniles called low-visibility decision making?

3 Is probable cause necessary before a search can legally be conducted in a school setting? Why or why not?

4 Under what conditions in certain states is a juvenile automatically transferred to the adult court system?

5 The presence of defense attorneys in juvenile courts has led to what changes? In what way have these changes made juvenile courts resemble adult courts?

6 What distinguishes the sentencing phase in juvenile versus adult courts?

7 Why is the age of onset an important factor in predicting juvenile criminal behavior?

8 What has been the relationship between alcohol and drug abuse and juvenile offenders?

9 What has been the statistical relationship between armed gang members and juvenile violent crime?

TEST PREPARATION ONLINE

Go to www.cjinaction.com for tools to aid you in studying for your exams. Click on *Online Reviews* under *Chapter Resources* for an interactive review of each major section of this chapter. Under *Chapter Resources,* you will also find the *Chapter Outline, Chapter Summary, Flashcards, Glossary, Learning Objectives, Lecture Presentations, Concept Builder, Essay Questions,* and a *Tutorial Quiz.* You can also test yourself with a game of *Concentration* or the *Crossword Puzzle.*

Web Resources

Go to www.cjinaction.com for a wealth of online resources. Explore the *Internet Activities* and *Class Project*s under *Chapter Resources.* Check out the *Web Links* to access the Web sites mentioned in the text, as well as many others. You can also access recent perspectives by clicking on *CJ in the News* and *Terrorism Update* under *Course Resources*. If you'd like some mentoring, click on *Board of Mentors* under *Book Resources*.

Search Online with InfoTrac College Edition

For additional information, explore InfoTrac College Edition, your online library that offers complete full-length articles from thousands of scholarly and popular publications. Click on *InfoTrac College Edition* under *Chapter Resources* at www.cjinaction.com for a list of key words and InfoTrac exercises. Use the passcode that came with your book.

Suggested Readings

Rosenheim, Margaret K., Franklin E. Zimring, David S. Tanenhaus, Bernadine Dohrn, and Adele Simmons, *A Century of Juvenile Justice,* Chicago: University of Chicago Press, 2002. The juvenile justice system has undergone a number of makeovers since the Illinois Juvenile Court Act of 1899. This work offers a comprehensive look at these changes, detailing not only the political forces that have shaped our ideas on juvenile justice, but the social and cultural ones as well. The editors also include essays on western European and Japanese approaches to juvenile crime, providing a context for understanding American successes and failures in this area.

Salzman, Mark, *True Notebooks,* New York: Knopf, 2003. When novelist Salzman was approached to teach a writing course at Central Juvenile Hall, a detention center for "high-risk" juvenile offenders in Los Angeles, he agreed—with reservations. Salzman soon warmed to his task, however, and this book reflects his experiences with his pupils, most of whom were waiting to be sent to juvenile correctional facilities or adult prisons. Their writing is often as bleak as their situations, but it does offer a clear picture of the life of a juvenile offender, including what it is like to be facing life behind bars.

Notes

1. Peter W. Greenwood, "Juvenile Crime and Juvenile Justice," in *Crime,* ed. James Q. Wilson and Joan Petersilia (San Francisco: ICS Press, 1995), 91.
2. Jennifer M. O'Connor and Lucinda K. Treat, "Getting Smart about Getting Tough: Juvenile Justice and the Possibility of Progressive Reform," *American Criminal Law Review* 33 (Summer 1996), 1299.
3. Eric K. Klein, "Dennis the Menace or Billy the Kid: An Analysis of the Role of Transfer to Criminal Court in Juvenile Justice," *American Criminal Law Review* 35 (Winter 1998), 371.
4. Bureau of Justice Statistics, *Sourcebook of Criminal Justice, 2001* (Washington, D.C.: U.S. Department of Justice, 2002), Table 2.58, page 139.
5. *In re Gault,* 387 U.S. 15 (1967).
6. Samuel Davis, *The Rights of Juveniles: The Juvenile Justice System,* 2d ed. (New York: C. Boardman Co., 1995), Section 1.2.
7. Cited in Anthony Platt, *The Child Savers* (Chicago: University of Chicago Press, 1969), 119.
8. 383 U.S. 541 (1966).
9. *Ibid.,* 556.
10. 387 U.S. 1 (1967).
11. 397 U.S. 358 (1970).
12. 421 U.S. 519 (1975).
13. 403 U.S. 528 (1971).
14. Andrew Murr and Karen Springen, "Death at a Very Early Age," *Newsweek* (August 28, 2000), 32.
15. Andrew Walkover, "The Infancy Defense in the New Juvenile Court," *UCLA Law Review* 31 (1984), 509–513.
16. Gary B. Melton, "Toward 'Personhood' for Adolescents: Autonomy and Privacy as Values in Public Policy," *American Psychology* 38 (1983), 99–100.
17. Research Network on Adolescent Development and Juvenile Justice, *Youth on Trial: A Developmental Perspective on Juvenile Justice* (Chicago: John D. & Catherine T. MacArthur Foundation, 2003), 1.
18. Richard E. Redding, "Juveniles Transferred to Criminal Court: Legal Reform Proposals Based on Social Science Research," *Utah Law Review* (1997), 709.
19. Howard N. Snyder and Melissa Sickmund, *Juvenile Offenders and Victims: A National Report* (Washington, D.C.: U.S. Department of Justice, 1995), 47.
20. 487 U.S. 815 (1988).
21. *Ibid.,* 822–823.
22. 492 U.S. 361, 371 (1989).
23. Office of Juvenile Justice and Delinquency Prevention, *Juveniles in Court* (Washington, D.C.: U.S. Department of Justice, June 2003), 2.
24. *Juveniles in Court,* 15.
25. Carl E. Pope and Howard N. Snyder, *Race as a Factor in Juvenile Arrests* (Washington, D.C.: Office of Juvenile Justice and Delinquency Prevention, April 2003), 1.
26. *Ibid.,* 4.
27. Sarah Lee Browning, "Race and Getting Hassled by the Police: A Research Note," *Police Studies* 17 (1994), 3.
28. George S. Bridges and Sara Steen, "Racial Disparities in Official Assessments of Juvenile Offenders," *American Sociological Review* 63 (1998), 554.
29. 469 U.S. 325 (1985).
30. *Ibid.,* 348.
31. *Vernonia School District v. Acton,* 515 U.S. 646 (1995).
32. 536 U.S. 822 (2002).
33. 422 U.S. 23 (1979).
34. Frederick Ward, Jr., "Prevention and Diversion in the United States," in *The Changing Faces of Juvenile Justice,* ed. V. Lorne Stewart (New York: New York University Press, 1978), 43.
35. President's Commission on Law Enforcement and Administration of Justice, *Task Force Report: Juvenile Delinquency and Youth Crime* (Washington, D.C.: U.S. Government Printing Office, 1967).
36. 42 U.S.C. Sections 5601–5778 (1974).
37. S'Lee Arthur Hinshaw II, "Juvenile Diversion: An Alternative to Juvenile Court," *Journal of Dispute Resolution* (1993), 305.

38. Rhode Island Gen. Laws Section 14-1-7.1 (1994 and Supp. 1996).

39. David S. Tanenhaus and Steven A. Drizin, "'Owing to the Extreme Youth of the Accused': The Changing Legal Response to Homicide," *Journal of Criminal Law and Criminology* (Spring/Summer 2002), 641.

40. Donna Bishop and Charles Frazier, "Consequences of Transfer," in *The Changing Borders of Juvenile Justice: Transfer of Adolescents to the Criminal Court,* ed. Jeffrey Fagan and Franklin E. Zimring (Chicago: University of Chicago Press, 2000), 237.

41. *Ibid.,* 248.

42. Jeffrey Fagan, "Separating the Men from the Boys: The Comparative Advantage of Juvenile versus Criminal Court Sanctions on Recidivism among Adolescent Felony Offenders," in *Serious, Violent, and Chronic Juvenile Offenders: A Sourcebook,* ed. James C. Howell, Barry A. Krisberg, David Hawkins, and John J. Wilson (Thousand Oaks, CA: Sage Publications, 1995).

43. 467 U.S. 253 (1984).

44. Barry C. Feld, "Criminalizing the American Juvenile Court," *Crime and Justice* 17 (1993), 227–254.

45. Barry C. Feld, "Abolish the Juvenile Court," *Journal of Criminal Law and Criminology* 88 (Fall 1997), 68.

46. Barry C. Feld, "Violent Youth and Public Policy: A Case Study of Juvenile Justice Law Reform," *Minnesota Law Review* 79 (May 1995), 965.

47. *Juveniles in Court,* 27.

48. Jullianne P. Sheffer, "Serious and Habitual Juvenile Offender Statutes: Reconciling Punishment and Rehabilitation within the Juvenile Justice System," *Vanderbilt Law Review* 48 (1995), 500–506.

49. Eric R. Lotke, "Youth Homicide: Keeping Perspective on How Many Children Kill," *Valparaiso University Law Review* 31 (Spring 1997), 395.

50. Bureau of Justice Statistics, *Prison and Jail Inmates at Midyear 2002* (Washington, D.C.: U.S. Department of Justice, April 2003), 5.

51. *Juveniles in Court,* 22.

52. Melissa Sickmund and Howard N. Snyder, *Juvenile Offenders and Victims: 1999 National Report* (Washington, D.C.: Office of Juvenile Justice and Delinquency Prevention, 1999), 182.

53. Melissa Sickmund, *Juvenile Residential Facility Census, 2000* (Washington, D.C.: Office of Juvenile Justice and Delinquency Prevention, December 2002), 2.

54. Troy L. Armstrong and David M. Altschuler, "Recent Developments in Programming of High-Risk Juvenile Parolees," in *Critical Issues in Crime and Justice,* ed. Albert Roberts (San Francisco: Sage Publications, 1994).

55. *Surveillance Summaries: Youth Risk Behavior Surveillance—United States, 2001* (Washington, D.C.: Centers for Disease Control and Prevention, June 28, 2002).

56. Federal Bureau of Investigation, *Crime in the United States, 2002* (Washington, D.C.: U.S. Department of Justice, 2003), Table 38, page 244.

57. Lori Dorfman and Vincent Schiraldi, "Media Delinquency," *Star-Ledger, NJ* (April 20, 2001), 19.

58. Howard N. Snyder, *Juvenile Arrests, 2000* (Washington, D.C.: Office of Juvenile Justice and Delinquency Prevention, November 2002), 1.

59. Alfred Blumstein, "Youth Violence, Guns, and Illicit Drug Markets," *NIJ Research Journal* (Washington, D.C.: National Institute of Justice, 1995).

60. Angie Cannon, "Kids Just Say No to Violence," *U.S. News & World Report* (November 1, 1999), 42.

61. Kimberly Kempf-Leonard and Lisa Sample, "Disparity Based on Sex: Is Gender-Specific Treatment Warranted?" *Justice Quarterly* 17 (2000), 89–128.

62. *Crime in the United States, 2002,* Table 33, page 239.

63. *Juveniles in Court,* 14.

64. Meda Chesney-Lind, "Are Girls Closing the Gender Gap in Violence?" *Criminal Justice* (Spring 2001), 20.

65. Sickmund and Snyder, 58.

66. Meda Chesney-Lind, *The Female Offender: Girls, Women, and Crime* (Thousand Oaks, CA: Sage Publications, 1997).

67. Marvin E. Wolfgang, *From Boy to Man, From Delinquency to Crime* (Chicago: University of Chicago Press, 1987).

68. Bureau of Justice Statistics, *Education and Correctional Trends* (Washington, D.C.: U.S. Department of Justice, January 2003), 1.

69. Travis Hirschi and Michael Gottfredson, "Age and the Explanation of Crime," *American Journal of Sociology* 89 (1982), 552–584.

70. David P. Farrington, "Offending from 10 to 25 Years of Age," in *Prospective Studies of Crime and Delinquency,* ed. Katherine Teilmann Van Dusen and Sarnoff A. Mednick (Boston: Kluwer-Nijhoff Publishers, 1983), 17.

71. *Juveniles in Court,* 29.

72. *Combating Underage Drinking, Fact Sheet #75* (Washington, D.C.: Office of Juvenile Justice and Delinquency Prevention, February 1998).

73. Office of National Drug Control Policy, *ONDCP Drug Policy Information Clearinghouse Fact Sheet* (Washington, D.C.: Executive Office of the President, June 2003), 1.

74. Fox Butterfield, "Teenage Drug Use Is Dropping, a Study Finds," *New York Times* (October 17, 2002), A23.

75. *Crime in the United States, 2002,* Table 32, page 238.

76. *Ibid.,* Table 34, page 240.

77. Lisette Blumhardt, "In the Best Interests of the Child: Juvenile Justice or Adult Retribution?" *University of Hawaii Law Review* (Winter 2000), 341.

78. National Mental Health Association, "Mental Health and Adolescent Girls in the Justice System" at http://www.nmha.org/children/justjuv/girlsjj.cfm.

79. *Collaboration, Coordination, and Cooperation: Helping Children Affected by Parental Addiction and Family Violence* (New York: Children of Alcoholics Foundation, 1996).

80. Ching-Tung Lung and Deborah Daro, *Current Trends in Child Abuse Reporting and Fatalities: The Results of the 1997 Annual Fifty-State Survey* (Chicago: National Committee to Prevent Child Abuse, 1998).

81. Polly E. Bijur, Matthew Kurzon, Mary Overpeck, and Peter C. Scheidt, "Parental Alcohol Use, Problem Drinking, and Child Injuries," *Journal of the American Medical Association* 267 (1992), 3166–3171.

82. David Huizinga, Rolf Loeber, and Terence Thornberry, *Urban Delinquency and Substance Abuse* (Washington, D.C.: Office of Juvenile Justice and Delinquency Prevention, 1993).

83. Grover Trask, "Defusing the Teenage Time Bomb," *Prosecutor* (March/April 1997), 29.

84. Cathy Spatz Widom, *The Cycle of Violence* (Washington, D.C.: National Institute of Justice, October 1992).

85. Office of Juvenile Justice and Delinquency Prevention, *1998 Youth Gang Survey* (Washington, D.C.: U.S. Department of Justice, November 2000), Table 9.

86. G. David Curry and Scott H. Decker, *Confronting Gangs: Crime and the Community* (Los Angeles: Roxbury, 1998).

87. Arlen Egly, Jr., *Highlights of the 1999 National Youth Gang Survey* (Washington, D.C.: Office of Juvenile Justice and Delinquency Prevention, November 2000), 1.

88. Martin Sanchez Jankowski, *Islands in the Street: Gangs and American Urban Society* (Berkeley: University of California Press, 1991), 37–47.

89. Scott H. Decker and B. Van Winkle, *Life in the Gang: Family, Friends, and Violence* (New York: Cambridge University Press, 1996).

90. Sara R. Battin, Karl G. Hill, Robert D. Abbott, Richard F. Catalano, and J. David Hawkins, "The Contribution of Gang Membership to Delinquency beyond Delinquent Friends," *Criminology* 36 (1998), 93–115.

91. Arlen Egly, Jr., and Aline K. Major, *Highlights of the 2002 National Youth Gang Survey* (Washington, D.C.: Office of Juvenile Justice and Delinquency Prevention, April 2003), 1.

92. Office of Juvenile Justice and Delinquency Prevention, *1998 Youth Gang Survey,* Table 34.

93. Karl G. Hill, Christina Lui, and J. David Hawkins, *Early Precursors of Gang Membership: A Study of Seattle Youth* (Washington, D.C.: Office of Juvenile Justice and Delinquency Prevention, December 2001).

94. Joseph F. Sheley and James D. Wright, *In the Line of Fire: Youth, Guns, and Violence in Urban America* (Hawthorne, NY: Aldine De Gruyter, 1995), 100.

95. Beth Bjerregaard and Alan J. Lizotte, "Gun Ownership and Gang Membership," *Journal of Criminal Law and Criminology* 86 (1995), 49.

96. Quoted in Gracie Bond Staples, "Guns in School," *Fort Worth Star-Telegram* (June 3, 1998), 1.

97. Office of Juvenile Justice and Delinquency Prevention, *1999 National Report Series: Juvenile Justice Bulletin— Kids and Guns* (Washington, D.C.: U.S. Department of Justice, March 2000), 4.

98. *Ethics of American Youth* (Marina del Rey, CA: Josephson Institute of Ethics, 2001).

99. *Crime in the United States, 2002,* Table 38, page 244.

100. Delbert Elliot, Norma J. Hatot, Paul Sirovatka, and Blair B. Potter, eds., *Youth Violence: A Report to the Surgeon General* (Washington, D.C.: U.S. Department of Health and Human Services, 2001), Chapter 2, Section 1.

101. *Crime in the United States, 2002,* Table 32, page 238.

102. "Minn. School Shooter Followed One Victim, Shot Him Again," *San Diego Union-Tribune* (September 26, 2003), A13.

103. "School Shooter Stalked Victim," *Duluth News-Tribune* (September 26, 2003), 1A.

104. U.S. Secret Service, *The Final Report and Findings of the Safe School Initiative: Implications for the Prevention of School Attacks in the United States* (Washington, D.C.: U.S. Department of Education, May 2002), 24.

105. Tonja R. Nansel, Mary Overpeck, Ramani S. Pilla, W. June Ruan, Bruce Simons-Morton, and Peter Scheidt, "Bullying Behaviors among U.S. Youth," *Journal of the American Medical Association* 285 (April 25, 2001), 2094.

106. Natalie Angier, "Bully for You: Why Push Comes to Shove," *New York Times* (May 20, 2001), Section 4, page 1.

107. Nancy Mitchell, "Colorado to Take Bullies by the Horn," *Rocky Mountain News* (October 25, 2001), 4A.

108. David Crary, "Anti-Bullying Programs Gain Favor and Funding," *Seattle Times* (March 11, 2001), A12.

109. Michael Janofsky, "Bill on Student Bullying Is Considered in Colorado," *New York Times* (March 19, 2001), A10.

110. U.S. Secret Service, 21.

111. Fox Butterfield, "Tips by Students Result in Arrests at 5 Schools," *New York Times* (March 8, 2001), A16.

112. National Center for Education Statistics, *Indicators of School Crime and Safety* (Washington, D.C.: U.S. Department of Education, October 2000), Table 13.2.

> **Chapter 16** <

The Ongoing War
against Illegal Dru

>chapter objectives<

After reading this chapter, you should be able to:

1 Explain why the criminal law concepts of *mala in se* and *mala prohibita* are necessary to understand drug laws.

2 Tell what happened to alcohol use and murder rates during Prohibition.

3 List the three factors in the learning process that cause first-time drug users to become multiple users.

4 Explain the 20-80 Rule as it applies to the use of psychoactives.

5 Contrast the medical model of addiction with the criminal model of addiction.

6 List federal agencies involved in drug law enforcement.

7 Summarize the three main legislative strategies to reduce illegal drug use.

8 Explain the *iron law of substitution.*

9 Identify some of the reasons law enforcement agencies may be likely to target members of minority groups when enforcing drug laws.

10 Outline the three major arguments against legalization.

Small-Town Crooks

O fficer Ron Jones of the Prentiss Police Department was shot in the abdomen just after he entered the back door of an apartment in Prentiss, Mississippi. Jones, who had been serving a search warrant for illegal drugs, died from his wounds, becoming the fourteenth homicide in Jefferson

A Mississippi Highway Patrol Honor Guardsman folds the American flag that was draped over the casket of police officer Ron Jones for presentation to Jones's family. One of five members of the Prentiss (Mississippi) Police Department, Jones was shot to death as he entered an apartment to serve a search warrant for illegal drugs.

AP Photo/Hattiesburg American, George Clark

Davis County in a two-year stretch. His killing gave the county, with only 14,000 residents, a higher murder rate than Detroit; Washington, D.C.; or New Orleans, the most dangerous cities in the United States.

The shift in the drug trade from large urban centers to rural America is one of the most significant trends in criminal justice over the past decade. While arrests for drug crimes in cities with more than 250,000 residents have fallen more than 11 percent in the past few years, they have risen more than 10 percent in areas with low population densities. Furthermore, the percentage of homicides that are drug related has declined by 50 percent in large cities, but it has tripled in rural areas. Among the many reasons offered to explain these trends are the limited resources of small-town law enforcement agencies, which allow producers of illicit drugs—particularly crack cocaine, methamphetamine, and marijuana—to operate without fear of apprehension. Jones was one of only five police officers in the Prentiss Police Department.

> **The awesome impact** of drugs on the criminal justice system has been evident throughout this textbook. According to one recent study, illegal drug and alcohol abuse and addiction played a role in the crimes committed by 80 percent of the over two million Americans behind bars.[1] Nearly half a million of those inmates were arrested for selling or using a banned drug substance. The illegal drug trade in the United States has reached $160 billion per year; worldwide the

industry amounts to $600 billion annually. Federal, state, and local governments spend over $40 billion a year for drug control, yet two leading indicators of law enforcement success—illegal drug price and availability—show little improvement. The effects of drugs and alcohol on society as a whole are also apparent. Three-fourths of all foster children are from families with drug- or alcohol-addicted parents. The nation's businesses lose 500 million workdays a year to alcoholism, and half of all workplace fatalities are linked to drugs and alcohol. By the eighth grade, 52 percent of all adolescents have consumed alcohol, 41 percent have smoked cigarettes, and 20 percent have used marijuana.[2]

For many Americans, these numbers call for greater enforcement of drug laws. They believe that illegal drugs are an insidious presence on the country's social and cultural landscape and support drastic measures for eradication. According to at least one New York narcotics officer, however, such efforts have the effectiveness of "a gnat biting a horse's behind."[3] In this chapter, we will try to determine whether the officer's pessimism is warranted by examining the United States's century-long struggle against illicit drugs. We will also discuss the tactics of the continuing "war on drugs," as well as assertions that such a war should never have been declared and can never be won. We will start by asking a deceptively simply question at the center of the debate: What is a drug?

▶ CONCEPT BUILDER
The "abuse" of illegal drugs is a significant problem in society and has had a tremendous impact on the criminal justice system. Go to the book's Web site for a more in-depth examination of this concept. Visit www.cjinaction.com for an interactive exploration of this key topic.

Drugs Defined

To use the broadest possible definition, a **drug** is any substance that modifies biological, psychological, or social behavior.[4] In popular terminology, however, the word *drug* has a more specific connotation. When people speak of the "drug" problem, or the war on "drugs," or "drug" abuse, they are referring specifically to illegal drugs. To be even more precise, they are referring to illegal **psychoactive drugs,** which affect the brain and alter consciousness or perception. Almost all the drugs that concern the criminal justice system are psychoactive.

Drug
Any substance that modifies behavior; in particular, an illegal substance with those properties.

Psychoactive Drugs
Chemicals that affect the brain, causing changes in emotions, perceptions, and behavior.

TYPES OF PSYCHOACTIVES

Psychoactives can be classified by their effects on the central nervous system. The different types of psychoactives are explained in the following overview.[5]

Opiates For more than six thousand years, humans have extracted **opiates** from the seed pod of the opium poppy. In harvesting the substance, the pod is sliced open, releasing a milky sap. The sap dries to form a resin called *opium*. Opium and its derivatives have the ability to block pain receptors in the brain and therefore have a variety of medical uses. The substance also produces a feeling of euphoria and reduction of anxiety, which explains its popularity as a pleasure drug.

Opiates may be ingested orally, smoked, sniffed, or injected. It is generally believed that opium smoking was brought to the United States in the mid–nineteenth century by Chinese laborers. The opium derivatives *morphine* and *codeine* were not taken full advantage of for their medicinal uses until 1853, when the perfection of the hypodermic syringe allowed delivery of the drugs directly into the bloodstream. Morphine was so widely used as a painkiller in the American Civil War (1861–1865) that many infantrymen became addicted—

Opiates
Drugs containing opium or its derivatives; have the effects of dulling sensations including pain and anxiety, producing a feeling of euphoria, and causing general inaction.

morphine addiction became known as the "soldier's disease." *Heroin*, a substitute for codeine and morphine, was created by Bayer Laboratories and marketed following the Civil War as nonaddictive. In fact, heroin—more fat soluble and therefore able to reach the brain more quickly—is two to three times more potent than morphine.

Stimulants   Acting on both the central nervous system (the spinal cord and the brain) and the peripheral nervous system (the muscles, glands, organs, and fibers that carry sensory information to the brain), **stimulants** produce feelings of well-being and mood elevation. The stimulant *cocaine* is the active ingredient in the South American coca plant. It is isolated from the leaves by soaking them in a mixture of water, potassium carbonate, and a petroleum product such as kerosene. The resulting paste is then dried and purified into a white powder, which can be snorted, or the paste itself can be smoked. In the 1970s, "freebasing"—a process in which the drug is vaporized and inhaled—became popular among cocaine users because it produced a more intense high. A cheaper, less complex method of freebasing led to the production of *crack cocaine* in the 1980s.

Amphetamine, originally developed in the 1920s to treat asthma sufferers, was found to be a stimulant in the 1930s and prescribed to narcoleptics, or individuals who involuntarily fall asleep. The drug was dispensed to soldiers in World War II to keep them alert during combat, which led to its popularization as a nonmedical substance that could be taken in pill form, via inhalants, or intravenously. *Nicotine,* a naturally occurring substance in the tobacco plant, and *caffeine,* found in coffee, tea, and soft drinks, are also stimulants.

Marijuana   The cannabis plant is the source of *marijuana,* the most widely used illegal drug in the United States today. Marijuana is a mixture produced by grinding the leaves and stem of the plant. Delta-9-tetrahydrocannabinol (THC), the active ingredient in marijuana, is rapidly absorbed from the surface of the lungs when the mixture is smoked, producing effects of mild sedation, euphoria, and, in rare cases, hallucination in the user. The Spanish probably imported cannabis to Central and South America in the sixteenth century because its strong fibers can be used to make rope. The plant is easily grown and cultivated (to the point where it has been called a weed), which has contributed to its widespread use.

Hallucinogens   A wide variety of plants and other natural products can be classified as **hallucinogens,** or substances that intensify sensory perception and in the process bring about hallucinations. The best-known hallucinogen is called *LSD,* after the substance lysergic acid diethylamide from which it is made. Synthesized in 1938, LSD rose in popularity during the 1960s as part of the then-prevailing youth culture. Only minuscule amounts of LSD (less than two-thousandths of a gram per kilogram of body weight) are needed to induce a hallucinatory state.

Stimulants
Drugs such as cocaine or amphetamine that stimulate the central nervous system, thereby quickening motor functions of the body.

Hallucinogens
Drugs that cause the user to experience alterations in sensory experiences, or hallucinations.

U.S. Customs agents stand guard by more than one thousand pounds of the drug Ecstasy—valued at $40,000,000—at the U.S. Customs House in Los Angeles, California. Ecstasy typically includes feelings of increased energy and euphoria, but in high doses the drug can sharply increase body temperature and in some instances lead to death by hyperthermia—a condition in which skeletal muscle breaks down and organs fail due to overheating.

AP Photo/Nick Ut

Other hallucinogens include *PCP (phencyclidine), mescaline* (taken from the peyote cactus), and *psilocybin* (taken from wild mushrooms). In the 1980s, new forms of hallucinogens known as *designer drugs* arrived. Produced by modifying the chemical structure of amphetamines, these drugs, such as Ecstasy, GHB, and "Foxy Methoxy," take on hallucinogenic properties.

Sedatives   **Sedatives** are able to reduce anxiety or induce sleep by depressing functions of the brain. Also known as "sleeping pills," *barbiturates* were the most popular form of sedatives in the first half of the twentieth century. Today, a different class of sedative, the *benzodiazepines,* has captured the market, with millions of prescriptions for Valium and Xanax being dispensed every year.

Alcohol   The most widely used drug in the United States, *alcohol,* in the form of alcoholic beverages, is consumed at least occasionally by approximately two-thirds of adult Americans.[6] Alcohol is unique in the sense that it acts as both a stimulant and a sedative, initially giving the user a feeling of euphoria before beginning to act as a depressant.

ILLICIT AND LICIT DRUGS

Most people do not consider alcohol—or nicotine or caffeine, for that matter—to be a drug. In one survey, for example, 95 percent of adults recognized heroin as a drug, but only 39 percent and 29 percent identified alcohol and nicotine, respectively, as drugs.[7] To a certain extent, then, the definition of drugs has been equated with **illicit drugs,** or those drugs whose sale and use have been made illegal. **Licit** (legal) **drugs** such as alcohol, caffeine, and nicotine are not seen as drugs, but as socially acceptable substances, if used in moderation and not by children. Furthermore, the common use of drugs for medical purposes—Americans spend approximately $180 billion for prescription drugs and billions more for over-the-counter drugs each year—is seen as enhancing our quality of life.[8]

Distinguishing between Licit and Illicit Drugs   Sometimes the line between licit and illicit is difficult to draw. According to health experts, for every person addicted to the illegal drug heroin, two people are addicted to legal prescription drugs such as oxycodone, hyrdocodone, codeine, and morphine.[9] Law enforcement agents also report a growing black market trade in OxyContin, a prescription drug used by terminal cancer patients to ease pain. Why has society prohibited the use of certain drugs, while allowing the use of others? The answer cannot be found in measuring the risk of harm caused by the substances. Both licit and illicit drugs, if abused, can have serious consequences for the health of the user. On an average day, four college students die in accidents involving alcohol, and another 1,370 suffer injuries related to drinking.[10]

Nor is illegality linked to the addictive quality of the drug. According to the American Medical Association, nicotine is the most addictive substance, with over two-thirds of people who smoke cigarettes becoming addicted.[11] The next most addictive drug is heroin, followed by cocaine, alcohol, amphetamines, and marijuana, in that order. The drug most widely associated with violent behavior, especially domestic violence, is alcohol.[12] One professor of preventive medicine has concluded that "there are no scientific . . . or medical bases on which the legal distinctions between various drugs are made."[13]

Sedatives
Drugs that slow the signals sent from the brain to other parts of the body, thereby inducing sleep or reducing anxiety.

Illicit Drugs
Certain drugs or substances whose use or sale has been declared illegal.

Licit Drugs
Legal drugs or substances, such as alcohol, coffee, and tobacco.

INFOTRAC KEYWORDS
illegal drug use

For more information, use this search term with InfoTrac College Edition, your online library at www.infotrac-college.com

> "Let us not forget who we are. Drug abuse is a repudiation of everything America is."
>
> —Ronald Reagan, former U.S. president (1986)

Society and the Law If drug laws are not based on science or medicine, on what are they based? To understand in part how the distinctions are made between illegal and legal drugs, we must turn to the concepts of criminal acts that are considered *mala in se,* or inherently evil, and *mala prohibita,* or deemed evil by the laws of society. From our discussion in Chapter 3, you will recall that acts such as murder and rape are *mala in se,* whereas those such as prostitution and gambling are *mala prohibita.* Taking a *mala prohibitum* view, certain drugs are characterized as illicit while others are not because of the presiding societal norms and values.

Society's norms and values are reflected in its laws, and the primary law for determining illicit drugs in the United States is the Controlled Substances Act (CSA), which is part of the Comprehensive Drug Abuse Prevention and Control Act of 1970.[14] The CSA specifies five hierarchical categories for drugs and the penalties for the manufacture, sale, distribution, possession, or consumption of these drugs, based on the substances' medical use, potential for abuse, and addictive qualities (see Figure 16.1). The CSA explicitly excludes "distilled spirits, wine, malt beverages, and tobacco" from the legal definition of a "controlled substance."[15] Therefore, alcohol and tobacco are legal not because they have pharmacological effects that are considerably different, or safer, than those of illicit drugs, but rather because the law, as supported by society, says so.[16]

ONLINE REVIEW *Go to the book's Web site for an interactive review of this section*

Prohibition in the United States

Government policies to limit and outlaw narcotics have a long and varied history, both in the United States and in other parts of the world. Nonetheless, drugs were not always regulated in this country to the extent that they are today. The general attitude of American society toward drugs has changed over the past century. With the notable exception of alcohol, many drugs were considered useful, medicinal substances in the 1800s. Cocaine was promoted as a remedy for tuberculosis, whooping cough, and asthma. Coca-Cola, introduced in 1886, was mar-

FIGURE 16.1 Schedules of Narcotics as Defined by the Federal Controlled Substances Act

The Comprehensive Drug Abuse Prevention and Control Act of 1970 continues to be the basis for the regulation of drugs in the United States. Substances named by the act were placed under direct regulation of the Drug Enforcement Administration (DEA). The act "ranks" drugs from I to V, with Schedule I drugs being the most heavily controlled and carrying the most severe penalties for abuse.

	CRITERIA	EXAMPLES
SCHEDULE I	Drugs with high abuse potential that are lacking therapeutic utility or adequate safety for use under medical supervision.	Marijuana, heroin, LSD, peyote, PCP, mescaline
SCHEDULE II	Drugs with high abuse potential that are currently accepted in medical practice despite high physical and psychological dependence potential.	Opium, cocaine, morphine, Benzedrine, methadone, methamphetamine
SCHEDULE III	Drugs with moderate abuse potential that are currently utilized in medical practice despite dependence potential.	Barbiturates, amphetamine
SCHEDULE IV	Drugs with low abuse potential that are currently accepted in medical practice despite limited dependence potential.	Valium, Darvon, Phenobarbital
SCHEDULE V	Drugs with minimal abuse potential that are currently used in medical practice despite limited dependence potential.	Cough medicine with small amounts of narcotic

Source: The Comprehensive Drug Abuse Prevention and Control Act of 1970.

keted as providing the benefits of coca without the dangers of alcohol. Opium was labeled "God's Own Medicine," and opiates were prescribed for a number of different ailments, including rheumatism, food poisoning, dysentery, and lockjaw.[17]

Under the U.S. Constitution, the states assumed responsibility for regulating and controlling the health profession, including pharmacological products. For most of the nineteenth century, the states chose to impose no controls whatsoever in this area.[18] As a result, the United States led the Western world in opium and morphine consumption and was, in Edward Brecher's words, a "dope fiend's paradise."[19] To the extent that addiction was seen as a problem, concern was primarily focused on drug use by middle-class housewives, who were prohibited from drinking alcohol by the social customs of the day.

THE HARRISON ACT

America's first comprehensive antidrug legislation, the Harrison Narcotic Drug Act of 1914,[20] was primarily a political act, driven by foreign policy concerns rather than by medical or criminal ones. The United States had recently colonized the Philippines, an island nation with a considerable opium-smuggling problem. At the same time, China had started a campaign against opium use in an attempt to modernize and wean its citizens off the drug. This campaign relied a great deal on limiting the drug supply in outside markets, which included the Philippines. Partly to control rampant opium smuggling in its new territory and partly to appease the Chinese government, which had been complaining about treatment of Chinese nationals in America, the United States led an international effort to combat *narcotics* trafficking.[21] (Narcotics are a class of drugs derived from the opium poppy and include opium, heroin, and morphine.)

INFOTRAC KEYWORDS

Controlled Substances Act

For more information, use this search term with InfoTrac College Edition, your online library at www.infotrac-college.com

These efforts culminated in the Hague Convention of 1912, in which twelve countries, including the United States, agreed to outlaw the international nonmedical opium trade. Certain American politicians—embarrassed that the United States was a signatory to an international trafficking ban without having a similar domestic law—urged Congress to pass legislation prohibiting the nonmedical use of narcotics. The resulting Harrison Act of 1914 banned the importation, sale, or possession of narcotics outside proper medical channels. To accomplish this goal, the act empowered the Internal Revenue Service to strictly control the sale of narcotics by placing a tax on such transfers—any such transfer that did not result in the tax being paid and was not authorized by an accredited physician became *de facto* illegal.

Interestingly, cocaine was included in the substances covered by the Harrison Act, even though it is not a narcotic (that is, it derives from the coca plant, not from opium poppies). Some historians believe that cocaine was willfully misclassified because of its usefulness as a propaganda tool to combat the apathetic views on drug criminalization held by many legislators.[22] The antidrug reformer Dr. Hamilton Wright, for example, informed Congress that "cocaine is often the direct incentive to the crime of rape ... [in] the South and other sections of the country."[23]

THE NATIONAL PROHIBITION ACT

In contrast to the *laissez-faire* attitude toward most drugs, the nineteenth century saw an active antialcohol movement. Between 1850 and 1855, thirteen states passed statutes prohibiting alcohol within their borders. Though all but five had repealed such legislation within a decade, public sentiment against the evils of

Two sisters, Florence Friermuth and Susie Friermuth Duffing pose after being arrested for illegally producing "moonshine" alcohol on their family farm near St. Paul, Minnesota in 1921. What incentives did people have to manufacture, transport, and sell alcohol during the period of Prohibition?

Prohibition

A period in American history, lasting from the passage of the Eighteenth Amendment in 1919 until its repeal in 1933, during which the production and consumption of alcohol were prohibited by federal law.

alcohol remained strong. Finally, in 1919, the passage of the National Prohibition Act (also known as the Volstead Act), which became our Eighteenth Amendment, made it illegal to manufacture, sell, and transport alcoholic beverages in the United States.

This period of **Prohibition** remains a crucial component in the debate over a society's proper response to the problem of addictive substances. For almost fourteen years until the Eighteenth Amendment was repealed by the Twenty-first Amendment, both the costs and benefits of prohibition policies were evident. Alcoholism and health problems attendant to alcohol use—such as death from cirrhosis of the liver—declined during Prohibition.[24] At the same time, the enormous profits to be made from illegally transporting and selling alcoholic beverages—a bottle of gin that sold for $1 in Ontario, Canada, was worth $6 across the border in Detroit—provided gangsters such as Al Capone sufficient incentive to use violent measures to protect their underground markets. Nationwide, the murder rate reached record levels.

The spread of lawlessness and corruption eventually turned public opinion against Prohibition, and the law was repealed in 1933. As might be predicted, alcoholism and alcohol-related abuses rose, while violent crime rates dropped. In fact, the country's murder rate declined eleven consecutive years after the repeal of Prohibition.[25]

THE MARIJUANA TAX ACT

Four years after Prohibition ended, Congress passed the Marijuana Tax Act, which outlawed the sale, possession, and use of marijuana.[26] The new law effectively added marijuana to the Harrison Act's list of illicit drugs. The timing of the law was not a coincidence. Though its euphoria-inducing effects were well known during the nineteenth century and the early part of the twentieth century, marijuana was primarily used as a remedy for ailments such as asthma.[27]

It was not until the 1920s that marijuana (still legal) began to be widely used for recreational purposes, in many cases as a replacement for criminalized alcoholic beverages.[28] During the decade, a number of states began to pass laws prohibiting the sale or use of marijuana, based primarily on concerns that the drug caused users to commit violent crimes. This worry was also the basis for the passage of the national law, and the image of the violent "dope fiend" dominated government efforts to increase restrictions on marijuana use into the 1950s.[29]

THE GATEWAY DRUG

Few people still believe that marijuana leads to violence; all available evidence shows that marijuana inhibits, rather than causes, aggressive behavior. Yet more people are arrested for marijuana-related crimes today than for those associated with any other drug (see Figure 16.2). The reason for restrictions against marijuana use is fairly straightforward: although marijuana does not directly lead to violence, use of the drug may have serious repercussions. First of all, those who smoke marijuana may suffer negative health consequences. Heavy marijuana use can damage the part of the brain that is crucial for learning and memory, and smoked marijuana contains twice as many carcinogens (agents that lead to cancer) as does smoked tobacco.[30]

Second, some members of the criminal justice system, as well as the scientific community, regard marijuana as a "gateway" drug that leads the user to experiment with, and possibly become addicted to, "harder" illegal substances. These observers feel that a person who uses marijuana will become socialized to the drug culture and more readily use cocaine and heroin. Though they are not universally accepted, a number of studies support this theory. The latest involved 311 sets of same-sex twins, including 136 identical twins, in which just one twin had smoked marijuana before the age of seventeen. The early marijuana smokers were found to be five times more likely than their siblings to use "harder" drugs, most commonly cocaine and other stimulants.[31] Researchers warned, however, that such findings do not prove that smoking marijuana somehow changes the user's brain to make him or her crave stronger drugs; many other factors could explain the correlation. The statistics are notable nonetheless, given that nearly 50 percent of all American high school seniors have experimented with marijuana.[32]

↗ ONLINE REVIEW *Go to the book's Web site for an interactive review of this section*

The Abuse of Drugs

Do we need the federal government to be so vigilant in enforcing drug laws? How you answer the question probably depends on how widespread you believe the problem of illicit drug use is.

DRUG USE EXAMINED

The main source of drug use data is the National Survey on Drug Use and Health, conducted annually by the National Institute on Drug Abuse. As can be seen in Figure 16.3 on the following page, only 8.3 percent of those surveyed had used an illicit drug in the past month. Even so, this means that a significant number of Americans—19.5 million—are regularly using illegal drugs, and the figure mushrooms when one considers licit substances such as alcohol (120 million users) and tobacco (71.5 million users).[33]

The Criminology of Drug Use   At first glance, the reason people use psychoactive drugs is obvious: such drugs give the user pleasure and provide a temporary escape for those who may feel tension or anxiety. Ultimately, however, such explanations are unsatisfactory because they fail to explain why some people use drugs while others do not. Several theories, some of which were discussed in Chapter 2, have been formulated to explain drug use. *Social disorganization theory* holds that rapid social change can cause people to become disaffiliated from mainstream society, causing them to turn to drugs. Subculture theory, particularly as applied to adolescents, sees drug use as the result of peer pressure. *Control theory* hypothesizes that a lack of social control, as provided by units such as the family or school, can lead to antisocial activity such as drug use.

Drugs and the "Learning Process"   Focusing on the question of why first-time drug users become multiple users (especially given that the first experience is often a negative one), sociologist Howard Becker sees three factors in the "learning process." He believes first-time users:

1 Learn the techniques of drug use.

2 Learn to perceive the pleasurable effects of drug use.

3 Learn to enjoy the social experience of taking drugs.[34]

"Drug misuse is not a disease, it is a decision, like the decision to step out in front of a moving car. You would call that not a disease but an error of judgment."

—Philip K. Dick, American author (1977)

FIGURE 16.2 Distribution of Arrests by Drug Violation

Approximately 1.6 million arrests for drug abuse violations were made in the United States in 2002. As you can see, more of these arrests concerned marijuana than any other illegal drug.

Source: Federal Bureau of Investigation, *Crime in the United States, 2002* (Washington, D.C.: U.S. Department of Justice, 2003), 232.

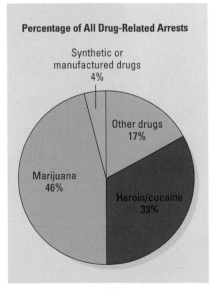

Percentage of All Drug-Related Arrests

Synthetic or manufactured drugs 4%

Other drugs 17%

Marijuana 46%

Heroin/cocaine 33%

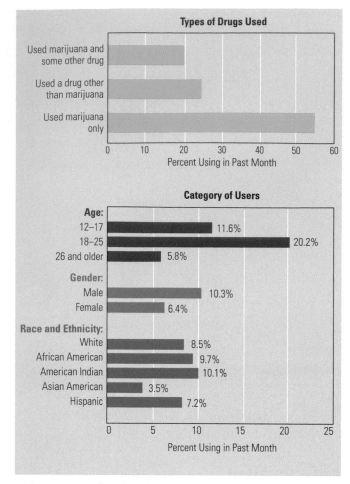

Types of Drugs Used

Percent Using in Past Month

Category of Users

Percent Using in Past Month

FIGURE 16.3. Drug Use in the United States

According to the National Survey on Drug Use and Health, approximately 20 million Americans, or 8.3 percent can be considered "illicit drug users." As you can see, most of these people used marijuana instead of other, stronger, drugs. Furthermore, eighteen- to twenty-five-year-olds were more likely to have used drugs than any other segment of the population.

Source: National Survey on Drug Use and Health, 2003.

Drug Abuse
The use of drugs that results in physical or psychological problems for the user, as well as disruption of personal relationships and employment.

Becker's assumptions are evident in a growing belief that positive images of drug use in popular culture "teach" adolescents that such behavior is not only acceptable but desirable. The entertainment industry, in particular, has been criticized for glamorizing various forms of drug use (see the feature *CJ and the Media—The Moral of the Story*).

DRUG ADDICTION AND DEPENDENCY

Another theory rests on the assumption that some people possess overly sensitive drug receptors in their brains and are therefore biologically disposed toward drug use.[35] Though there is little conclusive evidence that biological factors can explain initial drug experimentation, science has provided a great deal of insight into patterns of drug use. In particular, it has aided in understanding the difference between drug *use* and drug *abuse*. **Drug abuse** can be defined as the use of any drug—licit or illicit—that causes either physiological or psychological harm to the abuser or to third parties. Just as most people who drink beer or wine avoid abusing that drug, most users of controlled substances are not abusers. For most drugs, only between 7 and 20 percent of all users suffer from compulsive abuse.[36]

Despite their small numbers, drug abusers have a disparate impact on the drug market. The 20 percent of Americans, for example, who drink the most consume more than 80 percent of all alcoholic beverages sold in the United States. The data are similar for illicit substance abusers, leading to the conclusion that, to a large extent, abusers and addicts sustain the market for drugs.

Addiction Basics The most extreme abusers are addicted, or physically dependent on a drug. To understand the basics of addiction and physical dependence, one must understand the role of *dopamine* in the brain.[37] Dopamine is responsible for delivering pleasure signals to brain nerve endings in response to behavior—such as eating good food or engaging in sex—that makes us feel good. The bloodstream delivers drugs to the area of the brain that produces dopamine, thereby triggering a large amount of the neurotransmitter. Over time, the continued use of drugs physically changes the nerve endings, called receptors. To continue operating in the presence of large amounts of dopamine, the receptors become less sensitive, meaning that greater amounts of any particular drug are required to create the amount of dopamine needed for the same level of pleasure. When the supply of the drug is cut off, the brain strongly feels the lack of dopamine stimulation, and the abuser will suffer symptoms of withdrawal until the receptors readjust.

Addiction and physical dependence are interrelated, though not exactly the same. Those who are physically dependent on a drug suffer withdrawal symptoms when they stop using it, but after a certain time period they are generally able to emerge without further craving. Addicts, in contrast, continue to feel a need for the drug long after withdrawal symptoms have passed. Though some evidence

> The Moral of the Story

"People think [heroin is] all about misery and desperation and death," says the narrator of the film *Trainspotting,* "but what they forget is the pleasure of it. . . . Take the best orgasm you ever had, multiply it by a thousand, and you're still nowhere near it."

When *Trainspotting* was released in 1996, it was criticized for glamorizing heroin use. Such concerns were bolstered by research supporting the entertainment media's influence on the attitudes, behavior, and values of young consumers. Government researchers have found that illicit drugs were visually featured in 22 percent of films, 20 percent of television shows, and 3 percent of music videos (although nearly half of the songs in the videos mentioned drugs). Alcohol made an appearance in 93 percent of films, 77 percent of television shows, and 37 percent of music videos.

The problem, according to the researchers, is not the prevalence of these images in the media, but the "message" they send. Only 9 percent of the movies in which drugs were shown had a "negative" portrayal of drug use. Similarly, 90 percent of films and television shows that presented alcohol were favorable or neutral concerning the effects of the drug. When drugs and alcohol appeared in music videos, viewers were almost never discouraged from using them.

Historically, the entertainment industry has been just as likely to show the horrors of drug use as to glamorize it. Since the early days of cinema, films such as *Cocaine Fiends* (1939) and *Marihuana—Weeds with Roots in Hell* (1936) have shown drugs

as leading to a "downward spiral." Modern films such as *Permanent Midnight* (1998) and *Requiem for a Dream* (2000) echo this theme, telling stories of lives ruined by drug abuse. Even in *Trainspotting,* things turn out very badly for the drug-using characters. By the end of the film, the narrator is lamenting the "sickness" that comes with kicking the heroin habit: "Too ill to sleep. Too tired to stay awake, but the sickness is on its way. Sweat, chills, nausea. Pain and craving. A need like nothing else I've ever known will soon take hold of me. It's on its way."

From left, actors Johnny Lee Miller, Ewan McGregor, Kevin McKidd and Ewen Bremmer on the set of the British film Trainspotting, *which has been criticized for glamorizing drug and alcohol use.*

suggests that certain people are genetically predisposed to alcoholism,[38] researchers are still striving to determine whether some people are more likely to become addicts than others for biological reasons.

The Medical Model of Addiction   Since the late nineteenth century, the treatment and rehabilitation of addiction have played a role in determining the attitude society takes toward criminal drug abusers. Those who followed, and follow, the **medical model of addiction** believe that addicts are not criminals, but mentally or physically ill individuals who are forced into acts of petty crime to "feed their habit." Those who believe in the "enslavement theory of addiction" advocate treating addiction as a disease and hold that society should not punish addicts but attempt to rehabilitate them, as would be done for any other patients.[39]

THE DRUG-CRIME RELATIONSHIP

Although a number of organizations, including the American Medical Association, recognize alcoholism and other forms of drug dependence as diseases, the criminal justice system has tended to favor the **criminal model of**

Medical Model of Addiction
An approach to drug addiction that treats drug abuse as a mental illness and focuses on treating and rehabilitating offenders rather than punishing them.

Criminal Model of Addiction
An approach to drug abuse that holds that drug offenders harm society by their actions to the same extent as other criminals and should face the same punitive sanctions.

addiction over the medical model. The criminal model holds that drug abusers and addicts endanger society with their behavior and should be treated the same as any other citizens who commit crimes.[40] (See Figure 16.4 for research results on drug and alcohol use by criminals.)

Research Efforts The argument that drug use is an intricate part of criminal culture has been made since the 1920s. In the mid-1970s, the newly created National Institute on Drug Abuse and the National Institute of Justice estimated the number of arrestees and prisoners who used illicit drugs (mostly heroin and marijuana) at between 15 percent and 40 percent.[41] Later studies further cemented the drug-crime relationship. In the early 1990s, a team of researchers in Miami, Florida, interviewed 699 cocaine users and found that nearly 92 percent had criminal histories and 41.5 percent had participated in robberies. Furthermore, each member of the test group had committed hundreds of crimes in the ninety days before being interviewed (nearly 93 percent of which involved retail drug sales).[42] Today, nearly two-thirds of the inmates in federal prisons were incarcerated for a drug offense.[43]

Epidemiologist Paul Goldstein has devised three models to explain the relationship between drugs and crime:

> The *psychopharmacological model* holds that individuals act violently or criminally as a direct result of the drugs they have ingested.

> The *economically impulsive model* holds that drug abusers commit crimes to get the money to purchase drugs. According to the U.S. Department of Justice, 19 percent of state prisoners and 16 percent of federal prisoners said that they committed the crimes for which they were incarcerated in order to get money to buy drugs.[44]

> The *systemic model* suggests that violence is a by-product of the interpersonal relationships within the drug-using community, such as when a dealer is assaulted by a buyer for selling "bad" drugs.[45]

The strength of the drug-crime relationship has provided justification for increased law enforcement efforts to criminalize drug use and punish offenders of controlled substance laws. Indeed, the connection was cited as the reason overall crime rates fell in the mid-1990s, in conjunction with a similar downturn in the use of crack cocaine.[46]

Other Explanations Some observers, however, have questioned the conclusion that drug use causes crime. Instead, they contend, drug use and criminal activity both reflect the same willingness to deviate from established norms among certain members of society, labeled by sociologists as the *criminal subculture*.[47]

FIGURE 16.4 Committing Crime under the Influence of Drugs and Alcohol

For most crime categories, more than half of state prisoners and about one-third of federal prisoners said that they were under the influence of either drugs or alcohol when they committed the crime for which they were arrested.

Source: Adapted from Bureau of Justice Statistics, *Substance Abuse and Treatment, State and Federal Prisoners, 1997* (Washington, D.C.: U.S. Department of Justice, January 1999), Table 1, page 3.

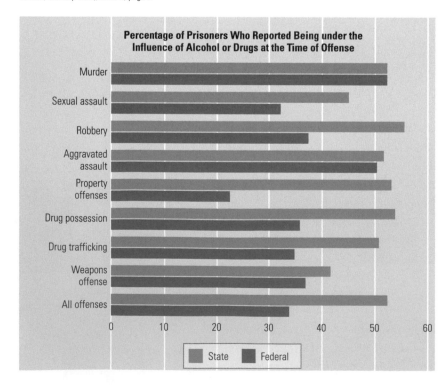

Furthermore, many believe that the violent and property crimes associated with illicit drugs take place "not because the drugs are drugs [but because] the drugs are illegal."[48] Seventy years ago, when alcohol was illegal in this country, the criminal gangs that controlled the alcohol trade used methods of violence similar to those associated with today's drug gangs. The fact that we

> no longer have drive-by shooting, turf wars and "cement shoes" in the alcohol business [is due to the fact that] alcohol today is legal—not because alcohol no longer intoxicates people, not because alcohol is no longer addicting, and not because alcohol dealers have suddenly developed a social conscience.[49]

◢ ONLINE REVIEW *Go to the book's Web site for an interactive review of this section*

Fighting the War on Drugs

The consumption of most illicit drugs is preceded by an act of voluntary exchange: a willing seller provides a willing buyer with the drug of choice. When a government decides to prohibit voluntary exchange, its officials must decide whether to target the seller or the buyer. For the past four decades, the American government has decided to focus on the seller, or supplier; therefore, the "war on drugs" is generally predicated on the idea of **supply-side enforcement.** As Figure 16.5 shows, the largest portion of the 2003 federal drug control budget went to law enforcement agencies, which are primarily concerned with reducing the supply of illegal drugs in this country. Only 27 percent was appropriated for treatment and prevention programs, which target the buyer by trying to reduce demand for illegal drugs.

LAW ENFORCEMENT EFFORTS

Federal, state, and local law agencies share responsibility for carrying out supply-side enforcement. In 1973, the federal Drug Enforcement Administration (DEA) was formed to restrict the supply of controlled substances through coordination with state and local agencies. Today, the DEA has more than four thousand officers and often works in tandem with local law enforcement agencies. The Controlled Substances Act gave the Federal Bureau of Investigation (FBI) concurrent jurisdiction with the DEA for domestic drug law enforcement. Along with the DEA and FBI, the Bureau of Customs and Border Protection, U.S. Customs, U.S. Coast Guard, U.S. Border Patrol, and branches of the U.S. military work to stem the flow of illegal drugs from other countries into the United States. Called *interdiction,* this process is discussed at length in the feature *Criminal Justice in Action— The Global Drug War* at the end of this chapter.

Most arrests for drug law violations take place at the local and state levels. About 90 percent of local law enforcement agencies regularly enforce drug laws, and in large U.S. cities (population of 250,000 or more), police departments assign an average of 123 officers to special drug units.[50] In general, the goals of local police with regard to illegal drug activity are as follows:

> To reduce the gang violence associated with the illegal drug trade.

Supply-Side Enforcement
The law enforcement strategy of combating the use of illegal drugs by concentrating on the suppliers of the drugs rather than the buyers. Thus, agents will focus on a single drug dealer rather than on his or her many clients.

FIGURE 16.5 Federal Drug Control Budget, 2003
The federal drug control budget for 2003 was triple the federal drug control budget of 1989. As you can see, the single largest item on the budget is domestic law enforcement.

Source: Office of National Drug Control Policy, *National Drug Control Strategy: 2003 Annual Report* (Washington, D.C.: Executive Office of the President, 2003).

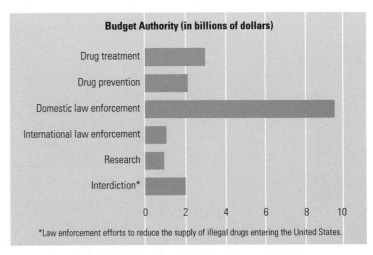

Budget Authority (in billions of dollars)

*Law enforcement efforts to reduce the supply of illegal drugs entering the United States.

NYT Pictures/Librado Romero

Drug smugglers use a variety of different methods to avoid interdiction efforts. One that is becoming more popular is paying poor men and women to swallow thumb-sized pellets of heroin wrapped in the cut-off fingers of surgical gloves. While this strategy makes it more difficult to find the drugs, it is also more dangerous for the "mule," or carrier. If the thin plastic covering the pellet ruptures, the heroin will spill into the carrier's stomach and can result in death. The body scanner shown here is being used in many international airports to stop this form of smuggling. Customs officers use it as an alternative to pat-down searches. According to one customs official, these searches focus on "high-risk flights" from "high-risk countries." How can such an attitude lead to complaints of racial and ethnic bias?

Asset Forfeiture Law
A statute that allows law enforcement agents to seize any equipment used in manufacturing, storing, or transporting illicit drugs and any profits or property gained from the sale of the drugs, as well as the drugs themselves.

> To control the street crimes committed by illegal drug users.

> To improve the quality of life in communities plagued by illegal drug use.

> To deter minors from using illegal drugs.

> To improve the physical, social, and economic well-being of illegal drug users.[51]

To accomplish these goals, police use tactics such as crackdowns, raids, and surveillance, discussed in Chapter 5. In some areas, concerted police activity has had a marked impact on drug abuse. As part of Tampa, Florida's Quick Uniformed Action against Drugs (QUAD) program, police constantly pressured sellers to change their sales venues and posed as buyers in "reverse sting" operations to confiscate illegal drugs. Six months after QUAD was initiated, street-corner drug dealing had been virtually eliminated in the targeted areas.[52]

LEGISLATIVE EFFORTS

Given public approval of increased sanctions against those who commit drug offenses, federal and state legislators have generally been willing, if not eager, to fortify existing drug laws. One Texas politician proposed cutting off a finger for each drug conviction. A peer from Delaware suggested flogging for drug felons, and William Bennett, former National Drug Policy director (or "drug czar"), voiced the opinion that drug dealers should be beheaded.[53] Though none of these propositions was taken seriously, recent legislation has provided law enforcement officers, prosecutors, and judges with a varied array of "weapons" to combat drug offenses, including the following:

> *Mandatory minimum sentencing laws.* As we discussed in Chapter 11, mandatory minimum sentencing laws remove discretion from judges by pre-determining the prison term for a crime depending on the circumstances surrounding that crime. In 1986, the Federal Sentencing Guidelines established minimum sentences for those found guilty of breaking federal drug laws. Federal law also provides that someone convicted of possessing or distributing one gram of crack cocaine will receive the same punishment as someone possessing or distributing one hundred grams of powder cocaine.[54] Furthermore, nearly every state has, at one point, passed its own mandatory minimum sentencing law for drug-related crimes.

> *Asset forfeiture laws.* An **asset forfeiture law** authorizes federal or state governments to seize contraband, drug manufacturing and storage equipment, and any item used to transport drugs. The goal of these laws is to combat the spread of drugs not only by arresting the traffickers, but also by confiscating the material used in the illegal operation. Federal and local law enforcement agencies seize more than $1 billion worth of cash and property each year under drug forfeiture statutes.

> *Child-protection laws.* To protect children from drug use and drug users, many legislatures have increased the penalties for drug offenses that involve minors. Under federal law, for example, any person convicted of selling a controlled substance to a person under eighteen years of age is subject to a sentence of up to twice the term and fine that would otherwise be authorized.

Recently, many states have begun to retreat from some of these tougher measures. In 2000, Utah voters changed the state's asset forfeiture law to stop law enforcement agencies from seizing property before the suspect has been proved guilty.[55] (The ballot initiative also required that all proceeds from asset forfeitures go to public schools rather than police departments.) Furthermore, between 1996 and 2002, forty-six states passed laws to ease penalties for drug offenses; the new laws provide for treatment instead of incarceration, permit those convicted of drug crimes to be eligible for public-assistance programs, or, as we shall discuss later in the chapter, allow marijuana use for medical reasons.[56]

PROSPECTS FOR SUCCESS

A study of homicides in New York offered the following breakdown of drug-related murders: they were overwhelmingly the result of the drug trade (74 percent), not of someone acting violently while under the influence of drugs nor of someone killing to get the money to purchase drugs.[57] Such data raise a central question about the nation's current illegal drug policy: Do drugs laws cause more harm than illegal drugs?[58]

Critics of American drug policy believe the answer is yes—that the "cure" of enforcement is worse than the "disease" of drug use. They offer a number of reasons for their stand, as summarized by professor of philosophy and law at Rutgers University Douglas N. Husak:

> The drug trade has created opportunities for a black market to flourish, which has greatly benefited organized crime. By keeping the prices of illegal drugs higher than they would be otherwise, law enforcement has provided a "subsidy" for drug dealers.

> The enormous profits have made corruption of law enforcement officials inevitable.

> Because the quality of illegal drugs is not regulated, consumers face risks of medical complications from "bad" drugs.

> Drugs are expensive not because of their production costs, but because of their illegality. Heroin is approximately 100 times more expensive and cocaine 20 times more expensive than they would be if the drugs were legal. As a result, users commit property crimes to obtain the funds necessary to purchase the drugs.

> Millions of otherwise law-abiding Americans have been labeled "criminals" because of drug use, with consequences throughout the criminal justice system.[59]

If this list represents some of the drawbacks of America's drug policy, what have been its benefits? Have supply-side enforcement tactics been successful? To answer that question, we must turn to the issue of illicit drug supply and price.

REDUCING THE SUPPLY OF ILLEGAL DRUGS

It is very difficult to "measure" the success of drug enforcement policies. After all, neither the sellers nor the buyers are eager to report their activities to official sources. If authorities are not certain of the total amount of drugs being manufactured and sold, then they can only guess as to the overall effect of their efforts. There is, however, a way to gauge these efforts: the price of illegal drugs on the street. This measurement is based on two assumptions:

1 If law enforcement agents are successful in incapacitating those who grow, refine, transport, and sell drugs, the amount of drugs available should drop.

The **U.S. Drug Enforcement Administration** is the nation's leading law enforcement agency in the fight against illegal drugs. To visit its Web site, click on *Web Links* under *Chapter Resources* at www.cjinaction.com

A device for making methamphetamine, otherwise known as meth, crank, ice, or tweek, is shown following a drug bust at a private home in Altamont, Tennessee. Because it is cheap and easy to manufacture and produces effects that can last as long as twelve hours (compared to, for example, thirty minutes for smoking cocaine), meth is considered a less expensive "high" than other drugs. In fact, law enforcement officials believe that a recent drop in the street price of heroin can be explained by the popularity of meth. Why would that be the case?

When the supply of a resource that many people want—whether it be diamonds, baseball cards, or drugs—decreases, the price should rise.

2 When authorities seize drugs and destroy the means of manufacturing and distributing them by arresting people in the drug business and confiscating equipment, drug lords must spend resources to rebuild their operations. If it become more expensive to make and distribute drugs, the dealers will pass these costs on to their customers, and the price should rise.

Therefore, if the price of illegal drugs is rising, then law enforcement agents know that they are having an impact. In reality, the opposite is taking place. According to many observers, the street price of illegal drugs has dropped dramatically since the beginning of the "war on drugs." According to the federal government, the price of a gram of cocaine was $201 in 1981 and roughly $51 in 2000. The price of a gram of heroin dropped even more dramatically, from nearly $1,207 in 1981 to $269 in 2000.[60] The price of marijuana has increased slightly, but the drug is much more potent than it was two decades ago, meaning that consumers are getting a more powerful product for relatively the same price.

The Substitution Effect Further complicating supply-side enforcement is the *iron law of substitution,* which holds that successful efforts to restrict the supply of one drug will lead to increased production and consumption of a substitute. As a corollary of this "law," whenever a drug is made illegal, more potent forms of the drug will drive less potent forms out of the market. Producers have a profit incentive to provide consumers with "more bang for the buck."[61] The smaller the "package," the less risk involved for both suppliers and consumers. Hence, it did not make economic sense to ship and sell beer when all alcohol was illegal.[62] During Prohibition, for example, America changed from a predominantly beer-drinking society to a hard-liquor one. Hard liquor can be more easily concealed because it has a greater potency and thus smaller quantities are needed for the same effect.

The identical process has been played out with cocaine replacing marijuana in the 1970s and crack replacing powder cocaine in the 1980s. Today, successful law enforcement efforts to reduce crack production have led to a resurgence in the use of methamphetamine, otherwise known as crank. The consequence of this substitution effect is that although law enforcement efforts may reduce the supply of a particular illicit drug in a particular place, they have been unsuccessful in reducing the supply of all illicit drugs on the national market.

The Darwinian Trafficker The substitution effect applies to drug suppliers as well as the illegal drugs themselves. For every "drug kingpin" or dealer that law enforcement manages to incarcerate, others are willing to take his or her place. The reason: few industries can match the profit incentive of the illegal drug market. In fact, successful apprehension of drug dealers may lead to what Jerome H. Skolnick calls "the Darwinian trafficker dilemma." According to Skolnick, law enforcement efforts succeed in capturing the marginal traffickers and dealers, leaving the most violent and efficient ones to dominate the market.[63] (The term *Darwinian* refers to the doctrine of English naturalist Charles Darwin [1809–1882]. Darwin believed that living things change and adapt to their environments. Consequently, any characteristic of an individual that allows it to better adapt to its environment will increase its chances of survival, as well as the chances of its offspring.)

For many, the negative consequences of our drug policy are most evident in low-income neighborhoods across the United States. The social and economic conditions of the inner cities seem designed to foster both illegal drug sellers and drug buyers. For those inner-city residents with ambition, mainstream educational and employment opportunities are less available. The only way to gain wealth and status seems to be through the drug trade. "Ambitious, energetic, inner-city youth are attracted to the underground economy precisely because they believe in the rags-to-riches American dream," notes anthropologist Phillipe Bourgeois.[64] Other residents of poor neighborhoods may react to their surrounding with despair, indifference, and a sense that the future holds no hope. (See the discussion of anomie theory in Chapter 2.) Such people are at high risk of turning to the induced euphoria of drug use to escape their surroundings.

The Ideal Environment   To a certain extent, then, inner cities are ideal environments for illegal drug activity and risky behavior. Law enforcement officers often react to this by converging on poor neighborhoods, where they make a disproportionate number of drug-related arrests. Because statistics tend to show that the majority of American drug users do not live in poor neighborhoods (see the feature *CJ in Focus—Myth versus Reality: Who Is Using Drugs?* on the next page), critics see these arrest rates as evidence of police bias.

Police Motivation   It is true that African Americans make up a high proportion of those charged and incarcerated for drug offenses. The targeting of inner cities for drug arrests may, however, be the result of selective enforcement rather than overt racism. Because of the low-income levels of those areas, residents are unlikely to hire expensive legal help to contest police action. A faulty drug arrest in a middle-class or wealthy neighborhood

> is apt to earn the police an expensive and embarrassing lawsuit by the wronged individual. The same mistake inflicted on the resident of an inner city will likely produce little more than a futile voice complaint. Quite simply, the inner city is an expedient locale for police to rack up impressive arrest numbers, with little fear for consequences if mistakes are made.[65]

Furthermore, because inner-city residents are often disconnected from the political process, elected officials will not suffer any negative consequences if they single out such areas for "get tough" police action.

ONLINE REVIEW *Go to the book's Web site for an interactive review of this section*

Alternatives to Prohibition

Considering the economic and social costs of "zero-tolerance" drug policies, many observers have called for liberalization of the nation's controlled substances laws. In general, these alternatives to prohibition fall into three broad categories: legalization, decriminalization, and harm reduction.

> Who Is Using Drugs?

Illegal drug abuse in the United States follows certain demographic patterns. In other words, people are more or less likely to abuse illegal drugs depending on factors such as their age, gender, race, or economic status. These patterns, however, do not necessarily match the expectations of many Americans.

The Myth

The stereotypical drug abuser is an uneducated, unemployed minority male living in a large city. This image is perpetuated by media coverage of drug use, which focuses on America's inner cities.

The Reality

The only aspect of the stereotype that is clearly supported by statistics is that drug abusers tend to be male. In 2003, according to the National Survey on Drug Use and Health, 10.3 percent of American men, compared to 6.4 percent of women, were users of illicit drugs. As for race, the study found that about 70 percent of all users were white, 13 percent African American,

and 10 percent Hispanic. These findings closely resemble those of prior years. Furthermore, eight of every ten illegal drug users are employed, and 75 percent of the demand for illegal drugs comes from middle-class users living in the suburbs.

As with many statistics, however, these do not tell the entire story of drug use. Though the overall number of white drug users dwarfs black users, the percentage of all African Americans who use drugs (9.7 percent) is slightly higher than for whites (8.5 percent). Furthermore, the negative consequences of drug use—loss of employment, family dislocation, overdose, death—are much greater for minorities than for whites. Researcher Jeffrey Kallan found that black males were almost twice as likely to die from illegal drug-related causes as whites.

FOR CRITICAL ANALYSIS

Kallan also found that people who have never been married have a significantly higher chance of dying from illegal drug use than those who have been married. What conclusion concerning illegal drug use and risky behavior can you draw from this finding? Also, what factors could explain higher mortality rates among African American users than white users?

LEGALIZATION

Legalization
The elimination or modification of federal and state laws that prohibit the manufacture, use, and sale of illegal drugs.

Believing that drug laws create worse evils than they solve, and that these same laws can never reduce illicit drug demand, some observers believe that illicit drugs should be made legal. In its most extreme form, **legalization** refers to the removal of all criminal sanctions on the sale and production of all psychoactive substances—with the exception of restrictions on sales to children.[66] Some see such a move as a panacea for many of the problems of the criminal justice system. Others, however, believe legalization is a risky proposition with consequences that cannot be predicted.

The Benefits of Legalization   Certain proponents of legalization cite the "peace dividend" that would come with the end of the "war on drugs." On the one hand, law enforcement agencies could eliminate costly drug enforcement programs. On the other hand, the state would reap a windfall in taxes on the controlled sale of substances previously available only on the black market. One expert concluded that the net economic gain for the United States would be $70 billion a year.[67] Other predicted benefits of legalization include:

> The reduction in drug prices to competitive levels, which means drug abusers and addicts would no longer require large sums of money to finance their drug use. This would reduce, if not eliminate (given the examples of alcohol and cigarettes), the need to steal money or engage in prostitution to acquire sufficient funds to cover one's habit.

> The end of violent crime associated with drug dealing, as black market organizations would be put out of business or forced to rely on less profitable criminal activities.

> A more efficient criminal justice system, as scarce law enforcement resources would be diverted away from drug offenses toward violent crimes, and the pressure on both overloaded court dockets and overcrowded prisons would be alleviated.[68]

Furthermore, as economist Milton Friedman has observed, legalization would improve the living conditions both in American inner cities and in drug-producing nations, whose corrupt political and law enforcement systems and high levels of violence can be attributed, at least in part, to America's demand for illicit drugs.[69]

INFOTRAC KEYWORDS
legalizing drugs
For more information, use this search term with InfoTrac College Edition, your online library at www.infotrac-college.com

Arguments against Legalization   Many observers insist that such a policy would cause more problems than it would solve. Given what we know about the "gateway effect," discussed earlier, they ask, how could we as a society justify making it easier for young people to obtain drugs? As an example, they point to cigarettes. Although tobacco products are generally prohibited to those under eighteen years of age, most teen-agers find little to stop them from smoking if they so desire. In general, opponents of legalization rely on three arguments, summarized by drug abuse researchers James A. Inciardi and Duane C. McBride:

> *The public-health and behavioral consequences argument.* If drugs such as marijuana, cocaine, and heroin were legalized, more people would use and abuse them. The abuse of these and other illicit drugs does negatively affect users' health, and the consequences could be significant. It is estimated that cigarette- and alcohol-related illnesses cause the deaths of 400,000 and 105,000 Americans each year, respectively.

> *The expanded-market argument.* Even with the restrictions imposed by government regulations, American alcohol and tobacco companies spend $5 billion a year on advertising. The goal of this advertising is to expand the market for their products, and one could assume the same would occur with legalized drugs. Furthermore, just as minors can often obtain cigarettes or alcoholic beverages, they are likely to have access to other legalized drugs.

> *The drugs and violence argument.* The United States already has a problem with alcohol-related violence. Although some drugs, notably marijuana, do not provoke aggressive behavior, others such as cocaine and certain hallucinogens do.[70]

Another argument against legalization warns that we do not know what the exact consequence of such an action would be. What happens if drugs are legalized and the results are unacceptable? Once instituted, legalization would be difficult to rescind. Finally, it would be a mistake to say that antidrug efforts have been a complete failure. Between 1985 and 1998, the number of Americans who reported illicit drug use within a month of being asked dropped from 12.1 percent to 8.3 percent,[71] and drug use among teen-agers hit an eight-year low in 2002.[72]

In Amsterdam, a customer smokes a marijuana cigarette in a coffeehouse. Law enforcement agencies generally turn a blind eye to cannabis use in these establishments, some two thousand of which are in operation in the city. This lax attitude encourages marijuana users from countries with harsher laws to flock to Amsterdam and has caused many of the Netherlands's neighbors to criticize its policies as contributing to drug use throughout northern Europe. What do you think would be the consequences if an American city or state took a similar stance on marijuana use?

Decriminalization
A policy that combines the elimination of criminal penalties on drug use with restrictions to discourage use such as high taxes and limitations on advertising of drugs.

DECRIMINALIZATION

"It would be strange," writes UCLA policy studies professor Mark Kleiman, "if one could not devise a set of laws and programs tighter than the light taxes and poorly enforced age restrictions to alcohol, yet much looser than the virtually total prohibition now applied to marijuana."[73] Kleiman, along with many other observers, advocates a middle ground between legalization and prohibition, generally known as **decriminalization.** In general, a decriminalization policy would:

> Place high taxes on the substance in question.

> Severely limit promotion of the substance, while using tax proceeds to finance public relations campaigns warning of its health risks.

> Restrict the sellers of the substance through governmental licensing.

> Restrict buyers by age and through strict sanctions for any public harm caused by abuse of the substance.[74]

Decriminalization at Home and Abroad   At times, decriminalization has had support in the United States. In 1972, for example, the Presidential Commission on Marijuana and Drug Abuse recommended the decriminalization of marijuana. In 2001, the Nevada legislature decriminalized small amounts of the drug.[75] A year later the state held a ballot initiative to legalize possession of up to three ounces of marijuana, but the measure was soundly defeated.

A number of Western European countries have adopted decriminalization policies, most notably the Netherlands, which has decriminalized "soft drugs" such as marijuana and hashish. Within the past few years, both Britain and Portugal have also limited or even eliminated criminal penalties for certain types of drug use. In 2003, much to the dismay of the U.S. government, Canadian lawmakers introduced legislation that would decriminalize possession of small amounts of marijuana. (For more information on this situation, see the feature *International CJ—The Border Dispute.*)

Medical Marijuana   To a certain extent, a number of states have already decriminalized marijuana use under certain circumstances. Since 1996, Alaska, Arizona, California, Colorado, Hawaii, Maine, Maryland, Nevada, Oregon, and Washington have passed voter initiatives that allow for the *medical use* of marijuana. For the most part, these laws allow people suffering from certain medical conditions to grow and possess marijuana as long as they have permission from a doctor to do so.

Medical marijuana laws have placed these states in direct conflict with the federal government, which does not recognize *any* legal uses of marijuana, designated a Schedule I illicit drug by the Controlled Substances Act. So, for example, in 2003 Californian Ed Rosenthal was tried in a federal district court and found guilty of marijuana cultivation and conspiracy. The federal prosecutors and jury rejected his defense that growing such plants was legal under the state's medicinal marijuana law.

Some federal judges have shown themselves to be sympathetic with state laws in this matter, however. The judge in Rosenthal's case refused to send him to federal prison for six and a half years, as the prosecutors requested, and instead sentenced him to one day in jail.[76] In 2002, the U.S. Court of Appeals for the Ninth

> The Border Dispute

According to a high-ranking Canadian government official, the Canadian and U.S. governments have the same goal of "zero use of marijuana." The Canadian government, in his opinion, is more realistic because it is willing to admit that—with 100,000 Canadians using the drug daily—efforts to combat marijuana have failed. New legislation proposed by the Canadian Parliament in 2003 reflects this reality. Under the proposed law, possession of half an ounce or less of marijuana would be punishable by a $150 fine (about $115 in U.S. currency), and the offender would not be given a criminal record. In other words, in Canada the punishment for possession of small amounts of pot would be essentially the same as for a speeding ticket.

Government officials in the United States expressed outrage at Canada's plans to relax its marijuana laws. "Marijuana is the most abused drug in our country," complained a spokesman for the U.S. Drug Enforcement Administration. "For Canada to decriminalize or legitimize marijuana means a greater availability of marijuana in Canada, which is going to cause individuals and organizations to try and smuggle the drug into the United States."

In fact, since security on the U.S.–Canada border was tightened in the wake of the September 11, 2001, terrorist attacks, the amount of marijuana seized by U.S. Customs agents has quadrupled. If the proposed legislation becomes law, U.S. officials warn that it would mean "more customs, more border patrols, more DEA," which would severely disrupt the $1 billion in legal trade that takes place every day along the four-thousand-mile U.S–Canada border.

FOR CRITICAL ANALYSIS
Canadian officials have gone to great lengths to assure the U.S. government that the proposed legislation does not reflect a "softening" attitude on illegal drugs. Indeed, the legislation would also increase the maximum sentence for those caught growing marijuana from seven years to fourteen years. What is the reasoning behind a strategy of punishing producers of drugs harshly while letting users off with the equivalent of a traffic ticket?

Circuit ruled that the federal government may not revoke the licenses of doctors who recommend marijuana to their patients in states with medical marijuana laws.[77] The United States Supreme Court subsequently declined to hear the federal government's appeal of this case. Although the Court's refusal to hear the appeal does not indicate that it agrees with the appellate court's decision (see Chapter 8), supporters of the decriminalization of marijuana for medicinal purposes were able to claim at least a temporary victory.

HARM REDUCTION

A third alternative accepts that a certain amount of drug use is inevitable and would focus drug policies on minimizing the harms for both the user and society that result from the activity. Ethan A. Nadelmann, director of the Lindesmith Center, a drug policy research institute, summarizes **harm reduction** strategy as follows:

> Rather than attempt to wean all illicit drug addicts off drugs by punitive means, harm reduction policies begin with the acknowledgement that some users cannot be persuaded to quit. These policies then seek to reduce the likelihood that they will contract or spread diseases such as hepatitis and AIDS, overdose on drugs of unknown purity and potency, or otherwise harm themselves or others.[78]

The "Wrong Message" Again, harm reduction policies have gained support in Western Europe. Switzerland has even passed legislation that makes heroin prescriptions to long-term addicts legal under certain circumstances. In the United

Drug Watch International and **Reform Coordination Network** have differing views on the legalization of drugs. Find their Web sites by clicking on *Web Links* under *Chapter Resources* at www.cjinaction.com

Harm Reduction
A drug policy based not on reducing use of illicit drugs but on reducing the crime and health problems associated with drug use.

States, such policies tend to be quite controversial, as opponents see them as "sending the wrong message" to potential drug users. In 1998, for example, despite findings by the U.S. Department of Health and Human Services that free needle exchange programs reduced the transmission of HIV among intravenous drug users, the federal government refused to lift a ban on federal funding for such programs. At the time of the decision, studies had found that 40 percent of new HIV infections in the United States were attributable to contaminated needles.[79]

Methadone Maintenance   Another controversial harm reduction program involves *methadone maintenance treatment*. Methadone is a synthetic narcotic that has some of the same physiological effects on the brain as heroin. Many physicians believe that it can be used to lessen the trauma of heroin withdrawal when administered at decreasing doses over a certain time period. Proponents of this treatment were disappointed and, in some cases, shocked when it became evident that methadone was not as safe for treating heroin addiction as had been thought. In Florida, methadone-related deaths increased from 209 in 2000 to 354 in 2001; another 254 users died in the first six months of 2002. Similar statistics have been reported in North Carolina and Maine, severely damaging hopes that methadone can play a significant role in harm reduction treatment.[80]

In 2002, the Food and Drug Administration approved two prescription drugs for heroin addicts: buprenorphine and buprenorphine-naloxone. Medical experts believe that because these drugs, unlike methadone, do not produce a "high," they do not encourage constant use and addiction. Furthermore, the new drugs have a much lower potential for overdose and withdrawal symptoms than does methadone. One physician has even predicted that the two new drugs are the first step toward drug addiction being treated like hypertension, diabetes, and other chronic diseases—"with a variety of medications prescribed at the doctor's office."[81]

⬆ONLINE REVIEW *Go to the book's Web site for an interactive review of this section*

Public Support for the War on Drugs

In certain countries such as Singapore and Malaysia, the sale of minuscule amounts of illicit drugs—as little as half an ounce of heroin or a hundred grams of marijuana—carries the death penalty. Though there is no evidence that a majority of Americans would favor such strict penalties (though they would certainly lessen the sale of drugs if applied uniformly), public opinion polls show that we would rather continue the "war on drugs" than liberalize drug policy. A recent poll conducted by the Pew Research Center for People and the Press found that although most Americans agree that U.S. antidrug efforts have failed, they support the continuation and expansion of such efforts.[82]

These survey results show that most Americans view the war on drugs as a moral issue rather than a legal, economic, or health-related one. Some observers blame this on the media, which they say overplay issues of crime and violence instead of addiction and treatment when dealing with the drug problem.[83] Others point out that, having started a "war" on drugs, to reduce law enforcement efforts would constitute a "surrender," an act with which Americans have never been comfortable. Whatever the reason, it seems clear that as long as our society considers illegal drugs a major danger to community values, the government will continue to take great efforts to eradicate them.

>The Global Drug War

In this chapter, we have focused mostly on domestic efforts to stop the consumption and sale of illegal drugs. The problem, however, is hardly limited to our national boundaries. A high percentage of the heroin, cocaine, marijuana, and amphetamines seized in the United States was smuggled across the Mexican border, mostly coming from sources in Central and South America. Southeast Asia has been a major source of illegal drugs in the past, and Africa is expected to be one in the future. The international illegal drug trade has been infiltrated by *narcoterrorists,* who finance their terrorist activities by participating in the drug trade. The ease with which funds can be transferred from country to country has contributed to *money laundering,* in which drug dealers convert illegally gained profits to cash using foreign businesses and banks. As we close this chapter, we will take a closer look at the challenges presented by the globalization of the illegal drug trade.

The Balloon Principle

On November 13, 2002, agents from the DEA and the U.S. Customs Service followed a forty-two-foot fishing boat called the *Sea'N Double* from open water to a private dock in the upscale neighborhood of Lighthouse Point in Broward County, Florida. On searching the vessel, the officers confiscated 771 pounds of cocaine. The seizure was not in itself extraordinary. In 2002, the Customs Service seized over 1.5 million pounds of illegal drugs. The significance of the incident was the route by which the boat entered American territory: from the Bahamian island of Grand Bahama. For the past two decades, South American drug trafficking organizations have primarily smuggled their contraband into the United States across the Mexican border, a reaction to law enforcement efforts to close the Bahamas/South Florida route in the 1970s. Now that attention is being focused on the overland route, especially with the increase in border security following the September 11, 2001, terrorist attacks, the traffickers have begun to revert to their old habits. Today,

about 35 percent of all cocaine smuggled into North America goes through the Caribbean, which has supplanted the Mexican border as the most popular route for the drug to enter the United States.[84]

When you press your finger on a balloon, the air inside pushes the balloon outward somewhere else. This *balloon principle* applies to the "war on drugs" as well. As can be seen from the above example, when law enforcement agents place pressure on one segment of the illicit drug trade, the market shifts to compensate. Given the overall scope of the international illegal drug market—estimated by the United Nations to have $600 billion in annual revenues, or 8 percent of total international trade—the balloon principle represents the single largest impediment to efforts to stop, or even slow, the flow of illegal drugs into the United States.

Interdiction Efforts

These efforts are extensive. Each year, $2 billion of federal funds go to interdiction programs. In the early 1980s, Vice President George H. W. Bush coordinated the National Narcotics Border Interdiction System, which linked the four military branches (Air Force, Navy, Army, and Marines) with local and federal law enforcement agencies to combat drug trafficking. The "militarization" of interdiction can be seen in efforts such as Operation Blast Furnace, during which U.S. Army Blackhawk helicopters attempted to destroy coca production labs in the South American country of Bolivia. In 1989, the U.S. military invaded Panama to arrest its president, Manuel Noriega, for violating federal drug trafficking laws.

The federal government also directs large amounts of foreign aid to *source-zone* countries, where illicit drugs are produced, with the understanding that the money is to be used to enhance local law enforcement efforts and provide alternative sources of income for drug-producing citizens. In recent years, the most significant efforts in this area have focused on Colombia. Since 1999, the United States has spent more than $2 billion to eradicate

Spectators in Kandahar, Afghanistan, watch as local police burn more than 650 pounds of opium and hashish. Afghanistan is the world's leading source for opium and heroin, and U.S. officials believe that proceeds from the sale of these drugs have been used to support international terrorism.

cocaine production in this South American country and has provided the Colombian government with more than eighty helicopters and fixed-wing aircraft to destroy coca crops. This strategy has resulted in the devastation of 300,000 acres of coca each year, and Colombian officials hope to double that number by 2005.

Despite this massive movement of government resources, the balloon principle has severely limited the effectiveness of the antidrug campaign in Colombia. With aerial fumigation focusing on Colombia, producers have simply shifted to other countries in the region. In neighboring Peru, for example, the coca crop expanded from 84,474 acres in 2000 to more than 125,000 acres in 2002.[85] Furthermore, Colombian farmers are shifting from coca plants to opium poppies, which are easier to grow in areas hidden from the view of crop-dusting airplanes. According to U.S. Customs officials, seizures of

Colombian heroin increased by 80 percent from 2001 to 2002.[86]

Greater Supply, Low Prices

The goal of interdiction is to reduce the supply of illegal drugs entering the United States, thereby raising the prices of the substances that do reach American streets. In fact, as noted earlier in the chapter, illegal drug prices have actually *dropped* as interdiction efforts have increased.

There are a number of reasons for this phenomenon. First, law enforcement agents seize only a small percentage of the illegal drugs that enter this country—10 percent, according to the DEA.[87] Second, the supply of drugs is expanding rapidly; estimates are that the world production of cocaine has more than doubled and the supply of heroin has more than tripled over the past decade. In other words, while the finger pressure on the balloon remains weak, the size of the balloon is rapidly expanding.

Third, the profits to be made in the illegal drug trade are often astounding. For instance, a kilogram of the high-grade heroin known as China White that can be purchased for $2,500 in the Southeast Asian country of Myanmar (formerly Burma) will sell for $200,000 in New York City.[88] Consequently, people are willing to take great risks to get illegal drugs into the United States and Western Europe.

A Matter of Climate and Economy

The coca bush, whose leaves provide the raw material for cocaine, is averse to below-freezing temperatures, but otherwise it will flourish in any climate that receives between 40 and 240 inches of rain annually. The opium poppy requires mild, sunny, and drier conditions, but the marijuana plant literally grows like a weed and can be found on every continent except Antarctica. Figure 16.6 lists the countries that are primarily responsible for producing and exporting the drugs that can be made using these three plants.

Illegal drug production depends on more than climate, however. As Figure 16.6 also shows, the major producers of coca, opium, and cannabis are among the world's materially poorer nations. The people who live in these countries have an economic incentive to grow illicit crops, and their governments do not have the resources to restrict the practice. In Afghanistan, for example, farmers can earn $4,000 from a plot (about eight-tenths of an acre) of opium poppies, compared to $500 for a legal crop such as wheat.[89] This general poverty restricts the United States's ability to offer foreign aid as an inducement to reduce production of illicit crops. The annual opium crop in Afghanistan is worth about $1.2 billion, as much as all the foreign aid the country received in 2002.[90] Finally, because law enforcement agents and government officials earn such low wages in these countries, they are more susceptible to corruption: according to Mexican authorities, major drug cartels in their country pay as much as $1 million a week in bribes.[91]

The Connection between the Drug Trade and Terrorism

The phenomenon of narcoterrorism is well documented. Guerrilla armies that engage in terrorism often rely on drug trafficking as their main source of income. The DEA has determined, for example, that Hezbollah—the militant Shiite group based in Lebanon that was responsible for the truck bombing of a U.S. Marine base in Beirut in 1983—has been using illegal drug profits to finance its operations for decades.[92] Following September 11, 2001, however, the practice has taken center stage, especially as Osama bin Laden is believed to have raised funds for his al Qaeda terrorist organization by smuggling heroin out of Afghanistan. "Lawlessness that breeds terrorism is also a fertile ground for the drug traf-

ficking that supports terrorism," said Attorney General John Ashcroft "To surrender to either of these threats is to surrender to both."[93]

Some observers believe that the connection is not quite so simple. A series of television advertisements produced by the federal government that aired in 2002 came under heavy criticism for exploiting the tragedy of September 11, 2001, as antidrug propaganda. In the ads, teen-agers and young adults admitted to buying illegal drugs and expressed remorse for having, at the same time, supported international terrorism. "I helped blow up a building," said one actor. As the Drug Policy Alliance pointed out at the time, federal authorities have yet to produce any evidence that proceeds from drug sales in the United States have gone to al Qaeda or any other Middle Eastern terrorist organization.[94]

Furthermore, the goals of fighting terrorism and fighting the drug trade can, at times, conflict with one another. During its final years in power in Afghanistan, for example, the Taliban government banned the cultivation of opium poppies. When a coalition of military forces led by the United States and Great Britain overthrew the Taliban in 2002, in large measure because of its support for terrorist groups in the Middle East, heroin production in Afghanistan skyrocketed. With most foreign resources in the country going to combat terrorist insurgencies, opium exports from Afghanistan are again threatening to flood the world with cheap heroin. "The fight against terrorism takes priority," pointed out one British government official. "The fight against narcotics comes in second."[95]

MAKING SENSE OF THE GLOBAL DRUG WAR

1 Should U.S. policymakers continue to see the drug program as a domestic problem? In other words, should we focus on decreasing the demand for illegal narcotics in the United States rather than trying to stem the supply from other countries? Why or why not?

2 Explain the different ways the "balloon principle" affects efforts to keep illegal drugs from entering this country.

3 According to one critic of U.S. drug policy, "If helping to put money in the pockets of drug dealers is akin to aiding terrorist causes, then by continuing to drive up the price of drugs the U.S. government is the biggest supporter of terrorism." Explain the rationale behind this assertion. Exaggeration aside, do you think there is any merit to the statement?

Chapter Summary

1 **Explain why the criminal law concepts of *mala in se* and *mala prohibita* are necessary to understand drug laws.** Because there are no clear-cut differences in risk of harm among certain psychoactives, to understand which are legal and which are illegal one must look to which drugs are considered *mala prohibita,* or inherently evil, depending on presiding societal norms and values. Basically, whatever psychoactives are deemed illegal by the Controlled Substances Act of 1970 and its amendments are therefore prohibited.

2 **Tell what happened to alcohol use and murder rates during Prohibition.** Alcohol abuse fell during most of the almost fourteen years of Prohibition, whereas violent crime and especially murder rates increased dramatically. After Prohibition was repealed, these two trends reversed themselves.

3 **List the three factors in the learning process that cause first-time drug users to become multiple users.** (a) They learn the techniques of drug use, (b) they learn to perceive the pleasurable effects of drug use, and (c) they learn to enjoy the social experience of taking drugs.

4 **Explain the 20-80 Rule as it applies to the use of psychoactives.** For most psychoactives, 20 percent of users consume about 80 percent of the total amount used.

5 **Contrast the medical model of addiction with the criminal model of addiction.** Those who support the former believe that addicts are not criminals but rather are mentally or physically ill individuals who are forced into acts of petty crime to "feed their habit." Those in favor of the criminal model of addiction believe that abusers and addicts endanger society with their behavior and should be treated like any other citizens who commit crimes.

6 **List federal agencies involved in drug law enforcement.** The Drug Enforcement Administration (DEA), Federal Bureau of Investigation (FBI), Bureau of Customs and Border Protection, U.S. Customs, U.S. Coast Guard, U.S. Border Patrol, and branches of the U.S. military.

7 **Summarize the three main legislative strategies to reduce illegal drug use.** (a) Mandatory minimum sentencing laws predetermine the prison sentence for individuals convicted of drug-related crimes; (b) asset forfeiture laws authorize law enforcement agencies to seize cash, equipment, and property used to produce and transport illegal drugs; and (c) child-protection laws increase the penalties for drug-related crimes when they involve minors.

8 **Explain the *iron law of substitution.*** Successful efforts to restrict the supply of one drug will lead to increased production and consumption of substitutes. The corollary to this "law" is that when a drug is made illegal, more potent forms of the drug drive less potent forms out of the market.

9 **Identify some of the reasons law enforcement agencies may be likely to target members of minority groups when enforcing drug laws.** Although sometimes attributed to racism, the high incidence of drug arrests in inner cities might be the result of selective enforcement. Resident of low-income neighborhoods are often unable to hire expensive lawyers to contest police action. Also, elected officials will probably not suffer negative publicity if they single out inner cities for "get tough" law enforcement strategies.

10 **Outline the three major arguments against legalization.** (a) Legalization would lead to increased use and abuse of the newly legalized drugs; (b) the market for newly legalized drugs would expand through advertising and word of mouth; and (c) violence would increase with the use of newly legalized drugs.

STORIES FROM THE STREET

Go to the Stories from the Street feature at www.cjinaction.com to hear Larry Gaines tell insightful stories related to this chapter and his experiences in the field.

1   On what basis is a distinction made between licit and illicit drugs?

2   Why did the murder rate rise during Prohibition and fall thereafter?

3   What role does dopamine play in the chemistry of addiction?

4   What are some of the reasons that illegal drug trafficking has grown so consistently?

5   What should happen to the price of successfully interdicted drugs, and why?

6   Why have we observed a resurgence in the use of methamphetamines ("crank")?

7   What is the distinction between legalization of illicit drugs and decriminalization?

8   What is the goal of a harm reduction strategy?

9   How does the balloon principle apply to the war on drugs?

10   Why are the major illegal drug production areas found in the world's materially poorer nations?

Go to www.cjinaction.com for tools to aid you in studying for your exams. Click on *Online Reviews* under *Chapter Resources* for an interactive review of each major section of this chapter. Under *Chapter Resources*, you will also find the *Chapter Outline*, *Chapter Summary*, *Flashcards*, *Glossary*, *Learning Objectives*, *Lecture Presentations*, *Concept Builder*, *Essay Questions*, and a *Tutorial Quiz*. You can also test yourself with a game of *Concentration* or the *Crossword Puzzle*.

Go to www.cjinaction.com for a wealth of online resources. Explore the *Internet Activities* and *Class Projects* under *Chapter Resources*. Check out the *Web Links* to access the Web sites mentioned in the text, as well as many others. You can also access recent perspectives by clicking on *CJ in the News* and *Terrorism Update* under *Course Resources*. If you'd like some mentoring, click on *Board of Mentors* under *Book Resources*.

For additional information, explore InfoTrac College Edition, your online library that offers complete full-length articles from thousands of scholarly and popular publications. Click on *InfoTrac College Edition* under *Chapter Resources* at www.cjinaction.com for a list of key words and InfoTrac exercises. Use the passcode that came with your book.

Chepesiuk, Ron, *The Bullet or the Bribe: Taking Down Colombia's Cali Drug Cartel*, Westport, CT: Praeger Publishers, 2003. The Cali Cartel, based in Colombia, was once the world's largest cocaine supplier, generating $8 billion a year in sales in the early 1990s. This book details the strategies employed by Colombian and U.S. law enforcement

agencies to combat and ultimately dismantle the organization. In the process, author Chepesiuk offers insights into the history of international drug trafficking, organized crime, and the consequences of U.S. drug policy.

Husak, Douglas N., *Drugs and Rights*, New York: Cambridge University Press,

2002. Do adults have a right to use drugs for recreational purposes? Husak, a professor of philosophy and law at Rutgers University, attempts to answer this question by comparing the harm caused by such drug use and the harm caused by laws criminalizing it. He concludes that most antidrug laws are unjustified and that the "war against drugs" violates the moral rights, if not the legal ones, of many Americans.

Notes

1. *Behind Bars: Substance Abuse and America's Prison Population* (New York: National Center on Addiction and Substance Abuse at Columbia University, 1998).

2. Jane J. Stein, ed., *Substance Abuse: The Nation's Number One Health Problem* (Princeton, NJ: The Robert Wood Johnson Foundation, February 2001), 23.

3. Quoted in Jerome H. Skolnick, "Rethinking the Drug Problem," in *Drugs, Crime, and Justice*, ed. Larry K. Gaines and Peter B. Kraska (Prospect Heights, IL: Waveland Press, 1997), 404.

4. Weldon Witters, Peter Venturelli, and Glen Hanson, *Drugs and Society*, 3d ed. (Boston: Jones & Bartlett, 1992), 4.

5. James E. Royce and David Scratchley, *Alcoholism and Other Drug Problems* (New York: Free Press, 1996), Chapters 1, 2, and 5.

6. National Center for Health Statistics, *Health, United States, 2003* (Washington, D.C.: Centers for Disease Control and Prevention, 2003), Table 65, page 224.

7. Referred to in Douglas N. Husak, *Drugs and Rights* (New York: Cambridge University Press, 2002), 21.

8. Charlotte Balcomb Lane, "Drugstore Clones," *Albuquerque Journal* (October 12, 2003), C1.

9. Richard Perez-Pena, "New Drug Promises Shift in Treatment for Heroin Addicts," *New York Times* (August 11, 2003), A1.

10. Task Force of the National Advisory Council on Alcohol Abuse and Alcoholism, *A Call to Action: Changing the Culture of Drinking at U.S. Colleges* (Washington, D.C.: National Institutes of Health, April 2002).

11. John Slade, "Health Consequences of Smoking: Nicotine Addiction," *Hearings before the Subcommittee on Health and the Environment of the House Committee on Energy and Commerce* (Washington, D.C.: U.S. Government Printing Office, 1988), 163–164.

12. Ethan Nadelmann, "Should We Legalize Drugs? History Answers: Yes," *American Heritage* (February/March 1993), 41.

13. Steven Jonas, "Solving the Drug Problem: A Public Health Approach to the Reduction of the Use and Abuse of Both Legal and Illegal Recreational Drugs," *Hofstra Law Review* 18 (1990), 753.

14. Codified as amended at 21 U.S.C. Sections 801–966 (1994).

15. Uniform Controlled Substances Act (1994), Section 201(h).

16. Husak, 25.

17. David F. Musto, *The American Disease: Origins of Narcotic Control* (New York: Oxford University Press, 1987), 1.

18. David F. Musto, "Opium, Cocaine, and Marijuana in American History," in *Drugs, Crime, and Justice*, ed. Larry K. Gaines and Peter B. Kraska (Prospect Heights, IL: Waveland Press, 1997), 22.

19. Edward M. Brecher, *Licit and Illicit Drugs* (Boston: Little, Brown, 1972), 3.

20. 38 Stat. 785 (1923).

21. Musto, "Opium, Cocaine, and Marijuana," 28–35.

22. Franklin E. Zimring and Gordon Hawkins, *The Search for Rational Drug Control* (New York: Cambridge University Press, 1992), 58–61.

23. Quoted in Erik Grant Luna, "Our Vietnam: The Prohibition Apocalypse," *DePaul Law Review* 46 (Winter 1997), 483.

24. P. Aaron and David F. Musto, "Temperance and Prohibition in America: A Historical Overview," in *Alcohol and Public Policy: Beyond the Shadow of Prohibition*, ed. Mark H. Moore and Dean R. Gerstein (Washington, D.C.: National Academy Press, 1981), 165.

25. Daniel K. Benjamin and Roger L. Miller, *Undoing Drugs: Beyond Legalization* (New York: Basic Books, 1991), 21.

26. 26 U.S.C.A. Section 4742(a)(2) (1937).

27. Zimring and Hawkins, 70.

28. Brecher, 409.

29. Duane C. McBride and Clyde B. McCoy, "The Drugs-Crime Relationship: An Analytical Framework," in *Drugs, Crime, and Justice*, ed. Larry K. Gaines and Peter B. Kraska (Prospect Heights, IL: Waveland Press, 1997), 91–92.

30. Gabriel G. Nahas and Nicholas A. Pace, "Marijuana as Chemotherapy Aid Poses Hazards," *New York Times* (December 4, 1993), 20.

31. Michael T. Lynskey, Andrew C. Heath, Kathleen K. Bucholz, Wendy S. Slutske, Pamela A. F. Madden, Elliot C. Nelson, Dixie J. Statham, and Nicholas G. Martin, "Escalation of Drug Use in Early-Onset Cannabis Users vs Co-twin Controls," *Journal of the American Medical Association* (January 22, 2003), 427-433.

32. National Institute of Drug Abuse, *Monitoring the Future: National Results on Adolescent Drug Use; Overview of Key Findings, 2002* (Washington, D.C.: U.S. Department of Health and Human Services, 2003), 8.

33. Substance Abuse and Mental Health Services Administration, *National Survey on Drug Use and Health, 2002* (Washington, D.C.: National Institute on Drug Abuse, 2003).

34. Howard S. Becker, *Outsiders: Studies in the Sociology of Deviance* (New York: Free Press, 1966).

35. Meyer Glantz and Roy Pickens, "Introduction and Overview," in *Vulnerability to Drug Abuse*, ed. Meyer Glantz and Roy Pickens (Washington, D.C.: American Psychological Association, 1992), 29–32.

36. Peter B. Kraska, "The Unmentionable Alternative: The Need for and the Argument Against the Decriminalization of Drug Laws," in *Drugs, Crime, and the Criminal Justice System*, ed. Ralph Weisheit (Cincinnati, OH: Anderson Publishing, 1990).

37. Anthony A. Grace, "The Tonic/Phasal Model of Dopamine System Regulation," *Drug and Alcohol Dependence* 37 (1995), 111.

38. Lawrence K. Altman, "Scientists See a Link between Alcoholism and a Specific Gene," *New York Times* (April 18, 1990), A1.

39. James A. Inciardi, *The War on Drugs: Heroin, Cocaine, and Public Policy* (Palo Alto, CA: Mayfield, 1986), 148.

40. *Ibid.*, 106.

41. Duane C. McBride, "The Relationship between Type of Drug Use and Arrest Charge in an Arrested Population," in *Drug Use and Crime* (Springfield, VA: National Technical Information Service, 1976), 409–418.

42. James A. Inciardi, Duane C. McBride, H. Virginia McCoy, and Dale D. Chitwood, "Recent Research on the Crack-Cocaine/Crime Connection," in *Studies in Crime and Crime Prevention* (Stockholm, Sweden: National Council for Crime Prevention), 63–82.

43. Bureau of Justice Statistics, *Federal Criminal Case Processing, 2001* (Washington, D.C.: U.S. Department of Justice, January 2003), 1.

44. Bureau of Justice Statistics, *Substance Abuse and Treatment, State and Federal Prisoners, 1997* (Washington, D.C.: U.S. Department of Justice, January 1999), 5.

45. Paul J. Goldstein, "The Drugs/Violence Nexus: A Tripartite Conceptual Framework," *Journal of Drug Issues* 15 (1985), 493–506.

46. Gordon Witkin, "The Crime Bust: What's behind the Dramatic Drop in Crime," *U.S. News & World Report* (May 25, 1998), 28–33, 36–37.

47. McBride and McCoy, 99.

48. Benjamin and Miller, 110.

49. *Ibid.*, 110-111.

50. Bureau of Justice Statistics, *Police Departments in Large Cities, 1990–2000* (Washington, D.C.: U.S. Department of Justice, May 2002), 7.

51. Mark H. Moore and Mark A. R. Kleiman, " The Police and Drugs," in *Drugs, Crime, and Justice*, ed. Larry K. Gaines and Peter B. Kraska (Prospect Heights, IL: Waveland Press, 1997), 229.

52. David M. Kennedy, "Closing the Market: Controlling the Drug Trade in Tampa, Florida," *National Institute of Justice Program Focus* (Washington, D.C.: U.S. Department of Justice, April 1993).

53. Quoted in Husak, 13.

54. United States Sentencing Commission Guidelines Manual Section 2D1.(c) (1994).

55. Mark Shurtleff, "Protecting Our Homes, Schools, and Neighborhoods," *Utah Bar Journal* (October 2000), 12.

56. Bill Piper, Matthew Briggs, Katharine Huffman, and Rebecca Lubot-Conk, *State of the States: Drug Policy Reforms, 1996–2002* (New York: Drug Policy Alliance, September 2003), i.

57. Paul J. Goldstein, "Crack and Homicide in New York City, 1988: A Conceptually Based Event Analysis," *Contemporary Drug Problems* 16 (1989), 662.

58. Husak, 18.

59. *Ibid.*, 53–58.

60. Office of National Drug Control Policy, *National Drug Control Strategy: 2001 Annual Report* (Washington, D.C.: Executive Office of the President of the United States, 2003), Table 41.

61. Steven B. Duke, "Drug Prohibition: An Unnatural Disaster," *Connecticut Law Review* 27 (Winter 1995), 571.

62. Skolnick, 414.

63. Skolnick, 412.

64. Phillipe Bourgeois, "Just Another Night on Crack Street," *New York Times Magazine* (November 12, 1989), 63.

65. Benjamin and Miller, 66.

66. Ethan A. Nadelmann, "The Case for Legalization," *Public Interest* (Summer 1992), 5.

67. Luna, 483.

68. James A. Inciardi and Duane C. McBride, "Debating the Legalization of Drugs," in *Handbook of Drug Control in the United States,* ed. James A. Inciardi (New York: Greenwood Press, 1990), 285–289.

69. Milton Friedman, "A Quarter-Century Later, 'War on Drugs' Is Still Misguided," *Seattle Post-Intelligencer* (January 15, 1998), A11.

70. Inciardi and McBride, 289–294.

71. *National Survey on Drug Use and Health, 2002.*

72. "Teenage Drug Use Drops to an 8-Year Low," *New York Times* (July 18, 2002), A17.

73. Mark A. R. Kleiman, "Neither Prohibition Nor Legalization: Grudging Toleration in Drug Control Policy," in *Drug Use and Drug Policy,* ed. Marilyn McShane and Frank P. Williams III (New York: Garland Publishing, 1997), 180.

74. *Ibid.,* 186–190.

75. A.B. 453, 2001 Leg., 71st Sess. (Nev. 2001).

76. Eric Bailey and Marcelo Rodriguez, "'Guru of Ganja' Gets a Day in Jail," *Los Angeles Times* (June 5, 2003), B1.

77. *Conant et al. v. Walters et al.,* 309 F.3d 629 (9th Cir. 2002).

78. Ethan A. Nadelmann, "Thinking Seriously about Alternatives to Drug Prohibition," *Daedalus* 121 (1992), 88.

79. Donna Shalala, "Report to the Committee on Appropriations of the Department of Labor, Health and Human Services, Education and Related Agencies," *Needle Exchange Programs in America: A Review of Published Studies and Ongoing Research* (Washington, D.C.: U.S. Department of Health and Human Services, 1997), 11.

80. Pam Belluck, "Methadone, Once the Way Out, Suddenly Grows as a Killer Drug," *New York Times* (February 9, 2003), A1.

81. Howard Markel, "For Addicts, Relief May Be an Office Visit Away," *New York Times* (October 27, 2002), Section 6, page 13.

82. The Pew Research Center for People and the Press, "Interdiction and Incarceration Still Top Remedies," March 21, 2001, at http://people-press.org/reports/display.php3?ReportID=16.

83. Peter Reuter, "Hawks Ascendant: The Punitive Trend of American Drug Policy," in *Drug Use and Drug Policy,* ed. Marilyn McShane and Frank P. Williams III (New York: Garland Publishing, 1997), 394.

84. Under Secretary of Defense for Policy, *The Cocaine Threat: A Hemispheric Perspective* (Washington, D.C.: U.S. Department of Defense, 2002), 3.

85. Juan Forero, "Farmers in Peru Are Turning Again to Coca Crop," *New York Times* (February 14, 2002), A3.

86. Juan Forero and Tim Weiner, "Latin American Poppy Fields Undermine U.S. Drug Battle," *New York Times* (June 8, 2003), Section 1, page 1.

87. *Drug Smuggling: Large Amounts of Illegal Drugs Not Seized by Federal Authorities* (Washington, D.C.: U.S. General Accounting Office, 1987).

88. Matthew Brzezinski, "Re-Engineering the Drug Business," *New York Times Magazine* (June 23, 2003), 27.

89. Scott Baldauf, "Afghan Military Tied to Drug Trade," *Christian Science Monitor* (September 4, 2003), 6.

90. *Ibid.*

91. "Mexico's Drug Menace," *Economist* (November 15, 1997), 38.

92. Deborah J. Daniels, "The Challenge of Domestic Terrorism to American Criminal Justice," *Corrections Today* (December 1, 2002), 66.

93. Thomas Ginsberg, "One Country, Two Wars," *Seattle Times* (December 23, 2002), A3.

94. Cathy Young, "Drugs and Terrorism and Insulting Ads," *Boston Globe* (January 13, 2002), A11.

95. Tim Golden, "U.S. Fears a Glut of Heroin from a Volatile Afghanistan," *New York Times* (April 1, 2002), A1.

Terrorism, Cyber Crime, and the Futu

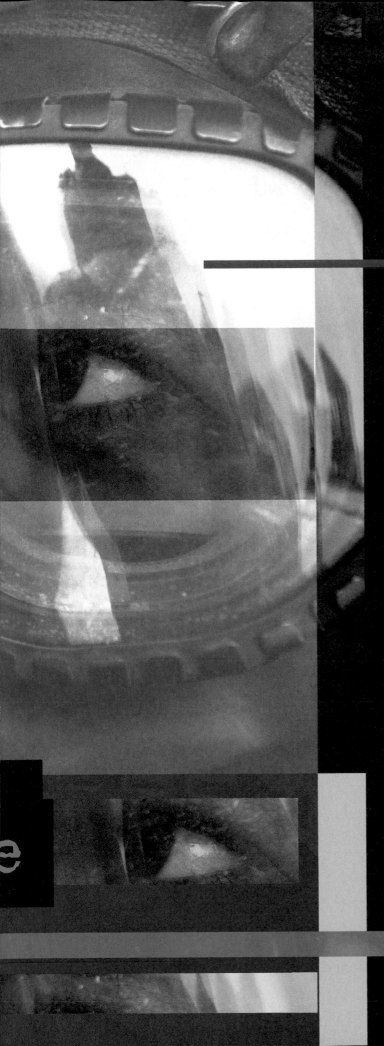

>chapter objectives<

After reading this chapter, you should be able to:

1 Explain why the Antiterrorism and Effective Death Penalty Act of 1996 (AEDPA) is an important legal tool against potential terrorists.

2 Describe the primary goals of an intelligence agency and indicate how it differs from an agency that focuses solely on law enforcement.

3 List some of the ways federal law enforcement can use aspects of immigration law to fight terrorism.

4 Indicate the three amendments to the U.S. Constitution that are cited most often by critics of the USA Patriot Act of 2001, and briefly explain why.

5 Explain how military tribunals differ from federal courts with regard to trials of suspected terrorists.

6 Distinguish cyber crime from "traditional" crime.

7 Explain the activities and purposes of most hackers.

8 Outline the three major reasons that the Internet is conducive to juvenile cyber crime.

9 Describe the challenges to enforcing online gambling laws.

10 Indicate some reasons why the database is seen as an important crime-fighting tool for the future of law enforcement.

Looking for Terrorism in Lackawanna

Lackawanna, a small town just south of Buffalo in upstate New York, was built in the early decades of the twentieth century to provide homes for employees at factories run by Bethlehem Steel. For years, the city attracted immigrants from countries as diverse as Ireland, Poland, and the Middle Eastern nation of Yemen. When the steel jobs dried up in the 1980s, many Yemenis stayed, forming a tight-knit community of about a thousand residents. In 2003, six members of this community—known as the "Lackawanna Six"—pled guilty to supporting terrorism. Their infraction? Attending an al Qaeda training camp in Afghanistan just before the September 11, 2001, attacks.

Galab   al-Bakri   Alwan   Goba   Mosed   Taher

Faysal Galab, Mukhtar al-Bakri, Sahim A. Alwan, Yahya Goba , Shafel Mosed, and Yasein Taher, who lived just blocks from each other in Lackawanna, New York, were convicted of providing "material support" to a terrorist organization for attending an al Qaeda training camp in Afghanistan.

Many trumpeted the arrests and conviction of the "Lackawanna Six" as an important victory in the "war" against terrorism. In his 2003 State of the Union address, President George W. Bush lauded law enforcement agents for having "broken" an al Qaeda cell in Lackawanna. The danger posed by these six young men, ranging in age from twenty-three to thirty, has not been established, however. Even though each of them admitted to visiting the terrorist training camp, all had returned to Lackawanna and gone on with their lives without any signs of carrying out illegal activities. In fact, Michael A. Battle, the federal prosecutor in the case, refused to call the "Lackawanna Six" a terrorist cell. "It's a heavy burden to prove," he said, "and I wasn't prepared to do that."

AP Photo

> **The case** of the "Lackawanna Six" represents a shift in the criminal justice system brought about by the new challenge of fighting terrorism. For a growing number of law enforcement agencies, the goal is no longer to solve crimes after they have occurred, but rather to prevent them from happening in the first place. Peter Ahearn, head of the Buffalo FBI office, described the strategy as follows: "If we don't know for sure they're going to do something, or not, we need to make sure that we prevent anything they may be planning, whether or not we know or don't know about it."[1]

Though Ahearn's strategy may seem somewhat confusing, it accurately represents the brave new world of law enforcement. Because of what journalist Fareed Zakaria has called the "democratization of violence," threats to the safety of Americans are coming from an ever-expanding array of sources. Pointing out

CONCEPT BUILDER

Anonymity is necessary for criminals to perpetrate their crimes without being apprehended. Does any one type of crime depend more on anonymity? Visit www.cjinaction. com for an interactive exploration of how such anonymity affects crime policies.

that Osama bin Laden gained technical knowledge for his biological weapons program by downloading documents from the Internet, Zakaria notes, "Today, if you want to find sources for anthrax, recipes for poison, or methods to weaponize chemicals, all you need is a good [Web] search engine."[2] In this final chapter, we will explore the impact terrorism and computer crimes have had on the criminal justice system and consider how these and other developments will affect the immediate future of law enforcement.

Law Enforcement and the "War" on Terrorism

In Chapter 4, we learned that criminal law generally requires intent and action; that is, a person must have both intended to commit a crime and taken some steps toward doing so. In most cases, criminal law also requires that a harm has been done and that the criminal act caused the harm. Consequently, the criminal justice system is structured to prove that these elements exist in any particular case, and the police and the courts spend a great deal of time trying to piece together events that have already taken place.

Combating terrorism requires, in contrast, that illegal acts be stopped before they occur.[3] As the September 11, 2001, attacks dramatically showed, we cannot afford to wait for terrorists to strike and then retroactively bring them to justice. The criminal justice system must, therefore, change in a fundamental way if it is to protect Americans effectively from terrorism. Whether this change is possible or, in some instances, desirable is perhaps the most important question in law enforcement today.

PROSECUTING TERRORISM

In the introduction to this chapter, we focused on the prosecution of the "Lackawanna Six." According to court records, a man named Kamal Derwish recruited them to take part in an al Qaeda boot camp in Afghanistan. At this camp, they were trained in weapons use, learning to operate rocket-propelled grenade launchers and firearms such as Kalashnikov machine guns, .9-millimeter handguns, and M-16 rifles. They were also exposed to anti-American propaganda films and lectures. Sahim Alwan, one of the "Six," met with Osama bin Laden three times and delivered a videotape to al Qaeda operatives in Pakistan.[4]

There was no evidence, however, that any of the six men had prior knowledge of the September 11, 2001, attacks, although they did hear rumors of "martyr operations" while at the camp. Furthermore, there was no evidence that they supported such operations.[5] In the end, what crimes had they committed? What harm had they caused?

Federal Law and Terrorism   The "Lackawanna Six" were prosecuted under the **Antiterrorism and Effective Death Penalty Act of 1996 (AEDPA).** Passed by Congress in response to the 1995 truck bombing of the Alfred P. Murrah Federal Building in Oklahoma City, Oklahoma, this law makes it a crime to provide "material support or resources" to any group that the United States has designated a

Counter-Terrorism serves as a clearinghouse for information concerning law enforcement and the "war" on terrorism. Find its Web site by clicking on *Web Links* under *Chapter Resources* at www.cjinaction.com

Antiterrorism and Effective Death Penalty Act of 1996 (AEDPA)
Legislation giving federal law enforcement officers the power to arrest and prosecute any individual who provides "material support or resources" to a "terrorist organization."

Visitors walk past the reflecting pool at the Oklahoma City National Memorial. On April 19, 1995, Timothy McVeigh exploded a truck bomb outside the Alfred P. Murrah Federal Building in Oklahoma City, killing 168 people in what was at the time the largest terror attack on American soil. In response, Congress passed the Antiterrorism and Effective Death Penalty Act (AEDPA). How is the AEDPA being used to combat terrorism in the wake of the events of September 11, 2001?

"terrorist organization."[6] The AEDPA is a critical legal tool in efforts to combat terrorism, as it permits law enforcement agents to arrest suspects even though no crime, in the traditional sense of the word, has taken place and no evident harm has been caused. In the words of Attorney General John Ashcroft, the act allows the government to "prevent first, prosecute second."[7]

Early Warning Systems In a sense, the AEDPA can be seen as part of an "early warning system" that the criminal justice system is in the process of creating to prevent terrorist attacks. As might be expected, technology is playing, and will continue to play, a crucial role in these efforts. In 2003, for example, federal officials unveiled two new bioterrorism warning systems.[8] The first would improve the ability of three thousand air-quality monitoring stations, already in place across the United States, to detect deadly pathogens that might signal the beginning of a biological attack. The second uses a computerized network to gather health data from a variety of sources, including physicians' reports, emergency room visits, and sales of particular medicines. Certain patterns in these data could signal that, for example, an area's water supply has been contaminated.

These types of monitoring systems will not, of course, be able to protect Americans from a biological attack. As in other areas of the criminal justice system, the bulk of the burden of preventing criminal terrorist actions will fall on federal and local law enforcement agencies. In many instances, this will require a redefining of the basic mission of law enforcement from apprehending and incarcerating criminals to detecting and stopping terrorist activity both in the United States and in foreign countries.[9] How quickly and effectively American law enforcement can make this adjustment will, to a large extent, determine how successful it is in the "war" against terrorism.

PREVENTING TERRORISM

Before September 11, 2001, terrorism was a relatively low priority for federal law enforcement officials. On September 10, 2001, the Department of Justice proposed to cut $65 million from a counterterrorism program that provides local and state law enforcement agencies with training and equipment. That same day, the department refused to endorse a request by the FBI for $58 million to hire four hundred new employees, including agents, analysts, and translators, to combat terrorism. Indeed, within the FBI, the terrorism "beat" was seen as less glamorous than other assignments such as bank robbery and police corruption.[10] Needless to say, this is no longer the case. In 2003, the federal government spent $41 billion to fight domestic terrorism, with $2.5 billion going to the FBI and Department of Justice.[11] The FBI has increased the number of agents assigned to terrorism from 535 to nearly 3,000, moving personnel from nonterrorism investigations such as narcotics and white-collar crime in the process (see Figure 17.1).

Cultural Changes   Perhaps the most dramatic change within the FBI brought on by the new emphasis on counterterrorism is in how the agency must *think about* fighting crime. According to Richard Shelby, a Republican senator from Alabama, the FBI is moving from a "federal police agency to an intelligence agency." This shift, said Shelby, marks a "big cultural change."[12] As noted earlier, a police agency works to solve crimes that have already been committed; in contrast, an **intelligence agency** works to prevent crimes by gathering information on potential criminals and criminal acts "in the planning stage."

The need to gather intelligence was behind the formation of the FBI's National Joint Terrorism Task Force in 2002. This organization acts as a clearinghouse for information gathered by eighty-four terrorist task forces spread across the United States. FBI agents are also becoming involved in intelligence gathering that was primarily the domain of local police and fire departments prior to September 11, 2001. In the summer of 2003, for example, two Washington, D.C.–based FBI agents were sent to investigate the possibility that someone had spread gasoline around an office building with the intention of starting a fire. As it turned out, the call was a false alarm caused by gas fumes from a car in the building's parking garage. "We no longer treat anything as routine," said J. Roger Morrison, who heads the National Joint Terrorism Task Force. "There's no threat, no complaint, no bit of information that's not addressed immediately."[13]

A New Intelligence Agency?   Some experts question whether the FBI can make the transition from law enforcement agency to intelligence agency. Duncan DeVille of Harvard University's John F. Kennedy School of Government points out that the FBI is divided into two disparate branches—one that deals with traditional crimes and one that focuses on counterintelligence.[14] Agents go back and forth between the two branches, meaning that one year an agent may be working on a bank robbery and the next she or he might be working on counterterrorism intelligence gathering. DeVille, and a number of other observers, believe this system promotes inefficiency by requiring agents who may have been trained to arrest drug dealers or fight organized crime to combat terrorism, and vice versa.

Even if the FBI *can* effectively protect the nation against terrorist attacks, *should* it be doing so? A number of politicians have begun to wonder whether the agency's new focus on terrorism has caused it to neglect its other crime-fighting duties. A study by the General Accounting Office found that drug

Intelligence Agency
An agency that is primarily concerned with gathering information on potential criminals and criminal acts in order to prevent crimes from occurring.

FIGURE 17.1 The Reallocation of FBI Field Agents
Following the September 11, 2001, attacks, federal government officials promised that the FBI would focus more of its resources on counterterrorism efforts. One aspect of this strategic shift has been the reassignment of FBI agents to the terrorism "beat" during a major transformation that took place in 2002.

Source: David M. Walker, *FBI Reorganization: Progress Made in Efforts to Transform, but Major Challenges Continue* (Washington, D.C.: General Accounting Office, June 18, 2003), 2.

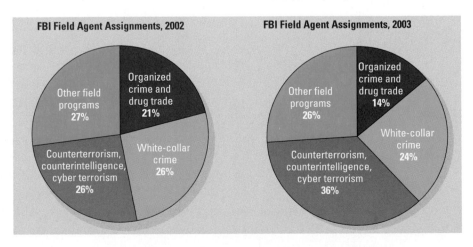

FBI Field Agent Assignments, 2002
- Organized crime and drug trade 21%
- White-collar crime 26%
- Counterterrorism, counterintelligence, cyber terrorism 26%
- Other field programs 27%

FBI Field Agent Assignments, 2003
- Organized crime and drug trade 14%
- White-collar crime 24%
- Counterterrorism, counterintelligence, cyber terrorism 36%
- Other field programs 26%

enforcement efforts by the FBI had "diminished significantly," with criminal referrals and prosecutions for federal drug crimes dropping about 15 percent between 2002 and 2003.[15] Furthermore, as we will discuss later in this section, local police officials are complaining that the FBI, by removing itself from the realm of traditional crime, has increased the burden on already short-handed local police departments.

These concerns have led DeVille and others to call for the FBI to be "split," with one segment of the agency retaining its jurisdiction over traditional crimes and the other becoming an intelligence agency based on the model of Great Britain's MI5.[16] (For a discussion of this agency, see the feature *International CJ—British Intelligence*.) In response to this need for a "terrorism-only" federal agency, the Terrorist Threat Integration Center began operations on May 1, 2003. The new center is designed to integrate all information on terrorism gathered by the FBI, Central Intelligence Agency (CIA), and U.S. Department of Homeland Security. Critics, however, worry that it will simply add another level of bureaucracy to an intelligence community already plagued by communication problems.[17]

THE ROLE OF IMMIGRATION LAW

One area in which federal law enforcement has not reduced its scope of operation as a result of the new focus on counterterrorism is immigration law. Even before September 11, 2001, federal agents and the federal courts were becoming more involved in immigration issues. The Illegal Immigration Reform and Responsibility Act of 1996 increased the range of crimes for which certain **aliens**—people living in the United States who are not U.S. citizens—could be removed from this country.[18] As a result, the number of noncitizen immigration offenders in federal prisons increased from just over 4,400 in 1996 to more than 13,100 in 2000.[19] Over the same period, as Figure 17.2 shows, the number of noncitizens deported from the United States because of criminal violations grew significantly as well.

Better Controls   Many law enforcement officials believe that U.S. immigration laws have not been sufficient to prevent domestic terrorist activity. This feeling was only exacerbated by the fact that all nineteen of the hijackers who carried out the September 11 attacks had entered the country on valid **visas,** the papers given to foreigners by the U.S. Department of State allowing them to visit the United States for a particular purpose. (At the time of the attacks, two of the hijackers were in violation of the terms of their visas and were therefore in the United States illegally.)

In an effort to better control the flow of potential terrorists into the United States, the Bush administration adopted a series of visa controls, most of which went into effect on August 1, 2003. These new regulations require face-to-face interviews for thousands of visitors from all Islamic countries

Alien

A person who is not a citizen of a given country and therefore may not enjoy the same protections as citizens of that country.

Visa

An endorsement made in a passport that allows the bearer to enter the country issuing the visa as long its conditions are followed.

FIGURE 17.2 Aliens Removed from the United States after Conviction, 1991–2002

Under U.S. immigration laws, aliens may be removed from the country after being convicted of a number of different crimes. Following passage of the Illegal Immigration Reform and Reponsibility Act of 1996, as this graph shows, federal law enforcement involvement in immigration law increased, as did the number of aliens removed because of criminal convictions.

Source: Bureau of Citizenship and Immigration Services, *2002 Statistical Yearbook* (Washington, D.C.: U.S. Department of Homeland Security, 2003), 19.

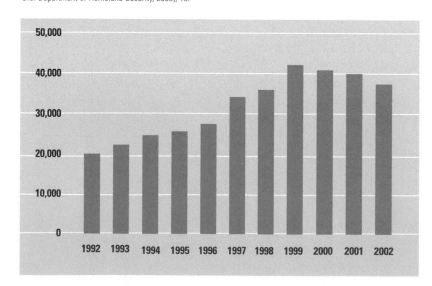

> British Intelligence

erhaps the most remarkable thing about MI5, the British domestic intelligence agency, is that for most of its history, it did not officially exist. Although the agency was formed in 1909 to protect English ports against German spies, no statute was ever passed to give it authority. In the eyes of the law, its employees were simply "ordinary citizens with no powers greater than anyone else" who happened to spend their time gathering intelligence in "defense of the Realm."

Britain was forced to draw up legislation recognizing MI5 (the MI stands for "military intelligence") in 1988, but the agency retains many of its shadowy aspects. MI5 agents have far-reaching surveillance powers to gather information about groups that may threaten Britain's security, including the ability to intercept communications, use informants and moles to infiltrate suspicious organizations, and electronically eavesdrop on a suspect's telephone calls and e-mails. Once the information is gathered, MI5 passes it on to the police. According to its Web site, MI5 cannot detain or arrest its targets, but seeks to "gain the advantage over [them] by covertly obtaining information."

In the wake of MI5's success in uncovering several terrorist plots, including one involving stores of the deadly toxin ricin in several London apartments, a number of U.S. politicians and policy observers called for an "MI5 solution" to problems in the American intelligence community. They wanted to "break down the walls" that seemed to separate the crime-fighting FBI from the intelligence-gathering CIA with a new agency modeled after MI5.

U.S. Secretary of Homeland Security Tom Ridge, who visited MI5's London headquarters, rejected the idea because of a rather large obstacle: the U.S. Constitution. MI5 agents can, for example, search any property as long as a superior agrees—there is no need to prove that any crime has been or will be committed. The ricin bust mentioned earlier was partly the result of e-mail monitoring that would have violated the Fourth Amendment to the U.S. Constitution. Furthermore, MI5's activities are not subject to judicial review, meaning that it is very difficult for citizens who may be unfairly targeted to seek help. Finally, some critics worry that a domestic spy agency modeled on MI5 would mark a return to the days when J. Edgar Hoover headed the FBI (from 1924 to 1972) and investigated citizens simply for speaking out against the government. Among Hoover's targets: civil rights leader Martin Luther King, Jr., and musician John Lennon.

FOR CRITICAL ANALYSIS
What steps could be taken to make sure that a domestic intelligence agency patterned after MI5 would not infringe on the constitutional rights of Americans?

---

and a number of non-Islamic ones, including South Korea and Brazil. An applicant's name will "trigger" a background check by the FBI if the person has been involved in one or more of two hundred scientific and technical specialties such as arms and munitions, nuclear technology, geography, and community development.[20] These background checks have caused lengthy delays in the issuance of visas, but, as one government official put it, "we do not believe that the issues at stake allow us the luxury of erring on the side of expeditious processing."[21]

Fewer Restrictions   Immigration law also helps federal law enforcement agents because it offers fewer procedural protections to noncitizens apprehended for **immigration violations** than criminal law provides for those suspected of criminal activity. Immigration violations include staying in the United States longer than the time specified on the visa, remaining in the country after the purpose for which the visa was issued has expired (for example, visitors on student visas must leave once their studies have finished), and crossing U.S. borders without obtaining a visa. Law enforcement agents do not have to meet the probable cause requirement (discussed in Chapter 7) when stopping a noncitizen for a violation of immigration law.[22] Furthermore, immigration arrestees are not guaranteed court-appointed counsel,[23] and federal law allows a person suspected of violating

Immigration Violations
Infractions of U.S. immigration laws, such as failing to comply with the terms of a visa, for which the punishment is often removal from the United States.

immigration law to be held for seven days before immigration or criminal charges are filed, and then indefinitely thereafter.[24]

These more lenient provisions allowed the federal government to hold some 750 men with Arab or Muslim backgrounds on immigration charges in its investigation of the September 11, 2001, attacks. By the fall of 2003, a handful of these suspects remained in custody; most of the others had been deported from the United States.

CHALLENGES FOR LOCAL LAW ENFORCEMENT

In general, only federal law enforcement agents have the authority to make arrests for immigration violations. In 2002, however, Florida officials completed an agreement with the U.S. Department of Justice that allows thirty-five state troopers, sheriff's deputies, and metropolitan police officers to arrest aliens who have violated the terms of their visas or entered the country illegally.[25]

For the most part, local police continue to resist the idea of using their resources to track down illegal immigrants. Twelve of the nineteen hijackers involved in the September 11, 2001, attacks had lived in Florida, however, spurring that state to adopt some of the terrorism prevention strategies now favored by federal law enforcement. Indeed, federal counterterrorism activities have had a significant "trickle-down" effect on local law enforcement, influencing both the role of local police in combating terrorism and the way they approach their traditional crime-fighting duties.

An Overwhelming Situation In the aftermath of September 11, 2001, many state and city police departments found their budgetary and personnel resources overwhelmed by the new security demands. The city of Boston found itself spending $100,000 a week on police overtime as officers responded to terrorism-related calls. Memphis city officials stationed officers at twenty-eight locations considered potential terrorist targets, including three bridges on the Mississippi River, at considerable additional cost. The human toll of fatigue and stress on individual officers caught between the need to provide counterterrorism security and fight traditional crimes has also been significant.[26]

"I think a good case could be made that this is war, and we're part of the front-line troops."
—John Timoney, Philadelphia police commissioner, commenting on the role of local police in combating terrorism (2001)

"This is it, point blank: The infrastructure cannot continue to support this substantive an increase of calls [regarding terrorism fears]," said Police Chief Theron Bowman of Arlington, Texas. "At the local level, we can't do it, and it's impacting our ability to deliver the same level of service for other noncrime-related things."[27] In Philadelphia, the number of drug-related murders increased 50 percent in the first month after September 11, 2001, a development attributed to the decision to move a number of narcotics detectives to uniformed patrols of city streets.[28]

Federal Help, or the Lack Thereof In the long run, local police departments will need the aid of federal law enforcement agencies to prepare adequately for terrorism prevention. To a certain extent, this aid has been forthcoming. FBI personnel have trained almost 30,000 state and local law enforcement officers in how to act as "first responders" to a terrorist attack involving chemical, biological, or nuclear weapons. The federal government has pledged $27 billion to local police departments for training and equipment such as biohazard suits and "terrorist-proof" communications systems.

For many, however, these efforts are insufficient. A 2003 report by the Council on Foreign Relations estimated that $125 billion in subsidies would be required for "first responders" such as local police, fire, and health officials.[29] That same year, the Homeland Security Preparedness Survey, distributed to more than 17,000 state, local, tribal, and federal law enforcement agencies by the International Association of Chiefs of Police, revealed high levels of dissatisfaction. Seventy-one percent of those responding indicated that their agency was either "somewhat" or "not at all" prepared to prevent a terrorist attack; 94 percent identified "critical incident response" training as their most urgent need.[30]

In 2003, an emergency responder, wearing protective clothing, examines several "victims" during a training exercise at a Massachusetts Bay Transit Authority train station in Cambridge, Massachusetts. The drill allowed local emergency personnel to work with the Massachusetts State Police and other law enforcement agencies in preparation for a possible bioterrorism attack.

Another area of concern for many local police officials is a lack of communication with federal agencies on terrorism-related subjects. In 2003, for example, Las Vegas police and sheriff's officials reacted angrily after the FBI failed to warn them of a potential danger—a videotape of the MGM Grand Hotel in the Nevada city had been found among other material belonging to an alleged terrorist cell in Dearborn, Michigan. Federal law enforcement officials face a dilemma when it comes to sharing "tips" on possible terrorist attacks, as most local law enforcement agents do not possess the security clearance to handle classified information. Continued efforts to better coordinate all of the nation's law enforcement agencies will be a crucial aspect of the "war" on terrorism.

ONLINE REVIEW *Go to the book's Web site for an interactive review of this section*

The Double-Edged Sword: Security versus Civil Liberties

The day after the September 11, 2001, terrorist attacks, President George W. Bush pledged that "we will not allow this enemy to win the war by changing our way of life or restricting our freedoms."[31] There is little doubt, however, that the Bush administration has adopted the crime control model in its approach to the war on terrorism. As you may recall from Chapter 1, in the crime control model the criminal justice system must be quick and efficient, with the courts operating on a "presumption of guilt," hampered as little as possible by the protection of individual rights.

In the interests of greater security, Americans appear willing to relinquish some personal freedoms: overwhelming majorities have indicated that they favor increased searches of people and their possessions at airports, office buildings, and other places.[32] At the same time, far smaller percentages are willing to accept monitoring of phone calls and Internet use,[33] and widespread criticism of the

USA Patriot Act of 2001 for infringing on civil liberties spurred Attorney General John Ashcroft to embark on a national tour to defend the law during the summer of 2003.

Judges in terrorism-related cases have also felt the pressure of conflicting demands. Magistrate Judge H. Kenneth Schroeder, Jr., who oversaw the "Lackawanna Six" case discussed in the introduction to this chapter, complained of having "some pretty restless, sleepless nights" trying to "balance the rights of the people of the community to be safe and the rights of the defendants."[34] As we have seen throughout this textbook, the need to balance the rights of society and the rights of the individual is a constant in the criminal justice system, and nowhere is this challenge more fraught with difficulty than in the "war" against terrorism.

THE USA PATRIOT ACT: RIGHTS DURING WARTIME

To a certain extent, the tension concerning civil liberties that has arisen as law enforcement agencies move to prevent terrorism is inevitable. The criminal justice system is designed to err on the side of the defendant; that is, it operates under the assumption that it is better for a guilty person to go free than for an innocent one to be convicted. Furthermore, criminal justice is a deliberative process: no matter how heinous the crime or certain the suspect's guilt, criminal law requires that certain procedures be followed.

These same rules do not apply, however, in a war, even an undeclared one such as the "war" on terrorism. The goal of a military operation is to destroy the enemy's forces, not to capture them and bring them to justice. The idea that an intelligence officer, having apprehended a terrorist suspect, should be required to read that person his or her *Miranda* rights, which include the right to remain silent and to be represented by counsel, strikes many as "ludicrous and highly counterproductive."[35] One senior military official—stationed in Afghanistan— believes the U.S. counterterrorism strategy should be as follows: "[A]s long as they want to send them here, we will kill them here. If they want to go somewhere else, we will kill them there."[36] Obviously, under the U.S. Constitution, law enforcement officials cannot take a similar view.

Military Alternatives The mixture of criminal law and military practice favored by the federal government has produced some interesting results. The U.S. Department of Justice, for example, refused to allow captured al Qaeda operatives to testify at the trial of suspected terrorist Zacarias Moussaoui for fear that national security would be compromised. The Constitution, as we learned in Chapter 10, gives defendants the right to produce witnesses whose testimony might demonstrate their innocence.

Another strategy that has caused consternation among constitutional scholars is the use of the **enemy combatant** designation by the Department of Justice. Once a suspect is given this label, he or she loses the right to a court hearing and representation by counsel. In the wake of September 11, 2001, hundreds of suspects were detained as enemy combatants, including several American citizens. According to Georgetown University law professor David Cole, this practice goes against one of the basic tenets of the criminal law: all suspects must be treated equally. "When [federal officials] feel they can win a criminal case, they'll go the

Enemy Combatant
A label given to certain persons suspected of terrorist activities by the U.S. government. Persons given this designation lose a number of rights provided by the U.S. Constitution.

criminal route," says Cole. "Where they feel they can't, where they don't have the evidence," the officials will turn to military alternatives such as enemy combatant status.[37] As Figure 17.3 shows, this can lead to inconsistency in the legal treatment of terrorist suspects.

Legislative Alternatives   The lightning rod for criticism of the Bush administration's conduct in the "war against terror" has been the USA Patriot Act. As mentioned earlier in this text, Congress passed this legislation after September 11, 2001, to provide law enforcement with the legal tools to prevent further terrorist attacks.[38] Critics of the act, such as Democratic Senator Russell Feingold of Wisconsin, believe that it has allowed terrorist-minded enemies of the United States "to win this battle without firing a shot."[39]

In the following sections, we will examine how the USA Patriot Act and several related government regulations intersect with the U.S. Constitution, particularly the Fourth, Fifth, and Sixth Amendments. We will also examine some of the justifications for these laws, as well as the complaints of those such as Senator Feingold who believe that they betray the spirit, if not the letter, of the Constitution.

THE FOURTH AMENDMENT AND MONITORING COMMUNICATIONS

The Fourth Amendment protects against unreasonable searches and seizures. According to the United States Supreme Court, the purpose of this amendment is to "prevent arbitrary and oppressive interference by enforcement officials with

FIGURE 17.3 Legal Treatment of Terrorist Suspects

As this summary shows, there is no single strategy in dealing with terrorist suspects. Two of these suspects who are American citizens are being held without access to an attorney, while two aliens have been provided with the protections of civilian courts. Many of the constitutional issues that have arisen over the treatment of terrorist suspects may be resolved in 2004 when the United States Supreme Court hears the cases of Yasser Esam Hamdi and other detainees.

	 JOHN WALKER LINDH	 YASSER ESAM HAMDI	 JOSE PADILLA	 ZACARIAS MOUSSAOUI	 RICHARD REID
Citizenship	U.S.	U.S.	U.S.	French	British
When taken into custody	November 2001	November 2001	May 2002	August 2001	December 2001
Charged with	Conspiracy to kill Americans, providing material support and resources to terrorist organization al Qaeda.	No charges filed. Held as "enemy combatant" after being captured as member of Taliban forces in Afghanistan.	No charges filed. Held as "enemy combatant" for taking part in a plot to detonate a "dirty bomb" in the United States.	Participating in an al Qaeda conspiracy, including the September 11, 2001, attacks and other planned terrorist acts in the United States.	Attempted murder and use of weapon of mass destruction for trying to detonate a bomb in his shoe on a commercial airline flight from Paris, France, to Miami, Florida.
Access to counsel?	Yes	No	No	Yes	Yes
Outcome of proceedings	Pled guilty in federal court, sentenced to twenty years in prison.	As of January 2004, still detained at U.S. Naval weapons station in Charleston, South Carolina.	As of January 2004, still detained at U.S. Naval weapons station in Charleston, South Carolina.	As of January 2004, Moussaoui's trial in federal court was ongoing.	Found guilty in federal court and sentenced to life in prison.

the privacy and personal security of individuals."[40] In practice, this has meant that a "neutral and detached" judge must, in most circumstances, decide whether a search of a suspect's person or property is warranted.[41]

The USA Patriot Act and Searches   The need for judicial approval before a search in terrorism cases came under quick criticism following the September 11, 2001, attacks. During the summer of that year, FBI agents in Minnesota had arrested Zacarias Moussaoui for immigration violations and sought a warrant to search his apartment and his laptop computer. Because FBI officials felt the agents had not established Moussaoui's involvement in terrorist activities, they did not ask a judge for a warrant until after September 11. According to a congressional report, the information on Moussaoui's computer would have helped to provide a "veritable blueprint for 9/11."[42]

In response, several sections of the USA Patriot Act make it easier for law enforcement agents to conduct searches. Previously, for example, if American intelligence agents wanted to monitor communications (telephones, e-mail, voice mail) to gather "foreign intelligence," they needed a court order based on probable cause that a crime had taken place or was about to take place. The USA Patriot Act amends the law to allow the FBI to obtain warrants for "terrorism" investigations, "chemical weapons" investigations, or "computer fraud and abuse" investigations as long as agents can prove that such actions have a "significant purpose."[43] In other words, no proof of criminal activity need be provided.

The USA Patriot Act and Surveillance   The USA Patriot Act also provides federal agents with "roving surveillance authority," allowing them to continue monitoring a terrorist suspect on the strength of an original warrant even if the suspect moves into another jurisdiction.[44] Previously, agents were required to obtain a new warrant from a judge in the new jurisdiction. Furthermore, the legislation makes it much easier for law enforcement agents to avoid the notification requirements of search warrants, meaning that a person whose home has been the target of a search and whose voice mails or computer records have been seized may not be informed of these activities until weeks after they have taken place.[45]

Experts worry that the USA Patriot Act makes it too "easy" for law enforcement agents and prosecutors to gather evidence. They warn that police may abuse the act by claiming that they need a warrant to gather foreign intelligence when, in fact, the goal of the investigation is nonterrorist criminal activity. Finally, because these warrants are obtained from special intelligence courts, they cannot be challenged—a crucial aspect of the adversarial process.[46]

THE FIFTH AMENDMENT AND INDEFINITE DETENTION

The Fifth Amendment holds that no person shall be deprived of life, liberty, or property, without due process of law. As we discussed in Chapter 4, to a large extent criminal law is designed to ensure that those charged with a crime are guaranteed due process. The question of how the due process clause applies to noncitizens or enemy combatants has not, however, been resolved. The USA Patriot Act requires the U.S. attorney general to take into custody any alien that he has "reasonable grounds" to believe has engaged in activity that "endangers the national security of the United States." If the alien is charged with a criminal

"As terrible as 9/11 was, it didn't repeal the Constitution."
—Rosemary S. Pooler, U.S. circuit judge (2003)

offense, the government can hold him or her for seven days without filing charges. If the alien is in custody for an immigration violation, the Constitution does not apply, and that person can be held indefinitely.[47]

The U.S. government has come under a great deal of international criticism for its policy regarding its detention center at the U.S. Naval Base in Guantánamo Bay, Cuba. The prison camp there has been used to detain more than six hundred prisoners captured during the American-led invasion of Afghanistan in 2001. Most of the detainees are either members of al Qaeda or fought for the Taliban. Because these detainees were captured during a military campaign and are not American citizens, the Fifth Amendment does not apply to their incarceration. (Indeed, one prisoner who was discovered to have been born in the United States was transferred to a Navy prison in Norfolk, Virginia.)

Many experts believe, however, that under international law they should be considered "prisoners of war" and accorded a number of rights under agreements signed by the United States—including the right to either a timely trial for war crimes or release.[48] The U.S. government has, instead, labeled them "unlawful combatants" and insisted that they may be held until the end of hostilities. Given the vague nature of "hostilities" under present circumstances, critics point out that those held at Guantánamo Bay could be detained without being charged and without access to legal representation for years.[49]

Detainees in orange jumpsuits sit in a holding area at the U.S. Naval Base located in Guantánamo Bay, Cuba. The base is serving as a holding facility for hundreds of suspected al Qaeda and Taliban operatives captured during U.S. military operations in Afghanistan. The U.S. government considers the detainees to be "unlawful combatants" and has denied them legal representation and the right to trial. Under what amendment(s) are such rights guaranteed to American citizens? Do you think non-American citizens who are in the custody of the U.S. military should be protected by our Constitution? Why or why not?

THE SIXTH AMENDMENT AND TRIAL RIGHTS

As you will recall from Chapter 10, the Sixth Amendment guarantees the right to the assistance of counsel. Antiterrorism regulations appear to restrict this right, in the minds of some, by inhibiting both the privacy that is assured in the attorney-client relationship and the ability to obtain the aid of a lawyer in the first place.

Limiting Counsel The United States Supreme Court has consistently held that the attorney-client privilege (see Chapter 9) is protected by the Constitution, even after the client's death.[50] In 2001, the U.S. Department of Justice imposed a new requirement on federal correctional facilities: all conversations between prisoners and their attorneys would be subject to monitoring if there is "reasonable suspicion" that the communication would be used to "further or facilitate" terrorist activities.[51] Like the provisions of the USA Patriot Act discussed above, this regulation does away with procedural safeguards that were designed to protect the due process rights of a suspect or prisoner; previously, a judge could allow such monitoring only after the government presented probable cause that criminal activity was occurring. Critics of the regulation also point out that there is no judicial review of the decision to monitor these communications, essentially giving the government free rein to infringe on an important right.[52]

Of course, one must have an attorney before the privilege can go into effect. Most of the aliens and enemy combatants detained during the investigation of the September 11 attacks had difficulty obtaining counsel, and in some instances, they were denied access to their attorneys. Albador Al-Hazmi, for example, a physician from San Antonio, Texas, was refused the opportunity to speak to his lawyer for several weeks after being taken into custody by federal agents in September 2001. Again, attorneys for the U.S. government denied that such treatment was illegal, as the suspects were either held for immigration violations or had been designated enemy combatants and, therefore, were not under the protection of the Constitution.

Military Tribunals Perhaps the most controversial step taken by the Bush administration was a presidential order stating that suspected terrorists would be tried in tribunals operated by the U.S. military, and not by civilian courts (described in Chapter 8).[53] In these military proceedings, there is no right to a trial by jury, as guaranteed by the Sixth Amendment. Instead, a panel of military officers acts in the place of a judge and jury and decides questions of "both fact and law." The traditional rules of evidence (see Chapter 10) do not apply; instead, any evidence is admissible if, in the opinion of the tribunal, it would help a reasonable person decide the issue at hand. Furthermore, only two-thirds of the panel must agree to convict, in contrast to the unanimous jury required in criminal trials.[54] (See Figure 17.4 for a list of the differences between military tribunals and regular criminal courts.)

Proponents of military tribunals raise a number of concerns with trying accused terrorists in civilian courts. Primarily, they believe that it would be difficult to protect classified information in an "open" court. They also worry that an accused terrorist might escape conviction on a "technicality" in a regular criminal court.[55] Of course, for critics of these measures, the lack of constitutional protections for the defendant is precisely the problem with military tribunals, as well as with many of the other legal weapons the federal government has given itself to combat terrorism.

THE ROLE OF THE COURTS

Federal law enforcement officials justify the USA Patriot Act, military tribunals, and other recent antiterror directives by pointing out that a congressional resolution passed on September 18, 2001, authorizes the president to use "all necessary and appropriate force" to fight terrorism.[56] Furthermore, according to FBI Director Robert S. Mueller III, these initiatives have helped federal law enforcement agents foil more than one hundred terrorist plots, both in the United States and abroad.[57] Critics contend, however, that the government has gone "too far." More than 150 communities across the nation have passed resolutions opposing the USA Patriot Act—in Amherst, Massachusetts, for example, town employees are prohibited from cooperating with any "investigations, interrogations, or arrest procedures" that are judged to violate civil rights or liberties.

As we have seen throughout this textbook, the court system is usually the final arbiter when it comes to balancing rights in the criminal justice system. To a certain extent, this has been the case with counterterrorism measures. Some courts have decided to "assume a deferential position" to governmental authority in a time of armed conflict, as the Fourth Circuit Court of Appeals did when it upheld a federal order denying enemy combatants the right to a lawyer.[58] Other courts have been less submissive. In 2002, a federal judge in New York held that enemy combatant Jose Padilla, accused of plotting to detonate a radioactive bomb in the United States, had a right to meet with his lawyer and offer evidence in his defense.[59] (See the feature *You Be the Judge— Does the U.S. Constitution Apply to "Terrorist Organizations"?* on the next page.)

	FEDERAL COURT	MILITARY TRIBUNAL
Right to Counsel	Defendant chooses an attorney, or, if the defendant cannot afford to pay for his or her defense, the government will provide counsel at no cost.	A military attorney is provided. Defendants can replace this attorney with a different military attorney of their own choosing or pay for a civilian attorney.
Standard of Proof	Guilt beyond a reasonable doubt.	Guilt beyond a reasonable doubt.
Vote Required for Verdict	Unanimous to convict and impose penalty.	Two-thirds vote required to convict. Decision to impose death penalty must be unanimous.
Composition of Jury	Twelve civilians.	Three to seven military officers. Seven members are required for death penalty cases.
Rules of Evidence	Federal rules of evidence, including limits on hearsay. (See Chapter 10.)	Evidence is admissible if it would "have probative value to a reasonable person."
Appeals	U.S. Court of Appeals and then the U.S. Supreme Court.	Review panel appointed by the Secretary of Defense. Panel members could be military officers or civilians temporarily appointed as officers.

FIGURE 17.4 Rules Comparison: Federal Criminal Courts and Military Tribunals

In 2002, the Bush administration announced the procedural rules for military tribunals. These special courts will primarily be used to try terrorist suspects captured during military maneuvers in Afghanistan and Iraq. These tribunals do not provide the same safeguards for defendants as do civilian courts, although the standard of proof for conviction is the same.

For more than two years after September 11, 2001, the United States Supreme Court declined to involve itself in the debate over the balance between individual liberties and national security. In November 2003, however, the Court agreed to hear a jurisdictional issue: should the U.S. government or civilian courts decide whether a person is being legally detained at the U.S. Naval Base in Guantánamo Bay? Early in 2004, the Court also agreed to hear an appeal of the Fourth Circuit decision mentioned above, but how actively it would intervene on behalf of individual rights was unclear. Indeed, in 1998 Chief Justice William Rehnquist published a book in which he forcefully argued that in wartime the balance between order and freedom should tip toward order.[60]

⬆ ONLINE REVIEW *Go to the book's Web site for an interactive review of this section*

Cyber Crime

In the days after the September 11, 2001, attacks, federal investigators had a difficult time determining the identities of the individuals who had hijacked the commercial airplanes. As it turned out, the hijackers had covered their tracks by stealing the identities of random individuals off the Internet and opening credit and bank accounts under the new names. There are other links between terrorism and the World Wide Web. A number of terrorist organizations operate Web sites to proselytize and raise funds. The FBI has publicly expressed concerns that information available on the Internet about energy infrastructures, water systems, uranium storage systems, and nuclear facilities might be used to the advantage of terrorist plotters. Federal law enforcement officials have found evidence that al Qaeda planned to breach computer programs operated by the U.S. military and commercial banking network, and both government and private officials acknowledge the threat of cyber terrorism.[61]

CRIME AND THE INTERNET

Cyber terrorism is, without question, a top concern for law enforcement. Most illegal activity on the Internet, however, is done not for ideological reasons but for economic ones. We will now examine the growing world of **computer crime,** which can be defined as any act that is directed against computers and computer parts, that uses computers as instruments of crime, or that involves computers and constitutes some form of abuse.[62] A number of white-collar crimes, discussed in Chapter 1, such as fraud, embezzlement, and the theft of intellectual property, are now committed with the aid of computers and are thus considered computer crimes. As we discuss this illegal activity, we will be using the term **cyber crime,** which covers any criminal activity occurring in the virtual community of the Internet.

Computer Crime
Any wrongful act that is directed against computers and computer parts or that involves wrongful use or abuse of computers or software.

Cyber Crime
A crime that occurs online, in the virtual community of the Internet, as opposed to the physical world.

It is very difficult, if not impossible, to tell how much cyber crime actually takes place. Often, people will never know that they have been the victims of a cyber crime. Furthermore, businesses sometimes do not report such crimes for fear of losing customer confidence. Nonetheless, reliable information on specific areas of cyber crime can be obtained from agencies such as the Internet Security Alliance, the National Institute for Standards and Technology, and the National Infrastructure Protection Center. We will rely on these sources for a great deal of the information in this section.

National Security Adviser Condoleezza Rice delivers the keynote speech at the Internet Policy Forum in Washington, D.C. Speakers at the forum discussed the security threats to the American people and the nation's economy posed by Internet "hackers" and other cyber criminals.

CYBER CRIMES AGAINST PERSONS AND PROPERTY

Most cyber crimes are not "new" crimes. Rather, they are existing crimes in which the Internet is the instrument of wrongdoing. When, for example, Michael Ian Campbell sent an e-mail to a Columbine High School student threatening to "finish what [had] begun," he was charged with making a threat across state lines.[63] The charge would have been the same if he had sent the message via regular mail. The challenge for law enforcement is to apply traditional laws, which were designed to protect persons from physical harm or to safeguard their physical property, to crimes committed in cyberspace. Here, we look at several types of activity that constitute "updated" crimes against persons and property—online consumer fraud, cyber theft, and cyber-stalking.

Cyber Consumer Fraud   The expanding world of e-commerce (buying and selling that takes place in cyberspace) has created many benefits for consumers. It has also led to some challenging problems, including fraud conducted via the Internet. In general, fraud is any misrepresentation knowingly made with the intention of deceiving another and on which a reasonable person would and does rely to her or his detriment. **Cyber fraud,** then, is fraud committed over the Internet. Scams that were once conducted solely by mail or phone can now be found online, and new technology has led to increasingly more creative ways to commit fraud. In 2003, for example, a California couple was indicted for operating a fraudulent online dating scheme in which they posed as Russian or Ukrainian women. Over three years, the pair stole $600,000 from nearly four hundred male victims.

No one knows the full extent of cyber fraud. Indications are that the practice is increasing with the growing use of the Internet. In 2000, the FBI and the National White Collar Crime Center formed the Internet Fraud Complaint Center (IFCC). In its first six months of operation, the IFCC received nearly 20,000 complaints and referred more than a quarter of them to law enforcement agencies for possible investigation.[64] In 2002, the IFCC received nearly 50,000 complaints of fraud. The complaints involved total losses of $54 million, triple the amount of only a year earlier.[65]

Cyber Fraud
Any misrepresentation knowingly made over the Internet with the intention of deceiving another and on which a reasonable person would and does rely to his or her detriment.

INFOTRAC KEYWORDS
cyber theft, computer crime
For more information, use these search terms with InfoTrac College Edition, your online library at www.infotrac-college.com

Online Auction Fraud   As you can see from Figure 17.5 on page 588, online auction fraud is the most widely reported form of consumer fraud on the Internet. In its most basic form, online auction fraud is a simple process. A person puts up an expensive item for auction, on either a legitimate or a fake auction site, and then

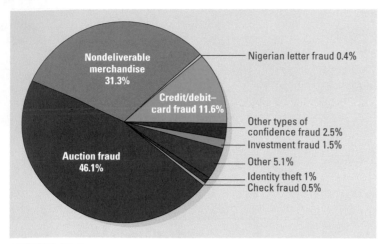

FIGURE 17.5
Fraudulent Activities Online

In 2001, the Internet Fraud Complaint Center referred 49,711 complaints to law enforcement agencies. As the graph shows, the largest number of these referrals concerned auction fraud.

Source: Internet Fraud Complaint Center, *Internet Fraud Report, January 1, 2002–December 31, 2002* (Washington, D.C.: Federal Bureau of Investigation and National White Collar Crime Center, 2003), 6.

Identity Theft

The theft of identity information, such as name, driver's license number, or Social Security number. The information is then usually used to access the victim's financial resources.

INFOTRAC KEYWORDS

identity theft

For more information, use this search term with InfoTrac College Edition, your online library at www.infotrac-college.com

refuses to send the product after receiving payment. Or, as a variation, the wrongdoer may provide the purchaser with an item that is worth less than the one offered in the auction.

Online Retail Fraud Somewhat similar to online auction fraud is online retail fraud, in which consumers pay directly (without bidding) for items that are never delivered. Because most online consumers will purchase items only from reputable, brand-name sites, criminals have had to take advantage of some of the complexities of cyberspace to lure unknowing customers.

Again, though determining the actual extent of online sales fraud is difficult, the anecdotal evidence suggests it is a substantial problem. In 2001, the FBI arrested a fraud ring of more than sixty persons believed to have cheated more than 56,000 consumers out of nearly $120 million. The fraud included charging entry fees to nonexistent online "shopping malls" and bogus investment schemes. Perhaps the most widespread and long-running Internet fraud is the "Nigerian letter fraud scam." In this scheme, targets are sent e-mails promising them a percentage if they will send money to help fictitious officials from the African country transfer millions of nonexistent dollars to Western banks. In 2002, victims in the United States paid $25 million to these criminals.[66]

Cyber Theft In cyberspace, thieves are not subject to the physical limitations of the "real" world. A thief can steal data stored in a networked computer with network access from anywhere on the globe. Only the speed of the connection and the thief's computer equipment limit the quantity of data that can be stolen. This freedom has led to a marked increase in **identity theft,** which occurs when the wrongdoer steals a form of identification—such as a name, date of birth, or Social Security number—and uses the information to access the victim's financial resources. This crime existed to a certain extent before widespread use of the Internet. Thieves would "steal" calling-card numbers by watching people using public telephones, or they would rifle through garbage to find bank account or credit-card numbers. The identity thief would then use the calling-card or credit-card number or withdraw funds from the victim's account until the theft was discovered.

The Internet has, however, turned identity theft into perhaps the fastest-growing financial crime in the United States. Primarily, it provides those who steal information offline with an easy medium for using items such as stolen credit-card numbers or e-mail addresses while protected by anonymity. Also, frequent Web surfers may be providing a wealth of information about themselves without knowing it. Many Web sites use "cookies" to collect data on those who visit their sites. The data can include the areas of the site the user visits and the links the user clicks on. Furthermore, Web browsers often store information such as the consumer's name and e-mail address. Finally, every time a purchase is made online, the item is linked to the purchaser's name, allowing Web retailers to amass a database of who is buying what.

As more consumers are discovering, information that can be collected can be stolen. A study released by the Federal Trade Commission reported that nearly 10 million people were the victims of identity theft in 2002. The cost was estimated at $5 billion to consumers and $48 billion to businesses and financial institutions such as banks, to say nothing of the nearly 300 million hours that Americans spent resolving the problems caused by identity theft.[67]

Cyber-Stalking   California passed the first stalking law in 1990, in response to the murders of six women by men who had harassed them. The law made it a crime to harass or follow a person while making a "credible threat" that puts the person in reasonable fear for her or his safety or the safety of the person's immediate family. Today, forty-five states have passed laws that criminalize **cyber-stalking**, which involves stalkers who find their victims through Internet chat rooms, Usenet groups and other bulletin boards, and e-mail. Some of the legislation requires a direct threat for prosecution, but Arizona's statute requires only that a victim be "seriously alarmed" or "annoyed."[68]

CYBER CRIMES IN THE BUSINESS WORLD

Just as cyberspace can be a dangerous place for consumers, it presents a number of hazards for businesses that wish to offer their services on the Internet. The same circumstances that enable companies to reach a wide number of consumers also leave them susceptible to cyber crime. The improper use of stolen credit cards online, for example, could cost businesses around the world more than $15 billion a year.[69] In 2000, an unknown person copied the credit-card numbers of more than 300,000 customers of CD Universe, an online music store. The thief then threatened to post the numbers on an open site unless the company paid $100,000. When CD Universe refused to cooperate with this extortion attempt, some of its customers' credit-card numbers did in fact turn up on a Web site that could be accessed by any Web surfer.

Hackers   The person who "broke into" CD Universe's database to steal the credit-card numbers is known as a hacker. A **hacker** is someone who uses one computer to break into another. Hackers who break into computers without authorization often commit cyber theft. In most cases, however, a hacker's principal aim is to prove how smart she or he is by gaining access to others' password-protected computers and causing data errors. Minnesota teen-ager Jeffrey Lee Parson, for example, was arrested for his role in spreading the "Blaster" worm through the Internet. A **worm** is a software program that is capable of reproducing itself as it spreads from one computer to the next. Blaster made its way through more than 500,000 computers. It appears that Parson did not have any concept of the damage that his worm would cause. "He was freaking out," said a friend. "I think he was surprised it got to the level it got to."[70]

The Scope of the Problem   At the same time the Blaster worm was winding its way through the World Wide Web, a virus called "SoBig" was declared the fastest harmful computer program ever. Like a worm, a **virus** reproduces itself, but unlike a worm, it must be attached to an "infected" host file to travel from one computer network to another. About a million copies of the SoBig virus were spotted within the first twenty-four hours of its existence.

Cyber-Stalking
The crime of stalking, committed in cyberspace. Generally, stalking consists of harassing a person and putting that person in reasonable fear for his or her safety or the safety of the person's immediate family.

Hacker
A person who uses one computer to break into another.

Worm
A computer program that can automatically replicate itself over a network such as the Internet and interfere with the normal use of a computer. A worm does not need to be attached to an existing file to move from one network to another.

Virus
A computer program that can replicate itself over a network such as the Internet and interfere with the normal use of a computer. A virus cannot exist as a separate entity and must attach itself to another program to move through a network.

Abraham Abdallah, a busboy in Brooklyn, New York, was arrested in 2001 after allegedly perpetrating the largest identity theft in the history of the Internet. Using a public library computer and a Web-enabled mobile phone, Abdallah accessed the private bank accounts of some of the wealthiest people in the United States. Taking advantage of information published in *Forbes* magazine, Abdallah was able to obtain some of his targets' Social Security numbers and gain access to their brokerage accounts. What are some other methods used to "steal" a person's identity?

Though the hackers and other "techies" who create worms and viruses are often romanticized as youthful rebels, they cause significant damage. A destructive program such as the SoBig virus often overloads a company's computer system, making e-mail and many other functions impossible until it is "cleaned out of the system." This cleansing process can cost between $100,000 and $5 million a day, depending on the size of the company affected. It is estimated that Blaster, SoBig, and other harmful programs caused $3.5 billion in damage to North American businesses in August 2003—the worst month on record.[71]

The Computer Crime and Security Survey polled 530 companies and large government institutions and found that 90 percent had suffered security breaches through computer-based means in 2002. Eighty percent suffered losses because of the breaches, costing more than $200 million to correct.[72] The number of hacking incidents reported to Carnegie Mellon University's CERT Coordination Center reached 82,094 that same year, up from 9,859 in 1999.[73] The actual amount of hacking is probably much larger; the FBI estimates that only 25 percent of all corporations that suffer security breaches report the incidents to a law enforcement agency.[74]

Juvenile Cyber Crime   Several years ago, a series of "hack attacks" were launched at some of the largest Internet companies, including Amazon.com and eBay. The sites either froze or significantly slowed down, causing nearly $2 billion in damages for the parent companies. While the FBI was searching for the hacker, one of its investigation chiefs joked that the companies' computer systems were so vulnerable that any fifteen-year-old with technological know-how could break into them.

As it turned out, the FBI agent was only a year off. The culprit was a sixteen-year-old Canadian high school dropout who was working as a kitchen worker in Montreal when he was arrested. The teen-ager, who went by the moniker of Mafiaboy, had uploaded software programs on Web sites in Europe and South Korea, from which he bombarded the American companies with e-mails. (To see how easy it is to wreak havoc on the Internet, see the feature *CJ and Technology—Scriptkiddies and the "Do-It-Yourself" Web Attack*.)

According to Assistant U.S. Attorney Joseph V. DeMarco, it should come as no surprise that Mafiaboy could cause so much damage. DeMarco believes that there are three main reasons why cyber crime is clearly suited to the habits and limitations of juveniles:

> *The enormous technological capacities of personal computers.* Most juvenile delinquents will never commit crimes more serious than shoplifting and other forms of petty theft. Advanced computer equipment and software, however, give these youth the ability to carry out complex criminal fraud and hacking schemes without leaving their bedrooms. Thus, computer technology has given juveniles the ability to "commit offenses that are disproportionate to their age." In addition, nearly 76 percent of all children have access to the Internet, either at home, at school, or through a library.[75]

> *The anonymity of the Internet.* The physical world denies juveniles the ability to commit many crimes. It would be very difficult, for example, for a fifteen-year-old to run a fraudulent auction in the flesh. The Internet, however, allows young people to depict themselves as adults, thereby opening up a

"There is a segment in society that views the unleashing of computer viruses as a challenge, a game. Far from it; it is a serious crime."

—Robert J. Cleary, lead prosecutor for the U.S. Attorney's office, New Jersey (1997)

> Scriptkiddies and the "Do-It-Yourself" Web Attack

After the mayor of Sneek in the northern Netherlands discovered that one of his constituents—a twenty-year-old who goes by the Web name OnTheFly—was responsible for the "Anna Kournikova" e-mail worm (which flooded the Internet in 2001), he promptly offered the young man a job with the city's information technology department. "It is obvious," the mayor said, "that [he] is very capable."

Experienced hackers scoffed at the mayor's comments. "A five-year-old can do what he did," said one. In fact, OnTheFly is known in the world of cyberspace as a "scriptkiddy," or someone who creates a virus by following directions from a "kit" taken from the Internet. The kit that OnTheFly used to create "Kournikova" was the VBS Worm Generator. This particular kit has been downloaded at least 15,000 times.

One observer compared creating a virus or worm from a kit to making brownies from a mix, "only easier." In essence, the scriptkiddy need only fill in the answers to a series of questions, such as the desired date for the virus to be released, the subject line of the e-mail message, and so forth. The program even has a box that can be checked next to "erase hard disk." All the person needs to do is check that box, and if an e-mail recipient opens the attachment, his or her hard drive will be erased. "To do this stuff is utterly trivial," said Peter G. Neumann, a scientist at a technological consulting firm. "Every other kid can do it."

In the Future

About 50,000 viruses are floating through the Internet, with hundreds more being created every day. Only a minuscule proportion of those—perhaps 0.03 percent—will ever do any damage, so the threat posed by scriptkiddies is relatively small. Experts are concerned, however, that someone may create a "supervirus," which would have the ability to attack certain components of a computer and spawn variations of itself to avoid detection and destruction. "[E]very year the situation gets worse," says one observer. "The Internet is just too complex to secure."

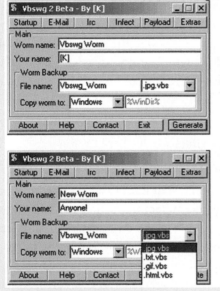

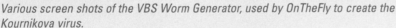

Various screen shots of the VBS Worm Generator, used by OnTheFly to create the Kournikova virus.

For more information on harmful computer programs and other CJ technologies, click on Crime and Technology *under* Book Resources *at* www.cjinaction.com

number of criminal possibilities that would otherwise be denied. Furthermore, the lack of a driver's license or the wealth necessary to travel does not limit a juvenile cyber delinquent's ability to commit far-reaching offenses, as we saw in the case of Mafiaboy.

> *The acceptance of hacking in youth culture.* A recent poll of nearly 50,000 elementary and middle school students conducted by Scholastic, Inc., found that nearly half of them did not consider hacking to be a crime.[76] Thus, DeMarco believes, there is an ethical "deficit" when it comes to youth and computer crimes: juveniles who would never consider robbery or burglary are not troubled by the prospect of committing cyber crimes.[77]

Intellectual Property
Property resulting from intellectual, creative processes.

Pirating Intellectual Property Online   Most people think of wealth in terms of houses, land, cars, stocks, and bonds. Wealth, however, also includes **intellectual property,** which consists of the products that result from intellectual, creative processes. The government provides various forms of protection for intellectual property such as copyrights and patents. These protections ensure that a person who writes a book or a song or creates a software program is financially rewarded if that product is sold in the marketplace.

Intellectual property such as books, films, music, and software is vulnerable to "piracy"—the unauthorized copying and use of the property. In the past, copying intellectual products was time consuming, and the quality of the pirated copies was clearly inferior. In today's online world, however, things have changed. Simply clicking a mouse can now reproduce millions of unauthorized copies, and pirated duplicates of copyrighted works obtained via the Internet are often exactly the same as the original, or close to it.

The Business Software Alliance estimates that 39 percent of all business software is pirated, costing software makers more than $12 billion in 2002.[78] The International Federation of the Phonographic Industry believes that 40 percent of recorded music is pirated.[79] In the United States, pirates can be prosecuted under the No Electronic Theft Act[80] and the Digital Millennium Copyright Act.[81] Global efforts are also under way to protect intellectual property. Private companies can also take advantage of civil law: in 2003, the Recording Industry Association of America sued 261 individuals who had downloaded music off the Internet for copyright infringement, with the promise of "thousands" more lawsuits if necessary to curtail the practice.

INFOTRAC KEYWORDS

online pornography, cyber crime

For more information, use these search terms with InfoTrac College Edition, your online library at www.infotrac-college.com

CYBER CRIMES AGAINST THE COMMUNITY

One of the greatest challenges cyberspace presents for law enforcement is how to enforce laws governing activities that are prohibited under certain circumstances but are not always illegal. Such laws generally reflect the will of the community, which recognizes behavior as acceptable under some circumstances and unacceptable under others. Thus, while it is legal in many areas to sell a pornographic video to a fifty-year-old, it is never legal to sell the same item to a fifteen-year-old. Similarly, placing a bet on a football game with a bookmaker in Las Vegas, Nevada, is legal, but placing a bet on a football game with a bookmaker in Cleveland, Ohio, is not. Of course, in cyberspace it is often impossible to know whether the customer buying porn is fifty or fifteen, or if the person placing the bet is from Las Vegas or Cleveland.

Consequently, the Internet has been a boon to both the pornography and the gambling industries. According to estimates, nearly 100,000 pornographic Web sites based in the United States generate about $1 billion in annual revenues.[82] Though no general figures are available, the Internet has undoubtedly also been a boon to those who produce and sell material depicting sexually explicit conduct involving a child—child pornography. Because it is so difficult to track Web-based child pornographers, courts and lawmakers have had a difficult time controlling the dissemination of this material via the Internet. We will explore these efforts in the chapter-ending *Criminal Justice in Action* feature.

The amount of money wagered online nearly doubled in a recent two-year period, increasing from $2.2 billion in 2000 to $4.1 billion in 2002.[83] In some states, certain forms of gambling, such as casino gambling or betting on horse and dog racing, are legal. This presents a jurisdictional quandary: can citizens in a state that does not allow gambling place online bets to a Web site located in a state that does? After all, states have no constitutional authority over activities that take place in other states. Complicating the problem is the fact that many Internet sites are located outside the United States in countries where Internet gambling is legal, and no state government has jurisdiction over activities that take place in other countries.

AP Photo/Jack Dempsey

Officials at World Wide Web Casinos headquarters in Antigua demonstrate some of their activities. Technology allows Internet users from all over the world to gamble online through companies such as World Wide Web Casinos outside the United States. World Wide Web Casinos has claimed that using its service "cannot be illegal because, despite their origination, bets will technically be placed on the computer at our off-shore land-based casino site that is legally licensed and taxed by the host government." Is this statement correct?

FIGHTING CYBER CRIME

Why not just pass a law that makes gambling in cyberspace illegal? In fact, five states—Illinois, Louisiana, Nevada, Oregon, and South Dakota—have specifically banned Internet gambling, and Congress is considering a similar step. Simply passing a law, however, does not guarantee that the law will be effectively enforced. With hundreds of millions of users reaching every corner of the globe, transferring unimaginable amounts of information almost instantaneously, the Internet has proved resistant to regulation. In the past, the U.S. government has generally adopted a "hands-off" attitude toward the Internet to promote the free flow of ideas and encourage the growth of electronic commerce. The terrorist attacks of September 11, 2001, seem to have changed this attitude. President Bush's efforts to increase homeland security included $722 million in funds to strengthen the nation's information security systems, a task in which law enforcement will play a crucial role.[84]

Jurisdictional Challenges Regardless of what type of cyber crime is being investigated, law enforcement agencies are often frustrated by problems of jurisdiction (noted briefly in the discussion of cyber gambling and explained more fully in Chapter 8). Jurisdiction is primarily based on physical geography—each country, state, and nation has jurisdiction, or authority, over crimes that occur within its boundaries. The Internet, however, destroys these traditional notions because geographic boundaries simply do not exist in cyberspace.[85]

To see how this can affect law enforcement efforts, let's consider a hypothetical cyber-stalking case. Phil, who lives in State A, has been sending e-mails containing graphic sexual threats to Stephanie, who lives in State B. Where has the crime taken place? Which police department has authority to arrest Phil, and which court system has authority to try him? To further complicate matters, what if State A has not yet added cyber-stalking to its criminal code, while State B has? Does that mean that Phil has not committed a crime in his home state, but has committed one in Stephanie's?

Federal Law Enforcement and Cyber Crime   Of course, federal law enforcement agencies have jurisdiction over all federal crimes, no matter in which state they may take place. Because of this freedom from jurisdictional restraints, the federal government has traditionally taken the lead in law enforcement efforts against cyber crime. This is not to say that little cyber crime prevention occurs on the local level. Most major metropolitan police departments have created special units to fight cyber crime. In general, however, only a handful of local police and sheriffs' departments have the resources to support a squad of cyber investigators.[86] (See the feature *Careers in CJ*.)

The Federal Bureau of Investigation   As the primary crime-fighting unit of the federal government, the FBI has taken the lead in law enforcement efforts against cyber crime. The FBI has the primary responsibility for enforcing all federal criminal statutes involving computer crimes. (See Figure 17.6 for a run-down of these laws.) In 1998, the Bureau oversaw the creation of the National Infrastructure Protection Center (NIPC), a Washington, D.C.–based agency charged with detecting and investigating cyber threats concerning the country's "critical infrastructures," such as transportation, energy, telecommunications, and financial networks.[87] Three years later, the FBI and the NIPC cosponsored Infragard, an organization that hopes to increase information sharing between law enforcement and private companies in order to combat cyber crime.

In 2000, responding to local police departments' inability to attend to problems of fraud, the FBI, along with the National White Collar Crime Center, launched the Internet Fraud Complaint Center (IFCC), discussed earlier in the chapter. The IFCC acts as a clearinghouse for accounts of Internet fraud reported by businesses and individuals at the agency's Web site (http://www.IFCCFBI.gov). The FBI also offers instruction in cyber crime prevention for local and state police officers at its training center in Quantico, Virginia.

FIGURE 17.6   Federal Laws and Computer Crime

18 U.S.C. Section 1030—It is a crime to do any of the following to and/or by means of a computer used by a financial institution, used by the federal government, or used in interstate or foreign commerce or communication:

1. gain unauthorized entry into a government computer and thereby discover information which is intended to remain confidential, information which the perpetrator either unlawfully discloses to someone not authorized to receive it or retains in violation of the law;
2. gain unauthorized entry to a computer and thereby gain access to information to which the perpetrator is not entitled to have access;
3. gain unauthorized access to a computer and thereby further the perpetration of a fraud;
4. cause damage to a computer as the result either of gaining unauthorized access to it or of inserting a program, code or information into the computer;
5. transmit, in interstate or foreign commerce, a threat to cause damage to a computer in order to extort money or property from a person or other legal entity.
6. traffic, with intent to defraud, in passwords which either permit unauthorized access to a government computer or affect interstate or foreign commerce; or

7. transmit in interstate or foreign commerce any threat to cause damage to a protected computer with intent to extort something of value.

18 U.S.C. Section 1462—It is a crime to use a computer to import obscene material into the United States.

18 U.S.C. Section 1463—It is a crime to transport obscene material in interstate or foreign commerce.

18 U.S.C. Section 2251—It is a crime to employ a minor or induce a minor to participate in making a visual depiction of a sexually explicit act if the depiction was created using materials that had been transported (including the transportation by computer) in interstate or foreign commerce.

18 U.S.C. Section 2252—It is a crime to transport child pornography in interstate or foreign commerce.

18 U.S.C. Section 1028—It is a crime to produce, transfer, or possess a device, including a computer, that is intended to be used to falsify identification documents.

Many traditional crimes encompass the use of a computer as well; for example, threatening the president's life or infringing a copyright.

Sources: Susan W. Brenner, "State Cybercrime Legislation in the United States of America: A Survey," *Richmond Journal of Law and Technology* 7 (Winter 2001), 1–5; and Heather Jacobson and Rebecca Green, "Computer Crimes," *American Criminal Law Review* (Spring 2002), 280–284.

> David Hendron Investigator High Technology Crime Task Force

One of the most challenging aspects of my job on the High Technology Crime Task Force in San Diego County is the technological sophistication of the cyber criminals. They use all the tricks imaginable. As a result, it can take tremendous patience to solve a case. For example, I've been working on one case for almost three years that involves a small group of people selling counterfeit software over several states, at a cost to the public of some $20 million.

These kinds of difficult investigations can involve hundreds of legal processes, such as grand jury subpoenas, search warrants, etc. I also have to make sure that I investigate suspect computers and networks in a way that complies with the search and seizure laws, while dealing with evidence that may be encrypted or hidden or protected in some way. For example, evidence may be linked to software time-bombs, Trojan horses, or other destruction devices. Also, the cyber criminals are very hard to find since they resort to aliases, phony addresses, and dead-end cell phone accounts. But the challenges are also what make it especially satisfying to see these individuals standing before judge and jury.

My first job in law enforcement was with the San Diego County Marshall's office (now in the Sheriff's Department)—and they hired me just after I left the Navy. I eventually moved up the ranks to become a detective with the San Diego Police Department. My interest in computer forensics was just developing when I worked on an assignment with the U.S. Secret Service. That assignment made me realize that this was the area I wanted to pursue.

The case involved a man studying for his Master's degree who was accused of plagiarizing his thesis. Apparently, he hid a gun in the lab and when he was brought before a team of professors to address their suspicions, he suddenly pulled out the gun and shot all three. Tragically, they all died. As part of the investigation, I did an extensive investigation of the suspect's computer and not only did I find copies of the thesis buried in different spots, but photo scans of the gun used in the shooting. This evidence helped convince jurors that the murders were premeditated, rather than the result of an impulsive rage or temporary insanity.

Courtesy of David Hendron

David Hendron

After this case, I decided I wanted to stay in high tech for the rest of my career in law enforcement. I've learned much on the job, but have also taken additional courses, and have a CRCD certificate (Certified Forensic Computer Examiner) that I earned through the International Association of Computer Investigative Specialists (IACIS).

A key ingredient to being successful as an investigator of cyber crimes is patience. You need to sift through mountains of data and go down many blind alleys before you can finally piece together the puzzle. Often the hours are long, and the demands on your time great. In addition, it's important that you can be self-directed and self-motivated because often no one but you is as deeply immersed in an individual case.

If you're interested in this field, you should focus on developing your knowledge and understanding of computers, as well as making sure you have a good background in criminal justice. In particular, you should gain understanding of so-called white-collar crime since that is the foundation of most cyber crime.

 Go to the Careers in Criminal Justice Interactive CD *for a video interview with David Hendron and for other profiles in the field of criminal justice.*

The United States Secret Service The USA Patriot Act greatly increased the Secret Service's role in fighting cyber crime. In the legal arena, the legislation gave the agency jurisidiction over some of the crimes listed in 18 U.S.C. Section 1030 (see Figure 17.6).[88] The Secret Service was authorized to develop a national network of electronic crime task forces based on the New York Electronic Crime Task Force, a collaboration among federal, state, and local law enforcement officers and a wide range of corporate sponsors. To date, the agency has established these task forces in Boston, San Francisco, Los Angeles, Chicago, Miami, Las Vegas, Washington, D.C., and Charlotte, North Carolina.

Private Efforts to Combat Cyber Crime The fact remains, however, that the federal government has very little regulatory oversight over the Internet. Hence, it has little choice but to rely on the voluntary efforts of private companies to secure their computer infrastructures. Although many federal officials do not believe private companies are being sufficiently diligent in this area, the fear of being "hacked" has spurred a billion-dollar industry that helps clients—either individuals or businesses—protect the integrity of their computer systems. Because every computer hooked up to the Internet is a potential security breach, these experts help devise elaborate and ever-changing password systems to ensure that only authorized users access data. They also install protective software such as firewalls and antivirus software, which can limit outside access to a computer or network. Because cyber criminals are constantly updating their technology, cyberspace security firms help their clients do the same with their defensive systems.

Perhaps the most successful and controversial way to protect computer information is to encrypt it. Through **encryption,** a message (plaintext) is transformed into something (ciphertext) that only the sender and receiver can understand. Unless a third party is able to "break the code," the information will stay secure. Encryption is particularly useful in protecting e-mails. Indeed, until recently the most widely used encryption program, known as P.G.P. for Pretty Good Privacy, was considered unbreakable. Several years ago, however, two cryptologists announced that the program may be flawed and would require a software fix called a "patch" to restore consumer confidence.

➤ ONLINE REVIEW *Go to the book's Web site for an interactive review of this section*

Encryption
The process by which a message is transmitted into a form or code that the sender and receiver intend third parties not to understand.

Criminal Justice: Looking to the Future

Some observers feel that the massive amount of illegal activity that occurs on the Internet is a sign of an inherent weakness that could be exploited by cyber terrorists. Richard A. Clarke, a former cyber security adviser for the U.S. Department of Homeland Security, warns of a possible "digital Pearl Harbor."[89] Cyber crime expert Chris Rouland believes the nation has been "lucky" that the authors of the viruses and worms that have caused so much economic damage were not "terribly malicious with their intent." Rouland points out that with minor changes, the Blaster worm could have "shut down major pieces of infrastructure."[90]

Others insist that such fears are overstated. A simulation of a possible "digital Pearl Harbor" carried out by the U.S. Naval War College determined that, though a Web-based attack on America could cause serious damage, anyone attempting such an attack would need five years of preparation and $200 million of funding.[91] As we have seen, much cheaper, easier, and similarly effective terrorist methods exist.

This does not mean, of course, that law enforcement agencies or private companies should be lax in protecting against possible security breaches on the Internet. Without question, the immediate future of the criminal justice system will be characterized by a focus on counterterrorism. These efforts are sure to inspire new technologies and strategies that will affect crime fighting beyond the sphere of terrorism.

Electronic fingerprint scanners such as the one shown below are an important part of the U.S. Department of Homeland Security's efforts to tighten security at entry points to the United States. The equipment allows border inspectors to check the identities of foreign visitors by comparing their fingerprints to the fingerprints of those on terrorist watch lists.

AP Photo/Stephen J. Boitano

REEMERGING TECHNOLOGY: THE DATABASE

We have discussed a number of technologies in this textbook, from infrared sensors that can "see" through walls to satellites that can track criminals from thousands of miles above the earth. For many criminal justice experts, however, the most exciting new crime-fighting technology has existed for years: the database.

"Talking" Computers   The arrests of Washington, D.C., area snipers John Allen Muhammad and John Lee Malvo were, in part, made possible because a federal database matched Malvo's fingerprints with those found on a murder scene in Alabama. Because crime computers in Alabama are not linked to those at the FBI, however, the link remained undiscovered for nearly a month, during which the snipers killed ten people. Almost every law enforcement agency in the United States, from the FBI to tiny local police departments, keeps information concerning its crime-fighting activities. The trick is to figure out a way for these various databases to "talk" with each other.

Efforts in this direction have intensified in the past few years. In 1995, the FBI created a database called the Violent Gang and Terrorist Organization File (VGTOF). The file now contains the names of more than seven thousand people suspected of being involved in street gangs or terrorist organizations, and most police officers are able to access VGTOF during routine traffic stops. In 2003, the Centers for Disease Control sponsored the creation of a National Violent Death Reporting System, which will create a database of the circumstances surrounding all suicides and homicides in six participating states. Scientists at the University of Arizona's Artificial Intelligence Lab are working on a computer code that would create a "[search engine] for law enforcement." This code, called Coplink, would allow different local police departments to enter names, weapons, and other elements of criminal behavior into a database that would provide matches for similar crimes in other areas of the country.

The Watch List   The "war" against terrorism has inspired significant interest in the benefits of database technology. In 2003, the U.S. Department of Homeland Security announced the creation of a "master watch list," a single database that will combine the knowledge of all the various federal law enforcement agencies that track potential terrorists. When fully functional, the database will offer "one-stop shopping" to police officers checking a suspect's criminal past and immigration officials who want to know the background of someone applying for a visa. (See Figure 17.7.)

The technology could also aid private companies in sensitive industries: the manager of a nuclear power plant, for example, could consult the master watch list before hiring a new employee. In addition, the federal government is sponsoring the Computer Assisted Passenger Prescreening System, known as CAPPS II. Plans for CAPPS II envision a system that will analyze passengers' past travel reservations, housing information, credit history, and family connections to determine if they represent a pattern that suggests ties to terrorism.[92]

State governments also recognize the benefits of counterterrorism databases. The Florida Department of Law Enforcement is

FIGURE 17.7

The "Master Watch List" of Terrorism Suspects

In order to better coordinate against terrorism, in 2003 federal intelligence and law enforcement officials announced the formation of a "master watch list" of suspected terrorists. This master list will combine the lists of the nine federal agencies, indicated below, that keep track of potential terrorist threats.

Central Intelligence Agency
Federal Bureau of Investigation
Air Force Office of Special Investigations
Bureau of Consular Affairs
Bureau of Immigration and Customs Enforcement
Bureau of Intelligence and Research
Marshals Service
National Central Bureau of Interpol
Transportation Security Administration

Source: General Accounting Office.

developing a program called the Multistate Anti-Terrorism Information Exchange—dubbed the Matrix—that combines criminal records with commercial files of American adults. Proponents of the Matrix believe it will help investigators discover links and patterns among people and events at a speed that will change the course of police work. "It is exactly how law enforcement worked yesterday, except it's extraordinarily faster,"[93] says the project's developer.

PRIVACY RIGHTS AND FEARS

"It's scary," said a Florida intelligence officer in appreciation of the Matrix program. "I mean, I can call up everything about you, your pictures and pictures of your neighbor."[94] Critics of the Matrix find databases that collect this kind of information not only "scary," but also unethical and, perhaps, unconstitutional. As we learned in Chapter 7, even though privacy as a fundamental right is not explicitly mentioned in the U.S. Constitution, the United States Supreme Court has found that some aspects of privacy, including certain personal communications, are constitutionally protected.[95] Furthermore, Congress has passed legislation preventing certain information about a person, such as financial background, from being released without the person's consent.[96]

Public Concerns   Provisions of the USA Patriot Act do allow for increased monitoring of financial and educational records.[97] Segments of the American public, however, do not seem as eager as the federal government to sacrifice their privacy in the name of greater security. Originally, for example, thirteen states agreed to take part in the Matrix project by providing organizers with their citizens' driver's license records, fingerprints, Social Security numbers, divorce records, and credit information.

See the Institute for Government Research for more information on the Multistate Anti-Terrorism Information Exchange. Find this Web site by clicking on *Web Link*s under *Chapter Resources* at www.cjinaction.com

AP Photo/N. Scott Trimble

Police officers watch over four men taken into custody in connection with a roadside shooting in Arizona. Four people were killed in the incident, which involved the transportation of illegal immigrants across the Mexican border. Violent crime associated with immigrant smuggling skyrocketed in the mid-2000s, a reflection of the high profits to be made by "people traffickers" in the Southwest United States.

By the winter of 2003, public complaints had forced six states to back out of the Matrix project. After Georgia took this step, one of its politicians said, "We should not allow our zeal to catch [terrorists to] lead us to start gathering, manipulating, and disseminating personal information on Georgia's citizens whom the government has no reason to believe have committed crimes."[98]

Data-Mining Dilemmas   In 2003, several angry citizens sued JetBlue Airways for violating its privacy policy after the company secretly turned over information on about 1.5 million of its passengers to an agency compiling data for CAPPS II. That same year, Congress refused to fund the U.S. military's Terrorism Awareness Program, which would have created a global data-surveillance system to collect travel, credit-card, medical, and other personal records of U. S. citizens and foreigners alike. Whatever the benefits of database technology, then, it seems that Americans are uncomfortable with "data-mining" programs that delve into their private lives to find patterns of terrorism.

DEVELOPMENTS AND TRENDS: PREDICTABLY UNPREDICTABLE

Counterterrorism efforts have indirectly led to a surge in violent crime along the Mexico–U.S. border. Traditionally, human smuggling operations in this area have involved only the smugglers, called *polleros* ("chicken ranchers") and their clients, called *pollos* ("chickens")—the Mexican citizens desperate to cross into the United States to find better jobs and other opportunities. With increased border patrols since September 11, 2001, it has become more difficult—and, consequently, more expensive—to carry out these smuggling operations. The price charged by the *polleros* to take *pollos* over the border has tripled since September 11, 2001, to more than $1,500.

One of the ironclad rules of law enforcement is that the more profitable a criminal activity is, the more criminals it will attract. In this case, the smuggling of people has become almost as lucrative as the smuggling of drugs, and the penalty is much less severe—months in prison versus years. As a result, a new player has joined the fray—the *bajadero* ("chicken stealer"), who kidnaps the illegal immigrants from their smugglers and holds them for ransom. In November 2003, four people were killed during a shoot-out between rival smuggling gangs just south of Phoenix, Arizona. Conflict between the *bajaderos* and the *polleros* is being blamed for a 45 percent rise in homicides and a 400 percent rise in kidnappings, home invasions, and extortion in southern Arizona between 2002 and 2003.[99]

As these new border wars show, the criminal justice system is not static. The landscape of law enforcement, the courts, and corrections is constantly changing and providing new challenges for those who make criminal justice their life's work. In this textbook, we have identified a number of these challenges, with terrorism being the most obvious. Other trends are also having a significant impact, however, including:

> The use of DNA evidence to convict and exonerate.

> The efforts to curb the costs of state prisons and jails, either by providing alternatives to incarceration or through the early release of those already serving time.

> The move to treat juvenile delinquents as adult offenders.

> The use of computers as instruments of crime.

These developments and countless others mean that the criminal justice system ten years from now will not be exactly the same as the one you have learned about in this textbook. This course has, however, provided you with a strong grasp of the fundamentals of criminal justice and hopefully has inspired you to consider a career in one of the most exciting and challenging fields of the new century.

↗ ONLINE REVIEW *Go to the book's Web site for an interactive review of this section*

>Child Pornography and the Internet

As we have seen in this chapter, the Internet has not—for the most part—created "new" crimes. Instead, it has made old crimes easier to commit. This is particularly true with regard to child pornography. Twenty years ago, those involved in the practice relied on mail and photography labs, providing the police with plenty of opportunities to gather and trace evidence. "Child pornography was pretty much eradicated in the 1980s," says the head of the U.S. Customs Service Cyber-Smuggling Center. "With the advent of the Internet," he adds, "it exploded."[100] In this *Criminal Justice in Action* feature, we will see how law enforcement agents have dealt with this explosion and discuss how the technology of the Internet both helps and hinders this process.

How Big Is the Problem?

The problem of child pornography on the Internet takes two general forms: (1) illegal exposure of children to sexual images or invitations online and (2) trafficking of photos and videos of children engaged in sexual acts. An indication of the prevalence of the first form can be found in data compiled by the Crimes against Children Research Center at the University of New Hampshire. One survey conducted by the organization found that 20 percent of the more than 1,500 ten- to seventeen-year-olds questioned had received at least one online sexual solicitation in the past year.[101] Another indicated that 25 percent of youths surfing the Internet are exposed to unwanted images of naked people or sexual behavior.[102]

As for the second form, in the past decade, a "community" of child pornographers has evolved, protected by the anonymity that the Internet offers. In 1996, the FBI was investigating 113 cases involving child pornography. By 2002, that figure had risen to 2,370 cases.[103]

These activities are also global in scope. Whereas twenty years ago an American or European interested in child pornography might have had to travel to a country where laws against it were not enforced, today he or she need only have access to a telephone connection. In the late 1990s, law enforcement agents in thirteen countries broke up the Wonderland Club, an immense child-pornography ring. Based in the United States, the Wonderland Club had more than two hundred members from forty-seven different countries.[104]

The Innocent Images Approach

Parents can take certain steps to protect their children from the worst of the Internet. A number of software programs have been designed to block out certain sites—including all chat rooms—and prevent children from keying in certain words. Given children's wide access to the Internet from a number of different computer systems (at school, at the library, at friends' homes), however, it is practically impossible to protect a child at all times. Consequently, the primary responsibility for fighting cyber porn rests with law enforcement agencies.

The FBI's Innocent Images unit has been particularly successful in apprehending online pedophiles. Using the anonymity that so often protects online pornographers, agents "hang out" in chat rooms, posing as either young children or sexual predators. In one such case, FBI agent Patricia Ferrante posed as One4Fun4U, a fourteen-year-old girl, in a chat room called "X Little Girl Gift." James Childress, a thirty-one-year-old Virginia resident using the screen name "Sylliboy," had several sexually graphic conversations with One4Fun4U and then arranged to meet her in a Maryland mall in order to have sex. When he appeared at the mall, Childress was arrested and eventually found guilty of traveling across state lines with the intent of engaging in sexual acts with a juvenile.[105]

Naughton and the "Fantasy Defense"

The prosecution rate for those arrested by Innocent Images agents is an impressive 95 percent.[106] Most of the defendants claim that they were entrapped by the FBI or other law enforcement agents (see Chapter 6 for a review of entrapment), but this defense has generally failed. In almost every instance, the defendant entered the chat room or made "first contact" with the victim/agent. A court will rarely find that the agent "cajoled" the defendant into action simply by pretending to be a child.[107]

At least one defendant in an online solicitation case has succeeded with the "fantasy defense," however. In that case, Patrick Naughton was arrested on the Santa Monica Pier in California as he waited to meet "KRISLA," whom he allegedly believed to be a thirteen-year-old girl, but who was in fact an FBI agent. Naughton had kept up a correspondence with KRISLA over the Internet for nine months and had told her that "he wanted to get [her] alone in his hotel room and have [her] strip naked for him."[108]

During the trial, Naughton argued that he never thought that KRISLA was actually thirteen years old, but always assumed that she was an adult woman who shared his "daughter/daddy" fantasy and was playing the role of a young girl. Therefore, he did not intend to have sex with an underage girl and had not committed a crime.

Patrick J. Naughton, left, successfully used the "fantasy defense" to avoid conviction on charges of online solicitation.

AP Photo/Lee Celano

Enough members of the jury believed Naughton, and he was acquitted.[109]

Virtually Illegal

The key to Naughton's successful defense was that those involved in the Internet culture understand that people online often do not represent themselves truthfully. Thus, Naughton could maintain that he was just involved in a fantasy courtship and had no way of knowing KRISLA's true age. This idea of the Internet as a fantasy world plays a large part in the latest controversy to arise regarding online child pornography: the depiction of "fake" minors engaged in sexual acts.

With current software programs, extremely lifelike digital images can be produced. Indeed, most Hollywood movies today use digital images, often without the viewer knowing that the images are "fake." When this relatively new and inexpensive technology is applied to pornography, the results are amazingly real. Suppose that a computer programmer, using just a computer and no human actors, creates a lifelike set of child actors and uses commands on the computer to have them engage in sexual acts. Has the programmer violated child-pornography laws?

In 1996, Congress passed the Child Pornography Prevention Act.[110] This act bans the distribution and possession of computer-generated images that appear to depict minors engaging in lewd and lascivious behavior. In *Ashcroft v. Free Speech Coalition* (2002),[111] the United States Supreme Court struck down the provisions of the law that related to "virtual" representations of child pornography. The Court held that these provisions violated the free speech protections of the First Amendment and that the "visual depiction" of teen-agers engaging in sexual activity is a "fact of modern society and has been a theme in art and literature throughout the ages."[112] The decision angered many observers—one politician complained that the Court had "sided with pedophiles over children"[113]—and will certainly not silence the debate over "virtual" child pornography.

MAKING SENSE OF CHILD PORNOGRAPHY ON THE INTERNET

1 Review the discussion of the mental requirements for committing a crime on pages 80–82 in Chapter 3. Do you think that Patrick Naughton, if he was indeed telling the truth, did not have the required *mens rea* to be charged with the intent to have sex with a minor?

2 What arguments can be made that the Child Pornography Prevention Act is contrary to the guarantee of freedom of speech in the U.S. Constitution? Do you agree with these arguments? Why or why not?

3 Does the government have a compelling interest in protecting children from "fake" pornography? In other words, how might banning virtual pornography protect "real" children?

INFOTRAC KEYWORDS
online child pornography
For more information, use this search term with InfoTrac College Edition, your online library at www.infotrac-college.com

Chapter Summary

1 **Explain why the Antiterrorism and Effective Death Penalty Act of 1996 (AEDPA) is an important legal tool against potential terrorists.** The AEDPA allows federal law enforcement officials to prosecute those suspected of providing "material support or resources" to any group that the U.S. government has designated a "terrorist organization." The act permits the arrest of a suspect who has not yet committed a criminal act, thereby allowing for preventive measures not usually available under criminal law.

2 **Describe the primary goals of an intelligence agency and indicate how it differs from an agency that focuses solely on law enforcement.** The primary goal of an intelligence agency is to prevent crime by gathering information on potential illegal acts before they occur. In contrast, a law enforcement agency devotes its resources to solving crimes that have already occurred and bringing those who committed those crimes to justice.

3 **List some of the ways federal law enforcement can use aspects of immigration law to fight terrorism.** Immigration law provides fewer procedural protections to suspected wrongdoers than does criminal law: (a) federal agents do not need to meet the probable cause requirement when detaining someone on suspicion of an immigration violation; (b) those arrested for violating immigration law are not guaranteed counsel; and (c) federal law allows a person suspected of violating immigration law to be held for seven days before being charged.

4 **Indicate the three amendments to the U.S. Constitution that are cited most often by critics of the USA Patriot Act of 2001, and briefly explain why.** (a) Critics see the act as infringing on the Fourth Amendment because it gives the federal government broader powers to monitor and search those suspected of supporting terrorism. (b) Critics believe the act allows for the indefinite detention of suspects in breach of the due process clause of the Fifth Amendment. (c) The USA Patriot Act and other government directives are seen as restricting the rights to counsel and a fair trial guaranteed by the Sixth Amendment.

5 **Explain how military tribunals differ from federal courts with regard to trials of suspected terrorists.** A defendant before a military tribunal does not enjoy the right to trial by jury; instead, a panel of military officers makes decisions of guilt and innocence. The traditional rules of evidence do not apply in military tribunals, which operate under a much more lenient standard of what evidence is allowed against the defendant. Also, military tribunals do not have to reach a unanimous verdict—only two-thirds of the panel must agree to find guilt.

6 **Distinguish cyber crime from "traditional" crime.** Most cyber crimes are not "new" types of crimes. Rather, they are traditional crimes committed

 STORIES FROM THE STREET
Go to the *Stories from the Street* feature at **www.cjinaction.com** to hear Larry Gaines tell insightful stories related to this chapter and his experiences in the field.

in cyberspace. Perpetrators of cyber crimes are often aided by certain aspects of the Internet, such as its ability to cloak the user's identity and its effectiveness as a conduit for transferring—or stealing—large amounts of information very quickly.

7 **Explain the activities and purposes of most hackers.** A hacker is someone who uses one computer to gain access to another computer. Sometimes a hacker's goal is to commit cyber theft. In most cases, however, a hacker's principal aim is to "show off" the ease with she or he can break into protected computer systems and cause errors.

8 **Outline the three major reasons that the Internet is conducive to juvenile cyber crime.** (a) Advanced computer equipment and software allow juveniles to commit crimes without leaving their homes; (b) the anonymity of cyberspace allows young people to commit crimes such as theft that would otherwise be almost impossible, given the limitations of size, money, and experience; and (c) hacking and other cyber crimes are often not recognized as unethical in youth culture.

9 **Describe the challenges to enforcing online gambling laws.** Although gambling is generally illegal in this country, almost anybody with a credit card can gamble online, regardless of his or her age or place of residence. Furthermore, many Internet gambling sites are physically based outside the United States, limiting the authority, or jurisdiction, of American law enforcement agencies and courts to control their actions.

10 **Indicate some reasons why the database is seen as an important crime-fighting tool for the future of law enforcement.** Almost every law enforcement agency in the United States keeps and updates a database with information on crimes, arrests, and other aspects of law enforcement in its jurisdiction. If law enforcement officers had the means to access the databases of other agencies and government organizations, it would allow them to "tap into" a wealth of crime information, aiding their investigative and preventive efforts immeasurably.

Key Terms

alien 576	cyber fraud 587	immigration violations 577
Antiterrorism and Effective Death Penalty Act of 1996 (AEDPA) 573	cyber-stalking 589	intellectual property 592
	encryption 596	intelligence agency 575
computer crime 586	enemy combatant 580	virus 589
cyber crime 586	hacker 589	visa 576
	identity theft 588	worm 589

Questions for Critical Analysis

1 What is the "big cultural change" that the FBI is facing in the aftermath of the September 11, 2001, terrorist attacks?

2 Why are some observers calling for the FBI to be "split"? What sort of new law enforcement agency would be created as a result of this split?

3 Why does the nature of online communication make it difficult to identify and prosecute those who commit cyber crimes?

4 How are the goals of a military operation different from those of a law enforcement investigation?

5 Why has the U.S. government been criticized for holding suspected terrorists at the U.S. Naval Base at Guantánamo Bay, Cuba? On what constitutional principle is this criticism based?

6 Consider the following situation: Melissa Chin is the sheriff of Jackson County, Missouri, population 1,434. Sheriff Chin has only two deputies at her disposal. Mae Brown, a resident of Jackson County, is receiving threatening e-mails from someone who has the cyberspace name of johndoe1313. Mae is certain that the sender is actually Matthew Green, her ex-husband. Matthew lives in Wilson County, Louisiana. What are some of the jurisdictional problems Sheriff Chin may face in investigating Matthew's possible involvement in cyber-stalking? What are some of the practical problems Sheriff Chin may encounter? How might she solve these problems?

7 How does encryption help protect information delivered via the Internet? Is this method foolproof?

8 Why did some states refuse to take part in the Multistate Anti-Terrorism Information System database program known as the Matrix?

9 How have counterterrorism efforts indirectly contributed to the rise of some violent crimes such as kidnapping and extortion in southern Arizona in recent years?

Notes

1. Matthew Purdy and Lowell Bergman, "Unclear Danger: Inside the Lackawanna Terror Case," *New York Times* (October 12, 2003), Section 1, page 1.

2. Fareed Zakaria, *Illiberal Democracy at Home and Abroad* (New York: W. W. Norton, 2003), 15.

3. Elisabeth Frater, "FBI Must Switch Gears to Prevent Terrorism, Experts Say," *National Journal* (October 9, 2001), 9.

4. Purdy and Bergman.

5. *Ibid.*

6. 18 U.S.C. Section 2339B(a)(1) (1996).

7. John Ashcroft, Testimony before the Senate Committee on the Judiciary, 107th Congress (September 25, 2001), available at http://www.usdoj.gov/ag/testimony/2001/0925AttorneyGeneralJohnAshcroftTestimonybeforetheSenateCommitteeontheJudiciary.htm.

8. "Feds Roll Out Anti-Bioterror Advances," *Law Enforcement News* (April 15, 2003), 8.

9. John W. Whitehead and Steven H. Aden, "Forfeiting 'Enduring Freedom' for 'Homeland Security': A Constitutional Analysis of the USA Patriot Act," *American University Law Review* (August 2002), 1086.

10. David Johnston and Don Van Natta, Jr., "Wary of Risk, Slow to Adapt, FBI Stumbles in Terror War," *New York Times* (June 2, 2002), Section 1, page 24.

11. AAAS R & D Funding Update, *Homeland Security R & D in the FY 2004 Budget* (Washington, D.C.: American Association for the Advancement of Science, October 1, 2003), 4.

12. Richard Shelby, statements made during appearance on *FOX News*, December 1, 2002.

13. Quoted in Toni Locy, "Anti-Terror Crew Chases Leads Big and Small," *USA Today* (October 8, 2003), 10A.

14. Duncan DeVille, "How to Split Up the Bipolar FBI," *New York Times* (June 18, 2002), A25.

15. David M. Walker, *FBI Reorganization: Progress Made in Efforts to Transform, but Major Challenges Continue* (Washington, D.C.: General Accounting Office, June 18, 2003), 17–18.

16. DeVille.

17. Dan Eggen, "Center to Assess Terrorist Threat: New Operation to Be Housed at CIA for Now," *Washington Post* (May 1, 2003), A10.

18. Pub. L. No. 104-208, 110 Stat. 3009 (1996).

19. Bureau of Justice Statistics, *Immigration Offenders in the Federal Criminal Justice System* (Washington, D.C.: U.S. Department of Justice, August 2002), 8.

20. Enhanced Border Security and Visa Reform Act, Pub. L. No. 107-173, 116 Stat. 543 (2002).

21. Janice L. Jacobs, deputy assistant secretary of state, quoted in Lee Hockstader, "Post 9/11 Visa Rules Keep Thousands from Coming to U.S.," *Washington Post* (November 11, 2003), A1.

22. *United States v. Martinez-Fuerte,* 428 U.S. 543, 566–567 (1976).

23. 8 U.S.C. Section 1362 (2000).

24. 8 U.S.C. Section 287.3 (2001).

25. "Give Us Your Tired, Your Poor . . . ," *Law Enforcement News* (March 15–31, 2002), 1.

26. Office of Community Oriented Policing Services, *Local Law Enforcement Responds to Terrorism* (Washington, D.C.: U.S. Department of Justice, 2002), 3.

27. Quoted in Jennifer Nislow, "Local Police Suffer Strain of Stretched Resources," *Law Enforcement News* (October 31, 2001), 11.

28. Kevin Sack, "Focus on Terror Creates Burden for the Police," *New York Times* (October 28, 2001), B4.

29. Warren Rudman, Richard A. Clarke, and Jamie F. Metzl, *Emergency Responders: Drastically Underfunded, Dangerously Unprepared* (New York: Council on Foreign Relations, 2003), 13.

30. "Unanswered Prayers: Police Officials Say Anti-Terror Needs Are Still Unmet," *Law Enforcement News* (September 15–31, 2003), 1.

31. "Remarks by the President in Photo Opportunity with National Security Team," The White House, Office of the Press Secretary at http://www.whitehouse.gov/news/releases/2001/09/20010912-4.html.

32. "Polls: Trade Some Freedom for Security," *Law Enforcement News* (September 15, 2001), 1.

33. *Ibid.*

34. Susan Sachs, "Murky Lives, Fateful Trip in Buffalo Terrorism Case," *New York Times* (September 20, 2002), A1.

35. Ronald J. Sievert, "War on Terrorism or Global Law Enforcement Operation?" *Notre Dame Law Review* (January 2003), 319.

36. Quoted in Michael Elliot, "Inside the Battle of Shah-i-Kot," *Time* (March 18, 2002), 38–39.

37. Quoted in Katharine Q. Seelye, "War on Terror Makes for Odd Twists in the Justice System," *New York Times* (June 23, 2002), Section 1, page 16.

38. Uniting and Strengthening America by Providing Appropriate Tools Required to Intercept and Obstruct Terrorism Act of 2001, Pub. L. No. 107-56, 115 Stat. 272 (2001).

39. Quoted in John Cloud, "Hitting the Wall," *Time* (November 5, 2001), 70.

40. *INS v. Delgado,* 466 U.S. 215 (1983).

41. *Johnson v. United States,* 33 U.S. 13–14 (1948).

42. Philip Shenon, "Senate Report on Pre-9/11 Failure Tells of Bungling at FBI," *New York Times* (August 28, 2002), A14.

43. USA Patriot Act, Pub. L. No. 107-156, Sections 201–202, 115 Stat. 272, 278 (2001).

44. USA Patriot Act, Section 206 (amending Section 105(c)(2)(B) of Foreign Intelligence Surveillance Act).

45. USA Patriot Act, Section 213.

46. Michael Hill, "Life, Liberty, and the Pursuit of Terrorists," *Baltimore Sun* (November 2, 2003), 1C.

47. USA Patriot Act, Section 412.

48. Geneva Convention Relative to the Treatment of Prisoners of War, 75 U.N.T.S. 287 Art. 84 (August 12, 1949).

49. Jamie Fellner, "Double Standards," *International Herald Tribune* (March 31, 2002), at http://hrw.org/editorials/2003/us033103.htm.

50. *Swidler & Berlin v. United States,* 524 U.S. 410 (1998).

51. 28 C.F.R. 501.3(d) (as amended, 2001).

52. American Civil Liberties Union, "Regarding Eavesdropping on Confidential Attorney-Client Communications," in Scott H. Decker, Leanne F. Alarid, and Charles M. Katz, eds., *Controversies in Criminal Justice* (Los Angeles: Roxbury Publishing Co., 2003), 85–93.

53. Military Order of November 11, 2001, "Detention, Treatment, and Trial of Certain Non-Citizens in the War Against Terror," 66 *Federal Register,* 57,833 (November 13, 2001).

54. *Military Commission Order No. 1* (Washington, D.C.: U.S. Department of Defense, March 21, 2002).

55. Spencer J. Crona and Neal A. Richardson, "Justice for War Criminals of Invisible Armies: A New Legal and Military Approach to Terrorism," *Oklahoma City University Law Review* 21 (1996), 371–374.

56. American Bar Association Task Force on Terrorism and the Law, *Report and Recommendations on Military Commissions, Army Law* (Washington, D.C.: American Bar Association, 2002), 11.

57. Richard B. Schmitt and Greg Krikorian, "Foot Soldiers on the Homeland Security Front," *Los Angeles Times* (April 21, 2003), A18.

58. Tom Jackman, "Judges Uphold U.S. Detention of Hamdi; Courts Must Yield to Military on 'Enemy Combatants' 4th Circuit Rules," *Washington Post* (January 9, 2003), A1.

59. Benjamin Weiser, "Judge Says Man Can Meet with Lawyer to Challenge Detention as Enemy Plotter," *New York Times* (December 5, 2002), A23.

60. William H. Rehnquist, *All the Laws but One: Civil Liberties in Wartime* (New York: Knopf, 1998).

61. Deborah J. Daniels, "The Challenge of Domestic Terrorism to American Criminal Justice," *Corrections Today* (December 1, 2002).

62. National Institute of Justice, *Computer Crimes: Criminal Justice Resource Manual* (Washington, D.C.: U.S. Department of Justice, 1989), 2.

63. Michael Janofsky, "Defense Cites an Addition to the Internet in Threat Case," *New York Times* (January 13, 2000), A18.

64. Internet Fraud Complaint Center, *IFCC 2001 Internet Fraud Report: January 1, 2001–December 31, 2001* (Washington, D.C.: Federal Bureau of Investigation and National White Collar Crime Center, 2003), 5.

65. Internet Fraud Complaint Center, *IFCC 2002 Internet Fraud Report: January 1, 2002–December 31, 2002* (Washington, D.C.: Federal Bureau of Investigation and National White Collar Crime Center, 2003), 3.

66. Brian Kates, "Nigeria Scam Cashes In on Crises," *New York Daily News* (August 24, 2003), 24.

67. Federal Trade Commission, *Identity Theft Survey Report* (McLean, VA: Synovate, September 2003), 6–7.

68. Arizona Revised Statute Ann. Section 2921(E) (West Supp. 1997).

69. Jonathan Rusch, *The Rising Tide of Internet Fraud* (Washington, D.C.: U.S. Department of Justice, 2001).

70. Brian Bakst, "Accused Web Attacker under House Arrest," *Associated Press Newswires* (August 30, 2003).

71. Jon Swartz, "Cops Take a Bite, or Maybe a Nibble, Out of Cybercrime," *USA Today* (September 2, 2003), B1.

72. *CSI/FBI Computer Crime and Security Survey* (San Francisco: Computer Security Institute, 2003), 1.

73. *CERT Coordination Center 2002 Annual Report* (Pittsburgh, PA: Carnegie Mellon University Software Engineering Institute, 2003).

74. Joy D. Russell, "Curbing Cybercrime," *VARBUSINESS* (May 14, 2001), 32.

75. Eric Newburger, *Home Computers and Internet Use in the United States: August 2000* (Washington, D.C.: U.S. Census Bureau, September 2001), 5.

76. Joseph V. DeMarco, *It's Not Just Fun and "War Games"—Juveniles and Computer Crimes* (Washington, D.C.: U.S. Department of Justice, 2001).

77. *Ibid.*

78. International Planning and Research Corporation, *Eighth Annual BSA Global Software Piracy Study: Trends in Software Piracy, 1994–2002* (Washington, D.C.: Business Software Alliance, 2003), 2–3.

79. *2002 IFPI Music Piracy Report* (London: International Federation of the Phonographic Industry, June 2002), 2.

80. 18 U.S.C. Section 23199(c) (1998).

81. 17 U.S.C. Sections 2301 *et seq.* (1998).

82. National Research Council, *Youth, Pornography, and the Internet* (Washington, D.C.: National Academies Press, 2002), 72.

83. Ira Sager, "The Underground Web," *Business Week* (September 2, 2002), 70.

84. http://www.whitehouse.gov/homeland/21st-technology. html.

85. *American Libraries Association v. Pataki*, 969 F.Supp. 168–169 (S.D.N.Y. 1997).

86. Alison Gerber, "Police Perplexed in Dealing with Cybercrime," *USA Today* (August 29, 2000), 5A.

87. Thomas T. Kubic, "Statement for the Record on the FBI's Perspective on the Cyber Crime Problem," delivered before the House Committee on the Judiciary Subcommittee on Crime (June 12, 2001).

88. Heather Jacobson and Rebecca Green, "Computer Crimes," *American Criminal Law Review* (Spring 2002), 283.

89. Quoted in Amy Harmon, "As Digital Vandals Disrupt the Internet, a Call for Oversight," *New York Times* (September 1, 2003), A1.

90. Quoted in Frank James, "Teen Held in Net Attack, but Bigger Fears Remain," *Chicago Tribune* (August 30, 2003), 1.

91. "The Mouse That Might Roar," *Economist* (October 26, 2002), 19.

92. Robert O'Harrow, Jr., "Profiling System Advances," *International Herald Tribune* (December 26, 2002), 9.

93. Quoted in Robert O'Harrow, Jr., "U.S. Backs Florida's New Counterterrorism Database," *Washington Post* (August 6, 2003), A1.

94. *Ibid.*

95. *Katz v. United States,* 389 U.S. 347, 350–351 (1967).

96. Privacy Act of 1974, 5 U.S.C. Section 552(a) (1999).

97. USA Patriot Act, Sections 355, 356, 358, 507.

98. Bob Barr, quoted in "Georgia Rejects Crime Database," *August Chronicle* (October 22, 2003), B6.

99. Charlie LeDuff, "After the Crossing, Danger to Migrants Isn't Over," *New York Times* (November 11, 2003), A1.

100. Rod Norland and Jeffrey Bartholet, "The Web's Dark Secret, " *Newsweek* (March 19, 2001), 46.

101. Kimberly Mitchell, David Finkelhor, and Janis Wolak, "Risk Factors for and Impact of Online Sexual Solicitation for Youth," *Journal of the American Medical Association* 285 (June 20, 2001), 3011.

102. Kimberly Mitchell, David Finkelhor, and Janis Wolak, "The Exposure of Youth to Unwanted Sexual Material on the Internet: A National Survey of Risk, Impact, and Prevention," *Youth and Society* 34 (2003), 330–358.

103. http://www.fbi.gov/hg/cid/cac/innocent/htm.

104. Michael Grunwald, "Global Internet Child Porn Ring Uncovered," *Washington Post* (September 3, 1998), A12; and Elaine Shannon, "Main Street Monsters," *Time* (September 14, 1998), 59.

105. *United States v. Childress,* 104 F.3d 47 (4th Cir. 1996).

106. Peter Gulotta, "An FBI Agent's Perspective" (July 31, 2000); see http://cbsnews.cbs.com/now/story/0,1597, 199217—412,00.html.

107. Donald S. Yamagimi, "Prosecuting Cyber Pedophiles," *Santa Clara Law Review* 41 (2001), 557–558.

108. *Ibid.,* 547.

109. *Ibid.,* 570.

110. 18 U.S.C. Section 2256.

111. 534 U.S. 234 (2002).

112. *Ibid.,* 246.

113. John Schwartz, "Swift, Passionate Reaction to a Pornography Ruling," *New York Times* (April 17, 2002), A16.

Appendix A
THE CONSTITUTION OF THE UNITED STATES

PREAMBLE

We the People of the United States, in Order to form a more perfect Union, establish Justice, insure domestic Tranquility, provide for the common defence, promote the general Welfare, and secure the Blessings of Liberty to ourselves and our Posterity, do ordain and establish this Constitution for the United States of America.

ARTICLE I

Section 1.   All legislative Powers herein granted shall be vested in a Congress of the United States, which shall consist of a Senate and House of Representatives.

Section 2.   The House of Representatives shall be composed of Members chosen every second Year by the People of the several States, and the Electors in each State shall have the Qualifications requisite for Electors of the most numerous Branch of the State Legislature.

No Person shall be a Representative who shall not have attained to the Age of twenty five Years, and been seven Years a Citizen of the United States, and who shall not, when elected, be an Inhabitant of that State in which he shall be chosen.

Representatives and direct Taxes shall be apportioned among the several States which may be included within this Union, according to their respective Numbers, which shall be determined by adding to the whole Number of free Persons, including those bound to Service for a Term of Years, and excluding Indians not taxed, three fifths of all other Persons. The actual Enumeration shall be made within three Years after the first Meeting of the Congress of the United States, and within every subsequent Term of ten Years, in such Manner as they shall by Law direct. The Number of Representatives shall not exceed one for every thirty Thousand, but each State shall have at Least one Representative; and until such enumeration shall be made, the State of New Hampshire shall be entitled to chuse three, Massachusetts eight, Rhode Island and Providence Plantations one, Connecticut five, New York six, New Jersey four, Pennsylvania eight, Delaware one, Maryland six, Virginia ten, North Carolina five, South Carolina five, and Georgia three.

When vacancies happen in the Representation from any State, the Executive Authority thereof shall issue Writs of Election to fill such Vacancies.

The House of Representatives shall chuse their Speaker and other Officers; and shall have the sole Power of Impeachment.

Section 3.   The Senate of the United States shall be composed of two Senators from each State, chosen by the Legislature thereof, for six Years; and each Senator shall have one Vote.

Immediately after they shall be assembled in Consequence of the first Election, they shall be divided as equally as may be into three Classes. The Seats of the Senators of the first Class shall be vacated at the Expiration of the second Year, of the second Class at the Expiration of the fourth Year, and of the third Class at the Expiration of the sixth Year, so that one third may be chosen every second Year; and if Vacancies happen by Resignation, or otherwise, during the Recess of the Legislature of any State, the Executive thereof may make temporary Appointments until the next Meeting of the Legislature, which shall then fill such Vacancies.

No Person shall be a Senator who shall not have attained to the Age of thirty Years, and been nine Years a Citizen of the United States, and who shall not, when elected, be an Inhabitant of that State for which he shall be chosen.

The Vice President of the United States shall be President of the Senate, but shall have no Vote, unless they be equally divided.

The Senate shall chuse their other Officers, and also a President pro tempore, in the Absence of the Vice President, or when he shall exercise the Office of President of the United States.

The Senate shall have the sole Power to try all Impeachments. When sitting for that Purpose, they shall be on Oath or Affirmation. When the President of the United States is tried, the Chief Justice shall preside: And no Person shall be convicted without the Concurrence of two thirds of the Members present.

Judgment in Cases of Impeachment shall not extend further than to removal from Office, and disqualification to hold and enjoy any Office of honor, Trust, or Profit under the United States: but the Party convicted shall nevertheless be liable and subject to Indictment, Trial, Judgment, and Punishment, according to Law.

Section 4.   The Times, Places and Manner of holding Elections for Senators and Representatives, shall be prescribed in each State by the Legislature thereof; but the Congress may at any time by Law make or alter such Regulations, except as to the Places of chusing Senators.

The Congress shall assemble at least once in every Year, and such Meeting shall be on the first Monday in December, unless they shall by Law appoint a different Day.

Section 5.   Each House shall be the Judge of the Elections, Returns, and Qualifications of its own Members, and a Majority of each shall constitute a Quorum to do Business; but a smaller Number may adjourn from day to day, and may be authorized to compel the Attendance of absent Members, in such Manner, and under such Penalties as each House may provide.

Each House may determine the Rules of its Proceedings, punish its Members for disorderly Behavior, and, with the Concurrence of two thirds, expel a Member.

Each House shall keep a Journal of its Proceedings, and from time to time publish the same, excepting such Parts as may in their Judgment require Secrecy; and the Yeas and Nays of the Members of either House on any question shall, at the Desire of one fifth of those Present, be entered on the Journal.

Neither House, during the Session of Congress, shall, without the Consent of the other, adjourn for more than three days, nor to any other Place than that in which the two Houses shall be sitting.

Section 6.   The Senators and Representatives shall receive a Compensation for their Services, to be ascertained by Law, and paid out of the Treasury of the United States. They shall in all Cases, except Treason, Felony and Breach of the Peace, be privileged from Arrest during their Attendance at the Session of their respective Houses, and in going to and returning from the same; and for any Speech or Debate in either House, they shall not be questioned in any other Place.

No Senator or Representative shall, during the Time for which he was elected, be appointed to any civil Office under the Authority of the United States, which shall have been created, or the Emoluments whereof shall have been increased during such time; and no Person holding any Office under the United States, shall be a Member of either House during his Continuance in Office.

Section 7.   All Bills for raising Revenue shall originate in the House of Representatives; but the Senate may propose or concur with Amendments as on other Bills.

Every Bill which shall have passed the House of Representatives and the Senate, shall, before it become a Law, be presented to the President of the United States; If he approve he shall sign it, but if not he shall return it, with his Objections to the House in which it shall have originated, who shall enter the Objections at large on their Journal, and proceed to reconsider it. If after such Reconsideration two thirds of that House shall agree to pass the Bill, it shall be sent together with the Objections, to the other House, by which it shall likewise be reconsidered, and if approved by two thirds of that House, it shall become a Law. But in all such Cases the Votes of both Houses shall be determined by Yeas and Nays, and the Names of the Persons voting for and against the Bill shall be entered on the Journal of each House respectively. If any Bill shall not be returned by the President within ten Days (Sundays excepted) after it shall have been presented to him, the Same shall be a Law, in like Manner as if he had signed it, unless the Congress by their Adjournment prevent its Return in which Case it shall not be a Law.

Every Order, Resolution, or Vote, to which the Concurrence of the Senate and House of Representatives may be necessary (except on a question of Adjournment) shall be presented to the President of the United States; and before the Same shall take Effect, shall be approved by him, or being disapproved by him, shall be repassed by two thirds of the Senate and House of Representatives, according to the Rules and Limitations prescribed in the Case of a Bill.

Section 8.   The Congress shall have Power To lay and collect Taxes, Duties, Imposts and Excises, to pay the Debts and provide for the common Defence and general Welfare of the United States; but all Duties, Imposts and Excises shall be uniform throughout the United States;

To borrow Money on the credit of the United States;

To regulate Commerce with foreign Nations, and among the several States, and with the Indian Tribes;

To establish an uniform Rule of Naturalization, and uniform Laws on the subject of Bankruptcies throughout the United States;

To coin Money, regulate the Value thereof, and of foreign Coin, and fix the Standard of Weights and Measures;

To provide for the Punishment of counterfeiting the Securities and current Coin of the United States;

To establish Post Offices and post Roads;

To promote the Progress of Science and useful Arts, by securing for limited Times to Authors and Inventors the exclusive Right to their respective Writings and Discoveries;

To constitute Tribunals inferior to the supreme Court;

To define and punish Piracies and Felonies committed on the high Seas, and Offenses against the Law of Nations;

To declare War, grant Letters of Marque and Reprisal, and make Rules concerning Captures on Land and Water;

To raise and support Armies, but no Appropriation of Money to that Use shall be for a longer Term than two Years;

To provide and maintain a Navy;

To make Rules for the Government and Regulation of the land and naval Forces;

To provide for calling forth the Militia to execute the Laws of the Union, suppress Insurrections and repel Invasions;

To provide for organizing, arming, and disciplining, the Militia, and for governing such Part of them as may be employed in the Service of the United States, reserving to the States respectively, the Appointment of the Officers, and the Authority of training the Militia according to the discipline prescribed by Congress;

To exercise exclusive Legislation in all Cases whatsoever, over such District (not exceeding ten Miles square) as may, by Cession of particular States, and the Acceptance of Congress, become the Seat of the Government of the United States, and to exercise like Authority over all Places purchased by the Consent of the Legislature of the State in which the Same shall be, for the Erection of Forts, Magazines, Arsenals, dock-Yards, and other needful Buildings;—And

To make all Laws which shall be necessary and proper for carrying into Execution the foregoing Powers, and all other Powers vested by this Constitution in the Government of the United States, or in any Department or Officer thereof.

Section 9. The Migration or Importation of such Persons as any of the States now existing shall think proper to admit, shall not be prohibited by the Congress prior to the Year one thousand eight hundred and eight, but a Tax or duty may be imposed on such Importation, not exceeding ten dollars for each Person.

The privilege of the Writ of Habeas Corpus shall not be suspended, unless when in Cases of Rebellion or Invasion the public Safety may require it.

No Bill of Attainder or ex post facto Law shall be passed.

No Capitation, or other direct, Tax shall be laid, unless in Proportion to the Census or Enumeration herein before directed to be taken.

No Tax or Duty shall be laid on Articles exported from any State.

No Preference shall be given by any Regulation of Commerce or Revenue to the Ports of one State over those of another: nor shall Vessels bound to, or from, one State be obliged to enter, clear, or pay Duties in another.

No Money shall be drawn from the Treasury, but in Consequence of Appropriations made by Law; and a regular Statement and Account of the Receipts and Expenditures of all public Money shall be published from time to time.

No Title of Nobility shall be granted by the United States: And no Person holding any Office of Profit or Trust under them, shall, without the Consent of the Congress, accept of any present, Emolument, Office, or Title, of any kind whatever, from any King, Prince, or foreign State.

Section 10. No State shall enter into any Treaty, Alliance, or Confederation; grant Letters of Marque and Reprisal; coin Money; emit Bills of Credit; make any Thing but gold and silver Coin a Tender in Payment of Debts; pass any Bill of Attainder, ex post facto Law, or Law impairing the Obligation of Contracts, or grant any Title of Nobility.

No State shall, without the Consent of the Congress, lay any Imposts or Duties on Imports or Exports, except what may be absolutely necessary for executing its inspection Laws: and the net Produce of all Duties and Imposts, laid by any State on Imports or Exports, shall be for the Use of the Treasury of the United States; and all such Laws shall be subject to the Revision and Controul of the Congress.

No State shall, without the Consent of Congress, lay any Duty of Tonnage, keep Troops, or Ships of War in time of Peace, enter into any Agreement or Compact with another State, or with a foreign Power, or engage in War, unless actually invaded, or in such imminent Danger as will not admit of delay.

ARTICLE II

Section 1.   The executive Power shall be vested in a President of the United States of America. He shall hold his Office during the Term of four Years, and, together with the Vice President, chosen for the same Term, be elected, as follows:

Each State shall appoint, in such Manner as the Legislature thereof may direct, a Number of Electors, equal to the whole Number of Senators and Representatives to which the State may be entitled in the Congress; but no Senator or Representative, or Person holding an Office of Trust or Profit under the United States, shall be appointed an Elector.

The Electors shall meet in their respective States, and vote by Ballot for two Persons, of whom one at least shall not be an Inhabitant of the same State with themselves. And they shall make a List of all the Persons voted for, and of the Number of Votes for each; which List they shall sign and certify, and transmit sealed to the Seat of the Government of the United States, directed to the President of the Senate. The President of the Senate shall, in the Presence of the Senate and House of Representatives, open all the Certificates, and the Votes shall then be counted. The Person having the greatest Number of Votes shall be the President, if such Number be a Majority of the whole Number of Electors appointed; and if there be more than one who have such Majority, and have an equal Number of Votes, then the House of Representatives shall immediately chuse by Ballot one of them for President; and if no Person have a Majority, then from the five highest on the List the said House shall in like Manner chuse the President. But in chusing the President, the Votes shall be taken by States,

the Representation from each State having one Vote; A quorum for this Purpose shall consist of a Member or Members from two thirds of the States, and a Majority of all the States shall be necessary to a Choice. In every Case, after the Choice of the President, the Person having the greater Number of Votes of the Electors shall be the Vice President. But if there should remain two or more who have equal Votes, the Senate shall chuse from them by Ballot the Vice President.

The Congress may determine the Time of chusing the Electors, and the Day on which they shall give their Votes; which Day shall be the same throughout the United States.

No person except a natural born Citizen, or a Citizen of the United States, at the time of the Adoption of this Constitution, shall be eligible to the Office of President; neither shall any Person be eligible to that Office who shall not have attained to the Age of thirty five Years, and been fourteen Years a Resident within the United States.

In Case of the Removal of the President from Office, or of his Death, Resignation or Inability to discharge the Powers and Duties of the said Office, the same shall devolve on the Vice President, and the Congress may by Law provide for the Case of Removal, Death, Resignation or Inability, both of the President and Vice President, declaring what Officer shall then act as President, and such Officer shall act accordingly, until the Disability be removed, or a President shall be elected.

The President shall, at stated Times, receive for his Services, a Compensation, which shall neither be increased nor diminished during the Period for which he shall have been elected, and he shall not receive within that Period any other Emolument from the United States, or any of them.

Before he enter on the Execution of his Office, he shall take the following Oath or Affirmation: "I do solemnly swear (or affirm) that I will faithfully execute the Office of President of the United States, and will to the best of my Ability, preserve, protect and defend the Constitution of the United States."

Section 2.   The President shall be Commander in Chief of the Army and Navy of the United States, and of the Militia of the several States, when called into the actual Service of the United States; he may require the Opinion, in writing, of the principal Officer in each of the executive Departments, upon any Subject relating to the Duties of their respective Offices, and he shall have Power to grant Reprieves and Pardons for Offenses against the United States, except in Cases of Impeachment.

He shall have Power, by and with the Advice and Consent of the Senate to make Treaties, provided two thirds of the Senators present concur; and he shall nominate, and by and with the Advice and Consent of the Senate, shall appoint Ambassadors, other public Ministers and Consuls, Judges of the supreme Court, and all other Officers of the United States, whose Appointments are not herein otherwise provided for, and which shall be established by Law; but the Congress may by Law vest the Appointment of such inferior Officers, as they think proper, in the President alone, in the Courts of Law, or in the Heads of Departments.

The President shall have Power to fill up all Vacancies that may happen during the Recess of the Senate, by granting Commissions which shall expire at the End of their next Session.

Section 3.   He shall from time to time give to the Congress Information of the State of the Union, and recommend to their Consideration such Measures as he shall judge necessary and expedient; he may, on extraordinary Occasions, convene both Houses, or either of them, and in Case of Disagreement between them, with Respect to the Time of Adjournment, he may adjourn them to such Time as he shall think proper; he shall receive Ambassadors and other public Ministers; he shall take Care that the Laws be faithfully executed, and shall Commission all the Officers of the United States.

Section 4.   The President, Vice President and all civil Officers of the United States, shall be removed from Office on Impeachment for, and Conviction of, Treason, Bribery, or other high Crimes and Misdemeanors.

ARTICLE III

Section 1.   The judicial Power of the United States, shall be vested in one supreme Court, and in such inferior Courts as the Congress may from time to time ordain and establish. The Judges, both of the supreme and inferior Courts, shall hold their Offices during good Behaviour, and shall, at stated Times, receive for their Services a Compensation, which shall not be diminished during their Continuance in Office.

Section 2.   The judicial Power shall extend to all Cases, in Law and Equity, arising under this Constitution, the Laws of the United States, and Treaties made, or which shall be made, under their Authority;—to all Cases affecting Ambassadors, other public Ministers and Consuls;—to all Cases of admiralty and maritime Jurisdiction;—to Controversies to which the United States shall be a Party;—to Controversies between two or more States;—between a State and Citizens of another State;—between Citizens of different States;—between Citizens of the same State claiming Lands under Grants of different States, and between a State, or the Citizens thereof, and foreign States, Citizens or Subjects.

In all Cases affecting Ambassadors, other public Ministers and Consuls, and those in which a State shall be a Party, the supreme Court shall have original Jurisdiction. In all the other Cases before mentioned, the supreme Court shall have appellate Jurisdiction, both as to Law and Fact, with such Exceptions, and under such Regulations as the Congress shall make.

The Trial of all Crimes, except in Cases of Impeachment, shall be by Jury; and such Trial shall be held in the State where the said Crimes shall have been committed; but when not committed within any State, the Trial shall be at such Place or Places as the Congress may by Law have directed.

Section 3.   Treason against the United States, shall consist only in levying War against them, or, in adhering to their Enemies, giving them Aid and Comfort. No Person shall be convicted of Treason unless on the Testimony of two Witnesses to the same overt Act, or on Confession in open Court.

The Congress shall have Power to declare the Punishment of Treason, but no Attainder of Treason shall work Corruption of Blood, or Forfeiture except during the Life of the Person attainted.

ARTICLE IV

Section 1.   Full Faith and Credit shall be given in each State to the public Acts, Records, and judicial Proceedings of every other State. And the Congress may by general Laws prescribe the Manner in which such Acts, Records and Proceedings shall be proved, and the Effect thereof.

Section 2. The Citizens of each State shall be entitled to all Privileges and Immunities of Citizens in the several States.

A Person charged in any State with Treason, Felony, or other Crime, who shall flee from Justice, and be found in another State, shall on Demand of the executive Authority of the State from which he fled, be delivered up, to be removed to the State having Jurisdiction of the Crime.

No Person held to Service or Labour in one State, under the Laws thereof, escaping into another, shall, in Consequence of any Law or Regulation therein, be discharged from such Service or Labour, but shall be delivered up on Claim of the Party to whom such Service or Labour may be due.

Section 3. New States may be admitted by the Congress into this Union; but no new State shall be formed or erected within the Jurisdiction of any other State; nor any State be formed by the Junction of two or more States, or Parts of States, without the Consent of the Legislatures of the States concerned as well as of the Congress.

The Congress shall have Power to dispose of and make all needful Rules and Regulations respecting the Territory or other Property belonging to the United States; and nothing in this Constitution shall be so construed as to Prejudice any Claims of the United States, or of any particular State.

Section 4. The United States shall guarantee to every State in this Union a Republican Form of Government, and shall protect each of them against Invasion; and on Application of the Legislature, or of the Executive (when the Legislature cannot be convened) against domestic Violence.

ARTICLE V

The Congress, whenever two thirds of both Houses shall deem it necessary, shall propose Amendments to this Constitution, or, on the Application of the Legislatures of two thirds of the several States, shall call a Convention for proposing Amendments, which, in either Case, shall be valid to all Intents and Purposes, as part of this Constitution, when ratified by the Legislatures of three fourths of the several States, or by Conventions in three fourths thereof, as the one or the other Mode of Ratification may be proposed by the Congress; Provided that no Amendment which may be made prior to the Year

One thousand eight hundred and eight shall in any Manner affect the first and fourth Clauses in the Ninth Section of the first Article; and that no State, without its Consent, shall be deprived of its equal Suffrage in the Senate.

ARTICLE VI

All Debts contracted and Engagements entered into, before the Adoption of this Constitution shall be as valid against the United States under this Constitution, as under the Confederation.

This Constitution, and the Laws of the United States which shall be made in Pursuance thereof; and all Treaties made, or which shall be made, under the Authority of the United States, shall be the supreme Law of the Land; and the Judges in every State shall be bound thereby, any Thing in the Constitution or Laws of any State to the Contrary notwithstanding.

The Senators and Representatives before mentioned, and the Members of the several State Legislatures, and all executive and judicial Officers, both of the United States and of the several States, shall be bound by Oath or Affirmation, to support this Constitution; but no religious Test shall ever be required as a Qualification to any Office or public Trust under the United States.

ARTICLE VII

The Ratification of the Conventions of nine States shall be sufficient for the Establishment of this Constitution between the States so ratifying the Same.

AMENDMENT I [1791]

Congress shall make no law respecting an establishment of religion, or prohibiting the free exercise thereof; or abridging the freedom of speech, or of the press; or the right of the people peaceably to assembly, and to petition the Government for a redress of grievances.

AMENDMENT II [1791]

A well regulated Militia, being necessary to the security of a free State, the right of the people to keep and bear Arms, shall not be infringed.

AMENDMENT III [1791]

No Soldier shall, in time of peace be quartered in any house, without the consent of the Owner, nor in time of war, but in a manner to be prescribed by law.

AMENDMENT IV [1791]

The right of the people to be secure in their persons, houses, papers, and effects, against unreasonable searches and seizures, shall not be violated, and no Warrants shall issue, but upon probable cause, supported by Oath or affirmation, and particularly describing the place to be searched, and the persons or things to be seized.

AMENDMENT V [1791]

No person shall be held to answer for a capital, or otherwise infamous crime, unless on a presentment or indictment of a Grand Jury, except in cases arising in the land or naval forces, or in the Militia, when in actual service in time of War or public danger; nor shall any person be subject for the same offence to be twice put in jeopardy of life or limb; nor shall be compelled in any criminal case to be a witness against himself, nor be deprived of life, liberty, or property, without due process of law; nor shall private property be taken for public use, without just compensation.

AMENDMENT VI [1791]

In all criminal prosecutions, the accused shall enjoy the right to a speedy and public trial, by an impartial jury of the State and district wherein the crime shall have been committed, which district shall have been previously ascertained by law, and to be informed of the nature and cause of the accusation; to be confronted with the witnesses against him; to have compulsory process for obtaining witnesses in his favor, and to have the Assistance of Counsel for his defence.

AMENDMENT VII [1791]

In Suits at common law, where the value in controversy shall exceed twenty dollars, the right of trial by jury shall be preserved, and no fact tried by jury, shall be otherwise reexamined in any Court of the United States, than according to the rules of the common law.

AMENDMENT VIII [1791]

Excessive bail shall not be required, nor excessive fines imposed, nor cruel and unusual punishments inflicted.

AMENDMENT IX [1791]

The enumeration in the Constitution, of certain rights, shall not be construed to deny or disparage others retained by the people.

AMENDMENT X [1791]

The powers not delegated to the United States by the Constitution, nor prohibited by it to the States, are reserved to the States respectively, or to the people.

AMENDMENT XI [1798]

The Judicial power of the United States shall not be construed to extend to any suit in law or equity, commenced or prosecuted against one of the United States by Citizens of another State, or by Citizens or Subjects of any Foreign State.

AMENDMENT XII [1804]

The Electors shall meet in their respective states, and vote by ballot for President and Vice-President, one of whom, at least, shall not be an inhabitant of the same state with themselves; they shall name in their ballots the person voted for as President, and in distinct ballots the person voted for as Vice-President, and they shall make distinct lists of all persons voted for as President, and of all persons voted for as Vice-President, and of the number of votes for each, which lists they shall sign and certify, and transmit sealed to the seat of the government of the United States, directed to the President of the Senate;—The President of the Senate shall, in the presence of the Senate and House of Representatives, open all the certificates and the votes shall then be counted;—The person having the greatest number of votes for President, shall be the President, if such number be a majority of the whole number of Electors appointed; and if no person have such majority, then from the persons having the highest numbers not exceeding three on the list of those voted for as President, the House of Representatives shall choose immediately, by ballot, the President. But in choosing the President, the votes shall be taken by states, the representation from each state having one vote; a quorum for this purpose shall consist of a member or members from two-thirds of the states, and a majority of all states shall be necessary to a choice. And if the House of Representatives shall not choose a President whenever the right of choice shall devolve upon them, before the fourth day of March next following, then the Vice-President shall act as President, as in the case of the death or other constitutional disability of the President.—The person having the greatest number of votes as Vice-President, shall be the Vice-President, if such number be a majority of the whole number of Electors appointed, and if no person have a majority, then from the two highest numbers on the list, the Senate shall choose the Vice-President; a quorum for the purpose shall consist of two-thirds of the whole number of Senators, and a majority of the whole number shall be necessary to a choice. But no person constitutionally ineligible to the office of President shall be eligible to that of Vice-President of the United States.

Amendment XIII [1865]

Section 1. Neither slavery nor involuntary servitude, except as a punishment for crime whereof the party shall have been duly convicted, shall exist within the United States, or any place subject to their jurisdiction.

Section 2. Congress shall have power to enforce this article by appropriate legislation.

Amendment XIV [1868]

Section 1. All persons born or naturalized in the United States, and subject to the jurisdiction thereof, are citizens of the United States and of the State wherein they reside. No State shall make or enforce any law which shall abridge the privileges or immunities of citizens of the United States; nor shall any State deprive any person of life, liberty, or property, without due process of law; nor deny to any person within its jurisdiction the equal protection of the laws.

Section 2. Representatives shall be apportioned among the several States according to their respective numbers, counting the whole number of persons in each State, excluding Indians not taxed. But when the right to vote at any election for the choice of electors for President and Vice President of the United States, Representatives in Congress, the Executive and Judicial officers of a State, or the members of the Legislature thereof, is denied to any of the male inhabitants of such State, being twenty-one years of age, and citizens of the United States, or in any way abridged, except for participation in rebellion, or other crime, the basis of representation therein shall be reduced in the proportion which the number of such male citizens shall bear to the whole number of male citizens twenty-one years of age in such State.

Section 3. No person shall be a Senator or Representative in Congress, or elector of President and Vice President, or hold any office, civil or military, under the United States, or under any State, who having previously taken an oath, as a member of Congress, or as an officer of the United States, or as a member of any State legislature, or as an executive or judicial officer of any State, to support the Constitution of the United States, shall have engaged in insurrection or rebellion against the same, or given aid or comfort to the enemies thereof. But Congress may by a vote of two-thirds of each House, remove such disability.

Section 4. The validity of the public debt of the United States, authorized by law, including debts incurred for payment of pensions and bounties for services in suppressing insurrection or rebellion, shall not be questioned. But neither the United States nor any State shall assume or pay any debt or obligation incurred in aid of insurrection or rebellion against the United States, or any claim for the loss or emancipation of any slave; but all such debts, obli-gations and claims shall be held illegal and void.

Section 5. The Congress shall have power to enforce, by appropriate legislation, the provisions of this article.

Amendment XV [1870]

Section 1. The right of citizens of the United States to vote shall not be denied or abridged by the United States or by any State on account of race, color, or previous condition of servitude.

Section 2. The Congress shall have power to enforce this article by appropriate legislation.

Amendment XVI [1913]

The Congress shall have power to lay and collect taxes on incomes, from whatever source derived, without apportionment among the several States, and without regard to any census or enumeration.

Amendment XVII [1913]

Section 1. The Senate of the United States shall be composed of two Senators from each State, elected by the people thereof, for six years; and each Senator shall have one vote. The electors in each State shall have the qualifications requisite for electors of the most numerous branch of the State legislatures.

Section 2. When vacancies happen in the representation of any State in the Senate, the executive authority of such State shall issue writs of election to fill such vacancies: *Provided,* That the legislature of any State may empower the executive thereof to make temporary appointments until the people fill the vacancies by election as the legislature may direct.

Section 3. This amendment shall not be so construed as to affect the election or term of any Senator chosen before it becomes valid as part of the Constitution.

AMENDMENT XVIII [1919]

Section 1. After one year from the ratification of this article the manufacture, sale, or transportation of intoxicating liquors within, the importation thereof into, or the exportation thereof from the United States and all territory subject to the jurisdiction thereof for beverage purposes is hereby prohibited.

Section 2. The Congress and the several States shall have concurrent power to enforce this article by appropriate legislation.

Section 3. This article shall be inoperative unless it shall have been ratified as an amendment to the Constitution by the legislatures of the several States, as provided in the Constitution, within seven years from the date of the submission hereof to the States by the Congress.

AMENDMENT XIX [1920]

Section 1. The right of citizens of the United States to vote shall not be denied or abridged by the United States or by any State on account of sex.

Section 2. Congress shall have power to enforce this article by appropriate legislation.

AMENDMENT XX [1933]

Section 1. The terms of the President and Vice President shall end at noon on the 20th day of January, and the terms of Senators and Representatives at noon on the 3d day of January, of the years in which such terms would have ended if this article had not been ratified; and the terms of their successors shall then begin.

Section 2. The Congress shall assemble at least once in every year, and such meeting shall begin at noon on the 3d day of January, unless they shall by law appoint a different day.

Section 3. If, at the time fixed for the beginning of the term of the President, the President elect shall have died, the Vice President elect shall become President. If the President shall not have been chosen before the time fixed for the beginning of his term, or if the President elect shall have failed to qualify, then the Vice President elect shall act as President until a President shall have qualified; and the Congress may by law provide for the case wherein neither a President elect nor a Vice President elect shall have qualified, declaring who shall then act as President, or the manner in which one who is to act shall be selected, and such person shall act accordingly until a President or Vice President shall have qualified.

Section 4. The Congress may by law provide for the case of the death of any of the persons from whom the House of Representatives may choose a President whenever the right of choice shall have devolved upon them, and for the case of the death of any of the persons from whom the Senate may choose a Vice President whenever the right of choice shall have devolved upon them.

Section 5. Sections 1 and 2 shall take effect on the 15th day of October following the ratification of this article.

Section 6. This article shall be inoperative unless it shall have been ratified as an amendment to the Constitution by the legislatures of three-fourths of the several States within seven years from the date of its submission.

AMENDMENT XXI [1933]

Section 1. The eighteenth article of amendment to the Constitution of the United States is hereby repealed.

Section 2. The transportation or importation into any State, Territory, or possession of the United States for delivery or use therein of intoxicating liquors, in violation of the laws thereof, is hereby prohibited.

Section 3. This article shall be inoperative unless it shall have been ratified as an amendment to the Constitution by conventions in the several States, as provided in the Constitution, within seven years from the date of the submission hereof to the States by the Congress.

AMENDMENT XXII [1951]

Section 1. No person shall be elected to the office of the President more than twice, and no person who has held the office of President, or acted as President, for more than two years of a term to which some other person was elected President shall be elected to the office of President more than once. But this Article shall not apply to any person holding the office of President when this Article was proposed by the Congress, and shall not prevent any person who may be holding the office of President, or acting as President, during the term within which this Article becomes operative from holding the office of President or acting as President during the remainder of such term.

Section 2. This article shall be inoperative unless it shall have been ratified as an amendment to the Constitution by the legislatures of three-fourths of the several States within seven years from the date of its submission to the States by the Congress.

AMENDMENT XXIII [1961]

Section 1. The District constituting the seat of Government of the United States shall appoint in such manner as the Congress may direct:

A number of electors of President and Vice President equal to the whole number of Senators and Representatives in Congress to which the District would be entitled if it were a State, but in no event more than the least populous state; they shall be in addition to those appointed by the states, but they shall be considered, for the purposes of the election of President and Vice President, to be electors appointed by a state; and they shall meet in the District and perform such duties as provided by the twelfth article of amendment.

Section 2. The Congress shall have power to enforce this article by appropriate legislation.

AMENDMENT XXIV [1964]

Section 1. The right of citizens of the United States to vote in any primary or other election for President or Vice President, for electors for President or Vice President, or for Senator or Representative in Congress, shall not be denied or abridged by the United States, or any State by reason of failure to pay any poll tax or other tax.

Section 2. The Congress shall have power to enforce this article by appropriate legislation.

AMENDMENT XXV [1967]

Section 1. In case of the removal of the President from office or of his death or resignation, the Vice President shall become President.

Section 2. Whenever there is a vacancy in the office of the Vice President, the President shall nominate a Vice President who shall take office upon confirmation by a majority vote of both Houses of Congress.

Section 3. Whenever the President transmits to the President pro tempore of the Senate and the Speaker of the House of Representatives his written declaration that he is unable to discharge the powers and duties of his office, and until he transmits to them a written declaration to the contrary, such powers and duties shall be discharged by the Vice President as Acting President.

Section 4. Whenever the Vice President and a majority of either the principal officers of the executive departments or of such other body as Congress may by law provide, transmit to the President pro tempore of the Senate and the Speaker of the House of Representatives their written declaration that the President is unable to discharge the powers and duties of his office, the Vice President shall immediately assume the powers and duties of the office as Acting President.

Thereafter, when the President transmits to the President pro tempore of the Senate and the Speaker of the House of Representatives his written declaration that no inability exists, he shall resume the powers and duties of his office unless the Vice President and a majority of either the principal officers of the executive department or of such other body as Congress may by law provide, transmit within four days to the President pro tempore of the Senate and the Speaker of the House of Representatives their written declaration that the President is unable to discharge the powers and duties of his office. Thereupon Congress shall decide the issue, assembling within forty-eight hours for that purpose if not in session. If the Congress, within twenty-one days after receipt of the latter written declaration, or, if Congress is not in session, within twenty-one days after Congress is required to assemble, determines by two-thirds vote of both Houses that the President is unable to discharge the powers and duties of his office, the Vice President shall continue to discharge the same as Acting President; otherwise, the President shall resume the powers and duties of his office.

Amendment XXVI [1971]

Section 1. The right of citizens of the United States, who are eighteen years of age or older, to vote shall not be denied or abridged by the United States or by any State on account of age.

Section 2. The Congress shall have power to enforce this article by appropriate legislation.

Amendment XXVII [1992]

No law, varying the compensation for the services of the Senators and Representatives, shall take effect, until an election of Representatives shall have intervened.

Appendix B

3.1 The court refused to throw out the charges. Although Emil was unconscious at the time his car struck the schoolgirls, he had earlier made the decision to get behind the wheel despite the knowledge that he suffered from epileptic seizures. In other words, the *actus reus* in this crime was not Emil's driving into the girls, but his decision to drive in the first place. That decision was certainly voluntary, and therefore satisfies the requirements of *actus reus*. Note that if Emil had never had an epileptic seizure before, and had no idea that he suffered from that malady, the court's decision would probably have been different. Source: *People v. Decina,* 138 N.E.2d 799 (1956). A briefed (summarized) version of this case can be found at **http://www.lectlaw.com/files/lws50.htm**. Scroll down the list to the case title to view the brief.

3.2 The court found that William could be charged with aggravated assault. With violent crimes such as murder or battery, the term *intent* includes not only what the defendant wanted to occur (in this case, William wanted to strike Sean with the wine bottle), but also those results that are practically certain to occur. Here, it does not matter that William did not intend for Sean to suffer permanent injury. Under the circumstances, William—being a reasonable person—was aware that hitting someone in the face with a blunt object is almost certain to cause serious harm, and he will be held responsible for that harm as if he intended it to happen. Source: *People v. Conley,* 543 N.E.2d 138 (1989).

4.1 A jury found that Bernhard had reasonably believed that he was in danger of being physically attacked, and acted reasonably to protect himself given what he thought was going to happen. Therefore, he was acquitted of all charges, save for one minor weapons violation. The case was very controversial, as many observers felt that the fact that Bernhard was white and his "assailants" were African American influenced the jury's decision. In other words, the jury might have felt that Bernhard's fear was reasonable only because of the racial make-up of the four young men. Source: *People v. Goetz,* 506 N.Y.S.2d 18 N.Y.,

(1986); and George P. Fletcher, *A Crime of Self-Defense: Bernhard Goetz and the Law on Trial,* New York: Free Press, 1988.

6.1 The jury acquitted the four police officers of all charges in the death of Amadou. Although the jurors later admitted being uncomfortable with the number of shots fired, they said that the law was clear: if the police officers were reasonable in feeling that their lives were endangered, they were justified in using deadly force. The jury found it reasonable that Sean, Ken, Rich, and Ed felt that Amadou was threatening them with a gun. The fact that they were mistaken in this belief is, under the law, irrelevant. Source: Jane Fritsch, "4 Officers in Diallo Shooting Are Acquitted of All Charges," *New York Times* (February 26, 2000), A1. CourtTV's Web site offers an extensive amount of information on this case at **http://www.courttv.com/national/diallo/index.html**.

7.1 The Court ruled that the evidence was valid, and could be presented against Harold. If the police officers had known, or should have known, that the third floor contained two apartments before they entered Harold's residence, then they would have been required to search only Larry's lodging. But, the Court said, "honest mistakes" by police officers do not equal an "unreasonable search" under the Fourth Amendment. Source: *Maryland v. Garrison,* 480 U.S. 79 (1987). The full text of this case can be found online at **http://laws.lp.findlaw.com/getcase/us/480/79.html**.

9.1 The court ruled that Noel was indigent and therefore had a right to free counsel, despite the fact that he owned a car worth more than potential lawyer's fees. The court reasoned that defendants should not be expected to sell necessities such as homes or cars in order to pay for a lawyer when they are obviously living on a low income. If Noel had owned a luxury automobile, the court probably would have ruled differently: people do not have a "fundamental right" to expensive automobiles, only those that get them from Point A to Point B. Source: *State v. Mickle,* 525 P.2d 1108 (1974).

10.1 The appeals court found that the prosecution had provided a "race-neutral" reason for dismissing the Rev. Robert Cook, and affirmed the defendant's conviction. The court agreed that religion-based professionals such as pastors, ministers, and rabbis tend to be more sympathetic, and that the trial court's decision to uphold the challenge was not "clearly erroneous." The subtext of this challenge is evident: the defendant's attorney felt that the fact that Rev. Robert Cook was a pastor was only a pretense to challenging his presence on the jury. The real reason was his race. This decision underscores a problem with the Supreme Court's ruling that peremptory challenges cannot be based on race: as long as attorneys can come up with another plausible reason for the challenge, members of racial minorities will continue to be discriminated against during *voir dire*. Source: Adam Liptak, "Court Rules That Lawyers May Keep Clergy Off Juries," *New York Times* (October 13, 2002), Section 1, page 31.

11.1 The trial judge, swayed by the arguments of the defendant's lawyer, sentenced Angela to eighty-nine days of community service and one day in jail. The Washington Supreme Court, however, overruled the sentence, saying that the trial judge's light sentence was not justified given the facts of the case. The Supreme Court said it was up to the state legislature, and not individual judges, to decide whether an "altruistic background" can be used as a reason for leniency. Source: "High Court Says Judge Can't Levy Light Sentence," *Seattle Times* (June 24, 1995), A10.

17.1 District Judge Robert M. Takasugi held that the law under which the Arab Americans were charged is unconstitutional. The judge rested his decision on the inability of groups designed as "terrorist" to challenge the designation. This, he said, violated the due process clause of the Constitution: "Because the government made its list of terrorist organizations in secret, without giving foreign groups a chance to defend themselves, the defendants are deprived of their liberty based on an unconstitutional designation that they could never challenges." Interestingly, this is the same law under which the "Lackawanna Six," described in the introduction to Chapter 17, were charged and convicted. Source: Greg Winter, "Judge Drops Case Against 7 Tied to Group Called Terrorist," *New York Times* (June 24, 2002), A13.

Appendix C

TABLE OF CASES

Glossary

A

Acquittal A declaration following a trial that the individual accused of the crime is innocent in the eyes of the law and thus absolved from the charges.

Actus Reus (pronounced *ak*-tus *ray*-uhs). A guilty (prohibited) act. The commission of a prohibited act is one of the two essential elements required for criminal liability, the other element being the intent to commit a crime.

Adjudicatory Hearing The process through which a juvenile court determines whether there is sufficient evidence to support the initial petition.

Administrative Law The body of law created by administrative agencies (in the form of rules, regulations, orders, and decisions) in order to carry out their duties and responsibilities.

Adversary System A legal system in which the prosecution and defense are opponents, or adversaries, and present their cases in the light most favorable to themselves. The court arrives at a just solution based on the evidence presented by the contestants and determines who wins and who loses.

Affidavit A written statement of facts, confirmed by the oath or affirmation of the party making it and made before a person having the authority to administer the oath or affirmation.

Age of Onset The age at which a juvenile first exhibits delinquent behavior. The earlier the age of onset, according to some observers, the greater the chance a person will become a career offender.

Aggravating Circumstances Any circumstances accompanying the commission of a crime that may justify a harsher sentence.

Aging Out A term used to explain the fact that criminal activity declines with age.

Alien A person who is not a citizen of a given country and therefore may not enjoy the same protections as citizens of that country.

***Allen* Charge** An instruction by a judge to a deadlocked jury with only a few dissenters that asks the jurors in the minority to reconsider the majority opinion.

Anomie A condition in which the individual suffers from the breakdown or absence of social norms. According to

this theory, this condition occurs when a person is disconnected from these norms or rejects them as inconsistent with his or her personal goals.

Antiterrorism and Effective Death Penalty Act of 1996 (AEDPA) Legislation giving federal law enforcement officers the power to arrest and prosecute any individual who provides "material support or resources" to a "terrorist organization."

Appeal The process of seeking a higher court's review of a lower court's decision for the purpose of correcting or changing the lower court's judgment or decision.

Appellate Courts Courts that review decisions made by lower courts, such as trial courts. Also known as courts of appeals.

Arraignment A court proceeding in which the suspect is formally charged with the criminal offense stated in the indictment. The suspect enters a plea (guilty, not guilty, *nolo contendere*) in response.

Arrest To take into custody a person suspected of criminal activity. Police may use only reasonable levels of force in making an arrest.

Arrest Warrant A written order, based on probable cause and issued by a judge or magistrate, commanding that the person named on the warrant be arrested by the police.

Asset Forfeiture Law A statute that allows law enforcement agents to seize any equipment used in manufacturing, storing, or transporting illicit drugs and any profits or property gained from the sale of the drugs, as well as the drugs themselves.

Attorney General The chief law officer of a state; also, the chief law officer of the nation.

Attorney-Client Privilege A rule of evidence requiring that communications between a client and his or her attorney be kept confidential, unless the client consents to disclosure.

Authentication Establishing the genuineness of an item that is to be introduced as evidence in a trial.

Authority The power designated to an agent of the law over a person who has broken the law.

Automatic Transfer The process by which a juvenile is transferred to adult court as a matter of state law. In some states, for example, a juvenile who is suspected of murder is automatically transferred to adult court.

B

Bail The amount or conditions set by the court to ensure that an individual accused of a crime will appear for further criminal proceedings. If the accused person proides bail, whether in cash or by means of a bail bond then she or he is released from jail.

Bail Bondsperson A businessperson who agrees, for a fee, to pay the bail amount if the accused fails to appear in court as ordered.

Bench Trial A trial conducted without a jury, in which a judge makes the determination of the defendant's guilt or innocence.

Beyond a Reasonable Doubt The standard used to determine the guilt or innocence of a person charged with a crime. To be guilty of a crime, a suspect must be proved guilty "beyond and to the exclusion of a reasonable doubt."

Bill of Rights The first ten amendments to the U.S. Constitution.

Blue Curtain A metaphorical term used to refer to the value placed on secrecy and the general mistrust of the outside world shared by many police officers.

Booking The process of entering a suspect's name, offense, and arrival time into the police log following her or his arrest.

Boot Camp A correctional facility based on militaristic principles of discipline and physical conditioning; reserved primarily for juvenile and first-time offenders serving terms of less than six months, with the ultimate goal of deterring further criminal behavior.

***Boykin* Form** A form that must be completed by a defendant who pleads guilty; the defendant states that she or he has done so voluntarily and with full comprehension of the consequences.

Broken Windows Theory Wilson and Kelling's theory that a neighborhood in disrepair signals that criminal activity is tolerated in the area. Thus, by cracking down on quality-of-life crimes, police can reclaim the neighborhood and encourage law-abiding citizens to live and work there.

Bureaucracy A hierarchically structured administrative organization that carries out specific functions.

C

Capital Punishment The use of the death penalty to punish wrongdoers for certain crimes.

Case Attrition The process through which prosecutors, by deciding whether or not to prosecute each person arrested, effect an overall reduction in the number of persons prosecuted. As a result, the number of persons convicted and sentenced is much smaller than the number of persons arrested.

Case Law The rules of law announced in court decisions. Case law includes the aggregate of reported cases that interpret judicial precedents, statutes, regulations, and constitutional provisions.

Challenge for Cause A *voir dire* challenge for which an attorney states the reason why a prospective juror should not be included on the jury.

Charge The judge's instructions to the jury following the attorneys' closing arguments; the charge sets forth the rules of law that the jury must apply in reaching its decision, or verdict.

Child Abuse Mistreatment of children by causing physical, emotional, or sexual damage without any plausible explanation, such as an accident.

Child Neglect A form of child abuse in which the child is denied certain necessities such as shelter, food, care, and love. Neglect is justification for a government agency to assume responsibility for a child in place of the parents or legal guardian.

Choice Theory A school of criminology that holds that wrongdoers act as if they weigh the possible benefits of criminal or delinquent activity against the expected costs of being apprehended. When the benefits are greater than the expected costs, the offender will make a rational choice to commit a crime or delinquent act.

Chronic Offender A delinquent or criminal who commits multiple offenses and is considered part of a small group of wrongdoers who are responsible for a majority of the antisocial activity in any given community.

Circumstantial Evidence Indirect evidence that is offered to establish, by inference, the likelihood of a fact that is in question.

Citizen Oversight The process by which citizens review complaints brought against individual police officers or police departments. The citizens often do not have the power to discipline misconduct, but can recommend that action be taken by police administrators.

Civil Law The branch of law dealing with the definition and enforcement of all private or public rights, as opposed to criminal matters.

Classical Criminology A school of criminology based on the belief that individuals have free will to engage in any behavior, including criminal behavior. To deter criminal behavior, society must hold wrongdoers responsible for their actions by punishing them.

Closing Arguments Arguments made by each side's attorney after the cases for the plaintiff and defendant have been presented.

Cohort A group of persons gathered for study because they share a certain characteristic, such as age, income, or criminal background.

Common Law The body of law developed from custom or judicial decisions in English and U.S. courts and not attributable to a legislature.

Community Policing A policing philosophy that emphasizes community support for and cooperation with the police in preventing crime. Community policing stresses a police role that is less centralized and more proactive than reform era policing strategies.

Computer Crime Any wrongful act that is directed against computers and computer parts or that involves wrongful use or abuse of computers or software.

Concurring Opinions Separate opinions prepared by judges who support the decision of the majority of the court but who want to make or clarify a particular point or to voice disapproval of the grounds on which the decision was made.

Confidential Informant (CI) A human source for police who provides information concerning illegal activity in which he or she is involved.

Conflict Model A criminal justice model in which the content of criminal law is determined by the groups that hold economic, political, and social power in a community.

Congregate System A nineteenth-century penitentiary system developed in New York in which inmates were kept in separate cells during the night but worked together in the daytime under a code of enforced silence.

Consensus Model A criminal justice model in which the majority of citizens in a society share the same values and beliefs. Criminal acts are those acts that conflict with these values and beliefs and are deemed harmful to society.

Consent Searches Searches by police that are made after the subject of the search has agreed to the action. In these situations, consent, if given of free will, validates a warrantless search.

Consolidation A corrections model in which the inmates who pose the highest security risk are housed in a single facility to separate them from the general prison population.

Constitutional Law Law based on the U.S. Constitution and the constitutions of the various states.

Continuum of Sanctions A corrections strategy in which offenders are not assigned a single punishment, but rather are initially sentenced based on their criminal acts and then moved toward harsher or more lenient forms of sanction depending on their behavior within the corrections system.

Control Theory A series of theories that assume that all individuals have the potential for criminal behavior, but are restrained by the damage that such actions would do to their relationships with family, friends, and members of the community. Criminality occurs when these bonds are broken or nonexistent.

Coroner The medical examiner of a county, usually elected by popular vote.

Corpus Delicti The body of circumstances that must exist for a criminal act to have occurred.

Courtroom Work Group The social organization consisting of the judge, prosecutor, defense attorney, and other court workers. The relationships among these persons have a far-reaching impact on the day-to-day operations of any court.

Crime Control Model A criminal justice model that places primary emphasis on the right of society to be protected from crime and violent criminals. Crime control values emphasize speed and efficiency in the criminal justice process; the benefits of lower crime rates outweigh any possible costs to individual rights.

Criminal Model of Addiction An approach to drug abuse that holds that drug offenders harm society by their actions to the same extent as other criminals and should face the same punitive sanctions.

Criminology The scientific study of crime and the causes of criminal behavior.

Cross-Examination The questioning of an opposing witness during trial.

Cultural Deviance Theory A branch of social structure theory based on the assumption that members of certain subcultures reject the values of the dominant culture through deviant behavior patterns.

Custodial Interrogation The questioning of a suspect after that person has been taken in custody. In this situation, the suspect must be read his or her *Miranda* rights before interrogation can begin.

Custody The forceful detention of a person, or the perception that a person is not free to leave the immediate vicinity.

Cyber Crime A crime that occurs online, in the virtual community of the Internet, as opposed to the physical world.

Cyber Fraud Any misrepresentation knowingly made over the Internet with the intention of deceiving another and on which a reasonable person would and does rely to his or her detriment.

Cyber Stalking The crime of stalking, committed in cyberspace. Generally, stalking consists of harassing a person and putting that person in reasonable fear for his or her safety or the safety of the person's immediate family.

D

Dark Figure of Crime A term used to describe the actual amount of crime that takes place. The "figure" is "dark," or impossible to detect, because a great number of crimes are never reported to the police.

Day Reporting Center A community-based corrections center to which offenders report on a daily basis for purposes of treatment, education, and incapacitation.

Deadly Force Force applied by a police officer that is likely or intended to cause death.

Decriminalization A policy that combines the elimination of criminal penalties on drug use with restrictions to discourage use such as high taxes and limitations on advertising of drugs.

Defense Attorney The lawyer representing the defendant.

Delegation of Authority The principles of command on which most police departments are based; personnel take orders from and are responsible to those in positions of power directly above them.

"Deliberate Indifference" A standard that must be met by inmates trying to prove that their Eighth Amendment rights were violated by a correctional facility. It occurs when prison officials are aware of harmful conditions of confinement but fail to take steps to remedy those conditions.

Departure A stipulation in many federal and state sentencing guidelines that allows a judge to adjust his or her sentencing decision based on the special circumstances of a particular case.

Deprivation Model A theory that inmate aggression is the result of the frustration inmates feel at being deprived of freedom, consumer goods, sex, and other staples of life outside the institution.

Detective The primary police investigator of crimes.

Detention The temporary custody of a juvenile in a state facility after a petition has been filed and before the adjudicatory process begins.

Detention Hearing A hearing to determine whether a juvenile should be detained, or remain detained, while waiting for the adjudicatory process to begin.

Determinate Sentencing A period of incarceration that is fixed by a sentencing authority and cannot be reduced by judges or other corrections officials.

Deterrence The strategy of preventing crime through the threat of punishment. Assumes that potential criminals will weigh the costs of punishments versus the benefits of the criminal act; therefore, punishments should be severe.

Differential Response A strategy for answering calls for service in which response time is adapted to the seriousness of the call.

Direct Evidence Evidence that establishes the existence of a fact that is in question without relying on inference.

Direct Examination The examination of a witness by the attorney who calls the witness to the stand to testify.

Direct Supervision Approach A process of prison and jail administration in which correctional officers are in continuous physical contact with inmates during the day.

Directed Patrol Patrol strategies that are designed to respond to a specific criminal activity at a specific time.

Discovery Formal investigation prior to trial. During discovery, the defense uses various methods to obtain information from the prosecution to prepare for trial.

Discretion The ability of individuals in the criminal justice system to make operational decisions based on personal judgment instead of formal rules or official information.

Discretionary Release The release of an inmate into a community supervision program at the discretion of the parole board within limits set by state or federal law.

Dispersion A corrections model in which high-risk inmates are spread throughout the general prison population, in the hopes that they will be absorbed without causing misconduct problems.

Disposition Hearing Similar to the sentencing hearing for adults, a hearing in which the juvenile judge or officer decides the appropriate punishment for a youth found to be delinquent or a status offender.

Dissenting Opinions Separate opinions in which judges disagree with the conclusion reached by the majority of the court and expand on their own views about the case.

Diversion In the context of corrections, a strategy to divert those offenders who qualify away from prison and jail and toward community-based and intermediate sanctions.

Diversion The removal of an alleged juvenile delinquent from the formal criminal or juvenile justice system and the referral of that person to a treatment or rehabilitation program.

Docket The list of cases entered on a court's calendar and thus scheduled to be heard by the court.

Double Jeopardy To twice place at risk (jeopardize) a person's life or liberty. The Fifth Amendment to the U.S. Constitution prohibits a second prosecution for the same criminal offense.

Drug Any substance that modifies behavior; in particular, an illegal substance with those properties.

Drug Abuse The use of drugs that results in physical or psychological problems for the user, as well as disruption of personal relationships and employment.

Dual Court System The separate but interrelated court system of the United States, made up of the courts on the national level and the courts on the state level.

Due Process Clause The provisions of the Fifth and Fourteenth Amendments to the Constitution that guarantee that no person shall be deprived of life, liberty, or property without due process of law. Similar clauses are found in most state constitutions.

Due Process Model A criminal justice model that places primacy on the right of the individual to be protected from the power of the government. Due process values hold that the state must prove a person's guilt within the confines of a process designed to safeguard personal liberties as enumerated in the Bill of Rights.

Duress Unlawful pressure brought to bear upon a person, causing the person to perform an act that he or she would not otherwise perform.

Durham Rule A test of criminal responsibility adopted in a 1954 case: "an accused is not criminally responsible if his unlawful act was the product of mental disease or mental defect."

Duty The moral sense of a police officer that she or he should apply authority in a certain manner.

E

Electronic Monitoring A technique of probation supervision in which the offender's whereabouts, though not his or her actions, are kept under surveillance by an electronic device; often used in conjunction with home confinement.

Encryption The process by which a message is transmitted into a form or code that the sender and receiver intend third parties not to understand.

Enemy Combatant A label given to certain persons suspected of terrorist activities by the U.S. government. Persons given this designation lose a number of rights provided by the U.S. Constitution.

Entrapment A defense in which the defendant claims that he or she was induced by a public official—usually an undercover agent or police officer—to commit a crime that he or she would otherwise not have committed.

Ethics The rules or standards of behavior governing a profession; aimed at ensuring the fairness and rightness of actions.

Evidence Anything that is used to prove the existence or nonexistence of a fact.

Exclusionary Rule A rule under which any evidence that is obtained in violation of the accused's rights under the Fourth, Fifth, and Sixth Amendments, as well as any evidence derived from illegally obtained evidence, will not be admissible in criminal court.

Exigent Circumstances Situations that require extralegal or exceptional actions by the police. In these circumstances, police officers are justified in not following procedural rules, such as those pertaining to search and arrest warrants.

Expert Witness A witness with professional training or substantial experience qualifying her or him to testify on a certain subject.

Extradition The surrender of a fugitive offender by one jurisdiction to another in which the offender has been convicted or is liable for punishment.

F

Federal Bureau of Investigation (FBI) The branch of the Department of Justice responsible for investigating violations of federal law. The bureau also collects national crime statistics and provides training and other forms of aid to local law enforcement agencies.

Federalism A form of government in which a written constitution provides for a division of powers between a central government and several regional governments. In the United States, the division of powers between the federal government and the fifty states is established by the Constitution.

Felony A serious crime punishable by death or by imprisonment in a federal or state corrections facility for more than a year.

Field Training The segment of a police recruit's training in which he or she is removed from the classroom and placed on the beat, under the supervision of a senior officer.

Forfeiture The process by which the government seizes private property attached to criminal activity.

Frisk A pat-down or minimal search by police to discover weapons; conducted for the express purpose of protecting the officer or other citizens, and not to find evidence of illegal substances for use in a trial.

Fruit of the Poisoned Tree Evidence that is acquired through the use of illegally obtained evidence and is therefore inadmissible in court.

Furlough Temporary release from a prison for purposes of vocational or educational training, to ease the shock of release, or for personal reasons.

G

General Patrol Patrol strategies that rely on police officers monitoring a certain area with the goal of detecting crimes in progress or preventing crime due to their presence. Also known as random or preventive patrol.

"Good Faith" Exception The legal principle, established through court decisions, that evidence obtained with the use of a technically faulty search warrant is admissible during trial if the police acted in good faith when they sought the warrant from a judge.

"Good Time" A reduction in time served by prisoners based on good behavior, conformity to rules, and other positive actions.

Graduated Sanctions The practical theory in juvenile corrections that a delinquent or status offender should receive a punishment that matches in seriousness the severity of the wrongdoing.

Grand Jury The group of citizens called to decide whether probable cause exists to believe that a suspect committed the crime with which she or he has been charged.

H

Habeas Corpus An order that requires correctional officials to bring an inmate before a court or a judge and explain why he or she is being held in prison.

Habitual Offender Laws Statutes that require lengthy prison sentences for those who are convicted of multiple felonies.

Hacker A person who uses one computer to break into another.

Halfway House A community-based form of early release that places inmates in residential centers and allows them to reintegrate with society.

Hallucinogens Drugs that cause the user to experience alterations in sensory experiences, or hallucinations.

"Hands-Off" Doctrine The unwritten judicial policy that favors noninterference by the courts in the administration of prisons and jails.

Harm Reduction A drug policy based not on reducing use of illicit drugs but on reducing the crime and health problems associated with drug use.

Hate Crime Law A statute that provides for greater sanctions against those who commit crimes motivated by animosity against an individual or a group based on race, ethnicity, religion, gender, sexual orientation, disability, or age.

Hearsay An oral or written statement made by an out-of-court declarant that is later offered in court by a witness (not the declarant) concerning a matter before the court. Hearsay usually is not admissible as evidence.

Home Confinement A community-based sanction in which offenders serve their terms of incarceration in their homes.

Hot Spots Concentrated areas of high criminal activity that draw a directed police response.

Hung Jury A jury whose members are so irreconcilably divided in their opinions that they cannot reach a verdict.

I

"Identifiable Human Needs" The basic human necessities that correctional facilities are required by the Constitution to provide to inmates. Beyond food, warmth, and exercise, the court system has been unable to establish exactly what these needs are.

Identity Theft The theft of identity information, such as name, driver's license number, or Social Security number. The information is then usually used to access the victim's financial resources.

Illicit Drugs Certain drugs or substances whose use or sale has been declared illegal.

Immigration Violations Infractions of U.S. immigration laws, such as failing to comply with the terms of a visa, for which the punishment is often removal from the United States.

Impeached As authorized by Article I of the Constitution, impeachment is voted on by the House of Representatives and then sent to the Senate for a vote to remove the president, vice president, or civil officers (such as federal judges) of the United States.

Incapacitation A strategy for preventing crime by detaining wrongdoers in prison, thereby separating them from the community and reducing criminal opportunities.

Inchoate Offenses Conduct deemed criminal without actual harm being done, provided that the harm that would have occurred is one the law tries to prevent.

Incident-Driven Policing A reactive approach to policing that emphasizes a speedy response to calls for service.

Indeterminate Sentencing An indeterminate term of incarceration in which a judge determines the minimum and maximum terms of imprisonment. When the minimum term is reached, the prisoner becomes eligible to be paroled.

Index Crimes Those crimes reported annually by the FBI in its Uniform Crime Report. Index crimes include murder, rape, robbery, aggravated assault, burglary, larceny, motor vehicle theft, and arson. Also known as Part I offenses.

Indictment A charge or written accusation, issued by a grand jury, that probable cause exists to believe that a named person has committed a crime.

"Inevitable Discovery" Exception The legal principle that illegally obtained evidence can be admitted in court if police using lawful means would have "inevitably" discovered it.

Information The formal charge against the accused issued by the prosecutor after a preliminary hearing has found probable cause.

Initial Appearance An accused's first appearance before a judge or magistrate following arrest; during the appearance, the defendant is informed of the charges, advised of the right to counsel, told the amount of bail, and given a date for the preliminary hearing.

Insanity A defense for criminal liability that asserts a lack of criminal responsibility. According to the law, a person cannot have the requisite state of mind to commit a crime if she or he did not know at the time of the act that it was wrong, or did not know the nature and quality of the act.

Intake Following referral of a juvenile to juvenile court by a police officer or other concerned party, the process by which an official of the court must decide whether to file a petition, release the juvenile, or place the juvenile under some other form of supervision.

Intellectual Property Property resulting from intellectual, creative processes.

Intelligence Agency An agency that is primarily concerned with gathering information on potential criminals and criminal acts in order to prevent crimes from occurring.

Intensive Supervision Probation (ISP) A punishment-oriented form of probation in which the offender is placed under stricter and more frequent surveillance and control by probation officers with limited caseloads.

Intermediate Sanctions Sanctions that are more restrictive than probation and less restrictive than imprisonment. Intended to alleviate pressure on overcrowded corrections facilities and understaffed probation departments.

Internal Affairs Unit (IAU) A division within a police department that receives and investigates complaints of wrongdoing by police officers.

Interrogation The direct questioning of a suspect to gather evidence of criminal activity and try to gain a confession.

Intoxication A defense for criminal liability in which the defendant claims that the taking of intoxicants rendered him or her unable to form the requisite intent to commit a criminal act.

Irresistible Impulse Test A test for the insanity defense under which a defendant who knew his or her action was wrong may still be found insane if he or she was nonetheless unable, as a result of a mental deficiency, to control the urge to complete it.

J

Jail A facility, usually operated by county government, used to hold persons awaiting trial or those who have been found guilty of misdemeanors.

Judicial Misconduct A general term describing behavior that diminishes public confidence in the judiciary. This behavior includes obviously illegal acts, such as bribery, and conduct that gives the appearance of impropriety, such as consorting with known felons.

Judicial Reprieve Temporary relief or the postponement of a sentence on the authority of a judge. In the United States, the judicial power to offer a reprieve has been limited by the Supreme Court.

Judicial Waiver The process in which the juvenile judge, based on the facts of the case at hand, decides that the alleged offender should be transferred to adult court.

Jurisdiction The authority of a court to hear and decide cases within an area of the law or a geographical territory.

Jury Nullification An acquittal of a defendant by a jury even though the evidence presented and the judge's instructions indicate that the defendant is guilty.

Jury Trial A trial before a judge and a jury.

Just Deserts A sanctioning philosophy based on the assertion that criminals deserve to be punished for breaking society's rules. The severity of the punishment should be determined by no other factor than the severity of the crime.

Justice of the Peace Established in fourteenth-century England, a government official who oversaw various aspects of local law enforcement. The post eventually became strictly identified with judicial matters.

Juvenile Delinquency Behavior that is illegal under federal or state law that has been committed by a person who is under an age limit specified by statute.

L

Labeling Theory The hypothesis that society creates crime and criminals by labeling certain behavior and certain people as deviant. The stigma that results from this social process excludes a person from the community, thereby increasing the chances that she or he will adopt the label as her or his identity and engage in a pattern of criminal behavior.

Lay Witness A witness who can truthfully and accurately testify on a fact in question without having specialized training or knowledge; an ordinary witness.

Learning Theory The hypothesis that delinquents and criminals must be taught both the practical and emotional skills necessary to partake in illegal activity.

Legalization The elimination or modification of federal and state laws that prohibit the manufacture, use, and sale of illegal drugs.

Licit Drugs Legal drugs or substances, such as alcohol, coffee, and tobacco.

Life Course Criminology The study of crime based on the belief that behavioral patterns developed in childhood can predict delinquent and criminal behavior later in life.

Lockdown A disciplinary action taken by prison officials in which all inmates are ordered to their quarters and nonessential prison activities are suspended.

Low-Visibility Decision Making A term used to describe the discretionary power police have in determining what to do with misbehaving juveniles. For the most part, this power goes unchallenged and unnoticed by citizens.

M

***M'Naughten* Rule** A common law test of criminal responsibility derived from *M'Naughten's* case in 1843 that relies on the defendant's inability to distinguish right from wrong.

Magistrate A public civil officer or official with limited judicial authority within a particular geographical area, such as the authority to issue an arrest warrant.

Mala in Se A descriptive term for acts that are inherently wrong, regardless of whether they are prohibited by law.

Mala Prohibita A descriptive term for acts that are made illegal by criminal statute and are not necessarily wrong in and of themselves.

Mandatory Release Release from prison that occurs when an offender has served the length of his or her sentence, with time taken off for good behavior.

Mandatory Sentencing Guidelines Statutorily determined punishments that must be applied to those who are convicted of specific crimes.

Master Jury List The list of citizens in a court's district from which a jury can be selected; often compiled from voter-registration lists, driver's license lists, and other sources.

Maximum-Security Prison A correctional institution designed and organized to control and discipline dangerous felons, as well as prevent escape, with intense supervision, cement walls, and electronic, barbed wire fences.

Medical Model A model of corrections in which the psychological and biological roots of an inmate's criminal behavior are identified and treated.

Medical Model of Addiction An approach to drug addiction that treats drug abuse as a mental illness and focuses on treating and rehabilitating offenders rather than punishing them.

Medium-Security Prison A correctional institution that houses less dangerous inmates and therefore uses less restrictive measures to avoid violence and escapes.

Mens Rea (pronounced *mehns* ray-uh). Mental state, or intent. A wrongful mental state is as necessary as a wrongful act to establish criminal liability.

Minimum-Security Prison A correctional institution designed to allow inmates, most of whom pose low security risks, a great deal of freedom of movement and contact with the outside world.

***Miranda* Rights** The constitutional rights of accused persons taken into custody by law enforcement officials. Following the United States Supreme Court's decision in *Miranda v. Arizona,* on taking an accused person into custody, the arresting officer must inform the person of certain constitutional rights, such as the right to remain silent and the right to counsel.

Misdemeanor Any crime that is not a felony; punishable by a fine or by confinement for up to a year.

Missouri Plan A method of selecting judges that combines appointment and election. Under the plan, the state governor or another government official selects judges from a group of nominees chosen by a nonpartisan committee. After a year on the bench, the judges face a popular election to determine whether the public wishes to keep them in office.

Mitigating Circumstances Any circumstances accompanying the commission of a crime that may justify a lighter sentence.

Motion for a Directed Verdict A motion requesting that the court grant judgment in favor of the defense on the ground that the prosecution has not produced sufficient evidence to support the state's claim.

N

Necessity A defense against criminal liability in which the defendant asserts that circumstances required her or him to commit an illegal act.

Negligence A failure to exercise the standard of care that a reasonable person would exercise in similar circumstances.

New-Generation Jail A type of jail that is distinguished architecturally from its predecessors by a design that encourages interaction between inmates and jailers and that offers greater opportunities for treatment.

Nolo Contendere Latin for "I will not contest it." A criminal defendant's plea, in which he or she chooses not to challenge, or contest, the charges brought by the government. Although the defendant may still be sentenced or fined, the plea neither admits nor denies guilt.

Nonpartisan Elections Elections in which candidates are presented on the ballot without any party affiliation.

O

Opening Statements The attorneys' statements to the jury at the beginning of the trial. Each side briefly outlines the evidence that will be offered during the trial and the legal theory that will be pursued.

Opiates Drugs containing opium or its derivatives; have the effects of dulling sensations including pain and anxiety, producing a feeling of euphoria, and causing general inaction.

Opinion A statement by the court expressing the reasons for its decision in a case.

Oral Arguments The verbal arguments presented in person by attorneys to an appellate court. Each attorney presents reasons why the court should rule in his or her client's favor.

Organized Crime A conspiratorial relationship between any number of persons engaged in the market for illegal goods or services, such as illicit drugs or firearms.

P

Pardon An act of executive clemency that overturns a conviction and erases mention of the crime from the person's criminal record.

Parens Patriae A doctrine that holds that the state has a responsibility to look after the well-being of children and to assume the role of parent if necessary.

Parole The conditional release of an inmate before his or her sentence has expired. The remainder of the sentence is served in the community under the supervision of correctional (parole) officers, and the offender can be returned to incarceration if he or she breaks the conditions of parole, as determined by a parole board.

Parole Board A body of appointed civilians that decides whether a convict should be granted conditional release before the end of his or her sentence.

Parole Contract An agreement between the state and the offender that establishes the conditions under which the latter will be allowed to serve the remainder of her or his prison term in the community.

Parole Grant Hearing A hearing in which the entire parole board or a subcommittee reviews information, meets the offender, and hears testimony from relevant witnesses to determine whether to grant parole.

Parole Guidelines Employed to remove discretion from the parole process, these guidelines attempt to measure the risks of an offender recidivating, and then use these measurements to determine whether early release will be granted and under what conditions.

Parole Revocation When a parolee breaks the conditions of parole, the process of withdrawing parole and returning the person to prison.

Part II Offenses All crimes recorded by the FBI that do not fall into the category of Part I offenses. Include both misdemeanors and felonies.

Partisan Elections Elections in which candidates are affiliated with and receive support from political parties; the candidates are listed in conjunction with their party on the ballot.

Patronage System A form of corruption in which the political party in power hires and promotes police officers, receiving job-related "favors" in return.

Penitentiary An early form of correctional facility that emphasized separating inmates from society and from each other so that they would have an environment in which to reflect on their wrongdoing and ponder their reformation.

Peremptory Challenges *Voir dire* challenges to exclude potential jurors from serving on the jury without any supporting reason or cause.

Petition The document filed with a juvenile court alleging that the juvenile is a delinquent or a status offender, and asking the court to either hear the case or transfer it to an adult court.

Plain View Doctrine The legal principle that objects in plain view of a law enforcement agent who has the right to be in a position to have that view may be seized without a warrant and introduced as evidence.

Plea Bargaining The process by which the accused and the prosecutor work out a mutually satisfactory conclusion to the case, subject to court approval. Usually, plea bargaining involves the defendant's pleading guilty to a lesser offense in return for a lighter sentence.

Podular Design The architectural style of the new-generation jail. Each "pod" consists of between twelve and twenty-four one-person cells and a communal "day-room" to allow for social interaction.

Police Corruption The abuse of authority by a law enforcement officer for personal gain.

Police Cynicism The suspicion that citizens are weak, corrupt, and dangerous. This outlook is the result of a police officer being constantly exposed to civilians at their worst and can negatively affect the officer's performance.

Police Subculture The values and perceptions that are shared by members of a police department and, to a certain extent, by all law enforcement agents. These values and perceptions are shaped by the unique and isolated existence of the police officer.

Positivism A school of social science that sees criminal and delinquent behavior as the result of biological, psychological, and social forces. Because wrongdoers are driven to deviancy by external factors, they should not be punished but treated to lessen the influence of those factors.

Precedent A court decision that furnishes an example of authority for deciding subsequent cases involving similar facts.

Predisposition Report A report prepared during the disposition process that provides the judge with relevant background material to aid in the disposition decision.

Preliminary Hearing An initial hearing in which a magistrate decides if there is probable cause to believe that the defendant committed the crime with which he or she is charged.

Presentence Investigative Report An investigative report on an offender's background that assists a judge in determining the proper sentence.

Presumptive Sentencing A sentencing strategy in which legislators set the average sentence that should be served for any particular crime, leaving judges with the ability to shorten or lengthen the sentence based on the circumstances of each case.

Pretrial Detainees Individuals who cannot post bail after arrest and are therefore forced to spend the time prior to their trial incarcerated in jail.

Pretrial Diversion Program An alternative to trial offered by a judge or prosecutor, in which the offender agrees to participate in a specified counseling or treatment program in return for withdrawal of the charges.

Preventive Detention The retention of an accused person in custody due to fears that she or he will commit a crime if released before trial.

Prison Code A system of social norms and values established by inmates to regulate behavior within the correctional institution.

Prisonization The socialization process through which a new inmate learns the accepted norms and values of the prison population.

Private Prisons Correctional facilities operated by private corporations instead of the government and, therefore, reliant on profit for survival.

Private Security The practice of private corporations or individuals offering services traditionally performed by police officers.

Probable Cause Reasonable grounds to believe the existence of facts warranting certain actions, such as the search or arrest of a person.

Probation A criminal sanction in which a convict is allowed to remain in the community rather than be imprisoned as long as she or he follows certain conditions set by the court.

Problem-Solving Policing A policing philosophy that requires police to identify potential criminal activity and develop strategies to prevent or respond to that activity.

Procedural Criminal Law Rules that define the manner in which the rights and duties of individuals may be enforced.

Procedural Due Process A provision in the Constitution that states that the law must be carried out in a fair and orderly manner.

Professional Model A style of policing advocated by August Vollmer and O. W. Wilson that emphasizes centralized police organizations, increased use of technology, and a limitation of police discretion through regulations and guidelines.

Prohibition A period in American history, lasting from the passage of the Eighteenth Amendment in 1919 until its repeal in 1933, during which the production and consumption of alcohol were prohibited by federal law.

Property Crime Crimes committed against property, including larceny/theft, burglary, and arson.

Prosecutorial Waiver A procedure in which juvenile court judges have the discretion to transfer a juvenile case to adult court, when certain predetermined conditions as to the seriousness of the offense and the age of the offender are met.

Psychoactive Drugs Chemicals that affect the brain, causing changes in emotions, perceptions, and behavior.

Public Defenders Court-appointed attorneys who are paid by the state to represent defendants who are unable to hire private counsel.

Public Order Crime Behavior that has been labeled criminal because it is contrary to shared social values, customs, and norms.

Public Prosecutors Individuals, acting as trial lawyers, who initiate and conduct cases in the government's name and on behalf of the people.

R

Rape Shield Law A state or federal law that disallows any evidence of an alleged sexual-assault victim's prior sexual conduct to be used against her or him in a criminal trial. These laws are designed to spare the victim the humiliation of irrelevant references to past sexual behavior that may improperly influence the jury.

Real Evidence Evidence that is brought into court and seen by the jury, as opposed to evidence that is described for a jury.

"Real Offense" The actual offense committed, as opposed to the charge levied by a prosecutor as the result of a plea bargain. Judges who make sentencing decisions based on the real offense are often seen as undermining the plea bargain process.

Reasonable Force The degree of force that is appropriate to protect the police officer or other citizens and is not excessive.

Rebuttal Evidence given to counteract or disprove evidence presented by the opposing party.

Rehabilitation The philosophy that society is best served when wrongdoers are not simply punished, but provided the resources needed to eliminate criminality from their behavioral pattern.

Reintegration A goal of corrections that focuses on preparing the offender for a return to the community unmarred by further criminal behavior.

Relative Deprivation The theory that inmate aggression is caused when freedoms and services that the inmate has come to accept as normal are decreased or eliminated.

Release on Recognizance (ROR) A judge's order that releases an accused from jail with the understanding that he or she will return for further proceedings of his or her own will; used instead of setting a monetary bond.

Relevant Evidence Evidence tending to make a fact in question more or less probable than it would be without the evidence. Only relevant evidence is admissible in court.

Residential Treatment Programs Government-run facilities for juveniles whose offenses are not deemed serious enough to warrant incarceration in a training school.

Response Time A measurement of police efficiency based on the rapidity with which calls for service are answered.

Retribution The philosophy that those who commit criminal acts should be punished based on the severity of the crime and that no other factors need be considered.

Rule of Four A rule of the United States Supreme Court that the Court will not issue a writ of *certiorari* unless at least four justices approve of the decision to hear the case.

S

Search The process by which police examine a person or property to find evidence that will be used to prove guilt in a criminal trial.

Search Warrant A written order, based on probable cause and issued by a judge or magistrate, commanding that police officers or criminal investigators search a specific person, place, or property to obtain evidence.

Searches and Seizures The legal term, as found in the Fourth Amendment of the U.S. Constitution, that generally refers to the searching for and the confiscating of evidence by law enforcement agents.

Searches Incidental to Arrests Searches for weapons and evidence of persons who have just been arrested. The fruit of such searches is admissible if any items found are within the immediate vicinity or control of the suspect.

Sedatives Drugs that slow the signals sent from the brain to other parts of the body, thereby inducing sleep or reducing anxiety.

Seizure The forcible taking of a person or property in response to a violation of the law.

Self-Defense The legally recognized privilege to protect one's self or property from injury by another. The privilege of self-defense protects only acts that are reasonably necessary to protect one's self or property.

Self-Reported Surveys A method of gathering crime data that relies on participants to reveal and detail their own criminal or delinquent behavior.

Sentencing Discrimination A situation in which the length of a sentence appears to be influenced by a defendant's race, gender, economic status, or other factor not directly related to the crime he or she committed.

Sentencing Disparity A situation in which those convicted of similar crimes do not receive similar sentences.

Sentencing Guidelines Legislatively determined guidelines that judges are required to follow when sentencing those convicted of specific crimes. These guidelines limit judicial discretion.

Separate Confinement A nineteenth-century penitentiary system developed in Pennsylvania in which inmates were kept separate from each other at all times, with daily activities taking place in individual cells.

Sheriff The primary law enforcement officer in a county, usually elected to the post by a popular vote.

Shire-Reeve The chief law enforcement officer in an early English shire, or county. The forerunner of the modern sheriff.

Shock Incarceration A short period of incarceration that is designed to deter further criminal activity by "shocking" the offender with the hardships of imprisonment.

Social Conflict Theories A school of criminology that views criminal behavior as the result of class conflict. Certain behavior is labeled illegal not because it is inherently criminal, but because the ruling class has an economic or social interest in restricting such behavior in order to protect the status quo.

Social Disorganization Theory The theory that deviant behavior is more likely in communities where social institutions such as the family, schools, and criminal justice system fail to exert control over the population.

Social Process Theories A school of criminology that considers criminal behavior to be the predictable result of a person's interaction with his or her environment. According to these theories, everybody has the potential for wrongdoing. Those who act upon this potential are conditioned to do so by family or peer groups, or institutions such as the media.

Social Reality of Crime The theory that criminal laws are designed by those in power (the rich) to help them keep power at the expense of those who do not have power (the poor). This would explain, for example, why the punishment for white-collar crime, mostly committed by members of the upper and middle classes, is less severe than the punishment for property and violent crimes, mostly committed by members of the lower class.

Socialization The process through which a police officer is taught the values and expected behavior of the police subculture.

Specialty Courts Lower courts that have jurisdiction over one specific area of criminal activity, such as illegal drugs or domestic violence.

Split Sentence Probation A sentence that consists of incarceration in a prison or jail, followed by a probationary period in the community.

Stare Decisis (pronounced *ster*-ay dih-*si-ses*). A common law doctrine under which judges are obligated to follow the precedents established under prior decisions.

Status Offender A juvenile who has been found to have engaged in behavior deemed unacceptable for those under a certain, statutorily determined age.

Statutory Law The body of law enacted by legislative bodies.

Stimulants Drugs such as cocaine or amphetamine that stimulate the central nervous system, thereby quickening motor functions of the body.

Stop A brief detention of a person by law enforcement agents for questioning. The agents must have a reasonable suspicion of the person before making a stop.

Strain Theory The assumption that crime is the result of frustration felt by individuals who cannot reach their financial and personal goals through legitimate means.

Strict Liability Certain crimes, such as traffic violations, in which the defendant is guilty regardless of her or his state of mind at the time of the act.

Subculture A group exhibiting certain values and behavior patterns that distinguish it from the dominant culture.

Substantial Capacity Test From the Model Penal Code, a test that states that a person is not responsible for criminal behavior if when committing the act "as a result of mental disease or defect he lacks substantial capacity either to appreciate the wrongfulness of his conduct or to conform his conduct to the requirements of the law."

Substantive Criminal Law Law that defines the rights and duties of individuals with respect to each other.

Substantive Due Process The constitutional requirement that laws used in accusing and convicting persons of crimes must be fair.

Supermax Prison A correctional facility reserved for those inmates who have extensive records of misconduct in maximum-security prisons; characterized by extremely strict control and supervision over the inmates, including extensive use of solitary confinement.

Supply-Side Enforcement The law enforcement strategy of combating the use of illegal drugs by concentrating on the suppliers of the drugs rather than the buyers. Thus, agents will focus on a single drug dealer rather than on his or her many clients.

Suspended Sentence A judicially imposed condition in which an offender is sentenced after being convicted of a crime, but is not required to begin the sentence immediately. The judge may revoke the suspended sentence and remit the offender to prison or jail if he or she does not follow certain conditions.

T

Technical Violation An action taken by a probationer that, although not criminal, breaks the terms of probation as designated by the court; can result in the revocation of probation and a return to prison or jail.

Ten Percent Cash Bail An alternative to traditional bail in which defendants may gain pretrial release by posting 10 percent of their bond amount to the court instead of seeking a bail bondsperson.

Terrorism The use or threat of violence to achieve political objectives.

Testimony Verbal evidence given by witnesses under oath.

Theory of Differential Association Sutherland's theory that criminality is the result of the values an individual is exposed to by family, friends, and other members of the community. When these values favor deviant behavior over conventional norms, criminal activity is more likely.

Time Served The period of time a person denied bail has spent in jail prior to his or her trial. If the suspect is found guilty and sentenced to a jail or prison term, the judge will often lessen the duration of the sentence based on the amount of time served as a pretrial detainee.

Tithing System In Anglo-Saxon England, a system of law enforcement in which groups of ten families, known as tithings, were collectively responsible for law and order within their groups.

Total Institution An institution, such as a prison, that provides all of the necessities for existence to those who live within its boundaries.

Training Schools Correctional institutions for juveniles found to be delinquent or status offenders.

Trial Courts Courts in which most cases usually begin and in which questions of fact are examined.

Truth-in-Sentencing Laws Legislative attempts to assure that convicts will serve approximately the terms to which they were initially sentenced.

U

Uniform Crime Report (UCR) An annual report compiled by the FBI to give an indication of criminal activity in the United States. The FBI collects data from local, state, and federal law enforcement agencies in preparing this report.

Utilitarianism An approach to ethical reasoning in which the "correct" decision is the one that results in the greatest amount of good for the greatest number of people affected by that decision.

V

Venire The group of citizens from which the jury is selected.

Verdict A formal decision made by the jury.

Victim Surveys A method of gathering crime data that directly surveys participants to determine their experiences as victims of crime.

Violent Crime Crimes committed against persons, including murder, rape, assault and battery, and robbery.

Virus A computer program that can replicate itself over a network such as the Internet and interfere with the normal use of a computer. A virus cannot exist as a separate entity and must attach itself to another program to move through a network.

Visa An endorsement made in a passport that allows the bearer to enter the country issuing the visa as long its conditions are followed.

Voir Dire The preliminary questions that the trial attorneys ask prospective jurors to determine whether they are biased or have any connection with the defendant or a witness.

W

Warden The prison official who is ultimately responsible for the organization and performance of a correctional facility.

Warrantless Arrest An arrest made without first seeking a warrant for the action; permitted under certain circumstances, such as when the arresting officer has witnessed the crime or has a reasonable belief that the suspect has committed a felony.

"Wedding Cake" Model A wedding cake-shaped model that explains why different cases receive different treatment in the criminal justice system. The cases at the "top" of the cake receive the most attention and have the greatest effect on public perception of criminal justice, while those cases at the "bottom" are disposed of quickly and virtually ignored by the media.

White-Collar Crime Nonviolent crimes committed by corporations and individuals to gain a personal or business advantage.

Widen the Net The criticism that intermediate sanctions designed to divert offenders from prison actually increase the number of citizens who are under the control and surveillance of the American corrections system.

Work Release Program Temporary release of convicts from prison for purposes of employment. The offenders may spend their days on the job, but must return to the correctional facility at night and during the weekend.

Worm A computer program that can automatically replicate itself over a network such as the Internet and interfere with the normal use of a computer. A worm can exist as a separate entity.

Writ of *Certiorari* A request from a higher court asking a lower court for the record of a case. In essence, the request signals the higher court's willingness to review the case.

Y

Youth Gangs Self-formed groups of youths with several identifiable characteristics, including a gang name and other recognizable symbols, a geographic territory, a leadership structure, a meeting pattern, and participation in illegal activities.

Index

Black, Freda, 324
Black, Hugo, 280, 348–349, 354
Black, Roy, 131
Black Muslims, 475, 483
Blacks. *See* African American(s)
Blackstone, Sir William, 109
Blackwell, Maurice J., 349
Block officers, 480
Blood, suspect identification and, 245
Blucker, Michael, 483
Blue curtain, 197
Bluffdale State Prison, 496
Blumberg, Abraham S., 297
Blumstein, Alfred, 440, 444, 532
Bobbit, Lorena, 353
Bolivia, coca production in, 563
Bonn, Robert L., 416
Booking, 245
Boot camps, 427–429
BOP. *See* Federal Bureau of Prisons
"Born criminal," 42–45
Boston House of Corrections, 408
Boston Nanny case, 341, 353
Boston Police Department, 141, 204
    diversity in, 176
Boudin, Kathy, 490
Bounty hunters, 302
Bourgeois, Phillipe, 557
Bouza, Anthony, 191
Bowker, Lee H., 474
Bowman, Theron, 578
Boykin form, 312
Brady Handgun Violence Prevention Act
    (Brady Bill)(1993), 66
Brain activity, crime and, 43–44, 45
"Brain mapping," 43–44, 45
Brandl, Steven G., 193
Bratton, William, 187
Brazil, visa controls and, 577
Brazoria County Detention Center, 455
Brecher, Edward, 547
Bremmer, Ewan, 551
Brennan, William, 386
Breyer, Charles, 8
Bribery of law enforcement officer, 203. *See*
    also Police corruption
Bridewell Palace, 437
Bridgeport (Connecticut) Police
    Department, 183–185
Bright, Stephen, 280, 383
Brockway, Zebulon, 439
Broken windows theory, 50, 51, 186
Brosnahan, James, 288
Brown, Bobby, 414
Brown, Diane, 282
Browne, Angela, 395

Browning, Kelly, 515
Brubaker, 449, 450
Brucker, Joseph, 343
Bryant, Kobe, 18, 130, 131, 132, 255
Buchter, Richard, 108
Building Blocks for Youth, 23
Bully problem, 534–536
Burden of proof. *See* Standard of proof
Burdine, Calvin Jerold, 281
Bureau of Alcohol, Tobacco, Firearms, and
        Explosives (ATF), 13, 145, 153
    fingerprinting firearms and, 66
    functions of, 155
    time on antiterrorism activities and, 29
Bureau of Citizenship and Immigration
        Services, 29, 150–151
Bureau of Customs and Border Protection
        (CBP), 151, 553
Bureau of Engraving and Printing, 153
Bureau of Immigration and Customs
        Enforcement (BICE), 151
Bureau of Justice Statistics, 38, 56, 91,
        375–376, 490
Bureau of Narcotics and Dangerous Drugs,
        154–155
Bureaucracy, 179–180
Burge, Tim, 345
Burger, Warren, 313–314
Burgess, Ernest, 46
Burma. *See* Myanmar
Bush, George H. W., 563
Bush, George W., 442
    Department of Homeland Security
        promoted by, 13, 29, 149, 151
    International Criminal Court and, 258
    judicial appointment and, 270
    military tribunals created by, 30, 129,
        585
    Posse Comitatus Act of 1878 and, 195
    Project Exile and, 62
    on racial profiling, 248
    sky marshal program and, 150
    USA Patriot Act and, 22, 30, 581
    war on terrorism and, 28–29, 129, 195,
        572, 576, 579, 581, 593
    on white-collar crime, 9, 10
Bush, Jeb, 385
Business Software Alliance, 592
Butler, Paul, 349
Byrd, James, Jr., 99, 328
Byrne, William, 341

C

Cabranes, José A., 371

Caffeine, 544
Calipatria State Prison, 449
Campbell, Aaron, 221
Campbell, Michael Ian, 587
Campos, Vincent, 449
Campus style of prison, 446
Camus, Albert, 443
Canada
    drug trafficking and, 151
    fingerprinting firearms in, 66
    illegal immigrants entering United
        States via, 151
    incarceration rate in, 436
    marijuana decriminalization proposals
        and, 560
Canetti, Elias, 23
Cannabis. *See* Marijuana
Cannibus Buyers' Cooperative, 8
Canons of Judicial Ethics, 274
Capital punishment, 382–394
    the American tradition of, 383–384
    arbitrariness and, 391–392
    automatic appeal requirement and, 350,
        392
    bifurcated process and, 386–387, 391
    as cruel and unusual, 265, 384, 386,
        389, 392
    debating, 388–392
    defined, 383
    deterrence and, 388–390
    discriminatory effect and, 392–394
    fairness concerns and, 394
    fallibility and, 390–391
    under the "Great Law," 437
    habeas corpus limitations and, 351
    immediate future of, 394
    juveniles and, 512
    methods of, 384
    mitigating circumstances and, 387–388
    recent downturn in use of, 394
    in the seventeenth and eighteenth
        centuries, 384
    Supreme Court and, 384–388
    trials involving, cost of, 280
    in the United States, 26
        1930 to present, 383
        extradition problems because of,
            209, 258
        by state, 1976-2000, 391
Capitalism, Marxism versus, 52
Capone, Al, 156, 548
CAPPS II (Computer Assisted
        Prescreening System), 597, 599
Cardozo, Benjamin, 338
Career criminals, 62–63
Carneak, Michael, 534

DATE DUE

GAYLORD   PRINTED IN U.S.A.